BASIC CONTRACT LAW
CONCISE EDITION

Tenth Edition

■ ■ ■

Lon L. Fuller
*Late Carter Professor of General Jurisprudence,
Harvard University*

Melvin Aron Eisenberg
*Jesse H. Choper Professor of Law Emeritus
University of California at Berkeley*

Mark P. Gergen
*Robert and Joann Burch D.P.
Professor of Tax Law and Policy
University of California at Berkeley*

AMERICAN CASEBOOK SERIES®

American Casebook Series is a trademark registered in the U.S. Patent and Trademark Office.

© West, a Thomson business, 2006
© 2013 LEG, Inc. d/b/a West Academic Publishing
© 2018 LEG, Inc. d/b/a West Academic
      444 Cedar Street, Suite 700
      St. Paul, MN 55101
      1-877-888-1330

West, West Academic Publishing, and West Academic are trademarks of West Publishing Corporation, used under license.

Printed in the United States of America

ISBN: 978-1-68328-567-0

ACKNOWLEDGMENTS

———

This book, *Basic Contract Law*, has a long and rich history. The first edition of the book, published in 1947, was authored by Lon Fuller, one of the greatest contracts and legal scholars of the twentieth century. Professor Robert Braucher, then of Harvard Law School and also the Reporter for the Restatement (Second) of Contracts, joined Fuller as a co-author of the second edition. Thereafter, however, Braucher left the book because he had been appointed as a judge on the Massachusetts Supreme Judicial Court, and Professor Melvin Eisenberg, of the University of California at Berkeley School of Law, took Braucher's place. Eisenberg then authored the third through the eighth editions. In 2012, Professor Mark Gergen, of the University of California at Berkeley School of Law, joined the book as a co-author of the ninth edition

———

It is impossible to acknowledge all those scholars, students, and law-school staff members whose influence has made itself felt in this book. First and foremost is Lon Fuller. Although Fuller passed away after publication of the third edition of this book, his designation as co-author has been retained through all subsequent editions because the book continues to reflect his seminal views on contract law. For the present, tenth, edition we also especially thank Toni Mendicino for her terrific work in helping to get the materials in the book ready for publication and overseeing the production of the book.

MELVIN ARON EISENBERG
MARK P. GERGEN

May 2018

SUMMARY OF CONTENTS

———

ACKNOWLEDGMENTS III

TABLE OF CASES XXV

TABLE OF UNIFORM COMMERCIAL CODE CITATIONS XXXIX

TABLE OF CITATIONS TO THE RESTATEMENT OF CONTRACTS XLI

TABLE OF CITATIONS TO THE RESTATEMENTS OF RESTITUTION XLV

Introduction 1

PART 1. WHAT PROMISES SHOULD THE LAW ENFORCE?— THE DOCTRINE OF CONSIDERATION

Chapter 1. Simple Donative Promises and the Elements of Form, Reliance, and Past Benefit Conferred 9
Section 1.   Simple Donative Promises 9
Section 2.   The Element of Form 16
Section 3.   The Element of Reliance 25
Section 4.   Promises Based on a Past Benefit Conferred ("Past Consideration") 42

Chapter 2. The Bargain Principle and Its Limits 57
Section 1.   The Bargain Principle 57
Section 2.   Duress and the Exploitation of Distress 69
Section 3.   Unconscionability 86
Section 4.   The Doctrine of Mutuality and the Illusory-Promise Rule 106
Section 5.   The Legal-Duty Rule; Modifications 120

Chapter 3. The Limits of Contract 139

PART 2. REMEDIES FOR BREACH OF CONTRACT

Chapter 4. An Introduction to Contract Damages 157

Chapter 5. The Expectation Measure 169
Section 1.   Breach of a Contract to Provide a Service or Good 169
Section 2.   Breach of a Contract to Pay Money for a Service or Good 193
Section 3.   Mitigation 204
Section 4.   Foreseeability 216
Section 5.   Certainty 224
Section 6.   Liquidated Damages 234

Chapter 6. Specific Performance 249

Chapter 7. Alternative Damage Measures............................**265**
Section 1.   Reliance Damages in a Bargain Context 265
Section 2.   The Restitution Measure 271
Section 3.   Disgorgement Damages 279

PART 3. ASSENT

Chapter 8. An Introduction to Interpretation........................**297**
Section 1.   Subjective and Objective Elements in Contract
   Interpretation 297
Section 2.   Problems of Interpreting Purposive Language................... 319

**Chapter 9. The Mechanics of a Bargain (I)—Offer and
   Revocation**..**331**
Section 1.   What Constitutes an Offer....................................... 331
Section 2.   Termination of the Offeree's Power of Acceptance: Lapse,
   Rejection, and Counter-Offer.. 348
Section 3.   Termination of the Offeree's Power of Acceptance:
   Revocation... 361

Chapter 10. The Mechanics of a Bargain (II)—Acceptance **387**
Section 1.   Form of Acceptance 387
Section 2.   When an Acceptance Is Effective (The Mailbox Rule) 396
Section 3.   Electronic Commerce.. 399
Section 4.   Silence as Acceptance.. 403
Section 5.   Restitution for a Benefit Conferred in the Mistaken Belief of
   the Existence of a Contract... 417

**Chapter 11. Indefiniteness, Preliminary Negotiations, and the
   Duty to Bargain in Good Faith**..**427**

PART 4. WRITTEN CONTRACTS

Chapter 12. The Parol Evidence Rule **465**
Section 1.   The Rule 465
Section 2.   Uses of Parol Evidence Not Precluded by the Rule.................. 483

Chapter 13. The Interpretation of Written Contracts.................**495**
Section 1.   Textualism v. Contextualism...................................... 495
Section 2.   The Role of Usage, Course of Dealing, and Course of
   Performance 509
Section 3.   The Duty of Good Faith.. 521

Chapter 14. Waiver and No Oral Modification Terms...................**535**
Section 1.   Waiver 536
Section 2.   No-Oral-Modification Terms...................................... 544

Chapter 15. Battle of the Forms.....................................**555**

Chapter 16. Consumer Form Contracts 577
Section 1.   "Shrinkwrap," "Clickwrap," and "Browsewrap" Agreements 580
Section 2.   UCC Rules Protecting Form-Takers 596
Section 3.   The Reasonable Expectations Doctrine.................................... 606
Section 4.   Company Policy Documents as Contracts 619

PART 5. MISTAKE AND UNEXPECTED CIRCUMSTANCES

Chapter 17. Mistake 637
Section 1.   Mechanical Errors ("Unilateral Mistakes") 637
Section 2.   Mistakes in Transcription; Reformation................................. 650
Section 3.   Mutual Mistakes (Shared Mistaken Assumptions)................... 654
Section 4.   Nondisclosure... 671

Chapter 18. The Effect of Unexpected Circumstances...................... 679

PART 6. CONDITIONS

Chapter 19. Constructive Conditions 705
Section 1.   Common Law Doctrines 706
Section 2.   Contracts for the Sale of Goods 726

Chapter 20. Express Conditions 739
Section 1.   Introduction 739
Section 2.   The Distinctions Between the Operation of a Promise and
             the Operation of a Condition 740
Section 3.   Problems of Interpretation in Distinguishing Between
             Conditions and Promises 748
Section 4.   Prevention; the Implication of a Duty to Fulfill a Condition..... 752
Section 5.   Conditions of Satisfaction 757
Section 6.   Excuse 765

Appendix. The Statute of Frauds 775
Section 1.   Introduction 776
Section 2.   The Text of the Original Statute 776
Section 3.   The Purpose of the Statute 778
Section 4.   How It Was Decided What Kinds of Contracts Should Be
             Required to Be in Writing.. 780
Section 5.   American Variations on the English Theme............................. 782
Section 6.   Judicial Interpretations of the Various Subsections of the
             Statute of Frauds—Introduction.. 783
Section 7.   Contracts for the Sale of an Interest in Land (Section 4(4))...... 783
Section 8.   Contracts for the Sale of Goods 785
Section 9.   Some Other Formal Requirements in the Uniform
             Commercial Code... 790
Section 10. Agreements Not to Be Performed Within One Year from the
             Making Thereof (Section 4(5)) 791
Section 11. The Suretyship Section (Section 4(2))—Generally................... 795

Section 12. The Suretyship Section Continued—"The Main Purpose Rule" 796

Section 13. The Suretyship Section Continued—Miscellaneous Problems 798

Section 14. Promises Made by Executors and Administrators (Section 4(1)) 799

Section 15. Contracts upon Consideration of Marriage (Section 4(3)) 800

Section 16. What Kind of Writing Will Satisfy the Statute 801

Section 17. Electronic Contracting and the Statute of Frauds 807

Section 18. Claims Available for Breach of an Oral Contract Within the Statute—Introduction 810

Section 19. Restitution 810

Section 20. Part Performance 812

Section 21. Promissory Estoppel 815

Section 22. The Effect of Non-Compliance—Legal Consequences of the Unenforceable Agreement 818

Section 23. Oral Rescission 821

Section 24. Oral Modifications 821

Section 25. The Interaction of the Statute of Frauds with the Parol Evidence Rule 824

Section 26. The Interaction of the Statute of Frauds with the Remedy of Reformation 825

Section 27. Pleading and Procedural Problems in Connection with the Statute 826

Section 28. A Glance Backward and Ahead 826

INDEX 831

TABLE OF CONTENTS

ACKNOWLEDGMENTS III

TABLE OF CASES XXV

TABLE OF UNIFORM COMMERCIAL CODE CITATIONS XXXIX

TABLE OF CITATIONS TO THE RESTATEMENT OF CONTRACTS XLI

TABLE OF CITATIONS TO THE RESTATEMENTS OF RESTITUTION XLV

Introduction 1
J. Rawls, A Theory of Justice 1
Thomas M. Scanlon, Promises and Practices 2
Gardner, Observations on the Course in Contracts 5

PART 1. WHAT PROMISES SHOULD THE LAW ENFORCE?— THE DOCTRINE OF CONSIDERATION

Chapter 1. Simple Donative Promises and the Elements of Form, Reliance, and Past Benefit Conferred 9
Section 1.   Simple Donative Promises 9
    Dougherty v. Salt 9
    Restatement, Second, Contracts §§ 1, 17, 71, 79 11
    Note on the Restatement of Contracts 11
    Note on the Concept of Consideration 12
    Note on Gifts 13
    Note on Donative Promises 14
Section 2.   The Element of Form 16
    Von Mehren, Civil-Law Analogues to Consideration: An Exercise in Comparative Analysis 16
    Note on the Channeling Function of Contract-Law Rules 17
    Schnell v. Nell 17
    Note on Statutes Applicable in Schnell v. Nell 20
    Note on Nominal Consideration 20
    Note on Form and the History of the Seal 22
Section 3.   The Element of Reliance 25
    Kirksey v. Kirksey 25
    Introductory Note on Promissory Estoppel 26
    Restatement, Second, Contracts § 90 28
    Feinberg v. Pfeiffer Co. 29
    Hayes v. Plantations Steel Co. 36
    Note on Contract Remedies and Consideration 37
    Goldstick v. ICM Realty 41

Section 4. Promises Based on a Past Benefit Conferred ("Past
    Consideration").. 42
    Restatement, Second, Contracts §§ 82, 83................................. 42
    Bankruptcy Code, 11 U.S.C. § 524 42
    Note on Traditional Exceptions to the Past Consideration Rule 42
    Mills v. Wyman.. 43
    Background Note on Mills v. Wyman 47
    Webb v. McGowin.. 47
    Webb v. McGowin.. 51
    Note on the Law of Unjust Enrichment...................................... 52
    Restatement, Second, Contracts § 86.. 54
    Restatement, Second, Contracts § 86, Illustrations 1, 2, 6, 10, 12, 13 ... 54
    American Law Institute, 42d Annual Proceedings 55
    Note on Past Consideration.. 55

Chapter 2. The Bargain Principle and Its Limits............................... 57
Section 1. The Bargain Principle 57
    Westlake v. Adams, C.P... 57
    Hamer v. Sidway 57
    Note on the Statute of Frauds 59
    Klockner v. Green.. 60
    De Cicco v. Schweizer... 61
    Note on Distinguishing a Conditional Bargain from a
        Conditional Donative Promise... 61
    Carlisle v. T & R Excavating, Inc.. 62
    Pennsy Supply, Inc. v. American Ash Recycling Corp. 64
    Restatement, Second, Contracts §§ 71, 72, 79.......................... 65
    Batsakis v. Demotsis.. 66
    B. Sweet-Escott, Greece—A Political and Economic Survey
        1939–1953 69
Section 2. Duress and the Exploitation of Distress 69
    Restatement, Second, Contracts §§ 175, 176............................. 69
    Totem Marine Tug & Barge, Inc. v. Alyeska Pipeline Service
        Company 69
    Unidroit Principles of International Commercial Contracts Art. 3.9 78
    Note on Unidroit.. 78
    Principles of European Contract Law § 4.108............................ 78
    Note on the Principles of European Contract Law 78
    Andreini v. Hultgren... 79
    Chouinard v. Chouinard 81
    Post v. Jones 83
    Eisenberg, The Bargain Principle and Its Limits 84
Section 3. Unconscionability 86
    Williams v. Walker-Thomas Furniture Co. 86
    Skilton & Helstad, Protection of the Installment Buyer of Goods
        Under the Uniform Commercial Code 91
    Restatement Contracts, Second § 208... 92

UCC § 2–302 92
Uniform Consumer Credit Code §§ 1.301, 5.108 92
Federal Trade Commission Regulations—Door-to-Door Sales 92
Note on the Uniform Commercial Code 92
Note on the Comments to the UCC 94
Pittsley v. Houser 94
Unidroit Principles of International Commercial Contracts Art. 3.10 ... 96
Principles of European Contract Law §§ 4.109, 4.110 96
Commission of the European Communities, Council Directive
    93/13/EEC 96
Maxwell v. Fidelity Financial Services, Inc. 96
Note on Classical and Modern Contract Law 103
Section 4.   The Doctrine of Mutuality and the Illusory-Promise Rule 106
Wood v. Lucy, Lady Duff-Gordon 110
Restatement, Second, Contracts § 77 111
Mattei v. Hopper 112
Harris v. Time, Inc. 113
Helle v. Landmark, Inc. 114
Lindner v. Mid-Continent Petroleum Corp. 114
Office Pavilion S. Florida, Inc. v. Asal Prods., Inc. 114
Section 5.   The Legal-Duty Rule; Modifications 120
Pollock, Principles of Contract 120
Shadwell v. Shadwell 120
Lingenfelder v. Wainwright Brewery Co. 120
Foakes v. Beer 125
Note on How Performance of a Modification Eliminates the Need for
    Consideration 127
Note on the Economic Justification for Restricting People's Power to
    Modify Contracts 128
Restatement, Second, Contracts § 89 129
Angel v. Murray 129
McCallum Highlands, Ltd. v. Washington Capital Dus, Inc. 134
Sugarhouse Finance Co. v. Anderson 136
UCC § 2–209 137
CISG Art. 29 137
Note on the CISG 137

Chapter 3. The Limits of Contract 139
Balfour v. Balfour 139
In re the Marriage of Witten 140
Note on Surrogate-Parenting Legislation 151
42 U.S. Code § 274. Prohibition of Organ Purchases 151
Radin, Market-Inalienability 152

PART 2. REMEDIES FOR BREACH OF CONTRACT

Chapter 4. An Introduction to Contract Damages 157
Restatement, Second, Contracts § 344 157
Hawkins v. McGee 157
Background Note on Hawkins v. McGee 161
Unidroit Principles of International Commercial Contracts Art. 7.4.2 163
Cooter & Eisenberg, Damages for Breach of Contract 163

Chapter 5. The Expectation Measure 169
Section 1.   Breach of a Contract to Provide a Service or Good 169
   (A)   Service Contracts.. 171
         Louise Caroline Nursing Home, Inc. v. Dix Construction Co. 171
         Peevyhouse v. Garland Coal & Mining Co. 173
         Note 181
         Restatement, Second, of Contracts § 348(2) 181
         Note on Possible Additional Facts in Peevyhouse 182
         H.P. Droher & Sons v. Toushin 183
         Eastern Steamship Lines, Inc. v. United States 184
         City School District of the City of Elmira v. McLane
             Construction Co. 185
         Advanced, Inc. v. Wilks 186
         Note on Damages When the Plaintiff Completes Work or
             Repairs a Defect 186
   (B)   Sales of Goods 187
         Note on Damages for the Seller's Breach of a Contract for the
             Sale of Goods 187
         UCC §§ 2–711(1), 2–712, 2–713, 2–714, 2–715(1), 2–723,
             2–724 187
         CISG Arts. 45, 49, 50, 74, 75, 76 187
         Continental Sand & Gravel, Inc. v. K & K Sand & Gravel, Inc. ... 187
         Manouchehri v. Heim 188
         Egerer v. CSR West, LLC 189
         J. White & R. Summers, Uniform Commercial Code 192
Section 2.   Breach of a Contract to Pay Money for a Service or Good 193
   (A)   Service Contracts.. 193
         Kearsarge Computer, Inc. v. Acme Staple Company, Inc. 193
         Restatement, Second, Contracts.................................. 197
         Wired Music, Inc. v. Clark 197
   (B)   Sales of Goods 198
         UCC §§ 2–501(1), 2–703, 2–704(1), 2–706, 2–708, 2–709,
             2–710, 2–723, 2–724 198
         CISG Arts. 61, 62, 64, 74, 75, 76 198
         Note on Seller's Damages Under the UCC 198
         Neri v. Retail Marine Corp. 199
         Lazenby Garages Ltd. v. Wright 203

Section 3. Mitigation.. 204
    Shirley MacLaine Parker v. Twentieth Century-Fox Film Corp. 204
    Restatement, Second, Contracts § 350.. 210
    Unidroit Principles of International Commercial Contracts
        Arts. 7.4.7, 7.4.8.. 210
    Principles of European Contract Law Arts. 9.504, 9.505 210
    Mr. Eddie, Inc. v. Ginsberg.. 210
    Southern Keswick, Inc. v. Whetherholt 211
    Note on Damages When the Plaintiff Fails to Mitigate 211
    Bomberger v. McKelvey 212
Section 4. Foreseeability... 216
    Hadley v. Baxendale 216
    Background Note on Hadley v. Baxendale 220
    Emerald Investments Ltd. Partnership v. Allmerican Financial Life
        Ins. and Annuity Co. 220
    Restatement, Second, Contracts § 351.. 221
    UCC §§ 2–713, 2–715(2).. 221
    CISG Art. 74 221
    Unidroit Principles of International Commercial Contracts
        Art. 7.4.4.. 221
    Principles of European Contract Law Art. 9.503 221
    Note on Limitations on Contract Damages 222
    Valentine v. General American Credit, Inc. 222
Section 5. Certainty 224
    Kenford Co. v. Erie County.. 224
    Note on Kenford.. 227
    Note on the New-Business Rule 228
    Rombola v. Cosindas 229
    Contemporary Mission, Inc. v. Famous Music Corp. 229
    UCC § 1–106(1).. 230
    Restatement, Second, Contracts § 352.. 230
    Unidroit Principles of International Commercial Contracts
        Art. 7.4.3.. 230
    Note on Loss of Chance 231
Section 6. Liquidated Damages 234
    NPS, LLC v. Minihane.. 234
    Lee Oldsmobile, Inc. v. Kaiden.. 238
    Norwalk Door Closer Co. v. Eagle Lock and Screw Co. 238
    UCC § 2–718(1).. 240
    Restatement, Second, Contracts § 356.. 240
    Unidroit Principles of International Commercial Contracts Art.
        7.4.13 240
    Principles of European Contract Law Art. 9.509 240
    Note on Liquidated Damages 240
    Note on Alternative-Performance Terms... 245

Chapter 6. Specific Performance **249**
Introductory Note 249
London Bucket Co. v. Stewart 251
Restatement, Second, Contracts §§ 359, 360 253
Unidroit Principles of International Commercial Contracts Arts. 7.2.1,
   7.2.2, 7.2.3 253
Principles of European Contract Law Arts. 9.101, 9.102, 9.103 253
Walgreen Co. v. Sara Creek Property Co. 254
UCC §§ 2–709, 2–716 259
CISG Arts. 46, 62 260
Note on Specific Performance of Contracts for the Sale of Goods 260
Note on Specific Performance of Contracts for the Sale of Land and
   Employment Contracts 261

Chapter 7. Alternative Damage Measures **265**
Section 1. Reliance Damages in a Bargain Context 265
   Security Stove & Mfg. Co. v. American Rys. Express Co. 265
   Anglia Television Ltd. v. Reed 269
   Beefy Trail, Inc. v. Beefy King Int'l, Inc. 270
   L. Albert & Son v. Armstrong Rubber Co. 270
Section 2. The Restitution Measure 271
   Osteen v. Johnson 271
   Restatement, Second, Contracts §§ 344, 345, 370, 371 274
   Restatement, Second, Contracts § 370, Illustrations 2, 5 274
   United States v. Algernon Blair, Inc. 275
   Restatement, Third, Restitution and Unjust Enrichment §§ 37, 38 277
   Note on Restitutionary and Reliance Damages 277
   Note on Expectation as a Cap on Reliance and Restitutionary
      Damages 278
Section 3. Disgorgement Damages 279
   United States Naval Institute v. Charter Communications, Inc. 279
   Laurin v. DeCarolis Construction Co. 283
   Restatement, Third, Restitution and Unjust Enrichment § 39 284
   Restatement, Third, Restitution and Unjust Enrichment § 39,
      Comments and Illustrations 284
   Kansas v. Nebraska 288
   Note on the Theory of Efficient Breach 288

PART 3. ASSENT

Chapter 8. An Introduction to Interpretation **297**
Section 1. Subjective and Objective Elements in Contract
   Interpretation 297
   Introductory Note 297
   Lucy v. Zehmer 298
   Restatement, Second, Contracts §§ 12, 16 303

Restatement, Second, Contracts § 16, Illustration 3 and Comments a
and b.. 303
Keller v. Holderman... 304
Raffles v. Wichelhaus... 304
Simpson, Contracts for Cotton to Arrive: The Case of the Two Ships
Peerless.. 306
Note on Mutual Misunderstanding.. 306
Oswald v. Allen... 308
Colfax Envelope Corp. v. Local No. 458–3M...................................... 308
Embry v. Hargadine, McKittrick Dry Goods Co................................. 309
Restatement, Second, Contracts §§ 20, 201....................................... 312
CISG Art. 8.. 312
Unidroit Principles of International Commercial Contracts Arts. 4.1,
4.2, 4.3... 312
Principles of European Contract Law Arts. 5.101, 5.102 313
Morales v. Sun Constructors, Inc. 313
Note on Objective and Subjective Elements in Interpretation 316
Section 2. Problems of Interpreting Purposive Language.......................... 319
Williams, Language and the Law—Part IV 319
Restatement, Second, Contracts § 204.. 321
Unidroit Principles of International Commercial Contracts Art. 4.8 ... 321
Spaulding v. Morse... 321
Beanstalk Group, Inc. v. AM General Corporation............................. 323

**Chapter 9. The Mechanics of a Bargain (I)—Offer and
Revocation.. 331**
Section 1. What Constitutes an Offer.. 331
Restatement, Second, Contracts § 24.. 331
CISG Art. 14(1).. 331
Unidroit Principles of International Commercial Contracts
Art. 2.1.2.. 332
Principles of European Contract Law § 2.201(1)................................. 332
Lonergan v. Scolnick 332
Lefkowitz v. Great Minneapolis Surplus Store 335
Sateriale v. R.J. Reynolds Tobacco Company...................................... 338
Restatement, Second, Contracts § 26.. 347
CISG Article 14(2) 348
Principles of European Contract Law Art. 2.201(2), (3) 348
Note on Offer and Acceptance 348
Section 2. Termination of the Offeree's Power of Acceptance: Lapse,
Rejection, and Counter-Offer... 348
Akers v. J.B. Sedberry, Inc. 348
Restatement, Second, Contracts §§ 38, 41.. 353
CISG Art. 17 353
Unidroit Principles of International Commercial Contracts
Arts. 2.1.5, 2.1.7... 353
Principles of European Contract Law Arts. 2.203, 2.206 353

Note on the Effect of the Rejection of an Offer 353
Ardente v. Horan 354
Rhode Island Dep't of Transportation v. Providence &
    Worcester R.R. 358
Restatement, Second, Contracts § 39 359
Restatement, Second, Contracts § 39, Illustrations 1–3 359
Restatement, Second, Contracts § 59 360
CISG Art. 19 360
Unidroit Principles of International Commercial Contracts
    Art. 2.1.11 360
Principles of European Contract Law Art. 2.208 360
Note on the Mirror-Image Rule 360
Restatement, Second, Contracts § 37 361

Section 3.   Termination of the Offeree's Power of Acceptance:
Revocation 361
Dickinson v. Dodds 361
Restatement, Second, Contracts §§ 42, 43 363
CISG Art. 16 364
Unidroit Principles of International Commercial Contracts
    Art. 2.1.4 364
Principles of European Contract Law Art. 2.202 364
Note on Contract Practice 364
Note on What Constitutes Receipt of a Written Acceptance 364
Restatement, Second, Contracts § 87(1) 365
1464-Eight, Ltd. & Millis Management Corp. v. Joppich 365
UCC § 2–205 370
Dodge, Teaching the CISG in Contracts 371
Restatement, Second, Contracts § 45 371
Ragosta v. Wilder 372
Note on Offers for Unilateral Contracts 376
Drennan v. Star Paving Co. 378
Restatement, Second, Contracts § 87(2) 383
Note on Restatement Second § 87(2) 383
Pavel Enterprises, Inc. v. A.S. Johnson Co. 384
Preload Technology, Inc. v. A.B. & J. Construction Co., Inc. 385
Allen M. Campbell Co. v. Virginia Metal Industries, Inc. 385

Chapter 10. The Mechanics of a Bargain (II)—Acceptance 387
Introductory Note 387
Section 1.   Form of Acceptance 387
Keller v. Bones 387
Restatement, Second, Contracts §§ 30, 56, 60 393
UCC § 2–206 393
Note on Acceptance by Promise or Performance 394
Bishop v. Eaton 394
Note on Requirement to Communicate Acceptance 395
Restatement, Second, Contracts § 56, Illustration 2 396

Section 2. When an Acceptance Is Effective (The Mailbox Rule) 396
    Restatement, Second, Contracts §§ 30, 49, 60, 63–68........................... 397
    UCC § 2–206(1)... 398
    CISG Arts. 15, 16, 18(2), 20, 22, 23, 24 398
    Unidroit Principles of International Commercial Contracts
        Arts. 2.1.3, 2.1.6(2), 2.1.7, 2.1.8, 2.1.10 398
    Principles of European Contract Law Arts. 2.205(1), 2.206 398
    Dodge, Teaching the CISG in Contracts.. 398
Section 3. Electronic Commerce.. 399
    Note on the Concept of "Record"... 399
    Note on Electronic Signature 399
    J.B.B. Investment Partners, Ltd. v. Fair 400
Section 4. Silence as Acceptance... 403
    McGurn v. Bell Microproducts, Inc. 404
    Restatement, Second, Contracts § 69... 413
    CISG Art. 18(1), (3) 413
    Unidroit Principles of International Commercial Contracts Art.
        2.1.6(3)... 413
    Principles of European Contract Law Art. 2.204(2)............................ 414
    Kukuska v. Home Mut. Hail-Tornado Ins. Co.................................. 414
    Hobbs v. Massasoit Whip Co. 415
    Austin v. Burge... 415
    39 U.S.C. § 3009 [Mailing of Unordered Merchandise] 416
    Note on Negative-Option Plans.. 416
    Note on the Significance of Unjust Enrichment and Loss Through
        Reliance in Cases Where Silence Is Treated as Acceptance.......... 417
Section 5. Restitution for a Benefit Conferred in the Mistaken Belief of
        the Existence of a Contract... 417
    Nursing Care Services, Inc. v. Dobos 417
    Note on Terminology and History... 420
    Note on the Two Types of Restitution Claims in the Principal Case.... 423

**Chapter 11. Indefiniteness, Preliminary Negotiations, and the
    Duty to Bargain in Good Faith.. 427**
Academy Chicago Publishers v. Cheever... 428
Peter Kurth, Book Review of Anita Miller, Uncollecting Cheever, the
    Family of John Cheever v. Academy Chicago Publisher 432
Ridgway v. Wharton.. 432
Rego v. Decker 433
Saliba-Kringlen Corp. v. Allen Engineering Co. 434
Restatement, Second, Contracts §§ 33, 34.. 435
UCC §§ 2–204, 2–305, 2–308, 2–309, 2–310.. 435
CISG Arts. 14(1), 31, 33, 55, 57, 58.. 435
Unidroit Principles of International Commercial Contracts
    Arts. 2.1.2, 2.1.13, 2.1.14, 5.1.7, 5.1.8, 6.1.1, 6.6.6 435
Principles of European Contract Law §§ 2.201(1), 6.104, 6.109, 7.01,
    7.102 435

Note on Gap-Fillers.. 435
Hawkland, Sales Contract Terms Under the UCC.................................... 436
Sateriale v. R.J. Reynolds Tobacco Company.. 436
Arbitron, Inc. v. Tralyn Broadcasting, Inc. 438
Channel Home Centers v. Grossman... 441
Unidroit Principles of International Commercial Contracts Art. 2.1.15...... 444
Principles of European Contract Law Art. 2.301 444
Teachers Insurance and Annuity Association of America v. Tribune Co..... 444
Venture Associates Corp. v. Zenith Data Systems Corp. 447
Note on the Availability of a Promissory Estoppel Claim or a Restitution
    Claim When a Contract Is Indefinite.. 447
Garwood Packaging, Inc. v. Allen & Company, Inc. 448
Hoffman v. Red Owl Stores, Inc. 454
Classic Cheesecake Company, Inc. v. JP Morgan Chase Bank, N.A............ 456

PART 4. WRITTEN CONTRACTS

Chapter 12. The Parol Evidence Rule 465
Section 1.   The Rule... 465
    Mitchill v. Lath 465
    Von Mehren, Civil Law Analogues to Consideration: An Exercise in
        Comparative Analysis 471
    James Bradley Thayer, A Preliminary Treatise on Evidence 471
    Calamari & Perillo, A Plea for a Uniform Parol Evidence Rule and
        Principles of Interpretation 472
    Restatement, Second, Contracts §§ 209, 210, 213, 214, 215, 216 474
    Braucher, Interpretation and Legal Effect in the Second
        Restatement of Contracts 474
    Interform Co. v. Mitchell Constr. Co... 475
    CISG Art. 8(3)... 475
    Dodge, Teaching the CISG in Contracts.. 476
    Unidroit Principles of International Law Art. 4.3 476
    Masterson v. Sine 476
    UCC § 2–202 481
    Interform v. Mitchell Constr. Co. 482
    Note on Merger Clauses... 482
    Unidroit Principles of International Commercial Contracts Art.
        2.1.17... 483
Section 2.   Uses of Parol Evidence Not Precluded by the Rule.............. 483
    Snyder v. Lovercheck 483
    Restatement, Second, Contracts § 214... 489
    Note on Exceptions to the Parol Evidence Rule 489
    Sisneros v. Citadel Broadcasting Co. 490

Chapter 13. The Interpretation of Written Contracts...................... 495
Section 1.   Textualism v. Contextualism.. 495
    Introductory Note.. 495

Holmes, The Theory of Legal Interpretation.. 495
Williston on Contracts 496
Restatement, First, Contracts § 231 496
Corbin on Contracts 496
Restatement, Second, Contracts § 212.. 496
Steuart v. McChesney... 497
Pacific Gas & Electric Co. v. G.W. Thomas Drayage & Rigging Co...... 503
Note on the New Literalism 507
Note—Is the Interpretation of Written Contracts a Question for the
    Judge or for the Jury? 508
Section 2.   The Role of Usage, Course of Dealing, and Course of
Performance in Interpretation 509
Foxco Industries, Ltd. v. Fabric World, Inc. 509
Restatement, Second, Contracts § 221, Illustration 2 513
Restatement, Second, Contracts § 222.. 513
Restatement, Second, Contracts § 222, Illustrations 1–3....................... 513
Hurst v. W.J. Lake & Co.. 514
Restatement, Second, Contracts § 220.. 515
UCC §§ 1–201(3), (12), 1–303, 2–208 515
Restatement, Second, Contracts §§ 219–223.. 515
CISG Art. 9 515
Unidroit Principles of International Commercial Contracts Art. 1.9 ... 515
Principles of European Contract Law Art. 1.105 516
Dennis Patterson, Good Faith, Lender Liability, and Discretionary
    Acceleration: Of Llewellyn, Wittgenstein, and the Uniform
    Commercial Code... 516
Nanakuli Paving and Rock Co. v. Shell Oil Co. 517
C-Thru Container Corp. v. Midland Mfg. Co.. 520
Section 3.   The Duty of Good Faith... 521
Market Street Associates v. Frey 521
Restatement, Second, Contracts § 205.. 528
Pre-2001 UCC Article 1, §§ 1–201(19), 1–203, UCC § 2–103(1)(b) 528
2001 Version of Article 1, § 1–201(20) 528
Note on the UCC Definitions of Good Faith 529
CISG Art. 7(1)... 529
Unidroit Principles of International Commercial Contracts Art. 1.7 ... 529
Principles of European Contract Law Art. 1.201 529
Seggebruch v. Stosor 530
Note on Criticism of the Doctrine.. 532

Chapter 14. Waiver and No Oral Modification Terms......................... 535
Section 1.   Waiver 536
Clark v. West 536
Restatement, Second, Contracts § 84.. 541
Restatement, Second, Contracts § 84, Illustrations 3, 4, 6.................... 541
Westinghouse Credit Corp. v. Shelton.. 542
Nassau Trust Co. v. Montrose Concrete Products Corp. 544

UCC §§ 1–306, 2–209(5).. 544
Section 2.   No-Oral-Modification Terms.................................... 544
   Wisconsin Knife Works v. National Metal Crafters.............. 544
   BMC Industries, Inc. v. Barth Industries, Inc. 553
   UCC § 2–209(1), (2), (4), (5) 554
   Unidroit Principles of International Commercial Contracts Art.
      2.1.18 554
   Principles of European Contract Law Art. 2.106 554

Chapter 15. Battle of the Forms... **555**
Note on the Battle of the Forms.. 557
UCC §§ 2–204(1), 2–204, 2–207 558
ABA Task Force Report on Article 2... 558
Note on What Constitutes an Acceptance Under UCC § 2–207 ... 559
CISG Art. 19.. 560
Unidroit Principles of International Commercial Contracts Arts. 2.1.12,
   2.1.22 560
Principles of European Contract Law Art. 2.209 560
Gardner Zemke Co. v. Dunham Bush, Inc. 560
Note on Gardner Zemke.. 570
Note on the Meaning of "Materially Alter" Under
   UCC § 2–207(2)(b) 570
Note on the "Expressly Made Conditional" Clause................... 572
Note on the Effect of Confirmations with Additional Terms...... 573
Transwestern Pipeline Co. v. Monsanto Co. 574
JOM, Inc. v. Adell Plastics, Inc. 575

Chapter 16. Consumer Form Contracts **577**
Llewellyn, The Common Law Tradition: Deciding Appeals........ 577
Section 1.   "Shrinkwrap," "Clickwrap," and "Browsewrap" Agreements 580
   DeFontes v. Dell, Inc.. 580
   ProCD, Inc. v. Zeidenberg.. 591
   Nguyen v. Barnes & Noble Inc. 592
   Note on Unconscionability and Waiver of Arbitration Clauses in
      Form Contracts... 596
Section 2.   UCC Rules Protecting Form-Takers 596
   UCC §§ 1–201(10), 2–302, 2–314, 2–316, 2–719(2), 2–719(3) 596
   Moscatiello v. Pittsburgh Contractors Equipment Co. 597
   Pierce v. Catalina Yachts, Inc. 605
Section 3.   The Reasonable Expectations Doctrine.................. 606
   Restatement, Second, Contracts § 211................................ 606
   Unidroit Principles of International Commercial Contracts
      Arts. 2.1.19, 2.1.22.. 606
   Principles of European Contract Law Art. 4.110 606
   Darner Motor Sales v. Universal Underwriters.................... 607
   Gordinier v. Aetna Casualty & Surety Co. 619

Section 4. Company Policy Documents as Contracts 619
    Anderson v. Douglas & Lomason Company 619
    Dyer v. Northwest Airlines Corporations 632

PART 5. MISTAKE AND UNEXPECTED CIRCUMSTANCES

Chapter 17. Mistake **637**
Section 1. Mechanical Errors ("Unilateral Mistakes") 637
    DePrince v. Starboard Cruise Services, Inc. 638
    In re UAL Corporation 648
    Restatement, Second, Contracts §§ 153, 154 649
    Note on Unilateral Mistake 649
Section 2. Mistakes in Transcription; Reformation 650
    Travelers Ins. Co. v. Bailey 650
    Restatement, Second, of Contracts § 155 653
    Chimart Associates v. Paul 654
Section 3. Mutual Mistakes (Shared Mistaken Assumptions) 654
    Sherwood v. Walker 656
    Nester v. Michigan Land & Iron Co. 662
    Everett v. Estate of Sumstad 663
    Restatement, Second, Contracts §§ 151, 152, 154 664
    Unidroit Principles of International Commercial Contracts Arts. 3.4,
        3.5, 3.18 664
    Principles of European Contract Law Art. 4.103 664
    Lenawee County Board of Health v. Messerly 664
    UCC §§ 2–312, 2–313, 2–314, 2–315 671
Section 4. Nondisclosure 671
    Hill v. Jones 671
    Restatement, Second, Contracts §§ 159, 161 676
    Restatement, Second, Contracts § 161, Illustrations 7, 10, 11 676
    Restatement, Second, Torts § 551, Illustrations 6, 8 677

Chapter 18. The Effect of Unexpected Circumstances **679**
Introductory Note 679
Taylor v. Caldwell 679
Tacit Assumptions—Continued 683
Ocean Tramp Tankers Corp. v. V/O Sovfracht 684
Mineral Park Land Co. v. Howard 685
Transatlantic Financing Corp. v. United States 686
Mishara Constr. Co. v. Transit-Mixed Concrete Corp. 690
UCC §§ 1–103, 2–509, 2–510, 2–613, 2–614, 2–615, 2–616 692
Restatement, Second, Contracts §§ 261–272 692
CISG Arts. 66–69 692
Unidroit Principles of International Commercial Contracts Arts. 6.2.1,
    6.2.2, 6.2.3, 7.1.7 692
Principles of European Contract Law Arts. 4.102, 6.111, 8.108 692
Albre Marble & Tile Co. v. John Bowen Co. 692

Note on the Equitable Apportionment of Losses Following Impossibility ... 695
Krell v. Henry.. 696
Wladis, Common Law and Uncommon Events: The Development of the
       Doctrine of Impossibility of Performance in English Contract Law 700
La Cumbre Golf & Country Club v. Santa Barbara Hotel Co. 701
Chase Precast Corp. v. John J. Paonessa Co. 701

PART 6. CONDITIONS

Chapter 19. Constructive Conditions **705**
Section 1.   Common Law Doctrines 706
    (A)   Substantial Performance 706
         Jacob & Youngs v. Kent 706
         R. Danzig, The Capability Problem in Contract Law 709
         Vincenzi v. Cerro 709
         O.W. Grun Roofing & Constr. Co. v. Cope 710
         Note on Restitution in Favor of a Plaintiff in Default 711
         Vines v. Orchard Hills, Inc. 712
         Restatement, Third, Restitution and Unjust Enrichment § 36..... 713
    (B)   Material Breach 713
         K & G Constr. Co. v. Harris 714
         Bartlett v. Bartlett 719
         Restatement, Second, Contracts §§ 237, 241, 242 720
         CISG Arts. 25, 49 721
         Unidroit Principles of International Commercial Contracts
            Arts. 7.3.1, 7.3.5, 7.3.6 721
         Principles of European Contract Law Arts. 9.301, 9.302,
            9.305, 9.307–309 721
         E. Allan Farnsworth, Contracts 721
         Note on Anticipatory Repudiation 722
         Wholesale Sand & Gravel, Inc. v. Decker 723
         Unique Systems, Inc. v. Zotos International, Inc. 725
         Thermo Electron Corp. v. Schiavone Construction Co. 725
Section 2.   Contracts for the Sale of Goods 726
         UCC §§ 2–508, 2–601, 2–608, 2–612 726
         CISG Arts. 35(1), 37, 45, 46, 48, 49 726
         J. White & R. Summers, Uniform Commercial Code 726
         Note on the Perfect-Tender Rule and the UCC 727
         Ramirez v. Autosport 729
         T.W. Oil, Inc. v. Consolidated Edison Co. 729
         Zabriskie Chevrolet v. Smith 735
         Manassas Autocars v. Couch 735

Chapter 20. Express Conditions **739**
Section 1.   Introduction 739
         Note on the Difference Between Promises and Conditions 739

Section 2.   The Distinctions Between the Operation of a Promise and the
Operation of a Condition.. 740
Oppenheimer & Co. v. Oppenheim, Appel, Dixon & Co. 740
Merritt Hill Vineyards, Inc. v. Windy Heights Vineyard, Inc. 746
Section 3.   Problems of Interpretation in Distinguishing Between
Conditions and Promises 748
Howard v. Federal Crop Insurance Corp. 748
Restatement, Second, Contracts § 227.. 752
Section 4.   Prevention; the Implication of a Duty to Fulfill a Condition..... 752
Johnson v. Coss 752
Section 5.   Conditions of Satisfaction 757
Introductory Note.. 757
McCartney v. Badovinac.. 758
Morin Building Products Co. v. Baystone Construction, Inc................. 758
Mattei v. Hopper 762
Fursmidt v. Hotel Abbey Holding Corp. 763
Restatement, Second, Contracts § 227, Illustrations 5–8..................... 764
Section 6.   Excuse 765
Aetna Casualty and Surety Co. v. Murphy 765
Restatement, Second, Contracts § 229... 771
Restatement, Second, Contracts § 229, Illustrations 1, 2..................... 771
Great American Ins. Co. v. C.G. Tate Construction Co. 772
Restatement, Second, Contracts § 230... 773
Restatement, Second, Contracts § 230, Illustrations 1, 2..................... 773
Restatement, Second, Contracts § 271... 773
Restatement, Second, Contracts § 271, Illustrations 1, 2..................... 773
Royal-Globe Insurance Co. v. Craven 774

Appendix. The Statute of Frauds **775**
Section 1.   Introduction 776
Section 2.   The Text of the Original Statute 776
Section 3.   The Purpose of the Statute 778
Section 4.   How It Was Decided What Kinds of Contracts Should Be
Required to Be in Writing.. 780
Section 5.   American Variations on the English Theme............................. 782
Section 6.   Judicial Interpretations of the Various Subsections of the
Statute of Frauds—Introduction.. 783
Section 7.   Contracts for the Sale of an Interest in Land (Section 4(4))...... 783
Section 8.   Contracts for the Sale of Goods 785
Section 9.   Some Other Formal Requirements in the Uniform
Commercial Code... 790
Section 10. Agreements Not to Be Performed Within One Year from the
Making Thereof (Section 4(5)) 791
Section 11. The Suretyship Section (Section 4(2))—Generally..................... 795
Section 12. The Suretyship Section Continued—"The Main
Purpose Rule" 796

Section 13. The Suretyship Section Continued—Miscellaneous
Problems 798
Section 14. Promises Made by Executors and Administrators
(Section 4(1)) 799
Section 15. Contracts upon Consideration of Marriage (Section 4(3)) 800
Section 16. What Kind of Writing Will Satisfy the Statute 801
Section 17. Electronic Contracting and the Statute of Frauds 807
Section 18. Claims Available for Breach of an Oral Contract Within the
Statute—Introduction 810
Section 19. Restitution 810
Section 20. Part Performance.. 812
Section 21. Promissory Estoppel... 815
Section 22. The Effect of Non-Compliance—Legal Consequences of the
Unenforceable Agreement 818
Section 23. Oral Rescission 821
Section 24. Oral Modifications 821
Section 25. The Interaction of the Statute of Frauds with the Parol
Evidence Rule 824
Section 26. The Interaction of the Statute of Frauds with the Remedy of
Reformation 825
Section 27. Pleading and Procedural Problems in Connection with the
Statute.. 826
Section 28. A Glance Backward and Ahead 826

INDEX... 831

TABLE OF CASES

The principal cases are in bold type.

1464-Eight, Ltd. & Millis Management Corp. v. Joppich, 365
A & H Corporation v. Bridgeport, 770
A & M Land Development Co. v. Miller, 668
A. Kemp Fisheries, Inc. v. Castle & Cook, Inc., 508
A.Z. v. B.Z., 140, 146
Academy Chicago Publishers v. Cheever, 428
Aceros Prefabricados, S.A. v. TradeArbed, Inc., 571, 573
Aceves v. U.S. Bank, N.A., 347
Action Engineering v. Martin Marietta Aluminum, 760
Adams v. Dell Computer Corp., 586
Adams v. Lindsell, 396
Adams v. Nichols, 690
Advanced, Inc. v. Wilks, 186
Aetna Casualty and Surety Co. v. Murphy, 765
Air Prods. & Chems. Inc. v. Fairbanks Morse, Inc., 568
Akers v. J.B. Sedberry, Inc., 348
ALA, Inc. v. CCAIR, Inc., 787
Alaska Airlines v. Stephenson, 816
Alaska Democratic Party v. Rice, 816
Alaska Packers' Ass'n v. Domenico, 131, 548
Albre Marble & Tile Co. v. John Bowen Co., 692
Alder v. Keighley, 218
Alexander v. Russo, 625
Algernon Blair, Inc., United States v., 275
Ali R. Ghahramani, M.D., P.A. v. Pablo A. Guzman, M.D., P.A., 642
Allen M. Campbell Co. v. Virginia Metal Industries, Inc., 385, 818
Allied Canners & Packers, Inc. v. Victor Packing Co., 190
Allied Chemical Corporation v. DeHaven, 135
Alligood v. Procter & Gamble Co., 341
Allington Towers N., Inc. v. Rubin, 117
All-Tech Telecom, Inc. v. Amway Corp., 452
Almadova v. State Farm Mutual Automobile Ins. Co., 611
Altman v. Blewett, 479

Amalgamated Ass'n of Street Electric Ry. & Motor Coach Employees of America v. Danielson, 648
American Airlines, Inc. v. Am. Coupon Exch., Inc., 341
American Home Improvement, Inc. v. MacIver, 101
American Industrial Sales Corp. v. Airscope, Inc., 479
American Soil Processing, Inc. v. Iowa Comprehensive Petroleum Underground Storage Tank Fund Board, 246
American Standard, Inc. v. Schectman, 185
AMPAT/Midwest, Inc. v. Illinois Tool Works Inc., 524, 525
Anderson v. Douglas & Lomason Company, 619
Anderson v. Liberty Lobby, Inc., 410
Anderson v. Onsager, 259
Andis v. Personett, 760
Andreini v. Hultgren, 79
Angel v. Murray, 129
Anglia Television Ltd. v. Reed, 269
Angus v. Scully, 695
Anstead v. Cook, 501
Appleton State Bank v. Lee, 734
Applied Genetics Intern., Inc. v. First Affiliated Securities, Inc., 488
Arbitron, Inc. v. Tralyn Broadcasting, Inc., 438
Architectural Metal Sys., Inc. v. Consolidated Sys., Inc., 627
Ardente v. Horan, 354, 358
Ardizonne v. Archer, 174
Armstrong v. Guy H. James Constr. Co., 356
Arnold Palmer Golf Co. v. Fuqua Industries Inc., 442
Arnold v. National Aniline & Chemical Co., 487
Asmus v. Pac. Bell, 346
AT&T Mobility LLC v. Concepcion, 596
Atkinson v. District Bond Co., 213
Austin Instrument, Inc. v. Loral Corp., 74
Austin v. Burge, 415

Axelson, Inc. v. McEvoy-Willis, a Division of Smith International (North Sea), Ltd., 588
A-Z Servicenter, Inc. v. Segall, 235, 236, 237
Babcock v. Bryant, 395
Baca v. Commissioner of Internal Revenue, 749
Bachman v. Easy Parking of America, 391
Badger State Lumber Co. v. G. W. Jones Lumber Co., 214
Baetjer v. New England Alcohol Co., 691
Baker v. Roberts, 19
Balfour v. Balfour, 139
Ballard v. Chavez, 491
Bank of Naperville v. Catalano, 648
Barber v. Old Republic Life Ins. Co., 611
Barngrover v. Pettigrew, 148
Barreto-Rivera v. Medina-Vargas, 409
Barrie School v. Patch, 237
Bartlett v. Bartlett, 719
Bartus v. Riccardi, 734
Basin Elec. Power Co-op., United States v., 632
Bates v. Southgate, 488
Batsakis v. Demotsis, 66
Batterman v. Pierce, 467
Batty v. Arizona State Dental Bd., 674
Baylies v. Vanden Boom, 486
Bayway Ref. Co. v. Oxygenated Mktg. & Trading A.G., 571
Bazak International Corp. v. Mast Industries, 806
Be In, Inc. v. Google Inc., 593
Beanstalk Group, Inc. v. AM General Corporation, 323
Bearbower v. Merry, 148
Beauty Time, Inc. v. VU Skin Systems, Inc., 327
Beck v. Farmers Ins. Exch., 80
Beefy Trail, Inc. v. Beefy King Int'l, Inc., 270
BellSouth Telecomm., Inc. v. Meeks, 645
Bennett v. Behring Corp., 646
Benson v. Williams, 148
Berthold Types Ltd. v. Adobe Systems Inc., 323
Best v. United States Bank, 245
Biakanja v. Irving, 382
Bigham v. Wabash-Pittsburg Terminal Ry. Co., 175
Bird v. Rozier, 488
Bischoff v. DirecTV, Inc., 585
Bishop v. Busse, 124
Bishop v. Eaton, 394

Blake v. Midland Railway Company, 218
Blanshan v. Russell, 10
Blaylock v. Akin, 134
BMC Industries, Inc. v. Barth Industries, Inc., 553
BMW of N. Am., Inc. v. Krathen, 644
Board of Control v. Burgess, 22
Boese-Hilburn Co. v. Dean Machinery Co., 568
Boeving v. Vandover, 260
Bogardus v. N.Y. Life Ins. Co., 707
Bolling v. Clevepak Corp., 628
Bomberger v. McKelvey, 212
Boomer v. Atlantic Cement Co., 258
Boothe v. Fitzpatrick, 49
Boston Plate & Window Glass Co. v. John Bowen Co., Inc., 691, 694
Boulay v. Impell Corp., 628
Bourque v. FDIC, 411
Brady v. Cassidy, 539
Brady v. Nally, 466
Brakeman v. Potomac Ins. Co., 769
Brauer v. Freccia, 766
Braun v. Northeast Stations & Servs., Inc., 625
Brazen v. Bell Atlantic Corp., 246
Brehaney v. Nordstrom, Inc., 80
Breyer, Estate of, 498
Bridges v. Ingram, 273
Broadway Photoplay Co. v. World Film Corp., 227
Brock v. Rogers and Babler, Inc., 77
Broemmer v. Abortion Serv. of Phoenix, 99
Brooks Building Tax Assessment Case, 503
Brower v. Gateway 2000, 585
Brower v. Gateway 2000, Inc., 585
Brown v. Branch, 449, 457
Brown v. Lamphear, 653
Brown-Marx Assocs. v. Emigrant Sav. Bank, 745
Brunold v. Glasser, 514
Brunzell Const. Co. v. G.J. Weisbrod, Inc., 382
Bruyn v. Russell, 10
Bryant v. Barton, 268
Buchannon v. Billings, 373
Buhl Foundation v. Board of Property Assessment, 503
Bullock v. Harwick, 356
Bump v. Robbins, 412
Burkle v. Superflow Mfg. Co., 793
Burlington Building & Loan Ass'n v. Cummings, 652
Bury v. Action Enterprises, Inc., 392
Busboom v. Smith, 178

Business Incentives Co. v. Sony Corp. of America, 82
Bustamante v. Intuit, Inc., 436
Butler v. Thomson, 531
Butler v. Walker Power, Inc., 621
Butler v. Westinghouse Elec. Corp., 630
C., M. & St. P. Ry. v. McCaull-Dinsmore Co., 268
C.R. Klewin, Inc. v. Flagship Properties, Inc., 792
Cairo, Inc. v. Crossmedia Servs., Inc., 594
Caldwell v. Cline, 624
California Lettuce Growers v. Union Sugar Co., 437, 477
Campbell Soup Co. v. Wentz, 88, 89
Capps v. Georgia Pacific Corporation, 74, 75
Cardamone v. University of Pittsburgh, 442
Carideo v. Dell, Inc., 586
Carlisle v. T & R Excavating, Inc., 62
Carlyle Apartments Joint Venture v. AIG Life Ins. Co., 245
Carnival Cruise Lines, Inc. v. Shute, 591
Carvel Corp. v. Diversified Mgmt. Group, Inc., 440
Causey v. Matson, 82
Cavanaugh v. Conway, 357
Central Trust Co. of New York v. Savannah & W.R. Co., 267
Chamberlain v. Parker, 178
Chambers v. Valley Nat'l Bank, 629
Champaign National Bank v. Landers Seed Co., 431
Channel Home Centers v. Grossman, 441
Chaplin v. Hicks, 231
Chapman v. Fargo, 226
Charbonnages de France v. Smith, 409
Chase Manhattan Bank v. First Marion Bank, 513
Chase Precast Corp. v. John J. Paonessa Co., 701
Chase v. Consolidated Foods Corp., 442
Chastain v. Texas Christian Missionary Society, 68
Chatlos Systems, Inc. v. National Cash Register Corp., 603
Chemetron Corp. v. McLouth Steel Corp., 551
Chesnick v. Saint Mary of Nazareth Hosp., 630
Chimart Associates v. Paul, 654
Chouinard v. Chouinard, 81

Chromo Mountain Ranch P'ship v. Gonzales, 492
Cincinnati Siemens-Lungren Gas Illuminating Co. v. Western Siemens-Lungren Co., 282
City School District of the City of Elmira v. McLane Construction Co., 185
Clabaugh v. Bottcher, 77
Clardy Mfg. Co. v. Marine Midland Business Loans Inc., 453
Clark v. West, 536
Classic Cheesecake Company, Inc. v. JP Morgan Chase Bank, N.A., 456
Cloud Corp. v. Hasbro, Inc., 401
Cobb v. Midwest Recovery Bureau Co., 543
Coca-Cola Co. v. Babyback's Int'l, Inc., 457
Coddington, State v., 674
Coggs v. Bernard, 682
Colfax Envelope Corp. v. Local No. 458–3M, 308
Colorado Management Corp. v. American Founders Life Insurance Co., 273
Columbia Iron Works & Dry-Dock Co. v. Douglas, 729
Columbia Nitrogen Corp. v. Royster Co., 513
Community College v. Community College, Society of the Faculty, 508
ConAgra, Inc. v. Bartlett Partnership, 391
Connelly v. Devoe, 131
Consolidated Foods Corp. v. United States, 327
Consolidation Services, Inc. v. KeyBank National Ass'n, 449
Contemporary Mission, Inc. v. Famous Music Corp., 227, 229
Conti v. Fisher, 355
Continental Sand & Gravel, Inc. v. K & K Sand & Gravel, Inc., 187
Cooper v. Government Employees Ins. Co., 769
Corman v. Musselman, 392
Costco Wholesale Corp. v. World Wide Licensing Corp., 822
Cowenhoven v. Ball, 540
Coyne v. Taber Partners I, 411
Crabtree v. Elizabeth Arden Sales Corp., 803
Cramer v. Grand Rapids Show Case Co., 225, 227
Crawford v. Pioneer Box & Lumber Co., 213, 214
Crisan's Estate, In re, 52

Crossland v. Nelson Auction Service, Inc., 134
Crouch v. Gutmann, 708
C-Thru Container Corp. v. Midland Mfg. Co., 520, 620
Cult Awareness Network, Inc., In re, 327
Cummings Props., LLC v. National Communications Corp., 235
Curry v. Estate of Thompson, 442
Dadourian Export Corp. v. United States, 307
Dairyland Mutual Ins. Co. v. Andersen, 613
Dakin & Co. v. Lee, 708
Daley v. People's Building, 89
Danann Realty Corp. v. Harris, 485
Daniels v. Newtown, 722
Daniels-Hall v. Nat'l Educ. Ass'n, 338
Darner Motor Sales, Inc. v. Universal Underwriters Ins. Co., 607
Daughetee v. Ohio Oil Co., 532
Davis v. Davis, 143
Davis v. New England Cotton Yarn Co., 159
De Cicco v. Schweizer, 61
de la Falaise v. Gaumont-British Picture Corp., 207
De Long v. County of Erie, 225
Dean Witter Reynolds Inc. v. Byrd, 583
DeCicco v. Schweizer, 10
DeFontes v. Dell, Inc., 580
Deitrick v. Sinnott, 627
Delaware & Hudson Canal Co. v. Penn. Coal Co., 531
deNeergaard v. Dillingham, 651
Denton v. Utley, 667, 669
DePrince v. Starboard Cruise Services, Inc., 638
Des Moines, City of v. Civil Serv. Comm'n, 623
Desmond-Dunne Co. v. Friedman-Doscher Co., 708
DF Activities Corp. v. Brown, 788
Di Mare v. Capaldi, 172
Diatom, Inc. v. Pennwalt Corp., 565, 569
Dickinson v. Dodds, 361
Digital Equipment Corp. v. Uniq Digital Technologies, Inc., 592
Discover Bank v. Superior Court, 596
Dispatch Automation, Inc. v. Richards, 326
Dittemore v. Dickey, 322
Doe v. United States, 344
Donovan v. RRL Corp., 340, 649

Dorton v. Collins & Aikman Corp., 565, 570, 572
Dougherty v. Salt, 9
Dowling v. Whites Lumber & Supply Co., 213
Draper v. Oswego Co. Fire R. Ass'n, 540
Drennan v. Star Paving Co., 378
Drew, United States v., 593
Driggs v. Dwight, 268
Duffy v. Brown, 488
Dunn v. Steubing, 539
Duprey v. Donahoe, 358
Durkin v. Cobleigh, 467
Durtsche v. American Colloid Co., 630
Dyer v. Northwest Airlines Corporations, 632
Earl of Chesterfield v. Janssen, 89
East Crossroads Center, Inc. v. Mellon-Stuart Co., 498
Eastern Bus Lines, Inc. v. Board of Education, 324
Eastern Forge Co. v. Corbin, 707
Eastern Steamship Lines, Inc. v. United States, 184
Easthampton L. & C. Co., Ltd. v. Worthington, 708
Easton v. Washington County Insurance Co., 501
Edelen v. Samuels & Co., 252
Edens v. Goodyear Tire & Rubber Co., 390
Edson v. Poppe, 49
Egerer v. CSR West, LLC, 189
Eighmie v. Taylor, 466, 469
Eldridge v. Evangelical Lutheran Good Samaritan Soc'y, 630
Embry v. Hargadine, McKittrick Dry Goods Co., 309, 627
Emerald Investments Ltd. Partnership v. Allmerican Financial Life Ins. and Annuity Co., 220, 222
Empire Gas Corp. v. American Bakeries Co., 526
English v. Fischer, 533
Equilease Corp. v. Hentz, 648
Equitable Trust Co. v. Western Pac. Ry., 722
Ernst v. Mechanics' & Metals Nat'l Bank, 627
Ersa Grae Corp. v. Fluor Corp., 436
Erskine v. Adeane, 467
Everett v. Estate of Sumstad, 663
Express Indus. & Terminal Corp., In re, 440
F.A. Bartlett Tree Expert Co. v. Hartney, 172
F.H. McGraw & Co. v. Sherman Plastering Co., 719

Fair v. General Finance Corp., 543
Fairbanks, Morse & Co. v.
    Consolidated Fisheries Co., 93
Falbe v. Dell, Inc., 586
Falczynski v. Amoco Oil Co., 628
Farash v. Sykes Datatronics, Inc., 811
Farhat v. Rassey, 669
Fauci v. Denehy, 691
Favorite v. Miller, 770
Federal Insurance Co. v. P.A.T.
    Homes, Inc., 611
Feinberg v. Pfeiffer Co., 29
Felte v. White, 498, 499
Fera v. Village Plaza, 228
Ferro v. Society of St. Pius X, 27
Ficara v. Belleau, 172
Filley v. Pope, 729
Fine Art Pictures Corp. v. Karzin, 214
Fink v. Cox, 10
Fire Ins. Ass'n. v. Wickham, 10
First National Bank of Cincinnati v.
    Pepper, 74
First National Bank of Logansport v.
    Logan Mfg. Co., 449
First National Exchange Bank of
    Roanoke v. Roanoke Oil Co., 302
First Options of Chicago, Inc. v.
    Kaplan, 583
Fisher v. Poole, 375
Flakus v. Schug, 486
*Florida Cranes, Inc. v. Florida East
    Coast Properties*, 646
Florida Ins. Guar. Ass'n v. Love, 644
FMC Finance Corp. v. Murphree, 603
Foakes v. Beer, 125
Fogel Refrigerator Co. v. Oteri, 500
Fogel v. Trustees of Iowa College, 622
Foltz v. First Trust & Sav. Bank, 23
Fontaine v. Industrial National Bank
    of Rhode Island, 543
Ford Motor Credit Co. v. Waters, 543
Fowler v. Mumford, 74
**Foxco Industries, Ltd. v. Fabric
    World, Inc., 509**
Frandsen v. Gerstner, 390
Frank's Maintenance & Eng'g, Inc. v.
    C.A. Roberts Co., 101
Fratello v. Socorro Electric
    Cooperative, Inc., 564
Freedman v. Chemical Construction
    Corporation, 792, 793
French v. Foods, Inc., 623
Frigaliment Importing Co. v. B.N.S.
    Intern. Sales Corp., 306
Frost v. Alward, 804
Fruhauf Southwest Garment Co. v.
    United States, 73
Fteja v. Facebook, Inc., 593

Fursmidt v. Hotel Abbey Holding
    Corp., 763
Gadsden Times v. Doe, 625
Gainesville Health Care Ctr., Inc. v.
    Weston, 646
Gallagher Switchboard Corp. v.
    Heckler Electric Co., 75
**Gardner Zemke Co. v. Dunham
    Bush, Inc., 560**
**Garwood Packaging, Inc. v. Allen
    & Company, Inc., 448**
Gasque v. Mooers Motor Car Co., 736
Gateway Co. v. Charlotte Theatres,
    Inc., 407
Gaybis v. Palm, 718
Gemini Investors III, L.P. v. Nunez,
    643
General Electric Capital Corp. v.
    Central Bank, 648
Gerber v. First National Bank of
    Lincolnwood, 74
Germantown Manufacturing Co. v.
    Rawlinson, 602
Gerson Electric Construction Co. v.
    Honeywell, Inc., 41
Gibson v. Cranage, 760
Gibson v. Neighborhood Health
    Clinics, Inc., 450
Gifford v. Commissioner of Public
    Health, 693
Gildea v. Kapenis, 627
Gillis v. Wells Fargo Bank, 401
Gillman v. Chase Manhattan Bank,
    101, 595
Ginsberg v. Northwest, Inc., 341
Glackin v. Bennett, 465
Glass Service Co. v. State Farm
    Mutual Auto. Ins. Co., 348
Glover v. Jewish War Veterans, 625
Godfrey v. Navratil, 676
Godfrey, Bassett & Kuykendall
    Architects, Ltd. v. Huntington
    Lumber & Supply Co., 492
Goebel v. Linn, 124
Gold Kist, Inc. v. Pillow, 552
Goldman v. McShain, 441
Goldstick v. ICM Realty, 41, 256, 451
Gonzales v. Internat. Assn. of
    Machinists, 207
Gordinier v. Aetna Casualty & Surety
    Co., 619
Graham v. Scissor-Tail, Inc., 99
Great American Ins. Co. v. C.G. Tate
    Construction Co., 769, 772
Great Lakes Constr. Co. v. Republic
    Creosoting Co., 276
Great Western Oil & Gas Company v.
    Mitchell, 180

Green River Bottling Co. v. Green River Corp., 327

Greenspun v. American Adhesives, Inc., 599

Greer v. Tweed, 88

Grenier v. Compratt Construction Co., 766

Grossman v. Schenker, 531

Groves v. John Wunder Co., 174, 175, 180

Gruen Industries, Inc. v. Biller, 453

Gulf Insurance Co. v. Grisham, 610

Gull Lab., Inc. v. Diagnostic Tech., Inc., 119

H.P. Droher & Sons v. Toushin, 183

Hadley v. Baxendale, 216

Hagarty v. William Akers, Jr. Co., 499

Hailpern v. Dryden, 667

Hale v. Ford Motor Credit Co., 543

Hall v. Wright, 680, 681

Hamer v. Sidway, 57

Hamilton v. First Baptist Elderly Hous. Found., 623

Hanson v. New Technology, Inc., 630

Harbor Ins. Co. v. Continental Bank Corp., 525

Hardesty v. Smith, 19

Hardie-Tynes Mfg. Co. v. Easton Cotton Oil Co., 159

Harleaux v. Wood, 390

Harper v. Cedar Rapids Television Co., 622

Harr v. Allstate Insurance Co., 612

Harris and Harris Const. Co. v. Crain and Denbo, Inc., 750

Harris v. Axline, 668, 669

Harris v. Clark, 10

Harris v. Nat. Union etc. Cooks, 207

Harris v. Time, Inc., 113, 341

Harrod v. Wineman, 622

Hartsville Oil Mill v. United States, 74

Hathaway v. Hudson, 669, 670

Hawkeye Land Co. v. Iowa Power & Light Co., 624

Hawkins Construction Co. v. Reiman Corp., 450

Hawkins v. McGee, 157

Hayes v. Plantations Steel Co., 36

Heacock v. Heacock, 148

Hearn v. Stevens & Bro., 111

Hecht Co. v. Bowles, 255

Hein v. Kerr-McGee Coal Corp., 629

Helle v. Landmark, Inc., 114

Henderson v. Hartford Accident & Indemnity Co., 750

Henningsen v. Bloomfield Motors, Inc., 88, 89, 90

Henry v. Thomas, 667

Hewett Grain & Provision Co. v. Spear, 803

Hicks v. Methodist Medical Ctr., 630

Hill v. Gateway 2000, Inc., 585, 586, 587, 596

Hill v. Jones, 671

Hillbrook Apartments, Inc. v. Nyce Crete Co., 442

Hines v. Overstock.com, Inc., 593

Hirsch Rolling Mill Co. v. Milwaukee & Fox River Valley Ry., 551

Hi-Valley Constructors, Inc. v. Heyser, 187

Hobbs v. Massasoit Whip Co., 415

Hoboken v. Bailey, 61

Hochster v. De La Tour, 722

Hoffman v. Porter, 51

Hoffman v. Red Owl Stores, Inc., 454

Hoffnagle v. McDonald's Corp., 621

Holmes v. Doan, 122

Holmes v. Roper, 10

Home Elec. Co. v. Underdown Heating & Air Conditioning Co., 385

Home Finance Co. v. Frazier, 543

Horning Co. v. Falconer Glass Industries, Inc., 572

Hoshaw v. Cosgriff, 314

Hotchkiss v. National City Bank of New York, 317, 505, 627

Houlton Citizens' Coalition v. Town of Houlton, 409

Howard Construction Co. v. Jeff-Coles Quarries, 806

Howard v. Federal Crop Insurance Corp., 748

Howsam v. Dean Witter Reynolds, Inc., 583

Hoyt R. Matise Co. v. Zurn, 358

Hudson v. Town & Country True Value Hardware, Inc., 95

Hughes v. Cornhusker Cas. Co., 390

Hume v. United States, 88, 89

Hunt v. I.B.M. Mid America Employees Fed. Credit Union, 628

Hunter v. Board of Trustees, 621

Hurd v. Dunsmore, 159

Hurst v. Lake & Co., Inc., 499

Hurst v. W.J. Lake & Co., 514

Hussey v. Robison, 31

Hutchison v. Tompkins, 245

Hyde v. The Dean of Windsor, 681

Idaho Power Co. v. Westinghouse Elec. Corp., 563

Indiana Tri-City Plaza Bowl, Inc. v. Estate of Glueck, 759, 760

Indianapolis Morris Plan Corporation v. Sparks, 88

Inman v. Clyde Hall Drilling Company, 76

Insurance Co. v. Norton, 540
Interform Co. v. Mitchell, 475, 482
Investors Premium Corp. v.
    Burroughs Corp., 630
Iowa Malleable Iron Co. v. Iowa
    Employment Sec. Comm'n, 624
Irons v. Rhode Island Ethics
    Commission, 591
Isaak v. Massachusetts Indemnity
    Life Ins. Co., 613
Ismert & Assocs., Inc. v. New England
    Mut. Life Ins. Co., 411, 412
Itek Corp. v. Chicago Aerial
    Industries, Inc., 442
J.B. v. M.B., 145
J.B.B. Investment Partners, Ltd. v.
    Fair, 400
J.C. Wyckoff & Associates, Inc. v.
    Standard Fire Ins. Co., 454
Jacob & Youngs v. Kent, 176, 185,
    706, 746, 768
James Baird Co. v. Gimbel Bros., 381
James T. Taylor & Son, Inc. v.
    Arlington Independent School
    District, 649
Jamison Coal & Coke Co. v. Goltra,
    260
Jamison's Estate, In re, 34
Janke Construction Co. v. Vulcan
    Materials Co., 450
Jason's Foods, Inc. v. Peter Eckrich &
    Sons, Inc., 551
Jaybe Constr. Co. v. Beco, Inc., 357
Jimenez v. Colorado Interstate Gas
    Co., 630
Joc Oil USA v. Consolidated Edison
    Co. of N.Y., 731
John Hancock Mutual Life Insurance
    Co. v. Dietlin, 357, 358
Johnson Controls, Inc. v. Bowes, 767,
    769
Johnson Enterprises of Jacksonville,
    Inc. v. FPL Group, Inc., 118
Johnson v. Capital City Ford Co., 337
Johnson v. Coss, 752
Johnson v. Davis, 675
Johnson v. McDonnell Douglas Corp.,
    628
Johnson v. Metcalfe, 718
Johnson v. Mobil Oil Corp., 100
Johnson v. Morton Thiokol, Inc., 629
Joiner v. Elrod, 390
JOM, Inc. v. Adell Plastics, Inc., 575
Jones v. Palace Realty Co., 750
Joseph Martin, Jr., Delicatessen, Inc.
    v. Schumacher, 439
Justice v. Lang, 531
K & C, Inc. v. Westinghouse Electric
    Corp., 603

K & G Constr. Co. v. Harris, 714
Kakalik v. Bernardo, 767
Kansas v. Nebraska, 288
Kass v. Kass, 143
Katz v. Pratt Street Realty Co., 357
Kazanjian v. New England Petroleum
    Corp., 441
Kearns v. Andree, 448
**Kearsarge Computer, Inc. v. Acme
    Staple Company, Inc., 193**
Keller v. Bones, 387, 389, 391, 392
Keller v. Holderman, 304
Kelly v. Marx, 236, 237, 245
Kendall v. Selvaggio, 235
Kendel v. Pontious, 390
Kenford Co. v. County of Erie, 224,
    225
Kennedy v. Panama, etc., Mail Co.,
    659
Keystone Engineering Corp. v. Sutter,
    719
Kham & Nate's Shoes No. 2, Inc. v.
    First Bank, 523, 525
Kidder v. Greenman, 408
Kiernan v. Dutchess Co. Mut.
    Insurance Co., 540
King Motors, Inc. v. Delfino, 239
Kinoshita v. Canadian P. Airlines,
    Ltd., 626
Kirkpatrick v. Temme, 186
Kirksey v. Kirksey, 25
Kitchin v. Mori, 713
Klocek v. Gateway, Inc., 584, 587
Klockner v. Green, 60
K-Mart Corp. v. Oriental Plaza, Inc.,
    255
Knarston v. Manhattan Life Ins. Co.,
    541
Knittel v. Security State Bank, 543
Koehring Co. v. Glowacki, 559
Koenen v. Royal Buick Co., 806
Kohl v. Bay Colony Club Condo., Inc.,
    646
Kramer v. Kramer, 10
Krell v. Codman, 450
Krell v. Henry, 696
Kristerin Dev. Co. v. Granson Inv.,
    626
Kristian v. Comcast Corp., 583
Kukuska v. Home Mut. Hail-Tornado
    Ins. Co., 414
Kumpf v. United Tel. Co., 630
L. Albert & Son v. Armstrong Rubber
    Co., 270
La Cumbre Golf & Country Club v.
    Santa Barbara Hotel Co., 701
La Salle Extension University v.
    Ogburn, 214
Laclede Gas Co. v. Amoco Oil Co., 260

Ladas v. Cal. State Auto. Ass'n, 437
LaFazia v. Howe, 486
LaFontaine v. Developers & Builders, Inc., 627
Laidlaw v. Organ, 523
Lamle v. Mattel, Inc., 401
Larson v. Johnson, 525
Lattimore v. Harsen, 122
Laurin v. DeCarolis Construction Co., 283
Lazenby Garages Ltd. v. Wright, 203
Lechuga v. Flanigan's Enters., Inc., 642
Lee Oldsmobile, Inc. v. Kaiden, 238
Lee v. Wood Products Credit Union, 543
Leeper v. Beltrami, 74
Lefkowitz v. Great Minneapolis Surplus Store, 335
Leigh v. Loyd, 674
Lemm v. Stillwater Land & Cattle Co., 506
Lemoge Electric v. San Mateo County, 382
Lenawee County Board of Health v. Messerly, 664, 666
Lenobel, Inc. v. Senif, 199
Leonard Pevar Co. v. Evans Prods. Co., 563
Leonard v. Pepsico, Inc., 341
Lerned v. Wannemacher, 804
LeRoy Dyal Co. v. Allen, 729
Lewis v. Fletcher, 370
Lewis v. Protective Security Life Ins. Co., 207
Lexington Prods. Ltd. v. B.D. Communications, 227
Licitra v. Gateway, Inc., 587
Lige Dickson Co. v. Union Oil Co., 818
Lindner v. Mid-Continent Petroleum Corp., 114
Linear Corp. v. Standard Hardware Co., 552
Lingenfelder v. Wainwright Brewing Co., 120, 131
Lingsch v. Savage, 675
Linnet v. Hitchcock, 442
Linz v. Schuck, 131
Litowitz, In re, 143
Locks v. Wade, 196
Lockwood v. Smigel, 789
Loeb & Co. v. Martin, 513
Lombardo v. Gasparini Excavating Co., 441, 442
London Bucket Co. v. Stewart, 251
Lonergan v. Scolnick, 332
Long v. Dell Inc., 580
Long v. Straus, 531

Lonnie Hayes & Sons Staves, Inc. v. Bourbon Cooperage Co., 806
Louise Caroline Nursing Home, Inc. v. Dix Construction Co., 171
Louisville Title Insurance Co. v. Surety Title & Guaranty Co., 74
Lowinson v. Newman, 732
Lucy v. Zehmer, 298, 303
Luing v. Peterson, 88
Luke v. Smith, 676
Lynn v. Taylor, 675
M. Ahern Co. v. John Bowen Co. Inc., 694
M.A. Mortenson Co. v. Timberline Software Corp., 585, 588
M.F. Kemper Const. Co. v. City of L.A., 382, 649
M.K. Metals v. Container Recovery Corp., 743
Mace v. Charleston Area Medical Ctr. Found., Inc., 629
Madison Tool & Die, Inc. v. ZF Sachs Automotive of America, Inc., 458
Major Mat Co. v. Monsanto Co., 450
Manassas Autocars v. Couch, 735
Mandel v. Liebman, 90
Manganaro Drywall, Inc. v. Penn-Simon Constr. Co., 235
Mangini v. Wolfschmidt, Ltd., 479
Mann v. Clowser, 176
Manouchehri v. Heim, 188
Market Street Associates v. Frey, 521
Marks v. Cowdin, 803, 804
Marks v. Gates, 101
Marr Enterprises, Inc. v. Lewis Refrigeration Co., 603
Marsh v. Blackman, 214
Marshall v. Broadhurst, 681
Martell Bros., Inc. v. Donbury, Inc., 724, 725
Martens v. Minnesota Mining and Manu. Co., 632
Martin v. Capital Cities Media, Inc., 628
Martin v. Phillips, 187
Mason & Dixon Lines, Inc. v. Glover, 454
Massman Const. Co. v. City Council of Greenville, 240
Masterson v. Sine, 476
Mattei v. Hopper, 112
Maxey v. Quintana, 493
Maxon Corp. v. Tyler Pipe Industries, Inc., 572
Maxton Bldrs. v. Lo Galbo, 746
Maxwell v. Fidelity Financial Services, Inc., 96
Mays v. Trump Indiana, Inc., 451

McBride v. City of Sioux City, 623
McCall Co. v. Wright, 110
McCallum Highlands, Ltd. v. Washington Capital Dus, Inc., 134
McCartney v. Badovinac, 758
McCarty v. Pheasant Run, Inc., 257
McGurn v. Bell Microproducts, Inc., 404
McIllmoil v. Frawley Motor Co., 438
McInerney v. Charter Golf, Inc., 453, 793
McKay v. Coleman, 668
McLaughlin v. Union Leader, 194
Mechanics' & Metals Nat'l Bank v. Ernst, 627
Mecurio v. Therm-O-Disc, Inc., 628
Meinhard v. Salmon, 523
Merritt Hill Vineyards v. Windy Heights Vineyard, 743, **746**
Merritt-Campbell, Inc. v. RxP Products, Inc., 119
Meyers v. Selznick Co., 509
Michaud v. McGregor, 131
Michigan City, City of v. Lake Air Corp., 259
Midland Hotel Corp. v. Reuben H. Donnelley Corp., 430
Miholevich v. Mid-West Mutual Auto Ins. Co., 223
Miller v. Benjamin, 707
Miller v. Miller, 148
Miller v. Robertson, 269
Milliken v. Western Union Tel. Co., 531
Mills v. Wyman, 43
Mineral Park Land Co. v. Howard, 685, 687
Minor v. Lillard, 31
Mirra Co. v. School Administrative District No. 35, 583
Mishara Constr. Co. v. Transit-Mixed Concrete Corp., 690
Mitchill v. Lath, 465
Mitsubishi Goshi Kaisha v. J. Aaron & Co., Inc., 729, 732
Monarco v. Lo Greco, 456, 816
Moore Brothers Co. v. Brown & Root, Inc., 754
Moore Burger, Inc. v. Phillips Petroleum Co., 818
Moore v. Morris, 641
Moore v. Stevens Coal Co., 499, 500
Moorpark, City of v. Moorpark Unified Sch. Dist., 340
Morales v. Sun Constructors, Inc., 313
Moran v. Standard Oil Co., 110
Morey v. Hoffman, 430
Morgan v. Griffith, 467

Morin Building Products Co. v. Baystone Construction, Inc., 525, **758**
Morrow v. Railroad, 268
Moscatiello v. Pittsburgh Contractors Equipment Co., 597
Moss v. Cogle, 357
Moss v. U.S. Secret Serv., 344
Mott v. Cline, 479
Mr. Eddie, Inc. v. Ginsberg, 210
Mueller v. Mineral Spring Co., 110
Mueller v. Union Pacific Railroad, 392
Multicare Medical Center v. State Social & Health Services, 374
Munroe v. Perkins, 122
Murphy v. Lischitz, 282
Murphy v. White Hen Pantry Co., 762
Mutual Life Ins. Co. of Baltimore v. Metzger, 653
Nanakuli Paving and Rock Co. v. Shell Oil Co., 517
Narragansett Improvement Co. v. United States, 276
Nassau Trust Co. v. Montrose Concrete Products Corp., 544
National City Bank v. Hotchkiss, 627
National Housing Indus. Inc. v. E.L. Jones Dev. Co., 674
National Oil & Pipe Line Co. v. Teel, 368
Nationwide Ins. Co. v. Gode, 769
Naumberg v. Young, 467
Neiss v. Ehlers, 450
Nelson v. Hamlin, 357
Neri v. Retail Marine Corp., 199
Nester v. Michigan Land & Iron Co., 662
Nettles v. Techplan Corp., 629
Neumiller Farms Inc. v. Cornett, 728
Nevada National Bank v. Huff, 543
New England Mutual Life Insurance Co. v. Jones, 652
New York Life Insurance Co. v. Kimball, 651
New York Life Insurance Co. v. Kwetkauskas, 314
New York Trust Co. v. Island Oil & Transp. Corp., 627
Newbery v. Wall, 804
Nguyen v. Barnes & Noble Inc., 592
Nielsen v. Adams, 486
Niles v. Hancock, 334
Norcross Brothers Co. v. Vose, 172
Norrington v. Wright, 727
Northern Indiana Public Service Co. v. Carbon County Coal Co., 255, 523
Northwest Fixture Co. v. Kilbourne & Clark Co., 240

Northwestern Engineering Co. v. Ellerman, 381

Norwalk Door Closer Co. v. Eagle Lock & Screw Co., 238, 767, 770

NPS, LLC v. Minihane, 234

Nursing Care Services, Inc. v. Dobos, 417

O.W. Grun Roofing & Constr. Co. v. Cope, 710

O'Malley v. Grady, 465

O'Quin v. Verizon Wireless, 585

Obde v. Schlemeyer, 675

Ocean Tramp Tankers Corp. v. V/O Sovfracht, 684, 688

Office Pavillion S. Florida, Inc. v. Asal Prods., Inc., 114

Okaw Drainage District v. National Distillers & Chemical Corp., 259

Olds v. Mapes-Reeves Const. Co., 196

Ollerman v. O'Rourke Co., 673

Omstead v. Dell, Inc., 586

One Ford Coach, United States v., 749

Oppenheimer & Co. v. Oppenheim, Appel, Dixon & Co., 740

Organ v. Stewart, 540

Osborn v. Phelps, 803

Osteen v. Johnson, 271

Oswald v. Allen, 308

Outlet Embroidery Co. v. Derwent Mills, 325

Pacific Gas & Electric Co. v. G.W. Thomas Drayage & Rigging Co., 503

Palmer v. Women's Christian Ass'n, 629

Panama, City of, 257

Paper Express, Ltd. v. Pfankuch Maschinen, 314

Parke v. Franco-American Trading Co., 539

Parks v. American Casualty Co. of Reading, PA, 610

Patton v. Mid-Continent Systems, Inc., 254

Paulink v. Am. Express Co., 314

Pavel Enterprises, Inc. v. A.S. Johnson Co., 384

Payne v. Lautz Bros., 342

Payne v. Sunnyside Community Hosp., 630

PDC Labs., Inc. v. Hach Co., 595

Pearson v. State Social Welfare Board, 505

Peck v. Requa, 122

Peeler v. United States Casualty Co., 772

Peevyhouse v. Garland Coal & Mining Co., 173

Pelatowski v. Black, 172

Pennsy Supply, Inc. v. American Ash Recycling Corp., 64

Pennsylvania Railroad Co. v. City of Louisville, 252

Perma Research & Devel. Co. v. Singer Co., 227

Peterson v. Browning, 80

Philpot v. Gruninger, 10

Phoenix Hermetic Co. v. Filtrine Mfg. Co., 110

Pierce v. Catalina Yachts, Inc., 605

Pierce v. Leasing International, Inc., 543

Pierce v. Staub, 767

Pimpinello v. Swift & Co., 315

Pioneer Investment Services Co. v. Brunswick Associates Limited Partnership, 648

Pittsley v. Houser, 94

Plasticrete Corporation v. American Policyholders Ins. Co., 766

Polaroid Corp. v. Rollins Envtl. Servs. (NJ), Inc., 407, 412

Pollstar v. Gigmania, Ltd., 594

Porter v. Commissioner of Internal Revenue, 34, 450

Post v. Jones, 83

Powell v. City of Newton, 402

Powell v. Howard, 172

Pratt v. Heartview Foundation, 632

Praxair, Inc. v. Hinshaw & Culbertson, 648

Preload Technology, Inc. v. A.B. & J. Construction Co., Inc., 385

Preston Law Firm, L.L.C. v. Mariner Health Care Mgmt. Co., 401

Pribil v. Ruther, 389, 390

Price v. Price, 375

Priebe & Sons, Inc. v. United States, 239

Printing Center of Texas, Inc. v. Supermind Publishing Co., 728

ProCD, Inc. v. Zeidenberg, 584, 589, 591

Procter & Gamble Distr. Co. v. Lawrence Amer. Field Warehousing Corp., 202, 203

Project Map, Inc. v. United States, 561

Providence Teachers' Union v. Providence School Committee, 583

Providence Washington Ins. Co. v. Beck, 172

Province Sec. Corp. v. Maryland Cas. Co., 172

Quashnock v. Frost, 673

R.J. Daum Const. Co. v. Child, 382

Rachid v. Perez, 642

Raffles v. Wichelhaus, 304

Ragosta v. Wilder, 372

Ralston Purina Co. v. McCollum, 818
Ramirez v. Autosport, 729
Randolph v. Castle, 811
Ranger Insurance Co. v. Phillips, 613
Ravitch v. Stollman Poultry Farms, Inc., 767
Ray v. Montgomery, 675
Raydon Exploration, Inc. v. Ladd, 358
Reaction Molding Technologies, Inc. v. General Elec. Co., 565
Rego v. Decker, 433
Renfroe v. Ladd, 818
Rental Development Corp. v. Lavery, 256
Reprosystem, V.B. v. SCRM Corp., 442, 444
Resource Management Co. v. Weston Ranch & Livestock Co., 101
Reynolds v. Philip Morris U.S.A., Inc., 342
Rhode Island Charities Trust v. Engelhard Corp., 326
Rhode Island Dep't of Transportation v. Providence & Worcester R.R., 358
Richards v. Powercraft Homes, Inc., 673
Richardson Lumber Co. v. Hoey, 667, 669
Richardson v. Davis, 213, 214
Richey v. Patrick, 484
Richter v. Union Land etc. Co., 479
Ricketts v. Scothorn, 27, 35
Ridgway v. Wharton, 432
Rivers v. Beadle, 477
Robert Gordon, Inc. v. Ingersoll-Rand Co., 381, 382
Robison v. Katz, 491
Rodemich v. State Farm Mutual Auto. Insurance Co., 611
Rohde v. Massachusetts Mut. Life Ins. Co., 755
Roland Machinery Co. v. Dresser Industries, Inc., 255
Rombola v. Cosindas, 229
Rose v. Spa Realty Associates, 552
Rosenthal Paper Co. v. Nat. Folding Box & Paper Co., 707
Rosnick v. Dinsmore, 451
Ross Systems v. Linden Dari-Delite, Inc., 74
Roto-Lith, Ltd. v. F.P. Bartlett & Co., 564
Rowe v. Peabody, 691
Royal-Globe Insurance Co. v. Craven, 774
Ruble v. Reich, 391
Rugg v. Minett, 682
Ruiz v. Moss Bros. Auto Group, Inc, 399

Russell v. Allerton, 111
Ryan v. Weiner, 103
S & M Rotogravure Service, Inc. v. Baer, 552
S. M. Wilson and Co. v. Smith International, Inc., 603
Saleemi v. Doctor's Associates, Inc., 596
Saliba-Kringlen Corp. v. Allen Engineering Co., 434
Sanchez v. Life Care Ctrs. of Am., Inc., 630
Sands, Taylor & Wood Co. v. Quaker Oats Co., 327
Sandy Valley & E.R. Co. v. Hughes, 175
Sateriale v. R.J. Reynolds Tobacco Company, 338, 436
Scaduto v. Orlando, 276
Schiffman v. Atlas Mill Supply, Inc., 127
Schlessinger v. Dickinson, 395
Schmidt v. Louisville & N.R. Co., 252
Schnell v. Nell, 17, 88
Scholes v. Lehmann, 450
Schrempp and Salerno v. Gross, 391
Schroeder v. Fageol Motors, Inc., 101
Schultze v. Goodstein, 708
Schwartzreich v. Bauman-Basch, Inc., 122
Schwasnick v. Blandin, 713
Scott v. United States, 88
Seale v. Bates, 273
Security Bank & Trust Co. v. Bogard, 450
Security Stove & Mfg. Co. v. American Rys. Express Co., 265
Seekings v. Jimmy GMC of Tucson, Inc., 100
Seggebruch v. Stosor, 530
Sellers v. Allstate Insurance Company, 610
Selmer Co. v. Blakeslee-Midwest Co., 548
Semelhago v. Paramadevan, 262
Semon, Bache & Co. v. Coppes, Zook & Mutschler Co., 760
Service Employees Int'l Local No. 55 v. Cedar Rapids Community Sch. Dist., 626
Shadwell v. Shadwell, 120
Shapiro Engineering Corp. v. Francis O. Day Co., 718
Shapiro v. Wells Fargo Realty Advisors, 631
Sherr v. Dell Inc., 586
Sherwood v. Walker, 656, 667, 668
Shirazi v. Greyhound Corp., 314

Shirley MacLaine Parker v. Twentieth Century-Fox Film Corp., 204
Shondel v. McDermott, 256
Sides v. Contemporary Homes, Inc., 196
Siegel v. Western Union Telegraph Co., 221
Silva v. Noble, 563
Sisneros v. Citadel Broadcasting Co., 490
Slattery v. Wells Fargo Armored Serv. Corp., 625
Smith v. General Finance Corp., 543
Smith v. Hughes, 311
Smith v. Westall, 791
Smoot v. Boise Cascade Corp., 631
Snyder v. Lovercheck, 483
Solar Motors v. First Nat. Bank of Chadron, 393
Sorenson v. Kennecott-Utah Copper Corp., 621
South Hampton Co. v. Stinnes Corp., 552
Southern Casualty v. Hughes, 613
Southern Cotton-Oil Co. v. Heflin, 213
Southern Idaho Pipe & Steel Co. v. Cal-Cut Pipe & Supply, Inc., 569
Southern Illinois Riverboat Casino Cruises, Inc. v. Triangle Insulation and Sheet Metal Co., 572
Southern Keswick, Inc. v. Whetherholt, 211
Southern Painting Co. v. United States, 276
Southwest Airlines Co. v. BoardFirst, LLC, 593
Soutier v. Kellerman, 515
Spadafora v. Carlo, 643
Spahr v. Hollingshead, 19
Sparks v. Republic Nat. Life Ins. Co., 612, 613, 614
Spaulding v. Morse, 321
Speed v. Bailey, 718
Spence v. Ham, 708
Sperry et al. v. O'Neill-Adams Co., 268
Sprague v. Sumitomo Forestry Co., Ltd., 191
Spring Hill Developers, Inc. v. Arthur, 459
Springer v. Weeks & Leo Co., 623
St. Peter v. Pioneer Theatre Corp., 625
Stacy v. Merchants Bank, 376
Stamato v. Stamato, 644
Stamen v. Metropolitan Life Insurance Co., 652
Standard Jury Instructions-Contract and Bus. Cases, In re, 644
Standard Oil Co. v. O'Hare, 392

Stanley-Bostitch, Inc. v. Regenerative Environmental Equipment Co., 583
State Property & Bldg. Comm'n v. H.W. Miller Constr. Co., 187
Stearns v. Emery-Waterhouse Co., 817, 818
Steinberg v. Chicago Medical School, 431
Steiner v. Mobil Oil Corp., 568
Steiner v. Thexton, 346
Stelmack v. Glen Alden Coal Co., 442
Stenzel v. Dell, Inc., 586
Step-Saver Data Systems, Inc. v. Wyse Technology, 573, 586
Steuart v. McChesney, 497
Stevenson v. Druley, 20
Stoddard v. Ill. Imp. Co., 532
Stone Mountain Properties, Ltd. v. Helmer, 759
Stone v. Blake, 652
Strano v. Carr & Carr, Inc., 419
Strickland v. Henry, 10
Strimiska v. Yates, 766
Strubbe v. Sonnenschein, 648
Stumpf v. Stumpf, 178
Sugarhouse Finance Co. v. Anderson, 136
Sully-Miller Contracting Co. v. Gledson/Cashman Construction, Inc., 340, 402
Sweeney v. Lewis Const. Co., 175
Symon v. J. Rolfe Davis, Inc., 420
T.W. Oil, Inc. v. Consolidated Edison Co., 729
TAL Fin. Corp. v. CSC Consulting, Inc., 235, 236
Taylor v. Caldwell, 679, 697
Taylor v. Thompson, 419
Teachers Insurance and Annuity Association of America v. Tribune Co., 444
Texas Gas Utilities Co. v. Barrett, 114
Textron, Inc. v. Aetna Casulty and Surety Co., 359
The Malcolm Baxter, Jr., 690
Thebest Laundry & Cleaning Co. v. Duffy, 531
Thermo Electron Corp. v. Schiavone Construction Co., 725
Theta Products, Inc. v. Zippo Mfg. Co., 787
Thompson v. Liquichimica of America, Inc., 442
Thompson-Starrett Co. v. La Belle Iron Works, 522, 525
Thrifticheck Service Corp. v. Commissioner, 327
Thumm v. Lohr, 31
Tibbitts v. Openshaw, 670

Tilbert v. Eagle Lock Co., 631
Tipper v. Great Lakes Chemical
Company, 419
Tipton County Farm Bureau
Cooperative Ass'n, Inc. v. Hoover,
452
Titus v. Glens Falls Ins. Co., 540
Tobin & Tobin Insurance Agency, Inc.
v. Zeskind, 419
**Totem Marine Tug & Barge, Inc. v.
Alyeska Pipeline Service
Company, 69**
Toussaint v. Blue Cross & Blue Shield
of Michigan, 626
**Transatlantic Financing Corp. v.
United States, 686**
Transwestern Pipeline Co. v.
Monsanto Co., 574
Travelers Ins. Co. v. Bailey, 650
Travers v. Spidell, 486
Trident Center v. Connecticut General
Life Ins. Co., 507
Trilco Terminal v. Prebilt Corp., 806
Tri-State Roofing Company of
Uniontown v. Simon, 74
Twin Forks Ranch, Inc. v. Brooks, 491
Tymshare, Inc. v. Covell, 524
U.S. Alliance Corp. v. Tobon, 644
U.S. Ecology, Inc. v. State, 347
U.S. Fibres, Inc. v. Proctor &
Schwartz, Inc., 552
UAL Corporation, In re, 648
Undersea Engineering & Construction
Co. v. International Telephone &
Telegraph Corp., 73
Unelko Corp. v. Prestone Products
Corp., 328
Union Carbide Corp. v. Oscar Mayer
Foods Corp., 572
Union Pacific Resources Co. v. Texaco,
Inc., 488
Unique Systems, Inc. v. Zotos
International, Inc., 725
United Drug Co. v. Theodore Rectanus
Co., 327
United Refining Co. v. Jenkins, 442
United States for Use of Susi
Contracting Co. v. Zara Contracting
Co., 275
**United States Naval Institute v.
Charter Communications, Inc.,
279**
United Steelworkers of America v.
Warrior & Gulf Navigation Co., 583
Universal C.I.T. Credit Corp. v.
Middlesboro Motor Sales, Inc., 543
Universal Inv. Co. v. Sahara Motor
Inn, Inc., 675

Universal Sales Corp. v. Cal. Press
Mfg. Co., 505, 506
Upton v. Tribilcock, 313, 413
Urban Plumbing and Heating Co. v.
United States, 73
Utschig v. McClone, 27
V'Soske v. Barwick, 445
Van Bibber v. Norris, 543
Van Buren v. Pima Community
College Dist. Bd., 674
Van Gulik v. Resource Development
Council for Alaska, 232
Van Tassell v. United Mktg. Grp.,
LLC, 593
Vanderpool v. Richardson, 223
Vaughn v. Ag Processing, Inc., 623
Venture Associates Corp. v. Zenith
Data Systems Corp., 447
Vickery v. Ritchie, 425
Vimar Seguros y Reaseguros, S.A. v.
M/V Sky Reefer, 591
Vincenzi v. Cerro, 709, 767
Volusia Cnty. v. Aberdeen at Ormond
Beach, L.P., 641
W. R. Grimshaw Co. v. Nevil C.
Withrow Co., 73
W.G. Taylor Co. v. Bannerman, 110
Wade v. Ford Motor Credit Co., 543
Wagner v. Graziano Construction Co.,
549
Wainscott v. Ossenkop, 619
Wakeman v. Wheeler & Wilson Mfg.
Co., 225
**Walgreen Co. v. Sara Creek
Property Co., 254**
Walker v. Syms, 514
Walton v. Waterhouse, 680
Ward v. Lyman, 653
Warden v. Jones, 779
Washington, State v., 642
Watkins v. Paul, 262
Weaver Bros., Inc. v. Chappel, 769
Weaver v. American Oil Co., 457
Webb v. McGowin, 47, 51
Webster v. Palm Beach Ocean Realty
Co., 487
Weisbrod v. Weisbrod, 23
Weiss v. Sheet Metal Fabricators, 718
Wells v. Holiday Inns, Inc., 348
Welsh v. Ford, 502
Wentworth v. Cock, 681
Western Farm Bureau Mut. Ins. Co. v.
Barela, 611
Western Geophysical Co. of Am. v.
Bolt Assocs., 227
Westinghouse Credit Corp. v. Shelton,
542
Westinghouse Elec. Corp. v. Nielsons,
Inc., 567

Westlake v. Adams, C.P., 57
Wheeler v. White, 447
Whelan v. Griffith Consumers
   Company, 687
White v. McLaren, 172
Whiteco Industries, Inc. v. Kopani,
   457
Whiting v. Stacy, 395
Wholesale Sand & Gravel, Inc. v.
   Decker, 723
Wiedeman v. Howell, 135
Wilkisius v. Sheehan, 314
Williams v. Lloyd, 682
Williams v. Ruben, 82
Williams v. Walker-Thomas
   Furniture Co., 86, 87, 103
Williamson v. Martz, 789
Wilson v. Lewiston Mill Co., 804
Wilson v. Odom, 117
Wilson v. Scampoli, 734
Wired Music, Inc. v. Clark, 197
Wisconsin & M. Ry. Co. v. Powers, 10
Wisconsin Knife Works v. National
   Metal Crafters, 544, 553
Witherbee v. Meyer, 225, 227
Witten, In re the Marriage of, 140
Woburn National Bank v. Woods, 316
Wolens v. Am. Airlines, Inc., 342
Wolfe v. Graether, 622
Wolowitz, State v., 101
Wolters v. King, 479
Wood v. Lucy, Lady Duff-Gordon,
   110, 526
Wood v. Mid-Valley Inc., 450
Woodbridge Place Apartments v.
   Washington Square Capital, Inc.,
   247
Woodbury v. Jones, 268
Woodman v. Blue Grass Land Co., 214
Woolley v. Hoffmann-La Roche, Inc.,
   626
Workman v. United Parcel Service,
   Inc., 450
World Enter., Inc. v. Midcoast
   Aviation Serv., Inc., 101
Worrall v. Munn, 284
Yakus v. United States, 255
Yeats v. Moody, 419
Yontz v. BMER Interprises, Inc., 450
Young Living Essential Oils, LC v.
   Marin, 532
Young v. Chicopee, 693, 694, 695
Zabriskie Chevrolet v. Smith, 734, 735
Zaltz v. JDATE, 593
Zappos.com, Inc. Customer Data Sec.
   Breach Litig., In re, 594
Zemco Mfg., Inc. v. Navistar Int'l
   Transp. Corp., 822
Zinn v. Ex-Cell-O Corp., 479

Zuckerman v. Transamerica Ins. Co.,
   612, 614

TABLE OF UNIFORM COMMERCIAL CODE CITATIONS

Art. 1 ....93, 528, 529, 790, 791
Art. 2 ...93, 94, 137, 529, 551, 562, 565,
   566, 568, 569, 570, 790, 828, 829
Art. 5 529
Art. 9 .... 93, 551
1–101 560
1–102 732
1–102(2)(b) 566
1–103 ....93, 94, 692, 818
1–106 192
1–106(1) 203, 230
1–201(3) 515, 546, 575
1–201(10) 592, 596, 769
1–201(12) 515
1–201(19) 528, 529, 728, 732
1–201(20) 528, 529, 728
1–201(27) 365
1–201(39) 546, 802
1–203 ....528, 728, 731, 735
1–204 100
1–204(2) 733
1–205(2) 512
1–205(4) 517
1–206 .... 790, 791, 827
1–209 560
1–303 515
1–304 728
1–306 544
2–101 560
2–102 93
2–103 560
2–103(1)(b) 528, 569, 732, 735
2–103(2) 728
2–104(1) 546, 787
2–105(1) 93
2–106 732
2–201 ....529, 785, 786, 788, 789, 790,
   803, 805, 806, 807, 809, 818, 821,
   822, 823, 828
2–201(1) 785, 786, 787, 789, 804,
   805, 806, 809
2–201(3)(c) 789
2–201(a) 828
2–202 ....481, 482, 512, 520, 521
2–202(a) 512
2–204 ....435, 558, 583, 584
2–204(1) 558
2–205 .... 370, 592
2–206 584
2–206(1) 94, 393, 398, 587
2–206(1)(b) 394

2–206(2) 396
2–207 .... 360, 558, 559, 560,
   562, 563, 564, 565, 566, 567, 569,
   570, 571, 572, 573, 574, 575, 584,
   586, 587
2–207(1) 94, 556, 563, 564, 565,
   567, 570, 572, 573, 574, 575, 576
2–207(2) 566, 567, 568, 569, 570,
   574, 575, 576
2–207(2)(a) 570, 574, 576
2–207(2)(b) 568, 570, 571, 572, 574
2–207(2)(c) 570, 574
2–207(3) 547, 567, 568, 570, 574,
   575, 576
2–207(4) 567
2–208 .... 515, 519
2–209 .... 137, 544, 548, 551, 584
2–209(1) 551, 554
2–209(2) 536, 546, 547, 548, 549,
   550, 551, 554, 592
2–209(3) 550, 551, 821, 822, 823
2–209(4) 547, 549, 550, 551, 553,
   554, 823
2–209(5) 550, 551, 553, 554, 823
2–209(42) 550
2–302 .... 92, 96, 99, 101, 596
2–302(5) 101
2–305 .... 435, 440
2–308 435
2–309 435
2–310 435
2–312 671
2–313 .... 567, 671
2–314 .... 567, 596, 671
2–315 671
2–316 596
2–316(2) 592, 769
2–316(3)(a) 551
2–501(1) 198
2–508 .... 726, 732
2–508(1) 728, 732
2–508(2) 728, 729, 731, 732, 735
2–509 692
2–509(2) 551
2–510 692
2–601 .... 726, 727, 729
2–608 .... 726, 727
2–610 .... 722, 725
2–612 .... 726, 727
2–612(2) 727
2–612(3) 727
2–613 692

2–614	692
2–614(1)	688
2–615	687, 689, 692, 696
2–616	692
2–703	198
2–704	202
2–704(1)	198
2–706	198
2–706(1)	198
2–708	198, 200, 201, 202
2–708(1)	198, 200
2–708(2)	199, 201, 202, 203
2–708(2)(b)	202
2–709	198, 259
2–710	198, 200, 202, 203
2–710(2)	200
2–711	192
2–711(1)	187
2–712	187, 190, 192, 193, 726
2–713	187, 190, 191, 192, 193, 221, 726
2–713(1)	190
2–713(2)	191
2–714	187, 726, 727
2–714(2)	188
2–715(1)	187
2–715(2)	221
2–715(2)(a)	221
2–716	259, 260
2–718	200, 571
2–718(1)	200, 240
2–718(2)	200, 711
2–718(2)(a)	200
2–718(2)(b)	200, 201
2–718(3)	200, 711
2–718(3)(a)	200, 201
2–719	571
2–719(2)	596, 605
2–719(3)	596
2–719(b)	605
2–719(c)	102, 605
2–723	187, 191, 198
2–724	187, 198
2–725	560
8–113	790
9–203	790
10–102	199

TABLE OF CITATIONS TO THE RESTATEMENT OF CONTRACTS

Restatement, First, Contracts
§ 2(1) 1
Restatement, First, Contracts
§ 20 356
Restatement, First, Contracts
§ 25 334
Restatement, First, Contracts
§ 35 351
Restatement, First, Contracts
§ 36 352
Restatement, First, Contracts
§ 40 351
Restatement, First, Contracts
§ 45 .... 377, 378, 380
Restatement, First, Contracts
§ 58 356
Restatement, First, Contracts
§ 84 21
Restatement, First, Contracts
§ 90 ....33, 163, 377, 378, 380,
381, 382, 434, 455
Restatement, First, Contracts
§ 161 523
Restatement, First, Contracts
§ 197 813
Restatement, First, Contracts
§ 208 .... 103, 803
Restatement, First, Contracts
§ 231 496
Restatement, First, Contracts
§ 240(1)(b).................................. 478
Restatement, First, Contracts
§ 261 750
Restatement, First, Contracts
§ 335 194
Restatement, First, Contracts
§ 346 196
Restatement, First, Contracts
§ 346(1)(a)(i) 176
Restatement, First, Contracts
§ 346(1)(a)(ii) 176
Restatement, First, Contracts
§ 347 276
Restatement, First, Contracts
§ 361 260
Restatement, First, Contracts
§ 406 122
Restatement, First, Contracts
§ 454 .... 687, 691
Restatement, First, Contracts
§ 457 689

Restatement, Second, Contracts
§ 1..11, 26
Restatement, Second, Contracts
§ 2(1) 747
Restatement, Second, Contracts
§ 12.. 303
Restatement, Second, Contracts
§ 16.. 303
Restatement, Second, Contracts
§ 17..11, 117
Restatement, Second, Contracts
§ 20.. 312
Restatement, Second, Contracts
§ 20(1) 318
Restatement, Second, Contracts
§ 22.. 626
Restatement, Second, Contracts
§ 24..331, 626
Restatement, Second, Contracts
§ 25.. 368
Restatement, Second, Contracts
§ 26.............................347, 441, 445
Restatement, Second, Contracts
§ 30.............................393, 397
Restatement, Second, Contracts
§ 32.. 394
Restatement, Second, Contracts
§ 32.2.. 13
Restatement, Second, Contracts
§ 33.................................... 431, 435
Restatement, Second, Contracts
§ 34.. 435
Restatement, Second, Contracts
§ 37.. 361
Restatement, Second, Contracts
§ 38.. 353
Restatement, Second, Contracts
§ 39.. 359
Restatement, Second, Contracts
§ 41.................................... 353, 392
Restatement, Second, Contracts
§ 42.. 363
Restatement, Second, Contracts
§ 43.. 363
Restatement, Second, Contracts
§ 45..................... 371, 374, 378, 383
Restatement, Second, Contracts
§ 49.. 397
Restatement, Second, Contracts
§ 51.. 624
Restatement, Second, Contracts
§ 54(1) 395

Restatement, Second, Contracts
§ 54(2) 395
Restatement, Second, Contracts
§ 55 61
Restatement, Second, Contracts
§ 56 .... 390, 393, 396
Restatement, Second, Contracts
§ 59 .... 360, 407
Restatement, Second, Contracts
§ 60 .... 393, 397
Restatement, Second, Contracts
§§ 63–68....................................... 397
Restatement, Second, Contracts
§ 64 396
Restatement, Second, Contracts
§ 68 364
Restatement, Second, Contracts
§ 69 .... 407, 412, 413
Restatement, Second, Contracts
§ 69(1) 412
Restatement, Second, Contracts
§ 69(1)(a)..................... 407, 408, 410
Restatement, Second, Contracts
§ 71 .... 11, 63, 65
Restatement, Second, Contracts
§ 71(1) 12, 374
Restatement, Second, Contracts
§ 71(2) 374
Restatement, Second, Contracts
§ 72 65
Restatement, Second, Contracts
§ 75 118
Restatement, Second, Contracts
§ 77 .... 107, 111, 118
Restatement, Second, Contracts
§ 79 .... 11, 65
Restatement, Second, Contracts
§ 82 42
Restatement, Second, Contracts
§ 83 42
Restatement, Second, Contracts
§ 84 541
Restatement, Second, Contracts
§ 86 56
Restatement, Second, Contracts
§ 87 ....43, 368, 369, 370
Restatement, Second, Contracts
§ 87(1) 365, 368
Restatement, Second, Contracts
§ 87(1)(a)...............365, 368, 369, 370
Restatement, Second, Contracts
§ 87(2) 371, 383
Restatement, Second, Contracts
§ 89 .... 129, 135
Restatement, Second, Contracts
§ 89(a)................................. 132, 133
Restatement, Second, Contracts
§ 90 ....28, 40, 43, 376, 817
Restatement, Second, Contracts
§ 90(1) 375, 449

Restatement, Second, Contracts
§ 111...800
Restatement, Second, Contracts
§ 112...796
Restatement, Second, Contracts
§§ 112–113 799
Restatement, Second, Contracts
§ 113...799
Restatement, Second, Contracts
§ 116....................................797, 798
Restatement, Second, Contracts
§ 124............................ 779, 800, 801
Restatement, Second, Contracts
§ 125...784
Restatement, Second, Contracts
§ 125(3) 813
Restatement, Second, Contracts
§ 127...784
Restatement, Second, Contracts
§ 128(1) 814
Restatement, Second, Contracts
§ 129...814
Restatement, Second, Contracts
§ 130............................ 792, 794, 814
Restatement, Second, Contracts
§ 131...804
Restatement, Second, Contracts
§ 133...779
Restatement, Second, Contracts
§ 134...802
Restatement, Second, Contracts
§ 139............................ 457, 816, 817
Restatement, Second, Contracts
§ 139(1) 456
Restatement, Second, Contracts
§ 141(2) 820
Restatement, Second, Contracts
§ 144...819
Restatement, Second, Contracts
§ 148...821
Restatement, Second, Contracts
§ 150...823
Restatement, Second, Contracts
§ 151....................................664, 667
Restatement, Second, Contracts
§ 152....................................664, 669
Restatement, Second, Contracts
§ 153............................ 645, 649, 674
Restatement, Second, Contracts
§ 154............. 645, 649, 664, 669, 670
Restatement, Second, Contracts
§ 154(a) 670
Restatement, Second, Contracts
§ 155...653
Restatement, Second, Contracts
§ 159...676
Restatement, Second, Contracts
§ 161....................................674, 676
Restatement, Second, Contracts
§ 164(1) 674

Restatement, Second, Contracts
§ 175 .... 69, 81
Restatement, Second, Contracts
§ 176 .... 69, 80, 81
Restatement, Second, Contracts
§ 176(2)(b)................................ 81
Restatement, Second, Contracts
§ 201 312
Restatement, Second, Contracts
§ 201(1)...................................... 319
Restatement, Second, Contracts
§ 201(2)...................................... 319
Restatement, Second, Contracts
§ 201(2)(b).................................. 317
Restatement, Second, Contracts
§ 203 615
Restatement, Second, Contracts
§ 204 321
Restatement, Second, Contracts
§ 205 .... 442, 528, 615
Restatement, Second, Contracts
§ 205(3)...................................... 747
Restatement, Second, Contracts
§ 206 615
Restatement, Second, Contracts
§ 208 .... 92, 615
Restatement, Second, Contracts
§ 209 474
Restatement, Second, Contracts
§ 210 474
Restatement, Second, Contracts
§ 211 ....606, 612, 614, 615, 616
Restatement, Second, Contracts
§ 211(1)...................................... 614
Restatement, Second, Contracts
§ 211(2)...................................... 614
Restatement, Second, Contracts
§ 211(3)...................................... 615
Restatement, Second, Contracts
§ 212 496
Restatement, Second, Contracts
§ 212(2)...................................... 509
Restatement, Second, Contracts
§ 213 474
Restatement, Second, Contracts
§ 214 .... 474, 488, 489
Restatement, Second, Contracts
§ 215 .... 474, 613
Restatement, Second, Contracts
§ 216 .... 474, 482
Restatement, Second, Contracts
§§ 219–223................................ 515
Restatement, Second, Contracts
§ 220 515
Restatement, Second, Contracts
§ 221 513
Restatement, Second, Contracts
§ 222 513
Restatement, Second, Contracts
§ 224 .... 743, 747

Restatement, Second, Contracts
§ 225(1) 747
Restatement, Second, Contracts
§ 227.................... 744, 752, 764, 767
Restatement, Second, Contracts
§ 227(1) 744, 767
Restatement, Second, Contracts
§ 228... 759
Restatement, Second, Contracts
§ 229........................... 744, 767, 771
Restatement, Second, Contracts
§ 230... 773
Restatement, Second, Contracts
§ 237.................... 709, 710, 720, 745
Restatement, Second, Contracts
§ 241(e)..................................... 710
Restatement, Second, Contracts
§ 245... 755
Restatement, Second, Contracts
§ 250........................... 724, 725, 726
Restatement, Second, Contracts
§ 250(b) 724
Restatement, Second, Contracts
§§ 261–272................................ 692
Restatement, Second, Contracts
§ 271... 773
Restatement, Second, Contracts
§ 272... 696
Restatement, Second, Contracts
§ 274... 719
Restatement, Second, Contracts
§ 318... 74
Restatement, Second, Contracts
§ 344................... 157, 274, 277, 713
Restatement, Second, Contracts
§ 345........................... 274, 277, 713
Restatement, Second, Contracts
§ 347... 282
Restatement, Second, Contracts
§ 348(2) 181
Restatement, Second, Contracts
§ 350... 210
Restatement, Second, Contracts
§ 351... 221
Restatement, Second, Contracts
§ 352... 230
Restatement, Second, Contracts
§ 356........................... 240, 246, 283
Restatement, Second, Contracts
§ 359... 253
Restatement, Second, Contracts
§ 360.................................. 253, 261
Restatement, Second, Contracts
§ 361... 246
Restatement, Second, Contracts
§ 367(1) 262
Restatement, Second, Contracts
§ 367(2) 263
Restatement, Second, Contracts
§ 370........................... 274, 277, 713

Restatement, Second, Contracts
  § 371 .... 274, 277, 713
Restatement, Second, Contracts
  § 551 674

TABLE OF CITATIONS TO THE RESTATEMENTS OF RESTITUTION

Restatement, Third, Restitution and
    Unjust Enrichment § 2 424
Restatement, Third, Restitution and
    Unjust Enrichment § 2(3) 423
Restatement, Third, Restitution and
    Unjust Enrichment § 2(4) ... 424, 425
Restatement, Third, Restitution and
    Unjust Enrichment § 9 425
Restatement, Third, Restitution and
    Unjust Enrichment § 20 .... 52, 56,
    423
Restatement, Third, Restitution and
    Unjust Enrichment § 25 56
Restatement, Third, Restitution and
    Unjust Enrichment § 36 ..... 277, 713
Restatement, Third, Restitution and
    Unjust Enrichment § 38(2)(b) ... 277,
    278
Restatement, Third, Restitution and
    Unjust Enrichment § 39 284
Restatement, Third, Restitution and
    Unjust Enrichment § 69 648
Restatement, First, Restitution and
    Unjust Enrichment § 116(a) 52

BASIC CONTRACT LAW
CONCISE EDITION

Tenth Edition

INTRODUCTION

∎ ∎ ∎

The law of contracts is, broadly speaking, the law of voluntary obligations; that is, obligations that arise because of an express or implied commitment—in particular, a promise. (In contrast, the law of torts, broadly speaking, involves obligations that are imposed upon persons without regard to any commitment they have made.) A promise may be defined as an expression of an intention to act or refrain from acting in a specified way, so made as to justify the person to whom the expression is addressed in understanding that a commitment has been made to that person. Restatement, First, of Contracts § 2(1). A person who makes a promise is called a *promisor*. A person to whom a promise is made is called a *promisee*.

Because contract law normally does not get off the ground unless there is a promise, or at least a promissory matrix, it is useful to begin the study of contract law with a brief treatment of the moral obligation that a promise imposes. Although it is widely accepted that there is a moral obligation to keep a promise, there has been a continuing debate over how to justify that obligation. The next two selections are important parts of that debate.

J. RAWLS, A THEORY OF JUSTICE
342–47 (1971).

. . . [T]he principle of fairness. . . . holds that a person is under an obligation to do his part as specified by the rules of an institution whenever he has voluntarily accepted the benefits of the scheme or has taken advantage of the opportunities it offers to advance his interests, provided that this institution is just or fair. . . .

. . . Now the principle of fidelity [to one's promise] is but a special case of the principle of fairness applied to the social practice of promising. . . .

. . . [B]y making a promise one invokes a social practice and accepts the benefits that it makes possible. What are these benefits and how does the practice work? To answer this question, let us assume that the standard reason for making promises is to set up and to stabilize small-scale schemes of cooperation, or a particular pattern of transactions. The role of promises is analogous to that which Hobbes attributed to the sovereign. Just as the sovereign maintains and stabilizes the system of social cooperation by publicly maintaining an effective schedule of penalties, so men in the absence of coercive arrangements establish and stabilize their private ventures by giving one another their word. Such ventures are often hard to initiate and to maintain. This is especially evident . . . in those instances where one person is to perform before the other. For this person may believe that the second party will not do his part, and therefore the scheme never gets going. It is subject to [this kind of instability] . . . even though the person to perform later would in fact carry through. Now in these situations there may be no way of assuring the party who is to perform first except by giving him a promise, that is, by putting oneself under an obligation to carry through later. Only in this way can the scheme be made secure so that both can gain from the benefits of their cooperation. The practice of promising exists for precisely this purpose; and so while we normally think of moral requirements as bonds laid upon us, they are sometimes deliberately self-imposed for our advantage. Thus promising is an act done with the public intention of deliberately incurring an obligation the existence of which in the circumstances will further one's ends. We want this obligation to exist and to be known to exist, and we want others to know that we recognize this tie and intend to abide by it. Having, then, availed ourselves of the practice for this reason, we are under an obligation to do as we promised by the principle of fairness.

———

THOMAS M. SCANLON, PROMISES AND PRACTICES
19 Philosophy & Public Affairs 199 (1990).*

Consider the following example, which I will call the case of the Guilty Secret. Suppose that you are visiting for a [fifteen-week] term at a university where you know almost no one, and at a party shortly after your arrival you are surprised to encounter Harold, whom you have not seen for years. Long ago, when you were young together, Harold did something that at the time he regarded as perfectly all right but that he now recalls with shame and embarrassment. It was not really that bad (you would not be violating any duty to others by failing to tell them about it), but Harold has come to be extremely sensitive about the incident. So, when the two of you are having a brief conversation apart from the rest of the party, he brings the matter up. "Remember that awful night in Chicago?" he asks. "I'll never forget it. The thought of how I behaved that night has haunted me ever since. It would be terribly embarrassing for me if anyone here were to learn of it. I know it seems as if I'm excessively concerned with this, but will you promise not to mention it to anyone while you are here?" Suppose that you do promise and Harold, looking much relieved, moves off in the direction of the bar. I assume that as a result of this encounter you now have two moral reasons not to tell the amusing story of that night in Chicago: you would be gratuitously injuring Harold, and you would be violating the obligation to him that you have just incurred. The question is how to account for this [second] obligation . . . It seems that Harold does not rely on the expectation you have created by taking or forgoing any action, because there is nothing he could do to shield himself from the embarrassment that would result from your telling the story. He can't leave town, and I am assuming that murder and bribery are ruled out. He's not that kind of guy. So there are no options that he is passing up as the days of your visit go by. There may have already been reliance of [some] kind. . . . If you had not promised so readily, Harold might have gotten down on his knees to plead with you or shown you pictures of his wife and children, whose happy lives, he believes, could be reduced to shambles by your loose lips. But, given that you promised to remain silent, he did not do these things. Even if there was reliance of this kind, however, it does not seem sufficiently important to be the basis of your obligation.

What is important is the value of assurance itself. It may seem that if you were to tell the Chicago story on the last night of your visit (having promised on the first night that you would not), your overall course of action would leave Harold better off than if you had told the story without having promised not to. After all, the promise gave him fifteen weeks of peace of mind. But this is to assume that the value of assurance is purely experiential, that it can be reduced to the values of freedom from worry, increased ability to sleep at night, and so on. I would maintain, however, that this assumption is false. What people in Harold's position, and many other positions, reasonably want is not mere freedom from worry; they also want certain things to happen (or, as in Harold's case, to not happen). They want to be given assurances, and they care about whether these assurances are genuine. One reason for caring is that they may rely on these assurances in deciding what to do. This is not, however, the only reason, as Harold's case demonstrates. Given the reasons which potential promisees have for wanting assurance, potential promisors have reason to want to be able to provide it. From the point of view of both potential promisees and potential promisors, then, it is reasonable to want a principle of fidelity that requires performance. . . . Such a principle can be stated as follows.

Principle F: If (1) A voluntarily and intentionally leads B to expect that A will do x (unless B consents to A's not doing x); (2) A knows that B wants to be assured of this; (3) A acts with the aim of providing this assurance, and has good reason to believe that he or she has done so; (4) B knows that A has the beliefs and intentions just described; (5) A intends for B to know this, and knows that B does know it; and (6) B knows that A has this knowledge and intent; then, in the absence of some special justification. A must do x unless B consents to x's not being done.

The fact that potential B's have reason to insist on such a duty of fidelity is in my view sufficient to establish it as a duty unless it would be reasonable for potential A's to reject such a principle. Would the duty described impose an unreasonable burden on those who create expectations in others? They could of course avoid bearing any burden at all simply by refraining from intentional creation of any expectations about their future conduct. This would be quite limiting if it meant that we could never tell people what we intend to do without being bound to seek their permission before changing course. But Principle F would not have this effect, since it applies only when A knows that B wants assurance, and when A has acted with the aim of supplying this assurance and has reason to believe that he or she has done so, and when this and other features of the situation are mutual knowledge. No one could reasonably object to a principle imposing, in such cases, at least a duty to warn at the time the expectation is created—to say, "This is my present intention, but of course I may change my mind," or to make this clear in some other way if it is not already clear in the context. Since the burden of such a duty to warn is so slight, one can hardly complain if failure to fulfill it leaves one open to the more stringent duty to perform or seek permission to substitute. But this is just the duty stated by Principle F, since the conditions of that principle specify that no such warning has been given and, indeed, that quite the opposite has occurred, since A has refrained from providing such a warning in situations in which he or she knows that the difference between an expectation qualified by that warning and one without that qualification is important to B.

When the conditions of Principle F are fulfilled, it would be wrong, in the absence of special justification, for the first party not to perform. In addition, the second party has a "right to rely" on this performance: that is, the second party has grounds for insisting that the first party fulfill the expectation he or she has created. . . .

Saying "I promise to . . . " normally binds one to do the thing promised, but it does not bind unconditionally or absolutely. It does not bind unconditionally because the binding force of promising depends on the conditions under which the promise is made: a promise may not bind if it was obtained by coercion or through deceit. It does not bind absolutely because, while a promise binds one against reconsidering one's intention simply on grounds of one's own convenience, it does not bind one to do the thing promised whatever the cost to oneself and others.

———

GARDNER, OBSERVATIONS ON THE COURSE IN CONTRACTS

1934.

"The ethical problems involved in the law of contracts result as I see them from four elementary ideas:

"(1) *The Tort Idea,* i.e. that one ought to pay for the injuries he does to another. As applied to promises this means that one ought to pay for losses which others suffer in reliance on his promises.

"(2) *The Bargain Idea,* i.e. that one who gets anything of value by promising to pay an agreed price for it ought to pay the seller the price he agreed.

"(3) *The Promissory Idea,* i.e. that promises are binding in their own nature and ought to be kept in all cases.

"(4) *The Quasi-Contractual Idea,* i.e. that one who receives anything of value from another ought to pay for it unless it came to him as a voluntary gift.

"These ideas, which at first seem trite and wholly harmonious, are in fact profoundly in conflict. The first and fourth proceed from the premise that justice is to be known after the event, and that it is the business of the court to correct whatever consequences of voluntary intercourse between men may be found to have turned out unjustly. The second and third proceed from the premise that justice is to be known before the event in transactions voluntarily entered into, and that it is the parties' business to settle the justice and injustice of their voluntary transactions at the start. The conflict between these two standpoints is perennial; it can be traced throughout the history of the law of contracts and noted in nearly every debatable contact question; there is no reason to think that it can ever be gotten rid of or to suppose that the present compromises of the issue will be any more permanent than the other compromises that have gone before."

PART 1

WHAT PROMISES SHOULD THE LAW ENFORCE?—THE DOCTRINE OF CONSIDERATION

■ ■ ■

The first great question of contract law is, what promises should and does the law enforce? This question is subsumed under the heading of *consideration,* and it is the question that will be addressed in Part I of this Book.

Part I consists of three Chapters. Chapter 1 primarily concerns the enforceability of donative promises, that is, promises to make a gift. Chapter 2 concerns bargain promises. Chapter 3 concerns the limits of contract as a technique for social ordering.

———

CHAPTER 1

SIMPLE DONATIVE PROMISES AND THE ELEMENTS OF FORM, RELIANCE, AND PAST BENEFIT CONFERRED

∎ ∎ ∎

SECTION 1. SIMPLE DONATIVE PROMISES

This Chapter has four sections. Section 1 considers *simple donative promises*, that is, promises that are made for affective reasons (such as love, friendship, or the like); that are not cast in a form to which modern contract law gives special significance; and that have not been demonstrably relied upon. Section 2 considers donative promises that are cast in a special form. Section 3 considers the effect of reliance. Section 4 considers promises based on a past benefit conferred that gives rise to a moral obligation to compensate the promisee for the benefit.

DOUGHERTY V. SALT
New York Court of Appeals, 1919.
227 N.Y. 200, 125 N.E. 94.

CARDOZO, J. The plaintiff, a boy of eight years, received from his aunt, the defendant's testatrix, a promissory note for $3,000 payable at her death or before. Use was made of a printed form, which contains the words "value received." How the note came to be given, was explained by the boy's guardian, who was a witness for his ward. The aunt was visiting her nephew. "When she saw Charley coming in, she said 'Isn't he a nice boy?' I answered her, yes, that he is getting along very nice, and getting along nice in school, and I showed where he had progressed in school, having good reports, and so forth, and she told me that she was going to take care of that child, that she loved him very much. I said, 'I know you do, Tillie, but your taking care of the child will be done probably like your brother and sister done, take it out in talk.' She said: 'I don't intend to take it out in talk, I would like to take care of him now.' I said, 'Well, that is up to you.' She said, 'Why can't I make out a note to him?' I said, 'You can, if you wish to.' She said, 'Would that be right?' And I said, 'I do not know, but I guess it would; I do not know why it would not.' And she said, 'Well, will you make out a note for me?' I said, 'Yes, if you wish me to,' and she said, 'Well, I wish

9

you would.'" A blank was then produced, filled out, and signed. The aunt handed the note to her nephew with these words, "You have always done for me, and I have signed this note for you. Now, do not lose it. Some day it will be valuable."

The trial judge submitted to the jury the question whether there was any consideration for the promised payment. Afterwards, he set aside the verdict in favor of the plaintiff, and dismissed the complaint. The Appellate Division, by a divided court, reversed the judgment of dismissal, and reinstated the verdict on the ground that the note was sufficient evidence of consideration.

We reach a different conclusion. The inference of consideration to be drawn from the form of the note has been so overcome and rebutted as to leave no question for a jury. This is not a case where witnesses summoned by the defendant and friendly to the defendant's cause, supply the testimony in disproof of value (Strickland v. Henry, 175 N.Y. 372). This is a case where the testimony in disproof of value comes from the plaintiff's own witness, speaking at the plaintiff's instance. The transaction thus revealed admits of one interpretation, and one only. The note was the voluntary and unenforceable promise of an executory gift (Harris v. Clark, 3 N.Y. 93; Holmes v. Roper, 141 N.Y. 64, 66). This child of eight was not a creditor, nor dealt with as one. The aunt was not paying a debt. She was conferring a bounty (Fink v. Cox, 18 Johns. 145). The promise was neither offered nor accepted with any other purpose. "Nothing is consideration that is not regarded as such by both parties" (Philpot v. Gruninger, 14 Wall. 570, 577; Fire Ins. Ass'n. v. Wickham, 141 U.S. 564, 579; Wisconsin & M. Ry. Co. v. Powers, 191 U.S. 379, 386; DeCicco v. Schweizer, 221 N.Y. 431, 438). A note so given is not made for "value received," however its maker may have labeled it. The formula of the printed blank becomes, in the light of the conceded facts, a mere erroneous conclusion, which cannot overcome the inconsistent conclusion of the law (Blanshan v. Russell, 32 App.Div. 103; affd., on opinion below, 161 N.Y. 629; Kramer v. Kramer, 181 N.Y. 477; Bruyn v. Russell, 52 Hun, 17). The plaintiff, through his own witness, has explained the genesis of the promise, and consideration has been disproved (Neg.Instr.Law, sec. 54; Consol.Laws, chap. 43).

We hold, therefore, that the verdict of the jury was contrary to law, and that the trial judge was right in setting it aside. . . .

HISCOCK, CH. J., CHASE, COLLIN, HOGAN, CRANE and ANDREWS, JJ., concur.

Judgment accordingly.

———

RESTATEMENT, SECOND, CONTRACTS §§ 1, 17, 71, 79

[See Selected Source Materials Supplement*]

NOTE ON THE RESTATEMENT OF CONTRACTS

The American Law Institute (ALI) is an organization composed of lawyers, judges, and legal academics. The ALI's objective is to promote the clarification and simplification of the law and its better adaptation to social needs. It has sought to achieve this objective in part by preparing Restatements of various branches of the common law, including Contracts.

The theory of the Restatements has changed somewhat over time. The introduction to the Restatement [First] of Contracts stated that "The function of the Institute is to state clearly and precisely in the light of the [courts'] decisions the principles and rules of the common law." The present theory is that the ALI "should feel obliged in [its] deliberations to give weight to all of the considerations that the courts, under a proper view of the judicial function, deem it right to weigh in theirs." Wechsler, The Course of the Restatements, 55 A.B.A.J. 147, 156 (1969).

The first Restatement of Contracts (hereafter cited as Restatement First) was published by the ALI in 1932. The Reporter was Samuel Williston of Harvard Law School. Williston was one of the leaders of a school of thought that is now called classical contract law. This school treated contract law as a set of axioms that were deemed to be self-evident, together with a set of subsidiary rules that were purportedly deduced from the axioms. Among the axioms of classical contract law were that bargains, and only bargains, constituted consideration; that bargains were formed by offer and acceptance; and that the remedy for breach of an enforceable promise was expectation damages.

Many of the original Restatements were eventually superseded by revised versions. Restatement, Second, of Contracts (hereafter cited as Restatement Second) was published in 1981. The Reporter for the first portion of Restatement Second was Robert Braucher, then of Harvard Law School. On Professor Braucher's appointment to the bench, he was succeeded as Reporter by Professor Allan Farnsworth of Columbia Law School.

Arthur Corbin of Yale Law School was, until his death, Consultant to the Restatement Second. From the 1920s through the 1960s, Williston and Corbin were the two giants of contract law. Each authored famous multi-volume treatises on contracts that are still in use. While Williston was a leader of the classical school of contract law, Corbin was instrumental in laying the foundation for modern contract law. To a significant extent, the differences in approach between Williston and Corbin are paralleled by differences in

---

*   References in this casebook to "Selected Source Materials Supplement" are to S. Burton & M. Eisenberg, Contract Law: Selected Source Materials (West Publishing Co.).

approach between Restatement First and Restatement Second. Restatement First had much that is admirable, and Restatement Second marks a considerable advance over Restatement First. However, both the theory of the Restatements and other factors often work to prevent a Restatement from setting out the best possible rule in any given area and the Restatements of Contracts are not exceptions.

———

NOTE ON THE CONCEPT OF CONSIDERATION

The term *consideration* may be conceived in two very different ways, one broad and one narrow. Under the *narrow* conception, consideration is equated with bargain. This conception, often referred to as the bargain theory of consideration, was adopted in Restatement First and continued in Restatement Second. Under the *broad* conception, consideration is simply a collective term for the set of elements that make promises legally enforceable. Bargain is one such element. As will be seen in subsequent Chapters, there are others, such as reliance.

In Restatement Second, this conception is embodied in section 71(1): "To constitute consideration, a performance or a return promise must be bargained for." The bargain theory of consideration can produce two kinds of distortions in contract law. The first concerns terminology. As will be seen in the balance of Part 1, a number of elements other than bargain should and do make promises legally enforceable. Restatement Second recognizes these elements, but only in sections that are grouped under a Topic called "Contracts [Enforceable] Without Consideration." The result is that under the terminology of Restatement Second, a promise needs consideration to be enforceable unless it does not need consideration to be enforceable.

The second distortion produced by the bargain theory of consideration is substantive. If consideration means the whole set of elements that make promises legally enforceable, the meaning of the term will be continually adjusted as it becomes socially desirable to add new elements or drop old ones. In contrast, the bargain theory of consideration suggests a closed system, in which all non-bargain promises are presumptively unenforceable. If taken seriously, such an approach tends to stifle the growth of the law.

The bargain theory of consideration is certainly not mandated by contract doctrine. On the contrary, the theory cannot account for many elements of enforceability, such as reliance, except by relegating these elements to the purgatory of Contracts [Enforceable] Without Consideration. Nor is the theory mandated by judicial decisions. A number of courts use the term consideration as equivalent to bargain, but many other courts use the term in its broader sense to embrace non-bargain elements, such as reliance, that make a promise enforceable.

———

NOTE ON GIFTS

The common law distinguishes between a gift and a promise to make a gift. As *Dougherty v. Salt* illustrates, a promise to make a gift is not enforceable as such. (However, as will be shown later in this Chapter, such a promise may be enforceable if other elements, such as reliance, are present.) In contrast, a completed gift is recognized by the law as a valid and binding legal transaction, which cannot be reversed by the donor in the absence of fraud or the like. Thus, if A promises to give B $1000 as a gift, A's promise is unenforceable absent reliance or some other special element. However, if A keeps her promise and gives B the $1000, A cannot recover the money; it belongs to B.

The classical way to make a gift is to deliver possession of the gift to the donee. However, that is not the only way. Normally, a person who owns personal property can make a gift of that property, even without delivering possession, by executing a signed writing in which the donor and the donee are identified, the subject matter of the gift is described, the nature of the interest given is specified, and the donor manifests an intention to make the gift by means of the instrument. (Such a writing is known as a deed of gift or an inter vivos document of transfer.) This rule is exemplified by two illustrations to Section 32.2 of the Restatement, Second, of the Law of Property (Donative Transfers) (1990):

> Illustration 3. O, by an inter vivos donative document of transfer, transfers the ownership of his watch to his son S. O continues to wear the watch after such transfer. S can demand possession of the watch at any time but does not. O dies. S requests the watch from the personal representatives of O's estate. S is entitled to the watch.

> Illustration 4. O, by an inter vivos donative document of transfer, transfers his stock in the X Company to his daughter D. The stock certificate is retained by O. After such transfer and before the stock certificate has been delivered to D or transferred to D's name on the books of the corporation, a dividend is declared. The dividend is made payable to O and received by O. D is entitled to the amount of the dividend check.

Notice that the technique of using a deed of gift will not work where the donor wants to make a gift of services, or to make a gift of personal property that she does not presently own, or to make only a future rather than a present gift.

There is at least one other way to make what is, in effect, a gift. A person may declare herself trustee of property she owns for the benefit of another—the beneficiary of the trust. Under the law of trusts, a person who makes such a declaration continues to hold legal title to the property, but beneficial ownership (that is, the right to enjoy the benefits of the property) vests in the beneficiary of the trust.

———

NOTE ON DONATIVE PROMISES

1.   Why does a person make a donative promise? Why does she not simply wait until the time when she expects to perform, and make the gift then, rather than committing herself in advance to make the gift?*

One possibility is that the promisor believes that she has better and worse instincts at different times; that her present intention to make the gift reflects his better instincts; and that if she does not commit herself to making the gift now, her worse instincts may keep her from actually making the gift later.

Another possibility is that the promisor hopes to derive satisfaction not only from the promisee's happiness and gratitude at the time the gift is actually made, but from the promisee's happiness and gratitude between the time the promise is made and the time the gift is made.

Still a third possibility is that the promisor wants to maximize the promisee's wealth or satisfaction. Making a promise before making the actual gift may create more wealth or satisfaction than making the gift without having made a promise. This is because if the promise is made before the gift is given, the promisee may be able to make plans on the basis of the promise that will enhance the value of the gift. For example, suppose Aunt intends to pay for Niece's college education, and Niece would not be able to afford college if Aunt did not pay. If Aunt keeps her intention to herself, Niece may plan her high school education to prepare herself for the job market rather than for college. If instead Aunt promises Niece a college education, Niece can take a curriculum in high school that prepares her for college. If she does, college will be more valuable to her than it would have been if she had not prepared for it. This is an example of a more general phenomenon. In reliance on a promise, a promisee may take an action that is intended to enhance the value of the promise. This is even more obvious in a commercial setting than in a donative setting. For example, suppose a band agrees with a promoter that it will play a concert in two months. The promoter can then take actions in reliance on the promise, such as advertising the concert, that will increase gate receipts from the concert and therefore increase the value of the band's promise. Reliance that increases the value of a promise is sometimes referred to as *beneficial reliance*.

2.   Donative promises may seem to comprise an exceptionally small segment of contract law. In fact, however, the treatment of donative promises is fundamental to contract doctrine, particularly consideration. Under classical contract law, the basic fault line in consideration ran at the boundary between bargain promises and "gratuitous" (donative) promises, because under the bargain theory of consideration every promise that was not a bargain promise was viewed as a gratuitous promise. "Gratuitous" was therefore virtually synonymous with "unenforceable," so that in a sense the main enterprise of

---

*   In this casebook, unless the context indicates otherwise, feminine pronouns will be used to refer to promisors, and masculine pronouns will be used to refer to promisees.

consideration in classical contract law doctrine was to separate out enforceable promises from donative promises.

The legal treatment of donative promises also carries heavy social freight. The concept that bargain promises are legally enforceable, while donative promises are not, implicates fundamental questions of social value. The enforceability of donative promises also bears directly on one of the deepest social questions of contract law: whether contract law should be based on (i) the deontological objective of ensuring that promisors keep their promises, because it is morally right that promises be kept; or (ii) more particular utilitarian objectives, such as compensating injured promisees and increasing social wealth.

In Consideration and Form, 41 Colum. L. Rev. 799 (1941), Lon Fuller posited various substantive and formal grounds—we might now say process grounds—for enforcing promises. The two process grounds were the provision of evidentiary safeguards that ensured that a promise had actually been made, and cautionary safeguards that prevented inconsiderate action by the promisor.

Simple donative promises fall short on both process grounds. First, they raise serious problems of proof: Because of the nature of such promises, a false claim that such a promise was made may often be found credible by a jury despite the absence of corroborating evidence. Second, simple donative promises raise serious problems of deliberativeness, because characteristically a donative promisor is emotionally involved with the promisee, and therefore may tend to look mainly to the promisee's interests rather than her own.

The substantive and process bases for enforcing, or not enforcing, any given kind of promise are interrelated. The stronger the substantive interest in enforcing a given kind of promise, the more the law can tolerate process concerns. Certainly there are some substantive reasons for enforcing simple donative promises. For example, a failure to keep a donative promise causes an injury to the promisee, in the form of disappointment. Moreover, gifts probably tend to move assets from persons with more wealth to persons with less. Furthermore, the enforcement of donative promises might increase the rate of beneficial reliance.

However, the strength of these substantive bases for enforcing simple donative promises is open to question. For example, although a non-relying donative promisee may suffer disappointment if the promise is broken, that injury seems relatively slight. Similarly, the social-welfare effects of making simple donative promises enforceable are indeterminate. Certainly, it is possible that more gifting would occur if simple donative promises were enforceable, because otherwise-unwilling donative promisors would be forced to keep their promises. However, it is also possible that making simple donative promises enforceable would result in less gifting: Many donative promisors make gifts only because they have earlier promised to do so, and many prospective donative promisors might refrain from making a promise in the first place if the promise was legally enforceable.

Moreover, just as a donative promisor has moral obligations, so too does a donative promisee. Suppose that a promisor lacks an objectively satisfactory excuse for not keeping a promise, but nevertheless does not want to perform. Perhaps the promisor has an excuse that he believes is satisfactory, although reasonable persons would not agree. Perhaps the promisor has simply changed his mind. Under the morality of *duty*, the promisor is obliged to keep his promise. Accordingly, in the world of commercial contracts, if the promisor has a duty to keep his promise, it is normally proper for the promisee to enforce the promise. In the world of gift, however, matters are not so straightforward. It may be wrong for a donative promisor to break a donative promise, but also wrong for the promisee to insist on performance, because under the morality of *aspiration*, where a donative promise is made for affective reasons, such as love or friendship, a donative promisee is often morally obliged to release a repenting promisor.

An article by Andrew Kull, Reconsidering Gratuitous Promises, 21 J. Legal Stud. 39 (1992), is instructive in this regard. Kull argues that simple donative promises should be enforceable. However, Kull also concludes that if, say, Uncle has made a donative promise to Nephew and later changes his mind, it might well be "unthinkable" for Nephew to sue Uncle. But if suit is unthinkable, how can enforceability be desirable? The principle that simple donative promises are unenforceable prevents the unthinkable from occurring, by capturing, as an enforceability regime would not, the promisee's moral obligation to release a repenting promisor from a simple, affective donative promise.

SECTION 2. THE ELEMENT OF FORM

Von Mehren, Civil-Law Analogues to Consideration: An Exercise in Comparative Analysis

72 Harv.L.Rev. 1009, 1016–1017 (1959)

"In French, German, and common-law thinking four general, interrelated concerns lead the systems to treat a given transaction type as unenforceable. There is a concern for evidentiary security, a desire to protect both the individual citizen and the courts against manufactured evidence and difficulties resulting from insufficiencies in the available proof. The individual must be safeguarded against his own rashness and the importuning of others. The enforceable obligation needs to be marked off or signalized so as to ensure an awareness on the individual's part that his action may have legal significance and to simplify the administration of justice. Finally, there is unwillingness to enforce transaction types considered suspect or of marginal value. To facilitate exposition, these four concerns will be referred to as evidentiary, cautionary, channeling, and deterrent policies."

NOTE ON THE CHANNELING FUNCTION
OF CONTRACT-LAW RULES

The channeling function referred to by von Mehren depends on the assumption that actors will know contract law, so that rules of contract law can in fact provide incentives and disincentives to engage in given kinds of behavior. However, experience suggests that most nonlawyers don't know contract law.

Whether actors are likely to know any given rule of contract law will depend in part on whether the rule is one that is probably relevant only to actors who regularly negotiate contracts, or is relevant even to actors who don't regularly negotiate contracts. However, even actors who regularly negotiate contracts are likely to know the relevant rules of contract law only if they are tutored by lawyers on those rules, or get into court on a repeated basis, or are normally counseled when they make contracts. In most cases, none of these conditions will prevail. For example, even lawyers who regularly draft contracts for a certain client are unlikely to tutor the client on contract law, except to the extent that a given contract raises minefield issues. This is especially true where the client is an organization and decision-making power over contracts is dispersed over a large number of different persons in the organization.

Whether it is likely that actors will know any given rule of contract law therefore must be determined on a rule-by-rule basis. There are some areas where it *is* likely that actors will either know the law in advance or will be counseled on the law when they make a contract. In such cases, contract law does provide incentives and disincentives. In other cases, it doesn't.

SCHNELL V. NELL

Supreme Court of Indiana, 1861.
17 Ind. 29, 79 Am.Dec. 453.

PERKINS, J. Action by J.B. Nell against Zacharias Schnell, upon the following instrument:

"This agreement, entered into this 13th day of February, 1856, between Zach. Schnell, of Indianapolis, Marion county, State of Indiana, as party of the first part, and J.B. Nell, of the same place, Wendelin Lorenz, of Stilesville, Hendricks county, State of Indiana, and Donata Lorenz, of Frickinger, Grand Duchy of Baden, Germany, as parties of the second part witnesseth: The said Zacharias Schnell agrees as follows: Whereas his wife, Theresa Schnell, now deceased, has made a last will and testament in which, among other provisions, it was ordained that every one of the above-named second parties, should receive the sum of $200; and whereas the said provisions of the will must remain a nullity, for the reason that no property, real or personal, was in the possession of the said Theresa Schnell, deceased, in her own name, at the time of her death, and all property held by Zacharias and Theresa Schnell jointly, therefore reverts to her husband; and whereas the said Theresa Schnell has also been a dutiful and loving wife to the said Zach. Schnell, and has materially aided him in the acquisition of all property, real and personal, now possessed by him; for, and in consideration of all this and the love and respect he bears to his wife; and, furthermore, in consideration of one cent, received by him of the second parties, he, the said Zach. Schnell, agrees to pay the above named sums of money to the parties of the second part, to wit: $200 to the said J.B. Nell; $200 to the said Wendelin Lorenz; and $200 to the said Donata Lorenz, in the following installments, viz., $200 in one year from the date of these presents; $200 in two years; and $200 in three years; to be divided between the parties in equal portions of $66²/₃ each year, or as they may agree, till each one has received his full sum of $200. And the said parties of the second part, for, and in consideration of this, agree to pay the above-named sum of money (one cent), and to deliver up to said Schnell, and abstain from collecting any real or supposed claims upon him or his estate, arising from the said last will and testament of the said Theresa Schnell, deceased. In witness whereof, the said parties have, on this 13th day of February, 1856, set hereunto their hands and seals. Zacharias Schnell. [Seal.] J.B. Nell. [Seal.] Wen. Lorenz. [Seal.]"

The complaint contained no averment of a consideration for the instrument, outside of those expressed in it; and did not aver that the one cent agreed to be paid, had been paid or tendered.

A demurrer to the complaint was overruled.

The defendant answered, that the instrument sued on was given for no consideration whatever.

He further answered, that it was given for no consideration, because his said wife, Theresa, at the time she made the will mentioned, and at the time of her death, owned neither separately, nor jointly with her husband, or anyone else (except so far as the law gave her an interest in her husband's property), any property, real or personal, etc. . . .

The court sustained a demurrer to these answers, evidently on the ground that they were regarded as contradicting the instrument sued on, which particularly set out the considerations upon which it was executed. But the instrument is latently ambiguous on this point. See Ind.Dig., p. 110.

The case turned below, and must turn here, upon the question whether the instrument sued on does express a consideration sufficient to give it legal obligation, as against Zacharias Schnell. It specifies three distinct considerations for his promise to pay $600:

(1) A promise, on the part of the plaintiffs, to pay him one cent.

(2) The love and affection he bore his deceased wife, and the fact that she had done her part, as his wife, in the acquisition of the property.

(3) The fact that she had expressed her desire, in the form of an inoperative will, that the persons named therein should have the sums of money specified.

The consideration of one cent will not support the promise of Schnell. It is true, that as a general proposition, inadequacy of consideration will not vitiate an agreement. Baker v. Roberts, 14 Ind. 552. But this doctrine does not apply to a mere exchange of sums of money of coin, whose value is exactly fixed, but to the exchange of something of, in itself, indeterminate value, for money, or, perhaps, for some other thing of indeterminate value. In this case had the one cent mentioned been some particular one cent, a family piece, or ancient, remarkable coin, possessing an indeterminate value, extrinsic from its simple value, a different view might be taken. As it is, the mere promise to pay six hundred dollars for one cent, even had the portion of that cent due from the plaintiff been tendered, is an unconscionable contract, void, at first blush, upon its face, if it be regarded as an earnest one. Hardesty v. Smith, 3 Ind. 39. The consideration of one cent is, plainly, in this case, merely nominal, and intended to be so. As the will and testament of Schnell's wife imposed no legal obligation upon him to discharge her bequests out of his property, and as she had none of her own, his promise to discharge them was not legally binding upon him, on that ground. A moral consideration, only, will not support a promise. Ind.Dig., p. 13. And for the same reason, a valid consideration for his promise cannot be found in the fact of a compromise of a disputed claim; for where such claim is legally groundless, a promise upon a compromise of it, or of a suit upon it, is not legally binding. Spahr v. Hollingshead, 8 Blackf. 415. There was no mistake of law or fact in this case, as the agreement admits the will inoperative and void. The promise was simply one to make a gift. The past services of his wife, and the love and affection he had borne her, are objectionable as legal considerations for Schnell's promise, on two grounds: (1) They are past considerations. Ind.Dig., p. 13. (2) The fact that Schnell loved his wife and that she had been industrious, constituted no consideration for his promise to pay J.B. Nell, and the Lorenzes, a sum of money. Whether, if his wife, in her lifetime had made a bargain with Schnell, that, in consideration of his promising to pay, after her death, to the persons named, a sum of money, she would be industrious, and worthy of his affection, such a promise would have been valid and consistent with public policy, we need not decide. Nor is the fact that Schnell now venerates the memory of his deceased wife a legal consideration for a promise to pay any third person money.

The instrument sued on, interpreted in the light of the facts alleged in the second paragraph of the answer, will not support an action. The demurrer to the answer should have been overruled. See Stevenson v. Druley, 4 Ind. 519.

Judgment reversed.

————

NOTE ON STATUTES APPLICABLE IN SCHNELL V. NELL

A statute in Indiana, which was in effect when *Schnell v. Nell* was decided, provided as follows: "A failure or want of consideration, in whole or in part, may be pleaded in any action, set-off or counter-claim upon or arising out of any specialty,* bond or deed, except instruments negotiable by the law merchant and negotiated before falling due." 2 Ind.Rev.Stats. 44–45 (1852). Another statute provided, "There shall be no difference in evidence between sealed and unsealed writings; and every writing not sealed, shall have the same force and effect that it would have if sealed. A writing under seal, except conveyances of real estate, or any interest therein, may therefore be changed, or altogether discharged, by a writing not under seal. An agreement in writing, without a seal, for the compromise or settlement of a debt, is as obligatory as if a seal were affixed." Id. § 492.

————

NOTE ON NOMINAL CONSIDERATION

The problem in *Schnell v. Nell* concerns what is now known as nominal consideration. Essentially, the term nominal consideration plays off the bargain theory of consideration. A bargain is a substantive transaction, consisting of an exchange in which each party views what she gives up as the *price* of what she gets. A transaction is said to involve nominal consideration when it has the form of a bargain but not the substance of a bargain, because it is clear that the promisor does not view what she gives up as the price of what she gets. So, for example, it is clear that in *Schnell v. Nell* the promisor, Schnell, did not view one cent as the price of his promise to pay $600. (It is possible that the promisees in *Schnell v. Nell* agreed to do other things, such as not bringing suit against Mrs. Schnell's estate, and that Schnell viewed these other things as the price of his promise. Even if that were the case,

————

*   A "specialty" is a contract under seal. (Footnote by eds.)

however, it remains true that Schnell did not view the one cent as the price of his promise.)

A basic axiom of the classical school of contract law was the bargain theory of consideration—that to constitute consideration a promise or performance must be bargained for. Ironically, however, as the bargain theory of consideration was actually elaborated by the classical school, it could be satisfied even though no bargain had been made: both Holmes and Restatement First took the view that the form of a bargain would suffice to make a promise enforceable. Holmes expressed his view in two well-known aphorisms:

Consideration is as much a form as a seal

and

[I]t is the essence of a consideration, that, by the terms of the agreement, it is given and accepted as the motive or inducement of the promise. Conversely, the promise must be made and accepted as the conventional motive or inducement for furnishing the consideration. The root of the whole matter is the relation of reciprocal conventional inducement, each for the other, between consideration and promise.

By the term *reciprocal inducement*, Holmes meant a bargain. By the term *conventional*, Holmes apparently meant a formal expression whose meaning and significance is artificially determined, like a bidding convention in the game of bridge. Thus, in Holmes's view, if the parties deliberately adopted the convention—that is, the form—of a bargain, the law would enforce their promises as though they had made an *actual* bargain.

Illustration 1 to Restatement First § 84 reflected the same idea:

A wishes to make a binding promise to his son B to convey to B Blackacre, which is worth $5000. Being advised that a gratuitous promise is not binding, A writes to B an offer to sell Blackacre for $1. B accepts. B's promise to pay $1 is sufficient consideration.

Restatement Second has retained the bargain definition of consideration. In two Illustrations, however, Restatement Second has reversed the position of Restatement First on nominal consideration, and adopted a test that requires a bargain in fact, rather than in form, to make a promise enforceable under the bargain principle:

4.   A desires to make a binding promise to give $1000 to his son B. Being advised that a gratuitous promise is not binding, A writes out and signs a false recital that B has sold him a car for $1000 and a promise to pay that amount. There is no consideration for A's promise.

5. A desires to make a binding promise to give $1000 to his son B. Being advised that a gratuitous promise is not binding, A offers to buy from B for $1000 a book worth less than $1. B accepts the offer knowing that the purchase of the book is a mere pretense. There is no consideration for A's promise to pay $1000.

Although Restatement Second rejects the concept of nominal consideration as a general principle, it does provide that nominal consideration makes a promise enforceable in two specific areas—options and guaranties. (An option is an offer accompanied by an enforceable promise to hold the offer open. A guarantee is a promise by A to C that if B doesn't pay B's debt to C, A will.) The cases in this area are not entirely consistent. The majority rule is that a mere recital of nominal consideration does not make an option binding. On the other hand, many of the cases hold that even the most negligible consideration will make an option enforceable if it is *paid*. See, e.g., Board of Control v. Burgess, 45 Mich.App. 183, 206 N.W.2d 256 (1973) ($1 nominal consideration not paid; option unenforceable; option would have been enforceable if the $1 had been paid). The reason for this distinction is not clear. If the consideration is really nominal, it is no less a form just because it is paid. Perhaps actual payment of nominal consideration is viewed as a better form than the mere recital of a bargain, because a physical transfer of money may have more psychological impact than a mere recital.

NOTE ON FORM AND THE HISTORY OF THE SEAL

The contract in *Schnell v. Nell* ended as follows: "In witness whereof, the said parties have . . .set hereunto their hands and seals. Zacharias Schnell. [Seal.] J.B. Nell. [Seal.] Wen. Lorenz. [Seal.]" Prior to statutory reforms in the 19th and early 20th centuries, a promise under seal occupied a special status in contract law, differing from an unsealed promise in a number of respects. The most important difference was that a promise under seal was enforceable even though it was donative.

Originally, a seal was an impression in wax, or some other medium, made by stamping the medium with a mold that was usually either part of a ring (a signet ring) or at the end of a handle. In its origin, the seal was a "natural formality"—that is, a promissory form that is popularly understood to carry legal significance—involving a writing, a ritual of hot wax, and a physical object, the signet ring, that personified its owner—elements that ensured both deliberation and proof.

The history of the seal can be summarized in terms of two movements: (1) A gradual "liberalization" of the requirement, from impressed wax, to an attached paper wafer, to a "scroll" in ink, to the printed word SEAL. (2) A gradual but widespread elimination of the special legal effects of the seal.[1] There is a close interrelation between these two movements. A sealed promise deserves special treatment, such as enforceability and a longer statute of limitations—only to the extent that the seal is socially recognized as a legal formality. Where the requirements for what constitutes a seal have been relaxed to the point of social meaninglessness, there is no longer any justification for giving a sealed promise a special effect.

However, the consequence of the widespread elimination of the special treatment of sealed promises is that in most states there is no longer available any legal device that can be employed with the certainty that it will bind a promisor to a promise when consideration is in doubt. Accordingly, the question arises whether the legislature should adopt, or the courts should recognize, some substitute formality that would have this effect.

The Uniform Commercial Code contains a number of provisions that dispense with consideration for certain types of contracts, including Section 2–205 on firm offers and Section 2–209(1) on contract modifications. Similarly, a series of New York statutes, enacted on the recommendation of the New York Law Revision Commission and now collected in N.Y. General Obligations Law §§ 5–1101 to 5–1115, 15–303, dispenses with consideration for certain types of promises—for example, promises to discharge a contract—if the promises are made in writing and signed. See Braucher, The Commission and The Law of Contracts, 40 Corn.L.Q. 696, 698–703 (1955). And many legislatures have adopted statutes which provide that a written instrument is presumptive evidence of consideration. See, e.g., Cal.Civ.Code § 1614.[2] Presumably, the presumption under these statutes is rebuttable, but even so these statutes can have a substantive effect, because it may sometimes be difficult to rebut the presumption, particularly where the promisor has died and suit is brought against his legal representative.

The narrow scope or effect of these statutes mean that they do not make a genuinely donative promise legally enforceable. The question arises, should the law recognize some new formality to play the role once played by the seal? An obvious candidate for this role is nominal consideration—that is, the *form* of a bargain—because it can be safely assumed that parties who falsely cast a nonbargain promise as a bargain do so for the express purpose of making the promise legally enforceable. A rule that nominal consideration makes a promise enforceable would have obvious benefits, but would also involve some

---

[1]   About two-thirds of the states have now adopted statutory provisions depriving the seal of its binding effect. The first of the two Indiana statutes quoted in the Note on Statutes Applicable in Schnell v. Nell, supra, is an example of one approach taken by these statutes, which is to allow a lack of consideration to be pleaded as a defense. The second Indiana statute quoted in that Note is an example of a second approach taken by these statutes, which is to abolish the distinction between sealed and unsealed instruments. See also, e.g. Cal.Civ.Code § 1629. Another approach is to abolish the use of a seal in contracts. See, e.g., Iowa Code Ann. § 537A.1.

[2]   The scope of the California statute has been narrowed by cases holding that the term "written instrument," as used in the statute, means a formal document, and does not include an ordinary letter. See Weisbrod v. Weisbrod, 27 Cal.App.2d 712, 81 P.2d 633 (1938); Foltz v. First Trust & Sav. Bank, 86 Cal.App.2d 59, 194 P.2d 135 (1948).

costs. Such a rule would render donative promises enforceable when the promisor included a recital of nominal consideration. Both morally and legally, however, an obligation created by a donative promise should normally be excused either by acts of the promisee amounting to ingratitude, or by a change in the personal circumstances of the promisor that render it improvident to keep the promise. If Uncle promises to give Nephew $20,000 in two years, and Nephew later wrecks Uncle's living room in an angry rage, Uncle should not remain obliged. The same result should ordinarily follow if Uncle suffers a serious financial setback and is barely able to take care of the needs of his immediate family, or if Uncle's wealth remains constant but his personal obligations significantly increase in an unexpected manner, as through illness or the birth of children.

Form alone cannot meet these problems. Thus the French and German Civil Codes, which provide special formalities that enable a donative promise to be made legally enforceable, also provide extensive treatment of ingratitude and improvidence as defenses. For example, under article 519(1) of the German Civil Code, a promisor may refuse to perform an otherwise-enforceable donative promise "insofar as, having regard to his other obligations, he is not in a position to fulfill the promise without endangering his own reasonable maintenance or the fulfillment of obligations imposed upon him by law to furnish maintenance to others." Under article 530(1), a donative promise may be revoked "if the donee, by any serious misconduct towards the donor or a close relative of the donor shows himself guilty of gross ingratitude." Similarly, under articles 960–966 of the French Civil Code, a donative promise made by a person with no living descendants is normally revoked by operation of law upon the birth of a child. Under articles 953 and 955, a donative promise can be revoked on the ground of ingratitude that involves serious cruelty, wrongs, or injuries.

As these rules suggest, the common law could not appropriately make donative promises enforceable solely on the basis of form unless the courts were also prepared to develop and administer a body of rules dealing with the problems of improvidence and ingratitude. Certainly such an enterprise is possible. It may be questioned, however, whether the benefits would be worth the costs. An inquiry into changed personal circumstances involves the measurement of wealth, lifestyle, dependents' needs, and even personal utilities. An inquiry into ingratitude involves the measurement of a maelstrom, because many or most donative promises arise in an intimate context in which emotions, motives, and cues are invariably complex and highly interrelated. Perhaps the civil-law style of adjudication is suited to wrestling with these kinds of inquiries, but they have held little appeal for common-law courts, which traditionally have been oriented toward inquiry into acts rather than into personal characteristics. Given these problems, the nonrecognition of a formality for making donative promises enforceable is understandable, if not preferable.

———

SECTION 3. THE ELEMENT OF RELIANCE

The cases in Sections 1 and 2 illustrate that the moral obligation to keep a promise is not a sufficient ground for concluding that there is a *legal* obligation to keep a promise. The moral obligation is a strong starting-point for concluding that there should be a legal obligation, because the courts should take moral norms into account in making law. It is not, however, conclusive, because in making legal rules a lawmaker must also consider social policy and administrative concerns, such as problems of proof.

More generally, that private conduct violates a moral norm does not alone justify the use of collective (governmental) resources to legally sanction the conduct. In some cases, like cutting in line, the injury caused by violation of a moral norm is not significant enough to justify a legal sanction. In other cases, like the failure to support aged parents who cannot support themselves, legal enforceability of a moral norm would intrude too far, without sufficient justification, into intimate areas better governed by social norms. In still other cases, legal enforceability of a moral norm would raise difficult problems of administrability. Thus as stated by Thomas Scanlon, "The fact that some action is morally required is not, in general, a sufficient justification for legal intervention to force people to do it; and the rationale for the law of contracts does not seem to be . . . an instance of the legal enforcement of morality."

The issue then is, what additional moral or policy elements, beyond the moral obligation to keep a promise, should make a given type of promise enforceable. This Section explores one such element: a significant injury to the promisee; in particular, a cost that the promisee incurs in reliance on the promise.

———

KIRKSEY V. KIRKSEY
Supreme Court of Alabama, 1845.
8 Ala. 131.

Assumpsit by defendant, against the plaintiff in error.

The plaintiff was the wife of defendant's brother, but had for some time been a widow, and had several children. In 1840, the plaintiff resided on public land, under a contract of lease, she had held over, and was comfortably settled, and would have attempted to secure the land she lived on. The defendant resided in Talladega county, some sixty or seventy miles off. On the 10th October, 1840, he wrote to her the following letter:

"Dear Sister Antillico,—Much to my mortification, I heard that brother Henry was dead, and one of his children. I know that your situation is one of grief and difficulty. You had a bad chance before, but a great deal worse now. I should like to come and see you, but cannot with convenience at present . . . I do not know whether you have a preference on the place you live on or not. If you had, I would advise you to obtain your preference, and sell the land and quit the country, as I understand it is very unhealthy, and I know society is very bad. If you will come down and see me, I will let you have a place to raise your family, and I have more open land than I can tend; and on the account of your situation, and that of your family, I feel like I want you and the children to do well."

Within a month or two after the receipt of this letter, the plaintiff abandoned her possession, without disposing of it, and removed with her family, to the residence of the defendant, who put her in comfortable houses, and gave her land to cultivate for two years, at the end of which time he notified her to remove, and put her in a house, not comfortable, in the woods, which he afterwards required her to leave.

A verdict being found for the plaintiff, for $200, the above facts were agreed, and if they will sustain the action, the judgment is to be affirmed, otherwise it is to be reversed.

ORMOND, J. The inclination of my mind is that the loss and inconvenience which the plaintiff sustained in breaking up and moving to the defendant's a distance of sixty miles is a sufficient consideration to support the promise to furnish her with a house and land to cultivate until she could raise her family. My brothers, however, think that the promise on the part of the defendant was a mere gratuity, and that an action will not lie for its breach.

The judgment of the court below must therefore be reversed, pursuant to the agreement of the parties.

INTRODUCTORY NOTE ON PROMISSORY ESTOPPEL

During the late nineteenth and early twentieth centuries, contract law was dominated by a school of thought now known as classical contract law. This school defined contract in its most general terms as a promise the law will enforce, a view that persists. See Restatement, Second, Contracts § 1. In classical contract law, the doctrine of consideration performed the essential task of determining what promises were legally enforceable. Classical contract law took it as axiomatic that only a bargain is consideration and that, accordingly, a donative promise could not be enforced. Cases like *Kirksey v. Kirksey* anticipated this axiom.

Even during the classical era, however, courts often found a way to allow a claim where a donative promise had been relied upon. Some cases used the doctrine of equitable estoppel. Ricketts v. Scothorn, 57 Neb. 51, 77 N.W. 365 (1898), is a leading case. Testator was distressed because his granddaughter had to work in a store. To enable her to give up her job, he delivered to her a promissory note for $2,000, saying "I have fixed out something that you have not got to work any more." In reliance on the note, the granddaughter quit work. Testator died without either paying or repudiating the note. The granddaughter brought suit on the note against the grandfather's executor, and the court held for the granddaughter. The court side-stepped the issue of whether reliance constituted consideration by concluding that reliance "estopped" (prevented) the executor from *pleading* a lack of consideration.

The approach taken in *Ricketts* drew on a doctrine known as *equitable estoppel* or *estoppel in pais*. The peculiar way the court used the doctrine follows from a maxim that equitable estoppel "operates always as a shield, never as a sword . . . [A]nd it does not of itself create new rights." Utschig v. McClone, 114 N.W.2d 854, 855 (Wis. 1962). Thus in *Ricketts* the court did not hold the grandfather's promissory note to be enforceable on the basis of equitable estoppel. Instead the court held the executor to be estopped from pleading a lack of consideration as a defense to a contract claim.

The use of equitable estoppel in *Ricketts* is difficult to square with another maxim of the doctrine. According to this maxim, equitable estoppel requires that the party asserting estoppel have relied on a misstatement of fact, and a misstatement of intent or a misstatement regarding a future event is not a basis for equitable estoppel. For example, in Ferro v. Society of St. Pius X, 149 P.3d 813 (Idaho), Ferro sought redress within his church after being slandered by a priest. A priest who took his side assured Ferro that the miscreant priest would be transferred and amends would be made by the church "to meet any damages." Relying on the priest's assurances, Ferro did not take legal action until the statute of limitations had run on his tort claim for defamation. The trial court allowed a claim by Ferro against the church, on the ground that the church was estopped from asserting the statute of limitations as a defense. The Idaho Supreme Court reversed on the ground that there could be no estoppel because the misstatement concerned a future event.

The doctrine of *promissory estoppel* is distinct from the doctrine of equitable estoppel in two respects. First, equitable estoppel generally is based on a statement of past or present fact that the defendant made to the plaintiff. In contrast, promissory estoppel is based on a promise concerning the future that the defendant made to the plaintiff. Second, equitable estoppel may help a plaintiff establish a cause of action against the defendant, but equitable estoppel is not a cause of action—a plaintiff cannot bring suit in equitable estoppel. In contrast, a plaintiff can bring suit in promissory estoppel.

Despite these differences, both doctrines turn on the core idea of reliance. More precisely, the two doctrines may be best understood as particular instances of a broader concept: When one person, A, uses words or actions that he knows or should know would induce another, B, to reasonably believe that A is committed to take a certain course of action, and A knows or should know that B will incur costs if A doesn't take action, A should take steps to ensure that if he doesn't take the action, B will not suffer a loss. See T.M. Scanlon, Promises and Practices, 19 Phil. & Pub. Affairs 199 (1990). Also both doctrines are technically considered to be equitable in nature. As a consequence, legal relief under both doctrines is discretionary, and not a matter of right. And disputed factual issue generally are resolved by a judge, and not a jury, under both doctrines.

In many states, promissory estoppel is pled as a cause of action, typically in conjunction with a claim for breach of contract. For example, in Toscano v. Greene Music, 124 Cal. App. 4th 685 (Cal. App. 2004), Toscano quit his job as general manager of a piano store in reliance on the defendant's offer of employment as general manager of another store When the defendant withdrew the offer Toscano sued for breach of contract and promissory estoppel, as well as on other theories. The breach of contract claim was dismissed on a motion for summary judgment, but the promissory estoppel claim was allowed to proceed to a bench trial, where Toscano prevailed. The doctrine of promissory estoppel is important in contract litigation and contract law because a promissory estoppel claim (or the doctrine) can avoid several impediments to recovery on a breach of contract claim. One of these impediments is the requirement of bargained for consideration.

The Restatement of Contracts does not treat promissory estoppel as a claim or action that is distinct from an action for breach of contract. Instead the doctrine is accounted for by several provisions that make reliance a basis for overcoming an impediment to recovery on a breach of contract claim. The most important of these provisions is Section 90, which was included to account for cases like *Ricketts v. Scothorn* where the doctrine of equitable estoppel was used to overcome the impediment of the absence of bargained for consideration. As adopted in Restatement First, Section 90 provided as follows:

> A promise which the promisor should reasonably expect to induce action or forbearance of a definite and substantial character on the part of the promisee and which does induce such action or forbearance is binding if injustice can be avoided only by enforcement of the promise.

The principal case that follows is a leading case applying § 90 and the doctrine of promissory estoppel to enforce a donative promise. A promissory estoppel claim fails in the note case. After you have read the principal case and the note case, you may find it useful to go back to *Kirksey v. Kirksey* and ask how a promissory estoppel claim would have fared in that case, had it been considered.

———

RESTATEMENT, SECOND, CONTRACTS § 90

[See Selected Source Materials Supplement]

FEINBERG v. PFEIFFER CO.
Missouri Court of Appeals, 1959.
322 S.W.2d 163.

DOERNER, COMMISSIONER. This is a suit brought in the Circuit Court of the City of St. Louis by plaintiff, a former employee of the defendant corporation, on an alleged contract whereby defendant agreed to pay plaintiff the sum of $200 per month for life upon her retirement. A jury being waived, the case was tried by the court alone. Judgment below was for plaintiff for $5,100, the amount of the pension claimed to be due as of the date of the trial, together with interest thereon, and defendant duly appealed.

The parties are in substantial agreement on the essential facts. Plaintiff began working for the defendant, a manufacturer of pharmaceuticals, in 1910, when she was but 17 years of age. By 1947 she had attained the position of bookkeeper, office manager, and assistant treasurer of the defendant, and owned 70 shares of its stock out of a total of 6,503 shares issued and outstanding. Twenty shares had been given to her by the defendant or its then president, she had purchased 20, and the remaining 30 she had acquired by a stock split or stock dividend. Over the years she received substantial dividends on the stock she owned, as did all of the other stockholders. Also, in addition to her salary, plaintiff from 1937 to 1949, inclusive, received each year a bonus varying in amount from $300 in the beginning to $2,000 in the later years.

On December 27, 1947, the annual meeting of the defendant's Board of Directors was held at the Company's offices in St. Louis, presided over by Max Lippman, its then president and largest individual stockholder. The other directors present were George L. Marcus, Sidney Harris, Sol Flammer, and Walter Weinstock, who, with Max Lippman, owned 5,007 of the 6,503 shares then issued and outstanding. At that meeting the Board of Directors adopted the following resolution, which because it is the crux of the case, we quote in full:

"The Chairman thereupon pointed out that the Assistant Treasurer, Mrs. Anna Sacks Feinberg, has given the corporation many years of long and faithful service. Not only has she served the corporation devotedly, but with exceptional ability and skill. The President pointed out that although all of the officers and directors sincerely hoped and desired that Mrs. Feinberg would continue in her present position for as long as she felt able, nevertheless, in view of the length of service which she has contributed provision should be made to afford her retirement privileges and benefits which should become a firm obligation of the corporation to be available to her whenever she should see fit to retire from active duty, however many years in the future such retirement may become effective. It was, accordingly, proposed that Mrs. Feinberg's salary which is presently $350.00 per month, be increased to $400.00 per month, and that Mrs. Feinberg would be given the privilege of retiring from active duty at any time she may elect to see fit so to do upon a retirement pay of $200.00 per month for life, with the distinct understanding that the retirement plan is merely being adopted at the present time in order to afford Mrs. Feinberg security for the future and in the hope that her active services will continue with the corporation for many years to come. After due discussion and consideration, and upon motion duly made and seconded, it was—

> "Resolved, that the salary of Anna Sacks Feinberg be increased from $350.00 to $400.00 per month and that she be afforded the privilege of retiring from active duty in the corporation at any time she may elect to see fit so to do upon retirement pay of $200.00 per month, for the remainder of her life."

At the request of Mr. Lippman his sons-in-law, Messrs. Harris and Flammer, called upon the plaintiff at her apartment on the same day to advise her of the passage of the resolution. Plaintiff testified on cross-examination that she had no prior information that such a pension plan was contemplated, that it came as a surprise to her, and that she would have continued in her employment whether or not such a resolution had been adopted. It is clear from the evidence that there was no contract, oral or written, as to plaintiff's length of employment, and that she was free to quit, and the defendant to discharge her, at any time.

Plaintiff did continue to work for the defendant through June 30, 1949, on which date she retired. In accordance with the foregoing resolution, the defendant began paying her the sum of $200 on the first of each month. Mr. Lippman died on November 18, 1949, and was succeeded as president of the company by his widow. Because of an illness, she retired from that office and was succeeded in October, 1953, by her son-in-law, Sidney M. Harris. Mr. Harris testified that while Mrs. Lippman had been president she signed the monthly pension check paid plaintiff, but fussed about doing so, and considered the payments as gifts. After his election, he stated, a new accounting firm employed by the defendant questioned the validity of the payments to plaintiff on several occasions, and in the Spring of 1956, upon its recommendation, he consulted the Company's then attorney, Mr. Ralph Kalish. Harris testified that both Ernst and Ernst, the accounting firm, and Kalish told him there was no need of giving plaintiff the money. He also stated that he had concurred in the view that the payments to plaintiff were mere gratuities rather than amounts due under a contractual obligation, and that following his discussion with the Company's attorney plaintiff was sent a check for $100 on April 1, 1956. Plaintiff declined to accept the reduced amount, and this action followed. Additional facts will be referred to later in this opinion.

Appellant's first assignment of error relates to the admission in evidence of plaintiff's testimony over its objection, that at the time of trial she was sixty-five and a half years old, and that she was no longer able to engage in gainful employment because of the removal of a cancer and the performance of a colocholecystostomy operation on November 25, 1957. Its complaint is not so much that such evidence was irrelevant and immaterial, as it is that the trial court erroneously made it one basis for its decision in favor of plaintiff. As defendant concedes, the error (if it was error) in the admission of such evidence would not be a ground for reversal, since, this being a jury-waived case, we are constrained by the statutes to review it upon both the law and the evidence, Sec. 510.310 RSMo 1949, V.A.M.S., and to render such judgment as the court below ought to have given. Section 512.160, Minor v. Lillard, Mo., 289 S.W.2d 1; Thumm v. Lohr, Mo.App., 306 S.W.2d 604. We consider only such evidence as is admissible, and need not pass upon questions of error in the admission and exclusion of evidence. Hussey v. Robison, Mo., 285 S.W.2d 603. However, in fairness to the trial court it should be stated that while he briefly referred to the state of plaintiff's health as of the time of the trial in his amended findings of fact, it is obvious from his amended grounds for decision and judgment that it was not, as will be seen, the basis for his decision.

Appellant's next complaint is that there was insufficient evidence to support the court's findings that plaintiff would not have quit defendant's employ had she not known and relied upon the promise of defendant to pay her $200 a month for life, and the finding that, from her voluntary retirement until April 1, 1956, plaintiff relied upon the continued receipt of the pension installments. The trial court so found, and, in our opinion, justifiably so. Plaintiff testified, and was corroborated by Harris, defendant's witness, that knowledge of the passage of the resolution was communicated to her on December 27, 1947, the very day it was adopted. She was told at that time by Harris and Flammer, she stated, that she could take the pension as of that day, if she wished. She testified further that she continued to work for another year and a half, through June 30, 1949; that at that time her health was good and she could have continued to work, but that after working for almost forty years she thought she would take a rest. Her testimony continued:

"Q. Now, what was the reason—I'm sorry. Did you then quit the employment of the company after you—after this year and a half?

"A. Yes.

"Q. What was the reason that you left?

"A. Well, I thought almost forty years, it was a long time and I thought I would take a little rest.

"Q. Yes.

"A. And with the pension and what earnings my husband had, we figured we could get along.

"Q. Did you rely upon this pension?

"A. We certainly did.

"Q. Being paid?

"A. Very much so. We relied upon it because I was positive that I was going to get it as long as I lived.

"Q. Would you have left the employment of the company at that time had it not been for this pension?

"A. No.

"Mr. Allen: Just a minute, I object to that as calling for a conclusion and conjecture on the part of this witness.

"The Court: It will be overruled.

"Q. (Mr. Agatstein continuing): Go ahead, now. The question is whether you would have quit the employment of the company at that time had you not relied upon this pension plan?

"A. No, I wouldn't.

"Q. You would not have. Did you ever seek employment while this pension was being paid to you—

"A. (interrupting): No.

"Q. Wait a minute, at any time prior—at any other place?

"A. No, sir.

"Q. Were you able to hold any other employment during that time?

"A. Yes, I think so.

"Q. Was your health good?

"A. My health was good."

It is obvious from the foregoing that there was ample evidence to support the findings of fact made by the court below.

We come, then, to the basic issue in the case. While otherwise defined in defendant's third and fourth assignments of error, it is thus succinctly stated in the argument in its brief: "... whether plaintiff has proved that she has a right to recover from defendant based upon a legally binding contractual obligation to pay her $200 per month for life."

It is defendant's contention, in essence, that the resolution adopted by its Board of Directors was a mere promise to make a gift, and that no contract resulted either thereby, or when plaintiff retired, because there was no consideration given or paid by the plaintiff. It urges that a promise to make a gift is not binding unless supported by a legal consideration; that the only apparent consideration for the adoption of the foregoing resolution was the "many years of long and faithful service" expressed therein; and that past services are not a valid consideration for a promise. Defendant argues further that there is nothing in the resolution which made its effectiveness conditional upon plaintiff's continued employment, that she was not under contract to work for any length of time but was free to quit whenever she wished, and that she had no contractual right to her position and could have been discharged at any time.

Plaintiff concedes that a promise based upon past services would be without consideration, but contends that there were two other elements which supplied the required element: First, the continuation by plaintiff in the employ of the defendant for the period from December 27, 1947, the date when the resolution was adopted, until the date of her retirement on June 30, 1949. And, second, her change of position, i.e., her retirement, and the abandonment by her of her opportunity to continue in gainful employment, made in reliance on defendant's promise to pay her $200 per month for life.

We must agree with the defendant that the evidence does not support the first of these contentions. There is no language in the resolution predicating plaintiff's right to a pension upon her continued employment. She was not required to work for the defendant for any period of time as a condition to gaining such retirement benefits. She was told that she could quit the day upon which the resolution was adopted, as she herself testified, and it is clear from her own testimony that she made no promise or agreement to continue in the employ of the defendant in return for its promise to pay her a pension. Hence there was lacking that mutuality of obligation which is essential to the validity of a contract. . . .

But as to the second of these contentions we must agree with plaintiff. . . .

Section 90 of the Restatement, Law of Contracts states that: "A promise which the promisor should reasonably expect to induce action or forbearance of a definite and substantial character on the part of the promisee and which does induce such action or forbearance is binding if injustice can be avoided only by enforcement of the promise." This doctrine has been described as that of "promissory estoppel," as distinguished from that of equitable estoppel or estoppel in pais, the reason for the differentiation being stated as follows:

> "It is generally true that one who has led another to act in reasonable reliance on his representations of fact cannot afterwards in litigation between the two deny the truth of the representations, and some courts have sought to apply this principle to the formation of contracts, where, relying on a gratuitous promise, the promisee has suffered detriment. It is to be noticed, however, that such a case does not come within the ordinary definition of estoppel. If there is any representation of an existing fact, it is only that the promisor at the time of making the promise intends to fulfill it. As to such intention there is usually no misrepresentation and if there is, it is not that which has injured the promisee. In other words, he relies on a promise and not on a misstatement of fact; and the term 'promissory' estoppel or something equivalent should be used to make the distinction." Williston on Contracts, Rev.Ed., Sec. 139, Vol. 1.

In speaking of this doctrine, Judge Learned Hand said in Porter v. Commissioner of Internal Revenue, 2 Cir., 60 F.2d 673, 675, that ". . . 'promissory estoppel' is now a recognized species of consideration."

As pointed out by our Supreme Court in In re Jamison's Estate, Mo., 202 S.W.2d 879, 887, it is stated in the Missouri Annotations to the Restatement under Section 90 that:

> " 'There is a variance between the doctrine underlying this section and the theoretical justifications that have been advanced for the Missouri decisions.' "

That variance, as the authors of the Annotations point out, is that:

> "This § 90, when applied with § 85, means that the promise described is a contract without any consideration. In Missouri the same practical result is reached without in theory abandoning the doctrine of consideration. In Missouri three theories have been advanced as ground for the decisions (1) *Theory of act for promise.* The induced 'action or forbearance' is the consideration for the promise. . . . (2) *Theory of promissory estoppel.* The induced 'action or forbearance' works an estoppel against the promisor. . . . (3) *Theory of bilateral contract.* When the induced 'action or forbearance' is begun, a promise to complete is implied, and we have an enforceable bilateral contract, the implied promise to complete being the consideration for the original promise." (Citing cases.)

Was there such an act on the part of plaintiff, in reliance upon the promise contained in the resolution, as will estop the defendant, and therefore create an enforceable contract under the doctrine of promissory estoppel? We think there was. One of the illustrations cited under Section 90 of the Restatement is: "2. A promises B to pay him an annuity during B's life. B thereupon resigns a profitable employment, as A expected that he might. B receives the annuity for some years, in the meantime becoming disqualified from again obtaining good employment. A's promise is binding." This illustration is objected to by defendant as not being applicable to the case at hand. The reason advanced by it is that in the illustration B became "disqualified" from obtaining other employment *before* A discontinued the payments, whereas in this case the plaintiff did not discover that she had cancer and thereby became unemployable until *after* the defendant had discontinued the payments of $200 per month. We think the distinction is immaterial. The only reason for the reference in the illustration to the disqualification of A is in connection with that part of Section 90 regarding the prevention of injustice. The injustice would occur regardless of when the disability occurred. Would defendant contend that the contract would be enforceable if the plaintiff's illness had been discovered on March 31, 1956, the day before it discontinued the payment of the $200 a month, but not if it occurred on April 2nd, the day after? Furthermore, there are more ways to become disqualified for work, or unemployable, than as the result of illness. At the time she retired plaintiff was 57 years of age. At the time the payments were discontinued she was over 63 years of age. It is a matter of common knowledge that it is virtually impossible for a woman of that age to find satisfactory employment, much less a position comparable to that which plaintiff enjoyed at the time of her retirement.

The fact of the matter is that plaintiff's subsequent illness was not the "action or forbearance" which was induced by the promise contained in the resolution. As the trial court correctly decided, such action on plaintiff's part was her retirement from a lucrative position in reliance upon defendant's promise to pay her an annuity or pension. In a very similar case, Ricketts v. Scothorn, 57 Neb. 51, 77 N.W. 365, 367, 42 L.R.A. 794, the Supreme Court of Nebraska said:

> ". . . Having intentionally influenced the plaintiff to alter her position for the worse on the faith of the note being paid when due, it would be grossly inequitable to permit the maker, or his executor, to resist payment on the ground that the promise was given without consideration."

The Commissioner therefore recommends, for the reasons stated, that the judgment be affirmed.

PER CURIAM.

The foregoing opinion by DOERNER, C., is adopted as the opinion of the court. The judgment is, accordingly, affirmed.

WOLFE, P.J., and ANDERSON and RUDDY, JJ., concur.

———

Hayes v. Plantations Steel Co.

438 A.2d 1091 (R.I.1982)

Plantations Steel Co. was founded by Hugo R. Mainelli, Sr., and Alexander A. Dimartino. Hayes was employed by Plantations from 1947 to 1972. In January 1972, Hayes announced his intention to retire in July because he had worked continuously for fifty-one years. Hayes was then sixty-five, and was Plantation's general manager, a position of considerable responsibility. About a week before his actual retirement, Hayes spoke with Hugo R. Mainelli Jr., an officer and a shareholder of Plantations. Mainelli Jr. said that the company "would take care" of Hayes, although there was no mention of a sum of money or a percentage of salary that Hayes would receive. Mainelli Jr.'s father, Hugo R. Mainelli Sr., authorized the first payment "as a token of appreciation for the many years of [Hayes's] service." It was implied that payments would continue on an annual basis, and it was Mainelli Jr.'s personal intention that the payments would continue for as long as he was around. Four annual payments of $5,000 each were made.

After Hayes's retirement, he visited Plantations each year to say hello and renew old acquaintances. During the course of his visits, Hayes would thank Mainelli Jr. for the previous check, and ask how long the checks would continue, so that he could plan an orderly retirement. In 1976, the DiMartinos assumed full control of Plantations as a result of a dispute between the two founding families. After 1976, the payments to Hayes were discontinued. A succession of several poor business years and the takeover by the DiMartino family contributed to the decision to stop the payments. Hayes brought suit. Held, for Plantations.

(Shea, J.) "[T]he important distinction between *Feinberg* and the case before us is that in *Feinberg* the employer's decision definitely shaped the thinking of the plaintiff. In this case the promise did not. It is not reasonable to infer from the facts that Hugo R. Mainelli, Jr., expected retirement to result from his conversation with Hayes. Hayes had given notice of his intention seven months previously. Here there was thus no inducement to retire which would satisfy the demands of § 90 of the Restatement. Nor can it be said that Hayes's refraining from other employment was 'action or forbearance of a definite and substantial character.' The underlying assumption of Hayes's initial decision to retire was that upon leaving the defendant's employ, he would no longer work. It is impossible to say that he changed his position any more so because of what Mainelli had told him in light of his own initial decision. These circumstances do not lead to a conclusion that injustice can be avoided only by enforcement of Plantations's promise. Hayes received $20,000 over the course of four years. He inquired each year about whether he could expect a check for the following year. Obviously, there was no absolute certainty on his part that the pension would continue. Furthermore, in the face of his uncertainty, the mere fact that payment for several years did occur is insufficient by itself to meet the requirements of reliance under the doctrine of promissory estoppel."

———

NOTE ON CONTRACT REMEDIES AND CONSIDERATION

The essential question considered in Part 1 of this casebook, under the heading *Consideration*, is what promises should and does the law enforce? On both a theoretical and a practical level, this question is inseparable from the issue, to what extent shall a particular kind of promise be enforced?

When issues of remedy are examined in detail (as they will be in Part 2), they present a great number of complexities and policy choices. At this point it is useful to examine some of these issues in a preliminary way.

Injury. One way to address the issue of damages for breach of an enforceable promise is to ask what injury the promisee has suffered. In a contract setting, the term "injury" to a promisee can have several different meanings. One meaning is that the promisee is worse off than he would have been if the promise had not been made. Another meaning is that the promisee is worse off than he would have been if the promise had been performed. The interests of a promisee that are invaded by these two different types of injuries are known as the reliance interest and the expectation interest, respectively.

These two distinct meanings of injury correspond to two distinct purposes of damages for breach of contract. *Reliance damages* have the purpose of restoring a promisee back to the position that he would have been in if the promise had not been made. If this purpose is perfectly achieved, a potential promisee is equally well off whether there is (i) no promise, or (ii) promise, breach, and payment of damages. *Expectation damages* have the purpose of placing a promisee forward to the position that he would have been in if the promise had been performed. If this purpose is perfectly achieved, the promisee is equally well off whether there is (i) promise and performance, or (ii) promise, breach, and payment of damages.*

Compensation. In our legal system, compensation is measured in money. Ideally, compensation is the sum of money that is sufficient to make the victim of an injury equally well off with the injury and the money as he would have been without the injury and the money. In this ideal sense, compensatory damages are the money equivalent of the injury. The idea of a money equivalent to an injury can be clarified with help from economic theory. Economists measure the well-being of individuals by the amount of satisfaction

---

* To keep matters simple, other contractual interests and remedies will not be considered in this Note.

they enjoy, and measure the well-being of firms by their profits. Compensation for an injury is "perfect" if it enables the victim to enjoy the same level of satisfaction (if an individual) or profits (if a firm) as would have prevailed without the injury. Computing compensatory damages involves comparing the victim's uninjured state with the injured state, in order to determine how much money is needed to make up the difference. (As a practical matter, an award of damages often falls well short of the ideal because money is an imperfect substitute for the victim's injury, and because the victim must accept whatever price a court or jury sets on her loss.)

Because there are two different conceptions of the uninjured state in a contract setting, there are also two different conceptions of compensation. Compensation for reliance requires an award such that the injured promisee will achieve the level of satisfaction or profits that would have been achieved if the promise had never been made. In contrast, compensation for expectation requires an award such that the injured party will achieve the level of satisfaction or profits that would have been achieved if the promise had been performed. Under the expectation conception of compensation, therefore, compensation is the amount required to make the promisee indifferent between performance and damages. (Expectation damages are properly described as compensatory because the promisor's wrong is breaking the promise, and the promisee's rightful position is the position he would have been in had the promise not been broken.)

Reliance damages. Let us focus here on the reliance conception. What compensation is necessary to put a relying promisee in a state just as good as he would have been in if the promise had not been made? When a promise is made, the promisee may rely upon it by incurring various financial and nonfinancial costs that cannot be fully recouped if the promise is broken. Broadly speaking, these costs fall into two classes—out-of-pocket costs and opportunity costs.

Out-of-pocket costs. Out-of-pocket costs are the costs incurred by a promisee in reliance on the promise prior to breach, less the value produced by those costs that can be realized after breach. To illustrate, assume that Aunt promises Niece that she will reimburse Niece for the cost of a $25,000 car. Niece purchases a car for $25,000 in cash on January 5, and immediately tells Aunt about the purchase. Aunt replies that she will not keep her promise. Niece's out-of-pocket costs are the difference between her outlay of $25,000 and the resale value of the car on January 5.

Opportunity costs. Engaging in one activity often entails forgoing an opportunity to engage in another. Opportunity costs are the surplus that the promisee would have enjoyed if he had taken the opportunity that the promise led him to forgo. More specifically, if, as a result of a breach, the injured party must purchase a substitute performance, the opportunity cost equals the difference between the price of the substitute performance and the best alternative contract price that was available to the party at the time of contracting. To illustrate, assume that at a time when Niece is about to buy a certain inexpensive make of car, Aunt promises Niece that if she purchases a certain more expensive make, Aunt will pay the full price. Niece begins shopping for the more expensive make of car, but before she makes the purchase, Aunt revokes her promise. Meanwhile, the less expensive make has gone up in price from $17,000 to $18,000. If Niece then purchases that make of car, she has suffered an opportunity cost of $1,000, because the promise led her to forgo buying that make when it cost $1,000 less.

With this background, let us return to the best measure of damages for breach of a relied-upon donative promise. *Dougherty v. Salt* teaches that a simple unrelied-upon donative promise is normally unenforceable. Section 90 of the Restatement teaches that reliance may make a donative promise enforceable. But to what *extent* should a relied-upon promise be enforceable? Or, to put it differently, what injury to a relying donative promisee should the law compensate? Since a relied-upon donative promise is enforced because, and only because, it has been relied upon, in the normal case the promise should be enforced to the extent of the reliance, that is, by a reliance (rather than an expectation) measure of damages. For reasons of policy or administrability, however, in at least some cases it might be desirable to employ an expectation measure as a surrogate for reliance. Indeed, when Restatement First was being debated on the floor of the ALI, Samuel Williston, the Reporter, went much further, and took the position that the expectation measure should be used in all Section 90 cases:

> MR. WILLISTON: . . . Johnny says, "I want to buy a Buick car." Uncle says, "Well, I will give you $1000." . . . [Uncle] knows that that $1000 is going to be relied on by the nephew for the purchase of a car. . . .

> [MR.] PRICKETT: May I ask the Reporter if in the example he gave of Johnny and the car, his uncle's promise would be enforceable when Johnny buys the car?

> MR. WILLISTON: I should say so, because the promise was made as a direct reply to Johnny's expression of a desire for a car. . . .

> MR. PRICKETT: Suppose Johnny pays no money down.

> MR. WILLISTON: If he has got the car and is liable for the price he gets the $1000 under this Section. . . .

> MR. PRICKETT: My idea is this: If he gets the car and pays no money down, if the car is taken away from him, has he suffered any substantial injury?

> MR. WILLISTON: Oh, I think he has, as long as he is liable for the price. . . .

> [MR.] TUNSTALL: . . . Suppose the car had been a Ford instead of a Buick, costing $600.

> . . . Johnny says, "I want to buy a Ford" and . . . not being familiar with the market price of a Ford, the uncle says, "I will give

you $1000." Now, is the uncle obligated for the $1000 or for the price of the Ford?

MR. WILLISTON: I think he might be bound for the $1000.

MR. COUDERT: . . . Please let me see if I understand it rightly. Would you say, Mr. Reporter, in your case of Johnny and the uncle, the uncle promising the $1000 and Johnny buying the car—say, he goes out and buys the car for $500—that uncle would be liable for $1000 or would he be liable for $500?

MR. WILLISTON: If Johnny had done what he was expected to do, or is acting within the limits of his uncle's expectation, I think the uncle would be liable for $1000; but not otherwise . . .

In Restatement Second, Section 90 was revised to explicitly negate Williston's view. This was accomplished by adding a new sentence to Section 90: "The remedy granted for breach may be limited as justice requires." The express purpose of this sentence is to permit the use of a reliance measure of damages in Section 90 cases.

This revision, while salutary, leaves open the following questions: (1) On what basis is it to be determined when justice requires the use of a reliance rather than an expectation measure? (2) Precisely how are reliance damages to be measured in a donative-promise context?

As applied to strictly financial interests, these questions often are relatively straightforward. If Aunt promises to give Niece $1200 for opera tickets during the 2006 season, and retracts her promise after Niece has purchased and used $600 worth of tickets, it seems clear that Aunt's liability should ordinarily be $600, not $1200. A court will not subtract Niece's non-financial benefit of attending the opera.

Sometimes a court will subtract a financial benefit realized by the promisee from relying on a promise from the promisee's out-of-pocket costs. For example, suppose Aunt promises to give Niece $25,000 for the purchase of a new car, to be paid in one year. Aunt retracts her promise, but only after Niece has purchased the car and driven it for six months. At the point of retraction, Niece's financial loss is the difference between $25,000 and the car's resale value. Though Niece could argue she should be entitled to keep the car and the entire $25,000 as compensation for some other loss she suffered in reliance on the promise, such as by giving up an apartment near a subway and taking an apartment that required a car.

Sometimes a promisee's reliance will involve a combination of nonfinancial opportunity costs and nonfinancial benefits. Suppose, for example, that Uncle promises to reimburse Nephew for his expenses, up to $12,000, for a four-week vacation in New York City. Nephew purchases a round-trip plane ticket for $900 and goes to New York. After he is there for a week, and has spent another $2,500 on hotels, meals, and entertainment, Uncle calls and says, "I'm not giving you any more money than you've already spent. Come back now, or pay for the rest of your vacation yourself." Nephew's financial loss at that point is only $3,400. But suppose that Nephew is entitled to only one four-week vacation each year, and except for Uncle's promise of a full four weeks in New York, Nephew would have gone backpacking with friends who have now set off without him. On these facts, Nephew has incurred a nonfinancial opportunity cost equal to the difference between the value he places on the vacation that he got and the value he places on the vacation that he lost out on. Assuming this opportunity cost was reasonably foreseeable, should Uncle be liable for this cost as well? If so, how should it be measured? One answer is that the best way to approximate this kind of cost may be to use the value of the promise that caused the promisee to forgo the opportunity. To put this differently, in cases where reliance damages are difficult to establish but obviously significant, the expectation measure may be used as a surrogate for reliance damages.

The vacation case also poses the problem of accounting for nonfinancial benefits. In an action by Nephew to recover his $3,400 financial loss, is Uncle entitled to an offset for the value of the enjoyment that Nephew derived from the trip? For these purposes, the value of a benefit to the promisee would ideally be the amount he would have been willing to pay for the benefit out of his own pocket. This amount will be very difficult to determine. Usually, it would be less than the cost of the benefit. Often, it would be considerably less, because a gift often consists of cash to purchase a luxury that the donee would not have purchased if he had been given cash to spend in anyway he chose. The difficulty of determining the amount that the promisee would have paid for such a benefit, coupled with the likelihood that in many cases the amount would be relatively small, suggests that nonfinancial or intangible benefits should often—perhaps ordinarily—be disregarded in determining a donative promisee's recovery.

———

Goldstick v. ICM Realty

788 F.2d 456 (7th Cir.1986)

(Posner, J.) "As a matter of strict logic one might suppose that the plaintiffs, even if they succeeded in establishing a promissory estoppel, would not necessarily be able to recover the value of the promise. . . . It would seem they would have to show their actual damages: what they gave up . . . in reliance on [the] promise. . . .

"This approach treats promissory estoppel as a tort doctrine for purposes of damages, though it is conventionally classified as a contract doctrine. . . . Some cases do award just the tort measure of damages in promissory estoppel cases, rather than giving the plaintiff the value of the promise, which he would be entitled to in a breach of contract action. . . . In Gerson Electric Construction Co. v. Honeywell, Inc., 117 Ill.App.3d 309, 312–13, 72 Ill.Dec. 851, 853, 453 N.E.2d 726, 728 (1983), however, the Illinois Appellate Court held that a plaintiff in a promissory estoppel case could recover damages for the profits he would have made had the defendant kept his promise—provided such an award was necessary to do justice to the plaintiff.

"There is much to be said for using the value of the promise as the measure of damages, simply on grounds of simplicity. . . . In addition, an expectation measure of damages will frequently cover opportunity costs (which are real, but not out-of-pocket, costs), that the reliance measure would miss. . . . "

SECTION 4. PROMISES BASED ON A PAST BENEFIT CONFERRED ("PAST CONSIDERATION")

Section 4 considers the enforceability of promises that are, for the most part, motivated by a moral obligation that preexists the promise. Such a promise is a special case of donative promise, in the sense that it is not bargained for. It differs from a simple donative promise, because a simple donative promise may *give rise* to a moral obligation but is not *based on* a preexisting moral obligation.

RESTATEMENT, SECOND, CONTRACTS §§ 82, 83

[See Selected Source Materials Supplement]

BANKRUPTCY CODE, 11 U.S.C. § 524

[See Selected Source Materials Supplement]

NOTE ON TRADITIONAL EXCEPTIONS TO THE PAST CONSIDERATION RULE

The rule that "past consideration" is no consideration had three exceptions under classical contract law. These cases are: (1) A promise to pay a debt barred by the statute of limitations. (2) A promise by an adult to pay a debt incurred when the adult was under legal age (so that the contract was not enforceable against her). (3) A promise to pay a debt that has been discharged in bankruptcy. (The practical significance of the bankruptcy case has been limited by § 524 of the Bankruptcy Code, which creates a number of hurdles that must be jumped to make such a promise enforceable, but the doctrinal significance of this case is likely to persist.)

In all three of these cases, the discussion in the traditional commentaries was not concerned with justifying the result, which was thought to need no justification, but in reconciling the result with the bargain theory of consideration. The standard explanation evaded the problem by finding consideration in the exchange that gave rise to the original debt, while giving effect to the later promise on grounds that did not require treating it as a contract. For example, it was said that in the case of the infant's contract, the original contract is not "void," but "voidable," and that when the infant, after coming of age, promises to perform it, he "affirms" the contract, and gives up his power to avoid it. Then in the case of the debt barred by the statute of limitations and the discharged bankrupt, it was said that the new promise of the debtor "waives" the defense of the statute or the discharge, and that a "waiver" does not require consideration.

An alternative explanation recognizes these cases as exceptions to the bargain theory of consideration and treats a moral obligation to pay for a benefit received as a legal basis for enforcing a promise to make that payment. Restatement Second of Contracts Section 87 takes such an approach, placing these cases alongside promissory estoppel (Section 90) under the heading "Contracts Without Consideration."

The remainder of this Chapter addresses the question whether these core cases stand by themselves or are instances of a more general principle under which a promise may be enforced to avoid unjust enrichment, even in the absence of bargained-for consideration or reliance. Answering this question requires a look at the law of unjust enrichment, which is the third major part of the law of private obligations alongside contract law and tort law.

MILLS V. WYMAN

Supreme Judicial Court of Massachusetts, 1825.
3 Pick. [20 Mass.] 207.

This was an action of assumpsit brought to recover a compensation for the board, nursing, & c., of Levi Wyman, son of the defendant, from the 5th to the 20th of February, 1821. The plaintiff then lived at Hartford, in Connecticut; the defendant, at Shrewsbury, in this county. Levi Wyman, at the time when the services were rendered, was about 25 years of age, and had long ceased to be a member of his father's family. He was on his return from a voyage at sea, and being suddenly taken sick at Hartford, and being poor and in distress, was relieved by the plaintiff in the manner and to the extent above stated. On the 24th of February, after all the expenses had been incurred, the defendant wrote a letter to the plaintiff, promising to pay him such expenses. There was no consideration for this promise, except what grew out of the relation which subsisted between Levi Wyman and the defendant, and Howe, J., before whom the cause was tried in the court of common pleas, thinking this not sufficient to support the action, directed a nonsuit. To this direction the plaintiff filed exceptions.

Parker, C.J. General rules of law established for the protection and security of honest and fair-minded men, who may inconsiderately make promises without any equivalent, will sometimes screen men of a different character from engagements which they are bound in *foro conscientiae* to perform. This is a defect inherent in all human systems of legislation. The rule that a mere verbal promise, without any consideration, cannot be enforced by action, is universal in its application, and cannot be departed from to suit particular cases in which a refusal to perform such a promise may be disgraceful.

The promise declared on in this case appears to have been made without any legal consideration. The kindness and services towards the sick son of the defendant were not bestowed at his request. The son was in no respect under the care of the defendant. He was twenty-five years old, and had long left his father's family. On his return from a foreign country, he fell sick among strangers, and the plaintiff acted the part of the good Samaritan, giving him shelter and comfort until he died. The defendant, his father, on being informed of this event, influenced by a transient feeling of gratitude, promises in writing to pay the plaintiff for the expenses he had incurred. But he has determined to break this promise, and is willing to have his case appear on record as a strong example of particular injustice sometimes necessarily resulting from the operation of general rules.

It is said a moral obligation is a sufficient consideration to support an express promise; and some authorities lay down the rule thus broadly; but upon examination of the cases we are satisfied that the universality of the rule cannot be supported, and that there must have been some preexisting obligation, which has become inoperative by positive law, to form a basis for an effective promise. The cases of debts barred by the statute of limitations, of debts incurred by infants, of debts of bankrupts, are generally put for illustration of the rule. Express promises founded on such preexisting equitable obligations may be enforced; there is a good consideration for them; they merely remove an impediment created by law to the recovery of debts honestly due, but which public policy protects the debtors from being compelled to pay. In all these cases there was originally a quid pro quo; and according to the principles of natural justice the party receiving ought to pay; but the legislature has said he shall not be coerced; then comes the promise to pay the debt that is barred, the promise of the man to pay the debt of the infant, of the discharged bankrupt to restore to his creditor what by the law he had lost. In all these cases there is a moral obligation founded upon an antecedent valuable consideration. These promises therefore have a sound legal basis. They are not promises to pay something for nothing; not naked pacts; but the voluntary revival or creation of obligation which before existed in natural law, but which had been dispensed with, not for the benefit of the party obliged solely, but principally for the public convenience. If moral obligation, in its fullest sense, is a good substratum for an express promise, it is not easy to perceive why it is not equally good to support an implied promise. What a man ought to do, generally he ought to be made to do, whether he promise or refuse. But the law of society has left most of such obligations to the interior forum, as the tribunal of conscience has been aptly called. Is there not a moral obligation upon every son who has become affluent by means of the education and advantages bestowed upon him by his father, to relieve that father from pecuniary embarrassment, to promote his comfort and happiness, and even to share with him his riches, if thereby he will be made happy? And yet such a son may, with impunity, leave such a father in any degree of penury above that which will expose the community in which he dwells, to the danger of being obliged to preserve him from absolute want. Is not a wealthy father under strong moral obligation to advance the interest of an obedient, well disposed son, to furnish him with the means of acquiring and maintaining a becoming rank in life, to rescue him from the horrors of debt incurred by misfortune? Yet the law will uphold him in any degree of parsimony, short of that which would reduce his son to the necessity of seeking public charity.

Without doubt there are great interests of society which justify withholding the coercive arm of the law from these duties of imperfect obligation, as they are called; imperfect, not because they are less binding upon the conscience than those which are called perfect, but because the wisdom of the social law does not impose sanctions upon them.

A deliberate promise, in writing, made freely and without any mistake, one which may lead the party to whom it is made into contracts and expenses, cannot be broken without a violation of moral duty. But if there was nothing paid or promised for it, the law, perhaps wisely, leaves the execution of it to the conscience of him who makes it. It is only when the party making the promise gains something, or he to whom it is made loses something, that the law gives the promise validity. And in the case of the promise of the adult to pay the debt of the infant, of the debtor discharged by the statute of limitations or bankruptcy, the principle is preserved by looking back to the origin of the transaction, where an equivalent is to be found. An exact equivalent is not required by the law; for there being a consideration, the parties are left to estimate its value: though here the courts of equity will step in to relieve from gross inadequacy between the consideration and the promise.

These principles are deduced from the general current of decided cases upon the subject as well as from the known maxims of the common law. The general position, that moral obligation is a sufficient consideration for an express promise, is to be limited in its application, to cases where at some time or other a good or valuable consideration has existed.

A legal obligation is always a sufficient consideration to support either an express or an implied promise; such as an infant's debt for necessaries, or a father's promise to pay for the support and education of his minor children. But when the child shall have attained to manhood, and shall have become his own agent in the world's business, the debts he incurs, whatever may be their nature, create no obligation upon the father; and it seems to follow, that his promise founded upon such a debt has no legally binding force.

The cases of instruments under seal and certain mercantile contracts, in which considerations need not be proved, do not contradict the principles above suggested. The first import a consideration in themselves, and the second belong to a branch of the mercantile law, which has found it necessary to disregard the point of consideration in respect to instruments negotiable in their nature and essential to the interests of commerce.

Instead of citing a multiplicity of cases to support the positions I have taken, I will only refer to a very able review of all the cases in the note in 3 Bos. & P. 249. The opinions of the judges had been variant for a long course of years upon this subject, but there seems to be no case in which it was nakedly decided, that a promise to pay the debt of a son of full age, not living with his father, though the debt were incurred by sickness which ended in the death of the son, without a previous request by the father proved or presumed, could be enforced by action.

It has been attempted to show a legal obligation on the part of the defendant by virtue of our statute, which compels lineal kindred in the ascending or descending line to support such of their poor relations as are likely to become chargeable to the town where they have their settlement. But it is a sufficient answer to this position, that such legal obligation does not exist except in the very cases provided for in the statute, and never until the party charged has been adjudged to be of sufficient ability thereto. We do not know from the report any of the facts which are necessary to create such an obligation. Whether the deceased had a legal settlement in this commonwealth at the time of his death, whether he was likely to become chargeable had he lived, whether the defendant was of sufficient ability, are essential facts to be adjudicated by the court to which is given jurisdiction on this subject. The legal liability does not arise until these facts have all been ascertained by judgment, after hearing the party intended to be charged.

For the foregoing reasons we are all of opinion that the nonsuit directed by the court of common pleas was right, and that judgment be entered thereon for costs for the defendant.

———

BACKGROUND NOTE ON MILLS V. WYMAN

Based on an analysis of original judicial and historical records, Professor Geoffrey Watson reports that Levi Wyman's "illness was a protracted one: by all accounts it lasted at least two weeks. Daniel Mills, the Good Samaritan who housed and cared for Levi Wyman, arranged for two men to guard Levi for four days and nights while Levi 'was in his derang'd state.' Levi was so sick that 'he leaped out of a chamber window to the imminent hazard of his life, and to the very great alarm of the family and the boarders.' . . . Mills also hired John Lee Comstock, a prominent Hartfort physician, to care for Wyman. Comstock found Levi 'in a state of indisposition' and, for some time 'in a state of delirium' that required two or three persons 'to prevent him from injuring himself.' [Mills's] expenses amounted to about twenty-two dollars—a considerable sum in those days—and included six dollars for fourteen days' board and lodging, three dollars for "Room pine and Candles," one dollar for a gallon of "Spirits," six dollars in expenses for the two men hired to restrain Levi, and six dollars for Dr. Comstock's fee." Wilson, In the Tribunal of Conscience: Mills v. Wyman Reconsidered, 71 Tul. L. Rev. 1749 (1997). (This article contains a wealth of other information about the facts and background of the case, including facts that suggest that Levi might actually have survived his illness and died much later.)

WEBB V. McGOWIN
Court of Appeals of Alabama, 1935.
27 Ala.App. 82, 168 So. 196.

Action by Joe Webb against N. Floyd McGowin and Joseph F. McGowin, as executors of the estate of J. Greeley McGowin, deceased. From a judgment of nonsuit, plaintiff appeals.

Reversed and remanded. . . .

BRICKEN, PRESIDING JUDGE. This action is in assumpsit. The complaint as originally filed was amended. The demurrers to the complaint as amended were sustained, and because of this adverse ruling by the court the plaintiff took a nonsuit, and the assignment of errors on this appeal are predicated upon said action or ruling of the court.

A fair statement of the case presenting the questions for decision is set out in appellant's brief, which we adopt.

"On the 3d day of August, 1925, appellant while in the employ of the W.T. Smith Lumber Company, a corporation, and acting within the scope of his employment, was engaged in clearing the upper floor of mill No. 2 of the company. While so engaged he was in the act of dropping a pine block from the upper floor of the mill to the ground below; this being the usual and ordinary way of clearing the floor, and it being the duty of the plaintiff in the course of his employment to so drop it. The block weighed about 75 pounds.

"As appellant was in the act of dropping the block to the ground below, he was on the edge of the upper floor of the mill. As he started to turn the block loose so that it would drop to the ground, he saw J. Greeley McGowin, testator of the defendants, on the ground below and directly under where the block would have fallen had appellant turned it loose. Had he turned it loose it would have struck McGowin with such force as to have caused him serious bodily harm or death. Appellant could have remained safely on the upper floor of the mill by turning the block loose and allowing it to drop, but had he done this the block would have fallen on McGowin and caused him serious injuries or death. The only safe and reasonable way to prevent this was for appellant to hold to the block and divert its direction in falling from the place where McGowin was standing and the only safe way to divert it so as to prevent its coming into contact with McGowin was for appellant to fall with it to the ground below. Appellant did this, and by holding to the block and falling with it to the ground below, he diverted the course of its fall in such way that McGowin was not injured. In thus preventing the injuries to McGowin appellant himself received serious bodily injuries, resulting in his right leg being broken, the heel of his right foot torn off and his right arm broken. He was badly crippled for life and rendered unable to do physical or mental labor.

"On September 1, 1925, in consideration of appellant having prevented him from sustaining death or serious bodily harm and in consideration of the injuries appellant had received, McGowin agreed with him to care for and maintain him for the remainder of appellant's life at the rate of $15 every two weeks from the time he sustained his injuries to and during the remainder of appellant's life; it being agreed that McGowin would pay this sum to appellant for his maintenance. Under the agreement McGowin paid or caused to be paid to appellant the sum so agreed on up until McGowin's death on January 1, 1934. After his death the payments were continued to and including January 27, 1934, at which time they were discontinued. Thereupon plaintiff brought suit to recover the unpaid installments accruing up to the time of the bringing of the suit. . . . "

The action was for the unpaid installments accruing after January 27, 1934, to the time of the suit.

The principal grounds of demurrer to the original and amended complaint are: (1) It states no cause of action; (2) its averments show the contract was without consideration; (3) it fails to allege that McGowin had, at or before the services were rendered, agreed to pay appellant for them; (4) the contract declared on is void under the statute of frauds.

The averments of the complaint show that appellant saved McGowin from death or grievous bodily harm. This was a material benefit to him of infinitely more value than any financial aid he could have received. Receiving this benefit, McGowin became morally bound to compensate appellant for the services rendered. Recognizing his moral obligation, he expressly agreed to pay appellant as alleged in the complaint and complied with this agreement up to the time of his death; a period of more than 8 years.

Had McGowin been accidentally poisoned and a physician, without his knowledge or request, had administered an antidote, thus saving his life, a subsequent promise by McGowin to pay the physician would have been valid. Likewise, McGowin's agreement as disclosed by the complaint to compensate appellant for saving him from death or grievous bodily injury is valid and enforceable.

Where the promisee cares for, improves, and preserves the property of the promisor, though done without his request, it is sufficient consideration for the promisor's subsequent agreement to pay for the service, because of the material benefit received. . . . Edson v. Poppe, 24 S.D. 466, 124 N.W. 441, 26 L.R.A. (N.S.) 534.

In Boothe v. Fitzpatrick, 36 Vt. 681, the court held that a promise by defendant to pay for the past keeping of a bull which had escaped from defendant's premises and been cared for by plaintiff was valid, although there was no previous request, because the subsequent promise obviated that objection; it being equivalent to a previous request. On the same principle, had the promisee saved the promisor's life or his body from grievous harm, his subsequent promise to pay for the services rendered would have been valid. Such service would have been far more material than caring for his bull. Any holding that saving a man from death or grievous bodily harm is not a material benefit sufficient to uphold a subsequent promise to pay for the service, necessarily rests on the assumption that saving life and preservation of the body from harm have only a sentimental value. The converse of this is true. Life and preservation of the body have material, pecuniary values, measurable in dollars and cents. Because of this, physicians practice their profession charging for services rendered in saving life and curing the body of its ills, and surgeons perform operations. The same is true as to the law of negligence authorizing the assessment of damages in personal injury cases based upon the extent of the injuries, earnings, and life expectancies of those injured.

In the business of life insurance, the value of a man's life is measured in dollars and cents according to his expectancy, the soundness of his body, and his ability to pay premiums. The same is true as to health and accident insurance.

It follows that if, as alleged in the complaint, appellant saved J. Greeley McGowin from death or grievous bodily harm, and McGowin subsequently agreed to pay him for the service rendered, it became a valid and enforceable contract.

It is well settled that a moral obligation is a sufficient consideration to support a subsequent promise to pay where the promisor has received a material benefit, although there was no original duty or liability resting on the promisor. [Extensive citation of cases omitted.]

The case at bar is clearly distinguishable from that class of cases where the consideration is a mere moral obligation or conscientious duty unconnected with receipt by promisor of benefits of a material or pecuniary nature. . . . Here the promisor received a material benefit constituting a valid consideration for his promise.

Some authorities hold that, for a moral obligation to support a subsequent promise to pay, there must have existed a prior legal or equitable obligation, which for some reason had become unenforceable, but for which the promisor was still morally bound. This rule, however, is subject to qualification in those cases where the promisor, having received a material benefit from the promisee, is morally bound to compensate him for the services rendered and in consideration of this obligation promises to pay. In such cases the subsequent promise to pay is an affirmance or ratification of the services rendered carrying with it the presumption that a previous request for the service was made. . . .

Under the decisions above cited, McGowin's express promise to pay appellant for the services rendered was an affirmance or ratification of what appellant had done raising the presumption that the services had been rendered at McGowin's request.

The averments of the complaint show that in saving McGowin from death or grievous bodily harm, appellant was crippled for life. This was part of the consideration of the contract declared on. McGowin was benefited. Appellant was injured. Benefit to the promisor or injury to the promisee is a sufficient legal consideration for the promisor's agreement to pay. . . .

Under the averments of the complaint the services rendered by appellant were not gratuitous. The agreement of McGowin to pay and the acceptance of payment by appellant conclusively shows the contrary.

The contract declared on was not void under the statute of frauds (Code 1923, § 8034).

From what has been said, we are of the opinion that the court below erred in the ruling complained of; that is to say, in sustaining the demurrer, and for this error the case is reversed and remanded.

Reversed and remanded.

Samford, Judge (concurring). The questions involved in this case are not free from doubt, and perhaps the strict letter of the rule, as stated by judges, though not always in accord, would bar a recovery by plaintiff, but following the principle announced by Chief Justice Marshall in Hoffman v. Porter, Fed.Cas. No. 6,577, 2 Brock. 156, 159, where he says, "I do not think that law ought to be separated from justice, where it is at most doubtful," I concur in the conclusions reached by the court.

WEBB V. McGOWIN

Supreme Court of Alabama, 1936.
232 Ala. 374, 168 So. 199.

Certiorari to Court of Appeals.

Petition of N. Floyd McGowin and Joseph F. McGowin, as executors of the estate of J. Greeley McGowin, deceased, for certiorari to the Court of Appeals to review and revise the judgment and decision of that court in Joe Webb v. McGowin, et al. Ex'rs, 168 So. 196. . . .

FOSTER, JUSTICE. . . .

The opinion of the Court of Appeals here under consideration recognizes and applies the distinction between a supposed moral obligation of the promisor, based upon some refined sense of ethical duty, without material benefit to him, and one in which such a benefit did in fact occur. We agree with that court that if the benefit be material and substantial, and was to the person of the promisor rather than to his estate, it is within the class of material benefits which he has the privilege of recognizing and compensating either by an executed payment or an executory promise to pay. The cases are cited in that opinion. The reason is emphasized when the compensation is not only for the benefits which the promisor received, but also for the injuries either to the property or person of the promisee by reason of the service rendered.

Writ denied.

ANDERSON, C.J., and GARDNER and BOULDIN, JJ., concur.[*]

------

[*] In The Capability Problem in Contract Law (2d ed. 2004), Richard Danzig and Geoffrey R. Watson report that after the decisions by Alabama's Court of Appeals and Supreme Court, upholding Webb's complaint against a demurrer, the case was settled for $900. There was some indication that the McGowin family also gave Webb the use of a home and several acres of land. Danzig and Watson further report that J. Greeley McGowin was the President of W.T. Smith Lumber Co. Id. at 159, 178–79. (Footnote by eds.)

NOTE ON THE LAW OF UNJUST ENRICHMENT

In *Mills v. Wyman*, if the son, Levi Wyman, had survived or left an estate, then Mills might well have had a claim against Levi or his estate for the cost of caring for Levi. See, e.g., *In re Crisan's Estate*, 107 N.W.2d 907 (Mich. 1961). Sosa Crisan was admitted to a public hospital unconscious and treated for 11 months until she died, never having regained consciousness. After her death, it was learned that she owned a home. The hospital then brought a claim against her estate for the value of the care rendered. The Michigan Supreme Court allowed the claim, answering in the affirmative the question "Will the law imply a promise to pay for emergency services rendered to an unconscious patient by a public hospital?"

This is an example of a promise implied in law. Such a promise is a legal fiction. The obligation is non-promissory and is dealt with by a body of law that has been variously described as quasi-contract, restitution, or the law of unjust enrichment. Obligation in contract generally is promise-based. Obligation in torts generally is harm-based. Obligation in the law of unjust enrichment generally is benefits-based.

Restatement, Third, Restitution and Unjust Enrichment addresses cases like *In re Crisan's Estate* in Section 20. This Section provides for restitution in a case of "professional services required for the protection of another's life or health . . . if the circumstances justify the decision to intervene without request." Restitution "is measured by a reasonable charge for the services in question."

The limitation to professional services makes restitution unavailable in a case like *Webb v. McGowin*. This limitation replaces a requirement in the first Restatement of Restitution that services be rendered "unofficiously and with intent to charge therefor." Restatement, [First] Restitution § 116(a). The Comment to the Third Restatement explain the new limitation:

> b.   *Professional services.* Emergency assistance rendered by a nonprofessional, however valuable, does not give rise to a claim in restitution under existing law. The result is that professional providers of medical assistance are routinely given an enforceable claim to compensation; while the nonprofessional rescuer or good Samaritan enjoys only such rewards as others may choose to bestow. . . .The claim by a rescuer to recover for injuries suffered in the course of the rescue is a particularly compelling one, but such a recovery reflects compensation and insurance principles, not principles of unjust enrichment.

> Practical concerns are often advanced to account for this difference in treatment. It is one thing to encourage professional intervention in emergencies, another to create financial incentives for would-be rescuers who might better remain on the sidelines. The problem of valuation is even more of an obstacle. Services of physicians, hospitals, and ambulance drivers are readily valued,

while emergency rescue by a bystander is literally priceless. The fact that it is impossible to assign a value to the rescue of human life explains why the rule of § 20 is limited to professional services while the rule of § 21 (protection of another's property) is not. Unsolicited intervention to protect a person's stray livestock or unmoored sailboat can be valued with relative ease, because it usually takes the form of services (by stables and dockyards) for which there is a market. The same difficulty explains the traditional refusal in admiralty to make any award in respect of "pure life salvage," in circumstances where salvage of property would be readily compensated.

The most important objection, in terms of its implications for broader restitution doctrine, is an even more basic one. The law does not require that every benefit be paid for. See § 2(1). A heroic rescue may confer a benefit of inestimable value, but it is likely to be purely altruistic in origin. The imposition of restitutionary liability in such circumstances—a principle that would become visible only when the claim was resisted—transforms an act of self-sacrifice into a contentious exchange of values. The law avoids these unedifying consequences by presuming that an emergency rescue is a gratuitous act. The heroic bystander receives nothing; the heroic professional receives a "reasonable and customary charge" for professional services, but nothing extra for heroism.

A claim under Section 20 would be against Levi or his estate and not the father. If Levi had been a minor, so that his father was under a legal duty to care for Levi, then Mills might well have had a restitution claim against the father under Section 22 of the Third Restatement ("Performance of Another's Duty").

If Levi had been Wyman's stray horse, and not Wyman's son, and had the horse survived, then Mills might well have had a restitution claim against Wyman under Section 21 of the Third Restatement ("Protection of Another's Property"). If Mills saved the horse's life, and if a dead horse was worthless to Wyman, then Wyman would have been obligated to reimburse Mills' cost of caring for the horse before Wyman could recover possession of his horse. Wyman could avoid the obligation to pay restitution by abandoning the horse (assuming he was under no legal duty to care for the horse). If the court is uncomfortable in requiring a defendant to pay to recover his own property, then it may impose a lien on the property, with the restitution claimant to be paid out of the proceeds of a sale of the property.

Webb v. McGowin makes an oblique appearance in the Third Restatement as Illustration 7 to Section 20. The Illustration concludes that while there is no restitution claim and "B's promise is unsupported by consideration. . .it may nevertheless be enforceable as a matter of contract law. (If such a promise is enforceable, B's recognition of the fact and value of the benefit conferred by A is a significant part of the rationale.)"

———

RESTATEMENT, SECOND, CONTRACTS § 86

[See Selected Source Materials Supplement]

———

RESTATEMENT, SECOND, CONTRACTS
§ 86, ILLUSTRATIONS 1, 2, 6, 10, 12, 13

1. A gives emergency care to B's adult son while the son is sick and without funds far from home. B subsequently promises to reimburse A for his expenses. The promise is not binding under this Section.

2. A lends money to B, who later dies. B's widow promises to pay the debt. The promise is not binding under this Section. . . .

6. A finds B's escaped bull and feeds and cares for it. B's subsequent promise to pay reasonable compensation to A is binding. . . .

10. A digs a well on B's land in performance of a bargain with B's tenant C. C is unable to pay as agreed, and B promises to pay A the reasonable value of the well. The promise is binding. . . .

12. A, a married woman of sixty, has rendered household services without compensation over a period of years for B, a man of eighty living alone and having no close relatives. B has a net worth of three million dollars and has often assured A that she will be well paid for her services, whose reasonable value is not in excess of $6,000. B executes and delivers to A a written promise to pay A $25,000 "to be taken from my estate." The promise is binding.

13. The facts being otherwise as stated in Illustration 12, B's promise is made orally and is to leave A his entire estate. A cannot recover more than the reasonable value of her services.

———

Query: Is there a world in which people would believe that a promise to reimburse a stranger for the costs of having cared for the promisor's bull (Ilustration 6) should be enforceable, but a promise to reimburse a stranger for the costs of having cared for the promisor's ill adult son (Illustration 1) should not be enforceable?

———

American Law Institute, 42d Annual Proceedings

273–74 (1965) (Comments of Professor Robert Braucher, the Reporter for the Restatement, Second, of Contracts)

"Section [86] is a new provision. . . .

". . . [W]ith the help of the Advisers we went into the cases where past consideration has been upheld, and it has been a traditional thing to say: Well, there is an orthodox view that past consideration does not make a promise binding; and then there is a scattering of cases which represents a minority view which holds that some kinds of past considerations—or sometimes it is called moral considerations—do make a promise binding.

"Actually, when you go through the cases in which this problem has been raised, it seemed to us that you discover that there is a principle, and so we have tried to capture the principle, although I think it is more of a principle than it is a rule.

"If you look at section [86], it bristles with non-specific concepts; in particular, the qualification that the promise is binding to the extent necessary to prevent injustice would be entirely at large if we did not add subsection (2) which refers to the concept of unjust enrichment.

"I think in the light of the comment the principle takes on meaning, and I think there is not a division here between a majority view and a minority view. One of the famous cases on this subject is the great case of Webb v. McGowin, which is summarily stated . . . as illustration 7.

"Now, that's in Alabama. The cases in Alabama were, I suppose, as firm as the cases anywhere in rejecting the notion of past consideration or moral obligation as consideration; and yet when this case came along the case was decided for the plaintiff, as described in this illustration, and I would suppose that, given those facts and that situation, this would be likely to happen in most courts. What you have, really, is a line of distinction between essentially gratuitous transactions and cases which are on the borderline of quasi-contracts, where promise removes the difficulty which otherwise would bar quasi-contractual relief.

"We strained quite a lot to phrase this as precisely as we could. I think you cannot make it more precise—certainly not very much more precise—than we have it in the black letter here, without getting into something that you are not all able to sustain. If you look through the cases, the cases are a wide variety of miscellany, but we think there is a principle. . . ."

NOTE ON PAST CONSIDERATION

Illustrations 1, 2, 6, 10, 12, 13, supra, are based on the law of contracts, and therefore turn in part on whether a promise was made. On the facts of some of the Illustrations, a remedy may also be available under the law of restitution, either in addition to the remedy under contract law or even though there is no remedy under contract law because no promise is made to pay for the benefit. For example, restitution may be available on the facts of Illustration 6, supra, even if the owner of the escaped bull did not promise to pay for its care. Traditionally restitution was not available on the facts of Illustration 10. However, restitution may be available under Restatement, Third, Restitution and Unjust Enrichment § 25 if the liability does not subject the land owner to a forced exchange (being forced to pay for an unrequested benefit), the contractor will not otherwise be compensated for the work, and the risk of non-payment is not allocated to the contractor by agreement. Restitution is not be available on the facts of the other Illustrations.

It is easy to explain why a promise to pay for an unrequested benefit should be enforced if an obligation exists to pay for the benefit under the law of unjust enrichment independent of the promise. More difficult to explain is why a more purely moral obligation is a basis for enforcing the promise in Illustration 12 but not Illustrations 1, 2, and 13. Sometimes the answer is that there is no moral obligation. If there is a moral obligation, then a further answer is unlikely to be found in the law of unjust enrichment because the defendant's promise largely obviates the usual reasons for not requiring a person who receives an unrequested benefit to make restitution. These reasons include preserving the finality of property dispositions, preserving the primacy of contract as a mechanism for exchange, and protecting the autonomy of a restitution defendant by not subjecting them to a forced exchange. This suggests the explanation why a promise to pay for a benefit received should not be enforceable lies in contract law and the general concerns that bear on the enforceability of promises, such as the evidentiary and cautionary concerns.

The use of the terminology "unjustly enriched" in Restatement, Second, of Contracts Section 86 creates the danger that courts will import into contract law requirements for a free standing unjust enrichment claim, such as the rule in Restatement, Third, Restitution and Unjust Enrichment § 20 limiting restitution to "professional services." If A has conferred a benefit on B, the benefit gives rise to a moral obligation in B to compensate A for its value, and B later promises to pay a specific sum to A in recognition of this moral obligation and the benefit, then A's promise should be binding unless evidentiary and cautionary concerns, or changed circumstances, justify not enforcing the promise. There is no difficulty in determining that a benefit was conferred on B, because B has so stated through her promise. For the same reason, there is little difficulty in determining whether the benefit gave rise to a moral obligation by B to make compensation. Finally, there is little difficulty in determining the value of the benefit to B, because B has set that value in her promise. Restatement, Third, Restitution and Unjust Enrichment § 20 precludes only an unjust enrichment claim in a case like *Webb v. McGowin*. It does speak to the availability of a contract claim.

CHAPTER 2

THE BARGAIN PRINCIPLE AND ITS LIMITS

∎ ∎ ∎

This Chapter introduces the major type of consideration, that is, the bargain. (Indeed, recall that under the terminology used by the Restatement and many courts, the terms "bargain" and "consideration" are almost equivalent.) The first several cases in Section 1 implicitly or explicitly set out the bargain principle, under which bargains are not only enforced, but enforced according to their terms. These cases also suggest, again explicitly or implicitly, some of the reasons that lie behind the bargain principle. Sections 2 and 3 explores the limits placed on the bargain principle by the doctrines of duress and unconscionability. Sections 4 and 5 explore two further, more technical limits on the bargain principle: the doctrine of mutuality and the legal-duty rule.

SECTION 1. THE BARGAIN PRINCIPLE

Westlake v. Adams, C.P.

5 C.B. (N.S.) 248, 265 (1858)

Byles, J., said: "It is an elementary principle, that the law will not enter into an inquiry as to the adequacy of the consideration. . . . The jury have, I think, made an end of the question [of consideration]; for they have found (as well they might) that the defendant received what he bargained for, and all that he bargained for."

HAMER V. SIDWAY
Court of Appeals of New York, 1891.
124 N.Y. 538, 27 N.E. 256.

Appeal from an order of the general term of the supreme court in the fourth judicial department, reversing a judgment entered on the decision of the court at special term in the county clerk's office of Chemung county on the 1st day of October, 1889. The plaintiff presented a claim to the executor of William E. Story, Sr., for $5,000 and interest from the 6th day of February, 1875. She acquired it through several mesne assignments from William E. Story, 2d. The claim being rejected by the executor, this action was brought. It appears that William E. Story, Sr., was the uncle of William E. Story, 2d; that at the celebration of the golden wedding of Samuel Story and wife, father and mother of William E. Story, Sr., on the 20th day of March, 1869, in the presence of the family and invited guests, he promised his nephew that if he would refrain from drinking, using tobacco, swearing, and playing cards or billiards for money until he became 21 years of age, he would pay him the sum of $5,000. The nephew assented thereto, and fully performed the conditions inducing the promise. When the nephew arrived at the age of 21 years, and on the 31st day of January, 1875, he wrote to his uncle, informing him that he had performed his part of the agreement, and had thereby become entitled to the sum of $5,000.

The uncle received the letter, and a few days later, and on the 6th day of February, he wrote and mailed to his nephew the following letter: "Buffalo, Feb. 6, 1875, W.E. Story, Jr.—Dear Nephew: Your letter of the 31st ult. came to hand all right, saying that you had lived up to the promise made to me several years ago. I have no doubt but you have, for which you shall have five thousand dollars, as I promised you. I had the money in the bank the day you was twenty-one years old that I intend for you, and you shall have the money certain. Now Willie, I do not intend to interfere with this money in any way till I think you are capable of taking care of it, and the sooner that time comes the better it will please me. I would hate very much to have you start out in some adventure that you thought all right and lose this money in one year. The first five thousand dollars that I got together cost me a heap of hard work. . . . This money you have earned much easier than I did, besides, acquiring good habits at the same time, and you are quite welcome to the money. Hope you will make good use of it. I was ten long years getting this together after I was your age. . . . Truly yours, W.E. Story. P.S. You can consider this money on interest."

The nephew received the letter, and thereafter consented that the money should remain with his uncle in accordance with the terms and conditions of the letter. The uncle died on the 29th day of January, 1887, without having paid over to his nephew any portion of the said $5,000 and interest.

PARKER, J. . . . The defendant contends that the contract was without consideration to support it, and therefore invalid. He asserts that the promisee, by refraining from the use of liquor and tobacco, was not harmed, but benefited; that that which he did was best for him to do, independently of his uncle's promise,—and insists that it follows that, unless the promisor was benefited, the contract was without consideration,—a contention which, if well founded, would seem to leave open for controversy in many cases whether that which the promisee did or omitted to do was in fact of such benefit to him as to leave no consideration to support the enforcement of the promisor's agreement. Such a rule could not be tolerated, and is without foundation in the law. The Exchequer Chamber in 1875 defined "consideration" as follows: "A valuable consideration, in the sense of the law, may consist either in some right, interest, profit, or benefit accruing to the one party, or some forbearance, detriment, loss, or responsibility given, suffered, or undertaken by the other." Courts "will not ask whether the thing which forms the consideration does in fact benefit the promisee or a third party, or is of any substantial value to any one. It is enough that something is promised, done, forborne, or suffered by the party to whom the promise is made as consideration for the promise made to him." Anson.Cont. 63. "In general a waiver of any legal right at the request of another party is a sufficient consideration for a promise." Pars.Cont. *444. "Any damage, or suspension, or forbearance of a right will be sufficient to sustain a promise." 2 Kent.Comm. (12th Ed.) *465. Pollock in his work on Contracts (page 166), after citing the definition given by the Exchequer Chamber, already quoted, says: "The second branch of this judicial description is really the most important one. 'Consideration' means not so much that one party is profiting as that the other abandons some legal right in the present, or limits his legal freedom of action in the future, as an inducement for the promise of the first."

Now, applying this rule to the facts before us, the promisee used tobacco, occasionally drank liquor, and he had a legal right to do so. That right he abandoned for a period of years upon the strength of the promise of the testator that for such forbearance he would give him $5,000. We need not speculate on the effort which may have been required to give up the use of those stimulants. It is sufficient that he restricted his lawful freedom of action within certain prescribed limits upon the faith of his uncle's agreement, and now, having fully performed the conditions imposed, it is of no moment whether such performance actually proved a benefit to the promisor, and the court will not inquire into it; but, were it a proper subject of inquiry, we see nothing in this record that would permit a determination that the uncle was not benefited in a legal sense. Few cases have been found which may be said to be precisely in point, but such as have been, support the position we have taken. . . .

Order appealed from reversed, and judgment of the special term affirmed.

————

NOTE ON THE STATUTE OF FRAUDS

William E. Story's original promise was not in writing. Did that affect the issue whether it was legally enforceable? The question, what promises must be in writing to be enforceable (or at least, to be enforceable in full), is addressed by a group of rules known as the Statute of Frauds. This casebook is designed so that Statute of Frauds problems are to be considered continuously, in the context of cases involving oral promises, rather than in one batch. To that end, an extended Note on the Statute of Frauds is set forth at Appendix A. You should study Appendix A at this point. Thereafter, whenever a case involves an oral promise you should turn to the relevant sections of Appendix A to consider the impact of the Statute of Frauds, if any, on that case.

———

Klockner v. Green

54 N.J. 230, 254 A.2d 782 (1969)

Plaintiffs Richard Klockner and Frances Klockner, the stepson and stepgranddaughter of Edyth Klockner, brought suit to enforce an alleged oral contract between Edyth and them to bequeath her estate to them in return for their services. The uncontradicted evidence at trial showed that Richard performed numerous services for his stepmother and that "Frances spent numerous nights with decedent when the latter felt fearful or alone, and also accompanied her on trips whenever she was needed." The evidence further showed that when Edyth discussed the disposition of her estate with Richard in June 1965 she "informed him that she wanted to compensate him for being so helpful, and that if he would agree to continue to look after her and continue to let Frances visit her, she would leave the real property to him and the balance of the estate to Frances." Edyth's long-time lawyer testified that she informed him of her decision, and that he redrafted her will in accordance with the decision in November 1965. Edyth died unexpectedly in 1966. She never signed the redrafted will out of a belief that it was a premonition of death. The trial court granted defendant's motion to dismiss at the conclusion of plaintiff's case, finding there was no consideration for Edyth's promise based on Richard and Frances' testimony "that they would have continued to perform the services for decedent even if she had not made the promises to compensate them." Reversed.

Although we recognize that alleged agreements to make a particular disposition of one's estate must be subjected to close scrutiny, we have no doubt that decedent here intended to obligate herself to bequeath her property to plaintiffs so long as they continued to serve her as they had prior to her promise. Such a promise, when acted upon, becomes a binding obligation. Decedent bargained for plaintiffs' services and obligated herself to bequeath the property to them when they performed. See 1 Corbin, Contracts, § 63 (1963).

The performance by plaintiffs need not have been induced solely by the offer of compensation. In the Restatement, Contracts § 55 (1932), it is indicated that if an act is requested by the offeror as consideration for a unilateral contract, the act need only be given with the intent of accepting the offer. The examples which illustrate that rule clearly encompass the instant case.

"A offers a reward for information leading to the conviction of a criminal. . . . B, . . . induced by motives of fear or public duty, would have given the information without hope of reward, but as there is an offer of reward he intends when he gives the information to accept the offer. There is a contract."

In the only New Jersey case discussing this rule, the Court of Errors and Appeals noted that once the contract has been legally concluded, in giving effect to that contract "the motive which induced the party to make the contract or perform it must always be immaterial." Mayor, etc. of Hoboken v. Bailey, 36 N.J.L. 490, 497 (E. & A. 1873). See also 1 Corbin, Contracts § 58 (1963) (recognizing the complexity of motivating causes in human action); Restatement, Second, Contracts § 55 (Tent. Draft No. 1, April 13, 1964) and § 84 (Tent. Draft No. 2, April 30, 1965).

————

De Cicco v. Schweizer

221 N.Y. 431, 117 N.E. 807 (1917)

(Cardozo, J.) "It will not do to divert the minds of others from a given line of conduct, and then to urge that because of the diversion the opportunity has gone by to say how their minds would otherwise have acted. If the tendency of the promise is to induce them to persevere, reliance and detriment may be inferred from the mere fact of performance. The springs of conduct are subtle and varied. One who meddles with them must not insist upon too nice a measure of proof that the spring which he released was effective to the exclusion of all others."

————

NOTE ON DISTINGUISHING A CONDITIONAL BARGAIN FROM A CONDITIONAL DONATIVE PROMISE

Bargain promises are made in a conditional form. For example, A may say to B, "If you mow my lawn, I will pay you $20." Donative promises may also be made in conditional form. For example, C may say to D, "If you select a car costing no more than $20,000, I will buy it for you as a graduation present." What's the difference between a bargain promise and a conditional donative promise? In the case of a bargain the parties view performance of the condition as the *price* of the promise. In the case of a gift the parties view performance of the condition as the *means* to make the gift, not as the price of the gift. Thus in the first example, B's act of mowing A's lawn is viewed by A and B as the price that B must pay to get $20 from A. (And, of course, $20 is viewed by A and B as the price that A must pay to get B to mow her lawn.) In contrast, in the second example, D's act of selecting a car is not viewed by C and D as a price D pays to get the gift, but as the means for making the gift.

How do we know whether fulfillment of a condition to a conditional promise is a bargained-for price or simply the means for making the gift? We make a judgment based on all the circumstances and on our knowledge of how people normally act. All this was well put by Williston, who formulated a now-famous hypothetical:

> It is of course ... possible to make a gratuitous conditional promise.... [A]ny event may be named in a promise as fixing the moment, on the happening of which a promisor (not as an exchange for the happening but as a mere coincidence in time) will perform a promise intended and understood to be gratuitous. The same thing, therefore, stated as the condition of a promise may or may not be consideration, according as a reasonable man would or would not understand that the performance of the condition was requested as the price or exchange for the promise. If a benevolent man says to a tramp, "if you go around the corner to the clothing shop there, you may purchase an overcoat on my credit," no reasonable person would understand that the short walk was requested as the consideration for the promise, but that in the event of the tramp going to the shop the promisor would make him a gift. Yet the walk to the shop is in its nature capable of being consideration. It is a legal detriment to the tramp to take the walk, and the only reason why the walk is not consideration is because on a reasonable interpretation, it must be held that the walk was not requested as the price of the promise, but was merely a condition of a gratuitous promise.

Williston on Contracts § 112 (3d ed. 1957).

––––––––

Carlisle v. T & R Excavating, Inc.

123 Ohio App.3d 277 (1997)

Plaintiff Janis Carlisle was married to Thomas Carlisle, who was sole owner of T & R Excavating, Inc. Plaintiff decided to build a preschool and kindergarten facility. In September 1992, T & R agreed in writing to do the excavation and site work for the project, estimating the cost to be $69,800 and promising in writing "All labor, equipment costs, overhead and profit, necessary for the completion of this project, totalling $40,000.00 will be provided at no cost to Wishing Well Preschool, Inc. The $29,800.00 allotted for materials will be billed to Wishing Well Preschool, Inc. at T & R Excavating's cost." The Carlisles separated in March 1993. T & R continued to work on the project until it abandoned the work in late May or early June. Plaintiff hired other contractors to complete the work and sued for damages. The trial court awarded $35,790.75 in damages. Reversed.

T & R's sole assignment of error is that the trial court incorrectly found that there was a contract between the parties, because their agreement lacked sufficient consideration and definiteness. It has asserted that its offer to do the excavation and site work for the preschool was in the nature of a gift or a favor, and was not supported by any legally sufficient consideration. In addition, it has asserted that the scope of the work it agreed to do was so uncertain that there could have been no meeting of the minds necessary to the formation of a contract.

. . . Under Ohio law, consideration consists of either a benefit to the promisor or a detriment to the promisee. To constitute consideration, the benefit or detriment must be "bargained for." Something is bargained for if it is sought by the promisor in exchange for his promise and is given by the promisee in exchange for that promise. See Restatement of the Law 2d, Contracts (1981) 172, Section 71. The benefit or detriment does not need to be great. In fact, a benefit need not even be actual, as in the nature of a profit, or be as economically valuable as whatever the promisor promises in exchange for the benefit; it need only be something regarded by the promisor as beneficial enough to induce his promise. Generally, therefore, a court will not inquire into the adequacy of consideration once it is found to exist.

Whether there is consideration at all, however, is a proper question for a court. Gratuitous promises are not enforceable as contracts, because there is no consideration. Restatement of Contracts, *supra*, 172–174, Section 71, Comments *a* and *b*. A written gratuitous promise, even if it evidences an intent by the promisor to be bound, is not a contract. Likewise, conditional gratuitous promises, which require the promisee to do something before the promised act or omission will take place, are not enforceable as contracts. Restatement of Contracts, *supra*, 174, Section 71, Comment *c*. While it is true, therefore, that courts generally do not inquire into the adequacy of consideration once it is found to exist, it must be determined in a contract case whether any "consideration" was really bargained for. If it was not bargained for, it could not support a contract. . .

Contrary to plaintiffs' position, nothing in the record shows any reasonable possibility that T & R bargained away the free excavation and site work services in exchange for the "benefit" of collecting from Wishing Well the materials costs that T & R had to pay someone else. Nor does it show any possibility that Ms. Carlisle reasonably believed that her promise to reimburse induced the promise for free services. At the time of the agreement, therefore, there was no contract, and T & R cannot be held liable on that basis. Rather, the record establishes only a conditional gratuitous promise. . . .

The only way Ms. Carlisle could have properly recovered the value of the services, therefore, is if she had argued and proved, under a theory of promissory estoppel, that she had reasonably relied to her detriment on T & R's promise. [Eds.: Promissory estoppel is the principle that reliance on a promise can make the promise enforceable, at least to the extent of the reliance, even though the promise is not bargained for. See Chapter 1 supra.] She has made no mention of detrimental reliance in her brief to this court, nor is it clear whether she was trying to argue it at trial. . .

The trial court found that Ms. Carlisle failed to prove that the delay in opening the preschool was attributable to T & R, and no other possible detriment other than delay-related expenses was suggested by Ms. Carlisle at trial. The fact that she may have relied on T & R's promise, as she testified, therefore, was not sufficient to recover under promissory estoppel, since she did not prove that the reliance was detrimental. Simply paying other workers to finish the job does not establish detrimental reliance, even if she was forced to pay much more than she would have had to pay if T & R had finished it. Such payment merely left her in the position she would have been in had T & R never made its promise, assuming she would have built the preschool even without that promise. Nowhere in the record is there a suggestion that she would not have built the preschool, or built it as she did, without relying on the promise of free services by T & R.

————

Pennsy Supply, Inc. v. American Ash Recycling Corp.

895 A.2d 595 (Pa. Superior Ct. 2006)

Defendant American Ash offered Treated Ash Aggregate ("AggRite') free of charge on a "first come, first served" basis to contractors such as Plaintiff, understanding the material would be used in paving work. Plaintiff's use of AggRite in paving saved Defendant the expense of disposing of AggRite, which was classified as hazardous waste material. Plaintiff's paving experienced cracking, which it attributed to defects in the AggRite, and Plaintiff was required to do remedial work, which included the removal and disposal of the AggRite. Plaintiff brought a breach of contract action against Defendant, seeking to recover the cost of removing and disposing of the AggRite. [Defendant] filed demurers, which the trial court granted, finding that "any alleged agreement between the parties is unenforceable for lack of consideration" and that "the facts as pleaded do not support an inference that disposal costs were part of any bargaining process *or* that American Ash offered the AggRite with an intent to avoid disposal costs." Reversed:

[W]e disagree with the trial court that the allegations of the Complaint show only that American Ash made a conditional gift of the AggRite to Pennsy. In paragraphs 8 and 9 of the Complaint, Pennsy alleged

American Ash actively promotes the use of AggRite as a building material to be used in base course of paved structures, and provides the material free of charge, in an effort to have others dispose of the material and thereby avoid incurring the disposal costs itself . . . American Ash provided the AggRite to Pennsy for use on the Project, which saved American Ash thousands of dollars in disposal costs it otherwise would have incurred.

Compl. ¶¶ 8, 9. Accepting these allegations as true and using the Holmesian formula for consideration [i.e., that the promise and the consideration are in a relation of reciprocal inducement], it is a fair interpretation of the Complaint that American Ash's promise to supply AggRite free of charge induced Pennsy to assume the detriment of collecting and taking title to the material, and critically, that it was this very detriment, whether assumed by Pennsy or some other successful bidder to the paving subcontract, which induced American Ash to make the promise to provide free AggRite for the project. Paragraphs 8–9 of the Complaint simply belie the notion that American Ash offered AggRite as a conditional gift to the successful bidder on the paving subcontract for which American Ash desired and expected nothing in return.

We turn now to whether consideration is lacking because Pennsy did not allege that American Ash's avoidance of disposal costs was part of any bargaining process between the parties. The Complaint does not allege that the parties discussed or even that Pennsy understood at the time it requested or accepted the AggRite that Pennsy's use of the AggRite would allow American Ash to avoid disposal costs. However, we do not believe such is necessary.

> The bargain theory of consideration does not actually require that the parties bargain over the terms of the agreement. . . . According to Holmes, an influential advocate of the bargain theory, what is required [for consideration to exist] is that the promise and the consideration be in 'the relation of reciprocal conventional inducement, each for the other.'

E. Allen Farnsworth, Farnsworth on Contracts § 2.6 (1990) (citing O. Holmes, The Common Law 293–94 (1881)); *see also* Restatement (Second) of Contracts § 71 (defining "bargained for" in terms of the Holmesian formula). Here, as explained above, the Complaint alleges facts which, if proven, would show the promise induced the detriment and the detriment induced the promise. This would be consideration.

———

RESTATEMENT, SECOND, CONTRACTS §§ 71, 72, 79

[See Selected Source Materials Supplement]

———

BATSAKIS v. DEMOTSIS
Court of Civil Appeals of Texas, 1949.
226 S.W.2d 673.

McGILL, JUSTICE. This is an appeal from a judgment of the 57th judicial District Court of Bexar County. Appellant was plaintiff and appellee was defendant in the trial court. The parties will be so designated.

Plaintiff sued defendant to recover $2,000 with interest at the rate of 8% per annum from April 2, 1942, alleged to be due on the following instrument, being a translation from the original, which is written in the Greek language:

"Peiraeus

"April 2, 1942

"Mr. George Batsakis

Konstantinou Diadohou # 7

Peiraeus

"Mr. Batsakis:

"I state by my present (letter) that I received today from you the amount of two thousand dollars ($2,000.00) of United States of America money, which I borrowed from you for the support of my family during these difficult days and because it is impossible for me to transfer dollars of my own from America.

"The above amount I accept with the expressed promise that I will return to you again in American dollars either at the end of the present war or even before in the event that you might be able to find a way to collect them (dollars) from my representative in America to whom I shall write and give him an order relative to this. You understand until the final execution (payment) to the above amount an eight per cent interest will be added and paid together with the principal.

"I thank you and I remain yours with respects.

"The recipient,

(Signed) Eugenia The. Demotsis."

Trial to the court without the intervention of a jury resulted in a judgment in favor of plaintiff for $750.00 principal, and interest at the rate of 8% per annum from April 2, 1942 to the date of judgment, totaling $1163.83, with interest thereon at the rate of 8% per annum until paid. Plaintiff has perfected his appeal.

The court sustained certain special exceptions of plaintiff to defendant's first amended original answer on which the case was tried, and struck therefrom paragraphs II, III and V. Defendant excepted to such action of the court, but has not cross-assigned error here. The answer, stripped of such paragraphs, consisted of a general denial contained in paragraph I thereof, and of Paragraph IV, which is as follows:

> "IV. That under the circumstances alleged in Paragraph II of this answer, the consideration upon which said written instrument sued upon by plaintiff herein is founded, is wanting and has failed to the extent of $1975.00, and defendant pleads specially under the verification hereinafter made the want and failure of consideration stated, and now tenders, as defendant has heretofore tendered to plaintiff, $25.00 as the value of the loan of money received by defendant from plaintiff, together with interest thereon.

> "Further, in connection with this plea of want and failure of consideration defendant alleges that she at no time received from plaintiff himself or from anyone for plaintiff any money or thing of value other than, as hereinbefore alleged, the original loan of 500,000 drachmae. That at the time of the loan by plaintiff to defendant of said 500,000 drachmae the value of 500,000 drachmae in the Kingdom of Greece in dollars of money of the United States of America, was $25.00, and also at said time the value of 500,000 drachmae of Greek money in the United States of America in dollars was $25.00 of money of the United States of America. The plea of want and failure of consideration is verified by defendant as follows."

The allegations in paragraph II which were stricken, referred to in paragraph IV, were that the instrument sued on was signed and delivered in the Kingdom of Greece on or about April 2, 1942, at which time both plaintiff and defendant were residents of and residing in the Kingdom of Greece, and

> "*Plaintiff* (emphasis ours) avers that on or about April 2, 1942 she owned money and property and had credit in the United States of America, but was then and there in the Kingdom of Greece in straitened financial circumstances due to the conditions produced by World War II and could not make use of her money and property and credit existing in the United States of America. That in the circumstances the plaintiff agreed to and did lend to defendant the sum of 500,000 drachmae, which at that time, on or about April 2, 1942, had the value of $25.00 in money of the United States of America. That the said plaintiff knowing defendant's financial distress and desire to return to the United States of America, exacted of her the written instrument plaintiff sues upon, which was a promise by her to pay to him the sum of $2,000.00 of United States of America money."

Plaintiff specially excepted to paragraph IV because the allegations thereof were insufficient to allege either want of consideration or failure of consideration, in that it affirmatively appears therefrom that defendant received what was agreed to be delivered to her, and that plaintiff breached no agreement. The court overruled this exception, and such action is assigned as error. Error is also assigned because of the court's failure to enter judgment for the whole unpaid balance of the principal of the instrument with interest as therein provided.

Defendant testified that she did receive 500,000 drachmas from plaintiff. It is not clear whether she received all the 500,000 drachmas or only a portion of them before she signed the instrument in question. Her testimony clearly shows that the understanding of the parties was that plaintiff would give her the 500,000 drachmas if she would sign the instrument. She testified:

"Q. . . . who suggested the figure of $2,000.00?

"A. That was how he asked me from the beginning. He said he will give me five hundred thousand drachmas provided I signed that I would pay him $2,000.00 American money."

The transaction amounted to a sale by plaintiff of the 500,000 drachmas in consideration of the execution of the instrument sued on, by defendant. It is not contended that the drachmas had no value. Indeed, the judgment indicates that the trial court placed a value of $750.00 on them or on the other consideration which plaintiff gave defendant for the instrument if he believed plaintiff's testimony. Therefore the plea of want of consideration was unavailing. A plea of want of consideration amounts to a contention that the instrument never became a valid obligation in the first place. . . .

Mere inadequacy of consideration will not void a contract. 10 Tex.Jur., Contracts, Sec. 89, p. 150; Chastain v. Texas Christian Missionary Society, Tex.Civ.App., 78 S.W.2d 728, loc. cit. 731(3), Wr. Ref.

Nor was the plea of failure of consideration availing. Defendant got exactly what she contracted for according to her own testimony. The court should have rendered judgment in favor of plaintiff against defendant for the principal sum of $2,000.00 evidenced by the instrument sued on, with interest as therein provided. We construe the provision relating to interest as providing for interest at the rate of 8% per annum. The judgment is reformed so as to award appellant a recovery against appellee of $2,000.00 with interest thereon at the rate of 8% per annum from April 2, 1942. Such judgment will bear interest at the rate of 8% per annum until paid on $2,000.00 thereof and on the balance interest at the rate of 6% per annum. As so reformed, the judgment is affirmed.

Reformed and affirmed.

B. Sweet-Escott, Greece—A Political and Economic Survey 1939–1953
93–96 (1954)

"It has been said that Greece suffered more heavily during the war than any other Allied country except Soviet Russia. From 1941 to 1944 the country was visited by famine, destruction, and inflation. Greece normally requires to import some 600,000 tons of grain a year. Most of this comes by sea. As soon as the Axis occupied Greece the usual sea routes ceased to be available—except those from the Black Sea and the Adriatic. And in any case there were few ships on which the Axis could lay their hands for feeding the country. Moreover, the only other main line of communication, the railway to Belgrade and Sofia, was fully occupied in supplying the Axis armies of occupation. Even if the Axis had been determined to maintain the existing standard of nutrition in Greece, it would have been a difficult task. As things were, the standard fell disastrously. It is estimated that the average daily diet in 1941, the worst of the three war winters, fell to 900 calories per person, and that it never exceeded 1,400 calories during the occupation. As the daily diet of a healthy man should be in the region of 3,000 calories, it is hardly surprising that Greece fell a prey to famine, especially in the towns. At one period in the winter of 1941–2 people were dying daily in the streets of Athens by the score. It will probably never be known how many perished of malnutrition and the diseases occasioned thereby, but the figure may well run into hundreds of thousands. . . . "

SECTION 2. DURESS AND THE EXPLOITATION OF DISTRESS

RESTATEMENT, SECOND, CONTRACTS §§ 175, 176

[See Selected Source Materials Supplement]

TOTEM MARINE TUG & BARGE, INC. V. ALYESKA PIPELINE SERVICE COMPANY

Supreme Court of Alaska, 1978.
584 P.2d 15.

BURKE, J.

This appeal arises from the superior court's granting of summary judgment in favor of defendants-appellees Alyeska Pipeline Services, et al.,

in a contract action brought by plaintiffs-appellants Totem Marine Tug &
Barge, Inc., Pacific, Inc., and Richard Stair.

The following summary of events is derived from the materials
submitted in the summary judgment proceedings below.

Totem is a closely held Alaska corporation which began operations in
March of 1975. Richard Stair, at all times relevant to this case, was vice-
president of Totem. In June of 1975, Totem entered into a contract with
Alyeska under which Totem was to transport pipeline construction
materials from Houston, Texas, to a designated port in southern Alaska,
with the possibility of one or two cargo stops along the way. In order to
carry out this contract, which was Totem's first, Totem chartered a barge
(The "Marine Flasher") and an ocean-going tug (the "Kirt Chouest"). These
charters and other initial operations costs were made possible by loans to
Totem from Richard Stair individually and Pacific, Inc., a corporation of
which Stair was principal stockholder and officer, as well as by guarantees
by Stair and Pacific.

By the terms of the contract, Totem was to have completed
performance by approximately August 15, 1975. From the start, however,
there were numerous problems which impeded Totem's performance of the
contract. For example, according to Totem, Alyeska represented that
approximately 1,800 to 2,100 tons of regular uncoated pipe were to be
loaded in Houston, and that perhaps another 6,000 or 7,000 tons of
materials would be put on the barge at later stops along the west coast.
Upon the arrival of the tug and barge in Houston, however, Totem found
that about 6,700 to 7,200 tons of coated pipe, steel beams and valves,
haphazardly and improperly piled, were in the yard to be loaded. This
situation called for remodeling of the barge and extra cranes and
stevedores, and resulted in the loading taking thirty days rather than the
three days which Totem had anticipated it would take to load 2,000 tons.
The lengthy loading period was also caused in part by Alyeska's delay in
assuring Totem that it would pay for the additional expenses, bad weather
and other administrative problems.

The difficulties continued after the tug and barge left Houston. It soon
became apparent that the vessels were travelling more slowly than
anticipated because of the extra load. In response to Alyeska's complaints
and with its verbal consent, on August 13, 1975, Totem chartered a second
tug, the "N. Joseph Guidry." When the "Guidry" reached the Panama
Canal, however, Alyeska had not yet furnished the written amendment to
the parties' contract. Afraid that Alyeska would not agree to cover the cost
of the second tug, Stair notified the "Guidry" not to go through the Canal.
After some discussions in which Alyeska complained of the delays and
accused Totem of lying about the horsepower of the first tug, Alyeska
executed the amendment on August 21, 1975.

By this time the "Guidry" had lost its preferred passage through the Canal and had to wait two or three additional days before it could go through. Upon finally meeting, the three vessels encountered the tail of a hurricane which lasted for about eight or nine days and which substantially impeded their progress.

The three vessels finally arrived in the vicinity of San Pedro, California, where Totem planned to change crews and refuel. On Alyeska's orders, however, the vessels instead pulled into port at Long Beach, California. At this point, Alyeska's agents commenced off-loading the barge, without Totem's consent, without the necessary load survey, and without a marine survey, the absence of which voided Totem's insurance. After much wrangling and some concessions by Alyeska, the freight was off-loaded. Thereafter, on or about September 14, 1975, Alyeska terminated the contract. Although there was talk by an Alyeska official of reinstating the contract, the termination was affirmed a few days later at a meeting at which Alyeska officials refused to give a reason for the termination.

Following termination of the contract, Totem submitted termination invoices to Alyeska and began pressing the latter for payment. The invoices came to something between $260,000 and $300,000. An official from Alyeska told Totem that they would look over the invoices but that they were not sure when payment would be made perhaps in a day or perhaps in six to eight months. Totem was in urgent need of cash as the invoices represented debts which the company had incurred on 10–30 day payment schedules. Totem's creditors were demanding payment and according to Stair, without immediate cash, Totem would go bankrupt. Totem then turned over the collection to its attorney, Roy Bell, directing him to advise Alyeska of Totem's financial straits. Thereafter, Bell met with Alyeska officials in Seattle, and after some negotiations, Totem received a settlement offer from Alyeska for $97,500. On November 6, 1975, Totem, through its president Stair, signed an agreement releasing Alyeska from all claims by Totem in exchange for $97,500.

On March 26, 1976, Totem, Richard Stair, and Pacific filed a complaint against Alyeska, which was subsequently amended. In the amended complaint, the plaintiffs sought to rescind the settlement and release on the ground of economic duress and to recover the balance allegedly due on the original contract. In addition, they alleged that Alyeska had wrongfully terminated the contract and sought miscellaneous other compensatory and punitive damages.

Before filing an answer, Alyeska moved for summary judgment against the plaintiffs on the ground that Totem had executed a binding release of all claims against Alyeska and that as a matter of law, Totem could not prevail on its claim of economic duress. In opposition, plaintiffs contended that the purported release was executed under duress in that Alyeska wrongfully terminated the contract; that Alyeska knew that Totem was faced with large debts and impending bankruptcy; that Alyeska withheld funds admittedly owed knowing the effect this would have on plaintiffs and that plaintiffs had no alternative but to involuntarily accept the $97,500 in order to avoid bankruptcy. Plaintiffs maintained that they had thus raised genuine issues of material fact such that trial was necessary, and that Alyeska was not entitled to judgment as a matter of law. Alyeska disputed the plaintiffs' assertions.

On November 30, 1976, the superior court granted the defendant's motion for summary judgment. This appeal followed. . .

II

As was noted above, a court's initial task in deciding motions for summary judgment is to determine whether there exist genuine issues of material fact. In order to decide whether such issues exist in this case, we must examine the doctrine allowing avoidance of a release on grounds of economic duress.

This court has not yet decided a case involving a claim of economic duress or what is also called business compulsion. At early common law, a contract could be avoided on the ground of duress only if a party could show that the agreement was entered into for fear of loss of life or limb, mayhem or imprisonment. 13 Williston on Contracts, § 1601 at 649 (3d ed. Jaeger 1970). The threat had to be such as to overcome the will of a person of ordinary firmness and courage. Id., § 1602 at 656. Subsequently, however, the concept has been broadened to include myriad forms of economic coercion which force a person to involuntarily enter into a particular transaction. The test has come to be whether the will of the person induced by the threat was overcome rather than that of a reasonably firm person. Id., § 1602 at 657.

At the outset it is helpful to acknowledge the various policy considerations which are involved in cases involving economic duress. Typically, those claiming such coercion are attempting to avoid the consequences of a modification of an original contract or of a settlement and release agreement. On the one hand, courts are reluctant to set aside agreements because of the notion of freedom of contract and because of the desirability of having private dispute resolutions be final. On the other hand, there is an increasing recognition of the law's role in correcting inequitable or unequal exchanges between parties of disproportionate bargaining power and a greater willingness to not enforce agreements which were entered into under coercive circumstances.

There are various statements of what constitutes economic duress, but as noted by one commentator, "The history of generalization in this field offers no great encouragement for those who seek to summarize results in any single formula." Dawson, Economic Duress An Essay in Perspective, 45 Mich.L.Rev. 253, 289 (1947). Section 492(b) of the Restatement of Contracts defines duress as:

> any wrongful threat of one person by words or other conduct that induces another to enter into a transaction under the influence of such fear as precludes him from exercising free will and judgment, if the threat was intended or should reasonably have been expected to operate as an inducement.

Professor Williston states the basic elements of economic duress in the following manner:

> 1.   The party alleging economic duress must show that he has been the victim of a wrongful or unlawful act or threat, and
>
> 2.   Such act or threat must be one which deprives the victim of his unfettered will.

13 Williston on Contracts, § 1617 at 704 (footnotes omitted).

Many courts state the test somewhat differently, eliminating use of the vague term "free will," but retaining the same basic idea. Under this standard, duress exists where: (1) one party involuntarily accepted the terms of another, (2) circumstances permitted no other alternative, and (3) such circumstances were the result of coercive acts of the other party. Undersea Engineering & Construction Co. v. International Telephone & Telegraph Corp., 429 F.2d 543, 550 (9th Cir. 1970); Urban Plumbing and Heating Co. v. United States, 408 F.2d 382, 389, 187 Ct.Cl. 15 (1969); W. R. Grimshaw Co. v. Nevil C. Withrow Co., 248 F.2d 896, 904 (8th Cir. 1957); Fruhauf Southwest Garment Co. v. United States, 111 F.Supp. 945, 951, 126 Ct.Cl. 51 (1953). The third element is further explained as follows:

> In order to substantiate the allegation of economic duress or business compulsion, the plaintiff must go beyond the mere showing of reluctance to accept and of financial embarrassment. There must be a showing of acts on the part of the defendant which produced these two factors. The assertion of duress must be proven by evidence that the duress resulted from defendant's wrongful and oppressive conduct and not by the plaintiff's necessities.

W. R. Grimshaw Co., supra, 111 F.Supp. at 904.

As the above indicates, one essential element of economic duress is that the plaintiff show that the other party by wrongful acts or threats, intentionally caused him to involuntarily enter into a particular transaction. Courts have not attempted to define exactly what constitutes a wrongful or coercive act, as wrongfulness depends on the particular facts in each case. This requirement may be satisfied where the alleged wrongdoer's conduct is criminal or tortious but an act or threat may also be considered wrongful if it is wrongful in the moral sense. Restatement of Contracts, § 492, comment (g); Gerber v. First National Bank of Lincolnwood, 30 Ill.App.3d 776, 332 N.E.2d 615, 618 (1975); Fowler v. Mumford, 48 Del. 282, 9 Terry 282, 102 A.2d 535, 538 (Del.Supr.1954).

In many cases, a threat to breach a contract or to withhold payment of an admitted debt has constituted a wrongful act. Hartsville Oil Mill v. United States, 271 U.S. 43, 49, 46 S.Ct. 389, 391, 70 L.Ed. 822, 827 (1926); Austin Instrument, Inc. v. Loral Corp., 29 N.Y.2d 124, 324 N.Y.S.2d 22, 25, 272 N.E.2d 533, 535 (1971); Capps v. Georgia Pacific Corporation, 253 Or. 248, 453 P.2d 935 (1969); See also 13 Williston, supra, § 1616A at 701. Implicit in such cases is the additional requirement that the threat to breach the contract or withhold payment be done in bad faith. See Louisville Title Insurance Co. v. Surety Title & Guaranty Co., 60 Cal.App.3d 781, 132 Cal.Rptr. 63, 76, 79 (1976); Restatement (Second) of Contracts, § 318 comment (e).

Economic duress does not exist, however, merely because a person has been the victim of a wrongful act; in addition, the victim must have no choice but to agree to the other party's terms or face serious financial hardship. Thus, in order to avoid a contract, a party must also show that he had no reasonable alternative to agreeing to the other party's terms, or, as it is often stated, that he had no adequate remedy if the threat were to be carried out. First National Bank of Cincinnati v. Pepper, 454 F.2d 626, 632–33 (2d Cir. 1972); Austin Instrument, supra, 324 N.Y.S.2d at 25, 272 N.E.2d at 535; Capps, supra; Ross Systems v. Linden Dari-Delite, Inc., 35 N.J. 329, 173 A.2d 258, 261 (1961); Leeper v. Beltrami, 53 Cal.2d 195, 1 Cal.Rptr. 12, 19, 347 P.2d 12, 19 (1959); Tri-State Roofing Company of Uniontown v. Simon, 187 Pa.Super. 17, 142 A.2d 333, 335–36 (1958). What constitutes a reasonable alternative is a question of fact, depending on the circumstances of each case. An available legal remedy, such as an action for breach of contract, may provide such an alternative. First National Bank of Cincinnati, supra; Austin Instrument, supra; Tri-State Roofing, supra. Where one party wrongfully threatens to withhold goods, services or money from another unless certain demands are met, the availability on the market of similar goods and services or of other sources of funds may also provide an alternative to succumbing to the coercing party's demands. Austin Instrument, supra; Tri-State Roofing, supra. Generally, it has been said that "(t)he adequacy of the remedy is to be tested by a practical standard which takes into consideration the exigencies of the situation in which the alleged victim finds himself." Ross Systems, 173 A.2d at 262. See also First National Bank of Cincinnati, supra at 634; Dalzell, Duress By Economic Pressure I, 20 N. Carolina L.Rev. 237, 240 (1942).

An available alternative or remedy may not be adequate where the delay involved in pursuing that remedy would cause immediate and irreparable loss to one's economic or business interest. For example, in Austin Instrument, supra, and Gallagher Switchboard Corp. v. Heckler Electric Co., 36 Misc.2d 225, 232 N.Y.S.2d 590 (N.Y.Sup.Ct.1962), duress was found in the following circumstances: A subcontractor threatened to refuse further delivery under a contract unless the contractor agreed to modify the existing contract between the parties. The contractor was unable to obtain the necessary materials elsewhere without delay, and if it did not have the materials promptly, it would have been in default on its main contract with the government. In each case such default would have had grave economic consequences for the contractor and hence it agreed to the modifications. In both, the courts found that the alternatives to agreeing to the modification were inadequate (i.e., suing for breach of contract or obtaining the materials elsewhere) and that modifications therefore were signed under duress and voidable.

Professor Dalzell, in Duress By Economic Pressure II, 20 N. Carolina L.Rev. 340, 370 (1942), notes the following with regard to the adequacy of legal remedies where one party refuses to pay a contract claim:

> Nowadays, a wait of even a few weeks in collecting on a contract claim is sometimes serious or fatal for an enterprise at a crisis in its history. The business of a creditor in financial straits is at the mercy of an unscrupulous debtor, who need only suggest that if the creditor does not care to settle on the debtor's own hard terms, he can sue. This situation, in which promptness in payment is vastly more important than even approximate justice in the settlement terms, is too common in modern business relations to be ignored by society and the courts.

This view finds support in Capps v. Georgia Pacific Corporation, 253 Or. 248, 453 P.2d 935 (1969). There, the plaintiff was owed $157,000 as a commission for finding a lessee for defendant's property but in exchange for $5,000, the plaintiff signed a release of his claim against defendant. The plaintiff sued for the balance of the commission, alleging that the release had been executed under duress. His complaint, however, was dismissed. On appeal, the court held that the plaintiff had stated a claim where he alleged that he had accepted the grossly inadequate sum because he was in danger of immediately losing his home by mortgage foreclosure and other property by foreclosure and repossession if he did not obtain immediate funds from the defendant. One basis for its holding was found in the following quote by a leading commentator in the area of economic duress:

> The most that can be claimed (regarding the law of economic duress) is that change has been broadly toward acceptance of a general conclusion that in the absence of specific countervailing factors of policy or administrative feasibility, restitution is

required of any excessive gain that results, in a bargain transaction, from impaired bargaining power, whether the impairment consists of economic necessity, mental or physical disability, or a wide disparity in knowledge or experience.

Dawson, Economic—Duress An Essay In Perspective, 45 Mich.L.Rev. 253, 289 (1947).[4]

III

Turning to the instant case, we believe that Totem's allegations, if proved, would support a finding that it executed a release of its contract claims against Alyeska under economic duress. Totem has alleged that Alyeska deliberately withheld payment of an acknowledged debt, knowing that Totem had no choice but to accept an inadequate sum in settlement of that debt; that Totem was faced with impending bankruptcy; that Totem was unable to meet its pressing debts other than by accepting the immediate cash payment offered by Alyeska; and that through necessity, Totem thus involuntarily accepted an inadequate settlement offer from Alyeska and executed a release of all claims under the contract. If the release was in fact executed under these circumstances,[5] we think that under the legal principles discussed above that this would constitute the type of wrongful conduct and lack of alternatives that would render the release voidable by Totem on the ground of economic duress. We would add that although Totem need not necessarily prove its allegation that Alyeska's termination of the contract was wrongful in order to sustain a claim of economic duress, the events leading to the termination would be probative as to whether Alyeska exerted any wrongful pressure on Totem and whether Alyeska wrongfully withheld payment from Totem.

---

[4]   This court expressed a similar view in Inman v. Clyde Hall Drilling Company, 369 P.2d 498, 500 (Alaska 1962). In response to a claim that a contract provision was unconscionable, it was said:

> In the absence of a constitutional provision or statute which makes certain contracts illegal or unenforceable, we believe it is the function of the judiciary to allow men to manage their own affairs in their own way. As a matter of judicial policy the court should maintain and enforce contracts, rather than enable parties to escape from the obligations they have chosen to incur.

> We recognize that 'freedom of contract' is a qualified and not an absolute right, and cannot be applied on a strict, doctrinal basis. An established principle is that a court will not permit itself to be used as an instrument of inequity and injustice. . . . In determining whether certain contractual provisions should be enforced, the court must look realistically at the relative bargaining positions of the parties in the framework of contemporary business practices and commercial life. If we find those positions are such that one party has unscrupulously taken advantage of the economic necessities of the other, then in the interest of justice as a matter of public policy we would refuse to enforce the transaction. But the grounds for judicial interference must be clear. Whether the court should refuse to recognize and uphold that which the parties have agreed upon is a question of fact upon which evidence is required. (footnotes omitted).

[5]   By way of clarification, we would note that Totem would not have to prove that Alyeska admitted to owing the precise sum Totem claimed it was owed upon termination of the contract but only that Alyeska acknowledged that it owed Totem approximately that amount which Totem sought.

One purpose of summary judgment, however, is to pierce the allegations in the pleadings in an effort to determine whether genuine issues of fact exist. As the moving party, Alyeska had the burden of showing that there were no such genuine issues and that it was entitled to judgment as a matter of law. E. g., Brock v. Rogers and Babler, Inc., 536 P.2d 778, 782 (Alaska 1975). Alyeska showed that Totem had executed the release, that Totem had been represented by counsel at the negotiating session leading to the settlement and release and that appellant Stair, who actually signed the release on behalf of Totem, was fully aware of the consequences of such a release. Such evidence, by itself, would have entitled Alyeska to summary judgment in its favor. As a matter of law, there is no doubt that a valid release of all claims arising under a contract will bar any subsequent claims based on that contract.

To avoid summary judgment once the moving party meets its burden, the non-moving party must produce competent evidence showing that there are issues of material fact to be tried. Id. The respondent must set forth specific facts showing that it could produce admissible evidence reasonably tending to dispute the movants evidence or establish an affirmative defense. Id. The court then must draw all reasonable inferences in favor of the non-moving party and against the movant. E. g., Clabaugh v. Bottcher, 545 P.2d 172, 175 n.5 (Alaska 1976).

. . . Our examination of the materials presented by Totem in opposition to Alyeska's motion for summary judgment leads us to conclude that Totem has made a sufficient factual showing as to each of the elements of economic duress to withstand that motion. There is no doubt that Alyeska disputes many of the factual allegations made by Totem[7] and drawing all inferences in favor of Totem, we believe that genuine issues of material fact exist in this case such that trial is necessary. Admittedly, Totem's showing was somewhat weak in that, for example, it did not produce the testimony of Roy Bell, the attorney who represented Totem in the negotiations leading to the settlement and release. At trial, it will probably be necessary for Totem to produce this evidence if it is to prevail on its claim of duress. However, a party opposing a motion for summary judgment need not produce all of the evidence it may have at its disposal but need only show that issues of material fact exist. 10 C. Wright and A. Miller, Federal Practice and Procedure: Civil, § 2727 at 546 (1973). Therefore, we hold that the superior court erred in granting summary judgment for appellees and remand the case to the superior court for trial in accordance with the legal principles set forth above. . . .

---

[7] For example, Alyeska has denied that it ever admitted to owing any particular sum to Totem and has disputed the truthfulness of Totem's assertions of impending bankruptcy. Other factual issues which remain unresolved include whether or not Alyeska knew of Totem's financial situation after termination of the contract and whether Alyeska did in fact threaten by words or conduct to withhold payment unless Totem agreed to settle.

REVERSED and REMANDED.

UNIDROIT PRINCIPLES OF INTERNATIONAL COMMERCIAL CONTRACTS ART. 3.9

[See Selected Source Materials Supplement]

NOTE ON UNIDROIT

In 1971, the governing council of the International Institute for the Unification of Private Law determined to include in its program a codification of the law of contracts. To this end, a Working Group consisting of academics, judges, and civil servants was created in 1980. The members of the Working Group were of different nationalities, but sat in their personal capacities, not to express the views of their governments. The ultimate result was the Unidroit Principles of International Commercial Contracts, which was finalized in 1994. The goal of the Unidroit Principles is to set forth general rules for international commercial contracts. The Principles are intended to enunciate communal principles and rules of existing legal systems, and to select the solutions that are best adapted to the special requirements of international commercial contracts. In preparing the Principles, particular attention was paid to recent codifications of contract and commercial law, including the UCC, the Restatement Second of Contracts, the Netherlands Civil Code, the 1985 Foreign Economic Contract Law of the People's Republic of China, the Draft New Civil Code of Quebec, and the Convention for the International Sale of Goods.

The Unidroit Principles are not intended for adoption by any country, and are not legally binding. Instead, they are a sort of international Restatement of Contract Law.

PRINCIPLES OF EUROPEAN CONTRACT LAW § 4.108

NOTE ON THE PRINCIPLES OF EUROPEAN CONTRACT LAW

The Principles of European Contract Law are the product of the Commission on European Contract Law, a body of lawyers drawn from all the member States of the European Union, under the chairmanship of Professor Ole Lando. The Principles are a response to a perceived need for a European Union-wide infrastructure of contract law. They are intended to reflect the common core of solutions to problems of contract law. In preparing the

Principles, the Commission drew on a wide range of legal materials from both within and outside Europe, including the Uniform Commercial Code and the Restatements of Contracts and of Restitution. Some of the provisions in the Principles reflect suggestions and ideas that have not yet materialized in the law of the European Union States. See Introduction, Principles of European Contract Law, parts I and II (1999).

———

Andreini v. Hultgren

860 P.2d 916 (Utah 1993)

After undergoing surgery on his right knee at Holy Cross Hospital, Andreini began to experience a "pins and needles" sensation in both hands, which also exhibited noticeable atrophy. His surgeon, Dr. Beck, told Andreini his condition was probably the result of lying in bed or hereditary. Another physician, Dr. Nord, diagnosed the source to be compression paralysis. Nord reported his findings to Beck, who offered to perform corrective surgery, and to get Holy Cross Hospital to waive its charges and to allow Andreini to pay Beck's fee over time. A week before the scheduled operation a nurse told Andreini the compression paralysis may have resulted from improper strapping of his wrists during surgery. The second operation was unsuccessful. Andreini sued Beck and Holy Cross for medical malpractice. They moved for summary judgment based on a release signed by Andreini before the second operation. The trial court found that Andreini had released both parties from liability and, as a matter of law, had not signed the form under duress. Reversed.

(Zimmerman, J.) "On July 9th, Andreini arrived at Holy Cross Hospital and was prepared for surgery. At some point between one-half to one hour before surgery was to begin, a Holy Cross employee presented Andreini with a release form and asked him to sign it. Andreini refused. The employee then arranged to have Beck talk to Andreini by phone. Beck told Andreini that he would not perform the surgery unless Andreini released both him and Holy Cross from future liability. Although visibly upset, Andreini signed the form and underwent the operation. The procedure was unsuccessful. Andreini has lost most of the dexterity in his hands and cannot perform any activity that requires grasping or holding. . . .

"Andreini argues that he has put into issue sufficient material facts to raise a jury question as to whether Beck's threat not to perform the corrective surgery was a breach of the duty of good faith and fair dealing and therefore constituted an improper threat. He also argues that he has raised a jury question as to whether he had any reasonable alternatives to signing the release. By making these arguments, Andreini hopes to meet the requirements established in sections 175(1) and 176(1)(d) of the Restatement, which would allow him to void the release.

"We first consider if Andreini adduced sufficient material facts as to whether defendants made an improper threat by breaching the duty of good faith and fair dealing. Under section 176(1)(d) of the Restatement, the breach of the duty of good faith and fair dealing must be "under a contract with the recipient." Id. § 176 & cmt. e, illus. 8–10. Therefore, to find a breach of the duty of good faith and fair dealing, there must be some type of preexisting contractual relationship. This is consistent with our case law. See Peterson v. Browning, 832 P.2d 1280, 1284 (Utah 1992); Beck v. Farmers Ins. Exch., 701 P.2d 795, 798 (Utah 1985); cf. Brehaney v. Nordstrom, Inc., 812 P.2d 49, 55 (Utah 1991). Andreini, however, does not explicitly allege that he and defendants entered into a contract before he was presented with and later signed the release. Consequently, Andreini may not rely on an alleged breach of good faith and fair dealing to claim duress for the first time on appeal.

"However, Andreini does make an argument that, fairly construed, appears to constitute an improper threat under section 176(2)(b) of the Restatement. Under this provision, an improper threat may be found when (i) "the resulting exchange is not on fair terms," and (ii) "the effectiveness of the threat in inducing the manifestation of assent is significantly increased by prior unfair dealing by the party making the threat." Restatement (Second) of Contracts § 176(2)(b) (1979). Andreini argues that Beck improperly induced him into signing the release by promising that the corrective surgery would fully restore the use of his hands. He avers that prior to entering the hospital for the corrective surgery, Beck told him that patients with similar injuries had recovered 50% use within two weeks and 100% use within two months as a result of surgery similar to that proposed. Andreini also points to language in the release itself suggesting full recovery: "I, EUGENE R. ANDREINI, will receive surgery to correct ulnar nerve palsy. . . . " (Emphasis added.) This evidence is sufficient to establish the legal possibility that the "resulting exchange"—defendants' unfulfilled promise to correct Andreini's injury exchanged for Andreini's release of all claims against defendants—is "not on fair terms" within the meaning of section 176(2) of the Restatement.

"However, to avoid summary judgment under section 176(2)(b)'s formulation of an "improper threat," there must also be sufficient evidence to raise a factual issue as to whether defendants had engaged in unfair dealing and whether this significantly increased the impropriety of their threat. Andreini argues that defendants acted in bad faith by promising him that the corrective surgery would result in his full recovery while neglecting to inform him until just prior to surgery that he would have to waive any claims he might have against them.

"Viewing the evidence in the light most favorable to Andreini, there is sufficient evidence to take this argument to the jury. We have already recited the evidence suggesting that defendants promised Andreini full recovery, and in Andreini's deposition, he testifies that he was not told until after he had been placed in a gown, shaved, and prepared for surgery that he would have to relinquish his rights. Andreini also testified that defendants were purposely noncommittal about the paralysis in his hands and its possible causes, even after Dr. Nord diagnosed his condition as compression paralysis. Moreover, Andreini averred that when he signed the release, his hands "were getting progressively worse" and "seemed to get worse each day." An expert affidavit submitted by Andreini indicates that time was, in fact, crucial to his recovery and suggests that Beck may have been aware that immediate surgery was necessary. Dr. Masud Seyal stated in the affidavit that "[a]fter the onset of Andreini's bilateral ulnar neuropathy, as diagnosed by R. David Beck, prompt surgical intervention was the recommended procedure" and the two-month delay "in performing the nerve transposition on July 9, 1987, likely denied Mr. Andreini a more substantial recovery." (Emphasis added.)

"Based on this evidence, a jury could find that defendants engaged in unfair dealing that significantly increased the effectiveness of their threat to refuse to undertake the corrective surgery. This conclusion is consistent with the Restatement's official commentary. Comment "f" states that section 176(2)(b) "is concerned with cases in which the party making the threat has by unfair dealing achieved an advantage over the recipient that makes his [or her] threat unusually effective. Typical examples involve manipulative conduct during the bargaining stage that leaves one person at the mercy of the other." Restatement (Second) of Contracts § 176 cmt. f (1979).

"Having determined that Andreini has adduced sufficient facts to raise a jury question as to whether defendants made an improper threat, we now consider if Andreini has mustered sufficient facts as to whether he had any reasonable alternatives to signing the release. Again, viewing the evidence in the light most favorable to Andreini, we think that a jury could find that Andreini had no reasonable alternatives under the attendant circumstances. See id. § 175 cmt. b. We acknowledge, as the trial court found, that Andreini could have left the hospital and that he was not in a life-threatening situation. However, there is evidence from which a jury could find that his alternatives were not reasonable. As mentioned earlier, Andreini averred that he was aware that his hands were getting progressively worse each day when he was confronted with the release and an expert affidavit suggests that immediate corrective surgery was indeed necessary to prevent further irreversible damage. When Andreini initially refused to sign the release, Beck allegedly told him that if he did not sign, Beck was "going to play hard ball" with him, which Andreini took to mean that defendants would not provide the corrective surgery regardless of who would pay for it. This evidence is sufficient to convince us that while Andreini may have had alternatives to signing the release form, there is a question of material fact as to whether those alternatives were reasonable."

———

Chouinard v. Chouinard

568 F.2d 430 (5th Cir.1978)

Arc Corporation was owned by Fred Chouinard; Fred's father, Al Chouinard; and Fred's twin brother, Ed Chouinard. Fred was the president and apparently ran the business. Over the years, the parties were in dispute concerning the precise nature of the ownership interests of Ed and Al. At one point, Ed concluded that he and Al each owned 37½ percent of Arc, and that the value of each of their interests was close to $500,000. These conclusions were not shared by Fred. In 1974, Arc got into substantial financial difficulties due in part to a bad decision by Fred, and needed new financing. Fred was able to obtain a financing commitment from the Heller Company, a commercial lender, but when Heller learned that Ed and Al each claimed a stock-ownership interest, Heller made it clear that it would not make a loan until the stock-ownership dispute was settled. Fred's attorney drafted a proposed agreement under which all parties would agree that Heller could make the loan, but no one would acknowledge anyone else's ownership claim. This proposal was apparently never put on the table, because the attorney for Ed and Al informed Fred's counsel that this was a good occasion to settle the ownership issue. Fred's counsel labeled that approach as blackmail, but Fred realized that the Heller loan was essential. Accordingly, he agreed to pay Ed and Al $95,000 each, mostly in the form of promissory notes, in exchange for releases by Ed and Al of all their claims to ownership in Arc. Fred then closed the loan with Heller and Arc obtained the needed funds. Subsequently, Fred brought suit to set the promissory notes aside. Held, for Ed and Al.

(Thornberry. J.) "While there is ample evidence of economic necessity and financial peril, neither the 'threat of considerable financial loss' nor 'impending bankruptcy' establish economic duress. Such economic stress must be attributable to the party against whom duress is alleged. 'Mere hard bargaining positions, if lawful, and the press of financial circumstances, not caused by the [party against whom the contract is sought to be voided], will not be deemed duress.' Business Incentives Co. v. Sony Corp. of America, 397 F.Supp. 63, 69 (S.D.N.Y.1975).

"The only possible claim of duress is that Ed and Al, recognizing the weakened state of the company, seized that opportunity to settle the long-standing dispute regarding stock-ownership. Because duress may not be implied merely from the making of a hard bargain, the question becomes whether the conduct of Ed and Al was wrongful. The law in Georgia and other jurisdictions makes clear that it was not, for the two men were merely asserting a legal right, i.e., their right to a certain share of the stock in the company. See Causey v. Matson, 215 Ga. 306, 110 S.E.2d 356 (1959); Williams v. Ruben, 216 Ga. 431, 117 S.E.2d 456 (1960). Fred admitted that Ed and Al were stockholders in the company, and the long-standing dispute was over the percentage of the company each owned. Thus, while there is no doubt that Fred was between the proverbial rock and a hard place, it is clear that his own actions put him there and that Ed and Al merely took advantage of the situation to insist upon settlement of the intrafamilial stock squabble. . . .

"We conclude, therefore, that there is simply no duress shown on this record, for one crucial element is missing: a wrongful act by the defendants to create and take advantage of an untenable situation. Ed and Al had nothing to do with the financial quagmire in which Fred found himself, and we cannot find duress simply because they refused to throw him a rope free of any 'strings.' "

———

Post v. Jones

60 U.S. (19 How.) 150, 15 L.Ed. 618 (1856)

The whaling vessel Richmond, with a nearly full cargo of whale oil, was inextricably run aground in a deserted area 5,000 miles from the nearest port of safety. Several days later, the whaling vessels Elizabeth Frith, Panama, and Junior came into the vicinity. These vessels did not have full cargoes, but the Richmond had more whale oil than the three vessels could take. At the instance of the Junior's captain, the Richmond's captain agreed to hold an auction for its oil. The Frith's captain bid $1 per barrel for as much as he needed, and the captains of the Panama and the Junior bid 75› per barrel. The three vessels took enough of the Richmond's oil to complete their cargoes, and returned to port with the oil and the Richmond's crew. The Richmond's owners then brought this action to recover part of the value of the oil taken by the Frith and the Panama, on the theory that while these vessels were entitled to salvage (a maritime concept under which one who saves property is entitled to a reward) for the oil they took, they were not entitled to keep the oil at the auction price. Held, for the owners of the Richmond.

(Grier, J.) "The contrivance of an auction sale, under such circumstances, where the master of the Richmond was hopeless, helpless, and passive—where there was no market, no money, no competition—where one party had absolute power, and the other no choice but submission where the vendor must take what is offered or get nothing—is a transaction which has no characteristic of a valid contract. It has been contended by the claimants that it would be a great hardship to treat this sale as a nullity, and thus compel them to assume the character of Salvors, because they were not bound to save this property, especially at so great a distance from any port of safety, and in a place where they could have completed their cargo in a short time from their own catchings, and where salvage would be no compensation for the loss of this opportunity. The force of these arguments is fully appreciated, but we think they are not fully sustained by the facts of the case. Whales may have been plenty around their vessels on the 6th and 7th of August, but, judging of the future from the past, the anticipation of filling up their cargo in the few days of the season in which it would be safe to remain, was very uncertain, and barely probable. The whales were retreating towards the North Pole, where they could not be pursued, and, though seen in numbers on one day, they would disappear on the next; and, even when seen in greatest numbers, their capture was uncertain. By this transaction, the vessels were enabled to proceed at once on their home voyage; and the certainty of a liberal salvage allowance for the property rescued will be ample compensation for the possible chance of greater profits, by refusing their assistance in saving their neighbor's property.

"It has been contended, also, that the sale was justifiable and valid, because it was better for the interests of all concerned to accept what was offered, than suffer a total loss. But this argument proves too much, as it would justify every sale to a salvor. Courts of admiralty will enforce contracts made for salvage service and salvage compensation, where the salvor has not taken advantage of his power to make an unreasonable bargain; but they will not tolerate the doctrine that a salvor can take the advantage of his situation, and avail himself of the calamities of others to drive a bargain; nor will they permit the performance of a public duty to be turned into a traffic of profit."

EISENBERG, THE BARGAIN PRINCIPLE AND ITS LIMITS
95 Harvard Law Review 741 (1982).

Suppose that *A* makes a bargain with *B* at a time when, through no fault of *B*, *A* is in a state of necessity that effectively compels him to enter into a bargain on any terms he can get—a condition that I shall refer to as distress. . . . [Take the following example:]

> *The Desperate Traveler. T,* a symphony musician, has been driving through the desert on a recreational trip, when he suddenly hits a rock jutting out from the sand. *T*'s vehicle is disabled and his ankle is fractured. He has no radio and little water, and will die if he is not soon rescued. The next day, *G,* a university geologist who is returning to Tucson from an inspection of desert rock formations, adventitiously passes within sight of the accident and drives over to investigate. *T* explains the situation and asks *G* to take him back to Tucson, which is sixty miles away. *G* replies that he will help only if *T* promises to pay him two-thirds of his wealth or $100,000, whichever is more. *T* agrees, but after they return to Tucson he refuses to keep his promise, and *G* brings an action to enforce it.

Under traditional contract doctrines, *T*'s promise would be enforceable to its full extent. He has made a bargain, and none of the orthodox contract defenses apply. The defense of duress might seem apposite, but traditionally that defense has required not only that the promisor was in distress, but that he was put in distress by a wrongful act or threat of the promisee. *G* did not put *T* in distress, and because the common law imposes no duty on strangers to rescue persons in distress even when life is at stake, *G*'s threat of refusing aid would probably not constitute a wrongful act within the meaning of this rule.

It seems clear, however, that [*T*'s promise, extracted through *G*'s distress,] should not be enforced to its full extent. Neither fairness nor efficiency, the two major props of the bargain principle, supports its application in such a case. In terms of fairness, our society posits, as part of its moral order, some degree of concern for others. In *The Desperate Traveler, G* has acted wrongly in treating *T* as simply an economic object.

The efficiency argument also fails. When a commodity is sold under perfect competition, the doctrine of distress would usually have no application, even to contracts for necessities. A sale at a perfectly competitive price would normally not be regarded as exploitive, because the price is generated by a mechanism that is conventionally regarded as fair, and normally equals the seller's opportunity cost and approximates the seller's marginal cost. Furthermore, traditional economic analysis suggests that such a price normally allocates supply to its highest-valued uses and encourages the appropriate amount of investment in productive capacity. *G,* however, is not a perfect competitor, but a monopolist. Full enforcement of promises like that made by *T* is not required to move rescue services to their highest-valued uses, and would have no measurable effect on the allocation of resources to rescue-capacity, since the rescue is adventitious, there are no other bidders for the rescue services at the time of the rescue, and prior to the accident there was no market on which the victim could have purchased a contingent contract to rescue. Indeed, there is an argument that full enforcement would be inefficient. If it were known that persons in distress could be required to pay the price demanded for adventitious rescue, however high, people either might be reluctant to engage in activity in which rescue is sometimes necessary or might spend on precautions an aggregate amount exceeding the cost of adventitious rescue.

. . . [O]ther mature legal systems . . . allow the courts to review bargains made under distress for fairness of terms. For example, section 138(2) of the German Civil Code provides that a transaction is void "when a person [exploits] the distressed situation, inexperience, lack of judgmental ability, or grave weakness of will of another to obtain the grant or promise of pecuniary advantages . . . which are obviously disproportionate to the performance given in return." French law is in accord. At home, it is well established in admiralty law that a contract for salvage services—that is, a contract to rescue a vessel or its cargo—is reviewable for fairness of terms if entered into while the promisor is in distress. . . . [as evidenced] in *Post v. Jones.* . . .

This . . . leaves open how to measure the promisee's recovery in such cases. Financial cost is one possibility. Such a solution, however, would often fail to recognize adequately the benefit conferred upon the promisor. Furthermore, a financial-cost rule might not provide a sufficient incentive to act. In *The Desperate Traveler,* for example, *G*'s financial cost is close to zero. Assuming *G* is under no legal duty to rescue *T,* he would have no economic incentive to perform the rescue if his recovery were limited to financial cost. The need for an economic incentive in such cases should not be overemphasized; most individuals in *G*'s position would be likely to rescue *T* whether they had an economic incentive to do so or not. Nevertheless, an economic incentive would probably be helpful at the margin. Admiralty again suggests a solution. Although it will not enforce unfair rescue contracts, it does provide ample compensation for rescuers under the principle of salvage. Recovery under this principle is viewed both as a reward and as an inducement. Accordingly, in measuring recovery the courts take into account the degree of danger to the rescued property; the value of the rescued property; the risk incurred by the salvors; their promptness, skill, and energy; the value of the property the salvor employed; the degree of danger to that property; and the salvor's time and labor. In more general terms, the recovery in distress cases involving an adventitious rescuer should not only compensate the promisee for all costs, tangible and intangible, but should also include a generous bonus to provide a clear incentive for action and compensation for the benefit conferred. Recovery measured in this way admits of no great precision, but that is not fatal in situations in which, by hypothesis, planning is not important. The viability of this approach is evidenced by the fact that it has stood the test of time in an area in which distress and adventitious rescue are common occurrences.

SECTION 3. UNCONSCIONABILITY

WILLIAMS V. WALKER-THOMAS FURNITURE CO.

United States Court of Appeals, District of Columbia Circuit, 1965.
121 U.S.App.D.C. 315, 350 F.2d 445.

J. SKELLY WRIGHT, CIRCUIT JUDGE. Appellee, Walker-Thomas Furniture Company, operates a retail furniture store in the District of Columbia. During the period from 1957 to 1962 each appellant in these cases purchased a number of household items from Walker-Thomas, for which payment was to be made in installments. The terms of each purchase were contained in a printed form contract which set forth the value of the purchased item and purported to lease the item to appellant for a stipulated monthly rent payment. The contract then provided, in substance, that title would remain in Walker-Thomas until the total of all the monthly payments made equaled the stated value of the item, at which time appellants could take title. In the event of a default in the payment of any monthly installment, Walker-Thomas could repossess the item.

The contract further provided that "the amount of each periodical installment payment to be made by [purchaser] to the Company under this present lease shall be inclusive of and not in addition to the amount of each installment payment to be made by [purchaser] under such prior leases, bills or accounts; *and all payments now and hereafter made by [purchaser] shall be credited pro rata on all outstanding leases, bills and accounts* due the Company by [purchaser] at the time each such payment is made." (Emphasis added.) The effect of this rather obscure provision was to keep a balance due on every item purchased until the balance due on all items, whenever purchased, was liquidated. As a result, the debt incurred at the time of purchase of each item was secured by the right to repossess all the items previously purchased by the same purchaser, and each new item purchased automatically became subject to a security interest arising out of the previous dealings.

On May 12, 1962, appellant Thorne purchased an item described as a Daveno, three tables, and two lamps, having total stated value of $391.10. Shortly thereafter, he defaulted on his monthly payments and appellee sought to replevy all the items purchased since the first transaction in 1958. Similarly, on April 17, 1962, appellant Williams bought a stereo set of stated value of $514.95.[1] She too defaulted shortly thereafter, and appellee sought to replevy all the items purchased since December, 1957. The Court of General Sessions granted judgment for appellee. The District of Columbia Court of Appeals affirmed, and we granted appellants' motion for leave to appeal to this court.

Appellants' principal contention, rejected by both the trial and the appellate courts below, is that these contracts, or at least some of them, are unconscionable and, hence, not enforceable. In its opinion in Williams v. Walker-Thomas Furniture Company, 198 A.2d 914, 916 (1964), the District of Columbia Court of Appeals explained its rejection of this contention as follows:

"Appellant's second argument presents a more serious question. The record reveals that prior to the last purchase appellant had reduced the balance in her account to $164. The last purchase, a stereo set, raised the balance due to $678. Significantly, at the time of this and the preceding purchases, appellee was aware of appellant's financial position. The reverse side of the stereo contract listed the name of appellant's social worker and her $218 monthly stipend from the government. Nevertheless, with full knowledge that appellant had to feed, clothe and support both herself and seven children on this amount, appellee sold her a $514 stereo set.

"We cannot condemn too strongly appellee's conduct. It raises serious questions of sharp practice and irresponsible business dealings. A review of the legislation in the District of Columbia

---

[1] At the time of this purchase her account showed a balance of $164 still owing from her prior purchases. The total of all the purchases made over the years in question came to $1,800. The total payments amounted to $1,400.

affecting retail sales and the pertinent decisions of the highest court in this jurisdiction disclose, however, no ground upon which this court can declare the contracts in question contrary to public policy. We note that were the Maryland Retail Installment Sales Act, Art. 83 §§ 128–153, or its equivalent, in force in the District of Columbia, we could grant appellant appropriate relief. We think Congress should consider corrective legislation to protect the public from such exploitive contracts as were utilized in the case at bar."

We do not agree that the court lacked the power to refuse enforcement to contracts found to be unconscionable. In other jurisdictions, it has been held as a matter of common law that unconscionable contracts are not enforceable.[2] While no decision of this court so holding has been found, the notion that an unconscionable bargain should not be given full enforcement is by no means novel. In Scott v. United States, 79 U.S. (12 Wall.) 443, 445, 20 L.Ed. 438 (1870), the Supreme Court stated:

> " . . . If a contract be unreasonable and unconscionable, but not void for fraud, a court of law will give to the party who sues for its breach damages, not according to its letter, but only such as he is equitably entitled to. . . . "[3]

Since we have never adopted or rejected such a rule, the question here presented is actually one of first impression.

Congress has recently enacted the Uniform Commercial Code, which specifically provides that the court may refuse to enforce a contract which it finds to be unconscionable at the time it was made. 28 D.C.Code § 2–302 (Supp. IV 1965). The enactment of this section, which occurred subsequent to the contracts here in suit, does not mean that the common law of the District of Columbia was otherwise at the time of enactment, nor does it preclude the court from adopting a similar rule in the exercise of its powers to develop the common law for the District of Columbia. In fact, in view of the absence of prior authority on the point, we consider the congressional adoption of § 2–302 persuasive authority for following the rationale of the cases from which the section is explicitly derived.[1] Accordingly, we hold

---

[2] Campbell Soup Co. v. Wentz, 3 Cir., 172 F.2d 80 (1948); Indianapolis Morris Plan Corporation v. Sparks, 132 Ind.App. 145, 172 N.E.2d 899 (1961); Henningsen v. Bloomfield Motors, Inc., 32 N.J. 358, 161 A.2d 69, 84–96, 75 A.L.R.2d 1 (1960). Cf. 1 Corbin, Contracts § 128 (1963).

[3] See Luing v. Peterson, 143 Minn. 6, 172 N.W. 692 (1919); Greer v. Tweed, N.Y.C.P., 13 Abb.Pr., N.S., 427 (1872); Schnell v. Nell, 17 Ind. 29 (1861); and see generally the discussion of the English authorities in Hume v. United States, 132 U.S. 406, 10 S.Ct. 134, 33 L.Ed. 393 (1889).

[1] See Comment, § 2–302, Uniform Commercial Code (1962). Compare Note, 45 Va.L.Rev. 583, 590 (1959), where it is predicted that the rule of § 2–302 will be followed by analogy in cases which involve contracts not specifically covered by the section. Cf. 1 State of New York Law Revision Commission, Report and Record of Hearings on the Uniform Commercial Code 108–110 (1954) (remarks of Professor Llewellyn).

that where the element of unconscionability is present at the time a contract is made, the contract should not be enforced.

Unconscionability has generally been recognized to include an absence of meaningful choice on the part of one of the parties together with contract terms which are unreasonably favorable to the other party.[6] Whether a meaningful choice is present in a particular case can only be determined by consideration of all the circumstances surrounding the transaction. In many cases the meaningfulness of the choice is negated by a gross inequality of bargaining power.[7] The manner in which the contract was entered is also relevant to this consideration. Did each party to the contract, considering his obvious education or lack of it, have a reasonable opportunity to understand the terms of the contract, or were the important terms hidden in a maze of fine print and minimized by deceptive sales practices? Ordinarily, one who signs an agreement without full knowledge of its terms might be held to assume the risk that he has entered a one-sided bargain.[8] But when a party of little bargaining power, and hence little real choice, signs a commercially unreasonable contract with little or no knowledge of its terms, it is hardly likely that his consent, or even an objective manifestation of his consent, was ever given to all the terms. In such a case the usual rule that the terms of the agreement are not to be questioned[9] should be abandoned and the court should consider whether

---

[6]   See Henningsen v. Bloomfield Motors, Inc., supra Note 2; Campbell Soup Co. v. Wentz, supra Note 2.

[7]   See Henningsen v. Bloomfield Motors, Inc., supra Note 2, 161 A.2d at 86, and authorities there cited. Inquiry into the relative bargaining power of the two parties is not an inquiry wholly divorced from the general question of unconscionability, since a one-sided bargain is itself evidence of the inequality of the bargaining parties. This fact was vaguely recognized in the common law doctrine of intrinsic fraud, that is, fraud which can be presumed from the grossly unfair nature of the terms of the contract. See the oft-quoted statement of Lord Hardwicke in Earl of Chesterfield v. Janssen, 28 Eng.Rep. 82, 100 (1751):

"... [Fraud] may be apparent from the intrinsic nature and subject of the bargain itself; such as no man in his senses and not under delusion would make...."

And cf. Hume v. United States, supra Note 3, 132 U.S. at 413, 10 S.Ct. at 137, where the Court characterized the English cases as "cases in which one party took advantage of the other's ignorance of arithmetic to impose upon him, and the fraud was apparent from the face of the contracts." See also Greer v. Tweed, supra Note 3.

[8]   See Restatement, Contracts § 70 (1932); Note, 63 Harv.L.Rev. 494 (1950). See also Daley v. People's Building, Loan & Savings Ass'n, 178 Mass. 13, 59 N.E. 452, 453 (1901), in which Mr. Justice Holmes, while sitting on the Supreme Judicial Court of Massachusetts, made this observation:

"... Courts are less and less disposed to interfere with parties making such contracts as they choose, so long as they interfere with no one's welfare but their own.... It will be understood that we are speaking of parties standing in an equal position where neither has any oppressive advantage or power...."

[9]   This rule has never been without exception. In cases involving merely the transfer of unequal amounts of the same commodity, the courts have held the bargain unenforceable for the reason that "in such a case, it is clear, that the law cannot indulge in the presumption of equivalence between the consideration and the promise." 1 Williston, Contracts § 115 (3d ed. 1957).

the terms of the contract are so unfair that enforcement should be withheld.[10]

In determining reasonableness or fairness, the primary concern must be with the terms of the contract considered in light of the circumstances existing when the contract was made. The test is not simple, nor can it be mechanically applied. The terms are to be considered "in the light of the general commercial background and the commercial needs of the particular trade or case."[11] Corbin suggests the test as being whether the terms are "so extreme as to appear unconscionable according to the mores and business practices of the time and place." 1 Corbin, op. cit. supra Note 2.[12] We think this formulation correctly states the test to be applied in those cases where no meaningful choice was exercised upon entering the contract.

Because the trial court and the appellate court did not feel that enforcement could be refused, no findings were made on the possible unconscionability of the contracts in these cases. Since the record is not sufficient for our deciding the issue as a matter of law, the cases must be remanded to the trial court for further proceedings.

So ordered.

DANAHER, CIRCUIT JUDGE (dissenting):

The District of Columbia Court of Appeals obviously was as unhappy about the situation here presented as any of us can possibly be. Its opinion in the *Williams* case, quoted in the majority text, concludes: "We think Congress should consider corrective legislation to protect the public from such exploitive contracts as were utilized in the case at bar."

My view is thus summed up by an able court which made no finding that there had actually been sharp practice. Rather the appellant seems to have known precisely where she stood.

There are many aspects of public policy here involved. What is a luxury to some may seem an outright necessity to others. Is public oversight to be required of the expenditures of relief funds? A washing machine, e.g., in the hands of a relief client might become a fruitful source of income. Many relief clients may well need credit, and certain business establishments will take long chances on the sale of items, expecting their pricing policies will afford a degree of protection commensurate with the risk. Perhaps a

---

[10] See the general discussion of "Boiler-Plate Agreements" in Llewellyn, The Common Law Tradition 362–371 (1960).

[11] Comment, Uniform Commercial Code [§ 2–302].

[12] See Henningsen v. Bloomfield Motors, Inc., supra Note 2; Mandel v. Liebman, 303 N.Y. 88, 100 N.E.2d 149 (1951). The traditional test as stated in Greer v. Tweed, supra Note 3, 13 Abb.Pr., N.S., at 429, is "such as no man in his senses and not under delusion would make on the one hand, and as no honest or fair man would accept, on the other."

remedy when necessary will be found within the provisions of the "Loan Shark" law, D.C.Code § § 26–601 et seq. (1961).

I mention such matters only to emphasize the desirability of a cautious approach to any such problem, particularly since the law for so long has allowed parties such great latitude in making their own contracts. I dare say there must annually be thousands upon thousands of installment credit transactions in this jurisdiction, and one can only speculate as to the effect the decision in these cases will have.

I join the District of Columbia Court of Appeals in its disposition of the issues.

———

Skilton & Helstad, Protection of the Installment Buyer of Goods Under the Uniform Commercial Code

65 Mich.L.Rev. 1465, 1476–81

"It appeared that from 1957 to 1962 Ora Lee Williams had made sixteen separate purchases of furniture and household appliances from the store, all on installment credit, and in each case had signed fine print bailment-lease contracts which provided for monthly rental payments and reserved title in the store until payment was made in full. Most of these purchases were made when a representative of the store came to her home. . . .

" . . . The seller maintained that it still had title to everything because, under the pro rata clause, a balance remained due on each item, despite Ora's payments of over $1,000. The store's records showed that of a combined total claim of $444 as of December 26, 1962, Ora still owed 25 cents on item 1, purchased December 23, 1957 (price $45.65); 3 cents on item 2, purchased December 31, 1957 (price $13.21); $2.34 on item 3, purchased August 12, 1958 (price $127.40); and similarly for subsequent purchases, with balances of $.96, $1.70, $2.86, $1.08, $7.21, $1.53, $2.38, $5.66, $10.32, and $1.61. The only claims which were significant in relation to the purchase price were for the last three purchases: an item for $254.95, on which a balance of $65.98 was claimed; the $514.95 stereo, on which a balance of $327.89 was claimed; and an item for $15.45, on which a balance of $12.60 was claimed. . . .

"Was there anything inherently wrong about what the seller did in Williams? Forget for the nonce that he was dealing with an impoverished buyer who asserted that she did not understand the pro rata plan and would not have bought the stereo had she known that the seller would continue to tie up all of her previous purchases. Is there any difference between this case and a case in which, to induce a loan or a credit sale, a person agrees to give the creditor a security interest in most of his personal property which he owns outright? Or in which he gives his creditor a security interest in all such property to secure the balance of a consolidated indebtedness? Is it simply the indirectness of what was done that raises questions? . . .

"The appellants in *Williams* . . . argued that to allow the store to utilize the pro-rata clause to enforce its claim upon so much of appellants' household goods would, in effect, subvert the policy of the statutes of the District of Columbia exempting household goods from attachment. Of course, the statutes on their face do not prevent creditors from taking security interests in such goods and then seizing them on default, but the point nevertheless has merit: if our exemption statutes are to accomplish their patent purpose of protecting debtors from complete impoverishment as a result of creditor action, their provisions should be correlated with statutory provisions restricting the use of such property as security in certain kinds of transactions. . . ."

RESTATEMENT CONTRACTS, SECOND § 208

[See Selected Source Materials Supplement]

UCC § 2–302

[See Selected Source Materials Supplement]

UNIFORM CONSUMER CREDIT CODE §§ 1.301, 5.108

[See Selected Source Materials Supplement]

FEDERAL TRADE COMMISSION REGULATIONS— DOOR-TO-DOOR SALES

[See Selected Source Materials Supplement]

NOTE ON THE UNIFORM COMMERCIAL CODE

The National Conference of Commissioners on Uniform State Laws (NCCUSL) consists of commissioners appointed by each state. NCCUSL recommends legislation to the states on subjects in which uniformity of law among the states is thought to be desirable. Among its successful projects was the Uniform Sales Act, drafted by Professor Williston.

In 1940, the idea of a Uniform Commercial Code was proposed to NCCUSL, to take the place of numerous disparate statutes, including the Uniform Sales Act, which had direct bearing on commercial transactions. Thereafter the UCC became a joint project of NCCUSL and the American Law

Institute (ALI), with Karl N. Llewellyn of Columbia Law School, and later of the University of Chicago Law School, as the Chief Reporter. The UCC was adopted by NCCUSL and the ALI in 1952, and comprehensively revised in 1956; further amendments were promulgated thereafter. It has now been enacted in forty-nine states and the District of Columbia. (Louisiana, whose law is based on a civil code, has not adopted the UCC as such. However, it has adopted most Articles of the UCC other than Article 2 ("Sales") and it has incorporated many of the concepts of Article 2 into its Civil Code.)

Many provisions of the UCC are of major interest in the study of contract law, and will be referred to in this book. Most of these provisions are in Article 2. The direct applicability of that Article is set out in UCC § 2–102, which provides that "Unless the context otherwise requires, this Article applies to transactions in goods. . . . " UCC § 2–105(1) defines "goods" to mean "all things (including specially manufactured goods) which are movable at the time of identification to the contract for sale other than the money in which the price is to be paid, investment securities . . . and things in action." Other UCC provisions of interest in the study of contract law are contained in Article 1 ("General Provisions") and Article 9 ("Secured Transactions"). Articles 1 and 2, and selected portions of Articles 3 and 9, are set forth in the Selected Source Materials Supplement.

In considering the UCC provisions referred to in this book, it should be borne in mind that even where a UCC provision is not directly applicable to a transaction—for example, where the provision is in Article 2 and the transaction involves services—the *principle* embodied in the provision may be applicable, so that the provision may serve as a source of law. "[P]rovisions of the Uniform Commercial Code which do not conflict with statute or settled case law are entitled to as much respect and weight as courts have been inclined to give the various Restatements. It, like the Restatements, has the stamp of approval of a large body of American Scholarship." Fairbanks, Morse & Co. v. Consolidated Fisheries Co., 190 F.2d 817, 822 n. 9 (3d Cir.1951). See generally Murray, The Spreading Analogy of Article 2 of the Uniform Commercial Code, 39 Fordham L.Rev. 447 (1971). For general discussion of the use of statutes as a source of law, see Landis, Statutes and the Sources of Law, *in* Harvard Legal Essays 213 (R. Pound ed. 1934); Pound, Sources and Forms of Law, pt. III, 22 Notre Dame Law. 1, 36–45 (1946).

Conversely, the UCC itself rests on the foundation of general law. Section 1–103 of the UCC, "Supplementary General Principles of Law Applicable," provides that "Unless displaced by the particular provisions of this Act, the principles of law and equity, including the law merchant and the law relative to capacity to contract, principal and agent, estoppel, fraud, misrepresentation, duress, coercion, mistake, bankruptcy, or other validating or invalidating cause shall supplement its provisions." As stated in PEB Study Group, Uniform Commercial Code Article 2—Preliminary Report 22–23 (1990), Section 1–103 gives rise to two questions:

. . . (1) Does the UCC displace the common law in a particular area: and, if not, (2) What common law principle should the court choose? A broader interpretive question is whether § 1–103 provides sufficient flexibility and guidance for the courts to develop principles within the framework of the UCC, without having to find and integrate other "principles of law and equity."

For example, Article 2 uses but does not define the term "offer." See Sections 2–206(1) and § 2–207 (1). Arguably, under Section 1–103 the UCC sections that use the term offer do not displace the common law definition of the term. Is a court bound willy nilly by whatever concept of offer is applicable in the state or may the court develop a definition which is consistent with the formation policies found in Article 2, Part 2? This is an important question for which there is no clear answer.

NOTE ON THE COMMENTS TO THE UCC

Each section of the UCC is accompanied by an Official Comment. A Comment may simply state the background of the relevant Section or explain the way in which the Section is related to other sections. Often, however, the Comment plays a substantive role, by explaining the intention of the Section, putting a gloss on the language of the Section, providing examples of how the Section operates, or in other ways. The courts normally give deference to the Comments, but the exact legal status of the Comments is not completely clear. It has been said that "In the great majority of cases, courts cite the Comments to support the application or purpose described in them. In some cases, however, courts specifically reject the Comments as authority for their propositions." Note, The Jurisprudence and Judicial Treatment of the Comments to the Uniform Commercial Code, 75 Cornell L.Rev. 962, 975 (1990).

Pittsley v. Houser

125 Idaho 820, 875 P.2d 232 (App.1994)

This was a contract for the purchase and installation of residential carpeting. On the issue whether the contract was governed by the UCC, the court said, "although there is little dispute that carpets are 'goods,' the transaction in this case also involved installation, a service. Such hybrid transactions, involving both goods and services, raise difficult questions about the applicability of the UCC. Two lines of authority have emerged to deal with such situations.

(Swanstrom, J.) "The first line of authority, and the majority position, utilizes the 'predominant factor' test. The Ninth Circuit, applying the Idaho

Uniform Commercial Code to the subject transaction, restated the predominant factor test as:

> The test for inclusion or exclusion is not whether they are mixed, but, granting that they are mixed, whether their predominant factor, their thrust, their purpose, reasonably stated, is the rendition of service, with goods incidentally involved (e.g., contract with artist for painting) or is a transaction of sale, with labor incidentally involved (e.g., installation of a water heater in a bathroom). . . .

"This test essentially involves consideration of the contract in its entirety, applying the UCC to the entire contract or not at all.

"The second line of authority . . . allows the contract to be severed into different parts, applying the UCC to the goods involved in the contract, but not to the nongoods involved, including . . . services as well as other nongoods assets and property. Thus, an action focusing on defects or problems with the goods themselves would be covered by the UCC, while a suit based on the service provided or some other nongoods aspect would not be covered by the UCC. . . .

"We believe the predominant factor test is the more prudent rule. Severing contracts into various parts, attempting to label each as goods or nongoods and applying different law to each separate part clearly contravenes the UCC's declared purpose 'to simplify, clarify and modernize the law governing commercial transactions.' . . . As the Supreme Court of Tennessee suggested in Hudson v. Town & Country True Value Hardware, Inc., 666 S.W.2d 51 (Tenn.1984), such a rule would, in many contexts, present 'difficult and in some instances insurmountable problems of proof in segregating assets and determining their respective values at the time of the original contract and at the time of resale, in order to apply two different measures of damages.' *Id.* at 54.

"Applying the predominant factor test to the case before us, we conclude that the UCC was applicable to the subject transaction. The record indicates that the contract between the parties called for '165 yds Masterpiece #2122—Installed' for a price of $4319.50. There was an additional charge for removing the existing carpet. The record indicates that Hilton paid the installers $700 for the work done in laying Pittsley's carpet. It appears that Pittsley entered into this contract for the purpose of obtaining carpet of a certain quality and color. It does not appear that the installation, either who would provide it or the nature of the work, was a factor in inducing Pittsley to choose Hilton as the carpet supplier. On these facts, we conclude that the sale of the carpet was the predominant factor in the contract, with the installation being merely incidental to the purchase."

———

UNIDROIT PRINCIPLES OF INTERNATIONAL COMMERCIAL CONTRACTS ART. 3.10

[See Selected Source Materials Supplement]

———

PRINCIPLES OF EUROPEAN CONTRACT LAW §§ 4.109, 4.110

[See Selected Source Materials Supplement]

———

COMMISSION OF THE EUROPEAN COMMUNITIES, COUNCIL DIRECTIVE 93/13/EEC

[See Selected Source Materials Supplement]

———

MAXWELL v. FIDELITY FINANCIAL SERVICES, INC.

Supreme Court of Arizona, En Banc, 1995.
184 Ariz. 82, 907 P.2d 51.

FELDMAN, CHIEF JUSTICE.

Elizabeth Maxwell petitions us to review a court of appeals opinion affirming a trial court ruling that the doctrine of novation barred Maxwell's claim that a contract was unconscionable and therefore unenforceable. See Maxwell v. Fidelity Fin. Servs., Inc., 179 Ariz. 544, 880 P.2d 1090 (Ct.App.1993). We granted review . . .

FACTS AND PROCEDURAL HISTORY

The facts, taken in the light most favorable to Maxwell, against whom summary judgment was granted, are that in December 1984, Elizabeth Maxwell and her then husband, Charles, were approached by Steve Lasica, a door-to-door salesman representing the now defunct National Solar Corporation (National). Lasica sold the Maxwells a solar home water heater for a total purchase price of $6,512. Although National was responsible for installation, the unit was never installed properly, never functioned properly, and was eventually declared a hazard, condemned, and ordered disconnected by the City of Phoenix. Thus, although the unit may have been intrinsically worthless, the question of unconscionability is determined as of the time the contract was made. A.R.S. § 47–2302. [U.C.C. § 2–302].

Financing for the purchase was accomplished through a loan to the Maxwells from Fidelity Financial Services, Inc. (Fidelity). The sale price was financed for a ten-year period at 19.5 percent interest, making the total cost nearly $15,000.

At the time of the transaction, Elizabeth Maxwell earned approximately $400 per month working part-time as a hotel maid and her husband earned approximately $1,800 per month working for the local paper. At Fidelity's request, an appraisal was made of the Maxwells' South Phoenix home, where they had resided for the preceding twelve years. The appraisal showed that the Maxwells lived in a modest neighborhood, that their 1,539 square foot home was in need of a significant amount of general repair and maintenance, and that its market value was approximately $40,000.

In connection with the financing transaction, Elizabeth Maxwell signed numerous documents, including a loan contract, a deed of trust, a truth-in-lending disclosure form, and a promissory note and security agreement. The effect of these documents was not only to secure the deferred purchase price with a lien on the merchandise sold, but also to place a lien on Maxwell's house as additional security for payment on the water heater contract. The forms and their terms were unambiguous and clearly indicated that Maxwell was placing a lien on her house. Included in the consumer credit contract between Maxwell and Fidelity was a clause expressly stating that Fidelity was subject to all claims by and defenses that Maxwell could assert against National.

Despite the fact that the water heater was never installed or working properly, Maxwell made payments on it for approximately three and one-half years, reducing the deferred purchase balance to $5,733. In 1988, Maxwell approached Fidelity to borrow an additional $800 for purposes unrelated to the original loan. In making this second loan, Fidelity required Maxwell to again sign a bundle of documents essentially identical to those she signed in 1984. Instead of simply adding $800 to Maxwell's outstanding balance on the 1984 contract, Fidelity created a new contract that included the unpaid balance of $5,733 on the 1984 loan, a term life insurance charge of $313, as well as the new $800 loan. In all, Maxwell financed the sum of $6,976 with this second loan. The terms of this latest loan also included interest at 19.5 interest and payments for a period of six years, making Maxwell's new payments, including interest, total nearly $12,000. The combined amount Maxwell would pay under the two contracts for a non-functioning water heater and the additional $800 loan thus totals approximately $17,000, or nearly one-half the value of her home.

Maxwell continued to make payments until 1990, when she brought this declaratory judgment action seeking, *inter alia*, a declaration that the 1984 contract was unenforceable on the grounds that it was unconscionable.

Following discovery, Fidelity moved for summary judgment asserting, among other things, that the statute of limitations had run on Maxwell's claim of unconscionability and, if not, that the 1988 contract worked a novation, thereby barring any action by Maxwell on the 1984 contract. Maxwell filed a memorandum in opposition to this motion and pointed to sworn testimony in her deposition, which Fidelity submitted with its motion, as raising genuine issues of material fact.

In a brief order, the trial court granted Fidelity's motion on the theory of novation. . . .

The court of appeals affirmed [partly on procedural grounds]. . . .

On review from summary judgment, the appellate court views the record in a light most favorable to the party opposing summary judgment (Maxwell) and will affirm only if no genuine issue of material fact exists. We therefore review this record to determine whether it could support a finding that Maxwell's claim of unconscionability was barred by the 1988 loan.

PRELIMINARY ISSUES

Before discussing the merits of Maxwell's petition, we must address. . . . [the issue, must Maxwell show an agency relationship between Fidelity and National to defeat Fidelity's motion for summary judgment]. . . .

The court of appeals found that Maxwell failed to establish an agency relationship between National and Fidelity. The court reasoned that, absent such a relationship, Maxwell could not defeat Fidelity's motion for summary judgment on grounds of novation. We fail to see the relationship between establishing agency and defeating a claim of novation or pursuing a claim of unconscionability in this case. Fidelity stands in the shoes of National by virtue of both federal law and the terms of the contract to which it is a party. The 1984 and 1988 consumer credit contracts between Maxwell and Fidelity clearly state, in bold face, capital letters:

> ANY HOLDER OF THIS CONSUMER CREDIT CONTRACT IS SUBJECT TO ALL CLAIMS AND DEFENSES WHICH THE DEBTOR COULD ASSERT AGAINST THE SELLER OF GOODS OR SERVICES OBTAINED WITH THE PROCEEDS HEREOF.

Thus, Maxwell need not establish an agency relationship between National and Fidelity to maintain a claim against Fidelity for unconscionability or to overcome Fidelity's claim of novation. . . .

Discussion

A. Unconscionability . . .

2. The Test for Unconscionability

The court of appeals found the 1984 contract valid because Maxwell "failed to raise a material issue of fact that the agreement evidenced by [the contract documents] was beyond her reasonable expectations or was unconscionable." It is not clear why the court of appeals applied the test of "reasonable expectations" as this test is more correctly associated with contracts of adhesion, not claims of unconscionability, and the issue of adhesion contracts was neither before the trial court nor briefed or argued on appeal. This court previously has noted the rule that "reasonable expectations" and unconscionability are two distinct grounds for invalidating or limiting the enforcement of a contract and has stated that "even if [the contract provisions are] consistent with the reasonable expectations of the party" they are unenforceable if they are oppressive or unconscionable. Broemmer v. Abortion Serv. of Phoenix, 173 Ariz. 148, 151, 840 P.2d 1013, 1016 (1992) (quoting Graham v. Scissor-Tail, Inc., 28 Cal.3d 807, 171 Cal.Rptr. 604, 611–12, 623 P.2d 165, 172–73 (1981)).

3. The History of Unconscionability . . .

. . . Although U.C.C. § 2–302 recognized and codified the amorphous equitable doctrine [of unconscionability], it did little to provide a set of rules for analyzing claims of unconscionability. Also lacking in the statutory recognition of unconscionability is a definition of that term. Courts and respected commentators alike have grappled with defining and applying unconscionability under the Code since its adoption. To this day, both groups remain divided on the proper method for doing so, though they share some common ground on defining such a test.

Within this common area, the elements of unconscionability can be ascertained to fulfill the Code's obvious intent of protecting against unconscionable contracts while not unnecessarily denying parties the benefit of their bargain. Although no litmus test exists, the cases do provide a reasonable, workable analysis.

4. Divisions of Unconscionability under the U.C.C.

This court previously has acknowledged that the unconscionability principle involves an assessment by the court of

> whether, in the light of the general commercial background and the commercial needs of the particular trade or case, the clauses involved are so one-sided as to be unconscionable under the circumstances existing at the time of the making of the contract. . . . The principle is one of the prevention of oppression

and unfair surprise . . . not of disturbance of allocation of risks because of superior bargaining power.

Seekings v. Jimmy GMC of Tucson, Inc., 130 Ariz. 596, 602, 638 P.2d 210, 216 (1981) (citations omitted). This somewhat circular articulation of the principle, however, is not readily applicable to the infinite variety of cases that may involve the doctrine of unconscionability.

The framework upon which the vast majority of courts construct their analysis consists of the well recognized division of unconscionability into substantive and procedural parts. See, e.g., James J. White & Robert S. Summers, 1 Uniform Commercial Code 204, N. 8 and cases cited therein; John D. Calamari & Joseph M. Perillo, Contracts 406 (3d ed. 1987). Professor Dobbs provides the following explanation of the difference between these two types:

> Procedural or process unconscionability is concerned with "unfair surprise," fine print clauses, mistakes or ignorance of important facts or other things that mean bargaining did not proceed as it should. Substantive unconscionability is an unjust or "one-sided" contract. Substantive unconscionability is important in two ways. First, substantive unconscionability sometimes seems sufficient in itself to avoid a term in the contract. Second, substantive unconscionability sometimes helps confirm or provide evidence of procedural unconscionability.

Dobbs, supra at 706 (footnote omitted). This dichotomy evolved from a distinction made by the late Professor Leff in his oft-cited article Unconscionability and The Code—The Emperor's New Clause, 115 U.Pa.L.Rev. 485, 487 (1967). In his article, Professor Leff distinguished between "bargaining naughtiness" (procedural unconscionability) and overly harsh terms (substantive unconscionability). Id.

Over the years, courts have refined the two divisions of unconscionability and identified several factors that are indicative of each. Procedural unconscionability was well-explained in Johnson v. Mobil Oil Corp.:

> Under the procedural rubric come those factors bearing upon . . . the real and voluntary meeting of the minds of the contracting party: age, education, intelligence, business acumen and experience, relative bargaining power, who drafted the contract, whether the terms were explained to the weaker party, whether alterations in the printed terms were possible, whether there were alternative sources of supply for the goods in question.

415 F.Supp. 264, 268 (E.D.Mich.1976) (internal quotations omitted). As Professors White and Summers have noted, procedural unconscionability

bears a strong resemblance to its "common-law cousins" of fraud and duress. White & Summers, supra at 204.

Substantive unconscionability concerns the actual terms of the contract and examines the relative fairness of the obligations assumed. Resource Management Co. v. Weston Ranch & Livestock Co., 706 P.2d 1028, 1041 (Utah 1985). Indicative of substantive unconscionability are contract terms so one-sided as to oppress or unfairly surprise an innocent party, an overall imbalance in the obligations and rights imposed by the bargain, and significant cost-price disparity. Id. (citations and internal quotations omitted).

We believe these authorities provide useful illustrations of both divisions of unconscionability under the U.C.C., although we do not restrict applicability of the doctrine to the factors outlined.

5. Application

The point of agreement by courts on the substantive-procedural elements also marks a point of departure in analyzing claims of unconscionability. See generally White & Summers, supra at 218–20. Many courts, perhaps a majority, have held that there must be some quantum of *both* procedural and substantive unconscionability to establish a claim, and take a balancing approach in applying them. Id. at 219. See also 2 William D. Hawkland, Uniform Commercial Code Series § 2–302:05 (1984) and cases cited therein. Other courts have held that it is sufficient if *either* is shown. See, e.g., Gillman v. Chase Manhattan Bank, N.A., 73 N.Y.2d 1, 537 N.Y.S.2d 787, 794, 534 N.E.2d 824, 829 (1988) ("While determinations of unconscionability are ordinarily based on the court's conclusion that both the procedural and substantive components are present . . . , there have been exceptional cases where a provision of the contract is so outrageous as to warrant holding it unenforceable on the ground of substantive unconscionability alone.") (citing State v. Wolowitz, 96 A.D.2d 47, 468 N.Y.S.2d 131 (1983)). In addition to the numerous courts holding that either procedural or substantive unconscionability is sufficient,[3] the leading commentators in this field have also endorsed this

---

[3] See, e.g., Resource Management Co. v. Weston Ranch & Livestock Co., 706 P.2d 1028, 1043 (Utah 1985) ("Gross disparity in terms, absent evidence of procedural unconscionability, can support a finding of unconscionability."); American Home Improvement, Inc. v. MacIver, 105 N.H. 435, 201 A.2d 886, 889 (1964) (relying explicitly on U.C.S. § 2–302 and finding unconscionable, based on price-value disparity, a contract requiring payment of $1,609 for goods and services valued at "far less"); World Enter., Inc. v. Midcoast Aviation Serv., Inc., 713 S.W.2d 606, 610 (Mo.App.1986) ("Unconscionability is defined as either procedural or substantive."); Frank's Maintenance & Eng'g, Inc. v. C.A. Roberts Co., 86 Ill.App.3d 980, 42 Ill.Dec. 25, 31–32, 408 N.E.2d 403, 409–10 (1980) ("Unconscionability can be either procedural or substantive or a combination of both.") (emphasis added). Cf. Schroeder v. Fageol Motors, Inc., 86 Wash.2d 256, 544 P.2d 20, 23 (1975) (en banc) (recognizing that cases fall within the two classifications of procedural and substantive unconscionability). Indeed, it has long been recognized that gross disparity in terms may satisfy the standard for unconscionability by itself. See Marks v. Gates, 154 F. 481, 483 (9th Cir.1907) (inadequacy of consideration sufficient ground for withholding specific performance if it is so gross as to render the contract unconscionable).

position. See White & Summers, supra at 220 (advocating the sufficiency of excessive price alone).

The cases that require a showing of both procedural and substantive unconscionability appear to be rather fact-specific, based more on the historical reluctance of courts to disturb contracts than on valid doctrinal underpinning.

> In some cases substantive unconscionability is found because the contract price is grossly excessive (or sometimes grossly inadequate). Most of these cases present additional elements such as actual misrepresentations, gross mistreatment of people who are already disadvantaged, or a subject matter such as premarital settlements that calls for intense state scrutiny by judges. In some of them, the substantive unconscionability really seems to be evidentiary only, that is, as confirming the conclusion that the process of bargaining was itself defective.

Dobbs, supra at 707 (footnote omitted) (emphasis added); see also Calamari & Perillo, supra at 406 ("[C]ontracts involving grossly unequal exchanges almost always involve some impropriety in the negotiating process or disability of a party."); White & Summers, supra at 218 ("Almost all of [the cases finding substantively unconscionable terms] exhibit creditor behavior that may be regarded as both procedurally and substantively unconscionable.").

Additional evidence that the dual requirement position is more coincidental than doctrinal is found within the very text of the statute on unconscionability, which explicitly refers to "the contract *or any clause* of the contract." A.R.S. § 47–2302 (emphasis added). Conspicuously absent from the statutory language is any reference to procedural aspects. That the U.C.C. contemplated substantive unconscionability alone to be sufficient is the most plausible reading of the language in § 47–2302, given that the Code itself provides for *per se* unconscionability if there exists, without more, a substantive term in the contract limiting consequential damages for injury to the person in cases involving consumer goods. See A.R.S. § 47–2719(c) [U.C.C. § 2–719(c)]. It is wholly inconsistent to assert that unconscionability under § 47–2302 requires some procedural irregularity when unconscionability under § 47–2719 clearly does not.

Therefore, we conclude that under A.R.S. § 47–2302, a claim of unconscionability can be established with a showing of substantive unconscionability alone, especially in cases involving either price-cost disparity or limitation of remedies. If only procedural irregularities are present, it may be more appropriate to analyze the claims under the doctrines of fraud, misrepresentation, duress, and mistake, although such irregularities can make a case of procedural unconscionability. See Resource Management Co., 706 P.2d at 1043.

However, we leave for another day the questions involving the remedy for procedural unconscionability alone. We conclude further that this case presents a question of at least substantive unconscionability to be decided by the trial court. From the face of it, we certainly cannot conclude that the contract as a whole is not unconscionable, given the $6,500 price of a water heater for a modest residence, payable at 19.5 percent interest, for a total time-payment price of $14,860.43. These facts present at least a question of grossly-excessive price, constituting substantive unconscionability. See Dobbs, supra at 707; White & Summers, supra at § 4–5 and cases cited therein. This contract is made even more harsh by its security terms, which, in the event of non-payment, permit Fidelity not only to repossess the water heater but foreclose on Maxwell's home. The apparent injustice and oppression in these security provisions not only may constitute substantive unconscionability but also may provide evidence of procedural unconscionability. See Dobbs, supra at 706–07 (citing Williams v. Walker-Thomas Furniture Co., 350 F.2d 445 (D.C.Cir.1965)).

Under the U.C.C. as enacted in A.R.S. § 47–2302, the court may "refuse enforcement of the contract altogether." Dobbs, supra at 705; Restatement § 208. The present factual record, before the statutorily required evidentiary hearing, certainly contains some evidence that the entire 1984 contract, including sale price, security provisions, and remedies, is unenforceable. . . .

CONCLUSION

. . . [W]e vacate the court of appeals' opinion, reverse the trial court's judgment, and remand to the trial court for proceedings consistent with this opinion and A.R.S. § 47–2302.

MOELLER, V.C.J., and CORCORAN and ZLAKET, JJ., concur.

[The opinion of Judge Martone, concurring in the judgment, is omitted.]

Still another approach to the problem of substantive unconscionability, implicitly suggested in Ryan v. Weiner, 610 A.2d 1377 (Del. Ch. 1992), is to enforce a transaction that seems shocking only if the benefited party can show that if the transaction is fully explained it is not shocking.

NOTE ON CLASSICAL AND MODERN CONTRACT LAW

From the middle of the nineteenth century until the first part of the twentieth century, contract law was dominated by a school of thought, now known as classical contract law, which found its central inspiration in

Christopher Columbus Langdell, Oliver Wendell Holmes, and Samuel Williston, and its central expression in Restatement First. Beginning in the middle of the twentieth century, modern contract law began to oust classical contract law. Today, classical contract law survives largely in the form of background rules that have been heavily eroded but not entirely superceded. The movement from classical to modern contract law has occurred in a variety of dimensions.

1.   *The nature of contract-law reasoning.* To begin with, there has been a shift in the nature of contract-law reasoning. Reasoning in common law areas, like contracts, may be substantive or formal. The premise of *substantive* legal reasoning is that the validity of a doctrine turns in part on normative considerations, that is, on the congruence of the doctrine with morals, policy, and experience. In contrast, the premise of *formal* legal reasoning is that law consists of doctrines that are autonomous from policy, morality, and experience—that doctrines are valid without regard to whether they are normatively justified.

Formal legal reasoning may be axiomatic, deductive, or both. *Axiomatic* legal reasoning takes as a premise that fundamental doctrines can be established on the ground that they are self-evident. In the strictest versions of axiomatic theories, such as classical contract law, no room is allowed for justifying doctrinal propositions on the basis of moral and policy propositions. So, for example, Langdell, speaking to the question whether an acceptance by mail was effective on dispatch or on receipt, said:

> The acceptance . . . must be communicated to the original offeror, and until such communication the contract is not made. It has been claimed that the purposes of substantial justice, and the interests of contracting parties as understood by themselves, will be best served by holding that the contract is complete the moment the letter of acceptance is mailed; and cases have been put to show that the contrary view would produce not only unjust but absurd results. The true answer to this argument is that it is irrelevant.

Deductive legal reasoning is based on the idea that many or most doctrines can be established solely by deduction from other, more fundamental doctrines that are taken as the major premises of syllogisms. As Holmes observed, disparagingly, axiomatic theories may easily be coupled with deductive theories: "I sometimes tell students that the law schools pursue an inspirational combined with a logical method, that is, the postulates are taken for granted upon authority without inquiry into their worth, and then logic is used as the only tool to develop the results."

Classical contract law was based on just such a coupling. It conceived contract law as a small set of core doctrines—axioms—that were justified on the ground that they were self-evident, and as a larger set of doctrines that were justified largely on the ground that they could be deduced from the core axioms. For example, it was an axiom of classical contract law that only bargain promises had consideration, that is, were enforceable (although exceptions were recognized for certain kinds of promises, such as those under seal, that were considered to be enforceable on strictly precedential, rather than principled, grounds).

In contrast to the formal reasoning of classical contract law, modern contract-law reasoning seeks to justify doctrines on the basis of policy, morality, and experience. Doctrines have an important role to play even in substantive legal reasoning, because of the social value that underlies doctrinal stability, but that value must always be weighed against the value of normative justification.

2.   *The deep structure of contract-law rules.* A second aspect of the movement from classical to modern contract law concerns the deep structure of contract-law rules. Legal rules can be ranged along various spectra. Four such spectra, which are particularly salient in contract law, will be discussed in the balance of this Note.

a.   *Objectivity/subjectivity.* One of these spectra runs from objectivity to subjectivity. A contract-law doctrine lies at the objective end of this spectrum if its application depends on a directly observable state of the world, and lies at the subjective end if its application depends on a mental state. For example, the classical-law rule that nominal consideration made a promise enforceable was objective, because it asked only whether there was the objective form of a bargain. In contrast, the modern rule that nominal consideration does not make a promise enforceable allows the courts to inquire whether the parties were actually (subjectively) bargaining for the consideration that is recited in their contract.

b.   *Standardization/individualization.* A second spectrum runs from standardization to individualization. A contract-law doctrine lies at the standardized end of this spectrum if its application depends on an abstract variable that is unrelated to the intentions of the parties or the particular circumstances of the transaction. A contract-law doctrine lies at the individualized end of this spectrum if its application depends on situation-specific variables that *are* related to intentions and circumstances. For example, application of the classical doctrine that adequacy of consideration will not be reviewed depends on a single variable—the presence of a bargain— that is deliberately designed to screen out all information concerning intentions and circumstances. In contrast, application of the modern doctrine of unconscionability depends on a number of situation-specific variables that are wholly concerned with that sort of information.

c.   *Static/dynamic.* A third spectrum runs from the static to the dynamic. A contract-law doctrine lies at the static end of this spectrum if its application turns entirely on what occurred at the moment in time when a contract was formed. A contract-law doctrine lies at the dynamic end if its application turns in significant part on a moving stream of events that precedes, follows, or constitutes the formation of a contract. For example, the bargain theory of consideration is static, because its application wholly depends on what occurs at the moment in time when the bargain was made.

In contrast, the reliance principle is dynamic, because its application turns on events after the promise is made. Similarly, the classical-contract-law legal-duty rule, which made many or most contract modifications unenforceable (see Section 5, infra) was static, because all rights and duties were frozen at the moment of contract formation. In contrast, a regime under which modifications are enforceable is dynamic, because it takes account the importance of voluntary reciprocity after contract formation.

d.   *Binary/multi-faceted.* A fourth spectrum runs from the binary to the multi-faceted. Contract law doctrines are binary if they organize the experience within their scope into two categories. Contract law doctrines are multi-faceted if they organize the experience within their scope into several categories. For example, recall that Williston argued that when it came to damages, the only choice in contract law was the binary choice between no damages and expectation damages. In contrast, modern contract law provides a multi-faceted menu of no damages, expectation damages, reliance damages, restitutionary damages, and disgorgement damages.

Classical contract law was a rigid rather than a supple instrument. It gave overriding priority to objective, standardized, static, and binary rules, which were often responsive to neither the actual objectives of the parties, the actual facts and circumstances of the parties' transaction, nor the dynamic character of contracts. In contrast, modern contact law pervasively (although not completely) consists of principles that are individualized, dynamic, multi-faceted, and, in appropriate cases, subjective. Many of the Chapters in this book illustrate the movement from classical to modern contract law along one or more of these dimensions.

SECTION 4. THE DOCTRINE OF MUTUALITY AND THE ILLUSORY-PROMISE RULE

The materials in this Section concern a technical restriction on the bargain principle that should be eliminated. In hundreds of American cases, it has been asserted as a general rule of contract law that both parties must be bound or neither is bound. This rule is called the doctrine of mutuality or the illusory promise rule. An illusory promise is an expression that seems like a promise, but isn't. A common form of the problem is as follows: two parties—call them A and B—enter into an agreement with the usual trappings of a contract. The agreement is in writing and has language that signifies an intent to be legally bound. The agreement will involve an exchange between A and B. A will commit to go through with the exchange at B's discretion. B will not commit to go through with the exchange, or B will make a promise that is illusory because he has the power to terminate the agreement. A breaches the contract. When B sues for breach of contract A will argue that the promise she made is unenforceable for want of mutuality or because the promise apparently made by B was illusory.

The Illustrations to Restatement Second of Contracts Section 77 show the rule in action:

> 1.   A offers to deliver to B at $2 a bushel as many bushels of wheat, not exceeding 5,000, as B may choose to order within the next 30 days. B accepts, agreeing to buy at that price as much as he shall order from A within that time. B's acceptance involves no promise by him, and is not consideration. . . .

> 2.   A promises B to act as B's agent for three years from a future date on certain terms; B agrees that A may so act, but reserves the power to terminate the agreement at any time. B's agreement is not consideration, since it involves no promise by him.

In Illustration 1, B makes no commitment because he only agrees to do whatever he may choose to do. In Illustration 2, B reserves the right to choose to terminate his apparent commitment at any time. In both cases B has not constrained his realm of choice.

Corbin, "The Effect of Options on Consideration," 4 Yale L.J. 571, 574 (1925), explains the logic behind the requirement:

> [T]he chief feature of contract law is that by an expression of his will to-day the promisor limits his freedom of voluntary choice in the future. Society controls his future action by affording the stimulus described as *compulsion.* With this element absent we are no longer dealing with what is called contract or with contract law. To fall within this field therefore, a promise must in its terms express a willingness to effect this limitation on freedom of choice. Thus, if A asks B to promise some future performance and B makes no answer, B has made no promise. This is true, even though when the future time arrives B may then be willing to perform as requested and may actually so perform. If, under these circumstances, A thinks that B has made a promise, he is under an illusion. The same is true if instead of making no answer B had replied, 'I predict that when the time comes I shall be willing to do what you ask.' A prediction of future willingness is not an expression of present willingness and is not a promise. To see a promise in it is to be under an illusion. We reach the same result if B's reply to A is, 'I promise to do as you ask if I please to do so when the time arrives.' In form this is a conditional promise, but the condition is the pleasure or future will of the promisor himself. The words used do not purport to effect any limitation upon the promisor's future freedom of choice. They do not lead the promisee to have an expectation of performance because of a present

expression of will. He may hope that a future willingness will exist; but he has no more reasonable basis for such a hope than if B had merely made a prediction or had said nothing at all. As a promise, B's words are mere illusion. Such an illusory promise is neither enforceable against the one making it, nor is it operative as a consideration for a return promise.

The doctrine of mutuality and the illusory-promise rule should be eliminated because it often is a person's interest to commit to an exchange without a commitment from the other party.* In Illustrations 1 and 2, the promisor, A, does not make a promise to B for nothing, as a gift. She makes it to advance her own interests, by increasing the probability of exchange. In Illustration 1, A must believe that B is unlikely to trade with her unless A agrees to allow B the choice of ordering as many bushels as he wants to at the stated price during the stated time. In Illustration 2, A must believe that B would be unlikely to retain her as his agent unless she agreed that B could terminate the arrangement at any time. In each Illustration, A presumably makes her promise because she believes that B's incentives to exchange with A, rather than with others, would be insufficient unless the promise is made. In effect, there is a disparity of information and incentives between A and B. A has confidence in the attractiveness of her performance, which she believes that B does not share. A therefore makes a promise to B that is intended to change B's incentives to exchange with A, so as to increase the probability of exchange. A does this by making a commitment that she believes will induce B to give A a *chance* to show that her performance is attractive, either by sampling A's performance or perhaps simply by giving more serious consideration to purchasing A's performance than he otherwise would be likely to do.

The value of a chance to increase the probability of exchange is widely evidenced: book clubs give free books for the opportunity to sell future books; developers give free vacations for the opportunity to present a sales pitch; retailers offer free prizes in promotional contests to induce customers to shop; direct sellers pay substantial amounts for mailing lists.

This proposition can be illustrated by the following hypothetical:

A, a third-year law student whose grades are only fair but whose confidence is great, interviews with the well-known Washington litigation firm, F, G & H. After the interview, which A feels went very well, she writes to F, G & H as follows:

---

* Williston acknowledged that for this reason the mutuality requirement did not follow from the bargain theory of consideration: "[That illusory promises] are frequently . . . so requested with intent to make a bargain cannot be successfully disputed. A contractor or seller is often so eager to obtain work, or a sale, that he will gladly subject himself to an absolute promise in return for one which leaves performance optional with the other party. This is most commonly illustrated in agreements to buy or sell goods where the quantity is fixed by the wishes of one of the parties." Williston on Contracts § 103b (Rev. ed. 1937).

Dear F, G & H:

I very much enjoyed meeting you at my recent interview. I know my grades are below the level F, G & H usually requires. However, I also know they are not a fair indicator of my skills, particularly in litigation. (As you may recall, I did exceptionally well in several moot court settings.) I am sure that if you gave me a chance you would be more than pleased with my work. In order to induce you to give me a chance I make the following offer: I will work for you for one year at $70,000 (one-half of your normal starting salary), beginning September 1. You may discharge me at any time, without notice, no questions asked.

Sincerely yours,

A

F, G & H concurs, and A begins work. After three months, however, A leaves for another job, over the firm's objection. F, G & H brings suit against A for breach of contract.

Under the doctrine of mutuality A would not be bound to her promise, because F, G & H made no promise to her. Clearly, however, A has made a bargain. If F, G & H had paid $500 for A's promise, her promise would clearly be enforceable. The act of giving A a chance to prove herself may be worth much more to A (and may cost F, G & H much more) than $500. A has received exactly what she bargained for, and should be bound by her promise.

The doctrine of mutuality is a creature of classical contract law. Although the rule is still on the books, it is being whittled away under modern contract law. One way to satisfy the requirement of mutuality is to characterize a transaction as a unilateral contract. In a bilateral contract, the parties exchange a promise for a promise. (For example, Seller promises to sell Buyer a used car for $2,000, delivery in three days, and Buyer promises to pay $2,000 on delivery.) In a unilateral contract, the parties exchange a promise for an act. (For example, A promises to pay B $50 for mowing A's lawn, and makes clear that only B's act of mowing the lawn, not B's promise to do so, will suffice.) In a unilateral contract, the party who exchanges an act for a promise (B, in the hypothetical) may never be bound, because he is not bound to do anything before he chooses to do the act and he may not be bound to do anything after he does the act. Thus suppose, in the hypothetical, that B mows the lawn. B was not bound to mow the lawn before he mowed it, and is not bound to A in any way after he mowed it. Nevertheless, A is bound to B. The requirement of mutuality is satisfied by B's performance. We begin with a case that illustrates another technique courts use to satisfy the requirement. We conclude with a case in which the court could easily have found the requirement satisfied, but chose not to.

———

WOOD v. LUCY, LADY DUFF-GORDON

Court of Appeals of New York, 1917.
222 N.Y. 88, 118 N.E. 214.

CARDOZO, J. The defendant styles herself "a creator of fashions." Her favor helps a sale. Manufacturers of dresses, millinery, and like articles are glad to pay for a certificate of her approval. The things which she designs, fabrics, parasols, and what not, have a new value in the public mind when issued in her name. She employed the plaintiff to help her to turn this vogue into money. He was to have the exclusive right, subject always to her approval, to place her indorsements on the designs of others. He was also to have the exclusive right to place her own designs on sale, or to license others to market them. In return she was to have one-half of "all profits and revenues" derived from any contracts he might make. The exclusive right was to last at least one year from April 1, 1915, and thereafter from year to year unless terminated by notice of 90 days. The plaintiff says that he kept the contract on his part, and that the defendant broke it. She placed her indorsement on fabrics, dresses, and millinery without his knowledge and withheld profits. He sues her for the damages, and the case comes here on demurrer.

The agreement of employment is signed by both parties. It has a wealth of recitals. The defendant insists, however, that it lacks the elements of a contract. She says that the plaintiff does not bind himself to anything. It is true that he does not promise in so many words that he will use reasonable efforts to place the defendant's indorsements and market her designs. We think, however, that such a promise is fairly to be implied. The law has outgrown its primitive stage of formalism when the precise word was the sovereign talisman, and every slip was fatal. It takes a broader view to-day. A promise may be lacking, and yet the whole writing may be "instinct with an obligation," imperfectly expressed (Scott, J., in McCall Co. v. Wright, 133 App.Div. 62, 117 N.Y.S. 775; Moran v. Standard Oil Co., 211 N.Y. 187, 198, 105 N.E. 217). If that is so, there is a contract.

The implication of a promise here finds support in many circumstances. The defendant gave an exclusive privilege. She was to have no right for at least a year to place her own indorsements or market her own designs except through the agency of the plaintiff. The acceptance of the exclusive agency was an assumption of its duties. Phoenix Hermetic Co. v. Filtrine Mfg. Co., 164 App.Div. 424, 150 N.Y.S. 193; W.G. Taylor Co. v. Bannerman, 120 Wis. 189, 97 N.W. 918; Mueller v. Mineral Spring Co., 88 Mich. 390, 50 N.W. 319. We are not to suppose that one party was to be placed at the mercy of the other. Hearn v. Stevens & Bro., 111 App.Div. 101, 106, 97 N.Y.S. 566; Russell v. Allerton, 108 N.Y. 288, 15 N.E. 391. Many other terms of the agreement point the same way. We are told at the outset by way of recital that:

> "The said Otis F. Wood possesses a business organization adapted to the placing of such indorsements as the said Lucy, Lady Duff-Gordon, has approved."

The implication is that the plaintiff's business organization will be used for the purpose for which it is adapted. But the terms of the defendant's compensation are even more significant. Her sole compensation for the grant of an exclusive agency is to be one-half of all the profits resulting from the plaintiff's efforts. Unless he gave his efforts, she could never get anything. Without an implied promise, the transaction cannot have such business "efficacy, as both parties must have intended that at all events it should have." Bowen, L.J., in the Moorcock, 14 P.D. 64, 68. But the contract does not stop there. The plaintiff goes on to promise that he will account monthly for all moneys received by him, and that he will take out all such patents and copyrights and trade-marks as may in his judgment be necessary to protect the rights and articles affected by the agreement. It is true, of course, as the Appellate Division has said, that if he was under no duty to try to market designs or to place certificates of indorsement, his promise to account for profits or take out copyrights would be valueless. But in determining the intention of the parties the promise *has* a value. It helps to enforce the conclusion that the plaintiff *had* some duties. His promise to pay the defendant one-half of the profits and revenues resulting from the exclusive agency and to render accounts monthly was a promise to use reasonable efforts to bring profits and revenues into existence. For this conclusion the authorities are ample.

The judgment of the Appellate Division should be reversed, and the order of the Special Term affirmed, with costs in the Appellate Division and in this court.

CUDDEBACK, MCLAUGHLIN, and ANDREWS, JJ., concur. HISCOCK, C.J., and CHASE and CRANE, JJ., dissent.

Judgment reversed, etc.

———

RESTATEMENT, SECOND, CONTRACTS § 77

[See Selected Source Materials Supplement]

———

Mattei v. Hopper

51 Cal.2d 119, 330 P.2d 625 (1958)

Plaintiff was a real-estate developer. He was planning to construct a shopping center on a tract adjacent to defendant's land, and wanted to acquire the defendant's land in connection with the development of the shopping center. For several months, a real-estate agent attempted to negotiate a purchase of defendant's land, on plaintiff's behalf, under terms agreeable to both parties. After several of plaintiff's proposals had been rejected by defendant because of the inadequacy of the price that plaintiff offered, defendant submitted an offer of $57,000, which plaintiff accepted.

The parties' written agreement was evidenced on a form of deposit receipt supplied by the real-estate agent. Under its terms, plaintiff was required to deposit $1000 with the real-estate agent, and was given 120 days to "examine the title and consummate the purchase." At the expiration of that period, the balance of the price was "due and payable upon tender of a good and sufficient deed of the property sold." The concluding paragraph of the deposit receipt provided: "Subject to Coldwell Banker & Company [a real-estate broker] obtaining leases satisfactory to the purchaser." Plaintiff wanted this clause, and the 120-day period, to make sure that he could arrange satisfactory leases of the shopping-center buildings prior to the time at which he was finally committed to pay the balance of the purchase price and take title to defendant's land.

Thereafter, defendant's attorney notified plaintiff that defendant would not sell her land under the terms contained in the deposit receipt. Subsequently, defendant was informed that satisfactory leases had been obtained by Coldwell Banker and that plaintiff offered to pay the balance of the purchase price. Defendant failed to tender the deed as provided in the deposit receipt. Plaintiff sued for damages, and defendant argued that the plaintiff's promise was illusory. Held, for plaintiff.

(Spence, J.) "While contracts making the duty of performance of one of the parties conditional upon his satisfaction would seem to give him wide latitude in avoiding any obligation and thus present serious consideration problems, such 'satisfaction' clauses have been given effect. They have been divided into two primary categories and have been accorded different treatment on that basis. First, in those contracts where the condition calls for satisfaction as to commercial value or quality, operative fitness, or mechanical utility, dissatisfaction cannot be claimed arbitrarily, unreasonably, or capriciously . . . and the standard of a reasonable person is used in determining whether satisfaction has been received. . . . Of the cited cases, two have expressly rejected the arguments that such clauses either rendered the contracts illusory . . . or deprived the promises of their mutuality of obligation. . . .

"[The] multiplicity of factors which must be considered in evaluating a lease shows that this case more appropriately falls within the second line of authorities dealing with 'satisfaction' clauses, being those involving fancy, taste, or judgment. Where the question is one of judgment, the promisor's determination that he is not satisfied, when made in good faith, has been held to be a defense to an action on the contract. . . . Although these decisions do not expressly discuss the issues of mutuality of obligation or illusory promises, they necessarily imply that the promisor's duty to exercise his judgment in good faith is an adequate consideration to support the contract. . . . "

———

Harris v. Time, Inc.

191 Cal.App.3d 449, 237 Cal.Rptr. 584 (1987)

Joshua Gnaizda, "the three-year-old son of a prominent Bay Area public interest attorney," received a letter from Time, Inc. The front of the envelope contained a small see-through window, which revealed part of the enclosed letter. The part of the letter that could be seen through the window contained a picture of a calculator watch under the following statement: "Joshua A. Gnaizda, I'll give you this versatile new calculator watch free just for opening this envelope before Feb. 15, 1985." However, the see-through window did not reveal the full text of the letter. Printed in the letter below the picture of the calculator watch, and not viewable through the see-through window, were the following additional words: "And mailing this certificate today!" The certificate required Joshua to purchase a subscription to *Fortune* magazine to receive the calculator watch.

Joshua's father demanded the calculator watch without purchasing a subscription to *Fortune*. Time refused. Joshua, acting through his father, then brought a class action for $15 million. Time argued there was no contract because the mere act of opening the envelope was valueless, and therefore did not constitute adequate consideration. The court rejected this argument.

(King, J.) " . . . It is basic modern contract law that, with certain exceptions not applicable here (such as illegality or preexisting legal duty), *any* bargained-for act or forbearance will constitute adequate consideration for a unilateral contract. . . . Courts will not require equivalence in the values exchanged or otherwise question the adequacy of the consideration. . . . If a performance is bargained for, there is no further requirement of benefit to the promisor or detriment to the promisee. . . .

"Moreover, the act at issue here—the opening of the envelope, with consequent exposure to Time's sales pitch—may have been relatively insignificant to the plaintiffs, but it was of great value to Time. At a time when our homes are bombarded daily by direct mail advertisements and solicitations, the name of the game for the advertiser or solicitor is to *get the recipient to open the envelope*. Some advertisers, like Time in the present case, will resort to ruse or trick to achieve this goal. From Time's perspective, the opening of the envelope was 'valuable consideration' in every sense of that phrase."

(The court nevertheless dismissed the action on the grounds that (i) members of the class other than Joshua had not given Time notice of performance, and (ii) Joshua fell within the legal maxim "de minimis non curat lex"—the law disregards trifles—embodied in Cal.Civil Code § 3533.)

———

Helle v. Landmark, Inc.

15 Ohio App.3d 1, 472 N.E.2d 765 (1984)

" 'The modern decisional tendency is against lending the aid of courts to defeat contracts on technical grounds of want of mutuality.' Texas Gas Utilities Co. v. Barrett (Tex.1970), 460 S.W.2d 409, 412. As a contract defense, the mutuality doctrine has become a faltering rampart to which a litigant retreats at his own peril."

———

Lindner v. Mid-Continent Petroleum Corp.

221 Ark. 241, 252 S.W.2d 631 (1952)

Lindner leased a filling station to Mid-Continent for three years, with an option in Mid-Continent to renew for two more years. Mid-Continent had the right to terminate the lease at any time on ten days' notice. Following an attempt by Lindner to cancel the lease, Mid-Continent brought suit to regain possession. Lindner defended on the ground that the lease lacked mutuality. Held, for Mid-Continent. "[T]he requirement of mutuality does not mean that the promisor's obligation must be exactly coextensive with that of the promisee. It is enough that the duty unconditionally undertaken by each party be regarded by the law as a sufficient consideration for the other's promise. . . . In this view it will be seen that Mid-Continent's option to cancel the lease upon ten days' notice to Mrs. Lindner is not fatal to the validity of the contract. This is not an option by which the lessee may terminate the lease at pleasure and without notice; at the very least the lessee bound itself to pay rent for ten days."

———

OFFICE PAVILION S. FLORIDA, INC. v. ASAL PRODS., INC.
District Court of Appeal of Florida, 2003.
849 So.2d 367.

Warner, J. Appellee, ASAL Products, Inc. ("ASAL"), an office supply wholesaler, sued appellant, Office Pavilion, an office supply company, for breach of a contract to supply chairs. Office Pavilion contended that the contract was unenforceable, as it was not supported by consideration and was indefinite. The trial court denied all motions directed to the enforceability of the contract, and after trial, the jury returned a substantial verdict in favor of ASAL. We hold, however, that the contract for the purchase of chairs was not enforceable and reverse.

Office Pavilion ("Pavilion") is a subsidiary of Herman Miller, Inc., a corporation which manufactures and distributes office furniture throughout the United States and Europe and is the exclusive distributor of Herman Miller office products in South Florida. Bernd Stier is a German wholesaler and reseller of office furniture and equipment mainly in Germany but also in other parts of Europe. Stier hired Oliver Asel, a former employee of Pavilion, and the two formed ASAL in Florida in order to facilitate purchasing Herman Miller keyboard trays from Pavilion to resell to Stier's customers in Europe.

Asel contacted Pavilion's sales manager, Gary Kemp, to negotiate a contract for the sale of keyboards. After months of negotiations, on December 23, 1998, they entered into a two-year contract for keyboard trays. The contract provided, in part:

2.   Purpose of Contract:

The parties agree that the purpose for entering into this agreement is for Pavilion to supply and ASAL to purchase from Pavilion products known as keyboard trays, and accessories for those keyboard trays.

3.   Delivery Times:

Pavilion agrees to supply ASAL with keyboard trays & accessories ordered by ASAL within 30 days of receipt of any orders up to 2,000 units per month and any accessories ordered by ASAL to supplement ordered units. A "unit" is defined, for purposes of this contract as a keyboard tray. An accessory is not a "unit" for purposes of calculating minimum and maximum order quantities.

4.   Quantities:

ASAL agrees to order a minimum of 1,000 units per year. Pavilion agrees to supply ASAL with any and all quantities ordered by ASAL up to a maximum of 2,000 units per month plus the accessories for those ordered units.

The contract further provided that the unit price would be established by a separate writing, which included volume discounts. ASAL placed three orders for keyboard trays in amounts between 100 and 150, for which ASAL timely paid and Pavilion timely delivered.

Approximately a month after the contract was signed, ASAL became interested in expanding its contract to include Herman Miller's Aeron chair, and Asel commenced negotiations with Kemp for this modification. While these negotiations were proceeding, ASAL marketed the chair in

January and February, in addition to the keyboard tray, to determine demand for the chair. On March 11, 1999, Kemp forwarded ASAL a letter regarding amending the parties' contract for the keyboard trays to include the Aeron chairs. The letter included the price for two Aeron chair models and indicated:

> The terms and conditions of the December 23, 1998 Contract and Amendment will apply to these chairs except for Paragraph 3 and 4, Delivery Times and Quantities. The following paragraph shall be added to the Contract and Amendment:

> Aeron Chair Delivery Times:

> Pavilion agrees to supply ASAL with Aeron chairs ordered by ASAL within its established manufacturing lead times. The lead time will normally be 6 weeks from receipt of orders until shipment to Pavilion. Shorter lead times are also available depending upon order quantity and fabric selection.

Like the keyboards, the attached price list allowed for volume discounts on the chairs. Later, the parties signed an addendum memorializing the pricing structure.

After the letter regarding the chairs was sent, ASAL purchased six chairs from Pavilion to display at a trade show in Germany. The show was such a success that ASAL immediately reevaluated its sales forecast and requested a meeting with Kemp. Asel wanted 2,450 chairs to cover sales orders from the show plus 30 chairs to use as samples. However, while ASAL wanted the chairs, it did not include a deposit with its order or specify model numbers for the chairs. Kemp replied that it could not fill the order because Herman Miller International would not approve the sale. Pavilion had authority from Herman Miller to supply its products to ASAL only for sale in Germany, and ASAL was expanding outside of Germany, contrary to Kemp's understanding of their original contract negotiations.

ASAL filed a breach of contract action, claiming as damages its lost profits for all expected sales under the contract for its two-year duration. While Pavilion admitted the existence of the keyboard contract, it defended against the much larger chair contract, contending that the agreement lacked consideration.

At trial, Kemp testified that he drafted the letter and addendum to expand the contract between the parties to include the chairs. He explained that the quantity paragraph from the keyboard tray contract was specifically excluded in his March 11th letter because "there was no minimum order quantities that were promised or that we agreed to for pricing for discounting purposes." He further explained that:

> Furniture industry agreements to purchase. [sic] They are not—They don't require you to purchase unless it would

specifically say you agree to by [sic] X amount. So historically what it is is [sic] it's a license—it's a hunting license, if you will, is what we used to call them in the industry, to try to go after business, but with no promise that you'd ever see any business from it.

However, Kemp said that even with the lack of a quantity term provision, if Pavilion received an order from ASAL, Pavilion would fill it "within whatever terms." Basically, with a hunting license, Pavilion "had no expectations of what would come from it." Based upon his negotiations with Asel, Kemp did not know when or if ASAL ever was going to place these orders because Asel had been indicating for several months that the "orders were coming."

Asel testified that he brought an order for 2,480 chairs and a check for $633,000 to the meeting with Kemp regarding the chairs. However, Kemp informed him that Herman Miller would not approve the agreement. Kemp then advised Asel to submit a smaller order, and Asel modified the amount to 1,000 chairs with a $255,000 deposit. However, that order also was not accepted. Kemp denied that Asel ever presented the $633,000 check at the meeting at which Kemp informed Asel of Herman Miller's rejection of his order. As to the smaller order, Asel's check for $255,000 was returned for insufficient funds, after which Pavilion rejected the order.

After the trial court denied Pavilion's motion for directed verdict with regard to the enforceability of the contract and on the speculative nature of the lost profits, the jury awarded ASAL $4,000,000 in damages. From this verdict and resulting judgment, Pavilion appeals.

Pavilion contends that the chair contract between the parties was legally unenforceable for lack of consideration. We agree. While the contract for keyboards obligated ASAL to purchase a minimum of 1,000 keyboards a year from Pavilion, there was no minimum quantity term for the chairs. Essentially, Pavilion agreed to fill orders as made by ASAL, but ASAL had no obligation to place any orders at all. As Kemp said, the "agreement" was a "hunting license" which allowed ASAL to look for customers of Pavilion's merchandise and then to place orders when it found them.

It is a fundamental principle of contract law that a promise must be supported by consideration to be enforceable. *See* Restatement (Second) of Contracts § 17 (1981) ("[T]he formation of a contract requires a bargain in which there is a manifestation of mutual assent to the exchange and a consideration.") Moreover, a modification of a contract must be supported with consideration. *See Wilson v. Odom,* 215 So.2d 37, 38 (Fla. 1st DCA 1968). In a contract where the parties exchange promises of performance, "[i]f either of those promises is illusory or unenforceable then there is no consideration for the other promise." *Allington Towers N., Inc. v. Rubin,*

400 So.2d 86, 87 (Fla. 4th DCA 1981). As stated by the Court of Appeals for the Eleventh Circuit applying Florida law:

> If, however, "one of the promises appears on its face to be so insubstantial as to impose no obligation at all on the promisor— who says, in effect, 'I will if I want to' "—then that promise may be characterized as an "illusory" promise . . . An illusory promise does not constitute consideration for the other promise, and thus the contract is unenforceable against either party.

Johnson Enter. of Jacksonville, Inc. v. FPL Group, Inc., 162 F.3d 1290, 1311 (11th Cir.1998) (citations omitted).

The Restatement of Contracts illustrates these contract principles. Section 75 acknowledges that "a promise which is bargained for is consideration if, *but only if,* the promised performance would be consideration." Restatement (Second) of Contracts § 75 (emphasis added). However, the Restatement further provides in Section 77, "[a] promise or apparent promise is not consideration if by its terms the promisor or purported promisor reserves a choice or alternative performances." The commentary to this section explains:

> Words of promise which by their terms make performance entirely optional with the "promisor" do not constitute a promise. . . Where the apparent assurance of performance is illusory, it is not consideration for the return promise.

Restatement, *supra* at § 77 cmt. a (citation omitted). As appellant noted in its brief, the Restatement contains an example of illusory promises explaining this principle which is analogous to the alleged contract between Pavilion and ASAL.

> A offers to deliver to B at $2 a bushel as many bushels of wheat, not exceeding 5,000 as B may choose to order within the next 30 days. B accepts, agreeing to buy at that price as much as he shall order from A within that time. B's acceptance involves no promise by him, and is not consideration.

Restatement, *supra* at § 77 cmt. a, illus. 1. Similarly, Pavilion agreed to sell to ASAL any chairs it chose to order at the price set forth in the price list. While ASAL may have agreed, its acceptance involved no promised performance and therefore did not constitute consideration to support the contract modification for the Aeron Chairs.

ASAL responds by maintaining that mutuality of obligation is unnecessary where other consideration is present in the contract; yet, it fails to point to any other consideration. It first cites to the parties' mutual promises in paragraph two of the contract for Pavilion to supply, and ASAL to buy, the chairs. Without the ensuing quantity term or price term, however, this "mutual promise" is illusory and unenforceable. Next, it maintains the consideration was the benefit Pavilion received from ASAL's ongoing marketing efforts and sales of the chairs. This "benefit" also does not constitute consideration. First, the contract does not obligate ASAL to market the chairs. Second, marketing the chairs actually benefits ASAL where it obtains orders from it. ASAL's marketing efforts did not obligate Pavilion to sell the chairs. *See, e.g., Gull Lab., Inc. v. Diagnostic Tech., Inc.,* 695 F.Supp. 1151, 1154 (D.Utah 1988) (holding agreement to actively market product did not supply consideration where contract failed to include requirement that purchaser had any obligation to buy a minimum quantity of product). Finally, ASAL asserts its implied promise to place future orders was consideration. Were that the case, then any promise to place orders with no obligation to do so would constitute consideration. The case law cited above rejects such an illusory promise.

Next, the parties' contract is unenforceable for lack of an essential term, the quantity of chairs ASAL must order. That a quantity term is essential to a contract for the sale of goods is illustrated by Florida's statute of frauds provisions adopted from the Uniform Commercial Code. [Section 2.201(a)], Florida Statutes (1997), provides that a contract for the sale of goods in excess of $500 must be in writing to be enforceable. "A writing is not insufficient because it omits or incorrectly states a term agreed upon but the contract is not enforceable under this paragraph *beyond the quantity of goods shown in such writing.* " . . . (emphasis added) . . . Therefore, without a quantity term, this contract would be unenforceable under this section. *See Merritt-Campbell, Inc. v. RxP Products, Inc.,* 164 F.3d 957, 962 (5th Cir.1999) ("[T]he only term that must appear in a writing to support an enforceable contract for the sale of goods is the quantity term."). Contrary to ASAL's argument, that pursuant to the statute the contract may still be enforceable if the parties admit the existence of the contract, the statute actually provides that a contract is enforceable, "[i]f the party against whom enforcement is sought admits in his or her pleading, testimony or otherwise in court that a contract for sale was made, but the contract is *not enforceable under this provision beyond the quantity of goods admitted.* " § 672.201(3)(b) (emphasis added). Not only did Pavilion not admit to an enforceable contract with respect to the sale of chairs, it did not admit any quantity of chairs governed by the contract. Therefore, the contract could not be enforceable under this exception.

Because the chair contract was illusory and unenforceable, and Pavilion did not breach the keyboard contract, the trial court erred in denying Pavilion's motion for directed verdict. We therefore reverse the final judgment and direct entry of a judgment in favor of Pavilion.

GUNTHER, J., and HARNAGE, HENRY H., ASSOCIATE JUDGE, concur.

———

SECTION 5. THE LEGAL-DUTY RULE; MODIFICATIONS

Just as classical contract law excluded illusory promises from the operation of the bargain principle, so too it excluded promises to perform an act that the promisor was already obliged to do. Under the *legal-duty rule* such a promise is not consideration, so that a bargain in which one party only promises to perform an act that he is already obliged to perform is unenforceable. The application of that rule in cases involving contract modifications, and the rule's erosion under modern contract law, is the subject of this Section.

———

Pollock, Principles of Contract

196 (9th ed. 1921)

" . . . [N]either the promise to do a thing nor the actual doing of it will be a good consideration if it is a thing which the party is already bound to do either by the general law or by a subsisting contract with the other party. It seems obvious that an express promise by A. to B. to do something which B. can already call on him to do can in contemplation of law produce no fresh advantage to B. or detriment to A."

———

Shadwell v. Shadwell

30 L.J.C.P. 145 (1860)

BYLES, J., said in this case: "The reason why the doing what a man is already bound to do is no consideration, is not only because such a consideration is in judgment of law of no value, but because a man can hardly be allowed to say that the prior legal obligation was not his determining motive."

———

LINGENFELDER V. WAINWRIGHT BREWERY CO.

Supreme Court of Missouri, 1891.
103 Mo. 578, 15 S.W. 844.

GANTT, P.J. This was an action by Phillip J. Lingenfelder and Leo Rassieur, executors of Edmund Jungenfeld against the Wainwright Brewery Company upon a contract for services as an architect. . . .

The controversy in the court below finally turned upon the single question whether or not, upon the facts found by the referee and the evidence returned by him, the deceased was entitled to commissions on the cost of the refrigerator plant. In considering the subject it should be borne in mind that Jungenfeld's contract with the brewery company was made on or about the 16th of June, 1883; that under and by it he undertook to design the buildings, and superintend their erection to completion; that the superintending or placing of machinery in the building was no part of his contract, and that the claim for commissions on the cost of the refrigerator plant is based solely on a subsequent promise, the facts of which are thus found and stated by the referee:

"[The refrigerator plant] was ordered not only without Mr. Jungenfeld's assistance, but against his wishes. He was in no way connected with its erection. Plaintiff's claim as to this item rests on a distinct ground, as to which I make the following finding of facts:

"Mr. Jungenfeld was president of the Empire Refrigerating Company, and was largely interested therein. The De la Vergne Ice-Machine Company was a competitor in business. Against Mr. Jungenfeld's wishes, Mr. Wainwright awarded the contract for the refrigerating plant to the De la Vergne Company. The brewery was at the time in process of erection, and most of the plans were made. When Mr. Jungenfeld heard that the contract was awarded he took away his plans, called off his superintendent on the ground, and notified Mr. Wainwright that he would have nothing more to do with the brewery. The defendant was in great haste to have its new brewery completed for divers reasons. It would be hard to find an architect to fill Mr. Jungenfeld's place, and the making of new plans and arrangements when another architect was found would involve much loss of time. Under these circumstances, Mr. Wainwright promised to give Mr. Jungenfeld five per cent on the cost of the De la Vergne ice machine if he would resume work. Mr. Jungenfeld accepted, and fulfilled the duties of superintending architect till the completion of the brewery.

"It is not clear to me how plaintiffs can bring their claim for this extra compensation on special agreement under their petition, which asks for the *quantum meruit* of Mr. Jungenfeld's labor; but I pass all questions of pleading, and treat the claim as properly before me, since it is desirable that this report should present findings as to the merits of all branches of the case.

"What was the consideration for defendant's promise to pay five per cent on the cost of the refrigerating plant, in addition to the regular charges?

"Plaintiffs submit two theories accounting for the consideration: (1) It is claimed that the transaction was the compromise of a doubtful claim. I do not find that Mr. Jungenfeld claimed that defendant had broken the contract, or intended to do so. I infer that Mr. Jungenfeld had confidently expected to get for his 'Empire Company' the contract for putting the refrigerating plant into the Wainwright brewery. When the De la Vergne machine was selected, he felt disappointed, aggrieved, angry; but I can find in the whole record no evidence that he ever claimed that any of his legal rights had been violated. With this understanding of the evidence, I find no basis for upholding defendant's promise to pay commission on this refrigerating plant as the compromise of any doubtful claim.

"(2) Plaintiffs also contend that the original contract between the parties was abrogated; that a new contract was entered into between the parties, differing from the old only in the fact that defendant was to pay a sum over and above the compensation agreed on in the discarded, original contract. The services to be performed (and thereafter actually performed) by Jungenfeld would, in this view, constitute a sufficient consideration. Such a principle has been recognized in a number of cases: Munroe v. Perkins, 9 Pick. 305; Holmes v. Doan, 9 Cush. 135; Lattimore v. Harsen, 14 Johns. 330; Peck v. Requa, 13 Gray 408. Without discussing the legal doctrine involved, (of the accuracy of which I may say, however, I am not convinced),* I do not think the case in hand warrants its application. I find in the evidence no substitution of one contract for another. As I understand the facts, and as I accordingly formally find, defendant promised Mr. Jungenfeld a bonus to resume work, and complete the original contract under the original terms. This case seems to me analogous to that of seamen who, when hired for a voyage, under threats of desertion in a foreign port receive promises of additional compensation. It has been uniformly held they could not recover. I accordingly submit that in my view defendant's promise to pay

---

* [Authors' Note: There was good authority under classical contract law that parties could avoid the legal duty rule by modifying a contract in two-steps. Step One is to agree to abrogate or rescind the old contract. Step Two is to enter into a new contract with the modified terms. This strategem works if the rescission of the old contract relieves both parties of a legal obligation for this satisfies the consideration requirement with respect to the release. See Restatement, First, Contracts § 406, Comment a (explaining "Where . . . there is a bilateral contract, and each party is still subject to some duty thereunder, the agreement of each party to surrender his rights under the contract affords sufficient consideration to the other for his corresponding agreement. . . . Adequacy of consideration is immaterial. . . . Therefore, since each party surrenders something which he might have retained, the agreement to rescind is effectual.") The release being effective, the reinstatement of whatever remaining obligation the beneficiary of the modification had under the old contract constitutes consideration because there is no pre-existing duty. For example, in Schwartzreich v. Bauman-Basch, Inc., 231 N.Y. 196, 131 N.E. 887 (1921), an agreement to increase an employee's weekly salary from $90 to $100 was held enforceable, with the jury being instructed that "the test question is whether by word or by act, either prior to or at the time of signing the $100 contract, these parties mutually agreed that the old contract from that instant should be null and void."]

Mr. Jungenfeld five per cent on the cost of the refrigerating plant was without consideration, and recommend that the claim be not allowed."

The referee's finding of fact is based on the testimony of Adolphus Busch, Philip Stock, Ellis Wainwright, and is amply borne out by the testimony. Upon this state of facts the referee was of opinion that the promise to pay the 5 per cent commissions on the cost of the refrigerator plant was void, and the claim should be rejected; whereas, the learned circuit judge was of opinion that the promise was good in law, and that the commission should be allowed; and this question of law is the sole matter presented by this record. . . .

Was there any consideration for the promise of Wainwright to pay Jungenfeld the 5 per cent on the refrigerator plant? If there was not, plaintiffs cannot recover the $3,449.75, the amount of that commission. The report of the referee and the evidence upon which it is based alike show that Jungenfeld's claim to this extra compensation is based upon Wainwright's promise to pay him this sum to induce him, Jungenfeld, to complete his original contract under its original terms. It is urged upon us by respondents that this was a new contract. New in what? Jungenfeld was bound by his contract to design and supervise this building. Under the new promise he was not to do any more or anything different. What benefit was to accrue to Wainwright? He was to receive the same service from Jungenfeld under the new, that Jungenfeld was bound to render under the original, contract. What loss, trouble, or inconvenience could result to Jungenfeld that he had not already assumed? No amount of metaphysical reasoning can change the plain fact that Jungenfeld took advantage of Wainwright's necessities, and extorted the promise of 5 per cent on the refrigerator plant as the condition of his complying with his contract already entered into. Nor was there even the flimsy pretext that Wainwright had violated any of the conditions of the contract on his part. Jungenfeld himself put it upon the simple proposition that "if he, an architect, put up the brewery, and another company put up the refrigerating machinery, it would be a detriment to the Empire Refrigerating Company," of which Jungenfeld was president. To permit plaintiff to recover under such circumstances would be to offer a premium upon bad faith, and invite men to violate their most sacred contracts that they may profit by their own wrong. "That a promise to pay a man for doing that which he is already under contract to do is without consideration" is conceded by respondents. The rule has been so long imbedded in the common law and decisions of the highest courts of the various states that nothing but the most cogent reasons ought to shake it. [Citation of cases omitted.] But "it is carrying coals to New Castle" to add authorities on a proposition so universally accepted, and so inherently just and right in itself.

The learned counsel for respondents do not controvert the general proposition. Their contention is, and the circuit court agreed with them, that when Jungenfeld declined to go further on his contract, that defendant then had the right to sue for damages, and, not having elected to sue Jungenfeld, but having acceded to his demand for the additional compensation, defendant cannot now be heard to say his promise is without consideration. While it is true Jungenfeld became liable in damages for the obvious breach of his contract we do not think it follows that defendant is estopped from showing its promise was made without consideration.

It is true that as eminent a jurist as Judge Cooley, in Goebel v. Linn, 47 Mich. 489, 11 N.W. 284, held that an ice company which had agreed to furnish a brewery with all the ice they might need for their business from November 8, 1879, until January 1, 1881, at $1.75 per ton, and afterwards, in May, 1880, declined to deliver any more ice unless the brewery would give it $3 per ton, could recover on a promissory note given for the increased price. Profound as is our respect for the distinguished judge who delivered that opinion, we are still of the opinion that his decision is not in accord with the almost universally accepted doctrine, and is not convincing, and certainly so much of the opinion as held that the payment by a debtor of a part of his debt then due would constitute a defense to a suit for the remainder is not the law of this state, nor, do we think, of any other where the common law prevails.

The case of Bishop v. Busse, 69 Ill. 403, is readily distinguishable from the case at bar. The price of brick increased very considerably, and the owner changed the plan of the building, so as to require nearly double the number. Owing to the increased price and change in the plans the contractor notified the party for whom he was building that he could not complete the house at the original prices, and thereupon a new arrangement was made and it is expressly upheld by the court on the ground that the change in the buildings was such a modification as necessitated a new contract.

Nothing we have said is intended as denying parties the right to modify their contracts, or make new contracts, upon new or different considerations, and binding themselves thereby. What we hold is that, when a party merely does what he has already obligated himself to do, he cannot demand an additional compensation therefor, and although by taking advantage of the necessities of his adversary he obtains a promise for more, the law will regard it as *nudum pactum,* and will not lend its process to aid in the wrong. So holding, we reverse the judgment of the circuit court of St. Louis to the extent that it allows the plaintiffs below (respondents here) the sum of $3,449.75, the amount of commission at 5 per cent on the refrigerator plant, and at the request of both sides we proceed to enter the judgment here which, in our opinion, the circuit court of St. Louis should have entered, and accordingly it is adjudged that the report of the referee be in all things approved, and that defendant have and recover of plaintiffs, as executors of Edmund Jungenfeld, the sum of $1,492.17, so found by the referee, with interest from March 9, 1887. All the judges of this division concur.

FOAKES V. BEER

In the House of Lords, 1884.
[1884] 9 App.Cas. 605.

[Dr. Foakes owed Julia Beer, £2090.19s. on a judgment. The parties entered into an agreement which, as interpreted by the Court of Appeal, provided that if Dr. Foakes would pay Mrs. Beer £500 at once, and the remainder of the principal in certain installments, Mrs. Beer would forgive the interest on the debt. This is a suit for the interest brought by Mrs. Beer against Dr. Foakes, alleging that if any agreement to forgive the interest was in fact entered, it was without consideration, since the consideration consisted only in Dr. Foakes' doing what he was already bound to do in paying the principal of the debt. Decision in the Court of Appeal went for Mrs. Beer.]

W.H. HOLL Q.C. for the appellant:—Apart from the doctrine of Cumber v. Wane [that £5 cannot be satisfaction of £15] there is no reason in sense or law why the agreement should not be valid, and the creditor prevented from enforcing his judgment if the agreement is performed. It may be much more advantageous to the creditor to obtain immediate payment of part of his debt than to wait to enforce payment, or perhaps by pressing his debtor to force him into bankruptcy with the result of only a small dividend. Moreover if a composition is accepted friends, who would not otherwise do so, may be willing to come forward to assist the debtor. And if the creditor thinks that the acceptance of part is for his benefit who is to say it is not? . . . It is every day practice for tradesmen to take less in satisfaction of a larger sum, and give discount, where there is neither custom nor right to take credit. . . . It has often been held that a sheet of paper or a stick of sealing wax is a sufficient consideration. . . . Here the agreement is not to take less than the debt, but to give time for payment of the whole without interest. Mankind have never acted on the doctrine of Cumber v. Wane, but the contrary; nay few are aware of it. By overruling it the House will only declare the universal practice to be good law as well as good sense.

[EARL OF SELBORNE, L.C. Whatever may be the ultimate decision of this appeal the House is much indebted to Mr. Holl for his exceedingly able argument.]

BOMPAS Q.C. (Gaskell with him) for the respondent: . . . There is a strong current of authority that what the law implies as a duty is no consideration. Therefore where a debt is due part payment is no reason for giving up the residue. The doctrine is too well settled to be now overthrown. . . . It is contrary to public policy to make the performance of a legal duty a good consideration. . . .

EARL OF SELBORNE L.C.: . . . [T]he question remains, whether the agreement is capable of being legally enforced. Not being under seal, it cannot be legally enforced against the respondent, unless she received consideration for it from the appellant, or unless, though without consideration, it operates by way of accord and satisfaction, so as to extinguish the claim for interest. What is the consideration? On the face of the agreement none is expressed, except a present payment of £500, on account and in part of the larger debt then due and payable by law under the judgment. The appellant did not contract to pay the future instalments of £150 each, at the time therein mentioned; much less did he give any new security, in the shape of negotiable paper, or in any other form. The promise de futuro was only that of the respondent, that if the half-yearly payments of £150 each were regularly paid, she would "take no proceedings whatever on the judgment." . . .

The question, therefore, is nakedly raised by this appeal, whether your Lordships are now prepared, not only to overrule, as contrary to law, the doctrine stated by Sir Edward Coke to have been laid down by all the judges of the Common Pleas in Pinnel's Case [that payment of a lesser sum on the day cannot be a satisfaction of a greater sum] . . . but to treat a prospective agreement, not under seal, for satisfaction of a debt, by a series of payments on account to a total amount less than the whole debt, as binding in law, provided those payments are regularly made. . . . The doctrine itself, as laid down by Sir Edward Coke, may have been criticised, as questionable in principle, by some persons whose opinions are entitled to respect, but it has never been judicially overruled; on the contrary I think it has always, since the sixteenth century, been accepted as law. If so, I cannot think that your Lordships would do right, if you were now to reverse, as erroneous, a judgment of the Court of Appeal, proceeding upon a doctrine which has been accepted as part of the law of England for 280 years. . . .

. . . It might be (and indeed I think it would be) an improvement in our law, if a release or acquittance of the whole debt, on payment of any sum which the creditor might be content to receive by way of accord and satisfaction (though less than the whole), were held to be, generally, binding, though not under seal; nor should I be unwilling to see equal force given to a prospective agreement, like the present, in writing though not under seal; but I think it impossible, without refinements which practically alter the sense of the word, to treat such a release or acquittance as supported by any new consideration. . . .

My conclusion is, that the order appealed from should be affirmed, and the appeal dismissed, with costs, and I so move your Lordships.

LORD BLACKBURN. . . .

What principally weighs with me in thinking that Lord Coke made a mistake of fact is my conviction that all men of business, whether merchants or tradesmen, do every day recognise and act on the ground that prompt payment of a part of their demand may be more beneficial to them than it would be to insist on their rights and enforce payment of the whole. Even where the debtor is perfectly solvent, and sure to pay at last, this often is so. Where the credit of the debtor is doubtful it must be more so. I had persuaded myself that there was no such long-continued action on this dictum as to render it improper in this House to reconsider the question. I had written my reasons for so thinking; but as they were not satisfactory to the other noble and learned Lords who heard the case, I do not now repeat them nor persist in them.

I assent to the judgment proposed, though it is not that which I had originally thought proper. . . .

LORD FITZGERALD. . . . I concur . . . that it would have been wiser and better if the resolution in Pinnel's Case had never been come to. . . . [but we] find the law to have been accepted as stated for a great length of time, and I apprehend that it is not now within our province to overturn it. . . .

NOTE ON HOW PERFORMANCE OF A MODIFICATION ELIMINATES THE NEED FOR CONSIDERATION

The absence of consideration is not grounds for reversing a modification where the modification has been performed. Thus, if in *Lingenfelder v. Wainwright Brewery Company*, supra, the architect, Jungenfeld, had obtained the additional payment he demanded upfront, before he resumed work, Wainwright Brewery Company could not have recovered the additional payment on the ground that there was no consideration for the additional payment under the legal-duty rule.[2] To recover a payment that it had made Wainwright Brewery Company could argue duress. The doctrine of duress is covered in Section 2, supra. Technically, duress is grounds for avoiding a

[2]   In *Foakes v. Beer*, supra, the defendant had fully paid the judgment in installments, as he had promised, when the plaintiff sued to recover the interest that she had agreed to forebear to induce him to pay the principal. Thus the court could have enforced the agreement on the technical ground that the consideration was not required because the agreement had been fully performed. This argument was accepted in Schiffman v. Atlas Mill Supply, Inc., 193 Cal. App.2d 847, 14 Cal. Rptr. 708 (1961). The plaintiff orally agreed to forgive a $4,000 debt owed to her by a family-owned corporation with the understanding other family members would also forgive debts owed them by the corporation, as a part of a plan to facilitate sale of the corporation to a third party to help her sick brother, who held the majority of the stock in the corporation. The court held the agreement was fully executed when the family members cancelled the debts and the third party purchased the corporation, so the issue of consideration was immaterial.

contract. A restitution claim is brought to recover a payment made under a void contract.

———

NOTE ON THE ECONOMIC JUSTIFICATION FOR RESTRICTING PEOPLE'S POWER TO MODIFY CONTRACTS

In an elegant article, Aivazian, Trebilock, and Penny explain how dynamic efficiency considerations may justify legal rules that restrict people's power to modify contracts:

> The nature of the apparent analytical paradox presented by contract modifications can be stated briefly. . . . If [most modification situations occur in a context in which one party seeks to exploit bargaining power he has obtained during the course of the relationship] . . . then it might be argued that the law should attempt to discourage extortionary, coercive, opportunistic or monopolistic behaviour by refusing to enforce most modifications, perhaps by means of a presumption of invalidity. . . . On the other hand, especially in commercial contexts where most litigated modification cases seem to arise, it might be argued that parties would typically not enter into modifications unless they both felt better off as a result relative to the position that would or might have been obtained without a modification. Hence, the law should respect the parties' assessment of what course of action best advances their joint welfare and enforce modifications, that is, apply a presumption of validity.

> . . . The paradox described above is the product of a tension between two competing sets of efficiency considerations, which in some cases require difficult trade-offs. . . . Static efficiency considerations will generally require that contract modifications be enforced on the grounds that the immediate contracting parties perceive mutual gains from recontracting that cannot, at the time modification is proposed, be realized as fully by any alternative strategy. On the other hand, dynamic efficiency considerations focus on the long-run incentives for contracting parties at large. . . . In the modification context, these dynamic efficiency considerations adopt an ex ante perspective, rather than the ex post perspective implicit in the static efficiency considerations. Adopting the former perspective, rules that impose no constraints on recontracting may increase the over-all costs of contracting by creating incentives for opportunistic behavior in cases where "holdup" possibilities arise during contract performance. . . . Thus, what is in the best interests of two particular contracting parties ex post contract formation when a modification is proposed and what is in the interests ex ante of contracting parties generally in terms of legally ordained incentives and constraints that minimize the over-all costs of contracting may lead to divergent policy perspectives.

Varouj A. Aivazian, et al., The Law of Contract Modifications: The Uncertain Quest for a Bench Mark of Enforceability, 22 Osgoode Hall L.J. 173, 174–75 (1984).

The authors use the terms "static" and "dynamic" in an economic sense. By static efficiency they mean the immediate welfare gains to the parties from a welfare-enhancing exchange that is made possible by enforcement of a modification. By dynamic efficiency they mean the general social welfare gains that result from a policy of not enforcing modifications when the prospect that a contract may be modified to their disadvantage deters people from exchange transactions that would be welfare enhancing. For example, it is in the immediate interest of both a creditor and a debtor for a creditor to have the legal power to take partial payment of a debt as satisfaction of the full debt. Using legal process to collect a debt imposes significant harms on a debtor and involves non-trivial costs to a creditor. But it may not be in the long-term interest of creditors and debtors generally for creditors to have this power, if the increase in the risk of less than full payment of a debt deters people who could extend credit and people who need credit from credit transactions that would be welfare enhancing.

Whether the benefits of a rule of not enforcing modifications outweigh the costs is an empirical question. For example, it is likely that firms that are in the business of extending credit agree to take partial payment in satisfaction of a debt only when it is in the long-term interest of the firm and their industry. Certainly these considerations cannot justify a blunt a rule like the pre-existing duty rule that is insensitive to the circumstances of a modification. They might justify something like the modern rules that enforce a modification when it is justified by changed circumstances and when the modification is not obtained by the use of coercion.

RESTATEMENT, SECOND, CONTRACTS § 89

[See Selected Source Materials Supplement]

ANGEL V. MURRAY
Supreme Court of Rhode Island, 1974.
113 R.I. 482, 322 A.2d 630.

ROBERTS, C.J. This is a civil action brought by Alfred L. Angel and others against John E. Murray, Jr., Director of Finance of the City of Newport, the city of Newport, and James L. Maher, alleging that Maher had illegally been paid the sum of $20,000 by the Director of Finance and praying that the defendant Maher be ordered to repay the city such sum. The case was heard by a justice of the Superior Court, sitting without a jury, who entered a judgment ordering Maher to repay the sum of $20,000 to the city of Newport. Maher is now before this court prosecuting an appeal.

The record discloses that Maher has provided the city of Newport with a refuse-collection service under a series of five-year contracts beginning in 1946. On March 12, 1964, Maher and the city entered into another such contract for a period of five years commencing on July 1, 1964, and terminating on June 30, 1969. The contract provided, among other things, that Maher would receive $137,000 per year in return for collecting and removing all combustible and noncombustible waste materials generated within the city.

In June of 1967 Maher requested an additional $10,000 per year from the city council because there had been a substantial increase in the cost of collection due to an unexpected and unanticipated increase of 400 new dwelling units. Maher's testimony, which is uncontradicted, indicates the 1964 contract had been predicated on the fact that since 1946 there had been an average increase of 20 to 25 new dwelling units per year. After a public meeting of the city council where Maher explained in detail the reasons for his request and was questioned by members of the city council, the city council agreed to pay him an additional $10,000 for the year ending on June 30, 1968. Maher made a similar request again in June of 1968 for the same reasons, and the city council again agreed to pay an additional $10,000 for the year ending on June 30, 1969.

The trial justice found that each such $10,000 payment was made in violation of law. . . . [H]e found that Maher was not entitled to extra compensation because the original contract already required him to collect all refuse generated within the city and, therefore, included the 400 additional units. The trial justice further found that these 400 additional units were within the contemplation of the parties when they entered into the contract. It appears that he based this portion of the decision upon the rule that Maher had a preexisting duty to collect the refuse generated by the 400 additional units, and thus there was no consideration for the two additional payments. . . .

A.

As previously stated, the city council made two $10,000 payments. The first was made in June of 1967 for the year beginning on July 1, 1967, and ending on June 30, 1968. Thus, by the time this action was commenced in October of 1968, the modification was completely executed. That is, the money had been paid by the city council, and Maher had collected all of the refuse. Since consideration is only a test of the enforceability of executory promises, the presence or absence of consideration for the first payment is unimportant because the city council's agreement to make the first payment was fully executed at the time of the commencement of this action. . . . However, since both payments were made under similar circumstances, our decision regarding the second payment (Part B, infra) is fully applicable to the first payment.

B.

It is generally held that a modification of a contract is itself a contract, which is unenforceable unless supported by consideration. . . .

The primary purpose of the preexisting duty rule is to prevent what has been referred to as the "hold-up game." See 1A Corbin . . . § 171. A classic example of the "hold-up game" is found in Alaska Packers' Ass'n v. Domenico, 117 F. 99 (9th Cir.1902). There 21 seamen entered into a written contract with Domenico to sail from San Francisco to Pyramid Harbor, Alaska. They were to work as sailors and fishermen out of Pyramid Harbor during the fishing season of 1900. The contract specified that each man would be paid $50 plus two cents for each red salmon he caught. Subsequent to their arrival at Pyramid Harbor, the men stopped work and demanded an additional $50. They threatened to return to San Francisco if Domenico did not agree to their demand. Since it was impossible for Domenico to find other men, he agreed to pay the men an additional $50. After they returned to San Francisco, Domenico refused to pay the men an additional $50. The court found that the subsequent agreement to pay the men an additional $50 was not supported by consideration because the men had a preexisting duty to work on the ship under the original contract, and thus the subsequent agreement was unenforceable.

Another example of the "hold-up game" is found in the area of construction contracts. Frequently, a contractor will refuse to complete work under an unprofitable contract unless he is awarded additional compensation. The courts have generally held that a subsequent agreement to award additional compensation is unenforceable if the contractor is only performing work which would have been required of him under the original contract. See, e.g., Lingenfelder v. Wainwright Brewing Co., 103 Mo. 578, 15 S.W. 844 (1891), which is a leading case in this area. . . .

These examples clearly illustrate that the courts will not enforce an agreement that has been procured by coercion or duress and will hold the parties to their original contract regardless of whether it is profitable or unprofitable. However, the courts have been reluctant to apply the preexisting duty rule when a party to a contract encounters unanticipated difficulties and the other party, not influenced by coercion or duress, voluntarily agrees to pay additional compensation for work already required to be performed under the contract. For example, the courts have found that the original contract was rescinded, Linz v. Schuck, 106 Md. 220, 67 A. 286 (1907); abandoned, Connelly v. Devoe, 37 Conn. 570 (1871), or waived, Michaud v. McGregor, 61 Minn. 198, 63 N.W. 479 (1895).

Although the preexisting duty rule has served a useful purpose insofar as it deters parties from using coercion and duress to obtain additional compensation, it has been widely criticized as a general rule of law. . . .

The modern trend appears to recognize the necessity that courts should enforce agreements modifying contracts when unexpected or unanticipated difficulties arise during the course of the performance of a contract, even though there is no consideration for the modification, as long as the parties agree voluntarily.

Under the Uniform Commercial Code, § 2–209(1), which has been adopted by 49 states, "[a]n agreement modifying a contract [for the sale of goods] needs no consideration to be binding." See G.L.1956 (1969 Reenactment) § 6A–2–209(1). Although at first blush this section appears to validate modifications obtained by coercion and duress, the comments to this section indicate that a modification under this section must meet the test of good faith imposed by the Code, and a modification obtained by extortion without a legitimate commercial reason is unenforceable.

The modern trend away from a rigid application of the preexisting duty rule is reflected by [§ 89(a)] of the American Law Institute's Restatement, Second, Law of Contracts. . . .

We believe that [§ 89(a)] is the proper rule of law and find it applicable to the facts of this case.[2] It not only prohibits modifications obtained by coercion, duress, or extortion but also fulfills society's expectation that agreements entered into voluntarily will be enforced by the courts.[3] See

---

[2]   The fact that these additional payments were made by a municipal corporation rather than a private individual does not, in our opinion, affect the outcome of this case. . . .

[3]   The drafters of [§ 89(a)] of the Restatement Second of the Law of Contracts use the following illustrations in comment (b) as examples of how this rule is applied to certain transactions:

"1.   By a written contract A agrees to excavate a cellar for B for a stated price. Solid rock is unexpectedly encountered and A so notifies B. A and B then orally agree that A will remove the rock at a unit price which is reasonable but nine times that used in computing the original price, and A completes the job. B is bound to pay the increased amount.

"2.   A contracts with B to supply for $300 a laundry chute for a building B has contracted to build for the government for $150,000. Later A discovers that he made an error as to the type of material to be used and should have bid $1,200. A offers to supply the chute for $1,000, eliminating overhead and profit. After ascertaining that other suppliers would charge more, B agrees. The new agreement is binding.

"3.   A is employed by B as a designer of coats at $90 a week for a year beginning November 1 under a written contract executed September 1. A is offered $115 a week by another employer and so informs B. A and B then agree that A will be paid $100 a week and in October execute a new written contract to that effect, simultaneously tearing up the prior contract. The new contract is binding.

"4.   A contracts to manufacture and sell to B 2,000 steel roofs for corn cribs at $60. Before A begins manufacture a threat of a nationwide steel strike raises the cost of steel about $10 per roof, and A and B agree orally to increase the price to $70 per roof. A thereafter manufactures and delivers 1,700 of the roofs, and B pays for 1,500 of them at the increased price without protest, increasing the selling price of the corn cribs by $10. The new agreement is binding.

generally Horwitz, The Historical Foundations of Modern Contract Law, 87 Harv.L.Rev. 917 (1974). Section [89(a)], of course, does not compel a modification of an unprofitable or unfair contract; it only enforces a modification if the parties voluntarily agree and if (1) the promise modifying the original contract was made before the contract was fully performed on either side, (2) the underlying circumstances which prompted the modification were unanticipated by the parties, and (3) the modification is fair and equitable.

The evidence, which is uncontradicted, reveals that in June of 1968 Maher requested the city council to pay him an additional $10,000 for the year beginning on July 1, 1968, and ending on June 30, 1969. This request was made at a public meeting of the city council, where Maher explained in detail his reasons for making the request. Thereafter, the city council voted to authorize the Mayor to sign an amendment to the [1964] contract which provided that Maher would receive an additional $10,000 per year for the duration of the contract. Under such circumstances we have no doubt that the city voluntarily agreed to modify the 1964 contract.

Having determined the voluntariness of this agreement, we turn our attention to the three criteria delineated above. First, the modification was made in June of 1968 at a time when the five-year contract which was made in 1964 had not been fully performed by either party. Second, although the 1964 contract provided that Maher collect all refuse generated within the city, it appears this contract was premised on Maher's past experience that the number of refuse-generating units would increase at a rate of 20 to 25 per year. Furthermore, the evidence is uncontradicted that the 1967–1968 increase of 400 units "went beyond any previous expectation." Clearly, the circumstances which prompted the city council to modify the 1964 contract were unanticipated. Third, although the evidence does not indicate what proportion of the total this increase comprised, the evidence does indicate that it was a "substantial" increase. In light of this, we cannot say that the council's agreement to pay Maher the $10,000 increase was not fair and equitable in the circumstances.

The judgment appealed from is reversed, and the cause is remanded to the Superior Court for entry of judgment for the defendants.

"5. A contracts to manufacture and sell to B 100,000 castings for lawn mowers at 50 cents each. After partial delivery and after B has contracted to sell a substantial number of lawn mowers at a fixed price, A notifies B that increased metal costs require that the price be increased to 75 cents. Substitute castings are available at 55 cents, but only after several months delay. B protests but is forced to agree to the new price to keep its plant in operation. The modification is not binding."

McCallum Highlands, Ltd. v. Washington Capital Dus, Inc.

66 F.3d 89 (5th Cir. 1995)

Susman and McCallum Highlands had a loan commitment from Washington Capital for $7,015,000 at an interest rate of 9.75% with an option to lower the interest rate through a buy-down process. Susman intended to use the loan to prepay an outstanding loan with a significantly higher interest rate. The lender agreed to waive a substantial prepayment penalty if Susman refinanced by April 30, 1991. After the commitment was made, Fannie Mae criticized another loan Washington Capital had made to Susman as too risky. One month before closing, Washington Capital told Susman it wanted to reduce the loan amount because of Fannie Mae's criticism, and "that they thought they could get out of the commitment through a loophole." Susman told Washington Capital he expected them to honor the commitment. To qualify under a Fannie Mae program, Susman had to formally select an interest rate by April 19. On April 18, Washington Capital told Susman that it would allow him to select an interest rate only if he would agree to accept a loan limited to $6,400,000 with no buy-down provision. Susman accepted these terms because he believed he needed to refinance the old loan to avoid bankruptcy. He later sued to avoid certain amended portions of the loan agreement, arguing that it was obtained by duress or that there was no consideration for the modification. The trial court granted Washington Capital's motion for summary judgment. Reversed.

The court began by explaining why the plaintiff could not establish economic duress under Texas law. The defendant's conduct was not economic duress, as Texas law defines it, because the defendants threat did not involve "an illegal exaction or a fraudulent deception," and because the plaintiff could not establish the defendant had created his financial predicament.

Turning to the issue of consideration, the court explained that the district court erred in treating the reduction in the loan amount as consideration for the modification. It explained that the plaintiff had not bargained for this. Finally the court held that consideration could not be found in the defendant giving up the right to assert its claim the loan commitment was not binding because of the absence of the evidence that this was honestly in dispute. The court then turned to the question of whether the modification was enforceable in the absence of consideration:

(Stewart, J.) "Because no bargained-for consideration was granted to Susman in exchange for his agreement to modify the loan commitment, the issue then becomes whether one of the exceptions to the requirement of new consideration applies. Parties can agree to first rescind an original agreement, and subsequently enter into a new one, thus avoiding the new-consideration requirement. *See Blaylock v. Akin*, 619 S.W.2d 207, 209 (Tex.Civ.App.— Texarkana, 1981, writ ref'd n.r.e.); *Crossland v. Nelson Auction Service, Inc.*, 424 S.W.2d 318, 319 (Tex.Civ.App.—Amarillo, 1967, writ ref'd n.r.e.). However, where an alleged rescission is coupled with a simultaneous re-entry into a new contract and the terms of that new contract are more favorable to only one of the parties, doubt is created as to the mutuality of the agreement to rescind the original contract. 3 Williston on Contracts § 7:37 (1992). Lurking beneath the surface in such cases is an implied threat by the promisor to withhold performance unless he receives the additional compensation or other changes he wants. *See id.* Moreover, this exception is based on circular logic because the validity of the new agreement depends upon the rescission while the validity of the rescission depends upon the new agreement. 1A Corbin on Contracts § 186 (1963). As a result, the validity of this exception to the preexisting duty rule has been questioned by a number of authorities. *See e.g.,* 3 Williston on Contracts § 7:37; 1A Corbin on Contracts § 186 (1963), Restatement (Second) of Contracts § 89 comment b (1981); John D. Calamari & Joseph M. Perillo, Contracts 206 (3d ed. 1987). Because the rescission of the original commitment occurred simultaneously with the creation of the amended loan agreement, and because the terms were more favorable to Washington than McCallum, the facts of this case place it neatly into the category of cases where this exception is most criticized.

"A more appropriate exception to the preexisting duty rule is presented in § 89 of the Restatement Second of Contracts:

> A promise modifying a duty under a contract not fully performed on either side is binding
>
> (a) if the modification is fair and equitable in view of circumstances not anticipated by the parties when the contract was made.

Restatement (Second) of Contracts § 89 (1981). Whether a modification is fair and equitable goes beyond absence of coercion and requires an objectively demonstrable reason for seeking a modification. *Id.* at § 89 cmt. b. The reason for modification must rest in circumstances not anticipated when the contract was made. *Id.* When such a reason is present, the relative financial strength of the parties, the formality with which the modification is made, the extent to which it is performed or relied on and other circumstances may be relevant to show or negate imposition or unfair surprise. *Id.*

"This exception to the requirement of new consideration for a modified contract is integrated into Texas law. *See Wiedeman v. Howell,* 276 S.W.2d 380, 383 (Tex.Civ.App.—Austin, 1955, writ ref'd n.r.e.); *Allied Chemical Corporation v. DeHaven,* 752 S.W.2d 155, 159 (Tex.App.—Houston [14 Dist.], 1988, writ denied). Fannie Mae's criticism of the earlier loan was such an unforeseen circumstance, but we conclude that, to use the language in the Restatement, the modification was not "fair and equitable" to McCallum."

———

Sugarhouse Finance Co. v. Anderson

610 P.2d 1369 (Utah 1980)

In December 1976, Sugarhouse recovered a judgment against Anderson for $2,423.86, plus interest, costs, and attorneys' fees, on account of an unpaid promissory note. Anderson failed to satisfy the judgment, and in January 1979 Sugarhouse served Anderson with an order in supplemental proceedings to collect the judgment. Two days after receiving this order, Anderson met with Petty, Sugarhouse's president, to discuss an alternative to full payment of the judgment. Anderson informed Petty of the existence of numerous outstanding obligations against him, including medical expenses incurred pursuant to treatment for injuries sustained in an automobile accident in 1978. He asserted that he was contemplating bankruptcy, which would result in Sugarhouse's judgment being discharged. The parties finally settled on a figure of $2,200 in full satisfaction of Sugarhouse's claim. Anderson agreed to borrow money from a third party to enable him to pay the $2,200. Anderson then gave Petty a check for this amount, but asked him not to negotiate the check immediately because there was some uncertainty as to the sufficiency of funds in Anderson's account to cover the check. Two days later, Anderson called to inform Sugarhouse that there were sufficient funds in the account to cover the check. Sugarhouse responded that it did not intend on going through with the settlement, and returned the check. Thereafter, Anderson filed a motion asking the court to order Sugarhouse to comply with the terms of the settlement. Held, for Anderson.

(Hall, J.) ". . . Where . . . the underlying claim is liquidated and certain as to amount, separate consideration must be found to support [an] accord; otherwise, the obligor binds himself to do nothing he was not already obligated to do, and the obligee's promise to accept a substitute performance is unenforceable. The original obligation in the present case being of a definite and undisputed amount, the question presented is whether or not separate consideration was given to support the accord reached by the parties. . . .

"It is to be noted that, in the present case, plaintiff held a judgment which had been outstanding for more than two years. Pursuant to the parties' conversation of January 31, 1979, defendant agreed that, for a release of the judgment upon payment of a lesser agreed amount, he would negotiate a loan with a third party to enable him to pay off the substitute obligation immediately. A check was given for the agreed amount at the conclusion of that conversation, and authorization to cash it followed two days later. In effect, defendant had agreed to transfer the debt, represented by plaintiff's judgment to a third party, thereby immediately satisfying the obligation owed to plaintiff. This was something defendant had no legal obligation to do; by law, plaintiff could only move by levy of execution against property already owned by the defendant—plaintiff could not legally require defendant to incur additional obligations to satisfy the judgment. By so doing, defendant deliberately incurred the detriment of surrendering his right to limit plaintiff's ability to obtain satisfaction of the underlying judgment, and bestowed upon plaintiff the benefit of immediate payment by means of the incurrence of additional indebtedness. We hold such action to constitute sufficient consideration to support the accord negotiated by the parties.

"We note, in addition, that this jurisdiction recognizes the doctrine of promissory estoppel, whereby an individual who has made a promise which the individual should reasonably expect to induce action or forbearance on the part of the promisee or a third person and which does induce such action or forbearance is estopped to deny or repudiate the promise should the promisee or some third party suffer detriment thereby. We note that, in the present case, defendant agreed to incur additional indebtedness pursuant to the terms of the accord, in reliance on plaintiff's promise to accept immediate payment of a lesser amount in full satisfaction of the underlying obligation. As such, plaintiff should now be estopped to deny or reject the promise made."

UCC § 2–209

[See Selected Source Materials Supplement]

CISG ART. 29

[See Selected Source Materials Supplement]

NOTE ON THE CISG

In 1969, the United Nations Commission on International Trade Law (UNCITRAL) appointed a Working Group to prepare a new draft of an international convention (treaty) on the sale of goods. The United States was an active participant in the Working Group. The ultimate result was the Convention for the International Sale of Goods (the CISG), which was adopted in 1980, and came into force in 1988 when it had been ratified by the requisite ten countries. The CISG is binding only in those countries that have ratified it. As of 2012, the CISG had been ratified by seventy-eight countries, including the United States, Canada, China, France, Germany, and Mexico.

Although in form the CISG is an international treaty, in substance it is a code, much like Article 2 of the UCC. Article 2 governs contracts for the sale of goods between a seller and a buyer in the United States. The CISG governs contracts for the sale of goods (with certain exclusions, such as consumer goods) between a seller and a buyer who have their places of business in different countries, both of which have ratified the CISG. Accordingly, if, for example, a seller with its place of business in the United States enters into a contract for the sale of goods to a buyer with its place of business in France, then unless the parties otherwise provide, the contract is governed by the provisions of the CISG.

Like the UCC, the CISG does not govern the issue whether a contract is substantively valid; that is, it does not govern matters such as fraud, capacity, duress, mistake, legality, or the like. However, the CISG does govern whether a contract satisfies requisite formal requirements, such as whether a contract is required to be in writing, and also governs such matters as whether a contract was formed and whether a contract is sufficiently definite to be enforceable.

———

CHAPTER 3

THE LIMITS OF CONTRACT

■ ■ ■

The term "contract" is ambiguous. The Restatement defines a contract as any legally enforceable promise. Under this definition, a relied-upon donative promise is a contract. For some purposes that is a useful definition, but in everyday life the term "contract" usually means an agreement—especially a legally enforceable agreement. The Chapters succeeding this one will deal for the most part with contracts consisting of commercial bargains, in which legal enforceability is pretty clearly appropriate. In contrast, the cases and materials in this Chapter concern situations in which contract—used in the sense of a legally enforceable bargain—may or may not be appropriate.

Balfour v. Balfour

2 K.B. 571, 578 (1919)

(Atkin, L.J.) "[I]t is necessary to remember that there are agreements between parties which do not result in contracts within the meaning of that term in our law. The ordinary example is where two parties agree to take a walk together, or where there is an offer and an acceptance of hospitality. Nobody would suggest in ordinary circumstances that those agreements result in what we know as a contract, and one of the most usual forms of agreement which does not constitute a contract appears to me to be the arrangements which are made between husband and wife. It is quite common, and it is the natural and inevitable result of the relationship of husband and wife, that the two spouses should make arrangements between themselves. . . . To my mind those agreements, or many of them, do not result in contracts at all, and they do not result in contracts even though there may be what as between other parties would constitute consideration for the agreement. The consideration, as we know, may consist either in some right, interest, profit or benefit accruing to one party, or some forbearance, detriment, loss or responsibility given, suffered or undertaken by the other. That is a well-known definition, and it constantly happens, I think, that such arrangements made between husband and wife are arrangements in which there are mutual promises, or in which there is consideration in form within the definition that I have mentioned. Nevertheless they are not contracts, and they are not contracts because the parties did not intend that they should be attended by legal consequences. . . . in respect of these promises each house is a domain into which the king's writ does not seek to run, and to which his officers do not seek to be admitted."

IN RE THE MARRIAGE OF WITTEN

Supreme Court of Iowa, 2003.
672 N.W.2d 768.

TERNUS, JUSTICE.

The primary issue raised on appeal of the district court's decree in this dissolution action is whether the court properly determined the rights of Arthur (known as Trip) and Tamera Witten with respect to the parties' frozen human embryos stored at a medical facility. While we agree with Tamera that the informed consent signed by the parties at the request of the medical facility does not control the current dispute between the donors over the use or disposition of the embryos, we reject Tamera's request that she be allowed to use the embryos over Trip's objection. Therefore, we affirm the trial court's order that neither party may use or dispose of the embryos without the consent of the other party. . . .

I.   BACKGROUND FACTS AND PROCEEDINGS.

The appellee, Arthur (Trip) Witten, and the appellant, Tamera Witten, had been married for approximately seven and one-half years when Trip sought to have their marriage dissolved in April 2002. One of the contested issues at trial was control of the parties' frozen embryos. During the parties' marriage they had tried to become parents through the process of in vitro fertilization. Because Tamera was unable to conceive children naturally, they had eggs taken from Tamera artificially fertilized with Trip's sperm. Tamera then underwent several unsuccessful embryo transfers in an attempt to become pregnant. At the time of trial seventeen fertilized eggs remained in storage at the University of Nebraska Medical Center (UNMC).[1]

Prior to commencing the process for in vitro fertilization, the parties signed informed consent documents prepared by the medical center. These documents included an "Embryo Storage Agreement," which was signed by Tamera and Trip as well as by a representative of UNMC. It provided in part:

---

[1]   No medical testimony was introduced at trial with respect to the cell stage of the parties' fertilized eggs. Therefore, while some cases refer to fertilized eggs in the early stages of division as "pre-zygotes" or "preembryos," we use the term "embryo" in discussing the present appeal, since that is the terminology used in the Wittens' contract with UNMC. This term is used interchangeably with the term "fertilized egg." [Ed.: Compare A.Z. v. B.Z., 431 Mass. 150, 752 N.E.2d 1051 (2000), where the court said "We use the term 'preembryo' to refer to the four-to-eight cell stage of a developing fertilized egg." *Id.* at footnote 1.]

Release of Embryos. The Client Depositors [Trip and Tamera] understand and agree that containers of embryos stored pursuant to this agreement will be used for transfer, release or disposition only with the signed approval of both Client Depositors. UNMC will release the containers of embryos only to a licensed physician recipient of written authorization of the Client Depositors.

The agreement had one exception to the joint-approval requirement that governed the disposition of the embryos upon the death of one or both of the client depositors. Another provision of the contract provided for termination of UNMC's responsibility to store the embryos upon several contingencies: (1) the client depositors' written authorization to release the embryos or to destroy them; (2) the death of the client depositors; (3) the failure of the client depositors to pay the annual storage fee; or (4) the expiration of ten years from the date of the agreement.

At trial, Tamera asked that she be awarded "custody" of the embryos. She wanted to have the embryos implanted in her or a surrogate mother in an effort to bear a genetically linked child. She testified that upon a successful pregnancy she would afford Trip the opportunity to exercise parental rights or to have his rights terminated. She adamantly opposed any destruction of the embryos, and was also unwilling to donate the eggs to another couple.

Trip testified at the trial that while he did not want the embryos destroyed, he did not want Tamera to use them. He would not oppose donating the embryos for use by another couple. Trip asked the court to enter a permanent injunction prohibiting either party from transferring, releasing, or utilizing the embryos without the written consent of both parties.

The district court decided the dispute should be governed by the "embryo storage agreement" between the parties and UNMC, which required both parties' consent to any use or disposition of the embryos. Enforcing this agreement, the trial court enjoined both parties "from transferring, releasing or in any other way using or disposing of the embryos . . . without the written and signed approval and authorization" of the other party.

Tamera has appealed the trial court's order, challenging only the court's resolution of the parties' dispute over the fertilized eggs. She claims the storage agreement is silent with respect to disposition or use of the embryos upon the parties' dissolution because there is no provision specifically addressing that contingency. Therefore, she argues, the court should have applied the "best interests [of the child]" test of Iowa Code chapter 598 (2001) and, pursuant to that analysis, awarded custody of the embryos to her. She makes the alternative argument that she is entitled to the fertilized eggs due to her fundamental right to bear children. Finally,

Tamera claims it would violate the public policy of this state if Trip were allowed to back out of his agreement to have children. She claims such an agreement is evidenced by his participation in the in vitro fertilization procedure. . . .

III. DISPOSITION OF EMBRYOS.

A. *Scope of storage agreement.* We first consider Tamera's contention that the storage agreement does not address the situation at hand. As noted earlier, the agreement had a specific provision governing control of the embryos if one or both parties died, but did not explicitly deal with the possibility of divorce. Nonetheless, we think the present predicament falls within the general provision governing "release of embryos," in which the parties agreed that the embryos would not be transferred, released, or discarded without "the signed approval" of both Tamera and Trip. This provision is certainly broad enough to encompass the decision-making protocol when the parties are unmarried as well as when they are married.

The only question, then, is whether such agreements are enforceable when one of the parties later changes his or her mind with respect to the proper disposition of the embryos. In reviewing the scarce case law from other jurisdictions on this point, we have found differing views of how the parties' rights should be determined. There is, however, abundant literature that has scrutinized the approaches taken to date. Some writers have suggested refinements of the analytical framework employed by the courts thus far; some have proposed an entirely new model of analysis. From these various sources, we have identified three primary approaches to resolving disputes over the disposition of frozen embryos, which we have identified as (1) the contractual approach, (2) the contemporaneous mutual consent model, and (3) the balancing test.

Tamera's argument that her right to bear children should override the parties' prior agreement as well as Trip's current opposition to her use of the embryos resembles the balancing test. As for Tamera's alternative argument, we have found no authority supporting a "best interests" analysis in determining the disposition of frozen embryos. Nonetheless, we will first consider whether chapter 598 requires application of that analysis under the circumstances presented by this case. Then, we will discuss and consider the three approaches suggested by decisions from other jurisdictions and the literature on this subject.

B. *"Best interests" test.* [The court began by considering the effect of an Iowa statute, § 598.41. This statute set forth various standards governing the award of child custody in a marital-dissolution case, including a requirement that any custody award reflect "the best interest of the child." The court held that the best-interest standard was not applicable to the issue at hand.] "First, we note the purposes of the 'best interest' standard set forth in that statute are to 'assure the child the opportunity for the maximum continuing physical and emotional contact with both parents' and to 'encourage parents to share the rights and responsibilities of raising the child.' Iowa Code § 598.41(1)(a). The principles developed under this statute are simply not suited to the resolution of disputes over the control of frozen embryos. Such disputes do not involve maximizing physical and emotional contact between both parents and the child; they involve the more fundamental decision of whether the parties will be parents at all. Moreover, it would be premature to consider which parent can most effectively raise the child when the "child" is still frozen in a storage facility. The principles of section 598.41 do not fit because what is really at issue here is not the custody of children as that concept is generally viewed and analyzed in dissolution cases. Rather, the issue here is who will have decision-making authority with respect to the fertilized eggs." . . .

C. *Enforcement of storage agreement.* We now consider the appropriateness of the trial court's decision to allow Tamera and Trip's agreement with the medical center to control the current dispute between them. As we noted above, there are three methods of analysis that have been suggested to resolve disputes over frozen embryos. We will discuss them separately.

1. *Contractual approach.* The currently prevailing view—expressed in three states—is that contracts entered into at the time of in vitro fertilization are enforceable so long as they do not violate public policy. *See* [*Kass v. Kass*, 91 N.Y.2d 554, 673 N.Y.S.2d 350, 696 N.E.2d 174, 179 (1998)] (stating agreements between donors "regarding disposition of pre-zygotes should generally be presumed valid and binding"); [*Davis v. Davis*, 842 S.W.2d 588 (Tenn. 1992)], 842 S.W.2d at 597 (holding agreement regarding disposition of embryos "should be considered binding"); *In re Litowitz,* 146 Wash.2d 514, 48 P.3d 261, 271 (2002) (enforcing parties' contract providing for disposition of preembryos after five years of storage).[2] The New York

---

[2] Application of the contractual approach in *Kass* resulted in enforcement of the parties' agreement that the fertilized eggs would be donated for research should the parties be "unable to make a decision regarding the disposition of [the] stored, frozen pre-zygotes." 696 N.E.2d at 176–77, 181. In *Litowitz,* the court permitted execution of the parties' previous agreement that the preembryos would be "disposed of" after five years. 48 P.3d at 271. The resolution of the divorcing couple's dispute was more complex in *Davis* because the parties did not have a contract addressing the disposition of any unused preembryos. 842 S.W.2d at 590. Noting that a "prior agreement concerning disposition should be carried out," the court concluded in the absence of such an agreement, "the relative interests of the parties in using or not using the preembryos must be weighed." *Id.* at 604. The court awarded the preembryos to the husband, concluding his interest in not becoming a parent outweighed his former wife's interest in donating the preembryos to another couple for implantation. *Id.* The court noted the issue might be closer if the wife had wanted to use the preembryos herself; but in view of the fact she had "a reasonable possibility of achieving parenthood by means other than use of the preembryos in question," she would not have prevailed even under those circumstances. *Id.*

Court of Appeals expressed the following rationale for this contractual approach:

> [It is] particularly important that courts seek to honor the parties' expressions of choice, made before disputes erupt, with the parties' over-all direction always uppermost in the analysis. Knowing that advance agreements will be enforced underscores the seriousness and integrity of the consent process. Advance agreements as to disposition would have little purpose if they were enforceable only in the event the parties continued to agree. To the extent possible, it should be the progenitors—not the State and not the courts—who by their prior directive make this deeply personal life choice.

Kass, 673 N.Y.S.2d 350, 696 N.E.2d at 180.

This approach has been criticized, however, because it "insufficiently protects the individual and societal interests at stake":

> First, decisions about the disposition of frozen embryos implicate rights central to individual identity. On matters of such fundamental personal importance, individuals are entitled to make decisions consistent with their contemporaneous wishes, values, and beliefs. Second, requiring couples to make binding decisions about the future use of their frozen embryos ignores the difficulty of predicting one's future response to life-altering events such as parenthood. Third, conditioning the provision of infertility treatment on the execution of binding disposition agreements is coercive and calls into question the authenticity of the couple's original choice. Finally, treating couples' decisions about the future use of their frozen embryos as binding contracts undermines important values about families, reproduction, and the strength of genetic ties.

[Carl H. Coleman, *Procreative Liberty and Contemporaneous Choice: An Inalienable Rights Approach to Frozen Embryo Disputes,*] 84 Minn. L.Rev. at 88–89. Another legal writer has echoed these concerns:

> Binding a couple to a prior disposition agreement has its roots in contract law. The primary advantage of treating the disposition of preembryos as a contract dispute is that it binds individuals to previous obligations, even if their priorities or values change. This advantage, while maximizing the efficiency of commercial transactions, is ill-suited to govern the disposition of human tissue with the potential to develop into a child. The potential of the embryo requires that couples be allowed to make contemporaneous decisions about the fate of the embryo that reflect their current values.

Christina C. Lawrence, Note, *Procreative Liberty and the Preembryo Problem: Developing a Medical and Legal Framework to Settle the Disposition of Frozen Embryos,* 52 Case W. Res. L.Rev. 721, 729 (2002) [hereinafter "Lawrence Note"]; *accord J.B. v. M.B.,* 170 N.J. 9, 783 A.2d 707, 718–19 (2001). In response to such concerns, one commentator has suggested an alternative model requiring contemporaneous mutual consent. We now examine that approach.

2. *Contemporaneous mutual consent.* The contractual approach and the contemporaneous mutual consent model share an underlying premise: "decisions about the disposition of frozen embryos belong to the couple that created the embryo, with each partner entitled to an equal say in how the embryos should be disposed." Coleman, 84 Minn. L.Rev. at 81. Departing from this common starting point, the alternative framework asserts the important question is "at what time does the partners' consent matter?" *Id.* at 91. Proponents of the mutual-consent approach suggest that, with respect to "decisions about intensely emotional matters, where people act more on the basis of feeling and instinct than rational deliberation," it may "be impossible to make a knowing and intelligent decision to relinquish a right in advance of the time the right is to be exercised." *Id.* at 98; *see also* Sara D. Petersen, Comment, *Dealing With Cryopreserved Embryos Upon Divorce: A Contractual Approach Aimed at Preserving Party Expectations,* 50 UCLA L.REV. 1065, 1090 & n. 156 (2003) (stating "surveys of couples that have stored frozen embryos suggest that they may be prone to changing their minds while their embryos remain frozen" and citing a study that found " '[o]f the 41 couples that had recorded both a pre-treatment and post-treatment decision about embryo disposition, only 12 (29%) kept the same disposition choice' " (citation omitted)). One's erroneous prediction of how she or he will feel about the matter at some point in the future can have grave repercussions. "Like decisions about marriage or relinquishing a child for adoption, decisions about the use of one's reproductive capacity have lifelong consequences for a person's identity and sense of self":

> When chosen voluntarily, becoming a parent can be an important act of self-definition. Compelled parenthood, by contrast, imposes an unwanted identity on the individual, forcing her to redefine herself, her place in the world, and the legacy she will leave after she dies. For some people, the mandatory destruction of an embryo can have equally profound consequences, particularly for those who believe that embryos are persons. If forced destruction is experienced as the loss of a child, it can lead to life-altering feelings of mourning, guilt, and regret.

Coleman, 84 Minn. L.Rev. at 96–97. To accommodate these concerns, advocates of the mutual-consent model propose "no embryo should be used by either partner, donated to another patient, used in research, or destroyed without the [contemporaneous] mutual consent of the couple that created the embryo." *Id.* at 110. Under this alternate framework,

> advance instructions would not be treated as binding contracts. If either partner has a change of mind about disposition decisions made in advance, that person's current objection would take precedence over the prior consent. If one of the partners rescinds an advance disposition decision and the other does not, the mutual consent principle would not be satisfied and the previously agreed-upon disposition decision could not be carried out. . . .
>
> When the couple is unable to agree to any disposition decision, the most appropriate solution is to keep the embryos where they are—in frozen storage. Unlike the other possible disposition decisions—use by one partner, donation to another patient, donation to research, or destruction—keeping the embryos frozen is not final and irrevocable. By preserving the status quo, it makes it possible for the partners to reach an agreement at a later time.

Id. at 110–12; *see also id.* at 89 (suggesting "the embryo would remain in frozen storage until the parties reach a new agreement, the embryo is no longer viable, or storage facilities are no longer available"); *accord* Lawrence Note, 52 Case W. Res. L.Rev. at 742. Although this model precludes one party's use of the embryos to have children over the objection of the other party, the outcome under the contractual approach and the balancing test would generally be the same. *See A.Z. v. B.Z.,* 431 Mass. 150, 725 N.E.2d 1051, 1057–58 (2000) ("As a matter of public policy, . . . forced procreation is not an area amenable to judicial enforcement."); *J.B.,* 783 A.2d at 717 (evaluating relative interests of parties in disposition of embryos, concluding husband should not be able to use embryos over wife's objection); *Davis,* 842 S.W.2d at 604 ("Ordinarily, the party wishing to avoid procreation should prevail."); Susan B. Apel, *Disposition of Frozen Embryos: Are Contracts the Solution?,* Vermont Bar Journal, March 2001, at 31 ("Some argue that the party seeking to avoid procreation should prevail, and indeed, this appears to be the one harmonizing rationale of the four reported cases.") [hereinafter "Apel"].

    3. *Balancing test.* The New Jersey Supreme Court appears to have adopted an analysis regarding the disposition of frozen human embryos that incorporates the idea of contemporaneous decision-making, but not that of mutual consent. In *J.B.,* the New Jersey court rejected the *Kass* and *Davis* contractual approach, noting public policy concerns in "[e]nforcement of a contract that would allow the implantation of preembryos at some future date in a case where one party has reconsidered his or her earlier acquiescence." 783 A.2d at 718. The court stated:

We believe that the better rule, and the one we adopt, is to enforce agreements entered into at the time in vitro fertilization is begun, *subject to the right of either party to change his or her mind about disposition up to the point of use or destruction of any stored preembryos.*

Id. at 719 (emphasis added). The court based its decision on "[t]he public policy concerns that underlie limitations on contracts involving family relationships." *Id.; see also A.Z.,* 725 N.E.2d at 1057–58 (refusing, in light of the same public policy concerns, to enforce an agreement that allowed the wife, upon the parties' separation, to use the couple's preembryos for implantation).

The New Jersey court did not, however, adopt the requirement for mutual consent as a prerequisite for any use or disposition of the preembryos. Rather, that court stated that "if there is a disagreement between the parties as to disposition . . . , the interests of both parties must be evaluated" by the court. *J.B.,* 783 A.2d at 719. This balancing test was also the default analysis employed by the Tennessee Supreme Court in *Davis* where the parties had not executed a written agreement. *See Davis,* 842 S.W.2d at 604 (holding in the absence of a prior agreement concerning disposition, "the relative interests of the parties in using or not using the preembryos must be weighed" by the court).

The obvious problem with the balancing test model is its internal inconsistency. *See generally* Lawrence Note, 52 Case W. Res. L.Rev. at 738 (suggesting "[t]he premise of the balancing test . . . is flawed"). Public policy concerns similar to those that prompt courts to refrain from enforcement of contracts addressing reproductive choice demand even more strongly that we not substitute the courts as decision makers in this highly emotional and personal area. Nonetheless, that is exactly what happens under the decisional framework based on the balancing test because the court must weigh the relative interests of the parties in deciding the disposition of embryos when the parties cannot agree. *See J.B.,* 783 A.2d at 719.

D. *Discussion.* With these alternative approaches in mind, we turn to the present case. . . .

[A]re prior agreements regarding the future disposition of embryos enforceable when one of the donors is no longer comfortable with his or her prior decision? We first note our agreement with other courts considering such matters that the partners who created the embryos have the primary, and equal, decision-making authority with respect to the use or disposition of their embryos. We think, however, that it would be against the public policy of this state to enforce a prior agreement between the parties in this highly personal area of reproductive choice when one of the parties has changed his or her mind concerning the disposition or use of the embryos.

Our statutes and case law evidence an understanding that decisions involving marital and family relationships are emotional and subject to change. For example, Iowa law imposes a seventy-two hour waiting period after the birth of a child before the biological parents can release parental rights. *See* Iowa Code § 600A.4(2)(*g*). In addition, although this court has not abolished claims for breach of promise to marry,[3] only recovery of monetary damages is permitted; the court will not force a party to actually consummate the marriage. *See* Herbert F. Goodrich, *Iowa Decisions on Breach of Marriage Promise,* 4 Iowa L. Bull. 166, 177 (1918). It has also long been recognized in this state that agreements for the purpose of bringing about a dissolution of marriage are contrary to public policy and therefore void. *Barngrover v. Pettigrew,* 128 Iowa 533, 535, 104 N.W. 904, 904 (1905) . . . .

This court has also expressed a general reluctance to become involved in intimate questions inherent in personal relationships. *See Miller v. Miller,* 78 Iowa 177, 179–80, 42 N.W. 641, 641 (1889). In *Miller,* we refused to enforce a contract between husband and wife that required, in part, each "to behave respectfully, and fairly treat the other." *Id.* at 180, 42 N.W. at 641. We explained our refusal on the following grounds:

> [J]udicial inquiry into matters of that character, between husband and wife, would be fraught with irreparable mischief, and forbidden by sound considerations of public policy.

> It is the genius of our laws, as well as of our civilization, that matters pertaining so directly and exclusively to the home, and its value as such, and which are so generally susceptible of regulation and control by those influences which surround it, are not to become matters of public concern or inquiry.

Id. at 182, 42 N.W. at 642; *accord Heacock v. Heacock,* 108 Iowa 540, 542, 79 N.W. 353, 354 (1899) ("Husband and wife cannot contract with each other to secure the performance of their marital rights and duties."). Certainly reproductive decisions are likewise not proper matters of judicial inquiry and enforcement.

We have considered and rejected the arguments of some commentators that embryo disposition agreements are analogous to antenuptial agreements and divorce stipulations, which courts generally enforce. *See* Apel, Vermont Bar Journal at 31. Whether embryos are viewed as having life or simply as having the potential for life, this characteristic or potential renders embryos fundamentally distinct from the chattels, real estate, and money that are the subjects of antenuptial agreements. Divorce stipulations are also distinguishable. While such agreements may address

---

[3]   This court has not had a breach-of-contract-to-marry case before it in over fifty years. *See Bearbower v. Merry,* 266 N.W.2d 128, 132 (Iowa 1978) (citing *Benson v. Williams,* 239 Iowa 742, 32 N.W.2d 813 (1948)).

custody issues, they are contemporaneous with the implementation of the stipulation, an attribute noticeably lacking in disposition agreements.

In addition to decisional and statutory authority supporting a public policy against judicial enforcement of personal decisions concerning marriage, family, and reproduction, our statutes also anticipate the effect of a couple's dissolution on their prior decisions. For example, Iowa Code section 633.271 provides that if a testator is divorced after making a will, "all provisions in the will in favor of the testator's spouse" are automatically revoked. Similarly, Iowa Code section 633.3107 revokes all provisions in a revocable trust in favor of the settlor's spouse upon divorce or dissolution of the marriage. Similar considerations make enforcement of contracts between partners involving such personal decisions as the use and disposition of their combined genetic material equally problematic. As noted by one commentator, embryos are originally created as "a mutual undertaking by [a] couple to have children together." Coleman, 84 Minn. L.Rev. at 83. Agreements made in that context are not always consistent with the parties' wishes once the mutual undertaking has ended.

We think judicial decisions and statutes in Iowa reflect respect for the right of individuals to make family and reproductive decisions based on their current views and values. They also reveal awareness that such decisions are highly emotional in nature and subject to a later change of heart. For this reason, we think judicial enforcement of an agreement *between a couple* regarding their future family and reproductive choices would be against the public policy of this state.

Our decision should not be construed, however, to mean that disposition agreements *between donors and fertility clinics* have no validity at all. We recognize a disposition or storage agreement serves an important purpose in defining and governing the relationship between the couple and the medical facility, ensuring that all parties understand their respective rights and obligations. *See A.Z.,* 725 N.E.2d at 1057 n. 22 ("We also recognize that agreements among donors and IVF clinics are essential to clinic operations."). In fact, it is this relationship, between the couple on the one side and the medical facility on the other, that dispositional contracts are intended to address. *See generally* Ellen A. Waldman, *Disputing Over Embryos: Of Contracts and Consents,* 32 Ariz. St. L.J. 897, 918 (2000) (noting "courts and most scholarly authorities would transform documents designed to record the transmission of medical information from clinic to couple, and the couple's acceptance of medical treatment, into a binding agreement between the couple itself"). Within this context, the medical facility and the donors should be able to rely on the terms of the parties' contract. *See A.Z.,* 725 N.E.2d at 1057 n. 22 (noting court's decision not to enforce agreement between partners is not an "impediment to the enforcement of such contracts by the clinics or by the donors against the clinics"); *J.B.,* 783 A.2d at 719.

In view of these competing needs, we reject the contractual approach and hold that agreements entered into at the time in vitro fertilization is commenced are enforceable and binding on the parties, "subject to the right of either party to change his or her mind about disposition up to the point of use or destruction of any stored embryo." *J.B.*, 783 A.2d at 719. This decisional model encourages prior agreements that can guide the actions of all parties, unless a later objection to any dispositional provision is asserted. It also recognizes that, *absent a change of heart by one of the partners,* an agreement governing disposition of embryos does not violate public policy. Only when one person makes known the agreement no longer reflects his or her current values or wishes is public policy implicated. Upon this occurrence, allowing either party to withdraw his or her agreement to a disposition that person no longer accepts acknowledges the public policy concerns inherent in enforcing prior decisions of a fundamentally personal nature. In fairness to the medical facility that is a party to the agreement, however, any change of intention must be communicated in writing to all parties in order to reopen the disposition issues covered by the agreement. *Id.*

That brings us, then, to the dilemma presented when one or both partners change their minds and the parties cannot reach a mutual decision on disposition. We have already explained the grave public policy concerns we have with the balancing test, which simply substitutes the court as decision maker. A better principle to apply, we think, is the requirement of contemporaneous mutual consent. Under that model, no transfer, release, disposition, or use of the embryos can occur without the signed authorization of both donors. If a stalemate results, the status quo would be maintained. The practical effect will be that the embryos are stored indefinitely unless both parties can agree to destroy the fertilized eggs. Thus, any expense associated with maintaining the status quo should logically be borne by the person opposing destruction. *See* Coleman, 84 Minn. L.Rev. at 112 ("The right to insist on the continued storage of the embryos should be dependent on a willingness to pay the associated costs.").

Turning to the present case, we find a situation in which one party no longer concurs in the parties' prior agreement with respect to the disposition of their frozen embryos, but the parties have been unable to reach a new agreement that is mutually satisfactory. Based on this fact, under the principles we have set forth today, we hold there can be no use or disposition of the Wittens' embryos unless Trip and Tamera reach an agreement.[4] Until then, the party or parties who oppose destruction shall be responsible for any storage fees. Therefore, we affirm the trial court's

---

[4]   We do not mean to imply that UNMC's obligation to store the embryos extends beyond the ten-year period provided in the parties' contract.

ruling enjoining both parties from transferring, releasing, or utilizing the embryos without the other's written consent. . . .

. . . DISPOSITION.

We affirm the trial court's decree [concerning the disposition of the embryos]. . . .

NOTE ON SURROGATE-PARENTING LEGISLATION

A number of states have adopted statutes concerning surrogacy. These statutes vary widely. For example, the District of Columbia, Indiana, Michigan, New York, and North Dakota either forbid surrogacy contracts or make such contracts void and unenforceable. See D.C. Code § 16–402; Indiana Code § 31–20–1–1; Mich. Comp. Laws § 722.855; N.Y. Dom. Rel. Law § 122; N.D. Cent. Code § 14–18–05. Arkansas allows surrogacy contracts. See Ark. Code § 9–10–201. Washington allows uncompensated surrogacy contracts. See Wash. Rev. Code §§ 26.26.210–260. New Mexico allows uncompensated surrogacy contracts and payment of the surrogate's medical and similar expenses. See N.M. Stat. §§ 32A–5–34(B), (F). Nebraska renders paid surrogacy contracts unenforceable, but says nothing about unpaid surrogacy. Neb. Rev. Stat. § 25–21,200. Nevada and Virginia allow unpaid surrogacy contracts but only where the prospective parents are married couples. See Nev. Rev. Stat. § 126.045; Va. Code § 20–158.

---

42 U.S. CODE § 274. PROHIBITION OF ORGAN PURCHASES

(a) *Prohibition.* It shall be unlawful for any person to knowingly acquire, receive, or otherwise transfer any human organ for valuable consideration for use in human transplantation if the transfer affects interstate commerce.

(b) *Penalties.* Any person who violates subsection (a) of this section shall be fined not more than $50,000 or imprisoned not more than five years, or both.

(c) *Definitions.* For purposes of subsection (a) of this section:

(1) The term "human organ" means the human (including fetal) kidney, liver, heart, lung, pancreas, bone marrow, cornea, eye, bone, and skin or any subpart thereof and any other human organ (or any subpart thereof, including that derived from a fetus) specified by the Secretary of Health and Human Services by regulation.

(2) The term "valuable consideration" does not include the reasonable payments associated with the removal, transportation, implantation, processing, preservation, quality control, and storage of a human organ or the expenses of travel, housing, and lost wages incurred by the donor of a human organ in connection with the donation of the organ. . . .

RADIN, MARKET-INALIENABILITY
100 Harvard L.Rev. 1849 (1987).*

Since the declaration of "unalienable rights" of persons at the founding of our republic, inalienability has had a central place in our legal and moral culture. Yet there is no one sharp meaning for the term "inalienable." Sometimes inalienable means nontransferable; sometimes only nonsalable. . . . In this Article I explore nonsalability, a species of inalienability I call market-inalienability. Something that is market-inalienable is not to be sold, which in our economic system means it is not to be traded in the market.

Controversy over what may be bought and sold—blood or babies—pervades our news. . . . About fifteen years ago, for example, Richard Titmuss advocated in his book, *The Gift Relationship,* that human blood should not be allocated through the market; others disagreed. More recently, Elisabeth Landes and Richard Posner suggested the possibility of a thriving market in infants, yet most people continue to believe that infants should not be allocated through the market. . . .

In [one] important set of meanings, inalienability is ascribed to an entitlement, right, or attribute that cannot be voluntarily transferred from one holder to another. Inalienability in these uses may mean nongiveable, nonsalable, or completely nontransferable. If something is nontransferable, the holder cannot designate a successor holder. Nongiveability and nonsalability are subsets of nontransferability. If something is inalienable by gift, it might be transferred by sale; if it is inalienable by sale, it might be transferred by gift. This nonsalability is what I refer to as market-inalienability. In precluding sales but not gifts, market-inalienability places some things outside the marketplace but not outside the realm of social intercourse.

Market-inalienability negates a central element of traditional property rights, which are conceived of as fully alienable. But market-inalienability differs from the nontransferability that characterizes many nontraditional property rights—entitlements of the regulatory and welfare

---

* This article now forms the basis of a book, Margaret Jane Radin, Contested Commodities (1996). (Footnote by ed.)

state—that are both nongiveable and nonsalable. [Examples are entitlements to social security and welfare benefits.] Market-inalienability also differs from the inalienability of other things, like voting rights, that seem to be moral or political duties related to a community's normative life; they are subject to broader inalienabilities that preclude loss as well as transfer. Unlike the inalienabilities attaching to welfare entitlements or political duties, market-inalienability does not render something inseparable from the person, but rather specifies that market trading may not be used as a social mechanism of separation. Finally, market-inalienability differs from the inalienability of things, like heroin, that are made nontransferable in order to implement a prohibition, because it does not signify that something is social anathema. Indeed, preclusion of sales often coexists with encouragement of gifts. For example, the market-inalienability of human organs does not preclude—and, indeed, may seek to foster—transfer from one individual to another by gift. . . .

Market-inalienability often expresses an aspiration for noncommodification. By making something nonsalable we proclaim that it should not be conceived of or treated as a commodity. When something is noncommodifiable, market trading is a disallowed form of social organization and allocation. We place that thing beyond supply and demand pricing, brokerage and arbitrage, advertising and marketing, stockpiling, speculation, and valuation in terms of the opportunity cost of production.

Market-inalienability poses for us more than the binary choice of whether something should be wholly inside or outside the market, completely commodified or completely noncommodified. Some things are completely commodified—deemed suitable for trade in a laissez-faire market. Others are completely noncommodified—removed from the market altogether. But many things can be described as incompletely commodified—neither fully commodified nor fully removed from the market. Thus, we may decide that some things should be market-inalienable only to a degree, or only in some aspects.

To appreciate the need to develop a satisfactory analysis of market-inalienability, consider the deeply contested issues of commodification that confront us. Infants and children, fetal gestational services, blood, human organs, sexual services, and services of college athletes are some salient things whose commodification is contested. Our division over whether to place a monetary equivalent on a spouse's professional degree or homemaker services in a divorce; or on various kinds of injuries in tort actions, such as loss of consortium, is another form of contest over commodification. Monetization—commodification—of clean air and water is likewise deeply contested. Moreover, debates about some kinds of regulation can be seen as contested incomplete commodification, with the contest being over whether to allow full commodification (a laissez-faire market regime) or something less. If we see the debates this way, residential rent control, minimum wage requirements, and other forms of price regulation, as well as residential habitability requirements, safety regulation, and other forms of product-quality regulation all become contests over the issue of commodification.

How are we to determine the extent to which something ought to be noncommodified, so that we can determine to what extent market-inalienability is justified? Because the question asks about the appropriate relationship of particular things to the market, normative theories about the appropriate social role of the market should be helpful in trying to answer it. We can think of such theories as ordered on a continuum stretching from universal noncommodification (nothing in markets) to universal commodification (everything in markets). On this continuum, Karl Marx's theory can symbolize the theoretical pole of universal noncommodification, and Richard Posner's can be seen as close to the opposite theoretical pole. . . .

Universal commodification undermines personal identity by conceiving of personal attributes, relationships, and philosophical and moral commitments as monetizable and alienable from the self. A better view of personhood should understand many kinds of particulars—one's politics, work, religion, family, love, sexuality, friendships, altruism, experiences, wisdom, moral commitments, character, and personal attributes—as integral to the self. To understand any of these as monetizable or completely detachable from the person—to think, for example, that the value of one person's moral commitments is commensurate or fungible with those of another, or that the "same" person remains when her moral commitments are subtracted—is to do violence to our deepest understanding of what it is to be human. . . .

———

PART 2

REMEDIES FOR BREACH
OF CONTRACT

■ ■ ■

Part 2 concerns remedies for breach of contract, chiefly in the bargain context.

An introductory Chapter, Chapter 4, explores the nature and theory of the expectation interest, which is the basis for the most characteristic remedy for breach of contract, expectation damages.

Chapter 5 considers the remedy of expectation damages in more detail.

Chapter 6 concerns the remedy of specific performance, under which a breaching party is ordered to perform the contract, rather than only to pay damages for breach.

Finally, Chapter 7 explores the use of alternative damage measures in a bargain context. These alternative damage measures include reliance damages, restitution damages, and disgorgement damages. The theory of efficient breach is considered in connection with disgorgement damages.

———

CHAPTER 4

AN INTRODUCTION TO CONTRACT DAMAGES

■ ■ ■

RESTATEMENT, SECOND, CONTRACTS § 344

[See Selected Source Materials Supplement]

———

HAWKINS V. MCGEE

Supreme Court of New Hampshire, 1929.
84 N.H. 114, 146 A. 641.

Assumpsit, against a surgeon for breach of an alleged warranty of the success of an operation. Trial by jury and verdict for the plaintiff. The writ also contained a count in negligence upon which a nonsuit was ordered, without exception.

[The defendant moved to have the verdict set aside on several grounds, one of them being that the damages awarded were excessive. The trial court ordered that the verdict be set aside unless the plaintiff would remit all damages in excess of $500. On the plaintiff's refusal to consent to a reduction, the trial court set the verdict aside as being "excessive and against the weight of the evidence." The plaintiff excepted to this ruling of the trial court; his exception and numerous exceptions taken by the defendant were transferred to the Supreme Court.]

BRANCH, J. The operation in question consisted in the removal of a considerable quantity of scar tissue from the palm of the plaintiff's right hand and the grafting of skin taken from the plaintiff's chest in place thereof. The scar tissue was the result of a severe burn caused by contact with an electric wire, which the plaintiff received about nine years before the time of the transactions here involved. There was evidence to the effect that before the operation was performed the plaintiff and his father went to the defendant's office, and that the defendant in answer to the question, "How long will the boy be in the hospital?" replied, "Three or four days, . . . not over four; then the boy can go home and it will be just a few days when he will go back to work with a perfect hand." Clearly this and other testimony to the same effect would not justify a finding that the doctor contracted to complete the hospital treatment in three or four days or that the plaintiff would be able to go back to work within a few days thereafter. The above statements could only be construed as expressions of opinion or predictions as to the probable duration of the treatment and plaintiff's resulting disability, and the fact that these estimates were exceeded would impose no contractual liability upon the defendant. The only substantial basis for the plaintiff's claim is the testimony that the defendant also said before the operation was decided upon, "I will guarantee to make the hand a hundred per cent perfect hand" or "a hundred per cent good hand." The plaintiff was present when these words were alleged to have been spoken, and, if they are to be taken at their face value, it seems obvious that proof of their utterance would establish the giving of a warranty in accordance with his contention.

The defendant argues, however, that, even if these words were uttered by him, no reasonable man would understand that they were used with the intention of entering into any "contractual relation whatever," and that they could reasonably be understood only "as his expression in strong language that he believed and expected that as a result of the operation he would give the plaintiff a very good hand." It may be conceded, as the defendant contends, that, before the question of the making of a contract should be submitted to a jury, there is a preliminary question of law for the trial court to pass upon, i.e. "whether the words could possibly have the meaning imputed to them by the party who founds his case upon a certain interpretation," but it cannot be held that the trial court decided this question erroneously in the present case. It is unnecessary to determine at this time whether the argument of the defendant, based upon "common knowledge of the uncertainty which attends all surgical operations," and the improbability that a surgeon would ever contract to make a damaged part of the human body "one hundred per cent perfect," would, in the absence of countervailing considerations, be regarded as conclusive, for there were other factors in the present case which tended to support the contention of the plaintiff. There was evidence that the defendant repeatedly solicited from the plaintiff's father the opportunity to perform this operation, and the theory was advanced by plaintiff's counsel in cross-examination of defendant that he sought an opportunity to "experiment on skin grafting," in which he had had little previous experience. If the jury accepted this part of plaintiff's contention, there would be a reasonable basis for the further conclusion that, if defendant spoke the words attributed to him, he did so with the intention that they should be accepted at their face value, as an inducement for the granting of consent to the operation by the plaintiff and his father, and there was ample evidence that they were so accepted by them. The question of the making of the alleged contract was properly submitted to the jury.

2.   The substance of the charge to the jury on the question of damages appears in the following quotation: "If you find the plaintiff entitled to

anything, he is entitled to recover for what pain and suffering he has been made to endure and for what injury he has sustained over and above what injury he had before." To this instruction the defendant seasonably excepted. By it, the jury was permitted to consider two elements of damage, (1) pain and suffering due to the operation, and (2) positive ill effects of the operation upon the plaintiff's hand. Authority for any specific rule of damages in cases of this kind seems to be lacking, but, when tested by general principle and by analogy, it appears that the foregoing instruction was erroneous.

"By 'damages,' as that term is used in the law of contracts, is intended compensation for a breach, measured in the terms of the contract." Davis v. New England Cotton Yarn Co., 77 N.H. 403, 404, 92 A. 732, 733. The purpose of the law is "to put the plaintiff in as good a position as he would have been in had the defendant kept his contract." 3 Williston Cont. § 1338; Hardie-Tynes Mfg. Co. v. Easton Cotton Oil Co., 150 N.C. 150, 63 S.E. 676, 134 Am.St.Rep. 899. The measure of recovery "is based upon what the defendant should have given the plaintiff, not what the plaintiff has given the defendant or otherwise expended." 3 Williston Cont. § 1341. "The only losses that can be said fairly to come within the terms of a contract are such as the parties must have had in mind when the contract was made, or such as they either knew or ought to have known would probably result from a failure to comply with its terms." Davis v. New England Cotton Yarn Co., 77 N.H. 403, 404, 92 A. 732, 733, Hurd v. Dunsmore, 63 N.H. 171.

The present case is closely analogous to one in which a machine is built for a certain purpose and warranted to do certain work. In such cases, the usual rule of damages for breach of warranty in the sale of chattels is applied and it is held that the measure of damages is the difference between the value of the machine if it had corresponded with the warranty and its actual value, together with such incidental losses as the parties knew or ought to have known would probably result from a failure to comply with its terms. . . .

We therefore conclude that the true measure of the plaintiff's damage in the present case is the difference between the value to him of a perfect hand or a good hand, such as the jury found the defendant promised him, and the value of his hand in its present condition, including any incidental consequences fairly within the contemplation of the parties when they made their contract. 1 Sutherland, Damages (4th Ed.) § 92. Damages not thus limited, although naturally resulting, are not to be given.

The extent of the plaintiff's suffering does not measure this difference in value. The pain necessarily incident to a serious surgical operation was a part of the contribution which the plaintiff was willing to make to his joint undertaking with the defendant to produce a good hand. It was a legal detriment suffered by him which constituted a part of the consideration given by him for the contract. It represented a part of the price which he was willing to pay for a good hand, but it furnished no test of the value of a good hand or the difference between the value of the hand which the defendant promised and the one which resulted from the operation.

It was also erroneous and misleading to submit to the jury as a separate element of damage any change for the worse in the condition of the plaintiff's hand resulting from the operation, although this error was probably more prejudicial to the plaintiff than to the defendant. Any such ill effect of the operation would be included under the true rule of damages set forth above, but damages might properly be assessed for the defendant's failure to improve the condition of the hand, even if there were no evidence that its condition was made worse as a result of the operation.

It must be assumed that the trial court, in setting aside the verdict, undertook to apply the same rule of damages which he had previously given to the jury, and, since this rule was erroneous, it is unnecessary for us to consider whether there was any evidence to justify his finding that all damages awarded by the jury above $500 were excessive.

3.   Defendant's requests for instructions were loosely drawn, and were properly denied. A considerable number of issues of fact were raised by the evidence, and it would have been extremely misleading to instruct the jury in accordance with defendant's request No. 2, that "The only issue on which you have to pass is whether or not there was a special contract between the plaintiff and the defendant to produce a perfect hand." Equally inaccurate was defendant's request No. 5, which reads as follows: "You would have to find, in order to hold the defendant liable in this case, that Dr. McGee and the plaintiff both understood that the doctor was guaranteeing a perfect result from this operation." If the defendant said that he would guarantee a perfect result, and the plaintiff relied upon that promise, any mental reservations which he may have had are immaterial. The standard by which his conduct is to be judged is not internal, but external. . . . Defendant's request number 7 was as follows: "If you should get so far as to find that there was a special contract guaranteeing a perfect result, you would still have to find for the defendant unless you further found that a further operation would not correct the disability claimed by the plaintiff." In view of the testimony that the defendant had refused to perform a further operation, it would clearly have been erroneous to give this instruction. The evidence would have justified a verdict for an amount sufficient to cover the cost of such an operation, even if the theory underlying this request were correct. . . .

New trial.

MARBLE, J., did not sit: the others concurred.

———

BACKGROUND NOTE ON HAWKINS V. MCGEE

The following background facts concerning Hawkins v. McGee (based on interviews and correspondence with the Hawkins family and a local lawyer) are reported in Roberts, Hawkins Case: A Hair-Raising Experience, Harvard Law School Record, March 17, 1978, at 1, 7, 13.

. . . George Hawkins was born in January, 1904—the second of Rose Wilkinson and Charles Augustus Hawkins' six children. . . .

One morning in 1915, 11-year-old George burned his right hand while preparing breakfast for his father on the family's wood-burning stove. At the time, George was trying to turn on the kitchen light to illuminate the stove, but an electrical storm the night before had damaged the wiring so that George received a severe shock. One of George's younger brothers, Howard Hawkins, now an insurance agent in Berlin, described George's initial scar as a "small pencil-size scar" which was between his thumb and index finger and did not substantially affect his use of the hand. Nevertheless, Charles Hawkins took his son George to skin specialists in Montreal after the accident; but there the doctors advised the Hawkinses against doing anything to restore the hand.

During this period, the family physician, Edward McGee, while treating one of George's younger brothers for pneumonia, also became aware of George's scarred hand. Later, in 1919, after returning from several years of medical service in Europe during World War I, McGee requested George and his parents to let him operate on the hand in order to restore it to "perfect" condition.

According to Dorothy St. Hilaire, George's younger sister, McGee claimed to have done a number of similar skin grafts on soldiers in Germany during the war, although he later admitted that he had really only observed such operations.

St. Hilaire recollects that McGee, in persuading George to undergo the surgery, emphasized the social problems which his scarred hand might create. McGee encouraged the Hawkinses to allow him to operate on the hand for three years, until finally George agreed shortly after his 18th birthday. . . .

McGee operated on George's hand in the St. Louis Hospital in Berlin in March of 1922. The skin graft operation was supposed to be quick, simple, and effective, and to require only a few days of hospitalization. Instead, St. Hilaire recalls that her brother bled very badly for several days. . . .

. . . George was, in the words of his brother Howard, "in the throes of death" for quite a while after the operation because of his extensive bleeding and the ensuing infection. Moreover, the post-operation scar covered his thumb and two fingers and was densely covered with hair. Howard Hawkins remembers that George's hand was partially closed up and continued to bleed periodically throughout his life. . . .

The jury only awarded the Hawkinses $3,000 for damages, and the final settlement was for $1,400 and lawyers fees. St. Hilaire believes the jurors, while at heart solidly behind the Hawkinses' cause, were afraid to return heavier damages against McGee because he was one of the more prominent physicians in the area. Charles Hawkins took the $1,400 and his injured son back to Montreal to see if any subsequent operations would alleviate George's deformity, but the doctors there said that the grafted skin was so tough that nothing more could be done. . . .

Hawkins' crippled hand affected his employment and outlook throughout his lifetime. After the operation, George Hawkins never returned to high school, even though, in Howard's opinion, "George was very bright, learned quickly, and had a pleasing personality." He was encouraged by his parents to finish school, but would not because, in his siblings' view, he was embarrassed by his hand.

George also gave up tennis and riflery after the operation, although previously he had won several medals as a marksman for the State Home Guard. Because of his hand, George was unable to perform any heavy manual labor or learn to type. He worked for many years in the printing division of the Brown Company, a pulp and paper manufacturer in Berlin, and later in a tire store. . . .

. . . According to his family members, George was always very sensitive about his hand and suffered lifelong emotional distress. His parents also grieved until their deaths because of the tragic and unnecessary crippling of their son's hand.

The Hawkins family was unaware of the widespread study of Hawkins v. McGee in law schools until, in 1964, Howard and Edith Hawkins' daughter Gail encountered the case early in her contracts course at Boston University Law School. Moreover, the Hawkins family did not know about the case's use in "The Paper Chase" contracts class scene until Edith Hawkins happened to see the 1972 movie during its first run.

Howard Hawkins, however, believes that George was somewhat aware of the case's importance before his 1958 death. Howard states: "I think he became aware of the importance of his case through a lawyer friend, an O. (Ovide) J. Coulombe. I think it gave him a sense of importance, in that this was bringing the facts out in the public eye, but this was only temporary, as he really lived with this incapacity all his life, and he did suffer mentally as well as physically."

———

UNIDROIT PRINCIPLES OF INTERNATIONAL COMMERCIAL CONTRACTS ART. 7.4.2

[See Selected Source Materials Supplement]

———

COOTER & EISENBERG, DAMAGES FOR BREACH OF CONTRACT

73 Calif.L.Rev. 1434 (1985).*

We now consider whether reliance or expectation damages should be preferred on breach of a bargain contract. In examining this question, we turn from problems of definition to problems of fairness and policy.

Fairness seems to require that a person who breaches a contract should pay compensation to the victim of breach for the injury he suffers as a result. But the meanings of the terms "compensation" and "injury" are fundamentally ambiguous. Under a reliance conception, the uninjured state is the condition the victim would have been in if he had not made the contract with the breaching party. Under an expectation conception, the uninjured state is the condition the victim would have been in if the breaching party had performed the contract. Which conception should govern is far from obvious.

In many cases, the issue of selecting between reliance and expectation damages is not significant, because the two measures will yield virtually identical damages. In particular . . . in a competitive market reliance damages normally will equal expectation damages [because the contract price promised by the wrongdoer will equal the forgone price at which the injured party could have contracted with a third party]. While it is true that few markets satisfy all the conditions of perfect competition, many come close enough so that the difference between expectation and reliance damages would be insignificant.

Often, however, the two measures may diverge significantly. This may occur, for example, in imperfectly competitive markets whose conditions differ materially from those of perfectly competitive markets. . . . The question of choice between competing conceptions of injury and compensation then becomes material. Traditionally, courts and commentators were united in holding that the expectation conception of injury governed in such cases. In fact, prior to the 1930's the reliance principle operated in only a covert manner. However, with the promulgation in 1932 of section 90 of the Restatement of Contracts, and the publication in 1934 of Fuller and Perdue's landmark article *The Reliance Interest in Contract Damages,* the reliance principle began to

———

*   The text is somewhat reorganized from the original. (Footnote by ed.)

undergo a process of steady and impressive growth. Until the last ten years or so, this growth served to expand liability in contract. Recently, however, some commentators have taken the position that the reliance principle should be used to reduce liability, by substituting the reliance conception for the expectation conception in the law of damages.

The reasons for this position are complex. Partly it is an attack on the very institution of contract: liability based on reliance may be conceptualized as liability in tort. It also results, however, from the apparent lack of a clear rationale for expectation damages. The reliance conception of injury reflects the basic intuition that if somebody is worse off than he was before, he has been hurt. The expectation conception reflects a much more subtle intuition, and indeed it is plausible to argue that the mere defeat of an expectation is not a very serious injury.

The question remains what measure of damages should be used in cases where expectation and reliance may materially diverge. We begin our analysis of that question with the concept of efficient contract terms.

Economists often distinguish between efficiency and distribution. For present purposes, efficiency concerns the amount of value created by a contract, and distribution concerns the division of that value between the parties. Economists say that a contract is efficient if its terms maximize the value that can be created by the contemplated exchange. Put differently, if a contract is inefficient, revising the inefficient terms can increase the value it creates.

The distinction between distribution and efficiency parallels a distinction between the price and nonprice terms of a contract. Adjusting *nonprice* terms often makes it possible to control a contract's efficiency. For example, suppose that a contract to make and sell a boat includes a term that imposes very high liquidated damages if Seller breaches. There are many types of precaution Seller can take to decrease the probability of breach, such as ordering materials well in advance, hiring extra workers to protect against someone's quitting or falling ill, and reserving dry-dock facilities needed in the final stages of construction. If the very high liquidated-damages term is enforceable, it may cause Seller to take excessive precaution, in the sense that the cost of the precaution to Seller is greater than the value to Buyer of the increased probability that Seller will perform. In that case, the liquidated damages term is inefficient. If, however, the term is modified by reducing the liquidated damages, the saving to Seller from taking less precaution would exceed the cost to Buyer of exposure to additional risk of nonperformance. This would result in a net increase in the value created by the contract.

The *price* term of a contract controls the distribution of the value that the contract creates. Revision of an inefficient nonprice term can produce an increase in value, and this increase can be distributed between the parties by adjusting the price term so that each party is better off. Thus in the boat case, an increase in value from adjusting the liquidated-damages provision, initially enjoyed by Seller, could be split with Buyer by lowering the price of the boat. The revised contract, containing lower liquidated damages and a lower price, would make both parties better off. Put differently, the original contract stipulates damages in the event of Seller's breach, thus creating a right in Buyer. If Seller is willing to pay more for a modification of this right than the price Buyer would demand, efficiency requires that the contract be modified. In this respect, the exchange of legal rights is no different than the exchange of ordinary commodities.

Under ideal conditions—that is, where negotiation and drafting are cost-free—self-interest compels a rational buyer and seller to create an efficient contract, so that the process of bargaining leads to the maximization of the value a contract creates. In practice, however, there are many obstacles to creating efficient contracts. For example, it is costly to write contract terms. Instead of including explicit terms covering all contingencies, therefore, most contracts leave many issues to be resolved by the courts in case an irreconcilable dispute should arise. Specifically, many contracts leave out terms covering damages for breach, and the courts, in effect, must fill in the contract with legal damages rules.

The damage rules that the courts apply to fill in contracts should be both fair and efficient. Contracts negotiated under ideal conditions will be efficient, and enforcing the terms of such contracts will usually be regarded as fair. Thus we take as a theorem that a damage rule is both fair and efficient if it corresponds to the terms that rational parties situated like the contracting parties would have reached when bargaining under ideal conditions.

The question then is, why might rational parties, who address the issue, choose an expectation measure over a reliance measure? One reason is administrative: it is usually easier to establish in court the value of performance than the extent of reliance. The very fact of reliance is often difficult to prove, as in cases where the reliance consists of passive inaction (such as failure to pursue alternatives) rather than a positive change of position. Even if the fact of reliance can be proved, reliance damages may be difficult to measure. In a noncompetitive market, for example, reliance damages would normally be calculated by the [victim's opportunity cost], which requires determining the forgone price. Often, however, the forgone price is very hard to determine, as where the buyer breaches and the commodity is so unusual that there is no way to establish exactly what the next-best alternative buyer would have paid. In contrast, expectation damages are based on the contract price, which is known, rather than the forgone price, which is speculative. This administrative consideration has implications for both fairness and efficiency. In terms of fairness, the difficulty of proving reliance damages might, paradoxically, result in a failure to protect the reliance interest unless an expectation measure is chosen. In terms of efficiency, a damage measure that was difficult to prove, and therefore unreliable, would undercut the goal of facilitating private planning.

An intimately related set of considerations has to do with the incentive effects of the expectation and reliance measures. Most contracts are made with the expectation of mutual gain. . . . The total gain to both parties—the surplus from exchange—is the value created by the contract. The terms of a contract have incentive effects upon behavior that influence how much value the contract will create. Accordingly, one index to whether a damage rule would have been agreed to by rational parties situated like the contracting parties, and bargaining under ideal conditions, is whether the rule provides incentives for efficient behavior. . . .

We begin with the incentive effects of damage measures on the decision whether to perform, that is, on the rate of breach. A contract involves a promise by at least one party, and it is always possible that events will induce a promisor to refuse to perform, either because performance has become unprofitable or because an alternative performance has become more profitable. If a promisor were liable only for the promisee's reliance damages, the value of the promisor's performance to the promisee would not enter into a purely self-interested calculation by the promisor whether to perform. In contrast, expectation damages place on the promisor the promisee's loss of his share of the contract's value in the event of breach, and thereby sweep that loss into the promisor's calculus of self-interest.

The effect of expectation damages on the promisor's calculations can be stated in terms of externalities. Economists say that an externality exists when one person imposes a cost upon another without paying for it. Incentives for performance are efficient if they compel a promisor to balance the cost to him of performing against the losses to himself and to others that will result if he does not perform. If the promisor does not perform, the promisee loses his share of the value of the contract. If the promisor is liable for that loss, he internalizes not only his own loss but the losses to the promisee that result from his failure to perform. In contrast, if the promisor is liable only for reliance damages, he will not internalize the full value of performance to the promisee. Thus expectation damages create efficient incentives for the promisor's performance, while reliance damages do not, unless they are identical to expectation damages.

By directly affecting the probability that the promisor will perform, the expectation measure has an indirect effect upon the promisee's behavior, which can be stated in terms of planning. Knowing that expectation damages give the promisor strong incentives to perform, the promisee will be more confident that his reliance on the promisor will not expose him to undue risk. The promisee can therefore plan more effectively, because once a contract is made he can order his affairs with the confidence that he will realize its value, whether by performance or damages. In contrast, under a regime of reliance damages, a promisee could plan only on the basis that if breach occurs the law will put him back to where he was when he started. Since planning is by nature forward-looking, this backward-looking nature of reliance damages would be a shaky foundation for ordering complex affairs. Furthermore, it is in the promisor's interest that the promisee be able to plan reliably, because the ability to do so will make the promisee willing to pay a higher price for the promise.

These ideas can also be expressed in institutional terms. The purpose of the social institution of bargain is to create joint value through exchange. In recognition of the desirability of creating value in this manner, the legal institution of contract supports the social institution of the bargain with official sanctions. It is rational to design the legal sanctions so that the joint value from exchange is maximized. This goal is achieved by protecting the expectation interest.

———

CHAPTER 5

THE EXPECTATION MEASURE

■ ■ ■

Chapter 5 considers damages rules that implement the basic principle of expectation damages, that is, the principle that upon breach of a bargain contract the injured party should be put in the position he would have been in if the contract had been performed. When that very general principle is applied to concrete, recurring kinds of cases, like breach of contracts for the sale of goods, much more specific rules are utilized. Section 1 examines the basic damage rules that apply to breach of a contract to provide a service or good when the plaintiff does not seek consequential damages (that is, damages that arise only in consequence of the plaintiff's special circumstances). Section 2 examines the basic damage rules that apply to a breach of a contract to pay for a service or a good. The remaining materials in this Chapter concern limits that the law sets on the principle of expectation damages. These include the innocent party's duty to mitigate (minimize) damages, the requirement that consequential damages were reasonably foreseeable at the time the contract was made, and the certainty with which damages must be established. The last Section of this Chapter concerns the test for the enforceability of liquidated-damages provisions, that is, contractual provisions in which the parties themselves fix damages for breach.

———

SECTION 1. BREACH OF A CONTRACT TO PROVIDE A SERVICE OR GOOD

This Section considers the basic rules (apart from the rule on consequential damages) that define the damages recoverable by a purchaser of a service or good when the seller fails to perform or renders deficient performance. The basic rules work best when the plaintiff obtains what he was promised from a third person through a reasonable substitute transaction—as by hiring a third person to perform the service, by purchasing the good from a third person, or by paying a third person to correct the deficiency in the service or the good. The rules measure expectation damages by the difference between the price of substitute and the unpaid balance of the contract price. These damages are easy to measure and give the plaintiff what he was promised if the substitute is equivalent to what he was promised. An equivalent substitute transaction can be thought of as a form of self-help specific performance: A purchaser who seeks specific performance seeks an order from the court to compel the seller to perform her contract as promised. A purchaser who engages in an equivalent substitute transaction obtains what he was promised in a voluntary transaction and then can be made close to whole by a damage award for the additional price he paid for the substitute.

When a reasonable substitute transaction is available to the purchaser, and the purchaser chooses to forego the transaction, then damages are likely to be measured by the difference between the price of the foregone substitute and the unpaid balance of the contract price. For example, in the case of breach of a contract to deliver a good that is available on the market, when the buyer does not cover by buying the good from a third party, the basic damage rule gives the buyer the difference between the market price of the good and the unpaid balance of the contract price. The premise is that if the buyer's loss from the breach were greater than this amount, then he would have covered by purchasing the good at the market price. A purchaser who fails to protect himself from a greater loss by an available substitute transaction may also run afoul of the duty to mitigate.

Problems arise when the purchaser cannot obtain what he was promised through a reasonable substitute transaction. When the breach is of a contract to deliver a unique asset a court will award specific performance, ordering the seller to deliver the asset, if the seller has the asset in hand and is able to deliver. But courts are reluctant to compel a defendant to perform a service, particularly when performance is complicated or involves an unreasonable cost.

Many of the cases in Section A involve a related problem. The defendant's breach of a contract to perform a service leaves the plaintiff with property that has a defect. The defect can be repaired but at what appears to be an unreasonable cost because the repair cost is significantly greater than the reduction in the market value of the property attributable to the defect. Under the American common law the basic damage rule that applies in this case generally requires that damages be measured either by the price of repairing the defect or by the reduction in the market value of the plaintiff's property attributable to the defect. Often the plaintiff's actual loss (defined as the amount of money that would give the plaintiff the same satisfaction as repairing the defect) is an amount between the price of repairing the defect and reduction in the market value of the plaintiff's property attributable to the defect. In some legal systems the court will estimate the plaintiff's actual loss and award damages for this amount. But this is not done under the American common law.

The cases in Section A illustrate a related point. While the expectation principle defines the goal of the damage rules examined in this Section the rules themselves generally measure damages by observable prices. Inevitably this can lead to over- or under-compensation, using the expectation principle as the benchmark. When a rule results in under-compensation an aggrieved purchaser generally may try to recover his uncompensated harm as consequential damages. But his claim for consequential damages will run into rules we examine in later Sections that preclude damages for losses that were unforeseeable at the time the contract was made or that cannot be quantified with sufficient certainty.

(A) SERVICE CONTRACTS

LOUISE CAROLINE NURSING HOME, INC. v. DIX CONSTRUCTION CO.

Supreme Judicial Court of Massachusetts, 1972.
362 Mass. 306, 285 N.E.2d 904.

Before TAURO, C.J., and REARDON, QUIRICO, BRAUCHER and HENNESSEY, JJ.

QUIRICO, JUSTICE.

This is an action of contract in which Louise Caroline Nursing Home, Inc. (Nursing Home) seeks damages from Dix Construction Corp. (Dix) for breach of a contract to build a nursing home. . . .

The case was referred to an auditor for hearing pursuant to a stipulation of the parties that his findings of fact would be final. After hearing the parties, the auditor filed a report in which he found generally: (1) that the Nursing Home had fulfilled all of its contractual obligations to Dix; (2) that Dix had committed a breach of its contractual obligations to the Nursing Home by failing, without justification, to complete the contract within the time agreed. . . . However, he further found that the Nursing Home "suffered no compensable damages as a result of the breach by Dix . . . in that the cost to complete the nursing home . . . was within the contract price . . . less what had been paid to Dix. . . ." . . .

. . . Two of the Nursing Home's objections relate to the measure of the damages applied by the auditor in reaching his conclusion that it suffered no "compensable damages." The rule of damages applied by the auditor was that if the cost of completing the contract by the use of a substitute contractor is within the contract price, less what had already been paid on the contract, no "compensable damages" have occurred. The Nursing Home argues that the proper rule of damages would entitle it to the difference between the value of the building as left by Dix and the value it would have had if the contract had been fully performed. Under this rule the Nursing Home contends that it was entitled to the "benefits of its bargain," meaning that if the fair market value of the completed building would have exceeded the contractual cost of construction, recovery should be allowed for this lost extra value. It bases this argument primarily upon our statement in Province Sec. Corp. v. Maryland Cas. Co., 269 Mass. 75, 94, 168 N.E. 252, 257, that "[i]t is a settled rule that the measure of damages where a contractor has failed to perform a contract for the construction of a building for business uses is the difference between the value of the building as left by the contractor and its value had it been finished according to contract. In other words the question is how much less was the building worth than it would have been worth if the contract had been fully performed. Powell v. Howard, 109 Mass. 192. White v. McLaren, 151 Mass. 553, 24 N.E. 911. Norcross Brothers Co. v. Vose, 199 Mass. 81, 95, 96, 85 N.E. 468. Pelatowski v. Black, 213 Mass. 428, 100 N.E. 831." This statement was probably not necessary to the court's decision in the *Province Sec. Corp.* case and, in any event, must be read in light of the cases cited by the court in support of it. All of these cases involved failure of performance in the sense of defective performance, as contrasted with abandonment of performance. In one of the cases, Pelatowski v. Black, 213 Mass. 428, 431, 100 N.E. 831, 832, the court expressly distinguished "cases where a contractor has abandoned his work while yet unfinished."

The fundamental rule of damages applied in all contract cases was stated by this court in Ficara v. Belleau, 331 Mass. 80, 82, 117 N.E.2d 287, 289, in the following language: "It is not the policy of our law to award damages which would put a plaintiff in a better position than if the defendant had carried out his contract. . . . 'The fundamental principle upon which the rule of damages is based is compensation. . . . Compensation is the value of the performance of the contract, that is, what the plaintiff would have made had the contract been performed.' F.A. Bartlett Tree Expert Co. v. Hartney, 308 Mass. 407, 412, 32 N.E.2d 237, 240. . . . The plaintiff is entitled to be made whole and no more."

Consonant with this principle we have held that in assessing damages for failure to complete a construction contract, "[t]he measure of the plaintiffs' damages (at least in the absence of other elements of damage, as, for example, for delay in construction, which the master has not found here) can be only in the amount of the reasonable cost of completing the contract and repairing the defendant's defective performance less such part of the contract price as has not been paid." Di Mare v. Capaldi, 336 Mass. 497, 502, 146 N.E.2d 517, 521. This principle was recently reiterated in Providence Washington Ins. Co. v. Beck, 356 Mass. 739, 255 N.E.2d 600. In the face of this principle the Nursing Home's arguments attempting to demonstrate the amount of alleged "benefits of its bargain" lost are to no avail. In any event, it should be noted that any such "benefits of its bargain" as would derive from obtaining a building worth much more than the actual costs of construction are preserved if the building can be completed at a total cost which is still within the contract price, less any amount which has already been paid on the contract. The auditor was correct in applying the "cost of completion" measure of damages which excluded any separate recovery for lost "benefits of its bargain."

The Nursing Home additionally contends that even under the rule of damages applied by the auditor they were entitled, in the words of the *DiMare* case, *supra,* to recover "other elements of damage, as, for example, for delay in construction." 336 Mass. at 502, 146 N.E.2d at 521. The short answer to this contention is the auditor's express statement, in his summary of the evidence, that "[t]here was no specific evidence as to the costs of delay, if any." . . .

. . . For the foregoing reasons the Nursing Home's exceptions to the denial of its motion to recommit the auditor's report and to the granting of Reliance's motion for entry of judgment in accordance with the auditor's report must be overruled.

Exceptions overruled.

PEEVYHOUSE v. GARLAND COAL & MINING CO.

Supreme Court of Oklahoma, 1962.
382 P.2d 109, cert. denied, 375 U.S. 906, 84 S.Ct. 196, 11 L.Ed.2d 145 (1963).

JACKSON, J. In the trial court, plaintiffs Willie and Lucille Peevyhouse sued the defendant, Garland Coal and Mining Company, for damages for breach of contract. Judgment was for plaintiffs in an amount considerably less than was sued for. Plaintiffs appeal and defendant cross-appeals.

In the briefs on appeal, the parties present their argument and contentions under several propositions; however, they all stem from the basic question of whether the trial court properly instructed the jury on the measure of damages.

Briefly stated, the facts are as follows: plaintiffs owned a farm containing coal deposits, and in November, 1954, leased the premises to defendant for a period of five years for coal mining purposes. A "strip-mining" operation was contemplated in which the coal would be taken from pits on the surface of the ground, instead of from underground mine shafts. In addition to the usual covenants found in a coal mining lease, defendant specifically agreed to perform certain restorative and remedial work at the end of the lease period. It is unnecessary to set out the details of the work to be done, other than to say that it would involve the moving of many thousands of cubic yards of dirt, at a cost estimated by expert witnesses at about $29,000.00. However, plaintiffs sued for only $25,000.00.

During the trial, it was stipulated that all covenants and agreements in the lease contract had been fully carried out by both parties, except the remedial work mentioned above; defendant conceded that this work had not been done.

Plaintiffs introduced expert testimony as to the amount and nature of the work to be done, and its estimated cost. Over plaintiffs' objections, defendant thereafter introduced expert testimony as to the "diminution in value" of plaintiffs' farm resulting from the failure of defendant to render performance as agreed in the contract—that is, the difference between the present value of the farm, and what its value would have been if defendant had done what it agreed to do.

At the conclusion of the trial, the court instructed the jury that it must return a verdict for plaintiffs, and left the amount of damages for jury determination. On the measure of damages, the court instructed the jury that it might consider the cost of performance of the work defendant agreed to do, "together with all of the evidence offered on behalf of either party".

It thus appears that the jury was at liberty to consider the "diminution in value" of plaintiffs' farm as well as the cost of "repair work" in determining the amount of damages.

It returned a verdict for plaintiffs for $5000.00—only a fraction of the "cost of performance", *but more than the total value of the farm even after the remedial work is done.*

On appeal, the issue is sharply drawn. Plaintiffs contend that the true measure of damages in this case is what it will cost plaintiffs to obtain performance of the work that was not done because of defendant's default. Defendant argues that the measure of damages is the cost of performance "limited, however, to the total difference in the market value before and after the work was performed".

It appears that this precise question has not heretofore been presented to this court. In Ardizonne v. Archer, 72 Okl. 70, 178 P. 263, this court held that the measure of damages for breach of a contract to drill an oil well was the reasonable cost of drilling the well, but here a slightly different factual situation exists. The drilling of an oil well will yield valuable geological information, even if no oil or gas is found, and of course if the well is a producer, the value of the premises increases. In the case before us, it is argued by defendant with some force that the performance of the remedial work defendant agreed to do will add at the most only a few hundred dollars to the value of plaintiffs' farm, and that the damages should be limited to that amount because that is all plaintiffs have lost.

Plaintiffs rely on Groves v. John Wunder Co., 205 Minn. 163, 286 N.W. 235, 123 A.L.R. 502. In that case, the Minnesota court, in a substantially similar situation, adopted the "cost of performance" rule as opposed to the "value" rule. The result was to authorize a jury to give plaintiff damages in the amount of $60,000, where the real estate concerned would have been worth only $12,160, even if the work contracted for had been done.

It may be observed that Groves v. John Wunder Co., supra, is the only case which has come to our attention in which the cost of performance rule has been followed under circumstances where the cost of performance greatly exceeded the diminution in value resulting from the breach of contract. Incidentally, it appears that this case was decided by a plurality rather than a majority of the members of the court.

Defendant relies principally upon Sandy Valley & E.R. Co. v. Hughes, 175 Ky. 320, 194 S.W. 344; Bigham v. Wabash-Pittsburg Terminal Ry. Co., 223 Pa. 106, 72 A. 318; and Sweeney v. Lewis Const. Co., 66 Wash. 490, 119 P. 1108. These were all cases in which, under similar circumstances, the appellate courts followed the "value" rule instead of the "cost of performance" rule. Plaintiff points out that in the earliest of these cases (Bigham) the court cites as authority on the measure of damages an earlier Pennsylvania *tort* case, and that the other two cases follow the first, with no explanation as to why a measure of damages ordinarily followed in cases sounding in tort should be used in contract cases. Nevertheless, it is of some significance that three out of four appellate courts have followed the diminution in value rule under circumstances where, as here, the cost of performance greatly exceeds the diminution in value.

The explanation may be found in the fact that the situations presented are artificial ones. It is highly unlikely that the ordinary property owner would agree to pay $29,000 (or its equivalent) for the construction of "improvements" upon his property that would increase its value only about ($300) three hundred dollars. The result is that we are called upon to apply principles of law theoretically based upon reason and reality to a situation which is basically unreasonable and unrealistic.

In Groves v. John Wunder Co., supra, in arriving at its conclusions, the Minnesota court apparently considered the contract involved to be analogous to a building and construction contract, and cited authority for the proposition that the cost of performance or completion of the building as contracted is ordinarily the measure of damages in actions for damages for the breach of such a contract.

In an annotation following the Minnesota case beginning at 123 A.L.R. 515, the annotator places the three cases relied on by defendant (Sandy Valley, Bigham and Sweeney) under the classification of cases involving "grading and excavation contracts".

We do not think either analogy is strictly applicable to the case now before us. The primary purpose of the lease contract between plaintiffs and defendant was neither "building and construction" nor "grading and excavation". It was merely to accomplish the economical recovery and marketing of coal from the premises, to the profit of all parties. The special provisions of the lease contract pertaining to remedial work were incidental to the main object involved.

Even in the case of contracts that are unquestionably building and construction contracts, the authorities are not in agreement as to the factors to be considered in determining whether the cost of performance rule or the value rule should be applied. The American Law Institute's Restatement of the Law, Contracts, Volume 1, Sections 346(1)(a)(i) and (ii) submits the proposition that the cost of performance is the proper measure of damages "if this is possible and does not involve *unreasonable economic waste*"; and that the diminution in value caused by the breach is the proper measure "if construction and completion in accordance with the contract would involve *unreasonable economic waste*". (Emphasis supplied.) In an explanatory comment immediately following the text, the Restatement makes it clear that the "economic waste" referred to consists of the destruction of a substantially completed building or other structure. Of course no such destruction is involved in the case now before us.

On the other hand, in McCormick, Damages, Section 168, it is said with regard to building and construction contracts that ". . . in cases where the defect is one that can be repaired or cured without *undue expense* "the cost of performance is the proper measure of damages, but where" . . . the defect in material or construction is one that cannot be remedied without *an expenditure for reconstruction disproportionate to the end to be attained* "(emphasis supplied) the value rule should be followed. The same idea was expressed in Jacob & Youngs, Inc. v. Kent, 230 N.Y. 239, 129 N.E. 889, 23 A.L.R. 1429, as follows:

"The owner is entitled to the money which will permit him to complete, unless the cost of completion is grossly and unfairly out of proportion to the good to be attained. When that is true, the measure is the difference in value."

It thus appears that the prime consideration in the Restatement was "economic waste"; and that the prime consideration in McCormick, Damages, and in Jacob & Youngs, Inc. v. Kent, supra, was the relationship between the expense involved and the "end to be attained"—in other words, the "relative economic benefit".

In view of the unrealistic fact situation in the instant case, and certain Oklahoma statutes to be hereinafter noted, we are of the opinion that the "relative economic benefit" is a proper consideration here. This is in accord with the recent case of Mann v. Clowser, 190 Va. 887, 59 S.E.2d 78, where, in applying the cost rule, the Virginia court specifically noted that " . . . the defects are remediable from a practical standpoint and the costs *are not grossly disproportionate to the results to be obtained*" (Emphasis supplied).

23 O.S.1961 §§ 96 and 97 provide as follows:

"§ 96. . . . Notwithstanding the provisions of this chapter, no person can recover a greater amount in damages for the breach of an obligation, than he would have gained by the full performance thereof on both sides. . . .

"§ 97. . . . Damages must, in all cases, be reasonable, and where an obligation of any kind appears to create a right to unconscionable and grossly oppressive damages, contrary to substantial justice no more than reasonable damages can be recovered."

Although it is true that the above sections of the statute are applied most often in tort cases, they are by their own terms, and the decisions of this court, also applicable in actions for damages for breach of contract. It would seem that they are peculiarly applicable here where, under the "cost of performance" rule, plaintiffs might recover an amount about nine times the total value of their farm. Such would seem to be "unconscionable and grossly oppressive damages, contrary to substantial justice" within the meaning of the statute. Also, it can hardly be denied that if plaintiffs here are permitted to recover under the "cost of performance" rule, they will receive a greater benefit from the breach than could be gained from full performance, contrary to the provisions of Sec. 96.

An analogy may be drawn between the cited sections, and the provisions of 15 O.S.1961 §§ 214 and 215. These sections tend to render void any provisions of a contract which attempt to fix the amount of stipulated damages to be paid in case of a breach, except where it is impracticable or extremely difficult to determine the actual damages. This results in spite of the agreement of the parties, and the obvious and well known rationale is that insofar as they exceed the actual damages suffered, the stipulated damages amount to a penalty or forfeiture which the law does not favor.

23 O.S.1961 §§ 96 and 97 have the same effect in the case now before us. *In spite of the agreement of the parties,* these sections limit the damages recoverable to a reasonable amount not "contrary to substantial justice"; they prevent plaintiffs from recovering a "greater amount in damages for the breach of an obligation" than they would have "gained by the full performance thereof".

We therefore hold that where, in a coal mining lease, lessee agrees to perform certain remedial work on the premises concerned at the end of the lease period, and thereafter the contract is fully performed by both parties except that the remedial work is not done, the measure of damages in an action by lessor against lessee for damages for breach of contract is ordinarily the reasonable cost of performance of the work; however, where the contract provision breached was merely incidental to the main purpose in view, and where the economic benefit which would result to lessor by full performance of the work is grossly disproportionate to the cost of performance, the damages which lessor may recover are limited to the diminution in value resulting to the premises because of the non-performance.

We believe the above holding is in conformity with the intention of the Legislature as expressed in the statutes mentioned, and in harmony with the better-reasoned cases from the other jurisdictions where analogous fact situations have been considered. It should be noted that the rule as stated does not interfere with the property owner's right to "do what he will with his own" (Chamberlain v. Parker, 45 N.Y. 569), or his right, if he chooses, to contract for "improvements" which will actually have the effect of reducing his property's value. Where such result is in fact contemplated by the parties, and is a main or principal purpose of those contracting, it would seem that the measure of damages for breach would ordinarily be the cost of performance.

The above holding disposes of all of the arguments raised by the parties on appeal.

Under the most liberal view of the evidence herein, the diminution in value resulting to the premises because of nonperformance of the remedial work was $300.00. After a careful search of the record, we have found no evidence of a higher figure, and plaintiffs do not argue in their briefs that a greater diminution in value was sustained. It thus appears that the judgment was clearly excessive, and that the amount for which judgment should have been rendered is definitely and satisfactorily shown by the record.

We are asked by each party to modify the judgment in accordance with the respective theories advanced, and it is conceded that we have authority to do so. 12 O.S.1961 § 952; Busboom v. Smith, 199 Okl. 688, 191 P.2d 198; Stumpf v. Stumpf, 173 Okl. 1, 46 P.2d 315.

We are of the opinion that the judgment of the trial court for plaintiffs should be, and it is hereby, modified and reduced to the sum of $300.00, and as so modified it is affirmed.

WELCH, DAVISON, HALLEY, and JOHNSON, JJ., concur.

WILLIAMS, C.J., BLACKBIRD, V.C.J., and IRWIN and BERRY, JJ., dissent.

IRWIN, JUSTICE (dissenting).

By the specific provisions in the coal mining lease under consideration, the defendant agreed as follows:

"... 7b Lessee agrees to make fills in the pits dug on said premises on the property line in such manner that fences can be placed thereon and access had to opposite sides of the pits.

"[7]c Lessee agrees to smooth off the top of the spoil banks on the above premises.

"7d Lessee agrees to leave the creek crossing the above premises in such a condition that it will not interfere with the crossings to be made in pits as set out in 7b.

. . .

"7f Lessee further agrees to leave no shale or dirt on the high wall of said pits. . . . "

Following the expiration of the lease, plaintiffs made demand upon defendant that it carry out the provisions of the contract and to perform those covenants contained therein.

Defendant admits that it failed to perform its obligations that it agreed and contracted to perform under the lease contract and there is nothing in the record which indicates that defendant could not perform its obligations. Therefore, in my opinion defendant's breach of the contract was wilful and not in good faith.

Although the contract speaks for itself, there were several negotiations between the plaintiffs and defendant before the contract was executed. Defendant admitted in the trial of the action, that plaintiffs insisted that the above provisions be included in the contract and that they would not agree to the coal mining lease unless the above provisions were included.

In consideration for the lease contract, plaintiffs were to receive a certain amount as royalty for the coal produced and marketed and in addition thereto their land was to be restored as provided in the contract.

Defendant received as consideration for the contract, its proportionate share of the coal produced and marketed and in addition thereto, the *right to use* plaintiffs' land in the furtherance of its mining operations.

The cost for performing the contract in question could have been reasonably approximated when the contract was negotiated and executed and there are no conditions now existing which could not have been reasonably anticipated by the parties. Therefore, defendant had knowledge, when it prevailed upon the plaintiffs to execute the lease, that the cost of performance might be disproportionate to the value or benefits received by plaintiff for the performance.

Defendant has received its benefits under the contract and now urges, in substance, that plaintiffs' measure of damages for its failure to perform should be the economic value of performance to the plaintiffs and not the cost of performance.

If a peculiar set of facts should exist where the above rule should be applied as the proper measure of damages, (and in my judgment those facts do not exist in the instant case) before such rule should be applied, consideration should be given to the benefits received or contracted for by the party who asserts the application of the rule.

Defendant did not have the right to mine plaintiffs' coal or to use plaintiffs' property for its mining operations without the consent of plaintiffs. Defendant had knowledge of the benefits that it would receive under the contract and the approximate cost of performing the contract. With this knowledge, it must be presumed that defendant thought that it would be to its economic advantage to enter into the contract with plaintiffs and that it would reap benefits from the contract, or it would have not entered into the contract.

Therefore, if the value of the performance of a contract should be considered in determining the measure of damages for breach of a contract, the value of the benefits received under the contract by a party who breaches a contract should also be considered. However, in my judgment, to give consideration to either in the instant action, completely rescinds and holds for naught the solemnity of the contract before us and makes an entirely new contract for the parties. . . .

In Great Western Oil & Gas Company v. Mitchell, Okl., 326 P.2d 794, we held:

> "The law will not make a better contract for parties than they themselves have seen fit to enter into, or alter it for the benefit of one party and to the detriment of the others; the judicial function of a court of law is to enforce a contract as it is written."

I am mindful of Title 23 O.S.1961 § 96, which provides that no person can recover a greater amount in damages for the breach of an obligation than he could have gained by the full performance thereof on both sides, except in cases not applicable herein. However, in my judgment, the above statutory provision is not applicable here.

In my judgment, we should follow the case of Groves v. John Wunder Company, 205 Minn. 163, 286 N.W. 235, 123 A.L.R. 502, which defendant agrees "that the fact situation is apparently similar to the one in the case at bar", and where the Supreme Court of Minnesota held:

> "The owner's or employer's damages for such a breach (i.e. breach hypothesized in 2d syllabus) are to be measured, not in respect to the value of the land to be improved, but by the reasonable cost of doing that which the contractor promised to do and which he left undone."

The hypothesized breach referred to states that where the contractor's breach of a contract is wilful, that is in bad faith, he is not entitled to any benefit of the equitable doctrine of substantial performance.

In the instant action defendant has made no attempt to even substantially perform. The contract in question is not immoral, is not tainted with fraud, and was not entered into through mistake or accident and is not contrary to public policy. It is clear and unambiguous and the parties understood the terms thereof, and the approximate cost of fulfilling the obligations could have been approximately ascertained. There are no conditions existing now which could not have been reasonably anticipated when the contract was negotiated and executed. The defendant could have performed the contract if it desired. It has accepted and reaped the benefits of its contract and now urges that plaintiffs' benefits under the contract be denied. If plaintiffs' benefits are denied, such benefits would inure to the direct benefit of the defendant.

Therefore, in my opinion, the plaintiffs were entitled to specific performance of the contract and since defendant has failed to perform, the proper measure of damages should be the cost of performance. Any other measure of damage would be holding for naught the express provisions of the contract; would be taking from the plaintiffs the benefits of the contract and placing those benefits in defendant which has failed to perform its obligations; would be granting benefits to defendant without a resulting obligation; and would be completely rescinding the solemn obligation of the contract for the benefit of the defendant to the detriment of the plaintiffs by making an entirely new contract for the parties.

I therefore respectfully dissent to the opinion promulgated by a majority of my associates.

———

NOTE

In a petition for rehearing, plaintiffs argued that the trial court had wrongfully excluded evidence that the diminution in the value of their farm was greater than $300, because the farm consisted not merely of the 60 acres covered by the coal-mining lease, but other lands as well. The court held, 5–4, that the evidence was properly excluded because the complaint related only to the 60 acres covered by the lease and the case had been tried and argued by plaintiffs on a cost-of-completion theory rather than a diminished-value theory.

———

RESTATEMENT, SECOND, OF CONTRACTS § 348(2)

[See Selected Source Materials Supplement]

———

NOTE ON POSSIBLE ADDITIONAL FACTS IN PEEVYHOUSE

1. The following excerpt from defendant's brief in *Peevyhouse* (as brought out by Professor Richard Danzig in unpublished materials) proposes an explanation why Garland, the defendant-appellee, did not perform the remedial work:

> A review of the testimony of the witness, G.B. Cumpton, will indicate that the defendant, at time of execution of the contract, had [a] good faith intention of complying with all of the terms; but, after partial performance, it became apparent that the amount of coal under the leased property was limited; and the operations were not extended far enough toward the southeastward to permit economic compliance with the terms of the lease requiring remedial work.

> Attention of the court is specifically invited to the following excerpt from the testimony of Mr. Cumpton: . . .

>> "Q. Now then, you were asked also by Mr. McConnell if when you executed this lease you intended to comply with the provisions for installing a fence. And I will ask you if you had been able economically to mine further coal toward the southeast, would you have been able to establish that fence on the spoil bank?

>> "A. Yes, we could have.

>> "Q. Having stopped when you ran out of coal down in here, can you now establish that fence line without putting in a very useless and expensive fill?

>> "A. No. . . . "

> From all the testimony of Mr. Cumpton and the engineer, Curry, it is obvious that the Appellee, at the inception of the contract, intended to comply with the terms; but, after it became economically impossible to complete performance of mining operations across the entire tract of land, construction of dikes for erection of fences became impracticable. Appellee went as far with performance of the remedial work as could reasonably be expected under the circumstances, without futile expenditure of money which would accomplish no constructive purpose.

> It is respectfully submitted that Appellee did not willfully, or in bad faith, enter into a contract which it did not intend to perform.

2. In Peevyhouse v. Garland Coal & Mining Co. Revisited: The Ballad of Willie and Lucille, 89 Nw.U.L.Rev. 1341 (1995), Professor Judith Maute reports that the Peevyhouses were reluctant to allow mining on their land, while Garland needed immediate access to the land to divert a creek from a neighboring piece of land that it was already mining. Thus the Peevyhouses had a relatively strong bargaining position. What they negotiated for was Garland's promise to do the restorative work on their land. The standard strip-

mining leases in the area did not contain provisions for restorative work. Instead, lessors typically received an up-front per-acre payment to compensate them for the damage that would be done to their land in the course of the mining. This amount would usually equal the total value of the land before mining began. The Peevyhouses were aware of this standard provision, and they had seen the damage done to their neighbors' land over the years. The Peevyhouses gave up the standard advance payment for surface damage, which in their case would have been $3,000, in return for Garland's promise to do the restorative work on their land.

Maute also questions Garland's claim, *supra,* that because the coal on the Peevyhouses' land was less accessible than Garland expected, the promised restoration was much more costly to implement than Garland expected.

H.P. Droher & Sons v. Toushin

250 Minn. 490, 85 N.W.2d 273 (1957)

This case was decided by the Minnesota court, which also decided Groves v. John Wunder Co., discussed in *Peevyhouse.* Droher agreed to build a house for the Toushins for an adjusted price of just under $44,000. When the house was completed, a steel post in the basement, which supported a beam on which the floor joists rested, was too low. As a result, the level of the floor, and of other parts of the house, sagged noticeably. To correct this defect it would have been necessary to jack up the beam. If that were done the plaster would crack and parts of the house would have to be rebuilt, so that the cost of repair would exceed $20,000. The diminution in the value of the house resulting from the defect was apparently much less than $20,000. Held, the diminished-value rule should be applied:

> . . . [The decision in Groves v. John Wunder Co.] was by a divided court, three members of the court concurring in the opinion, two dissenting, and two taking no part. The majority opinion is based, at least in part, on the fact that the breach of the contract was wilful and in bad faith. . . .

> It would seem that the better rule and the one followed by a majority of the courts is that, where there is a substantial good-faith effort to perform the contract but there are defects of such a nature that the contract has not been performed according to its terms, which defects can be remedied without the destruction of a substantial part of the building, the owner is entitled to recover the cost of making the work conform to the contract but, where it appears that the cost of remedying the defects is grossly disproportionate to the benefits to be derived therefrom, the owner is entitled to recover the difference between the value of the property as it would have been if the contract had been performed according to its terms and the value in its condition as constructed. Cases such as we have here,

where the evidence establishes a substantial good-faith performance, are to be distinguished from those where there has been a wilful failure to perform at all, such as we had in Groves v. John Wunder Co. . . .

Eastern Steamship Lines, Inc. v. United States

125 Ct.Cl. 422, 112 F.Supp. 167 (1953)

During World War II, The United States Government chartered the steamship *Acadia* as a troop transport. The charter provided:

> Clause 7. . . . Before redelivery, the Charterer [that is, the Government], at its own expense, and on its time, shall restore the Vessel to at least as good condition and class as upon delivery, ordinary wear and tear excepted, and do all work and make all repairs necessary to satisfy any outstanding classification or steamboat inspection requirements necessary to place her in such condition and class. . . . [provided] that at the Charterer's option, redelivery of the Vessel to the Owner may be made prior to satisfying such requirements or prior to completion of such repairs or work, in which event the Charterer shall pay to the Owner the amount reasonably expended to place the Vessel in such class and condition. . . .

After the war, the owner sued the government for $4,000,000, which the owner claimed to be due under Clause 7 as the estimated cost of restoring the *Acadia* to its pre-war condition. The Government claimed that it was not bound to pay more than $2,000,000, the estimated value of the ship after restoration. The court rejected the owner's claim:

> [We will assume, based on the evidence] that after some $4,000,000 had been spent in restoring the ship, it would be worth $2,000,000. . . .
>
> . . . According to the plaintiff's interpretation [of the charter] the Government has now become obligated to pay it $4,000,000. Candor compels the plaintiff to say that it will not feel obliged to spend the $4,000,000 when it gets it, to restore the *Acadia*. Common sense and reality tell us that it will not so spend the money, since after the expenditures it would have only a $2,000,000 ship. The result would be that the Government would pay out $2,000,000 more than the plaintiff had lost by the Government's chartering and use of its ship. The extra $2,000,000 would not be a subsidy to get ships built or sailing. The *Acadia* would still rust at anchor. We decline to . . . produce such a result.
>
> . . . We think that neither party anticipated what actually happened, *viz.* that the market for old ships on the one hand, and the

market for labor and materials, on the other, would be such as to make the restoration of old ships a useless and wasteful expenditure of public funds. . . .

The plaintiff has urged that, regardless of the waste of public money that would be entailed by compelling the Government to pay $4,000,000 when the plaintiff's loss is $2,000,000 the weight of authority is that what is "nominated in the bond" will be compelled, regardless of economic waste. We think that is not the law. . . .

. . . The case will be assigned to a commissioner of this court for trial upon the question of the value of the *Acadia*.

City School District of the City of Elmira v. McLane Construction Co.

85 A.D.2d 749, 445 N.Y.S.2d 258 (1981)

In 1976, the Elmira school district contracted with McLane Construction Company for the construction of a swimming-pool building, which was to feature a roof consisting of natural-wood decking supported by laminated-wood beams. The appearance of the beams was central to the aesthetics of the architectural scheme, which contrasted the natural beauty of the beams with the relatively stark unfinished concrete that comprised the balance of the structure. Even the effectiveness of the indirect lighting system employed in the building depended on the appearance of beams. Because the building was to be a showplace and the site of large regional swimming competitions, the design was intentionally dramatic. It was contemplated that the beams, properly treated, would be essentially maintenance-free. However, Weyerhauser Company, which supplied the beams, and was aware of the school district's plans and specifications, used a method of treating the beams that it knew would result in staining and discoloration, and the beams became permanently discolored.

The school district sued Weyerhauser and recovered a verdict of $357,000, based on the cost of replacing the beams. On appeal, Weyerhauser argued that damages should have been limited to $3,000, the difference between the value of the structure as built and its value if the beams had been as agreed upon. Held, for the school district.

"[W]here the contractor's performance has been incomplete or defective, the usual measure of damages is the reasonable cost of replacement or completion (*American Std. v. Schectman*, 80 A.D.2d 318, 321, 439 N.Y.S.2d 529). That rule does not apply if the contractor performs in good faith but defects nevertheless exist and remedying them could entail economic waste. Then, diminution in value becomes the proper measure of damages. A classic illustration of when the general rule is abandoned in favor of this exception is *Jacob & Youngs v. Kent*, 230 N.Y. 239, 129 N.E. 889, where the contractor did not use the brand of pipe specified in the contract, but other brands of like quality. Inasmuch as the cost of replacing the pipe was grievously out of proportion to any damages actually suffered by the house owner, the proper award was the nominal difference in value of the house with and without the specified brand of pipe.

"But Weyerhaeuser does not come within this exception, for here the defect, in relation to the entire project, was not of inappreciable importance. One of the school district's principal objectives was to have an aesthetically prepossessing structure, and that goal has by all accounts been frustrated. Moreover, as the facts already recited indicate, Weyerhaeuser's conduct cannot be said to be innocent oversight or inattention. . . ."

———

Advanced, Inc. v. Wilks

711 P.2d 524 (Alaska 1985)

(Rabinowitz, C.J.) "An owner's recovery is not necessarily limited to diminution in value whenever that figure is less than the cost of repair. It is true that in a case where the cost of repair exceeds the damages under the value formula, an award under the cost of repair measure may place the owner in a better economic position than if the contract had been fully performed, since he could pocket the award and then sell the defective structure. On the other hand, it is possible that the owner will use the damage award for its intended purpose and turn the structure into the one originally envisioned. He may do this for a number of reasons, including personal esthetics or a hope for increased value in the future. If he does this his economic position will equal the one he would have been in had the contractor fully performed. The fact finder is the one in the best position to determine whether the owner will actually complete performance, or whether he is only interested in obtaining the best immediate economic position he can. In some cases, such as where the property is held solely for investment, the court may conclude as a matter of law that the damage award can not exceed the diminution in value. Where, however, the property has special significance to the owner and repair seems likely, the cost of repair may be appropriate even if it exceeds the diminution in value."

———

NOTE ON DAMAGES WHEN THE PLAINTIFF COMPLETES WORK OR REPAIRS A DEFECT

When the plaintiff pays to complete work not finished by the defendant courts routinely award the cost of completion without questioning the reasonableness of the plaintiff's decision to complete the work. See, e.g., Kirkpatrick v. Temme, 654 P.2d 1011 (Nev. 1982) (awarding $84,333.73 spent to complete construction where contract price was $175,000 despite defendant's testimony that the work was 80% compete and that he could have finished for $39,200, when the owner and the architect testified that the original plans and specifications were followed). While there is less authority for the point, the same seems to be true when the plaintiff repairs defective work. See, e.g., Hi-Valley Constructors, Inc. v. Heyser, 428 P.2d 354 (Colo. 1967) (awarding cost of repainting exterior of home). If the plaintiff does additional work, then only the amount the plaintiff would have paid for the original work, or to repair the defect, is recovered. See, e.g., Martin v. Phillips, 440 A.2d 1124 (N.H. 1982). Alternatively, the enhanced value from the additional work may be subtracted. State Prop. & Bldg. Comm'n v. H.W. Miller Constr. Co., 385 S.W.2d 211 (Ky. 1964).

(B) SALES OF GOODS

NOTE ON DAMAGES FOR THE SELLER'S BREACH OF A CONTRACT FOR THE SALE OF GOODS

The remedies for breach of a contract for the sale of goods are governed by the Uniform Commercial Code. A buyer's remedies for breach by the seller fall into two broad categories—specific relief (in which the buyer is awarded the actual goods) and damages. Specific relief will be covered in Chapter 6, *infra.*

The buyer's damage remedies, in turn, fall into several subcategories. One subcategory consists of the buyer's remedies when the seller fails to deliver or the buyer properly rejects the goods or rightfully revokes his acceptance (UCC §§ 2–712, 2–713). A second subcategory consists of the buyer's remedies when the buyer has accepted the goods, and cannot or does not want to rightfully revoke his acceptance, but the goods are defective (UCC § 2–714). Typically, such an action is for breach of warranty.

UCC §§ 2–711(1), 2–712, 2–713, 2–714, 2–715(1), 2–723, 2–724

[See Selected Source Materials Supplement]

CISG ARTS. 45, 49, 50, 74, 75, 76

[See Selected Source Materials Supplement]

Continental Sand & Gravel, Inc. v. K & K Sand & Gravel, Inc.

755 F.2d 87 (7th Cir.1985)

Defendant sold the land and assets of a sand and gravel pit to plaintiff for a total price of $650,000. The sale included certain mobile equipment (front-loaders, cranes, and so forth). The contract allocated $50,000 of the total price to the equipment. Defendant made various express warranties concerning the equipment. The warranties were breached, and plaintiff sued for damages. The trial court awarded $104,206.75, the cost of repairs to bring the equipment up to the warranted condition. Affirmed.

(Cudahy, J.) "Defendants argue that, since the clear bargain of the parties was to sell and purchase the mobile equipment for $50,000, the plaintiff is only entitled to receive an amount of damages that represents the diminution in value from the purchase price as the result of the breach of warranty. In other words, defendants contend that the maximum amount of recoverable damages is the difference between the fair market value of the equipment as accepted, which they define as $50,000, and the fair market value of the equipment in the defective condition. Under this method of computing damages, Continental would be entitled to recover no more than the $50,000 purchase price, and as little as nothing, depending on the court's assessment of the value of the equipment in the defective condition. . . .

"The court below rejected this argument, and instead applied section 2–714 (2) of the Illinois Uniform Commercial Code, . . . which provides that damages generally should represent the difference between the value of the goods at the time of acceptance and the value they would have had if they had been as warranted. The court stated that under this section the cost of repair is the proper standard. This was the correct approach under Illinois law, as well as under the general commercial law. . . . As the district court noted, it is not unusual for damages in a breach of warranty case to exceed the purchase price of the goods. . . . This result is logical, since to limit recoverable damages by the purchase price, as defendants suggest, would clearly deprive the purchaser of the benefit of its bargain in cases in which the value of the goods as warranted exceeds that price. Thus we find that the district court properly computed the damages recoverable for the defendants' breach of the warranties."

Manouchehri v. Heim

123 N.M. 439, 941 P.2d 978 (N.M. Ct. App. 1997)

"Although [U.C.C. §] 2–714 (2) sets the measure of direct damages for breach of warranty as the difference between the value of the goods as warranted and the value of the goods as accepted, often that difference can be approximated by the cost to repair the goods so that they conform to the warranty. For example, if it costs $200 to fix [a] machine so that it performed as [warranted,] then one could assume that the unrepaired machine (the 'goods accepted') was worth $200 less than the repaired machine (the goods 'as warranted'). Thus, the cost of repair is commonly awarded as the direct damages."

EGERER V. CSR WEST, LLC

Court of Appeals of Washington, 2003.
116 Wash.App. 645, 67 P.3d 1128.

BECKER, C.J.

Appellant CSR West breached a contract to supply fill for land development. Issues on appeal include the calculation of damages based on "hypothetical cover". . . . We affirm in all respects.

According to unchallenged findings of fact entered after a bench trial, Robert Egerer owned a 10 acre parcel of land in Skagit County that he planned to develop into commercial property. The property required a considerable amount of fill to make it suitable for development.

Egerer first purchased fill material in 1995, when he contracted at the rate of $1.10 per cubic yard to have Wilder Construction haul to his property some material being excavated from the shoulders of Interstate 5 as a part of a highway improvement project. In its suitability to serve as structural fill, the shoulder material resembled a gravel known as "pit run", but it was cheaper than pit run because it contained asphalt grindings.

Beyond what Wilder Construction could supply, Egerer needed roughly 17,000 cubic yards of fill material. In May 1997, Egerer learned that CSR West had contracted with the Washington State Department of Transportation to excavate material from the shoulder areas of Interstate 5 near Lake Samish. He met with John Grisham, CSR's sales manager, and they reached an agreement to have CSR transport "all" the shoulder excavations from the project to Egerer's site at the rate of $.50 per cubic yard.

CSR brought fill material to Egerer's property on only two nights: July 9 and 10, 1997. Shortly thereafter, the Department of Transportation issued a change order that allowed CSR to use the excavated shoulder material in the reconstruction of the shoulder area. It was more profitable for CSR to supply the material for the State's use than to fulfill its contract with Egerer. CSR excavated a total of 16,750 cubic yards of material during its work on the shoulder project in 1997, and supplied virtually all of it to the Department of Transportation.

Egerer did not purchase replacement fill at the time of the breach in July 1997. Asked about this at trial, he explained that it would have been too expensive, and he also did not think there was time to find replacement fill and get it onto his property before the end of the summer. Egerer said that his window of opportunity to place fill on the property was June through September, before the weather became too wet. In January and February 1998, he obtained price quotes for pit run ranging from $8.25 per cubic yard to $9.00 per cubic yard. These prices exceeded Egerer's budget, and he did not contract for replacement fill at that time either.

In the summer of 1999, Egerer learned of an unexpected landslide at a gravel pit not far from his property. The company agreed to sell Egerer the unwanted slide material at a cost of $6.39 per cubic yard, including the cost of hauling and spreading.

Egerer filed suit in November 2000, alleging that CSR breached its contract by failing to deliver all the excavated shoulder material in the summer of 1997. After a bench trial, the court found breach. The court then turned to the Uniform Commercial Code to determine the measure of damages. CSR raises several legal issues with respect to the award of damages. . . .

Where a seller fails to make delivery of goods sold to a buyer, the buyer has two alternative remedies under the Uniform Commercial Code. One is the remedy of "cover": the buyer may purchase substitute goods and recover as damages the difference between the cost of this cover and the contract price, provided the buyer covers in good faith and without unreasonable delay. U.C.C. § 2–712.* The other, a complete alternative, is damages for non-delivery, also known as "hypothetical cover"[1]: the buyer may recover as damages from the seller "the difference between the market price at the time when the buyer learned of the breach and the contract price". U.C.C. § 2–713. This measure applies only when and to the extent that the buyer does not cover. Uniform Commercial Code Comment 5, § 2–713. "The general baseline adopted in this section uses as a yardstick the market in which the buyer would have obtained cover had he sought that relief." U.C.C. Comment 1, § 2–713. "The market or current price to be used in comparison with the contract price under this section is the price for goods of the same kind and in the same branch of trade." U.C.C. Comment 2, § 2–713.

The court determined that Egerer was limited to damages for non-delivery under section 2–713: "Mr. Egerer is limited to damages reflecting the difference between CSR contract price and the price he could have obtained replacement material for at the time of the breach in 1997. *See* U.C.C. § 2–713(1) and Comment 3." The court found that Egerer could have obtained replacement material at the time of the breach for a cost of $8.25 per cubic yard—a price quoted to Egerer in early 1998. The court calculated his damages for the non-delivery of fill to be $129,812.50, which was the

---

* For simplicity, citations to the UCC have been inserted in place of citations to the counterpart sections of the Washington UCC. (Footnote by edsed.)

[1] *Allied Canners & Packers, Inc. v. Victor Packing Co.,* 162 Cal.App.3d 905, 911–12, 209 Cal.Rptr. 60, 61 (1984).

** The more conventional name for the damages that the court refers to as "hypothetical cover" is "market-price damages." (Footnote by edsed.)

difference between the market price of $8.25 per cubic yard and the contract price of $.50 per cubic yard.

CSR accepts the trial court's decision to apply the remedy furnished by section 2–713, but contends the court erred by calculating damages based on a market price of $8.25 per cubic yard for pit run. CSR argues that $8.25 was not "the price for goods of the same kind" (as U.C.C. Comment 2 calls for) because pit run is a product superior to shoulder excavations containing asphalt grindings. CSR further argues that $8.25 was not "the market price at the time when the buyer learned of the breach" (as section 2–713 calls for) because the breach was in July 1997 and the $8.25 price was as of six months later—in January, 1998. CSR takes the position that the trial court should instead have used the $1.10 per cubic yard price reflected in Egerer's 1995 contract with Wilder Construction, because that was the only evidence in the record of a price for shoulder excavations. Use of the much higher price for pit run resulted in a windfall for Egerer, according to CSR.

The trial court expressly relied on Comment 3 to U.C.C. 2–713 in determining that $8.25 per cubic yard was the price for which Egerer could have obtained replacement material at the time of the breach. That comment states in part, "When the current market price under this section is difficult to prove the section on determination and proof of market price is available to permit a showing of a comparable market price or, where no market price is available, evidence of spot sale prices is proper." U.C.C. Comment 3, § 2–713. The section on determination and proof of market price provides,

> If evidence of a price prevailing at the times or places described in this Article is not readily available the price prevailing within any reasonable time before or after the time described or at any other place which in commercial judgment or under usage of trade would serve as a reasonable substitute for the one described may be used, making any proper allowance for the cost of transporting the goods to or from such other place.

U.C.C. § 2–723 (2).

A court is granted a "reasonable leeway" in measuring market price under section 2–723. *Sprague v. Sumitomo Forestry Co., Ltd.,* 104 Wash.2d 751, 760, 709 P.2d 1200 (1985). Contrary to CSR's argument, a trial court may use a market price for goods different in quality from those for which the buyer contracted. That possibility is encompassed in the reference to "price ... which in commercial judgment or under usage of trade would serve as a reasonable substitute for the one described". And section 2–723 expressly permits looking to a price "prevailing within any reasonable time before or after the time described."

We conclude the trial court did not misapply the law in concluding that the January 1998 price for pit run was the relevant market price. The court found the 1998 quotes for replacement material and hauling "were reasonable and customary", and noted that CSR "did not offer evidence that suitable replacement material was available at a lower price at the time of breach." There was testimony that shoulder excavation material, though cheap when available, is rarely available. John Grisham, CSR's sales manager, acknowledged that it would have been difficult for Egerer to locate an alternative supplier of shoulder excavations in 1997 because "quantities like that are few and far between". Grisham said he was unaware of any other pit in the area that would have had similar material available at a price anywhere near $.50 per cubic yard in the summer of 1997. Egerer's eventual purchase in 1999 was possible only because of the landslide that unexpectedly deposited unwanted fill material in a local gravel pit. If Egerer had covered at the time of the breach, higher-priced pit run would have been a reasonable substitute for the shoulder excavations. . . .

Affirmed.

WE CONCUR: SCHINDLER, COX, JJ.

———

J. White & R. Summers, Uniform Commercial Code

220–21 (5th ed. 2000)

"We come now to the problem of a buyer who has covered but who seeks to ignore 2–712 and sue for a larger contract-market differential under 2–713. On first reading, it seems that he can disregard 2–712; section 2–711 tells buyers that they can 'cover' or they can recover damages for nondelivery under 2–713. Commenting on the relationship between 2–712 and 2–713, Judge Peters has argued that an aggrieved buyer who purchases goods 'in substitution' may disregard 2–712 and seek recovery under the contract-market differential of 2–713. However, this interpretation allows a buyer to learn of a breach on September 2 when the market is at $25,000, wait until September 15 to cover, when the market is at $23,000, and then sue under 2–713 for the higher damages of contract-market differential, all contrary to the general principle of 1–106 (in as good a position as if the other party had performed and no more). Moreover comment 5 to 2–713 indicates that a buyer who has covered may not use 2–713:

> The present section provides a remedy which is *completely alternative* to cover under the preceding section and applies only *when and to the extent that the buyer has not covered.* (Emphasis added.)

> If the Code's goal is to put the buyer in the same position as though there had been no breach, and if 2–712 will accomplish that

goal but 2–713 will do so only by coincidence, why not force the covering buyer to use 2–712? There is no room for punitive damages here. . . . Notwithstanding Judge Peters' arguments concerning the statutory history . . . both the message of Comment 5 to 2–713 and the policy of the Code properly deny the covering buyer any use of 2–713. . . . Of course, whether purchases following seller's breach are cover purchases may be a disputed question of fact. If the facts at trial show cover, 2–712 applies. If the facts do not show cover, 2–713 applies.

SECTION 2. BREACH OF A CONTRACT TO PAY MONEY FOR A SERVICE OR GOOD

This Section considers the basic rules that define the damages recovered by a seller of a service or good when the purchaser breaches. When the plaintiff has fully performed he is entitled to the contract price as damages, plus interest when there is a statute providing pre-judgment interest. When the plaintiff has not fully performed damages generally are the unpaid balance of the contract price minus the cost avoided by the plaintiff as a result of not completing performance. Profit made by the plaintiff in another transaction may also be subtracted, if the plaintiff would not have made the profit but for the breach.

(A) SERVICE CONTRACTS

KEARSARGE COMPUTER, INC. V. ACME STAPLE COMPANY, INC.
Supreme Court of New Hampshire, 1976.
116 N.H. 705, 366 A.2d 467.

Opinion

KENISON, CHIEF JUSTICE.

This appeal results from cross actions by Kearsarge Computer, Inc., against Acme Staple Company, Inc., and by Acme against Kearsarge. Both actions relate to a certain data processing contract between the parties. Kearsarge sought payment for goods and services sold and delivered and damages for breach of contract. Acme also sued for breach of contract and alleged that, following termination of the contract, Kearsarge retained certain property owned by Acme. The cases were consolidated for a hearing on the merits before Master Earl J. Dearborn, Esquire, who held in favor of Kearsarge on all ultimate issues in both cases and awarded Kearsarge

$12,313.22, plus interest and costs. Loughlin, J., approved the master's report and reserved and transferred the defendant's exceptions.

Under a one-year contract which began June 11, 1971, Kearsarge performed electronic data processing services for Acme for twenty-five dollars per computer hour or $2,000 per month whichever was greater. At a January 7, 1972 meeting between the parties, Acme terminated the contract on the grounds that Kearsarge's performance was unsatisfactory. In a letter dated January 10, 1972, Kearsarge requested information regarding the alleged data processing errors and any losses therefrom. Acme responded that such information had been sufficiently provided at the meeting. On April 12, 1972, Kearsarge served pretrial discovery interrogatories upon Acme one of which read:

'Please state in precise detail the alleged breaches by Kearsarge of the contract between it and Acme dated April 5, 1971, which resulted in Acme's alleged termination of said contract on January 7, 1972, giving the date of each alleged breach.'

In response, Acme listed eleven incidents of alleged breach in the degree of detail requested.

At trial the master refused to permit Acme to introduce evidence of any breaches other than those listed in the answer to the interrogatory. . . . The first issue in this case is whether the master erred in excluding Acme's evidence. . . .

[The Court held the master did not err in excluding the evidence because "subjecting Kearsarge to the surprise of undisclosed evidence so late in the trial would be contrary to the purpose of pretrial discovery."]

The second issue is whether the master erred in awarding Kearsarge the full balance of the contract price. If the defendant's breach saves expense to the plaintiff, the plaintiff will recover the contract price minus the savings. McLaughlin v. Union Leader, 99 N.H. 492, 500, 116 A.2d 489, 496 (1955); Restatement of Contracts § 335 (1932); 5 A. Corbin, Contracts § 1038 (1964). The parties agree that if termination of the contract caused no savings or pecuniary advantage to Kearsarge, recovery is the full contract price.

Acme contends that Kearsarge did experience certain savings and that the master erred in not reducing the damages accordingly. However, Acme's breach did not result in substantial savings to Kearsarge. The plaintiff would not have spent significantly more on salaries, machine rental, or other overhead expenses if it continued to provide Acme with data processing services. With respect to labor costs, if a plaintiff cannot reduce his work force because of the breach, no savings result. 5 A. Corbin, supra at § 1038 at 239–40. Extensive testimony makes clear that no layoffs were possible in this case because each of Kearsarge's three employees performed separate functions. The payroll decrease subsequent to Acme's termination occurred only because the employees voluntarily accepted a drastic reduction in wages so that Kearsarge could stay in business. Such survival tactics cannot properly be classified as savings. Kearsarge's operating costs—notably the rentals on computers and other equipment— were substantially fixed. The reduction of output due to the breach did not result in savings. Id., R. Posner, Economic Analysis of the Law 59 n.7 (1972).

At the time of the breach, the only performance left on Kearsarge's part was the actual running of the data processing equipment and the delivery of the results to Acme. The cost of performance was the cost of paper, electricity and transportation of data to and from the offices of the parties. In suits for breach of contracts to sell advertising, courts hold that the costs of ink, paper and typographical composition are negligible and allow plaintiffs to recover the full contract price. Cases cited in Annot., 17 A.L.R.2d 968, 973 (1951). Similarly, the costs of performance [in this case] were trivial in relation to the contract price. Because the breach did not relieve Kearsarge of a costly burden, the master did not err in rewarding Kearsarge the full contract price. Restatement, supra at § 335, Comment b; 5 A. Corbin, supra at § 1038.

The fact that the plaintiff did not introduce evidence of the cost of paper, electricity and delivery of data does not bar recovery because the defendant has the burden of proving savings. Restatement, supra at § 335, Ill. 5. The general rule is:

> If the plaintiff's required expenditures are of cash or material, the tendency is to put the burden of allegation and proof of the amount thereof on him, but if his expenditures would be of time or labor, the burden is normally placed on the defendant. The court usually decides whether the plaintiff's performance requires an outlay of money or material from the nature of the contract, without a specific raising of the point by the parties. Annot., 17 A.L.R.2d 968, 972 (1951).

It is clear from the facts of this case that Kearsarge's performance did not require substantial cash outlays or materials as in the cases upon which the defendant relies.

After Acme terminated the contract, Kearsarge increased its efforts to secure new business. Acme's position is that at least some of the income from the new business should mitigate the damages. The general rule is that '(g)ains made by the injured party on other transactions after the breach are never to be deducted from the damages that are otherwise recoverable, unless such gains could not have been made, had there been no breach.' 5 A. Corbin, supra at § 1041; see D. Dobbs, Remedies § 3.6 at 183–84, § 12.6 at 827 (1973). In a suit for breach of a personal services contract, the wages obtained by the plaintiff-employee from a substitute job are deducted from the amount of damages if the earnings of the second income would not have been possible but for the breach. Id.; 11 Williston, Contracts § 1358 (3d ed. W. Jaeger 1968); Annot., 15 A.L.R. 751 (1921). In contrast, no deduction is allowed if the plaintiff sells to a third party a product that can be produced according to demand. The theory is that the second sale would have occurred even if the defendant did not breach his contract. See Locks v. Wade, 36 N.J.Super. 128, 114 A.2d 875 (App.Div.1955); J. Calamari & J. Perillo, Contracts § 217 (1970); 5 A. Corbin, supra at § 1041.

A contract for computer data processing services is neither a contract purely for personal services nor a contract for the sale of goods. It is an enterprise that involves a combination of personal skills and labor, materials, equipment and time. In these respects, a contract for data processing services is similar to a construction contract or a contract for the sale of advertising layouts. The law with respect to these contracts is clear. When a party refuses to allow a builder to perform, the builder's profits on contracts entered into after the breach do not mitigate the damages unless the first contract required the builder's personal services to such an extent that concurrent performance of another contract would be impossible. Olds v. Mapes-Reeves Const. Co., 177 Mass. 41, 58 N.E. 478 (1900); Sides v. Contemporary Homes, Inc., 311 S.W.2d 117 (Mo.App.1958); Restatement of Contracts § 346, Comment f on subsection (2) (1932); J. Calamari & J. Perillo, supra at § 217; Annot., 15 A.L.R. 751, 761 (1921). Likewise, when a purchaser of advertising space breaches his contract, the advertiser who is not limited by a specific number of pages recovers the full contract price. D. Dobbs, supra at § 3.6 at 183 n.2; Annot., 17 A.L.R.2d 968, 973 (1951). The reason is that, like manufacturing, these businesses are deemed to be expandable. The law presumes that they can accept a virtually unlimited amount of business so that income generated from accounts acquired after the breach does not mitigate the plaintiff's damages. 5 A. Corbin, Contracts § 1041 (1964). We hold that in the absence of evidence to the contrary a data processing contract does not involve unique personal services to such an extent that when the provider of such services seeks new business after a breach of contract, the income from such new business mitigates the damages owed to him by the breaching party. There is no evidence that Kearsarge could not render service to its new clients but for Acme's breach.

Finally, although the master found that Kearsarge's errors may have been justifiable, the contract unequivocally states that Kearsarge would be liable for its errors. Acme expended at least $837.75 in correcting mistakes in Kearsarge's work. Under the contract, Acme was entitled to this amount. Thus, Kearsarge's damages in the sum of $12,313.22 plus interest and costs shall be reduced by $837.75.

So ordered.

BOIS, J., did not sit; the others concurred.

Restatement, Second, Contracts

§ 347, Illustrations 6, 7

"6.　A contracts to build a house for B for $100,000. When it is partly built, B repudiates the contract and A stops work. A would have to spend $60,000 more to finish the house. The $60,000 cost avoided by A as a result of not having to finish the house is subtracted from the $100,000 price lost in determining A's damages. A has a right to $40,000 in damages from B, less any progress payments that he has already received.

"7.　The facts being otherwise as stated in Illustration 6, A has bought materials that are left over and that he can use for other purposes, saving him $5,000. The $5,000 cost avoided is subtracted in determining A's damages, resulting in damages of only $35,000 rather than $40,000."

Wired Music, Inc. v. Clark

26 Ill.App.2d 413, 168 N.E.2d 736 (1960)

Wired Music distributed recorded music to various locations, through direct wires rented from the telephone company. Clark executed a contract with Wired Music providing for three years of service at $24.30 per month. The contract provided that there could be no assignment without Wired Music's written consent.

After seventeen months, Clark moved his business and discontinued the service. The tenant who rented the space formerly occupied by Clark requested the right to take an assignment of Clark's contract, but Wired Music refused. Thereafter, the new tenant entered into a new contract for Wired Music's service at the same location and at a higher monthly charge. Wired Music sued Clark for its lost profits, based on the contract price to Clark minus Wired Music's costs for renting the telephone wires. Clark argued that Wired Music failed to show damages, because under the contract with the new tenant, Wired Music would realize more revenue from Clark's former location than it would have received from Clark. The trial court entered judgment for Wired Music in an amount that reflected the contract price for nineteen months minus the wire charges that Wired Music would have had to pay during that period to fulfill its contract with Clark. Affirmed.

[T]he evidence is uncontradicted that plaintiff could supply any number of additional customers without incurring further expenses except for wire rental. If defendant's contention were adopted by this court, it would have the effect of denying to the plaintiff the benefit of his bargain. This case is not at all like the situation where a plaintiff has one house to rent or one car to sell or a fixed quantity of personal property or real estate. Here, plaintiff has so far as the evidence shows, an unlimited supply of music, limited in its distributions only by the number of contracts which plaintiff can secure.

———

(B) SALES OF GOODS

———

UCC §§ 2–501(1), 2–703, 2–704(1), 2–706, 2–708, 2–709, 2–710, 2–723, 2–724

[See Selected Source Materials Supplement]

———

CISG ARTS. 61, 62, 64, 74, 75, 76

[See Selected Source Materials Supplement]

———

NOTE ON SELLER'S DAMAGES UNDER THE UCC

The damage rules in § 2–706 and § 2–708(1) generally apply when the seller has the goods on hand in limited quantity. For example, these rules apply to the sale by an owner of a used car or the sale by a farmer of a crop. Typically the seller will resell the goods to a third person and recover damages under § 2–706, and the main element of damages will be the unpaid contract price minus the resale price. The seller can also recover incidental damages, as described in § 2–710. A seller cannot recover consequential damages under the UCC. The rule in § 2–708(1) generally applies when the seller chooses not to resell the goods, or resells the goods in a transaction that does not comply with the requirements for damages based on the resale under § 2–706(1). The action for the price in § 2–709 generally applies when the seller cannot reasonably be expected to resell the goods.

The damage rule in § 2–708(2) was intended to cover several different types of cases in which the rules in §§ 2–706 and 2–708(1) would not make the seller whole. These include the lost-volume seller and the seller who does not complete production of the goods.

———

NERI V. RETAIL MARINE CORP.

Court of Appeals of New York, 1972.
30 N.Y.2d 393, 334 N.Y.S.2d 165, 285 N.E.2d 311.

GIBSON, JUDGE. The appeal concerns the right of a retail dealer to recover loss of profits and incidental damages upon the buyer's repudiation of a contract governed by the Uniform Commercial Code. This is, indeed, the correct measure of damage in an appropriate case and to this extent the code (§ 2–708, subsection [2]) effected a substantial change from prior law, whereby damages were ordinarily limited to "the difference between the contract price and the market or current price".[1] Upon the record before us, the courts below erred in declining to give effect to the new statute and so the order appealed from must be reversed.

The plaintiffs contracted to purchase from defendant a new boat of a specified model for the price of $12,587.40, against which they made a deposit of $40. They shortly increased the deposit to $4,250 in consideration of the defendant dealer's agreement to arrange with the manufacturer for immediate delivery on the basis of "a firm sale", instead of the delivery within approximately four to six weeks originally specified. Some six days after the date of the contract plaintiffs' lawyer sent to defendant a letter rescinding the sales contract for the reason that plaintiff Neri was about to undergo hospitalization and surgery, in consequence of which, according to the letter, it would be "impossible for Mr. Neri to make any payments". The boat had already been ordered from the manufacturer and was delivered to defendant at or before the time the attorney's letter was received. Defendant declined to refund plaintiffs' deposit and this action to recover it was commenced. Defendant counterclaimed, alleging plaintiffs' breach of the contract and defendant's resultant damage in the amount of $4,250, for which sum defendant demanded judgment. Upon motion, defendant had summary judgment on the issue of liability tendered by its counterclaim; and Special Term directed an assessment of damages, upon which it would be determined whether plaintiffs were entitled to the return of any portion of their down payment.

Upon the trial so directed, it was shown that the boat ordered and received by defendant in accordance with plaintiffs' contract of purchase was sold some four months later to another buyer for the same price as that negotiated with plaintiffs. From this proof the plaintiffs argue that defendant's loss on its contract was recouped, while defendant argues that but for plaintiffs' default, it would have sold two boats and have earned two profits instead of one. Defendant proved, without contradiction, that its profit on the sale under the contract in suit would have been $2,579 and that during the period the boat remained unsold incidental expenses

---

[1]   Personal Property Law, Consol.Laws, c. 41, § 145, repealed by Uniform Commercial Code, § 10–102 (L.1962, ch. 553, eff. Sept. 27, 1964); Lenobel, Inc. v. Senif, 252 App.Div. 533, 300 N.Y.S. 226.

aggregating $674 for storage, upkeep, finance charges and insurance were incurred. Additionally, defendant proved and sought to recover attorneys' fees of $1,250.

The trial court found "untenable" defendant's claim for loss of profit, inasmuch as the boat was later sold for the same price that plaintiffs had contracted to pay; found, too, that defendant had failed to prove any incidental damages; further found "that the terms of section 2–718, subsection 2(b), of the Uniform Commercial Code are applicable and same make adequate and fair provision to place the sellers in as good a position as performance would have done" and, in accordance with paragraph (b) of subsection (2) thus relied upon, awarded defendant $500 upon its counterclaim and directed that plaintiffs recover the balance of their deposit, amounting to $3,750. The ensuing judgment was affirmed, without opinion, at the Appellate Division, 37 A.D.2d 917, 326 N.Y.S.2d 984, and defendant's appeal to this court was taken by our leave.

The issue is governed in the first instance by section 2–718 of the Uniform Commercial Code which provides, among other things, that the buyer, despite his breach, may have restitution of the amount by which his payment exceeds: (a) reasonable liquidated damages stipulated by the contract or (b) absent such stipulation, 20% of the value of the buyer's total performance or $500, whichever is smaller (§ 2–718, subsection [2], pars. [a], [b]). As above noted, the trial court awarded defendant an offset in the amount of $500 under paragraph (b) and directed restitution to plaintiffs of the balance. Section 2–718, however, establishes, in paragraph (a) of subsection (3), an alternative right of offset in favor of the seller, as follows: "(3) The buyer's right to restitution under subsection (2) is subject to offset to the extent that the seller establishes (a) a right to recover damages under the provisions of this Article other than subsection (1)".

Among "the provisions of this Article other than subsection (1)" are those to be found in section 2–708, which the courts below did not apply. Subsection (1) of that section provides that "the measure of damages for non-acceptance or repudiation by the buyer is the difference between the market price at the time and place for tender and the unpaid contract price together with any incidental damages provided in this Article (Section 2–710), but less expenses saved in consequence of the buyer's breach." However, this provision is made expressly subject to subsection (2), providing: "(2) If the measure of damages provided in subsection (1) is inadequate to put the seller in as good a position as performance would have done then the measure of damages is the profit (including reasonable overhead) which the seller would have made from full performance by the buyer, together with any incidental damages provided in this Article (Section 2–710), due allowance for costs reasonably incurred and due credit for payments or proceeds of resale."

The provision of the code upon which the decision at Trial Term rested (§ 2–718, subsection [2], par. [b]) does not differ greatly from the corresponding provisions of the prior statute (Personal Property Law, § 145–a, subd. 1, par. [b]), except as the new act includes the alternative remedy of a lump sum award of $500. Neither does the present reference (in § 2–718, subsection [3], par. [a]) to the recovery of damages pursuant to other provisions of the article differ from a like reference in the prior statute (Personal Property Law, § 145–a, subd. 2, par. [a]) to an alternative measure of damages under section 145 of that act; but section 145 made no provision for recovery of lost profits as does section 2–708 (subsection [2]) of the code. The new statute is thus innovative and significant and its analysis is necessary to the determination of the issues here presented.

Prior to the code, the New York cases "applied the 'profit' test, contract price less cost of manufacture, only in cases where the seller [was] a manufacturer or an agent for a manufacturer" (1955 Report of N.Y.Law Rev.Comm., vol. 1, p. 693). Its extension to retail sales was "designed to eliminate the unfair and economically wasteful results arising under the older law when fixed price articles were involved. This section permits the recovery of lost profits in all appropriate cases, which would include all standard priced goods." (Official Comment 2, McKinney's Cons.Laws of N.Y., Book 62½, Part 1, p. 605, under Uniform Commercial Code, § 2–708.) Additionally, and "[i]n all cases the seller may recover incidental damages" (id., Comment 3). The buyer's right to restitution was established at Special Term upon the motion for summary judgment, as was the seller's right to proper offsets, in each case pursuant to section 2–718; and, as the parties concede, the only question before us, following the assessment of damages at Special Term, is that as to the proper measure of damage to be applied. The conclusion is clear from the record—indeed with mathematical certainty—that "the measure of damages provided in subsection (1) is inadequate to put the seller in as good a position as performance would have done" (Uniform Commercial Code, § 2–708, subsection [2]) and hence—again under subsection (2)—that the seller is entitled to its "profit (including reasonable overhead) . . . together with any incidental damages . . ., due allowance for costs reasonably incurred and due credit for payments or proceeds of resale."

It is evident, first, that this retail seller is entitled to its profit and, second, that the last sentence of subsection (2), as hereinbefore quoted, referring to "due credit for payments or proceeds of resale" is inapplicable to this retail sales contract.[2] Closely parallel to the factual situation now

---

2 The concluding clause, "due credit for payments or proceeds of resale", is intended to refer to "the privilege of the seller to realize junk value when it is manifestly useless to complete the operation of manufacture" (Supp. No. 1 to the 1952 Official Draft of Text and Comments of the Uniform Commercial Code, as Amended by the Act of the American Law Institute of the National Conference of Commissioners on Uniform Laws [1954], p. 14). The commentators who have considered the language have uniformly concluded that "the reference is to a resale as scrap under

before us is that hypothesized by Dean Hawkland as illustrative of the operation of the rules: "Thus, if a private party agrees to sell his automobile to a buyer for $2,000, a breach by the buyer would cause the seller no loss (except incidental damages, i.e., expense of a new sale) if the seller was able to sell the automobile to another buyer for $2000. But the situation is different with dealers having an unlimited supply of standard-priced goods. Thus, if an automobile dealer agrees to sell a car to a buyer at the standard price of $2000, a breach by the buyer injures the dealer, even though he is able to sell the automobile to another for $2000. If the dealer has an inexhaustible supply of cars, the resale to replace the breaching buyer costs the dealer a sale, because, had the breaching buyer performed, the dealer would have made two sales instead of one. The buyer's breach, in such a case, depletes the dealer's sales to the extent of one, and the measure of damages should be the dealer's profit on one sale. Section 2–708 recognizes this, and it rejects the rule developed under the Uniform Sales Act by many courts that the profit cannot be recovered in this case." (Hawkland, Sales and Bulk Sales [1958 ed.], pp. 153–154; and see Comment, 31 Fordham L.Rev. 749, 755–756.)

The record which in this case establishes defendant's entitlement to damages in the amount of its prospective profit, at the same time confirms defendant's cognate right to "any incidental damages provided in this Article (Section 2–710)"[3] (Uniform Commercial Code, § 2–708, subsection [2]). From the language employed it is too clear to require discussion that the seller's right to recover loss of profits is not exclusive and that he may recoup his "incidental" expenses as well (Proctor & Gamble Distr. Co. v. Lawrence Amer. Field Warehousing Corp., 16 N.Y.2d 344, 354, 266 N.Y.S.2d 785, 792, 213 N.E.2d 873, 878). Although the trial court's denial of incidental damages in the uncontroverted amount of $674 was made in the context of its erroneous conclusion that paragraph (b) of subsection (2) of section 2–718 was applicable and was "adequate . . . to place the sellers in as good a position as performance would have done", the denial seems not to have rested entirely on the court's mistaken application of the law, as there was an explicit finding "that defendant completely failed to show that it suffered any incidental damages." We find no basis for the court's conclusion with respect to a deficiency of proof inasmuch as the proper items of the $674 expenses (being for storage, upkeep, finance charges and

---

. . . Section 2–704" (1956 Report of N.Y.Law Rev.Comm., p. 397; 1955 Report of N.Y.Law Rev.Comm., vol. 1, p. 761; New York Annotations, McKinney's Cons.Laws of N.Y., Book 62½, Part 1, p. 606, under Uniform Commercial Code, § 2–708; 1 Willier and Hart, Bender's Uniform Commercial Code Service, § 2–708, pp. 1–180—1–181). Another writer, reaching the same conclusion, after detailing the history of the clause, says that " 'proceeds of resale' previously meant the resale value of the goods in finished form; now it means the resale value of the components on hand at the time plaintiff learns of breach" (Harris, Seller's Damages, 18 Stanf.L.Rev. 66,104).

[3] Incidental damages to an aggrieved seller include any commercially reasonable charges, expenses or commissions incurred in stopping delivery, in the transportation, care and custody of goods after the buyer's breach, in connection with return or resale of the goods or otherwise resulting from the breach (Uniform Commercial Code, § 2–710).

insurance for the period between the date performance was due and the time of the resale) were proven without objection and were in no way controverted, impeached or otherwise challenged, at the trial or on appeal. Thus the court's finding of a failure of proof cannot be supported upon the record and, therefore, and contrary to plaintiffs' contention, the affirmance at the Appellate Division was ineffective to save it.

The trial court correctly denied defendant's claim for recovery of attorney's fees incurred by it in this action. Attorney's fees incurred in an action such as this are not in the nature of the protective expenses contemplated by the statute (Uniform Commercial Code, § 1–106, subd. [1] ; § 2–710; § 2–708, subsection [2]) and by our reference to "legal expense" in Procter & Gamble Distr. Co. v. Lawrence Amer. Field Warehousing Corp. (16 N.Y.2d 344, 354–355, 266 N.Y.S.2d 785, 792–793, 213 N.E.2d 873, 878–879, supra), upon which defendant's reliance is in this respect misplaced.

It follows that plaintiffs are entitled to restitution of the sum of $4,250 paid by them on account of the contract price less an offset to defendant in the amount of $3,253 on account of its lost profit of $2,579 and its incidental damages of $674.

The order of the Appellate Division should be modified, with costs in all courts, in accordance with this opinion, and, as so modified, affirmed.

FULD, C.J., and BURKE, SCILEPPI, BERGAN, BREITEL, and JASEN, JJ., concur.

Ordered accordingly.

———

Lazenby Garages Ltd. v. Wright

[1976] 2 All E.R. 770, [1976] 1 W.L.R. 459 (Ct.App. Eng. 1976)

(Lord Denning, M.R.) "Mr. Wright works on the land. On February 19, 1974 he went to the showrooms of motor dealers called Lazenby Garages Ltd. He saw some secondhand cars there. He agreed to buy a BMW 2002. He signed a contract to pay £1,670 for it. It was to be delivered to him on March 1, 1974. He went back home to his wife and told her about it. She persuaded him not to buy it. So next day he went back to the garage and said he would not have it after all. They kept it there offering it for re-sale. Two months later on April 23, 1974 they re-sold it for £1,770, that is, for £100 more than Mr. Wright was going to pay.

"Notwithstanding this advantageous re-sale, the garage sued Mr. Wright for damages. They produced evidence that they had themselves bought the car secondhand on 14th February 1974, that is five days before Mr. Wright had come in and agreed to buy it. They said that they had bought it for £1,325. He had agreed to buy it from them for £1,670. So they had lost £345 and they claimed that sum as damages.

"In answer Mr. Wright said: 'You haven't lost anything; you've sold it for a higher price.' The garage people said that they were dealers in secondhand cars; that they had had a number of cars of this sort of age and type, BMW 2002s; and that they had lost the sale of another car. They said that, if Mr. Wright had taken this car, they would have been able to sell one of those other cars to the purchaser. So they had sold one car less and were entitled to profit accordingly. . . .

". . . Now there is an appeal to this court. The cases show that if there are a number of new cars, all exactly of the same kind, available for sale, and the dealers can prove that they sold one car less than they otherwise would have done, they would be entitled to damages amounting to their loss of profit on the one car. . . .

"But it is entirely different in the case of a secondhand car. Each secondhand car is different from the next, even though it is the same make. The sales manager of the garage admitted in evidence that some secondhand cars, of the same make, even of the same year, may sell better than others of the same year. Some may sell quickly, others sluggishly. You simply cannot tell why. But they are all different.

"In the circumstances the cases about new cars do not apply. . . . "

SECTION 3. MITIGATION

SHIRLEY MACLAINE PARKER V. TWENTIETH CENTURY-FOX FILM CORP.

California Supreme Court, 1970.
3 Cal.3d 176, 89 Cal.Rptr. 737, 474 P.2d 689.

BURKE, J. Defendant Twentieth Century-Fox Film Corporation appeals from a summary judgment granting to plaintiff the recovery of agreed compensation under a written contract for her services as an actress in a motion picture. As will appear, we have concluded that the trial court correctly ruled in plaintiff's favor and that the judgment should be affirmed.

Plaintiff is well known as an actress, and in the contract between plaintiff and defendant is sometimes referred to as the "Artist." Under the contract, dated August 6, 1965, plaintiff was to play the female lead in defendant's contemplated production of a motion picture entitled "Bloomer

Girl."[*] The contract provided that defendant would pay plaintiff a minimum "guaranteed compensation" of $53,571.42 per week for 14 weeks commencing May 23, 1966, for a total of $750,000. Prior to May 1966 defendant decided not to produce the picture and by a letter dated April 4, 1966, it notified plaintiff of that decision and that it would not "comply with our obligations to you under" the written contract.

By the same letter and with the professed purpose "to avoid any damage to you," defendant instead offered to employ plaintiff as the leading actress in another film tentatively entitled "Big Country, Big Man" (hereinafter, "Big Country"). The compensation offered was identical, as were 31 of the 34 numbered provisions or articles of the original contract.[1] Unlike "Bloomer Girl," however, which was to have been a musical production, "Big Country" was a dramatic "western type" movie. "Bloomer Girl" was to have been filmed in California; "Big Country" was to be produced in Australia. Also, certain terms in the proffered contract varied from those of the original.[2] Plaintiff was given one week within which to

---

[*]   Victor Goldberg reports that *Bloomer Girl* was an adaptation of a stage musical written by Harold Arlen and Yip Harburg, which ran for 654 performances on Broadway in the mid-1940's. Harburg's son summarized the play's plot and political themes as follows:

> *Bloomer Girl* concerns the political activities of Amelia (renamed Dolly) Bloomer and the effect they have on a pre-Civil War family of her brother-in-law, hoopskirt king Horace Applegate, and his feminist daughter, Evalina. Evalina is the youngest and only remaining unmarried Applegate daughter; her older sisters are all married to company salesmen, and as *Bloomer Girl* begins, Horace is trying to unify business and family by encouraging his chief Southern salesman, Jefferson Calhoun, to court Evalina. On the eve of the Civil War, *Bloomer Girl* centers around Evalina's tutelage of Jeff in matters of gender and racial equality. Evalina, Dolly, and the other feminists of Cicero Falls not only campaign against Applegate's hoopskirts and sexism but also stage their own version of Uncle Tom's Cabin and conceal a runaway slave—Jeff's own manservant, Pompey. It was, said Yip, a show about "the indivisibility of human freedom."

> *Bloomer Girl* interweaves the issues of black and female equality and war and peace with the vicissitudes of courtship and pre-Civil War politics. . . . [I]t was at no point an escapist entertainment. . . .

Goldberg, "Bloomer Girl Revisited or how to Frame an Unmade Picture," 1998 *Wisconsin Law Review* 1051 (1998) (quoting Harold Meyerson and Ernie Harburg, *Who Put the Rainbow in* The Wizard of Oz? *Yip Harburg, Lyricist* (1993). (Footnote by edsed.)

[1]   Among the identical provisions was the following found in the last paragraph of Article 2 of the original contract: "We [defendant] shall not be obligated to utilize your [plaintiff's] services in or in connection with the Photoplay hereunder, our sole obligation, subject to the terms and conditions of this Agreement, being to pay you the guaranteed compensation herein provided for."

[2]   Article 29 of the original contract specified that plaintiff approved the director already chosen for "Bloomer Girl" and that in case he failed to act as director plaintiff was to have approval rights of any substitute director. Article 31 provided that plaintiff was to have the right of approval of the "Bloomer Girl" dance director, and Article 32 gave her the right of approval of the screenplay. Defendant's letter of April 4 to plaintiff, which contained both defendant's notice of breach of the "Bloomer Girl" contract and offer of the lead in "Big Country," eliminated or impaired each of those rights. It read in part as follows: "The terms and conditions of our offer of employment are identical to those set forth in the 'Bloomer Girl' Agreement, Articles 1 through 34 and Exhibit A to the Agreement, except as follows:

> "1. Article 31 of said Agreement will not be included in any contract of employment regarding 'Big Country, Big Man' as it is not a musical and it thus will not need a dance director.

accept; she did not and the offer lapsed. Plaintiff then commenced this action seeking recovery of the agreed guaranteed compensation.

The complaint sets forth two causes of action. The first is for money due under the contract; the second, based upon the same allegations as the first, is for damages resulting from defendant's breach of contract. Defendant in its answer admits the existence and validity of the contract, that plaintiff complied with all the conditions, covenants and promises and stood ready to complete the performance, and that defendant breached and "anticipatorily repudiated" the contract. It denies, however, that any money is due to plaintiff either under the contract or as a result of its breach, and pleads as an affirmative defense to both causes of action plaintiff's allegedly deliberate failure to mitigate damages, asserting that she unreasonably refused to accept its offer of the leading role in "Big Country."

Plaintiff moved for summary judgment under Code of Civil Procedure section 437c, the motion was granted, and summary judgment for $750,000 plus interest was entered in plaintiff's favor. This appeal by defendant followed.

The familiar rules are that the matter to be determined by the trial court on a motion for summary judgment is whether facts have been presented which give rise to a triable factual issue. The court may not pass upon the issue itself. Summary judgment is proper only if the affidavits or declarations in support of the moving party would be sufficient to sustain a judgment in his favor and his opponent does not by affidavit show facts sufficient to present a triable issue of fact. . . .

The general rule is that the measure of recovery by a wrongfully discharged employee is the amount of salary agreed upon for the period of service, less the amount which the employer affirmatively proves the employee has earned or with reasonable effort might have earned from other employment. . . . However, before projected earnings from other employment opportunities not sought or accepted by the discharged employee can be applied in mitigation, the employer must show that the other employment was comparable, or substantially similar, to that of which the employee has been deprived; the employee's rejection of or failure to seek other available employment of a different or inferior kind

---

"2. In the 'Bloomer Girl' agreement, in Articles 29 and 32, you were given certain director and screenplay approvals and you had preapproved certain matters. Since there simply is insufficient time to negotiate with you regarding your choice of director and regarding the screenplay and since you already expressed an interest in performing the role in 'Big Country, Big Man,' we must exclude from our offer of employment in 'Big Country, Big Man' any approval rights as are contained in said Articles 29 and 32; however, we shall consult with you respecting the director to be selected to direct the photoplay and will further consult with you with respect to the screenplay and any revisions or changes therein, provided, however, that if we fail to agree . . . the decision of . . . [defendant] with respect to the selection of a director and to revisions and changes in the said screenplay shall be binding upon the parties to said agreement."

may not be resorted to in order to mitigate damages. (Gonzales v. Internat. Assn. of Machinists (1963) 213 Cal.App.2d 817, 822–824 [29 Cal.Rptr. 190]; Harris v. Nat. Union etc. Cooks, Stewards (1953) 116 Cal.App.2d 759, 761 [254 P.2d 673]. . . . de la Falaise v. Gaumont-British Picture Corp., 39 Cal.App.2d 46 [103 P.2d 447 (1940)]. . . .

　　In the present case defendant has raised no issue of *reasonableness of efforts* by plaintiffs to obtain other employment; the sole issue is whether plaintiff's refusal of defendant's substitute offer of "Big Country" may be used in mitigation. Nor, if the "Big Country" offer was of employment different or inferior when compared with the original "Bloomer Girl" employment, is there an issue as to whether or not plaintiff acted reasonably in refusing the substitute offer. Despite defendant's arguments to the contrary, no case cited or which our research has discovered holds or suggests that reasonableness is an element of a wrongfully discharged employee's option to reject, or fail to seek, different or inferior employment lest the possible earnings therefrom be charged against him in mitigation of damages.[5]

　　Applying the foregoing rules to the record in the present case, with all intendments in favor of the party opposing the summary judgment motion—here, defendant—it is clear that the trial court correctly ruled that plaintiff's failure to accept defendant's tendered substitute employment could not be applied in mitigation of damages because the offer of the "Big Country" lead was of employment both different and inferior, and that no factual dispute was presented on that issue. The mere circumstance that "Bloomer Girl" was to be a musical review calling upon plaintiff's talents as a dancer as well as an actress, and was to be produced in the City of Los Angeles, whereas "Big Country" was a straight dramatic role in a "Western Type" story taking place in an opal mine in Australia, demonstrates the difference in kind between the two employments; the female lead as a

---

　　[5]　Instead, in each case the reasonableness referred to was that of the *efforts* of the employee to obtain other employment that was not different or inferior; his right to reject the latter was declared as an unqualified rule of law. Thus Gonzales v. Internat. Assn. of Machinists, supra, 213 Cal.App.2d 817, 823–824, holds that the trial court correctly instructed the jury that plaintiff union member, a machinist, was required to make "such *efforts* as the average [member of his union] desiring employment would make at that particular time and place" (italics added); but, further, that the court *properly rejected* defendant's *offer of proof of the availability of other kinds* of employment at the same or higher pay than plaintiff usually received and all outside the jurisdiction of his union, as plaintiff could not be required to accept different employment or a non-union job.

　　In Harris v. Nat. Union etc. Cooks, Stewards, supra, 116 Cal.App.2d 759, 761, the issues were stated to be, inter alia, whether comparable employment was open to each plaintiff employee, and if so whether each plaintiff made a *reasonable effort* to secure such employment. It was held that the trial court *properly sustained an objection to an offer to prove a custom of accepting a job in a lower rank* when work in the higher rank was not available, as "The duty of mitigation of damages . . . does not require the plaintiff 'to seek or to accept other employment of a different or inferior kind.' " . . .

　　See also: Lewis v. Protective Security Life Ins. Co. (1962) 208 Cal.App.2d 582, 584 [25 Cal.Rptr. 213]: "*honest effort* to find similar employment. . . . " (Italics added.) . . .de la Falaise v. Gaumont-British Picture Corp., supra, 39 Cal.App.2d 461, 469: "reasonable effort."

dramatic actress in a western style motion picture can by no stretch of imagination be considered the equivalent of or substantially similar to the lead in a song-and-dance production.

Additionally, the substitute "Big Country" offer proposed to eliminate or impair the director and screenplay approvals accorded to plaintiff under the original "Bloomer Girl" contract (see fn. 2, ante), and thus constituted an offer of inferior employment. No expertise or judicial notice is required in order to hold that the deprivation or infringement of an employee's rights held under an original employment contract converts the available "other employment" relied upon by the employer to mitigate damages, into inferior employment which the employee need not seek or accept. (See Gonzales v. Internat. Assn. of Machinists, supra, 213 Cal.App.2d 817, 823–824; and fn. 5. . . .)

Statements found in affidavits submitted by defendant in opposition to plaintiff's summary judgment motion, to the effect that the "Big Country" offer was not of employment different from or inferior to that under the "Bloomer Girl" contract, merely repeat the allegations of defendant's answer to the complaint in this action, constitute only conclusionary assertions with respect to undisputed facts, and do not give rise to a triable factual issue so as to defeat the motion for summary judgment. . . .

In view of the determination that defendant failed to present any facts showing the existence of a factual issue with respect to its sole defense—plaintiff's rejection of its substitute employment offer in mitigation of damages—we need not consider plaintiff's further contention that for various reasons, including the provisions of the original contract set forth in footnote 1, ante, plaintiff was excused from attempting to mitigate damages.

The judgment is affirmed.

McComb, J., Peters, J., Tobriner, J., Kaus, J.,* and Roth, J.,** concurred.

Sullivan, Acting C.J. (dissenting). The basic question in this case is whether or not plaintiff acted reasonably in rejecting defendant's offer of alternate employment. The answer depends upon whether that offer (starring in 'Big Country, Big Man') was an offer of work that was substantially similar to her former employment (starring in 'Bloomer Girl') or of work that was of a different or inferior kind. To my mind this is a factual issue which the trial court should not have determined on a motion for summary judgment. The majority have not only repeated this error but have compounded it by applying the rules governing mitigation of damages

---

   *   Assigned by the Acting Chairman of the Judicial Council.

  ** Assigned by the Acting Chairman of the Judicial Council.

in the employer-employee context in a misleading fashion. Accordingly, I respectfully dissent.

The familiar rule requiring a plaintiff in a tort or contract action to mitigate damages embodies notions of fairness and socially responsible behavior which are fundamental to our jurisprudence. Most broadly stated, it precludes the recovery of damages which, through the exercise of due diligence, could have been avoided. Thus, in essence, it is a rule requiring reasonable conduct in commercial affairs. This general principle governs the obligations of an employee after his employer has wrongfully repudiated or terminated the employment contract. Rather than permitting the employee simply to remain idle during the balance of the contract period, the law requires him to make a reasonable effort to secure other employment. He is not obliged, however, to seek or accept any and all types of work which may be available. Only work which is in the same field and which is of the same quality need be accepted.

Over the years the courts have employed various phrases to define the type of employment which the employee, upon his wrongful discharge, is under an obligation to accept. Thus in California alone it has been held that he must accept employment which is 'substantially similar' . . . 'comparable employment' . . . employment 'in the same general line of the first employment' . . . 'equivalent to his prior position' . . . 'employment in a similar capacity' . . . employment which is 'not * * * of a different or inferior kind.' . . .

For reasons which are unexplained, the majority cite several of these cases yet select from among the various judicial formulations which contain one particular phrase, 'Not of a different or inferior kind,' with which to analyze this case. I have discovered no historical or theoretical reason to adopt this phrase, which is simply a negative restatement of the affirmative standards set out in the above cases, as the exclusive standard. Indeed, its emergence is an example of the dubious phenomenon of the law responding not to rational judicial choice or changing social conditions, but to unrecognized changes in the language of opinions or legal treatises. However, the phrase is a serviceable one and my concern is not with its use as the standard but rather with what I consider its distortion.

The relevant language excuses acceptance only of employment which is of a Different kind. . . . It has never been the law that the mere existence of Differences between two jobs in the same field is sufficient, as a matter of law, to excuse an employee wrongfully discharged from one from accepting the other in order to mitigate damages. Such an approach would effectively eliminate any obligation of an employee to attempt to minimize damage arising from a wrongful discharge. The only alternative job offer an employee would be required to accept would be an offer of his former job by his former employer. . . .

I believe that the approach taken by the majority (a superficial listing of differences with no attempt to assess their significance) may subvert a valuable legal doctrine. The inquiry in cases such as this should not be whether differences between the two jobs exist (there will always be differences) but whether the differences which are present are substantial enough to constitute differences in the Kind of employment or, alternatively, whether they render the substitute work employment of an Inferior kind.

It seems to me that this inquiry involves, in the instant case at least, factual determinations which are improper on a motion for summary judgment. Resolving whether or not one job is substantially similar to another or whether, on the other hand, it is of a different or inferior kind, will often (as here) require a critical appraisal of the similarities and differences between them in light of the importance of these differences to the employee. This necessitates a weighing of the evidence, and it is precisely this undertaking which is forbidden on summary judgment. . . .

MOSK, J., did not participate.

RESTATEMENT, SECOND, CONTRACTS § 350

[See Selected Source Materials Supplement]

UNIDROIT PRINCIPLES OF INTERNATIONAL COMMERCIAL CONTRACTS ARTS. 7.4.7, 7.4.8

[See Selected Source Materials Supplement]

PRINCIPLES OF EUROPEAN CONTRACT LAW ARTS. 9.504, 9.505

[See Selected Source Materials Supplement]

Mr. Eddie, Inc. v. Ginsberg

430 S.W.2d 5 (Tex.Civ.App.1968)

Ginsberg was wrongfully dismissed by defendant early in the term of a three-year employment contract. Immediately after the dismissal Ginsberg took another job, which he held for thirty-four weeks, earning $13,760. After Ginsberg left that job, he spent $1,340 unsuccessfully seeking further employment. Held, Ginsberg was entitled to recover his remaining salary under his contract with defendant, minus the $13,760 earned on the other job, but plus the $1,340 he unsuccessfully expended in looking for further employment. As to the $1,340 expense, the court said, "the rule in such cases is . . . as follows: 'The expenses for which a recovery may be had include necessary and reasonable disbursements made in an effort to avoid or mitigate the injurious consequences of the defendant's wrong. . . . if such expenses are the result of a prudent attempt to minimize damages they are recoverable even though the result is an aggravation of the damages rather than a mitigation.' "

Southern Keswick, Inc. v. Whetherholt

293 So.2d 109 (Fla.App.1974)

This was an action for breach of an employment contract. The jury was instructed, "[It is] the general rule that employment of different or inferior nature cannot be used in reduction of damages." Reversed. "While we would agree that a wrongfully discharged employee is not obliged to *seek* employment of a different or inferior nature, if he in fact *obtains* such employment within the contract period his earnings should be used in mitigation of damages. The foregoing charge was therefore clearly wrong. . . . " (Emphasis added.)

NOTE ON DAMAGES WHEN THE PLAINTIFF FAILS TO MITIGATE

A plaintiff who fails to mitigate does not recover damages for the avoidable loss. Rockingham County v. Luten Bridge Co., 35 F.2d 301 (1929), illustrates. Defendant county rescinded a contract for construction of bridge before the erection of the bridge was commenced. Plaintiff had spent $1,900 on labor and material at the time of the attempted rescission. Plaintiff ignored the attempted rescission, completed the bridge, and sued for the contract price of $18,301. The disputed issues in the case involved the validity of a series of conflicting actions taken by a divided board of county commissioners. The bridge contract had been approved by a 3–2 majority of the board. One member of the majority resigned and then tried to withdraw his resignation. The clerk ignored the withdrawal then appointed a new commissioner, who voted with the previous minority to rescind the contract. The court of appeal held that the rescission of the contract by the newly constituted majority of the board was valid and then turned to the issue of damages.

> . . . [W]e do not think that, after the county had given notice, while the contract was still executory, that it did not desire the bridge built and would not pay for it, plaintiff could proceed to build it and recover the contract price. It is true that the county had no right to rescind the contract, and the notice given plaintiff amounted to a breach on its part; but, after plaintiff had received notice of the breach, it was its duty to do nothing to increase the damages flowing

therefrom. If A enters into a binding contract to build a house for B, B, of course, has no right to rescind the contract without A's consent. But if, before the house is built, he decides that he does not want it, and notifies A to that effect, A has no right to proceed with the building and thus pile up damages. His remedy is to treat the contract as broken when he receives the notice, and sue for the recovery of such damages as he may have sustained from the breach, including any profit which he would have realized upon performance, as well as any other losses which may have resulted to him. In the case at bar, the county decided not to build the road of which the bridge was to be a part, and did not build it. The bridge, built in the midst of the forest, is of no value to the county because of this change of circumstances. When, therefore, the county gave notice to the plaintiff that it would not proceed with the project, plaintiff should have desisted from further work. It had no right thus to pile up damages by proceeding with the erection of a useless bridge. . . .

. . . It follows that there was error in directing a verdict for plaintiff for the full amount of its claim. The measure of plaintiff's damage, upon its appearing that notice was duly given not to build the bridge, is an amount sufficient to compensate plaintiff for labor and materials expended and expense incurred in the part performance of the contract, prior to its repudiation, plus the profit which would have been realized if it had been carried out in accordance with its terms. . . .

———

Bomberger v. McKelvey

35 Cal.2d 607, 220 P.2d 729 (1950)

Defendants purchased twelve lots in Modesto, California to construct a building and parking facility for a grocery store. Two of these lots were acquired from plaintiffs for $60,000. Upon the two lots was an old commercial building occupied by a tenant, the Hills, who paid $300 per month rent as well as some residential structures. Plaintiffs assigned the tenant's lease to Defendant on conveyance of the two lots. Plaintiffs reserved title to the residential structures, which it agreed to remove from the property. Defendants agreed to pay plaintiffs $3,500 to demolish and remove the commercial building. Defendants also agreed to pay the Hills $4,000 to surrender the lease. It was understood that plaintiffs intended to salvage plate glass and skylights from this building to use in a new store plaintiffs had agreed to construct for the Hills.

These events occurred in 1946 when there was a shortage of construction materials. Defendant was unable to get materials to construct the store and parking lot, so it instructed plaintiffs not to demolish the old building. Plaintiffs disregarded this instruction, asserting they needed the plate glass and skylights to complete the new store they were constructing for the Hills.

Plaintiffs removed the plate glass and skylights from the old building, and then after the Hills vacated, demolished the old building. Defendants refused to pay the agreed price of $3,500 due upon demolition of the old building or the $2,500 due to the Hills upon the surrender of the lease. The Hills assigned this claim to plaintiffs. The trial court entered a judgment for plaintiffs for $6,000, finding the plaintiffs had fully performed their agreement and that the sum promised to the Hills became due and payable when the Hills moved to the new building. Defendants appealed arguing plaintiffs disregard of their instruction not to demolish the old building was a breach of the duty to mitigate. Affirmed.

(Gibson, C.J) "It is the general rule in California and in practically all other jurisdictions that either party to an executory contract has the power to stop performance of the contract by giving notice or direction to that effect, subjecting himself to liability for damages, and upon receipt of such notice the other party cannot continue to perform and recover damages based on full performance. Richardson v. Davis, 116 Cal.App. 388, 2 P.2d 860; Atkinson v. District Bond Co., 5 Cal.App.2d 738, 745, 43 P.2d 867; See Crawford v. Pioneer Box & Lumber Co., 105 Cal.App. 760, 765, 288 P. 694 et seq.; 5 Williston on Contracts, Rev.Ed. 1937, § 1298, pp. 3693–3695; 12 Am.Jur. 979–980. This is an application of the principle that a plaintiff must mitigate damages so far as he can without loss to himself. See 5 Williston on Contracts, Rev.Ed.1937, § 1298, p. 3694.

"The reason for this rule is twofold: Ordinarily a plaintiff is interested only in the profit he will make from his contract, and if he receives this he obtains the full benefit of his bargain; on the other hand, performance by the plaintiff might be useless to the defendant, although he would have to pay the entire contract price if the plaintiff were permitted to perform, and this would inflict damage on the defendant without benefit to the plaintiff. See 5 Williston on Contracts, Rev.Ed.1937, § 1298, p. 3694; Dowling v. Whites Lumber & Supply Co., 170 Miss. 267, 154 So. 703, 705. If these reasons are not present, the rule is not applied. For example, where the plaintiff is not interested solely in profit from the agreement but must proceed with the work in order to fulfill contract obligations to others, or where refraining from performance might involve closing a factory, damages may be inadequate and the plaintiff may have a right to continue performance. Southern Cotton-Oil Co. v. Heflin, 5 Cir., 99 F. 339; 5 Williston on Contracts, Rev.Ed.1937, § 1299, p. 3696. It has likewise been held that where a contractor has started work and has reached a point where it would be impracticable to attempt to make a reasonable estimate of damages, or where to complete the work will diminish damages or at least not enhance them, the contractor may go forward and complete performance. Dowling v. Whites Lumber & Supply Co., 170 Miss. 267, 154 So. 703. In the Restatement of Contracts, Comment a on section 336, it is said that 'It is not reasonable to expect the plaintiff to avoid harm if at the time for action it appears that the attempt may cause other serious harm. He need not enter into other risky contracts, incur unreasonable inconvenience or expense, disorganize his business, or put himself in a humiliating position or in one involving loss of honor and respect.'

"The general rule is also subject to the jurisdiction of equity to order specific performance of the contract, and, apparently in recognition of this principle, it has been held that in cases where damages will not afford adequate compensation and where specific performance will lie, the plaintiff may continue to perform, in spite of a notice to stop, and thereafter recover on the basis of his continued performance. Marsh v. Blackman, N.Y.Supreme Court, 50 Barb. 329; Fine Art Pictures Corp. v. Karzin, Mo.App., 29 S.W.2d 170, 173; see Woodman v. Blue Grass Land Co., 125 Wis. 489, 494, 103 N.W. 236, 237, 104 N.W. 920; Badger State Lumber Co. v. G. W. Jones Lumber Co., 140 Wis. 73, 121 N.W. 933, 934; 17 C.J.S., Contracts, § 473, p. 979; 12 Am.Jur. 980; cf. La Salle Extension University v. Ogburn, 174 N.C. 427, 93 S.E. 986, 988, Ann.Cas.1918C, 887. In the Fine Art Pictures decision the court stated that this is one of the necessary exceptions to the rule. 29 S.W.2d at page 173.

"In the present case the trial court granted relief similar to that which has been allowed under this exception to the general rule. The court determined that plaintiffs acted properly in performing the contract on their part and that, having performed, they were entitled to the full amount of $6,000 due under the agreement. In the light of the foregoing, we must consider whether the facts bring this case within the reasons underlying the general rule or the reasons for the exception, and we must determine whether there is sufficient evidence to show that plaintiffs would have been entitled to specific performance and that damages would have been inadequate.

"Unlike the situations presented in Richardson v. Davis, 116 Cal.App. 388, 2 P.2d 860, and Crawford v. Pioneer Box & Lumber Co., 105 Cal.App. 760, 288 P. 694, relied upon by defendants, the agreement involved here did not provide simply for the payment of money in return for the performance of services. As we have seen, it was contemplated that plaintiffs were to keep all salvaged material. During the negotiations for the agreement they informed defendants that they planned to use as much of this material as they could in constructing the new building for the Hills, and, in reliance on the contract, they altered the plans for the new building to permit use of the glass and skylights from the old one. These materials were then scarce, and sheet metal for the skylights was under priority. There was testimony that it would take from 90 to 120 days to obtain new glass and skylights, and some other glass required for the new building did not arrive until about five months after it was ordered. Except for the glass and skylights the new building was completed sometime in October, and the lack of these materials left it exposed to the weather and apparently unsuitable for occupation by the Hills. Thus it is obvious that an essential element of the rule giving one party the power to stop performance by giving notice not to perform is lacking here since plaintiffs were not interested solely in the profit to be derived from tearing down the old building and selling the salvage, but they had an additional interest in obtaining actual performance of the agreement so that they could secure scarce materials and complete the new building.

"The fact that the agreement involved property which was scarce and under priority is of particular importance in the present case. There are analogous decisions in other jurisdictions holding that a purchaser does not have an adequate remedy at law and may obtain specific performance of a contract to sell materials if he needs them in his business and cannot obtain them or their equivalent within the local marketing area. . . .

"Under these circumstances the trial court could properly conclude that inability to obtain the salvage from the old building would seriously interfere with completion of the new building, that equivalent materials could not then be secured by plaintiffs, and that in an action for breach of contract damages would be difficult to ascertain and would be inadequate.

"Defendants argue that plaintiffs were not entitled to proceed with performance because they could have covered up the holes in the new building with boards to protect it from the weather until new glass and skylights could be obtained and, further, that the glass and skylights from the old building, even if required, could have been removed without tearing down the entire structure. Boarding up the new building, however, would have rendered it unusable for an indefinite period. Also, removal of part of the old building without demolition of the remainder was not authorized by the agreement, and there is nothing in the record to indicate that defendants had suggested or would have consented to such a step, even though they knew that the need for the glass and skylights was the principal reason for plaintiffs' insistence upon full performance of the contract. All of these factors were, of course, to be considered by the trial court in passing upon the propriety of plaintiffs' conduct, and we cannot say as a matter of law that plaintiffs were required to adopt one of the solutions now mentioned by defendants.

"Defendants introduced testimony that the value of the old building, if allowed to remain on the property for continued use, was $26,250, and they contend that demolition of such a valuable structure was not justified by plaintiffs' need for the salvage, which, it is asserted, could have been replaced for $540. Regardless of the weight to be given this testimony, however, the trial court could properly consider the facts that defendants had purchased the property for construction of a chain grocery store, that they had made a lease to the chain store operators by which they agreed to deliver possession of lots 15 and 16 for use as a parking lot with all improvements removed, and that for this reason the building had little if any value for continued use on the property. On the other hand the value of the salvage to plaintiffs was enhanced by their need of materials for the new building."

SECTION 4. FORESEEABILITY

HADLEY V. BAXENDALE
In the Court of Exchequer, 1854.
9 Exch. 341.

. . . At the trial before Crompton, J., at the last Gloucester Assizes, it appeared that the plaintiffs carried on an extensive business as millers at Gloucester; and that, on the 11th of May, their mill was stopped by a breakage of the crank shaft by which the mill was worked. The steam-engine was manufactured by Messrs. Joyce & Co., the engineers, at Greenwich, and it became necessary to send the shaft as a pattern for a new one to Greenwich. The fracture was discovered on the 12th, and on the 13th the plaintiffs sent one of their servants to the office of the defendants, who are the well-known carriers trading under the name of Pickford & Co., for the purpose of having the shaft carried to Greenwich. The plaintiffs' servant told the clerk that the mill was stopped, and that the shaft must be sent immediately; and in answer to the inquiry when the shaft would be taken, the answer was, that if it was sent up by twelve o'clock any day, it would be delivered at Greenwich on the following day. On the following day the shaft was taken by the defendants before noon, for the purpose of being conveyed to Greenwich, and the sum of £2, 4s. was paid for its carriage for the whole distance; at the same time the defendants' clerk was told that a special entry, if required, should be made to hasten its delivery. The delivery of the shaft at Greenwich was delayed by some neglect; and the consequence was, that the plaintiffs did not receive the new shaft for several days after they would otherwise have done and the working of their mill was thereby delayed, and they thereby lost the profits they would otherwise have received.[*]

On the part of the defendants, it was objected that these damages were too remote, and that the defendants were not liable with respect to them. The learned Judge left the case generally to the jury, who found a verdict with £25 damages beyond the amount paid into Court.[**]

WHATELEY, in last Michaelmas Term, obtained a rule nisi for a new trial, on the ground of misdirection.

KEATING and DOWDESWELL (Feb. 1) showed cause. The plaintiffs are entitled to the amount awarded by the jury as damages. These damages are not too remote, for they are not only the natural and necessary

---

[*] In The Capability Problem in Contract Law (2d ed. 2004), Richard Danzig and Geoffrey R. Watson set out the following statement from the Assize Report in August 8, 1853, edition of The Times of London: "[I]nstead of being forwarded by wagon immediately, [the crankshaft] was kept for several days in London, and was at length forwarded by water on the 20th, along with many tons of iron goods which had been consigned to the same parties." Id. at 59 n. 5. (Footnote by eds.)

[**] According to the report of the case, the amount which the defendant had paid into court was £25. See 9 Exch.Rep. at 343. (Footnote by edsed.)

consequence of the defendants' default, but they are the only loss which the plaintiffs have actually sustained. The principle upon which damages are assessed is founded upon that of rendering compensation to the injured party. . . .

[PARKE, B. The sensible rule appears to be that which has been laid down in France, and which is declared in their code—Code Civil, liv, iii, tit. iii. ss. 1149, 1150, 1151, and which is thus translated in Sedgwick [on Damages, p. 67]: "The damages due to the creditor consist in general of the loss that he has sustained, and the profit which he has been prevented from acquiring, subject to the modifications hereinafter contained. The debtor is only liable for the damages foreseen, or which might have been foreseen, at the time of the execution of the contract, when it is not owing to his fraud that the agreement has been violated. Even in the case of non-performance of the contract, resulting from the fraud of the debtor, the damages only comprise so much of the loss sustained by the creditor, and so much of the profit which he has been prevented from acquiring, as directly and immediately results from the non-performance of the contract."] If that rule is to be adopted, there was ample evidence in the present case of the defendants' knowledge of such a state of things as would necessarily result in the damage the plaintiffs suffered through the defendants' default. . . .

[. . . MARTIN, B. Take the case of the non-delivery by a carrier of a delicate piece of machinery, whereby the whole of an extensive mill is thrown out of work for a considerable time; if the carrier is to be liable for the loss in that case, he might incur damages to the extent of 10,000*l*. . . .] These extreme cases, and the difficulty which consequently exists in the estimation of the true amount of damages, supports the view for which the plaintiffs contend, that the question is properly for the decision of a jury, and therefore that this matter could not properly have been withdrawn from their consideration. . . .

WHATELEY, WILLES, and PHIPSON, in support of the rule (Feb. 2). It has been contended, on the part of the plaintiffs, that the damages found by the jury are a matter fit for their consideration; but still the question remains, in what way ought the jury to have been directed? It has been also urged, that, in awarding damages, the law gives compensation to the injured individual. But it is clear that complete compensation is not to be awarded; for instance, the non-payment of a bill of exchange might lead to the utter ruin of the holder, and yet such damage could not be considered as necessarily resulting from the breach of contract, so as to entitle the party aggrieved to recover in respect of it. Take the case of the breach of a contract to supply a rick-cloth, whereby and in consequence of bad weather the hay, being unprotected, is spoiled, that damage would not be recoverable. Many similar cases might be added. . . . Sedgwick says [p. 28], "In regard to the quantum of damages, instead of adhering to the term compensation, it would be far more accurate to say, in the language of

Domat, which we have cited above, 'that the object is to discriminate between that portion of the loss which must be borne by the offending party and that which must be borne by the sufferer.' The law in fact aims not at the satisfaction but at a division of the loss." . . . This therefore is a question of law, and the jury ought to have been told that these damages were too remote; and that, in the absence of the proof of any other damage, the plaintiffs were entitled to nominal damages only. . . .

The judgment of the Court was now delivered by ALDERSON, B.

We think that there ought to be a new trial in this case; but, in so doing, we deem it to be expedient and necessary to state explicitly the rule which the Judge, at the next trial, ought, in our opinion, to direct the jury to be governed by when they estimate the damages.

It is, indeed, of the last importance that we should do this; for, if the jury are left without any definite rule to guide them, it will, in such cases as these, manifestly lead to the greatest injustice. The Courts have done this on several occasions; and, in Blake v. Midland Railway Company, 18 Q.B. 93, the Court granted a new trial on this very ground, that the rule had not been definitely laid down to the jury by the learned Judge at Nisi Prius.

"There are certain established rules," this Court says, in Alder v. Keighley, 15 M. & W. 117, "according to which the jury ought to find." And the Court, in that case, adds: "and here there is a clear rule, that the amount which would have been received if the contract had been kept, is the measure of damages if the contract is broken."

Now we think the proper rule in such a case as the present is this:— Where two parties have made a contract which one of them has broken, the damages which the other party ought to receive in respect of such breach of contract should be such as may fairly and reasonably be considered either arising naturally, i.e., according to the usual course of things, from such breach of contract itself, or such as may reasonably be supposed to have been in the contemplation of both parties, at the time they made the contract, as the probable result of the breach of it. Now, if the special circumstances under which the contract was actually made were communicated by the plaintiffs to the defendants, and thus known to both parties, the damages resulting from the breach of such a contract, which they would reasonably contemplate, would be the amount of injury which would ordinarily follow from a breach of contract under these special circumstances so known and communicated. But, on the other hand, if these special circumstances were wholly unknown to the party breaking the contract, he, at the most, could only be supposed to have had in his contemplation the amount of injury which would arise generally, and in the great multitude of cases not affected by any special circumstances, from such a breach of contract. For, had the special circumstances been known, the parties might have specially provided for the breach of contract by special terms as to the damages in that case; and of this advantage it would be very unjust to deprive them. Now the above principles are those by which we think the jury ought to be guided in estimating the damages arising out of any breach of contract. It is said, that other cases such as breaches of contract in the non-payment of money, or in the not making a good title to land, are to be treated as exceptions from this, and as governed by a conventional rule. But as, in such cases, both parties must be supposed to be cognizant of that well-known rule, these cases may, we think, be more properly classed under the rule above enunciated as to cases under known special circumstances, because there both parties may reasonably be presumed to contemplate the estimation of the amount of damages according to the conventional rule. Now, in the present case, if we are to apply the principles above laid down, we find that the only circumstances here communicated by the plaintiffs to the defendants at the time the contract was made, were, that the article to be carried was the broken shaft of a mill, and that the plaintiffs were the millers of that mill. But how do these circumstances [show] reasonably that the profits of the mill must be stopped by an unreasonable delay in the delivery of the broken shaft by the carrier to the third person? Suppose the plaintiffs had another shaft in their possession put up or putting up at the time, and that they only wished to send back the broken shaft to the engineer who made it; it is clear that this would be quite consistent with the above circumstances, and yet the unreasonable delay in the delivery would have no effect upon the intermediate profits of the mill. Or, again, suppose that, at the time of the delivery to the carrier, the machinery of the mill had been in other respects defective, then, also, the same results would follow. Here it is true that the shaft was actually sent back to serve as a model for a new one, and that the want of a new one was the only cause of the stoppage of the mill, and that the loss of profits really arose from not sending down the new shaft in proper time, and that this arose from the delay in delivering the broken one to serve as a model. But it is obvious that, in the great multitude of cases of millers sending off broken shafts to third persons by a carrier under ordinary circumstances, such consequences would not, in all probability, have occurred; and these special circumstances were here never communicated by the plaintiffs to the defendants. It follows, therefore, that the loss of profits here cannot reasonably be considered such a consequence of the breach of contract as could have been fairly and reasonably contemplated by both the parties when they made this contract. For such loss would neither have flowed naturally from the breach of this contract in the great multitude of such cases occurring under ordinary circumstances, nor were the special circumstances, which, perhaps, would have made it a reasonable and natural consequence of such breach of contract, communicated to or known by the defendants. The Judge ought, therefore, to have told the jury, that, upon the facts then before them, they ought not to take the loss of profits into consideration at all in estimating the damages. There must therefore be a new trial in this case.

Rule absolute.

————

BACKGROUND NOTE ON HADLEY V. BAXENDALE

Who was Hadley? Who was Baxendale? And what caused the delay? These and other questions concerning the players and the play are extensively addressed in Danzig, Hadley v. Baxendale: A Study in the Industrialization of the Law, 4 J.Leg.Stud. 249 (1975). A brief extract follows:

> In Gloucester, England, on Thursday, May 12, 1853, the engine shaft at City Flour Mills broke, preventing the further milling of corn. On May 13, the mill proprietors, Joseph and Jonah Hadley, dispatched an employee to Pickford and Co., "common carriers," to inquire as to the fastest means of conveying the shaft to W. Joyce and Co., Greenwich, where it would serve as a model for the crafting of a new shaft. . . . The shaft was delivered to Pickfords on Saturday, May 14, but it did not, in fact, reach W. Joyce and Co. until the 21st, because at the last stage of the voyage the shaft was shipped with a consignment of iron bound for Joyce and Co. by canal rather than by rail. . . . When Pickfords refused to make good these losses, the Hadleys brought suit . . . naming Joseph Baxendale, the London-based managing director of Pickford's, as the defendant. (Baxendale was personally liable for the failings of his unincorporated business.)
> . . .

Id. at 251.

————

Emerald Investments Ltd. Partnership v. Allmerican Financial Life Ins. and Annuity Co.

516 F.3d 612 (7th Cir. 2008)

(Posner, J.) ". . . *Hadley* and the cases following it . . . are cases about special handling. The Hadleys owned a flour mill. The millshaft broke, and the Hadleys hired Baxendale to transport the broken millshaft to a shop that, using the broken millshaft as a model, would make a new one. Because the Hadleys had no spare, the mill was shut down until the new millshaft arrived, and they incurred substantial losses. The receipt of the new shaft was delayed as a result of a breach by Baxendale of its contract of carriage. The court held that the Hadleys could not recover the profits they had lost because of the delay. Had they wanted Baxendale to take special care to get the new millshaft to them by the contractually specified deadline, they should have negotiated for that care, that special handling; undoubtedly Baxendale would have demanded a higher price.

"An Illinois case illustrates this point. The plaintiff in Siegel v. Western Union Telegraph Co., 312 Ill.App. 86, 37 N.E.2d 868 (1941), had delivered $200 to Western Union with instructions to transmit it to a friend of the plaintiff's. The money was to be bet (legally) on a horse, but this was not disclosed in the instructions to Western Union, which misdirected the money order; as a result it did not reach the friend until after the race was over-in which the horse that the plaintiff had intended to bet on won and would have paid $1650. The plaintiff sued Western Union for the $1450 in lost profit (which was conceded-there was no question that he would have bet on the horse that won), and failed on the authority of Hadley v. Baxendale, 37 N.E.2d at 871. Or imagine a professional photographer who after spending months in the Himalayas taking pictures to be used in advertising mountain-climbing gear drops off his roll of film at the nearest Walgreens when he returns to the United States and Walgreen loses it, and he sues Walgreen for his lost profits. He would lose. Had he wanted Walgreen to guarantee that the film would be properly developed and returned to him, he should have negotiated for such a guaranty; failing that, he should have taken an extra roll of film with him on his expedition or had the film developed by a firm catering to professional photographers."

————

RESTATEMENT, SECOND, CONTRACTS § 351

[See Selected Source Materials Supplement]

————

UCC §§ 2–713, 2–715(2)

[See Selected Source Materials Supplement]

————

CISG ART. 74

[See Selected Source Materials Supplement]

————

UNIDROIT PRINCIPLES OF INTERNATIONAL COMMERCIAL CONTRACTS ART. 7.4.4

[See Selected Source Materials Supplement]

————

PRINCIPLES OF EUROPEAN CONTRACT LAW ART. 9.503

[See Selected Source Materials Supplement]

NOTE ON LIMITATIONS ON CONTRACT DAMAGES

Fuller and Perdue, The Reliance Interest in Contract Damages, 46 Yale L.J. 52, 84 (1936), concludes that Hadley v. Baxendale "may be said to stand for two propositions: (1) that it is not always wise to make the defaulting promisor pay for all the damage which follows as a consequence of his breach, and (2) that specifically the proper test for determining whether particular items of damage should be compensable is to inquire whether they should have been foreseen by the promisor at the time of the contract. The first aspect of the case is much more important than the second. In its first aspect the case bears an integral relation to the very bases of contract liability. It declares in effect that just as it is wise to refuse enforcement altogether to some promises (considerationless, unaccepted, 'social' promises, etc.) so it is wise not to go too far in enforcing those promises which are deemed worthy of legal sanction."

As the cases in this Chapter illustrate, many of the principles governing damages for breach of contract reflect a tension between that idea and the idea that contract damages should put the injured party in as good a position as that in which he would have been put by full performance of the contract.

Valentine v. General American Credit, Inc.

420 Mich. 256, 362 N.W.2d 628 (1984)

(Levin, J.) "Valentine may not recover mental distress damages for breach of the employment contract, although such damages may have been foreseeable and she might not be "made whole" absent an award of mental distress damages. . . .

"[T]he general rule, with few exceptions, is to "uniformly den[y]" recovery for mental distress damages although they are "foreseeable within the rule of *Hadley v. Baxendale*." The rule barring recovery of mental distress damages—a gloss on the generality of the rule stated in *Hadley v. Baxendale*—is fully applicable to an action for breach of an employment contract.

"The denial of mental distress damages, although the result is to leave the plaintiff with less than a full recovery, has analogy in the law. The law does not generally compensate for all losses suffered. Recovery is denied for attorney's fees, for mental anguish not accompanied by physical manifestation, and "make-whole" or full recovery has been denied where the cost of performance exceeds the value to the promisee. The courts have not, despite "make whole" generalizations regarding the damages recoverable, attempted to provide compensation for all losses. Instead, specific rules have been established that provide for the calculation of the damages recoverable in particular kinds of actions. In contract actions, the market price is the general standard.

"In determining what damages are recoverable, the courts of this state have qualified the general rule, pursuant to which mental distress damages for breach of contract are not recoverable, with a narrow exception. Rather than look to the foreseeability of loss to determine the applicability of the exception, the courts have considered whether the contract "has elements of personality" and whether the "damage suffered upon the breach of the agreement is capable of adequate compensation by reference to the terms of the contract.

"The narrow scope of those verbal formulas appears on consideration of the limited situations in which this Court has allowed the recovery of mental distress damages for breach of contract. In *Vanderpool v. Richardson,* 52 Mich. 336, 17 N.W. 936 (1883), recovery was allowed for breach of a promise to marry. In *Stewart v. Rudner,* 349 Mich. 459, 84 N.W.2d 816 (1957), a doctor who failed to fulfill his promise to deliver a child by caesarean section was required to pay mental distress damages. In *Miholevich v. Mid-West Mutual Auto Ins. Co.,* 261 Mich. 495, 246 N.W. 202 (1933), the plaintiff, who was jailed for failure to pay a liability judgment, recovered mental distress damages from an insurer who had failed to pay the judgment.

"Loss of a job is not comparable to the loss of a marriage or a child and generally results in estimable monetary damages. In *Miholevich,* the breach resulted in a deprivation of personal liberty.

"An employment contract will indeed often have a personal element. Employment is an important aspect of most persons' lives, and the breach of an employment contract may result in emotional distress. The primary purpose in forming such contracts, however, is economic and not to secure the protection of personal interests. The psychic satisfaction of the employment is secondary.

"Mental distress damages for breach of contract have not been awarded where there is a market standard by which damages can be adequately determined. Valentine's monetary loss can be estimated with reasonable certainty according to the terms of the contract and the market for, or the market value of, her service. Mental distress damages are not awarded an employee found to have been wrongfully discharged in violation of a collective bargaining agreement.

"We conclude, because an employment contract is not entered into primarily to secure the protection of personal interests and pecuniary damages can be estimated with reasonable certainty, that a person discharged in breach of an employment contract may not recover mental distress damages."

———

SECTION 5. CERTAINTY

KENFORD CO. v. ERIE COUNTY
New York Court of Appeals, 1986.
67 N.Y.2d 257, 502 N.Y.S.2d 131, 493 N.E.2d 234.

PER CURIAM.

The issue in this appeal is whether a plaintiff, in an action for breach of contract, may recover loss of prospective profits for its contemplated 20-year operation of a domed stadium which was to be constructed by defendant County of Erie (County).

On August 8, 1969, pursuant to a duly adopted resolution of its legislature, the County of Erie entered into a contract with Kenford Company, Inc. (Kenford) and Dome Stadium, Inc. (DSI) for the construction and operation of a domed stadium facility near the City of Buffalo. The contract provided that construction of the facility by the County would commence within 12 months of the contract date and that a mutually acceptable 40-year lease between the County and DSI for the operation of said facility would be negotiated by the parties and agreed upon within three months of the receipt by the County of preliminary plans, drawings and cost estimates. It was further provided that in the event a mutually acceptable lease could not be agreed upon within the three-month period, a separate management contract between the County and DSI, as appended to the basic agreement, would be executed by the parties, providing for the operation of the stadium facility by DSI for a period of 20 years from the completion of the stadium and its availability for use.

Although strenuous and extensive negotiations followed, the parties never agreed upon the terms of a lease, nor did construction of a domed facility begin within the one-year period or at any time thereafter. A breach of the contract thus occurred and this action was commenced in June 1971 by Kenford and DSI.

Prolonged and extensive pretrial and preliminary proceedings transpired throughout the next 10 years, culminating with the entry of an order which affirmed the grant of summary judgment against the County on the issue of liability and directed a trial limited to the issue of damages (*Kenford Co. v. County of Erie*, 88 A.D.2d 758, *lv dismissed* 58 N.Y.2d 689). The ensuing trial ended some nine months later with a multimillion dollar jury verdict in plaintiffs' favor.* An appeal to the Appellate Division

---

*   Editors' note. The plaintiffs originally sought lost profits on the management contract plus lost profits on land they acquired surrounding the stadium, including lost profits on planned developments (parking, a theme park, office buildings, and a baseball franchise) and appreciation in land value. The plaintiffs donated the land for the stadium to the county. The trial court held lost profits on the planned developments on peripheral land were too speculative but allowed the claims for lost profits on the management contract and appreciation in value of peripheral land. The jury awarded $25.6 million for lost profits on the management contract and $18 million for resulted in a modification of the judgment. That court reversed portions of the judgment awarding damages for loss of profits and for certain out-of-pocket expenses incurred, and directed a new trial upon other issues (*Kenford Co. v. County of Erie,* 108 A.D.2d 132). On appeal to this court, we are concerned only with that portion of the verdict which awarded DSI money damages for loss of prospective profits during the 20-year period of the proposed management contract, as appended to the basic contract. That portion of the verdict was set aside by the Appellate Division and the cause of action dismissed. The court concluded that the use of expert opinion to present statistical projections of future business operations involved the use of too many variables to provide a rational basis upon which lost profits could be calculated and, therefore, such projections were insufficient as a matter of law to support an award of lost profits. We agree with this ultimate conclusion, but upon different grounds.

Loss of future profits as damages for breach of contract have been permitted in New York under long-established and precise rules of law. First, it must be demonstrated with certainty that such damages have been caused by the breach and, second, the alleged loss must be capable of proof with reasonable certainty. In other words, the damages may not be merely speculative, possible or imaginary, but must be reasonably certain and directly traceable to the breach, not remote or the result of other intervening causes (*Wakeman v. Wheeler & Wilson Mfg. Co.,* 101 N.Y. 205). In addition, there must be a showing that the particular damages were fairly within the contemplation of the parties to the contract at the time it was made (*Witherbee v. Meyer,* 155 N.Y. 446). If it is a new business seeking to recover for loss of future profits, a stricter standard is imposed for the obvious reason that there does not exist a reasonable basis of experience upon which to estimate lost profits with the requisite degree of reasonable certainty (*Cramer v. Grand Rapids Show Case Co.,* 223 N.Y. 63; 25 CJS, Damages, § 42[b]).

These rules must be applied to the proof presented by DSI in this case. We note the procedure for computing damages selected by DSI was in accord with contemporary economic theory and was presented through the testimony of recognized experts. Such a procedure has been accepted in this State and many other jurisdictions (*see, De Long v. County of Erie,* 60 N.Y.2d 296). DSI's economic analysis employed historical data, obtained

---

lost appreciation in the value of the peripheral land. It also awarded $6 million as out-of-pocket expenses. Only the claim for $25.6 million lost profits on the management contract is addressed by the New York Court of Appeals in this decision. The case came back to the Court in 1989 on the claim for lost appreciation in the value of peripheral land, which was reduced from $18 million to $6.5 million on retrial. The Court held the damages could not be recovered under the New York version of the foreseeability rule, which limits damages to "what liability the defendant fairly may be supposed to have assumed consciously, or to have warranted the plaintiff reasonably to suppose that it assumed, when the contract was made." Kenford Company, Inc. v. County of Erie, 537 N.E.2d 176, 179 (N.Y. 1989). This rule also makes a brief appearance in this decision as an alternative ground for the result.

from the operation of other domed stadiums and related facilities throughout the country, which was then applied to the results of a comprehensive study of the marketing prospects for the proposed facility in the Buffalo area. The quantity of proof is massive and, unquestionably, represents business and industry's most advanced and sophisticated method for predicting the probable results of contemplated projects. Indeed, it is difficult to conclude what additional relevant proof could have been submitted by DSI in support of its attempt to establish, with reasonable certainty, loss of prospective profits. Nevertheless, DSI's proof is insufficient to meet the required standard.

The reason for this conclusion is twofold. Initially, the proof does not satisfy the requirement that liability for loss of profits over a 20-year period was in the contemplation of the parties at the time of the execution of the basic contract or at the time of its breach (*see, Chapman v. Fargo,* 223 N.Y. 32; 36 N.Y.Jur.2d, Damages, §§ 39, 40, at 66–70). Indeed, the provisions in the contract providing remedy for a default do not suggest or provide for such a heavy responsibility on the part of the County. In the absence of any provision for such an eventuality, the commonsense rule to apply is to consider what the parties would have concluded had they considered the subject. The evidence here fails to demonstrate that liability for loss of profits over the length of the contract would have been in the contemplation of the parties at the relevant times.

Next, we note that despite the massive quantity of expert proof submitted by DSI, the ultimate conclusions are still projections, and as employed in the present day commercial world, subject to adjustment and modification. We of course recognize that any projection cannot be absolute, nor is there any such requirement, but it is axiomatic that the degree of certainty is dependent upon known or unknown factors which form the basis of the ultimate conclusion. Here, the foundations upon which the economic model was created undermine the certainty of the projections. DSI assumed that the facility was completed, available for use and successfully operated by it for 20 years, providing professional sporting events and other forms of entertainment, as well as hosting meetings, conventions and related commercial gatherings. At the time of the breach, there was only one other facility in this country to use as a basis of comparison, the Astrodome in Houston. Quite simply, the multitude of assumptions required to establish projections of profitability over the life of this contract require speculation and conjecture, making it beyond the capability of even the most sophisticated procedures to satisfy the legal requirements of proof with reasonable certainty.

The economic facts of life, the whim of the general public and the fickle nature of popular support for professional athletic endeavors must be given great weight in attempting to ascertain damages 20 years in the future. New York has long recognized the inherent uncertainties of predicting profits in the entertainment field in general (*see, Broadway Photoplay Co. v. World Film Corp.,* 225 N.Y. 104) and, in this case, we are dealing, in large part, with a new facility furnishing entertainment for the public. It is our view that the record in this case demonstrates the efficacy of the principles set forth by this court in *Cramer v. Grand Rapids Show Case Co.* (223 N.Y. 63, *supra*), principles to which we continue to adhere. In so doing, we specifically reject the "rational basis" test enunciated in *Perma Research & Dev. Co. v. Singer Co.* (542 F.2d 111, *cert. denied* 429 U.S. 987) and adopted by the Appellate Division.

Accordingly, that portion of the order of the Appellate Division being appealed from should be affirmed.

CHIEF JUDGE WACHTLER and JUDGES MEYER, ALEXANDER, TITONE and KANE* concur in Per Curiam opinion; JUDGES SIMONS, KAYE and HANCOCK, JR., taking no part.

Order insofar as appealed from affirmed, with costs.

NOTE ON KENFORD

At the end of the opinion in *Kenford,* the court stated that "we specifically reject the 'rational basis' test enunciated in *Perma Research* . . . and adopted by the Appellate Division." The passage of the Appellate Division opinion to which the Court of Appeals referred, reads as follows:

> . . . In [Perma Research & Devel. Co. v. Singer Co., 402 F.Supp. 881, affd. 542 F.2d 111, cert. den. 429 U.S. 987, 97 S.Ct. 507, 50 L.Ed.2d 598, the court held that lost profits for a new venture] may be awarded if plaintiff establishes three elements: that the lost profits are the direct and proximate result of the breach; that profits were contemplated by the parties; and that there is a rational basis on which to calculate the lost profits (Perma Research & Devel. Co. v. Singer Co. . . .). The first two criteria reflect the lost profits test applicable to established businesses as enunciated in Witherbee v. Meyer, 155 N.Y. 446, 449–450, 50 N.E. 58. . . . What the court did in Perma Research, in essence, was to add a third requirement for new businesses by requiring them to establish some rational basis on which to calculate the lost profits. . . . The Perma Research test has been subsequently employed in the Second Circuit (Lexington Prods. Ltd. v. B.D. Communications, 677 F.2d 251, 253; Western Geophysical Co. of Am. v. Bolt Assocs., 584 F.2d 1164, 1172 . . . Contemporary Mission v. Famous Music Corp., 557 F.2d 918, 926. . . .)

----

*   Designated pursuant to N.Y. Constitution, article VI, § 2.

————

NOTE ON THE NEW-BUSINESS RULE

In the past, a major application of the uncertainty principle was the new-business rule. This rule prohibits recovery of lost profits that a plaintiff claims would have been generated by a proposed new business, on the ground that in such cases profits are too speculative. (In one typical fact pattern, the plaintiff had leased premises for its new business from the defendant, who then broke the lease before the plaintiff even moved in.) The new-business rule still surfaces in some cases, but there is a definite trend toward abrogating the rule and reconstruing the older cases as resting only on the particular facts involved, rather than on a special rule. For example, in Fera v. Village Plaza, Inc., 396 Mich. 639, 242 N.W.2d 372 (1976), the plaintiffs executed a ten-year lease for a "book and bottle" shop in the defendants' proposed shopping center. Later, the plaintiffs were refused their space because the defendants had misplaced the lease and rented the space to other tenants. The plaintiffs brought suit, claiming lost profits. The jury returned a verdict against the defendants for $200,000. The Court of Appeals (an intermediate appellate court) reversed, partly on the basis of the new-business rule. The Michigan Supreme Court reinstated the jury verdict:

> [Earlier Michigan cases] should not be read as stating a rule of law which prevents *every* new business from recovering anticipated lost profits for breach of contract. The rule is merely an application of the doctrine that "[i]n order to be entitled to a verdict, or a judgment, for damages for breach of contract, the plaintiff must lay a basis for a reasonable estimate of the extent of his harm, measured in money." 5 Corbin on Contracts, § 1020, p. 124. The issue becomes one of sufficiency of proof. . . .
>
> The Court of Appeals based its opinion reversing the jury's award on two grounds: First, that a new business cannot recover damages for lost profits for breach of a lease. We have expressed our disapproval of that rule. Secondly, the Court of Appeals held plaintiffs barred from recovery because the proof of lost profits was entirely speculative. We disagree. . . .
>
> While we might have found plaintiffs' proofs lacking had we been members of the jury, that is not the standard of review we employ. As a reviewing court we will not invade the fact finding of the jury or remand for entry of judgment unless the factual record is so clear that reasonable minds may not disagree. This is not the situation here. . . .

————

Rombola v. Cosindas

351 Mass. 382, 220 N.E.2d 919 (1966)

Rombola agreed to train, maintain, and race Cosindas's horse, Margy Sampson, for the period November 8, 1962, to December 1, 1963. Rombola was to pay all expenses and receive 75% of all gross purses, and Cosindas was to receive the remaining 25%. In the winter of 1962–63, Rombola maintained and trained the horse at his stable, and in the following spring and summer he raced her twenty-five times. In fall 1963, Rombola entered Margy Sampson in six stake races—races in which the owners of the horses put up money that is added to the track's payoff—to be held at a Suffolk Downs meet ending December 1. Before the meet began, Cosindas took possession of Margy Sampson, and thereby deprived Rombola of his right to race her. The horse was not raced again until after December 1. Rombola sued Cosindas for breach of contract, and the trial judge directed a verdict for Cosindas on the ground that Rombola's damages were too uncertain. Reversed.

... In the year of the contract, of the twenty-five races in which the horse was entered by Rombola, she had won ten and shared in the purse money in a total of twenty races, earning, in all, purses approximating $12,000. In the year following the expiration of Rombola's contract with Cosindas, the horse raced twenty-nine times and won money in an amount almost completely consistent percentagewise with the money won during the period of the contract. . . .

We think . . . that Rombola would be entitled to show substantial damages on the theory of loss of prospective profits. . . . [Margy Sampson] had already proved her ability both prior to and while under Rombola's management and training, over an extended period of time, against many competitors and under varying track conditions. Her consistent performance in the year subsequent to the breach negates any basis for an inference of a diminution in ability or in earning capacity at the time of the Suffolk Downs meet. While it is possible that no profits would have been realized if Margy Sampson had participated in the scheduled stake races, that possibility is inherent in any business venture. . . .

————

Contemporary Mission, Inc. v. Famous Music Corp.

557 F.2d 918 (2d Cir.1977)

Famous Music failed to perform a contract with Contemporary Mission, under which Famous Music agreed to pay a royalty to Contemporary Mission in return for the master tape recording of *Virgin* (a rock opera) and the exclusive right to manufacture and sell records made from the master. Under the agreement, Famous Music was obliged to release at least four separate single records from *Virgin*.

Under the doctrine of *Wood v. Lucy* (Chapter 2, Section 3, *supra*), Famous Music had an obligation to use reasonable efforts to promote *Virgin* on a nationwide basis. Prior to the breach, one of the singles from *Virgin* had reached number 80 on the hot soul record charts, and later it reached number 61. At the trial, Contemporary Mission offered a statistical analysis of every song that had reached number 61 during 1974. This analysis showed that 76 percent of the 324 songs that had reached number 61 ultimately reached the top 40; 65 percent reached the top 30; 51 percent reached the top 20; 34 percent reached the top 10; 21 percent reached the top 5; and 10 percent reached number 1. Contemporary Mission also was prepared to offer the testimony of an expert witness who could have converted these measures of success into projected sales figures and lost royalties. The trial judge excluded all this evidence on the ground that it was speculative. Held, the evidence should have been admitted.

"... This is not a case in which the plaintiff sought to prove hypothetical profits from the sale of a hypothetical record at a hypothetical price in a hypothetical market. . . . [T]he record was real, the price was fixed, the market was buying and the record's success, while modest, was increasing. Even after the promotional efforts ended, [and] the record was withdrawn from the marketplace, it was carried, as a result of its own momentum, to an additional 10,000 sales and to a rise from approximately number 80 on the 'Hot Soul Singles' chart of Billboard magazine to number 61. It cannot be gainsaid that if someone had continued to promote it, and if it had not been withdrawn from the market, it would have sold more records than it actually did. Thus, it is certain that Contemporary suffered some damage in the form of lost royalties. . . ."

UCC § 1–106(1)

[See Selected Source Materials Supplement]

RESTATEMENT, SECOND, CONTRACTS § 352

[See Selected Source Materials Supplement]

UNIDROIT PRINCIPLES OF INTERNATIONAL COMMERCIAL CONTRACTS ART. 7.4.3

[See Selected Source Materials Supplement]

NOTE ON LOSS OF CHANCE

When a breach of contract deprives the plaintiff of a valuable opportunity upon which a price can be set that price can be used as the measure of damages, rather than trying to predict how the opportunity would have played out. For example, take a case where a contestant who has properly qualified for a contest is wrongfully disqualified by the contest's promoter, and it cannot be determined whether the contestant would have won a prize if he had not been disqualified. In such a case, the promoter's breach has clearly caused a loss to the contestant: Before the promoter acted wrongfully, the contestant had a chance to win the contest; after the promoter acted wrongfully, the contestant did not have the chance. As a result of the promoter's wrongful act, therefore, the contestant has lost an asset—the chance to win the contest—and the promoter should be liable for the value of that asset. By way of analogy, suppose that Burgle steals a lottery ticket owned by Jones. Burgle should be liable to Jones for the value of the ticket even though the ticket was not a winner. Similarly, if the promoter of a contest wrongfully disqualified a contestant, the promoter should be liable to the contestant for the value of the contestant's chance even though that chance was significantly less than 50%.

The leading case is Chaplin v. Hicks, [1911] 2 K.B. 786, decided by the English Court of Appeal in 1911. Hicks, a well-known actor and theater manager, ran a contest for actresses. The prizes were theatrical engagements. The not-very-appealing rules of the contest were as follows: Contestants would send photographs of themselves to Hicks, who would divide England into ten districts and would publish, in a newspaper in each district, photographs of the candidates he had selected. Newspaper readers would then vote for the contestants they considered to be the most beautiful. Hicks would thereafter interview fifty finalists, consisting of the five candidates in each district who had the highest votes. From these fifty finalists, Hicks would select twelve winning contestants, who would receive the theatrical engagements.

Chaplin became one of the fifty finalists, but Hicks did not give her an interview. Chaplin then brought an action against Hicks for the loss of her chance of being selected as one of the twelve winners. At trial, she was awarded damages of £100. The Court of Appeal affirmed. Lord Justice Moulton stated:

> Is expulsion from a limited class of competitors an injury? To my mind there can be only one answer to that question; it is an injury and may be a very substantial one. Therefore the plaintiff starts with an unchallengeable case of injury, and the damages given in respect of it should be equivalent to the loss. . . .

> . . . Is there any such rule as that, where the result of a contract depends on the volition of an independent party, the law shuts its eyes to the wrong and says that there are no damages? Such a rule, if it existed, would work great wrong. Let us take the case of a man under a contract of service to serve as a second-class clerk for five years at a salary of £200 a year, which expressly provides that, at the end of that period, out of every five second-class clerks two first-class

clerks will be chosen at a salary of £500 a year. If such a clause is embodied in the contract, it is clear that a person thinking of applying for the position would reckon that he would have the advantage of being one of five persons from whom the two first-class clerks must be chosen, and that might be a very substantial portion of the consideration for his appointment. If, after he has taken the post and worked under the contract of service, the employers repudiate the obligation, is he to have no remedy? He has sustained a very real loss, and there can be no possible reason why the law should not leave it to the jury to estimate the value of that of which he has been deprived. Where by contract a man has a right to belong to a limited class of competitors, he is possessed of something of value, and it is the duty of the jury to estimate the pecuniary value of that advantage if it is taken from him.

Moulton's opinion did not state with precision how the value of a contestant's chance should be measured. In cases like lottery tickets, in which there is an established market for the chance, the value of the chance is normally its market price. When there is no established market, the value of the chance is the price that a willing buyer of the chance would pay to a willing seller. This approach was implied in the opinion of Lord Justice Vaughan Williams, concurring in Chaplin v. Hicks:

> It is true that no market [for the chance to win the contest] can be said to exist. None of the fifty competitors could have gone into the market and sold her right; her right was a personal right and incapable of transfer. But a jury might well take the view that such a right, if it could have been transferred, would have been of such a value that every one would recognize that a good price could be obtained for it.

Typically, in the absence of a market price, what a willing buyer would pay a willing seller should be based on the expected value of the chance. So, for example, in Van Gulik v. Resource Development Council for Alaska, 695 P.2d 1071 (Alaska 1985), a promoter had staged a lottery. Under the lottery's rules, the contestants' tickets were to be drawn from a bin, one by one. The last ticket drawn would win the grand prize of $10,000. When only three tickets, owned by A, B, and C, remained in the bin, the lottery operators mistakenly, and in breach of the contest rules, drew the tickets owned by B and C simultaneously, and overlooked the fact that A's ticket was still in the bin. When they realized their mistake, the operators then compounded their breach by wrongfully drawing all the lottery tickets all over again. A brought suit. If the lottery operators had drawn only B's ticket, or only C's ticket, as they should have done, the last two tickets would have either been those of A and B or A and C. Accordingly, at the time of the breach A had a 50% chance of winning $10,000. The court gave A the choice of either (i) $5,000 in damages, based on the expected value of his chance at the time of the breach, or (ii) participation in a re-drawing involving only his ticket and one other.

A claim for the loss of profits can be treated as a special case of a claim for the loss of a chance, that is, the chance to make a profit. Just as the damages of a person who holds an explicit chance, like a contestant, can be measured by the value of the chance of winning at the time of breach, so too in the lost-profits case the plaintiff's damages could be measured by the value of the chance of profits at the time of breach. Accordingly, the plaintiff would recover the amount that a buyer would have paid for a pre-breach assignment of the plaintiff's right to earn profits under the contract.

The problem is how to measure the market value of such a right when, as in *Kenford*, there is no actual market in which identical rights are freely traded. The answer is that a right is an asset, and financial economics provides a well-established methodology, known as the Capital Asset Pricing Model (CAPM, pronounced cap-em) for determining the value of assets whose value is based on prospective returns. To apply CAPM, the *expected cash flow* of an income-producing asset (that is, roughly speaking, the income that can be expected to be generated by the asset, minus the expenses required to generate that income) is calculated by determining the various possible cash flows that the asset may yield, multiplying each cash flow by its probability, and summing the result. The value of the asset is then calculated, based on (i) the expected cash flow and (ii) a formula that turns in large part on the risk rates implicitly assigned by the stock market to corporations that are in the kind of business the asset involves. So, for example, in deciding how much to pay for a movie theater, an investor using CAPM basically would apply, to the theater's expected cash flow, the risk rate implicitly assigned by the stock market to corporations engaged in the movie-theater business.

As the methodology of financial economics shows, therefore, the fact that projected profits are risky and uncertain does not prevent the valuation of an income-producing asset—it could not; virtually all such assets have risky and uncertain returns. Instead, risk and uncertainty is impounded into the value of the assets, first in weighting the cash flows the asset may produce, and then in determining the risk rates to apply to the expected cash flow based on that weighting.

A contract is a special type of income-producing asset. Its value can be determined in the same way as the value of any other such asset. Thus if in *Kenford* there was a 40% probability of a $10 million cash flow to Dome over the twenty-year term of the management agreement, a 30% probability of a $30 million cash flow, and a 30% probability of a $40 million cash flow, the expected cash flow to Dome would be $25 million (40% of $10 million, plus 30% of $30 million, plus 30% of $40 million). Damages would be calculated by applying the appropriate risk rate to the expected cash flow. A court that believes profits under a contract to be uncertain would therefore not deny recovery of profits, but instead would assign very low probabilities to very unlikely cash flows, assign a high risk rate, or both.

SECTION 6. LIQUIDATED DAMAGES

NPS, LLC v. MINIHANE

Supreme Judicial Court of Massachusetts, 2008.
451 Mass. 417, 886 N.E.2d 670.

COWIN, J.

In this case we decide whether an acceleration clause in a ten-year license agreement for luxury seats for New England Patriots professional football games at Gillette Stadium is enforceable. The agreement requires the purchaser of the license to pay, upon default, the amounts due for all years remaining on the license. The plaintiff contends that the clause is a lawful liquidated damages provision; the defendant, who defaulted in the first year of the agreement, argues that it is an unlawful penalty. A judge in the Superior Court agreed with the defendant and refused to enforce the provision. Because we conclude the provision is enforceable, we modify the judgment accordingly.

Background. The judge issued his ruling on the liquidated damages provision from the bench without detailed findings of fact. Most of the underlying facts, however, are not in dispute, as indicated by the joint stipulation of the parties. We supplement these facts with those that were found or implied by the judge. The plaintiff, NPS, LLC (NPS), is the developer of Gillette Stadium (stadium), the home field of the New England Patriots professional football team (Patriots). In 2002, while the stadium was still under construction, NPS entered into an agreement with the defendant, Paul Minihane, for the purchase of a ten-year license for two luxury seats in the Club Level III section. The agreement called for the defendant to pay $3,750 per seat annually for each of the ten seasons from 2002 to 2011. The agreement included a liquidated damages provision, set forth in the margin,[2] which provides that in the event of a default, including failure to pay any amount due under the license agreement, the payments would be accelerated so that the defendant would be required to pay the balance for all the years remaining on the contract. Upon executing the agreement, the defendant paid a $7,500 security deposit; he later made a

---

[2] "15. *Default.* The following shall constitute an 'Event of Default' under this Agreement: (i) Licensee fails to pay when due any amounts to be paid by Licensee pursuant to the Agreement .... In the event of any such Event of Default, Owner may, at its option: (a) withhold distribution of tickets to Licensee for games and/or other Stadium Events until such time as such default is cured; and/or (b) terminate the rights of Licensee under the Agreement after giving Licensee not less than twenty (20) days prior written notice of such default or breach .... In the event that Licensee shall not have cured the default or breach specified in said notice by the date specified in said notice, Owner may terminate the right of Licensee to the use and possession of the Club Seats and all other rights and privileges of Licensee under the Agreement and declare the entire unpaid balance of the License Fee (which for the purposes hereof shall include the total aggregate unpaid balance of the annual License Fees for the remainder of the Term) immediately due and payable, whereupon Owner shall have no further obligation of any kind to Licensee. Owner shall have no duty to mitigate any damages incurred by it as a result of a default by Licensee hereunder. . . . ."

payment of $2,000 toward the license fee for the 2002 season. Although he or his guests attended all but one of the 2002 preseason and regular season Patriots games at the stadium using the tickets for the Club Seats, he made no further payments.

After giving notice to the defendant, NPS accelerated the payments and filed a complaint in the Superior Court seeking the full amount due under the contract. After a bench trial, the judge ruled that the liquidated damages provision was unenforceable because the amount due was "grossly disproportionate to a reasonable estimate of actual damages made at the time of contract formation." After taking further evidence on the issue of actual damages, the judge issued a memorandum of decision and order in which he awarded damages to NPS in the amount of $6,000. This appeal followed, and we transferred the case to this court on our own motion.

We accept the judge's findings of fact unless they are clearly erroneous. *Kendall v. Selvaggio,* 413 Mass. 619, 620, 602 N.E.2d 206 (1992). "On the other hand, to ensure that the ultimate findings and conclusions are consistent with the law, we scrutinize without deference the legal standard which the judge applied to the facts." *Id.* at 621, 602 N.E.2d 206. Whether a liquidated damages provision in a contract is an unenforceable penalty is a question of law. *Manganaro Drywall, Inc. v. Penn-Simon Constr. Co.,* 357 Mass. 653, 656, 260 N.E.2d 182 (1970). The burden of showing that a liquidated damages provision is unenforceable rests with the party challenging enforcement of the provision (here, the defendant), *TAL Fin. Corp. v. CSC Consulting, Inc.,* 446 Mass. 422, 423, 844 N.E.2d 1085 (2006), and we resolve reasonable doubts in favor of the aggrieved party (here, NPS). *Cummings Props., LLC v. National Communications Corp.,* 449 Mass. 490, 494, 869 N.E.2d 617 (2007).

It is well settled that "a contract provision that clearly and reasonably establishes liquidated damages should be enforced, so long as it is not so disproportionate to anticipated damages as to constitute a penalty." *TAL Fin. Corp. v. CSC Consulting, Inc., supra* at 431, 844 N.E.2d 1085. A liquidated damages provision will usually be enforced, provided two criteria are satisfied: first, that at the time of contracting the actual damages flowing from a breach were difficult to ascertain; and second, that the sum agreed on as liquidated damages represents a "reasonable forecast of damages expected to occur in the event of a breach." *Cummings Props., LLC v. National Communications Corp., supra* at 494, 869 N.E.2d 617. Where damages are easily ascertainable, and the amount provided for is grossly disproportionate to actual damages or unconscionably excessive, the court will award the aggrieved party no more than its actual damages. *A-Z Servicenter, Inc. v. Segall,* 334 Mass. 672, 675, 138 N.E.2d 266 (1956). Since there is "no bright line separating an agreement to pay a reasonable measure of damages from an unenforceable penalty clause," *TAL Fin. Corp.*

v. CSC Consulting, Inc., supra, the reasonableness of the measure of anticipated damages depends on the circumstances of each case. *A-Z Servicenter, Inc. v. Segall, supra.* In assessing reasonableness, we look to the circumstances at the time of contract formation; we do not take a "second look" at the actual damages after the contract has been breached. *Kelly v. Marx,* 428 Mass. 877, 878, 705 N.E.2d 1114 (1999).

In this case, the trial judge found that, at the time the parties entered into the license agreement, the harm resulting from a possible breach was difficult to ascertain. That finding was supported by the evidence, which indicated that the damages sustained by NPS would vary depending on the demand for tickets at the time of breach. Although the Patriots had won their first Super Bowl championship in 2002, shortly before the parties entered into their agreement, the demand for luxury stadium seats was then and remains variable and depends, according to the evidence, on the current performance of the team, as well as other factors, such as the popularity of the players and the relative popularity of other sports, that are unpredictable at the time of contract. Therefore, to predict at the time of contract how long it would take NPS to resell the defendant's seat license would be extremely difficult, if not impossible.

The judge went on to find, however, that the sum provided for in the agreement—acceleration of all payments for the remaining term of the contract—was "grossly disproportionate to a reasonable estimate of actual damages made at the time of contract formation." That finding was not supported by the evidence. It is the defendant's burden to show that the amount of liquidated damages is "unreasonably and grossly disproportionate to the real damages from a breach" or "unconscionably excessive." See *TAL Fin. Corp. v. CSC Consulting, Inc., supra* at 423, 844 N.E.2d 1085; *A-Z Servicenter, Inc. v. Segall, supra* at 675, 138 N.E.2d 266. Having presented little evidence beyond his assertion that the contract as a whole was unconscionable, the defendant in this case has not sustained that burden.

The liquidated damages provision here is similar to one we upheld in *Cummings Props., LLC v. National Communications Corp., supra* (*Cummings*). In that case, a tenant who defaulted on a commercial lease was required by the terms of the agreement to pay the entire amount of rent remaining under the lease. *Id.* at 491–492, 869 N.E.2d 617. The judge here did not have the benefit of our decision in *Cummings,* which was issued more than a year after the trial in this case; however, for present purposes, we see no meaningful distinction between the two provisions.

In upholding the liquidated damages provision in *Cummings,* we noted that "to the extent that the liquidated damages amount represented the agreed rental value of the property over the remaining life of the lease, decreasing in amount as the lease term came closer to expiration, it appears to be a reasonable anticipation of damages that might accrue from the nonpayment of rent." *Id.* at 496–497, 869 N.E.2d 617. The same is true here. This, like *Cummings,* is a case where the damages were difficult to estimate at the outset, and the defendant is required to pay no more than the total amount he would have paid had he performed his obligations under the agreement. The sum provided for therefore bears a reasonable relationship to the anticipated actual damages resulting from a breach. It anticipates a worst-case scenario, that is, NPS's inability to resell the seat for the remaining term of the license.[7] However, the defendant has not shown that this outcome is sufficiently unlikely that it renders the amount grossly disproportionate to a reasonable estimate of actual damages.

The defendant stood to receive a substantial benefit from this agreement: guaranteed luxury seating for all Patriots home games, as well as a hedge against future price increases over ten years. He was not deprived of an opportunity to learn and consider the terms of the agreement. Those terms may be harsh, especially when, as here, the breach occurred early in the life of the agreement. But the defendant has not shown that in the circumstances they are "unreasonably and grossly disproportionate to the real damages from a breach." *A-Z Servicenter, Inc. v. Segall,* 334 Mass. 672, 675, 138 N.E.2d 266 (1956).

On appeal, the parties have not raised the issue whether, if the liquidated damages provision is enforced, mitigation should be considered. However, because mitigation was raised (albeit obliquely) in the defendant's amended answer to the complaint, and because we hold that the liquidated damages provision is enforceable, we consider the issue, which appears to be one of first impression in Massachusetts.

We will follow the rule in many other jurisdictions and hold that, in the case of an enforceable liquidated damages provision, mitigation is irrelevant and should not be considered in assessing damages. When parties agree in advance to a sum certain that represents a reasonable estimate of potential damages, they exchange the opportunity to determine actual damages after a breach, including possible mitigation, for the "peace of mind and certainty of result" afforded by a liquidated damages clause. *Kelly v. Marx,* 428 Mass. 877, 881, 705 N.E.2d 1114 (1999), quoting *Kelly v. Marx,* 44 Mass.App.Ct. 825, 833, 694 N.E.2d 869 (1998) (Spina, J., dissenting). In such circumstances, to consider whether a plaintiff has mitigated its damages not only is illogical, but also defeats the purpose of liquidated damages provisions. See *Barrie School v. Patch,* 401 Md. 497, 513–514, 933 A.2d 382 (2007) (sum that stipulates damages in advance

---

[7] We note in passing that there was evidence at trial that NPS in fact had not been able to resell the defendant's seat, some four years after the defendant committed a breach of the agreement. Although Kelly v. Marx, 428 Mass. 877, 878, 705 N.E.2d 1114 (1999), prevents our consideration of this fact, it suggests that it was not unduly pessimistic to think that NPS might have difficulty reselling the defendant's seat in the event of breach.

"replaces any determination of actual loss," so that if liquidated damages provision is enforceable, court need not consider mitigation). Since the liquidated damages provision at issue here is enforceable, the question is irrelevant.

Conclusion. The ruling of the Superior Court that the liquidated damages provision of the license agreement is unenforceable is set aside, and the judgment is modified to award NPS the total amount of unpaid license fees due under the agreement, $65,500, plus interest. As so modified, the judgment is affirmed.

So ordered.

———

Lee Oldsmobile, Inc. v. Kaiden

32 Md.App. 556, 363 A.2d 270 (1976)

Lee Oldsmobile dealt in Rolls-Royces as part of its business operations. Kaiden learned that Lee had on order, as a part of its allotted 1973 quota of ten or eleven Rolls-Royces, a car of the style and color she wanted, and in August 1973 she sent Lee a $5,000 deposit on the purchase of this car for $29,500. Lee then sent Kaiden an order form, which she signed and returned. The order form contained a clause providing that Lee had the right, upon failure or refusal of the purchaser to accept delivery of the motor vehicle, to retain as liquidated damages any cash deposit made by the purchaser. Apparently there was a dispute concerning the date of delivery, and on November 21, Kaiden notified Lee that she had purchased another Rolls elsewhere, and instructed that her order be canceled. On November 29, Lee notified Kaiden that the car was ready for delivery. She declined to accept and demanded the return of her deposit. Lee refused, and later sold the Rolls to another purchaser. Held, Kaiden was entitled to recover the amount of her deposit, minus actual damages.

"We reject the application of the liquidated damage clause in the present case ... because it is clear that the actual damages are capable of accurate estimation. We do not say this from hindsight made possible because the actual figures claimed were in evidence. We say it because at the time the contract was made, it was clear that the nature of any damages which would result from a possible future breach was such that they would be easily ascertainable. . . . "

———

Norwalk Door Closer Co. v. Eagle Lock and Screw Co.

153 Conn. 681, 220 A.2d 263 (1966)

Norwalk and Eagle had a contract to manufacturer door closers exclusively for Norwalk, using tools, dies, patterns, and equipment provided by Norwalk. The contract had a seven-year term and provided that Eagle would pay $100,000 liquidated damages, if Eagle terminated the agreement, ceased operations, or there was a change in ownership. Eagle was acquired by new owners in breach of this term. Norwalk sued seeking liquidated damages. The trial court held the liquidated damage term was unenforceable, finding that Norwalk suffered no harm as a result of the change in ownership as the new owners employed the same local management and continued production "without loss to Norwalk of either business or time." Affirmed.

(Alcorn, J.) ". . . '[N]o provision in a contract for the payment of a fixed sum as damages, whether stipulated for as a penalty or as liquidated damages, will be enforced in a case where the court sees that no damage has been sustained.' See also King Motors, Inc. v. Delfino, supra, 136 Conn. 498, 72 A.2d 233. This principle finds approval in comment (e) of the Restatement, 1 Contracts § 339, where it is stated that '(i)f the parties honestly but mistakingly suppose that a breach will cause harm that will be incapable or very difficult of accurate estimation, when in fact the breach causes no harm at all or none that is incapable of accurate estimation without difficulty, their advance agreement fixing the amount to be paid as damages for breach * * * is not enforceable.' See also Priebe & Sons, Inc. v. United States, 332 U.S. 407, 412, 68 S.Ct. 123, 92 L.Ed. 32. This is not to say that any burden is placed on a plaintiff to prove actual damage in order to recover under a valid contract for liquidated damages. The proposition is only that equitable principles will be invoked to deny recovery when the facts make it apparent that no damage has been suffered.

"The principle is based on justice and fairness. 'The probable injury that the parties had reason to foresee is a fact that largely determines the question whether they made a genuine pre-estimate of that injury; but the justice and equity of enforcement depend also upon the amount of injury that has actually occurred.' 5 Corbin, contracts § 1063. For a collection of cases on the general subject see the annotation in 34 A.L.R. 1336.

"The circumstances which the parties might reasonably foresee at the time of making a contract could, in any given case, be vastly different from the circumstances which actually exist when a court is called upon to enforce the contract. It is not the function of the court to determine by hindsight the reasonableness of the expectation of the parties at the time the contract was made, but it is the function of the court at the time of enforcement to do justice. In the ordinary contract action the court determines the just damages from evidence offered. In a valid contract for liquidated damages, the parties are permitted, in order to avoid the uncertainties and time-consuming effort involved, to estimate in advance the reasonably probable foreseeable damages which would arise in the event of a default. Implicit in the transaction is the premise that the sum agreed upon will be within the fair range of those just damages which would be called for and provable had the parties resorted to proof. Consequently, if the damage envisioned by the parties never occurs, the whole premise of their agreed estimate vanishes, and, even if the contract was to be construed as one for liquidated damages rather than one for a penalty, neither justice nor the intent of the parties is served by enforcement. To enforce it would amount in reality to the infliction of a penalty. Massman Const. Co. v.

City Council of Greenville, Miss., 147 F.2d 925, 928 (5th Cir.); Northwest Fixture Co. v. Kilbourne & Clark Co., 128 F. 256, 261 (9th Cir.)

"Under the facts of the present case, where the court has found that Norwalk is continuing its business without having been harmed, and substantially as it did before the breach, neither justice nor reason permit it to recover $100,000 in damages."

———

UCC § 2–718(1)

[See Selected Source Materials Supplement]

———

RESTATEMENT, SECOND, CONTRACTS § 356

[See Selected Source Materials Supplement]

———

UNIDROIT PRINCIPLES OF INTERNATIONAL COMMERCIAL CONTRACTS ART. 7.4.13

[See Selected Source Materials Supplement]

———

PRINCIPLES OF EUROPEAN CONTRACT LAW ART. 9.509

[See Selected Source Materials Supplement]

———

NOTE ON LIQUIDATED DAMAGES

All courts agree on the principle that liquidated-damages provisions should be given special judicial scrutiny, although the formulation of the principle varies. In contrast, many commentators have criticized this principle. Most of the critiques have an implicit or explicit three-part structure: (1) They begin by assuming that the major justification for the principle that liquidated-damages provisions should be given special scrutiny is that such provisions lend themselves to blameworthy exploitation of one party by the other, and consequent one-sidedness, in a way that other types of contract provisions do not. (2) They then argue that this justification will not hold. (3) They conclude that the principle is therefore unjustified. So, for example, Goetz and Scott argue that the principle of special scrutiny of liquidated-damages provisions arose in a historical context in which protections against fraud and duress were not available. Given the modern development of unconscionability as a unifying unfairness principle, they suggest, the law should simply collapse the treatment of liquidated damages into that principle. Charles J. Goetz & Robert E. Scott, Liquidated Damages, Penalties and the Just Compensation Principle: Some Notes on an Enforcement Model and a Theory of Efficient Breach, 77 Colum. L. Rev. 554, 592 (1977).

The assumption that special scrutiny of liquidated-damages provisions is justified primarily by a special potential for blameworthy exploitation and one-sidedness does reflect the courts' rhetoric, which is cast in terms of whether or not such provisions are "penalties," and therefore suggests a concern with advantage-taking and oppression. In fact, however, the justification for the special scrutiny of liquidated-damages provisions is not that such provisions are specially amenable to blameworthy exploitation and one-sidedness, but that such provisions are systematically likely to reflect the limits of human cognition.

Classical contract law was based on a rational-actor model of psychology. Under this model, actors who make decisions in the face of uncertainty rationally maximize their subjective expected utility, with all future benefits and costs properly discounted to present value. A great body of theoretical and empirical work in cognitive psychology within the last thirty or forty years has shown that rational-actor psychology often lacks explanatory power. Although rational-actor psychology is the foundation of the standard economic model of choice, the empirical evidence shows that this model often diverges from the actual psychology of choice, due to limits of cognition. As Amos Tversky and Daniel Kahneman point out, expected-utility (rational-actor) theory "emerged from a logical analysis of games of chance rather than from a psychological analysis of risk and value. The theory was conceived as a normative model of an idealized decision maker, not as a description of the behavior of real people." Amos Tversky & Daniel Kahneman, Rational Choice and the Framing of Decisions, 59 J. Bus. S251 (1986).

In contrast to rational-actor psychology, modern cognitive psychology recognizes various limits of cognition. For purposes of contract law, three kinds of limits of cognition are especially salient: bounded rationality, irrational disposition, and defective capability.

1. Bounded Rationality

To begin with, an actor may not even consider the choice that would maximize his utility, because actors limit their search for and their processing (evaluating and deliberating on) of choices. If the costs of searching for and processing information were zero, and human information-processing capabilities were perfect, then an actor contemplating a decision would make a comprehensive search for relevant information, would process perfectly all the information he acquired, and would then make the best possible substantive decision—the decision that, as of the time made, was better than all the alternative decisions the actor might have made if he had complete knowledge and perfect processing abilities, and which would therefore maximize the actor's subjective expected utility.

In reality, of course, searching for and processing information does involve costs, in the form of time, energy, and perhaps money. Most actors either do not want to expend the resources required for comprehensive search and processing or recognize that comprehensive search and processing would not be achievable at any realistic cost. Actors therefore put boundaries on the amount of search and processing they engage in before making decisions. To put it differently, actors often consciously choose to be in a state of *rational ignorance*—"rational," because the incremental cost of achieving complete knowledge concerning and deliberating on a decision would be more than the expected gain from making the decision with complete rather than partial knowledge. So, for example, a patient may seek a second or perhaps a third doctor's opinion about treatment, but no more, because he believes it unlikely that consulting an extra five, ten, or fifteen doctors will not improve the quality of his choice of treatment sufficiently to justify spending the extra time and money.

Furthermore, our abilities to process information and arrive at decisions are constrained by limitations of computational ability, ability to calculate consequences, ability to organize and utilize memory, and the like. Hence, actors will often process imperfectly even the information they do acquire. Such imperfections in human processing ability scale up as decisions become more complex and involve more permutations.

Accordingly, human rationality is normally bounded both by limited information and limited information-processing ability.

2. *Irrational Disposition*

Next, actors are unrealistically optimistic as a systematic matter. (Lawyers do not realize this, because they are trained to be systematically pessimistic.) The dispositional characteristic of undue optimism is strikingly illustrated in a study by Lynn Baker and Robert Emery, appropriately titled, When Every Relationship Is Above Average, 17 Law and Hum. Behav. 439 (1993). Baker and Emery asked subjects who were about to get married to report on their own divorce-related prospects as compared to the divorce-related prospects of the general population. The disparities between perceptions concerning the prospects of the general population and the prospects of the subjects were enormous, and were almost invariably in the direction of optimism. For example, the subjects correctly estimated that fifty percent of American couples will eventually divorce. In contrast, the subjects estimated that their own chance of divorce was zero. Similarly, the subjects' median estimate of what percentage of spouses pay all court-ordered alimony was forty percent. In contrast, 100 percent of the subjects predicted that their own spouse would pay all court-ordered alimony.

3.   Defective Capability

Finally, cognitive psychology has established that actors use certain decision-making rules (heuristics) that yield systematic errors: "[T]he deviations of actual behavior from the normative model are too widespread to be ignored, too systematic to be dismissed as random error, and too fundamental to be accommodated by relaxing the normative system." Tversky & Kahneman, supra, at S252. For example, actors make decisions on the basis of data that is readily available to their memory, rather than on the basis of all the relevant data. This is known as the availability heuristic. Accordingly, actors systematically give undue weight to instantiated evidence as compared to general statements, to vivid evidence as compared to pallid evidence, and to concrete evidence as compared to abstract evidence. Similarly, actors are systematically insensitive to sample size, and erroneously take small samples as representative samples.

Another defect in capability concerns the ability of actors to make rational comparisons between present and future states. For example, the sample consisting of present events is often wrongly taken to be representative, and therefore predictive, of future events. Actors also systematically give too little weight to future benefits and costs as compared to present benefits and costs. Thus Martin Feldstein concludes that "some or all individuals have, in Pigou's . . . words, a 'faulty telescopic faculty' that causes them to give too little weight to the utility of future consumption." Feldstein, The Optimal Level of Social Security Benefits, 100 Q. J. Econ. 303, 307 (1985).

A defect of capability related to faulty telescopic faculties is the systematic underestimation of risks. Based on the work of cognitive psychologists, Kenneth Arrow observes that "[i]t is a plausible hypothesis that individuals are unable to recognize that there will be many surprises in the future; in short, as much other evidence tends to confirm, there is a tendency to underestimate uncertainties." Arrow, Risk Perception in Psychology and Economics, 20 Econ. Inquiry 1, 5 (1982). In fact, empirical evidence shows that actors often not only underestimate but ignore low-probability risks.

4.   Liquidated-Damages Provisions

The limits of cognition have a special bearing on liquidated-damages provisions. To begin with, bounded rationality and rational ignorance play an important role here. Contracting parties normally will find it relatively easy to evaluate proposed performance terms—terms that specify what performance the party is required to render—such as subject matter, quantity, and price. In contrast, at the time a contract is made it is often impracticable, if not impossible, to imagine all the scenarios of breach. Similarly, the inherent complexity of determining the application of a liquidated-damages provision to every possible breach scenario will often exceed actors' information-processing abilities.

Even on the doubtful assumption that a contracting party could imagine all breach scenarios, and determine the application of a liquidated-damages provision to every possible scenario, the benefits of extensive search and information processing on these issues will often seem to be very low as compared to the costs. A party who contracts to buy or sell a commodity normally expects to perform. Accordingly, the expected benefits of deliberating very carefully on performance terms are compelling, and the costs of such deliberation usually do not outweigh the expected benefits. In contrast, a party often will not expect that a liquidated-damages provision will ever come into play against him, partly because he intends to perform and partly because experience will tell him that in general there is a high rate of performance of contracts. For example, if contracts are performed at least ninety-five percent of the time (which observation suggests is likely), all the costs of processing the more remote applications of a liquidated-damages provision would have to be taken into account, but the benefits of such processing would have to be discounted by ninety-five percent. The resulting cost-benefit ratio will often provide a substantial disincentive for processing every possible application of a liquidated-damages provision, even if it were in fact possible to imagine every such application. As a result, contracting parties are often likely to not completely think through liquidated-damages provisions, and are therefore often unlikely to fully understand the full implications of such provisions.

The problem of irrational disposition also bears significantly on liquidated-damages provisions. Because actors tend to be unrealistically optimistic, a contracting party will probably believe that his performance is more likely, and his breach less likely, than is actually the case. Accordingly, unrealistic optimism will reduce even further the deliberation that actors give to liquidated-damages provisions.

Finally, defective capabilities have particular relevance to liquidated-damages provisions. The availability heuristic may lead a contracting party to give undue weight to his present intention to perform, which is vivid and concrete, as compared with the abstract possibility that future circumstances may lead him to breach. Because actors tend to take the sample of present evidence as unduly representative of the future, a contracting party is apt to overestimate the extent to which his present intention to perform is a reliable predictor of his future intention. Because actors have faulty telescopic faculties, a contracting party is likely to overvalue the benefit of the prospect of performance, which will normally begin to occur in the short term, as against the cost of breach, which will typically occur, if at all, only down the road. Because actors tend to underestimate risks, a contracting party is likely to underestimate the risk that a liquidated-damages provision will take effect.

The rationale for giving special scrutiny to liquidated-damages provisions affects the point of time on which the scrutiny is focused. If the justification for giving special scrutiny to liquidated-damages provisions is that such provisions are especially subject to blameworthy exploitation and one-sidedness, the scrutiny should be focused on the time the contract is made—a forward-looking test. In contrast, if the justification for special scrutiny is that parties often make cognitive errors in adopting such provisions, the scrutiny should be focused on the time of breach—a second-look test, which compares the liquidated damages with actual loss, on the ground that a gross discrepancy between forecast and result suggests that the liquidated-damages provision was a product of limited or defective cognition.

About half the states hold that the enforceability of liquidated-damages provisions is to be determined at the time the contract is made, and about half the states hold that enforceability of such provisions is to be determined, or also determined, at the time of the breach. See Kelly v. Marx, 44 Mass.App.Ct. 825, 694 N.E.2d 869 (1998), reversed, Kelly v. Marx, 428 Mass. 877, 705 N.E.2d 1114 (1999). However, even courts that purport to employ only a forward-looking test may apply a second-look test in the guise of relief against forfeiture, unconscionability, or the like. See, e.g., Hutchison v. Tompkins, 259 So.2d 129 (Fla. 1972).

NOTE ON ALTERNATIVE-PERFORMANCE TERMS

A contract may give the promisor the option to choose among alternative performances. This can include an option to pay a stipulated sum of money in lieu of some other performance. For example, a multi-year employment contract might give either party the option to buy out of the balance of the contract by paying a stipulated sum of money.

A genuine alternative-performance term is not subject to the rule prohibiting punitive liquidated damages. Best v. United States Bank, 303 Or. 557, 739 P.2d 554 (1987), gives the usual rationale. The plaintiffs challenged the fee charged by their bank for processing nonsufficient fund (NSF) checks. The bank had increased the fee from $3 to $5 per check. The plaintiffs presented evidence the new fee was two or three times the bank's NSF processing costs. Among the grounds for challenging the fee was that it was an unlawful penalty. This challenge failed because there was no agreement "not to write NSF checks. . . . There being no agreement, there could be no unlawful penalty for breach of the agreement."

In Carlyle Apartments Joint Venture v. AIG Life Ins. Co., 333 Md. 265, 635 A.2d 366 (1994), the borrower, Carlyle, sought to pre-pay a high interest commercial loan without paying a steep agreed prepayment fee, by arguing (i) prepayment was a breach because there was no right to prepay a fixed term loan under Maryland law, (ii) the fee was a liquidated damage term and (iii) as a liquidated-damage term it was void as a penalty. The court rejected the argument at the first step, holding prepayment was an option and not a breach. Among the authorities Carlyle relied upon was Whitman, Mortgage Prepayment Clauses: An Economic and Legal Analysis, 40 UCLA L. Rev. 851 (1993). Professor Whitman argued that "Essentially, prepayment fees are nothing more than liquidated damage clauses." Id. at 871. He went on to argue the fee should be enforced because it promotes economic efficiency, notwithstanding the legal rule. The court refused Carlyle's invitation to "give an economic interpretation to the loan contract in order to pronounce the prepayment clause a liquidated damage clause . . . " It continued: "[L]enders ordinarily should be able to predict the legal result that language employed by them in their loan contracts will achieve. No universal principle unifies the legal and economic analysis of all transactions, and the legal form selected for a transaction may control, despite its equivalency with some other form of transaction." 333 Md. at 279, 635 A.2d at 373.

Restatement, Second, Contracts § 356, Comment c ["Disguised penalties"] cautions:

> Sometimes parties attempt to disguise a provision for a penalty by using language that purports to make payment of the amount an alternative performance under the contract, that purports to offer a discount for prompt performance, or that purports to place a valuation on property to be delivered. Although the parties may in good faith contract for alternative performances and fix discounts or valuations, a court will look to the substance of the agreement to determine whether this is the case or whether the parties have attempted to disguise a provision for a penalty that is unenforceable under this Section. In determining whether a contract is one for alternative performances, the relative value of the alternatives may be decisive.

On the other hand, if a payment obligation is denominated as liquidated damages, then it seems it will be treated as such. In Brazen v. Bell Atlantic Corp., 695 A.2d 43 (Del. 1997), the termination-fee provisions in a corporate merger agreement stated that the $550 million fee "constitute liquidated damages and not a penalty." An attempt to characterize the fee as an alternative-performance term to avoid a challenge that it was a penalty was rejected: "counsel for Bell Atlantic explained that the liquidated damage language was 'boilerplate' terminology for termination fees in merger transactions such as this one. So be it . . . . [T]he parties to this merger cannot disown their own language." Id. at 48 n. 9. The form chosen was not fatal because the court went on to find the fee was not void as a penalty.

Whether a payment obligation is denominated as liquidated damages or as an alternative-performance term can matter for reasons other than whether the term will have to pass scrutiny under the penalty rule. If ordinary damages are inadequate, then the plaintiff can waive liquidated damages (assuming it was not agreed to be the exclusive remedy) and obtain an order compelling specific performance. Restatement § 361. Under an alternative-performance term the obligor has the power to choose between performance and payment. Another difference is that supervening events that make performance impracticable may absolve a party from liability to pay liquidated damages. They do not absolve a party from liability to render an alternative performance. This was the issue in American Soil Processing, Inc. v. Iowa Comprehensive Petroleum Underground Storage Tank Fund Board, 586 N.W.2d 325 (1998), which has an extended analysis of the difference between the two types of terms.

Similar issues are raised by the ability to cast a deposit paid towards the purchase of property as the price of an option to purchase the property. A term stating that a buyer forfeits the deposit on breach may be invalidated as a penalty. On the other hand, if the payment is the price of a genuine option, then there is no requirement that the amount be a reasonable estimate of the seller's anticipated or actual loss in the event the buyer allows the option to lapse. For an extended analysis of the proper characterization of a loan commitment fee, see Woodbridge Place Apartments v. Washington Square Capital, Inc., 965 F.2d 1249 (7th Cir. 1992).

CHAPTER 6

SPECIFIC PERFORMANCE

■ ■ ■

INTRODUCTORY NOTE

Chapter 6 concerns the remedy of specific performance. Under this remedy, the court, instead of ordering the breaching party to pay damages, orders the breaching party to perform the contract.

The historical background. For centuries the English administration of justice was characterized by the peculiarity that there were two systems of courts administering two different bodies of law. What may be called the "regular" court system consisted of the courts of common law, which had jurisdiction over "actions at law," and administered "regular" law. The other system consisted of courts of "equity" or "chancery," which had jurisdiction over "suits in equity," and applied a body of principles that came to be called "equity." (Note the double linguistic usages involved here. "Law" used: (1) in a broad sense to mean the principles for administering justice, which includes both common law and equity, or (2) in a narrower sense, to mean the principles applied by the common law courts. "Equity" used: (1) in a broad sense, to mean fairness, or (2) in a narrower sense, to mean the established principles administered by a specific system of courts.)

In general, the English equity or chancery courts acted to remedy defects in the rules administered by the common law courts. The equity courts did not have a general jurisdiction over all kinds of disputes; their function was to act in those cases where "the legal remedy was inadequate," that is, where according to the notions of the time, the regular or common law courts did not give the kind of relief that the plaintiff ought to have.

One of the great defects of common law courts was that except in certain extraordinary cases, the procedure in those courts did not contemplate *ordering* the defendant to do anything. If a creditor sued his debtor for £10 and was awarded a judgment at law, the judgment did not take the form of an order commanding the debtor to pay his debt. Instead, in its traditional form the judgment recited that it was "considered that the plaintiff do recover against the defendant his debt." Enforcement of the judgment was accomplished not by commanding the defendant to pay, but by directing the sheriff to levy execution on the defendant's property if the defendant did not pay, so that the plaintiff's claim could be satisfied out of this property.

Where the plaintiff was complaining of a breach of contract by the defendant, this defect prevented the courts from ordering the defendant to perform his promise. Thus, if Seller contracted to convey Blackacre to Buyer, and then broke his promise, there was no way in which Buyer, by appealing to the common law courts, could get a deed to Blackacre, even though Seller had a perfectly good title to the land and was wholly capable of carrying out her contract. Accordingly, the only relief Buyer could obtain from a common law court was an award of money damages. However, in such a case Buyer could successfully appeal to a court of equity, alleging that his legal remedy (money damages) was inadequate. The equity court would issue a decree ordering Seller to execute a deed in Buyer's favor. If Seller refused to obey this order, she would put herself in contempt of court and be subject to fine or imprisonment.

There are other situations, though, where an appeal to equity to enforce a contract would fail. To put the plainest kind of case, suppose that Seller had sold and delivered a horse to Buyer for $500, and that Buyer, although having ample funds to do so, refused to pay the promised price of the horse. Here conceivably Seller might get a certain spiritual satisfaction out of an order commanding Buyer to pay his debt—an order that the common law courts would not issue. On the other hand, the common law courts would ensure the promised price for Seller through a levy of execution on Buyer's goods. Accordingly in this case the legal remedy was deemed to be adequate, and a suit by Seller in an equity court would be denied.

In other cases, equity refused to enforce contracts not because the legal remedy was adequate, but because it was considered unwise for one or another reasons to attempt specific enforcement. For example, a famous opera singer agrees to sing in the plaintiff's opera house for three months and then breaks her contract. Here the opera-house proprietor may with much justice assert that his legal remedy of damages is inadequate; an award of money can scarcely be treated as an adequate substitute for actual performance. At the same time, there are obvious objections to attempting to compel a star to sing against her will. Accordingly, this is a case where a court of equity would deny specific performance despite a recognition that the monetary relief granted by the common law courts is an inadequate form of relief.

The relation of law and equity in the United States today. Specific performance is a type of injunction. It is usually said that a showing of irreparable injury is required for an injunction. Outside of contract law, some injuries—here, injury means no more than a violation of a legal right—are considered irreparable by their nature. Examples include a continuing trespass to land, a continuing nuisance, and a continuing violation of an individual's civil liberties. In contract law, specific performance of a contract generally requires a particularized showing of the inadequacy of damages. However, for certain types of contracts—in particular, contracts for the sale of land—such a showing is not required.

A plaintiff who establishes the inadequacy of damages is not *entitled* to specific performance. The remedy is discretionary. Discretionary factors include: performance would impose an undue burden on the defendant;

enforcement of the order would impose an undue burden on the court; performance or compulsion is contrary to public policy; or the contract is unconscionable.

Today, most American states no longer have separate courts of law and equity. Instead, in most states the same judges administer both bodies of law. This does not mean, however, that the two bodies of law are not to a considerable extent still kept distinct in the thinking of lawyers and judges. If a plaintiff asks the court to issue an order directing the defendant to perform her promise—say, to comply with a covenant not to compete—such a suit will be tested by principles and rules called "equity" and derived historically from the English chancery courts. In some jurisdictions, the suit will in fact be labeled as a "suit in equity" even though the judge who tries the suit has the power to try "actions at law" as well. Even in those jurisdictions where no label is attached to the suit to indicate whether it is "at law" or "in equity," the rules applied to the suit will be "equity" rules if the case involves a demand for an order directing the defendant to specifically perform. An important consequence in most states is that there is no right to a jury trial in a suit in equity.

LONDON BUCKET CO. v. STEWART
Court of Appeals of Kentucky, 1951.
314 Ky. 832, 237 S.W.2d 509.

STANLEY, COMMISSIONER. This is an appeal from a judgment decreeing specific performance of a contract to properly furnish and install a heating system for a large motel. The basic contention of the appellant, London Bucket Company, is that the remedy of specific performance will not lie for breach of this type of contract.

The chancellor overruled a demurrer to the petition and this is the first assignment of error. Stewart's petition set out the contract, the pertinent parts of which are as follows: "The parties of the first part agree and bind themselves to furnish and install (subletting installation) in said building the following equipment. . . . " The only standard as to the quality of work to be performed was that the defendant was to "guarantee to heat this said court to 75 degrees in winter, and to supervise all work," etc. The plaintiff alleged that the defendant "soon thereafter and within one year installed a plant in an incompleted, unskilled unworkmanlike manner, never finishing same, and of such size, type and inferior quality of materials that same does not to a reasonable degree perform the purpose contemplated." The petition further states: "Plaintiff here now demands of the court of equity that defendant be compelled to specifically perform the terms of said contract and complete said installation and furnish the type of furnace provided in said contract and all the things necessary to properly heat said building and rooms and same to be done forthwith, before the fall of cold weather."

The plaintiff prayed that "immediate specific performance be adjudged" and also asked $8,250 damages for faulty and negligent construction and resulting expense, loss of business, etc. On being required to elect his remedy, he chose specific performance and dismissed without prejudice his action for damages.

The defendant, among other defenses, pleaded there had been a mutual cancellation of the contract insofar as it covered the completion of the job. Upon sharply conflicting evidence, but with some documents strongly supporting the plaintiff's contention, the court found as a fact that there had been no such cancellation. This was an issue necessary to be decided before deciding there could be a decree of specific performance.

The court decreed: "The defendant is hereby mandatorily ordered and directed to comply with the terms of said contract, in its entirety. He shall proceed diligently so to do and continue its obligation, assumed by it under the said contract, therein specifically set out."

No matter what the evidence may have been, the plaintiff's legal right could be no greater than that which the basic facts pleaded authorized. So if the demurrer should have been sustained to his pleading which undertook to state his whole case, that is all the court need consider. In other words, if the plaintiff did not state a cause of action for specific performance, the demurrer should have been sustained instead of overruled. That is the way the trial court treated the case except to find that the work done was defective, the heating system was not properly functioning, and the job was incomplete. In his opinion, the court recognized the difficulty of the question whether the contract and the conditions were such as required specific performance. He considered the familiar principle that such an equitable decree will not be adjudged unless the ordinary common law remedy of damages for a breach of contract is an inadequate and incomplete remedy for injuries arising from the failure to carry out its terms. Edelen v. Samuels & Co., 126 Ky. 295, 103 S.W. 360. The court concluded, nevertheless, that this case was within Schmidt v. Louisville & N.R. Co., 101 Ky. 441, 41 S.W. 1015, 19 Ky.Law Rep. 666, 38 L.R.A. 809, and Pennsylvania Railroad Co. v. City of Louisville, 277 Ky. 402, 126 S.W.2d 840.

It seems to us the two cases are not altogether apt. In the *Schmidt* case it was held a decree of specific performance to operate the railroad under the terms of the lease for the benefit of both holders was proper since there was no adequate remedy at law. The *Pennsylvania Railroad* Case was a suit to declare the rights of the parties and to require several railroad companies to proceed with the elimination of grade crossings as they had contracted to do. Both cases involve matters of great magnitude and were of public interest and welfare. In each case the court in effect said, "Proceed to do what you contracted to do." There was no question of partial or incomplete or faulty performance of a building contract. The *Schmidt* case is distinguished in the leading case of Edelen v. Samuels & Co., supra. In the present case the decree was in effect to direct a building contractor to go back, correct defective work and complete its job. It is the general rule that contracts for building construction will not be specifically enforced because ordinarily damages are an adequate remedy and, in part, because of the incapacity of the court to superintend the performance. 9 Am.Jur., Building and Construction Contracts, § 124; 58 C.J. 1046. The case at bar is not within the exceptions to the rule or of the class where specific performance should be decreed. 49 Am.Jur., Specific Performance, § 12. That there may be difficulty in proving the damages as appellee suggests, is not enough to put the case within the exceptions.

Under our conclusion that specific performance should not have been decreed, the decision on the issue of cancellation of the contract must follow it. This will leave the question open in the common-law action for damages should it be filed.

Wherefore, the judgment is reversed.

RESTATEMENT, SECOND, CONTRACTS §§ 359, 360

[See Selected Source Materials Supplement]

UNIDROIT PRINCIPLES OF INTERNATIONAL COMMERCIAL CONTRACTS ARTS. 7.2.1, 7.2.2, 7.2.3

[See Selected Source Materials Supplement]

PRINCIPLES OF EUROPEAN CONTRACT LAW ARTS. 9.101, 9.102, 9.103

[See Selected Source Materials Supplement]

WALGREEN CO. v. SARA CREEK PROPERTY CO.

United States Court of Appeals, Seventh Circuit, 1992.
966 F.2d 273.

POSNER, CIRCUIT JUDGE.

This appeal from the grant of a permanent injunction raises fundamental issues concerning the propriety of injunctive relief. 775 F.Supp. 1192 (E.D.Wis.1991). The essential facts are simple. Walgreen has operated a pharmacy in the Southgate Mall in Milwaukee since its opening in 1951. Its current lease, signed in 1971 and carrying a 30-year, 6-month term, contains, as had the only previous lease, a clause in which the landlord, Sara Creek, promises not to lease space in the mall to anyone else who wants to operate a pharmacy or a store containing a pharmacy. . . .

In 1990, fearful that its largest tenant—what in real estate parlance is called the "anchor tenant"—having gone broke was about to close its store, Sara Creek informed Walgreen that it intended to buy out the anchor tenant and install in its place a discount store operated by Phar-Mor Corporation, a "deep discount" chain, rather than, like Walgreen, just a "discount" chain. Phar-Mor's store would occupy 100,000 square feet, of which 12,000 would be occupied by a pharmacy the same size as Walgreen's. The entrances to the two stores would be within a couple of hundred feet of each other.

Walgreen filed this diversity suit for breach of contract against Sara Creek and Phar-Mor and asked for an injunction against Sara Creek's letting the anchor premises to Phar-Mor. After an evidentiary hearing, the judge found a breach of Walgreen's lease and entered a permanent injunction against Sara Creek's letting the anchor tenant premises to Phar-Mor until the expiration of Walgreen's lease. He did this over the defendants' objection that Walgreen had failed to show that its remedy at law—damages—for the breach of the exclusivity clause was inadequate. Sara Creek had put on an expert witness who testified that Walgreen's damages could be readily estimated, and Walgreen had countered with evidence from its employees that its damages would be very difficult to compute, among other reasons because they included intangibles such as loss of goodwill.

Sara Creek reminds us that damages are the norm in breach of contract as in other cases. Many breaches, it points out, are "efficient" in the sense that they allow resources to be moved into a more valuable use. Patton v. Mid-Continent Systems, Inc., 841 F.2d 742, 750–51 (7th Cir.1988). Perhaps this is one—the value of Phar-Mor's occupancy of the anchor premises may exceed the cost to Walgreen of facing increased competition. If so, society will be better off if Walgreen is paid its damages, equal to that cost, and Phar-Mor is allowed to move in rather than being kept out by an injunction. That is why injunctions are not granted as a matter of course, but only when the plaintiff's damages remedy is inadequate. Northern Indiana Public Service Co. v. Carbon County Coal Co., 799 F.2d 265, 279 (7th Cir.1986). Walgreen's is not, Sara Creek argues; the projection of business losses due to increased competition is a routine exercise in calculation. Damages representing either the present value of lost future profits or (what should be the equivalent . . .) the diminution in the value of the leasehold have either been awarded or deemed the proper remedy in a number of reported cases for breach of an exclusivity clause in a shopping-center lease. . . . Why, Sara Creek asks, should they not be adequate here?

Sara Creek makes a beguiling argument that contains much truth, but we do not think it should carry the day. For if, as just noted, damages have been awarded in some cases of breach of an exclusivity clause in a shopping-center lease, injunctions have been issued in others. . . . The choice between remedies requires a balancing of the costs and benefits of the alternatives. Hecht Co. v. Bowles, 321 U.S. 321, 329, 64 S.Ct. 587, 591, 88 L.Ed. 754 (1944); Yakus v. United States, 321 U.S. 414, 440, 64 S.Ct. 660, 674, 88 L.Ed. 834 (1944). The task of striking the balance is for the trial judge, subject to deferential appellate review in recognition of its particularistic, judgmental, fact-bound character. K-Mart Corp. v. Oriental Plaza, Inc., 875 F.2d 907, 915 (1st Cir.1989). As we said in an appeal from a grant of a preliminary injunction—but the point is applicable to review of a permanent injunction as well—"The question for us [appellate judges] is whether the [district] judge exceeded the bounds of permissible choice in the circumstances, not what we would have done if we had been in his shoes." Roland Machinery Co. v. Dresser Industries, Inc., 749 F.2d 380, 390 (7th Cir.1984).

The plaintiff who seeks an injunction has the burden of persuasion— damages are the norm, so the plaintiff must show why his case is abnormal. . . . [W]hen, as in this case, the issue is whether to grant a permanent injunction, . . . the burden is to show that damages are inadequate. . . .

The benefits of substituting an injunction for damages are twofold. First, it shifts the burden of determining the cost of the defendant's conduct from the court to the parties. If it is true that Walgreen's damages are smaller than the gain to Sara Creek from allowing a second pharmacy into the shopping mall, then there must be a price for dissolving the injunction that will make both parties better off. Thus, the effect of upholding the injunction would be to substitute for the costly processes of forensic fact determination the less costly processes of private negotiation. Second, a premise of our free-market system, and the lesson of experience here and abroad as well, is that prices and costs are more accurately determined by the market than by government. A battle of experts is a less reliable method of determining the actual cost to Walgreen of facing new competition than negotiations between Walgreen and Sara Creek over the price at which Walgreen would feel adequately compensated for having to face that competition.

That is the benefit side of injunctive relief but there is a cost side as well. Many injunctions require continuing supervision by the court, and that is costly. . . . This ground was . . . stressed in Rental Development Corp. v. Lavery, 304 F.2d 839, 841–42 (9th Cir.1962), a case involving a lease. Some injunctions are problematic because they impose costs on third parties. Shondel v. McDermott, 775 F.2d 859, 868 (7th Cir.1985). A more subtle cost of injunctive relief arises from the situation that economists call "bilateral monopoly," in which two parties can deal only with each other: the situation that an injunction creates. Goldstick v. ICM Realty, 788 F.2d 456, 463 (7th Cir.1986) . . . The sole seller of widgets selling to the sole buyer of that product would be an example. But so will be the situation confronting Walgreen and Sara Creek if the injunction is upheld. Walgreen can "sell" its injunctive right only to Sara Creek, and Sara Creek can "buy" Walgreen's surrender of its right to enjoin the leasing of the anchor tenant's space to Phar-Mor only from Walgreen. The lack of alternatives in bilateral monopoly creates a bargaining range, and the costs of negotiating to a point within that range may be high. Suppose the cost to Walgreen of facing the competition of Phar-Mor at the Southgate Mall would be $1 million, and the benefit to Sara Creek of leasing to Phar-Mor would be $2 million. Then at any price between those figures for a waiver of Walgreen's injunctive right both parties would be better off, and we expect parties to bargain around a judicial assignment of legal rights if the assignment is inefficient. R.H. Coase, "The Problem of Social Cost," 3 J. Law & Econ. 1 (1960). But each of the parties would like to engross as much of the bargaining range as possible—Walgreen to press the price toward $2 million, Sara Creek to depress it toward $1 million. With so much at stake, both parties will have an incentive to devote substantial resources of time and money to the negotiation process. The process may even break down, if one or both parties want to create for future use a reputation as a hard bargainer; and if it does break down, the injunction will have brought about an inefficient result. All these are in one form or another costs of the injunctive process that can be avoided by substituting damages.

The costs and benefits of the damages remedy are the mirror of those of the injunctive remedy. The damages remedy avoids the cost of continuing supervision and third-party effects, and the cost of bilateral monopoly as well. It imposes costs of its own, however, in the form of diminished accuracy in the determination of value, on the one hand, and of the parties' expenditures on preparing and presenting evidence of damages, and the time of the court in evaluating the evidence, on the other. The weighing up of all these costs and benefits is the analytical procedure that is or at least should be employed by a judge asked to enter a permanent injunction, with the understanding that if the balance is even the injunction should be withheld. The judge is not required to explicate every detail of the analysis and he did not do so here, but as long we are satisfied that his approach is broadly consistent with a proper analysis we shall affirm; and we are satisfied here. The determination of Walgreen's damages would have been costly in forensic resources and inescapably inaccurate. . . . The lease had ten years to run. So Walgreen would have had to project its sales revenues and costs over the next ten years, and then project the impact on those figures of Phar-Mor's competition, and then discount that impact to present value. All but the last step would have been fraught with uncertainty.

. . . It is difficult to forecast the profitability of a retail store over a decade, let alone to assess the impact of a particular competitor on that profitability over that period. Of course one can hire an expert to make such predictions, Glen A. Stankee, "Econometric Forecasting of Lost Profits: Using High Technology to Compute Commercial Damages," 61 Fla.B.J. 83 (1987), and if injunctive relief is infeasible the expert's testimony may provide a tolerable basis for an award of damages. We cited cases in which damages have been awarded for the breach of an exclusivity clause in a shopping-center lease. But they are awarded in such circumstances not because anyone thinks them a clairvoyant forecast but because it is better to give a wronged person a crude remedy than none at all. It is the same theory on which damages are awarded for a disfiguring injury. No one thinks such injuries readily monetizable, City of Panama, 101 U.S. 453, 464, 25 L.Ed. 1061 (1880); McCarty v. Pheasant Run, Inc., 826 F.2d 1554, 1557 (7th Cir.1987); Marcus L. Plant, "Damages for Pain and Suffering," 19 Ohio St.L.J. 200, 205–06 (1958), but a crude estimate is better than letting the wrongdoer get off scot-free (which, not incidentally, would encourage more such injuries). Randall R. Bovbjerg et al., "Valuing Life and Limb in Tort: Scheduling 'Pain and Suffering,'" 83 Nw.U.L.Rev. 908 (1989). Sara Creek presented evidence of what happened (very little) to Walgreen when Phar-Mor moved into other shopping malls in which Walgreen has a pharmacy, and it was on the right track in putting in comparative evidence. But there was a serious question whether the other malls were actually comparable to the Southgate Mall, so we cannot conclude, in the face of the district judge's contrary conclusion, that the existence of comparative evidence dissolved the difficulties of computing damages in this case. Sara Creek complains that the judge refused to compel Walgreen to produce all the data that Sara Creek needed to demonstrate the feasibility of forecasting Walgreen's damages. Walgreen resisted, on grounds of the confidentiality of the data and the cost of producing the massive data that Sara Creek sought. Those are legitimate grounds; and the cost (broadly conceived) they expose of pretrial discovery, in turn presaging complexity at trial, is itself a cost of the damages remedy that injunctive relief saves.

Damages are not always costly to compute, or difficult to compute accurately. In the standard case of a seller's breach of a contract for the sale of goods where the buyer covers by purchasing the same product in the market, damages are readily calculable by subtracting the contract price from the market price and multiplying by the quantity specified in the contract. But this is not such a case and here damages would be a costly and inaccurate remedy; and on the other side of the balance some of the costs of an injunction are absent and the cost that is present seems low. The injunction here, like one enforcing a covenant not to compete (standardly enforced by injunction . . ., is a simple negative injunction— Sara Creek is not to lease space in the Southgate Mall to Phar-Mor during the term of Walgreen's lease—and the costs of judicial supervision and enforcement should be negligible. There is no contention that the injunction will harm an unrepresented third party. It may harm Phar-Mor but that harm will be reflected in Sara Creek's offer to Walgreen to dissolve the injunction. (Anyway Phar-Mor is a party.) The injunction may also, it is true, harm potential customers of Phar-Mor—people who would prefer to shop at a deep-discount store than an ordinary discount store—but their preferences, too, are registered indirectly. The more business Phar-Mor would have, the more rent it will be willing to pay Sara Creek, and therefore the more Sara Creek will be willing to pay Walgreen to dissolve the injunction.

The only substantial cost of the injunction in this case is that it may set off a round of negotiations between the parties. In some cases, illustrated by Boomer v. Atlantic Cement Co., 26 N.Y.2d 219, 309 N.Y.S.2d 312, 257 N.E.2d 870 (1970), this consideration alone would be enough to warrant the denial of injunctive relief. The defendant's factory was emitting cement dust that caused the plaintiffs harm monetized at less than $200,000, and the only way to abate the harm would have been to close down the factory, which had cost $45 million to build. An injunction against the nuisance could therefore have created a huge bargaining range (could, not would, because it is unclear what the current value of the factory was), and the costs of negotiating to a point within it might have been immense. If the market value of the factory was actually $45 million, the plaintiffs would be tempted to hold out for a price to dissolve the injunction in the tens of millions and the factory would be tempted to refuse to pay anything more than a few hundred thousand dollars. Negotiations would be unlikely to break down completely, given such a bargaining range, but they might well be protracted and costly. There is nothing so dramatic here. Sara Creek does not argue that it will have to close the mall if enjoined from leasing to Phar-Mor. Phar-Mor is not the only potential anchor tenant. . . .

To summarize, the judge did not exceed the bounds of reasonable judgment in concluding that the costs (including forgone benefits) of the damages remedy would exceed the costs (including forgone benefits) of an injunction. We need not consider whether, as intimated by Walgreen, exclusivity clauses in shopping-center leases should be considered presumptively enforceable by injunctions. Although we have described the choice between legal and equitable remedies as one for case-by-case determination, the courts have sometimes picked out categories of case in which injunctive relief is made the norm. The best-known example is specific performance of contracts for the sale of real property. Anderson v. Onsager, 155 Wis.2d 504, 455 N.W.2d 885 (1990); Okaw Drainage District v. National Distillers & Chemical Corp., 882 F.2d 1241, 1248 (7th Cir.1989); Anthony T. Kronman, "Specific Performance," 45 U.Chi.L.Rev. 351, 355 and n. 20 (1978). The rule that specific performance will be ordered in such cases as a matter of course is a generalization of the considerations discussed above. Because of the absence of a fully liquid market in real property and the frequent presence of subjective values (many a homeowner, for example, would not sell his house for its market value), the calculation of damages is difficult; and since an order of specific performance to convey a piece of property does not create a continuing relation between the parties, the costs of supervision and enforcement if specific performance is ordered are slight. The exclusivity clause in Walgreen's lease relates to real estate, but we hesitate to suggest that every contract involving real estate should be enforceable as a matter of course by injunctions. Suppose Sara Creek had covenanted to keep the entrance to Walgreen's store free of ice and snow, and breached the covenant. An injunction would require continuing supervision, and it would be easy enough if the injunction were denied for Walgreen to hire its own ice and snow remover and charge the cost to Sara Creek. Cf. City of Michigan City v. Lake Air Corp., 459 N.E.2d 760 (Ind.App.1984). On the other hand, injunctions to enforce exclusivity clauses are quite likely to be justifiable by just the considerations present here—damages are difficult to estimate with any accuracy and the injunction is a one-shot remedy requiring no continuing judicial involvement. So there is an argument for making injunctive relief presumptively appropriate in such cases, but we need not decide in this case how strong an argument.

AFFIRMED.

HARLINGTON WOOD, JR., SENIOR CIRCUIT JUDGE, concurring.

I gladly join in the affirmance reached in Judge Posner's expert analysis.

UCC §§ 2–709, 2–716

[See Selected Source Materials Supplement]

CISG ARTS. 46, 62

[See Selected Source Materials Supplement]

NOTE ON SPECIFIC PERFORMANCE OF CONTRACTS FOR THE SALE OF GOODS

The traditional pre-UCC rule, inherited from the English legal system, was that in the case of a contract for the sale of goods, neither the buyer nor the seller could ordinarily get specific performance unless the goods were "unique." If goods were not unique, then the buyer could cover, and damages for the additional cost of cover were deemed an adequate remedy. On the other hand, where a contract was for the sale of a unique item, such as a painting or an heirloom, cover on the market was by hypothesis not possible, and specific performance would be granted by a court of equity.

Today, specific performance of contracts for the sale of goods is largely governed by UCC § 2–716, which authorizes specific performance "where the goods are unique or in other proper circumstances." The Official Comment explains "this Article seeks to further a more liberal attitude than some courts have shown in connection with the specific performance of contracts of sale." Laclede Gas Co. v. Amoco Oil Co., 522 F.2d 33 (8th Cir. 1975), is an example. The case involved a contract to supply propane gas to Laclede, for use in residential developments until the developments were supplied with natural gas, which might not occur for as much as 10 to 15 years. The court granted specific performance even though propane in and of itself is not unique:

"It is axiomatic that specific performance will not be ordered when the party claiming breach of contract has an adequate remedy at law. Jamison Coal & Coke Co. v. Goltra, 143 F.2d 889, 894 (8th Cir.), cert. denied, 323 U.S. 769, 65 S.Ct. 122, 89 L.Ed. 615 (1944). This is especially true when the contract involves personal property as distinguished from real estate.

"However, in Missouri, as elsewhere, specific performance may be ordered even though personalty is involved in the 'proper circumstances.' Mo.Rev.Stat. § 400.2–716 (1); Restatement, Contracts, supra, § 361. And a remedy at law adequate to defeat the grant of specific performance 'must be as certain, prompt, complete, and efficient to attain the ends of justice as a decree of specific performance.' . . .

"One of the leading Missouri cases allowing specific performance of a contract relating to personalty because the remedy at law was inadequate is Boeving v. Vandover, 240 Mo.App. 117, 218 S.W.2d 175, 178 (1949). In that case the plaintiff sought specific performance of a contract in which the defendant had promised to sell him an automobile. At that time (near the end of and shortly after World War II) new cars were hard to come by, and the court held that specific performance was a proper remedy since a new car 'could not be obtained elsewhere except at considerable expense, trouble or loss, which cannot be estimated in advance.'

"We are satisfied that Laclede has brought itself within this practical approach taken by the Missouri courts. As Amoco points out, Laclede has propane immediately available to it under other contracts with other suppliers. And the evidence indicates that at the present time propane is readily available on the open market. However, this analysis ignores the fact that the contract involved in this lawsuit is for a long-term supply of propane to these subdivisions. The other two contracts under which Laclede obtains the gas will remain in force only until March 31, 1977, and April 1, 1981, respectively; and there is no assurance that Laclede will be able to receive any propane under them after that time. Also it is unclear as to whether or not Laclede can use the propane obtained under these contracts to supply the Jefferson County subdivisions, since they were originally entered into to provide Laclede with propane with which to 'shave' its natural gas supply during peak demand periods.[4] Additionally, there was uncontradicted expert testimony that Laclede probably could not find another supplier of propane willing to enter into a long-term contract such as the Amoco agreement, given the uncertain future of worldwide energy supplies. And, even if Laclede could obtain supplies of propane for the affected developments through its present contracts or newly negotiated ones, it would still face considerable expense and trouble which cannot be estimated in advance in making arrangements for its distribution to the subdivisions."

―――――

NOTE ON SPECIFIC PERFORMANCE OF CONTRACTS FOR THE SALE OF LAND AND EMPLOYMENT CONTRACTS

1. *Contracts for the sale of land.* It is well settled that in a contract for the sale of land, the buyer can get a decree specifically ordering the seller to execute a deed in his favor. In most states, the seller can also get a decree ordering the buyer to take title to the land and pay the agreed price. Restatement Second § 360, Comment e.

The traditional rationale of the rule that a *buyer* of land can get specific performance is that damages are inadequate in such cases because: (1) The value of land is always to some extent conjectural, since land usually does not have a clearly defined market price; and (2) Every piece of land is to some extent unique, and therefore the buyer cannot with an award of money damages go out on the market and buy a piece of land exactly like that promised him by the defaulting seller. Statutes now provide for self-executing

―――――

[4]   During periods of cold weather, when demand is high, Laclede does not receive enough natural gas to meet all this demand. It, therefore, adds propane to the natural gas it places in its distribution system. This practice is called "peak shaving."

decrees in such cases; such a decree has the effect of a deed, and can be recorded in the Registry of Deeds.

Today, the concept that every piece of real property is unique seems questionable. A few cases recognize this reality and criticize the traditional rule. For example, in Semelhago v. Paramadevan, [1996] 136 D.L.R. (4th) 1, decided by the Canadian Supreme Court, the seller breached a contract to sell a home. Although the case did not involve a decree of specific performance, the court forcefully pointed out that not all real estate is unique:

> While at one time the common law regarded every piece of real estate to be unique, with the progress of modern real estate development this is no longer the case. Both residential, business and industrial properties are mass produced much in the same way as other consumer products. If a deal falls through for one property, another is frequently, though not always, readily available. It is no longer appropriate, therefore, to maintain a distinction in the approach to specific performance as between realty and personalty. It cannot be assumed that damages for breach of contract for the purchase and sale of real estate will be an inadequate remedy in all cases. . . .

Similarly, in Watkins v. Paul, 95 Idaho 499, 511 P.2d 781 (1973), the court refused, on similar grounds, to order specific performance of an option to purchase a tract of land:

> The evidence fails to show that the plaintiffs need the land in question for any particular, unique purpose, which is one of the main reasons for granting specific performance; on the contrary, the plaintiffs' own evidence shows that they seek to obtain the land only so that they may resell it for profit. Under these circumstances, specific performance would bring the plaintiffs no greater relief than would damages in the amount of their lost profit.

Traditionally, a *seller* of land also is entitled to specific performance without a showing that damages are an inadequate remedy. Ordinarily, however, a decree in favor of the seller ordering the buyer to pay money is not enforced by contempt. Instead, the decree provides that if the purchase price is not paid by a certain time, the right of the buyer to "redeem" the land by paying the purchase price is cut off, or "foreclosed." If the buyer does not complete the purchase in the time ordered, then the seller retains the land and has a judgment for the purchase price.

2.   *Employment contracts.* Employment contracts are not specifically enforced at the suit of either the employee or the employer. Restatement Second § 367(1). The objections to specific performance here do not lie in a notion that monetary relief is an adequate substitute for the promised performance. Rather, they stem from a belief that it is unwise to attempt to extract, from an unwilling party, a performance involving personal relations. In some cases, the courts, although they will not order the employee to work for the employer, will enjoin the employee from working for a competitor Often,

such an injunction could be tantamount to ordering specific performance, because if the employee cannot work for a competitor, she will not be able to earn a living, and therefore will be indirectly forced to work for her original employer. Accordingly, Restatement Second § 367(2) adopts the rule that "[a] promise to render personal service exclusively for one employer will not be enforced by an injunction against serving another if its probable result will be to compel a performance involving personal relations the enforced continuance of which is undesirable or will be to leave the employee without other reasonable means of making a living."

CHAPTER 7

ALTERNATIVE DAMAGE MEASURES

■ ■ ■

This Chapter considers three damage measures that may be used in a bargain context as an alternative to the expectation measure.

Section 1 concerns the reliance measure as a remedy for breach in a bargain context. (Recall from Chapter 1 that the reliance measure may also be used in a donative context.) As pointed out earlier, the name of this measure is something of a misnomer. Calling it the *cost* measure would be more accurate, and would make it easier to understand the measure's dynamics.

Section 2 concerns cases in which the aggrieved party elects to rescind the contract and bring a claim for restitutionary damages against the party in breach.

Section 3 concerns cases in which the aggrieved party has a claim for the profit the breaching party made by the breach. These are described as disgorgement damages.

SECTION 1. RELIANCE DAMAGES IN A BARGAIN CONTEXT

SECURITY STOVE & MFG. CO. V. AMERICAN RYS. EXPRESS CO.
Kansas City Court of Appeals, Missouri, 1932.
227 Mo.App. 175, 51 S.W.2d 572.

BLAND, J. This is an action for damages for the failure of defendant to transport, from Kansas City to Atlantic City, New Jersey, within a reasonable time, a furnace equipped with a combination oil and gas burner. The cause was tried before the court without the aid of a jury, resulting in a judgment in favor of plaintiff in the sum of $801.50 and interest, or in a total sum of $1,000.00. Defendant has appealed.

The facts show that plaintiff manufactured a furnace equipped with a special combination oil and gas burner it desired to exhibit at the American Gas Association Convention held in Atlantic City in October, 1926. The president of plaintiff testified that plaintiff engaged space for the exhibit for the reason "that the Henry L. Dougherty Company was very much interested in putting out a combination oil and gas burner; we had just developed one, after we got through, better than anything on the market and we thought this show would be the psychological time to get in contact with the Dougherty Company"; that "the thing wasn't sent there for sale but primarily to show"; that at the time the space was engaged it was too late to ship the furnace by freight so plaintiff decided to ship it by express, and, on September 18th, 1926, wrote the office of the defendant in Kansas City, stating that it had engaged a booth for exhibition purposes at Atlantic City, New Jersey, from the American Gas Association, for the week beginning October 11th; that its exhibit consisted of an oil burning furnace, together with two oil burners which weighed at least 1,500 pounds; that, "In order to get this exhibit in place on time it should be in Atlantic City not later than October the 8th. What we want you to do is to tell us how much time you will require to assure the delivery of the exhibit on time."

Mr. Bangs, chief clerk in charge of the local office of the defendant, upon receipt of the letter, sent Mr. Johnson, a commercial representative of the defendant, to see plaintiff. Johnson called upon plaintiff taking its letter with him. Johnson made a notation on the bottom of the letter giving October 4th, as the day that defendant was required to have the exhibit in order for it to reach Atlantic City on October 8th.

On October 1st, plaintiff wrote the defendant at Kansas City, referring to its letter of September 18th, concerning the fact that the furnace must be in Atlantic City not later than October 8th, and stating what Johnson had told it, saying: "Now Mr. Bangs, we want to make doubly sure that this shipment is in Atlantic City not later than October 8th and the purpose of this letter is to tell you that you can *have your truck call for the shipment between 12 and 1 o'clock on Saturday, October 2nd for this.*" (Italics plaintiff's.) On October 2nd, plaintiff called the office of the express company in Kansas City and told it that the shipment was ready. Defendant came for the shipment on the last mentioned day, received it and delivered the express receipt to plaintiff. The shipment contained 21 packages. Each package was marked with stickers backed with glue and covered with silica of soda, to prevent the stickers being torn off in shipping. Each package was given a number. They ran from 1 to 21.

Plaintiff's president made arrangements to go to Atlantic City to attend the convention and install the exhibit, arriving there about October 11th. When he reached Atlantic City he found the shipment had been placed in the booth that had been assigned to plaintiff. The exhibit was set up, but it was found that one of the packages shipped was not there. This missing package contained the gas manifold, or that part of the oil and gas burner that controlled the flow of gas in the burner. This was the most important part of the exhibit and a like burner could not be obtained in Atlantic City.

Wires were sent and it was found that the stray package was at the "over and short bureau" of defendant in St. Louis. Defendant reported that the package would be forwarded to Atlantic City and would be there by Wednesday, the 13th. Plaintiff's president waited until Thursday, the day the convention closed, but the package had not arrived at the time, so he closed up the exhibit and left. About a week after he arrived in Kansas City, the package was returned by the defendant. . . .

The petition upon which the case was tried alleges that " . . . relying upon defendant's promise and the promises of its agents and servants, that said parcels would be delivered at Atlantic City by October 8th, 1926, if delivered to defendant by October 4th, 1926, plaintiff herein hired space for an exhibit at the American Gas Association Convention at Atlantic City, and planned for an exhibit at said Convention and sent men in the employ of this plaintiff to Atlantic City to install, show and operate said exhibit, and that these men were in Atlantic City ready to set up this plaintiff's exhibit at the American Gas Association Convention on October 8th, 1926." . . .

Plaintiff asked damages, which the court in its judgment allowed as follows: $147.00 express charges (on the exhibit); $45.12 freight on the exhibit from Atlantic City to Kansas City; $101.39 railroad and pullman fares to and from Atlantic City, expended by plaintiff's president and a workman taken by him to Atlantic City; $48.00 hotel room for the two; $150.00 for the time of the president; $40.00 for wages of plaintiff's other employee and $270.00 for rental of the booth, making a total of $801.51. . . .

We think, under the circumstances in this case, that it was proper to allow plaintiff's expenses as its damages. Ordinarily the measure of damages where the carrier fails to deliver a shipment at destination within a reasonable time is the difference between the market value of the goods at the time of the delivery and the time when they should have been delivered. But where the carrier has notice of peculiar circumstances under which the shipment is made, which will result in an unusual loss by the shipper in case of delay in delivery, the carrier is responsible for the real damage sustained from such delay if the notice given is of such character, and goes to such extent, in informing the carrier of the shipper's situation, that the carrier will be presumed to have contracted with reference thereto. Central Trust Co. of New York v. Savannah & W.R. Co. (C.C.) 69 F. 683, 685. . . .

Defendant contends that plaintiff "is endeavoring to achieve a return of the status quo in a suit based on a breach of contract. Instead of seeking to recover what he would have had, had the contract not been broken, plaintiff is trying to recover what he would have had, had there never been any contract of shipment"; that the expenses sued for would have been incurred in any event. It is no doubt, the general rule that where there is a breach of contract the party suffering the loss can recover only that which he would have had, had the contract not been broken, and this is all the cases decided upon which defendant relies, including C., M. & St. P. Ry. v. McCaull-Dinsmore Co., 253 U.S. 97, 100, 40 S.Ct. 504, 64 L.Ed. 801. But this is merely a general statement of the rule and is not inconsistent with the holdings that, in some instances, the injured party may recover expenses incurred in relying upon the contract, although such expenses would have been incurred had the contract not been breached. See Morrow v. Railroad, 140 Mo.App. 200, 212, 213, 123 S.W. 1034; Bryant v. Barton, 32 Neb. 613, 616, 49 N.W. 331; Woodbury v. Jones, 44 N.H. 206; Driggs v. Dwight, 17 Wend. (N.Y.) 71, 31 Am.Dec. 283.

In Sperry et al. v. O'Neill-Adams Co. (C.C.A.) 185 F. 231, the court held that the advantages resulting from the use of trading stamps as a means of increasing trade are so contingent that they cannot form a basis on which to rest a recovery for a breach of contract to supply them. In lieu of compensation based thereon the court directed a recovery in the sum expended in preparation for carrying on business in connection with the use of the stamps. The court said, loc. cit. 239:

> "Plaintiff in its complaint had made a claim for lost profits, but, finding it impossible to marshal any evidence which would support a finding of exact figures, abandoned that claim. Any attempt to reach a precise sum would be mere blind guesswork. Nevertheless a contract, which both sides conceded would prove a valuable one, had been broken and the party who broke it was responsible for resultant damage. In order to carry out this contract, the plaintiff made expenditures which otherwise it would not have made. . . . The trial judge held, as we think rightly, that plaintiff was entitled at least to recover these expenses to which it had been put in order to secure the benefits of a contract of which defendant's conduct deprived it." . . .

The case at bar was [not] to recover damages for loss of profits by reason of the failure of the defendant to transport the shipment within a reasonable time, so that it would arrive in Atlantic City for the exhibit. There were no profits contemplated. The furnace was to be shown and shipped back to Kansas City. There was no money loss, except the expenses, that was of such a nature as any court would allow as being sufficiently definite or lacking in pure speculation. Therefore, unless plaintiff is permitted to recover the expenses that it went to, which were a total loss to it by reason of its inability to exhibit the furnace and equipment, it will be deprived of any substantial compensation for its loss. The law does not contemplate any such injustice. It ought to allow plaintiff, as damages, the loss in the way of expenses that it sustained, and which it would not have been put to if it had not been for its reliance upon the defendant to perform its contract. There is no contention that the exhibit would have been entirely valueless and whatever it might have accomplished defendant knew of the circumstances and ought to respond for whatever damages plaintiff suffered. In cases of this kind the method of estimating the damages should be adopted which is the most definite and certain and which best achieves the fundamental purpose of compensation. 17 C.J. p. 846; Miller v. Robertson, 266 U.S. 243, 257, 45 S.Ct. 73, 78, 69 L.Ed. 265. Had the exhibit been shipped in order to realize a profit on sales and such profits could have been realized, or to be entered in competition for a prize, and plaintiff failed to show loss of profits with sufficient definiteness, or that he would have won the prize, defendant's cases might be in point. But as before stated, no such situation exists here.

While it is true that plaintiff already had incurred some of these expenses, in that it had rented space at the exhibit before entering into the contract with defendant for the shipment of the exhibit and this part of plaintiff's damages, in a sense, arose out of a circumstance which transpired before the contract was even entered into, yet, plaintiff arranged for the exhibit knowing that it could call upon defendant to perform its common law duty to accept and transport the shipment with reasonable dispatch. The whole damage, therefore, was suffered in contemplation of defendant performing its contract, which it failed to do, and would not have been sustained except for the reliance by plaintiff upon defendant to perform it. It can, therefore, be fairly said that the damages or loss suffered by plaintiff grew out of the breach of the contract, for had the shipment arrived on time, plaintiff would have had the benefit of the contract, which was contemplated by all parties, defendant being advised of the purpose of the shipment.

The judgment is affirmed.

All concur.

Anglia Television Ltd. v. Reed

[1971] 3 All.E.R. 690 (C.A. 1971))

Anglia Television Ltd wanted to make a film for television entitled "The Man in the Wood," which portrayed an American man married to an English woman. Before Anglia selected the leading man, it arranged for a place where the filming was to occur; employed a director, a designer, and a stage manager; and involved itself in much expense. For the leading man, Anglia required a strong actor capable of holding the film together. It eventually decided upon Robert Reed, an American with a very high reputation as an actor, and by telephone conversation the parties agreed that Reed would come to England and star in the film for a fee of $581,050 and expenses. Reed later repudiated the contract because of a mixup in his bookings. Anglia tried hard to find a substitute but could not do so and abandoned the film. It then sued Reed for its out-of-pocket expenses on the film of $582,750, including almost $581,900 incurred before the contract was made. Held (per Denning, L.J), Anglia was entitled to recover all of its expenses:

> [I]t is plain that, when Mr. Reed entered into this contract, he must have known perfectly well that much expenditure had already been incurred on director's fees and the like. He must have contemplated—or, at any rate, it is reasonably to be imputed to him— that if he broke his contract, all that expenditure would be wasted, whether or not it was incurred before or after the contract. He must pay damages for all the expenditure so wasted and thrown away. . . . It is true that, if the defendant had never entered into the contract, he would not be liable, and the expenditure would have been incurred by the plaintiff without redress; but, the defendant having made his contract and broken it, it does not lie in his mouth to say he is not liable, when it was because of his breach that the expenditure has been wasted.

Beefy Trail, Inc. v. Beefy King Int'l, Inc.

267 So.2d 853 (Fla.Dist.App.1972)

(Owen, J., concurring in part and dissenting in part) "Essentially, the rationale [for granting reliance damages in a bargain context] is this: Normally, had the contract's performance not been prevented by the defendant, and the contract had been a profitable one for the plaintiff, the plaintiff would have recovered over the life of the contract a gain, sufficient not only to fully reimburse him for his expenditures, but also to yield an excess which would be the profit. Since the amount of the gross receipts (i.e., the gain) cannot be determined with the requisite degree of certainty, the amount of the profit cannot be determined and therefore cannot be allowed in the recovery. *But the amount of the gain which would have reimbursed plaintiff for the expenditures incurred in preparation and part performance can be determined by and to the extent of these expenditures,* and therefore *this amount can be allowed in the recovery.*" (Emphasis in original.)

L. Albert & Son v. Armstrong Rubber Co.

178 F.2d 182 (2d Cir.1949)

(L. HAND, J.) Seller agreed to sell to Buyer four machines designed to recondition old rubber. Seller breached the contract, and Buyer claimed as damages the expenses that it had incurred in reliance upon Seller's promise, including $3000 for the cost of a foundation it had laid for the machines. In the course of his opinion, Hand discussed as follows the issues involved by the possibility that if the contract had been completed it would have resulted in a loss to the plaintiff:

> . . . The Buyer . . . asserts that it is . . . entitled to recover the cost of the foundation upon the theory that what it expended in reliance upon the Seller's performance was a recoverable loss. In cases where the venture would have proved profitable to the promisee, there is no reason why he should not recover his expenses. On the other hand, on those occasions in which the performance would not have covered the promisee's outlay, such a result imposes the risk of the promisee's contract upon the promisor. . . . It is often very hard to learn what the value of the performance would have been; and it is a common expedient, and a just one, in such situations to put the peril of the answer upon that party who by his wrong has made the issue relevant to the rights of the other. On principle therefore the proper solution would seem to be that the promisee may recover his outlay in preparation for the performance, subject to the privilege of the promisor to reduce it by as much as he can show that the promisee would have lost, if the contract had been performed. . . .

SECTION 2. THE RESTITUTION MEASURE

If a breach of contract is material, then the promisee may elect to rescind the contract and recover the value of performance he rendered (less benefits received) through a restitution claim. Typically, although not invariably, a restitution claim is brought for breach when expectation damages are too uncertain. While nominally restitutionary, this type of claim does not depend on unjust enrichment. The claim is similar the claim for reliance damages when expectation damages are uncertain. The differences are: (i) restitution claim is for a subset of the plaintiff's reliance costs (it does not include the plaintiff's costs of preparing to perform or opportunity costs); and (ii) the defendant is not allowed to reduce damages by showing the plaintiff would not have recovered costs he incurred to perform had the contract not been breached. In some jurisdictions restitutionary damages may even exceed the contract price.

OSTEEN V. JOHNSON
Colorado Court of Appeals, 1970.
473 P.2d 184.

DUFFORD, JUDGE . . . This was an action for breach of an oral contract. Trial was to the court, which found that the plaintiffs had paid the sum of $2,500. In exchange, the defendant had agreed to "promote" the plaintiffs' daughter, Linda Osteen, as a singer and composer of country-western music. More specifically, it was found that the defendant had agreed to advertise Linda through various mailings for a period of one year; to arrange and furnish the facilities necessary for Linda to record several songs; to prepare two records from the songs recorded; to press and mail copies of one of the records to disc jockeys throughout the country; and, if the first record met with any success, to press and mail out copies of the second record.

The trial court further found that the defendant did arrange for several recording sessions, at which Linda recorded four songs. A record was prepared of two of the songs, and 1,000 copies of the record were then pressed. Of the pressed records, 340 copies were mailed to disc jockeys, 200 were sent to the plaintiffs, and the remainder were retained by the defendant. Various mailings were made to advertise Linda; flyers were sent to disc jockeys throughout the country; and Linda's professional name was advertised in trade magazines. The record sent out received a favorable review and a high rating in a trade magazine.

Upon such findings the trial court concluded that the defendant had substantially performed the agreement. However, a judgment was entered in favor of the plaintiffs in the sum of $1.00 and costs on the basis that the defendant had wrongfully caused the name of another party to appear on the label of the record as co-author of a song which had been written solely by Linda. The trial court also ordered the defendant to deliver to the plaintiffs certain master tapes and records in the defendant's possession.

1.   RIGHT OF RESTITUTION

Although plaintiffs' reasons are not clearly defined, they argue here that the award of damages is inadequate, and that the trial court erred in concluding that the defendant had substantially performed the agreement. However, no evidence was presented during the trial of the matter upon which an award of other than nominal damages could be based. In our opinion, the remedy which plaintiffs proved and upon which they can rely is that of restitution. See 5 A. Corbin, Contracts § 996. This remedy is available where there has been a contract breach of vital importance, variously defined as a substantial breach or a breach which goes to the essence of the contract. See 5 A. Corbin, Contracts § 1104, where the author writes:

> "In the case of a breach by non-performance, . . . the injured party's alternative remedy by way of restitution depends upon the extent of the non-performance by the defendant. The defendant's breach may be nothing but a failure to perform some minor part of his contractual duty. Such a minor non-performance is a breach of contract and an action for damages can be maintained. The injured party, however, can not maintain an action for restitution

of what he has given the defendant unless the defendant's non-performance is so material that it is held to go to the 'essence'. . . . A minor breach by one party does not discharge the contractual duty of the other party; and the latter being still bound to perform as agreed can not be entitled to the restitution of payments already made by him or to the value of other part performances rendered." . . .

2.   BREACH OF CONTRACT

The essential question here then becomes whether any breach on the part of the defendant is substantial enough to justify the remedy of restitution. Plaintiffs argue that the defendant breached the contract in the following ways: First, the defendant did not promote Linda for a period of one year as agreed; secondly, the defendant wrongfully caused the name of another party to appear on the label as co-author of the song which had been composed solely by Linda; and thirdly, the defendant failed to press and mail out copies of the second record as agreed.

The first argument is not supported by the record. Plaintiffs brought the action within the one-year period for which the contract was to run. There was no evidence that during this period the defendant had not continued to promote Linda through the use of mailings and advertisements. Quite obviously the mere fact that the one-year period had not ended prior to the commencement of the action does not justify the conclusion that the defendant had breached the agreement. Plaintiffs' second argument overlooks the testimony offered on behalf of the defendant that listing the other party as co-author of the song would make it more likely that the record would be played by disc jockeys.

The plaintiffs' third argument does, however, have merit. It is clear from the record and the findings of the trial court that the first record had met with some success. It is also clear that copies of the second record were neither pressed nor mailed out. In our opinion the failure of the defendant to press and mail out copies of the second record after the first had achieved some success constituted a substantial breach of the contract and, therefore, justifies the remedy of restitution. Seale v. Bates, 145 Colo. 430, 359 P.2d 356; Colorado Management Corp. v. American Founders Life Insurance Co., 145 Colo. 413, 359 P.2d 665; Bridges v. Ingram, 122 Colo. 501, 223 P.2d 1051. Both parties agree that the essence of their contract was to publicize Linda as a singer of western songs and to make her name and talent known to the public. Defendant admitted and asserted that the primary method of achieving this end was to have records pressed and mailed to disc jockeys. . . .

3.   DETERMINING DAMAGES

It is clear that the defendant did partially perform the contract and, under applicable law, should be allowed compensation for the reasonable value of his services. See 5 A. Corbin, Contracts § 1114, where the author writes:

> "[A]ll courts are in agreement that restitution by the defendant will not be enforced unless the plaintiff returns in some way what he has received as a part performance by the defendant."

It shall, therefore, be the ultimate order of this court that prior to restoring to the plaintiffs the $2,500 paid by them to the defendant further proceedings be held during which the trial court shall determine the reasonable value of the services which the defendant rendered on plaintiffs' behalf.

The judgment is reversed, and this case is remanded with directions that a new trial be held to determine the one issue of the amount to which the plaintiffs are entitled by way of restitution. Such amount shall be the $2,500 paid by plaintiffs to defendant less the reasonable value of the services which the defendant performed on behalf of plaintiffs.

COYTE and PIERCE, JJ., concur.

————

RESTATEMENT, SECOND, CONTRACTS §§ 344, 345, 370, 371

[See Selected Source Materials Supplement]

————

RESTATEMENT, SECOND, CONTRACTS § 370, ILLUSTRATIONS 2, 5

2.   A contracts to sell B a machine for $100,000. After A has spent $40,000 on the manufacture of the machine but before its completion, B repudiates the contract. A cannot get restitution of the $40,000 because no benefit was conferred on B. . . .

5.   A, a social worker, promises B to render personal services to C in return for B's promise to educate A's children. B repudiates the contract after A has rendered part of the services. A can get restitution from B for the services, even though they were not rendered to B, because they conferred a benefit on B. . . .

————

UNITED STATES v. ALGERNON BLAIR, INC.

United States Court of Appeals, Fourth Circuit, 1973.
479 F.2d 638.

CRAVEN, CIRCUIT JUDGE. May a subcontractor, who justifiably ceases work under a contract because of the prime contractor's breach, recover in quantum meruit the value of labor and equipment already furnished pursuant to the contract irrespective of whether he would have been entitled to recover in a suit on the contract? We think so, and, for reasons to be stated, the decision of the district court will be reversed.

The subcontractor, Coastal Steel Erectors, Inc., brought this action under the provisions of the Miller Act, 40 U.S.C.A. § 270a et seq., in the name of the United States against Algernon Blair, Inc., and its surety, United States Fidelity and Guaranty Company. Blair had entered a contract with the United States for the construction of a naval hospital in Charleston County, South Carolina. Blair had then contracted with Coastal to perform certain steel erection and supply certain equipment in conjunction with Blair's contract with the United States. Coastal commenced performance of its obligations, supplying its own cranes for handling and placing steel. Blair refused to pay for crane rental, maintaining that it was not obligated to do so under the subcontract. Because of Blair's failure to make payments for crane rental, and after completion of approximately 28 percent of the subcontract, Coastal terminated its performance. Blair then proceeded to complete the job with a new subcontractor. Coastal brought this action to recover for labor and equipment furnished.

The district court found that the subcontract required Blair to pay for crane use and that Blair's refusal to do so was such a material breach as to justify Coastal's terminating performance. This finding is not questioned on appeal. The court then found that under the contract the amount due Coastal, less what had already been paid, totaled approximately $37,000. Additionally, the court found Coastal would have lost more than $37,000 if it had completed performance. Holding that any amount due Coastal must be reduced by any loss it would have incurred by complete performance of the contract, the court denied recovery to Coastal. While the district court correctly stated the " 'normal' rule of contract damages,"[1] we think Coastal is entitled to recover in quantum meruit.

In United States for Use of Susi Contracting Co. v. Zara Contracting Co., 146 F.2d 606 (2d Cir.1944), a Miller Act action, the court was faced with a situation similar to that involved here—the prime contractor had

---

[1]   Fuller & Perdue, The Reliance Interest in Contract Damages, 46 Yale L.J. 52 (1936); Restatement of Contracts § 333 (1932).

unjustifiably breached a subcontract after partial performance by the subcontractor. The court stated:

> For it is an accepted principle of contract law, often applied in the case of construction contracts, that the promisee upon breach has the option to forego any suit on the contract and claim only the reasonable value of his performance.

146 F.2d at 610. The Tenth Circuit has also stated that the right to seek recovery under quantum meruit in a Miller Act case is clear.[3] Quantum meruit recovery is not limited to an action against the prime contractor but may also be brought against the Miller Act surety, as in this case. Further, that the complaint is not clear in regard to the theory of a plaintiff's recovery does not preclude recovery under quantum meruit. Narragansett Improvement Co. v. United States, 290 F.2d 577 (1st Cir.1961). A plaintiff may join a claim for quantum meruit with a claim for damages from breach of contract.

In the present case, Coastal has, at its own expense, provided Blair with labor and the use of equipment. Blair, who breached the subcontract, has retained these benefits without having fully paid for them. On these facts, Coastal is entitled to restitution in quantum meruit:

> The "restitution interest," involving a combination of unjust impoverishment with unjust gain, presents the strongest case for relief. If, following Aristotle, we regard the purpose of justice as the maintenance of an equilibrium of goods among members of society, the restitution interest presents twice as strong a claim to judicial intervention as the reliance interest, since if A not only causes B to lose one unit but appropriates that unit to himself, the resulting discrepancy between A and B is not one unit but two.

Fuller & Perdue, The Reliance Interest in Contract Damages, 46 Yale L.J. 52, 56 (1936).[6]

The impact of quantum meruit is to allow a promisee to recover the value of services he gave to the defendant irrespective of whether he would have lost money on the contract and been unable to recover in a suit on the contract. Scaduto v. Orlando, 381 F.2d 587, 595 (2d Cir.1967). The measure of recovery for quantum meruit is the reasonable value of the performance, Restatement of Contracts § 347 (1932); and recovery is undiminished by any loss which would have been incurred by complete performance. 12 Williston on Contracts § 1485, at 312 (3d ed. 1970). While the contract price may be evidence of reasonable value of the services, it does not measure

---

[3]   Southern Painting Co. v. United States, 222 F.2d 431, 433 (10th Cir.1955). See also Great Lakes Constr. Co. v. Republic Creosoting Co., 139 F.2d 456 (8th Cir.1943) (dealing with a prior statute).

[6]   This case also comes within the requirements of the Restatements for recovery in quantum meruit. Restatement, Restitution § 107 (1937); Restatement, Contracts §§ 347–357 (1932).

the value of the performance or limit recovery. Rather, the standard for measuring the reasonable value of the services rendered is the amount for which such services could have been purchased from one in the plaintiff's position at the time and place the services were rendered.

Since the district court has not yet accurately determined the reasonable value of the labor and equipment use furnished by Coastal to Blair, the case must be remanded for those findings. When the amount has been determined, judgment will be entered in favor of Coastal, less payments already made under the contract. Accordingly, for the reasons stated above, the decision of the district court is

Reversed and remanded with instructions.

_____

RESTATEMENT, THIRD, RESTITUTION AND UNJUST ENRICHMENT §§ 37, 38

[See Selected Source Materials Supplement]

_____

NOTE ON RESTITUTIONARY AND RELIANCE DAMAGES

In theory, restitutionary and reliance damages are distinguishable: restitutionary damages are based on the market value of the performance rendered by the plaintiff; reliance damages are based on costs incurred by the plaintiff. Thus costs in preparing to perform may be recovered under the reliance measure in appropriate cases, but may not be recovered under the restitution measure. The frequent difficulty of distinguishing preparation from performance sometimes blurs this distinction.

Traditionally, restitutionary damages for breach have been viewed as benefit-based, that is, as based on the market value of the benefit rendered to the breaching party. However, under Restatement, Third, Restitution and Unjust Enrichment, restitutionary damages for breach of contract are not benefit-based. Instead, the measure of these damages is "the market value of the plaintiff's uncompensated contractual performance." Indeed, Restatement, Third, Restitution and Unjust Enrichment § 38(2)(b) avoids the term restitution, to describe this type of damages, and instead describes them as performance-based damages. (Caution: This terminology is relatively new, although it accurately describes what courts tend to do. Many and perhaps most courts continue to use the benefit-based terminology.)

_____

NOTE ON EXPECTATION AS A CAP ON RELIANCE AND RESTITUTIONARY DAMAGES

Algernon Blair allows a promisee in a losing contract that has been breached by the promisor to recover restitutionary damages in excess of the contract price. This could be an important difference between reliance and restitutionary damages. Recall that in L. Albert & Son v. Armstrong Rubber Co., Section 1, supra, Learned Hand said that expectation damages set a cap on reliance damages. Later cases and the Restatement agree.

Restatement Third, Restitution and Unjust Enrichment § 38(2)(b) rejects the result in *Algernon Blair*. Under the rule stated, restitutionary (performance-based) damages in a bargain contest may not exceed "the price of such performance as determined by reference to the parties' agreement." Comment d explains:

> . . . [S]ome authorities allow recovery 'off the contract,' unlimited by contract price; but this Restatement rejects that outcome. By capping the damage calculation at the contract rate (where such rate may be determined) § 38(2)(b) prevents these plaintiffs as well from electing performance-based damages as a means of escape from an unfavorable bargain.

> The contrary rule, allowing damages measured by the value of performance unlimited by the contract price, permits the injured party to reallocate or revalue risks that it is the function of contract to price and to assign. Such an outcome is contrary to fundamental objectives of contract law and inconsistent with the other remedies for breach of contract, all of which take the parties' agreement as the benchmark by which the plaintiff's remedies are measured.

A contract-price cap is not quite the same as an expectation-damages-measure cap. A contract price cap allows a contractor to recover its costs incurred up to the contract price, or up to the pro-rated contract price if a court adopts this embellishment of the rule. An expectation-damages-measure cap will not allow a contractor to recover costs incurred if the defendant can show the plaintiff would have not recouped those costs had the plaintiff completed performance.

The logic behind this is apparent if you consider the legal position of a contractor who has partially completed a construction contract at the time of the defendant's breach. The contractor has the option to sue for expectation damages if it can prove its cost to complete is less than the balance due (unpaid contract price minus expense saved). If the cost to complete is uncertain or difficult to prove, then the contractor may forgo a claim for expectation damages and sue for all of its costs incurred (including costs of preparing to perform), through a reliance claim, or it may sue for the cost of the work done to date, through a restitution claim. The damages may not exceed the unpaid balance of the contract price whichever form of claim is brought under the rule in the Restatement Third of Restitution. If the contractor brings a reliance claim, then the defendant is allowed to prove the cost to complete exceeds the unpaid balance of the contract price, meaning the contractor would have incurred a loss had the contract not been breached. The restitution claim allows the contractor to take off the table the issue of its cost to complete, if the contractor is willing to narrow its claim to the cost of work done to date, and forego a claim for costs of preparing to perform.

The logic behind this is even clearer in a case like *Osteen v. Johnson* where the plaintiff sues to recover money paid the defendant for work the defendant did not do or did poorly. Johnson could not defeat the Osteens claim to restitution of the money they paid him to produce a second record by showing that the second record would have been an embarrassment. On the other hand, if the Osteens had sought reliance damages, such as money they had paid musicians to play at the recording session, then Johnson would have been allowed to try to establish the second record would have been an embarrassment, and so this money would have been wasted.

SECTION 3. DISGORGEMENT DAMAGES

UNITED STATES NAVAL INSTITUTE V. CHARTER COMMUNICATIONS, INC.

United States Court of Appeals, Second Circuit, 1991.
936 F.2d 692.

Before KEARSE, WINTER and ALTIMARI, CIRCUIT JUDGES.

KEARSE, CIRCUIT JUDGE:

This case returns to us following our remand in *United States Naval Institute v. Charter Communications, Inc.,* 875 F.2d 1044 (2d Cir.1989) ("*Naval I*"), to the United States District Court for the Southern District of New York, Pierre N. Leval, *Judge,* for the fashioning of relief in favor of plaintiff United States Naval Institute ("Naval") against defendant Charter Communications, Inc., and Berkley Publishing Group (collectively "Berkley"), for breach of an agreement with respect to the publication of the paperback edition of *The Hunt For Red October* ("*Red October*" or the "Book"). On remand, the district court awarded Naval $35,380.50 in damages, $7,760.12 as profits wrongfully received by Berkley, and $15,319.27 as prejudgment interest on the damages awarded, plus costs. Naval appeals from so much of the judgment as failed to award a greater amount as profits, denied prejudgment interest on the profits awarded, and refused to award attorney's fees under the Copyright Act of 1976, 17 U.S.C. § 101 *et seq.* (1988) (the "Copyright Act" or the "Act"). Berkley cross-appeals from the judgment as a whole and from such parts of it as awarded moneys to Naval. For the reasons below, we reverse the award of profits; we affirm the award of damages, the award of prejudgment interest, and the denial of attorney's fees.

I.   BACKGROUND

The events leading to this action are fully set forth in *Naval I,* 875 F.2d at 1045–47, and will be summarized here only briefly. Naval, as the assignee of the author's copyright in *Red October,* entered into a licensing agreement with Berkley in September 1984 (the "Agreement"), granting Berkley the exclusive license to publish a paperback edition of the Book "not sooner than October 1985." Berkley shipped its paperback edition to retail outlets early, placing those outlets in position to sell the paperback prior to October 1985. As a result, retail sales of the paperback began on September 15, 1985, and early sales were sufficiently substantial that the Book was near the top of paperback bestseller lists before the end of September 1985.

Naval commenced the present action when it learned of Berkley's plans for early shipment, and it unsuccessfully sought a preliminary injunction. After trial, the district judge dismissed the complaint. He ruled that Berkley had not breached the Agreement because it was entitled, in accordance with industry custom, to ship prior to the agreed publication date. On appeal, we reversed. Though we upheld the district court's finding that the Agreement did not prohibit the early shipments themselves, we concluded that if the "not sooner than October 1985" term of the Agreement had any meaning whatever, it meant at least that Berkley was not allowed to cause such voluminous paperback retail sales prior to that date, and that Berkley had therefore breached the Agreement. *Naval I,* 875 F.2d at 1049–51. Accordingly, we remanded for entry of a judgment awarding Naval appropriate relief.

On the remand, Naval asserted that it was entitled to recovery for copyright infringement, and it sought judgment awarding it all of Berkley's profits from pre-October 1985 sales of the Book; it estimated those profits at $724,300. It also requested prejudgment interest, costs, and attorney's fees. Berkley, on the other hand, challenged Naval's right to any recovery at all, contending, *inter alia,* that Berkley could not be held liable for copyright infringement since the Agreement had made it the exclusive licensee of the paperback edition copyright as of September 14, 1984; it argued that Naval therefore had at most a claim for breach-of-contract but that Berkley could not be held liable on that basis because Naval had disavowed its pursuit of a contract claim. Berkley also argued that the profits attributed to it by Naval were inflated, and it opposed any award of prejudgment interest or attorney's fees.

In a Memorandum and Order dated July 17, 1990, 1990 WL 104027 ("July 17 Order"), the district judge rejected Berkley's claim that "its premature publication of the paperback edition constituted only a contract violation and not an infringement of Naval's copyright." *Id.* at 8. He found that Naval's copyright was infringed by the early publication because, though "the *extent* of the breach was a relatively trivial matter of two weeks of sales, the *term* breached was crucial to the scope of the license, as it governed when the license would take effect." *Id.* (emphasis in original). He concluded that Naval was entitled to recover damages for copyright infringement, comprising actual damages suffered by Naval plus Berkley's profits "attributable to the infringement," 17 U.S.C. § 504(b).

The court calculated Naval's "actual damages from Berkley's wrongful pre-October 'publication'" as the profits Naval would have earned from hardcover sales in September 1985 if the competing paperback edition had not then been offered for sale. July 17 Order at 8. Noting the downward trend of hardcover sales of the Book from March through August 1985, the court found that there was no reason to infer that Naval's September 1985 sales would have exceeded its August 1985 sales. The court calculated Naval's lost sales as the difference between the actual hardcover sales for those two months, and awarded Naval $35,380.50 as actual damages.

The district judge held that Berkley's profits "attributable to the infringement" were only those profits that resulted from "sales to customers who would not have bought the paperback but for the fact it became available in September." July 17 Order at 10. He found that most of the September paperback sales were made to buyers who would not have bought a hardcover edition in September, and therefore only those September sales that displaced hardcover sales were attributable to the infringement. Berkley's profit on the displacing copies totaled $7,760.12, and the court awarded that amount to Naval.

The court awarded Naval prejudgment interest (totaling $15,319.27) on the $35,380.50 awarded as actual damages but denied such interest on the award of Berkley's profits. It also denied Naval's request for attorney's fees.

Judgment was entered accordingly, and these appeals followed.

II. DISCUSSION . . .

A. *Naval's Claim of Copyright Infringement . . .*

The Agreement between Naval and Berkley, headed "Agreement made this 14th day of September 1984," granted Berkley, in & 1, "the exclusive right to publish and reproduce, distribute and sell English-language paperback editions" of the Book in the United States and certain other areas. Paragraph 2 of the Agreement stated that "[t]he term of this license will begin on the date written above"; it stated that the term of the license would continue until at least five years after the date of Berkley's "first publication" of the Book. Paragraph 4 provided that Berkley was to publish the paperback edition "not sooner than October 1985."

These provisions contradict the district court's finding that Berkley's publication date "governed when the license would take effect." Paragraph 2 provided that the license took effect on "the date written above"; since September 14, 1984, was the only date mentioned in the Agreement prior to & 3, the license term began on that date. Further, & 2's distinct references to (a) "the date written above" to define the start of the license term, and (b) Berkley's "first publication" date to anchor the continuation of the license term reveal that the parties deliberately did not define the start of the term by Berkley's first publication date. Thus, according to the express provisions of the Agreement, Berkley became the owner of the right to publish the paperback edition of the book in September 1984 and remained the owner of that right for at least five years after its first publication of that edition in 1985. Its publication of that edition in 1985 therefore could not constitute copyright infringement. . . .

B.   Contract Damages

Our ruling that Naval is not entitled to recover under the Copyright Act does not, as Berkley would have it, require the entry of judgment in favor of Berkley. Though Berkley argues that Naval had abandoned its contract claim for money damages prior to trial, we thereafter ruled in *Naval I* that Naval was entitled to recover for breach of contract. . . . Our ruling in *Naval I* that Naval was entitled to recover for breach of the Agreement is the law of the case. . . .

As Naval has renounced any effort at rescission and has accepted Berkley's payments of substantial copyright royalties for paperback sales under the Agreement, plainly the relief to which Naval is entitled on its meritorious breach-of-contract claim is money damages.

The damages awarded by the district court on remand had two components: (1) Naval's lost profits resulting from Berkley's early publication of the paperback edition of the Book, and (2) Berkley's profits attributable to its assumed infringement. For the reasons discussed above, the latter component of the award cannot stand. The former component, however, may properly measure damages under a breach-of-contract theory.

Since the purpose of damages for breach of contract is to compensate the injured party for the loss caused by the breach, 5 *Corbin On Contracts* '1002, at 31 (1964), those damages are generally measured by the plaintiff's actual loss, *see, e.g., Restatement (Second) of Contracts* § 347 (1981). While on occasion the defendant's profits are used as the measure of damages, *see, e.g., Cincinnati Siemens-Lungren Gas Illuminating Co. v. Western Siemens-Lungren Co.,* 152 U.S. 200, 204–07, 14 S.Ct. 523, 525–26, 38 L.Ed. 411 (1894); *Murphy v. Lischitz,* 183 Misc. 575, 577, 49 N.Y.S.2d 439, 441 (Sup.Ct.N.Y. County 1944), *aff'd mem.,* 268 A.D. 1027, 52 N.Y.S.2d 943 (1st Dep't), *aff'd mem.,* 294 N.Y. 892, 63 N.E.2d 26 (1945), this generally occurs when those profits tend to define the plaintiff's loss, for an award of the defendant's profits where they greatly exceed the plaintiff's loss and there has been no tortious conduct on the part of the defendant would tend to be punitive, and punitive awards are not part of the law of contract damages. *See generally Restatement (Second) of Contracts* § 356 comment *a* ("The central objective behind the system of contract remedies is compensatory, not punitive."); *id.* comment *b* (agreement attempting to fix damages in amount vastly greater than what approximates actual loss would be unenforceable as imposing a penalty); *id.* § 355 (punitive damages not recoverable for breach of contract unless conduct constituting the breach is also a tort for which such damages are recoverable).

Here, the district court found that Berkley's alleged $724,300 profits did not define Naval's loss because many persons who bought the paperback in September 1985 would not have bought the book in hardcover but would merely have waited until the paperback edition became available. This finding is not clearly erroneous. . . .

[The court then held that Naval had proved with sufficient certainty the damages of $33,380.50 awarded by the trial court as the profits Naval would have earned on hardcover sales in September 1985 if the paperback edition had not then been offered for sale.]

CONCLUSION

. . . For the foregoing reasons, we reverse so much of the judgment as granted Naval $7,760.12 as an award of Berkley's profits. In all other respects, the judgment is affirmed.

No costs.

Laurin v. DeCarolis Construction Co.

372 Mass. 688, 363 N.E.2d 675 (1977)

In March 1971, the Laurins agreed to purchase a home that DeCarolis was then constructing. The home was situated on a well-wooded lot. Prior to the closing, the Laurins found that after the contract had been signed, DeCarolis had bulldozed many of the trees on the property. The Laurins ordered DeCarolis to desist, but DeCarolis continued to bulldoze trees and also removed gravel and loam worth $6480. The Laurins paid the purchase price of $26,900 at the closing, and then sued DeCarolis for the value of the trees, gravel, and loam that DeCarolis had removed.

The case was tried by a master, who concluded that the Laurins were the "equitable owners" of the property from and after the signing of the agreement, so that DeCarolis had unlawfully converted the trees, gravel, and loam. In other words, the master reasoned that the Laurins were entitled to disgorgement under a property theory. The Massachusetts Supreme Judicial

Court rejected this reasoning, on the ground that under Massachusetts law, "the rights of the purchaser of real property prior to closing are contract rights rather than property rights." Accordingly, the Court concluded, "[this] case must be decided, not as [an] action for injury to or conversion of property, but as a claim for a deliberate and willful breach of contract. . . . "

This left the contract theory. The problem was that taking the trees, gravel, and loam had not diminished the value of the property. Therefore, although DeCarolis had made a gain from breach, the Laurins had not suffered a loss. Nevertheless, the Court held that the Laurins were entitled to disgorgement, because DeCarolis should not be allowed to retain its gains from a willful breach of contract:

> . . . Particularly where the defendant's breach is deliberate and willful, we think damages limited to diminution in value of the premises may sometimes be seriously inadequate. "Cutting a few trees on a timber tract, or taking a few hundred tons of coal from a mine, might not diminish the market value of the tract, or of the mine, and yet the value of the wood or coal, severed from the soil, might be considerable. The wrongdoer would, in the cases instanced, be held to pay the value of the wood and coal, and he could not shield himself by showing that the property from which it was taken was, as a whole, worth as much as it was before." *Worrall v. Munn, 53 N.Y. 185, 190 (1873)*. This reasoning does not depend for its soundness on the holding of a property interest, as distinguished from a contractual interest, by the plaintiffs. Nor is it punitive; it merely deprives the defendant of a profit wrongfully made, a profit which the plaintiff was entitled to make. . . .

RESTATEMENT, THIRD, RESTITUTION AND UNJUST ENRICHMENT § 39

[See Selected Source Materials Supplement]

RESTATEMENT, THIRD, RESTITUTION AND UNJUST ENRICHMENT § 39, COMMENTS AND ILLUSTRATIONS

Comment b. Opportunistic breach. The common rationale of every instance in which restitution allows a recovery of profits from wrongdoing, in the contractual context or any other, is the reinforcement of an entitlement that would be inadequately protected if liability for interference were limited to provable damages. Cases in which restitution reaches the profits from a breach of contract are those in which the promisee's contractual position is vulnerable to abuse. Vulnerability in this context stems from the difficulty that the promisee may face in recovering, as compensatory damages, a full equivalent of the performance for which the promisee has bargained. A promisor who was permitted to exploit the shortcomings of the promisee's damage remedy could accept the price of the promised performance, then deliver something less than what was promised. Such an outcome results in unjust enrichment as between the parties. The mere possibility of such an outcome undermines the stability of any contractual exchange in which one party's performance may be neither easily compelled nor easily valued.

A promisor who recognizes this possibility and attempts to profit by it commits what is here called an "opportunistic breach." The label suggests the reasons why a breach of this character is condemned, but there is no requirement under this section that the claimant prove the motivation of the breaching party.

In countering this form of opportunism, the rule of § 39 reinforces the contractual position of the vulnerable party and condemns a form of conscious advantage-taking that is the equivalent, in the contractual context, of an intentional and profitable tort. A restitution claim in response to a profitable tort typically operates to protect property from deliberate interference: standard examples include the claim to profits from trespass or infringement. . . . The rule of § 39 extends an analogous protection to contract rights, where what the wrongdoer seeks to acquire is not "property" but the modification or release of his own contractual obligation. The two situations have much in common. Confronted with a situation—in either context—in which the appropriate course of action would be to negotiate regarding legal entitlements, the wrongdoer takes without asking. The opportunistic calculation in either setting is that the wrongdoer's anticipated liability in damages is less than the anticipated cost of the entitlement, were it to be purchased from the claimant in a voluntary transaction. Restitution (through the disgorgement remedy) seeks to defeat this calculation, reducing the likelihood that the conscious disregard of another's entitlement can be more advantageous than its negotiated acquisition. . . .

The broader function of disgorgement in the Illustrations that follow is not merely to frustrate conscious wrongdoers but to reinforce the stability of the contract itself, enhancing the ability of the parties to negotiate for a contractual performance that may not be easily valued in money. The result is to expand the range of transactions for which parties may effectively bargain. The point is seen by considering the position of the parties at the bargaining stage. Where the value of the promised performance is easily demonstrated—and substitutes are readily available—it may be plausible to attribute to the parties an understanding that the promisor shall be free, as a practical matter, to elect between performance and payment of damages. In other transactions . . . the proposition that the promisor should be free to choose whether or not to perform would be incompatible with fundamental objectives of the promisee, ultimately making it impossible to fix a price for the promisor's contractual obligation. Absent an enforceable agreement on liquidated damages, the bargain in question is then less likely to be made.

Not by coincidence, the contractual entitlements that are vulnerable in the manner just described are those for which the promisee would most often be entitled to protection by injunction, or to a remedy by specific performance; or in which well-advised parties would most often provide by contract (where permitted to do so) for liquidated damages or specific enforceability. Disgorgement by the rule of this section serves the same contract-reinforcing objectives as the devices just mentioned, at a different stage of contractual performance.

c.   *Adequacy of a remedy in damages.* If the promisee's contractual entitlement is adequately protected by a judgment for money damages, there is no claim to restitution by the rule of this section. (If the promisee's contractual entitlement is adequately compensated by an award of damages, there is no remedial vulnerability to be exploited, no opportunism, and no unjust enrichment.) The adequacy of a damage remedy in particular circumstances is a determination for the court, applying its governing law to its own understanding of the case before it; but § 39(2) provides the standard baseline of the inquiry. . . .

Illustrations:

2.   Vendor and Purchaser agree on a sale of Blackacre for $100,000. The contract expressly provides that existing timber and gravel are to be conveyed with the property. Vendor removes timber and gravel which he sells for a net gain of $10,000. Purchaser takes title and commences an action against Vendor. Under local law, the contract of sale gives Purchaser no interest in the property prior to conveyance: accordingly, Purchaser has no action for conversion, being limited to the available remedies for breach of contract. Purchaser is entitled to recover $10,000 from Vendor by the rule of this section. It is irrelevant that the removal of timber and gravel did not appreciably diminish the value of Blackacre. . . .

5.   Landowner and Mining Company enter a contract for strip-mining. The agreement authorizes Mining Company to remove coal from Blackacre in exchange for payment of a specified royalty per ton. A further provision of the agreement, included at Landowner's insistence, obliges Mining Company to restore the surface of Blackacre to its preexisting contours on the completion of mining operations. Mining Company removes the coal from Blackacre, pays the stipulated royalty, and repudiates its obligation to restore the land. In Landowner's action against Mining Company it is established that the cost of restoration would be $25,000, and that the diminution in the value of Blackacre if the restoration is not

performed would be negligible. The contract is not affected by mistake or impracticability. The cost of restoration is in line with what Mining Company presumably anticipated, and the available comparisons suggest that Mining Company took this cost into account in calculating the contractual royalty. Landowner is entitled to recover $25,000 from Mining Company . . . . It is not a condition to Landowner's recovery in restitution that the money be used to restore Blackacre. . .

7. City contracts with Firefighters' Association for fire protection services to be furnished during the ensuing 12 months. The contract specifies the number of men, horses, and wagons to be kept in readiness at specified times and places, and the contract price is negotiated as a function thereof. After the 12 months have elapsed and the full contract price has been paid, City discovers that Association consistently devoted fewer men, horses, and wagons to City's fire protection than the numbers required by contract. Association acted in deliberate breach of its contractual obligations, calculating—accurately as it turned out—that the resources specified by contract were in excess of City's firefighting needs. In consequence, Association saved $100,000 over the life of its contract with City; while City suffered no increased loss from fire as a result of Association's disregard of the contract specifications. City is entitled to recover $100,000 from Association by the rule of this section. . . .

9. A licensing agreement between Coca-Cola and Bottler provides that products produced under license shall be manufactured in strict conformity to Coca-Cola's specifications, one of which calls for the use of cane sugar as the sweetening ingredient. In the course of renegotiating various aspects of the licensing agreement, Bottler asks to be allowed to substitute artificial sweeteners for sugar in the manufacture of certain licensed products. The parties fail to reach agreement on this point, and the amendment to the license resulting from their negotiations omits any modification of the product specifications. Acting in conscious disregard of its contractual obligations, Bottler substitutes low-cost artificial sweetener for sugar in the manufacture of licensed products. The products manufactured from these different materials are for all practical purposes indistinguishable. By the time the practice comes to light, Bottler has saved $5 million by the use of the less expensive ingredients. Coca-Cola may require Bottler to disgorge $5 million by the rule of this section. It is not a condition of recovery that Coca-Cola prove damages as a result of Bottler's breach. . . .

Kansas v. Nebraska

135 S.Ct. 1042 (2015)

Nebraska was dilatory in implementing measures to decrease groundwater pumping that it knew were necessary to ensure it did not take more than its allotted share of water under an interstate compact with Kansas. The measures it took might have sufficed had there been prodigious amounts of rain. Instead there was drought. As a result the consumption of water by its residents exceeded its allocation under the compact with Kansas by 17 percent in 2005 and 2006. Kansas filed a claim in the U.S. Supreme Court, which has original jurisdiction over such matters. The Court appointed a special master who, after two years of proceedings, awarded Kansas $3.7 million compensatory damages and $1.8 million in "partial disgorgement" for the excess water taken by Nebraska in 2005–2006. Nebraska's gain from the breach exceeded Kansas' loss because "an acre-foot of water is substantially more valuable on farmland in Nebraska than in Kansas." The special master estimated Nebraska's gain was "several multiples" of Kansas' loss, which translates to a figure larger than $11.1 million. The special master found disgorgement to be appropriate because "Nebraska 'knowingly exposed Kansas to a substantial risk 'of receiving less water than the Compact provided, and so 'knowingly failed' to comply with the obligations." The master justified the $1.8 million award for disgorgement, and declined Kansas' request for an injunction, citing Nebraska's good faith efforts to bring itself into compliance with the compact after 2005–2006. Nebraska appealed, challenging the award of disgorgement damages. Kansas appealed asking for greater damages, among other things.

A divided Court affirmed the judgment. The majority held disgorgement damages were appropriate, though Nebraska did not deliberately breach the compact, because "Nebraska recklessly gambled with Kansas's rights, consciously disregarding a substantial probability that its actions would deprive Kansas of the water to which it was entitled." As for Kansas' request for full disgorgement, the majority held disgorgement need not be "all or nothing," and partial disgorgement will suffice when it "will serve to stabilize a compact by conveying an effective message to a breaching party that it must work hard to meet its future obligations." Three Justices dissented, arguing disgorgement was not justified because there was no "deliberate breach."

NOTE ON THE THEORY OF EFFICIENT BREACH

A well-known theory in the law and economics of contract is the theory of efficient breach. This theory holds that breach of contract is efficient, and therefore desirable, if the promisor's gain from breach, after payment of expectation damages, will exceed the promisee's loss from breach. Probably the best-known exposition of the theory is that given by Richard Posner in his book,

Economic Analysis of Law. This exposition has changed somewhat over the eight editions of that book. Here is the core of the exposition in the first edition:

> . . . [I]n some cases a party [to a contract] would be tempted to breach the contract simply because his profit from breach would exceed his expected profit from completion of the contract. If his profit from breach would also exceed the expected profit to the other party from completion of the contract, and if damages are limited to loss of expected profit, there will be an incentive to commit a breach. There should be.

Although the theory of efficient breach is typically presented in very generalized terms, in fact the theory can only be properly understood and evaluated in the context of paradigm cases to which it might meaningfully be applied. The most salient paradigm is the Overbidder Paradigm. In this Paradigm, a seller who has contracted to sell a commodity to a buyer breaches the contract in order to sell the commodity to a third party who comes along later and offers a higher price.

The Resale Paradigm is the poster child of the theory of efficient breach. Proponents of the theory, including Posner, typically include an illustration based on this Paradigm as part of their argument for the theory. Here is the centerpiece illustration of the theory of efficient breach in the first edition of Posner's *Economic Analysis of Law*:

> . . . I sign a contract to deliver 100,000 custom-ground widgets at $.10 apiece to A, for use in his boiler factory. After I have delivered 10,000, B comes to me, explains that he desperately needs 25,000 custom-ground widgets at once since otherwise he will be forced to close his pianola factory at great cost, and offers me $.15 apiece for 25,000 widgets. I sell him the widgets and as a result do not complete timely delivery to A, who sustains $1000 in damages from my breach. Having obtained an additional profit of $1250 on the sale to B, I am better off even after reimbursing A for his loss. Society is also better off. Since B was willing to pay me $.15 per widget, it must mean that each widget was worth at least $.15 to him. But it was worth only $.14 to A—$.10, what he paid, plus $.04 ($1000 divided by 25,000), his expected profit. Thus the breach resulted in a transfer of the 26,000 widgets from a lower valued to a higher valued use.

There are two major criteria under which the theory of efficient breach needs to be evaluated. One is whether the predicates of the theory are correct; the other is whether, if the predicates are correct, application of the theory would promote efficiency. The theory would be valid only if it satisfies both criteria.

Predicates. The theory of efficient breach rests on two basic predicates, both of which feature in Posner's illustration. The first predicate is that the expectation measure makes the promisee indifferent between performance and damages. This predicate is incorrect because expectation damages do not have that effect. For example, expectation damages are based on objective rather than subjective value; the recovery of a buyer's lost profits under the expectation measure is often cut off by the principle of Hadley v. Baxendale, the certainty rule, or both (see Chapter 5, infra); expectation damages do not include legal fees and other costs of litigation; and prejudgment interest for breach of contract is often not awarded, and when awarded is almost invariably less than the time value of the gains that the promisee would have made from performance.

The second predicate of the theory of efficient breach is that at the time of the perform-or-breach decision, the promisor knows the value that the promisee places on the promisor's performance. In the context of the Overbidder Paradigm, this predicate is incorrect because a seller will seldom know what value the buyer puts on a promisor's performance. At least in the case of differentiated commodities (which is the only case to which the theory of efficient breach is relevant), at the time of contract formation a buyer will rarely if ever tell a seller what profits he expects to make from a contract, because a seller could use that information to lever up the price. Even if the buyer did disclose that information, the seller would normally have no way of knowing what profits the buyer expected to make at the time of the perform-or-breach decision, because between the time of contract formation and the time of that decision, markets may have shifted, or the buyer may have increased his potential profits through investment in beneficial reliance such as advertising or the purchase of complimentary commodities.

Efficiency. Even assuming, counterfactually, that the predicates of the theory of efficient breach were correct, the encouragement of breach in the Overbidder Paradigm would decrease rather than promote efficiency. The efficiency justification of the theory is that if a seller's gain on sale to an overbidder exceeds the buyer's loss, breach is an instrument for transferring a commodity to a higher-valued use. However, in a world without transaction costs, commodities will always flow to higher-valued uses, so that if the overbidder values the commodity more than the buyer, he will end up with the commodity even under a performance regime, that is, a regime in which performance of a contract is normally required. Commodities will also normally flow to higher-valued uses in a world *with* transaction costs. If a third party values the commodity more than the buyer, and knows the buyer's identity, he will purchase from the buyer either an assignment of the contract or the commodity itself. If the third party does not know the buyer's identity, a rational seller will either negotiate with the buyer to be released from the contract, so that she can sell to the overbidder, or will sell the overbidder's identity to the buyer, or the buyer's identity to the overbidder. Posner more or less admitted that if an overbidder values the contracted-for commodity more than the buyer, the overbidder will end up with the commodity even if the seller is not allowed to breach, and fell back on an argument that the transaction costs of moving a commodity to an overbidder will be less in an efficient-breach regime than in a performance regime. However, it is impossible to establish that the transaction costs of moving commodities to higher-valued uses would be less under an efficient-breach regime than under a performance regime. Indeed, given the cost of litigation, the transaction costs of such movements would almost certainly be greater in an efficient-breach regime than in a performance regime.

In short, in the context of the Overbidder Paradigm there is no convincing efficiency justification for the theory of efficient breach. Moreover, if the theory was widely followed it would lead to inefficiency, by remaking the parties' contract, reducing the rewards for planning and investing, and weakening the contracting system.

Remaking Contracts. The efficiency of a contract rule can usually be measured by asking whether it is the rule that well-informed contracting parties would normally agree upon if bargaining were cost-free. There is an easy way to determine whether the theory of efficient breach corresponds to what contracting parties in the Overbidder Paradigm would normally agree upon. Suppose a seller and a buyer have negotiated a contract under which the seller agrees to sell a differentiated commodity to buyer—say, a home to live in, or a used machine that the buyer will employ as a factor of production. As the parties are about to sign a written contract, the seller says, "In all honesty, I should tell you that although I have no present intention to breach this contract, neither do I have a present intention to perform. If a better offer comes along, I will take it and pay you expectation damages. In fact, I will begin actively looking for a better offer right after we sign this contract. Let's insert a provision that recognizes that I will do just that."

What would be the buyer's likely response? Under the theory of efficient breach, the buyer would say, "Of course, I expect no more." Experience strongly suggests, however, that in real life most buyers would be surprised if not shocked by such a statement, and would either walk away; insist on an explicit contractual provision stating that the seller has a present intent to perform and that any profit on breach and resale will go to buyer; or demand a payment, in the form of a reduced price, for the seller's right to resell. Buyers will react this way because normally one of the very points of a bargain promise is to convince the promisee that the promisor has an intent to perform.

Moreover, at the time a contract for the sale of a differentiated commodity is made, the buyer and the seller know that an overbid might later be forthcoming. Because the buyer and the seller know this, the buyer will need to pay the seller an implicit premium for taking the risk of forgoing an overbid. The amount of this premium will be the expected value of an overbid, based on a rough probability-weighted average of potential overbid prices. To put this differently, if the seller is economically rational, her price will include a premium paid by the buyer to ensure that the seller will take the contracted-for commodity off the market—a premium equal to the reduction in price that the buyer would demand for giving the seller a right to resell to an overbidder. Allowing the seller to obtain and retain the amount of this premium would take from the buyer a right that he has bought and paid for, and inefficiently remake the parties' contract.

Reducing the rewards for planning and investing. The theory of efficient breach also inefficiently reduces the rewards for planning and investing. Where the buyer's damages are based on the difference between contract price and market price, the seller will gain from breach only if the price paid by the overbidder exceeds the market price. There are two basic reasons why an overbidder might pay more than market price.

First, market price is an inexact construct based on extrapolations from comparable transactions, and the overbidder may be willing to pay a price in excess of the extrapolated price. In that case the theory has no positive efficiency implication: there is no reason to believe that the overbidder values the commodity more highly than the buyer, because the buyer might also have been willing to pay a price in excess of the price.

Second, the overbidder may have a strategic need for the commodity that leads him to place a higher value on the commodity than anyone else, and the extrapolated price is almost certain to be less than that value. However, if the third party had a strategic need for the commodity when he made his overbid, he probably had a prospect of the strategic need when the contract between the buyer and the seller was made. The question then arises, why didn't the overbidder make a contract with the seller at that time? The answer to this question is likely to involve issues of foresight and investment. For example, it often may be that the buyer foresaw a future need for the commodity, and therefore was willing to invest in a contract for production of the commodity at a time when the overbidder lacked the foresight, was unwilling to make the investment, or both. Or, it may be that the commodity essentially consists of productive capacity, and the buyer foresaw a future need for that capacity, and was willing to invest in a contract to lock up that capacity, at a time when the overbidder lacked the foresight, was unwilling to make the investment, or both.

In either type of case, the overbidder may be willing to pay more than the extrapolated price because the supply or productive capacity that he needs has now become highly constrained. However, providing the seller with an incentive to sell the commodity to the overbidder in either type of case would deny the buyer the benefit of his foresight and investment. Efficient incentives should be just the other way around. The law should reward the ant, not the grasshopper. It is the buyer who has earned the opportunity to acquire the commodity, by having foresight and investing when the third party was either not smart enough or willing enough to do so. Accordingly, in such cases too, the theory of efficient breach would have efficiency costs, because it would reduce the rewards for planning and investing.

Weakening the contracting system. There is a third way the theory of efficient breach, if widely followed, would reduce efficiency. The theory of efficient breach is based on a static and short-run approach to the issue of breach, because it addresses only the efficiency of performing or breaching an individual contract. In contrast, a dynamic long-run approach to the issue of breach addresses the efficiency of the contracting system as a whole. From that perspective, the theory of efficient breach is inefficient because if widely followed it would diminish the efficiency of that system.

The efficiency of the contracting system does not rest, as the theory of efficient breach implies, solely on legal remedies. Rather, the efficiency of the contracting system rests on a tripod whose legs are legal remedies, reputational constraints, and the internalization of social norms—in particular, the moral norm of promise keeping. These three legs are mutually supportive. Legal rules rest in significant part on social norms, reputational effects rest principally on social norms, and moral norms are reinforced by legal rules and supported by reputational effects.

All three of these legs are necessary to ensure the reliability of the contracting system. Legal rules are not alone sufficient, because dispute settlement under law is expensive and chancy. The moral norm of promise keeping is not alone sufficient, because not all actors fully internalize moral norms and there are limits on the power of norms. Reputational effects are not alone sufficient, because they are fully effective only if third parties have reliable knowledge concerning a promisor's history of breach, and this kind of information is hard to come by, both because many breaches do not become widely known and because many promisors will often claim that they had a valid excuse for not performing.

Because all three legs are necessary to support the efficiency of the contracting system, anything that weakens one leg seriously threatens the efficiency of the system. The theory of efficient breach, if widely adopted, would do precisely that, because the effect of the theory is to remove the moral force of promising in a bargain context. The moral meaning of making a promise is to commit yourself to take a given action in the future even if, when the action is due to be taken, all things considered you do not wish to take it. The theory of efficient breach turns this upside down. Under that theory, if you don't wish to take a promised action when it is due because, all things considered, you believe that the cost to you of taking the action would exceed the gain to the promisee, you not only needn't, but *shouldn't* keep the promise. As Posner states, if the seller's gain from breach will exceed the buyer's loss, then "if damages are limited to loss of expected profit, there will be an incentive to commit breach. *There should be.*"

In short, the theory of efficient breach, if widely adopted, would increase the need to resort to litigation, which is very expensive, as opposed to achieving performance of contracts through the internalization of the moral norm of promise keeping, which is very inexpensive; would lead contracting parties to make greater use of costly noncontractual measures to ensure performance, such as self-enforcing deposits; and would diminish the force of reputational constraints, because reputational constraints rest in part on a moral basis.

To summarize, in the context of the Overbidder Paradigm the theory of efficient breach is inefficient in three major respects. First, the theory would inefficiently remake the parties' contract by converting a contract under which the seller agrees to provide a commodity, and to not search for or sell to an overbidder, into a contract that allows and indeed encourages sellers to both search for and sell to an overbidder. Second, the theory would reduce the rewards for planning and investing, by encouraging sellers to transfer commodities away from buyers who have planned and invested, to overbidders who have done neither. Third, the theory would reduce the efficiency of the contracting system by seriously weakening one of the three legs upon which that efficiency rests.

———

PART 3

ASSENT

■ ■ ■

The most common forms of contracts are bargains. A bargain entails mutual manifested assent. What constitutes mutual manifested assent for purposes of the law of contracts is a very difficult issue. That issue is considered in Part 3.

Part 3 begins with Chapter 8, which concerns the basic principles of interpretation in contract law. Although problems of interpretation run through all areas of contract law, they are most salient when the issue is whether a person manifested assent to a contract or to a term.

Although bargains can be formed in more than one way, they are most commonly formed by an offer followed by an acceptance. Chapters 9 and 10 concern problems of offer and acceptance—problems such as what constitutes an offer, whether and when offers are revocable, and what kind of acceptance an offer requires.

Chapter 11 concerns the problems that arise where the terms of an agreement are indefinite or not final.

CHAPTER 8

AN INTRODUCTION TO INTERPRETATION

■ ■ ■

This Chapter concerns the interpretation of contractual language. The Chapter consists of two Sections.

Section 1 introduces the role of subjective and objective elements in contract interpretation.

Section 2 concerns the problems of interpreting purposive language.

Special rules of interpretation are sometimes applied when a contract is in writing. These rules will be considered later, in Chapters 12 and 13, because they reflect policies that give primacy to written expressions of intent.

SECTION 1. SUBJECTIVE AND OBJECTIVE ELEMENTS IN CONTRACT INTERPRETATION

INTRODUCTORY NOTE

It is very commonly asserted that a contract requires a meeting of the minds. In many contexts this statement is scarcely objectionable. For example, if A offers to sell his bicycle to B for $90, and B says that he accepts provided A will reduce the price to $80, it is obvious that no contract has as yet been entered. One may quite properly justify this conclusion by saying that there has been no meeting of the minds. On the other hand, difficulties will arise if the requirement of a meeting of the minds is taken literally and applied indiscriminately. In Europe there has been much discussion of the problem of a mental reservation. Could a defendant who had signed a contract with the apparent intention of binding himself escape liability by showing that at the time of the signing he had made a mental reservation that he should not be bound? It is obvious that this defense should not be allowed; so obvious is this conclusion that the question has not even been discussed in the case-oriented literature of the common law.

But there are questions of practical import that do present real difficulty, including cases where effective communication fails because one party misinterprets the intention of the other. In these cases, the question may arise whether a verbal or written expression may be affected by a state of mind that accompanied it. A major theme running through Part III is the tension, in such cases, between subjective intent (state of mind, or what a party "really" meant) and objective intent (what the party seemed to have meant).

It is sometimes concluded that what a party objectively means is not a question of intent at all. This conclusion rests on a confusion of thought concerning the meaning of intent, as is shown by the analogy of legislation. Under our constitutional system, the courts are generally subservient to the legislature. If Congress has properly enacted a law falling within the field of its competence, the courts are bound to follow and apply this law. With respect to the statute, the court's function is conceived as being subordinate. This constitutional relation between courts and statutes is commonly expressed by saying that the intent of the legislature governs the interpretation of a statute. Yet it is generally recognized that the intent that the court must respect is a formalized thing, and not the actual inner intent of particular legislators. A statute becomes law only after it has been enacted in accordance with certain rules; when these rules have been followed the statute stands as law even though Senator Sorghum confides to his dinner partner that he was asleep when the bill was read and did not know what he was voting for.

Similarly, it is sometimes concluded that by emphasizing objective intent, contract law makes no place for subjective intent. This conclusion is equally flawed. The attitude that our courts take toward private agreements rests upon a kind of tacitly accepted constitution. This constitution, like that which regulates the relation of the courts to statutes, is a multi-faceted concept. When that is recognized, there is no longer any need to be disturbed by the fact that judges sometimes hold a person to an agreement he did not subjectively intend and at the same time insist that their purpose in enforcing contracts is to carry out the intention of the parties. Similar paradoxes, proceeding from similar causes, are to be found in most human institutions. The rules of an athletic association, for example, may be intended to ensure that the official record shall go to the fastest runner. At the same time these rules may operate to exclude the fastest runner from the record because his achievement occurred under conditions not satisfying the association's standards. No one argues from this that the association has placed itself in a self-contradictory position, and must either abandon its rules for establishing records or cease pretending that it is interested in the speed of runners. There is as little reason to force upon the law of contracts a similar either-or alternative with regard to the treatment of intent.

LUCY v. ZEHMER

Supreme Court of Appeals of Virginia, 1954.
196 Va. 493, 84 S.E.2d 516.

BUCHANAN, JUSTICE. This suit was instituted by W.O. Lucy and J.C. Lucy, complainants, against A.H. Zehmer and Ida S. Zehmer, his wife, defendants, to have specific performance of a contract by which it was alleged the Zehmers had sold to W.O. Lucy a tract of land owned by A.H. Zehmer in Dinwiddie County containing 471.6 acres, more or less, known as the Ferguson farm, for $50,000. J.C. Lucy, the other complainant, is a brother of W.O. Lucy, to whom W.O. Lucy transferred a half interest in his alleged purchase.

The instrument sought to be enforced was written by A.H. Zehmer on December 20, 1952, in these words: "We hereby agree to sell to W.O. Lucy the Ferguson Farm complete for $50,000.00, title satisfactory to buyer," and signed by the defendants, A.H. Zehmer and Ida S. Zehmer.

The answer of A.H. Zehmer admitted that at the time mentioned W.O. Lucy offered him $50,000 cash for the farm, but that he, Zehmer considered that the offer was made in jest; that so thinking, and both he and Lucy having had several drinks, he wrote out "the memorandum" quoted above and induced his wife to sign it; that he did not deliver the memorandum to Lucy, but that Lucy picked it up, read it, put it in his pocket, attempted to offer Zehmer $5 to bind the bargain, which Zehmer refused to accept, and realizing for the first time that Lucy was serious, Zehmer assured him that he had no intention of selling the farm and that the whole matter was a joke. Lucy left the premises insisting that he had purchased the farm.

Depositions were taken and the decree appealed from was entered holding that the complainants had failed to establish their right to specific performance, and dismissing their bill. The assignment of error is to this action of the court.

W.O. Lucy, a lumberman and farmer, thus testified in substance: He had known Zehmer for fifteen or twenty years and had been familiar with the Ferguson farm for ten years. Seven or eight years ago he had offered Zehmer $20,000 for the farm which Zehmer had accepted, but the agreement was verbal and Zehmer backed out. On the night of December 20, 1952, around eight o'clock, he took an employee to McKenney, where Zehmer lived and operated a restaurant, filling station and motor court. While there he decided to see Zehmer and again try to buy the Ferguson farm. He entered the restaurant and talked to Mrs. Zehmer until Zehmer came in. He asked Zehmer if he had sold the Ferguson farm. Zehmer replied that he had not. Lucy said, "I bet you wouldn't take $50,000.00 for that place." Zehmer replied, "Yes, I would too; you wouldn't give fifty." Lucy said he would and told Zehmer to write up an agreement to that effect. Zehmer took a restaurant check and wrote on the back of it, "I do hereby agree to sell to W.O. Lucy the Ferguson Farm for $50,000 complete." Lucy told him he had better change it to "We" because Mrs. Zehmer would have to sign it too. Zehmer then tore up what he had written, wrote the agreement quoted above and asked Mrs. Zehmer, who was at the other end of the counter ten or twelve feet away, to sign it. Mrs. Zehmer said she would for $50,000 and signed it. Zehmer brought it back and gave it to

Lucy, who offered him $5 which Zehmer refused, saying, "You don't need to give me any money, you got the agreement there signed by both of us."

The discussion leading to the signing of the agreement, said Lucy, lasted thirty or forty minutes, during which Zehmer seemed to doubt that Lucy could raise $50,000. Lucy suggested the provision for having the title examined and Zehmer made the suggestion that he would sell it "complete, everything there," and stated that all he had on the farm was three heifers.

December 20 was on Saturday. Next day Lucy telephoned to J.C. Lucy and arranged with the latter to take a half interest in the purchase and pay half of the consideration. On Monday he engaged an attorney to examine the title. The attorney reported favorably on December 31 and on January 2 Lucy wrote Zehmer stating that the title was satisfactory, that he was ready to pay the purchase price in cash and asking when Zehmer would be ready to close the deal. Zehmer replied by letter, mailed on January 13, asserting that he had never agreed or intended to sell.

Mr. and Mrs. Zehmer were called by the complainants as adverse witnesses. Zehmer testified in substance as follows.

He bought this farm more than ten years ago for $11,000. He had had twenty-five offers, more or less, to buy it, including several from Lucy, who had never offered any specific sum of money. He had given them all the same answer, that he was not interested in selling it. On this Saturday night before Christmas it looked like everybody and his brother came by there to have a drink. He took a good many drinks during the afternoon and had a pint of his own. When he entered the restaurant around eight-thirty Lucy was there and he could see that he was "pretty high." He said to Lucy, "Boy, you got some good liquor, drinking, ain't you?" Lucy then offered him a drink. "I was already high as a Georgia pine, and didn't have any more better sense than to pour another great big slug out and gulp it down, and he took one too."

After they had talked a while Lucy asked whether he still had the Ferguson farm. He replied that he had not sold it and Lucy said, "I bet you wouldn't take $50,000.00 for it." Zehmer asked him if he would give $50,000 and Lucy said yes. Zehmer replied, "You haven't got $50,000.00 in cash." Lucy said he did and Zehmer replied that he did not believe it. They argued "pro and con for a long time," mainly about "whether he had $50,000 in cash that he could put up right then and buy that farm."

Finally, said Zehmer, Lucy told him if he didn't believe he had $50,000, "you sign that piece of paper here and say you will take $50,000.00 for the farm." He, Zehmer, "just grabbed the back off of a guest check there" and wrote on the back of it. At that point in his testimony Zehmer asked to see what he had written to "see if I recognize my own handwriting." He examined the paper and exclaimed, "Great balls of fire, I got 'Firgerson' for

Ferguson. I have got satisfactory spelled wrong. I don't recognize that writing if I would see it, wouldn't know it was mine."

After Zehmer had, as he described it, "scribbled this thing off," Lucy said, "Get your wife to sign it." Zehmer walked over to where she was and she at first refused to sign but did so after he told her that he "was just needling him [Lucy], and didn't mean a thing in the world, that I was not selling the farm." Zehmer then "took it back over there . . . and I was still looking at the dern thing. I had the drink right there by my hand, and I reached over to get a drink, and he said, 'Let me see it.' He reached and picked it up, and when I looked back again he had it in his pocket and he dropped a five dollar bill over there, and he said, 'Here is five dollars payment on it.' . . . I said, 'Hell no, that is beer and liquor talking. I am not going to sell you the farm. I have told you that too many times before.'" [Mrs. Zehmer's testimony was comparable to that of Mr. Zehmer. She added that after Lucy said, "All right, get your wife to sign it." Zehmer came back to where she was standing and said, "You want to put your name to this?" She said "No," but he said in an undertone, "It is nothing but a joke," and she signed it.] . . .

The defendants insist that the evidence was ample to support their contention that the writing sought to be enforced was prepared as a bluff or dare to force Lucy to admit that he did not have $50,000; that the whole matter was a joke; that the writing was not delivered to Lucy and no binding contract was ever made between the parties. . . .

In his testimony Zehmer claimed that he "was high as a Georgia pine," and that the transaction "was just a bunch of two doggoned drunks bluffing to see who could talk the biggest and say the most." That claim is inconsistent with his attempt to testify in great detail as to what was said and what was done. It is contradicted by other evidence as to the condition of both parties. . . . It was in fact conceded by defendants' counsel in oral argument that under the evidence Zehmer was not too drunk to make a valid contract. . . .

The appearance of the contract, the fact that it was under discussion for forty minutes or more before it was signed; Lucy's objection to the first draft because it was written in the singular, and he wanted Mrs. Zehmer to sign it also; the rewriting to meet that objection and the signing by Mrs. Zehmer; the discussion of what was to be included in the sale, the provision for the examination of the title, the completeness of the instrument that was executed, the taking possession of it by Lucy with no request or suggestion by either of the defendants that he give it back, are facts which furnish persuasive evidence that the execution of the contract was a serious business transaction rather than a casual, jesting matter as defendants now contend. . . .

If it be assumed, contrary to what we think the evidence shows, that Zehmer was jesting about selling his farm to Lucy and that the transaction was intended by him to be a joke, nevertheless the evidence shows that Lucy did not so understand it but considered it to be a serious business transaction and the contract to be binding on the Zehmers as well as on himself. . . .

Not only did Lucy actually believe, but the evidence shows he was warranted in believing, that the contract represented a serious business transaction and a good faith sale and purchase of the farm.

In the field of contracts, as generally elsewhere, "We must look to the outward expression of a person as manifesting his intention rather than to his secret and unexpressed intention. 'The law imputes to a person an intention corresponding to the reasonable meaning of his words and acts.'" First Nat. Exchange Bank of Roanoke v. Roanoke Oil Co., 169 Va. 99, 114, 192 S.E. 764, 770.

At no time prior to the execution of the contract had Zehmer indicated to Lucy by word or act that he was not in earnest about selling the farm. They had argued about it and discussed its terms, as Zehmer admitted, for a long time. Lucy testified that if there was any jesting it was about paying $50,000 that night. The contract and the evidence show that he was not expected to pay the money that night. Zehmer said that after the writing was signed he laid it down on the counter in front of Lucy. Lucy said Zehmer handed it to him. In any event there had been what appeared to be a good faith offer and a good faith acceptance, followed by the execution and apparent delivery of a written contract. Both said that Lucy put the writing in his pocket and then offered Zehmer $5 to seal the bargain. Not until then, even under the defendants' evidence, was anything said or done to indicate that the matter was a joke. Both of the Zehmers testified that when Zehmer asked his wife to sign he whispered that it was a joke so Lucy wouldn't hear and that it was not intended that he should hear.

The mental assent of the parties is not requisite for the formation of a contract. If the words or other acts of one of the parties have but one reasonable meaning, his undisclosed intention is immaterial except when an unreasonable meaning which he attaches to his manifestations is known to the other party. Restatement of the Law of Contracts, Vol. I, § 71, p. 74. . . .

So a person cannot set up that he was merely jesting when his conduct and words would warrant a reasonable person in believing that he intended a real agreement. 17 C.J.S., Contracts, § 47, p. 390; Clark on Contracts, 4 ed., § 27, at p. 54.

Whether the writing signed by the defendants and now sought to be enforced by the complainants was the result of a serious offer by Lucy and a serious acceptance by the defendants, or was a serious offer by Lucy and an acceptance in secret jest by the defendants, in either event it constituted a binding contract of sale between the parties.

Defendants contend further, however, that even though a contract was made, equity should decline to enforce it under the circumstances. These circumstances have been set forth in detail above. They disclose some drinking by the two parties but not to an extent that they were unable to understand fully what they were doing. There was no fraud, no misrepresentation, no sharp practice and no dealing between unequal parties. The farm had been bought for $11,000 and was assessed for taxation at $6,300. The purchase price was $50,000. Zehmer admitted that it was a good price. There is in fact present in this case none of the grounds usually urged against specific performance. . . .

The complainants are entitled to have specific performance of the contract sued on. The decree appealed from is therefore reversed and the cause is remanded for the entry of a proper decree requiring the defendants to perform the contract in accordance with the prayer of the bill.

Reversed and remanded.

RESTATEMENT, SECOND, CONTRACTS §§ 12, 16

[See Selected Source Materials Supplement]

RESTATEMENT, SECOND, CONTRACTS § 16, ILLUSTRATION 3 AND COMMENTS A AND B

Illustration 3.   A has been drinking heavily. B, who has also been drinking, meets A, offers to buy A's farm for $50,000, a fair price, and offers A a drink which A accepts. In drunken exhilaration A, as a joke, writes out and signs a memorandum of agreement to sell, gets his wife to sign it, and delivers it to B, who understands the transaction as a serious one. A's intoxication is no defense to B's suit for specific performance. . .

Comment a. Because drunkenness has both voluntary and compulsive aspects, the courts have been ambivalent toward it as an incapacity defense. A way of avoiding the problem is to focus on the conduct of the other party and the fairness of the contract. This was the approach taken in Lucy v. Zehmer, 196 Va. 493, 84 S.E.2d 516 (1954). If one party takes advantage of the other's drunkenness and an unfair contract is entered into, a stronger case is made under the fraud, overreaching and unconscionability concepts than under capacity concepts, because the critical factor appears to be the conduct of the sober party, rather than the inability of the drunkard. In extreme cases, no manifestation of assent may occur, but otherwise, the problem seems closer to that of persons of mild mental retardation or dull normal intelligence where extra protection should be given rather than capacity denied. . . .

b.   *What contracts are voidable.* The standard of competency in intoxication cases is the same as that in cases of mental illness. A contract made by a person who is so drunk he does not know what he is doing is voidable if the other party has reason to know of the intoxication. Where there is some understanding of the transaction despite intoxication, avoidance depends on a showing that the other party induced the drunkenness or that the consideration was inadequate or that the transaction departed from the normal pattern of similar transactions; if the particular transaction in its result is one which a reasonably competent person might have made, it cannot be avoided even though entirely executory.

Keller v. Holderman

11 Mich. 248, 83 Am.Dec. 737 (1863)

Suit against the maker of a check for $300, which had been given in return for an old silver watch, worth about $15. The court said, "when the court below found as a fact that 'the whole transaction between the parties was a frolic and a banter, the plaintiff not expecting to sell, nor the defendant to buy the watch at the sum for which the check was drawn,' the conclusion should have been that no contract was ever made by the parties, and the finding should have been that no cause of action existed upon the check to the plaintiff."

RAFFLES V. WICHELHAUS
In the Court of Exchequer, 1864.
2 Hurl. & C. 906.

Declaration. For that it was agreed between the plaintiff and the defendants, to wit, at Liverpool, that the plaintiff should sell to the defendants, and the defendants buy of the plaintiff, certain goods, to wit, 125 bales of Surat cotton, guaranteed middling fair merchant's dhollorah, to arrive ex Peerless from Bombay; and that the cotton should be taken from the quay, and that the defendants would pay the plaintiff for the same at a certain rate, to wit, at the rate of 17¼ d. per pound, within a certain time then agreed upon after the arrival of the said goods in England. Averments: that the said goods did arrive by the said ship from Bombay in

England, to wit, at Liverpool, and the plaintiff was then and there ready and willing and offered to deliver the said goods to the defendants, etc. Breach: that the defendants refused to accept the said goods or pay the plaintiff for them.

Plea. That the said ship mentioned in the said agreement was meant and intended by the defendant to be the ship called the Peerless, which sailed from Bombay, to wit, in October; and that the plaintiff was not ready and willing, and did not offer to deliver to the defendants any bales of cotton which arrived by the last-mentioned ship, but instead thereof was only ready and willing, and offered to deliver to the defendants 125 bales of Surat cotton which arrived by another and different ship, which was also called the Peerless, and which sailed from Bombay, to wit, in December.

Demurrer, and joinder therein.

Milward, in support of the demurrer. The contract was for the sale of a number of bales of cotton of a particular description, which the plaintiff was ready to deliver. It is immaterial by what ship the cotton was to arrive, so that it was a ship called the Peerless. The words "to arrive ex Peerless," only mean that if the vessel is lost on the voyage, the contract is to be at an end. [Pollock, C.B. It would be a question for the jury whether both parties meant the same ship called the Peerless.] That would be so if the contract was for the sale of a ship called the Peerless; but it is for the sale of cotton on board a ship of that name. [Pollock, C.B. The defendant only bought that cotton which was to arrive by a particular ship. It may as well be said, that if there is a contract for the purchase of certain goods in warehouse A., that is satisfied by the delivery of goods of the same description in warehouse B.] In that case there would be goods in both warehouses; here it does not appear that the plaintiff had any goods on board the other Peerless. [Martin, B. It is imposing on the defendant a contract different from that which he entered into. Pollock, C.B. It is like a contract for the purchase of wine coming from a particular estate in France or Spain, where there are two estates of that name.] The defendant has no right to contradict by parol evidence, a written contract good upon the face of it. He does not impute misrepresentation or fraud, but only says that he fancied the ship was a different one. Intention is of no avail, unless stated at the time of the contract. [Pollock, C.B. One vessel sailed in October and the other in December.] The time of sailing is no part of the contract.

Mellish (Cohen with him), in support of the plea. There is nothing on the face of the contract to show that any particular ship called the Peerless was meant; but the moment it appears that two ships called the Peerless were about to sail from Bombay there is a latent ambiguity, and parol evidence may be given for the purpose of showing that the defendant meant one Peerless and the plaintiff another. That being so, there was no consensus ad idem, and therefore no binding contract. He was then stopped by the Court.

PER CURIAM. There must be judgment for the defendants.

Judgment for the defendants.

————

Simpson, Contracts for Cotton to Arrive: The Case of the Two Ships *Peerless*

11 Cardozo L. Rev. 287, 295 (1989)

"There were reports of at least eleven ships called *Peerless* sailing the seven seas at the time [of the *Peeerless* case], for the name was a popular one. The *Mercantile Navy List* for 1863 lists nine British registered sailing vessels of that name, their ports of registration being London, Aberystwyth, Dartmouth, Greenock, Halifax, Windsor (Nova Scotia), Hull, and Liverpool, which boasted two such ships. There were also two American ships named *Peerless* from Boston and Baltimore. The existence of so many vessels of the same or a similar name could obviously cause confusion in shipping movement reports. There was nothing unusual however in this state of affairs. Ships commonly shared the same name, particularly popular names such as *Annie*. But the two vessels with which we are concerned can readily be identified as the two which were registered at Liverpool. At the time it was the practice in the shipping press to differentiate vessels bearing the same name by the names of their captains, not, as one might expect, by using their unique registered number."

————

NOTE ON MUTUAL MISUNDERSTANDING

Today, *Raffles v. Wichelhaus* generally is described as a case of mutual misunderstanding. In almost all of the cases covered in this chapter there is a misunderstanding either about the existence of a contract or about a material term. In *Raffles*, the misunderstanding was about a material term: whether the contract was for cotton on a vessel sailing from Bombay in October or in December. In *Lucy v. Zehmer*, if you believe Zehmer's testimony (the Virginia Supreme Court did not), the misunderstanding was about the existence of a contract: whether the sale was made in jest. *Lucy v. Zehmer* illustrates the law's usual way of handling a misunderstanding, which is to adopt the understanding of the party who is less at fault; this is the party who holds the more reasonable understanding. The label *mutual misunderstanding* is reserved for cases in which neither party is more at fault. *Raffles* illustrates the law's usual response in such cases.

Frigaliment Importing Co. v. B.N.S. Intern. Sales Corp., 190 F. Supp. 116 (S.D.N.Y. 1960), is a modern variation on *Raffles*. The contract was for the sale of chicken. The New York seller thought it could fill the contract with older and larger birds more precisely described as stewing chicken or fowl. The Swiss buyer thought it was buying younger and smaller birds more precisely described as broilers or fryers. The trial judge was Henry Friendly, one of the most respected jurists of the mid-20th century. His opinion carefully reviews the relevant evidence, including the correspondence between the parties, the parties' testimony of what they understood chicken to mean, the definition of chicken in authoritative sources, such as dictionaries and government regulations, and expert testimony on trade usage. The concluding passages in the opinion identify another relevant consideration and summarize the key factual findings:

> Defendant makes a further argument based on the impossibility of its obtaining broilers and fryers at the 33 cents price offered by plaintiff for the 2 ½–3 lbs. birds. There is no substantial dispute that, in late April, 1957, the price for 2 ½–3 lbs. broilers was between 35 and 37 cents per pound, and that when defendant entered into the contracts, it was well aware of this and intended to fill them by supplying fowl in these weights. It claims that plaintiff must likewise have known the market since plaintiff had reserved shipping space on April 23, three days before plaintiff's cable to Stovicek, or, at least, that Stovicek was chargeable with such knowledge. It is scarcely an answer to say, as plaintiff does in its brief, that the 33 cents price offered by the 2 ½–3 lbs. "chickens" was closer to the prevailing 35 cents price for broilers than to the 30 cents at which defendant procured fowl. Plaintiff must have expected defendant to make some profit—certainly it could not have expected defendant deliberately to incur a loss. . . .

> When all the evidence is reviewed, it is clear that defendant believed it could comply with the contracts by delivering stewing chicken in the 2 ½–3 lbs. size. Defendant's subjective intent would not be significant if this did not coincide with an objective meaning of "chicken." Here it did coincide with one of the dictionary meanings, with the definition in the Department of Agriculture Regulations to which the contract made at least oblique reference, with at least some usage in the trade, with the realities of the market, and with what plaintiff's spokesman had said. Plaintiff asserts it to be equally plain that plaintiff's own subjective intent was to obtain broilers and fryers; the only evidence against this is the material as to market prices and this may not have been sufficiently brought home. In any event it is unnecessary to determine that issue. For plaintiff has the burden of showing that "chicken" was used in the narrower rather than in the broader sense, and this it has not sustained.

The following year, Judge Friendly stated that *Frigaliment* might better have been placed on the ground of failure of the minds to meet, under *Raffles v. Wichelhaus*, "with the loss still left on the plaintiff because defendant's not unjustifiable change of position. . . ." Dadourian Export Corp. v. United States, 291 F.2d 178, 187 n. 4. (2d Cir.1961) (dissenting opinion). The reason the loss was left on the plaintiff (the buyer) was that it had paid the contract price for the first shipment of stewing hen and was seeking damages for breach of warranty. The plaintiff might have done better had it pled in the alternative that if the contract was not for broilers, then there was no contract (as in *Raffles*), and it was entitled to recover, in a restitution claim, the difference between the price it paid and the market price of fowl less the defendant's shipping costs. See Chapter 10.

Oswald v. Allen

417 F.2d 43 (2d Cir.1969)

Oswald, a coin collector from Switzerland, was interested in Allen's collection of Swiss coins. In April 1964, Oswald was in the United States and the parties drove to the Newburgh Savings Bank, where two of Allen's coin collections were located. Oswald first examined the coins in Allen's Swiss Coin Collection, and was then shown several valuable Swiss coins from Allen's Rarity Coin Collection. Oswald took notes on each collection. On the parties' return from the bank, a price of $50,000 was agreed upon for Allen's collection of Swiss coins. However, Oswald thought he was buying all of Allen's Swiss coins, while Allen thought she was selling only the Swiss Coin Collection, but not the Swiss coins in the Rarity Coin Collection. The evidence showed that each collection had its own key number, and was housed in a labeled cigar box. Oswald, however, testified that he did not know that some of the Swiss coins he examined were in a separate Collection. Held, no contract was formed. "Even though the mental assent of the parties is not requisite for the formation of a contract . . . the facts . . . clearly place this case within the small group of exceptional cases in which there is 'no sensible basis for choosing between conflicting understandings.' . . . The rule of Raffles v. Wichelhaus is applicable here."

Colfax Envelope Corp. v. Local No. 458–3M

20 F.3d 750 (7th Cir.1994)

"*Raffles* and *Oswald* were cases in which neither party was blameable for the mistake. . . . If neither party can be assigned the greater blame for the misunderstanding, there is no nonarbitrary basis for deciding which party's understanding to enforce, so the parties are allowed to abandon the contract without liability. . . . These are not cases in which one party's understanding is more reasonable than the other's. Compare Restatement . . . § 20(2)(b). If rescission were permitted in that kind of case, the enforcement of every contract would be at the mercy of a jury, which might be persuaded that one of the parties had genuinely held an idiosyncratic idea of its meaning, so that there had been, in fact, no meeting of the minds."

EMBRY V. HARGADINE, MCKITTRICK DRY GOODS CO.

St. Louis Court of Appeals, Missouri, 1907.
127 Mo.App. 383, 105 S.W. 777.

Action by Charles R. Embry against the Hargadine-McKittrick Dry Goods Company. From a judgment for defendant, plaintiff appeals. Reversed and remanded.

GOODE, J. We dealt with this case on a former appeal (115 Mo.App. 130, 91 S.W. 170). It has been retried, and is again before us for the determination of questions not then reviewed. The appellant was an employee of the respondent company under a written contract to expire December 15, 1903, at a salary of $2,000 per annum. His duties were to attend to the sample department of respondent, of which he was given complete charge. It was his business to select samples for the traveling salesmen of the company, which is a wholesale dry goods concern, to use in selling goods to retail merchants.

Appellant contends that on December 23, 1903, he was re-engaged by respondent, through its president, Thos. H. McKittrick, for another year at the same compensation and for the same duties stipulated in his previous written contract. On March 1, 1904, he was discharged, having been notified in February that, on account of the necessity of retrenching expenses, his services and that of some other employees would no longer be required.

The respondent company contends that its president never re-employed appellant after the termination of his written contract, and hence that it had a right to discharge him when it chose. The point with which we are concerned requires an epitome of the testimony of appellant and the counter testimony of McKittrick, the president of the company, in reference to the alleged re-employment.

Appellant testified: That several times prior to the termination of his written contract on December 15, 1903, he had endeavored to get an understanding with McKittrick for another year, but had been put off from time to time. That on December 23d, eight days after the expiration of said contract, he called on McKittrick, in the latter's office, and said to him that as appellant's written employment had lapsed eight days before, and as there were only a few days between then and the 1st of January in which to seek employment with other firms, if respondent wished to retain his services longer he must have a contract for another year, or he would quit respondent's service then and there. That he had been put off twice before and wanted an understanding or contract at once so that he could go ahead without worry. That McKittrick asked him how he was getting along in his department, and appellant said he was very busy, as they were in the height of the season getting men out—had about 110 salesmen on the line and others in preparation. That McKittrick then said: "Go ahead, you're all right. Get your men out, and don't let that worry you." That appellant took McKittrick at his word and worked until February 15th without any question in his mind. It was on February 15th that he was notified his services would be discontinued on March 1st.

McKittrick denied this conversation as related by appellant, and said that, when accosted by the latter on December 23d he (McKittrick) was working on his books in order to get out a report for a stockholders' meeting, and, when appellant said if he did not get a contract he would leave, that he (McKittrick) said: "Mr. Embry, I am just getting ready for the stockholders' meeting to-morrow. I have no time to take it up now. I have told you before I would not take it up until I had these matters out of the way. You will have to see me at a later time. I said: 'Go back upstairs and get your men out on the road.' I may have asked him one or two other questions relative to the department, I don't remember. The whole conversation did not take more than a minute."

Embry also swore that, when he was notified he would be discharged, he complained to McKittrick about it, as being a violation of their contract, and McKittrick said it was due to the action of the board of directors, and not to any personal action of his, and that others would suffer by what the board had done as well as Embry. Appellant requested an instruction to the jury setting out, in substance, the conversation between him and McKittrick according to his version, and declaring that those facts, if found to be true, constituted a contract between the parties that defendant would pay plaintiff the sum of $2,000 for another year, provided the jury believed from the evidence that plaintiff commenced said work believing he was to have $2,000 for the year's work. This instruction was refused, but the court gave another embodying in substance appellant's version of the conversation, and declaring it made a contract "if you (the jury) find both parties thereby intended and did contract with each other for plaintiff's employment for one year from and including December 23, 1903, at a salary of $2,000 per annum." Embry swore that, on several occasions when he spoke to McKittrick about employment for the ensuing year, he asked for a renewal of his former contract, and that on December 23d, the date of the alleged renewal, he went into Mr. McKittrick's office and told him his contract had expired, and he wanted to renew it for a year, having always worked under year contracts. Neither the refused instruction nor the one given by the court embodied facts quite as strong as appellant's testimony, because neither referred to appellant's alleged statement to McKittrick that unless he was re-employed he would stop work for respondent then and there.

It is assigned for error that the court required the jury, in order to return a verdict for appellant, not only to find the conversation occurred as appellant swore, but that both parties intended by such conversation to contract with each other for plaintiff's employment for the year from

December 1903, at a salary of $2,000. If it appeared from the record that there was a dispute between the parties as to the terms on which appellant wanted re-employment, there might have been sound reason for inserting this clause in the instruction; but no issue was made that they split on terms; the testimony of McKittrick tending to prove only that he refused to enter into a contract with appellant regarding another year's employment until the annual meeting of stockholders was out of the way. Indeed as to the proposed terms McKittrick agrees with Embry, for the former swore as follows: "Mr. Embry said he wanted to know about the renewal of his contract. Said if he did not have the contract made he would leave." As the two witnesses coincided as to the terms of the proposed re-employment, there was no reason for inserting the above mentioned clause in the instruction in order that it might be settled by the jury whether or not plaintiff, if employed for one year from December 23, 1903, was to be paid $2,000 a year. Therefore it remains to determine whether or not this part of the instruction was a correct statement of the law in regard to what was necessary to constitute a contract between the parties; that is to say, whether the formation of a contract by what, according to Embry, was said, depended on the intention of both Embry and McKittrick. Or, to put the question more precisely: Did what was said constitute a contract of re-employment on the previous terms irrespective of the intention or purpose of McKittrick?

Judicial opinion and elementary treatises abound in statements of the rule that to constitute a contract there must be a meeting of the minds of the parties, and both must agree to the same thing in the same sense. Generally speaking, this may be true; but it is not literally or universally true. That is to say, the inner intention of parties to a conversation subsequently alleged to create a contract cannot either make a contract of what transpired, or prevent one from arising, if the words used were sufficient to constitute a contract. In so far as their intention is an influential element, it is only such intention as the words or acts of the parties indicate; not one secretly cherished which is inconsistent with those words or acts. . . .

In Smith v. Hughes, L.R. 6 Q.B. 597, 607, it was said: "If, whatever a man's real intention may be, he so conducts himself that a reasonable man would believe that he was assenting to the terms proposed by the other party, and that other party upon that belief enters into the contract with him, the man thus conducting himself would be equally bound as if he had intended to agree to the other party's terms." . . .

In view of those authorities, we hold that, though McKittrick may not have intended to employ Embry by what transpired between them according to the latter's testimony, yet if what McKittrick said would have been taken by a reasonable man to be an employment, and Embry so understood it, it constituted a valid contract of employment for the ensuing year.

The next question is whether or not the language used was of that character, namely, was such that Embry, as a reasonable man, might consider that he was re-employed for the ensuing year on the previous terms, and act accordingly. We do not say that in every instance it would be for the court to pronounce on this question, because, peradventure, instances might arise in which there would be such an ambiguity in the language relied on to show an assent by the obligor to the proposal of the obligee that it would be for the jury to say whether a reasonable mind would take it to signify acceptance of the proposal. . . . Embry was demanding a renewal of his contract, saying he had been put off from time to time and that he had only a few days before the end of the year in which to seek employment from other houses, and that he would quit then and there unless he was re-employed. McKittrick inquired how he was getting along with the department, and Embry said they, i.e., the employees of the department, were very busy getting out salesmen. Whereupon McKittrick said: "Go ahead, you are all right. Get your men out, and do not let that worry you." We think no reasonable man would construe that answer to Embry's demand that he be employed for another year, otherwise than as an assent to the demand, and that Embry had the right to rely on it as an assent. . . . The answer was unambiguous, and we rule that if the conversation was according to appellant's version, and he understood he was employed, it constituted in law a valid contract of re-employment, and the court erred in making the formation of a contract depend on a finding that both parties intended to make one. . . .

The judgment is reversed, and the cause remanded. All concur.

RESTATEMENT, SECOND, CONTRACTS §§ 20, 201

[See Selected Source Materials Supplement]

CISG ART. 8

[See Selected Source Materials Supplement]

UNIDROIT PRINCIPLES OF INTERNATIONAL COMMERCIAL CONTRACTS ARTS. 4.1, 4.2, 4.3

[See Selected Source Materials Supplement]

PRINCIPLES OF EUROPEAN CONTRACT LAW ARTS. 5.101, 5.102

[See Selected Source Materials Supplement]

Morales v. Sun Constructors, Inc.

541 F.3d 218 (3d Cir. 2008)

As a condition to his employment, Juan Morales, "a Spanish-speaking welder who resided in St. Croix, United States Virgin Islands," was required to sign a 13-page hourly employment agreement that was presented to him at the end of a 2½-hour orientation conducted entirely in English. Morales was given some help at the orientation:

> The Sun employee who conducted the orientation, Mr. Langner, asked Jose Hodge (Hodge), a bilingual applicant who was also present at the orientation, and whom Morales knew, to explain to Morales what Langner was saying and help him fill out the documents. Hodge testified that he generally understands about eighty-five percent of what is said and written in English. He also stated that Morales did not ask him what he was signing and that he did not specifically explain the arbitration clause to Morales. Mr. Langner stated that he did explain the arbitration provisions in English and that, during the orientation, Hodge was speaking to Morales in a foreign language. . . .

Morales was fired by Sun after a year. When he brought a suit for wrongful termination in the District Court, Sun filed a motion to have the proceedings stayed pending arbitration. The District Court denied the motion, determining Morales had not assented to the arbitration clause. The Third Circuit reversed and remanded with instructions to enter a stay pending arbitration.

(Chagares, J.) "The Supreme Court has observed: "It will not do for a man to enter into a contract, and, when called upon to respond to its obligations, to say that he did not read it when he signed it, or did not know what it contained." *Upton v. Tribilcock,* 91 U.S. 45, 50, 23 L.Ed. 203 (1875). The "integrity of contracts demands" that this principle "be rigidly enforced by the courts." 1 Richard A. Lord, *Williston on Contracts* § 4:19 (4th ed.2008). As one noted treatise explains:

> According to the objective theory of contract formation, what is essential is not assent, but rather what the person to whom a manifestation is made is justified as regarding as assent. Thus, if an offeree, in ignorance of the terms of an offer, so acts or expresses itself as to justify the other party in inferring assent, and this action or expression was of such a character that a reasonable person in the

position of the offeree should have known it was calculated to lead
the offeror to believe that the offer had been accepted, a contract will
be formed in spite of the offeree's ignorance of the terms of the offer.
The most common illustration of this principle is the situation when
one who is ignorant of the language in which a document is written,
or who is illiterate, executes a writing proposed as a contract under a
mistake as to its contents. Such a person is bound, in the absence of
fraud, if the person does not require the document to be read to
him. . .

Id. See New York Life Ins. Co. v. Kwetkauskas, 63 F.2d 890, 891 (3d Cir.1933)
(recognizing that "[i]t is true that an illiterate man may bind himself by
contract by negligently failing to learn the contents of an instrument which he
has executed"); *Hoshaw v. Cosgriff,* 247 F. 22, 26 (8th Cir.1917) (holding that
every contracting party has the duty "to learn and know the contents of a
contract before he signs and delivers it"). . . .

"Morales, in essence, requests that this Court create an exception to the
objective theory of contract formation where a party is ignorant of the language
in which a contract is written. We decline to do so. In the absence of fraud, the
fact that an offeree cannot read, write, speak, or understand the English
language is immaterial to whether an English-language agreement the offeree
executes is enforceable. *See Paper Express, Ltd. v. Pfankuch Maschinen,* 972
F.2d 753, 757 (7th Cir.1992) (addressing a contract dispute between an Illinois
corporation and a German corporation and holding that parties should be held
to contracts, even if the contracts are in foreign languages or the parties cannot
read or understand the contracts due to blindness or illiteracy); *Shirazi v.
Greyhound Corp.,* 145 Mont. 421, 401 P.2d 559, 562 (1965) (holding Iranian
student subject to limitation contained in baggage receipt and stating that "[i]t
was incumbent upon [the plaintiff], who knew of his own inability to read the
English language, to acquaint himself with the contents of the ticket"); *Paulink
v. Am. Express* Co., 265 Mass. 182, 163 N.E. 740, 741 (1928) (stating that
"plaintiff was bound by the terms [of foreign bills of exchange], in the absence
of deceit on the part of the defendant, even though not understanding their
purport and ignorant of the English language"); *Wilkisius v. Sheehan,* 258
Mass. 240, 155 N.E. 5, 6 (1927) (holding that Lithuanian husband and wife,
who did not speak or understand English and used an interpreter to contract
for an exchange of real estate, were bound by the terms of the agreement
because "their failure to understand these details was not due to fraudulent
acts on the part of the defendant but to their own inability to read, write, speak
or understand the English language, and to the incapacity of the interpreter").

"Morales is not claiming fraud, . . . and he is not alleging that Sun
misrepresented the contents of the Agreement to him. . . ."

(Fuentes, J., dissenting) "No one disputes that Sun asked Hodge to
translate the Employment Agreement for Morales, who did not read English.
And no one disputes that Hodge failed to translate the arbitration clause in the
Agreement. On this basis, I disagree with my colleagues' conclusion that the

parties here manifested mutual assent to the arbitration clause of the Agreement, and I would therefore affirm the District Court's decision.

"The majority opens its opinion by asserting that this case "requires us to determine whether an arbitration clause is enforceable where one party is ignorant of the language in which the agreement is written." Maj. Op. at 220. The problem, however, is not simply Morales' ignorance of the language. The gravamen of this case is that Sun—the other party to the Agreement—took upon itself the task of translating the Agreement for Morales and, in doing so, failed to convey the entire contents of the Agreement. What we must determine is whether this failure resulted in a lack of mutual assent; I believe that it did.

"The law is clear that a party may not be relieved of his or her obligations pursuant to a contract solely because he or she cannot understand the language in which that contract is written. However, the law is also clear that there are certain circumstances where a person's inability to comprehend the language in which a contract is written may result in a lack of mutual assent. . . .

"The majority appears to agree that there can be such "special circumstances," but suggests that these circumstances exist *only* in a case where a fraud has been perpetuated. Maj. Op. at 223. I do not think that this is correct. In *New York Life,* the court noted that an illiterate signer will be held to a contract if he or she negligently failed to learn its contents; it does not automatically follow that an illiterate signer who is unaware of the contents of a contract but did not act in a negligent fashion will similarly be held to that contract unless he or she was a victim of fraud. 63 F.2d at 891. In *Pimpinello v. Swift & Co.,* another case cited by the majority, the court found that if a signer is "illiterate, or blind, or ignorant of the alien language of the writing" and the contents of a contract "are *misread or misinterpreted* to him" or her, the writing would be considered void unless the signer had acted negligently. 253 N.Y. 159, 163, 170 N.E. 530 (1930) (emphasis added). The court did not suggest that the contents would need to be *intentionally* "misread or misinterpreted" in order to void the writing. . . .

"Here, although Morales does not allege that Sun acted fraudulently, he does allege that Hodge, who was translating the document at Sun's direction, failed to inform Morales that the Agreement contained an arbitration clause. Importantly, Sun does not dispute the following factual findings made by the District Court: (1) Morales was unable to read the contract; (2) Sun assigned Hodge, a coworker who himself was not fluent in English, to translate the document for Morales; (3) Hodge, in translating the document, neglected to translate the arbitration clauses; and (4) as a result of Hodge's incomplete translation, Morales was not aware that the Agreement contained an arbitration clause. (App.3–5.) I also note, as does the majority, that the record demonstrates that Sun was under pressure to hire Morales in an expedient manner, and urged him to accept Hodge's translation and to sign the Agreement immediately. Maj. Op. at 220–221. . . .

"If the facts of this case were different, I might adopt the majority's position. For example, if Sun had simply handed the Agreement to Morales and indicated that it was Morales' responsibility to find a translator, and Morales had employed a incompetent translator who failed to translate the arbitration clause, I would agree that Morales was bound by the Agreement. However, when Sun made the decision to insert itself between Morales and the contract, it created a situation where lack of mutual assent could, and did, occur. Because I do not believe it was negligent or otherwise improper for Morales to rely upon the translation provided by Sun, and because Morales was not informed in the course of that translation that the Agreement contained an arbitration clause, I agree with the District Court that Morales did not "manifest an intention" to be bound by the arbitration clause."

NOTE ON OBJECTIVE AND SUBJECTIVE ELEMENTS IN INTERPRETATION

Recall that one difference between classical contract law and modern contract law is that classical contract law tended to be objective and standardized, while modern contract law tends to include subjective and individualized elements as well. This difference is particularly striking in the area of interpretation. Classical contract law adopted a theory of interpretation that was purely, or almost purely, objective. As stated in Woburn National Bank v. Woods, 77 N.H. 172, 89 A. 491 (1914):

> A contract involves what is called a meeting of the minds of the parties. But this does not mean that they must have arrived at a common mental state touching the matter in hand. The standard by which their conduct is judged and their rights are limited is not internal but external. In the absence of fraud or incapacity, the question is: What did the party say and do? "The making of a contract does not depend upon the state of the parties' minds; it depends upon their overt acts."

The strict objectivism of classical contract law is also reflected in well-known passages by Williston and Learned Hand. According to Williston:

> It is even conceivable that a contract shall be formed which is in accordance with the intention of neither party. If a written contract is entered into, the meaning and effect of the contract depends on the construction given the written language by the court, and the court will give that language its natural and appropriate meaning; and, if it is unambiguous, will not even admit evidence of what the parties may have thought the meaning to be.

1 Samuel Williston, The Law of Contracts § 95, at 181–82 (1st ed. 1920.) And according to Learned Hand:

> A contract has, strictly speaking, nothing to do with the personal, or individual, intent of the parties. A contract is an obligation attached by the mere force of law to certain acts of the parties, usually words, which ordinarily accompany and represent a known intent. If, however, it were proved by twenty bishops that either party, when he used the words, intended something else than the usual meaning which the law imposes upon them, he would still be held, unless there were some mutual mistake, or something else of the sort. Of course, if it appear by other words, or acts, of the parties, that they attribute a peculiar meaning to such words as they use in the contract, that meaning will prevail, but only by virtue of the other words, and not because of their unexpressed intent.

> . . . [W]hatever was the understanding in fact of the banks [in this case] . . . of the legal effect of this practice between them, it is of not the slightest consequence, unless it took form in some acts or words, which, being reasonably interpreted, would have such meaning to ordinary men. . . . Yet the question always remains for the court to interpret the reasonable meaning to the acts of the parties, by word or deed, and no characterization of its effect by either party thereafter, however truthful, is material. . . .

Hotchkiss v. National City Bank, 200 F. 287, 293–94 (S.D.N.Y.1911), aff'd 201 F. 664 (2d Cir.1912), aff'd 231 U.S. 50, 34 S.Ct. 20, 58 L.Ed. 115 (1913).

However, contract law is a functional instrument, whose purpose is to effectuate the objectives of parties to a promissory transaction, provided appropriate conditions (such as consideration) are satisfied, and subject to appropriate constraints (such as unconscionability). Accordingly, the principles of interpretation should be responsive not only to objective elements but, where appropriate, to the parties' subjective intentions. Under modern contract law, that is just the case, as illustrated by four central modern principles of interpretation:

> *Principle I: If the parties subjectively attach different meanings to an expression, neither party knows that the other attaches a different meaning, and the two meanings are not equally reasonable, the more reasonable meaning prevails.*

Principle I is adopted in Restatement Second § 201(2)(b):

> Where the parties have attached different meanings to a promise or agreement or a term thereof, it is interpreted in accordance with the meaning attached by one of them if at the time the agreement was made. . . .

> (b)   that party had no reason to know of any different meaning attached by the other, and the other had reason to know the meaning attached by the first party.

Principle I is based in significant part on the concept of liability for fault. A is at fault—is negligent—if he uses an expression that he should realize would lead a reasonable person in B's position to understand that A attaches a given meaning, Beta, to the expression, when in fact A attaches meaning Alpha to the expression. If B attaches meaning Beta to the expression, and thereby suffers wasted reliance or the defeat of a legitimate expectation when A insists on meaning Alpha, A should compensate B.

Although *Principle I* is primarily objective, it has a subjective element as well. The more reasonable meaning will prevail only if one of the parties has actually (subjectively) attached that meaning to the expression.

> *Principle II: If the parties subjectively attach different meanings to an expression, neither party knows that the other attaches a different meaning, and the two meanings are equally reasonable, neither meaning prevails.*

Principle II is adopted in the Restatement Second § 20(1):

> There is no manifestation of mutual assent to an exchange if the parties attach materially different meanings to their manifestations and
>
> > (a) neither party knows or has reason to know the meaning attached by the other; or
> >
> > (b) each party knows or each party has reason to know the meaning attached by the other.

Principle II is consistent with *Principle I.* If parties to a promissory transaction subjectively attach different meanings to their expressions, and in attaching these different meanings both parties are either equally fault-free or equally at fault, there is no reason why one meaning rather than the other should prevail. *Principle II* is associated with Raffles v. Wichelhaus, the *Peerless* case. To preserve the classical-school program, Holmes argued that the result in *Peerless* could be explained by objective theory. "The true ground of the decision was not that each party meant a different thing from the other ... but that each said a different thing. The plaintiff offered one thing, the defendant expressed his assent to another." Holmes, The Common Law 309 (1881). But if both parties subjectively meant the December Peerless, Buyer should have been deemed in breach; and if both parties subjectively meant the October Peerless, Seller should have been deemed in breach. Holmes had it backwards: the result in *Peerless* is correct because the parties meant different things, not because the parties said different things.

> *Principle III: If the parties subjectively attach the same meaning to an expression, that meaning prevails even though it is unreasonable.*

Principle III squarely reverses the strict objectivism of classical contract law, under which the subjective intention of the parties was irrelevant even if mutually held. Again, the objectivists had it wrong. Where both parties attach the same unreasonable meaning to an expression, both parties may have been at fault in their use of language, but the fault caused no injury. Indeed, a party who in litigation presses a meaning that he did not attach to his expression at the time of contract-formation is himself at fault.

Principle III is adopted in Restatement Second § 201(1). That section provides that "[w]here the parties have attached the same meaning to a promise or agreement or a term thereof, it is interpreted in accordance with that meaning." Under section 201(1), reasonableness becomes relevant only where there is not a mutually held subjective meaning. Thus, Restatement Second stands the classical school's position on its head, by giving primacy to mutually held subjective interpretation, and resorting to an objective or reasonable meaning only in the absence of a mutually held subjective meaning.

> *Principle IV: If the parties, A and B, attach different meanings, Alpha and Beta, to an expression, and A knows that B attaches meaning Beta, but B does not know that A attaches meaning Alpha, the meaning Beta prevails even if it is less reasonable than the meaning Alpha.*

Principle IV is adopted in Restatement Second § 201(2):

> Where the parties have attached different meanings to a promise or agreement or a term thereof, it is interpreted in accordance with the meaning attached by one of them if at the time the agreement was made
>
> (a) that party did not know of any different meaning attached by the other, and the other knew the meaning attached by the first party. . . .

Principle IV, which is largely subjective, is supported by a fault analysis. B may have been at fault in attaching meaning Beta to the expression, but A was more at fault in allowing B to proceed on the basis of an interpretation that A knew B held, at least when B did not know that A held a different interpretation.

––––––––

SECTION 2. PROBLEMS OF INTERPRETING PURPOSIVE LANGUAGE

WILLIAMS, LANGUAGE AND THE LAW—PART IV
61 L.Q.Rev. 384, 400–404 (1945).

[A distinction must] be made between (a) the literal or primary meaning of the words, and (b) the ulterior meaning i.e., the meaning, other than the literal meaning, intended to be conveyed by the speaker when he uttered the words, or the meaning, other than the literal meaning, attributed by a hearer to the speaker. . . .

. . . For example a tactless host looks out of the window and says to his guest: "It has stopped raining." The guest mistakenly takes this to be an oblique hint that he is desired to leave. Here it may be said that while the meaning of the words to the host is "It has stopped raining" . . . the meaning to the guest is both this . . . and also "Please go". . . .

It has already been remarked that the Courts will generally enforce consequences logically implied in the language of contracts, wills, statutes, and other legal documents and transactions. The point now to be noticed is that the legal doctrine of implied terms goes much farther than this. Judges are accustomed to read into documents and transactions many terms that are not logically implied in them. As an academic matter non-logical implication may be classified into three kinds: (i) of terms that the parties (the plural shall throughout include the singular) probably had in mind but did not trouble to express; (ii) of terms that the parties, whether or not they actually had them in mind, would probably have expressed if the question had been brought to their attention; and (iii) of terms that the parties, whether or not they had them in mind or would have expressed them if they had foreseen the difficulty, are implied by the Court because of the Court's view of fairness or policy or in consequence of rules of law. Of these three kinds of non-logical implication (i) is an effort to arrive at actual intention; (ii) is an effort to arrive at hypothetical or conditional intention— the intention that the parties would have had if they had foreseen the difficulty; (iii) is not concerned with the intention of the parties except to the extent that the term implied by the Court may be excluded by an expression of positive intention to the contrary.

. . . [O]nly in case (i) does the implication amount to a declaration by the Court of ulterior meaning in the sense already defined; in the other two cases the so-called implication is in reality an addition by the Court to the meaning of the parties. . . .

We pass to a consideration of . . . types (ii) and (iii). It is common form among judges to deny that they ever read into a contract or other document anything other than what, in their view, the parties actually intended; and occasionally they have even gone so far as to say that the implication must be collected from the words of the document itself. These statements cannot be taken seriously. It is true that the declaration of presumed actual intention is the commonest form of implication; but it is not the only form. Courts frequently import into a document terms that are not logically implied in it, and that the parties probably did not think about: or, to say the least, such terms are imported whether or not in the particular case it is probable that the parties thought about them. . . .

The view may perhaps be held that this particular process is not very happily called "implication." It is not so much the interpretation of a pre-existing and expressed intent as legislation amending or supplementing the expressed intent. Terms so read into the contract might better be called "constructive" than "implied." However, this is simply a question of nomenclature; and in any case no fixed nomenclature can be maintained in practice, because terms of classes (i) (ii) and (iii) merge into each other. . . .

This brings me to my last point, which is that it is a matter of taste whether implied terms of classes (ii) and (iii) be styled implied terms or rules of law. They are in fact merely rules of law that apply in the absence of an expression of contrary intent: whether we choose to call them implied terms or not is simply a matter of terminology. . . .

———

RESTATEMENT, SECOND, CONTRACTS § 204

[See Selected Source Materials Supplement]

———

UNIDROIT PRINCIPLES OF INTERNATIONAL COMMERCIAL CONTRACTS ART. 4.8

[See Selected Source Materials Supplement]

———

SPAULDING V. MORSE

Supreme Judicial Court of Massachusetts, 1947.
322 Mass. 149, 76 N.E.2d 137.

DOLAN, JUSTICE. [George and Ruth Morse were married in 1921. In 1932, Ruth obtained a decree of divorce which made provision for the custody and support of the Morse's two children, Richard and Merilyn. Subsequently, disputes arose between the Morses. As a result, in 1937 they entered into an agreement "intended to supersede in so far as the provisions herein contained are concerned" the provisions made in the decree for the benefit of Ruth, Richard, and Merilyn. The agreement provided that George would make a lump sum payment to Ruth, in installments, as alimony, that Ruth would have custody of Richard, and that George would have custody of Merilyn. In addition, a trustee was appointed for Richard, and it was agreed that George "shall and will pay to the said trustee in trust for his said minor son Richard the sum of twelve hundred dollars ($1,200) per year . . . until the entrance of Richard D. Morse into some college, university or higher institution of learning beyond the completion of the high school grades, and thereupon, instead of said payments, amounting to twelve hundred dollars ($1,200) yearly, he shall and will then pay to the trustee payments in the sum of twenty-two hundred dollars ($2,200) per year for a period of said higher education but not more than four years. . . . "

[Richard completed high school in February 1946, and was immediately inducted into the Army. The trustee brought this action to require George to continue paying $100 a month for Richard while he was in the Army. The trial court held for the trustee, and ordered George to pay $1,500 (the amount which had accrued since Richard's induction) and to continue paying $100 per month to the trustee "until such time, if any, as [Richard] enters college, and, thereupon, and for a period not to exceed four (4) years thereafter, to pay the sum of twenty-two hundred dollars ($2,200) per year to the . . . [plaintiff] payable in monthly payments." George appealed.]

"Every instrument in writing is to be interpreted, with a view to the material circumstances of the parties at the time of the execution, in the light of the pertinent facts within their knowledge and in such manner as to give effect to the main end designed to be accomplished. . . . [The] instrument is to be so construed as to give effect to the intent of the . . . [parties] as manifested by the words used illumined by all the attendant factors, unless inconsistent with some positive rule of law or repugnant to other terms of the instrument. An omission to express an intention cannot be supplied by conjecture. But, if the instrument as a whole produces a conviction that a particular result was fixedly desired although not expressed by formal words, that defect may be supplied by implication and the underlying intention . . . may be effectuated, provided it is sufficiently declared by the entire instrument." Dittemore v. Dickey, 249 Mass. 95, 104, 105, 144 N.E. 57, 60. . . .

Examining the instrument before us, guided by the settled rule of interpretation set forth above, it is manifest that the main purpose of the parents of Richard was to arrive at an agreement for his maintenance and education and to provide security therefor. At the time of the execution of the agreement he was almost ten years of age. His custody had already been awarded to his mother by the decree of divorce of the Nevada court, concerning the validity of which no question is raised. This being so, it is a fair inference that in so far as Richard was concerned his maintenance and education were the main purposes sought to be accomplished by the trust agreement, the parties to the agreement having in mind his age and recognizing the necessity of his being supported during the years to come, and of his being properly educated in a manner appropriate to the defendant's financial ability and station in life. The instrument specifically provided that the payments to be made by the defendant to the trustee for Richard's benefit should "be applied by . . . [his mother] or the trustee upon or toward the maintenance and education and benefit of said Richard, so long as she shall maintain and educate said Richard to the satisfaction of the said trustee." But, as appears by the agreed facts and the record, the education of Richard was interrupted by the second World War and his induction into the armed forces of the United States on February 6, 1946, the day following the completion of his high school grades on February 5, 1946. Since then he had been continuously, and at the time of the hearing and order for decree in the court below was, in the service of the armed forces of the nation. Thus he was actually under the command of his superior officers in that service, his maintenance was provided for during the period here involved by the government, and he was not in the actual custody of his mother and was not a student in any higher institution of learning. Thus neither of the main objects for which the defendant had bound himself to provide existed within the meaning of the trust instrument during the period for which the plaintiff claims payment. In these circumstances we are of opinion that the proper construction of the trust instrument is that the defendant is not required under its terms to perform provisions for the maintenance and education of Richard while he was or is in the armed service of the United States. . . .

It follows from what we have said that the decree entered by the judge must be reversed and that instead a final decree must be entered after rescript dismissing the bill with costs of the appeal.

So ordered.

BEANSTALK GROUP, INC. v. AM GENERAL CORPORATION

United States Court of Appeals, Seventh Circuit, 2002.
283 F.3d 856.

POSNER, J. Beanstalk, which serves owners of intellectual property by negotiating licenses of their property, brought this diversity suit for breach of its contract with AM General; the substantive issues are governed by the law of Indiana. The contract, called a "representation agreement," appointed Beanstalk an agent of AM General to obtain licenses to use the latter's "HUMMER" trademark. When the contract was made in 1997, AM General was the manufacturer of the Humvee, a military vehicle that is the successor to the jeep and like the jeep is also sold in a version intended for the civilian market, under the name "Hummer." Beanstalk named General Motors as an additional defendant for reasons that will appear in a moment. The district judge granted the defendants' motion to dismiss the complaint (to which Beanstalk had attached the representation agreement) for failure to state a claim. Fed.R.Civ.P. 12(b)(6). Since the representation agreement was part of a pleading rather than submitted separately, the judge could consider it without converting the defendants' motion to one for summary judgment. Fed.R.Civ.P. 12(c); *Berthold Types Ltd. v. Adobe Systems Inc.*, 242 F.3d 772, 775 (7th Cir.2001).

The agreement made Beanstalk AM General's "sole and exclusive nonemployee representative" for the purpose of licensing the Hummer trademark and entitled Beanstalk to 35 percent of the "gross receipts . . . received on Owner's [AM General's] behalf . . . under any License Agreements" made while the representation agreement was in force. Each license agreement "shall provide for all payments thereunder to be made to Beanstalk on Owner's behalf," and Beanstalk is required to account quarterly to AM General for "all gross receipts actually received during the preceding calendar quarter under any License Agreements." AM General is given "the absolute right to veto, without cause and at its sole discretion," any proposed license, including renewals. "License agreement" is defined as "any agreement or arrangement, whether in the form of a license or otherwise, granting merchandising or other rights in the Property," which in turn is defined to mean trademarks and related rights. The contract, which is assignable (though by Beanstalk only with AM's consent) and contains an integration clause, was to continue until the end of 2000.

The agreement was drafted by Beanstalk, but this fact has little interpretive significance since AM General is a commercially sophisticated party represented by counsel. Most courts now agree with this exception to the principle that contracts are to be construed against the party that drafted it. . . There are holdouts, illustrated by *Eastern Bus Lines, Inc. v. Board of Education,* 7 Conn.App. 581, 509 A.2d 1071, 1073–74 (1986), where the court, quoting an earlier opinion, said that "the party who actually does the writing of an instrument will presumably be guided by his own interests and goals in the transaction. He may choose shadings of expression, words more specific or more imprecise, according to the dictates of these interests." No doubt; but the other party, if commercially sophisticated and represented by counsel, will insist on clarification. Indiana has yet to take a stand on the exception . . . No matter . . . We add that the rule is in practice a makeweight rather than a tie breaker.

Beanstalk set about obtaining agreements for the licensing of the Hummer trademark. In 1999, however, two years into the representation agreement with Beanstalk, AM General entered into a joint-venture agreement with General Motors under which GM would design and engineer a new version of the Hummer, would make an interest-free loan of $235 million to AM General for the construction of a factory to manufacture the new version, would promise to buy a minimum number of the new vehicles, would obtain an option to buy up to 40 percent of AM General's common stock—and would acquire the Hummer trademark. GM informed Beanstalk that it had not assumed any of AM General's obligations under the representation agreement and that it would not compensate Beanstalk for any license agreements made or renewed after the effective date of the joint-venture agreement.

Beanstalk argues that the agreement between AM General and GM, although of course not labeled a license agreement, was one because it transferred the Hummer trademark to GM and thus was an "agreement or arrangement, whether in the form of a license or otherwise, granting merchandising or other rights in the Property"; for the transfer gave GM the right, indeed the exclusive right, to merchandise the Hummer trademark, that is, the "Property." The contract thus is clear, Beanstalk argues—the joint venture was an "agreement" that "grant[ed]" GM "merchandising . . . rights" in the Hummer trademark and it did not have to be "in the form of a license" because the representation agreement says "in the form of a license *or otherwise* "-and under accepted principles of contract law we should look no further. Beanstalk wants 35 percent of so much of the consideration running from GM to AM General as represents the value of the Hummer trademark. We do not know what the consideration was, or what that value is, because no evidence has been taken—in fact, the joint-venture agreement is not even in the record, though the sketch we have just given of its terms is not contested.

Beanstalk is correct that written contracts are usually enforced in accordance with the ordinary meaning of the language used in them and without recourse to evidence, beyond the contract itself, as to what the parties meant. This presumption simplifies the litigation of contract disputes and, more important, protects contracting parties against being blindsided by evidence intended to contradict the deal that they thought they had graven in stone by using clear language. It is a strong presumption, motivated by an understandable distrust in the accuracy of litigation to reconstruct contracting parties' intentions, but it is rebuttable—here by two principles of contract interpretation that are closely related in the setting of this suit. The first is that a contract will not be interpreted literally if doing so would produce absurd results, in the sense of results that the parties, presumed to be rational persons pursuing rational ends, are very unlikely to have agreed to seek. . .

This is an interpretive principle, not a species of paternalism. "The letters between plaintiff and defendant were from one merchant to another. They are to be read as businessmen would read them, and only as a last resort are to be thrown out altogether as meaningless futilities. . . If literalness is sheer absurdity, we are to seek some other meaning whereby reason will be instilled and absurdity avoided." *Outlet Embroidery Co. v. Derwent Mills,* 254 N.Y. 179, 172 N.E. 462, 463 (1930) (Cardozo, C.J.). "There is a long tradition in contract law of reading contracts sensibly; contracts—certainly business contracts of the kind involved here—are not parlor games but the means of getting the world's work done. . . True, parties *can* contract for preposterous terms. If contract language is crystal clear or there is independent extrinsic evidence that something silly was actually intended, a party may be held to its bargain, absent some specialized defense." *Rhode Island Charities Trust v. Engelhard Corp.*, 267 F.3d 3, 7 (1st Cir.2001); see also *Dispatch Automation, Inc. v. Richards,* 280 F.3d 1116, 1118–19 (7th Cir.2002). The second principle is that a contract must be interpreted as a whole. . . Sentences are not isolated units of meaning, but take meaning from other sentences in the same document.

The second principle thus is linguistic; the first reflects the fact that interpretation is a cultural as well as a linguistic undertaking. To interpret a contract or other document, it is not enough to have a command of the grammar, syntax, and vocabulary of the language in which the document is written. One must know something about the practical as well as the purely verbal context of the language to be interpreted. In the case of a commercial contract, one must have a general acquaintance with commercial practices. This doesn't mean that judges should have an M.B.A. or have practiced corporate or commercial law, but merely that they be alert citizens of a market-oriented society so that they can recognize absurdity in a business context. A blinkered literalism, a closing of one's eyes to the obvious, can produce nonsensical results, as this case illustrates. Beanstalk is in the business of merchandising trademarks. If, while the representation agreement was in effect, a toy company wanted to make a toy Hummer, Beanstalk was authorized to grant the toy company a license in exchange for a fee that it would split 35/65 with AM General. The joint-venture agreement was not that kind of arrangement. It was not an arrangement for the promotion of AM General's trademark. By the agreement creating the joint venture, AM General essentially transferred the Hummer business to General Motors, retaining a role limited to manufacturing, in a factory built with GM's money, a vehicle designed by, engineered by, and to be marketed by (that is the significance of the transfer of the trademark) GM. Quite apart from the option that GM also received to buy a large, doubtless controlling interest in AM General, it's as if AM General had sold its entire business, including its manufacturing assets and all its trademarks, to GM.

Beanstalk is not a business broker. It had nothing to do with the joint venture and indeed didn't even know about it until after it took place. The parties could hardly have intended that Beanstalk should get a commission if AM General decided, as in effect it did, to get out of the Hummer business. A business would not contract to pay an agent for work that the agent did not do but that the business did itself. Beanstalk and AM General must have known when they signed the representation agreement that if AM General ever sold its Hummer business, the trademark would go with it, as the purchaser would need it in order to identify the product, while AM General would no longer have any need or use for it. Indeed, AM General would have nothing to attach the trademark to—and a trademark is an identifier, not a freestanding piece of intellectual property; hence the rule that a trademark cannot be sold in gross, that is, without the assets that create the product that it identifies. 15 U.S.C. § 1060; *United Drug Co. v. Theodore Rectanus Co.,* 248 U.S. 90, 97, 39 S.Ct. 48, 63 L.Ed. 141 (1918); *In re Cult Awareness Network, Inc.,* 151 F.3d 605, 608 n. 1 (7th Cir.1998); *Green River Bottling Co. v. Green River Corp.,* 997 F.2d 359, 362 (7th Cir.1993); *Sands, Taylor & Wood Co. v. Quaker Oats Co.,* 978 F.2d 947, 956 (7th Cir.1992); *Beauty Time, Inc. v. VU Skin Systems, Inc.,* 118 F.3d 140, 150 (3d Cir.1997). The parties would hardly have intended Beanstalk to obtain a commission on the sale of the business merely because the sale would *inevitably* include the trademark. And they would not have wanted to burden the sale with the added cost of allocating the purchase price between the trademark and the other assets involved in the sale, as Beanstalk claims they must do in order to compute the commission to which it is entitled on the joint venture. (Such allocations may be required for tax purposes. See *Thrifticheck Service Corp. v. Commissioner,* 287 F.2d 1, 2, 3–4 (2d Cir.1961) (Friendly, J.). We are not told whether that was the case with the AM General-GM joint venture.)

The unreasonableness of Beanstalk's position can be seen most clearly by imagining that the joint venture had taken place the day after the representation agreement between Beanstalk and AM General went into effect. Then on Beanstalk's interpretation it would be entitled to 35 percent of the entire value of the Hummer trademark even though it had made absolutely no contribution to that value. That makes no sense; it is apparent that the definition of "License Agreement" in the representation agreement covers any agreement that has the function or character of a trademark licensing agreement even if the word "license" or a cognate term does not appear; the sale of a business is an agreement of an entirely different character. "[The] issue of whether a transfer of the use of a trademark is a sale or a license for tax purposes is a thorny one, and has not always been consistently solved in the courts. The basic problem is to determine the extent to which the transferor retains proprietary rights in the transferred asset. If the transferor retains sufficient proprietary rights, the transfer must be considered a license rather than a sale . . . We do not suggest that [the] nomenclature [used in the contract] should be finally determinative of the distinction between a license and a sale." *Consolidated Foods Corp. v. United States,* 569 F.2d 436, 437, 442 (7th Cir.1978). Indeed not.

Beanstalk ignores relevant provisions of the contract, one of which engages Beanstalk to be AM General's "sole and exclusive *non-employee* representative," implying that AM General's employees can negotiate license agreements without going through Beanstalk. Beanstalk agrees with this interpretation, as it must (there is no possible ambiguity), but claims that even when an employee of AM General negotiates such an agreement with no involvement by Beanstalk, Beanstalk is entitled to 35 percent of the revenues that AM General obtains under the agreement. No reason is given why AM General would compensate Beanstalk for services rendered wholly by AM General's own employees, whom it must compensate. That would be paying double for the same service.

Further ignored are the provisions keying Beanstalk's commissions to gross receipts "received"—obviously by Beanstalk—"on Owner's [that is, AM General's] behalf" and requiring Beanstalk to account to AM General periodically for the gross receipts of the license agreements. This implies that Beanstalk would receive receipts only for license agreements that it negotiated. The implication is reinforced by the fact that the representation agreement contains no provision for compensating Beanstalk out of receipts received directly by AM General, for example under a license agreement negotiated by an employee of AM General.

Beanstalk goes so far as to argue that, whoever negotiates the license agreement, the receipts generated by it must be paid in the first instance to Beanstalk to enable it to take its 35 percent cut off the top. Beanstalk thus is arguing that not 35 percent but 100 percent of the consideration that GM paid AM General for the joint-venture agreement that represented the value of the Hummer trademark had to be paid to Beanstalk. Beanstalk's argument amounts to saying that if Chrysler hired it to license the Chrysler trademarks and then sold its entire automobile business to Daimler for $10 billion, Beanstalk would be entitled to an immediate cash receipt of $10 billion, from which it would deduct 35 percent of the value of the Chrysler trademarks and then remit the balance to Chrysler. Absurd.

Against all this it might be argued that to disregard a contractual term, whether on the basis that interpreting it literally would yield absurd results or that other terms in the contract alter the disputed term's apparent meaning, requires evidence and thus cannot be done on a motion to dismiss. Not so. For when we said earlier that the interpretation of a contract is a cultural as well as a linguistic undertaking, we did not add that the materials of interpretation are limited to literal meanings on the one hand and trial-type evidence on the other. The cultural background that a judge brings to the decision of a contract case includes as we said a general knowledge of how the world operates, including the commercial world, and this knowledge, precisely because it is general rather than being knowledge of the specific facts of the case ("adjudicative facts"), can show that the literal interpretation of a particular contractual term would be unsound, in which event no evidence need be taken. *Unelko Corp. v. Prestone Products Corp.,* 116 F.3d 237, 240 (7th Cir.1997).

It would be different if Beanstalk, instead of standing on the literal terms of the representation agreement—on quicksand, in other words— wanted to present evidence to show that the agreement means what it says it means. The only evidence it wants to present is that before selling the

Hummer business to GM, AM General approached Beanstalk and asked for an express exclusion from the representation agreement of any agreement "for the purpose of producing motor vehicles" even if such an agreement included a transfer of trademark rights. But of course. It was simple prudence for AM General to try to head off this lawsuit. It doesn't follow that the lawsuit has any merit. Indeed, to penalize AM General for attempting an amicable resolution of a potential dispute in advance would violate the spirit of the rule that makes settlement offers inadmissible in an adjudication on the merits. See Fed.R.Evid. 408.

With our conclusion that there was no breach of contract, Beanstalk's other claims collapse . . .

As for GM's having told Beanstalk that it will not pay any commissions on license agreements that are renewed, GM was entitled as the owner of the "Property" to veto any license agreements, including renewals, that Beanstalk might propose. Even if GM remains bound by the representation agreement, which it does not, because the agreement did not require AM General to assign its duties under it to an assignee of the "Property" covered by the agreement, the veto power granted the represented party excuses GM from any duty to renew any license agreements negotiated by Beanstalk.

[The dissenting opinion of Rovner, J., is omitted]

———

CHAPTER 9

THE MECHANICS OF A BARGAIN (I)— OFFER AND REVOCATION

■ ■ ■

Most bargains are formed by the process of offer and acceptance. Because a bargain is enforceable by expectation damages at the moment it is formed, without regard to whether it has been relied upon, the rules that govern the offer-and-acceptance process often play a central role in contract disputes. These issues are the subject of Chapters 9 and 10.

Chapter 9 focuses on offers. It consists of three Sections:

Section 1 concerns the issue, what constitutes an offer. If it is determined that a party has made an offer, the legal consequence is to create in the offeree a power of acceptance—that is, a power to conclude a bargain, and therefore a legally enforceable contract, by accepting the offer. Section 2 concerns three kinds of events that can terminate a power of acceptance: lapse of the offer; rejection of the offer; and the making of a counter-offer (or some legal equivalent) by the offeree. Finally, Section 3 concerns the power of an offeror to terminate the offeree's power of acceptance by revoking the offer.

SECTION 1. WHAT CONSTITUTES AN OFFER

RESTATEMENT, SECOND, CONTRACTS § 24

[See Selected Source Materials Supplement]

CISG ART. 14(1)

[See Selected Source Materials Supplement]

UNIDROIT PRINCIPLES OF INTERNATIONAL COMMERCIAL CONTRACTS ART. 2.1.2

[See Selected Source Materials Supplement]

PRINCIPLES OF EUROPEAN CONTRACT LAW § 2.201(1)

[See Selected Source Materials Supplement]

LONERGAN V. SCOLNICK

California Court of Appeal, Fourth District, 1954.
129 Cal.App.2d 179, 276 P.2d 8.

BARNARD, PRESIDING JUSTICE. This is an action for specific performance or for damages in the event specific performance was impossible.

The complaint alleged that on April 15, 1952, the parties entered into a contract whereby the defendant agreed to sell, and plaintiff agreed to buy a 40-acre tract of land for $2,500; that this was a fair, just and reasonable value of the property; that on April 28, 1952, the defendant repudiated the contract and refused to deliver a deed; that on April 28, 1952, the property was worth $6,081; and that plaintiff has been damaged in the amount of $3,581. The answer denied that any contract had been entered into, or that anything was due to the plaintiff.

By stipulation the issue of whether or not a contract was entered into between the parties was first tried, reserving the other issues for a further trial if that became necessary. The issue as to the existence of a contract was submitted upon an agreed statement, including certain letters between the parties, without the introduction of other evidence.

The stipulated facts are as follows: During March, 1952, the defendant placed an ad in a Los Angeles paper reading, so far as material here, "Joshua Tree vic. 40 acres, . . . need cash, will sacrifice." In response to an inquiry resulting from this ad the defendant, who lived in New York, wrote a letter to the plaintiff dated March 26, briefly describing the property, giving directions as to how to get there, stating that his rock-bottom price was $2,500 cash, and further stating that "This is a form letter." On April 7, the plaintiff wrote a letter to the defendant saying that he was not sure he had found the property, asking for its legal description, asking whether the land was all level or whether it included certain jutting rock hills, and suggesting a certain bank as escrow agent "should I desire to purchase the land." On April 8, the defendant wrote to the plaintiff saying "From your description you have found the property"; that this bank "is O.K. for escrow agent"; that the land was fairly level; giving the legal description; and then saying, "If you are really interested, you will have to decide fast, as I expect to have a buyer in the next week or so." On April 12, the defendant sold the property to a third party for $2,500. The plaintiff received defendant's letter of April 8 on April 14. On April 15 he wrote to the defendant thanking him for his letter "confirming that I was on the right land", stating that he would immediately proceed to have the escrow opened and would deposit $2,500 therein "in conformity with your offer", and asking the defendant to forward a deed with his instructions to the escrow agent. On April 17, 1952, the plaintiff started an escrow and placed in the hands of the escrow agent $100, agreeing to furnish an additional $2,400 at an unspecified time, with the provision that if the escrow was not closed by May 15, 1952, it should be completed as soon thereafter as possible unless a written demand for a return of the money or instruments was made by either party after that date. It was further stipulated that the plaintiff was ready and willing at all times to deposit the $2,400.

The matter was submitted on June 11, 1953. On July 10, 1953, the judge filed a memorandum opinion stating that it was his opinion that the letter of April 8, 1952, when considered with the previous correspondence, constituted an offer of sale which offer was, however, qualified and conditioned upon prompt acceptance by the plaintiff; that in spite of the condition thus imposed, the plaintiff delayed more than a week before notifying the defendant of his acceptance; and that since the plaintiff was aware of the necessity of promptly communicating his acceptance to the defendant his delay was not the prompt action required by the terms of the offer. Findings of fact were filed on October 2, 1953, finding that each and all of the statements in the agreed statement are true, and that all allegations to the contrary in the complaint are untrue. As conclusions of law, it was found that the plaintiff and defendant did not enter into a contract as alleged in the complaint or otherwise, and that the defendant is entitled to judgment against the plaintiff. Judgment was entered accordingly, from which the plaintiff has appealed.

The appellant contends that the judgment is contrary to the evidence and to the law since the facts, as found, do not support the conclusions of law upon which the judgment is based. It is argued that there is no conflict in the evidence, and this court is not bound by the trial court's construction of the written instruments involved; that the evidence conclusively shows that an offer was made to the plaintiff by the defendant, which offer was accepted by the mailing of plaintiff's letter of April 15; that upon receipt of defendant's letter of April 8 the plaintiff had a reasonable time within which to accept the offer that had been made; that by his letter of April 15 and his starting of an escrow the plaintiff accepted said offer; and that the agreed statement of facts establishes that a valid contract was entered into between the parties. In his briefs the appellant assumes that an offer was made by the defendant, and confined his argument to contending that the evidence shows that he accepted that offer within a reasonable time.

There can be no contract unless the minds of the parties have met and mutually agreed upon some specific thing. This is usually evidenced by one party making an offer which is accepted by the other party. Section 25 of the Restatement, Law on Contracts reads:

"If from a promise, or manifestation of intention, or from the circumstances existing at the time, the person to whom the promise or manifestation is addressed knows or has reason to know that the person making it does not intend it as an expression of his fixed purpose until he has given a further expression of assent, he has not made an offer."

The language used in Niles v. Hancock, 140 Cal. 157, 73 P. 840, 842, "It is also clear from the correspondence that it was the intention of the defendant that the negotiations between him and the plaintiff were to be purely preliminary," is applicable here. The correspondence here indicates an intention on the part of the defendant to find out whether the plaintiff was interested, rather than an intention to make a definite offer to the plaintiff. The language used by the defendant in his letters of March 26 and April 8 rather clearly discloses that they were not intended as an expression of fixed purpose to make a definite offer, and was sufficient to advise the plaintiff that some further expression of assent on the part of the defendant was necessary.

The advertisement in the paper was a mere request for an offer. The letter of March 26 contains no definite offer, and clearly states that it is a form letter. It merely gives further particulars, in clarification of the advertisement, and tells the plaintiff how to locate the property if he was interested in looking into the matter. The letter of April 8 added nothing in the way of a definite offer. It merely answered some questions asked by the plaintiff, and stated that if the plaintiff was really interested he would have to act fast. The statement that he expected to have a buyer in the next week or so indicated that the defendant intended to sell to the first-comer, and was reserving the right to do so. From this statement, alone, the plaintiff knew or should have known that he was not being given time in which to accept an offer that was being made but that some further assent on the part of the defendant was required. Under the language used the plaintiff was not being given a right to act within a reasonable time after receiving the letter; he was plainly told that the defendant intended to sell to another, if possible, and warned that he would have to act fast if he was interested in buying the land.

Regardless of any opinion previously expressed, the court found that no contract had been entered into between these parties, and we are in accord with the court's conclusion on that controlling issue. The court's construction of the letters involved was a reasonable one, and we think the most reasonable one, even if it be assumed that another construction was possible.

The judgment is affirmed.

GRIFFIN and MUSSELL, JJ., concur.

———

LEFKOWITZ V. GREAT MINNEAPOLIS SURPLUS STORE
Supreme Court of Minnesota, 1957.
251 Minn. 188, 86 N.W.2d 689.

MURPHY, JUSTICE. This is an appeal from an order of the Municipal Court of Minneapolis denying the motion of the defendant for amended findings of fact, or, in the alternative, for a new trial. The order for judgment awarded the plaintiff the sum of $138.50 as damages for breach of contract.

This case grows out of the alleged refusal of the defendant to sell to the plaintiff a certain fur piece which it had offered for sale in a newspaper advertisement. It appears from the record that on April 6, 1956, the defendant published the following advertisement in a Minneapolis newspaper:

> "Saturday 9 A.M. Sharp
> 3 Brand New
> Fur Coats
> Worth to $100
> First Come
> First Served
> $1 Each"

On April 13, the defendant again published an advertisement in the same newspaper as follows:

> "Saturday 9 A.M.
> 2 Brand New Pastel
> Mink 3-Skin Scarfs
> Selling for $89.50
> Out they go
> Saturday.
> Each. . . . $1.00
> 1 Black Lapin Stole
> Beautiful,
> worth $139.50. . . . $1.00

First Come

First Served"

The record supports the findings of the court that on each of the Saturdays following the publication of the above-described ads the plaintiff was the first to present himself at the appropriate counter in the defendant's store and on each occasion demanded the coat and the stole so advertised and indicated his readiness to pay the sale price of $1. On both occasions, the defendant refused to sell the merchandise to the plaintiff, stating on the first occasion that by a "house rule" the offer was intended for women only and sales would not be made to men, and on the second visit that plaintiff knew defendant's house rules.

The trial court properly disallowed plaintiff's claim for the value of the fur coats since the value of these articles was speculative and uncertain. The only evidence of value was the advertisement itself to the effect that the coats were "Worth to $100.00," how much less being speculative especially in view of the price for which they were offered for sale. With reference to the offer of the defendant on April 13, 1956, to sell the "1 Black Lapin Stole . . . worth $139.50 . . . " the trial court held that the value of this article was established and granted judgment in favor of the plaintiff for that amount less the $1 quoted purchase price.

1.   The defendant contends that a newspaper advertisement offering items of merchandise for sale at a named price is a "unilateral offer" which may be withdrawn without notice. He relies upon authorities which hold that, where an advertiser publishes in a newspaper that he has a certain quantity or quality of goods which he wants to dispose of at certain prices and on certain terms, such advertisements are not offers which become contracts as soon as any person to whose notice they may come signifies his acceptance by notifying the other that he will take a certain quantity of them. Such advertisements have been construed as an invitation for an offer of sale on the terms stated, which offer, when received, may be accepted or rejected and which therefore does not become a contract of sale until accepted by the seller; and until a contract has been so made, the seller may modify or revoke such prices or terms. . . .

The defendant relies principally on Craft v. Elder & Johnston Co. supra. In that case, the court discussed the legal effect of an advertisement offering for sale, as a one-day special, an electric sewing machine at a named price. The view was expressed that the advertisement was (38 N.E.2d 417, 34 Ohio L.A. 605) "not an offer made to any specific person but was made to the public generally. Thereby it would be properly designated as a unilateral offer and not being supported by any consideration could be withdrawn at will and without notice." It is true that such an offer may be withdrawn before acceptance. Since all offers are by their nature unilateral because they are necessarily made by one party or on one side in the negotiation of a contract, the distinction made in that decision between a unilateral offer and a unilateral contract is not clear. On the facts before us we are concerned with whether the advertisement constituted an offer, and, if so, whether the plaintiff's conduct constituted an acceptance.

There are numerous authorities which hold that a particular advertisement in a newspaper or circular letter relating to a sale of articles may be construed by the court as constituting an offer, acceptance of which would complete a contract. . . .

The test of whether a binding obligation may originate in advertisements addressed to the general public is "whether the facts show that some performance was promised in positive terms in return for something requested." 1 Williston, Contracts (Rev. ed.) § 27.

The authorities above cited emphasize that, where the offer is clear, definite, and explicit, and leaves nothing open for negotiation, it constitutes an offer, acceptance of which will complete the contract. The most recent case on the subject is Johnson v. Capital City Ford Co., La.App., 85 So.2d 75, in which the court pointed out that a newspaper advertisement relating to the purchase and sale of automobiles may constitute an offer, acceptance of which will consummate a contract and create an obligation in the offeror to perform according to the terms of the published offer.

Whether in any individual instance a newspaper advertisement is an offer rather than an invitation to make an offer depends on the legal intention of the parties and the surrounding circumstances. Annotation, 157 A.L.R. 744, 751; 77 C.J.S. Sales § 25b; 17 C.J.S. Contracts § 389. We are of the view on the facts before us that the offer by the defendant of the sale of the Lapin fur was clear, definite, and explicit, and left nothing open for negotiation. The plaintiff having successfully managed to be the first one to appear at the seller's place of business to be served, as requested by the advertisement, and having offered the stated purchase price of the article, he was entitled to performance on the part of the defendant. We think the trial court was correct in holding that there was in the conduct of the parties a sufficient mutuality of obligation to constitute a contract of sale.

2.   The defendant contends that the offer was modified by a "house rule" to the effect that only women were qualified to receive the bargains advertised. The advertisement contained no such restriction. This objection may be disposed of briefly by stating that, while an advertiser has the right at any time before acceptance to modify his offer, he does not have the right, after acceptance, to impose new or arbitrary conditions not contained in the published offer. . . .

Affirmed.

––––––

SATERIALE V. R.J. REYNOLDS TOBACCO COMPANY

United States Court of Appeals, Ninth Circuit, 2012.
697 F.3d 777.

FISHER, CIRCUIT JUDGE.

R.J. Reynolds Tobacco Company (RJR) operated a customer rewards program, called Camel Cash, from 1991 to 2007. Under the terms of the program, RJR urged consumers to purchase Camel cigarettes, to save Camel Cash certificates included in packages of Camel cigarettes, to enroll in the program and, ultimately, to redeem their certificates for merchandise featured in catalogs distributed by RJR. The plaintiffs allege that, in reliance on RJR's actions, they purchased Camel cigarettes, enrolled in the program and saved their certificates for future redemption. They allege that in 2006 RJR abruptly ceased accepting certificates for redemption, making the plaintiffs' unredeemed certificates worthless. The plaintiffs brought this action for breach of contract, promissory estoppel and violation of two California consumer protection laws. The district court dismissed the action for failure to state a claim. We affirm in part, reverse in part and remand. We hold that the plaintiffs have adequately alleged claims for breach of contract and promissory estoppel, but affirm dismissal of the plaintiffs' claims under the Unfair Competition Law and the Consumer Legal Remedies Act.

I. BACKGROUND

The plaintiffs appeal from a dismissal for failure to state a claim. *See* Fed.R.Civ.P. 12(b)(6). For purposes of a motion to dismiss, we accept all well-pleaded allegations of material fact as true and construe them in the light most favorable to the nonmoving party. *See Daniels-Hall v. Nat'l Educ. Ass'n,* 629 F.3d 992, 998 (9th Cir.2010). We thus recite the facts as they appear in the plaintiffs' third amended complaint. This factual background is based on the *allegations* of the plaintiffs' complaint. Whether the plaintiffs' allegations are true has not been decided.

RJR initiated the Camel Cash customer loyalty program in 1991. Compl. ¶ 24. RJR represented on Camel Cash certificates, packages of Camel cigarettes and in the media that customers who saved the certificates—called C-Notes—could exchange them for merchandise according to terms provided in a catalog. *Id.* The C-Notes stated:

> USE THIS NEW C-NOTE AND THE C-NOTES YOU'VE BEEN SAVING TO GET THE BEST GOODS CAMEL HAS TO OFFER. CALL 1-800-CAMEL CASH (1800-266-3522) for a free catalog. Offer restricted to smokers 21 years of age or older. Value 1/1000 of 1¢. Offer good only in the USA, and void where restricted or prohibited by law. Check catalog for expiration date. Limit 5 requests for a catalog per household.

Id. ¶ 26. According to the complaint, "Certain (but not all) of the Camel Cash catalogs state[d] that Reynolds could terminate the Camel Cash program without notice." *Id.* ¶ 32.

The plaintiffs are 10 individuals who joined the Camel Cash program by purchasing RJR's products and filling out and submitting signed registration forms to RJR. *Id.* ¶¶ 27, 48. RJR sent each plaintiff a unique enrollment number that was used in communications between the parties. *Id.* ¶ 27. These communications included catalogs RJR distributed to the plaintiffs containing merchandise that could be obtained by redeeming Camel Cash certificates. *Id.*

From time to time, RJR issued a new catalog with merchandise offered in exchange for Camel Cash, either upon request, or by mailing catalogs to consumers enrolled in the program. *Id.* ¶ 28. The number of Camel Cash certificates needed to obtain merchandise varied from as little as 100 to many thousands. *Id.* ¶ 29. This encouraged consumers to buy more packages of cigarettes together with Camel Cash and also to save or obtain Camel Cash certificates to redeem them for more valuable items. *Id.*

RJR honored the program from 1991 to 2006, and during that time Camel's share of the cigarette market nearly doubled, from approximately 4 percent to more than 7 percent. *Id.* ¶¶ 3, 34. In October 2006, however, RJR mailed a notice to program members announcing that the program would terminate as of March 31, 2007. *Id.* ¶ 32. The termination notice stated:

> As a loyal Camel smoker, we [sic] wanted to tell you our Camel Cash program is expiring. C-Notes will no longer be included on packs, which means whatever Camel Cash you have is among the last of its kind.
>
> Now this isn't happening overnight—there'll be plenty of time to redeem your C-Notes before the program ends. In fact, you'll have from OCTOBER '06 though MARCH '07 to go to camelsmokes.com to redeem your C-Notes. Supplies will be limited, so it won't hurt to get there before the rush.

Id. ¶ 33 & ex. A.

The announcement advised members that they could continue to redeem their C-Notes until March 2007. Beginning in October 2006, however, RJR allegedly stopped printing and issuing catalogs and told consumers that it did not have any merchandise available for redemption. *Id.* ¶¶ 34, 48. Several of the plaintiffs attempted, without success, to redeem C-Notes or obtain a catalog during the final six months of the program. *Id.* ¶ 49. The plaintiffs had saved hundreds or thousands of Camel Cash certificates that they were unable to redeem. *Id.* ¶ 11.

In November 2009, the plaintiffs filed a class action complaint against RJR. They allege breach of contract, promissory estoppel and violations of two California consumer protection laws, the Unfair Competition Law (UCL), Cal. Bus. & Prof.Code § 17200 *et seq.*, and the Consumer Legal Remedies Act (CLRA), Cal. Civ.Code § 1750 *et seq.* The district court dismissed the action under Rule 12(b)(6), and the plaintiffs timely appealed. . . .

III. BREACH OF CONTRACT

We begin by addressing whether the plaintiffs have stated a claim for breach of contract. The plaintiffs do not dispute that RJR had the right to terminate the Camel Cash program effective March 31, 2007, but allege that RJR breached a contract by refusing to redeem C-Notes during the six months preceding program termination. Compl. ¶¶ 6–7. RJR challenges the plaintiffs' contract claim on four grounds: the absence of an offer, indefiniteness, lack of mutuality of obligation (premised on RJR's right to terminate its contractual obligations) and untimeliness. We address RJR's contentions in turn.

A. Existence of an Offer

"An offer is the manifestation of willingness to enter into a bargain, so made as to justify another person in understanding that his assent to that bargain is invited and will conclude it." *Donovan v. RRL Corp.,* 26 Cal.4th 261, 109 Cal.Rptr.2d 807, 27 P.3d 702, 709 (2001) (quoting *City of Moorpark v. Moorpark Unified Sch. Dist.,* 54 Cal.3d 921, 1 Cal.Rptr.2d 896, 819 P.2d 854, 860 (1991)) (internal quotation marks omitted). "The determination of whether a particular communication constitutes an operative offer, rather than an inoperative step in the preliminary negotiation of a contract, depends upon all the surrounding circumstances." *Id.* "[T]he pertinent inquiry is whether the individual to whom the communication was made had reason to believe that it was intended as an offer." *Id.* The issue here is whether the C-Notes, read in isolation or in combination with the catalogs, may have constituted an offer.

1. *Bilateral Contract*

As an initial matter, we are not persuaded that the plaintiffs have alleged the existence of an offer to enter into a *bilateral* contract. "A bilateral contract consists of mutual promises made in exchange for each other by each of the two contracting parties." *Sully-Miller Contracting Co. v. Gledson/Cashman Constr., Inc.,* 103 Cal.App.4th 30, 126 Cal.Rptr.2d 400, 403 (2002) (quoting Corbin on Contracts § 1.23 (rev. ed. 1993)) (internal quotation marks omitted). Both sides of the bargain must have made promises. Here, the plaintiffs have identified an alleged promise by RJR (to allow customers to redeem Camel Cash certificates for rewards), but they have not pointed to any promise they made to RJR. Nor do they argue that RJR sought a return promise in exchange for its own promise to allow consumers to exchange C-Notes for merchandise. They argue instead the requirements for a bilateral contract are met because they agreed to certain terms and conditions when they enrolled in the Camel Cash program. *See* Appellants' Reply Brief at 9; Compl. ¶ 26. Nothing in the complaint, however, suggests that these terms were anything more than *conditions* that the plaintiffs were required to satisfy to trigger RJR's duty to perform, as opposed to promises that the plaintiffs were bound to perform to avoid incurring their own contractual liability. "A condition is an event . . . which must occur . . . before performance under a contract becomes due." Restatement (Second) of Contracts (hereinafter Restatement) § 224 (1981). A promise, by contrast, "is an express or implied declaration in a contract that raises a duty to perform and subjects the promisor to liability for breach for failure to do so." 13 Richard A. Lord, *Williston on Contracts* (hereinafter Williston) § 38:5 (4th ed. 2012). The plaintiffs have not alleged that they were bound to do anything. They therefore have not alleged the existence of an offer to enter into a bilateral contract.[1]

2. *Unilateral Contract*

We reach a different conclusion as to the plaintiffs' theory that RJR made an offer to enter into a *unilateral* contract. In contrast to a bilateral contract, a unilateral contract involves the exchange of a promise for a performance. *See Harris v. Time, Inc.,* 191 Cal.App.3d 449, 237 Cal.Rptr. 584, 587 (1987). The offer is accepted by rendering a performance rather than providing a promise. *See* Restatement § 45 cmt. a. "Typical illustrations are found in offers of rewards or prizes. . . ." *Id.*

RJR argues that its C-Notes, whether read in isolation or in combination with the catalogs, were not offers, but invitations to make an offer. RJR relies on the common law's general rule that "[a]dvertisements of goods by display, sign, handbill, newspaper, radio or television are not ordinarily intended or understood as offers to sell." *Id.* § 26 cmt. b. RJR emphasizes that two judicial decisions have applied this general rule to customer rewards programs similar to the Camel Cash program, *see Leonard v. Pepsico, Inc.,* 88 F.Supp.2d 116, 122–27 (S.D.N.Y.1999); *Alligood v. Procter & Gamble Co.,* 72 Ohio App.3d 309, 594 N.E.2d 668, 668–70 (1991) (per curiam), and urges us to apply the rule here as well. We decline to do so.

First, it is not clear that the common law rule upon which RJR relies applies under California law. *See Donovan,* 109 Cal.Rptr.2d 807, 27 P.3d at 710 (stating that "[t]his court has not previously applied the common

---

[1] It is, of course, possible for a consumer rewards program to involve a bilateral contract. Frequent flyer programs, for example, may be governed by membership agreements that impose contractual duties on both sides of the bargain, exposing airlines and travelers alike to potential contractual liability. *See, e.g., Ginsberg v. Northwest, Inc.,* 653 F.3d 1033, 1035, 1040 (9th Cir.2011); *Am. Airlines, Inc. v. Am. Coupon Exch., Inc.,* 721 F.Supp. 61, 63 (S.D.N.Y.1989). Here, however, the plaintiffs have not alleged an offer or contract involving reciprocal duties, and therefore they have not alleged a bilateral contract.

law rules upon which defendant relies, including the rule that advertisements generally constitute invitations to negotiate rather than offers," observing that "such rules . . . have been criticized on the ground that they are inconsistent with the reasonable expectations of consumers and lead to haphazard results," citing Melvin Aron Eisenberg, *Expression Rules in Contract Law and Problems of Offer and Acceptance,* 82 Cal. L. Rev. 1127, 1166–72 (1994), and concluding that "[i]n the present case . . . we need not consider the viability of the black-letter rule regarding the interpretation of advertisements").

Second, even assuming California law incorporates the common law rule, that rule includes an exception for offers of a reward, including offers of a reward for the redemption of coupons. As a leading contract law treatise explains,

> It is very common, where one desires to induce many people to action, to offer a reward for such action by general publication in some form. A statement that plausibly makes an offer of this kind must be reasonably interpreted according to its terms and the surrounding circumstances. If the statement, properly interpreted, calls for the performance or commencement of performance of specific acts, action in accordance with such an interpretation will close a contract or make the offer irrevocable. There are many cases of an offer of a reward for the capture of a person charged with crime, for desired information, for the return of a lost article, for the winning of a contest, or *for the redemption of coupons.* In addition, advertisements placed by buyers inviting sellers to ship goods without prior communication are clear cases of offers. The contracts so made are almost always unilateral.

Corbin on Contracts (hereinafter Corbin) § 2.4 (2012) (emphasis added) (footnotes omitted). RJR does not discuss this exception, relying instead on *Leonard* and *Alligood.* Several courts, however, have applied the exception to customer rewards programs. *See, e.g., Payne v. Lautz Bros.,* 166 N.Y.S. 844, 845–46, 848 (N.Y.City Ct.1916) (reward coupons included with packages of soap wrappers), *aff'd without opinion,* 168 N.Y.S. 369 (N.Y.Sup.), *aff'd without opinion,* 185 A.D. 904, 171 N.Y.S. 1094 (1918), *cited with approval in* Corbin § 2.4 n.14; *Reynolds v. Philip Morris U.S.A., Inc.,* No. 05–cv–1876 (S.D.Cal. June 5, 2007) (order denying defendant's motion for summary judgment) (reward points obtained by purchasing Marlboro cigarettes), *rev'd on other grounds,* 332 Fed.Appx. 397 (9th Cir.2009); *Wolens v. Am. Airlines, Inc.,* 157 Ill.2d 466, 193 Ill.Dec. 172, 626 N.E.2d 205, 208 (1993) (reward miles awarded for flying on American

Airlines), *rev'd on other grounds,* 513 U.S. 219, 115 S.Ct. 817, 130 L.Ed.2d 715 (1995).[2]

Like these courts, we see no justification for applying the general common law rule, rather than the common law exception, to circumstances such as those presented here. The common law rule that advertisements ordinarily do not constitute offers arose to address a specific problem—the potential for over-acceptance—not applicable here. Professor Farnsworth explains that an offer ordinarily does not exist

> when a proposal for a limited quantity has been sent to more persons than its maker could accommodate. . . . Otherwise, supposing a shopkeeper were sold out of a particular class of goods, thousands of members of the public might crowd into the shop and demand to be served, and each one would have a right of action against the proprietor for not performing his contract. A customer would not usually have reason to believe that the shopkeeper intended exposure to the risk of a multitude of acceptances resulting in a number of contracts exceeding the shopkeeper's inventory.

E. Allan Farnsworth, *Contracts* (hereinafter Farnsworth) § 3.10, at 134 (4th ed. 2004) (footnote and internal quotation marks omitted). This problem arises in the case of ordinary advertisements for the sale of goods or services, but not here. First, RJR's ostensible purpose in promoting the Camel Cash program was not to sell a limited inventory, but to induce as many consumers as possible to purchase Camel cigarettes. Second, RJR could not have been trapped into a situation in which acceptances exceeded inventory. RJR alone decided how many C-Notes to distribute, so it exercised absolute control over the number of acceptances. As Farnsworth explains, "if the very nature of a proposal restricts its maker's potential liability to a reasonable number of people, there is no reason why it cannot be an offer." *Id.* at 135.

For these reasons, we find no reason to presume that RJR's communications did not constitute an offer merely because they were addressed to the general public in the form of advertisements. The

---

[2] *Payne* found an enforceable unilateral contract where the defendant advertised that it would give a round-trip train ticket to consumers who collected 25 coupons from the defendant's soap packages and redeemed them for the train tickets (or other merchandise in the defendant's rewards catalogs) at the defendant's stores. *See* 166 N.Y.S. at 844–48. In *Reynolds,* the court held that a genuine issue of material fact existed regarding whether the plaintiff accepted an offer to enter into a unilateral contract by purchasing Marlboro cigarettes, clipping Marlboro Miles certificates, saving the certificates and eventually mailing a sufficient number of certificates to Philip Morris to exchange for products. *See Reynolds v. Philip Morris U.S.A., supra,* at 8. In *Wolens,* the Illinois Supreme Court recognized a contractual relationship between American Airlines and members of its frequent flyer program, stating, "When a member earns frequent flyer miles by flying on American or by doing business with American affiliates, a contractual relationship is formed which vests the frequent flyer with the right to earn specific travel awards." 193 Ill.Dec. 172, 626 N.E.2d at 208.

operative question under California law, therefore, is simply "whether the advertiser, in clear and positive terms, promised to render performance in exchange for something requested by the advertiser, and whether the recipient of the advertisement reasonably might have concluded that by acting in accordance with the request a contract would be formed." *Donovan,* 109 Cal.Rptr.2d 807, 27 P.3d at 710. Construing the complaint in the light most favorable to the plaintiffs, and drawing all reasonable inferences from the complaint in the plaintiffs' favor, *see Moss v. U.S. Secret Serv.,* 572 F.3d 962, 969 (9th Cir.2009); *Doe v. United States,* 419 F.3d 1058, 1062 (9th Cir.2005), we conclude that the plaintiffs have adequately alleged the existence of an offer to enter into a unilateral contract, whereby RJR promised to provide rewards to customers who purchased Camel cigarettes, saved Camel Cash certificates and redeemed their certificates in accordance with the catalogs' terms.

We reach this conclusion in light of the totality of the circumstances surrounding RJR's communications to consumers: the repeated use of the word "offer" in the C-Notes; the absence of any language disclaiming the intent to be bound; the inclusion of specific restrictions in the C-Notes ("Offer restricted to smokers 21 years of age or older"; "Offer good only in the USA, and void where restricted or prohibited by law"; "Check catalog for expiration date"; "Limit 5 requests for a catalog per household"); the formal enrollment process, through which consumers submitted registration forms and RJR issued enrollment numbers; and the substantial reliance expected from consumers.[3] *Donovan* explains that under the common law "advertisements have been held to constitute offers where they invite the performance of a specific act without further communication and leave nothing for negotiation." 109 Cal.Rptr.2d 807, 27 P.3d at 710. These requirements are satisfied here. RJR's alleged offer invited the performance of specific acts (saving C-Notes and redeeming them for rewards in accordance with the catalog) without further communication, and leaving nothing for negotiation.

RJR properly emphasizes that the alleged offer left aspects of RJR's performance to RJR's discretion. The offer did not specify when future catalogs would be issued, what rewards merchandise they would include,

---

[3]   The plaintiffs' substantial reliance distinguishes this case from cases involving garden-variety advertisements. To take advantage of the Camel Cash program, consumers were expected to purchase Camel cigarettes and accumulate Camel Cash certificates for a period of weeks, months or even years. *See* Compl. ¶ 29 (alleging that "[t]he number of Camel Cash certificates needed to obtain merchandise . . . varied from as little as one hundred to many thousands," and noting that RJR "further encouraged plaintiffs and other Class members to collect their Camel Cash (as opposed to redeeming them as soon as possible) because merchandise listed in defendant's catalogs for redemption by a greater number of coupons was disproportionately more valuable than the merchandise which could be redeemed by fewer coupons"). Citing an offer for a reward as an example, Corbin explains that "a proposal is likely to be deemed to be an offer if it is foreseeable that the addressee of the proposal will rely upon it." Corbin § 2.2. This is so because a member of the public is unlikely to undertake substantial reliance in the absence of a binding commitment from the offeror—i.e., on the mere chance that the offeror will perform.

what quantities of merchandise would be available or how many C-Notes would be required to exchange for particular items. The plaintiffs, however, do not allege that these were essential terms. *See* Compl. ¶ 31 ("[I]t was not a contract to obtain a specific item or good, such as a 'Joe Camel' jacket or ashtray."). Instead, they allege a contract the essence of which was their general right to redeem their Camel Cash certificates, during the life of the program, for whatever rewards merchandise RJR made available, with RJR's discretion limited only by the implied duty of good faith performance. The presence of discretion thus does not preclude the existence of an offer.

[Section III-B of the opinion addressing the indefiniteness issue is set out in Chapter 11.]

C.   Mutuality of Obligation & RJR's Right to Terminate

RJR argues that the plaintiffs' contract claim must be dismissed for lack of mutuality of obligation because RJR had an unrestricted right to terminate the Camel Cash program at will, and without notice. The complaint discusses RJR's right to terminate the Camel Cash program in three paragraphs:

Plaintiffs do not dispute that defendant had the right to terminate the Camel Cash program. However, defendant made a deliberate and calculated choice to waive any right to terminate the program "without notice" and instead provided six months prior notice. Thus, during that six-month period, from approximately October 2006 through March 2007, defendant was obligated to comply with the terms of its contract with plaintiffs. . . .

Also, the breach of contract alleged is *not* that Reynolds was prohibited from terminating the program but that, during the program's duration, Reynolds had the obligation to perform through the program's termination date. Certain (but not all) of the Camel Cash catalogs state that Reynolds could terminate the Camel Cash program without notice. Defendant, however, waived any right to terminate without notice when, on or about October 1, 2006, it announced by mailing a notice to program members, that the program would terminate as of March 31, 2007. Namely, defendant gave notice of termination and represented that plaintiffs could redeem their Camel Cash certificates for six months. . . .

> 54. In or about October 2006, defendant announced that it was terminating the Camel Cash program as of March 31, 2007. Thus, the contract was in effect until March 31, 2007 when defendant terminated the program.

Compl. ¶¶ 6, 32, 54.

Given our conclusion that the plaintiffs have alleged an offer to enter into a unilateral rather than a bilateral contract, RJR's reliance on mutuality of obligation necessarily fails: that doctrine does not apply to unilateral contracts. *See, e.g., Asmus v. Pac. Bell,* 23 Cal.4th 1, 96 Cal.Rptr.2d 179, 999 P.2d 71, 78 (2000) ("In the unilateral contract context, there is no mutuality of obligation."). RJR's argument nonetheless raises important questions about the viability of the plaintiffs' contract claim. If, in fact, RJR reserved an *unrestricted* right to terminate the Camel Cash program, *without notice,* then the plaintiffs' contract claim may well be untenable.

First, a reservation of an unrestricted right to terminate could have precluded RJR's communications from constituting an offer. As Corbin explains, if an offeror expressly reserves not only the right to revoke the offer at will and without notice, but also the *unrestricted right not to perform,* then the offer is not legally effective as an offer at all: "A purported offer that reserves the power to withdraw at will even after an acceptance should not be described as an offer at all, but as an invitation to submit an offer." Corbin § 2.19.[8]

Second, if RJR reserved an unrestricted right to terminate the Camel Cash program at any time and without notice, then RJR's promise to perform could be deemed illusory, and hence unenforceable. As Farnsworth explains, when a promise "appears on its face to be so insubstantial as to impose no obligation at all on the promisor—who says, in effect, 'I will *if* I want to' "—the promise is not enforceable. Farnsworth § 2.13, at 75. Accordingly, an enforceable termination clause that gives a promisor an unrestricted power to terminate a contract at any time, without notice, renders the promise illusory and unenforceable, at least so long as the purported contract remains wholly executory.

Either of the foregoing principles could possibly serve to defeat the plaintiffs' contract claim here. The complaint, however, does not definitively allege that RJR reserved an *unrestricted* right to terminate its duty to perform. The complaint alleges only that "[c]*ertain* (but not all) of the Camel Cash catalogs state that Reynolds could terminate the Camel Cash program without notice." Compl. ¶ 32 (emphasis added). The complaint, moreover, alleges that RJR "waived any right to terminate without notice when, on or about October 1, 2006, it announced by mailing a notice to program members, that the program would terminate as of March 31, 2007." *Id.* Dismissal is therefore unwarranted on the current record. . .

---

[8]   It does not appear that the plaintiffs' beginning of performance (by purchasing Camel cigarettes and saving C-Notes) would alter that result. It is true as a general matter that an offeree's part performance may render an offer to enter into a unilateral contract irrevocable. *See Steiner v. Thexton,* 48 Cal.4th 411, 106 Cal.Rptr.3d 252, 226 P.3d 359, 368 (2010); Restatement § 45(1). That default principle, however, does not apply when the offer expressly reserves the right to revoke notwithstanding the offeror's beginning of performance. *See* Restatement § 45 cmt. b.

IV. PROMISSORY ESTOPPEL

Under California law, the elements of promissory estoppel are (1) a promise clear and unambiguous in its terms; (2) reliance by the party to whom the promise is made; (3) the reliance must be both reasonable and foreseeable; and (4) the party asserting the estoppel must be injured by his reliance. *See U.S. Ecology, Inc. v. State,* 129 Cal.App.4th 887, 28 Cal.Rptr.3d 894, 905 (2005).

Here, the parties chiefly dispute the first element—whether the plaintiffs have adequately alleged that RJR made a promise clear and unambiguous in its terms. We conclude this element is satisfied: the C-Notes promised consumers that if they saved C-Notes and redeemed them for rewards merchandise in accordance with the catalog, RJR would provide the merchandise. These terms are neither unclear nor ambiguous. *See Aceves v. U.S. Bank, N.A.,* 192 Cal.App.4th 218, 120 Cal.Rptr.3d 507, 514–15 (2011) (holding that a bank's promise—to work with the plaintiff on a mortgage reinstatement and loan modification if the plaintiff no longer pursued relief in bankruptcy court—was a clear and unambiguous promise to negotiate, even though it left open the terms of any loan modification agreement that might be discussed). RJR correctly points out that its communications were unspecific as to precisely what merchandise would be offered in future catalogs. The plaintiffs, however, do not rest their promissory estoppel claim on an alleged promise to provide particular merchandise.

The plaintiffs' promissory estoppel claim, though, is subject to the same definiteness requirement as their breach of contract claim. *See id.* at 514. This claim therefore rises or falls with the contract claim. Given that we have concluded that the alleged contract is sufficiently definite to survive a motion to dismiss, we vacate dismissal of the promissory estoppel claim as well. If further proceedings demonstrate that the contract claim fails for indefiniteness, the promissory estoppel claim will likely fail for the same reason. . . .

VIII. CONCLUSION

We affirm dismissal of the plaintiffs' UCL and CLRA claims. We reverse dismissal of the plaintiffs' breach of contract and promissory estoppel claims.

The parties shall bear their own costs on appeal.

AFFIRMED IN PART, REVERSED IN PART AND REMANDED.

———

RESTATEMENT, SECOND, CONTRACTS § 26

[See Selected Source Materials Supplement]

CISG ARTICLE 14(2)

[See Selected Source Materials Supplement]

PRINCIPLES OF EUROPEAN CONTRACT LAW ART. 2.201(2), (3)

[See Selected Source Materials Supplement]

NOTE ON OFFER AND ACCEPTANCE

Everyday life gives rise to recurring kinds of arrangements that might or might not be considered to be contracts. For example, a hotel reservation has been held to be a contract binding on the hotel, even where the guest has not guaranteed the reservation. Wells v. Holiday Inns, Inc., 522 F.Supp. 1023 (W.D.Mo.1981). On the other hand, in Glass Service Co. v. State Farm Mutual Auto. Ins. Co., 530 N.W.2d 867 (Minn.App.1995), the court held that appointments made by customers with an auto glass-repair company did not constitute contracts. In the course of its opinion the court said, "We do not believe people intend to be legally bound when they make reservations at a restaurant, or schedule appointments to have their car repaired, their hair cut, or their teeth checked. Nor is it likely that the providers of such services perceive the customers to be bound or intend to be legally bound themselves by scheduling appointments."

SECTION 2. TERMINATION OF THE OFFEREE'S POWER OF ACCEPTANCE: LAPSE, REJECTION, AND COUNTER-OFFER

AKERS V. J.B. SEDBERRY, INC.
Court of Appeals of Tennessee, 1955.
39 Tenn.App. 633, 286 S.W.2d 617, cert. denied by Tenn.S.Ct.

FELTS, JUDGE. These two consolidated causes are before us upon a writ of error sued out by J.B. Sedberry, Inc., and Mrs. M.B. Sedberry, defendants below, to review a decree of the Chancery Court, awarding a recovery against them in favor of each of the complainants, Charles William Akers and William Gambill Whitsitt, for damages for breach of a contract of employment. . . .

J.B. Sedberry, Inc., was a Tennessee corporation with its principal place of business at Franklin, Tennessee. Mrs. M.B. Sedberry owned practically all of its stock and was its president and in active charge of its affairs. It was engaged in the business of distributing "Jay Bee" hammer mills, which were manufactured for it under contract by Jay Bee Manufacturing Company, a Texas corporation, whose plant was in Tyler, Texas, and whose capital stock was owned principally by L.M. Glasgow and B.G. Byars.

On July 1, 1947, J.B. Sedberry, Inc., by written contract, employed complainant Akers as Chief Engineer for a term of five years at a salary of $12,000 per year, payable $1,000 per month, plus 1% of its net profits for the first year, 2% the second, 3% the third, 4% the fourth, and 5% the fifth year. His duties were to carry on research for his employer, and to see that the Jay Bee Manufacturing Company, Tyler, Texas, manufactured the mills and parts according to proper specifications. Mrs. M.B. Sedberry guaranteed the employer's performance of this contract.

On August 1, 1947, J.B. Sedberry, Inc., by written contract, employed complainant Whitsitt as Assistant Chief Engineer for a term of five years at a salary of $7,200 per year, payable $600 per month, plus 1% of the corporation's net profits for the first year, 2% for the second, 3% for the third, 4% for the fourth, and 5% for the fifth year. His duties were to assist in the work done by the Chief Engineer. Mrs. M.B. Sedberry guaranteed the employer's performance of this contract.

Under Mrs. Sedberry's instructions, Akers and Whitsitt moved to Tyler, Texas, began performing their contract duties in the plant of the Jay Bee Manufacturing Company, continued working there, and were paid under the contracts until October 1, 1950, when they ceased work, under circumstances hereafter stated. . . .

[After the employment contracts were made, Mrs. Sedberry acquired the stock of Jay Bee from Glasgow and Byars, and installed a new manager, A.M. Sorenson.] There soon developed considerable friction between Sorenson and complainants Akers and Whitsitt. The Jay Bee Manufacturing Company owed large sums to the Tyler State Bank & Trust Co.; and the bank's officers, fearing the company might fail under Sorenson's management, began talking to Akers and Whitsitt about the company's financial difficulties. . . .

While these matters were pending, Akers and Whitsitt flew to Nashville and went to Franklin to talk with Mrs. Sedberry about them. They had a conference with her at her office on Friday, September 29, 1950, lasting from 9:30 a.m. until 4:30 p.m. As they had come unannounced, and unknown to Sorenson, they felt Mrs. Sedberry might mistrust them; and at the outset to show their good faith, they offered to resign, but she did not accept their offer. Instead, she proceeded with them in discussing the operation and refinancing of the business.

Testifying about this conference, Akers said that, at the very beginning, to show their good faith, he told Mrs. Sedberry that they would offer their resignations on a ninety-day notice, provided they were paid according to the contract for that period; that she pushed the offers aside—"would not accept them", but went into a full discussion of the business; that nothing was thereafter said about the offers to resign; and that they spent the whole day discussing the business, Akers making notes of things she instructed him to do when he got back to Texas.

Whitsitt testified that . . . [Mrs. Sedberry]. . . . did not accept the offer, but proceeded with the business, and nothing further was said about resigning.

Mrs. Sedberry testified that Akers and Whitsitt came in and "offered their resignations"; that they said they could not work with Sorenson and did not believe the bank would go along with him; and that "they said if it would be of any help to the organization they would be glad to tender their resignation and pay them what was due them." She further said that she "did not accept the resignation", that she "felt it necessary to contact Mr. Sorenson and give consideration to the resignation offer." But she said nothing to complainants about taking the offer under consideration.

On cross-examination she said that in the offer to resign "no mention was made of any ninety-day notice". Asked what response she made to the offer she said, "I treated it rather casually because I had to give it some thought and had to contact Mr. Sorenson." She further said she excused herself from the conference with complainants, went to another room, tried to telephone Sorenson in Tyler, Texas, but was unable to locate him.

She then resumed the conference, nothing further was said about the offers to resign, nothing was said by her to indicate that she thought the offers were left open or held under consideration by her. But the discussion proceeded as if the offers had not been made. She discussed with complainants future plans for refinancing and operating the business, giving them instructions, and Akers making notes of them.

Following the conference, complainants, upon Mrs. Sedberry's request, flew back to Texas to proceed to carry out her instructions. . . .

On Monday, October 2, 1950, Mrs. Sedberry sent to complainants similar telegrams, signed by "J.B. Sedberry, Inc., by M.B. Sedberry, President", stating that their resignations were accepted, effective immediately. We quote the telegram to Akers, omitting the formal parts:

"Account present unsettled conditions which you so fully are aware we accept your kind offer of resignation effective immediately. Please discontinue as of today with everyone employed in Sedberry, Inc., Engineering Department, discontinuing all expenses in this department writing." . . .

While this said she was "writing", she did not write. . . .

[Akers then wrote] that he was amazed to get her telegram, and called her attention to the fact that no offer to resign by him was open or outstanding when she sent the telegram; that while he had made a conditional offer to resign at their conference on September 29, she had immediately rejected the offer, and had discussed plans for the business and had instructed him and Whitsitt as to things she wanted them to do in the business on their return to Tyler.

This letter further stated that Akers was expecting to be paid according to the terms of his contract until he could find other employment that would pay him as much income as that provided in his contract, and that if he had to accept a position with less income, he would expect to be paid the difference, or whatever losses he suffered by her breach of the contract. [Whitsitt wrote a similar letter.] . . .

As it takes two to make a contract, it takes two to unmake it. It cannot be changed or ended by one alone, but only by mutual assent of both parties. A contract of employment for a fixed period may be terminated by the employee's offer to resign, provided such offer is duly accepted by the employer. . . .

An employee's tender of his resignation, being a mere offer is, of course, not binding until it has been accepted by the employer. Such offer must be accepted according to its terms and within the time fixed. The matter is governed by the same rules as govern the formation of contracts. . . .

An offer may be terminated in a number of ways, as, for example, where it is rejected by the offeree, or where it is not accepted by him within the time fixed, or, if no time is fixed, within a reasonable time. An offer terminated in either of these ways ceases to exist and cannot thereafter be accepted. 1 Williston on Contracts (1936), secs. 50A, 51, 53, 54; 1 Corbin on Contracts (1950), secs. 35, 36; 1 Restatement, Contracts, §§ 35, 40.

The question what is a reasonable time, where no time is fixed, is a question of fact, depending on the nature of the contract proposed, the usages of business and other circumstances of the case. Ordinarily, an offer made by one to another in a face to face conversation is deemed to continue only to the close of their conversation, and cannot be accepted thereafter.

The rule is illustrated by Restatement Contracts § 40, Illustration 2, as follows:

"2. While A and B are engaged in conversation, A makes B an offer to which B then makes no reply, but a few hours later meeting A again, B states that he accepts the offer. There is no contract unless the offer or the surrounding circumstances indicate that the offer is intended to continue beyond the immediate conversation." . . .

Professor Corbin says:

> "When two negotiating parties are in each other's presence, and one makes an offer to the other without indicating any time for acceptance, the inference that will ordinarily be drawn by the other party is that an answer is expected at once. . . . If, when the first reply is not an acceptance, the offeror turns away in silence, the proper inference is that the offer is no longer open to acceptance." 1 Corbin on Contracts (1950), section 36, p. 111.

The only offer by Akers and Whitsitt to resign was the offer made by them in their conversation with Mrs. Sedberry. They made that offer at the outset, and on the evidence it seems clear that they expected an answer at once. Certainly, there is nothing in the evidence to show that they intended the offer to continue beyond that conversation; and on the above authorities, we think the offer did not continue beyond that meeting.

Indeed, it did not last that long, in our opinion, but was terminated by Mrs. Sedberry's rejection of it very early in that meeting. While she did not expressly reject it, and while she may have intended, as she says, to take the offer under consideration, she did not disclose such an intent to complainants; but, by her conduct, led them to believe she rejected the offer, brushed it aside, and proceeded with the discussion as if it had not been made.

> "An offer is rejected when the offeror is justified in inferring from the words or conduct of the offeree that the offeree intends not to accept the offer or to take it under further advisement (Rest. Contracts sec. 36)." 1 Williston on Contracts, section 51.

So, we agree with the Trial Judge that when defendants sent the telegrams, undertaking to accept offers of complainants to resign, there was no such offer in existence; and that this attempt of defendants to terminate their contract was unlawful and constituted a breach for which they are liable to complainants. . . .

Finally, defendants contend that if complainants are entitled to any recovery at all, such recovery should have been limited to the ninety-day period from and after October 2, 1950, because complainants themselves admitted that they had offered to resign upon ninety days notice with pay for that period.

The answer to this contention is that their offer to resign on ninety days notice was not accepted, but had terminated, and there was no offer in existence when Mrs. Sedberry undertook to accept their offers of resignation. Such attempt by defendants to terminate their contract was unlawful and was a breach for which they become liable for the measure of recovery as above stated. . . .

All of the assignments of error are overruled and the decree of the Chancellor is affirmed. . . .

The causes are remanded to the Chancery Court for further proceedings not inconsistent with this opinion.

HICKERSON and SHRIVER, JJ., concur.

––––––––

RESTATEMENT, SECOND, CONTRACTS §§ 38, 41

[See Selected Source Materials Supplement]

––––––––

CISG ART. 17

[See Selected Source Materials Supplement]

––––––––

UNIDROIT PRINCIPLES OF INTERNATIONAL COMMERCIAL CONTRACTS ARTS. 2.1.5, 2.1.7

[See Selected Source Materials Supplement]

––––––––

PRINCIPLES OF EUROPEAN CONTRACT LAW ARTS. 2.203, 2.206

[See Selected Source Materials Supplement]

––––––––

NOTE ON THE EFFECT OF THE REJECTION OF AN OFFER

A recurring problem in the area of offer and acceptance concerns the issue whether an expression by an offeree in response to an offer terminates the offeree's power of acceptance. The underlying question in determining whether an offeree's response terminates his power of acceptance is whether the offeror would reasonably understand that the response serves to take the offer off the table. If an offer is taken off the table the offeree has nothing to accept, any more than if the offer had never been made or had lapsed. Furthermore, an offeror is likely to rely on his understanding that the offer has been taken off the table. For example, suppose an offer states that it will be open for ten days. During those ten days, the offeror may begin steps to prepare for performance based on his assessment of the probability of acceptance by the offeree. Suppose now that as a result of an expression used by the offeree on the second day, the offeror reasonably believes the offer has been taken off the table. In that case, the offeror will take no further steps to prepare for performance, and may arrange his affairs on the basis that he will not be entering into the proposed contract. Alternatively, the offeror may make a new offer to a third party that he would not have made in the absence of the offeree's expression. If the offeree then tries to accept on the tenth day, the offeror would be caught short. Moreover, it would be difficult if not impossible for the offeror to prove that he would have acted differently in the absence of the offeree's expression, because the offeror's response to the offeree's expression may consist of nonaction or of action that is not related to the expression in an obvious way.

The issue then is, what kinds of expressions by an offeree will lead an offeror to reasonably believe that the offer is off the table. To a very large extent, the law of offer and acceptance deals with this issue through a series of categorical rules, rather than by application of the general principles of interpretation on a case-by-case basis. Under one of these rules, a rejection terminates the offeree's power of acceptance even if the rejection is communicated before the offer would otherwise have lapsed. It is easy to justify this rule, because it seems virtually certain that under the general principles of interpretation a rejection would be understood by the offeror to take the offer off the table. Although it is conceivable that in a few cases the general principles of interpretation would lead to a different result—because, for example, neither party subjectively viewed the rejection as taking the offer off the table—such a scenario is so unlikely that a categorical rule is supported by administrative considerations. It should be stressed, however, that even in this relatively easy case, the categorical rule represents a choice. A rejection terminates the power of acceptance, not because a rejection must logically terminate the power of acceptance, but because giving that effect to a rejection is justified by prudential considerations.

ARDENTE V. HORAN

Supreme Court of Rhode Island, 1976.
117 R.I. 254, 366 A.2d 162.

DORIS, JUSTICE. Ernst P. Ardente, the plaintiff, brought this civil action in Superior Court to specifically enforce an agreement between himself and William A. and Katherine L. Horan, the defendants, to sell certain real property. The defendants filed an answer together with a motion for summary judgment pursuant to Super.R.Civ.P. 56. Following the submission of affidavits by both the plaintiff and the defendants and a hearing on the motion, judgment was entered by a Superior Court justice for the defendants. The plaintiff now appeals.

In August 1975, certain residential property in the city of Newport was offered for sale by defendants. The plaintiff made a bid of $250,000 for the property which was communicated to defendants by their attorney. After defendants' attorney advised plaintiff that the bid was acceptable to defendants, he prepared a purchase and sale agreement at the direction of defendants and forwarded it to plaintiff's attorney for plaintiff's signature. After investigating certain title conditions, plaintiff executed the agreement. Thereafter plaintiff's attorney returned the document to defendants along with a check in the amount of $20,000 and a letter dated September 8, 1975, which read in relevant part as follows:

> "My clients are concerned that the following items remain with the real estate: a) dining room set and tapestry wall covering in dining room; b) fireplace fixtures throughout; c) the sun parlor furniture. I would appreciate your confirming that these items are a part of the transaction, as they would be difficult to replace."

The defendants refused to agree to sell the enumerated items and did not sign the purchase and sale agreement. They directed their attorney to return the agreement and the deposit check to plaintiff and subsequently refused to sell the property to plaintiff. This action for specific performance followed.

In Superior Court, defendants moved for summary judgment on the ground that the facts were not in dispute and no contract had been formed as a matter of law.[1] The trial justice ruled that the letter quoted above constituted a conditional acceptance of defendants' offer to sell the property and consequently must be construed as a counteroffer. Since defendants never accepted the counteroffer, it followed that no contract was formed, and summary judgment was granted. . . .

The plaintiff assigns several grounds for appeal in his brief. He urges first that summary judgment was improper because there existed a genuine issue of fact. The factual question, according to plaintiff, was whether the oral agreement which preceded the drafting of the purchase and sale agreement was intended by the parties to take effect immediately to create a binding oral contract for the sale of the property.

We cannot agree with plaintiff's position. A review of the record shows that the issue was never raised before the trial justice. The plaintiff did not, in his affidavit in opposition to summary judgment or by any other means, bring to the attention of the trial court any facts which established the existence of a relevant factual dispute. Indeed, at the hearing on the motion plaintiff did not even mention the alleged factual dispute which he

---

[1]   Although the contract would appear to be within the statute of frauds, defendants did not raise this defense in the trial court, nor do they raise it here. Where a party makes no claim to the benefit of the statute, the court sua sponte will not interpose it for him. Conti v. Fisher, 48 R.I. 33, 36, 134 A. 849, 850 (1926).

now claims the trial justice erred in overlooking. The only issue plaintiff addressed was the proper interpretation of the language used in plaintiff's letter of acceptance. This was solely a question of law. . . .

The plaintiff's second contention is that the trial justice incorrectly applied the principles of contract law in deciding that the facts did not disclose a valid acceptance of defendants' offer. Again we cannot agree.

The trial justice proceeded on the theory that the delivery of the purchase and sale agreement to plaintiff constituted an offer by defendants to sell the property. Because we must view the evidence in the light most favorable to the party against whom summary judgment was entered, in this case plaintiff, we assume as the trial justice did that the delivery of the agreement was in fact an offer.[3]

The question we must answer next is whether there was an acceptance of that offer. The general rule is that where, as here, there is an offer to form a bilateral contract, the offeree must communicate his acceptance to the offeror before any contractual obligation can come into being. A mere mental intent to accept the offer, no matter how carefully formed, is not sufficient. The acceptance must be transmitted to the offeror in some overt manner. Bullock v. Harwick, 158 Fla. 834, 30 So.2d 539 (1947); Armstrong v. Guy H. James Constr. Co., 402 P.2d 275 (Okl.1965); 1 Restatement, Contracts § 20 (1932). See generally 1 Corbin, Contracts § 67 (1963). A review of the record shows that the only expression of acceptance which was communicated to defendants was the delivery of the executed purchase and sale agreement accompanied by the letter of September 8. Therefore it is solely on the basis of the language used in these two documents that we must determine whether there was a valid acceptance. Whatever plaintiff's unexpressed intention may have been in sending the documents is irrelevant. We must be concerned only with the language actually used, not the language plaintiff thought he was using or intended to use.

There is no doubt that the execution and delivery of the purchase and sale agreement by plaintiff, without more, would have operated as an acceptance. The terms of the accompanying letter, however, apparently conditioned the acceptance upon the inclusion of various items of personalty. In assessing the effect of the terms of that letter we must keep in mind certain generally accepted rules. To be effective, an acceptance must be definite and unequivocal. "An offeror is entitled to know in clear terms whether the offeree accepts his proposal. It is not enough that the words of a reply justify a probable inference of assent." 1 Restatement, Contracts § 58, comment a (1932). The acceptance may not impose

---

[3] The conclusion that the delivery of the agreement was an offer is not unassailable in view of the fact that defendants did not sign the agreement before sending it to plaintiff, and the fact that plaintiff told defendants' attorney after the agreement was received that he would have to investigate certain conditions of title before signing the agreement. If it was not an offer, plaintiff's execution of the agreement could itself be no more than an offer, which defendants never accepted.

additional conditions on the offer, nor may it add limitations. "An acceptance which is equivocal or upon condition or with a limitation is a counteroffer and requires acceptance by the original offeror before a contractual relationship can exist." John Hancock Mut. Life Ins. Co. v. Dietlin, 97 R.I. 515, 518, 199 A.2d 311, 313 (1964). Accord, Cavanaugh v. Conway, 36 R.I. 571, 587, 90 A. 1080, 1086 (1914).

However, an acceptance may be valid despite conditional language if the acceptance is clearly independent of the condition. Many cases have so held. Williston states the rule as follows:

> "Frequently an offeree, while making a positive acceptance of the offer, also makes a request or suggestion that some addition or modification be made. So long as it is clear that the meaning of the acceptance is positively and unequivocally to accept the offer whether such request is granted or not, a contract is formed." 1 Williston, Contracts § 79 at 261–62 (3d ed.1957).

Corbin is in agreement with the above view. 1 Corbin, supra, § 84 at 363–65. Thus our task is to decide whether plaintiff's letter is more reasonably interpreted as a qualified acceptance or as an absolute acceptance together with a mere inquiry concerning a collateral matter.

In making our decision we recognize that, as one text states, "The question whether a communication by an offeree is a conditional acceptance or counter-offer is not always easy to answer. It must be determined by the same common-sense process of interpretation that must be applied in so many other cases." 1 Corbin, supra § 82 at 353. In our opinion the language used in plaintiff's letter of September 8 is not consistent with an absolute acceptance accompanied by a request for a gratuitous benefit. We interpret the letter to impose a condition on plaintiff's acceptance of defendants' offer. The letter does not unequivocally state that even without the enumerated items plaintiff is willing to complete the contract. In fact, the letter seeks "confirmation" that the listed items "are a part of the transaction". Thus, far from being an independent, collateral request, the sale of the items in question is explicitly referred to as a part of the real estate transaction. Moreover, the letter goes on to stress the difficulty of finding replacements for these items. This is a further indication that plaintiff did not view the inclusion of the listed items as merely collateral or incidental to the real estate transaction.

A review of the relevant case law discloses that those cases in which an acceptance was found valid despite an accompanying conditional term generally involved a more definite expression of acceptance than the one in the case at bar. E.g., Moss v. Cogle, 267 Ala. 208, 101 So.2d 314 (1958); Jaybe Constr. Co. v. Beco, Inc., 3 Conn.Cir. 406, 216 A.2d 208, 212 (1965); Katz v. Pratt Street Realty Co., 257 Md. 103, 262 A.2d 540 (1970); Nelson

v. Hamlin, 258 Mass. 331, 155 N.E. 18 (1927); Duprey v. Donahoe, 52 Wash.2d 129, 323 P.2d 903 (1958).

Accordingly, we hold that since the plaintiff's letter of acceptance dated September 8 was conditional, it operated as a rejection of the defendants' offer and no contractual obligation was created.

The plaintiff's appeal is denied and dismissed, the judgment appealed from is affirmed and the case is remanded to the Superior Court.

PAOLINO, J., did not participate.

———

Rhode Island Dep't of Transportation v. Providence & Worcester R.R.

674 A.2d 1239 (R.I.1996)

P & W owned a parcel of waterfront property in East Providence, Rhode Island. There were railroad tracks on the property. A statute, Rhode Island G.L. § 39–6.1–9, provided that "All rail properties within the state offered for sale by any railway corporation . . . shall be offered for sale to the state in the first instance at the lowest price at which the railway corporation is willing to sell. . . . The state shall have a period of not more than thirty (30) days from receipt of the notification to accept the offer." P & W entered into a Real Estate Sales Agreement to sell the property to Promet for $100,000, subject to the State's option. Under the agreement with Promet, P & W was required to remove the tracks from the property. Pursuant to the statute, P & W then offered the property to the State for $100,000. The relevant State official accepted the offer in writing, but added, "Of course, you understand that certain wording in the Real Estate Sales Agreement [with Promet] relating to 'buyer' and obligations concerning the removal of track would be inappropriate to the purpose of the State's purchase." P & W claimed that no contract had been formed because the State's response was a conditional acceptance. Held, for the State:

> This Court has held that a valid acceptance "must be definite and unequivocal," Ardente v. Horan, 117 R.I. 254, 259, 366 A.2d 162, 165 (1976), and that an "acceptance which is equivocal or upon condition or with a limitation is a counteroffer and requires acceptance by the original offeror before a contractual relationship can exist." John Hancock Mutual Life Insurance Co. v. Dietlin, 97 R.I. 515, 518, 199 A.2d 311, 313 (1964). It is not equivocation, however, "if the offeree merely puts into words that which was already reasonably implied in the terms of the offer." 1 Corbin on Contracts, § 3.32 at 478–79 (rev. ed.1993). It is further the case that "an acceptance must receive a reasonable construction" and that "the mere addition of a collateral or immaterial [matter] will not prevent the formation of a contract." Raydon Exploration, Inc. v. Ladd, 902 F.2d 1496, 1500 (10th Cir.1990). See also Hoyt R. Matise Co. v. Zurn, 754 F.2d 560, 566 (5th Cir.1985) ("[t]o transmogrify a purported

acceptance into a counteroffer, it must be shown that the acceptance differs in some material respect from the offer").

The state's letter of acceptance points out that the name of the buyer in the original agreement would have to be changed. In our opinion, this statement simply reflected the obvious necessity to replace "the state" for "Promet" as the named buyer in the deed. Moreover, the letter's reference to P & W's obligation to Promet to remove tracks from the property as "inappropriate to the purpose of the State's purchase" did not add any terms or conditions to the contract but, instead, constituted a clear benefit to P & W. In pointing out that the "wording" that obligated P & W to remove tracks would be "inappropriate" in an agreement between P & W and the state, the state, in fact, relieved P & W from the obligation and expense it otherwise would have incurred in selling the property to Promet. When an offeree, in its acceptance of an offer, absolves the offeror of a material obligation, the "rules of contract construction and the 'rules of common sense'" preclude construing that absolution as an additional term that invalidates the acceptance. Textron, Inc. v. Aetna Casualty and Surety Co., 638 A.2d 537, 541 (R.I.1994). . . .

Therefore, we concur with the trial justice who found that the state validly accepted the option extended to it by P & W.

RESTATEMENT, SECOND, CONTRACTS § 39

[See Selected Source Materials Supplement]

RESTATEMENT, SECOND, CONTRACTS § 39, ILLUSTRATIONS 1–3

1. A offers B to sell him a parcel of land for $5,000, stating that the offer will remain open for thirty days. B replies, "I will pay $4800 for the parcel," and on A's declining that, B writes, within the thirty day period, "I accept your offer to sell for $5,000." There is no contract unless A's offer was [an option supported by consideration], or unless A's reply to the counter-offer manifested an intention to renew his original offer.

2. A makes the same offer to B as that stated in Illustration 1, and B replies, "Won't you take less?" A answers, "No." An acceptance thereafter by B within the thirty-day period is effective. B's inquiry was not a counter-offer, and A's original offer stands.

3. A makes the same offer to B as that stated in Illustration 1. B replies "I am keeping your offer under advisement, but if you wish to close

the matter at once I will give you $4800." A does not reply, and within the thirty-day period B accepts the original offer. B's acceptance is effective.

———

RESTATEMENT, SECOND, CONTRACTS § 59

[See Selected Source Materials Supplement]

———

CISG ART. 19

[See Selected Source Materials Supplement]

———

UNIDROIT PRINCIPLES OF INTERNATIONAL COMMERCIAL CONTRACTS ART. 2.1.11

[See Selected Source Materials Supplement]

———

PRINCIPLES OF EUROPEAN CONTRACT LAW ART. 2.208

[See Selected Source Materials Supplement]

———

NOTE ON THE MIRROR-IMAGE RULE

Under classical contract law, the rule that a conditional acceptance terminates the power of acceptance was accompanied by a closely connected rule known as the mirror-image or ribbon-matching rule. Under that rule if a purported acceptance varied from the offer in any respect, no matter how minor, no contract was formed. Under modern contract law, the bite of this rule has been softened in two respects. First, UCC § 2–207 applies a special rule in the case of contracts for the sale of goods. Although section 2–207 is not limited in terms to form offers and form acceptances, it is obviously designed primarily to deal with the problems presented by forms, and normally is applied only to forms. UCC § 2–207 will be considered in Chapter 15, infra. Second, Comment a to Restatement Second § 59, which builds on UCC § 2–207, and is supported by some case law, provides that "a definite and seasonal expression of acceptance is operative despite the statement of additional or different terms if the acceptance is not made to depend on assent to the additional or different terms." This leaves open how a court is to determine whether in any given case the acceptance is or is not made to depend on assent to the additional or different terms.

———

RESTATEMENT, SECOND, CONTRACTS § 37

[See Selected Source Materials Supplement]

———

SECTION 3. TERMINATION OF THE OFFEREE'S POWER OF ACCEPTANCE: REVOCATION

DICKINSON V. DODDS

In the Court of Appeal, Chancery Division, 1876.
2 Ch.Div. 463.

On Wednesday, the 10th of June, 1874, the defendant John Dodds signed and delivered to the plaintiff, George Dickinson, a memorandum, of which the material part was as follows:

> "I hereby agree to sell to Mr. George Dickinson the whole of the dwellinghouses, garden ground, stabling, and outbuildings thereto belonging, situate at Croft, belonging to me, for the sum of £800. As witness my hand this tenth day of June, 1874.
>
> [Signed] John Dodds."

> "P.S.—This offer to be left over until Friday, 9 o'clock a.m. J.D. (the twelfth), 12th June, 1874.
>
> [Signed] J. Dodds."

The bill alleged that Dodds understood and intended that the plaintiff should have until Friday, 9 a.m., within which to determine whether he would or would not purchase, and that he should absolutely have until that time the refusal of the property at the price of £800, and that the plaintiff in fact determined to accept the offer on the morning of Thursday, the 11th of June, but did not at once signify his acceptance to Dodds, believing that he had the power to accept it until 9 a.m. on the Friday.

In the afternoon of the Thursday the plaintiff was informed by a Mr. Berry that Dodds had been offering or agreeing to sell the property to Thomas Allan, the other defendant. Thereupon the plaintiff, at about half past seven in the evening, went to the house of Mrs. Burgess, the mother-in-law of Dodds, where he was then staying, and left with her a formal acceptance in writing of the offer to sell the property. According to the evidence of Mrs. Burgess this document never in fact reached Dodds, she having forgotten to give it to him.

On the following (Friday) morning, at about seven o'clock, Berry, who was acting as agent for Dickinson, found Dodds at the Darlington railway station, and handed to him a duplicate of the acceptance by Dickinson, and explained to Dodds its purport. He replied that it was too late, as he had sold the property. A few minutes later Dickinson himself found Dodds entering a railway carriage, and handed him another duplicate of the notice of acceptance, but Dodds declined to receive it, saying: "You are too late. I have sold the property."

It appeared that on the day before, Thursday, the 11th of June, Dodds had signed a formal contract for the sale of the property to the defendant Allan for £800, and had received from him a deposit of £40.

The bill in this suit prayed that the defendant Dodds might be decreed specifically to perform the contract of the 10th of June, 1874; that he might be restrained from conveying the property to Allan; that Allan might be restrained from taking any such conveyance; that, if any such conveyance had been or should be made, Allan might be declared a trustee of the property for, and might be directed to convey the property to, the plaintiff; and for damages.

The cause came on for hearing before Vice Chancellor Bacon on the 25th of January, 1876. [It was his opinion that Dodds could withdraw only by giving notice to Dickinson, in spite of Cooke v. Oxley, 3 T.R. 653, and that the contract took effect by the doctrine of relation back as of the time of the offer and hence was prior to the sale to Allan. He therefore decreed specific performance in favor of the plaintiff. From the decision both of the defendants appealed.]

JAMES, L.J., after referring to the document of the 10th of June, 1874, continued:

The document, though beginning "I hereby agree to sell," was nothing but an offer, and was only intended to be an offer, for the plaintiff himself tells us that he required time to consider whether he would enter into an agreement or not. Unless both parties had then agreed, there was no concluded agreement then made; it was in effect and substance only an offer to sell. The plaintiff, being minded not to complete the bargain at that time, added this memorandum: "This offer to be left over until Friday, 9 o'clock a.m. 12th June, 1874." That shows it was only an offer. There was no consideration given for the undertaking or promise, to whatever extent it may be considered binding, to keep the property unsold until 9 o'clock on Friday morning; but apparently Dickinson was of opinion, and probably Dodds was of the same opinion, that he (Dodds) was bound by that promise, and could not in any way withdraw from it, or retract it, until 9 o'clock on Friday morning, and this probably explains a good deal of what afterwards took place. But it is clear settled law, on one of the clearest principles of law, that this promise, being a mere nudum pactum, was not binding, and that at any moment before a complete acceptance by Dickinson of the offer, Dodds was as free as Dickinson himself.

Well, that being the state of things, it is said that the only mode in which Dodds could assert that freedom was by actually and distinctly saying to Dickinson, "Now I withdraw my offer." It appears to me that there is neither principle nor authority for the proposition that there must be an express and actual withdrawal of the offer, or what is called a retraction. It must, to constitute a contract, appear that the two minds were at one, at the same moment of time, that is, that there was an offer continuing up to the time of the acceptance. If there was not such a continuing offer, then the acceptance comes to nothing. Of course it may well be that the one man is bound in some way or other to let the other man know that his mind with regard to the offer has been changed; but in this case, beyond all question, the plaintiff knew that Dodds was no longer minded to sell the property to him as plainly and clearly as if Dodds had told him in so many words, "I withdraw the offer." This is evident from the plaintiff's own statements in the bill.

The plaintiff says in effect that, having heard and knowing that Dodds was no longer minded to sell to him and that he was selling or had sold to some one else, thinking that he could not in point of law withdraw his offer, meaning to fix him to it, and endeavoring to bind him: "I went to the house where he was lodging, and saw his mother-in-law, and left with her an acceptance of the offer, knowing all the while that he had entirely changed his mind. I got an agent to watch for him at 7 o'clock the next morning, and I went to the train just before 9 o'clock, in order that I might catch him and give him my notice of acceptance just before 9 o'clock, and when that occurred he told my agent, and he told me, 'You are too late,' and he then threw back the paper." It is to my mind quite clear that before there was any attempt at acceptance by the plaintiff, he was perfectly well aware that Dodds had changed his mind, and that he had in fact agreed to sell the property to Allan. It is impossible, therefore, to say there was ever that existence of the same mind between the two parties which is essential in point of law to the making of an agreement. I am of opinion, therefore, that the plaintiff has failed to prove that there was any binding contract between Dodds and himself. . . .

[The bill] will be dismissed with costs.

[The concurring opinion of Mellish, L.J., is omitted.]

RESTATEMENT, SECOND, CONTRACTS §§ 42, 43

[See Selected Source Materials Supplement]

CISG ART. 16

[See Selected Source Materials Supplement]

––––––––––

UNIDROIT PRINCIPLES OF INTERNATIONAL COMMERCIAL CONTRACTS ART. 2.1.4

[See Selected Source Materials Supplement]

––––––––––

PRINCIPLES OF EUROPEAN CONTRACT LAW ART. 2.202

[See Selected Source Materials Supplement]

––––––––––

NOTE ON CONTRACT PRACTICE

In 1988, Professor Russell Weintraub sent a questionnaire to the general counsels of 182 corporations of various sizes, asking for their company's views on certain contracts issues. Weintraub, A Survey of Contract Practice and Policy, 1992 Wisc.L.Rev. 1. Several questions in the survey concerned firm offers. The results were as follows: 76% of the respondents reported that their companies received firm offers. Of these, 95% reported that they relied on the firm offers they received. Correspondingly, 73% percent of the respondents reported that their companies made firm offers to other companies. Of these, 97% reported that they expected offerees to rely on their firm offers.

––––––––––

NOTE ON WHAT CONSTITUTES RECEIPT OF A WRITTEN ACCEPTANCE

What was the legal effect of leaving a written acceptance with Dodds's mother-in-law, assuming Dickinson still had power to accept? Restatement, Second, Contracts § 68 provides that "A written revocation, rejection, or acceptance is received when the writing comes into the possession of the person addressed, or of some person authorized by him to receive it for him, or when it is deposited in some place which he has authorized as the place for this or similar communications to be deposited for him." Illustration 1 to § 68 is as follows:

A sends B by mail an offer dated from A's house and states as a condition of the offer that an acceptance must be received within three days. B mails an acceptance which reaches A's house and is delivered to a servant or is deposited in a mail box at the door within three days; but A has been called away from home and does not personally receive the letter for a week. There is a contract.

Under UCC § 1–201(27), "a notice or notification received by an organization is effective for a particular transaction from the time when it is brought to the attention of the individual conducting that transaction, and in any event from the time when it would have been brought to his attention if the organization had exercised due diligence. . . . "

See also Note on Electronic Commerce, Chapter 10, infra.

RESTATEMENT, SECOND, CONTRACTS § 87(1)

[See Selected Source Materials Supplement]

1464-EIGHT, LTD. & MILLIS MANAGEMENT CORP. V. JOPPICH

Supreme Court of Texas, 2004.
154 S.W.3d 101.

COLEMAN, J. The question presented is whether section 87(1)(a) of the Restatement (Second) of Contracts should be incorporated into the common law of Texas. *See* 3 Williston & Lord, A Treatise on the Law of Contracts § 7:23 (4th ed. 1992) ("As far as option contracts are concerned, the Restatement (Second) has taken the position, adopted by some common law courts, that a false recital of nominal consideration is sufficient to support the irrevocability of an offer so long as the underlying exchange is fair and the offer is to be accepted within a reasonable time.").

The petitioners, citing section 87(1)(a) of the Restatement (Second) of Contracts, assert that the respondent's offer to sell real property should be binding as an option contract because the offer was in writing and signed by the respondent, acknowledged the receipt of a nominal consideration of ten dollars, and proposed an exchange on fair terms within a reasonable time. The respondent, contending that the parties' written option agreement is unenforceable, asserts that the agreement lacks consideration because the recited nominal consideration was never actually paid, and that the offer was revoked before it was properly accepted.

In this case of first impression, we agree with the petitioners that the nonpayment of the recited nominal consideration does not preclude enforcement of the parties' written option agreement. Therefore, we will reverse and remand.

I

In July 1997, Gail Ann Joppich entered into an earnest money contract with 1464-Eight, Ltd. and Millis Management Corporation (collectively "Millis") under which Joppich agreed to buy, and Millis agreed to convey, an undeveloped residential lot located in a subdivision being developed by Millis. The purchase price was $65,000. An addendum attached to the earnest money contract provided:

> All Lots being sold in Shiloh Lake Estates Subdivision are being sold pursuant to an Option Agreement to be executed by Buyer and Seller at closing that shall survive closing and provide Seller with an option to purchase the Property from the Buyer at a price equal to 90% of the sale price herein if Buyer fails to commence construction of a private residence on the Property within 18 months from the date of closing.

At the closing later the same month, Millis executed a special warranty deed conveying the lot to Joppich. In addition, the parties executed a separate four-page document entitled "Option Agreement." The notarized document, which was signed by both Joppich and Millis, provided:

> 1. *Grant of Option.* In consideration of the sum of Ten and No/100 ($10.00) Dollars ("Option Fee") paid in cash by Developer, the receipt and sufficiency of which is hereby acknowledged and confessed, Purchaser hereby grants to Developer the exclusive right and option to purchase [the Property]. This Option may be exercised at any time from and after January 21, 1999.

> 2. *Purchase Price.* The total purchase price for the Property shall be [$58,500] and shall be due and payable at closing.

> 3. *Expiration Date.* This Option shall automatically expire at 5:00 o'clock p.m. on the date which is five (5) years after the date of execution and recording in the Office of the County Clerk of Fort Bend County, Texas unless prior to the expiration date this Option is exercised by Developer.

> 4. *Termination.* This Option shall automatically terminate on the date that Purchaser, or Purchaser's assigns, commence construction of a primary residence which has been approved by [the appropriate committee].

The Option Agreement did not contain an express statement regarding whether the parties intended the offer to sell real property to be revocable or irrevocable.

In October 1999, Joppich filed suit against Millis, seeking a declaratory judgment that the Option Agreement was unenforceable. In her original petition, Joppich asserted that "[a]lthough the Option

Agreement states that a sum of Ten and No/100 dollars was given to Plaintiff in consideration for granting the option, this sum was not then nor has it ever been tendered to nor paid to Plaintiff," and she requested that "the Court declare that the Agreement granting the exclusive right and option to purchase [the Property] to the Developer is void and unenforceable for lack of consideration or alternatively, failure of consideration." Millis answered with a general denial.

In September 2000, Millis filed a counterclaim seeking specific performance, damages, and attorney's fees, asserting:

> Counter Defendant failed to begin construction of a primary residence on the property, therefore, Counter Plaintiffs sent notice of their exercising of the option to Counter Defendant on September 4, 1999. . . Counter Defendant refused and continues to refuse to convey the property pursuant to the terms of the option.

Joppich answered with a general denial. In addition, . . . the answer . . . set forth the affirmative defenses of lack of consideration and failure of consideration.

In January 2001, Joppich moved for final summary judgment . . . from Defendants to Plaintiff and she revoked the Option Agreement before consideration had in fact passed, the Option Agreement is void and unenforceable." In her affidavit, which was attached to the motion, Joppich stated: "The Option Agreement states that a sum of Ten and No/100 dollars was given to me in consideration for granting Defendants the right to repurchase the property under certain conditions. This sum was not then nor has it ever been tendered to or paid to me."

Millis responded to Joppich's motion and, in the same document, moved for partial summary judgment. . .

In February 2001, the trial court denied Joppich's motion for final summary judgment and granted Millis's motion for partial summary judgment. In May 2001, the trial court rendered a final judgment declaring that the Option Agreement was enforceable, requiring Joppich to sell the property in compliance with the terms of the Option Agreement, and awarding attorney's fees to Millis.

In the court of appeals, both sides characterized the consideration recited in the Option Agreement as "nominal." . . .

In December 2002, the court of appeals reversed and remanded, concluding that "summary judgment for [Millis] was improper." 96 S.W.3d 614, 617. Because it sustained her first issue, the court of appeals did not address Joppich's other issues.

In this Court, Millis asserts that "[t]he court of appeals' holding that failure to deliver the nominal consideration recited in an option contract precludes its enforcement directly conflicts with the modern view reflected in the Restatement (Second) of Contracts." In response, Joppich argues that "[t]he Restatement shows that its view is not the modern view but is in fact the minority view consisting of one and possibly two states." Joppich does not dispute Millis's contention, made in both its petition for review and its brief on the merits, that the Option Agreement satisfies section 87(1)(a) of the Restatement (Second) of Contracts, including its requirement that an offer propose an exchange on fair terms within a reasonable time.

II

"[A] promise to give an option is valid if supported by an independent consideration. For example, if a sum of money be paid for the option, the promisee may, at his election, enforce the contract." *Nat'l Oil & Pipe Line Co. v. Teel,* 95 Tex. 586, 68 S.W. 979, 980 (1902); *see also* Restatement (Second) of Contracts § 25 (1981) ("An option contract is a promise which meets the requirements for the formation of a contract and limits the promisor's power to revoke an offer."). . .

Section 87(1) of the Restatement (Second) of Contracts provides:

(1) An offer is binding as an option contract if it

(a) is in writing and signed by the offeror, recites a purported consideration for the making of the offer, and proposes an exchange on fair terms within a reasonable time; or

(b) is made irrevocable by statute.

Restatement (Second) of Contracts § 87(1) (1981).

The official comment to section 87 states:

b. Nominal consideration. Offers made in consideration of one dollar paid or promised are often irrevocable under Subsection (1)(a). . .

[A] nominal consideration is regularly held sufficient to support a short-time option proposing an exchange on fair terms. The fact that the option is an appropriate preliminary step in the conclusion of a socially useful transaction provides a sufficient substantive basis for enforcement, and a signed writing taking a form appropriate to a bargain satisfies the desiderata of form. In the absence of statute, however, the bargaining form is essential: a payment of one dollar by each party to the other is so obviously not a bargaining transaction that it does not provide even the form of an exchange.

    c. False recital of nominal consideration. A recital in a written agreement that a stated consideration has been given is evidence of that fact as against a party to the agreement, but such a recital may ordinarily be contradicted by evidence that no such consideration was given or expected. See § 218. In cases within Subsection (1)(a), however, the giving and recital of nominal consideration performs a formal function only. The signed writing has vital significance as a formality, while the ceremonial manual delivery of a dollar or a peppercorn is an inconsequential formality. In view of the dangers of permitting a solemn written agreement to be invalidated by oral testimony which is easily fabricated, therefore, the option agreement is not invalidated by proof that the recited consideration was not in fact given. A fictitious rationalization has sometimes been used for this rule: acceptance of delivery of the written instrument conclusively imports a promise to make good the recital, it is said, and that promise furnishes consideration. Compare § 218. But the sound basis for the rule is that stated above.

Id. § 87 cmts. b-c (illustrations omitted).

The illustration following comment c states:

    3. A executes and delivers to B a written agreement "in consideration of one dollar in hand paid" giving B an option to buy described land belonging to A for $15,000, the option to expire at noon six days later. The fact that the dollar is not in fact paid does not prevent the offer from being irrevocable.

Id. § 87 cmt. c, illus. 3.

The authors of the national treatises on contracts have generally endorsed section 87(1)(a) of the Restatement (Second) of Contracts. For example, *Corbin on Contracts* states:

    [Restatement (Second)] has synthesized [cases upholding nominal consideration for options] into a new doctrine, categorizing . . . option contracts—where the formal requisites are met—as enforceable contracts without consideration. The reason for giving special treatment to options and guaranties is their presumptive utility as ancillaries to bargain transactions. . .

    Consideration is designed primarily to protect promisors from their own donative promises. Options, however, are one commercial step in a commercial deal. A number of cases have followed the forthright approach taken by the Restatement (Second). Indeed, it may be urged that the Restatement fails to lead the way to more progressive reform. Having recognized the value of the enforceability of options as commercial devices, it still insists on the fictional recital of a purported consideration. Such fictional charades should not be a part of a mature legal system. Commercial promises such as options and credit guaranties should be enforceable without consideration.

2 Perillo & Bender, Corbin on Contracts § 5.17 (rev. ed.1995). . .

In addition, the authors of law review commentary have agreed that the nonpayment of a recited nominal consideration should not preclude enforcement of a written option agreement. . .

III

The position taken by section 87(1)(a) of the Restatement (Second) of Contracts is admittedly the minority position among the limited number of state supreme courts that have addressed the question. *See, e.g., Lewis v. Fletcher,* 101 Idaho 530, 617 P.2d 834, 835 (1980) (holding that a written option agreement that contains a fictional recital of a nominal consideration is unenforceable for lack of consideration) . . . Nevertheless, we are persuaded that the position of the Restatement (Second) of Contracts, which is supported by a well-articulated and sound rationale, represents the better approach. *See, e.g.,* Restatement (Second) of Contracts § 87 cmt. b (1981) ("The fact that the option is an appropriate preliminary step in the conclusion of a socially useful transaction provides a sufficient substantive basis for enforcement, and a signed writing taking a form appropriate to a bargain satisfies the desiderata of form."); Gordon, *Consideration and the Commercial-Gift Dichotomy,* 44 Vand. L.Rev. 283, 293–94 (1991) ("Option contracts are related to economic exchanges— transactions based on self-interest, not altruism. Moreover, people expect that option contracts are serious and binding commitments.") (footnote omitted).

IV

Based on the foregoing analysis, we reverse the court of appeals's judgment and remand the case to the court of appeals for further proceedings.

[The concurring opinion of Chief Justice Jefferson and Justice Brister are omitted.]

———

UCC § 2–205

[See Selected Source Materials Supplement]

———

Dodge, Teaching the CISG in Contracts

50 J. Leg. Ed. 72 (2000)

"Under the common law, an offer is freely revocable, even if the offeror has promised to hold it open, unless that promise is supported by consideration or reliance. The UCC, of course, changes this rule, allowing a merchant to make an irrevocable offer—a "firm offer"—without the need for consideration. But the UCC's firm-offer rule contains a number of restrictions: the offeror must be a merchant; the offer must be in a signed writing; the offer must contain an "assurance that it will be held open"; and the period of irrevocability may not exceed three months.

"CISG Article 16 allows an offeror to make a firm offer without these limitations:

(1)   Until a contract is concluded an offer may be revoked if the revocation reaches the offeree before he has dispatched an acceptance.

(2)   However, an offer cannot be revoked:

(a)   if it indicates, whether by stating a fixed time for acceptance or otherwise, that it is irrevocable; or

(b)   if it was reasonable for the offeree to rely on the offer as being irrevocable and the offeree has acted in reliance on the offer.

"As one can see, Article 16 does not require that the offeror be a merchant or that the offer be in a signed writing, and there is no limit on the period of irrevocability. Article 16 does not even require an express assurance that the offer will be held open. It requires only that the offer 'indicate that it is irrevocable' and it makes clear that an offer may do this 'by stating a fixed time for acceptance.' If an offer simply stated that it would expire after thirty days, the UCC would not treat the offer as 'firm' and would allow the offeror to revoke before the thirty days were up. The CISG, on the other hand, would treat the offer as being irrevocable during the thirty-day period. Article 16(2)(b), like Restatement (Second) § 87(2), provides for an offer to become irrevocable because of the offeree's reliance.

"Article 16 reflects a compromise between the civil law tradition, which presumes that offers are irrevocable, and the common law tradition, which presumes the opposite. Article 16(1) provides that offers are revocable, as under the common law, but Article 16(2) creates broad exceptions that will lead many offers to be irrevocable in practice."

———

RESTATEMENT, SECOND, CONTRACTS § 45

[See Selected Source Materials Supplement]

RAGOSTA V. WILDER

Supreme Court of Vermont, 1991.
156 Vt. 390, 592 A.2d 367.

Before ALLEN, C.J., and PECK, GIBSON, DOOLEY and MORSE, JJ.

PECK, JUSTICE.

Defendant appeals from a judgment ordering him to convey to plaintiffs a piece of real property known as "The Fork Shop." Defendant argues that the court improperly found that a binding contract existed and that it misapplied the doctrine of equitable estoppel. He also contends that the ruling cannot be upheld under promissory estoppel principles since the court failed to examine the extent to which enforcement of defendant's promise to sell was required to prevent injustice. Because the trial court's ruling cannot stand on contract or equitable estoppel grounds and because the court's analysis of promissory estoppel is inextricably bound in its contractual analysis, we reverse and remand the cause for further proceedings consistent with the principles expressed herein.

In 1985, plaintiffs became interested in purchasing "The Fork Shop" from defendant, but preliminary negotiations between the parties were fruitless. In 1987, plaintiffs learned that defendant was again considering selling "The Fork Shop," [and] mailed him a letter offering to purchase the property along with a check for $2,000 and began arrangements to obtain the necessary financing. By letter dated September 28, 1987, defendant returned the $2,000 check explaining that he had two properties "up for sale" and that he would not sign an acceptance to plaintiffs' offer because "that would tie up both these properties until [there was] a closing." In the letter, he also made the following counter-offer:

> I will sell you The Fork Shop and its property as listed in book 35, at page 135 of the Brookfield Land Records on 17 April 1972, for $88,000.00—(Eighty-eight thousand dollars), at anytime up until the 1st of November 1987 that you appear with me at the Randolph National Bank with said sum. At which time they will give you a certified deed to this property or to your agent as directed, providing said property has not been sold.

On October 1st, the date plaintiffs received the letter, they called defendant. The court found that during the conversation plaintiffs told defendant that "the terms and conditions of his offer were acceptable and that they would in fact prepare to accept the offer." Defendant assured plaintiffs that there was no one else currently interested in purchasing "The Fork Shop."

On October 6th, plaintiffs informed defendant that they would not close the sale on October 8th as discussed previously but that they would come to Vermont on October 10th. On October 8th, defendant called plaintiffs and informed them that he was no longer willing to sell "The Fork Shop." The trial court found that, at that time, defendant was aware plaintiffs "had processed their loan application and were prepared to close." Plaintiffs informed defendant that they would be at the Randolph National Bank at 10:00 a.m. on October 15th with the $88,000 purchase price and in fact appeared. Defendant did not. Plaintiffs claim they incurred $7,499.23 in loan closing costs.

Plaintiffs sued for specific performance arguing that defendant had contracted to sell the property to them. They alleged moreover that defendant knew they would have to incur costs to obtain financing for the purchase but assured them that the sale would go through and that they relied on his assurances.

The trial court concluded that defendant "made an offer in writing which could only be accepted by performance prior to the deadline." It concluded further that defendant could not revoke his offer on October 8th because plaintiffs, relying on the offer, had already begun performance and that defendant should be estopped from revoking the offer on a theory of equitable estoppel. It ordered defendant to convey to plaintiffs "The Fork Shop" for $88,000. This appeal followed.

I.

Plaintiffs claim that defendant's letter of September 28, 1987 created a contract to sell "The Fork Shop" to them unless the property was sold to another buyer. Rather, defendant's letter contains an offer to sell the property for $88,000, which the trial court found could only be accepted "by performance prior to the deadline," and a promise to keep the offer open unless the property were sold to another buyer. Defendant received no consideration for either promise. In fact, defendant returned plaintiffs' check for $2,000 which would have constituted consideration for the promise to keep the offer open, presumably because he did not wish to make a firm offer. Thus, the promise to keep the offer to sell open was not enforceable and, absent the operation of equitable estoppel, defendant could revoke the offer to sell the property at any time before plaintiffs accepted it. See *Buchannon v. Billings,* 127 Vt. 69, 75, 238 A.2d 638, 642 (1968) ("An option is a continuing offer, and *if supported by a consideration,* it cannot be withdrawn before the time limit.") (emphasis added).

Plaintiffs argue that the actions they undertook to obtain financing, which were detrimental to them, could constitute consideration for the promise to keep the offer to sell open. Their argument is unconvincing. Although plaintiffs are correct in stating that a detriment may constitute consideration, they ignore the rule that "[t]o constitute consideration, a performance or a return promise must be bargained for." Restatement (Second) of Contracts § 71(1) (1981). "A performance or return promise is bargained for if it is sought by the promisor in exchange for his promise and is given by the promisee in exchange for that promise." *Id.* at § 71(2). Plaintiffs began to seek financing even before defendant made a definite offer to sell the property. Whatever detriment they suffered was not in exchange for defendant's promise to keep the offer to sell open.

The trial court ruled that the offer to sell "The Fork Shop" could only be accepted by performance but concluded that in obtaining financing plaintiffs began performance and that therefore defendant could not revoke the offer to sell once plaintiffs incurred the cost of obtaining financing. Section 45 of the Restatement (Second) of Contracts provides that "[w]here an offer invites an offeree to accept by rendering a performance and does not invite a promissory acceptance, an option contract is created when the offeree tenders or begins the invited performance or tenders a beginning of it." However, "[w]hat is begun or tendered must be part of the actual performance invited in order to preclude revocation under this Section." *Id.* at comment f.

Here, plaintiffs were merely engaged in preparation for performance. The court itself found only that "plaintiffs had changed their position in order to tender performance." At most, they obtained financing and assured defendant that they would pay; plaintiffs never tendered to defendant or even began to tender the $88,000 purchase price. Thus, they never accepted defendant's offer and no contract was ever created. See *Multicare Medical Center v. State Social & Health Services,* 114 Wash.2d 572, 584, 790 P.2d 124, 131 (1990) ("under a unilateral contract, an offer cannot be accepted by promising to perform; rather, the offeree must accept, if at all, by performance, and the contract then becomes executed").*

II.

Defendant claims next that the court was not justified in applying equitable estoppel in this case. We agree.

One who invokes the doctrine of equitable estoppel has the burden of establishing each of its constituent elements. Four essential elements must be established: first, the party to be estopped must know the facts; second, the party being estopped must intend that his conduct shall be acted upon or the acts must be such that the party asserting the estoppel has a right to believe it is so intended; third, the latter must be ignorant of the true

---

* Because defendant specified that the manner of acceptance would be performance, plaintiffs' argument that they accepted defendant's offer over the telephone must fail. In fact, plaintiffs admitted in their depositions that they were very worried that the property would be sold to someone else prior to closing. Thus, they should have understood that they had no enforceable contract until closing.

facts; and finally, the party asserting the estoppel must rely on the conduct of the party to be estopped to his detriment.

Fisher v. Poole, 142 Vt. 162, 168, 453 A.2d 408, 411–12 (1982) (citations omitted).

Equitable estoppel is inapplicable here because there were no facts known to defendant but unknown to plaintiffs. Plaintiffs cannot have acted on an understanding that defendant would definitely convey the property to them. On its face, defendant's offer stated only that he would convey the property to plaintiffs if he did not convey it to another party first. The trial court acknowledged that if defendant had sold "The Fork Shop" to another party plaintiffs would not have been entitled to relief. Thus, plaintiffs had no assurance that defendant would definitely convey the property to them even if on October 1st defendant told them that there was no one else interested in buying the property at that time. Moreover, plaintiffs engaged in obtaining financing for the purchase even before defendant made any offer to them whatsoever. They understood, at the time they obtained financing for the transaction, that they were assuming a risk that they would be unable to purchase the property in question. Since the plaintiffs had not tendered performance and did not establish the elements for the application of equitable estoppel, defendant was entitled to withdraw his offer when he did.

III.

In the course of analyzing the case under part performance and equitable estoppel theories, the trial court cited promissory estoppel principles. It noted, "Plaintiffs relied on the conduct of the Defendant to their detriment when they prepared for and tendered performance" and concluded that defendant's conduct induced plaintiffs to begin performance by obtaining financing.

A promise which the promisor should reasonably expect to induce action or forbearance on the part of the promisee or a third person and which does induce such action or forbearance is binding if injustice can be avoided only by enforcement of the promise. The remedy granted for breach may be limited as justice requires.

Restatement (Second) of Contracts § 90(1). This principle is distinct from part performance since the action or forbearance involved need not constitute part performance. While the court's order cannot be upheld under a part performance theory, its ruling may be appropriate on promissory estoppel grounds. We cannot affirm the order on those grounds, however, because the trial court, in ruling that the promise must be enforced, erroneously relied on a part performance theory. Cf. *Price v. Price,* 149 Vt. 118, 122, 541 A.2d 79, 82 (1987) (order must be reversed and remanded where court may have relied on inappropriate considerations for its ruling). Under promissory estoppel, plaintiffs are entitled to enforcement of defendant's promise only if the promise induced them to take action "of a definite and substantial character," and if "injustice [*can*] *be avoided only* by enforcement of the promise." *Stacy v. Merchants Bank*, 144 Vt. 515, 521, 482 A.2d 61, 64 (1984) (emphasis added) (citing Restatement (Second) of Contracts § 90).

On remand the court shall consider the case under promissory estoppel only and determine what remedy, if any, is necessary to prevent injustice. In making this determination the court should consider the fact that plaintiffs incurred the expense of obtaining financing although they could not be certain that the property would be sold to them. . . .

Reversed and the cause remanded for further proceedings consistent with the principles expressed herein.

NOTE ON OFFERS FOR UNILATERAL CONTRACTS

The court in *Ragosta* drew a sharp distinction between *preparing* to perform an act pursuant to an offer for a unilateral contract and *beginning* to perform the act. To understand why the court drew this distinction, it is necessary to briefly trace the doctrinal history concerning an offer for a unilateral contract—that is, an offer for a contract to be formed by the exchange of a promise (in the form of an offer) and an act, rather than an offer for a contract to be formed by an exchange of promises.

It was a rule of classical contract law that an offer for a unilateral contract could be revoked at any time before the designated act had been completed, even if performance of the act had begun. This rule was exemplified in a pair of famous hypotheticals. In one, A says to B, "I will give you $100 if you walk across the Brooklyn Bridge." After B has walked halfway across the bridge, A overtakes B and revokes. In the other, A offers B $50 to climb a flagpole. After B has climbed halfway up the flagpole, A calls out to B and revokes. The result under classical contract law was the same in both hypotheticals: the revocation was effective, on the ground that an offer for a unilateral contract is revocable until performance of the act has been completed even if performance had begun. Too bad for B.

The unilateral-contract rule defeated the reasonable expectations of offerees. Tiersma has put this point very well:

> [N]o reasonable person would intentionally create the sort of agreement that the traditional theory of unilateral contracts assumes. Suppose that a person, asserting his freedom to contract and his mastery over his offer, specifically intends to make a promise that will bind him not at the time he makes it, but only after the other party has completed a particular act in exchange. In other words, this promisor wishes to create the traditional unilateral contract. For

example, he might tell the offeree that if she paints his house, he will—once she is finished—commit himself to paying her $1000. He makes it clear that he does not wish to be bound until she is completely finished, explaining to her that before she is finished he may revoke with impunity. What rational person would even buy the paint if she believed the speaker had not committed himself? The fact of the matter . . . is that very reasonable people spend substantial time and money doing the sorts of things that unilateral contracts attempt to induce them to do. The only rational explanation for such behavior is that people believe the speaker is in fact committed then and there to paying the price if the conditions of the offer are met.

Peter Meijes Tiersma, Reassessing Unilateral Contracts: The Role of Offer, Acceptance and Promise, 26 U.C. Davis L. Rev. 1, 29 (1992).

Furthermore, the unilateral-contract rule was against the interests of offerors as a class. An actor makes an offer for a unilateral contract because she thinks her interests are best served by such an offer. It is in the interests of an actor who makes an offer for a unilateral contract that the offeree act under the offer—otherwise, the offer would not be made—and correspondingly that the offeree begin acting as quickly as reasonably possible. If, however, offers for unilateral contracts were revocable before performance was completed, offerees would not act under such offers, or at least would act at a much lower rate, because of the substantial risks of forfeiture that such action would entail if the offeror revokes before the act has been completed.

The framers of Restatement First—in particular, Williston, as the Reporter—understood that the unilateral-contract rule was unsatisfactory. However, Williston had to square this with the requirement of bargained-for consideration. The result was Section 45 of the First Restatement, which provided:

> If an offer for a unilateral contract is made, and part of the consideration requested in the offer is given or tendered by the offeree in response thereto, the offeror is bound by a contract, the duty of immediate performance of which is conditional on the full consideration being given or tendered within the time stated in the offer, or, if no time is stated therein, within a reasonable time.

Section 45 was conceptualized as bargain-based, not reliance based. If it had been conceptualized as reliance-based, then the problem could have been solved with Section 90. But this would have made enforcement discretionary. Instead, the beginning of performance was—and under Restatement Second still is—conceptualized as completing an option contract, enforceable by expectation damages. The theory is as follows: an offer for a unilateral contract carries with it an implied promise that if part of the requested performance is given or tendered, the offeror will not revoke the offer. Rendering (or tendering) part performance completes a bargain for that promise. This makes the promise enforceable as an option under the bargain theory of consideration.

In order to maintain this conceptualization, the text and comment of Section 45, as formulated in both the First and Second Restatements, drew a sharp distinction between beginning to perform and preparing to perform. Under Section 45 of Restatement First, beginning to perform completed a bargain and therefore made the offeror's promise to hold the offer open enforceable. In contrast, action by the offeree other than beginning to perform had no effect under Section 45, because it would not complete a Section 45 bargain—although the Comment to Restatement First added that such action could have an effect under Section 90, which is not bargain based:

> The main offer [for a unilateral contract] includes as a subsidiary promise, necessarily implied, that if part of the requested performance is given, the offeror will not revoke his offer. . . . Part performance . . . may thus furnish consideration for the subsidiary [promise]. Moreover, merely acting in justifiable reliance on an offer may in some cases serve as sufficient reason for making a promise binding (see § 90).

Section 45 of Restatement Second carries forward the approach of Restatement First.

The distinction between beginning to perform and preparing to perform is not easy to justify. For example, suppose A offers B $10,000 to B if B produces a solution to a famous mathematical problem. B begins by developing some new techniques that will be needed to solve the problem, but will also have independent significance. Has B prepared to perform or has he begun to perform? And why should it matter? As James Gordley observes, under the preparation-versus-performance distinction, if the offeree takes one step on the Brooklyn Bridge the offeror is bound, but if the offeree engages in massive preparations to get ready to cross the Bridge, the offeror is not bound. James Gordley, Enforcing Promises, 82 Cal. L. Rev. 547, 605 (1995).

DRENNAN v. STAR PAVING CO.

Supreme Court of California, 1958.
51 Cal.2d 409, 333 P.2d 757.

TRAYNOR, JUSTICE. Defendant appeals from a judgment for plaintiff in an action to recover damages caused by defendant's refusal to perform certain paving work according to a bid it submitted to plaintiff.

On July 28, 1955, plaintiff, a licensed general contractor, was preparing a bid on the "Monte Vista School Job" in the Lancaster school district. Bids had to be submitted before 8:00 p.m. Plaintiff testified that it was customary in that area for general contractors to receive the bids of subcontractors by telephone on the day set for bidding and to rely on them in computing their own bids. Thus on that day plaintiff's secretary, Mrs. Johnson, received by telephone between fifty and seventy-five subcontractors' bids for various parts of the school job. As each bid came in, she wrote it on a special form, which she brought into plaintiff's office. He then posted it on a master cost sheet setting forth the names and bids of all subcontractors. His own bid had to include the names of subcontractors who were to perform one-half of one per cent or more of the construction work, and he had also to provide a bidder's bond of ten per cent of his total bid of $317,385 as a guarantee that he would enter the contract if awarded the work.*

Late in the afternoon, Mrs. Johnson had a telephone conversation with Kenneth R. Hoon, an estimater for defendant. He gave his name and telephone number and stated that he was bidding for defendant for the paving work at the Monte Vista School according to plans and specifications and that his bid was $7,131.60. At Mrs. Johnson's request he repeated his bid. Plaintiff listened to the bid over an extension telephone in his office and posted it on the master sheet after receiving the bid form from Mrs. Johnson. Defendant's was the lowest bid for the paving. Plaintiff computed his own bid accordingly and submitted it with the name of defendant as the subcontractor for the paving. When the bids were opened on July 28th, plaintiff's proved to be the lowest, and he was awarded the contract.

On his way to Los Angeles the next morning plaintiff stopped at defendant's office. The first person he met was defendant's construction engineer, Mr. Oppenheimer. Plaintiff testified: "I introduced myself and he immediately told me that they had made a mistake in their bid to me the night before, they couldn't do it for the price they had bid, and I told him I would expect him to carry through with their original bid because I had used it in compiling my bid and the job was being awarded them. And I would have to go and do the job according to my bid and I would expect them to do the same."

Defendant refused to do the paving work for less than $15,000. Plaintiff testified that he "got figures from other people" and after trying for several months to get as low a bid as possible engaged L & H Paving Company, a firm in Lancaster, to do the work for $10,948.60.

The trial court found on substantial evidence that defendant made a definite offer to do the paving on the Monte Vista job according to the plans and specifications for $7,131.60, and that plaintiff relied on defendant's bid in computing his own bid for the school job and naming defendant therein as the subcontractor for the paving work. Accordingly, it entered judgment

---

* Under a "bidder's" or "bid" bond, a Surety promises the person who is receiving bids (the "Obligee"), that if the bidder is awarded the contract but refuses to enter into it, the Surety will pay damages up to a stipulated amount (called "the penalty") that is set in the bond. (Footnote by ed.)

for plaintiff in the amount of $3,817.00 (the difference between defendant's bid and the cost of the paving to plaintiff) plus costs.

Defendant contends that there was no enforceable contract between the parties on the ground that it made a revocable offer and revoked it before plaintiff communicated his acceptance to defendant.

There is no evidence that defendant offered to make its bid irrevocable in exchange for plaintiff's use of its figures in computing his bid. Nor is there evidence that would warrant interpreting plaintiff's use of defendant's bid as the acceptance thereof, binding plaintiff, on condition he received the main contract, to award the subcontract to defendant. In sum, there was neither an option supported by consideration nor a bilateral contract binding on both parties.

Plaintiff contends, however, that he relied to his detriment on defendant's offer and that defendant must therefore answer in damages for its refusal to perform. Thus the question is squarely presented: Did plaintiff's reliance make defendant's offer irrevocable?

Section 90 of the Restatement of Contracts states: "A promise which the promisor should reasonably expect to induce action or forbearance of a definite and substantial character on the part of the promisee and which does induce such action or forbearance is binding if injustice can be avoided only by enforcement of the promise." This rule applies in this state. . . .

Defendant's offer constituted a promise to perform on such conditions as were stated expressly or by implication therein or annexed thereto by operation of law. (See 1 Williston, Contracts [3rd ed.], § 24A, p. 56, § 61, p. 196.) Defendant had reason to expect that if its bid proved the lowest it would be used by plaintiff. It induced "action . . . of a definite and substantial character on the part of the promisee."

Had defendant's bid expressly stated or clearly implied that it was revocable at any time before acceptance we would treat it accordingly. It was silent on revocation, however, and we must therefore determine whether there are conditions to the right of revocation imposed by law or reasonably inferable in fact. In the analogous problem of an offer for a unilateral contract, the theory is now obsolete that the offer is revocable at any time before complete performance. Thus section 45 of the Restatement of Contracts provides: "If an offer for a unilateral contract is made, and part of the consideration requested in the offer is given or tendered by the offeree in response thereto, the offeror is bound by a contract, the duty of immediate performance of which is conditional on the full consideration being given or tendered within the time stated in the offer, or, if no time is stated therein, within a reasonable time." In explanation, comment *b* states that the "main offer includes as a subsidiary promise, necessarily implied, that if part of the requested performance is given, the offeror will not revoke his offer, and that if tender is made it will be accepted. Part performance or tender may thus furnish consideration for the subsidiary promise. Moreover, merely acting in justifiable reliance on an offer may in some cases serve as sufficient reason for making a promise binding (see § 90)."

Whether implied in fact or law, the subsidiary promise serves to preclude the injustice that would result if the offer could be revoked after the offeree had acted in detrimental reliance thereon. Reasonable reliance resulting in a foreseeable prejudicial change in position affords a compelling basis also for implying a subsidiary promise not to revoke an offer for a bilateral contract.

The absence of consideration is not fatal to the enforcement of such a promise. It is true that in the case of unilateral contracts the Restatement finds consideration for the implied subsidiary promise in the part performance of the bargained-for exchange, but its reference to section 90 makes clear that consideration for such a promise is not always necessary. The very purpose of section 90 is to make a promise binding even though there was no consideration "in the sense of something that is bargained for and given in exchange." (See 1 Corbin, Contracts 634 et seq.) Reasonable reliance serves to hold the offeror in lieu of the consideration ordinarily required to make the offer binding. In a case involving similar facts the Supreme Court of South Dakota stated that "we believe that reason and justice demand that the doctrine [of section 90] be applied to the present facts. We cannot believe that by accepting this doctrine as controlling in the state of facts before us we will abolish the requirement of a consideration in contract cases, in any different sense than an ordinary estoppel abolishes some legal requirement in its application. We are of the opinion, therefore, that the defendants in executing the agreement [which was not supported by consideration] made a promise which they should have reasonably expected would induce the plaintiff to submit a bid based thereon to the Government, that such promise did induce this action, and that injustice can be avoided only by enforcement of the promise." Northwestern Engineering Co. v. Ellerman, 69 S.D. 397, 408, 10 N.W.2d 879, 884; see also, Robert Gordon, Inc. v. Ingersoll-Rand Co., 7 Cir., 117 F.2d 654, 661; cf. James Baird Co. v. Gimbel Bros., 2 Cir., 64 F.2d 344.

When plaintiff used defendant's offer in computing his own bid, he bound himself to perform in reliance on defendant's terms. Though defendant did not bargain for this use of its bid neither did defendant make it idly, indifferent to whether it would be used or not. On the contrary it is reasonable to suppose that defendant submitted its bid to obtain the subcontract. It was bound to realize the substantial possibility that its bid would be the lowest, and that it would be included by plaintiff in his bid. It was to its own interest that the contractor be awarded the general contract; the lower the subcontract bid, the lower the general contractor's bid was likely to be and the greater its chance of acceptance and hence the greater defendant's chance of getting the paving subcontract. Defendant had reason not only to expect plaintiff to rely on its bid but to want him to. Clearly defendant had a stake in plaintiff's reliance on its bid. Given this interest and the fact that plaintiff is bound by his own bid, it is only fair that plaintiff should have at least an opportunity to accept defendant's bid after the general contract has been awarded to him.

It bears noting that a general contractor is not free to delay acceptance after he has been awarded the general contract in the hope of getting a better price. Nor can he reopen bargaining with the subcontractor and at the same time claim a continuing right to accept the original offer. See, R.J. Daum Const. Co. v. Child, Utah, 247 P.2d 817, 823. In the present case plaintiff promptly informed defendant that plaintiff was being awarded the job and that the subcontract was being awarded to defendant.

Defendant contends, however, that its bid was the result of mistake and that it was therefore entitled to revoke it. It relies on the rescission cases of M.F. Kemper Const. Co. v. City of Los Angeles, 37 Cal.2d 696, 235 P.2d 7, and Brunzell Const. Co. v. G.J. Weisbrod, Inc., 134 Cal.App.2d 278, 285 P.2d 989. See also, Lemoge Electric v. San Mateo County, 46 Cal.2d 659, 662, 297 P.2d 638. In those cases, however, the bidder's mistake was known or should have been known to the offeree, and the offeree could be placed in status quo. Of course, if plaintiff had reason to believe that defendant's bid was in error, he could not justifiably rely on it, and section 90 would afford no basis for enforcing it. Robert Gordon, Inc. v. Ingersoll-Rand, Inc., 7 Cir., 117 F.2d 654, 660. Plaintiff, however, had no reason to know that defendant had made a mistake in submitting its bid, since there was usually a variance of 160 per cent between the highest and lowest bids for paving in the desert around Lancaster. He committed himself to performing the main contract in reliance on defendant's figures. Under these circumstances defendant's mistake, far from relieving it of its obligation, constitutes an additional reason for enforcing it, for it misled plaintiff as to the cost of doing the paving. Even had it been clearly understood that defendant's offer was revocable until accepted, it would not necessarily follow that defendant had no duty to exercise reasonable care in preparing its bid. It presented its bid with knowledge of the substantial possibility that it would be used by plaintiff; it could foresee the harm that would ensue from an erroneous underestimate of the cost. Moreover, it was motivated by its own business interest. Whether or not these considerations alone would justify recovery for negligence had the case been tried on that theory (see Biakanja v. Irving, 49 Cal.2d 647, 650, 320 P.2d 16), they are persuasive that defendant's mistake should not defeat recovery under the rule of section 90 of the Restatement, Contracts. As between the subcontractor who made the bid and the general contractor who reasonably relied on it, the loss resulting from the mistake should fall on the party who caused it. . . .

There is no merit in defendant's contention that plaintiff failed to state a cause of action, on the ground that the complaint failed to allege that plaintiff attempted to mitigate the damages or that they could not have been mitigated. Plaintiff alleged that after defendant's default, "plaintiff had to procure the services of the L & H Co. to perform said asphaltic paving for the sum of $10,948.60." Plaintiff's uncontradicted evidence showed that he spent several months trying to get bids from other subcontractors and that he took the lowest bid. Clearly he acted reasonably to mitigate damages. In any event any uncertainty in plaintiff's allegation as to damages could have been raised by special demurrer. Code Civ.Proc. § 430, subd. 9. It was not so raised and was therefore waived. Code Civ.Proc. § 434.

The judgment is affirmed.

GIBSON, C.J., and SHENK, SCHAUER, SPENCE and McCOMB, JJ., concur.

RESTATEMENT, SECOND, CONTRACTS § 87(2)

[See Selected Source Materials Supplement]

NOTE ON RESTATEMENT SECOND § 87(2)

At first glance, it is not easy to see how the operation of Restatement Second § 87(2) differs from that of Section 45, since both sections concern offers that have been relied upon. In the view of those who prepared Restatement Second, the difference is rooted in the distinction discussed in the Note on Offers for Unilateral Contracts, *supra*, between beginning to perform and preparing to perform. According to the Comment to Section 45, that section (which applies only to offers for unilateral contracts) is applicable to beginning to perform, but not to preparing to perform. The Comment goes on to say, however, that "Preparations to perform may . . . constitute justifiable reliance sufficient to make the offeror's promise binding under Section 87(2)."

Thus the framers of the Restatement apparently believed that where an offeree has actually begun to perform pursuant to an offer for a unilateral contract, he should automatically be entitled to expectation damages, while in other cases of reliance on an offer, the offeree may appropriately be limited to reliance damages. According to the Comment to Section 87(2), "[i]f the beginning of performance is a reasonable mode of acceptance, it makes the offer *fully enforceable* under § 45 . . .; if not, the offeror commonly has no reason to expect part performance before acceptance. But circumstances may be such that the offeree must undergo substantial expense, or undertake substantial commitments, or forego alternatives, in order to put himself in a position to accept by either promise or performance. . . . Full-scale enforcement of the offered contract is not necessarily appropriate in such cases." (Emphasis added.)

Pavel Enterprises, Inc. v. A.S. Johnson Co.

342 Md. 143, 674 A.2d 521 (1996)

(Karwacki, J.) "The *Drennan* decision has been very influential. Many states have adopted the reasoning used by Justice Traynor. . . .

"Despite the popularity of the *Drennan* reasoning, the case has subsequently come under some criticism. The criticism centers on the lack of symmetry of detrimental reliance in the bid process, in that subcontractors are bound to the general, but the general is not bound to the subcontractors. The result is that the general is free to bid shop,[13] bid chop,[14] and to encourage bid peddling,[15] to the detriment of the subcontractors. One commentator described the problems that these practices create:

'Bid shopping and peddling have long been recognized as unethical by construction trade organizations. These "unethical," but common practices have several detrimental results. First, as bid shopping becomes common within a particular trade, the subcontractors will pad their initial bids in order to make further reductions during post-award negotiations. This artificial inflation of subcontractor's offers makes the bid process less effective. Second, subcontractors who are forced into post-award negotiations with the general often must reduce their sub-bids in order to avoid losing the award. Thus, they will be faced with a Hobson's choice between doing the job at a loss or doing a less than adequate job. Third, bid shopping and peddling tend to increase the risk of loss of the time and money used in preparing a bid. This occurs because generals and subcontractors who engage in these practices use, without expense, the bid estimates prepared by others. Fourth, it is often impossible for a general to obtain bids far enough in advance to have sufficient time to properly prepare his own bid because of the practice, common among many subcontractors, of holding sub-bids until the last possible moment in order to avoid pre-award bid shopping by the general. Fifth, many subcontractors refuse to submit bids for jobs on which they expect bid shopping. As a result, competition is reduced,

---

[13] Bid shopping is the use of the lowest subcontractor's bid as a tool in negotiating lower bids from other subcontractors post-award.

[14] "The general contractor, having been awarded the prime contract, may pressure the subcontractor whose bid was used for a particular portion of the work in computing the overall bid on the prime contract to reduce the amount of the bid." . . .

[15] An unscrupulous subcontractor can save estimating costs, and still get the job by not entering a bid or by entering an uncompetitive bid. After bid opening, this unscrupulous subcontractor, knowing the price of the low sub-bid, can then offer to perform the work for less money, precisely because the honest subcontractor has already paid for the estimate and included that cost in the original bid. This practice is called bid peddling.

and, consequently, construction prices are increased. Sixth, any price reductions gained through the use of post-award bid shopping by the general will be of no benefit to the awarding authority, to whom these price reductions would normally accrue as a result of open competition before the award of the prime contract. Free competition in an open market is therefore perverted because of the use of post-award bid shopping.'

". . . These problems have caused at least one court to reject promissory estoppel in the contractor-subcontractor relationship. Home Elec. Co. v. Underdown Heating & Air Conditioning Co., 86 N.C.App. 540, 358 S.E.2d 539 (1987). . . . But other courts, while aware of the limitations of promissory estoppel, have adopted it nonetheless. . . . "

––––––

Preload Technology, Inc. v. A.B. & J. Construction Co., Inc.

696 F.2d 1080, 1089 (5th Cir.1983)

(Garwood, J.) "Another limitation on the doctrine of promissory estoppel in [suits by a general contractor alleging reliance on a subcontractor's bid] is the prohibition against 'bid shopping,' 'bid chiseling' and related practices sometimes engaged in by general contractors after they have been awarded the general contract and before they subcontract the particular part of the work in dispute. . . . 'Bid shopping' commonly refers to a general contractor's seeking of bids from subcontractors other than the one whose bid amount the general used in calculating its own bid, and often involves the general's informing the other subcontractors of the amount of the low bid and inviting them to undercut it. 'Bid chiseling' usually refers to the general contractor's attempt to negotiate a lower price than that bid from the subcontractor whose bid figure the general employed in calculating its own bid, frequently by threatening to subcontract the work to a third party. . . . When these practices are engaged in, recovery by the general contractor under § 90 may be denied on a variety of theories, viz: that the general contractor did not in fact rely on the subcontractor's bid, or failed to accept it within a reasonable time, or rejected it by a counter-offer, or, perhaps more persuasively, because in such circumstances there is a failure to meet § 90's requirement that 'injustice can be avoided only by enforcement of the promise.' "

––––––

Allen M. Campbell Co. v. Virginia Metal Industries, Inc.

708 F.2d 930 (4th Cir.1983)

Campbell, a general contractor, proposed to bid on a contract to construct housing. Virginia Metal telephoned Campbell and quoted a price to supply hollow metal doors and frames required by the contract plans and specifications. Campbell was awarded the contract, but Virginia Metal backed out of its bid. Campbell sued. The case was governed by North Carolina law.

Held, Virginia Metal was bound to its bid under the theory of promissory estoppel. Although the bid was oral, the UCC Statute of Frauds was not a defense, because under North Carolina law promissory estoppel overcomes the Statute of Frauds.

———

CHAPTER 10

THE MECHANICS OF A BARGAIN (II)—ACCEPTANCE

■ ■ ■

INTRODUCTORY NOTE

This Chapter concerns the rules on acceptance and some related issues. Under classical contract law the fundamental requirement for a response to an offer to be treated as an acceptance is that the response must unequivocally manifest the offeree's assent to the offeror's terms. See *Ardente v. Horan*, supra Chapter 9. Section 1 of this Chapter concerns additional issues involving the form of acceptance and the requirement that acceptance be communicated to the offeror. Section 2 concerns when an acceptance is effective. This is the subject of the "mail box" rule. Section 3 concerns the extension of contract law to electronic commerce. Section 4 concerns the rules that determine when silence is acceptance. A contract that is based on the parties' actions, and not their expressions, is sometimes described as an "implied-in-fact contract." Section 5 concerns the action in the law of restitution when the plaintiff renders a benefit to the defendant in the mistaken belief in the existence of a contract.

―――――

SECTION 1. FORM OF ACCEPTANCE

KELLER V. BONES
Supreme Court of Nebraska, 2000.
260 Neb. 202, 615 N.W.2d 883.

STEPHAN, J.

This is an action for specific performance of a real estate purchase agreement brought by Dean Keller (the buyer) against Calvin R. Bones and Audrey J. Bones (the sellers). The district court for Lincoln County, Nebraska, granted the sellers' motion for summary judgment, finding that no contract existed between the parties due to the sellers' failure to communicate their acceptance within the time prescribed in the buyer's offer. The Nebraska Court of Appeals affirmed. On further review, we conclude that a binding contract was formed by the parties and, therefore, reverse.

BACKGROUND

The following recitation of the pertinent facts is taken from the Nebraska Court of Appeals' opinion, Keller v. Bones, 8 Neb.App. 946, 948–49, 604 N.W.2d 847, 850 (2000):

> The material facts in this case are undisputed. Calvin R. Bones and Audrey J. Bones are the trustees of the Calvin R. and Audrey J. Bones Family Trust. The trust owns, inter alia, a ranch in Lincoln County, Nebraska, which is the subject of this dispute. On June 11, 1997, the Boneses listed the ranch for sale with a real estate agent in North Platte, Nebraska, called Agri Affiliates, Inc. (agent). According to the listing agreement between the Boneses and their agent, if the listing sold to the current tenants, Lydic Brothers, the agent would receive only a 1-percent commission. On the other hand, if the listing sold to anyone else, the agent would receive a 6-percent commission.

> On July 17, 1997, Dean Keller submitted an offer to buy the ranch to the agent in the form of a "Real Estate Purchase Agreement" (offer) and made an earnest money deposit of $49,000 payable to the agent. The offer was for $490,000 and by its own terms would be withdrawn if not accepted by July 21 at 5 p.m. At 4:53 p.m. on July 21, the Boneses faxed a signed copy of the offer to their agent. Paragraph 15 of the offer states in part that "[u]pon execution by Seller, this agreement shall become a binding contract." Loren Johnson, the agent's representative, did not telephone Keller to inform him of the Boneses' acceptance until 5:12 p.m. on July 21 and did so by leaving a voice message on Keller's answering machine.

> On July 22, 1997, Don Lydic, a representative of Lydic Brothers, informed the Boneses and the agent that Lydic Brothers would match Keller's offer for the ranch. The Boneses wanted to accept Don Lydic's offer and sell the ranch to Lydic Brothers. Later that same day, the agent asked Keller if he would be willing to release the Boneses from the agreement and "back out" of the deal. Keller refused and asserted that he wanted to go forward with the sale.

> The Boneses unequivocally informed Keller on December 5, 1997, that they would not sell the ranch to him. After the Boneses failed to close on December 10, 1997—the date set in the offer—Keller brought suit against the Boneses seeking specific performance and other relief.

All parties filed motions for summary judgment. On January 5, 1999, the district court entered summary judgment for the sellers, finding that no valid contract was formed because the sellers' acceptance was not communicated to the buyer until after the deadline set forth in the offer had expired. The district court therefore dismissed the buyer's petition.

The buyer appealed the judgment of dismissal to the Nebraska Court of Appeals, alleging that the trial court erred in (1) finding that the sellers' acceptance must be communicated to the buyer prior to the expiration of the offer, contrary to the language in the offer, and (2) finding that the buyer did not waive the late communication of the acceptance. The Court of Appeals affirmed, finding our decision in Pribil v. Ruther, 200 Neb. 161, 262 N.W.2d 460 (1978), controlling. The court noted that under Pribil, neither the sellers' act of signing the offer nor the act of faxing a signed copy to their agent constituted the requisite "communication" of the acceptance to the buyer to form a binding contract. The court maintained that the message left by the sellers' agent on the buyer's answering machine did not constitute the requisite communication because it was not in writing as required by the offer, was made after the 5 p.m. deadline, and was not delivered personally or by registered mail, as further required by the offer.

The Court of Appeals also determined that "[t]here was no communication from [the buyer] to the [sellers] or their agent which could be interpreted either as a waiver of the [sellers'] failure to accept within the time specified or as an acceptance of a counteroffer." Keller v. Bones, 8 Neb.App. 946, 953, 604 N.W.2d 847, 853 (2000). The court maintained that even if Nebraska law allowed the buyer to make a waiver, the buyer did not comply with a provision in his own offer which required waivers to be in writing. Thus, the Court of Appeals affirmed the order of the district court, finding that no contract existed between the parties.

ASSIGNMENTS OF ERROR

In petitioning for further review, the buyer assigns, summarized and restated, that the Court of Appeals erred (1) in determining that Pribil v. Ruther, supra, controlled; (2) in determining that no valid contract existed between the parties; (3) in determining that an acceptance of his offer could not be governed by the language of the contract, and instead required an actual communication of the sellers' acceptance to him; (4) in determining that a valid contract between the buyer and the sellers was not created by their subsequent communications and course of dealing with each other following the expiration of the stated deadline in the buyer's original offer; (5) in determining that no contract was formed after the buyer waived the late communication of the sellers' acceptance, or, in the alternative, that the buyer could effectuate a waiver in writing only; and (6) in affirming the district court's order granting summary judgment in favor of the sellers. . . .

ANALYSIS

The Court of Appeals determined that under Pribil v. Ruther, 200 Neb. 161, 262 N.W.2d 460 (1978), a communicated acceptance was required in order to form a binding contract. In Pribil, we stated that "[a]n express contract is proved by evidence of a definite offer and unconditional acceptance. Where the offer requires a promise on the part of the offeree, a communicated acceptance is essential." 200 Neb. at 163, 262 N.W.2d at 462. The Court of Appeals reached its determination notwithstanding language in the offer dispensing with the notice requirement. The relevant provisions of the buyer's offer provide as follows:

> "12. [T]he Buyer and Seller each acknowledge that this agreement, when signed, becomes a LEGALLY BINDING CONTRACT . . . 15. . . . Buyer acknowledges that this agreement is not binding until accepted by the Seller. Upon execution by Seller, this agreement shall become a binding contract."

The purchase agreement which formed the basis of the buyer's offer in Pribil did not contain a provision similar to that contained in the buyer's offer in this case, which provides that the agreement becomes a binding contract upon execution.

Although we have adhered to the general principle that the offeror is master of the offer, see Hughes v. Cornhusker Cas. Co., 235 Neb. 656, 456 N.W.2d 765 (1990), we have never addressed the issue of whether an offer may dispense with a notice of acceptance. We note that several jurisdictions have recognized that an acceptance need not be communicated to form a binding contract where the language of the offer dispenses with this requirement. See, Edens v. Goodyear Tire & Rubber Co., 858 F.2d 198 (4th Cir.1988) (stating offeror entitled to notification of acceptance unless offer indicates contrary intention); Frandsen v. Gerstner, 26 Utah 2d 180, 487 P.2d 697 (1971) (concluding express terms of offer may modify general rule requiring communication of acceptance); Harleaux v. Wood, 542 So.2d 747 (La.App.1989) (concluding contract became binding upon offeree's signature because by terms of offer, parties altered general rule that contract is not perfected until notice of acceptance is received); Joiner v. Elrod, 716 S.W.2d 606, 609 (Tex.App.1986) (stating because "notification of acceptance is required for the benefit of the person who makes the offer, the person who makes the offer may dispense with notice to himself"). See, also, 1 Arthur L. Corbin, Corbin on Contracts § 3.13 (Joseph M. Perillo rev. ed. 1993 & Cum.Supp.2000); Restatement (Second) of Contracts § 56 (1981). But see Kendel v. Pontious, 261 So.2d 167 (Fla.1972) (concluding where offer stated it would become binding upon signing by both parties, offeree was nonetheless required to communicate its acceptance).

We need not decide whether to recognize an exception to the rule requiring a communicated acceptance in this case because we find uncontroverted evidence that the sellers' acceptance was communicated to the buyer, thereby establishing a binding contract. The Court of Appeals determined that

> [the buyer's] offer required that the [the sellers] accept in writing by 5 p.m. on July 21, 1997, through registered mail or delivering the acceptance to [the buyer] personally. Additionally, paragraph 15 of the offer states in part, "Time is of the essence of this agreement and each and every provision hereof." The voice message left on [the buyer's] answering machine was not in writing, occurred after the deadline, and was not delivered by the means specified in the offer; thus, it could not constitute an acceptance.

Keller v. Bones, 8 Neb.App. 946, 952, 604 N.W.2d 847, 852 (2000). The terms of the buyer's offer required only that the offer be signed by the 5 p.m. deadline, not that it be communicated prior to that time as found by the Court of Appeals. The offer is silent with respect to the manner and time for communication of acceptance. Paragraph 4 of the offer provides that "[t]his document constitutes an offer to purchase the Property. In the event this offer is not accepted by Seller on or before July 21, 1997 at 5 o'clock p.m., this offer shall be deemed revoked and the deposit shall be refunded to Buyer." Paragraphs 12 and 15 of the offer, when read together, define "acceptance" to mean when the document is signed. Paragraph 15 provides, "Buyer acknowledges that this agreement is not binding until accepted by the Seller. Upon execution by Seller, this agreement shall become a binding contract." (Emphasis supplied.) Paragraph 12 provides, "Buyer and Seller each acknowledge that this agreement, when signed, becomes a LEGALLY BINDING CONTRACT." (Emphasis supplied.) (Emphasis in original.)

A contract which is written in clear and unambiguous terms is not subject to interpretation or construction; rather, the intent of the parties must be determined from the contents of the contract, and the contract must be enforced according to its terms. ConAgra, Inc. v. Bartlett Partnership, 248 Neb. 933, 540 N.W.2d 333 (1995); Schrempp and Salerno v. Gross, 247 Neb. 685, 529 N.W.2d 764 (1995). A contract is viewed as a whole in order to construe it. Ruble v. Reich, 259 Neb. 658, 611 N.W.2d 844 (2000); Bachman v. Easy Parking of America, 252 Neb. 325, 562 N.W.2d 369 (1997).

Construing the language of the buyer's offer, we conclude that the 5 p.m. deadline applies only to the time by which the sellers were required to sign the document in order to indicate their acceptance. The sellers signed the buyer's offer at 4:53 p.m. on July 21, 1997, prior to the deadline stated in the offer. Accordingly, the sellers' acceptance was timely, leaving only the question of whether it was communicated to the buyer in an effective and timely manner.

Upon signing the buyer's offer, the sellers faxed it to their agent at 4:53 p.m. As we noted in Pribil v. Ruther, 200 Neb. 161, 262 N.W.2d 460 (1978), delivery to a seller's agent is not delivery to a buyer and does not put the acceptance beyond the seller's control. Consequently, the question is whether any other communication by the sellers or their agent to the buyer qualifies as notice of acceptance. See, Corman v. Musselman, 232 Neb. 159, 439 N.W.2d 781 (1989) (holding principal is bound by, and liable for, acts which his agent does within actual or apparent authority from principal and within scope of agent's employment); Mueller v. Union Pacific Railroad, 220 Neb. 742, 371 N.W.2d 732 (1985) (same); Bury v. Action Enterprises, Inc., 197 Neb. 38, 246 N.W.2d 724 (1976) (same).

The first communication between the parties occurred at 5:12 p.m. on July 21, 1997, when the sellers' agent left a voice message on the buyer's answering machine informing him that the sellers had accepted his offer. The Court of Appeals concluded that the message left on the buyer's answering machine was not a proper communication of the acceptance because it was "not in writing, occurred after the deadline, and was not delivered by the means specified in the offer." Keller v. Bones, 8 Neb.App. 946, 952, 604 N.W.2d 847, 852 (2000). In reaching this conclusion, the Court of Appeals was in part referring to paragraph 16 of the offer, which provides, "All notices and other communications given hereunder shall be in writing and shall be delivered personally or sent by registered mail, addressed to Buyer or Seller as below." Viewing the language of the offer as a whole, we interpret this provision as applying to all notices and other communications arising after the formation of a binding contract. Thus, this provision in the offer does not apply to communication of the sellers' acceptance, and as such, an oral communication of the sellers' acceptance was effective.

As noted, there is no language in the buyer's offer specifying the time or manner for communication of the acceptance. To the extent the offer does not speak to a time within which communication of the acceptance must be made, a reasonable time is used. See, Restatement (Second) of Contracts § 41 at 109 (1981) (stating that "[a]n offeree's power of acceptance is terminated at the time specified in the offer, or, if no time is specified, at the end of a reasonable time"); Standard Oil Co. v. O'Hare, 126 Neb. 11, 252 N.W. 398 (1934) (stating in case where contract did not specify time within which acceptance must be made, before offer could ripen into contract, it must be accepted, and notice of its acceptance be given to offeror within reasonable time).

Here, the sellers' agent left a message on the buyer's answering machine indicating the sellers' acceptance of the buyer's offer only 19 minutes after the sellers signed the offer and 12 minutes after the 5 p.m. signing deadline. It cannot be said that the sellers' communication of acceptance was not made within a reasonable time.

Moreover, the interpretation given to a contract by the parties themselves while engaged in the performance of it is one of the best indications of true intent and should be given great, if not controlling, influence. Solar Motors v. First Nat. Bank of Chadron, 249 Neb. 758, 545 N.W.2d 714 (1996). From the moment the sellers signed the purchase agreement, both they and the buyer acted in a manner consistent with the existence of a binding contract between them. For example, on July 22, 1997, the agent, at the sellers' request, telephoned the buyer to inquire whether he would "back out" of the deal, and the buyer refused to do so. Moreover, on that same day, the agent, acting under his express authority, cashed the buyer's earnest money deposit check, which he told the buyer he would do only after the sellers had accepted his offer. Also, on July 25, the sellers sent a letter to their agent indicating their intent to have the agent disclose to the buyer, pursuant to their responsibility under the agreement, certain defects of the property. Based on these uncontroverted facts, we conclude as a matter of law that the sellers' acceptance was properly and timely communicated to the buyer so as to form a binding contract.

CONCLUSION

For the reasons discussed above, we conclude that the Court of Appeals erred in affirming the district court's order granting summary judgment in favor of the sellers because the sellers' acceptance was *timely* communicated to the buyer so as to create a valid and binding contract. Therefore, we reverse the judgment of the Court of Appeals and remand the cause with directions to reverse the judgment of the district court and remand the cause for further proceedings consistent with this opinion.

Reversed and remanded with directions.

––––––––

RESTATEMENT, SECOND, CONTRACTS §§ 30, 56, 60

[See Selected Source Materials Supplement]

––––––––

UCC § 2–206

[See Selected Source Materials Supplement]

NOTE ON ACCEPTANCE BY PROMISE OR PERFORMANCE

Restatement Second § 32 provides that "In case of doubt an offer is interpreted as inviting the offeree to accept either by promising to perform what the offer requests or by rendering the performance, as the offeree chooses." Relatedly, UCC § 2–206(1)(b) provides that "an order or other offer to buy goods for prompt or current shipment shall be construed as inviting acceptance either by a prompt promise to ship or by the prompt or current shipment of conforming or non-conforming goods." When the offeree accepts an offer of a bilateral contract by rendering performance she undertakes an obligation to perform in accordance with the offer. An offeree who ships non-conforming goods can avoid the shipment being treated as both an acceptance and a breach by seasonably notifying the buyer that the shipment "is offered only as an accommodation to the buyer."

Bishop v. Eaton

161 Mass. 496, 37 N.E. 665 (1894)

In December, 1886, defendant in a letter to plaintiff said "If Harry needs more money, let him have it, or assist him to get it, and I will see that it is paid." Harry was defendant's brother and was connected in business with plaintiff. Defendant lived in Nova Scotia; Harry and plaintiff lived in Illinois. On January 7, 1887, plaintiff signed a $200 note for Harry as surety. Plaintiff immediately sent a letter to defendant stating that the note had been given and the amount. Defendant testified that he never received the letter.

(Knowlton, J.) "[T]his was not a proposition which was to become a contract only upon the giving of a promise for the promise, and it was not necessary that the plaintiff should accept it in words, or promise to do anything before acting upon it. It was an offer which was to become effective as a contract upon the doing of the act referred to. It was an offer to be bound in consideration of an act to be done, and in such a case the doing of the act constitutes the acceptance of the offer and furnishes the consideration. Ordinarily there is no occasion to notify the offerer of the acceptance of such an offer, for the doing of the act is a sufficient acceptance, and the promisor knows that he is bound when he sees that action has been taken on the faith of his offer. But if the act is of such a kind that knowledge of it will not quickly come to the promisor, the promisee is bound to give him notice of his acceptance within a reasonable time after doing that which constitutes the acceptance. In such a case it is implied in the offer that, to complete the contract, notice shall be given with due diligence, so that the promisor may know that a contract has been made. But where the promise is in consideration of an act to be done, it becomes binding upon the doing of the act so far that the promisee cannot be affected by a subsequent withdrawal of it, if within a reasonable time afterward he notifies the promisor. In accordance with these principles, it has been held in cases like the present, where the guarantor would not know of himself, from the nature of the transaction, whether the offer has been accepted or not, that he is not bound without notice of the acceptance, seasonably given after the performance which constitutes the consideration. Babcock v. Bryant, 12 Pick. 133; Whiting v. Stacy, 15 Gray, 270; Schlessinger v. Dickinson, 5 Allen, 47.

"In the present case the plaintiff seasonably mailed a letter to the defendant, informing him of what he had done in compliance with the defendant's request, but the defendant testified that he never received it, and there is no finding that it ever reached him. The judge ruled, as matter of law, that upon the facts found, the plaintiff was entitled to recover, and the question is thus presented whether the defendant was bound by the acceptance when the letter was properly mailed, although he never received it.

"When an offer of guaranty of this kind is made, the implication is that notice of the act which constitutes an acceptance of it shall be given in a reasonable way. What kind of a notice is required depends upon the nature of the transaction, the situation of the parties, and the inferences fairly to be drawn from their previous dealings, if any, in regard to the matter. If they are so situated that communication by letter is naturally to be expected, then the deposit of a letter in the mail is all that is necessary. If that is done which is fairly to be contemplated from their relations to the subject-matter and from their course of dealing, the rights of the parties are fixed, and a failure actually to receive the notice will not affect the obligation of the guarantor.

"The plaintiff in the case now before us resided in Illinois, and the defendant in Nova Scotia. The offer was made by letter, and the defendant must have contemplated that information in regard to the plaintiff's acceptance or rejection of it would be by letter. It would be a harsh rule which would subject the plaintiff to the risk of the defendant's failure to receive the letter giving notice of his action on the faith of the offer. We are of opinion that the plaintiff, after assisting Harry to get the money, did all that he was required to do when he seasonably sent the defendant the letter by mail informing him of what had been done."

————

NOTE ON REQUIREMENT TO COMMUNICATE ACCEPTANCE

As a general rule, when an offeree accepts by promise she is expected to make a reasonable effort to communicate the acceptance to the offeror. *Keller v. Bones*, supra, discusses one exception to this rule: when the offeror expressly dispenses with notice of acceptance. Restatement Second § 54(1) provides that "Where an offer invites an offeree to accept by rendering a performance, no notification is necessary to make such an acceptance effective unless the offer requests such a notification." The rule in § 54(2) qualifies this by requiring the offeree to "exercise reasonable diligence to notify the offeror of acceptance" when the offeree "has reason to know that the offeror has no adequate means of learning of the performance with reasonable promptness and certainty." UCC § 2–206(2) is similar.

———

Restatement, Second, Contracts § 56, Illustration 2

"A makes written application for life insurance through an agent for B Insurance Company, pays the first premium, and is given a receipt stating that the insurance "shall take effect as of the date of approval of the application" at B's home office. Approval at the home office in accordance with B's usual practice is an acceptance of A's offer even though no steps are taken to notify A."

———

SECTION 2. WHEN AN ACCEPTANCE IS EFFECTIVE (THE MAILBOX RULE)

The issue often arises in contract law whether a given type of communication is effective when it is dispatched or when it is received. The rules that govern this issue were formulated when the basic modes of communication were face to face and by mail or, somewhat later, by telephone and telegram. The rules that developed were as follows: Except for acceptances, contractual communications are normally effective when received. If an acceptance is given face to face or "by telephone or other medium of substantially instantaneous two-way communication," it is also effective when received. See Restatement Second § 64. However, if an acceptance is transmitted through a medium, such as regular mail, that is not substantially instantaneous two-way communication then the acceptance is effective when dispatched unless the offeror specifies otherwise. (Presumably, the same rule would be applied to private express-mail services, such as FedEx.) This rule is known as the *mailbox rule* or the *dispatch rule*. The rule is often associated with a famous English case, Adams v. Lindsell, 1 Barn. & Ald. 681 (K.B. 1818).

Application of the mailbox rule arises in a variety of contexts. Two follow.

1. *Crossed revocation and acceptance.* The paradigm case for application of the mailbox rule is a crossed revocation and acceptance. For example, assume that A makes an offer by mail to B on June 1. The course of post is two days, so that B receives the offer on June 3. B promptly accepts by mail that day, and his acceptance reaches A on June 5. Meanwhile, on June 2, A has sent B a revocation, which reaches B on June 4. Here A's revocation was dispatched before B's acceptance was

dispatched, and was received before B's acceptance was received. Nevertheless, under the mailbox rule a contract is formed, because a revocation is effective only when received (on June 4) while an acceptance is effective when dispatched (on June 3).

An argument in favor of the mailbox rule in this context is that it pushes up the beginning of performance to the earliest possible date. Suppose, for example, that as in the hypothetical, the course of post is two days, and the offeree is to perform before the offeror. Under the mailbox rule, an offeree can safely begin to perform as soon as he dispatches his acceptance. If we assume that, as seems likely, most offerors do not revoke, then offerors as a class may prefer the mailbox rule, because it is usually in the interests of offerors that performance begin as soon as possible.

2. *Delay or failure of transmission.* A different question is presented when a mailed acceptance is either delayed or fails to reach the offeror. For example, suppose that Seller offers by mail to sell Blackacre to Buyer, and gives Buyer five days in which to accept. Buyer promptly dispatches a letter of acceptance, but the letter miscarries and never reaches Seller. Seller waits ten days, and having had no word from Buyer, assumes that Buyer is no longer interested and sells Blackacre to someone else. Buyer, who has no reason to anticipate that his acceptance will fail to reach Seller, disposes of the premises now in his possession, in the expectation of occupying Blackacre. Is there a contract?

Delay or failure cases are commonly dealt with under the mailbox rule, on the theory that the cases turn on the same issue as crossed-revocation-and-acceptance cases—namely, when does an acceptance take effect. It is apparent, however, that delay and failure cases involve different considerations than those involved in the crossed-revocation-and-acceptance context. In crossed-revocation-and-acceptance cases, the offeror knows that the offeree decided to accept. In delay or failure cases, the offeror is likely to believe that the offeree decided not to accept. Accordingly, if an acceptance takes effect on dispatch in the delay and failure cases, it must either be for reasons other than those that apply to the crossed-revocation-and-acceptance case, or because it is thought wise to avoid nuances and complexities by establishing a categorical rule to cover all types of cases in which the issue is when an acceptance takes effect.

———

RESTATEMENT, SECOND, CONTRACTS §§ 30, 49, 60, 63–68

[See Selected Source Materials Supplement]

———

UCC § 2–206(1)

[See Selected Source Materials Supplement]

———

CISG ARTS. 15, 16, 18(2), 20, 22, 23, 24

[See Selected Source Material Supplement]

———

UNIDROIT PRINCIPLES OF INTERNATIONAL COMMERCIAL CONTRACTS ARTS. 2.1.3, 2.1.6(2), 2.1.7, 2.1.8, 2.1.10

[See Selected Source Materials Supplement]

———

PRINCIPLES OF EUROPEAN CONTRACT LAW ARTS. 2.205(1), 2.206

[See Selected Source Materials Supplement]

———

Dodge, Teaching the CISG in Contracts

50 J. Leg. Ed. 72 (2000)

"Under the common law, acceptances are effective upon dispatch, even if they never reach the offeror. This rule performs two functions: it protects the offeree against the possibility of revocation once the acceptance is dispatched, and it places the risk of a lost communication on the offeror. In contrast to the common law mailbox rule, Article 18(2) of the CISG adopts a receipt rule: 'An acceptance of an offer becomes effective at the moment the indication of assent reaches the offeror.' But this provision must be read in conjunction with Article 16(1), which says that 'an offer may be revoked if the revocation reaches the offeree before he has dispatched an acceptance' (emphasis added). In other words, once the offeree has dispatched an acceptance, the offeror may no longer revoke, but if the acceptance is lost in the mail there is no contract. So the CISG and the common law both protect the offeree against the possibility of revocation once the acceptance is dispatched, but the CISG places the risk of a lost communication on the offeree rather than the offeror.

———

SECTION 3. ELECTRONIC COMMERCE

NOTE ON THE CONCEPT OF "RECORD"

With the advent of electronic contracting, the term "record" has been introduced into contract discourse. Under the Electronic Signatures in Global and National Commerce Act and the Uniform Electronic Transactions Act, "record" means "information that is inscribed on a tangible medium or that is stored in an electronic or other medium and is retrievable in perceivable form." "Electronic record," a special type of record, means "a record created, generated, sent, communicated, received, or stored by electronic means." The Comments to Section 2 (Definitions) of the Uniform Electronic Transactions Act state:

> 10. **"Record."** This is a standard definition designed to embrace all means of communicating or storing information except human memory. It includes any method for storing or communicating information, including "writings." A record need not be indestructible or permanent, but the term does not include oral or other communications which are not stored or preserved by some means. Information that has not been retained other than through human memory does not qualify as a record . . .

> 6. **"Electronic record."** An electronic record is a subset of the broader defined term "record." It is any record created, used or stored in a medium other than paper. . . .

Information processing systems, computer equipment and programs, electronic data interchange, electronic mail, voice mail, facsimile, telex, telecopying, scanning, and similar technologies all qualify as electronic under this Act. Accordingly information stored on a computer hard drive or floppy disc, facsimiles, voice mail messages, messages on a telephone answering machine, audio and video tape recordings, among other records, all would be electronic records under this Act.

NOTE ON ELECTRONIC SIGNATURE

At one time, it may have been open to question whether an electronic writing or signature satisfied any rule that was applicable to the relevant transaction and required a writing, a signature, or both. That issue has now been resolved by the Uniform Electronic Transactions Act ("UETA") and the Electronic Signatures in Global and National Communications Act ("E-Sign"), both of which validate electronic records and signatures. These statutes reflect the modern widespread use of electronic communications in commerce. When challenged the authenticity of an electronic signature can be established by circumstantial evidence of reasonable security procedures, such as a unique login ID and password to access a web site. Ruiz v. Moss Bros. Auto Group, Inc,

232 Cal. App.4th 836, 181 Cal. Rptr.3d 781 (2014), holds that when an employee swore that he could not recall being presented with or signing a modification of an on-line employee handbook, a conclusory assertion by a Human Resources manager that electronic signature of agreement to arbitrate dispute and to waive class action was that of employee was insufficient to establish authenticity. The court added that "the burden of authenticating an electronic signature is not great." The following note case shows that what constitutes a signature also depends on the purpose of a signature requirement.

———

J.B.B. Investment Partners, Ltd. v. Fair

232 Cal. App.4th 974, 181 Cal. Rptr.3d 154 (2014)

Plaintiffs were investors in companies managed by Fair, a retired member of the California bar. They accused Fair and the companies of fraud. On July 4, 2013, plaintiffs' attorney, Russo, sent an unsigned settlement offer to Fair by e-mail. The offer required that Fair stipulate to a judgment of $350,000 and demanded that Fair make full disclosure of information to demonstrate that the companies were not "a Ponzi or Ponzi-like scheme," and to demonstrate that alleged misrepresentations and non-disclosures "are, in fact, simply at most a negligent mistake on your part." The July 4 offer concluded:

> WE require a YES or NO on this proposal; you need to say 'I accept'. . . . Anything less shifts all focus to the litigation and to the Court Orders we will seek now as well as in the future as well as the subpoenas we will serve. . . . It is now up to you to decide whether you would rather resolve this amicably or not. Let me know your decision.

On July 5, there were a flurry of communications between Fair, Russo, and one of the plaintiffs using email, voicemail, and text messages. The plaintiffs also filed their lawsuit on the 5th. In one email Russo stated:

> This confirms full agreement; I will work on the formal settlement paperwork which will conform to the settlement agreement made today based on the 10 numbered paragraphs below with no admission of liability or wrongdoing by anyone. I will seek to get that settlement paperwork to you for review by Monday with the goal of getting it all finalized and signed next week. The settlement is otherwise binding under [Code of Civil Procedure section] 664.6. . . .

Russo shortly followed this email with a text message: "I have accepted by phone and [e-mail]. Stop proceeding. I said accept which is same as 'agreed.' You must stop and you must tell the court we have an agreement." The plaintiffs prepared a settlement agreement, which they mailed to Fair. He never signed the agreement.

On August 6, 2013, plaintiffs moved to enforce the settlement agreement, presenting the July 4 offer and the July 5 e-mail, voice mail, and text messages. Russo testified that he had not read the July 4 offer before replying, and that his messages "simply signified his good faith and desire to work out a settlement." The trial court found "that there was an agreement struck on July 5th", and that Russo's printed name at the end of his e-mail, combined with the corroborating voice mails, satisfied the requirement of Code of Civil Procedure section 664.6 that a settlement outside the presence of the court be "in a writing signed by the parties." Reversed.

(Kline, P.J.) "We agree that a printed name or some other symbol might, under specific circumstances, be a signature under UETA and might satisfy the even more rigorous requirements under Code of Civil Procedure section 664.6. Courts in other jurisdictions that have adopted a version of UETA have concluded that names typed at the end of e-mails *can* be electronic signatures. (See, e.g., *Preston Law Firm, L.L.C. v. Mariner Health Care Mgmt. Co.* (5th Cir. 2010) 622 F.3d 384, 391 [affirming that "[e]mails can qualify as the signed writings needed to form contracts" under Louisiana's UETA]; *Cloud Corp. v. Hasbro, Inc.* (7th Cir. 2002) 314 F.3d 289, 295–296 [holding that "the sender's name on an e-mail satisfies the signature requirement of the [Illinois] statute of frauds" and noting that it would be a valid signature under the federal Electronic Signatures in Global and National Commerce Act (15 U.S.C. § 7001 et seq.) as well]; see also [*Lamle v. Mattel, Inc.*, 394 F.3d 1355 (Fed. Cir. 2005)] [e-mail was written prior to the enactment of California's UETA but court opined that inclusion of individual's name on e-mail would be valid signature under California's UETA]; *Gillis v. Wells Fargo Bank* (E.D. Mich. 2012) 875 F.Supp.2d 728, 734–735 [signed letter and e-mail messages that included the sender's salutation were sufficient to satisfy statute of frauds].)

"The trial court's analysis was incomplete. Attributing the name on an e-mail to a particular person and determining that the printed name is "[t]he act of [this] person" is a necessary prerequisite but is insufficient, by itself, to establish that it is an "electronic signature." (§ 1633.9, subd. (a).) As counsel and the court seemed unaware, UETA defines the term "electronic signature." Subdivision (h) of section 1633.2 states that " '[e]lectronic signature' means an electronic sound, symbol, or process attached to or logically associated with an electronic record and *executed or adopted by a person with the intent to sign the electronic record*." (Italics added; see CACI No. 380 [party suing to enforce an agreement formalized by electronic means must prove "based on the context and surrounding circumstances, including the conduct of the parties, that the parties agreed to use [e.g., e-mail] to formalize their agreement" (italics omitted)].)

"We have independently reviewed the record and conclude, as a matter of law, that it does not show that Fair printed his name at the end of his e-mail with any intent to formalize an electronic transaction. Indeed, substantial evidence in the record refutes such a finding.

"Whether the parties agree to conduct a transaction by electronic means is determined from the context and surrounding circumstances, including the parties' conduct" (§ 1633.5, subd. (b).) The absence of an explicit agreement to conduct the transaction by electronic means is not determinative; however, it is a relevant factor to consider.

"Plaintiffs argue that the July 4 offer expressly contemplated acceptance by electronic means as it specified that Fair needed to say, "I accept." They also cite Fair's testimony that he personally typed his name and that he refused to sign the July 11 writing because he had simply changed his mind. Plaintiffs' evidence is legally insufficient.

"The exchange of e-mail messages shows that the parties clearly agreed to negotiate the terms of the settlement by e-mail, but plaintiffs did not demonstrate, as they must (§ 1633.5, subd. (b)), that the parties ever agreed to conduct transactions by electronic means or that Fair intended with his printed name at the end of his e-mail to sign electronically the July 4 offer. The July 4 offer did not contain any statement indicating that the parties agreed to enter into a final settlement by electronic means. The plain language of the July 4 offer made it clear that no signature was being requested as the offer included no signature line or signature block, contained no signature by any of the plaintiffs, and advised that future paperwork was forthcoming. The last section in the July 4 offer provided that "[t]he Settlement paperwork would be drafted. . . . " Additionally, this section advised that plaintiffs require "a YES or NO on this proposal; you need to say 'I accept.' " (Italics added.) The last sentence in this section stated: "Let me know your decision." None of these sentences in the July 4 offer supports a conclusion that the parties agreed that Fair's agreement to the proposal was an agreement to sign a legally binding settlement. (See [*Sully-Miller Contracting Co. v. Gledson/Cashman Construction, Inc.* (2002) 103 Cal.App.4th 30, 37, [126 Cal.Rptr.2d 400] [a party's signature added "to a document that does not call for it" is not a signed writing under Code of Civil Procedure section 664.6 because "[a] party's signature fails to convey" knowledge and express consent "unless it is contained in a document that was clearly intended by that party to be a binding settlement agreement"]; *Powell v. City of Newton* (2010) 364 N.C. 562, [703 S.E.2d 723, 727–728] [applying North Carolina's UETA and concluding that the parties did not agree to the use of electronic signatures "[i]n light of the express indication by [one party] that [the other party] should sign and forward the [agreements]"].) Moreover, Fair's subsequent voicemail and text messages from his cell phone did not indicate that he intended for his e-mail to be a signature to the electronic record as he simply stated that he "agree [d] with" or accepted Russo's terms.

"Subsequently, the statements of plaintiffs' counsel provided further evidence that no party considered the July 4 offer attached to the July 5 e-mail a final document requiring a signature. Russo stated that Fair's response "confirms full agreement" and he promised to work "on the formal settlement paperwork" and "get the settlement paperwork" for Fair's review "with the goal of getting it all finalized and signed next week." He added that the "settlement is otherwise binding under" Code of Civil Procedure section 664.6, but the settlement could not be binding without all of the parties' signatures. Halliburton sent Fair an e-mail on July 19, 2013, stating in relevant part: "It's a good thing we have a settlement, then; let's put pen to paper and close it." "We are not going to stay anything until we have a signed deal."

"In contrast to the July 4 offer, the July 11 writing included a signature line at the end of the settlement agreement. Additionally, it specified that an electronic signature could be used. The July 11 writing provided: "This Settlement Agreement may be signed and delivered by facsimile and in counter-parts. It may also be electronically signed by each of the Parties through the use of EchoSign, DocuSign, or such other commercially available electronic signature software which results in confirmed signatures delivered electronically to each of the Parties, which shall be treated as an original as though in-signed by officers or other duly authorized representatives of each Party." No similar language was in the July 4 offer and, as already stressed, the July 4 offer did not indicate that a printed name at the bottom of an e-mail would be an electronic signature.

"Accordingly, we conclude that the evidence in the record is as a matter of law insufficient to establish that Fair signed electronically a settlement agreement. Since Fair's printed name was not a signature under UETA, the trial court erred when it concluded that Fair's printed name at the bottom of the e-mail satisfied the strict signature requirements under Code of Civil Procedure section 664.6."

SECTION 4. SILENCE AS ACCEPTANCE

This section concerns the rules that treat an offeree's silence in response to an offer as acceptance of the offer. In the principal case the question is whether a offeror's silence in response to a counter-offer is acceptance of a changed term in the counter-offer when the original offeror did not read the counter-offer. You will see this issue again in Chapter 15 when we take up the battle of the forms The rules in Restatement § 69 on when silence constitutes acceptance generally focus on a simpler problem, defining when a party who accepts property or services tacitly agrees to pay.

McGurn v. Bell Microproducts, Inc.

United States Courts of Appeals, First Circuit, 2002.
284 F.3d 86.

Lipez, Circuit Judge.

This case requires us to evaluate the district court's application of an exception to the general rule that silence does not constitute acceptance of the terms of a contract offer.

I.

Bell Microproducts, Inc. (Bell) mailed George R. McGurn a signed offer of employment, which stipulated that if McGurn was terminated without cause during the first twelve months of his employment with Bell he would receive a severance package worth $120,000. In countersigning and returning the offer letter, McGurn crossed out the word "twelve" and replaced it with "twenty-four." McGurn initialed his alteration, but otherwise did nothing to call it to Bell's attention. Bell terminated McGurn thirteen months later and refused to pay him the severance package on the ground that the twelve-month period stipulated in the offer letter had passed, and that McGurn's replacement of "twelve" with "twenty-four" was a counteroffer which Bell had never accepted.

McGurn filed an action in the Massachusetts Superior Court to collect the compensation he claimed Bell owed him under the contract, and Bell removed the case to federal district court on the basis of diversity of citizenship. The parties agree that Massachusetts law governs this dispute. Presented with cross-motions for summary judgment, the district court granted summary judgment for McGurn, finding that Bell's silence in response to McGurn's counteroffer constituted an acceptance of the 24-month termination clause. We find that conclusion premature. The import of Bell's silence cannot be decided as a matter of law on a motion for summary judgment because of genuine issues of material fact about whether Bell knew or should have known of McGurn's counteroffer. We therefore vacate the district court's judgment and remand for further proceedings.

II.

Except as noted, the following facts are undisputed. Bell Microproducts is a distributor of semiconductor parts and components with headquarters in San Jose, California. McGurn is a resident of Massachusetts. In March of 1997, Bell's President, Donald Bell, met with McGurn, who at the time was gainfully employed elsewhere, to discuss the position of Vice President for the Eastern Region at Bell. McGurn said that if he came to work for Bell he would require a written contract that included a "termination clause" stipulating that he would receive six months salary and half his commissions in the event that he was fired.

During the next few months McGurn communicated several times with Bill Murphy, the Bell official to whom McGurn would report, and expressed interest in pursuing the position.

Based on these discussions, Murphy's secretary prepared an offer letter and delivered it to Linda Teague, Bell's Director of Human Resources. Teague dated the letter June 10, 1997, signed it, and mailed it to McGurn. Upon receipt of the letter, McGurn telephoned Murphy to discuss the offer and the absence of a termination clause. McGurn then had a series of telephone conversations with Donald Bell in which a termination clause was discussed. On June 29, McGurn requested a termination clause that would remain in force as long as he worked for Bell. However, he also said to Donald Bell that he would consider one that was limited to the first twenty four months of his employment. According to McGurn, Donald Bell replied that a twenty-four month termination clause would be acceptable.

Teague then drafted a second offer letter, in consultation with Donald Bell, which she signed and dated July 1, 1997. The letter included a termination clause stipulating that "[i]f your status as an employee with Bell Microproducts is terminated within the first 12 months of employment for any reason other than gross misconduct, upon termination you will receive a six-month severance package." In response, McGurn drafted his own proposed offer letter, dated July 2, 1997, which included a paragraph on termination "for cause," defined as conviction of a felony or gross negligence or misconduct on the job, and a paragraph on termination "without cause," which was open-ended:

> [T]he Company may terminate your employment without cause. In such event, you will continue to receive your base salary for a period of six (6) months following your termination of employment, [and] . . . you will receive an additional lump-sum amount equal to $40,000 or 50% of annual incentive.

McGurn faxed his proposed offer letter to Murphy.

McGurn's next contact with Bell was his receipt of an offer letter dated July 3, 1997, signed by Teague. The letter included the following paragraph on termination without cause (we have underlined the material change from McGurn's July 2 proposal):

> [T]he Company may terminate your employment without cause. In *the event that this occurs within your first twelve months of employment,* you will continue to receive your base salary for a period of six (6) months following your termination of employment, [and] . . . you will receive an additional lump-sum amount equal to $40,000 or 50% of annual incentive.

The letter concluded with Teague's request that McGurn "sign an acknowledgment of this offer of employment and return to me for our files." The following appeared under Teague's signature:

> I acknowledge my acceptance of the offer as described above and my start date will be _____.
>
> Signed _____ Date _____

McGurn signed his name and entered "7–8–97" in the other two blank spaces. In addition, he crossed out the word "twelve" in the termination clause, inserted "twenty four" directly above it, and initialed the change. The alteration was in the center of the second page of the two-page letter, five inches above McGurn's signature. McGurn returned the letter to Teague (or possibly to Murphy), and started work on July 8, 1997.

McGurn advised no one at Bell that he had modified the July 3 offer letter, and Teague, Murphy, and Donald Bell all deny having viewed the letter upon its return. The Human Resources Department did receive the letter, but Teague testified that she herself would only have been notified if the letter had *not* been received, as McGurn could not have been paid unless a countersigned copy of the offer letter was in Bell's files. Although there is no direct evidence that anyone in the Human Resources Department examined the returned letter, there was evidence that it was Bell's practice to check that returned offer letters had been signed by the employee.

In or around April of 1998, Brian Clark (Murphy's successor at Bell) concluded that McGurn's performance was not satisfactory. At some point after Clark made this determination, but before he fired McGurn on August 3, 1998, Murphy discovered McGurn's alteration of the offer letter, and discussed it with Teague and Donald Bell. Upon learning of his termination on August 3, 1998, after approximately 13 months at Bell, McGurn conveyed to Clark his belief that his contract included a two-year termination clause. Clark disagreed, and Bell refused to pay the amounts specified in the termination clause.

McGurn sued Bell for breach of contract in the Superior Court of Middlesex County, Massachusetts. Based on diversity of citizenship, Bell removed the case to federal district court. 28 U.S.C. § 1332(a)(1). The parties filed cross-motions for summary judgment. In a Memorandum and Order dated February 15, 2001, the district court granted McGurn's motion and denied Bell's motion. The district court found that McGurn's alteration of the July 3 offer letter constituted a counteroffer which, in the circumstances of this case, Bell had accepted by its silence. The court entered judgment for McGurn in the amount of $120,000 plus interest, and Bell filed a timely notice of appeal.

III.

The parties agree that McGurn's alteration of Bell's offer letter constituted a rejection of that offer and created a counteroffer. *See Restatement (Second) of Contracts* § 59 (1981) ("A reply to an offer which purports to accept it but is conditional on the offeror's assent to terms additional to or different from those offered is not an acceptance but is a counter-offer."). What is in dispute is whether Bell accepted McGurn's counteroffer. The district court concluded that it did because Bell should have known about the change made by McGurn, and hence its silence constituted an acceptance of McGurn's counteroffer:

> Although no one on behalf of the defendant signed McGurn's counteroffer, the defendant admits it received the offer and accepted McGurn's services for thirteen months. A presumably sophisticated employer who receives a signed letter of engagement from a prospective employee and fails to read the letter, particularly after weeks of negotiation, does so at its own peril. Thus, in the circumstances of this case, the defendant's failure to read the terms of the offer [does] not preclude the formation of a contract. The defendant accepted the terms of the plaintiff's offer when it decided to and did employ the plaintiff for thirteen months.

Urging a different theory than the "should have known" theory adopted by the district court, McGurn argues that Bell's silence in the face of his counteroffer amounted to an acceptance because Bell knew that McGurn had amended the termination clause, but gave no indication that it rejected the change. Bell denies that it knew about McGurn's alteration of the offer letter.

As a general rule, silence in response to an offer to enter into a contract does not constitute an acceptance of the offer. *See Restatement (Second) of Contracts* § 69 cmt. a ("Acceptance by silence is exceptional."); *Polaroid Corp. v. Rollins Envtl. Servs. (NJ), Inc.,* 416 Mass. 684, 624 N.E.2d 959, 964 (1993) (noting that "silence does not ordinarily manifest assent"). There is, however, an exception to the rule against acceptance by silence "[w]here an offeree takes the benefit of offered services with reasonable opportunity to reject them and reason to know that they were offered with the expectation of compensation."[2] *Restatement (Second) of Contracts* § 69(1)(a).

In *Gateway Co. v. Charlotte Theatres, Inc.,* 297 F.2d 483 (1st Cir.1961), a case in many respects similar to this one, the defendant had sent the

---

[2]   Although the *Restatement* exception, by its terms, addresses a situation in which the offeree advances no payment at all in exchange for the offeror's services, the district court concluded correctly that the exception also applies when there is a dispute about the nature or extent of required compensation. *See Polaroid,* 624 N.E.2d at 964 (applying the exception to a dispute over whether a waste disposal contract included an indemnification clause).

plaintiff two copies of a document which reduced to writing an oral agreement for the defendant to install air conditioning in the plaintiff's movie theater, with one copy to be countersigned and returned. *Id.* at 485. The plaintiff signed, but also inserted a provision that the work would be performed by a certain date. *Id.* The plaintiff returned the countersigned contract with a cover letter noting its "understanding" that the work would be performed by that date (although the letter made no reference to the alteration of the contract itself). *Id.* at 485–86. We stated that "[i]n the absence of actual knowledge [of the alteration of the contract], the test is whether there was reason for [the defendant] to suppose that such addition might have been made." *Id.* at 486. We held that because of the cover letter flagging the issue, defendant's silence could constitute acceptance of plaintiff's counteroffer.

Importantly, we also noted in *Gateway* that "absent the [cover] letter, the case would seem more like" *Kidder v. Greenman,* 283 Mass. 601, 187 N.E. 42 (1933). *Gateway,* 297 F.2d at 486. In *Kidder,* a tenant had signed and returned a lease to her landlord with the understanding that the landlord would fill in certain blank spaces pursuant to an oral agreement. The landlord then completed the lease so as to include a term contrary to the oral understanding, signed it, and returned it to the tenant, who "did not look at the lease at the time she received it except to slit the envelope and see it contained a lease." *Kidder,* 187 N.E. at 45 (internal quotation marks omitted). The court declined to enforce the disputed term against the tenant on the ground that she "had no reason to think that the [landlord] had not completed the lease in the authorized manner and, therefore, [had] no occasion to examine it, when it was returned to her, to see if he had done so." *Id.* at 48. The *Kidder* court concluded that "[i]n these circumstances the doctrine that a person who accepts an instrument . . . without reading it . . . is charged with knowledge of [its] contents is not applicable." *Id.* (citations omitted).

We distill from the *Restatement* and the *Gateway* and *Kidder* precedents the legal rule in Massachusetts that silence in response to an offer may constitute an acceptance if an offeree who takes the benefit of offered services knew or had reason to know of the existence of the offer, and had a reasonable opportunity to reject it. *See Restatement (Second) of Contracts* § 69(1)(a); *Gateway,* 297 F.2d at 485–86; *Kidder,* 187 N.E. at 48. We turn now to the application of that rule in this case.

IV.

Under Federal Rule of Civil Procedure 56(c), a court may enter summary judgment if the record "show[s] that there is no genuine issue as to any material fact and that the moving party is entitled to a judgment as a matter of law." We review the district court's grant of summary judgment de novo, and examine the record in the light most favorable to the party against whom summary judgment had been entered, drawing all reasonable inferences in that party's favor. *Barreto-Rivera v. Medina-Vargas*, 168 F.3d 42, 45 (1st Cir.1999). We note that "disputes about whether a contract has or has not been formed as the result of words and conduct over a period of time . . . present interpretive issues traditionally understood to be for the trier of fact." *Charbonnages de France v. Smith*, 597 F.2d 406, 414–15 (4th Cir.1979). This is so unless "the manifestations of intention of both parties to be bound, or of either not to be bound, are so unequivocal as to present no genuine issue of fact." *Id.* at 415.

A.   The District Court's Opinion

In response to Bell's assertion that it did not notice McGurn's alteration of the offer letter until just before his termination, the district court observed that "absent fraud, a party to a contract is bound by the terms of the contract whether or not he read them." The court added: "It will not do for a man to enter into a contract, and, when called upon to respond to its obligations, to say that he did not read it when he signed it, or did not know what it contained." The district court's legal proposition is sound, but inapposite to this case. The disputed term was added to the offer *after Bell had signed it.* The relevant question is why, as a matter of law, Bell should be expected to *re-read* an offer it had written and signed, upon its return with McGurn's countersignature.

In response to that question, the district court declared that "[a] presumably sophisticated employer who receives a signed letter of engagement from a prospective employee and fails to read the letter, particularly after weeks of negotiation, does so at its own peril." Although the logic of this generalization has some appeal, its generality is an insurmountable problem. Unless the record establishes that Bell knew or had reason to know that McGurn had modified what Bell had written—and the district court points to no facts in the record that would support such a conclusion—we cannot say that Bell's silence, as a matter of law, constituted an acceptance of McGurn's counteroffer.

Although we decline to endorse the district court's generalization, "we may affirm [a summary judgment] order on any ground revealed by the record." *Houlton Citizens' Coalition v. Town of Houlton*, 175 F.3d 178, 184 (1st Cir.1999). We therefore examine the record to see if, drawing all reasonable inferences in Bell's favor, the evidence nevertheless compels the conclusion that responsible officials at Bell knew or should have known about McGurn's counteroffer far enough in advance of his termination that Bell had a reasonable opportunity to reject the 24-month termination clause if it wished to avoid being bound. Summary judgment for McGurn would be proper if Bell had actual or constructive knowledge of McGurn's counteroffer at the time he returned the offer letter, or if, when Clark discovered the counteroffer, he had a "reasonable opportunity to reject" it before he fired McGurn, but instead continued to "take[ ] the benefit of [McGurn's] services" without speaking up. *Restatement (Second) of Contracts* § 69(1)(a).

There are three possible grounds for affirmance suggested by the record, two involving alleged actual knowledge and one involving constructive knowledge. We examine them in turn.

B.   Prominence of the Alteration

McGurn argues that Bell had actual knowledge of the alteration of the offer letter at the time of its return. Although McGurn advances no direct evidence that anyone at Bell noticed his revision of the termination clause, he points out that the alteration was made on the same page that bore his signature, which Bell acknowledges an unknown employee checked pursuant to company policy. McGurn infers from this that the unknown employee "had to have seen the change" in the duration of the termination clause, because "one's eyes are immediately drawn to the change made by McGurn and his initials above that change."

While an inference that Bell "had to have seen the change" would be permissible based on the evidence in the record—the alteration was in the center of the very page McGurn had signed—we cannot say that a factfinder would be required to conclude that the Bell employee who checked for McGurn's signature must have noticed McGurn's alteration of the termination clause half-way up the page. That is, the evidence that a Bell employee must have seen McGurn's alteration is not "so one-sided that [McGurn] must prevail as a matter of law." *Anderson v. Liberty Lobby, Inc.,* 477 U.S. 242, 252, 106 S.Ct. 2505, 91 L.Ed.2d 202 (1986).

C.   Clark's Discovery

Clark declared that he examined the countersigned offer letter and discovered what McGurn had done "[a]t some point after making [the] decision [to terminate McGurn], but before the actual termination." The record only establishes that this discovery was made during or after April of 1998, and before McGurn was fired in August of 1998. McGurn argues that once Bell discovered his counteroffer it had an obligation to speak up if it wished to reject it. Bell points out, however, that Clark "could have discovered the altered document as late as the day before" he fired McGurn. Whatever the merits of McGurn's legal argument on this point—a matter as to which we take no view—this factual uncertainty precludes summary judgment for McGurn based on Clark's actual knowledge of McGurn's counteroffer.

D.   Teague's Responsibility

We also examine the record for evidence that Teague (Bell's Director of Human Resources), or an employee in her department acting on her behalf, should have determined if the returned offer letter had been modified. Teague had participated in the negotiations with McGurn. She stated at her deposition that "Bill Murphy and I worked together on all of these offer letters," and Donald Bell testified that he "consult[ed] with Linda [Teague]" during the drafting of the letter. The July 3 offer letter from Bell to McGurn was signed by Teague, and indicated that McGurn should return the countersigned copy *to her*. Under these circumstances, a jury might conclude that McGurn could reasonably have expected Teague (or Murphy) to inspect the document upon its return. Moreover, the offer set out in Bell's letter was not a mere reduction to writing of a previous oral agreement; it was a step in a negotiation which Bell had no reason to assume had been concluded. Although Teague requested that McGurn simply sign and return the letter unamended, the evidence supports the inference that she had no basis for assuming he would do so. Instead, she should have checked the document to ensure that he had not made further changes.

Although an inference that Teague should have examined the returned offer letter with greater care would be permissible based on the evidence in the record, the evidence, again, does not compel such an inference. Bell disputes the notion that Teague (or her subordinates) had any reason to check the returned offer letter for unauthorized modifications, and a factfinder might conclude that Teague had no reason to inspect the letter absent any indication from McGurn that he had revised a material term.[5]

We have stated that "[o]rdinarily the question of whether a contract has been made . . . is for the jury," *Ismert & Assocs., Inc. v. New England Mut. Life Ins. Co.,* 801 F.2d 536, 541 (1st Cir.1986), except where "[t]he words and actions that allegedly formed a contract [are] so clear themselves that reasonable people could not differ over their meaning," *Bourque v. FDIC,* 42 F.3d 704, 708 (1st Cir.1994) (internal quotation marks omitted). When, as is the case here, "the facts support plausible but conflicting inferences on a pivotal issue in the case, the judge may not choose between those inferences at the summary judgment stage." *Coyne v. Taber Partners I,* 53 F.3d 454, 460 (1st Cir.1995); *accord* 10A Charles Alan Wright, Arthur R. Miller & Mary Kay Kane, *Federal Practice and Procedure* § 2725 at 433–37 (3d ed. 1998) ("[I]f the evidence presented on [a] motion [for summary judgment] is subject to conflicting interpretations,

---

[5] Because the July 3 offer letter was signed by Teague, and McGurn returned it to Teague (or Bill Murphy), we need not be detained by Bell's argument that the low-level employee who examined the returned letter lacked the authority to bind the corporation (with his silence) on the question of McGurn's termination clause. Teague having requested that McGurn return the letter *to her,* it would be no defense for her to say that a subordinate in her office who lacked the authority to bind the corporation opened the letter and failed to show it to her. *See Gateway,* 297 F.2d at 486 & n. 4 (holding corporation responsible for contents of letter addressed to its president but read by a secretary). To accept Bell's argument on this point would be to penalize McGurn for Teague's failure to read her own mail. The same logic applies if McGurn returned the letter to Murphy, as he suggested he might have done.

or reasonable people might differ as to its significance, summary judgment is improper.") (footnotes omitted).

V.

In sum, drawing all reasonable inferences in Bell's favor, as we must in reviewing the district court's entry of summary judgment against Bell, we cannot say that the facts in the record compel a conclusion that Bell noticed or should have noticed McGurn's modification of Bell's offer letter, and that its silence, therefore, constituted an acceptance of McGurn's offer. Instead, those issues must be resolved by the factfinder at a trial.

Judgment vacated. Remanded for further proceedings consistent with this opinion. Each party to bear his or its own costs.

SELYA, CIRCUIT JUDGE (dubitante).

I write separately because I doubt that the court's opinion reflects either the practicalities of the case at hand or the result that the Supreme Judicial Court (SJC) would reach.

The critical facts are undisputed. McGurn's counteroffer—the letter containing his modification of the termination clause—was received at Bell's headquarters in the ordinary course and routed by it to its human resources department. That letter formed the basis for the company's treatment of McGurn as an employee and remained part of the corporate personnel records for the duration of his employment. Given these facts, the case turns on whether Bell should be said to have accepted McGurn's counteroffer.

While no official of the company ever said "I accept" in so many words, acceptance can occur by silence under certain circumstances. *See, e.g., Ismert & Assocs., Inc. v. New Engl. Mut. Life Ins. Co.,* 801 F.2d 536, 541–42 (1st Cir.1986); *Polaroid Corp. v. Rollins Envtl. Servs. (NJ), Inc.,* 416 Mass. 684, 624 N.E.2d 959, 964 (1993); *see also* Restatement (Second) of Contracts § 69 (1981). One such set of circumstances, pertinent here, is when an offeree fails to reply to an offer yet takes the benefit of the offered services with reasonable opportunity to reject them and reason to know that they were tendered in the expectation of a particular consideration. *See* Restatement (Second) of Contracts § 69(1). In such a situation, it would be manifestly unjust for an offeree to reap the benefit of the services without letting the offeror know that it had no intention of paying the remuneration that the offeror expected to receive. *Id.,* cmt. b. Thus, fundamental fairness permits silence to operate as an acceptance.

This principle is part of the warp and woof of Massachusetts contract law. *See Polaroid,* 624 N.E.2d at 964; *Bump v. Robbins,* 24 Mass.App.Ct. 296, 509 N.E.2d 12, 18–19 (1987). On the facts of record here, I think it likely that the SJC would find, as did the able district judge, that Bell implicitly assented to (and, therefore, should be bound by) the terms of

McGurn's counteroffer. After all, Bell unreservedly accepted McGurn's services, having reason to know *from its own files* that those services were being rendered with an expectation that the terms of the counteroffer (including the amended termination clause) would be fulfilled.

To be sure, Bell tells us that, even though it employed McGurn for thirteen months *pursuant to the letter that set out the terms of his counteroffer,* no one in its employ noticed the modification. But there is no hint here of chicanery on McGurn's part, and I doubt that ignorance induced by a party's own negligence or lassitude is a basis for escaping from contractual obligations. To the contrary, the acceptance of offered services, under circumstances in which the beneficiary of those services ought to have known that the provider expected to be compensated for them in a certain way, is the functional equivalent of express assent. *See Bump,* 509 N.E.2d at 18–19. This case seems to fit within the contours of that rule.

To sum up, I believe that a party should not be able to insulate itself from ex contractu liability by professing that it neglected to read the very document essential for the formation of the contract, especially when that document has reposed in its own files at all relevant times. Were the law otherwise and the majority's view taken to its logical extreme, an offeree could completely redefine its responsibilities by the simple expedient of claiming that it was not aware of what its own records plainly showed. I doubt that the SJC would countenance so counterintuitive a result. *Cf. Upton v. Tribilcock,* 91 U.S. 45, 50, 23 L.Ed. 203 (1875) (observing that "[i]t will not do for a man to enter into a contract, and, when called upon to respond to its obligations, to say that he did not . . . know what it contained. If this were permitted, contracts would not be worth the paper on which they are written"). Given this doubt, I respectfully decline to join the court's opinion.

RESTATEMENT, SECOND, CONTRACTS § 69

[See Selected Source Materials Supplement]

CISG ART. 18(1), (3)

[See Selected Source Materials Supplement]

UNIDROIT PRINCIPLES OF INTERNATIONAL COMMERCIAL CONTRACTS ART. 2.1.6(3)

[See Selected Source Materials Supplement]

PRINCIPLES OF EUROPEAN
CONTRACT LAW ART. 2.204(2)

[See Selected Source Materials Supplement]

Kukuska v. Home Mut. Hail-Tornado Ins. Co.

204 Wis. 166, 235 N.W. 403 (1931)

On July 3, Kukuska, a farmer, applied to an agent of the Home Mutual Hail-Tornado Insurance Company for hail insurance. Kukuska received no communication from the company or its agent until 11 A.M. on August 1, when he was informed that his application was declined. That afternoon, Kukuska's crops were severely damaged by hail. "Other insurance companies were writing hail insurance, and, if the plaintiff had been notified of the rejection of his application within a reasonable time, he could have protected himself against such loss. It is well known that the months of July and August constitute the most hazardous period for hailstorms in the locality where plaintiff's crops were situated." Kukuska brought suit against the company for the loss occasioned by the hailstorm. Held, for Kukuska:

It is significant that the insured does not take the first step in the process which leads to the making of a contract of insurance. . . . [The insurer in this case] required the application to be made upon blanks furnished by it. By the terms of the application, which was required to be made according to the by-laws, the applicant agreed to pay all just assessments and to be governed and abide by the rules, regulations, and by-laws of the company. He was required to pay the amount of the premium in advance. If the application were accepted, he agreed that the policy should run from the date of the application, July 2, 1928, rather than from the date of the acceptance when made. By the soliciting, making and receiving of the application, the parties had entered into some kind of a consensual relationship. . . .

Under such circumstances, having in view the nature of the risk against which the insurer seeks protection, is there not a duty upon the insurer to act upon the application within a reasonable time? Can the insurer, having preempted the field, retain control of the situation and the applicant's funds indefinitely? Does not the very nature of the transaction impose upon the insurer a duty to act? It is considered that there is a duty. If the insurer is under such a duty and fails to perform the duty within a reasonable time and, as a consequence, the applicant sustains damage, it is not vastly important that the legal relationship be placed in a particular category. If we say it is contractual, that is, there is an implied agreement under the circumstances on the part of the insurer to act within a reasonable time, or, having a duty to act, the insurer negligently fails in the performance of that duty, or that the duty springs out of a consensual relationship, and is therefore in the nature of a quasi contractual liability, is not vitally important. Each view finds some support in the cases. . . .

————

Hobbs v. Massasoit Whip Co.

158 Mass. 194, 33 N.E. 495 (1893)

Without receiving any specific order for them, the plaintiff had on four or five occasions shipped eelskins to the defendant, for which the defendant had paid. The plaintiff then shipped further eelskins. The defendant retained these eelskins for some months without communicating with the plaintiff, but after a destruction of the skins, the defendant refused to pay for them. The plaintiff sued for the price of the skins. Held, for the plaintiff. The past dealings of the parties were such that the plaintiff had a kind of "standing offer" for eelskins. ". . . Even if the offer was not such that the contract was made as soon as skins corresponding to its terms were sent, sending them did impose on the defendant a duty to act about them; and silence on its part, coupled with a retention of the skins for an unreasonable time, might be found by the jury to warrant the plaintiff in assuming that they were accepted, and thus to amount to an acceptance."

————

Austin v. Burge

156 Mo.App. 286, 137 S.W. 618 (1911)

This was an action for the subscription price of a newspaper. The defendant's father-in-law had given him a two-year subscription to the newspaper, but the publisher continued mailing the newspaper to defendant after the subscription expired. The defendant twice paid bills for the subscription price, but each time he directed the newspaper to be stopped. The publisher nevertheless continued to mail the newspaper to the defendant, and the defendant continued to receive and read the newspaper, until finally he moved to another state. The trial court gave judgment for the defendant. Reversed:

> It is certain that one cannot be forced into contractual relations with another and that therefore he cannot, against his will, be made the debtor of a newspaper publisher. But it is equally certain that he may cause contractual relations to arise by necessary implication from his conduct. . . . In this case defendant admits that, notwithstanding he ordered the paper discontinued at the time when he paid a bill for it, yet plaintiff continued to send it, and he continued to take it from the post office to his home. This was an acceptance and

use of the property, and, there being no pretense that a gratuity was intended, an obligation arose to pay for it. . . .

The preparation and publication of a newspaper involves much mental and physical labor, as well as an outlay of money. One who accepts the paper, by continuously taking it from the post office, receives a benefit and pleasure arising from such labor and expenditure as fully as if he had appropriated any other product of another's labor, and by such act he must be held liable for the subscription price.

———

39 U.S.C. § 3009 [MAILING OF UNORDERED MERCHANDISE]

[See Selected Source Materials Supplement]

———

NOTE ON NEGATIVE-OPTION PLANS

A negative-option plan is a promotional technique that is similar in some respects to the sending of unordered merchandise. This type of plan is defined in a Federal Trade Commission rule to mean "a contractual plan or arrangement under which a seller periodically sends to subscribers an announcement which identifies merchandise (other than annual supplements to previously acquired merchandise) it proposes to send to subscribers to such plan, and the subscribers thereafter receive and are billed for the merchandise identified in each such announcement, unless by a date or within a time specified by the seller with respect to each such announcement the subscribers, in conformity with the provisions of such plan, instruct the seller not to send the identified merchandise." 16 C.F.R. § 425.1. Among the most familiar examples are book and record clubs. In contract-law terms, negative-option plans differ significantly from the sending of unordered merchandise, because the consumer normally contracts in advance, for consideration (in the form of a bonus for joining), to be bound by the plan's terms. The FTC's rule does not prohibit such plans. Instead, the rule requires clear disclosure of the plan's material terms and imposes certain minimal regulation, such as a requirement that the subscriber be given at least ten days in which to instruct the seller not to mail the current selection.

———

NOTE ON THE SIGNIFICANCE OF UNJUST ENRICHMENT AND LOSS THROUGH RELIANCE IN CASES WHERE SILENCE IS TREATED AS ACCEPTANCE

Three kinds of cases in which an offeree remains silent after receiving an offer may be distinguished: (1) Cases where the offeree enriches himself by silently appropriating the benefit of something offered to him. (2) Cases where the offeror changes her position either because she assumes that her offer has been accepted, or because, as in *Kukuska*, supra, the very act of making the offer requires her to forgo other opportunities to covering her needs. (3) Cases where there is no enrichment of the offeree, and no detrimental reliance by the offeror, but where the offeror forms an expectation of profit on the assumption that a contract has been concluded through the offeree's silence. Assuming that the facts bearing on the apparent meaning of silence are in other respects the same in all three situations, it is clear that a court will be more likely to give relief in (1) than in (2), and that (2) in turn makes a stronger appeal to judicial sympathy than (3). The problem of silence as acceptance is analyzed in these terms in Laufer, Silence as Acceptance: A Critique, 1939, 7 Duke Bar Ass'n Jour. 87.

———

SECTION 5. RESTITUTION FOR A BENEFIT CONFERRED IN THE MISTAKEN BELIEF OF THE EXISTENCE OF A CONTRACT

This section concerns the claim in the law of restitution or unjust enrichment when A confers a benefit on B in the mistaken belief of the existence of a contract with B. In the principal case the defendant did not know, or have to reason to know, she was expected to pay for a benefit provided her by the plaintiff. This precludes recovery by the plaintiff on a theory of implied-in-fact contract.

———

NURSING CARE SERVICES, INC. v. DOBOS
District Court of Appeal of Florida, Fourth District, 1980.
380 So.2d 516.

HURLEY, JUDGE.

Plaintiff, Nursing Care Services, Inc., appeals from that part of a final judgment which disallowed compensation for certain nursing care services. Our review of the record reveals substantial uncontradicted testimony supporting plaintiff's theory of recovery and thus we remand for entry of an amended final judgment.

Mary Dobos, the defendant, was admitted to Boca Raton Community Hospital with an abdominal aneurysm. Her condition was sufficiently serious to cause her doctor to order around-the-clock nursing care. The hospital implemented this order by calling upon the plaintiff which provides individualized nursing services.

Mrs. Dobos received nursing care which in retrospect can be divided into three periods: (1) two weeks of in-hospital care; (2) forty-eight hour post-release care; and (3) two weeks of at-home care. The second period of care (the forty-eight hour post-release care) was removed as an issue at trial when Mrs. Dobos conceded that she or her daughter authorized that period of care. The total bill for all three periods came to $3,723.90; neither the reasonableness of the fee, the competency of the nurses, nor the necessity for the services was contested at trial.

The gist of the defense was that Mrs. Dobos never signed a written contract nor orally agreed to be liable for the nursing services. Testifying about the in-hospital care, she said, "Dr. Rosen did all the work. I don't know what he done (sic), and he says, I needed a nurse." It is undisputed that Mrs. Dobos was mentally alert during her at-home recuperation period. Asked if she ever tried to fire the nurses or dispense with their care, she replied, "I didn't. I didn't know who—I thought maybe if they insist, the doctors insist so much, I thought the Medicare would take care of it, or whatever. I don't know."

After a non-jury trial, the court granted judgment for the plaintiff in the sum of $248.00, the cost of the forty-eight hour post-release care. It declined to allow compensation for the first and third periods of care, saying,

> ". . . [T]here certainly was a service rendered, but based on the total surrounding circumstances, I don't think there is sufficient communications and dealings with Mrs. Dobos to make sure that she knew that she would be responsible for those services rendered. . . ."

We concur in the trial court's determination that the plaintiff failed to prove an express contract or a contract implied in fact. It is our view, however, that the uncontradicted testimony provided by plaintiff and defendant alike, clearly established a contract implied in law which entitles the plaintiff to recover.

Contracts implied in law, or as they are more commonly called "quasi contracts", are obligations imposed by law on grounds of justice and equity. Their purpose is to prevent unjust enrichment. Unlike express contracts or contracts implied in fact, quasi contracts do not rest upon the assent of the contracting parties. See generally, 28 Fla.Jur., Restitution and Implied Contracts.

One of the most common areas in which recovery on a contract implied in law is allowed is that of work performed or services rendered. The rationale is that the defendant would be unjustly enriched at the expense of the plaintiff if she were allowed to escape payment for services rendered or work performed. There is, however, an important limitation. Ordinarily liability is imposed to pay for services rendered by another only when the person for whose benefit they were rendered requested the services or knowingly and voluntarily accepted their benefits. *Yeats v. Moody,* 128 Fla. 658, 175 So. 719 (1937); *Strano v. Carr & Carr, Inc.,* 97 Fla. 150, 119 So. 864 (1929); *Taylor v. Thompson,* 359 So.2d 14 (Fla. 1st DCA 1978); and *Tobin & Tobin Insurance Agency, Inc. v. Zeskind,* 315 So.2d 518 (Fla. 3d DCA 1975).

The law's concern that needless services not be foisted upon the unsuspecting has led to the formulation of the "officious intermeddler doctrine." It holds that where a person performs labor for another without the latter's request or implied consent, however beneficial such labor may be, he cannot recover therefor. *Tipper v. Great Lakes Chemical Company,* 281 So.2d 10 (Fla.1973). A notable exception to this rule, however, is that of emergency aid:

> A person who has supplied things or services to another, although acting without the other's knowledge or consent, is entitled to restitution therefore from the other if he acted unofficiously and with intent to charge therefore, and the things or services were necessary to prevent the other from suffering serious bodily harm or pain, and the person supplying them had no reason to know that the other would not consent to receiving them, if mentally competent, and it was impossible for the other to give consent or, because of extreme youth or mental impairment, the other's consent would have been immaterial. 66 Am.Jur.2d, Restitution and Implied Contract, § 23.

In the case at bar it is unclear whether Mrs. Dobos, during the period of in-hospital care, understood or intended that compensation be paid. Her condition was grave. She had been placed in the hospital's intensive care unit and thereafter had tubes and other medical equipment attached to her body which necessitated special attention. She was alone, unable to cope and without family assistance. It is worthy of note that at no point during the litigation was there any question as to the propriety of the professional judgment that the patient required special nursing care. To the contrary, the record demonstrates that the in-hospital nursing care was essential to Mrs. Dobos' health and safety. Given these circumstances it would be unconscionable to deny the plaintiff recovery for services which fall squarely within the emergency aid exception. *Tipper v. Great Lakes Chemical Company,* supra.

The third period of care is less difficult. It is unquestioned that during the at-home recuperation, Mrs. Dobos was fully aware of her circumstances and readily accepted the benefits conferred. Given such facts, we believe the rule set down in *Symon v. J. Rolfe Davis, Inc.,* 245 So.2d 278, 279 (Fla. 4th DCA 1971) must govern:

> It is well settled that where services are rendered by one person for another which are knowingly and voluntarily accepted, the law presumes that such services are given and received in expectation of being paid for, and will imply a promise to pay what they are reasonably worth.

A patient's unannounced misconception that the cost of accepted services will be paid by an insurer or Medicare does not absolve her of responsibility to bear the cost of the services.

As a postscript we note that Mrs. Dobos' home recuperation was interrupted by her readmission to the hospital with an apparent heart attack. In this age of burgeoning malpractice actions it is not idle conjecture to ponder what her legal position might have been had the plaintiff unilaterally terminated its services at a time of vital need. To its credit, it did not and therefore it is entitled to just compensation. Accordingly, we remand the cause to the trial court with instructions to enter an amended final judgment for the plaintiff in the sum of $3,723.90 plus interest and court costs.

It is so ordered.

ANSTEAD and LETTS, JJ., concur.

NOTE ON TERMINOLOGY AND HISTORY

Various names are used to denote the non-contractual claim in the principal case: quasi-contract, implied-in-law contract, quantum meruit, restitution, and unjust enrichment. There is a great deal of history behind this welter of names.

At an early time, the English common law settled into a *formulary* system. Under this system, a plaintiff could obtain a judicial remedy only if the transaction giving rise to his grievance came within (or could, through a legal fiction, be made to come within) an established form of action or *writ*. The principal writs for enforcing what we think of as a contract were covenant and debt. *Covenant* could be brought for cases in which the contract was under seal. *Debt* could be brought for cases in which the plaintiff had fully performed a contract that involved (i) a quid pro quo and (ii) a promise to pay a "sum certain," which the defendant had refused to pay. Accordingly, covenant was a *formal* contract action, because it was based on a form—the seal—while debt was an action based on a *half-completed exchange.*

Covenant and debt were burdened with archaic procedures, and were gradually superseded by a new form of action, known as *assumpsit*. The earliest assumpsit cases were pled using the writ *trespass on the case*. This was a non-formulaic writ with two basic parts. The second part was a description of the defendant's harmful conduct. This was preceded by a "whereas" clause that explained why the harmful conduct should be actionable. This form of pleading was useful for a lawyer who wanted to bring a novel claim or a claim for which there was no formulaic pleading, for it enabled a lawyer to tell the client's story in the whereas clause. Hearing the story, a sympathetic court might allow the claim despite its novelty. Among the grounds for imposing liability for harmful conduct was that a defendant had undertaken or assumed an obligation to care for the plaintiff's person, property, or money. It should not be surprising that from early times the common law recognized an action when there was *invited reliance, negligence, and harm*. These cases are antecedents to the modern negligence action alongside cases in which the plaintiff pled a duty as a matter of custom or the defendant taking control of a dangerous instrumentality, and not as a matter of assumpsit (invited reliance). These assumpsit cases also are antecedents to the doctrine of promissory estoppel.

Over time assumpsit came to be used as a general claim for breach of contract. The pleading of assumpsit also became formulaic. At first a plaintiff was allowed to avoid the archaic limitations on debt by pleading *indebitatus assumpsit* (the defendant *"being indebted, undertook to pay"*). The action was on the promise to pay, and not the original debt, avoiding a supposed early common-law rule that the same set of facts could not give rise to more than one form of action. For some time, it was held that assumpsit would not lie against a debtor who had *not* made a separate and later promise to pay her debt, "for if he assumed at the time of the contract then debt lies, and not assumpsit; but if he assumed after the contract, then an action lies upon the assumpsit." (Manwood, C.B. in Anon., Dailson 84 pl. 35, 1572.) However, the pressure for a more complete device to avoid the archaic restrictions of the action of debt continued, and was reinforced by the desire of the King's Bench court to increase its powers by expanding the scope of assumpsit (that court being excluded from jurisdiction over actions in debt). Accordingly, King's Bench began to allow assumpsit in cases where the action of debt would lie, even in the absence of a later promise by the debtor to pay.

This attempt to relieve the plaintiff in assumpsit from the burden of proving a later promise was for a while thwarted by the Exchequer Chamber, but finally "all the justices of England" were brought together to consider *Slade's Case* (4 Coke 92b.), and decided, in 1602, that the practice of King's Bench should be upheld. The allegation that the defendant had made a new promise to pay was treated as a legal fiction, which the defendant was not permitted to deny and the plaintiff was not required to prove. However, the defendant could deny that the transaction that was claimed to be the basis of the defendant's obligation occurred, or could argue that even if the transaction did occur, it gave rise to no legal obligation.

A comparable development led to the use of indebitatus assumpsit where a person had made an implied-in-fact promise to pay for a benefit and later made an express promise to pay. For example, suppose that a tailor, at the request of his customer, made and delivered a suit, there being no agreement on the amount the customer would pay. Here the tailor could not bring an action of covenant, because there was no promise under seal; could not bring an action of debt, because there was no "sum certain"; and, at first, could not bring an action of assumpsit, because there was no express promise by the customer—although such a promise could readily be implied in fact, since it is implicit in the customer's request. That being so, the tailor was left remediless. Of this result, Ames wrote, "The lawyer of today, familiar with the ethical character of the law as now administered, can hardly fail to be startled when he discovers how slowly the conception of a promise implied in fact, as the equivalent of an express promise, made its way in our law." (From early on, the customer would have had a claim for damages against the tailor, if the work was done negligently, in trespass on the case based on assumpsit.)

The injustice of denying a remedy to one in the tailor's position when the customer refused to pay for work competently done was so manifest that it could be expected that the English courts would, despite the restrictions of the formulary system, find some way of protecting his interest. For understandable reasons, the development occurred along the following lines: It was first held that if the customer *later* made an express promise to pay a certain amount, this promise could be enforced in assumpsit—the benefit conferred in the past, at the customer's request, being treated as consideration for this promise.

Once the later promise was treated as a fiction, the way was open to bringing non-promise based claims to avoid unjust enrichment. The plaintiff would allege that: (1) As a result of certain conduct (for example, the payment of money to the defendant by mistake), the defendant had been unjustly enriched at the plaintiff's expense; and (2) the defendant had thereafter promised to pay the plaintiff the amount of this enrichment. The defendant could deny that the conduct described in the first allegation had occurred, or could deny that the conduct resulted in the defendant's being unjustly enriched. However, the defendant was not permitted to deny the second allegation that the defendant had later made a new promise to pay, because that allegation was fictional. Hence the name *contract implied in law*, that is, transactions that are *not* contractual but are brought in assumpsit—a contract action—through the legal fiction that the defendant made a new promise to pay the amount by which she had been unjustly enriched.

Quantum meruit ("as much as he deserved") is a common count (that is, a common and recurring type of claim) in assumpsit for work and labor. The common counts were different formulaic ways of pleading assumpsit. Originally this count was used in cases where the promise to pay was explicit or reasonably implicit. But the fictitious nature of the promise that was pled gave the count a broader range. For example, in a case reported in 1744 a home builder was unable to recover on his contract because the house did not comply with the promised specifications. The court allowed the claim on quantum meruit, leaving it to the jury to decide a fair payment for the work done.

The recognition of restitution or unjust enrichment as a general field of obligation alongside contract and tort is a relatively recent development. The titles of a few canonical works on the topic reflect the welter of names. The first common law treatise on the topic is Keener, Treatise on the Law of Quasi-Contracts (1893). The full title of the first restatement on the subject is Restatement of the Law of Restitution, Quasi-Contracts, and Constructive Trusts (1936). The concept of unjust enrichment appears in Section 1: "A person who has been unjustly enriched at the expense of another is required to make restitution to the other." There is no second restatement, but following the American Law Institute's practice concerning the titles of Restatements, the successor to the first restatement is Restatement, Third, Restitution and Unjust Enrichment (2011). The term *unjust enrichment* appears in the title and throughout Restatement Third. However, Comment *b* to Section 1 urges against treating unjust enrichment as a principle, while suggesting another name for the field: "The concern of restitution is not, in fact, with unjust enrichment in any such broad sense, but with a narrower set of circumstances giving rise to what might more appropriately be called *unjustified enrichment*. Compared to the open-ended implications of the term 'unjust enrichment,' instances of unjustified enrichment are both predictable and objectively determined, because the justification in question is not moral but legal." The wisdom of trying to detach this area of law from morality is doubtful.

NOTE ON THE TWO TYPES OF RESTITUTION CLAIMS IN THE PRINCIPAL CASE

Two different types of restitution and unjust enrichment claims are involved in *Dobos*.

1. *The two weeks of in-hospital care.* This claim is covered by the rule of Restatement, Third, Restitution and Unjust Enrichment § 20, which allows a claim for the reasonable market price of "professional services required for the protection of another's life or health . . . if the circumstances justify the decision to intervene without request." See Note on the Law of Unjust Enrichment in Chapter 1, Section 4. Generally when one person voluntarily confers an unrequested benefit to another person the benefactor has no claim in restitution against the beneficiary. Thus Restatement, Third, Restitution and Unjust Enrichment § 2(3) provides: "There is no liability in restitution for an unrequested benefit voluntarily conferred, unless the circumstances of the transaction justify the claimant's intervention in the absence of a contract." The incapacity of Dobos during the two weeks justified the unrequested intervention.

2. *The two weeks of at-home care.* This claim presents a much more difficult issue under the law of restitution. The plaintiff's claim would be that

it provided Dobos this care in the mistaken belief it had a contract with Dobos to pay for the service. The trial court found that Dobos did not know that she was expected to pay for the at-home care. Thus this is a case of misunderstanding. As you have seen, when there is a misunderstanding about the existence or terms of an agreement, the objective principle of interpretation resolves the misunderstanding against the party who is more at fault. For example, Painter paints the exterior of Owner's house while Owner is absent, reasonably believing that Owner has ordered him to proceed. Actually Owner did not intend to order the work and was undecided about the color. The principle of objective interpretation casts the loss from the misunderstanding on Owner by finding a contract to pay for the work if Owner reasonably appeared to order Painter to proceed. If nothing was said about price, then a reasonable price will be implied.

But what if Painter was more at fault because he was unreasonable in thinking Owner had ordered the work? Painter does not have a contract claim. But Painter may have a restitution claim to avoid unjust enrichment. The principle precluding restitution for unrequested benefits voluntarily conferred does not bar the claim. Benefits conferred by mistake are not considered voluntarily conferred. For example, a restitution claim is available to recover a mistaken payment of cash so long as the recipient has not changed his position in the good faith belief the cash was his, such as by spending the cash on something other than a necessity. That a mistake is a product of carelessness or negligence does not preclude a restitution claim.

Two other limiting principles in Restatement, Third, Restitution and Unjust Enrichment § 2 potentially apply when a plaintiff seeks restitution for the value of a benefit conferred in the mistaken belief of the existence of a contract. Section 2(2) provides: "A valid contract defines the obligation of the parties as to matters within its scope, displacing to that extent any inquiry into unjust enrichment." In *Dobos*, this principle would cut off the plaintiff's restitution claim for the two weeks of at-home care if the court had found there was a contract absolving Dobos from an obligation to pay for the at-home care because the plaintiff had reason to know Dobos believed she would not be charged for the service.

Sometimes a contract will not dispose of a possible unjust enrichment claim. For example. Painter has a contract with Owner's next-door neighbor but he gets the address wrong and mistakenly paints the exterior of Owner's house while Owner is absent. There is no contract between Painter and Owner so the claim is not barred by the principle in § 2(2). But the claim may still run afoul of the principle in Restatement, Third, Restitution and Unjust Enrichment § 2(4): "Liability in restitution may not subject an innocent recipient to a forced exchange: in other words, an obligation to pay for a benefit that the recipient should have been free to refuse." Unless there are unusual facts that make the benefit to Owner clear and quantifiable, this principle casts the loss from the mistake on Painter so long as Owner is "an innocent recipient."

The plaintiff's claim against *Dobos* for the in-home care would be covered by the principle in § 2(4) if the court found there was no contract either obligating Dobos to pay for the in-home care or absolving Dobos from obligation to pay for the in-home care. This is possible if Dobos did not know or have reason to know the plaintiff expected to be paid, and if the plaintiff did not know or have reason to know Dobos expected she would not be charged for the service. Restatement, Third, Restitution and Unjust Enrichment § 9 (Benefits Other Than Money) provides rules to implement the principle in § 2(4). These rules would require either that Dobos "has revealed a willingness to pay for the benefit" or that Dobos "has been spared an otherwise necessary expense."

Vickery v. Ritchie, 202 Mass. 247, 88 N.E. 835 (1909), illustrates the application of the first of these two rules in a case of mutual misunderstanding. An architect duped a property owner and a contractor to proceed with a project to construct a bath house on the owner's land. The architect misled the owner to believe that the price was $23,200 and the contractor to believe that the price was $33,721. The deception was discovered after the work was completed. At trial, the value of the improvement was established to be $22,000 and the "fair value" of the contractor's labor and materials was established to be $33,499.30. Today an architect generally acts as agent for the owner so the loss would be cast on the owner. In the case the architect was considered an agent for both parties so it was a case of mutual misunderstanding. The court awarded $33,499.30, treating the claim as a run-of-the-mill quantum-meruit claim. Restatement First and Restatement Third take the position that the appropriate measure of damages is $23,200, which is what the owner agreed to pay for the building. The Restatement Third explains this does not impose a "forced exchange" on the owner for he agreed to pay this price. See id. § 10, Illustration 27. Query whether the result subjects the architect to a "forced exchange" of his services for $23,200 rather than $33,721?

CHAPTER 11

INDEFINITENESS, PRELIMINARY NEGOTIATIONS, AND THE DUTY TO BARGAIN IN GOOD FAITH

■ ■ ■

One of the axioms of classical contract law was that a contract is formed by offer and acceptance. This axiom was at the center of several clusters of rules. One of these clusters concerned preliminary negotiations, indefiniteness, further-document-to-follow provisions, agreements to agree, and the duty to negotiate in good faith. The rules in this cluster are the subject of this Chapter.

One set of the rules in this cluster concerned the characterization and effect of expressions looking toward the formation of a bargain. Under classical contract law, such expressions were characterized as either an offer or acceptance, on the one hand, or as preliminary negotiations, on the other. This was a binary, static characterization, in which an expression either had an immediate legal effect or no legal effect. An offer had the immediate legal effect of creating a power of acceptance in the offeree, and an acceptance had the immediate legal effect of concluding a contract. In contrast, preliminary negotiations had no legal effect. This binary characterization was reflected in binary outcomes: no liability up to the time at which an acceptance of an offer occurred; full liability for expectation damages thereafter.

Another set of rules in this cluster concerned the indefiniteness of agreements. The relationship between the basic rules of offer and acceptance and the rules concerning indefiniteness was not always clear. A basic rule of offer and acceptance is that an expression will not constitute an offer unless it is sufficiently definite. But why then should contract law have another rule about the indefiniteness of *agreements*? If an expression is not sufficiently definite to constitute an offer, no contract can be formed. If an expression is sufficiently definite to constitute an offer, and the offeree assents, what room is left to argue that a resulting agreement is too indefinite?

One possible answer to this question is that the concept of indefiniteness of agreements reflects the brute fact that many contracts are not formed by an offer-and-acceptance sequence, but by simultaneous actions, like signing a contract, shaking hands, concurring that "It's a deal," or the like. In such cases, whether one of the parties used an expression that was sufficiently definite to constitute an offer is usually irrelevant. Instead, indefiniteness bears on whether parties to a joint expression that looks like an agreement reasonably believed that they had concluded the bargaining process, or were still in preliminary negotiations—preliminary, that is, to the conclusion of an agreement. In addition, indefiniteness may be relevant because even if the parties believed they had concluded the bargaining process, the resulting agreement may be too indefinite to allow the courts to fashion a remedy for its breach.

Still another set of rules in this cluster involved fact patterns in which the parties made an agreement that would look as if it were a completed bargain except for the fact that the parties included in the agreement a provision that contemplated a further, more elaborate document. Often, the original agreement would be sufficiently definite to be enforceable but for the presence of such a provision. The question then is, what is the legal significance of the provision? The rule of classical contract law again was binary and static: If the parties intended the further document to be only an evidentiary memorial of the terms of their original agreement (for example, to tie together various pieces of correspondence), and the original agreement was otherwise sufficiently definite, then the original agreement was enforceable. If, however, the parties intended not to be bound unless and until the further document was executed, so that the further document was to be the consummation of their negotiations, then the original agreement was unenforceable. Accordingly, the parties' contemplation of a further document, which did not eventuate either (1) prevented the formation of a contract, in which case there was no liability, or (2) did not, in which case there was a contract on the terms of the original agreement.

Finally, classical contract law did not recognize a duty to negotiate in good faith. On the contrary, it adopted the rule that an agreement to agree was unenforceable, which by implication precluded an obligation to negotiate in good faith.

As will be seen in this Chapter, in regard to these issues modern contract law has made important dynamic departures from the binary, static offer-and-acceptance model of classical contract law.

———

ACADEMY CHICAGO PUBLISHERS v. CHEEVER
Supreme Court of Illinois, 1991.
144 Ill.2d 24, 161 Ill.Dec. 335, 578 N.E.2d 981.

JUSTICE HEIPLE delivered the opinion of the court:

This is a suit for declaratory judgment. It arose out of an agreement between the widow of the widely published author, John Cheever, and

Academy Chicago Publishers. Contact between the parties began in 1987 when the publisher approached Mrs. Cheever about the possibility of publishing a collection of Mr. Cheever's short stories which, though previously published, had never been collected into a single anthology. In August of that year, a publishing agreement was signed which provided, in pertinent part:

> "Agreement made this 15th day of August 1987, between Academy Chicago Publishers or any affiliated entity or imprint (hereinafter referred to as the Publisher) and Mary W. Cheever and Franklin H. Dennis of the USA (hereinafter referred to as Author).

> Whereas the parties are desirous of publishing and having published a certain work or works, tentatively titled *The Uncollected Stories of John Cheever* (hereinafter referred to as the Work):

* * *

> 2. The Author will deliver to the Publisher on a mutually agreeable date one copy of the manuscript of the Work as finally arranged by the editor and satisfactory to the Publisher in form and content.

* * *

> 5. Within a reasonable time and a mutually agreeable date after delivery of the final revised manuscript, the Publisher will publish the Work at its own expense, in such style and manner and at such price as it deems best, and will keep the Work in print as long as it deems it expedient; but it will not be responsible for delays caused by circumstances beyond its control."

Academy and its editor, Franklin Dennis, assumed the task of locating and procuring the uncollected stories and delivering them to Mrs. Cheever. Mrs. Cheever and Mr. Dennis received partial advances for manuscript preparation. By the end of 1987, Academy had located and delivered more than 60 uncollected stories to Mrs. Cheever. Shortly thereafter, Mrs. Cheever informed Academy in writing that she objected to the publication of the book and attempted to return her advance.

Academy filed suit in the circuit court of Cook County in February 1988, seeking a declaratory judgment: (1) granting Academy the exclusive right to publish the tentatively titled, "The Uncollected Stories of John Cheever"; (2) designating Franklin Dennis as the book's editor; and (3) obligating Mrs. Cheever to deliver the manuscript from which the work was to be published. The trial court entered an order declaring, *inter alia:* (1) that the publishing agreement executed by the parties was valid and enforceable; (2) that Mrs. Cheever was entitled to select the short stories to be included in the manuscript for publication; (3) that Mrs. Cheever would comply with her obligations of good faith and fair dealing if she delivered a manuscript including at least 10 to 15 stories totaling at least 140 pages; (4) Academy controlled the design and format of the work to be published, but control must be exercised in cooperation with Mrs. Cheever.

Academy appealed the trial court's order, challenging particularly the declaration regarding the minimum story and page numbers for Mrs. Cheever's compliance with the publishing agreement, and the declaration that Academy must consult with defendant on all matters of publication of the manuscript.

The appellate court affirmed the decision of the trial court with respect to the validity and enforceability of the publishing agreement and the minimum story and page number requirements for Mrs. Cheever's compliance with same. The appellate court reversed the trial court's declaration regarding control of publication, stating that the trial court erred in considering extrinsic evidence to interpret the agreement regarding control of the publication, given the explicit language of the agreement granting exclusive control to Academy. (200 Ill.App.3d 677, 146 Ill.Dec. 386, 558 N.E.2d 349.) Appeal is taken in this court pursuant to Supreme Court Rule 315(a) (134 Ill.2d R. 315(a)).

The parties raise several issues on appeal; this matter, however, is one of contract and we confine our discussion to the issue of the validity and enforceability of the publishing agreement.

While the trial court and the appellate court agreed that the publishing agreement constitutes a valid and enforceable contract, we cannot concur. The principles of contract state that in order for a valid contract to be formed, an "offer must be so definite as to its material terms or require such definite terms in the acceptance that the promises and performances to be rendered by each party are reasonably certain." (1 Williston, Contracts §§ 38 through 48 (3d ed. 1957); 1 Corbin, Contracts §§ 95 through 100 (1963).) Although the parties may have had and manifested the intent to make a contract, if the content of their agreement is unduly uncertain and indefinite no contract is formed. 1 Williston § 37; 1 Corbin § 95.

The pertinent language of this agreement lacks the definite and certain essential terms required for the formation of an enforceable contract. (*Midland Hotel Corp. v. Reuben H. Donnelley Corp.* (1987), 118 Ill.2d 306, 113 Ill.Dec. 252, 515 N.E.2d 61.) A contract "is sufficiently definite and certain to be enforceable if the court is enabled from the terms and provisions thereof, under proper rules of construction and applicable principles of equity, to ascertain what the parties have agreed to do." (*Morey v. Hoffman* (1957), 12 Ill.2d 125, 145 N.E.2d 644.) The provisions of the subject publishing agreement do not provide the court with a means of determining the intent of the parties.

Trial testimony reveals that a major source of controversy between the parties is the length and content of the proposed book. The agreement sheds no light on the minimum or maximum number of stories or pages necessary for publication of the collection, nor is there any implicit language from which we can glean the intentions of the parties with respect to this essential contract term. The publishing agreement is similarly silent with respect to who will decide which stories will be included in the collection. Other omissions, ambiguities, unresolved essential terms and illusory terms are: No date certain for delivery of the manuscript. No definition of the criteria which would render the manuscript satisfactory to the publisher either as to form or content. No date certain as to when publication will occur. No certainty as to style or manner in which the book will be published nor is there any indication as to the price at which such book will be sold, or the length of time publication shall continue, all of which terms are left to the sole discretion of the publisher.

A contract may be enforced even though some contract terms may be missing or left to be agreed upon, but if the essential terms are so uncertain that there is no basis for deciding whether the agreement has been kept or broken, there is no contract. (*Champaign National Bank v. Landers Seed Co.* (1988), 165 Ill.App.3d 1090, 116 Ill.Dec. 742, 519 N.E.2d 957, Restatement (Second) of Contracts § 33 (1981).) Without setting forth adequate terms for compliance, the publishing agreement provides no basis for determining when breach has occurred, and, therefore, is not a valid and enforceable contract.

An enforceable contract must include a meeting of the minds or mutual assent as to the terms of the contract. (*Midland Hotel,* 118 Ill.2d at 313, 113 Ill.Dec. 252, 515 N.E.2d 61.) It is not compelling that [whether?] the parties share a subjective understanding as to the terms of the contract; the parties' conduct may indicate an agreement to the terms of same. (*Steinberg v. Chicago Medical School* (1977), 69 Ill.2d 320, 13 Ill.Dec. 699, 371 N.E.2d 634.) In the instant case, however, no mutual assent has been illustrated. The parties did not and do not share a common understanding of the essential terms of the publishing agreement.

In rendering its judgment, the trial court supplied minimum terms for Mrs. Cheever's compliance, including story and page numbers. It is not uncommon for a court to supply a missing material term, as the reasonable conclusion often is that the parties intended that the term be supplied by implication. However, where the subject matter of the contract has not been decided upon and there is no standard available for reasonable implication, courts ordinarily refuse to supply the missing term. (1 Williston § 42; 1 Corbin § 100.) No suitable standard was available for the trial court to apply. It is our opinion that the trial court incorrectly supplied minimum compliance terms to the publishing agreement, as the agreement did not constitute a valid and enforceable contract to begin with. As noted above, the publishing agreement contains major unresolved uncertainties. It is not the role of the court to rewrite the contract and spell out essential elements not included therein.

In light of our decision that there was no valid and enforceable contract between the parties, we need not address other issues raised on appeal. For the foregoing reasons, the decisions of the trial and appellate courts in this declaratory judgment action are reversed.

Reversed.

JUSTICES CLARK and FREEMAN took no part in the consideration or decision of this opinion.

———

Peter Kurth, Book Review of Anita Miller, Uncollecting Cheever, the Family of John Cheever v. Academy Chicago Publisher

Salon, November 25, 1998

" 'Uncollecting Cheever' is the blow-by-blow account of the Cheevers' famous legal battle with Academy Chicago, a small Midwestern publishing house owned and run by [Anita] Miller and her husband, Jordan, who in 1988 hoped to publish a volume of Cheever's previously uncollected short stories. The idea for the book came from Franklin Dennis, a New York book publicist who did work for the Millers and was also a neighbor of the Cheevers in Ossining. Mary Cheever at first agreed to the project, signing a contract and receiving half of a $1,500 token advance for what she later insisted she had envisioned as 'a small edition for libraries, for students,' and not a major commercial work. Only when Franklin Dennis had unearthed more than 60 Cheever stories from magazines and anthologies, and when paperback rights to the collection were sold for $225,500 in advance of publication, did the Cheevers—and, for that matter, the Millers—realize that they might have 'a gold mine' on their hands. Mary Cheever tried to break the contract; the Millers responded with a lawsuit to enforce its terms; the Cheevers countered with a suit to protect their copyright, and one of the great literary court battles was born."

———

Ridgway v. Wharton

6 Clark's H.L. Cases 238, 305–306 (1856)

Lord Wensleydale said: "An agreement to be finally settled must comprise all the terms which the parties intend to introduce into the agreement. An agreement to enter into an agreement upon terms to be afterwards settled between the parties is a contradiction in terms. It is absurd to say that a man enters into an agreement till the terms of that agreement are settled. Until those terms are settled he is perfectly at liberty to retire from the bargain."

————

Rego v. Decker

482 P.2d 834 (Alaska 1971)

(Rabinowitz, J.) "Regarding the rule requiring reasonable certainty and its application to particular factual situations, [our cases] demonstrate that:

> The dream of a mechanical justice is recognized for what it is— only a dream and not even a rosy or desirable one.

"In general it has been said that the primary underlying purpose of the law of contracts is the attempted 'realization of reasonable expectations that have been induced by the making of a promise.' In light of this underlying purpose, two general considerations become relevant to solution of reasonable certainty-specific performance problems. On the one hand, courts should fill gaps in contracts to ensure fairness where the reasonable expectations of the parties are fairly clear. The parties to a contract often cannot negotiate and draft solutions to all the problems which may arise. Except in transactions involving very large amounts of money or adhesion contracts to be imposed on many parties, contracts tend to be skeletal, because the amount of time and money needed to produce a more complete contract would be disproportionate to the value of the transaction to the parties. Courts would impose too great a burden on the business community if the standards of certainty were set too high. On the other hand, the courts should not impose on a party any performance to which he did not and probably would not have agreed. Where the character of a gap in an agreement manifests failure to reach an agreement rather than a sketchy agreement, or where gaps cannot be filled with confidence that the reasonable expectations of the parties are being fulfilled, then specific enforcement should be denied for lack of reasonable certainty.

"Several other considerations affect the standard of certainty. A greater degree of certainty is required for specific performance than for damages, because of the difficulty of framing a decree specifying the performance required, as compared with the relative facility with which a breach may be perceived for purposes of awarding damages. Less certainty is required where the party seeking specific performance has substantially shifted his position in reliance on the supposed contract, than where the contract is wholly unperformed on both sides."

————

Saliba-Kringlen Corp. v. Allen Engineering Co.

15 Cal.App.3d 95, 92 Cal.Rptr. 799 (1971)

Saliba, a general contractor, was awarded a freeway-construction contract. Allen, an electrical subcontractor, had submitted the low bid to Saliba for the electrical work, but refused to honor its bid, and Saliba was forced to subcontract out the electrical work at a price in excess of Allen's bid. Saliba sued Allen, who defended on the ground that its bid was too indefinite to form the basis of a contract, since it stated only the price. Held, for Saliba:

It is undisputed that the customary practice in the construction industry is for the general contractor who is awarded a contract to enter into a written contract with the subcontractor, which written contract embraces far more than the price which the subcontractor has bid by telephone. The additional matters would include such things as whether the subcontractor would furnish a bond, who would provide for insurance, how payments would be made and many other matters. Although the provisions other than price are not identical in all subcontracts generally or in electrical subcontracts particularly, price is the principal item as is evident from the fact (as shown by the evidence) that seldom does a general contractor fail to reach an agreement with the subcontractor whose bid is low. Defendant asserts that it should not be held to its bid price because the general contractor could not have known that the general contractor and defendant would have reached an agreement on the terms of the subcontract.

While a prospective subcontractor could submit a bid by way of a written proposed subcontract including not only the price but all other details, we are not aware that this is ever done. The customary bid is made, as it was here, by a brief telephone call in which only the price is stated. If defendant's position is correct, there would never be an occasion to invoke section 90 of the Restatement, Contracts by a general contractor against a prospective subcontractor. Even a subcontractor who did not make a mistake in his bid price but who desired to avoid doing the work because of increased costs, other commitments or any other reason could claim that his bid is not binding because it is incomplete. But California has not taken that position. In *Drennan* the bid was one of price only and it is obvious that the general contractor would have entered into a written subcontract with the prospective subcontractor containing terms other than price. The Supreme Court nevertheless held that the subcontractor's bid was binding. The same rule must be applied here.

It should be noted that here the lack of an electrical subcontract between the general contractor and defendant was not due to the failure of the parties negotiating in good faith to arrive at the terms other than price. We do not intimate what our conclusion would be had that been the case. Here, as in *Drennan,* the parties did not get around to discussing contract provisions because defendant made it clear that it would not do the work at the price bid regardless of the other contractual provisions.

––––––

RESTATEMENT, SECOND, CONTRACTS §§ 33, 34

[See Selected Source Materials Supplement]

––––––

UCC §§ 2–204, 2–305, 2–308, 2–309, 2–310

[See Selected Source Materials Supplement]

––––––

CISG ARTS. 14(1), 31, 33, 55, 57, 58

[See Selected Source Materials Supplement]

––––––

UNIDROIT PRINCIPLES OF INTERNATIONAL COMMERCIAL CONTRACTS ARTS. 2.1.2, 2.1.13, 2.1.14, 5.1.7, 5.1.8, 6.1.1, 6.6.6

[See Selected Source Materials Supplement]

––––––

PRINCIPLES OF EUROPEAN CONTRACT LAW §§ 2.201(1), 6.104, 6.109, 7.01, 7.102

[See Selected Source Materials Supplement]

––––––

NOTE ON GAP-FILLERS

The UCC provisions cross-referenced above are generally referred to as gap-fillers, because they fill gaps that parties may leave in a contract for the sale of goods. The UCC gap-filler provisions are default rules; that is, background rules that the law reads into a contract in the absence of, but only in the absence of, the parties' actual agreement on the relevant issues. (In contrast, mandatory rules, such as the principles of consideration, cannot be supplanted by the parties' agreement.)

The theory of how default rules should be constructed is contested. Most commentators take the position that with certain exceptions, default rules should be based on the agreement parties probably would have reached if they had addressed the relevant issues. This approach leaves open two possible conceptions. Under one conception, the default rule should be the term that reasonable persons in the positions of the parties probably would have agreed to if they had addressed the relevant issue when they made their contract. Under an alternative conception, the default rule should be the term that the actual parties probably would have agreed to if they had addressed the issue. The second conception takes into account the bargaining power and risk-averseness of the actual parties, the intensity with which the parties hold their positions, and the like. The first conception is much more attractive, because it would be extremely difficult to determine the actual parties' relative bargaining power, degree of risk-averseness, intensity, and the like at the time they made their contract, and even if those elements could be determined, it would be highly problematic how those elements would have played out in the negotiation of any given issue.

———

Hawkland, Sales Contract Terms Under the UCC

17 U.C.C.L.J. 195, 207 (1985)

"The rationale underlying the use of statutory [gap-filler] terms is that they represent ordinary understanding about common matters and therefore most likely would have been used by the parties had they considered the term when they made their agreement. In short, statutory terms presuppose that the parties have omitted, through haste, ignorance, or forgetfulness, a routine term that subsequently has become important and that the fairest method to fill that missing term is to impose upon them the kind of term that normally is used by most parties in common, unexceptional deals."

———

SATERIALE V. R.J. REYNOLDS TOBACCO COMPANY
United States Court of Appeals, Ninth Circuit, 2012.
697 F.3d 777.

[Other parts of the opinion are in Chapter 9, supra.]

RJR argues that, even if there was an offer, any contract arising from it would be too indefinite to be enforced. To be enforceable under California law, a contract must be sufficiently definite "for the court to ascertain the parties' obligations and to determine whether those obligations have been performed or breached." *Bustamante v. Intuit, Inc.,* 141 Cal.App.4th 199, 45 Cal.Rptr.3d 692, 699 (2006) (quoting *Ersa Grae Corp. v. Fluor Corp.,* 1 Cal.App.4th 613, 2 Cal.Rptr.2d 288, 294 (1991)) (internal quotation marks omitted). "The terms of a contract are reasonably certain if they provide a basis for determining the existence of a breach and for giving an appropriate remedy." *Id.* (quoting Restatement § 33(2)) (internal quotation marks omitted).

1. *Existence of a Breach*

The first of these requirements is satisfied here. The plaintiffs do not claim that they were entitled to particular merchandise, but that RJR was required to make reasonable quantities of rewards merchandise available during the life of the Camel Cash program—a duty RJR allegedly breached by failing to make *any* merchandise available after October 1, 2006. This alleged breach is readily discernible. *See* Restatement § 33 cmt. b ("[T]he degree of certainty required may be affected by the dispute which arises and by the remedy sought. Courts decide the disputes before them, not other hypothetical disputes which might have arisen.").[5]

2. *Giving an Appropriate Remedy*

The second requirement—that the contract provide a basis for giving an appropriate remedy—presents a closer question. As noted, RJR exercised considerable discretion in deciding what rewards would be offered. We cannot know precisely what merchandise the plaintiffs might have received had RJR fully performed its obligations, an uncertainty that could inhibit the process of determining a remedy. *See Bustamante,* 45 Cal.Rptr.3d at 699 ("[T]he limits of performance must be sufficiently defined to provide a rational basis for the assessment of damages." (quoting *Ladas v. Cal. State Auto. Ass'n,* 19 Cal.App.4th 761, 23 Cal.Rptr.2d 810, 814 (1993)) (internal quotation marks omitted)).

It is not clear, however, that damages could not be rationally assessed here. RJR's internal documents assigned C-Notes values, such as 15 cents per $1 note, that might afford a basis for assessing damages. In the alternative, RJR's final rewards catalog and pre-breach performance might provide a basis for giving an appropriate remedy.

We should not lightly conclude, especially at this early stage in the proceedings, that there is no basis for determining an appropriate remedy where, as here, the allegations suggest that the parties intended to contract. *See Cal. Lettuce Growers,* 289 P.2d at 790 ("The law does not favor, but leans against, the destruction of contracts because of uncertainty; and it will, if feasible, so construe agreements as to carry into

---

[5]   That the alleged contract afforded RJR some discretion in performing does not compel the conclusion that the alleged contract is too indefinite to be enforced. *See* Restatement § 34 cmt. a ("If the agreement is otherwise sufficiently definite to be a contract, it is not made invalid by the fact that it leaves particulars of performance to be specified by one of the parties."); Corbin § 4.4 ("[T]he fact that one of the parties reserves the power of fixing or varying the price or other performance is not fatal if the exercise of this power is subject to prescribed or implied limitations, as that the variation . . . must be reasonable or in good faith." (footnote omitted)); *Cal. Lettuce Growers, Inc. v. Union Sugar Co.,* 45 Cal.2d 474, 289 P.2d 785, 791 (1955) ("[W]here a contract confers on one party a discretionary power affecting the rights of the other, a duty is imposed to exercise that discretion in good faith and in accordance with fair dealing.").

effect the reasonable intentions of the parties if that can be ascertained."
(*quoting McIllmoil v. Frawley Motor Co.*, 190 Cal. 546, 213 P. 971, 972
(1923))); Corbin § 4.1 ("If the parties have concluded a transaction in which
it appears that they intend to make a contract, the court should not
frustrate their intention if it is possible to reach a fair and just result, even
though this requires a choice among conflicting meanings and the filling of
some gaps that the parties have left."). Here, the allegations of the
complaint support the inference that the parties intended to contract. The
plaintiffs enrolled in the Camel Cash program, purchased Camel cigarettes
and collected Camel Cash certificates. RJR accepted the plaintiffs'
registration forms, issued them enrollment numbers, performed under the
program for 15 years and, according to internal RJR documents, treated
outstanding C-Notes as a binding obligation and an outstanding financial
liability. According to the documents, RJR closely monitored its exposure
under the program, and even went so far as to create a financial reserve to
cover that exposure—actions consistent with a legally binding
commitment.

We also consider the plaintiffs' substantial reliance on RJR's promises,
as well as the substantial benefits RJR accrued by virtue of consumers'
reliance on the Camel Cash program. Corbin explains that, "[i]f one party
has greatly benefited by part performance or if one party has relied
extensively on the agreement, the court should go to great lengths to find
a construction of the agreement that will salvage it." Corbin § 4.3 (footnotes
omitted). For these reasons, dismissal for indefiniteness is unwarranted.

————

Arbitron, Inc. v. Tralyn Broadcasting, Inc.

400 F.3d 130 (2d Cir. 2005)

Arbitron had a five-year license agreement (1997 to 2002) to provide
listener-demographics data to Trayln for its single radio station at a monthly
rate of $1,729.57. The data would be more valuable to Trayln if it acquired
additional stations in the same market or an adjacent market. The agreement
covered this possibility with an escalation clause, which gave Arbitron the
right to increase the fee in the event Trayln (or its successor) acquired
additional stations. Trayln also agreed to inform Arbitron in this event. In
June 1999, JMD purchased Trayln's station. The purchase agreement assigned
the Arbitron license agreement to JMD. JMD and Trayln did not inform
Arbitron of the assignment, as required by the license agreement. Nor did they
inform Arbitron that JMD owned four additional radio stations in the same
market. In June 2000, Arbitron learned of these events. It notified JMD that
it was exercising its right to increase the monthly licensing fee by five to reflect
the five JMD stations that could now share Arbitron's listener data. JMD
refused to pay. Arbitron sued for breach, seeking the quintupled fee from June
1999 to the end of the contract's five year term. The district court granted

summary judgment for JMD, concluding that because "[n]either the escalation clause in ¶ 11, nor any other section of the Agreement, contains any basis for determining the new rate to be paid Arbitron in the event changes in ownership occur, the License Agreement's escalation clause was unenforceably vague under New York law." Reversed.

(Calabresi, J.) "[W]e conclude that the escalation clause is enforceable under the common law of New York. This is so because the clause before us is not an "agreement to agree," under which future negations between the parties must occur, but is instead an acknowledgment that, if certain conditions arise in the future, *no* new agreement is required before Arbitron may set new license terms. Such an agreement is not unenforceably vague under New York's common law.

"The seminal New York precedent on unenforceably indefinite contracts is *Joseph Martin, Jr., Delicatessen, Inc. v. Schumacher,* 52 N.Y.2d 105, 436 N.Y.S.2d 247, 417 N.E.2d 541 (1981). There, the Court of Appeals was faced with an agreement between a landlord and a tenant to lease a commercial space for five years at a monthly rate beginning at $500 and escalating over five years to $650, with the option to renew the lease for another five-year term at a rent to be determined by the parties. At the close of the lease's five-year term, the landlord sought to increase the rent from $650 to $900 monthly. Surprised, the tenant employed an assessor, who appraised the market value of the premises at no more than $550 per month. The tenant sued for specific performance, seeking a new five-year lease at the fair market rate of $550. *Id.* at 108, 436 N.Y.S.2d 247, 417 N.E.2d 541. In resolving the case, the *Delicatessen* majority recognized that the U.C.C., as implemented by the New York legislature, counseled in favor of supplying missing price terms to save and enforce the agreement, and that the terms supplied by a court under the U.C.C. would correspond to a good's fair market value. *Id.* at 111, 436 N.Y.S.2d 247, 417 N.E.2d 541 (discussing predecessors to N.Y. U.C.C. § 2–305 in New York law). Nevertheless, because the New York statute's terms made clear that leases or contracts for the sale of real property were not covered by the U.C.C., the Court of Appeals refused to enforce the agreement. It concluded that

> it is rightfully well settled *in the common law of contracts in this State that a mere agreement to agree, in which a material term is left for future negotiations, is unenforceable.* This is *especially true* of the amount to be paid for the sale or lease of real property. The rule applies *all the more,* and not the less, when, as here, the extraordinary remedy of specific performance is sought.

52 N.Y.2d at 109–10, 436 N.Y.S.2d 247, 417 N.E.2d 541 (all emphases added) (internal citations omitted). . . .

"The escalation clause, unlike the promise to set a future rent rate collectively in *Delicatessen,* does not require the parties to reach an "agreement" on price at some point in the future. That is, the escalation clause is not an "agreement to agree." *Delicatessen,* 52 N.Y.2d at 109, 436 N.Y.S.2d 247, 417 N.E.2d 541. Instead, like the contract in *Cobble Hill,* it is a mechanism for objectively setting material terms in the future without further negotiations between both parties. It does so, moreover, with "sufficient evidence that both parties intended that [pricing] arrangement." *Express Indus.*, 93 N.Y.2d at 590, 693 N.Y.S.2d 857, 715 N.E.2d 1050. The escalation clause clearly and unambiguously states that, in the event that Tralyn or its successors acquired new radio stations in the same (or an adjacent) geographic market, "Arbitron may redetermine its Gross Annual Rate for the Data, Reports and Services licensed hereunder . . . effective the first of the month following [the acquisition]." The escalation clause further provides, in unambiguous language, that Arbitron may exercise this power to "redetermine" the license fee "[n]otwithstanding Station's failure to notify Arbitron" that an acquisition had occurred.

"The intent of the parties is manifest in the language of the agreement. Both Arbitron and Tralyn explicitly agreed that Arbitron was authorized to adjust the license fee in the event that Tralyn or its successors began to operate additional stations. This fact makes the instant case very different from those disputes in which courts are faced with "no objective evidence" of a shared intent to permit one party to set prices in the future. *See [In Re Express Indus. & Terminal Corp.,* 93 N.Y.2d 584, 693 N.Y.S.2d 857, 715 N.E.2d 1050 (1999)] And it in no way leads a court enforcing the contract to "impos[e] its own conception of what the parties should or might have undertaken." *Delicatessen,* 52 N.Y.2d at 109, 436 N.Y.S.2d 247, 417 N.E.2d 541. Accordingly, we conclude that the district court erred in holding the License Agreement's escalation clause "impenetrably vague" under New York law. . .

"It is not clear whether, under New York law, a license agreement of the sort at issue in this case constitutes a contract for the sale of goods, or is otherwise governed by the U.C.C. We note, however, that were this section of New York's commercial code applied to the License Agreement, then the escalation clause would undoubtedly be a valid contract term under New York law; it would simply establish "[a] price to be fixed by the seller," and would be enforceable so long as that price was fixed "in good faith." N.Y. U.C.C. § 2–305. But the applicability of the U.C.C. to the license agreement before is not something we need to decide today.

"Because we believe that the License Agreement's escalation clause is not inconsistent with New York law, we conclude that the district court erred in granting summary judgment to JMD. We therefore vacate the district court's order and remand the case for further proceedings. On remand, the district court may wish to consider whether Arbitron has exercised its authority under the escalation clause in "good faith" within the meaning of N.Y. U.C.C. § 2–305 (which, as we have previously noted, may or may not apply to a "license" of this sort), or more generally, in a manner consistent with Arbitron's implied duty of fair dealing under New York law. *See, e.g., Carvel Corp. v. Diversified Mgmt. Group, Inc.,* 930 F.2d 228, 230 (2d Cir.1991) ("Under New York law, every contract contains an implied covenant of good faith and fair dealing."). We express no opinion on either question."

Channel Home Centers v. Grossman

795 F.2d 291 (3rd Cir. 1986)

On December 11, 1984, Channel signed a letter of intent with Grossman to lease space in a mall Grossman was acquiring to redevelop. The letter, which was drafted by Channel, required Grossman to withdraw the space from the rental market and made execution of the lease contingent on approval by Channel's parent corporation, Grace.* In the two months following execution of the letter, "both parties initated procedures directed toward satisfaction of lease contingencies." Drafts of the lease were exchanged. "Detailed marketing plans were developed [by Channel], building plans drafted, delivery schedules were prepared and materials and equipment deemed necessary for the store were purchased." While this was occurring, Grossman was approached by a competitor of Channel, Mr. Good Buys, seeking space in the mall. On February 6, 1985, Grossman notified Channel that he was terminating negotiations on the lease. On February 7, he signed a lease with Mr. Good Buys. Channel brought an action for breach of contract. The district court dismissed the action, finding "(1) the letter of intent (1) did not bind the parties to any obligation; (2) was unenforceable for lack of consideration . . . ." Held, reversed:

(Becker, J) "It is hornbook law that evidence of preliminary negotiations or an agreement to enter into a binding contract in the future does not alone constitute a contract. See *Goldman v. McShain,* 432 Pa. 61, 68, 247 A.2d 455, 458 (1968); *Lombardo v. Gasparini Excavating Co.,* 385 Pa. 388, 392, 123 A.2d 663, 666 (1956); *Kazanjian v. New England Petroleum Corp.,* 332 Pa.Super. 1, 7, 480 A.2d 1153, 1157 (1984); *see* Restatement (Second) of Contracts § 26 (1979). Appellees believe that this doctrine settles this case, but, in so arguing, appellees misconstrue Channel's contract claim. Channel does not contend

---

* The preliminary agreement described the leased property and included the lease term and rent, the lessee's renewal options, and the parties' obligations with respect to taxes, maintenance, and repairs. The first paragraph and concluding paragraphs of the letter provided as follows:

The Channel Home Centers Division of Grace Retail Corporation has approved the leasing of a store at the above described location subject to the terms and conditions of this letter. The purpose of this letter is to express the understanding under which an Agreement of Lease, prepared by Tenant, but in a mutually satisfactory form, is to be executed by the owner of the Shopping Center, as Landlord and Grace Retail Corporation, as Tenant.

. . .

Execution of the Agreement of Lease by Landlord and Tenant is specifically subject to each of the following:

    a.   *Tenant's authority:* Approval by Tenant's parent corporation, W.R. Grace & Co., and its Retail Group, of the essential business terms of the Agreement of Lease;

. . .

A store opening date during the first half of 1985 is planned. Lease preparation, obtaining the sign permits and approvals described above and delivery of possession of the Store to Tenant would commence immediately and proceed to achieve that estimated opening date. To induce the Tenant to proceed with the leasing of this Store, you will withdraw the Store from the rental market, and only negotiate the above described leasing transaction to completion.

that the letter of intent is binding as a lease or an agreement to enter into a lease. Rather, it is Channel's position that this document is enforceable as a mutually binding obligation *to negotiate in good faith.* By unilaterally terminating negotiations with Channel and precipitously entering into a lease agreement with Mr. Good Buys, Channel argues, Grossman acted in bad faith and breached his promise to "withdraw the Store from the rental market and only negotiate the above-described leasing transaction to completion." . . .

"Under Pennsylvania law, the test for enforceability of an agreement is whether both parties have manifested an intention to be bound by its terms and whether the terms are sufficiently definite to be specifically enforced. *Lombardo v. Gasparini Excavating Co.,* 385 Pa. 388, 393, 123 A.2d 663, 666; *Linnet v. Hitchcock,* 324 Pa.Super. 209, 214, 471 A.2d 537, 540. Additionally, of course, there must be consideration on both sides. *Stelmack v. Glen Alden Coal Co.,* 339 Pa. 410, 14 A.2d 127 (1940); *Cardamone v. University of Pittsburgh,* 253 Pa.Super. 65, 384 A.2d 1228 (1978). Consideration "confers a benefit upon the promisor or causes a detriment to the promisee and must be an act, forbearance or return promise bargained for and given in exchange for the original promise." *Curry v. Estate of Thompson,* 332 Pa.Super. 364, 371, 481 A.2d 658, 661 (1984).

"Although no Pennsylvania court has considered whether an agreement to negotiate in good faith may meet these conditions, the jurisdictions that have considered the issue have held that such an agreement, if otherwise meeting the requisites of a contract, is an enforceable contract. *See, e.g., Thompson v. Liquichimica of America, Inc.,* 481 F.Supp. 365, 366 (E.D.N.Y.1979); ("Unlike an agreement to agree, which does not constitute a closed proposition, an agreement to use best efforts [or to negotiate in good faith] is a closed proposition, discrete and actionable."); *accord Reprosystem, B.V. v. SCM Corp.,* 727 F.2d 257, 264 (2d Cir.1984); *Chase v. Consolidated Foods Corp.,* 744 F.2d 566, 571 (7th Cir.1984); *Arnold Palmer Golf Co. v. Fuqua Industries Inc.,* 541 F.2d 584 (6th Cir.1976); *Itek Corp. v. Chicago Aerial Industries, Inc.,* 248 A.2d 625 (Del.1968); Restatement (Second) of Contracts § 205 comment (c) (1979) ("Good faith in negotiation"); *see generally* Kessler and Fine, *Culpa in Contrahendo, Bargaining in Good Faith, and Freedom of Contract; a Comparative Study,* 77 Harv.L.Rev. 401 (1964). We are satisfied that Pennsylvania would follow this rule. Applying Pennsylvania law, then, we must ask (1) whether both parties manifested an intention to be bound by the agreement; (2) whether the terms of the agreement are sufficiently definite to be enforced; and (3) whether there was consideration.

"In determining the parties' intentions concerning the letter of intent, we must examine the entire document and the relevant circumstances surrounding its adoption. *United Refining Co. v. Jenkins,* 410 Pa. 126, 137, 189 A.2d 574, 580 (1963); *Hillbrook Apartments, Inc. v. Nyce Crete Co.,* 237 Pa.Super. 565, 572, 352 A.2d 148, 151 (1975). The letter of intent, signed by both parties, provides that "[t]o induce the Tenant [Channel] to proceed with the leasing of the Store, you [Grossman] will withdraw the Store from the rental market, and only negotiate the above described leasing transaction to completion." . . . The agreement thus contains an unequivocal promise by Grossman to withdraw the store from the rental market and to negotiate the proposed leasing transaction with Channel to completion.

"Evidence of record supports the proposition that the parties intended this promise to be binding. After the letter of intent was executed, both Channel and the Grossmans initiated procedures directed toward satisfaction of lease contingencies. Channel directed its parent corporation to prepare a draft lease; Channel planning representatives visited the lease premises to obtain measurements for architectural alterations, renovations, and related construction. Channel developed extensive marketing plans; delivery schedules were prepared and material and equipment deemed necessary for the store were purchased. The Grossmans applied to the township zoning committee for permission to erect Channel signs at various locations on the mall property. Channel submitted a draft lease on January 11, 1985, and the parties, through correspondence and telephone conversations and on-site visits, exhibited an intent to move toward a lease as late as January 23, 1985. . . . Accordingly, the letter of intent and the circumstances surrounding its adoption both support a finding that the parties intended to be bound by an agreement to negotiate in good faith.

"We also believe that Grossman's promise to "withdraw the Store from the rental market and only negotiate the above described leasing transaction to completion," viewed in the context of the detailed letter of intent (which covers most significant lease terms), is sufficiently definite to be specifically enforced, provided that Channel submitted sufficient legal consideration in return.

"Appellees argue that "[n]o money or thing of value was paid, either at the time of the letter or at any other time that would convert an agreement to negotiate into some enforceable type of contract." Brief of Appellees at 16. We disagree. It seems clear that the execution and tender of the letter of intent by Channel was of substantial value to Frank Grossman. At the time the letter of intent was executed, Grossman was in the process of obtaining financing for his purchase of the mall. When it became apparent to Grossman that Channel—a major corporate tenant—was seriously interested in leasing the mall site, he requested that Channel sign a letter of intent which, as Grossman put it, could be shown to "other people, banks or whatever with a view to getting permanent financing." App. at 366a–367a. Fully aware of Grossman's desire to obtain financing, Channel sought to solidify its bargaining position by requesting that Grossman also sign the letter of intent and promise to "withdraw the store from the rental market and only negotiate the above-described leasing transaction to completion." There being evidence that value passed from each party to the other, we conclude that the record would support a finding that Channel's execution and tender of the letter of intent conferred a bargained for benefit on Grossman which was valid consideration for Grossman's return promise to negotiate in good faith."

———

UNIDROIT PRINCIPLES OF INTERNATIONAL COMMERCIAL CONTRACTS ART. 2.1.15

[See Selected Source Materials Supplement]

———

PRINCIPLES OF EUROPEAN CONTRACT LAW ART. 2.301

[See Selected Source Materials Supplement]

———

Teachers Insurance and Annuity Association of America v. Tribune Co.

670 F.Supp. 491 (S.D.N.Y. 1987)

(Leval, J.): ". . . There has been much litigation over preliminary agreements. It is difficult to generalize about their legal effect. They cover a broad scope ranging in innumerable forms and variations from letters of intent which presuppose that no binding obligations will be placed upon any party until final contract documents have been signed, to firm binding commitments which, notwithstanding a need for a more detailed documentation of agreement, can bind the parties to adhere in good faith to the deal that has been agreed. As is commonly the case with contract disputes, prime significance attaches to the intentions of the parties and to their manifestations of intent. Labels such as 'letter of intent' or 'commitment letter' are not necessarily controlling although they may be helpful indicators of the parties' intentions. Notwithstanding the intention of the parties at the time, if the agreement is too fragmentary, in that it leaves open terms of too fundamental importance, it may be incapable of sustaining binding legal obligation. Furthermore, the conclusion that a preliminary agreement created binding obligations does not necessarily resolve disputes because it leaves open the further question of the nature, scope and extent of the binding obligations.

"A primary concern for courts in such disputes is to avoid trapping parties in surprise contractual obligations that they never intended. Ordinarily in contract negotiations, enforceable legal rights do not arise until either the expression of mutual consent to be bound, or some equivalent event that marks acceptance of offer. Contractual liability, unlike tort liability, arises from consent to be bound (or in any event from the manifestation of consent). It is fundamental to contract law that mere participation in negotiations and discussions does not create binding obligation, even if agreement is reached on all disputed terms. More is needed than agreement on each detail, which is overall agreement (or offer and acceptance) to enter into the binding contract.[7]

---

    [7] *See Winston v. Mediafare Entertainment Corp.,* 777 F.2d 78 (2d Cir.1985); *R.G. Group v. Horn & Hardart Co.,* 751 F.2d 69 (2d Cir.1984); *Reprosystem, B.V. v. SCM Corp.,* 727 F.2d 257 (2d Cir.), *cert. denied,* 469 U.S. 828, 105 S.Ct. 110, 83 L.Ed.2d 54 (1984).

Nor is this principle altered by the fact that negotiating parties may have entered into letters of intent or preliminary agreements if those were made with the understanding that neither side would be bound until final agreement was reached. The Court of Appeals in several recent cases has stressed the importance of recognizing the freedom of negotiating parties from binding obligations, notwithstanding their having entered into various forms of non-binding preliminary assent. Those decisions have underlined various indicia that can be helpful in making the determination whether a manifestation of preliminary assent amounted to a legally binding agreement.*

"Notwithstanding the importance of protecting negotiating parties from involuntary judicially imposed contract, it is equally important that courts enforce and preserve agreements that were intended as binding, despite a need for further documentation or further negotiation. It is, of course, the aim of contract law to gratify, not to defeat, expectations that arise out of intended contractual agreement, despite informality or the need for further proceedings between the parties.

"Preliminary contracts with binding force can be of at least two distinct types. One occurs when the parties have reached complete agreement (including the agreement to be bound) on all the issues perceived to require negotiation. Such an agreement is preliminary only in form—only in the sense that the parties desire a more elaborate formalization of the agreement. The second stage is not necessary; it is merely considered desirable. As the Court of Appeals stated with respect to such preliminary agreements in *V'Soske v. Barwick,* 404 F.2d 495, 499 (2d Cir.), *cert. denied,* 394 U.S. 921, 89 S.Ct. 1197, 22 L.Ed.2d 454 (1969), 'the mere fact that the parties contemplate memorializing their agreement in a formal document does not prevent their informal agreement from taking effect prior to that event. . . . Restatement (Second) of Contracts, § 26 (then Tent.Draft No. 1, 1964); 1 Corbin on Contracts § 30 (1950); 1 Williston on Contracts § 28 (3d ed. 1957).'

"The second and different sort of preliminary binding agreement is one that expresses mutual commitment to a contract on agreed major terms, while recognizing the existence of open terms that remain to be negotiated. Although the existence of open terms generally suggests that binding agreement has not been reached, that is not necessarily so. For the parties can bind themselves to a concededly incomplete agreement in the sense that they accept a mutual commitment to negotiate together in good faith in an effort to reach final agreement within the scope that has been settled in the preliminary agreement. To differentiate this sort of preliminary agreement from the first,

---

* [These factors were summarized as follows in *Winston,* supra note 7.

. . . We have articulated several factors that help determine whether the parties intended to be bound in the absence of a document executed by both sides. The court is to consider (1) whether there has been an express reservation of the right not to be bound in the absence of a writing; (2) whether there has been partial performance of the contract; (3) whether all of the terms of the alleged contract have been agreed upon; and (4) whether the agreement at issue is the type of contract that is usually committed to writing.

(Footnote by ed.)]

it might be referred to as a binding preliminary commitment. Its binding obligations are of a different order than those which arise out of the first type discussed above. The first type binds both sides to their ultimate contractual objective in recognition that that contract has been reached, despite the anticipation of further formalities. The second type—the binding preliminary commitment—does not commit the parties to their ultimate contractual objective but rather to the obligation to negotiate the open issues in good faith in an attempt to reach the alternate objective within the agreed framework. In the first type, a party may lawfully demand performance of the transaction even if no further steps have been taken following the making of the 'preliminary' agreement. In the second type, he may not. What he may demand, however, is that his counter-party negotiate the open terms in good faith toward a final contract incorporating the agreed terms. This obligation does not guarantee that the final contract will be concluded if both parties comport with their obligation, as good faith differences in the negotiation of the open issues may prevent a reaching of final contract. It is also possible that the parties will lose interest as circumstances change and will mutually abandon the negotiation. The obligation does, however, bar a party from renouncing the deal, abandoning the negotiations, or insisting on conditions that do not conform to the preliminary agreement.

"... In seeking to determine whether such a preliminary commitment should be considered binding, a court's task is, once again, to determine the intentions of the parties at the time of their entry into the understanding, as well as their manifestations to one another by which the understanding was reached. Courts must be particularly careful to avoid imposing liability where binding obligation was not intended. There is a strong presumption against finding binding obligation in agreements which include open terms, call for future approvals and expressly anticipate future preparation and execution of contract documents. Nonetheless, if that is what the parties intended, courts should not frustrate their achieving that objective or disappoint legitimately bargained contract expectations.

"Giving legal recognition to preliminary binding commitments serves a valuable function in the marketplace, particularly for relatively standardized transactions like loans. It permits borrowers and lenders to make plans in reliance upon their preliminary agreements and present market conditions. Without such legal recognition, parties would be obliged to expend enormous sums negotiating every detail of final contract documentation before knowing whether they have an agreement, and if so, on what terms. At the same time, a party that does not wish to be bound at the time of the preliminary exchange of letters can very easily protect itself by not accepting language that indicates a 'firm commitment' or 'binding agreement.'"

———

Venture Associates Corp. v. Zenith Data Systems Corp.

96 F.3d 275 (7th Cir.1996)

(Posner, J.) "Damages for breach of an agreement to negotiate may be, although they are unlikely to be, the same as the damages for breach of the final contract that the parties would have signed had it not been for the defendant's bad faith. If, quite apart from any bad faith, the negotiations would have broken down, the party led on by the other party's bad faith to persist in futile negotiations can recover only his reliance damages—the expenses he incurred by being misled, in violation of the parties' agreement to negotiate in good faith, into continuing to negotiate futilely. But if the plaintiff can prove that had it not been for the defendant's bad faith the parties would have made a final contract, then the loss of the benefit of the contract is a consequence of the defendant's bad faith, and, provided that it is a foreseeable consequence, the defendant is liable for that loss—liable, that is, for the plaintiffs consequential damages. . . . The difficulty, which may well be insuperable, is that since by hypothesis the parties had not agreed on *any* of the terms of their contract, it may be impossible to determine what those terms would have been and hence what profit the victim of bad faith would have had. . . . But this goes to the practicality of the remedy, not the principle of it. Bad faith is deliberate misconduct, whereas many breaches of 'final' contracts are involuntary— liability for breach of contract being, in general, strict liability. It would be a paradox to place a lower ceiling on damages for bad faith than on damages for a perfectly innocent breach, though a paradox that the practicalities of proof may require the courts in many or even all cases to accept."

NOTE ON THE AVAILABILITY OF A PROMISSORY ESTOPPEL CLAIM OR A RESTITUTION CLAIM WHEN A CONTRACT IS INDEFINITE

Under classical contract law the rigorous nature of the requirement of definiteness could result in a court finding an agreement insufficiently definite to be enforced as a contract even though the parties intended to enter into a contract and one party had performed, or prepared to perform, in reliance on the existence of the contract. From early on courts used the law of restitution to allow the plaintiff to recover performance-based damages in these cases. Once the doctrine of promissory estoppel was developed courts used it to allow the plaintiff to recover reliance-based damages.

Wheeler v. White, 398 S.W.2d 93 (1965), illustrates the use of promissory estoppel. White promised to provide money to Wheeler to finance construction of improvements on land owned by Wheeler, either by procuring a loan from a third party or lending his own money The parties executed a written agreement stating the amount of the loan, the term, the maximum interest rate, and the commission Wheeler was to pay White. Relying on the agreement, and acting on White's advice to get started with the project, Wheeler demolished an old structure on the property. White refused to perform his agreement. Wheeler tried to borrow money elsewhere but could not. He sued for breach of contract. The court held the agreement was insufficiently definite to be "specifically enforceable," but that the doctrine of promissory estoppel could be used to estop White "from denying the enforceability of the promise."

Kearns v. Andree, 107 Conn. 181, 139 A. 695 (1928), illustrates the use of restitution. The defendant refused to honor an oral agreement to purchase a house owned by the plaintiff. At the defendant's request, the plaintiff had made alterations in the house that reduced its value. The court held that the work done was sufficient to take the contract out of the statute of frauds but the agreement was unenforceable on the ground of indefiniteness. The parties had agreed the defendant would finance part of the purchase price with a mortgage from a third party but they did not specify the mortgagee or the terms of the mortgage. The plaintiff was held entitled to recover damages for his costs in making the requested alterations on a restitution claim. But he was not allowed to recover his cost in restoring the house to its original condition. The plaintiff would have recovered these costs as well on a promissory estoppel claim (assuming he acted reasonably in restoring the house to its original condition).

Under modern contract law a court should find the contract in these cases to be sufficiently definite to determine the defendant had breached his contract. The indefiniteness of the contract might still bear on the court's choice of a remedy. For example, in *Kearns* a court might decline to grant the plaintiff specific performance because of the absence of an agreement on the terms of the mortgage to finance part of the purchase price. The inability of the plaintiff in *Wheeler* to cover by borrowing money elsewhere might well lead to the same result with the plaintiff recovering reliance damages as a surrogate for speculative expectation damages.

GARWOOD PACKAGING, INC. V. ALLEN & COMPANY, INC.

United States Court of Appeals, Seventh Circuit, 2004.
378 F.3d 698.

POSNER, CIRCUIT JUDGE.

This is a diversity suit, governed by Indiana law, in which substantial damages are sought on the basis of promissory estoppel. The suit pits Garwood Packaging, Inc., which created a packaging system designed to increase the shelf life of fresh meat, and its two principals, Garwood and McNamara, against Allen & Company (an investment company) and a vice-president of Allen named Martin. We shall refer to the plaintiffs collectively as "GPI" and the defendants collectively as "Allen." The district court granted summary judgment in favor of Allen and dismissed the suit. . . .

GPI had flopped in marketing its food-packaging system and by 1993 had run up debts of $3 million and was broke. It engaged Martin to help find investors. After an initial search turned up nothing, Martin told GPI that Allen (Martin's employer, remember) would consider investing $2 million of its own money in GPI if another investor could be found who would make a comparable investment. The presence of the other investor would reduce the risk to Allen not only by augmenting GPI's assets but also by validating Allen's judgment that GPI might be salvageable, because it would show that someone else was also willing to bet a substantial sum of money on GPI's salvation. To further reduce its risk Allen decided to off-load half its projected $2 million investment on other investors.

Martin located a company named Hobart Corporation that was prepared to manufacture $2 million worth of GPI packaging machines in return for equity in the company. Negotiations with Hobart proved arduous, however. There were two sticking points: the amount of equity that Hobart would receive and the obtaining of releases from GPI's creditors. Hobart may have been concerned that unless the creditors released GPI the company would fail and Hobart wouldn't be able to sell the packaging systems that it manufactured. Or it may have feared that the creditors would assert liens in the systems. All that is clear is that Hobart insisted on releases. They were also important to the other investors whom Allen wanted to bring into the deal, the ones who would contribute half of Allen's offered $2 million.

Martin told Garwood and McNamara (GPI's principals) that he would see that the deal went through "come hell or high water." Eventually, however, Allen decided not to invest, the deal collapsed, and GPI was forced to declare bankruptcy. The reason for Allen's change of heart was that the investors who it thought had agreed to put up half of "Allen's" $2 million had gotten cold feet. When Allen withdrew from the deal, no contract had been signed and no agreement had been reached on how much stock either Allen or Hobart would receive in exchange for their contributions to GPI. Nor had releases been obtained from the creditors.

GPI's principal claim on appeal, and the only one we need to discuss (the others fall with it), is that Martin's unequivocal promise to see the deal through to completion bound Allen by the doctrine of promissory estoppel, which makes a promise that induces reasonable reliance legally enforceable. *Brown v. Branch,* 758 N.E.2d 48, 52 (Ind.2001); *First National Bank of Logansport v. Logan Mfg. Co.,* 577 N.E.2d 949, 954 (Ind.1991); *Consolidation Services, Inc. v. KeyBank National Ass'n,* 185 F.3d 817, 822 (7th Cir.1999) (Indiana law); *Restatement (Second) of Contracts* § 90(1) (1981); 1 E. Allan Farnsworth, *Farnsworth on Contracts* § 2.19 (3d ed.2004). If noncontractual promises were never enforced, reliance on their being enforceable would never be reasonable, so let us consider why the law might want to allow people to rely on promises that do not create actual contracts and whether the answer can help GPI.

The simplest answer to the "why" question is that the doctrine merely allows reliance to be substituted for consideration as the basis for making a promise enforceable. *First National Bank of Logansport v. Logan Mfg. Co., supra,* 577 N.E.2d at 954; *Workman v. United Parcel Service, Inc.,* 234 F.3d 998, 1001 (7th Cir.2000); *Consolidation Services, Inc. v. KeyBank National Ass'n, supra,* 185 F.3d at 822; *Porter v. Commissioner,* 60 F.2d 673, 675 (2d Cir.1932) (L.Hand, J.). On this view promissory estoppel is really just a doctrine of contract law. The most persuasive reason for the requirement of consideration in the law of contracts is that in a system in which oral contracts are enforceable—and by juries, to boot—the requirement provides some evidence that there really *was* a promise that was intended to be relied on as a real commitment. *Gibson v. Neighborhood Health Clinics, Inc.,* 121 F.3d 1126, 1131 (7th Cir.1997); *Scholes v. Lehmann,* 56 F.3d 750, 756 (7th Cir.1995); *Krell v. Codman,* 154 Mass. 454, 28 N.E. 578 (Mass.1891) (Holmes, J.); Lon L. Fuller, "Consideration and Form," 41 *Colum. L.Rev.* 799, 799–801 (1941). Actual reliance, in the sense of a costly change of position that cannot be recouped if the reliance turns out to have been misplaced, is substitute evidence that there may well have been such a promise. *Consolidation Services, Inc. v. KeyBank National Ass'n, supra,* 185 F.3d at 822; *Yontz v. BMER Interprises, Inc.,* 91 Ohio App.3d 202, 632 N.E.2d 527, 530 (1993). The inference is especially plausible in a commercial setting, because most businesspeople would be reluctant to incur costs in reliance on a promise that they believed the promisor didn't consider himself legally bound to perform.

In other words, reasonable reliance is seen as nearly as good a reason for thinking there really was a promise as bargained-for reliance is. In many such cases, it is true, no promise was intended, or intended to be legally enforceable; in those cases the application of the doctrine penalizes the defendant for inducing the plaintiff to incur costs of reliance. The penalty is withheld if the reliance was unreasonable; for then the plaintiff's wound was self-inflicted—he should have known better than to rely.

A relevant though puzzling difference between breach of contract and promissory estoppel as grounds for legal relief is that while the promise relied on to trigger an estoppel must be definite in the sense of being clearly a promise and not just a statement of intentions, *Security Bank & Trust Co. v. Bogard,* 494 N.E.2d 965, 968–69 (Ind.App.1986); *Wood v. Mid-Valley Inc.,* 942 F.2d 425, 428 (7th Cir.1991) (Indiana law); *Major Mat Co. v. Monsanto Co.,* 969 F.2d 579, 582–83 (7th Cir.1992), its terms need not be as clear as a contractual promise would have to be in order to be enforceable. E.g., *Janke Construction Co. v. Vulcan Materials Co.,* 527 F.2d 772, 777 (7th Cir.1976) (Wisconsin law); *Hawkins Construction Co. v. Reiman Corp.,* 245 Neb. 131, 511 N.W.2d 113, 117 (1994); *Neiss v. Ehlers,*

135 Or.App. 218, 899 P.2d 700, 707 (1995). Indiana may go furthest in this direction: "Even though there were insufficient terms for the enforcement of an express oral contract, and unfulfilled pre-existing conditions prohibiting recovery for breach of a written contract . . ., we are not precluded from finding a promise under these circumstances. Indeed, it is precisely under such circumstances, where a promise is made but which is not enforceable as a 'contract,' that the doctrine of promissory estoppel is recognized." *First National Bank of Logansport v. Logan Mfg. Co., supra,* 577 N.E.2d at 955.

The reason for this difference between breach of contract and promissory estoppel is unclear. A stab at an explanation is found in *Rosnick v. Dinsmore,* 235 Neb. 738, 457 N.W.2d 793, 800 (1990), where the court said that "promissory estoppel only provides for damages as justice requires and does not attempt to provide the plaintiff damages based upon the benefit of the bargain. The usual measure of damages under a theory of promissory estoppel is the loss incurred by the promisee in reasonable reliance on the promise, or 'reliance damages.' Reliance damages are relatively easy to determine, whereas the determination of 'expectation' or 'benefit of the bargain' damages available in a contract action requires more detailed proof of the terms of the contract." The only problem with this explanation is that its premise is mistaken; if the promise giving rise to an estoppel is clear, the plaintiff will usually be awarded its value, which would be the equivalent of the expectation measure of damages in an ordinary breach of contract case. *Goldstick v. ICM Realty,* 788 F.2d 456, 463–64 (7th Cir.1986); *Restatement, supra,* § 90 comment d. The rationale in both cases is that the benefit of the contract to the promisee is a good proxy for the opportunities that he forewent in making the contract. *Walters v. Marathon Oil Co.,* 642 F.2d 1098, 1100–01 (7th Cir.1981); L.L. Fuller & William R. Perdue, Jr., "The Reliance Interest in Contract Damages: 1," 46 *Yale L.J.* 52, 60 (1936) ("physicians with an extensive practice often charge their patients the full office call fee for broken appointments. Such a charge looks on the face of things like a claim to the promised fee; it seems to be based on the 'expectation interest'. Yet the physician making the charge will quite justifiably regard it as compensation for the loss of the opportunity to gain a similar fee from a different patient"). Of course, if the promise is unclear, damages will be limited to expenses incurred in reasonable reliance on the vague promise, *First National Bank of Logansport v. Logan Mfg. Co., supra,* 577 N.E.2d at 952, 955–56, but that would be equally true in a breach of contract case in which the promise that the defendant had broken was unclear.

But even though the court is "not precluded from finding a promise" by its vagueness, *id.* at 955, the vaguer the alleged promise the less likely it is to be found to *be* a promise. *Mays v. Trump Indiana, Inc.,* 255 F.3d 351, 358–59 (7th Cir.2001) (Indiana law); *All-Tech Telecom, Inc. v. Amway*

Corp., 174 F.3d 862, 868–69 (7th Cir.1999); *Restatement, supra,* § 33(3) and comment f. And if it is *really* vague, the promisee would be imprudent to rely on it—he wouldn't know whether reliance was worthwhile. The broader principle, which the requirement that the promise be definite and at least minimally clear instantiates, is that the promisee's reliance must be reasonable; if it is not, then not only is he the gratuitous author of his own disappointment, but probably there wasn't really a promise, or at least a promise intended or likely to induce reliance. The "promise" would have been in the nature of a hope or possibly a prediction rather than a commitment to do something within the "promisor's" power to do ("I promise it will rain tomorrow"); and the "promisee" would, if sensible, understand this. He would rely or not as he chose but he would know that he would have to bear the cost of any disappointment.

We note, returning to the facts of this case, that there was costly reliance by GPI, which forewent other opportunities for salvation, and by Garwood and McNamara, who moved from Indiana to Ohio to be near Hobart's plant where they expected their food-packaging system to be manufactured, and who forgave their personal loans to GPI and incurred other costs as well. The reliance was on statements by Martin, of which "come hell or high water" was the high water mark but is by no means an isolated example. If GPI's evidence is credited, as it must be in the procedural posture of the case, Martin repeatedly confirmed to GPI that the deal would go through, that Allen's commitment to invest $2 million was unconditional, that the funding would be forthcoming, and so on; and these statements induced the plaintiffs to incur costs they would otherwise not have done.

But were these real promises, and likely to be understood as such? Those are two different questions. A person may say something that he intends as merely a prediction, or as a signal of his hopes or intentions, but that is reasonably understood as a promise, and if so, as we know (this is the penal or deterrent function of promissory estoppel), he is bound. *Tipton County Farm Bureau Cooperative Ass'n, Inc. v. Hoover,* 475 N.E.2d 38, 42 (Ind.App.1985). But what is a reasonable, and indeed actual, understanding will often depend on the knowledge that the promisee brings to the table. McNamara, with whom Martin primarily dealt, is a former investment banker, not a rube. He knew that in putting together a deal to salvage a failing company there is many a slip 'twixt cup and lips. Unless blinded by optimism or desperation he *had* to know that Martin could not mean *literally* that the deal would go through "come hell or high water," since if Satan or a tsunami obliterated Ohio that would kill the deal. Even if Allen had dug into its pockets for the full $2 million after the investors who it had hoped would put up half the amount defected, the deal might well not have gone through because of Hobart's demands and because of the creditors. GPI acknowledges that the Internal Revenue

Service, one of its largest creditors, wouldn't give a release until paid in full. Some of GPI's other creditors also intended to fight rather than to accept a pittance in exchange for a release. Nothing is more common than for a deal to rescue a failing company to fall apart because all the creditors' consent to the deal cannot be obtained—that is one of the reasons for bankruptcy law. Again these were things of which McNamara was perfectly aware.

The problem, thus, is not that Martin's promises were indefinite, which they were not if GPI's evidence is credited, but that they could not have been reasonably understood by the persons to whom they were addressed (mainly McNamara, the financial partner in GPI) to *be* promises rather than expressions of optimism and determination. *Security Bank & Trust Co. v. Bogard, supra,* 494 N.E.2d at 968–69; *Workman v. United Parcel Service, Inc., supra,* 234 F.3d at 1001–02; *Wood v. Mid-Valley Inc., supra,* 942 F.2d at 428; *Major Mat Co. v. Monsanto Co., supra,* 969 F.2d at 582–83. To move to Ohio, to forgive personal loans, to forgo other searches for possible investors, and so forth were in the nature of gambles on the part of GPI and its principals. They may have been reasonable gambles, in the sense that the prospects for a successful salvage operation were good enough that taking immediate, even if irrevocable, steps to facilitate and take advantage of the expected happy outcome was prudent. But we often reasonably rely on things that are not promises. A farmer plants his crops in the spring in reasonable reliance that spring will be followed by summer rather than by winter. There can be reasonable reliance on statements as well as on the regularities of nature, but if the statements are not reasonably understood as legally enforceable promises there can be no action for promissory estoppel.

Suppose McNamara thought that there was a 50 percent chance that the deal would go through and believed that reliance on that prospect would cost him $100,000, but also believed that by relying he could expect either to increase the likelihood that the deal would go through or to make more money if it did by being able to start production sooner and that in either event the expected benefit of reliance would exceed $100,000. Then his reliance would be reasonable even if not induced by enforceable promises. The numbers are arbitrary but the example apt. GPI and its principals relied, and may have relied reasonably, but they didn't rely on Martin's "promises" because those were not promises reasonably understood as such by so financially sophisticated a businessman as McNarama. *McInerney v. Charter Golf, Inc.,* 176 Ill.2d 482, 223 Ill.Dec. 911, 680 N.E.2d 1347, 1352–53 (1997); *Gruen Industries, Inc. v. Biller,* 608 F.2d 274, 281–82 (7th Cir.1979); *Clardy Mfg. Co. v. Marine Midland Business Loans Inc.,* 88 F.3d 347, 358, 360–61 (5th Cir.1996). So we see now that the essence of the doctrine of promissory estoppel is not that the plaintiff have reasonably relied on the defendant's promise, but that he have reasonably relied on its *being* a promise in the sense of a legal commitment, and not a mere prediction or aspiration or bit of puffery.

One last point. Ordinarily the question whether a plaintiff reasonably understood a statement to be a promise is a question of fact and so cannot be resolved in summary judgment proceedings. But if it is clear that the question can be answered in only one way, there is no occasion to submit the question to a jury. See *Mason & Dixon Lines, Inc. v. Glover,* 975 F.2d 1298, 1303–05 (7th Cir.1992); *J.C. Wyckoff & Associates, Inc. v. Standard Fire Ins. Co.,* 936 F.2d 1474, 1493 (6th Cir.1991). This, we believe, is such a case.

Affirmed.

——

Hoffman v. Red Owl Stores, Inc.

26 Wis.2d 683, 133 N.W.2d 267 (1965)

Plaintiff Hoffman owned and operated a successful bakery in Wautoma, Wisconsin. Defendant Red Owl's divisional manager, Lukowitz, persuaded Hoffman to apply for a Red Owl grocery store franchise in a larger town. Hoffman repeatedly told Lukowitz that he had only $18,000 capital to invest in a store. Lukowitz repeatedly assured him this amount would be sufficient. To get experience in running a grocery store, Hoffman bought the assets of a small grocery in Wautoma, which he ran successfully for several months in 1961 before selling the store. In September 1961, Hoffman paid $1,000 for an option on a lot for a grocery store in Chilton. In November 1961, Hoffman sold his bakery on Lukowitz's advice, retaining the equipment for the grocery. He also moved his family. All of this Hoffman did on Lukowitz's advice.

During Fall and early Winter 1961 Hoffman met with Red Owl's people to negotiate the terms of the franchise agreement. During these meetings a credit manager informed Hoffman that he would need more than the $18,000 capital Lukowitz had assured him would suffice. Hoffman borrowed $13,000 from his father-in-law to obtain the additional capital. Initially Red Owl's credit manager told Hoffman this could be treated as a lowest-priority unsecured loan, but at the last minute he was told it had to be a gift. When Hoffman refused to ask his father-in-law to make a gift of the money negotiations terminated.

Hoffman sued Red Owl for breach of contract, seeking as damages his expenses and lost income. The jury awarded Hoffman $20,000 damages, the major element of which was a $16,735 loss on the sale of Wautoma store. The trial court granted a new trial on damages with respect to this loss. Affirmed, instructing that on retrial damages with respect to the loss on the sale of the Wautoma store should be measured by the difference between the sales price and the fair market value.

(Currie, C.J.) "We determine that there was ample evidence to sustain the answers of the jury to the questions of the verdict with respect to the promissory representations made by Red Owl, Hoffman's reliance thereon in the exercise of ordinary care, and his fulfillment of the conditions required of him by the terms of the negotiations had with Red Owl.

"There remains for consideration the question of law raised by defendants that agreement was never reached on essential factors necessary to establish a contract between Hoffman and Red Owl. Among these were the size, cost, design, and layout of the store building; and the terms of the lease with respect to rent, maintenance, renewal, and purchase options. This poses the question of whether the promise necessary to sustain a cause of action for promissory estoppel must embrace all essential details of a proposed transaction between promisor and promisee so as to be the equivalent of an offer that would result in a binding contract between the parties if the promisee were to accept the same.

"Originally the doctrine of promissory estoppel was invoked as a substitute for consideration rendering a gratuitous promise enforceable as a contract. See Williston, Contracts (1st ed.), p. 307, sec. 139. In other words, the acts of reliance by the promisee to his detriment provided a substitute for consideration. If promissory estoppel were to be limited to only those situations where the promise giving rise to the cause of action must be so definite with respect to all details that a contract would result were the promise supported by consideration, then the defendants' instant promises to Hoffman would not meet this test. However, sec. 90 of Restatement, 1 Contracts, does not impose the requirement that the promise giving rise to the cause of action must be so comprehensive in scope as to meet the requirements of an offer that would ripen into a contract if accepted by the promisee. Rather the conditions imposed are:

(1) Was the promise one which the promisor should reasonably expect to induce action or forbearance of a definite and substantial character on the part of the promisee?

(2) Did the promise induce such action or forbearance?

(3) Can injustice be avoided only by enforcement of the promise?

"We deem it would be a mistake to regard an action grounded on promissory estoppel as the equivalent of a breach of contract action. As Dean Boyer points out, it is desirable that fluidity in the application of the concept be maintained. 98 University of Pennsylvania Law Review (1950), 459, at page 497. While the first two of the above listed three requirements of promissory estoppel present issues of fact which ordinarily will be resolved by a jury, the third requirement, that the remedy can only be invoked where necessary to avoid injustice, is one that involves a policy decision by the court. Such a policy decision necessarily embraces an element of discretion.

"We conclude that injustice would result here if plaintiffs were not granted some relief because of the failure of defendants to keep their promises which induced plaintiffs to act to their detriment."

———

Classic Cheesecake Company, Inc. v. JP Morgan Chase Bank, N.A.

546 F.3d 839 (7th Cir. 2008)

Plaintiff Classic sought a loan from defendant bank to establish a distribution center in Las Vegas to serve hotels and casinos. Classic's principals met with Dowling, a vice president of a local loan office of the bank, on July 27, 2004, to pitch the loan. On September 17 Dowling told Classic the loan was a "go," while asking for additional documents to speed up the confirmation process. Dowling did not tell Classic that her superior had initially declined to approve the loan on August 19, citing various concerns. Dowling continued to assure Classic that the loan would be approved until October 12, when she told them the loan had been turned down. Classic sued for breach of an oral promise to make a loan, claiming "the breach delayed it from seeking loans elsewhere for a critical two and a half months and that as a result of the delay it . . . . incurred in the aggregate a loss of more than $1 million." The district court granted defendant's motion to dismiss because of an absence of a writing to satisfy a provision of the Indiana statute of frauds requiring that agreements to lend money be in writing. Ind.Code § 26–2–9–5. Affirmed.

(Posner, J.) "[T]he question becomes whether the bank's conduct could have been found to inflict an "unjust and unconscionable injury and loss" and so trump the bank's defense based on the statute of frauds. To answer the question requires us to explore the provenance of a phrase at once vague (what does "unjust and unconscionable" mean?) and redundant (how does "injury" differ from "loss"?).

"The statute of frauds has long been controversial. The Farnsworth treatise says that "it has been the subject of constant erosion." 2 E. Allan Farnsworth, *Farnsworth on Contracts* § 6.1, p. 107 (3d ed.2004). The particular erosive process that culminates in the doctrine of "unjust and unconscionable injury and loss" began—where else?—in an opinion by Justice Traynor, *Monarco v. Lo Greco,* 35 Cal.2d 621, 220 P.2d 737 (1950), that allowed the statute of frauds to be circumvented by a claim of promissory estoppel. . . . Importantly, however, Justice Traynor limited the use of promissory estoppel to defeat the statute of frauds: only if "either an unconscionable injury or unjust enrichment would result from refusal to enforce" an oral promise would a defense based on the statute of frauds be negated. 220 P.2d at 741.

"The *Monarco* opinion, like so many of Justice Traynor's innovations, caught on. 2 Farnsworth, *supra,* § 6.12, p. 206. Eventually it was picked up— and expanded—by the *Restatement (Second) of Contracts* (1981), which in section 139(1) allows promissory estoppel to defeat the statute of frauds "if injustice can be avoided only by enforcement of the [oral] promise." This notably loose formulation has been influential too, 2 Farnsworth, *supra,* § 6.12, pp. 206–13—but not in Indiana. "Indiana courts have declined to embrace § 139 [of the *Restatement*], but have recognized the possibility of relief for 'injustice' in limited circumstances, while defining it much more narrowly than in § 139." *Coca-Cola Co. v. Babyback's Int'l, Inc.,* 841 N.E.2d 557, 569 (Ind.2006).

"Indiana's formula is as follows:

> In order to establish an estoppel to remove the case from the operation of the Statute of Frauds, the party must show [ ] that the other party's refusal to carry out the terms of the agreement has resulted not merely in a denial of the rights which the agreement was intended to confer, but the infliction of an unjust and unconscionable injury and loss.

> In other words, neither the benefit of the bargain itself, nor mere inconvenience, incidental expenses, etc. short of a reliance injury so substantial and independent as to constitute an unjust and unconscionable injury and loss are sufficient to remove the claim from the operation of the Statute of Frauds.

Id., quoting *Brown v. Branch, supra,* 758 N.E.2d at 52, which in turn was quoting *Whiteco Industries, Inc. v. Kopani,* 514 N.E.2d 840, 845 (Ind.App.1987).

"The formula itself—"unjust and unconscionable injury and loss"—does not tell us much, and it has not been further elaborated by the Indiana courts. Comparison with Justice Traynor's formula—"either an unconscionable injury or unjust enrichment"—deepens the mystery. The Traynor formula suggests two grounds for getting around the statute of frauds: unjust gain to the promisor or "unconscionable" injury to the promisee. . . .

"We can at least set aside any issue of unjust enrichment in this case. The bank made no money in its dealings with Classic and gained no other advantage; all it gained was this lawsuit against it. And anyway, to invoke the doctrine of unconscionability Classic would have to show that it had been taken advantage of because of its obvious ignorance or desperate circumstances, e.g., *Weaver v. American Oil Co.,* 257 Ind. 458, 276 N.E.2d 144, 146 (1971), and there is nothing like that here. . . .

"We can get some help from the case law. In *Monarco,* the *fons et origo* of the doctrine that the Indiana courts call "unjust and unconscionable injury and loss," there was both a big loss and unjust enrichment. When the plaintiff reached 18 and wanted to leave home and make his own way in the world, his mother and stepfather promised him that if he stayed and worked on the family farm they would leave almost all their property (which was in joint tenancy) to him. He stayed, and worked hard, receiving in exchange only room and board and spending money. The farm prospered. But when the stepfather died 20 years later, he left his half interest in the farm to his own grandson.

220 P.2d at 738–39. The element of unjust enrichment lay in the fact that the plaintiff had worked the farm for slight compensation for 20 years (giving up among other things the opportunity to obtain an education beyond high school) in the expectation that he would be well compensated when either his mother or his stepfather died. The farm had done well, in part no doubt because of the plaintiff's undercompensated efforts—his "sweat equity." So the grandson was indeed unjustly enriched. The plaintiff's having the rug pulled out from under him after working for 20 years for slight remuneration faintly echoed Laban's fraud on his son-in-law Jacob. After promising the hand of his younger daughter, Rachel, to Jacob in marriage in return for seven years' service to him, Laban tricked Jacob—whose work had enriched Laban—into marrying Laban's elder daughter, Leah, instead. Jacob was compelled to serve Laban for another seven years in order to be permitted to marry Rachel. As in *Monarco*, there was both unjust enrichment of the oral promisor and heavy loss to the promisee—seven more years of unpaid labor. . . .

"Only two cases (one a federal district court diversity case governed by Indiana law) have allowed a claim based on the Indiana formula to survive a motion for summary judgment, though in neither case did the plaintiff ultimately prevail. . . .

"In the diversity case, *Madison Tool & Die, Inc. v. ZF Sachs Automotive of America, Inc.,* 2007 WL 2286130 (S.D.Ind. Aug.7, 2007), the defendant orally agreed to make the plaintiff its auto parts supplier. To induce the plaintiff to retool its facilities so that it could supply the parts, the defendant announced that it was not working with any other suppliers and would therefore need the plaintiff to begin production within 30 days. So the plaintiff went out and bought a special machine for $415,000 to produce the parts for the defendant. The plaintiff made test parts for the defendant with the new machine, but rather than ordering any parts the defendant assured the plaintiff for three years that it would begin ordering parts soon. Yet it never did, and at the end of the period declared that it would not be using the plaintiff as a supplier after all.

"In the other case, *Keating v. Burton,* 545 N.E.2d 35 (Ind.App.1989), the defendant orally agreed to hire the plaintiff as a full-time employee with an option to purchase 49 percent of the defendant's company after three years of employment. In reliance on the agreement the plaintiff went to work for the defendant and claimed to have shut down his own company, which had been growing. (The court eventually found that the plaintiff had not abandoned his business entirely. But for purposes of getting a fix on Indiana law, all that matters is the evidence that was before the court when it decided not to grant summary judgment to the defendant.) After the plaintiff had been working for the defendant's company for a year and a half, the defendant so limited the plaintiff's responsibilities that he quit.

"These cases are not as dramatic as *Monarco* or *Genesis* 29 and do not involve (so far as appears) substantial gain to the (oral) promisor. But there is a family resemblance, which helps us to understand the scope and operation of the Indiana formula as elaborated in the second paragraph of the indented quotation from *Babyback's* and as paraphrased in *Spring Hill Developers, Inc. v. Arthur,* 879 N.E.2d 1095, 1103 (Ind.App.2008), as follows: the "injury must be not only (1) independent from the benefit of the bargain and resulting incidental expenses and inconvenience, but also (2) so substantial as to constitute an unjust and unconscionable injury." The benefit of the bargain would be what the promisee hoped to gain from the promise, which in *Madison* would have been the profit from selling auto parts to the defendant and in *Keating* the 49 percent share of the defendant's company. The plaintiffs lost those expectancies of course, but they suffered other losses as well—the cost of the machine in *Madison* that the plaintiff would not have bought had it not been for the oral promise and in *Keating* the plaintiff's alleged loss of his company. And those losses were significant in relation to the plaintiffs' net worth, satisfying the second part of the Indiana formula.

"But what these cases really show is the mercury-like slipperiness of the Indiana formula, as of the *Monarco* formula as well. The "benefit of the bargain" is contract-speak for the expected profit from performing a contract; the "independent" loss of which the *Spring Hill* opinion spoke is the reliance loss—the expenses a party incurs to perform the contract. The plaintiff in *Madison* incurred the expense of the machine in reliance on the defendant's promise, and likewise with the plaintiff's giving up his business in *Keating*. A promise plus a reliance loss is what you need for promissory estoppel, yet the Indiana Supreme Court refused in *Babyback's* to endorse a *general* exception to the statute of frauds for promissory estoppel. 841 N.E.2d at 568–70; see *Spring Hill Developers, Inc. v. Arthur, supra,* 879 N.E.2d at 1100–04. So the whole weight of the doctrine of "unjust and unconscionable injury and loss" falls on the gravity of the injury, and the decisive distinction between *Monarco, Madison,* and *Keating* (and for that matter Jacob's grievance) on the one hand and the present case on the other hand is simply the duration of the injury in those cases relative to this one: 20 years, 3 years, 1.5 years, and 7 years (Jacob's case), versus in our case at most 2.5 months but more likely 3.5 weeks—the time that elapsed between Dowling's telling Classic on September 17 that the deal was a "go" and on October 12 that the loan application had been rejected. The more protracted the period during which reliance costs are being incurred, the stronger the inference that the oral promise was as the plaintiff represents it to be; for had there been no promise the plaintiff's conduct—his immense reliance cost relative to his resources—would have been incomprehensible.

"Remember that the objection to placing promissory estoppel outside the statute of frauds is that it is too easy for a plaintiff to incur reliance costs in order to bolster his claim of an oral promise. The objection is attenuated if the reliance is so extensive that it is unlikely that the plaintiff would have undertaken it (buying an expensive specialized machine or giving up a growing company) merely to bolster a false claim. He might of course have misunderstood the "promisor" or been gambling on getting a contract, but courts seem not to think those possibilities likely enough to warrant a sterner rule. The compromise that the courts strike between the value of protecting reasonable reliance and the policy that animates the statute of frauds is to require a party that wants to get around the statute of frauds to prove an *enhanced* promissory estoppel, and the enhancement consists of proving a kind or amount of reliance unlikely to have been incurred had the plaintiff not had a good-faith belief that he had been promised remuneration.

"This seems to us a better understanding of the "unjust and unconscionable" rule than ascribing it to judicial indignation at dishonorable behavior by promisors. It is a strength rather than a weakness of contract law that it generally eschews a moral conception of transactions. Liability for breach of contract is strict, rather than based (as tort liability generally is) on fault; punitive damages are unavailable even for deliberate breaches (and again note the contrast with tort law); and specific performance is exceptional—and when the only remedy for a breach of contract is compensatory damages, a promisor has in effect an option to perform or pay damages rather than a duty to perform (the duty the civil law expresses by the phrase *pacta sunt servanda*). Even such contract doctrines as "good faith," "best efforts," and "duress," which have a moral ring, seem aimed not at vindicating the moral law but at protecting each party to a contract from the other party's taking advantage of a temporary monopoly (not in an antitrust sense) that contracts often create when the performance of the parties is not simultaneous. . . .

"Even though the behavior of the defendants in *Monarco* and the other cases we have discussed may well shock the conscience, the outcomes of those cases are defensible on the practical ground of protecting reasonable reliance in situations (and this is key) in which the contention that the reliance was induced by an oral promise is credible. The formulas the cases use to describe these situations, however, are not illuminating. Holmes warned that "the law is full of phraseology drawn from morals, and by the mere force of language continually invites us to pass from one domain to the other without perceiving it, as we are sure to do unless we have the boundary constantly before our minds." O.W. Holmes, "The Path of the Law," 10 *Harv. L.Rev.* 457, 459–60 (1897). Ruminating on the meaning of "unjust" and "unconscionable" will not separate the cases we have discussed from this case; reflection on reliance will.

"The duration of reliance in the present case was much shorter than in the other cases that we have discussed, and the reliance is more easily imagined as based on hope than on a promise. And not all of it could be considered *reasonable* reliance, which is the only kind that can support a claim of promissory estoppel and *a fortiori* an invocation of the enhanced promissory-estoppel doctrine of the Indiana cases. The only reasonable reliance that the plaintiffs placed on Dowling's assurances was to cure (for less than $20,000) a delinquency somewhat earlier than they would otherwise have been forced to do. For the plaintiffs to treat the bank loan as a certainty because they were told by the bank officer whom they were dealing with that it would be approved was unreasonable, especially if, as the plaintiffs' damages claim presupposes, the need for the loan was urgent. Rational businessmen know that there is many a slip 'twixt cup and lips, that a loan is not approved until it is approved, that if a bank's employee tells you your loan application will be approved that is not the same as telling you it has been approved, and that if one does not have a loan commitment in writing yet the need for the loan is urgent one had better be negotiating with other potential lenders at the same time. The level of reliance that could be thought to have been reasonable in this case was not comparable to that involved in the other cases. In the end, this case turns out to be a routine promissory estoppel case, and that is not enough in Indiana to defeat a defense of statute of frauds."

———

PART 4

WRITTEN CONTRACTS

∎ ∎ ∎

This Part takes up issues that generally arise when there is a written contract.

Chapter 12 concerns cases in which A and B have entered into a written contract, and A claims that prior to, or contemporaneously with, making the written contract, the parties entered into a separate agreement that concerned the same subject matter as the written contract, but was not intended to be superseded by the written contract. The treatment of such alleged separate agreements—and more specifically, the issue whether evidence concerning such agreements is admissible—is governed by the *parol evidence rule*.

Chapter 13 considers the issue whether, in the admissibility of evidence concerning the *interpretation* of a contract, it should make a difference that the contract is in writing; and if so, what difference it should make. This issue is analytically separate from the issue governed by the parol evidence rule, which concerns the admissibility of evidence concerning whether the parties had a *separate agreement* that was superseded by the written agreement. Special consideration is given to how trade usage, course of performance, and course of dealing bear on the interpretation of a contract. Chapter 13 also takes up the duty of good faith, which can be understood as a principle of contract interpretation.

Chapter 14 concerns how conduct subsequent to the execution of a written contract can operate as a waiver of rights under the contract. It also concerns the effect of a contract having a no oral modification clause when there is an oral modification.

Chapter 15 and 16 concerns issues that are generally associated with commercial and consumer form contracts. Chapter 15 concerns what is called "the battle of the forms." This refers to the situation in which two firms trade forms in a transaction and neither party signifies assent to doing business based on terms in the other party's form. Chapter 16 concerns consumer form contracts. In these cases a firm typically presents an individual consumer or employee with a form with boilerplate terms. The individual may or may not sign the form. Invariably, the individual does not read boilerplate terms in the form. As you will see, American law tilts in favor of the firm and against the individual in this situation.

CHAPTER 12

THE PAROL EVIDENCE RULE

■ ■ ■

Section 1 of this Chapter takes up the parol evidence rule. Section 2 concerns uses of parol evidence not precluded by the rule.

SECTION 1. THE RULE

MITCHILL V. LATH

Court of Appeals of New York, 1928.
247 N.Y. 377, 160 N.E. 646, 68 A.L.R. 239.

Action by Catherine C. Mitchill against Charles Lath and another. Judgment of Special Term in plaintiff's favor, directing specific performance of an agreement to remove an icehouse, was affirmed by the Appellate Division (220 App.Div. 776, 221 N.Y.S. 864), and defendants appeal. Judgments of Appellate Division and Trial Term reversed, and complaint dismissed.

ANDREWS, J. In the fall of 1923 the Laths owned a farm. This they wished to sell. Across the road, on land belonging to Lieutenant Governor Lunn, they had an icehouse which they might remove. Mrs. Mitchell looked over the land with a view to its purchase. She found the icehouse objectionable. Thereupon "the defendants orally promised and agreed, for and in consideration of the purchase of their farm by the plaintiff, to remove the said icehouse in the spring of 1924." Relying upon this promise, she made a written contract to buy the property for $8,400, for cash and a mortgage and containing various provisions usual in such papers. Later receiving a deed, she entered into possession, and has spent considerable sums in improving the property for use as a summer residence. The defendants have not fulfilled their promise as to the icehouse, and do not intend to do so. We are not dealing, however, with their moral delinquencies. The question before us is whether their oral agreement may be enforced in a court of equity.

This requires a discussion of the parol evidence rule—a rule of law which defines the limits of the contract to be construed. Glackin v. Bennett, 226 Mass. 316, 115 N.E. 490. It is more than a rule of evidence, and oral testimony, even if admitted, will not control the written contract (O'Malley

v. Grady, 222 Mass. 202, 109 N.E. 829), unless admitted without objection (Brady v. Nally, 151 N.Y. 258, 45 N.E. 547). It applies, however, to attempts to modify such a contract by parol. It does not affect a parol collateral contract distinct from and independent of the written agreement. It is, at times, troublesome to draw the line. Williston, in his work on Contracts (section 637) points out the difficulty. "Two entirely distinct contracts," he says, "each for a separate consideration, may be made at the same time, and will be distinct legally. Where, however, one agreement is entered into wholly or partly in consideration of the simultaneous agreement to enter into another, the transactions are necessarily bound together. . . . Then if one of the agreements is oral and the other in writing, the problem arises whether the bond is sufficiently close to prevent proof of the oral agreement." That is the situation here. It is claimed that the defendants are called upon to do more than is required by their written contract in connection with the sale as to which it deals.

The principle may be clear, but it can be given effect by no mechanical rule. As so often happens, it is a matter of degree, for, as Prof. Williston also says, where a contract contains several promises on each side it is not difficult to put any one of them in the form of a collateral agreement. If this were enough, written contracts might always be modified by parol. Not form, but substance, is the test.

In applying this test, the policy of our courts is to be considered. We have believed that the purpose behind the rule was a wise one, not easily to be abandoned. Notwithstanding injustice here and there, on the whole it works for good. Old precedents and principles are not to be lightly cast aside, unless it is certain that they are an obstruction under present conditions. New York has been less open to arguments that would modify this particular rule, than some jurisdictions elsewhere. Thus in Eighmie v. Taylor, 98 N.Y. 288, it was held that a parol warranty might not be shown, although no warranties were contained in the writing.

Under our decisions before such an oral agreement as the present is received to vary the written contract, at least three conditions must exist: (1) The agreement must in form be a collateral one; (2) it must not contradict express or implied provisions of the written contract; (3) it must be one that parties would not ordinarily be expected to embody in the writing, or, put in another way, an inspection of the written contract, read in the light of surrounding circumstances, must not indicate that the writing appears "to contain the engagements of the parties, and to define the object and measure the extent of such engagement." Or, again, it must not be so clearly connected with the principal transaction as to be part and parcel of it.

The respondent does not satisfy the third of these requirements. It may be, not the second. We have a written contract for the purchase and sale of land. The buyer is to pay $8,400 in the way described. She is also to pay her portion of any rents, interest on mortgages, insurance premiums, and water meter charges. She may have a survey made of the premises. On their part, the sellers are to give a full covenant deed of the premises as described, or as they may be described by the surveyor, if the survey is had, executed, and acknowledged at their own expense; they sell the personal property on the farm and represent they own it; they agree that all amounts paid them on the contract and the expense of examining the title shall be a lien on the property; they assume the risk of loss or damage by fire until the deed is delivered; and they agree to pay the broker his commissions. Are they to do more? Or is such a claim inconsistent with these precise provisions? It could not be shown that the plaintiff was to pay $500 additional. Is it also implied that the defendants are not to do anything unexpressed in the writing?

That we need not decide. At least, however, an inspection of this contract shows a full and complete agreement, setting forth in detail the obligations of each party. On reading it, one would conclude that the reciprocal obligations of the parties were fully detailed. Nor would his opinion alter if he knew the surrounding circumstances. The presence of the icehouse, even the knowledge that Mrs. Mitchill thought it objectionable, would not lead to the belief that a separate agreement existed with regard to it. Were such an agreement made it would seem most natural that the inquirer should find it in the contract. Collateral in form it is found to be, but it is closely related to the subject dealt with in the written agreement—so closely that we hold it may not be proved. . . .

We do not ignore the fact that authorities may be found that would seem to support the contention of the appellant. Such are Erskine v. Adeane (1873) L.R. 8 Ch.App. 756, and Morgan v. Griffith (1871) L.R. 6 Exch. 70, where although there was a written lease a collateral agreement of the landlord to reduce the game was admitted. In this state, Wilson v. Deen might lead to the contrary result. Neither are they approved in New Jersey. Naumberg v. Young, 44 N.J.Law, 331, 43 Am.Rep. 380. Nor in view of later cases in this court can Batterman v. Pierce, 3 Hill, 171, be considered an authority. A line of cases in Massachusetts, of which Durkin v. Cobleigh, 156 Mass. 108, 30 N.E. 474, 17 L.R.A. 270, 32 Am.St.Rep. 436, is an example, have to do with collateral contracts made before a deed is given. But the fixed form of a deed makes it inappropriate to insert collateral agreements, however closely connected with the sale. This may be cause for an exception. Here we deal with the contract on the basis of which the deed to Mrs. Mitchill was given subsequently, and we confine ourselves to the question whether its terms may be modified. . . .

It is argued that what we have said is not applicable to the case as presented. The collateral agreement was made with the plaintiff. The contract of sale was with her husband, and no assignment of it from him appears. Yet the deed was given to her. It is evident that here was a transaction in which she was the principal from beginning to end. We must treat the contract as if in form, as it was in fact, made by her.

Our conclusion is that the judgment of the Appellate Division and that of the Special Term should be reversed and the complaint dismissed, with costs in all courts.

LEHMAN, J. (dissenting). I accept the general rule as formulated by Judge Andrews. I differ with him only as to its application to the facts shown in the record. The plaintiff contracted to purchase land from the defendants for an agreed price. A formal written agreement was made between the sellers and the plaintiff's husband. It is on its face a complete contract for the conveyance of the land. It describes the property to be conveyed. It sets forth the purchase price to be paid. All the conditions and terms of the conveyance to be made are clearly stated. I concede at the outset that parol evidence to show additional conditions and terms of the conveyance would be inadmissible. There is a conclusive presumption that the parties intended to integrate in that written contract every agreement relating to the nature or extent of the property to be conveyed, the contents of the deed to be delivered, the consideration to be paid as a condition precedent to the delivery of the deeds, and indeed all the rights of the parties in connection with the land. The conveyance of that land was the subject-matter of the written contract, and the contract completely covers that subject.

The parol agreement which the court below found the parties had made was collateral to, yet connected with, the agreement of purchase and sale. It has been found that the defendants induced the plaintiff to agree to purchase the land by a promise to remove an icehouse from land not covered by the agreement of purchase and sale. No independent consideration passed to the defendants for the parol promise. To that extent the written contract and the alleged oral contract are bound together. The same bond usually exists wherever attempt is made to prove a parol agreement which is collateral to a written agreement. Hence "the problem arises whether the bond is sufficiently close to prevent proof of the oral agreement." See Judge Andrews' citation from Williston on Contracts, § 637.

Judge Andrews has formulated a standard to measure the closeness of the bond. Three conditions, at least, must exist before an oral agreement may be proven to increase the obligation imposed by the written agreement. I think we agree that the first condition that the agreement "must in form be a collateral one" is met by the evidence. I concede that this condition is met in most cases where the courts have nevertheless excluded evidence of the collateral oral agreement. The difficulty here, as in most cases, arises in connection with the two other conditions.

The second condition is that the "parol agreement must not contradict express or implied provisions of the written contract." Judge Andrews voices doubt whether this condition is satisfied. The written contract has been carried out. The purchase price has been paid; conveyance has been made; title has passed in accordance with the terms of the written contract. The mutual obligations expressed in the written contract are left unchanged by the alleged oral contract. When performance was required of the written contract, the obligations of the parties were measured solely by its terms. By the oral agreement the plaintiff seeks to hold the defendants to other obligations to be performed by them thereafter upon land which was not conveyed to the plaintiff. The assertion of such further obligation is not inconsistent with the written contract, unless the written contract contains a provision, express or implied, that the defendants are not to do anything not expressed in the writing. Concededly there is no such express provision in the contract, and such a provision may be implied, if at all, only if the asserted additional obligation is "so clearly connected with the principal transaction as to be part and parcel of it," and is not "one that the parties would not ordinarily be expected to embody in the writing." The hypothesis so formulated for a conclusion that the asserted additional obligation is inconsistent with an implied term of the contract is that the alleged oral agreement does not comply with the third condition as formulated by Judge Andrews. In this case, therefore, the problem reduces itself to the one question whether or not the oral agreement meets the third condition.

I have conceded that upon inspection the contract is complete. "It appears to contain the engagements of the parties, and to define the object and measure the extent of such engagement;" it constitutes the contract between them, and is presumed to contain the whole of that contract. Eighmie v. Taylor, 98 N.Y. 288. That engagement was on the one side to convey land; on the other to pay the price. The plaintiff asserts further agreement based on the same consideration to be performed by the defendants after the conveyance was complete, and directly affecting only other land. It is true, as Judge Andrews points out, that "the presence of the icehouse, even the knowledge that Mrs. Mitchill thought it objectionable, would not lead to the belief that a separate agreement existed with regard to it"; but the question we must decide is whether or not, *assuming* an agreement was made for the removal of an unsightly icehouse from one parcel of land as an inducement for the purchase of another parcel, the parties would ordinarily or naturally be expected to embody the agreement for the removal of the icehouse from one parcel in the written agreement to convey the other parcel. Exclusion of proof of the oral agreement on the ground that it varies the contract embodied in the writing may be based only upon a finding or presumption that the written contract was intended to cover the oral negotiations for the removal of the icehouse which lead up to the contract of purchase and sale. To determine what the writing was intended to cover, "the document alone will not suffice. What it was intended to cover cannot be known till we know what there was to cover. The question being whether certain subjects of negotiation were intended to be covered, we must compare the writing and the negotiations before we can determine whether they were in fact covered." Wigmore on Evidence (2d Ed.) § 2430.

The subject-matter of the written contract was the conveyance of land. The contract was so complete on its face that the conclusion is inevitable that the parties intended to embody in the writing all the negotiations covering at least the conveyance. The promise by the defendants to remove the icehouse from other land was not connected with their obligation to convey except that one agreement would not have been made unless the other was also made. The plaintiff's assertion of a parol agreement by the defendants to remove the icehouse was completely established by the great weight of evidence. It must prevail unless that agreement was part of the agreement to convey and the entire agreement was embodied in the writing.

The fact that in this case the parol agreement is established by the overwhelming weight of evidence is, of course, not a factor which may be considered in determining the competency or legal effect of the evidence. Hardship in the particular case would not justify the court in disregarding or emasculating the general rule. It merely accentuates the outlines of our problem. The assumption that the parol agreement was made is no longer obscured by any doubts. The problem, then, is clearly whether the parties are presumed to have intended to render that parol agreement legally ineffective and nonexistent by failure to embody it in the writing. Though we are driven to say that nothing in the written contract which fixed the terms and conditions of the stipulated conveyance suggests the existence of any further parol agreement, an inspection of the contract, though it is complete on its face in regard to the subject of the conveyance, does not, I think, show that it was intended to embody negotiations or agreements, if any, in regard to a matter so loosely bound to the conveyance as the removal of an icehouse from land not conveyed.

The rule of integration undoubtedly frequently prevents the assertion of fraudulent claims. Parties who take the precaution of embodying their oral agreements in a writing should be protected against the assertion that other terms of the same agreement were not integrated in the writing. The limits of the integration are determined by the writing, read in the light of the surrounding circumstances. A written contract, however complete, yet covers only a limited field. I do not think that in the written contract for the conveyance of land here under consideration we can find an intention to cover a field so broad as to include prior agreements, if any such were made, to do other acts on other property after the stipulated conveyance was made.

In each case where such a problem is presented, varying factors enter into its solution. Citation of authority in this or other jurisdictions is useless, at least without minute analysis of the facts. The analysis I have made of the decisions in this state leads me to the view that the decision of the courts below is in accordance with our own authorities and should be affirmed.

CARDOZO, C.J., and POUND, KELLOGG and O'BRIEN, JJ., concur with ANDREWS, J.

LEHMAN, J., dissents in opinion in which CRANE, J., concurs.

Judgment accordingly.

Von Mehren, Civil Law Analogues to Consideration: An Exercise in Comparative Analysis

72 Harv.L.Rev. 1009, 1011–1012 (1959)

"One or more of the interested parties often think that a contractual obligation will be more readily enforced if it is formally divorced from the environment and the motives that produced it. Civil-law theorists, especially the German writers, have discussed such a divorcement in terms of whether the legal system permits an 'abstract' obligation. . . . [I]n all jurisdictions, a transaction can also be rendered partially abstract by embodying it in an integrating agreement."

James Bradley Thayer, A Preliminary Treatise on Evidence

428–429 (1898)

Commenting on an opinion of Chief Justice Holt, Thayer remarked: "The Chief Justice here retires into that lawyer's Paradise where all words have a fixed, precisely ascertained meaning; where men may express their purposes, not only with accuracy, but with fulness; and where, if the writer has been careful, a lawyer, having a document referred to him, may sit in his chair, inspect the text, and answer all questions without raising his eyes. Men have dreamed of attaining for their solemn muniments of title such an absolute security; and some degree of security they have encompassed by giving strict definitions and technical meanings to words and phrases, and by rigid rules of construction. But the fatal necessity of looking outside the text in order to identify persons and things, tends steadily to destroy such illusions and to reveal the essential imperfection of language, whether spoken or written."

CALAMARI & PERILLO, A PLEA FOR A UNIFORM PAROL EVIDENCE RULE AND PRINCIPLES OF INTERPRETATION
42 Indiana L.J. 333 (1967).

Any reader of advance sheets is well aware that most of the contract decisions reported do not involve offer and acceptance or other subjects usually explored in depth in a course in contracts but rather involve the parol evidence rule and questions of interpretation, topics given scant attention in most courses in contracts. . . . Much of the fog and mystery surrounding these subjects stems from the fact that there is basic disagreement as to the meaning and effect of the parol evidence rule and as to the appropriate goals to be achieved by the process of contractual interpretation. The cases and treatises of the contract giants tend to conceal this conflict. While frequently masking disagreement by using the same terminology, Professors Williston and Corbin are often poles apart in the meaning they attach to the same term. Often starting from what superficially appear to be the same premises, they frequently advocate different results in similar fact situations. The polarity of their views reflects conflicting value judgments as to policy issues that are as old as our legal system and that are likely to continue as long as courts of law exist. Although many writers and courts have expressed their views on the subject and have made major contributions to it, concentration on the analyses of Professors Williston and Corbin will point up the fundamental bases upon which the conflicting cases and views rest.

THE AREA OF SUBSTANTIAL AGREEMENT

There is a rule of substantive law which states that whenever contractual intent is sought to be ascertained from among several expressions of the parties, an earlier tentative expression will be rejected in favor of a later expression that is final. More simply stated, the contract made by the parties supersedes tentative promises made in earlier negotiations. Consequently, in determining the content of the contract, the earlier tentative promises are irrelevant.

The parol evidence rule comes into play only when the last expression is in writing. Professor Corbin states the rule as follows: "When two parties have made a contract and have expressed it in a writing to which they have both assented as the complete and accurate integration of that contract, evidence, whether parol or otherwise, of antecedent understandings and negotiations will not be admitted for the purpose of varying or contradicting the writing." Professor Williston's formulation is not to the contrary: "Briefly stated," he writes, "this rule requires, in the absence of fraud, duress, mutual mistake, or something of the kind, the exclusion of extrinsic evidence, oral or written, where the parties have reduced their agreement to an integrated writing." Both agree that this, too, is a rule of substantive law that also operates as an exclusionary rule of evidence merely because prior understandings are irrelevant to the process of determining the content of the final contract. The similarity between the parol evidence rule and the rule stated in the preceding paragraph is obvious. The main and important difference is that where the last expression is not in writing the jury determines whether the parties intended the second expression to supersede the first. This is to say that this question of intention is determined as is any other question of intention stemming from oral transactions. Where the later expression is in writing, however, this question is usually determined by the trial judge. At an early date it was felt (and the feeling strongly remains) that writings require the special protection that is afforded by removing this issue from the province of unsophisticated jurors.

THE PAROL EVIDENCE RULE: THE MAJOR AREA OF CONFLICT

Apparent agreement by Professors Williston and Corbin, except as noted, on the rules stated above conceals real conflict. The battleground upon which they express disagreement is a major one: the concept of total integration. This, of course, is the area in which most of the cases arise. Both assert that the existence of a total integration depends on the intention of the parties. . . . It appears, however, that in this context they use the term "intent" in ways that are remarkably dissimilar. A typical fact situation will illustrate this. *A* agrees to sell and *B* agrees to purchase Blackacre for $10,000. The contract is in writing and in all respects appears complete on its face. Prior to the signing of the contract *A,* in order to induce *B's* assent, orally promises him in the presence of a number of reputable witnesses that if *B* will sign the contract, *A* will remove an unsightly shack on *A's* land across the road from Blackacre. May this promise be proved and enforced? This depends upon whether the writing is a total integration.

Williston argues that if the intention to have a total integration were to be determined by the ordinary process of determining intention, the parol evidence rule would be emasculated. He points out that the mere existence of the collateral oral agreement would conclusively indicate that the parties intended only a partial integration and that the only question that would be presented is whether the alleged prior or contemporaneous agreement was actually made. This would be a question of fact for the jury, thus eliminating the special protection which the trial judge should afford the writing. . . .

. . . [Williston therefore suggests that] where the writing appears to be a complete instrument expressing the rights and obligations of both parties, it is deemed a total integration unless the alleged additional terms were such as might naturally be made as a separate agreement by parties situated as were the parties to the written contract.

Professor Corbin has an easy task in demolishing the Willistonian approach. In treating the matter of integration as a question of intent, as

Professor Williston purports to do, he shows the absurdity of excluding all relevant evidence of intent except the writing itself. But . . . Williston, and [courts that follow his view] are unconcerned about the true intention of the parties. Rather, shorn of rote language of fiction indicating a search for intention, they are advocating and applying a rule of form. Since (and even before) the common law had its genesis, there has been a deeply-felt belief that transactions will be more secure, litigation will be reduced, and the temptation to perjury will be removed, if everyone will only use proper forms for his transactions. The Statute of Wills and the Statute of Frauds are but examples of this belief. Professor Corbin, by attacking the apparent arguments of Williston's position has not expressly come to grips with the substance of his position. This is not to suggest that either he or Professor Williston have been unaware of the true nature of their disagreement. Rather, they seem for the most part to have been content not to make explicit the basis of their differing views. . . .

The debate involves the question: is the public better served by giving effect to the parties' entire agreement written and oral, even at the risk of injustice caused by the possibility of perjury and the possibility that superseded documents will be treated as operative, or does the security of transactions require that, despite occasional injustices, persons adopting a formal writing be required, on the penalty of voidness of their oral and written side agreements, to put their entire agreement in the formal writing. . . .

_____

RESTATEMENT, SECOND, CONTRACTS
§§ 209, 210, 213, 214, 215, 216

[See Selected Source Materials Supplement]

_____

Braucher, Interpretation and Legal Effect in the Second Restatement of Contracts

81 Colum.L.Rev. 13, 17 (1981)

"The core of the 'parol evidence rule' is stated in section 213: a binding integrated agreement discharges inconsistent prior agreements, and a binding completely integrated agreement discharges prior agreements within its scope. These statements, however, merely point to the obvious conclusion; the difficulties arise in determining whether there is an integrated agreement, whether, if so, it is completely or only partially integrated, and whether the prior agreement is consistent with the integrated agreement or within its scope. Those determinations are made in accordance with all relevant evidence, and require interpretation both of the integrated agreement and of the prior agreement. They are made by the court, not by the trier of fact."

Interform Co. v. Mitchell Constr. Co.

575 F.2d 1270, 1275–77 (9th Cir.1978)

(Sneed, J.) "In practice . . . the difference between the [Corbin and Williston] views is less significant than one might imagine. A writing, which ordinarily and naturally would be an integrated one, generally is one the parties thereto intended to be integrated. Also, the meaning to which the reasonably intelligent person would subscribe generally is that to which the parties did subscribe. . . .

"There are, however, significant differences between the two views. To suggest none exist would reduce the debate between their respective leading protagonists, Williston with regard to the first and Corbin the second, to a triviality. The debate is not that. It relates, as indicated, to the attitude with which judges should approach written contracts. Williston requires the judge to ascertain the legal relations between the parties by reference to those associated with the 'forms' (that is, the natural and normal integration practices and the meaning of words that reasonably intelligent people would employ) to which they should adhere and from which they depart at their peril. Calamari & Perillo 104–05; Williston §§ 633, 638–39. Corbin, on the other hand, directs the judge to fix the legal relations between the parties in accordance with their intention even when the 'forms' they employed suggest otherwise. Corbin §§ 538–42A. A judge, guided by Williston . . . would impose upon the parties the terms of the [contractual documents] as understood by the reasonably intelligent person if [those documents] appear complete and any additional terms ordinarily and naturally would have been included therein. Williston §§ 638–39; Calamari & Perillo 105. A judge, guided by Corbin, would impose upon the parties the agreement that the evidence indicates they in fact reached. . . .

"It is unlikely that any jurisdiction will inflexibly adopt one approach to the exclusion of the other; each is likely to influence the conduct of judges and the disposition of cases. However, it must be acknowledged that the influence of Corbin's way is stronger now . . ., than when he and Williston grappled during the drafting of the American Law Institute's first Restatement, Contracts. . . . "

CISG ART. 8(3)

[See Selected Source Materials Supplement]

Dodge, Teaching the CISG in Contracts

50 J. Leg. Ed. 72 (2000)

"Under the parol evidence rule found in both the common law and the UCC, the parties may not contradict the terms of a final written agreement with evidence of prior or contemporaneous negotiations or agreements. CISG Article 8(3), by contrast, directs a court interpreting a contract to give 'due consideration . . . to all relevant circumstances of the case including the negotiations, any practices which the parties have established between themselves, usages and any subsequent conduct of the parties.' In other words, the CISG lacks a parol evidence rule and allows a court interpreting a written contract to consider not just trade usage, course of dealing, and course of performance, but even the parties' prior negotiations."

UNIDROIT PRINCIPLES OF INTERNATIONAL LAW ART. 4.3

[See Selected Source Materials Supplement]

MASTERSON v. SINE

Supreme Court of California, 1968.
68 Cal.2d 222, 65 Cal.Rptr. 545, 436 P.2d 561.

TRAYNOR, CHIEF JUSTICE.

Dallas Masterson and his wife Rebecca owned a ranch as tenants in common. On February 25, 1958, they conveyed it to Medora and Lu Sine by a grant deed "Reserving unto the Grantors herein an option to purchase the above described property on or before February 25, 1968" for the "same consideration as being paid heretofore plus their depreciation value of any improvements Grantees may add to the property from and after two and a half years from this date." Medora is Dallas' sister and Lu's wife. Since the conveyance Dallas has been adjudged bankrupt. His trustee in bankruptcy and Rebecca brought this declaratory relief action to establish their right to enforce the option.

The case was tried without a jury. Over defendants' objection the trial court admitted extrinsic evidence that by "the same consideration as being paid heretofore" both the grantors and the grantees meant the sum of $50,000 and by "depreciation value of any improvements" they meant the depreciation value of improvements to be computed by deducting from the total amount of any capital expenditures made by defendants grantees the amount of depreciation allowable to them under United States income tax regulations as of the time of the exercise of the option.

The court also determined that the parol evidence rule precluded admission of extrinsic evidence offered by defendants to show that the parties wanted the property kept in the Masterson family and that the option was therefore personal to the grantors and could not be exercised by the trustee in bankruptcy.

The court entered judgment for plaintiffs, declaring their right to exercise the option, specifying in some detail how it could be exercised, and reserving jurisdiction to supervise the manner of its exercise and to determine the amount that plaintiffs will be required to pay defendants for their capital expenditures if plaintiffs decide to exercise the option.

Defendants appeal. They contend that the option provision is too uncertain to be enforced and that extrinsic evidence as to its meaning should not have been admitted. The trial court properly refused to frustrate the obviously declared intention of the grantors to reserve an option to repurchase by an overly meticulous insistence on completeness and clarity of written expression. (See California Lettuce Growers v. Union Sugar Co. (1955) 45 Cal.2d 474, 481, 289 P.2d 785, 49 A.L.R.2d 496; Rivers v. Beadle (1960) 183 Cal.App.2d 691, 695–697, 7 Cal.Rptr. 170.) It properly admitted extrinsic evidence to explain the language of the deed. . . . to the end that the consideration for the option would appear with sufficient certainty to permit specific enforcement. . . . The trial court erred, however, in excluding the extrinsic evidence that the option was personal to the grantors and therefore nonassignable.

When the parties to a written contract have agreed to it as an "integration"—a complete and final embodiment of the terms of an agreement—parol evidence cannot be used to add to or vary its terms. . . . When only part of the agreement is integrated, the same rule applies to that part, but parol evidence may be used to prove elements of the agreement not reduced to writing. . . .

California cases have stated that whether there was an integration is to be determined solely from the face of the instrument . . . and that the question for the court is whether it "appears to be a complete . . . agreement. . . . " . . . Neither of these strict formulations of the rule, however, has been consistently applied. The requirement that the writing must appear incomplete on its face has been repudiated in many cases where parol evidence was admitted "to prove the existence of a separate oral agreement as to any matter on which the document is silent and which is not inconsistent with its terms"—even though the instrument appeared to state a complete agreement. . . . Even under the rule that the writing alone is to be consulted, it was found necessary to examine the alleged collateral agreement before concluding that proof of it was precluded by the writing alone. (See 3 Corbin, Contracts (1960) § 582, pp. 444–446.) It is therefore evident that "The conception of a writing as wholly and intrinsically self-determinative of the parties' intent to make it a sole memorial of one or seven or twenty-seven subjects of negotiation is an impossible one." (9 Wigmore, Evidence (3d ed. 1940) § 2431, p. 103.) For example, a promissory note given by a debtor to his creditor may integrate all their present contractual rights and obligations, or it may be only a minor part of an underlying executory contract that would never be discovered by examining the face of the note.

In formulating the rule governing parol evidence, several policies must be accommodated. One policy is based on the assumption that written evidence is more accurate than human memory. . . . This policy, however, can be adequately served by excluding parol evidence of agreements that directly contradict the writing. Another policy is based on the fear that fraud or unintentional invention by witnesses interested in the outcome of the litigation will mislead the finder of facts. . . .

Evidence of oral collateral agreements should be excluded only when the fact finder is likely to be misled. The rule must therefore be based on the credibility of the evidence. One such standard, adopted by section 240(1)(b) of the Restatement [First] of Contracts, permits proof of a collateral agreement if it "is such an agreement as might *naturally* be made as a separate agreement by parties situated as were the parties to the written contract." (Italics added; see McCormick, Evidence (1954) § 216, p. 441; see also 3 Corbin, Contracts (1960) § 583, p. 475, § 594, pp. 568–569; 4 Williston, Contracts (3d ed. 1961) § 638, pp. 1039–1045.) The draftsmen of the Uniform Commercial Code would exclude the evidence in still fewer instances: "If the additional terms are such that if agreed upon, they would *certainly* have been included in the document in the view of the court, then evidence of their alleged making must be kept from the trier of fact." (Com. 3, § 2–202, italics added.)[1]

The option clause in the deed in the present case does not explicitly provide that it contains the complete agreement, and the deed is silent on the question of assignability. Moreover, the difficulty of accommodating the formalized structure of a deed to the insertion of collateral agreements makes it less likely that all the terms of such an agreement were included. (See 3 Corbin, Contracts (1960) § 587; 4 Williston, Contracts (3d ed. 1961) § 645; 70 A.L.R. 752, 759 (1931); 68 A.L.R. 245 (1930).) The statement of the reservation of the option might well have been placed in the recorded deed solely to preserve the grantors' rights against any possible future

---

[1]   Corbin suggests that, even in situations where the court concludes that it would not have been natural for the parties to make the alleged collateral oral agreement, parol evidence of such an agreement should nevertheless be permitted if the court is convinced that the unnatural actually happened in the case being adjudicated. (3 Corbin, Contracts, § 485, pp. 478, 480; cf. Murray, The Parol Evidence Rule: A Clarification (1966) 4 Duquesne L.Rev. 337, 341–342.) This suggestion may be based on a belief that judges are not likely to be misled by their sympathies. If the court believes that the parties intended a collateral agreement to be effective, there is no reason to keep the evidence from the jury.

purchasers and this function could well be served without any mention of the parties' agreement that the option was personal. There is nothing in the record to indicate that the parties to this family transaction, through experience in land transactions or otherwise, had any warning of the disadvantages of failing to put the whole agreement in the deed. This case is one, therefore, in which it can be said that a collateral agreement such as that alleged "might naturally be made as a separate agreement." *A fortiori,* the case is not one in which the parties "would certainly" have included the collateral agreement in the deed.

It is contended, however, that an option agreement is ordinarily presumed to be assignable if it contains no provisions forbidding its transfer or indicating that its performance involves elements personal to the parties. (Mott v. Cline (1927) 200 Cal. 434, 450, 253 P. 718; Altman v. Blewett (1928) 93 Cal.App. 516, 525, 269 P. 751.) The fact that there is a written memorandum, however, does not necessarily preclude parol evidence rebutting a term that the law would otherwise presume. In American Industrial Sales Corp. v. Airscope, Inc., supra, 44 Cal.2d 393, 397–398, 282 P.2d 504, we held it proper to admit parol evidence of a contemporaneous collateral agreement as to the place of payment of a note, even though it contradicted the presumption that a note, silent as to the place of payment, is payable where the creditor resides. (For other examples of this approach, see Richter v. Union Land etc. Co. (1900) 129 Cal. 367, 375, 62 P. 39 [presumption of time of delivery rebutted by parol evidence]; Wolters v. King (1897) 119 Cal. 172, 175–176, 51 P. 35 [presumption of time of payment rebutted by parol evidence]; Mangini v. Wolfschmidt, Ltd., supra, 165 Cal.App.2d 192, 198–201, 331 P.2d 728 [presumption of duration of an agency contract rebutted by parol evidence]; Zinn v. Ex-Cell-O Corp. (1957) 148 Cal.App.2d 56, 73–74, 306 P.2d 1017; see also Rest., Contracts, § 240, com. c.)[3] Of course a statute may preclude parol evidence to rebut a statutory presumption. . . . Here, however, there is no such statute. In the absence of a controlling statute the parties may provide that a contract right or duty is nontransferable. . . . Moreover, even when there is no explicit agreement—written *or* oral—that contractual duties shall be personal, courts will effectuate a presumed intent to that effect if the circumstances indicate that performance by substituted person would be different from that contracted for. . . .

In the present case defendants offered evidence that the parties agreed that the option was not assignable in order to keep the property in the Masterson family. The trial court erred in excluding that evidence.

---

[3]   Counsel for plaintiffs direct our attention to numerous cases that they contend establish that parol evidence may never be used to show a collateral agreement contrary to a term that the law presumes in the absence of an agreement. In each of these cases, however, the decision turned upon the court's belief that the writing was a complete integration and was no more than an application of the rule that parol evidence cannot be used to vary the terms of a completely integrated agreement. . . .

The judgment is reversed.

PETERS, TOBRINER, MOSK, and SULLIVAN, JJ., concur.

Dissenting Opinion

BURKE, JUSTICE.

I dissent. . . .

The opinion permits defendants to establish by parol testimony that their grant to their brother (and brother-in-law) of a written option, absolute in terms, was nevertheless agreed to be nonassignable by the grantee (now a bankrupt), and that therefore the right to exercise it did not pass, by operation of the bankruptcy laws, to the trustee for the benefit of the grantee's creditors.

And how was this to be shown? By the proffered testimony of the bankrupt optionee himself! Thereby one of his assets (the option to purchase defendants' California ranch) would be withheld from the trustee in bankruptcy and from the bankrupt's creditors. Understandably the trial court, as required by the parol evidence rule, did not allow the bankrupt by parol to so contradict the unqualified language of the written option.

The court properly admitted parol evidence to explain the intended meaning of the "same consideration" and "depreciation value" phrases of the written option to purchase defendants' land, as the intended meaning of those phrases was not clear. However, there was nothing ambiguous about the *granting* language of the option and not the slightest suggestion in the document that the option was to be nonassignable. Thus, to permit such words of limitation to be added by parol is to *contradict* the absolute nature of the grant, and to directly violate the parol evidence rule.

Just as it is unnecessary to state in a deed to "lot X" that the house located thereon goes with the land, it is likewise unnecessary to add to "I grant an option to Jones" the words *"and his assigns"* for the option to be assignable. . . . California statutes expressly declare that it *is* assignable, and only if I add language in writing showing my intent to withhold or restrict the right of assignment may the grant be so limited. Thus, to seek to restrict the grant by parol is to *contradict* the written document in violation of the parol evidence rule. . . .

[D]espite the law which until the advent of the present majority opinion has been firmly and clearly established in California and relied upon by attorneys and courts alike, that parol evidence may not be employed to vary or contradict the terms of a written instrument, the majority now announce that such evidence 'should be excluded only when the fact finder is likely to be misled,' and that 'The rule must therefore be based on the *credibility* of the evidence.' (Italics added.) But was it not, inter alia, to avoid misleading the fact finder, and to further the introduction of only the evidence which is most likely to be credible (the written document), that the Legislature adopted the parol evidence rule as a part of the substantive law of this state?

Next, in an effort to implement this newly promulgated 'credibility' test, the majority opinion offers a choice of two 'standards': one, a 'certainty' standard, quoted from the Uniform Commercial Code, and the other a 'natural' standard found in the Restatement of Contracts, and concludes that at least for purposes of the present case the 'natural' viewpoint should prevail. . . .

In an effort to provide justification for applying the newly pronounced 'natural' rule to the circumstances of the present case, the majority opinion next attempts to account for the silence of the writing in this case concerning assignability of the option, by asserting that 'the difficulty of accommodating the formalized structure of a deed to the insertion of collateral agreements makes it less likely that all the terms of such an agreement were included.' What difficulty would have been involved here, to add the words 'this option is nonassignable'? . . .

[T]he majority assert that 'There is nothing in the record to indicate that the parties to this family transaction, through experience in land transactions or otherwise, had any warning of the disadvantages of failing to put the whole agreement in the deed.' (Italics added.) The facts of this case, however, do not support such claim of naivete. The grantor husband (the bankrupt businessman) testified that as none of the parties were attorneys 'we wanted to contact my attorney * * * which we did. * * * The wording in the option was obtained from (the attorney). * * * I told him what my discussion was with the Sines (defendant grantees) and he wanted * * * a little time to compose it * * *. And, then this (the wording provided by the attorney) was taken to the title company at the time Mr. and Mrs. Sine and I went in to complete the transaction.' The witness was an experienced businessman who thus demonstrated awareness of the wisdom of seeking legal guidance and advice in this business transaction, and who did so. Wherein lies the naive family transaction postulated by the majority? . . .

McCOMB, J., concurs.

Rehearing denied; McCOMB and BURKE, JJ., dissenting.

———

UCC § 2–202

[See Selected Source Materials Supplement]

———

Interform v. Mitchell Constr. Co.

575 F.2d 1270, 1277 (9th Cir. 1978)

(Sneed, J.) ". . . [UCC § 2–202] reflects Corbin's influence. It precludes contradiction of 'confirmatory memoranda' by prior or contemporaneous oral agreements when the writing was *intended* by the parties as a final expression of their agreement' and permits the introduction of consistent additional terms 'unless the court finds the writing to have been *intended* also as a complete and exclusive statement of the terms of the agreement.' (Italics added). The focus plainly is on the intention of the parties, not the integration practices of reasonable persons acting normally and naturally. This is Corbin's focus. Furthermore, [Official Comment 1 rejects] certain rules more applicable to Williston's approach than to Corbin's. . . . "

NOTE ON MERGER CLAUSES

Many written contracts contain provisions that state that the written contract is the entire contract between the parties. These provisions are known as "merger" or "integration" clauses because they say, in effect, that all agreements between the parties have been merged or integrated into the writing. Typically these are boilerplate provisions—that is, they are standardized provisions that are routinely inserted by the drafting lawyer into every contract the lawyer writes—even when the principals have not specifically negotiated such a provision—and usually appear at the end of the contract with other standardized provisions, like provisions that set out the addresses to which notices should be sent.

The law on what effect should be given to merger clauses is messy. In some cases they have been given a great deal of weight; in some they have been given little weight; and in some the courts have said that the weight to be given such provisions depends on the circumstances. The muddiness of the case law is reflected in the muddiness of Restatement Second § 216, Comment e:

> e.   *Written term excluding oral terms ("merger" clause).* Written agreements often contain clauses stating that there are no representations, promises or agreements between the parties except those found in the writing. Such a clause may negate the apparent authority of an agent to vary orally the written terms, and if agreed to is likely to conclude the issue whether the agreement is completely integrated. Consistent additional terms may then be excluded even though their omission would have been natural in the absence of such a clause. But such a clause does not control the question whether the writing was assented to as an integrated agreement, the scope of the writing if completely integrated, or the interpretation of the written terms.

UNIDROIT PRINCIPLES OF INTERNATIONAL COMMERCIAL CONTRACTS ART. 2.1.17

[See Selected Source Materials Supplement]

SECTION 2. USES OF PAROL EVIDENCE NOT PRECLUDED BY THE RULE

SNYDER V. LOVERCHECK

Supreme Court of Wyoming 1999.
992 P.2d 1079.

TAYLOR, JUSTICE, Retired.

Believing himself to have been shortchanged in the purchase of a wheat farm, appellant filed suit against the sellers, both real estate agents, and his agent's employer. The district court granted summary judgment in favor of all defendants on all of appellant's claims. The district court awarded costs to all defendants, and awarded attorney's fees to the sellers. Finding the district court's disposition on the motions for summary judgment to be correct, we affirm. . .

In the fall of 1995, Snyder began searching for a suitable wheat farm. To facilitate his search, he contacted and employed Hayek, a real estate agent employed by The Property Exchange. Hayek contacted Ron Lovercheck of Bear Mountain Land Company (Ron) and discussed O.W. and Margaret Lovercheck's (the Loverchecks) farm in Goshen County. Hayek, Ron, and Snyder toured the farm on November 5, 1995. The crops were planted but not growing when they toured the farm. Ron did mention that there had been some problems with rye in the past, expressing his belief that the problem was minor. Snyder left the meeting with the understanding that the problem was confined to about 100 of the 1,960 acres.

The following day, Ron, through Hayek, informed Snyder that he had spoken with the former owner of the farm, Ray Headrick (Headrick). Headrick stated that the acreage in question had always produced more wheat than the county average. Headrick also showed Ron the areas where the rye problem was at its worst. Those areas comprised about 100 acres total, and Headrick said that those areas could grow as much as twenty to twenty-five percent rye. Snyder returned to view the property on ten to twelve occasions after the initial tour.

Eventually, Snyder made an offer on the property, and negotiations ensued. On February 16, 1996, Snyder and the Loverchecks entered into a contract for sale of the farm. The contract, drafted by Hayek on Wyoming Real Estate Commission Forms, expressly provided that:

> Purchaser is not relying upon any representations of the Seller or Seller's agents or sub-agents as to any condition which Purchaser deems to be material to Purchaser's decision to purchase this property[.]

This language mirrors the language in a statement of condition of the property completed by the Loverchecks at Snyder's request. The contract also contained an "as is" clause, a merger clause, a liberal inspection clause, and a specific objection procedure. Snyder stated in his deposition that he read parts of the contract, but not the above-quoted language.

The purchase price for the farm was $526,500.00, and the parties closed on May 10, 1996. According to Snyder, when the crops came up the rye problem was not minor, but rather he estimates that there is rye on 1,800 acres, over a third of which was 100% infected. The affidavit of Snyder's expert stated that the extensive rye problem decreased the value of the farm to only $392,000.00.

Snyder filed suit alleging that the Loverchecks breached the contract for sale, that Ron and the Loverchecks negligently and fraudulently misrepresented the extent of the rye problem, that Ron's fraudulent misrepresentations entitled Snyder to punitive damages, and that Hayek and The Property Exchange breached their duty to delete and/or explain the waiver language quoted above. The district court granted summary judgment in favor of all appellees. The district court awarded the Loverchecks $12,811.09 in attorney's fees and $819.90 in costs, and awarded $8,746.12 in costs to Ron. This timely appeal followed. . .

The district court found that neither Ron nor the Loverchecks had breached the contract, and that the punitive damages claim fell with the underlying claims. Snyder makes no argument to this Court that such determinations were erroneous; rather, he relies solely on the contention that the Loverchecks, through Ron, negligently and fraudulently represented to Snyder that the rye problem was minor and manageable. The Loverchecks respond that the disclaimer clause in the contract for sale precludes Snyder from asserting such claims. The district court considered the common elements of both causes of action,[1] and held that Snyder could not assert reliance upon the representations of either Ron or the

---

[1] The elements of a negligent misrepresentation claim are: false information supplied in the course of one's business for the guidance of others in their business; failure to exercise reasonable care in obtaining or relating the information; and pecuniary loss resulting from justifiable reliance thereon. *Richey v. Patrick,* 904 P.2d 798, 802 (Wyo.1995); *Duffy v. Brown,* 708 P.2d 433, 437 (Wyo.1985); Restatement of Torts (Second) § 552 at 126–27 (1977).

The elements of a claim for fraud are: "a false representation made by the defendant which is relied upon by the plaintiff to his damage, the asserted false representation must be made to induce action, and the plaintiff must reasonably believe the representation to be true." *Duffy,* 708 P.2d at 437.

Loverchecks. We, however, find the two causes of action sufficiently distinguishable to merit independent analysis.

...FRAUDULENT MISREPRESENTATION

The effect of merger and disclaimer clauses on pre-contractual misrepresentations poses significant questions of public policy. There are two prevailing views on the subject. One school of thought focuses on the sanctity of the right to contract, and holds that a party is bound by a specific disclaimer even if the contract was fraudulently obtained. The other school of thought latches on to the age-old proposition that fraud vitiates all contracts, and holds that a party to a contract is not bound by a disclaimer if it was fraudulently obtained. Wyoming subscribes to the latter view.

The Loverchecks ask us to adopt the reasoning of *Danann Realty Corp. v. Harris,* 184 N.Y.S.2d 599, 5 N.Y.2d 317, 157 N.E.2d 597, 598 (1959), where the New York Court of Appeals considered "whether the plaintiff can possibly establish from the facts alleged in the complaint * * * reliance upon the misrepresentations * * *." In *Danann Realty Corp.,* the contract provided:

> "The Purchaser has examined the premises agreed to be sold and is familiar with the physical condition thereof. The Seller has not made and does not make any representations as to the physical condition, rents, leases, *expenses, operation* or any other matter or thing affecting or related to the aforesaid premises, except as herein specifically set forth, and the Purchaser hereby *expressly acknowledges that no such representations have been made, and the Purchaser further acknowledges that it has inspected the premises and agrees to take the premises 'as is'* * * *. It is understood and agreed that all understandings and agreements heretofore had between the parties hereto are merged in this contract, which alone fully and completely expresses their agreement, *and that the same is entered into after full investigation, neither party relying upon any statement or representation*, not embodied in this contract, made by the other. The Purchaser has inspected the buildings standing on said premises and is thoroughly acquainted with their condition."

Danann Realty Corp., 184 N.Y.S.2d 599, 157 N.E.2d at 598 (emphasis in original). That court recognized a difference between a general merger clause and a specific disclaimer of reliance, noting that general merger clauses do not preclude a claim of fraud in the inducement. The New York Court of Appeals went on to say:

> Here, however, plaintiff has in the plainest language announced and stipulated that it is not relying on any representations as to the very matter as to which it now claims it was defrauded. Such a specific disclaimer destroys the allegations in plaintiff's

complaint that the agreement was executed in reliance upon these contrary oral representations * * *.

and,

If the language here used is not sufficient to estop a party from claiming that he entered the contract because of fraudulent representations, then no language can accomplish that purpose. To hold otherwise would be to say that it is impossible for two businessmen dealing at arm's length to agree that the buyer is not buying in reliance on any representations of the seller as to a particular fact.

Danann Realty Corp., 184 N.Y.S.2d 599, 157 N.E.2d at 599, 600.

Danann Realty Corp. has been followed by other courts, but has been limited in its applicability to situations where the disclaimer is specifically tailored. In *LaFazia v. Howe,* 575 A.2d 182, 186 (R.I.1990), the Supreme Court of Rhode Island applied the reasoning of *Danann Realty Corp.* to a disclaimer specifically denying reliance upon the seller's representations as to the profitability of the business being sold. However, in *Travers v. Spidell,* 682 A.2d 471, 473 (R.I.1996) (per curiam), the court found that a merger-and-disclaimer clause was insufficient to invoke the rule where it did not specifically discuss the location or boundaries of the well in issue. Another path of evolution has been to dilute *Danann Realty Corp.* into a balancing test where the disclaimer is a factor to be considered in determining reliance. *See Flakus v. Schug,* 213 Neb. 491, 329 N.W.2d 859, 863 (1983), *overruled on other grounds sub nom., Nielsen v. Adams,* 223 Neb. 262, 388 N.W.2d 840 (1986).

Although not cited by the parties, we found that this issue is not unprecedented in Wyoming, and we choose to follow our long-established rule. Our decision to do so is not solely based on consideration of the doctrine of stare decisis, but also our finding that the rule in Wyoming more appropriately balances the competing interests of justice and freedom of contract.

In *Baylies v. Vanden Boom,* 40 Wyo. 411, 278 P. 551, 552 (1929), the parties negotiated an exchange of a hotel in Kansas City, Missouri for a ranch in Uinta County. The parties entered into an agreement which provided:

"In the telegram of acceptance of proposition of the exchange of properties said telegram mentioned certain representations made by Bert L. Cook, Henry J. Vanden Boom, having no way of knowing whether to concur in his agents' representations, said representations are herewith set out, and constitute the only representations made."

Baylies, 278 P. at 553–54. The memorandum went on to list several representations, and was signed by both parties. *Id.* at 554. After taking over management of the hotel, Baylies discovered that several of the representations made to him, and not contained within the agreement, were untrue. *Id.* at 552. Baylies sued to rescind the contract, and Vanden Boom asserted that Baylies was precluded from asserting reliance upon any representations not contained within the memorandum. *Id.* at 551–52.

We considered the rule analogous to *Danann Realty Corp.* that was in use at the time in several jurisdictions, and exemplified by Massachusetts cases.

> "The Massachusetts cases emphasize the desirability of certainty in the contractual relations of those who have made a definite agreement, and if they say that they contract without regard to prior representations and that prior utterances have not been an inducement to their consent, any occasional damage to the individual caused by antecedent fraud is thought to be outweighed by the advantage of certainty and freedom from attacks, which would in the majority of cases be unfounded where such provisions were in the agreement."

Baylies, 278 P. at 555 (*quoting Arnold v. National Aniline & Chemical Co.,* 20 F.2d 364 (2nd Cir.1927)). We found, however, that competing considerations outweighed any interest in certainty. " 'A perpetrator of fraud cannot close the lips of his innocent victim by getting him blindly to agree in advance not to complain against it.' " *Baylies,* 278 P. at 556 (*quoting Webster v. Palm Beach Ocean Realty Co.,* 16 Del.Ch. 15, 139 A. 457 (1927)). We held that Baylies was not precluded from proving that he relied upon the fraudulent misrepresentations notwithstanding the fact that he had signed the memorandum. *Baylies,* 278 P. at 557.

The Massachusetts Supreme Court has subsequently adopted the rule to which we subscribe, and has succinctly stated the policy behind the rule:

> In the realm of fact it is entirely possible for a party knowingly to agree that no representations have been made to him, while at the same time believing and relying upon representations which in fact have been made and in fact are false but for which he would not have made the agreement. To deny this possibility is to ignore the frequent instances in everyday experience where parties accept, often without critical examination, and act upon agreements containing somewhere within their four corners exculpatory clauses in one form or another, but where they do so, nevertheless, in reliance upon the honesty of supposed friends, the plausible and disarming statements of salesmen, or the customary course of business. To refuse relief would result in opening the

door to a multitude of frauds and in thwarting the general policy
of the law.

Bates v. Southgate, 308 Mass. 170, 31 N.E.2d 551, 558 (1941).

Moreover, such a rule comports with the well-established exceptions
to the parol evidence rule. That rule dictates that when the meaning of a
contract is unambiguous, extrinsic evidence is not admitted to contradict
the plain meaning of the terms used by the parties. *Union Pacific Resources
Co. v. Texaco, Inc.,* 882 P.2d 212, 220 (Wyo.1994). We depart from the parol
evidence rule only if parol evidence is used to establish a separate and
distinct contract, a condition precedent, ***fraud***, mistake or repudiation.
Applied Genetics Intern., Inc. v. First Affiliated Securities, Inc., 912 F.2d
1238, 1245 (10th Cir.1990); Restatement of Contracts (Second) § 214
(1981).

Therefore, we decline to adopt the reasoning of *Danann Realty Corp.,*
and hold that Snyder is not precluded from asserting a claim for fraudulent
misrepresentation by either the merger or disclaimer clauses. While the
district court's decision on this issue was incorrect, it is well established
that a district court judgment may be affirmed on any proper legal grounds
supported by the record. *Bird v. Rozier,* 948 P.2d 888, 892 (Wyo.1997).

"A plaintiff who alleges fraud must do so clearly and distinctly, and
fraud will not be imputed to any party when the facts and circumstances
out of which it is alleged to arise are consistent with honesty and purity of
intention." *Duffy v. Brown,* 708 P.2d 433, 437 (Wyo.1985). Fraud must be
established by clear and convincing evidence, and will never be presumed.
Id.

In the present case, Snyder presented no evidence to the district court
consistent with fraud. Ron expressed his belief about the extent of the rye
problem, and immediately sought a more informed opinion. No accusation
has been made that Headrick's appraisal of the rye problem was based on
anything other than his observations or was intentionally misleading. No
one prevented Snyder from inspecting the land, and, in fact, he visited the
land at least ten times before he agreed to the purchase. The facts of this
case do not even approach the elevated burden of proof necessary to
establish a claim of fraud. Summary judgment was properly granted on
this issue. . . .

[The court affirmed summary judgment for the defendants on the
negligent misrepresentation claim, adopting a rule that a seller owes no
duty of care to a buyer to ensure the accuracy of a representation made by
the seller, or to warn the buyer not to rely, when the contract clearly and
unambiguously allocates the risk in question to the buyer. The court also
affirmed summary judgment for the broker Hayek on Snyder's malpractice
claim. The court declined to affirm on the ground pressed by Hayek, which
was "that Snyder waived the breach of duty by signing the contract." The

opinion observes: "It is inconceivable to this Court that a broker can escape liability for failing to advise his client of the consequences of signing a document by allowing the client to sign the very document that the broker failed to explain ... [S]uch a rule ... provides no protection for the unsophisticated and unwary consumer who places his trust in his paid agent." The court instead affirmed on the ground that "the undisputed facts in this case are such that no genuine question of material fact could be raised. Snyder is not the typical first-time home buyer who might benefit from a detailed explanation of all the terms contained in a contract for sale. Snyder fancies himself a sophisticated purchaser... Snyder read the document, and expressed neither concern nor confusion about the language. Hayek was justified in believing that ... the contract was understandable and acceptable to Snyder."]

... Summary judgment was properly granted as to all claims ... By this decision, the balance of rights between sellers, buyers, and broker is maintained. Buyers may assert claims if they have been defrauded in their purchase; however, simple negligence will not relieve a buyer from a poor bargain. Brokers, entrusted with great responsibility to protect their client's interests, must explain the contracts they present in a manner commensurate with the sophistication of their clients. Accordingly, the judgment of the district court is affirmed on the motions for summary judgment ...

RESTATEMENT, SECOND, CONTRACTS § 214

[See Selected Source Materials Supplement]

NOTE ON EXCEPTIONS TO THE PAROL EVIDENCE RULE

The disagreement between Corbin and Williston discussed in the excerpt from Calamari & Perillo, *supra*, was over whether a court should consider all relevant evidence in deciding whether the written contract was intended to be an integration. Williston sided with the majority in *Mitchill v. Lath*; Corbin with the dissent. It is uncontroversial that the rule does not preclude the use of parol evidence for a variety of other purposes, including to establish fraud, mutual misunderstanding, or mistake, to establish a basis for reformation, or for purpose of interpretation. Within each of these bodies of law there are rules that enable judges to screen out dubious claims that protect the integrity of written contracts. Rules on interpretation are considered in Section 2.

Sisneros v. Citadel Broadcasting Co.

140 N.M. 266, 142 P.3d 34 (N.M. App. 2006)

Plaintiff Sisneros worked as a radio personality for defendant Citadel for over twenty years under a series of employment agreements. The last of these agreements was entered in September 2002. When presented with a draft of this agreement Sisneros demanded and Citadel agreed to eliminate a provision (paragraph 26(h)) requiring arbitration of disputes. Sisneros did not object to another provision (paragraph 22) that required arbitration of disputes "in accordance with, and to the extent provided in, the standard arbitration procedure in the Company's employee handbook." The handbook included a term requiring arbitration of all disputes between an employee and the company. In 2003 Citadel terminated Sisneros without cause. Sisneros filed a lawsuit asserting various claims, including breach of contract and misuse of his name and persona for commercial gain. The trial court granted Citadel's motion to compel arbitration. Reversed.

(Fry, J.) "Plaintiff contends that the parties expressly agreed they would not be compelled to arbitrate their disputes. He claims that even though paragraph 22 of the employment agreement sets forth an agreement to arbitrate, this paragraph does not reflect the understanding of the parties before they entered into the agreement.

"Plaintiff claims the parties agreed that language referring to compulsory arbitration would be removed from the final employment agreement. To support this claim before the district court, Plaintiff submitted two affidavits stating that (1) during negotiations over the employment agreement, Plaintiff objected to the draft agreement's paragraph 26(h), which waived his right to litigate in court any disputes arising out of the agreement, and told Citadel's representatives that compulsory arbitration would be a "deal breaker"; (2) Citadel agreed to remove all language referring to compulsory arbitration; (3) Citadel's representatives provided Plaintiff with a revised employment agreement and told him that the compulsory arbitration requirement had been removed; and (4) based on these representations and his review of paragraph 26(h) of the revised agreement, which no longer required compulsory arbitration, Plaintiff agreed to the revised agreement. Based on these affidavits, Plaintiff argues that the evidence was insufficient that the parties intended to enter into an arbitration agreement or, in the alternative, the contract was ambiguous on the subject. He contends that Citadel misrepresented its agreement to remove the arbitration requirement in order to induce him to sign the contract.

"Citadel counters that paragraph 22 remained part of the final agreement and clearly set forth an agreement to arbitrate according to the standard arbitration procedures in the handbook. Citadel claims that (1) evidence extrinsic to the employment agreement is not admissible to establish any understandings reached before the parties signed the agreement; (2) Plaintiff had a duty to ascertain the contents of what he was signing and cannot now object to the writing that he signed; (3) Plaintiff failed to establish an element of his claim, which is that Citadel intentionally deceived Plaintiff; and (4) even if a misrepresentation induced Plaintiff to sign the agreement, Plaintiff affirmed or ratified the agreement by accepting six months of paychecks after he was terminated, as provided in the agreement. We address each of Citadel's arguments in turn.

"1. Extrinsic Evidence

"Citadel contends that "evidence outside of the 'four corners' of a written contract . . . is *only* admissible at this stage to show the language actually used by the parties in a contract is ambiguous." Therefore, Citadel continues, Plaintiff cannot rely on evidence of what occurred prior to the signing of the agreement in order to support his claim that Citadel misrepresented the substance of the agreement. We do not agree. "Extrinsic evidence is admissible to establish that the [contract] did not express the true agreement of the parties, even if the inconsistency cannot be detected on the face of the [contract] and becomes clear only in light of surrounding circumstances." *Twin Forks Ranch, Inc. v. Brooks,* 120 N.M. 832, 835, 907 P.2d 1013, 1016 (Ct.App.1995). If Citadel's argument were correct, it would be virtually impossible to show mistake or misrepresentation in the contract context.

"2. Duty to Read Before Signing

"It is the general rule that a person has a duty to read a contract and familiarize himself with its contents, *see Ballard v. Chavez,* 117 N.M. 1, 3, 868 P.2d 646, 648 (1994), and Plaintiff does not contend that he had no opportunity to review the final version of the contract prior to signing it. However, this general rule is not absolute. In order to understand the limitations on the general rule, we first review the law regarding misrepresentation in the contract context.

"Misrepresentations by one party as to a writing can make a contract voidable by the other party. *See Restatement* § 164 (describing the circumstances under which a misrepresentation makes a contract voidable). In order for this to occur, the recipient of the misrepresentation must show that (1) there was a misrepresentation that was (2) material or fraudulent and which (3) induced the recipient to enter into the agreement, and that (4) the recipient's reliance on the misrepresentation was justified. *See Robison v. Katz,* 94 N.M. 314, 319, 610 P.2d 201, 206 (Ct.App.1980) (stating that rescission of a contract "should be granted a party who, in entering a contract, justifiably relied on a misrepresentation of a material fact"); *Restatement* ch. 7 at 425 (listing similar elements to support voiding a contract). Citadel's argument regarding Plaintiff's duty to read the agreement involves the first and third elements—whether there was a misrepresentation and if so, whether Plaintiff justifiably relied on it.

"A misrepresentation is an assertion that is not in accord with the facts." *Id.* at 424. A misrepresentation includes the situation where one party knows that the other party is mistaken as to the content of a writing and yet fails to correct this mistake. *Id.* § 161 cmt. E. (stating that a party is expected to correct the mistaken understanding of the other party as to the contents of a writing); *Chromo Mountain Ranch P'ship v. Gonzales,* 101 N.M. 298, 299, 681 P.2d 724, 725 (1984); *see also* I E. Allan Farnsworth, *Farnsworth on Contracts* § 4.11 (3d ed.2004) (explaining that a misrepresentation can include a false representation "as to the contents or legal effect of a writing that is to evidence or embody the contract"). Plaintiff's affidavits about the pre-contract negotiations reasonably give rise to an inference that Citadel knew Plaintiff was unwilling to agree to compulsory arbitration and told Plaintiff the employment agreement had been changed to remove the arbitration provision even though the stated change had not been made. It is for the fact finder to determine whether to accept or reject this inference after considering all the evidence.

"As for whether Plaintiff was justified in relying on Citadel's statements, a contract may be voidable even when a party fails to use care in reading the writing and thus does not discover the mistake, depending on the circumstances. *Restatement* § 161 cmt. E; *see also Godfrey, Bassett & Kuykendall Architects, Ltd. V. Huntington Lumber & Supply Co.,* 584 So.2d 1254, 1259 (Miss.1991) (stating that "[w]here one party's false representations induce another party to contract, negligence of the second party cannot be raised to bar relief to him"). "A recipient's fault in not knowing or discovering the facts before making the contract does not make his reliance unjustified unless it amounts to a failure to act in good faith and in accordance with reasonable standards of fair dealing." *Restatement* § 172. Our Supreme Court, in a case involving mutual mistake, recognized this notion that failure to read a writing does not necessarily bar a contracting party from a remedy. *Ballard,* 117 N.M. at 3, 868 P.2d at 648 ("[A] mutual mistake . . . can be subject to reformation . . . despite the fact that each party to a contract has a duty to read and familiarize himself with the contents of the contract.").

"The *Restatement's* discussion of misrepresentation and fault contains an illustration closely tracking Plaintiff's allegations:

> A and B reach an understanding that they will execute a written contract containing terms on which they have agreed. A prepares a writing containing essential terms different from those agreed upon and induces B to sign it by telling him that it contains the agreed terms and that it is not necessary for him to read it. [B's] . . . reliance is justified since his fault does not amount to a failure to act in good faith . . . [or] fair dealing. The contract is voidable by B. In the alternative he may have the writing reformed.

"§ 172 cmt. a, illus. 1. The evaluation of fault and the recipient's failure to discover a mistake in the writing is fact-specific and includes consideration of the conduct of both parties. The inquiry includes a consideration of the recipient's "peculiar qualities and characteristics" and whether he knew the representation was false. *Id.* § 172 cmt. b.

"Thus, contrary to Citadel's argument, the existence of Plaintiff's duty to read the agreement before signing it does not end the inquiry. Plaintiff has produced evidence giving rise to factual inferences that could reasonably support the determination that his failure to read the agreement was justified by Citadel's conduct. It was improper for the district court to resolve these factual issues by entering summary judgment.

"3. Intentional Fraud

"Citadel argues that Plaintiff must prove that Citadel intentionally deceived Plaintiff to survive summary judgment. We are not persuaded. As we have already noted, Plaintiff does not appear to claim that Citadel's misrepresentations were fraudulent. In addition, our case law makes it clear that a misrepresentation can result in the voiding or rescission of a contract "irrespective of the good or bad faith of the party making the misrepresentation." *Robison,* 94 N.M. at 319, 610 P.2d at 206; *see also Maxey v. Quintana,* 84 N.M. 38, 41, 499 P.2d 356, 359 (Ct.App.1972) ("Rescission may be effected without regard to the good faith with which a misrepresentation is made."). The *Restatement* explains that the recipient of a misrepresentation may void the contract regardless of whether the misrepresentation was intentionally made to mislead. *See* § 164(1) (stating that a contract is voidable "[i]f a party's manifestation of assent is induced by *either a fraudulent or a material misrepresentation* by the other party upon which the recipient is justified in relying" (emphasis added)); § 162 cmt. a (explaining that a fraudulent misrepresentation "must not only be consciously false but must also be intended to mislead another"). However, if a misrepresentation is non-fraudulent, the recipient is entitled to void the contract only if the misrepresentation is material. *Id.* cmt. c. Thus, the question for the fact finder in the present case, assuming Citadel made a misrepresentation, is whether the misrepresentation was material, not whether it was intentional."

———

CHAPTER 13

THE INTERPRETATION OF WRITTEN CONTRACTS

■ ■ ■

SECTION 1. TEXTUALISM V. CONTEXTUALISM

INTRODUCTORY NOTE

The parol evidence rule does not preclude the use of extrinsic evidence (that is, evidence that is outside the four corners of a written agreement) for the purpose of *interpreting* a written agreement. However, classical contract law used another rule, the plain meaning (or four corners) rule to limit the use of extrinsic evidence in interpreting written agreements. Under this rule, extrinsic evidence cannot be introduced to help interpret a written contract unless the contract is ambiguous on its face. Some courts continue to adhere to the plain meaning rule. Other courts have abandoned the rule and adopted a rule that instructs a judge to consider all credible extrinsic evidence before determining whether a contract is susceptible to a non-literal interpretation.

There are substantive differences between the parol evidence rule and the plain meaning rule, because the two rules preclude the use of different types of evidence. The parol evidence rule precludes evidence of certain prior or contemporaneous separate agreements. The plain meaning rule precludes all extrinsic evidence when the writing is deemed unambiguous. This category is broader than prior or contemporaneous separate agreements. For example, evidence of the circumstances surrounding the making of a contract should not be precluded by the parol evidence rule but may be precluded by the plain meaning rule.

Holmes, The Theory of Legal Interpretation

12 Harv.L.Rev. 417 (1899)

"I do not suppose that you could prove, for purposes of construction as distinguished from avoidance, an oral declaration or even an agreement that words in a dispositive instrument making sense as they stand should have a different meaning from the common one; for instance, that the parties to a contract orally agreed that when they wrote five hundred feet it should mean one hundred inches, or that Bunker Hill Monument should signify Old South Church."

Williston on Contracts

3d ed., § 95

"It is even conceivable that a contract may be formed which is in accordance with the intention of neither party. If a written contract is entered into, the meaning and effect of the contract depends on the interpretation given the written language by the court. The court will give that language its natural and appropriate meaning; and, if the words are unambiguous, will not even admit evidence of what the parties may have thought the meaning to be."

Restatement, First, Contracts § 231

Illustration 2: "A and B are engaged in buying and selling shares of stock from one another and agree orally for the purpose of concealing the nature of their dealings that in transactions between them the word 'buy' shall be used to mean 'sell,' and that the word 'sell' shall be used to mean 'buy.' A sends a written offer to B to 'sell' certain shares of stock. B, having in mind the oral agreement, accepts the offer and tenders the shares to A. On A's refusal to accept the tender, B brings an action against him. B cannot recover, unless reformation is had of the writings. The private oral agreement cannot make 'buy' mean 'sell,' though a private agreement may give to a word which has no inconsistent meaning, a meaning in accordance with the agreement."

Corbin on Contracts

Supp. § 572b (1971)

"No contract should ever be interpreted and enforced with a meaning that neither party gave it."

Restatement, Second, Contracts § 212

Illustration 4: "A and B are engaged in buying and selling shares of stock from each other, and agree orally to conceal the nature of their dealings by using the word 'sell' to mean 'buy' and using the word 'buy' to mean 'sell.' A sends a written offer to B to 'sell' certain shares, and B accepts. The parties are bound in accordance with the oral agreement."

STEUART V. MCCHESNEY
Supreme Court of Pennsylvania, 1982.
498 Pa. 45, 444 A.2d 659.

Before O'BRIEN, C.J., and ROBERTS, NIX, LARSEN, FLAHERTY, MCDERMOTT and HUTCHINSON, JJ.

OPINION OF THE COURT

FLAHERTY, JUSTICE.

This is an appeal from an Order of the Superior Court which reversed a Decree of the Court of Common Pleas of the Thirty-Seventh Judicial District construing a Right of First Refusal affecting the sale of certain real property.

On June 8, 1968, the appellant, Lepha I. Steuart, and her husband, James A. Steuart (now deceased), executed an agreement granting to the appellees, William C. McChesney and Joyce C. McChesney, husband and wife, a Right of First Refusal on a parcel of improved farmland. The agreement provided:

(a) During the lifetime of said Steuarts, should said Steuarts obtain a Bona Fide Purchaser for Value, the said McChesneys may exercise their right to purchase said premises at a value equivalent to the market value of the premises according to the assessment rolls as maintained by the County of Warren and Commonwealth of Pennsylvania for the levying and assessing of real estate taxes; provided, however, that the date of valuation shall be that upon which the said Steuarts notify said McChesneys, in writing, of the existence of a Bona Fide Purchaser.

On July 6, 1977, the subject property was appraised by a real estate broker at a market value of $50,000. Subsequently, on October 10, 1977 and October 13, 1977 respectively, appellant received bona fide offers of $35,000 and $30,000 for the land. Upon receiving notice of these offers, the appellees sought to exercise their right to purchase the property by tendering $7,820. This amount was exactly twice the assessed value of the property as listed on the tax rolls maintained in Warren County, it being the practice in that County to value real estate for tax assessment purposes at 50% of market value. The tender was refused, however, by appellant, who then commenced an action in equity seeking to cancel the Right of First Refusal, or, in the alternative, to have the agreement construed as requiring that the exercise price be that of a bona fide third party offer or fair market value as determined independently of assessed value. Appellees, requesting a conveyance of the subject premises for $7,820, sought specific performance.

The primary issue on appeal concerns the price at which the Right of First Refusal may be exercised. The Court of Common Pleas, after hearing testimony, held that the formula of twice the assessed value was intended to serve as "a mutual protective minimum price for the premises rather than to be the controlling price without regard to a market third party offer." The agreement was, therefore, construed as granting appellees a preemptive right to purchase the land for $35,000, the amount of the first bona fide offer received. The Superior Court reversed, holding that the plain language of the agreement required that assessed market value, alone, determine the exercise price. We agree.

It is well established that the intent of the parties to a written contract is to be regarded as being embodied in the writing itself, and when the words are clear and unambiguous the intent is to be discovered only from the express language of the agreement. *Estate of Breyer,* 475 Pa. 108, 379 A.2d 1305 (1977); *Felte v. White,* 451 Pa. 137, 302 A.2d 347 (1973). . . . As this Court stated in *East Crossroads Center, Inc. v. Mellon-Stuart Co.,* 416 Pa. at 230–231, 205 A.2d at 866, "[w]hen a written contract is clear and unequivocal, its meaning must be determined by its contents alone. It speaks for itself and a meaning cannot be given to it other than that expressed. Where the intention of the parties is clear, there is no need to resort to extrinsic aids or evidence." Hence, where language is clear and unambiguous, the focus of interpretation is upon the terms of the agreement as *manifestly expressed,* rather than as, perhaps, silently intended.

Application of the plain meaning rule of interpretation has, however, been subjected to criticism as being unsound in theory. "The fallacy consists in assuming that there is or ever can be *some one real* or absolute meaning." 9 Wigmore, *Evidence* § 2462 (Chadbourn rev. 1981). "[S]ome of the surrounding circumstances always must be known before the meaning of the words can be plain and clear; and proof of the circumstances may make a meaning plain and clear when in the absence of such proof some other meaning may also have seemed plain and clear." 3 Corbin, *Contracts* § 542 (1960). "It is indeed desirable that it be made as difficult as is reasonably feasible for an unscrupulous person to establish a meaning that was foreign to what was in fact understood by the parties to the contract. However, this result can be achieved without the aid of an inflexible rule." Murray, *Contracts,* § 110 (1974).

While adhering to the plain meaning rule of construction, this Court, too, has cautioned:

> We are not unmindful of the dangers of focusing only upon the words of the writing in interpreting an agreement. A court must be careful not to "retire into that lawyer's Paradise where all words have a fixed, precisely ascertained meaning; where men

may express their purposes, not only with accuracy, but with fullness; and where, if the writer has been careful, a lawyer, having a document referred to him, may sit in his chair inspect the text, and answer all questions without raising his eyes." Thayer, Preliminary Treatise on Evidence 428, quoted in 3 Corbin on Contracts § 535 n. 16 (1960).

Estate of Breyer, 475 Pa. at 115, 379 A.2d at 1309 n. 5 (1977). Indeed, whether the language of an agreement is clear and unambiguous may not be apparent without cognizance of the context in which the agreement arose:

> The flexibility of or multiplicity in the meaning of words is the principal source of difficulty in the interpretation of language. Words are the conduits by which thoughts are communicated, yet scarcely any of them have such a fixed and single meaning that they are incapable of denoting more than one thought. In addition to the multiplicity in meaning of words set forth in the dictionaries there are the meanings imparted to them by trade customs, local uses, dialects, telegraphic codes, etc. One meaning crowds a word full of significance, while another almost empties the utterance of any import.

Hurst v. Lake & Co., Inc., 141 Or. 306, 310, 16 P.2d 627, 629 (1932), quoted in 4 Williston, *Contracts* § 609 (3d ed. 1961).

Nevertheless, the rationale for interpreting contractual terms in accord with the plain meaning of the language expressed is multifarious, resting in part upon what is viewed as the appropriate role of the courts in the interpretive process: "[T]his Court long ago emphasized that '[t]he parties [have] the right to make their own contract, and it is not the function of this Court to re-write it, or to give it a construction in conflict with . . . the accepted and plain meaning of the language used.' *Hagarty v. William Akers, Jr. Co.,* 342 Pa. 236, 20 A.2d 317 (1941)." *Felte v. White,* 451 Pa. at 144, 302 A.2d at 351. " 'It is not the province of the court to alter a contract by construction or to make a new contract for the parties; its duty is confined to the interpretation of the one which they have made for themselves, without regard to its wisdom or folly.' [13 C.J. § 485, p. 524]" *Moore v. Stevens Coal Co.,* 315 Pa. 564, 568, 173 A. 661, 662 (1934).

In addition to justifications focusing upon the appropriate role of the courts in the interpretive process, the plain meaning approach to construction has been supported as generally best serving the ascertainment of the contracting parties' mutual intent. "When the parties have reduced their agreement to writing, the writing is to be taken to be the final expression of their intention." 17A C.J.S. *Contracts* § 296(2). "Where the contract evidences care in its preparation, it will be presumed that its words were employed deliberately and with intention." 17A C.J.S.

Contracts § 296(2). "In determining what the parties intended by their contract, the law must look to what they clearly expressed. Courts in interpreting a contract do not assume that its language was chosen carelessly." *Moore v. Stevens Coal Co.,* 315 Pa. at 568, 173 A. at 662. Neither can it be assumed that the parties were ignorant of the meaning of the language employed. *See Fogel Refrigerator Co. v. Oteri,* 391 Pa. 188, 137 A.2d 225, 231 (1958).

Accordingly, the plain meaning approach enhances the extent to which contracts may be relied upon by contributing to the security of belief that the final expression of *consensus ad idem* will not later be construed to import a meaning other than that clearly expressed. *Cf.* McCormick, *The Parol Evidence Rule as a Procedural Device for Control of the Jury,* 41 Yale L.J. 365, 365–366 (1932). Likewise, resort to the plain meaning of language hinders parties dissatisfied with their agreement from creating a myth as to the true meaning of the agreement through subsequently exposed extrinsic evidence. Absent the plain meaning rule, nary an agreement could be conceived, which, in the event of a party's later disappointment with his stated bargain, would not be at risk to having its true meaning obfuscated under the guise of examining extrinsic evidence of intent. Even if the dissatisfied party in good faith believed that the agreement, as manifest, did not express the *consensus ad idem,* his post hoc judgment would be inclined to be colored by belief as to what should have been, rather than what strictly was, intended. Hence, the plain meaning approach to interpretation rests upon policies soundly based, and the judiciousness of that approach warrants reaffirmation.

In the instant case, the language of the Right of First Refusal, viewed in context, is express and clear and is, therefore, not in need of interpretation by reference to extrinsic evidence. The plain meaning of the agreement in question is that if, during the lifetime of the appellant, a bona fide purchaser for value should be obtained, the appellees may purchase the property "at a value equivalent to the market value of the premises according to the assessment rolls as maintained by the County of Warren and Commonwealth of Pennsylvania for the levying and assessing of real estate taxes." Indeed, a more clear and unambiguous expression of the Right of First Refusal's exercise price would be onerous to conceive. By conditioning exercise of the Right of First Refusal upon occurrence of the triggering event of there being obtained a bona fide offer, protection was afforded against a sham offer, made not in good faith, precipitating exercise of the preemptive right. The clear language of the agreement, however, in no manner links determination of the exercise price to the magnitude of the bona fide offer received through that triggering mechanism.

Were the present agreement to be regarded as ambiguous, so as to enable a court to consider extrinsic evidence of the meaning intended, as was done in the Court of Common Pleas, the policy of resorting to extrinsic evidence only when confronted with unclear or ambiguous language would be enervated. Certainly, the words of the Right of First Refusal are not indefinite, doubtful, or uncertain in their signification, so as to be regarded as unclear. Nor is the language reasonably or fairly susceptible to being understood in more than one sense so as to be regarded as ambiguous. "A patent ambiguity is that which appears on the face of the instrument, and arises from the defective, obscure, or insensible language used." *Black's Law Dictionary* 105 (rev. 4th ed. 1968). In contrast, a latent ambiguity arises from extraneous or collateral facts which make the meaning of a written agreement uncertain although the language thereof, on its face, appears clear and unambiguous. *Easton v. Washington County Insurance Co.,* 391 Pa. 28, 137 A.2d 332 (1957). "The usual instance of a latent ambiguity is one in which a writing refers to a particular person or thing and is thus apparently clear on its face, but upon application to external objects is found to fit two or more of them equally." *Id.* at 35, 137 A.2d at 336. In holding that an ambiguity is present in an agreement, a court must not rely upon a strained contrivancy to establish one; scarcely an agreement could be conceived that might not be unreasonably contrived into the appearance of ambiguity. Thus, the meaning of language cannot be distorted to establish the ambiguity. *Anstead v. Cook,* 291 Pa. 335, 337, 140 A. 139, 140 (1927). The instant agreement, not being reasonably susceptible to being understood in more than one sense, whether by patent or latent ambiguity, does not present language in need of extrinsic clarification.

By construing the clause in question to merely signify that the exercise price be, *in effect, "not less than"* the market value of the premises according to the assessment rolls, the Court of Common Pleas ignored the clearly expressed intent that the exercise price be "*equivalent* to the market value of the premises according to the assessment rolls." To no extent is the term "equivalent", meaning "equal",[3] interchangeable with "not less than", and, since the parties specified the former, they shall be deemed to have intended the same. Hence, any divergence between the exercise price and the bona fide offer cannot be eliminated by construction where no ambiguity exists. Nor is there freedom, under the guise of construction, to redraft the Right of First Refusal simply because of the realization, at the time when rights under the agreement are to be exercised, that the market price according to the assessment rolls falls substantially short of the bona fide offers received.

Appellant contends that, based upon equitable considerations, specific performance at the assessed market value of $7,820 should be denied; in

---

[3]   "Equivalent carries with it the idea of value in some way (Latin *aequus,* equal, plus *valere,* to be strong or valuable). When something adds up to something else in value or worth or significance or importance, the two are said to be equivalent the one to the other; when two or more things are exactly the same they are properly said to be equal. *Equal* is the simpler term, and applies to simpler considerations." J.B. Opdycke, *Mark My Words,* at 568–569 (1940).

particular, the divergence between assessed market value and the amount of the bona fide offers assertedly renders an award of specific performance inequitable. As this Court has established, however, " '[i]nadequacy of consideration is not ground for refusing to decree specific performance of a contract to convey real estate, unless there is evidence of fraud or unfairness in the transaction sufficient to make it inequitable to compel performance . . .' *Welsh v. Ford,* 282 Pa. 96, 99, 127 A. 431, 432 (1925). . . . "

. . . . Appellant alleges that an attorney employed solely by the appellees drafted the Right of First Refusal agreement, and that she was unfairly induced to enter the agreement without representation of her interests. This position ignores, however, an express finding of fact by the Court of Common Pleas, amply supported by testimony of record, that at the time of the preliminary negotiation and drafting of the agreement the parties were all represented by the same attorney. Hence, appellant's assertion is without merit.

Order affirmed.

ROBERTS, J., files a dissenting opinion in which LARSEN, J., joins.

ROBERTS, JUSTICE, dissenting.

I dissent. Although the contract at issue mandates that appellees may purchase appellant's property at "the market value of the premises according to the assessment rolls as maintained by the County of Warren . . .," it is by no means clear that $7,820 is the price which appellees should pay.

The omission from the contract of a specific future purchase price was intentional because, according to the draftsman, the parties "wanted to reflect either increase or decrease of the assessed value as of [the] time" of appellees' exercise of the option to buy. To assure the accuracy and currency of this "reflection" of the change in assessed value, the parties provided that "the date of valuation shall be that upon which the said Steuarts notify said McChesneys, in writing, of the existence of a Bona Fide purchaser."

Written notice of appellant's receipt of an offer for the property was delivered to appellees on or about October 25, 1977. At that time, the assessed value of the property, as recorded on the tax rolls of Warren County, was $3,910, or 50% of the "market value" of $7,820. However, from the testimony of the draftsman, it would appear that the property had not been reassessed since 1972, when the assessed value was increased by only $405.

Section 602 of the Fourth to Eighth Class County Assessment Law provides:

"It shall be the duty of the chief assessor to assess, rate and value all subjects and objects of local taxation . . . according to the actual value thereof. . . . [R]eal property shall be assessed at a value based upon an established predetermined ratio . . . not exceeding seventy-five per centum (75%) of its actual value or the price for which the same would separately bona fide sell. . . . "

72 P.S. § 5453.602(a) (1964). As this Court stated in *Brooks Building Tax Assessment Case,* 391 Pa. 94, 97, 137 A.2d 273, 274 (1958),

"[t]he term 'actual value' means 'market value' [citing cases]. And market value has been defined as the price which a purchaser, willing but not obliged to buy, would pay an owner, willing but not obliged to sell, taking into consideration all uses to which the property is adapted and might in reason be applied."

Accord, *Buhl Foundation v. Board of Property Assessment,* 407 Pa. 567, 570, 180 A.2d 900, 902 (1962).

Here, where appellant received bona fide offers of $30,000, $35,000, and $50,000 for her property, there can be no doubt that the actual value of appellant's property in 1977 was at least four times greater than the value according to the outdated assessment on the Warren County tax rolls. It is the height of unfairness to grant appellees' requested decree for specific performance at a price based on a valuation which took place in 1972. In effect, appellees are receiving a substantial windfall simply because Warren County has apparently failed to maintain accurate assessments "according to the actual value" of appellant's property, as required by law.

In these circumstances, I would remand this case to the Court of Common Pleas of Warren County for a determination of what the proper assessed value of appellant's property would have been on October 25, 1977, the "date of valuation," with directions to enter a decree of specific performance in favor of appellees at a "market value" based upon that determination.

LARSEN, J., joins in this dissenting opinion.

PACIFIC GAS & ELECTRIC CO. v. G.W. THOMAS DRAYAGE & RIGGING CO.
Supreme Court of California, 1968.
69 Cal.2d 33, 69 Cal.Rptr. 561, 442 P.2d 641.

TRAYNOR, CHIEF JUSTICE. Defendant appeals from a judgment for plaintiff in an action for damages for injury to property under an indemnity clause of a contract.

In 1960 defendant entered into a contract with plaintiff to furnish the labor and equipment necessary to remove and replace the upper metal cover of plaintiff's steam turbine. Defendant agreed to perform the work "at [its] own risk and expense" and to "indemnify" plaintiff "against all loss, damage, expense and liability resulting from . . . injury to property, arising out of or in any way connected with the performance of this contract." Defendant also agreed to procure not less than $50,000 insurance to cover liability for injury to property. Plaintiff was to be an additional named insured, but the policy was to contain a cross-liability clause extending the coverage to plaintiff's property.

During the work the cover fell and injured the exposed rotor of the turbine. Plaintiff brought this action to recover $25,144.51, the amount it subsequently spent on repairs. During the trial it dismissed a count based on negligence and thereafter secured judgment on the theory that the indemnity provision covered injury to all property regardless of ownership.

Defendant offered to prove by admissions of plaintiff's agents, by defendant's conduct under similar contracts entered into with plaintiff, and by other proof that in the indemnity clause the parties meant to cover injury to property of third parties only and not to plaintiff's property.[1] Although the trial court observed that the language used was "the classic language for a third party indemnity provision" and that "one could very easily conclude that . . . its whole intendment is to indemnify third parties," it nevertheless held that the "plain language" of the agreement also required defendant to indemnify plaintiff for injuries to plaintiff's property. Having determined that the contract had a plain meaning, the court refused to admit any extrinsic evidence that would contradict its interpretation.

When a court interprets a contract on this basis, it determines the meaning of the instrument in accordance with the " . . . extrinsic evidence of the judge's own linguistic education and experience." (3 Corbin on Contracts (1960 ed.) [1964 Supp. § 579, p. 225, fn. 56].) The exclusion of testimony that might contradict the linguistic background of the judge reflects a judicial belief in the possibility of perfect verbal expression. (9 Wigmore on Evidence (3d ed. 1940) § 2461, p. 187.) This belief is a remnant of a primitive faith in the inherent potency and inherent meaning of words.

The test of admissibility of extrinsic evidence to explain the meaning of a written instrument is not whether it appears to the court to be plain and unambiguous on its face, but whether the offered evidence is relevant to prove a meaning to which the language of the instrument is reasonably susceptible. . . .

---

[1] Although this offer of proof might ordinarily be regarded as too general to provide a ground for appeal . . . since the court repeatedly ruled that it would not admit extrinsic evidence to interpret the contract and sustained objections to all questions seeking to elicit such evidence, no formal offer of proof was required. . . .

A rule that would limit the determination of the meaning of a written instrument to its four-corners merely because it seems to the court to be clear and unambiguous, would either deny the relevance of the intention of the parties or presuppose a degree of verbal precision and stability our language has not attained.

Some courts have expressed the opinion that contractual obligations are created by the mere use of certain words, whether or not there was any intention to incur such obligations.[4] Under this view, contractual obligations flow, not from the intention of the parties but from the fact that they used certain magic words. Evidence of the parties' intention therefore becomes irrelevant.

In this state, however, the intention of the parties as expressed in the contract is the source of contractual rights and duties.[5] A court must ascertain and give effect to this intention by determining what the parties meant by the words they used. Accordingly, the exclusion of relevant, extrinsic evidence to explain the meaning of a written instrument could be justified only if it were feasible to determine the meaning the parties gave to the words from the instrument alone.

If words had absolute and constant referents, it might be possible to discover contractual intention in the words themselves and in the manner in which they were arranged. Words, however, do not have absolute and constant referents. "A word is a symbol of thought but has no arbitrary and fixed meaning like a symbol of algebra or chemistry,. . . ." (Pearson v. State Social Welfare Board (1960) 54 Cal.2d 184, 195, 5 Cal.Rptr. 553, 559, 353 P.2d 33, 39.) The meaning of particular words or groups of words varies with the " . . . verbal context and surrounding circumstances and purposes in view of the linguistic education and experience of their users and their hearers or readers (not excluding judges). . . . A word has no meaning apart from these factors; much less does it have an objective meaning, one true meaning." (Corbin, The Interpretation of Words and the Parol Evidence Rule (1965) 50 Cornell L.Q. 161, 187.) Accordingly, the meaning of a writing " . . . can only be found by interpretation in the light of all the circumstances that reveal the sense in which the writer used the words. The exclusion of parol evidence regarding such circumstances merely because the words do not appear ambiguous to the reader can easily lead to the attribution to a written instrument of a meaning that was never intended. [Citations omitted.]" (Universal Sales Corp. v. Cal. Press Mfg. Co., supra, 20 Cal.2d 751, 776, 128 P.2d 665, 679 (concurring opinion); see

---

[4] "A contract has, strictly speaking, nothing to do with the personal, or individual, intent of the parties. A contract is an obligation attached by the mere force of law to certain acts of the parties, usually words, which ordinarily accompany and represent a known intent." (Hotchkiss v. National City Bank of New York (S.D.N.Y.1911) 200 F. 287, 293. . . .)

[5] "A contract must be so interpreted as to give effect to the mutual intention of the parties as it existed at the time of contracting, so far as the same is ascertainable and lawful." (Civ.Code, § 1636 . . .)

also, e.g., Garden State Plaza Corp. v. S.S. Kresge Co. (1963) 78 N.J.Super. 485, 189 A.2d 448, 454. . . .

Although extrinsic evidence is not admissible to add to, detract from, or vary the terms of a written contract, these terms must first be determined before it can be decided whether or not extrinsic evidence is being offered for a prohibited purpose. The fact that the terms of an instrument appear clear to a judge does not preclude the possibility that the parties chose the language of the instrument to express different terms. That possibility is not limited to contracts whose terms have acquired a particular meaning by trade usage, but exists whenever the parties' understanding of the words used may have differed from the judge's understanding.

Accordingly, rational interpretation requires at least a preliminary consideration of all credible evidence offered to prove the intention of the parties.[7] (Civ.Code, § 1647; Code Civ.Proc. § 1860; see also 9 Wigmore on Evidence, op. cit. supra, § 2470, fn. 11, p. 227.) Such evidence includes testimony as to the "circumstances surrounding the making of the agreement . . . including the object, nature and subject matter of the writing . . ." so that the court can "place itself in the same situation in which the parties found themselves at the time of contracting." (Universal Sales Corp. v. Cal. Press Mfg. Co., supra, 20 Cal.2d 751, 761, 128 P.2d 665, 671; Lemm v. Stillwater Land & Cattle Co., supra, 217 Cal. 474, 480–481, 19 P.2d 785.) If the court decides, after considering this evidence, that the language of a contract, in the light of all the circumstances, is "fairly susceptible of either one of the two interpretations contended for. . . ." . . . extrinsic evidence relevant to prove either of such meanings is admissible.[8]

In the present case the court erroneously refused to consider extrinsic evidence offered to show that the indemnity clause in the contract was not intended to cover injuries to plaintiff's property. Although that evidence was not necessary to show that the indemnity clause was reasonably susceptible of the meaning contended for by defendant, it was nevertheless relevant and admissible on that issue. Moreover, since that clause was reasonably susceptible of that meaning, the offered evidence was also admissible to prove that the clause had that meaning and did not cover

---

[7] When objection is made to any particular item of evidence offered to prove the intention of the parties, the trial court may not yet be in a position to determine whether in the light of all of the offered evidence, the item objected to will turn out to be admissible as tending to prove a meaning of which the language of the instrument is reasonably susceptible or inadmissible as tending to prove a meaning of which the language is not reasonably susceptible. In such case the court may admit the evidence conditionally by either reserving its ruling on the objection or by admitting the evidence subject to a motion to strike. (See Evid.Code, § 403.)

[8] Extrinsic evidence has often been admitted in such cases on the stated ground that the contract was ambiguous (e.g., Universal Sales Corp. v. Cal. Press Mfg. Co., supra, 20 Cal.2d 751, 761, 128 P.2d 665). This statement of the rule is harmless if it is kept in mind that the ambiguity may be exposed by extrinsic evidence that reveals more than one possible meaning.

injuries to plaintiff's property. Accordingly, the judgment must be reversed. . . .

PETERS, MOSK, BURKE, SULLIVAN, and PEEK, JJ., concur.

MCCOMB, J., dissents.

———

NOTE ON THE NEW LITERALISM

The debate over the merits of the plain meaning rule continues. Judge Kozinksi defended the rule in Trident Center v. Connecticut General Life Ins. Co., 847 F.2d 564 (9th Cir.1988):

> Trident argues . . . that, even if the language of the contract appears to be unambiguous, the deal the parties actually struck is in fact quite different. . . Under traditional contract principles, extrinsic evidence is inadmissible to interpret, vary or add to the terms of an unambiguous integrated written instrument. See 4 S. Williston, supra p. 5, § 631, at 948–49; 2 B. Witkin, California Evidence § 981, at 926 (3d ed. 1986).

> Trident points out, however, that California does not follow the traditional rule. Two decades ago the California Supreme Court in Pacific Gas & Electric Co. v. G.W. Thomas Drayage & Rigging Co., 69 Cal.2d 33, 442 P.2d 641, 69 Cal.Rptr. 561 (1968), turned its back on the notion that a contract can ever have a plain meaning discernible by a court without resort to extrinsic evidence. . . .

> *Pacific Gas* casts a long shadow of uncertainty over all transactions negotiated and executed under the law of California. As this case illustrates, even when the transaction is very sizeable, even if it involves only sophisticated parties, even if it was negotiated with the aid of counsel, even if it results in contract language that is devoid of ambiguity, costly and protracted litigation cannot be avoided if one party has a strong enough motive for challenging the contract. While this rule creates much business for lawyers and an occasional windfall to some clients, it leads only to frustration and delay for most litigants and clogs already overburdened courts.

> It also chips away at the foundation of our legal system. By giving credence to the idea that words are inadequate to express concepts, Pacific Gas undermines the basic principle that language provides a meaningful constraint on public and private conduct. If we are unwilling to say that parties, dealing face to face, can come up with language that binds them, how can we send anyone to jail for violating statutes consisting of mere words lacking 'absolute and constant referents'? How can courts ever enforce decrees, not written in language understandable to all, but encoded in a dialect reflecting only the 'linguistic background of the judge'? Can lower courts ever

be faulted for failing to carry out the mandate of higher courts when 'perfect verbal expression' is impossible? Are all attempts to develop the law in a reasoned and principled fashion doomed to failure as 'remnant[s] of a primitive faith in the inherent potency and inherent meaning of words'? Be that as it may. While we have our doubts about the wisdom of *Pacific Gas*, we have no difficulty understanding its meaning, even without extrinsic evidence to guide us. As we read the rule in California, we must reverse and remand to the district court in order to give plaintiff an opportunity to present extrinsic evidence as to the intention of the parties in drafting the contract. It may not be a wise rule we are applying, but it is a rule that binds us.

A different panel of the United States Courts of Appeals for the Ninth Circuit described the impact of *Pacific Gas* in more modest terms in A. Kemp Fisheries, Inc. v. Castle & Cook, Inc., 852 F.2d 493, n. 2 (9th Cir. 1988):

> The broad language in *Trident* suggests that under California law courts must always admit extrinsic evidence to determine the meaning of disputed contract language. *Trident* held only that courts may not dismiss on the pleadings when one party claims that extrinsic evidence renders the contract ambiguous. The case must proceed beyond the pleadings so that the court may consider the evidence. If, after considering the evidence, the court determines that the contract is not reasonably susceptible to the interpretation advanced, the parol evidence rule operates to exclude the evidence. The court may then decide the case on a motion for summary judgment. *See Trident* at 570 n. 6. The court decided this case on a fully developed record.

————

NOTE—IS THE INTERPRETATION OF WRITTEN CONTRACTS A QUESTION FOR THE JUDGE OR FOR THE JURY?

It is commonly said that questions of fact are for the jury and questions of law are for the judge. A more realistic statement would be that questions that the legal system assigns to the jury are *called* questions of fact, and questions that the legal system assigns to the judge are *called* questions of law. Within this verbal framework, it has long been the general rule that the interpretation of written contracts is a question of law even though "in actuality [such interpretation involves] a factual, not a legal, decision. . . . This fact-finding function exercised by the court is denominated a 'question of law' . . . not because analytically it is a question of law but rather to indicate that it is the trial judge, not the jury, to whom the law assigns the responsibility for deciding the matter." Community College v. Community College, Society of the Faculty, 473 Pa. 576, 375 A.2d 1267 (1977).

Traditionally, there has been an exception to this general rule—that is, the interpretation of written contracts has been given to the trier of fact—

where the court deems the agreement ambiguous; the meaning of the agreement turns on evidence extrinsic to the agreement; and the credibility of that evidence is at issue. In Meyers v. Selznick Co., 373 F.2d 218 (2d Cir.1966), Judge Friendly forcefully supported a liberalization of this exception under which questions of interpretation are for the trier of fact *whenever* evidence extrinsic to the written instrument is relevant to its interpretation, even though there is no issue as to the credibility of the evidence, but merely as to its significance:

> Whether determination of meaning be regarded as a question of fact, a question of law, or just itself, reliance on the jury to resolve ambiguities in the light of extrinsic evidence seems quite as it should be, save where the form or subject-matter of a particular contract outruns a jury's competence. . . . Resolution of [issues involving the determination of meaning] may hinge in no small degree on notions of fairness—the very kind of decision laymen are ideally equipped to make.

This view is adopted in Restatement Second § 212(2), which provides that "A question of interpretation of an integrated agreement is to be determined by the trier of fact if it depends on the credibility of extrinsic evidence or on a choice among reasonable inferences to be drawn from extrinsic evidence. Otherwise a question of interpretation of an integrated agreement is to be determined as a question of law."

SECTION 2. THE ROLE OF USAGE, COURSE OF DEALING, AND COURSE OF PERFORMANCE IN INTERPRETATION

FOXCO INDUSTRIES, LTD. V. FABRIC WORLD, INC.

United States Court of Appeals, Fifth Circuit, 1979.
595 F.2d 976.

TJOFLAT, CIRCUIT JUDGE:

In this diversity action Foxco Industries, Ltd. (Foxco), a Delaware corporation, following a jury trial recovered a $26,000 judgment against Fabric World, Inc. (Fabric World), an Alabama corporation, for breaching a contract to purchase certain knitted fabric goods and refusing to pay for merchandise previously purchased. [On appeal, Fabric World argues that] the district court erred in admitting into evidence published standards of the Knitted Textile Association to establish the meaning of a disputed contract term. For the reasons set forth below, we reject the [argument] of Fabric World and affirm.

I

Foxco is in the business of manufacturing knitted fabrics for sale to retail fabric stores and the garment industry. Foxco's principal place of business is in New York City; it has never formally qualified to do business in Alabama. Fabric World is engaged in the retail fabric business and operates a chain of stores in a number of states; its headquarters is in Huntsville, Alabama.

There are two seasons in the fabric industry, a spring season and a fall season. Before the beginning of each season Foxco displays for customers samples of the line of fabrics it will manufacture that season. Customer orders are accepted only from the fabric shown on display. Foxco's manufacturing operation is limited to filling these orders; no fabrics are manufactured merely to be held as inventory. There was some conflict in the testimony as to whether fabric specially knit for one customer, such as Fabric World, could be resold to another customer.

Foxco sells some of its goods to retail fabric stores through manufacturers' representatives, operating on a commission basis, who sell the lines of numerous manufacturers. Foxco furnishes each representative with samples and a price list. Larger retail store customers, such as Fabric World, are handled personally by Foxco's sales manager, Allen Feller, a salaried employee, who supervises all retail fabric store sales. He has responsibility over the approximately twenty-six manufacturers' representatives carrying the Foxco line.

Foxco has never maintained an office in Alabama. At the time of the transactions giving rise to this action, its manufacturers' representative in Alabama was a resident of the state. Foxco's sales manager, Feller, made periodic trips to Alabama to meet with this representative and to obtain orders from Fabric World and Kennemer Company, another large fabric retailer. At the beginning of each season Feller would meet with the manufacturers' representative for two or three days so that the new line of fabrics could be previewed and discussed. In 1974, Foxco's gross sales approximated $14,000,000; Alabama accounted for in excess of $100,000 of that amount. A substantial portion of the Alabama business was with Fabric World, from which three separate orders were obtained.

On April 22, 1974, Feller traveled to Huntsville to show Fabric World the new fall line. His meeting with Glenn Jameson, Fabric World's president, culminated in a written order for "first quality" goods. A dispute subsequently arose regarding the quality of the goods sent to fill the order, and Fabric World refused to pay for the portion of the goods it considered defective.

On October 21, 1974, Feller returned to Huntsville to show Jameson the line for the following spring season. Jameson voiced no complaint about the quality of the goods received pursuant to the previous April 22 order.

In fact, he gave Feller a new order, in writing, for 12,000 yards of first quality fabric, at a price of $36,705, to be delivered by January 15, 1975.

A few weeks after the October 21 order was placed, the textile industry began to experience a precipitous decline in the price of yarn. Because of a drop in the price of finished goods, Fabric World wrote Foxco on November 15, 1974, and cancelled its October 21 order. Foxco immediately replied, stating that the manufacture of the order was substantially completed and that it could not accept the cancellation. On November 27, 1974, Foxco's attorney wrote Fabric World that if the goods were not accepted they would be finished and sold and Fabric World sued for the difference between the contract price and the sales price received by Foxco. On December 3, 1974, Fabric World agreed to accept the order, but threatened to return the entire shipment if it contained one flaw. Foxco, believing that it was impossible to produce an order of this magnitude without a single flaw, decided it would not ship the order (which was completed a short time later).

Fabric World established that in December 1974 the fair market value of the October order was approximately 20% less than the contract price. However, Foxco made no attempt to sell the goods from the time Fabric World cancelled the order until September 1975, when the goods had dropped 50% In value. In that month Foxco sold at a private sale without notice to Fabric World approximately 7,000 yards from the order for an average price of between $1.50 and $1.75 per yard, a total consideration of $10,119.50. By the time of trial in April 1976, Foxco had on hand about 5,000 yards of the order worth between $1.25 and $1 per yard, or about $6,250.

During the course of the trial there was much testimony regarding the meaning of the term first quality goods used in the contracts between Foxco and Fabric World. The testimony on behalf of Fabric World was that it meant fabric containing no flaws. Foxco introduced evidence, over the objection of Fabric World, in the form of an exhibit containing standards for finished knitted goods promulgated by the Knitted Textile Association, a large textile industry group to which Foxco belongs. These standards indicated that certain types and amounts of flaws were permissible in first quality fabric. Fabric World is not a member of that association and claimed it had no knowledge of the standards adopted by the association's members. One ground for Fabric World's present appeal is its contention that the standards of a trade association of which it had no knowledge are not admissible to show the meaning of the undefined and disputed contract term "first quality" goods. . . .

Fabric World's [claims] that the district court erred in admitting into evidence the definition of first quality goods contained in the Standards for Finished Knitted Fabrics of the Knitted Textile Association. It contends that it is not a member of the Knitted Textile Association, was unaware of its existence until the time of trial, and that that group's standards were inadmissible because they were a custom or usage of the trade of which Fabric World had no knowledge. We find no error in the trial court's ruling.

A major issue in this case is what was meant by the term "first quality." Under the traditional application of the parol evidence rule, Fabric World's contention may have merit: the private, subjective intent of one party to a contract may well be irrelevant in determining the meaning of a contract term unless it is shown that that intent was communicated to the other party. See Levie, Trade Usage and Custom under the Common Law and the Uniform Commercial Code, 40 N.Y.U.L.Rev. 1101 (1965). In this case there is no direct evidence, as Fabric World argues, that it was put on notice that usage and custom, as embodied in the industry standards, would be used to define the meaning of first quality. Under Alabama sales law, however, that Fabric World did not know of the industry's usage and custom or of the standards in question is of no moment; the parties to a contract such as the one in issue are presumed to have intended the incorporation of trade usage in striking their bargain. U.C.C. section 2–202, Ala.Code tit. 7, § 7–2–202 (1977), explicitly provides that trade usages may help explain or supplement contract terms.[8] As stated in the comment to that provision,

> [Section 2–202(a)] makes admissible evidence of course of dealing, usage of trade and course of performance to explain or supplement the terms of any writing stating the agreement of the parties in order that the true understanding of the parties as to the agreement may be reached. *Such writings are to be read on the assumption that* the course of prior dealings between the parties *and the usages of trade were taken for granted when the document was phrased. Unless carefully negated they have become an element of the meaning of the words used.*

Id., Official Comment (emphasis added). Section 1–205(2) . . . defines trade usages. It provides in part that

> A usage of trade is any practice or method of dealing having such regularity of observance in a place, vocation or trade as to

---

8   Section 2–202 states:

    Final written expression: Parol or extrinsic evidence.

    Terms with respect to which the confirmatory memoranda of the parties agree or which are otherwise set forth in a writing intended by the parties as a final expression of their agreement with respect to such terms as are included therein may not be contradicted by evidence of any prior agreement or of a contemporaneous oral agreement but may be explained or supplemented:

        (a) By course of dealing or usage of trade (section 7–1–205) or by course of performance (section 7–2–208); and

        (b) By evidence of consistent additional terms unless the court finds the writing to have been intended also as a complete and exclusive statement of the terms of the agreement.

justify an expectation that it will be observed with respect to the transaction in question. The existence and scope of such a usage are to be proved as facts.

It further states: "A course of dealing between parties and any usage of trade in the vocation or trade in which they are engaged or of which they are or should be aware give particular meaning to and supplement or qualify terms of an agreement." . . . There was uncontroverted testimony that the Knitted Textile Association is an industry group with over 1500 members. Its standards could certainly qualify as trade usages, and thus were admissible notwithstanding Fabric World's unawareness of them. Loeb & Co. v. Martin, 295 Ala. 262, 327 So.2d 711, 715 (1976). See Columbia Nitrogen Corp. v. Royster Co., 451 F.2d 3 (4th Cir. 1971); Chase Manhattan Bank v. First Marion Bank, 437 F.2d 1040 (5th Cir. 1971); Southern Concrete Services, Inc. v. Mableton Contractors, Inc., 407 F.Supp. 581 (N.D.Ga.1975), aff'd 569 F.2d 1154 (5th Cir. 1978).

. . . Accordingly, the judgment of the district court is AFFIRMED.

RESTATEMENT, SECOND, CONTRACTS § 221, ILLUSTRATION 2

2.   A, an ordained rabbi, is employed by B, an orthodox Jewish congregation, to officiate as cantor at specified religious services. At the time the contract is made, it is the practice of such congregations to seat men and women separately at services, and a contrary practice would violate A's religious beliefs. At a time when it is too late for A to obtain substitute employment, B adopts a contrary practice. A refuses to officiate. The practice is part of the contract, and A is entitled to the agreed compensation.

RESTATEMENT, SECOND, CONTRACTS § 222

[See Selected Source Materials Supplement]

RESTATEMENT, SECOND, CONTRACTS § 222, ILLUSTRATIONS 1–3

1.   A contracts to sell B 10,000 shingles. By usage of the lumber trade, in which both are engaged, two packs of a certain size constitute 1,000, though not containing that exact number. Unless otherwise agreed, 1,000 in the contract means two packs.

2.   A contracts to sell B 1,000 feet of San Domingo mahogany. By usage of dealers in mahogany, known to A and B, good figured mahogany of a certain density is known as San Domingo mahogany, though it does not come from San Domingo. Unless otherwise agreed, the usage is part of the contract. . . .

3.   A and B enter into a contract for the purchase and sale of "No. 1 heavy book paper guaranteed free from ground wood." Usage in the paper trade may show that this means paper not containing over 3% ground wood.

————

Hurst v. W.J. Lake & Co.

141 Or. 306, 16 P.2d 627 (1932)

Buyer and Seller made a contract for the sale of 350 tons of horse meat scraps, "minimum 50% protein," for $50 per ton. Under the contract, if any of the scraps tested at "less than 50% of protein" Buyer was to receive a discount of $5.00 per ton. About 170 tons contained less than 50% protein; of these, 140 tons contained 49.53 to 49.96% protein. Buyer took a $5.00 discount on the entire 170 tons. Seller claimed that Buyer was entitled to a discount on only 30 tons, because under a usage of trade the terms "minimum 50% protein" and "less than 50% protein," when used in a contract for the sale of horse meat scraps, meant that a protein content of not less than 49.5% was equal to a content of 50% protein. The trial court granted Buyer's motion for judgment on the pleadings. Reversed.

(Bean, C.J.) "The flexibility of or multiplicity in the meaning of words is the principal source of difficulty in the interpretation of language. Words are the conduits by which thoughts are communicated, yet scarcely any of them have such a fixed and single meaning that they are incapable of denoting more than one thought. In addition to the multiplicity in meaning of words set forth in the dictionaries there are the meanings imparted to them by trade customs, local uses, dialects, telegraphic codes, etc. One meaning crowds a word full of significance, while another almost empties the utterance of any import. The various groups above indicated are constantly amplifying our language; in fact, they are developing what may be called languages of their own. Thus one is justified in saying that the language of the dictionaries is not the only language spoken in America. For instance, the word, 'thousand' as commonly used has a very specific meaning; it denotes ten hundreds or fifty scores, but the language of the various trades and localities has assigned to it meanings quite different from that just mentioned. Thus in the bricklaying trade a contract which fixes the bricklayer's compensation at "$5.25 a thousand" does not contemplate that he need lay actually one thousand bricks in order to earn $5.25 but that he should build a wall of a certain size: Brunold v. Glasser, 25 Misc. 285 (53 N.Y.S. 1021); Walker v. Syms, 118 Mich. 183 (76 N.W. 320). In the lumber industry a contract requiring the delivery of 4,000 shingles will be fulfilled by the delivery of only 2,500 when it appears that by trade custom two packs of a certain size are regarded as 1,000 shingles and that, hence, the delivery of eight packs fulfills the contract, even though they contain only 2,500 shingles by actual count: Soutier v. Kellerman, 18 Mo. 509. And where the custom of locality considers 100 dozen as constituting a thousand, one who has 19,200 rabbits upon a warren under an agreement for their sale at the price of 60 pounds for each thousand rabbits will be paid for only 16,000 rabbits: Smith v. Wilson, 3 Barn. & Adol. 728. . . .

". . . We believe that it is safe to assume, in the absence of evidence to the contrary, that when tradesmen employ trade terms they attach to them their trade significance. If, when they write their trade terms into their contracts, they mean to strip the terms of their special significance and demote them to their common import, it would seem reasonable to believe that they would so state in their agreement. Otherwise, they would refrain from using the trade term and express themselves in other language."

––––––

Restatement, Second, Contracts § 220

Illustration 9: ". . . A promises to sell and B to buy a certain quantity of 'white arsenic' for a stated price. The parties contract with reference to a usage of trade that 'white arsenic' includes arsenic colored with lamp black. The usage is part of the contract."

––––––

UCC §§ 1–201(3), (12), 1–303, 2–208

[See Selected Source Materials Supplement]

––––––

RESTATEMENT, SECOND, CONTRACTS §§ 219–223

[See Selected Source Materials Supplement]

––––––

CISG ART. 9

[See Selected Source Materials Supplement]

––––––

UNIDROIT PRINCIPLES OF INTERNATIONAL COMMERCIAL CONTRACTS ART. 1.9

[See Selected Source Materials Supplement]

PRINCIPLES OF EUROPEAN
CONTRACT LAW ART. 1.105

[See Selected Source Materials Supplement]

Dennis Patterson, Good Faith, Lender Liability, and Discretionary
    Acceleration: Of Llewellyn, Wittgenstein, and the Uniform Commercial
    Code

68 Tex. L. Rev. 169, 187–192 (1989)

" . . .Williston and Llewellyn differed fundamentally on the proper role
and function of law in regulating commerce. For Williston, contract was the
apotheosis of theory, a pure conceptual edifice. By the 1930s, the Uniform Sales
Act (Williston's statute) was to Llewellyn's mind hopelessly antiquated both in
form and substance. Llewellyn's goal, first manifested in three successive
drafts of a revised Uniform Sales Act and ultimately realized (with some
compromises) in the Code, was to replace the offer- acceptance-consideration
model of contract with one more in keeping with the realities of commercial
practice. The cornerstone of the new conceptualism of the Code was the concept
of agreement. . .

"In the Code concept of agreement, Llewellyn reacted against two salient
aspects of Willistonian formalism: (1) that contract terms might have a plain
meaning, and (2) that written contract terms have priority over all unwritten
expressions of agreement. . . In Llewellyn's view . . . the meaning of the
agreement did not depend, in the first instance, on the existence or content of
a writing. Instead, meaning derived from an interpretation of 'language and by
implication from other circumstances, including course of dealing or usage of
trade or course of performance,' considered together, each an aspect of the total
context. The context, and not an a priori rule, determined the weight accorded
any one aspect.

"Llewellyn's embrace of the commercial context challenged . . .
common-law sales doctrine. Under the common law, neither custom nor trade
usage could be introduced as evidence to contradict the written terms of an
agreement. The Uniform Sales Act afforded little relief from this orthodoxy,
providing merely that trade usage could displace express terms only if the
parties intended it to. The argument is viciously circular. Resort to terms or
sources of meaning outside the express terms of the contract was allowable
only if the parties intended such reference. The language of the agreement,
however, was the sole expression of the parties' intent.

"In the 1941 draft of the Revised Uniform Sales Act, Llewellyn sought to
put the confusion to rest. The 1941 Act provided that trade usage and course

of dealing were no longer the stepchildren of the writing: their significance for the question of contract interpretation was now guaranteed.

> 'Between merchants, the usage of trade, or of a particular trade, and any course of dealing between the parties, are presumed to be the background which the parties have presupposed in their bargaining and have intended to read into the particular contract; and express words are to be construed, where that is reasonable, as consistent with, rather than as a displacement of, such usage and course of dealing.'

"Llewellyn's concept of agreement thus integrated trade usage and course of dealing with the written terms of the parties. Now, a court could not answer the question of what the parties meant by their agreement without first understanding the meaning of the commercial practice from which their agreement arose.

"Llewellyn's conceptual revolution was not universally embraced. After the completion of the New York Law Revision Commission hearings, Professor Edwin Patterson of the Columbia University Law School prepared a report recommending 'amendment of section 1–205(4) to insure that express terms would always dominate usage of trade and course of dealing.' . . .

"Professor Patterson never gave up in his attempt to reorient judicial thinking to the classical model. In 1964, fully eight years after having his perspective rejected by the New York Law Revision Commission, Patterson wrote the following:

> 'The Commercial Code seeks to express the requirement of reasonableness along with a statement as to which source of interpretation prevails when they are in conflict with each other: [text of section 1–205(4)]. An alleged usage which contradicts express terms of the contract is to be rejected. A course of dealing between these parties is more likely to express their expectations than a conflicting usage that may be the practice of other persons.' "

Nanakuli Paving and Rock Co. v. Shell Oil Co.

664 F.2d 772 (9th Cir. 1981)

Prior to 1963, there were two major paving contractors on Oahu: Nanakuli and Hawaiian Bitumals ("H.B."). Of these, H.B. was by far the largest, in part because it had a special relationship with Chevron, which supplied asphalt, a major element in paving construction. Shell Oil, like Chevron, was a major worldwide oil company, but partly because of the relationship between H.B. and Chevron, Shell had only a small percentage of the asphalt market in Hawaii and had no asphalt terminals in Hawaii.

In 1963, Nanakuli and Shell entered into a five-year contract under which Nanakuli agreed to buy its asphalt requirements from Shell, and Shell agreed to supply these requirements. The contract gave Nanakuli an assured source of supply, so that it could compete on equal terms with H.B., and gave Shell the potential for drastically expanding its asphalt sales in Hawaii. In 1969, a new contract was executed. The term of this contract was until December 31, 1975, at which point each party had an option to cancel on 6 months' notice.

In February 1976, Nanakuli sued Shell for breach of the 1969 contract. That contract provided that the price of asphalt to Nanakuli would be "Shell's posted price at the time of delivery"—that is, the price Shell posted, at the time of delivery, for sale to all buyers. Nanakuli argued that notwithstanding this price term, Nanakuli was entitled to "price protection" under both trade usage and course of performance, and that Shell had breached the contract by refusing to give such protection. "Price protection" means that a supplier will not increase the price charged to a contractor, despite an increase in the supplier's posted price, without advance notice, and instead will apply the posted price that is in place at the time the contractor made a bid, and that is incorporated by the contractor into its bid, long enough to allow the contractor to order the asphalt needed on the job. Nanakuli claimed that Shell breached the 1969 contract in January 1974 by failing to price protect Nanakuli on 7,200 tons of asphalt when Shell raised the price for asphalt from $44 to $76.

At trial, Nanakuli presented "extensive evidence" of a trade practice of price protection that was not contradicted by Shell. This included evidence aggregate suppliers routinely price protected Nanakuli and H.B.; Chevron routinely price protected H.B.; and Chevron "price protected Nanakuli on the island of Molokai, where Nanakuli purchased its asphalt from Chevron." The evidence covered periods both prior and subsequent to the 1969 contract. "None of the aggregate companies had a contract with Nanakuli expressly stating price protection would be given. . ." Chevron's contract with H.B. "provided that the price to H.B. would be a given percentage of the price Chevron set for a specified crude oil in California. No mention was made of price protection in the written contract between H.B. and Chevron." Nanakuli presented course of performance evidence that Shell price protected it in Oahu twice under the 1969 contract, in 1970 and 1971. Nanakuli also presented evidence Shell price protected it in Oahu subsequent to the dispute in 1977 and 1978.

The district court admitted all of this evidence, much of it over objection by Shell. The district court excluded some evidence Nanakuli sought to present, including evidence Shell price protected Nanakuli prior to the 1969 contract, and testimony by Nanakuli managers of their understanding. "The principal reason the judge initially refused to allow any such testimony . . . was his belief that there was no ambiguity in the express price term of 'posted price at time of delivery.'" Notwithstanding these qualms, the district court submitted the case to the jury, which returned a verdict of $220,880 for Nanakuli. The district court set aside the verdict, and granted Shell's motion for judgment n.o.v. Nanakuli appealed. Held, judgment vacated and jury verdict reinstated:

"... Shell protested that the jury could not have found that those two instances of price protection [in 1970 and 1971] amounted to a course of performance of its 1969 contract, relying on two Code comments. First, one instance does not constitute a course of performance. 'A single occasion of conduct does not fall within the language of this section. . . .' Haw.Rev.Stat. § 490:2–208, Comment 4. Although the Comment rules out one instance, it does not further delineate how many acts are needed to form a course of performance. The prior occasions here were only two, but they constituted the only occasions before 1974 that would call for such conduct. In addition, the language used by a top asphalt official of Shell in connection with the first price protection of Nanakuli indicated that Shell felt that Nanakuli was entitled to some form of price protection. On that occasion in 1970 Blee, who had negotiated the contract with Nanakuli and was familiar with exactly what terms Shell was bound to by that agreement, wrote of the need to 'bargain' with Nanakuli over the extent of price protection to be given, indicating that some price protection was a legal right of Nanakuli's under the 1969 agreement.

"Shell's second defense is that the Comment expresses a preference for an interpretation of waiver.

> 3.   Where it is difficult to determine whether a particular act merely sheds light on the meaning of the agreement or represents a waiver of a term of the agreement, the preference is in favor of "waiver" whenever such construction, plus the application of the provisions on the reinstatement of rights waived . . . , is needed to preserve the flexible character of commercial contracts and to prevent surprise or other hardship.

Id., Comment 3. The preference for waiver only applies, however, where acts are ambiguous. It was within the province of the jury to determine whether those acts were ambiguous, and if not, whether they constituted waivers or a course of performance of the contract. . . .

"Perhaps one of the most fundamental departures of the Code from prior contract law is found in the parol evidence rule and the definition of an agreement between two parties. Under the U.C.C., an agreement goes beyond the written words on a piece of paper. ' 'Agreement' means the bargain of the parties in fact as found in their language or by implication from other circumstances including course of dealing or usage of trade or course of performance as provided in this chapter (sections 490:1–205 and 490:2–208).' *Id.* § 490:1–201 (3). Express terms, then, do not constitute the entire agreement, which must be sought also in evidence of usages, dealings, and performance of the contract itself. . . .

"... Since the agreement of the parties is broader than the express terms and includes usages, which may even add terms to the agreement, and since the commercial background provided by those usages is vital to an understanding of the agreement, we follow the Code's mandate to proceed on the assumption that the parties have included those usages unless they cannot reasonably be construed as consistent with the express terms.

"... Here the evidence was overwhelming that all suppliers to the asphaltic paving trade price protected customers under the same types of circumstances. Chevron's contract with H.B. was a similar long-term supply contract between a buyer and seller with very close relations, on a form supplied by the seller, covering sales of asphalt, and setting the price at seller's posted price, with no mention of price protection. . . .

"Because the stock printed forms cannot always reflect the changing methods of business, members of the trade may do business with a standard clause in the forms that they ignore in practice. If the trade consistently ignores obsolete clauses at variance with actual trade practices, a litigant can maintain that it is reasonable that the courts also ignore the clauses. . . .

"*Kirst,* [Usage of Trade and Course of Dealing: Subversion of the UCC Theory, [1977] U.Ill.L. Forum 811] at 824. *Levie,* [Trade Usage and Custom . . . , 40 N.Y.U.L.Rev. 1101 (1965)], at 1112, writes, 'Astonishing as it will seem to most practicing attorneys, under the Code it will be possible in some cases to use custom to contradict the written agreement.' . . ."

The court also held that in light of the universal practice in the asphaltic paving trade of giving advance notice of a price increase, Shell could not have exercised good faith in raising its price by $32, effective January 1, in a letter written on December 31 and only received on January 4.

———

C-Thru Container Corp. v. Midland Mfg. Co.

533 N.W.2d 542 (Iowa 1995)

C-Thru and Midland entered into a contract under which Midland purchased bottle-making equipment from C-Thru. Under the contract, Midland could pay for the equipment by supplying commercially acceptable bottles to C-Thru. If Midland failed to supply the bottles, C-Thru could demand the purchase price of the equipment in cash. C-Thru claimed that Midland had breached the contract by being incapable of producing commercially acceptable bottles, and demanded that Midland pay the purchase price of the equipment. Midland contended that it had not breached the contract because C-Thru had not ordered any bottles. C-Thru responded that the practice in the bottling industry was that before the purchaser places an order, the bottle manufacturer provides sample bottles to verify that it is capable of producing commercially acceptable bottles, and that C-Thru had not provided such samples. C-Thru argued that evidence of this practice was inadmissible under the parol evidence rule, because the contract was complete and unambiguous. Held, evidence that there was such a practice was admissible.

We first reject Midland's argument that evidence of trade usage is admissible only when the contract is ambiguous. There is no such requirement in [UCC § 2–202]. Moreover, the official comment to [§ 2–202] . . . states that this section "definitely rejects" a requirement that the language of the contract be ambiguous as a condition precedent to the admission of trade-usage evidence. . . .

We also hold that even a "complete" contract may be explained or supplemented by parol evidence of trade usages.[1] . . . As the official comment to section 2–202 states, commercial sales contracts "are to be read on the assumption that the course of prior dealings between the parties and the usages of trade were taken for granted when the document was phrased." U.C.C. § 2–202 cmt. 2 (1977). Therefore, even a completely integrated contract may be supplemented by practices in the industry that do not contradict express terms of the contract.

That brings us to the remaining argument made by Midland— that C-Thru may not use parol evidence to add a new term to the agreement. Section [2–202] says that when parol evidence shows a usage of trade that does not contradict a contract term, the evidence is admissible to "supplement" the contract. We look to the common meaning of the word "supplement." . . . "Supplement" means "to add . . . to." Webster's Third New Int'l Dictionary 2297 (1993). Consequently, the trade-usage evidence upon which C-Thru relies is admissible even though it adds a new term to the contract. White & Summers, § 3–3 (usage of trade may itself constitute a contract term).

———

SECTION 3. THE DUTY OF GOOD FAITH

MARKET STREET ASSOCIATES V. FREY
United States Court of Appeals, Seventh Circuit, 1991.
941 F.2d 588.

[Market Street Associates acquired the leasehold interest in a shopping center owned by General Electric Pension Trust under a 25-year sale leaseback agreement. Market Street Associates acquired the property in 1987 when there were six years left to run on the lease. Under the sale leaseback agreement, the lessee could request the lessor (the pension trust) finance improvements costing at least $250,000. If such a request was made, then the pension trust agreed to negotiate in good faith to provide financing, and, if negotiations failed, then after 60 days, the lessee had an option to purchase the property for the original price increased 6% per annum. In 1988 Market Street Associates sought to buy the property from the pension trust, acting through its General Partner, Orenstein. David Erb, the responsible official at the pension trust, failed to return Orenstein's calls, and eventually quoted a price ($3 million) that Orenstein

---

[1]   The contract here stated that "[t]his agreement constitutes the entire agreement between C-Thru and Midland and supersedes any and all prior agreements between them."

thought was much too high. At this point Orenstein made a formal request for $2 million financing, but never mentioning the lease nor the relevant provision of the lease providing the contingent buy-out option. Erb peremptorily rejected this request, explaining that the pension trust was not interested in financing projects of less than $7 million. Orenstein replied that he would look elsewhere for financing. The next communication from Orenstein to Erb was sent immediately after the 60 day period ended. It was a notice that Market Street Associates was exercising the buy-out option at a price of $1 million.]

POSNER, CIRCUIT JUDGE . . . .

The pension trust refused to sell, and this suit to compel specific performance followed. Apparently the price computed by the formula in paragraph 34 is only $1 million. The market value must be higher, or Market Street Associates wouldn't be trying to coerce conveyance at the paragraph 34 price; whether it is as high as $3 million, however, the record does not reveal.

The district judge granted summary judgment for the pension trust on two grounds that he believed to be separate although closely related. The first was that, by failing in its correspondence with the pension trust to mention paragraph 34 of the lease, Market Street Associates had prevented the negotiations over financing that are a condition precedent to the lessee's exercise of the purchase option from taking place. Second, this same failure violated the duty of good faith . . . . In support of both grounds the judge emphasized a statement by Orenstein in his deposition that it had occurred to him that Erb mightn't know about paragraph 34, though this was unlikely (Orenstein testified) because Erb or someone else at the pension trust would probably check the file and discover the paragraph and realize that if the trust refused to negotiate over the request for financing, Market Street Associates, as Penney's assignee, would be entitled to walk off with the property for (perhaps) a song. The judge inferred that Market Street Associates didn't want financing from the pension trust—that it just wanted an opportunity to buy the property at a bargain price and hoped that the pension trust wouldn't realize the implications of turning down the request for financing. Market Street Associates should, the judge opined, have advised the pension trust that it was requesting financing pursuant to paragraph 34, so that the trust would understand the penalty for refusing to negotiate. . . .

So we must consider the meaning of the contract duty of "good faith." The Wisconsin cases are cryptic as to its meaning though emphatic about its existence, so we must cast our net wider. We do so mindful of Learned Hand's warning, that "such words as 'fraud,' 'good faith,' 'whim,' 'caprice,' 'arbitrary action,' and 'legal fraud' . . . obscure the issue." Thompson-Starrett Co. v. La Belle Iron Works, 17 F.2d 536, 541 (2d Cir.1927). Indeed they do. . . . The particular confusion to which the vaguely moralistic overtones of "good faith" give rise is the belief that every contract establishes a fiduciary relationship. A fiduciary is required to treat his principal as if the principal were he, and therefore he may not take advantage of the principal's incapacity, ignorance, inexperience, or even naivete. . . . Meinhard v. Salmon, 249 N.Y. 458, 463–64, 164 N.E. 545, 546 (1928) (Cardozo, C.J.). If Market Street Associates were the fiduciary of General Electric Pension Trust, then (we may assume) it could not take advantage of Mr. Erb's apparent ignorance of paragraph 34, however exasperating Erb's failure to return Orenstein's phone calls was and however negligent Erb or his associates were in failing to read the lease before turning down Orenstein's request for financing.

But it is unlikely that Wisconsin wishes, in the name of good faith, to make every contract signatory his brother's keeper, especially when the brother is the immense and sophisticated General Electric Pension Trust, whose lofty indifference to small (= < $7 million) transactions is the signifier of its grandeur. In fact the law contemplates that people frequently will take advantage of the ignorance of those with whom they contract, without thereby incurring liability. Restatement, supra, § 161, comment d. The duty of honesty, of good faith even expansively conceived, is not a duty of candor. You can make a binding contract to purchase something you know your seller undervalues. Laidlaw v. Organ, 15 U.S. (2 Wheat.) 178, 181 n. 2, 4 L.Ed. 214 (1817); . . . Anthony T. Kronman, "Mistake, Disclosure, Information, and the Law of Contracts," 7 J. Legal Stud. 1 (1978).

That of course is a question about formation, not performance, and the particular duty of good faith under examination here relates to the latter rather than to the former. But even after you have signed a contract, you are not obliged to become an altruist toward the other party and relax the terms if he gets into trouble in performing his side of the bargain. Kham & Nate's Shoes No. 2, Inc. v. First Bank, 908 F.2d 1351, 1357 (7th Cir.1990). Otherwise mere difficulty of performance would excuse a contracting party—which it does not. Northern Indiana Public Service Co. v. Carbon County Coal Co., 799 F.2d 265, 276–78 (7th Cir.1986). . . .

But it is one thing to say that you can exploit your superior knowledge of the market—for if you cannot, you will not be able to recoup the investment you made in obtaining that knowledge—or that you are not required to spend money bailing out a contract partner who has gotten into trouble. It is another thing to say that you can take deliberate advantage of an oversight by your contract partner concerning his rights under the contract. Such taking advantage is not the exploitation of superior knowledge or the avoidance of unbargained-for expense; it is sharp dealing. Like theft, it has no social product, and also like theft it induces costly defensive expenditures, in the form of overelaborate disclaimers or investigations into the trustworthiness of a prospective contract partner, just as the prospect of theft induces expenditures on locks. See generally Steven J. Burton, "Breach of Contract and the Common Law Duty to Perform in Good Faith," 94 Harv.L.Rev. 369, 393 (1980).

The form of sharp dealing that we are discussing might or might not be actionable as fraud or deceit. That is a question of tort law and there the rule is that if the information is readily available to both parties the failure of one to disclose it to the other, even if done in the knowledge that the other party is acting on mistaken premises, is not actionable. . . Before the contract is signed, the parties confront each other with a natural wariness. Neither expects the other to be particularly forthcoming, and therefore there is no deception when one is not. Afterwards the situation is different. The parties are now in a cooperative relationship the costs of which will be considerably reduced by a measure of trust. So each lowers his guard a bit, and now silence is more apt to be deceptive. Cf. AMPAT/Midwest, Inc. v. Illinois Tool Works Inc., 896 F.2d 1035, 1040–41 (7th Cir.1990).

Moreover, this is a contract case rather than a tort case, and conduct that might not rise to the level of fraud may nonetheless violate the duty of good faith in dealing with one's contractual partners and thereby give rise to a remedy under contract law. Burton, supra, at 372 n. 17. This duty is, as it were, halfway between a fiduciary duty (the duty of *utmost* good faith) and the duty merely to refrain from active fraud. Despite its moralistic overtones it is no more the injection of moral principles into contract law than the fiduciary concept itself is. Tymshare, Inc. v. Covell, 727 F.2d 1145, 1152 (D.C.Cir.1984). . . It would be quixotic as well as presumptuous for judges to undertake through contract law to raise the ethical standards of the nation's business people. The concept of the duty of good faith like the concept of fiduciary duty is a stab at approximating the terms the parties would have negotiated had they foreseen the circumstances that have given rise to their dispute. The parties want to minimize the costs of performance. To the extent that a doctrine of good faith designed to do this by reducing defensive expenditures is a reasonable measure to this end, interpolating it into the contract advances the parties' joint goal.

It is true that an essential function of contracts is to allocate risk, and would be defeated if courts treated the materializing of a bargained-over, allocated risk as a misfortune the burden of which is required to be shared between the parties (as it might be within a family, for example) rather than borne entirely by the party to whom the risk had been allocated by mutual agreement. But contracts do not just allocate risk. They also (or some of them) set in motion a cooperative enterprise, which may to some extent place one party at the other's mercy. "The parties to a contract are embarked on a cooperative venture, and a minimum of cooperativeness in the event unforeseen problems arise at the performance stage is required even if not an explicit duty of the contract." AMPAT/Midwest, Inc. v. Illinois Tool Works, Inc., supra, 896 F.2d at 1041. The office of the doctrine of good faith is to forbid the kinds of opportunistic behavior that a mutually dependent, cooperative relationship might enable in the absence of rule. " 'Good faith' is a compact reference to an implied undertaking not to take opportunistic advantage in a way that could not have been contemplated at the time of drafting, and which therefore was not resolved explicitly by the parties." Kham & Nate's Shoes No. 2, Inc. v. First Bank, supra, 908 F.2d at 1357. The contractual duty of good faith is thus not some newfangled bit of welfare-state paternalism or (pace Duncan Kennedy, "Form and Substance in Private Law Adjudication," 89 Harv.L.Rev. 1685, 1721 (1976)) the sediment of an altruistic strain in contract law, and we are therefore not surprised to find the essentials of the modern doctrine well established in nineteenth-century cases . . .

The emphasis we are placing on postcontractual versus precontractual conduct helps explain the pattern that is observed when the duty of contractual good faith is considered in all its variety, encompassing not only good faith in the *performance* of a contract but also good faith in its *formation*, Summers, supra, at 220–32, and in its enforcement. Harbor Ins. Co. v. Continental Bank Corp., 922 F.2d 357, 363 (7th Cir.1990). The formation or negotiation stage is precontractual, and here the duty is minimized. It is greater not only at the performance but also at the enforcement stage, which is also postcontractual. "A party who hokes up a phony defense to the performance of his contractual duties and then when that defense fails (at some expense to the other party) tries on another defense for size can properly be said to be acting in bad faith." Id.; see also Larson v. Johnson, 1 Ill.App.2d 36, 46, 116 N.E.2d 187, 191–92 (1953). At the formation of the contract the parties are dealing in present realities; performance still lies in the future. As performance unfolds, circumstances change, often unforeseeably; the explicit terms of the contract become progressively less apt to the governance of the parties' relationship; and the role of implied conditions—and with it the scope and bite of the good-faith doctrine—grows.

We could of course do without the term "good faith," and maybe even without the doctrine. We could, as just suggested, speak instead of implied conditions necessitated by the unpredictability of the future at the time the contract was made. Farnsworth, "Good Faith Performance and Commercial Reasonableness under the Uniform Commercial Code," 30 U.Chi.L.Rev. 666, 670 (1963). Suppose a party has promised work to the promisee's "satisfaction." As Learned Hand explained, "he may refuse to look at the work, or to exercise any real judgment on it, in which case he has prevented performance and excused the condition." Thompson-Starrett Co. v. La Belle Iron Works, supra, 17 F.2d at 541. See also Morin Building Products Co. v. Baystone Construction, Inc., 717 F.2d 413, 415 (7th Cir.1983). That is, it was an implicit condition that the promisee examine the work to the extent necessary to determine whether it was satisfactory; otherwise the performing party would have been placing himself at the complete mercy of the promisee. The parties didn't write this condition into the contract either because they thought such behavior unlikely or failed to foresee it altogether. In just the same way—to switch to another familiar example of the operation of the duty of good faith—parties to a requirements contract surely do not intend that if the price of the product covered by the contract rises, the buyer shall be free to increase his "requirements" so that he can take advantage of the rise in the market price over the contract price to resell the product on the open market at a guaranteed profit. Empire Gas Corp. v. American Bakeries Co., 840 F.2d 1333 (7th Cir.1988). If they fail to insert an express condition to this effect, the court will read it in, confident that the parties would have inserted the condition if they had known what the future held. Of similar character is the implied condition that an exclusive dealer will use his best efforts to promote the supplier's goods, since otherwise the exclusive feature of the dealership contract would place the supplier at the dealer's mercy. Wood v. Duff-Gordon, 222 N.Y. 88, 118 N.E. 214 (1917) (Cardozo, J.).

But whether we say that a contract shall be deemed to contain such implied conditions as are necessary to make sense of the contract, or that a contract obligates the parties to cooperate in its performance in "good faith" to the extent necessary to carry out the purposes of the contract, comes to much the same thing. They are different ways of formulating the overriding purpose of contract law, which is to give the parties what they would have stipulated for expressly if at the time of making the contract they had had complete knowledge of the future and the costs of negotiating and adding provisions to the contract had been zero.

. . . The dispositive question in the present case is simply whether Market Street Associates tried to trick the pension trust and succeeded in doing so. If it did, this would be the type of opportunistic behavior in an ongoing contractual relationship that would violate the duty of good faith performance however the duty is formulated. There is much common sense in Judge Reynolds' conclusion that Market Street Associates did just that. The situation as he saw it was as follows. Market Street Associates didn't want financing from the pension trust (initially it had looked elsewhere, remember), and when it learned it couldn't get the financing without owning the property, it decided to try to buy the property. But the pension trust set a stiff price, so Orenstein decided to trick the pension trust into selling at the bargain price fixed in paragraph 34 by requesting financing and hoping that the pension trust would turn the request down without noticing the paragraph. His preliminary dealings with the pension trust made this hope a realistic one by revealing a sluggish and hidebound bureaucracy unlikely to have retained in its brontosaurus's memory, or to be able at short notice to retrieve, the details of a small lease made twenty years earlier. So by requesting financing without mentioning the lease Market Street Associates might well precipitate a refusal before the pension trust woke up to paragraph 34. It is true that Orenstein's second letter requested financing "pursuant to the lease." But when the next day he received a reply to his first letter indicating that the pension trust was indeed oblivious to paragraph 34, his response was to send a lulling letter designed to convince the pension trust that the matter was closed and could be forgotten. The stage was set for his thunderbolt: the notification the next month that Market Street Associates was taking up the option in paragraph 34. Only then did the pension trust look up the lease and discover that it had been had.

The only problem with this recital is that it construes the facts as favorably to the pension trust as the record will permit, and that of course is not the right standard for summary judgment. The facts must be construed as favorably to the nonmoving party, to Market Street Associates, as the record permits (that Market Street Associates filed its own motion for summary judgment is irrelevant, as we have seen). When that is done, a different picture emerges. On Market Street Associates' construal of the record, $3 million was a grossly excessive price for the property, and while $1 million might be a bargain it would not confer so great a windfall as to warrant an inference that if the pension trust had known about paragraph 34 it never would have turned down Market Street Associates' request for financing cold. And in fact the pension trust may have known about paragraph 34, and either it didn't care or it believed that unless the request mentioned that paragraph the pension trust would incur no liability by turning it down. Market Street Associates may have assumed and have been entitled to assume that in reviewing a request for financing from one of its lessees the pension trust would take the time to read the lease to see whether it bore on the request. Market Street Associates did not desire financing from the pension trust initially—that is undeniable—yet when it discovered that it could not get financing elsewhere unless it had the title to the property it may have realized that it would have to negotiate with the pension trust over financing before it could hope to buy the property at the price specified in the lease.

On this interpretation of the facts there was no bad faith on the part of Market Street Associates. It acted honestly, reasonably, without ulterior motive, in the face of circumstances as they actually and reasonably appeared to it. The fault was the pension trust's incredible inattention, which misled Market Street Associates into believing that the pension trust had no interest in financing the improvements regardless of the purchase option. We do not usually excuse contracting parties from failing to read and understand the contents of their contract; and in the end what this case comes down to—or so at least it can be strongly argued—is that an immensely sophisticated enterprise simply failed to read the contract. On the other hand, such enterprises make mistakes just like the rest of us, and deliberately to take advantage of your contracting partner's mistake during the performance stage (for we are not talking about taking advantage of superior knowledge at the formation stage) is a breach of good faith. To be able to correct your contract partner's mistake at zero cost to yourself, and decide not to do so, is a species of opportunistic behavior that the parties would have expressly forbidden in the contract had they foreseen it. The immensely long term of the lease amplified the possibility of errors but did not license either party to take advantage of them.

The district judge jumped the gun in choosing between these alternative characterizations. The essential issue bearing on Market Street Associates' good faith was Orenstein's state of mind, a type of inquiry that ordinarily cannot be concluded on summary judgment, and could not be here. If Orenstein believed that Erb knew or would surely find out about paragraph 34, it was not dishonest or opportunistic to fail to flag that paragraph, or even to fail to mention the lease, in his correspondence and (rare) conversations with Erb, especially given the uninterest in dealing with Market Street Associates that Erb fairly radiated. To decide what Orenstein believed, a trial is necessary. As for the pension trust's intimation that a bench trial (for remember that this is an equity case, since the only relief sought by the plaintiff is specific performance) will add no illumination beyond what the summary judgment proceeding has done, this overlooks the fact that at trial the judge will for the first time have a chance to see the witnesses whose depositions he has read, to hear their testimony elaborated, and to assess their believability.

The judgment is reversed and the case is remanded for further proceedings consistent with this opinion.

REVERSED AND REMANDED.

––––––

RESTATEMENT, SECOND, CONTRACTS § 205

[See Selected Source Materials Supplement]

––––––

PRE-2001 UCC ARTICLE 1, §§ 1–201(19), 1–203, UCC § 2–103(1)(b)

2001 VERSION OF ARTICLE 1, § 1–201(20)

[See Selected Source Materials Supplement]

––––––

NOTE ON THE UCC DEFINITIONS OF GOOD FAITH

The UCC is promulgated by the National Conference of Commissioners on Uniform State Law (NCCUSL) and the American Law Institute (ALI). However, the UCC is only effective to the extent it is adopted by state legislatures. Prior to 2001, Section 1–201 (19) of Article 1 (General Provisions) defined good faith narrowly, to mean "honesty in fact in the conduct or transaction concerned." In contrast, Section 2–201 of Article 2 (Sale of Goods) defined good faith broadly, to mean, in the case of a merchant, "honesty in fact and the observance of reasonable commercial standards of fair dealing in the trade."

In 2001, NCCUSL and the ALI promulgated a revised official version of UCC Article 1. Section 1–201 (20) of the revised official version of Article 1 defined good faith broadly, for all Articles of the UCC except Article 5, to mean "honesty in fact and the observance of reasonable commercial standards of fair dealing." The adoption of this broad definition in the revised official version of Article 1 rendered superfluous the broad definition of good faith in the official version of Article 2. Accordingly, that definition was deleted from the official version of Article 2. Prof. Keith Rowley reports that as of July 1, 2011, forty states had adopted the revised official version of Article 1. Of these forty, eleven did not adopt the definition of good faith in revised Article 1 and retained the prior definition of good faith in Article 2.

CISG ART. 7(1)

[See Selected Source Materials Supplement]

UNIDROIT PRINCIPLES OF INTERNATIONAL COMMERCIAL CONTRACTS ART. 1.7

[See Selected Source Materials Supplement]

PRINCIPLES OF EUROPEAN CONTRACT LAW ART. 1.201

[See Selected Source Materials Supplement]

SEGGEBRUCH V. STOSOR

Appellate Court of Illinois, 1941.
309 Ill. App. 385, 33 N.E.2d 159.

O'CONNOR, J. June 29, 1939, plaintiff filed a forcible detainer suit against defendant to recover possession of certain premises in Chicago Heights which were improved with a brick building used as a gasoline station. In the complaint it is alleged defendant was to pay 1 1/4 cents for each gallon of gasoline sold as rental for the premises; that defendant had performed all the covenants of the lease, paid the monthly rent which was approximately $140 a month up to May 1, 1939; that shortly prior to that date defendant acquired an adjoining lot and erected another gasoline station thereon which he continued to operate from May 1, and abandoned the operation of the gas station on plaintiff's premises, except occasionally defendant sold a few gallons of gasoline. Plaintiff claimed $1000 was due under the terms of the lease. . . .

April 23, 1940, the case was heard before the court without a jury and a decree entered which found the equities in favor of plaintiff; that defendant had maliciously failed and refused to operate the gasoline station on plaintiff's premises for the purpose of defrauding her; that there was due and owing plaintiff $147.50 a month from May 1, 1939, to the date of the entry of the decree. The decree further found the court had theretofore entered judgment at law in the forcible detainer case in plaintiff's favor and against defendant that she recover possession of the premises and it was decreed that plaintiff recover from defendant $1696.25. Defendant appeals from that part of the decree awarding plaintiff $1696.25. No appeal was taken from the judgment entered in the forcible detainer case.

Defendant contends he had a right to construct and conduct a station on the adjoining premises because, as stated by counsel, "No minimum rental is fixed and there is no agreement that the defendant will not conduct the same business at any other address"—that since the lease contained no provision on this question defendant was at liberty to conduct the gasoline station on the adjoining premises.

In deciding the case the chancellor said: "The parties hereto entered into a written lease for the premises and as a rental it is provided" that defendant would pay plaintiff 1 1/4 cents for each gallon of gasoline "sold from the premises each month during the term * * * During the term created by the lease the Defendant built another station immediately adjoining this particular station and began to operate the new place.

"The pleadings admit that prior to his occupation of the new station there was sold an average of 12,000 gallons of gas at the station operated under the lease and that immediately after the new station began to be operated the sale of gas in the old place dropped to some 200 gallons a month. The Defendant on the witness stand admits there was no change in the volume of sale at the place so that since the operation of the new station the sales in the two places have reached about the same as the sales in the old place when it was operated alone.

"In an undertaking such as we have here the lessee undertakes to operate the premises in such a way as to reasonably produce the rental contemplated by the parties at the time the contract was entered into, and that he will not by his own act deprive the Plaintiff of her share of the bargain to which she would be reasonably entitled if the premises continued in the condition in which it was rented without hinderance on the part of the Defendant.

"Here the Defendant willfully and deliberately and purely with the intention of injuring the Plaintiff built himself a station right next door and transferred to the new place. Now he stands before the Court and says there is nothing in my contract that I will not cheat the Plaintiff by building my own station next door thereby depriving her of income under the lease. Of course, there is not. Certainly the Plaintiff could not foresee such a possibility and the law will not stand by and allow such an evident wrong to be committed without finding some remedy. The law will treat the income from the new place as belonging to the old, especially since the evidence clearly shows there was no change in the volume."

We agree with the statement of the chancellor and while there was no express covenant in the lease, it was clearly implied that defendant would use reasonable diligence in operating the gas station on plaintiff's premises.

In Thebest Laundry & Cleaning Co. v. Duffy, 293 Ill.App. 252, 12 N.E.2d 235, in passing on a contract we said: "In Grossman v. Schenker, 206 N.Y. 466 [100 N.E. 39], the court said (p. 469 [p. 40]): 'A contract includes not only what the parties said but also what is necessarily to be implied from what they said. (Milliken v. Western Union Tel. Co., 110 N.Y. 403, 408 [18 N.E. 251, 1 L.R.A. 281].) Thus the words "cash on delivery" with no other promise to pay "imply a promise and create an obligation" to make payment upon delivery. (Justice v. Lang, supra [42 N.Y. 493, 1 Am.Rep. 576].) So the word "sold" in a written agreement implies not only a contract to sell but also a contract to buy (Butler v. Thomson, 92 U.S. 412, 414 [23 L.Ed. 684]); and a contract to buy with no express promise to sell implies the latter obligation. ([Delaware &] Hudson Canal Co. v. Penn. Coal Co., 75 U.S. (8 Wall.) 276, 289 19 L.Ed. 349].) "What is implied in an express contract is as much a part of it as what is expressed" (Bishop on Contracts (2d Ed.), sec. 241); for "the law is a silent factor in every contract." (Long v. Straus, 107 Ind. 94, 95 [6 N.E. 123, 7 N.E. 763, 57 Am.Rep. 87].)'"

And our Supreme Court many years ago announced the law as above stated. Daughetee v. Ohio Oil Co., 263 Ill. 518, 105 N.E. 308; Stoddard v. Ill. Imp. Co., 275 Ill. 199, 113 N.E. 913.

In the Daughetee case, the court construed an oil and gas lease, by which the lessee was given the exclusive right to explore plaintiff's land for gas and oil, to mean that the lessee was required to use reasonable diligence to develop oil and gas on the lands. And in the Stoddard case where lands were leased for a stone quarry it was held that the lessee should quarry stone with reasonable diligence for a term covered by the lease if the stone could be found and quarried at a profit, and that if the lessee retained possession of the property but quarried no stone he was liable in damages for the amount of stone at the price fixed in the lease which could by reasonable diligence have been quarried and sold at a profit.

The decree of the Circuit Court of Cook County is affirmed.

Decree affirmed.

NOTE ON CRITICISM OF THE DOCTRINE

Young Living Essential Oils, LC v. Marin, 366 P.3d 814 (Utah 2011), warns that "judicial inference of contract terms is also fraught with peril, as its misuse threatens commercial certainty and breeds costly litigation." The opinion continues:

> With these concerns in mind, we have set a high bar for the invocation of a new covenant. Under our cases, the court may recognize a covenant of good faith and fair dealing where it is clear from the parties' "course of dealings" or a settled custom or usage of trade that the parties undoubtedly would have agreed to the covenant if they had considered and addressed it. No such covenant may be invoked, however, if it would create obligations "inconsistent with express contractual terms." These limitations likewise protect the reliance interests of the parties to a contract and foreclose the imposition of a code of commercial morality rooted merely in judicial sensibilities. Where the court adopts a covenant enshrined in a settled custom or usage of trade, it is simply endorsing a universal standard that the parties would doubtless have adopted if they had thought to address it by contract. Where the parties themselves have agreed to terms that address the circumstance that gave rise to their dispute, by contrast, the court has no business injecting its own sense of what amounts to "fair dealing." By enforcing these standards and limitations, our cases preserve the core role of the covenant of good faith while controlling against its misuse to the detriment of commercial security and reliance.

Marin was a distributor of Young Living products. He argued Young Living had breached a promise to provide him promotional materials, and that this breach excused his failure to meet performance guarantees. Young Living prevailed in the district court on a motion for summary judgment with "the court holding that the parol-evidence rule barred extrinsic evidence of a condition not set forth in the parties' integrated contract and that such a condition could not be inferred through the covenant of good faith and fair dealing." The rejected evidence was an affidavit from Marin attesting to repeated representations and a shared understanding that promotional materials would be supplied. Marin argued the representations, some of which were subsequent to the execution of the distributorship agreement, constituted a "course of dealing." The court replied:

> Marin misperceives the kind of "course of dealing" evidence that is relevant to establishing a covenant of good faith and fair dealing. The covenant is not a license for the judiciary to codify standards of altruism that a party may have held itself to in the course of its contract performance. Young Living may have expressed a willingness to provide marketing materials to Marin, but that does not itself establish a binding legal covenant to do so. To sustain a new covenant, evidence of "course of dealing" would have to conform to the core terms of the legal doctrine, by demonstrating a settled, longstanding pattern of dealing that the parties unquestionably would have relied on (but failed to memorialize) in entering into their contract. If Young Living for years provided new product to its distributors on the first of every month, for example, but suddenly withheld such product until the 20th of the month despite the existence of a monthly sales quota, it might make sense to deem Young Living to have breached a covenant informed by the parties' longstanding course of dealing. That is not at all what is presented by Marin here, however, and his claim fails despite his invocation of the "course of dealing" terminology.

English v. Fischer, 660 S.W.2d 521, 522 (Tex. 1983), rejects the doctrine entirely:

> A basis for the judgments below was the adoption of a novel theory of law enunciated only by California courts. That theory holds that in every contract there is an implied covenant that neither party will do anything which injures the right of the other party to receive the benefits of the agreement. The courts below call this a covenant of "good faith and fair dealing."

> This concept is contrary to our well-reasoned and long-established adversary system which has served us ably in Texas for almost 150 years. Our system permits parties who have a dispute over a contract to present their case to an impartial tribunal for a determination of the agreement as made by the parties and embodied in the contract itself. To adopt the laudatory sounding theory of "good

faith and fair dealing" would place a party under the onerous threat of treble damages should he seek to compel his adversary to perform according to the contract terms as agreed upon by the parties. The novel concept advocated by the courts below would abolish our system of government according to settled rules of law and let each case be decided upon what might seem "fair and in good faith," by each fact finder. This we are unwilling to do.

Some of this criticism appears to be directed at the <u>tort</u> of bad faith breach of contract. California law at the time was unusual in allowing a tort claim with possible punitive damages for bad faith breach outside the insurance context, and in particular for bad faith termination of an at-will employee.

———

CHAPTER 14

WAIVER AND NO ORAL MODIFICATION TERMS

■ ■ ■

This Chapter concerns the waiver doctrine and the effect of a provision in a written contract that the contract cannot be modified except by a writing. An express waiver of a contract right is similar to a contract modification relinquishing a right in that both involve an expression by the right-holder of an intent to forego the right. But express waiver requires much less in the way of formality—there is no need for consideration or for a writing to satisfy the Statute of Frauds. Waiver can also be tacit. An insurer who receives timely oral notification of a claim by an insured who does not remind the insured that the policy requires written notification is likely to be held to have tacitly waived the condition requiring written notification.

A waiver is less permanent than a modification. A waiver affecting an executory part of a contract may be retracted unless the retraction would be unjust in view of the other party's change of position in reliance on the waiver. Also courts are reluctant to find a waiver of a material right in the absence of a clear expression of intent by the right-holder to waive the right.

The rules of classical contract law that give priority to a written contract in determining manifest intent do not apply when a party claims a written contract was modified or that a right was waived. The parol evidence rule applies only to agreements made before and, if the alleged agreement is oral, contemporaneously with, a written contract that constitutes an integration. The rule therefore is inapplicable to a *later* agreement that modifies a written contract. The plain meaning rule prevents the use of evidence of course of performance to interpret an unambiguous term in a written contract. But the rule does not prevent the use of such evidence to establish waiver or to establish a modification, since these do not involve interpreting the written contract.

Often, a written contract includes a provision that the contract cannot be modified except by a writing—a sort of private Statute of Frauds. Such provisions are sometimes referred to as n.o.m. (no oral modification) clauses. The general rule at common law was that an oral modification was enforceable, notwithstanding an n.o.m. clause. The theory was that: (1)

Parties can, by later contracts, change their earlier contracts. (2) An oral modification is a later contract. (3) An implied provision of the later contract is to abrogate the n.o.m. provision of the earlier contract. Section 2–209(2) changes this rule. It provides that if a contract for the sale of goods includes an n.o.m. clause, then modifications of the contract must be in writing. Section 2–209(4) qualifies this rules by providing that an attempt at modification that does not satisfy Section 2–209(2) "can operate as a waiver."

———

SECTION 1. WAIVER

CLARK V. WEST
Court of Appeals of New York, 1908.
193 N.Y. 349, 86 N.E. 1.

On February 12, 1900, the plaintiff and defendant entered into a written contract, under which the former was to write and prepare for publication for the latter a series of law books, the compensation for which was provided in the contract. After the plaintiff had completed a three-volume work known as "Clark & Marshall on Corporations," the parties disagreed. The plaintiff claimed that the defendant had broken the contract by causing the book to be copyrighted in the name of a corporation which was not a party to the contract, and he brought this action to recover what he claims to be due him, for an accounting and other relief. The defendant demurred to the complaint on the ground that it did not state facts sufficient to constitute a cause of action. The Special Term overruled the demurrer, but upon appeal to the Appellate Division that decision was reversed, and the demurrer sustained. [125 App.Div. 654, 110 N.Y.S. 110.]

Those portions of the contract which are germane to the present stage of the controversy are as follows: The plaintiff agreed to write a series of books relating to specified legal subjects. The manuscript furnished by him was to be satisfactory to the defendant. The plaintiff was not to write or edit anything that would interfere with the sale of books to be written by him under the contract, and he was not to write any other books unless requested so to do by the defendant, in which latter event he was to be paid $3,000 a year. The contract contained a clause which provided that "the first party (the plaintiff) agrees to totally abstain from the use of intoxicating liquors during the continuance of this contract, and the payment to him in accordance with the terms of this contract of any money in excess of $2 per page is dependent on the faithful performance of this as well as the other conditions of this contract. . . ." In a later paragraph it further recited that, "in consideration of the above promises of the first party (the plaintiff), the second party (the defendant) agrees to pay to the first party $2 per page, . . . on each book prepared by the first party under this contract and accepted by the second party, and if said first party abstains from the use of intoxicating liquor and otherwise fulfills his agreements as hereinbefore set forth, he shall be paid an additional $4 per page in manner hereinbefore stated." This was followed by a specification of the method and times of payment. . . .

The plaintiff in his complaint alleges completion of the work on Corporations and publication thereof by the defendant, the sale of many copies thereof from which the defendant received large net receipts, the number of pages it contained (3,469), for which he had been paid at the rate of $2 per page, amounting to $6,938, and that defendant has refused to pay him any sum over and above that amount, or any sum in excess of $2 per page. Full performance of the agreement on plaintiff's part is alleged, except that he "did not totally abstain from the use of intoxicating liquor during the continuance of said contract; but such use by the plaintiff was not excessive and did not prevent or interfere with the due and full performance by the plaintiff of all the other stipulations in said contract." The complaint further alleges a waiver on the part of the defendant of the plaintiff's stipulation to totally abstain from the use of intoxicating liquors, as follows: "(12) That defendant waived plaintiff's breach of the stipulation to totally abstain from the use of intoxicating liquors during the continuance of said contract; that long prior to the completion of said manuscript on Corporations, and its delivery to and acceptance by the defendant, the defendant had full knowledge and well knew of plaintiff's said use of intoxicating liquor during the continuance of said contract, but nevertheless acquiesced in and failed to object thereto, and did not terminate the contract on account thereof; that with full knowledge of said breach by the plaintiff defendant continued to exact and require of the plaintiff performance of all the other stipulations and conditions of said contract, and treated the same as still in force, and continued to receive, and did receive, installments of manuscript under said contract, and continued to make and did make payments to plaintiff by way of advancements, and finally accepted and published said manuscript as aforesaid; that at no time during the performance of said contract by the plaintiff did the defendant notify or intimate to the plaintiff that defendant would insist upon strict compliance with said stipulation to totally abstain from the use of intoxicating liquor, or that defendant intended to take advantage of plaintiff's said breach, and on account and by reason thereof refuse to pay plaintiff the royalty stipulated in said contract; that, on the contrary, and with full knowledge of plaintiff's said use of intoxicating liquors, defendant repeatedly avowed and represented to the plaintiff that he was entitled to and would receive said royalty payment, and plaintiff believed and relied on said representation, and in reliance thereon continued in the performance of said contract until the time of the breach thereof by the defendant, as hereinafter specifically alleged, and at all times during the writing of said treatise on Corporations, and after as well as before publication thereof, as aforesaid, it was mutually understood, agreed, and intended by the parties hereto that, notwithstanding plaintiff's said use of intoxicating liquors, he was nevertheless entitled to receive and would receive said royalty as the same accrued under said contract." The defendant's breach of the contract is then alleged, which is claimed to consist in his having taken out a copyright upon the plaintiff's work on Corporations in the name of a publishing company which had no relation to the contract, and the relief asked for is that the defendant be compelled to account, and that the copyright be transferred to the plaintiff, or that he recover its value.

The appeal is by permission of the Appellate Division, and the following questions have been certified to us: (1) Does the complaint herein state facts sufficient to constitute a cause of action? (2) Under the terms of the contract alleged in the complaint, is the plaintiff's total abstinence from the use of intoxicating liquors a condition precedent which can be waived so as to render defendant liable upon the contract notwithstanding plaintiff's use of intoxicating liquors? (3) Does the complaint herein allege facts constituting a valid and effective waiver of plaintiff's nonperformance of such condition precedent?

WERNER, J. . . . Briefly stated, the defendant's position is that the stipulation as to plaintiff's total abstinence is the consideration for the payment of the difference between $2 and $6 per page, and therefore could not be waived except by a new agreement to that effect based upon a good consideration; that the so-called waiver alleged by the plaintiff is not a waiver, but a modification of the contract in respect of its consideration. The plaintiff, on the other hand, argues that the stipulation for his total abstinence was merely a condition precedent, intended to work a forfeiture of the additional compensation in case of a breach, and that it could be waived without any formal agreement to that effect based upon a new consideration.

The subject-matter of the contract was the writing of books by the plaintiff for the defendant. The duration of the contract was the time necessary to complete them all. The work was to be done to the satisfaction of the defendant, and the plaintiff was not to write any other books except those covered by the contract unless requested so to do by the defendant, in which latter event he was to be paid for that particular work by the year. The compensation for the work specified in the contract was to be $6 per page, unless the plaintiff failed to totally abstain from the use of intoxicating liquors during the continuance of the contract, in which event he was to receive only $2 per page. That is the obvious import of the contract construed in the light of the purpose for which it was made, and in accordance with the ordinary meaning of plain language. It is not a contract to write books in order that the plaintiff shall keep sober, but a contract containing a stipulation that he shall keep sober so that he may write satisfactory books. When we view the contract from this standpoint, it will readily be perceived that the particular stipulation is not the consideration for the contract, but simply one of its conditions which fits in with those relating to time and method of delivery of manuscript, revision of proof, citation of cases, assignment of copyrights, keeping track of new cases and citations for new editions, and other details which might be waived by the defendant, if he saw fit to do so. This is made clear, it seems to us, by the provision that, "in consideration of the above promises," the defendant agrees to pay the plaintiff $2 per page on each book prepared by him, and if he "abstains from the use of intoxicating liquor and otherwise fulfills his agreements as hereinbefore set forth, he shall be paid an additional $4 per page in manner hereinbefore stated." The compensation of $2 per page, not to exceed $250 per month, was an advance or partial payment of the whole price of $6 per page, and the payment of the two-thirds, which was to be withheld pending the performance of the contract, was simply made contingent upon the plaintiff's total abstention from the use of intoxicants during the life of the contract. . . .

It is obvious that the parties thought that the plaintiff's normal work was worth $6 per page. That was the sum to be paid for the work done by the plaintiff, and not for total abstinence. If the plaintiff did not keep to the condition as to total abstinence, he was to lose part of that sum. . . . This, we think, is the fair interpretation of the contract, and it follows that the stipulation as to the plaintiff's total abstinence was nothing more nor less than a condition precedent. If that conclusion is well founded, there can be no escape from the corollary that this condition could be waived; and, if it was waived, the defendant is clearly not in a position to insist upon the forfeiture which his waiver was intended to annihilate. The forfeiture must stand or fall with the condition. If the latter was waived, the former is no longer a part of the contract. Defendant still has the right to counterclaim for any damages which he may have sustained in consequence of the plaintiff's breach, but he cannot insist upon strict performance. Dunn v. Steubing, 120 N.Y. 232, 24 N.E. 315; Parke v. Franco-American Trading Co., 120 N.Y. 51, 56, 23 N.E. 996; Brady v. Cassidy, 145 N.Y. 171, 39 N.E. 814.

This whole discussion is predicated, of course, upon the theory of an express waiver. We assume that no waiver could be implied from the defendant's mere acceptance of the books and his payment of the sum of $2 per page without objection. It was the defendant's duty to pay that amount in any event after acceptance of the work. The plaintiff must stand upon his allegation of an express waiver, and if he fails to establish that he cannot maintain his action.

The theory upon which the defendant's attitude seems to be based is that, even if he has represented to the plaintiff that he would not insist upon the condition that the latter should observe total abstinence from intoxicants, he can still refuse to pay the full contract price for his work. The inequity of this position becomes apparent when we consider that this contract was to run for a period of years, during a large portion of which the plaintiff was to be entitled only to the advance payment of $2 per page; the balance being contingent, among other things, upon publication of the books and returns from sales. Upon this theory the defendant might have waived the condition while the first book was in process of production, and yet, when the whole work was completed, he would still be in a position to insist upon the forfeiture because there had not been strict performance. Such a situation is possible in a case where the subject of the waiver is the very consideration of a contract (Organ v. Stewart, 60 N.Y. 413, 420), but not where the waiver relates to something that can be waived. In the case at bar, as we have seen, the waiver is not of the consideration or subject-matter, but of an incident to the method of performance. The consideration remains the same. The defendant has had the work he bargained for, and it is alleged that he has waived one of the conditions as to the manner in which it was to have been done. He might have insisted upon literal performance, and then he could have stood upon the letter of his contract. If, however, he has waived that incidental condition, he has created a situation to which the doctrine of waiver very precisely applies.

The cases which present the most familiar phases of the doctrine of waiver are those which have arisen out of litigation over insurance policies where the defendants have claimed a forfeiture because of the breach of some condition in the contract (Insurance Co. v. Norton, 96 U.S. 234, 24 L.Ed. 689; Titus v. Glens Falls Ins. Co., 81 N.Y. 410; Kiernan v. Dutchess Co. Mut. Insurance Co., 150 N.Y. 190, 44 N.E. 698), but it is a doctrine of general application which is confined to no particular class of cases. A "waiver" has been defined to be the intentional relinquishment of a known right. It is voluntary and implies an election to dispense with something of value, or forego some advantage which the party waiving it might at its option have demanded or insisted upon (Herman on Estoppel & Res Adjudicata, vol. 2, p. 954; Cowenhoven v. Ball, 118 N.Y. 234, 23 N.E. 470), and this definition is supported by many cases in this and other states. In the recent case of Draper v. Oswego Co. Fire R. Ass'n, 190 N.Y. 12, 16, 82 N.E. 755, Chief Judge Cullen, in speaking for the court upon this subject, said: "While that doctrine and the doctrine of equitable estoppel are often confused in insurance litigation, there is a clear distinction between the two. A 'waiver' is the voluntary abandonment or relinquishment by a party of some right or advantage. As said by my Brother Vann in the Kiernan Case, 150 N.Y. 190, 44 N.E. 698: 'The law of waiver seems to be a technical doctrine, introduced and applied by the court for the purpose of defeating forfeitures. . . . While the principle may not be easily classified, it is well established that, if the words and acts of the insurer reasonably justify the conclusion that with full knowledge of all the facts it intended to abandon or not to insist upon the particular defense afterwards relied upon, a verdict or finding to that effect establishes a waiver, which, if it once exists, can never be revoked.' The doctrine of equitable estoppel, or estoppel in pais, is that a party may be precluded by his acts and conduct from asserting a right to the detriment of another party who, entitled to rely on such conduct, has acted upon it. . . . As already said, the doctrine of waiver is to relieve against forfeiture. It requires no consideration for a waiver, nor any prejudice or injury to the other party." To the same effect, see Knarston v. Manhattan Life Ins. Co., 140 Cal. 57, 73 P. 740.

It remains to be determined whether the plaintiff has alleged facts which, if proven, will be sufficient to establish his claim of an express waiver by the defendant of the plaintiff's breach of the condition to observe total abstinence. In the 12th paragraph of the complaint, the plaintiff alleges facts and circumstances which we think, if established, would prove defendant's waiver of plaintiff's performance of that contract stipulation. . . .

The three questions certified should be answered in the affirmative, the order of the Appellate Division reversed, the interlocutory judgment of the Special Term affirmed, with costs in both courts, and the defendant be permitted to answer the complaint within 20 days upon payment of costs.

RESTATEMENT, SECOND, CONTRACTS § 84

[See Selected Source Materials Supplement]

RESTATEMENT, SECOND, CONTRACTS § 84, ILLUSTRATIONS 3, 4, 6

3.   A employs B to build a house, promising to pay therefor $10,000 on the production of a certificate from A's architect, C, stating that the work has been satisfactorily completed. B builds the house but the work is defective in certain trivial particulars. C refuses to give B a certificate. A says to B, "My architect rightfully refuses to give you a certificate but the defects are not serious; I will pay you the full price which I promised." A is bound to do so, and has no power to restore the requirement of the condition.

4.   A, an insurance company, insures B's house for $5000 against loss by fire. The insurance policy provides that it shall be payable only if B gives written notification of any loss within thirty days after its occurrence. An insured loss occurs and B gives only oral notification thereof within thirty days. A tells him, either before or after the lapse of thirty days from the

loss, that this notification is sufficient. A cannot thereafter rely upon B's failure to give written notification as an excuse for failure to pay for the loss. . . .

6. In Illustration 4, A can restore the requirement of the condition by notifying B of his intention to do so if there still remains a reasonable time for the occurrence of the condition before the expiration of the thirty-day period, unless such action would be unjust in view of a material change of position by B in reliance on A's waiver. If a reasonable time does not remain, A cannot restore the requirement of the condition by extending the time.

Westinghouse Credit Corp. v. Shelton

645 F.2d 869 (1981)

Shelton purchased a mobile home in May 1974, agreeing to pay principal and interest totaling $22,662.71 in 144 installments of $157.38 on the 25th day of every month beginning with June 25, 1974. The dealer assigned the note to Westinghouse. Shelton's payments were habitually late by one, two, and even three months. Westinghouse accepted the late payments. In April 1978, after Shelton failed to make the payments due January, February, and March 1978, Westinghouse filed a complaint that declared Shelton in default, accelerated full payment of the principal remaining due, and requested a writ of replevin to permit repossession of the mobile home. The district court granted Westinghouse's motion for summary judgment. Reversed.

(Seymour, J.) "When Westinghouse filed suit in April 1978 and requested replevin relief, Shelton was indisputedly in default. Also not contested is the fact Westinghouse accepted all late payments in the course of the contract's performance from June 1974 to December 1977, and that almost all of the roughly 40 installments covering this period were paid late. This toleration, Shelton argues, precluded Westinghouse from suddenly declaring default without first apprising Shelton of its insistence on strict compliance with the contract's timeliness terms. Whether or to what extent Shelton was actually apprised of such insistence is a fact vigorously disputed by the parties. Shelton argues this dispute precluded the grant of summary judgment. We conclude that beyond just the question of notification to Shelton, the overall issue whether in this case the parties' course of performance worked a waiver of one or more terms in their contract is a question for the factfinder. Summary judgment was therefore inappropriate. . . .

"Absent an "anti-waiver" clause such as paragraph 6 in Shelton's contract,* courts have uniformly held that a creditor may not fall into a pattern

---

* "The waiver or indulgence of any default by the Buyer of any provision of this Agreement or any promissory note which it secures shall not operate as a waiver of any subsequent default by the Buyer of such provision or as a waiver of any of the other rights of (Westinghouse) herein. Time shall be deemed the essence of this Agreement."

of accepting delinquent installments and then suddenly declare default, without first apprising the debtor of his insistence on strict compliance with the terms of the contract. See, e. g., Knittel v. Security State Bank, 593 P.2d 92, 95–96 (Okl.1979); Lee v. Wood Products Credit Union, 275 Or. 445, 551 P.2d 446, 448 (1976); Nevada National Bank v. Huff, 582 P.2d 364, 369 (Nev.1978). See also Ga.Code Ann. § 20–116 (where parties' course of performance departs from terms of contract, reasonable notice must be given of intention to rely on exact terms of agreement and until such notice departure deemed quasi new agreement). But courts have split over the significance of the parties' course of performance when the contract includes an "anti-waiver" provision, which in effect tells the debtor that the creditor's toleration of one or more defaults should not be taken to mean the creditor would indulge others.

"Some have construed the "anti-waiver" clause strictly according to its terms, thus conclusively precluding a creditor's pattern of accepting late payments from operating as a modification or waiver of the contract's default provisions. See Hale v. Ford Motor Credit Co., 374 So.2d 849, 853 (Ala.1979); Fair v. General Finance Corp., 147 Ga.App. 706, 250 S.E.2d 9 (1978); Universal C.I.T. Credit Corp. v. Middlesboro Motor Sales, Inc., 424 S.W.2d 409, 411 (Ct.App.Ky.1968); Home Finance Co. v. Frazier, 380 S.W.2d 91, 93 (Ky.1964).

"But the weight of authority, and the view we think Oklahoma state courts would follow, is that an "anti-waiver" clause, like any other term in the contract, is itself subject to waiver or modification by course of performance and that whether such waiver or modification has occurred is a question for the factfinder. See Smith v. General Finance Corp., 243 Ga. 500, 255 S.E.2d 14, 15 (1979) (disapproving of Fair v. General Finance Corp., 147 Ga.App. 706, 250 S.E.2d 9); Pierce v. Leasing International, Inc., 142 Ga.App. 371, 235 S.E.2d 752, 754–55 (1977); Van Bibber v. Norris, 404 N.E.2d 1365, 1373–74 (Ct.App.Ind.1980); Cobb v. Midwest Recovery Bureau Co., 295 N.W.2d 232, 237 (Minn.1980). Cf. 12A Okla.Stat.Ann. § 1–205 & Official Comment 2. See also Wade v. Ford Motor Credit Co., 455 F.Supp. 147, 150 (E.D.Mo.1978) (pattern of accepting late payments operates as waiver of default as to previously accepted payments, but not as to yet unaccepted payments); Fontaine v. Industrial National Bank of Rhode Island, 111 R.I. 6, 298 A.2d 521, 523–24 (1973) (acceptance of late payments operates as absolute waiver of contract's default provision as to accepted payments and precludes creditor's declaration of default after timely payments have intervened); Ford Motor Credit Co. v. Waters, 273 So.2d 96, 100 (Ct.App.Fla.1973).

"In Shelton's case the question is whether Westinghouse, by accepting late payments as it did, waived its right to strictly enforce not only the contract's time terms, but also the "anti-waiver" clause itself. Shelton should have the opportunity to prove, if he can, that Westinghouse's conduct in toto regarding timeliness was so pervasive that in the eyes of a reasonable debtor it "spoke louder than (the) word," Van Bibber, 404 N.E.2d at 1374, of the "anti-waiver" clause, which in effect counseled against reliance on conduct indulging default. If waiver by Westinghouse of the contract's timeliness and "anti-waiver" terms were found, the question whether or to what extent Westinghouse apprised

Shelton, before taking him to court in April 1978, of its insistence upon strict adherence to the contract's terms would bear upon whether Westinghouse effectively retracted its waiver. See 12A Okla.Stat.Ann. § 2–209(5). In view of these fact questions, we must vacate the district court's summary judgment and the dismissal of Shelton's counterclaim, and remand for further proceedings."

———

Nassau Trust Co. v. Montrose Concrete Products Corp.

56 N.Y.2d 175, 451 N.Y.S.2d 663, 436 N.E.2d 1265 (1982), reargument denied 57 N.Y.2d 674, 454 N.Y.S.2d 1032, 439 N.E.2d 1247 (1982)

"Modification . . . requires consideration. . . . [In contrast, waiver does not rest] upon consideration or agreement. A modification, because it is an agreement based upon consideration, is binding according to its terms and may only be withdrawn by agreement. . . . A waiver, to the extent that it has been executed, cannot be expunged or recalled . . . but, not being a binding agreement, can, to the extent that it is executory, be withdrawn, provided the party whose performance has been waived is given notice of withdrawal and a reasonable time after notice within which to perform. . . . "

———

UCC §§ 1–306, 2–209(5)

[See Selected Source Materials Supplement]

———

SECTION 2. NO-ORAL-MODIFICATION TERMS

WISCONSIN KNIFE WORKS V. NATIONAL METAL CRAFTERS

United States Court of Appeals for the Seventh Circuit, 1986
781 F.2d 1280 (7th Cir. 1986).

POSNER, CIRCUIT JUDGE:

. . . Wisconsin Knife Works, having some unused manufacturing capacity, decided to try to manufacture spade bits for sale to its parent, Black & Decker, a large producer of tools, including drills. A spade bit is made out of a chunk of metal called a spade bit blank; and Wisconsin Knife Works had to find a source of supply for these blanks. National Metal Crafters was eager to be that source. After some negotiating, Wisconsin Knife Works sent National Metal Crafters a series of purchase orders on the back of each of which was printed, "Acceptance of this Order, either by acknowledgment or performance, constitutes an unqualified agreement to the following." A list of "Conditions of Purchase" follows, of which the first is, "No modification of this contract, shall be binding upon Buyer [Wisconsin Knife Works] unless made in writing and signed by Buyer's authorized representative. Buyer shall have the right to make changes in the Order by a notice, in writing, to Seller." There were six purchase orders in all, each with the identical conditions. National Metal Crafters acknowledged the first two orders (which had been placed on August 21, 1981) by letters that said, "Please accept this as our acknowledgment covering the above subject order," followed by a list of delivery dates. The purchase orders had left those dates blank. Wisconsin Knife Works filled them in, after receiving the acknowledgments, with the dates that National Metal Crafters had supplied in the acknowledgments. There were no written acknowledgments of the last four orders (placed several weeks later, on September 10, 1981). Wisconsin Knife Works wrote in the delivery dates that National Metal Crafters orally supplied after receiving purchase orders in which the space for the date of delivery had again been left blank.

Delivery was due in October and November 1981. National Metal Crafters missed the deadlines. But Wisconsin Knife Works did not immediately declare a breach, cancel the contract, or seek damages for late delivery. Indeed, on July 1, 1982, it issued a new batch of purchase orders (later rescinded). By December 1982 National Metal Crafters was producing spade bit blanks for Wisconsin Knife Works under the original set of purchase orders in adequate quantities, though this was more than a year after the delivery dates in the orders. But on January 13, 1983, Wisconsin Knife Works notified National Metal Crafters that the contract was terminated. By that date only 144,000 of the more than 281,000 spade bit blanks that Wisconsin Knife Works had ordered in the six purchase orders had been delivered.

Wisconsin Knife Works brought this breach of contract suit, charging that National Metal Crafters had violated the terms of delivery in the contract that was formed by the acceptance of the six purchase orders. National Metal Crafters replied that the delivery dates had not been intended as firm dates. It also counterclaimed for damages for (among other things) the breach of an alleged oral agreement by Wisconsin Knife Works to pay the expenses of maintaining machinery used by National Metal Crafters to fulfill the contract. The parties later stipulated that the amount of these damages was $30,000.

The judge ruled that there had been a contract but left to the jury to decide whether the contract had been modified and, if so, whether the modified contract had been broken. The jury found that the contract had been modified and not broken. Judgment was entered dismissing Wisconsin Knife Works' suit and awarding National Metal Crafters $30,000 on its counterclaim. Wisconsin Knife Works has appealed from the dismissal of its suit. The appeal papers do not discuss the counterclaim, and the effect on it of our remanding the case for further proceedings on Wisconsin Knife Works' claim will have to be resolved on remand.

The principal issue is the effect of the provision in the purchase orders that forbids the contract to be modified other than by a writing signed by an authorized representative of the buyer. The theory on which the judge sent the issue of modification to the jury was that the contract could be modified orally or by conduct as well as by a signed writing. National Metal Crafters had presented evidence that Wisconsin Knife Works had accepted late delivery of the spade bit blanks and had cancelled the contract not because of the delays in delivery but because it could not produce spade bits at a price acceptable to Black & Decker.

Section 2–209(2) of the Uniform Commercial Code provides that "a signed agreement which excludes modification or rescission except by a signed writing cannot be otherwise modified or rescinded, but except as between merchants such a requirement on a form supplied by the merchant must be separately signed by the other party." . . . The meaning of this provision and its proviso is not crystalline and there is little pertinent case law. One might think that an agreement to exclude modification except by a signed writing must be signed in any event by the party against whom the requirement is sought to be enforced, that is, by National Metal Crafters, rather than by the party imposing the requirement. But if so the force of the proviso ("but except as between merchants . . .") becomes unclear, for it contemplates that between merchants no separate signature by the party sought to be bound by the requirement is necessary. A possible reconciliation, though not one we need embrace in order to decide this case, is to read the statute to require a separate signing or initialing of the clause forbidding oral modifications, as well as of the contract in which the clause appears. There was no such signature here; but it doesn't matter; this was a contract "between merchants." Although in ordinary language a manufacturer is not a merchant, "between merchants" is a term of art in the Uniform Commercial Code. It means between commercially sophisticated parties (see UCC § 2–104(1); White & Summers, Handbook of the Law Under the Uniform Commercial Code 345 (2d ed. 1980)), which these were.

Of course there must still be a "signed agreement" containing the clause forbidding modification other than by a signed writing, but there was that (see definition of "agreement" and of "signed" in UCC §§ 1–201(3), (39)). National Metal Crafters' signed acknowledgments of the first two purchase orders signified its assent to the printed conditions and naturally and reasonably led Wisconsin Knife Works to believe that National Metal Crafters meant also to assent to the same conditions should they appear in any subsequent purchase orders that it accepeted. Those subsequent orders were accepted, forming new contracts on the same conditions as the old, by performance—that is, by National Metal Crafters' beginning the manufacture of the spade bit blanks called for by the orders. See UCC § 2–207(3). So there was an agreement, signed by National Metal Crafters, covering all the purchase orders. The fact that the delivery dates were not on the purchase orders when received by National Metal Crafters is nothing of which it may complain; it was given carte blanche to set those dates.

When National Metal Crafters had difficulty complying with the original specifications for the spade bit blanks, Wisconsin Knife Works modified them; and National Metal Crafters argues that the engineering drawings containing those modifications are the written modification that section 2–209(2), if applicable, calls for. In fact these particular modifications seem to fall within the clause of the contract that allows the buyer (Wisconsin Knife Works) to modify the specifications by notice. The context of this clause makes clear that such notice is not the written modification to which the previous sentence refers. But in any event there was no modification of the delivery dates. The "pert charts" which National Metal Crafters supplied Wisconsin Knife Works, and which showed new target dates for delivery, do not purport to modify the contract and were not signed by Wisconsin Knife Works.

We conclude that the clause forbidding modifications other than in writing was valid and applicable and that the jury should not have been allowed to consider whether the contract had been modified in some other way. This may, however, have been a harmless error. Section 2–209(4) of the Uniform Commercial Code provides that an "attempt at modification" which does not satisfy a contractual requirement that modifications be in writing nevertheless "can operate as a waiver." Although in instructing the jury on modification the judge did not use the word "waiver," maybe he gave the substance of a waiver instruction and maybe therefore the jury found waiver but called it modification. Here is the relevant instruction:

> Did the parties modify the contract? The defendant bears the burden of proof on this one. You shall answer this question yes only if you are convinced to a reasonable certainty that the parties modified the contract.

> If you determine that the defendant had performed in a manner different from the strict obligations imposed on it by the contract, and the plaintiff by conduct or other means of expression induced a reasonable belief by the defendant that strict enforcement was not insisted upon, but that the modified performance was satisfactory and acceptable as equivalent, then you may conclude that the parties have assented to a modification of the original terms of the contract and that the parties have agreed that the different mode of performance will satisfy the obligations imposed on the parties by the contract.

To determine whether this was in substance an instruction on waiver we shall have to consider the background of section 2–209, the Code provision on modification and waiver.

Because the performance of the parties to a contract is typically not simultaneous, one party may find himself at the mercy of the other unless the law of contracts protects him. Indeed, the most important thing which that law does is to facilitate exchanges that are not simultaneous by preventing either party from taking advantage of the vulnerabilities to which sequential performance may give rise. If A contracts to build a highly idiosyncratic gazebo for B, payment due on completion, and when A completes the gazebo B refuses to pay, A may be in a bind—since the resale value of the gazebo may be much less than A's cost—except for his right to sue B for the price. Even then, a right to sue for breach of contract, being costly to enforce, is not a completely adequate remedy. B might therefore go to A and say, "If you don't reduce your price I'll refuse to pay and put you to the expense of suit"; and A might knuckle under. If such modifications are allowed, people in B's position will find it harder to make such contracts in the future, and everyone will be worse off.

The common law dealt with this problem by refusing to enforce modifications unsupported by fresh consideration. See, e.g., Alaska Packers' Ass'n v. Domenico, 117 Fed. 99 (9th Cir.1902), discussed in Selmer Co. v. Blakeslee-Midwest Co., 704 F.2d 924, 927 (7th Cir.1983). Thus in the hypothetical case just put B could not have enforced A's promise to accept a lower price. But this solution is at once overinclusive and underinclusive—the former because most modifications are not coercive and should be enforceable whether or not there is fresh consideration, the latter because, since common law courts inquire only into the existence and not the adequacy of consideration, a requirement of fresh consideration has little bite. B might give A a peppercorn, a kitten, or a robe in exchange for A's agreeing to reduce the contract price, and then the modification would be enforceable and A could no longer sue for the original price. See White & Summers, supra, at 47; Farnsworth, Contracts 271–78 (1982).

The draftsmen of the Uniform Commercial Code took a fresh approach, by making modifications enforceable even if not supported by consideration (see section 2–209(1)) and looking to the doctrines of duress and bad faith for the main protection against exploitive or opportunistic attempts at modification, as in our hypothetical case. See UCC § 2–209, official comment 2. But they did another thing as well. In section 2–209(2) they allowed the parties to exclude oral modifications. National Metal Crafters argues that two subsections later they took back this grant of power by allowing an unwritten modification to operate as a waiver.

The common law did not enforce agreements such as section 2–209(2) authorizes. The "reasoning" was that the parties were always free to agree orally to cancel their contract and the clause forbidding modifications not in writing would disappear with the rest of the contract when it was cancelled. "The most ironclad written contract can always be cut into by the acetylene torch of parol modification supported by adequate proof." Wagner v. Graziano Construction Co., 390 Pa. 445, 448, 136 A.2d 82, 83–84 (1957). This is not reasoning; it is a conclusion disguised as a metaphor. It may have reflected a fear that such clauses, buried in the fine print of form contracts, were traps for the unwary; a sense that they were unnecessary because only modifications supported by consideration were enforceable; and a disinclination to allow parties in effect to extend the reach of the Statute of Frauds, which requires only some types of contract to be in writing. But the framers of the Uniform Commercial Code, as part and parcel of rejecting the requirement of consideration for modifications, must have rejected the traditional view; must have believed that the protection which the doctrines of duress and bad faith give against extortionate modifications might need reinforcement—if not from a requirement of consideration, which had proved ineffective, then from a grant of power to include a clause requiring modifications to be in writing and signed. An equally important point is that with consideration no longer required for modification, it was natural to give the parties some means of providing a substitute for the cautionary and evidentiary function that the requirement of consideration provides; and the means chosen was to allow them to exclude oral modifications.

If section 2–209(4), which as we said provides that an attempted modification which does not comply with subsection (2) can nevertheless operate as a "waiver," is interpreted so broadly that any oral modification is effective as a waiver notwithstanding section 2–209(2), both provisions become superfluous and we are back in the common law—only with not even a requirement of consideration to reduce the likelihood of fabricated or unintended oral modifications. A conceivable but unsatisfactory way around this result is to distinguish between a modification that substitutes a new term for an old, and a waiver, which merely removes an old term. On this interpretation National Metal Crafters could not enforce an oral term of the allegedly modified contract but could be excused from one of the written terms. This would take care of a case such as Alaska Packers, where seamen attempted to enforce a contract modification that raised their wages, but would not take care of the functionally identical case where seamen sought to collect the agreed-on wages without doing the agreed-on work. Whether the party claiming modification is seeking to impose an onerous new term on the other party or to wriggle out of an onerous term that the original contract imposed on it is a distinction without a difference. We can see that in this case. National Metal Crafters, while claiming that Wisconsin Knife Works broke their contract as orally modified to extend the delivery date, is not seeking damages for that breach. But this is small comfort to Wisconsin Knife Works, which thought it had a binding contract with fixed delivery dates. Whether called modification or waiver, what National Metal Crafters is seeking to do is to nullify a key term other than by a signed writing. If it can get away with this merely by testimony about an oral modification, section 2–209(2) becomes very nearly a dead letter.

The path of reconciliation with subsection (4) is found by attending to the precise wording of (4). It does not say that an attempted modification "is" a waiver; it says that "it can operate as a waiver." It does not say in what circumstances it can operate as a waiver; but if an attempted modification is effective as a waiver only if there is reliance, then both sections 2–209(2) and 2–209(4) can be given effect. Reliance, if reasonably induced and reasonable in extent, is a common substitute for consideration in making a promise legally enforceable, in part because it adds something in the way of credibility to the mere say-so of one party. The main purpose of forbidding oral modifications is to prevent the promisor from fabricating a modification that will let him escape his obligations under the contract; and the danger of successful fabrication is less if the promisor has actually incurred a cost, has relied. There is of course a danger of bootstrapping— of incurring a cost in order to make the case for a modification. But it is a risky course and is therefore less likely to be attempted than merely testifying to a conversation; it makes one put one's money where one's mouth is.

We find support for our proposed reconciliation of subsections (2) and (4) in the secondary literature. See Eisler, Oral Modification of Sales Contracts Under the Uniform Commercial Code: The Statute of Frauds Problem, 58 Wash. U.L.Q. 277, 298–302 (1980); Farnsworth, supra, at 476–77; 6 Corbin on Contracts 211 (1962). It is true that 2 Anderson on the Uniform Commercial Code § 2–209:42 (3d ed. 1982), opines that reliance is not necessary for an attempted modification to operate as a waiver, but he does not explain his conclusion or provide any reason or authority to support it. This provision was quoted along with other material from Anderson in Double-E Sportswear Corp. v. Girard Trust Bank, 488 F.2d 292, 295 (3d Cir.1973), but there was no issue of reliance in that case. 2 Hawkland, Uniform Commercial Code Series § 2–209:05, at p. 138 (1985), remarks, "if clear factual evidence other than mere parol points to that conclusion [that an oral agreement was made altering a term of the contract], a waiver may be found. In the normal case, however, courts should be careful not to allow the protective features of sections 2–209(2) and (3) to be nullified by contested parol evidence." (Footnote omitted.) The instruction given by the judge in this case did not comply with this test, but in any event we think a requirement of reliance is clearer than a requirement of "clear factual evidence other than mere parol."

Our approach is not inconsistent with section 2–209(5), which allows a waiver to be withdrawn while the contract is executory, provided there is no "material change of position in reliance on the waiver." Granted, in (5) there can be no tincture of reliance; the whole point of the section is that a waiver may be withdrawn unless there is reliance. But the section has a different domain from section 2–209(4). It is not limited to attempted modifications invalid under subsections (2) or (3); it applies, for example, to an express written and signed waiver, provided only that the contract is still executory. Suppose that while the contract is still executory the buyer writes the seller a signed letter waiving some term in the contract and then, the next day, before the seller has relied, retracts it in writing; we have no reason to think that such a retraction would not satisfy section 2–209(5), though this is not an issue we need definitively resolve today. In any event we are not suggesting that "waiver" means different things in (4) and (5); it means the same thing; but the effect of an attempted modification as a waiver under (4) depends in part on (2), which (4) (but not 5)) qualifies. Waiver and estoppel (which requires reliance to be effective) are frequently bracketed. See, e.g., Chemetron Corp. v. McLouth Steel Corp., 522 F.2d 469, 472–73 (7th Cir.1975); Hirsch Rolling Mill Co. v. Milwaukee & Fox River Valley Ry., 165 Wis. 220, 161 N.W. 741 (1917).

The statute could be clearer; but the draftsmen were making a big break with the common law in subsections (1) and (2), and naturally failed to foresee all the ramifications of the break. The innovations made in Article 9 of the UCC were so novel that the article had to be comprehensively revised only ten years after its promulgation. See Appendix II to the 1978 Official Text of the Uniform Commercial Code. Article 2 was less innovative, but of course its draftsmanship was not flawless—what human product is? Just a few months ago we wrestled with the mysterious and apparently inadvertent omission of key words in the middle subsection of another section of Article 2. See Jason's Foods, Inc. v. Peter Eckrich & Sons, Inc., 774 F.2d 214 (7th Cir.1985) (section 2–509(2)). Another case of gap-filling in Article 2 is discussed in White & Summers, supra, at 450 (section 2–316(3)(a)). But as a matter of fact we need go no further than section 2–209(5) to illustrate the need for filling gaps in Article 2. In holding that that section allows the retraction of a waiver of the Statute of Frauds, the Third Circuit said in Double-E Sportswear Corp. v. Girard Trust Bank, supra, 488 F.2d at 297 n. 7, "We have found it necessary to fill the interstices of the code," because of "a drafting oversight."

We know that the draftsmen of section 2–209 wanted to make it possible for parties to exclude oral modifications. They did not just want to give "modification" another name—"waiver." Our interpretation gives effect to this purpose. It is also consistent with though not compelled by the case law. There are no Wisconsin cases on point. Cases from other jurisdictions are diverse in outlook. Some take a very hard line against allowing an oral waiver to undo a clause forbidding oral modification. See, e.g., South Hampton Co. v. Stinnes Corp., 733 F.2d 1108, 1117–18 (5th Cir.1984) (Texas law); U.S. Fibres, Inc. v. Proctor & Schwartz, Inc., 358 F.Supp. 449, 460 (E.D.Mich.1972), aff'd, 509 F.2d 1043 (6th Cir.1975) (Pennsylvania law). Others allow oral waivers to override such clauses, but in most of these cases it is clear that the party claiming waiver had relied to his detriment. See, e.g., Gold Kist, Inc. v. Pillow, 582 S.W.2d 77, 79–80 (Tenn.App.1979) (where this feature of the case is emphasized); Linear Corp. v. Standard Hardware Co., 423 So.2d 966 (Fla.App.1982); cf. Rose v. Spa Realty Associates, 42 N.Y.2d 338, 343–44, 397 N.Y.S.2d 922, 925–26, 366 N.E.2d 1279, 1282–83 (1977). In cases not governed by the Uniform Commercial Code, Wisconsin follows the common law rule that allows a contract to be waived orally (unless within the Statute of Frauds) even though the contract provides that it can be modified only in writing. See, e.g., S & M Rotogravure Service, Inc. v. Baer, 77 Wis.2d 454, 468–69, 252 N.W.2d 913, 920 (1977). But of course the Code, which is in force in Wisconsin as in every other state (with the partial exception of Louisiana), was intended to change this rule for contracts subject to it.

Missing from the jury instruction on "modification" in this case is any reference to reliance, that is, to the incurring of costs by National Metal Crafters in reasonable reliance on assurances by Wisconsin Knife Works that late delivery would be acceptable. And although there is evidence of such reliance, it naturally was not a focus of the case, since the issue was cast as one of completed (not attempted) modification, which does not require reliance to be enforceable. National Metal Crafters must have incurred expenses in producing spade bit blanks after the original delivery dates, but whether these were reliance expenses is a separate question. Maybe National Metal Crafters would have continued to manufacture spade bit blanks anyway, in the hope of selling them to someone else. It may be significant that the stipulated counterclaim damages seem limited to the damages from the breach of a separate oral agreement regarding the maintenance of equipment used by National Metal Crafters in fulfilling the contract. The question of reliance cannot be considered so open and shut as to justify our concluding that the judge would have had to direct a verdict for National Metal Crafters, the party with the burden of proof on the issue. Nor, indeed, does National Metal Crafters argue that reliance was shown as a matter of law.

There is no need to discuss most of the other alleged errors in the conduct of the trial; they are unlikely to recur in a new trial. We do however point out that Wisconsin Knife Works' objections to the introduction of parol evidence have no merit once the issue is recast as one of waiver. The purpose of the parol evidence rule is to defeat efforts to vary by oral evidence the terms of a written instrument that the parties intended to be the fully integrated expression of their contract; it has no application when the issue is whether one of the parties later waived strict compliance with those terms. . . .

When a jury instruction is erroneous there must be a new trial unless the error is harmless. On the basis of the record before us we cannot say that the error in allowing the jury to find that the contract had been modified was harmless; but we do not want to exclude the possibility that it might be found to be so, on motion for summary judgment or otherwise, without the need for a new trial. Obviously National Metal Crafters has a strong case both that it relied on the waiver of the delivery deadlines and that there was no causal relationship between its late deliveries and the cancellation of the contract. We just are not prepared to say on the record before us that it is such a strong case as not to require submission to a jury.

REVERSED AND REMANDED.

[Judge Easterbrook's dissenting opinion is omitted.]

———

BMC Industries, Inc. v. Barth Industries, Inc.

160 F.3d 1322 (11th Cir.1998), certiorari denied, 526 U.S. 1132, 119 S.Ct. 1807, 143 L.Ed.2d 1010 (1999)

(Tjoflat, J.) "As an initial matter, we must determine whether, under the UCC, waiver must be accompanied by detrimental reliance. . . . [C]ourts disagree on whether the UCC retains this requirement. We conclude, however, that the UCC does not require consideration or detrimental reliance for waiver of a contract term.

"Our conclusion follows from the plain language of subsections [2–209(4)] and (5). While subsection (4) states that an attempted modification that fails may still constitute a waiver, subsection (5) provides that the waiver may be retracted unless the non-waiving party relies on the waiver. Consequently, the statute recognizes that waivers may exist in the absence of detrimental reliance—these are the retractable waivers referred to in subsection (5). Only this interpretation renders meaning to subsection (5), because reading subsection (4) to require detrimental reliance for all waivers means that waivers would never be retractable. See Wisconsin Knife Works v. National Metal Crafters, 781 F.2d 1280, 1291 (7th Cir.1986) (Easterbrook, J., dissenting) (noting that reading a detrimental reliance requirement into the UCC would eliminate the distinction between subsections (4) and (5)). Subsection (5) would therefore be meaningless.

"Although [some] courts have held that waiver requires reliance under the UCC, those courts have ignored the UCC's plain language. The leading case espousing this view of waiver is Wisconsin Knife Works v. National Metal Crafters, 781 F.2d 1280 (7th Cir.1986) . . . in which a panel of the Seventh Circuit addressed a contract that included a term prohibiting oral modifications, and considered whether an attempted oral modification could instead constitute a waiver. Writing for the majority, Judge Posner concluded that the UCC's subsection (2), which gives effect to 'no oral modification' provisions, would become superfluous if contract terms could be waived without detrimental reliance. Judge Posner reasoned that if attempted oral modifications that were unenforceable because of subsection (2) were nevertheless enforced as waivers under subsection (4), then subsection (2) is 'very nearly a dead letter.' Id. at 1286. According to Judge Posner, there must be some difference between modification and waiver in order for both subsections (2) and (4) to have meaning. This difference is waiver's detrimental reliance requirement.

"Judge Posner, however, ignores a fundamental difference between modifications and waivers: while a party that has agreed to a contract modification cannot cancel the modification without giving consideration for the cancellation, a party may unilaterally retract its waiver of a contract term provided it gives reasonable notice. The fact that waivers may unilaterally be retracted provides the difference between subsections (2) and (4) that allows both to have meaning. We therefore conclude that waiver under the UCC does not require detrimental reliance."

UCC § 2–209(1), (2), (4), (5)

[See Selected Source Materials Supplement]

UNIDROIT PRINCIPLES OF INTERNATIONAL COMMERCIAL CONTRACTS ART. 2.1.18

[See Selected Source Materials Supplement]

PRINCIPLES OF EUROPEAN CONTRACT LAW ART. 2.106

[See Selected Source Materials Supplement]

CHAPTER 15

BATTLE OF THE FORMS

■ ■ ■

The problems raised by form contracts have been a major preoccupation of contract-law scholars since the middle of the twentieth century. The primary areas of concern have been the enforceability of preprinted terms and the import of preprinted terms in determining whether a form sent in response to an offer constitutes an acceptance.

The phenomenon of rational ignorance plays a powerful role in both concerns. The provisions of a contract can be divided into performance and nonperformance terms. Performance terms specify the performance each party must render. All other provisions are normally nonperformance terms. The most important types of performance terms concern the description of the subject-matter of the contract, quantity, price, delivery terms, and payment terms. Nonperformance terms cover a wide range of issues, such as how and when notice of default must be given, limitations on warranties, excuse, and so forth. Most preprinted terms are nonperformance terms that concern low-probability future risks. Nonperformance terms also address matters that are peripheral to the main subject-matter of the contract, such as the right to collect and use an individual's personal data.

Call a party who prepares a form contract a form-giver, and a party who receives a form contract a form-taker. A form-giver typically offers a package consisting of a commodity (using that term in a broadly defined manner, to include goods, realty, and services) and a form contract that states the terms on which the commodity will be purchased or sold. Each part of the package, in turn, consists of a number of attributes: The commodity has physical attributes, such as size, shape, and color. The form contract has business and legal attributes, most of which are nonperformance terms. Typically, the most important performance terms—description, quantity, price, delivery, payment—will be custom-tailored to each transaction, and individually filled into the form. In contrast, the nonperformance terms and the less important performance terms (such as provisions concerning crating or notice of shipment) will typically be preprinted.

To make an optimum substantive decision, a form-taker who is choosing between a variety of commodities of a given type would carefully deliberate not only on the characteristics of the commodities, but also on the business and legal attributes of each form contract that is coupled with each commodity that he is considering. Analyzing all the terms of a form contract in this manner, however, will often be unduly costly. First, a form contract often contains a very large number of terms. Form insurance contracts, for example, often contain forty, fifty, or more terms. Moreover, the meaning and effect of the preprinted terms will very often be inaccessible to laypersons. In part, this is because the terms are often written in highly technical prose. Even if the terms are written clearly, however, the form-taker usually will be unable fully to understand their effects, because preprinted terms characteristically vary the form-taker's baseline legal rights, and most form-takers do not know their baseline legal rights. The verbal and legal obscurity of preprinted terms renders the cost of searching out and deliberating on the preprinted terms of various form contracts exceptionally high. In contrast, the low probability that these nonperformance terms will ever come into play heavily discounts the benefits of search and deliberation.

Furthermore, the length and complexity of a form contract is often not correlated to the dollar value of the transaction. Often, therefore, the cost of thorough search and deliberation on preprinted terms, let alone the cost of legal advice about the meaning and effect of the terms, would be prohibitive in relation to the benefits. A rational form-taker faced with preprinted terms whose effect he knows he will find difficult or impossible to fully understand, which involve risks that probably will never mature, which are unlikely to be worth the cost of search and deliberation, and which probably aren't subject to negotiation in any event, will typically decide to remain ignorant of many or most preprinted terms.

There is, however, a fundamental imbalance in this respect between the form-taker and the form-giver. For the form-taker, any given form contract is normally a one-shot transaction. This is one reason why the costs of searching and deliberating on the preprinted terms, or of retaining a lawyer to evaluate them, will normally far exceed the benefits of search and deliberation. For the form-giver, however, a form contract is a high-volume, repeat transaction. Thus, a rational form-giver will spend a significant amount of time and money, including money for legal services, to prepare a form contract that is optimal from his perspective. These asymmetrical incentives almost always work to heavily slant form contracts in favor of form-givers.

The law has responded to these problems through Section 2–207 of the Uniform Commercial Code, and through the common law doctrines of unfair surprise and reasonable expectations, and through related rules in the Uniform Commercial Code, which sharply limit the effect of preprinted terms in the contexts of contract formation and contract enforceability, respectively. The former issue is the subject of this Chapter. The latter issue is the subject of Chapter 16.

NOTE ON THE BATTLE OF THE FORMS

When goods are supplied by a commercial seller to a commercial buyer, in most cases there is no document covering the transaction that is called on its face a "contract." Often the buyer will send to the seller a form that the buyer calls a "purchase order." At the bottom of this form, or on the reverse side, there will appear certain preprinted terms, often loosely designated in the form as "conditions." These terms may be fairly extensive, and include shipping instructions, provisions making the order cancellable for delays in delivery, provisions covering crating charges, provisions for the arbitration of disputes, etc. Usually the purchase-order form will state that the order is given subject to the conditions stated. Generally the purchase order will request an acknowledgment, although occasionally the word acceptance is used. The buyer sometimes hopefully provides a tear sheet or a separate form, requesting the seller to sign and return this form as an acknowledgment of the order.

Often the seller, instead of accepting the buyer's purchase order, or returning the buyer's acknowledgment form, sends the buyer the seller's own form, frequently called a sales order. Or the first document may be a sales order sent by the seller to the buyer. This will be like the buyer's purchase order, and will itself be subject to certain preprinted terms or "conditions" printed at the bottom or on the back.

The chances that the preprinted terms in the sales order will coincide with those in the purchase order are negligible. Sometimes, to strengthen its position, the seller will repeat its terms (or perhaps a different set of terms) on an invoice that is sent when the goods are shipped, stating that the goods are shipped "subject to the following conditions." The buyer, anticipating that the seller will decorate the back of its invoice with fine print, may stipulate in its purchase order that if the terms stated in the invoice do not agree with the buyer's purchase order, the terms of the purchase order will control.

The result is that instead of an orderly negotiation of the terms of the sale, we have the parties engaged in a *battle of the forms*, each jockeying for position and each attempting to get the other to indicate assent to its form. Sometimes a seller's sales order is signed by the buyer, and a buyer's purchase order is signed by the seller. Thus, the same transaction is covered by two different forms, stipulating inconsistent terms. More commonly, neither party is willing to sign the other's form, so that each party states in writing its terms of the sale, but neither expressly indicates assent to the terms proposed by the other.

The battle of the forms had a special bite under the mirror-image (or ribbon-matching) rule of classical contract law. Under this rule, any difference between an offer and a purported acceptance, no matter how minor, prevented the formation of a contract. Since the seller's form and the buyer's form seldom if ever matched, the exchange of a purchase order and a sales order (or counterpart forms) would seldom if ever constitute a contract under the mirror-image rule.

But the matter did not end there. Under another common law rule, an offer can be accepted by conduct. Putting the two rules together, if no contract was formed by the exchange of forms because the two forms were not identical, but the seller shipped the goods and the buyer accepted them, a contract was deemed to have been made, consisting of the terms in whichever form was sent last. The theory was that the first form was an offer, the responding form was a counter-offer, and the goods were shipped and accepted pursuant to that counter-offer. For example, suppose the buyer began a transaction by sending a purchase order, and the seller responded by sending back a nonconforming sales order. Under the mirror-image rule, there would be no contract at that point. However, the sales order would not be without legal effect; instead, under traditional principles it would be a counter-offer. Now suppose the seller shipped the goods and the buyer accepted the shipment. The buyer was deemed to have accepted pursuant to the sales order/counter-offer, so that the terms of the resulting contract were those set by the seller. Similarly, suppose the seller began a transaction be sending a sales order, the buyer responded with a nonconforming purchase order, the seller shipped the goods, and the buyer accepted the shipment. In that case, the terms of the contract would be those set in the purchase order, because the buyer's nonconforming purchase order would be a counter-offer, and the seller's shipment would be deemed an acceptance of that counter-offer. This analysis was often called the last-shot approach, because if the goods were shipped and accepted, the terms of the contract were those set by whichever party fired the last shot in the battle of the forms.

UCC §§ 2–204(1), 2–204, 2–207

[See Selected Source Materials Supplement]

ABA Task Force Report on Article 2

16 Del.J.Corp.Law. 981, 1063–64 (1991)

"The premise that underlies [UCC] section 2–207 is that pre-printed boilerplate terms in each party's form are not read. Indeed, they cannot reasonably be expected to be read by the other party."

NOTE ON WHAT CONSTITUTES AN
ACCEPTANCE UNDER UCC § 2–207

UCC § 2–207 applies only if there has been a "definite and [seasonable] expression of acceptance," but leaves open what constitutes a definite and seasonable expression of acceptance. In most cases under § 2–207 the offeror has sent a form to the offeree; the offeree has returned to the offeror another form whose individualized (non-preprinted) terms match the individualized terms of the offer; virtually no other terms match; and the courts have explicitly or implicitly held that the return form nevertheless constitutes an "expression of acceptance" under § 2–207. Indeed, that is the paradigm case at which § 2–207 was directed.

Where, however, the parties don't employ forms, even a small difference between the offer and the response may prevent a response from being an acceptance under § 2–207, at least if the parties have been bargaining about that difference.

For example, in Koehring Co. v. Glowacki, 77 Wis.2d 497, 253 N.W.2d 64 (1977), Koehring circulated a letter listing nine items of surplus machinery that were available for sale at its plant on an "as is, where is" basis. The term "as is, where is" meant that the buyer would bear the cost and risk of loading the machinery onto its truck. Glowacki telephoned Koehring, inquiring as to price. Koehring responded that Glowacki must bid $16,500, and that the bid must be in the form of a telegram. Glowacki telegraphed a bid of only $16,000. Koehring called Glowacki, reiterating that the bid must be $16,500. Glowacki then sent a second telegram, which bid $16,500, but including the statement "FOB [free on board], our truck, your plant, loaded." The term "FOB . . . loaded" meant that the seller would bear the cost and risk of loading the machinery onto the buyer's truck. Koehring responded with a telegram "accepting" the bid, but restating that the machinery was sold "as is, where is." In a suit by Koehring, the court held that no contract had been formed:

> As the trial court properly held in the present case, before we reach the question of additional or different terms added to a contract, we must first inquire whether or not any contract ever existed. Here the defendant's telegram was an offer to purchase at a price of $16,500 "FOB, our truck, your plant, loaded." Plaintiff's response was a counteroffer to sell at the price of $16,500 on an "as is, where is" basis. There was no "meeting of the minds" or agreement of the parties prior to the exchange of telegrams. No such "meeting of the minds" or agreement resulted from the exchange of telegrams. This being so, we do not reach the issue as to whether additional or differing terms do or do not destroy an agreement of the parties since there is no valid contract in the first place.

> In the case before us, we deal with an initial and continuing absence of agreement between the parties as to whether the sales price included loading risks and costs. The second telegram of defendant, offering $16,500 "FOB, our truck, your plant, loaded," was

an offer. The responding telegram of plaintiff, all tools sold on an "as is, where is" basis, while labeled an acceptance, was actually a rejection of the defendant's offer and a counteroffer. This being the situation, it follows, as the trial court concluded, that there was here no contract or agreement between these two parties either preceding or derived from their exchange of telegrams.

———

CISG ART. 19

[See Selected Source Materials Supplement]

———

UNIDROIT PRINCIPLES OF INTERNATIONAL COMMERCIAL CONTRACTS ARTS. 2.1.12, 2.1.22

[See Selected Source Materials Supplement]

———

PRINCIPLES OF EUROPEAN CONTRACT LAW ART. 2.209

[See Selected Source Materials Supplement]

———

GARDNER ZEMKE CO. v. DUNHAM BUSH, INC.

Supreme Court of New Mexico, 1993.
115 N.M. 260, 850 P.2d 319.

FRANCHINI, JUSTICE.

This case involves a contract for the sale of goods and accordingly the governing law is the Uniform Commercial Code—Sales, as adopted in New Mexico. NMSA 1978, §§ 55–2–101 to–2–725 (Orig.Pamp. & Cum.Supp.1992) (Article 2). In the course of our discussion, we will also refer to pertinent general definitions and principles of construction found in NMSA 1978, Sections 55–1–101 to–1–209 (Orig.Pamp. & Cum.Supp.1992). Section 55–2–103 (4). The case presents us with our first opportunity to consider a classic "battle of the forms" scenario arising under Section 55–2–207. Appellant Gardner Zemke challenges the trial court's judgment that a Customer's Acknowledgment (Acknowledgment) sent by appellee manufacturer Dunham Bush, in response to a Gardner Zemke Purchase Order (Order), operated as a counteroffer, thereby providing controlling warranty terms under the contract formed by the parties. We find merit in appellants' argument and remand for the trial court's reconsideration.

I.

Acting as the general contractor on a Department of Energy (DOE) project, Gardner Zemke issued its Order to Dunham Bush for air-conditioning equipment, known as chillers, to be used in connection with the project. The Order contained a one-year manufacturer's warranty provision and the requirement that the chillers comply with specifications attached to the Order. Dunham Bush responded with its preprinted Acknowledgment containing extensive warranty disclaimers, a statement that the terms of the Acknowledgment controlled the parties' agreement, and a provision deeming silence to be acquiescence to the terms of the Acknowledgment.

The parties did not address the discrepancies in the forms exchanged and proceeded with the transaction. Dunham Bush delivered the chillers, and Gardner Zemke paid for them. Gardner Zemke alleges that the chillers provided did not comply with their specifications and that they incurred additional costs to install the nonconforming goods. Approximately five or six months after start up of the chillers, a DOE representative notified Gardner Zemke of problems with two of the chillers. In a series of letters, Gardner Zemke requested on-site warranty repairs. Through its manufacturer's representative, Dunham Bush offered to send its mechanic to the job site to inspect the chillers and absorb the cost of the service call only if problems discovered were within any component parts it provided. Further, Dunham Bush required that prior to the service call a purchase order be issued from the DOE, to be executed by Dunham Bush for payment for their services in the event their mechanic discovered problems not caused by manufacturing defects. Gardner Zemke rejected the proposal on the basis that the DOE had a warranty still in effect for the goods and would not issue a separate purchase order for warranty repairs.

Ultimately, the DOE hired an independent contractor to repair the two chillers. The DOE paid $24,245.00 for the repairs and withheld $20,000.00 from its contract with Gardner Zemke.[1] This breach of contract action then ensued, with Gardner Zemke alleging failure by Dunham Bush to provide equipment in accordance with the project plans and specifications and failure to provide warranty service.

II.

On cross-motions for summary judgment, the trial court granted partial summary judgment in favor of Dunham Bush, ruling that its Acknowledgment was a counteroffer to the Gardner Zemke Order and that

---

[1] The government has the right to set off the remaining $4,245.00 from any other Gardner Zemke government contract. *See Project Map, Inc. v. United States*, 203 Ct.Cl. 52, 486 F.2d 1375 (1973) (per curiam).

the Acknowledgment's warranty limitations and disclaimers were controlling. Gardner Zemke filed an application for interlocutory appeal from the partial summary judgment in this Court, which was denied. A bench trial was held in December 1991, and the trial court again ruled the Acknowledgment was a counter-offer which Gardner Zemke accepted by silence and that under the warranty provisions of the Acknowledgment, Gardner Zemke was not entitled to damages.

On appeal, Gardner Zemke raises two issues: (1) the trial court erred as a matter of law in ruling that the Acknowledgment was a counteroffer; and (2) Gardner Zemke proved breach of contract and contract warranty, breach of code warranties, and damages.

III.

Karl N. Llewellyn, the principal draftsman of Article 2, described it as "[t]he heart of the Code." Karl N. Llewellyn, *Why We Need the Uniform Commercial Code,* 10 U.Fla.L.Rev. 367, 378 (1957). Section 2–207 is characterized by commentators as a "crucial section of Article 2" and an "iconoclastic Code section." *Bender's Uniform Commercial Code Service* (Vol. 3, Richard W. Duesenberg & Lawrence P. King, Sales & Bulk Transfers Under The Uniform Commercial Code) § 3.01 at 3–2 (1992). Recognizing its innovative purpose and complex structure Duesenberg and King further observe Section 2–207 "is one of the most important, subtle, and difficult in the entire Code, and well it may be said that the product as it finally reads is not altogether satisfactory." *Id.* § 3.02 at 3–13.

Section 55–2–207 provides:

(1) A definite and seasonable expression of acceptance or a written confirmation which is sent within a reasonable time operates as an acceptance even though it states terms additional to or different from those offered or agreed upon, unless acceptance is expressly made conditional on assent to the additional or different terms.

(2) The additional terms are to be construed as proposals for addition to the contract. Between merchants such terms become part of the contract unless:

    (a) the offer expressly limits acceptance to the terms of the offer;

    (b) they materially alter it; or,

    (c) notification of objection to them has already been given or is given within a reasonable time after notice of them is received.

(3) Conduct by both parties which recognizes the existence of a contract is sufficient to establish a contract for sale although the writings of the parties do not otherwise establish a contract. In such

case the terms of the particular contract consist of those terms on which the writings of the parties agree, together with any supplementary terms incorporated under any other provisions of this act [this chapter].

Relying on Section 2–207(1), Gardner Zemke argues that the trial court erred in concluding that the Dunham Bush Acknowledgment was a counteroffer rather than an acceptance. Gardner Zemke asserts that even though the Acknowledgment contained terms different from or in addition to the terms of their Order, it did not make acceptance expressly conditional on assent to the different or additional terms and therefore should operate as an acceptance rather than a counteroffer.

At common law, the "mirror image" rule applied to the formation of contracts, and the terms of the acceptance had to exactly imitate or "mirror" the terms of the offer. *Idaho Power Co. v. Westinghouse Elec. Corp.*, 596 F.2d 924, 926 (9th Cir.1979). If the accepting terms were different from or additional to those in the offer, the result was a counteroffer, not an acceptance. *Id.; see also Silva v. Noble*, 85 N.M. 677, 678–79, 515 P.2d 1281, 1282–83 (1973). Thus, from a common law perspective, the trial court's conclusion that the Dunham Bush Acknowledgment was a counteroffer was correct.

However, the drafters of the Code "intended to change the common law in an attempt to conform contract law to modern day business transactions." *Leonard Pevar Co. v. Evans Prods. Co.*, 524 F.Supp. 546, 551 (D.Del.1981). As Professors White and Summers explain:

> The rigidity of the common law rule ignored the modern realities of commerce. Where preprinted forms are used to structure deals, they rarely mirror each other, yet the parties usually assume they have a binding contract and act accordingly. Section 2–207 rejects the common law mirror image rule and converts many common law counteroffers into acceptances under 2–207(1).

James J. White & Robert S. Summers, *Handbook of the Law Under the Uniform Commercial Code* § 1–3 at 29–30 (3d ed. 1988) (footnotes omitted).

On its face, Section 2–207(1) provides that a document responding to an offer and purporting to be an acceptance will be an acceptance, despite the presence of additional and different terms. Where merchants exchange preprinted forms and the essential contract terms agree, a contract is formed under Section 2–207(1). Duesenberg & King, § 3.04 at 3–47 to–49. A responding document will fall outside of the provisions of Section 2–207(1) and convey a counteroffer, only when its terms differ radically from the offer, or when "acceptance is expressly made conditional on assent to the additional or different terms"—whether a contract is formed under Section 2–207(1) here turns on the meaning given this phrase.

Dunham Bush argues that the language in its Acknowledgment makes acceptance expressly conditional on assent to the additional or different terms set forth in the Acknowledgment. The face of the Acknowledgment states:

> IT IS UNDERSTOOD THAT OUR ACCEPTANCE OF THIS ORDER IS SUBJECT TO THE TERMS AND CONDITIONS ENUMERATED ON THE REVERSE SIDE HEREOF, IT BEING STRICTLY UNDERSTOOD THAT THESE TERMS AND CONDITIONS BECOME A PART OF THIS ORDER AND THE ACKNOWLEDGMENT THEREOF.

The following was among the terms and conditions on the reverse side of the Acknowledgment.

> Failure of the Buyer to object in writing within five (5) days of receipt thereof to Terms of Sale contained in the Seller's acceptance and/or acknowledgment, or other communications, shall be deemed an acceptance of such Terms of Sale by Buyer.

In support of its contention that the above language falls within the "expressly conditional" provision of Section 2–207, Dunham Bush urges that we adopt the view taken by the First Circuit in *Roto-Lith, Ltd. v. F.P. Bartlett & Co.,* 297 F.2d 497 (1st Cir.1962). There, Roto-Lith sent an order for goods to Bartlett, which responded with an acknowledgment containing warranty disclaimers, a statement that the acknowledgment reflected the terms of the sale, and a provision that if the terms were unacceptable Roto-Lith should notify Bartlett at once. *Id.* at 498–99. Roto-Lith did not protest the terms of the acknowledgment and accepted and paid for the goods. The court held the Bartlett acknowledgment was a counteroffer that became binding on Roto-Lith with its acceptance of the goods, reasoning that "a response which states a condition materially altering the obligation solely to the disadvantage of the offeror" falls within the "expressly conditional" language of 2–207(1). *Id.* at 500.

Dunham Bush suggests that this Court has demonstrated alliance with the principles of *Roto-Lith* in *Fratello v. Socorro Electric Cooperative, Inc.,* 107 N.M. 378, 758 P.2d 792 (1988). *Fratello* involved the terms of a settlement agreement in which one party sent the other party a proposed stipulated order containing an additional term. In the context of the common law, we cited *Roto-Lith* in support of the proposition that the additional term made the proposed stipulation a counteroffer. *Fratello,* 107 N.M. at 381, 758 P.2d at 795.

We have never adopted *Roto-Lith* in the context of the Code and decline to do so now. While ostensibly interpreting Section 2–207(1), the First Circuit's analysis imposes the common law doctrine of offer and acceptance on language designed to avoid the common law result. *Roto-Lith* has been almost uniformly criticized by the courts and commentators as an aberration on Article 2 jurisprudence. *Leonard Pevar Co.,* 524 F.Supp. at 551 (and cases cited therein); Duesenberg & King, § 3.05[1] at 3–61 to–62; White & Summers, § 1–3 at 36–37.

Mindful of the purpose of Section 2–207 and the spirit of Article 2, we find the better approach suggested in *Dorton v. Collins & Aikman Corp.,* 453 F.2d 1161 (6th Cir.1972). In *Dorton,* the Sixth Circuit considered terms in acknowledgment forms sent by Collins & Aikman similar to the terms in the Dunham Bush Acknowledgment. The Collins & Aikman acknowledgments provided that acceptance of orders was subject to the terms and conditions of their form, together with at least seven methods in which a buyer might acquiesce to their terms, including receipt and retention of their form for ten days without objection. *Id.* at 1167–68.

Concentrating its analysis on the concept of the offeror's "assent," the Court reasoned that it was not enough to make acceptance expressly conditional on additional or different terms; instead, the expressly conditional nature of the acceptance must be predicated on the offeror's "assent" to those terms. *Id.* at 1168. The Court concluded that the "expressly conditional" provision of Section 2–207(1) "was intended to apply only to an acceptance which clearly reveals that the offeree is unwilling to proceed with the transaction unless he is assured of the offeror's assent to the additional or different terms therein." *Id.* This approach has been widely accepted. *Diatom, Inc. v. Pennwalt Corp.,* 741 F.2d 1569, 1576–77 (10th Cir.1984); *Reaction Molding Technologies, Inc. v. General Elec. Co.,* 588 F.Supp. 1280, 1288 (E.D.Pa.1984); *Idaho Power Co.,* 596 F.2d at 926–27.

We agree with the court in *Dorton* that the inquiry focuses on whether the offeree clearly and unequivocally communicated to the offeror that its willingness to enter into a bargain was conditioned on the offeror's "assent" to additional or different terms. An exchange of forms containing identical dickered terms, such as the identity, price, and quantity of goods, and conflicting undickered boilerplate provisions, such as warranty terms and a provision making the bargain subject to the terms and conditions of the offeree's document, however worded, will not propel the transaction into the "expressly conditional" language of Section 2–207(1) and confer the status of counteroffer on the responsive document.

While *Dorton* articulates a laudable rule, it fails to provide a means for the determination of when a responsive document becomes a counteroffer. We adopt the rule in *Dorton* and add that whether an acceptance is made expressly conditional on assent to different or additional terms is dependent on the commercial context of the transaction. Official Comment 2 to Section 55–2–207 suggests that "[u]nder this article a proposed deal which in commercial understanding has in fact been closed is recognized as a contract." While the comment applies broadly and envisions recognition of contracts formed under a variety of circumstances, it guides us to application of the concept of "commercial understanding" to the question of formation. *See* 2 William D. Hawkland, *Uniform Commercial Code Series* § 2–207:02 at 160 (1992) ("The basic question is whether, in commercial understanding, the proposed deal has been closed.").

Discerning whether "commercial understanding" dictates the existence of a contract requires consideration of the objective manifestations of the parties' understanding of the bargain. It requires consideration of the parties' activities and interaction during the making of the bargain; and when available, relevant evidence of course of performance, Section 55–2–208; and course of dealing and usage of the trade, Section 55–1–205. The question guiding the inquiry should be whether the offeror could reasonably believe that in the context of the commercial setting in which the parties were acting, a contract had been formed. This determination requires a very fact specific inquiry. *See* John E. Murray, Jr., *Section 2–207 Of The Uniform Commercial Code: Another Word About Incipient Unconscionability,* 39 U.Pitt.L.Rev., 597, 632–34 (1978) (discussing *Dorton* and identifying the commercial understanding of the reasonable buyer as the "critical inquiry").

Our analysis does not yield an iron clad rule conducive to perfunctory application. However, it does remain true to the spirit of Article 2, as it calls the trial court to consider the commercial setting of each transaction and the reasonable expectations and beliefs of the parties acting in that setting. *Id.* at 600; § 55–1–102(2)(b) (stating one purpose of the act is "to permit the continued expansion of commercial practices through custom, usage and agreement of the parties").

The trial court's treatment of this issue did not encompass the scope of the inquiry we envision. We will not attempt to make the factual determination necessary to characterize this transaction on the record before us. Not satisfied that the trial court adequately considered all of the relevant factors in determining that the Dunham Bush Acknowledgment functioned as a counteroffer, we remand for reconsideration of the question.

In the event the trial court concludes that the Dunham Bush Acknowledgment constituted an acceptance, it will face the question of which terms will control in the exchange of forms. In the interest of judicial economy, and because this determination is a question of law, we proceed with our analysis.

IV.

The Gardner Zemke Order provides that the "[m]anufacturer shall replace or repair all parts found to be defective during initial year of use at no additional cost." Because the Order does not include any warranty terms, Article 2 express and implied warranties arise by operation of law.

Section 55–2–313 (express warranties), § 55–2–314 (implied warranty of merchantability), § 55–2–315 (implied warranty of fitness for a particular purpose). The Dunham Bush Acknowledgment contains the following warranty terms.

> WARRANTY: We agree that the apparatus manufactured by the Seller will be free from defects in material and workmanship for a period of one year under normal use and service and when properly installed: and our obligation under this agreement is limited solely to repair or replacement at our option, at our factories, of any part or parts thereof which shall within one year from date of original installation or 18 months from date of shipment from factory to the original purchaser, whichever date may first occur be returned to us with transportation charges prepaid which our examination shall disclose to our satisfaction to have been defective. THIS AGREEMENT TO REPAIR OR REPLACE DEFECTIVE PARTS IS EXPRESSLY IN LIEU OF AND IS HEREBY DISCLAIMER OF ALL OTHER EXPRESS WARRANTIES, AND IS IN LIEU OF AND IN DISCLAIMER AND EXCLUSION OF ANY IMPLIED WARRANTIES OF MERCHANTABILITY AND FITNESS FOR A PARTICULAR PURPOSE, AS WELL AS ALL OTHER IMPLIED WARRANTIES, IN LAW OR EQUITY, AND OF ALL OTHER OBLIGATIONS OR LIABILITIES ON OUR PART. THERE ARE NO WARRANTIES WHICH EXTEND BEYOND THE DESCRIPTION HEREOF. . . . Our obligation to repair or replace shall not apply to any apparatus which shall have been repaired or altered outside our factory in any way.

The one proposition on which most courts and commentators agree at this point in the construction of the statute is that Section 2–207(3) applies only if a contract is not found under Section 2–207(1). *Dorton*, 453 F.2d at 1166; Duesenberg & King, § 3.03[1] at 3–40; 2 Hawkland, § 2–207:04 at 178–79; White & Summers, § 1–3 at 35. However, there are courts that disagree even with this proposition. *See Westinghouse Elec. Corp. v. Nielsons, Inc.*, 647 F.Supp. 896 (D.Colo.1986) (dealing with different terms, finding a contract under 2–207(1) and proceeding to apply 2–207(2) and 2–207(3)).

The language of the statute makes it clear that "additional" terms are subject to the provisions of Section 2–207(2). However, a continuing controversy rages among courts and commentators concerning the treatment of "different" terms in a Section 2–207 analysis. While Section 2–207(1) refers to both "additional or different" terms, Section 2–207(2) refers only to "additional" terms. The omission of the word "different" from Section 55–2–207(2) gives rise to the questions of whether "different" terms are to be dealt with under the provisions of Section 2–207(2), and if not, how they are to be treated. That the terms in the Acknowledgment are "different" rather than "additional" guides the remainder of our inquiry and requires that we join the fray. Initially, we briefly survey the critical and judicial approaches to the problem posed by "different" terms.

One view is that, in spite of the omission, "different" terms are to be analyzed under Section 2–207(2). 2 Hawkland, § 2–207:03 at 168. The foundation for this position is found in Comment 3, which provides "[w]hether or not additional or different terms will become part of the agreement depends upon the provisions of Subsection (2)." Armed with this statement in Comment 3, proponents point to the ambiguity in the distinction between "different" and "additional" terms and argue that the distinction serves no clear purpose. *Steiner v. Mobil Oil Corp.,* 20 Cal.3d 90, 141 Cal.Rptr. 157, 165–66 n. 5, 569 P.2d 751, 759–60 n. 5 (1977); *Boese-Hilburn Co. v. Dean Machinery Co.,* 616 S.W.2d 520, 527 (Mo.Ct.App.1981). Following this rationale in this case, and relying on the observation in Comment 4 that a clause negating implied warranties would "materially alter" the contract, the Dunham Bush warranty terms would not become a part of the contract, and the Gardner Zemke warranty provision, together with the Article 2 warranties would control. § 55–2–207(2)(b).

Another approach is suggested by Duesenberg and King who comment that the ambiguity found in the treatment of "different" and "additional" terms is more judicially created than statutorily supported. While conceding that Comment 3 "contributes to the confusion," they also admonish that "the Official Comments do not happen to be the statute." Duesenberg & King, § 3.05 at 3–52. Observing that "the drafters knew what they were doing, and that they did not sloppily fail to include the term 'different' when drafting subsection (2)," Duesenberg and King postulate that a "different" term in a responsive document operating as an acceptance can never become a part of the parties' contract under the plain language of the statute. *Id.* § 3.03[1] at 3–38.

The reasoning supporting this position is that once an offeror addresses a subject it implicitly objects to variance of that subject by the offeree, thereby preventing the "different" term from becoming a part of the contract by prior objection and obviating the need to refer to "different" terms in Section 55–2–207(2). *Id.* § 3.05[1] at 3–77; *Air Prods. & Chems. Inc. v. Fairbanks Morse, Inc.,* 58 Wis.2d 193, 206 N.W.2d 414, 423–25 (1973). Professor Summers lends support to this position. White & Summers, § 1–3 at 34. Although indulging a different analysis, following this view in the case before us creates a result identical to that flowing from application of the provisions of Section 2–207(2) as discussed above—the Dunham Bush warranty provisions fall out, and the stated Gardner Zemke and Article 2 warranty provisions apply.

Yet a third analysis arises from Comment 6, which in pertinent part states:

> Where clauses on confirming forms sent by both parties conflict each party must be assumed to object to a clause of the other conflicting with one on the confirmation sent by himself. As a result the requirement that there be notice of objection which is found in Subsection (2) is satisfied and the conflicting terms do not become a part of the contract. The contract then consists of the terms originally expressly agreed to, terms on which the confirmations agree, and terms supplied by this act, including Subsection (2).

The import of Comment 6 is that "different" terms cancel each other out and that existing applicable code provisions stand in their place. The obvious flaws in Comment 6 are the use of the words "confirming forms," suggesting the Comment applies only to variant confirmation forms and not variant offer and acceptance forms, and the reference to Subsection 55–2–207(2)—arguably dealing only with "additional" terms—in the context of "different" terms. Of course, Duesenberg and King remind us that Comment 6 "is only a comment, and a poorly drawn one at that." Duesenberg & King, § 3.05[1] at 3–79.

The analysis arising from Comment 6, however, has found acceptance in numerous jurisdictions including the Tenth Circuit. *Daitom, Inc. v. Pennwalt Corp.,* 741 F.2d 1569, 1578–79 (10th Cir.1984). Following a discussion similar to the one we have just indulged, the court found this the preferable approach. *Id.* at 1579; *accord Southern Idaho Pipe & Steel Co. v. Cal-Cut Pipe & Supply, Inc.,* 98 Idaho 495, 567 P.2d 1246, 1254–55 (1977), *appeal dismissed and cert. denied,* 434 U.S. 1056, 98 S.Ct. 1225, 55 L.Ed.2d 757 (1978). Professor White also finds merit in this analysis. White & Summers, § 1–3 at 33–35. Application of this approach here cancels out the parties' conflicting warranty terms and allows the warranty provisions of Article 2 to control.

We are unable to find comfort or refuge in concluding that any one of the three paths drawn through the contours of Section 2–207 is more consistent with or true to the language of the statute. We do find that the analysis relying on Comment 6 is the most consistent with the purpose and spirit of the Code in general and Article 2 in particular. We are mindful that the overriding goal of Article 2 is to discern the bargain struck by the contracting parties. However, there are times where the conduct of the parties makes realizing that goal impossible. In such cases, we find guidance in the Code's commitment to fairness, Section 55–1–102(3); good faith, Sections 55–1–203 & –2–103 (1)(b); and conscionable conduct, Section 55–2–302.

While Section 2–207 was designed to avoid the common law result that gave the advantage to the party sending the last form, we cannot conclude that the statute was intended to shift that advantage to the party sending the first form. Such a result will generally follow from the first two analyses discussed. We adopt the third analysis as the most even-handed resolution of a difficult problem. We are also aware that under this analysis even though the conflicting terms cancel out, the Code may provide a term similar to one rejected. We agree with Professor White that "[a]t least a term so supplied has the merit of being a term that the draftsmen considered fair." White & Summers, § 1–3 at 35.

Due to our disposition of this case, we do not address the second issue raised by Gardner Zemke. On remand, should the trial court conclude a contract was formed under Section 2–207(1), the conflicting warranty provisions in the parties' forms will cancel out, and the warranty provisions of Article 2 will control.

IT IS SO ORDERED.

BACA, J., and PATRICIO M. SERNA, DISTRICT JUDGE (sitting by designation).

NOTE ON GARDNER ZEMKE

The rule approved in *Gardner Zemke,* that when a contract is formed under UCC § 2–207, conflicting terms in the offer and acceptance cancel each other out, is commonly referred to as the knockout rule, because under the rule conflicting terms knock each other out of the contract. In Dorton v. Collins & Aikman Corp., 453 F.2d 1161 (6th Cir.1972), the court applied the knockout rule where one of the conflicting terms was implied, rather than express.

NOTE ON THE MEANING OF "MATERIALLY ALTER" UNDER UCC § 2–207(2)(b)

Notwithstanding the knockout rule, a contract formed under UCC § 2–207 (1) may include important terms that are neither in both forms, supplied by other provisions of Article 2, nor supplied by trade usage. In particular, important terms may be added by an acceptance, if the offeror fails to either (1) expressly limit acceptance to the terms of the offer under (subsection (2)(a)), (2) object to the added terms in the acceptance under (subsection (2)(c)), or (3) include contrary terms in the offer so that both the offeror's terms and the offeree's added terms drop away under the knockout rule.

It is true that under subsection (2)(b), a term that is added by an acceptance does not become part of the contract if the term would "materially alter" the contract. Furthermore, in general usage a term in a contract would be considered "material" if it had economic significance or would be likely to affect a party's decision whether to enter into the contract. Accordingly, if the language of subsection (2)(b) was given its ordinary meaning, an added term that is economically significant, or would be likely to affect a party's decision whether to enter into the contract, would be excluded under that subsection. However, the Official Comment to Section 2–207 utilizes a different test for materiality—whether the added term would result in surprise or hardship. So, for example, the comment states:

> 4. Examples of typical clauses which would normally "materially alter" the contract and so result in surprise or hardship if incorporated without express awareness by the other party are: a clause negating such standard warranties as that of merchantability or fitness for a particular purpose in circumstances in which either warranty normally attaches ... [or] a clause requiring that complaints be made in a time materially shorter than customary or reasonable.

> 5. Examples of clauses which involve no element of unreasonable surprise and which therefore are to be incorporated in the contract unless notice of objection is seasonably given are: a clause setting forth and perhaps enlarging slightly upon the seller's exemption due to supervening causes beyond his control, similar to those covered by the provision of this Article on merchant's excuse by failure of presupposed conditions or ... a clause fixing a reasonable time for complaints within customary limits ...; a clause providing for interest on overdue invoices or fixing the seller's standard credit terms where they are within the range of trade practice and do not limit any credit bargained for; a clause limiting the right of rejection for defects which fall within the customary trade tolerances for acceptance "with adjustment" or otherwise limiting remedy in a reasonable manner (see Sections 2–718 and 2–719).

Relying on the test and illustrations set out in the Official Comment, a number of cases have upheld the inclusion of additional terms in an acceptance, even though the terms were material in the ordinary sense of that term, on the ground that they did not result in surprise or hardship. For example, in Aceros Prefabricados, S.A. v. TradeArbed, Inc., 282 F.3d 92 (2d Cir. 2002), the court held that an added term in the acceptance that required all disputes to be arbitrated did not result in a material alteration of the contract under subsection (2)(b):

> A material alteration is one that would "result in surprise or hardship if incorporated without express awareness by the other party." ... U.C.C. § 2–207 cmt. 4; *Bayway Ref. [Co. v. Oxygenated Mktg. & Trading A.G.*, 215 F.3d 219,] 224 (2d. Cir. 2000). Surprise includes both a subjective element of what a party actually knew and an objective element of what a party should have known. *Id.* We have

stated that "[a] profession of surprise and raised eyebrows are not enough." *Id.* Instead, "[t]o carry [its] burden . . . [the nonassenting] party must establish that, under the circumstances, it cannot be presumed that a reasonable merchant would have consented to the additional term." *Id.*

Similarly, in Southern Illinois Riverboat Casino Cruises, Inc. v. Triangle Insulation and Sheet Metal Co., 302 F.3d 667 (7th Cir. 2002), the court held that the addition of a term in an acceptance that significantly limited the buyer's remedies did not result in a material alteration of the contract under Subsection 2(b).

Another issue in this context is the meaning of the "hardship" test in the Comment to section 2–207. Most cases have treated "hardship" as a criterion that is independent of surprise in determining whether a term constitutes a material alteration under UCC § 2–207(2)(b). For example, in Maxon Corp. v. Tyler Pipe Industries, Inc., 497 N.E.2d 570 (Ind.App. 1986), the court said:

> . . . [E]ven if Tyler [the offeror] was not surprised by the indemnity clause in Maxon's invoice, the clause is nevertheless a material alteration if its incorporation without Tyler's express awareness would result in hardship.

> There can be no doubt that Maxon's indemnity clause would impose serious hardship if incorporated without Tyler's express awareness. By its very nature, a clause which shifts liability from a negligent party to an innocent party imposes hardship. Accordingly, we hold that Maxon's indemnity clause constitutes a material alteration as a matter of law.

Similarly, in Horning Co. v. Falconer Glass Industries, Inc., 730 F.Supp. 962 (S.D.Ind.1990), the court held that although a term limiting consequential damages was not surprising because of industry practice, the term did not become part of the contract, because it would result in hardship.

Some cases, however, suggest or imply that if an added term is not surprising it will not be deemed to cause hardship. Union Carbide Corp. v. Oscar Mayer Foods Corp., 947 F.2d 1333 (7th Cir. 1991); cf *Aceros,* supra.

NOTE ON THE "EXPRESSLY MADE CONDITIONAL" CLAUSE

Under section 2–207, the inclusion of an "expressly made conditional" or "conditional-assent" provision in a response to an offer can have significant consequences. The question then arises, what kind of language is necessary to constitute such a provision? Some courts have effectively held that unless language in a response to an offer virtually tracks the expressly made conditional clause of UCC § 2–207(1) it will not be treated as a conditional assent under that section. In Dorton v. Collins & Aikman Corp., 453 F.2d 1161 (6th Cir.1972), cited with approval in *Gardner Zemke,* the court said, "In order to fall within [the conditional-assent] proviso, it is not enough that an acceptance is expressly conditional on additional or different terms; rather, an acceptance must be *expressly* conditional on the offeror's *assent* to those terms. Viewing the Subsection (1) proviso within the context of the rest of that Subsection and within the policies of Section 2–207 itself, we believe that it was intended to apply only to an acceptance which clearly reveals that the offeree is unwilling to proceed with the transaction unless he is assured of the offeror's assent to the additional or different terms therein. . . . That the acceptance is predicated on the offeror's assent must be 'directly and distinctly stated or expressed rather than implied or left to inference.' Webster's Third International Dictionary (defining 'express')."

Other courts have taken a less stringent view. For example, in Step-Saver Data Systems, Inc. v. Wyse Technology, 939 F.2d 91 (3d Cir.1991), the court said:

> To determine whether a writing constitutes a conditional acceptance, courts have established [various] tests. . . .
>
> [Under one approach an acceptance is] conditional when certain key words or phrases are used, such as a written confirmation stating that "the terms of the confirmation are the only ones upon which we will accept orders." [Another] approach requires the offeree to demonstrate an unwillingness to proceed with the transaction unless the additional or different terms are included in the contract.
>
> Although we are not certain that these . . . two approaches would generate differing answers, we adopt the [latter] approach for our analysis because it best reflects the understanding of commercial transactions developed in the UCC. . . .

NOTE ON THE EFFECT OF CONFIRMATIONS WITH ADDITIONAL TERMS

It may come as a surprise that under UCC § 2–207, it is possible for additional terms to become part of a contract even if the terms are not proposed until after the contract is made. As pointed out in Aceros Prefabricados, S.A. v. TradeArbed ["TA"], 282 F.3d 92 (2d Cir. 2002):

> Under [the UCC] an expression of acceptance or written confirmation that sets forth terms in addition to those initially agreed upon will not defeat formation of a binding contract. Instead, a contract will be found and the additional terms . . . are then treated as "proposals" for addition to the contract. . . . [Emphasis added.] An Official Comment to section 2–207 makes clear the applicability of that provision to these two situations:
>
> > Under this Article a proposed deal which in commercial understanding has in fact been closed is recognized as a contract.

Therefore, any additional matter contained *either in the writing intended to close the deal or in a later confirmation* falls within subsection (2) and must be regarded as a proposal for an added term. . . .

. . . U.C.C. § 2–207 cmt. 2. Therefore, were we to find that the contract between Aceros and TA was formed on January 12, as Aceros claims and as the district court held, then the three confirmation orders would constitute written confirmations stating terms additional to the January 12 agreement, and analysis would proceed under section 2–207(2).*

Were we to agree instead with TA's argument that each of its order confirmations served as a separate acceptance of individual prior offers by Aceros to purchase steel, the confirmations would then constitute acceptances proposing additional terms and analysis would likewise proceed under section 2–207 (2), albeit of three individual contracts. Both contract formation scenarios lead us to the same conclusion regarding the [effect of the additional term].

Of course, an additional term in a confirmation, like an additional term in an acceptance, will not become part of a contract if it is excluded under section 2–207(2) (a), (b), or (c), or by the knockout rule.

Transwestern Pipeline Co. v. Monsanto Co.

46 Cal.App.4th 502, 53 Cal.Rptr.2d 887 (1996)

Monsanto sold a lubricant called Turbinol to Texas Eastern during a twelve-year period. The Turbinol was sold for use by Texas Eastern's subsidiary, Transwestern, a pipeline company. It turned out that Turbinol contained PCBs, a chemical that poses a substantial risk of environmental contamination. Some of the PCBs ended up in a pipeline owned by SoCalGas. Transwestern paid SoCalGas's cleanup costs, and then sued Monsanto for indemnification.

Monsanto's acceptances of Texas Eastern's purchase orders for Turbinol had been expressly made conditional on Turbinol's assent to the additional terms in Monsanto's sales-invoice forms. These forms disclaimed liability for consequential damages, and limited the buyer's damages to the purchase price. Monsanto contended that no contract was formed under UCC §§ 2–207(1) and (2), because of the expressly-made-conditional provisions, and that under § 2–207 (3) the provisions in the sales invoices became "supplementary terms" of the contracts as a result of the parties' course of dealing over a twelve-year period. Held, for Transwestern:

(Johnson, A.J.) "We agree with Monsanto [that] the 'supplementary terms' referred to in section [2–207(3)] may include terms incorporated as a result of

---

*　　Emphasis by the court. (Footnote by ed.)

the parties' course of dealing. Subdivision (3) refers to 'supplementary terms incorporated under any other provisions of this code.' Section [1–201], subdivision (3) defines an 'agreement' as: "[T]he bargain of the parties in fact as found in their language or by implication from other circumstances including course of dealing . . .

"Thus, the issue boils down to whether the exchange of forms containing inconsistent provisions as to liability and remedies, over a long period of time, can 'fairly be regarded as establishing a common basis of understanding' between the parties as to their respective liability and remedies.

"Common sense tells us the mere exchange of forms containing inconsistent terms, for however long a period, cannot establish a common understanding between the parties as to which set of conflicting terms is part of their contract. Although Monsanto repeatedly stated in its invoices its acceptance was conditioned on assent to its liability limiters, Texas Eastern never expressed such assent. Moreover, Texas Eastern's purchase orders repeatedly stated terms and conditions which contained no limitations on Monsanto's liability. Under these circumstances, we see no reason why Monsanto's form disclaiming liability and limiting Texas Eastern's remedies should be accepted over Texas Eastern's form which contained no such limitations. Each party is equally entitled to claim its terms and conditions constituted the parties' 'course of dealing.' . . . Furthermore, the fact this battle of the forms went on for 12 years makes Monsanto's argument even less tenable. The longer such a battle continues, the more obvious it is the parties have not reached an agreement over the terms in dispute."

———

JOM, Inc. v. Adell Plastics, Inc.

193 F.3d 47, 53 (1st Cir. 1999)

"Section 2–207 . . . affords three main avenues to contract formation. . . . First, if the parties exchange forms with divergent terms, yet the seller's invoice does not state that its acceptance is made 'expressly conditional' on the buyer's assent to any additional or different terms in the invoice, a contract is formed, and its precise terms are determined through recourse to the three-part test in § 2–207(2).

"Second, if the seller does make its acceptance 'expressly conditional' on the buyer's assent to any additional or divergent terms in the seller's invoice, the invoice is merely a counteroffer, and a contract is formed [under § 2–207(1)] only when the buyer expresses its affirmative acceptance of the seller's counteroffer. Unlike the 'mirror image' rule at common law, however, the seller's invoice is not deemed 'expressly conditional' under § 2–207 merely because its terms do not *match* the terms of the buyer's offer. Rather, to be deemed 'expressly conditional,' the seller's invoice must place the buyer on unambiguous notice that the invoice is a mere counteroffer. *See* 1 James J.

White & Robert S. Summers, Uniform Commercial Code § 1–3 at 20 (4th ed. 1995) (noting that 'express conditionality' is '*not* easily invoked').

"Finally, where for any reason the exchange of forms does not result in contract formation (*e.g.,* the buyer 'expressly limits acceptance to the terms of [its offer]' under § 2–207(2)(a), or the buyer does not accept the seller's counteroffer under the second clause of § 2–207(1)), a contract nonetheless is formed [under § 2–207(3)] if their *subsequent conduct*—for instance, the seller ships and the buyer accepts the goods—demonstrates that the parties *believed* that a binding agreement had been formed. The terms of their agreement would then be determined under the 'default' test in § 2–207(3), which implicitly incorporates the criteria prescribed in § 2–207(2)."

———

CHAPTER 16

CONSUMER FORM CONTRACTS

■ ■ ■

This Chapter concerns rules that often are associated with consumer form contracts though the rules are of more general applicability. In the "battle of the forms," generally both parties are firms and each firm argues its form governs a transaction. In the cases considered in this Chapter, generally one party is an individual and the other party is a firm. The Chapter begins with cases in which a firm seeks to hold an individual to a term in its form that the individual has not read. Section 1 concerns rules that treat everyday actions, such as purchasing a good in a package that contains a form, as the legal equivalent of signing the form. Section 2 concerns UCC rules that guard against unfair surprise and protect reasonable expectations. Section 3 concerns the common law reasonable expectations doctrine and related doctrines. The Chapter closes in Section 4 with cases in which an individual seeks to enforce a term in a document that was promulgated by a firm as a statement of the firm's policies and practices.

––––––––––

LLEWELLYN, THE COMMON LAW TRADITION: DECIDING APPEALS
362–371 (1960).

The impetus to the form-pad is clear, for any business unit: by standardizing terms, and by standardizing even the spot on the form where any individually dickered term appears, one saves all the time and skill otherwise needed to dig out and record the meaning of variant language; one makes check-up, totaling, follow-through, etc., into routine operations; one has duplicates (in many colors) available for the administration of a multidepartment business; and so on more. The content of the standardized terms accumulates experience, it avoids or reduces legal risks and also confers all kinds of operating leeways and advantages, all without need of either consulting counsel from instance to instance or of bargaining with the other parties. Not to be overlooked, either, is the tailoring of the crude misfitting hand-me-down pattern of the "general law" "in the absence of agreement" to the particular detailed working needs of your own line of business—whether apartment rentals, stock brokerage, international grain trade, installment selling of appliances, flour milling, sugar beet raising, or insurance. It would be a heartwarming scene, a triumph of private attention to what is essentially private self-government in the lesser transactions of life or in those areas too specialized for the blunt, slow tools of the legislature—if only all businessmen and all their lawyers would be reasonable.

But power, like greed, if it does not always corrupt, goes easily to the head. So that the form-agreements tend either at once or over the years, and often by whole lines of trade, into a massive and almost terrifying jug-handled character; the one party lays his head into the mouth of a lion— either, and mostly, without reading the fine print, or occasionally in hope and expectation (not infrequently solid) that it will be a sweet and gentle lion. The more familiar instances, perhaps, are the United Realtors' Standard Lease, almost any bank's collateral note or agreement, almost any installment sale form, an accident insurance policy, a steamship ticket, a beet sugar refinery contract with a farmer or a flour miller's with its customer; or, on a lesser scale, the standard nonwarranty given by seed companies or auto manufacturers. In regard to such, one notes four things: (1) sometimes language which seems at first sight horrifying may have good human and economic stimulus; thus, suits for loss of crop before a farmer jury are pretty terrible things to face for the price of a few bags of seed; and (2) there are crooked claims and there are irrationally unreasonable ones—each with its jury risk—as well as solid ones; and only a clause which in law bars the claim absolutely can free an outfit like an insurance company to deal fairly though "in its discretion" with the latter class. On the other hand, (3) boiler-plate clauses can and often do run far beyond any such need or excuse, sometimes . . . involving flagrant trickery; and (4) not all "dominant" parties are nice lions, and even nice lions can make mistakes.

There is a fifth and no less vital thing to note: Where the form is drawn with a touch of Mr. Dooley's "gentlemanly restraint," or where, as with the overseas grain contracts or the Pacific Coast dried fruit contracts or the Worth Street Rules on textiles, two-fisted bargainers on either side have worked out in the form a balanced code to govern the particular line or trade or industry, there is every reason for a court to assume both fairness and wisdom in the terms, and to seek in first instance to learn, understand, and fit both its own thinking and its action into the whole design. Contracts of this kind (so long as reasonable in the net) are a road to better than official-legal regulation of our economic life. . . .

. . . [T]he true answer to the whole problem seems, amusingly, to be one which could occur to any court or any lawyer, at any time, as readily as to a scholar who had spent a lifetime on the subject—though I doubt if it could occur to anyone without the inquiry and analysis in depth which we owe to the scholarly work.

The answer, I suggest, is this: Instead of thinking about "assent" to boilerplate clauses, we can recognize that so far as concerns the specific, there is no assent at all. What has in fact been assented to, specifically, are the few dickered terms, and the broad type of the transaction, and but one thing more. That one thing more is a blanket assent (not a specific assent) to any not unreasonable or indecent terms the seller may have on his form, which do not alter or eviscerate the reasonable meaning of the dickered terms. The fine print which has not been read has no business to cut under the reasonable meaning of those dickered terms which constitute the dominant and only real expression of agreement. . . .

The queer thing is that where the transaction occurs without the fine print present, courts do not find this general line of approach too hard to understand: thus . . . [I cannot] see a court having trouble, where a short memo agrees in due course to sign "our standard contract," in rejecting an outrageous form as not being fairly within the reasonable meaning of the term. The clearest case to see is the handing over of a blank check: no court, judging as between the parties, would fail to reach for the circumstances, in determining whether the amount filled in had gone beyond the reasonable.

Why, then, can we not face the fact where boiler-plate is present? There has been an arm's length deal, with dickered terms. There has been accompanying that basic deal another which, if not on any fiduciary basis, at least involves a plain expression of confidence, asked and accepted, with a corresponding limit on the powers granted: the boiler-plate is assented to en bloc, "unsight, unseen," on the implicit assumption and to the full extent that (1) it does not alter or impair the fair meaning of the dickered terms when read alone, and (2) that its terms are neither in the particular nor in the net manifestly unreasonable and unfair. Such is the reality, and I see nothing in the way of a court's operating on that basis, to truly effectuate the only intention which can in reason be worked out as common to the two parties, granted good faith. And if the boiler-plate party is not playing in good faith, there is law enough to bar that fact from benefiting it. We had a hundred years of sales law in which any sales transaction with explicit words resulted in two several contracts for the one consideration: that of sale, and the collateral one of warranty. The idea is applicable here, for better reason: any contract with boiler-plate results in *two* several contracts: the *dickered* deal, and the collateral one of *supplementary* boiler-plate.

Rooted in sense, history, and simplicity, it is an answer which could occur to anyone.

———

SECTION 1. "SHRINKWRAP," "CLICKWRAP," AND "BROWSEWRAP" AGREEMENTS

DeFontes v. Dell, Inc.

Supreme Court of Rhode Island, 2009.
984 A.2d 1061.

WILLIAMS, RETIRED CHIEF JUSTICE. The defendants, Dell, Inc. f/k/a Dell Computer Corp. (Dell), Dell Catalog Sales LP (Dell Catalog), Dell Marketing LP (Dell Marketing), QualxServ, LLC (QualxServ), and BancTec, Inc. (BancTec), collectively (defendants), appeal from a Superior Court order denying their motion to stay proceedings and compel arbitration. This case is the first of two companion cases now before this Court. *See Long v. Dell Inc.*, No.2007–346–M.P., 984 A.2d 1074 (R.I., filed Dec. 14, 2009). It arises out of a long-frustrated putative class-action suit brought against the defendants. For the reasons set forth below, we affirm the judgment of the Superior Court.

I

Facts and Travel

This litigation began on May 16, 2003, when Mary E. DeFontes, individually and on behalf of a class of similarly situated persons, brought suit against Dell, alleging that its collection of taxes from them on the purchase of Dell optional service contracts violated the Deceptive Trade Practices Act, G.L.1956 chapter 13.1 of title 6. Ms. DeFontes asserted that service contracts, such as the option service contract offered by Dell, were not taxable within the State of Rhode Island. Nicholas Long joined the suit as a plaintiff, and an amended complaint was filed on July 16, 2003, that also added Dell subsidiaries Dell Catalog and Dell Marketing, and two service providers, QualxServ and BancTec as defendants.

Dell is an international computer hardware and software corporation. Within the Dell corporate umbrella, Dell Catalog and Dell Marketing primarily are responsible for selling computers via the internet, mail-order catalogs, and other means to individual and business consumers. Dell ships these orders throughout all fifty states from warehouses located in Texas and Tennessee. As part of these purchases, Dell offers consumers an optional service contract for on-site repair of its products, with Dell often acting as an agent for third-party service providers, including BancTec and QualxServ. Parties opting to purchase a service contract are charged a "tax," which is either paid to the State of Rhode Island directly or collected by the third-party service provider and then remitted to the state.

The two initial plaintiffs, Ms. DeFontes and Mr. Long, engaged in slightly different transactions. Ms. DeFontes purchased her computer through Dell Catalog and selected a service contract with BancTec. She paid a total of $950.51, of which $13.51 was characterized as tax on the service contract. Mr. Long purchased his computer through Dell Marketing and opted for a service contract managed by Dell. In total, he paid $3,037.73, out of which $198.73 was designated as tax paid on the service contract. There is no allegation that Dell improperly retained any of the collected tax. Several months after plaintiffs filed their amended complaint, defendants filed a motion to stay proceedings and compel arbitration, citing an arbitration provision within the parties' purported agreements.[2] The defendants argued that the arbitration provision was part of a "Terms and Conditions Agreement," which they contended plaintiffs had accepted by accepting delivery of the goods. Specifically, they averred that plaintiffs had three separate opportunities to review the terms and conditions agreement, to wit, by selecting a hyperlink on the Dell website, by reading the terms that were included in the acknowledgment/invoice that was sent to plaintiffs sometime after they placed their orders, or by reviewing the copy of the terms Dell included in the packaging of its computer products.

The hearing justice issued a written decision on January 29, 2004. He first addressed which state law to apply to the parties' dispute. After determining that the choice-of-law provision included in the terms and conditions agreement, which identified Texas as the controlling jurisdiction, was enforceable, he then analyzed whether the parties had, in fact, agreed to be bound by the terms and conditions agreement. The hearing justice found that although plaintiffs had three opportunities to review the terms, none was sufficient to give rise to a contractual obligation. First, he noted that plaintiffs could have reviewed the terms and conditions agreement had they clicked a hyperlink that appeared on Dell's website. The hearing justice found, however, that this link was "inconspicuously located at the bottom of the webpage" and insufficient to

---

[2]   The arbitration clause in Ms. DeFontes' "Terms and Conditions Agreement," quoted by the hearing justice in his decision, provided,

"ANY CLAIM, DISPUTE, OR CONTROVERSY (WHETHER IN CONTRACT, TORT, OR OTHERWISE, WHETHER PREEXISTING, PRESENT OR FUTURE, AND INCLUDING STATUTORY, COMMON LAW, INTENTIONAL TORT AND EQUITABLE CLAIMS) AGAINST DELL, its agents, employees, successors, assigns or affiliates * * * arising from or relating to this Agreement, its interpretation, or the breach, termination or validity thereof, the relationships which result from this Agreement (including, to the full extent permitted by applicable law, relationships with third parties who are not signatories to this Agreement), Dell's advertising, or any related purchase SHALL BE RESOLVED EXCLUSIVELY AND FINALLY BY BINDING ARBITRATION ADMINISTERED BY THE NATIONAL ARBITRATION FORUM (NAF) under its Code of Procedure then in effect * * *. The arbitration * * * will be limited solely to the dispute or controversy between Customer and Dell * * *. Any award of the arbitrator(s) shall be final and binding on each of the parties, and may be entered as a judgment in any court of competent jurisdiction."

The arbitration provision in the terms and conditions agreement sent to Mr. Long contained substantially similar language.

place customers on notice of the terms and conditions.[3] Nevertheless, the hearing justice noted that the terms and conditions agreement also appeared both in the acknowledgment that Dell sent to plaintiffs when they placed their orders and later within the packaging when the computers were delivered.

The hearing justice noted that "courts generally recognize that shrinkwrap agreements,[5] paper agreements enclosed within the packaging of an item, are sufficient to put consumers on inquiry notice of the terms and conditions of a transaction." He also observed, however, that shrinkwrap agreements generally contain an express disclaimer that explains to consumers that they can reject the proposed terms and conditions by returning the product. The crucial test, according to the hearing justice, was "whether a reasonable person would have known that return of the product would serve as rejection of those terms." He looked to the introductory language of the terms and conditions agreement, which he quoted as follows,[6]

> **"PLEASE READ THIS DOCUMENT CAREFULLY! IT CONTAINS VERY IMPORTANT INFORMATION ABOUT YOUR RIGHTS AND OBLIGATIONS, AS WELL AS LIMITATIONS AND EXCLUSIONS THAT MAY APPLY TO YOU. THIS DOCUMENT CONTAINS A DISPUTE RESOLUTION CLAUSE.**

> "This Agreement contains the terms and conditions that apply to purchases by Home, Home Office, and Small Business customers from the Dell entity named on the invoice ('Dell'). By accepting delivery of the computer systems, related products, and/or services and support, and/or other products described on that invoice. [sic] You ('Customer') agrees [sic] to be bound by and accepts [sic] these terms and conditions * * * These terms and conditions are subject to change without prior written notice at any time, in Dell's sole discretion."

The hearing justice found that this language was insufficient to give a reasonable consumer notice of the method of rejection. He found that defendants' failure to include an express disclaimer meant that they could

---

[3] We also note that Mr. Long appears to have purchased his computer over the telephone and it is unclear from the record whether he viewed the Dell website in relation to his purchase.

[5] A "shrinkwrap agreement" refers to the common commercial practice of including additional terms and conditions either on the outside of a package or within it when it is shipped to the consumer. Often these packages are covered in plastic or cellophane which must be breached to open.

[6] The hearing justice appears to have conflated the slightly different language of the terms and conditions agreements sent to Mr. Long and Ms. DeFontes. Although similar, some differences do exist. Significantly, the documents sent to Ms. DeFontes contained an express disclaimer advising her that "[i]f for any reason Customer is not satisfied with a Dell-branded hardware system, Customer may return the system under the terms and conditions of Dell's Total Satisfaction Return Policy * * * "

not prove that plaintiffs "knowingly consent[ed]" to the terms and conditions of the agreement. Accordingly, the hearing justice found that Plaintiffs could not be compelled to enter arbitration. . . .

II

Discussion

We review the trial court's denial of a motion to compel arbitration *de novo. See Kristian v. Comcast Corp.,* 446 F.3d 25, 31 (1st Cir.2006). The parties acknowledge that because their transactions involved interstate commerce, the Federal Arbitration Act (FAA) is applicable. *See* 9 U.S.C. §§ 1 through 16. Congress enacted the FAA to "overrule the judiciary's longstanding refusal to enforce agreements to arbitrate." *Dean Witter Reynolds Inc. v. Byrd,* 470 U.S. 213, 219–20, 105 S.Ct. 1238, 84 L.Ed.2d 158 (1985). It requires enforcement of privately negotiated arbitration agreements "save upon such grounds as exist at law or in equity for the revocation of any contract." 9 U.S.C. § 2. Thus, once a court is "satisfied that the making of the agreement for arbitration or the failure to comply therewith is not an issue" it "shall make an order directing the parties to proceed to arbitration in accordance with the terms of the agreement." 9 U.S.C. § 4.

Yet, the United States Supreme Court has been equally insistent that "arbitration is a matter of contract and a party cannot be required to submit to arbitration any dispute which he has not agreed so to submit." *Howsam v. Dean Witter Reynolds, Inc.,* 537 U.S. 79, 83, 123 S.Ct. 588, 154 L.Ed.2d 491 (2002) (quoting *United Steelworkers of America v. Warrior & Gulf Navigation Co.,* 363 U.S. 574, 582, 80 S.Ct. 1347, 4 L.Ed.2d 1409 (1960)); *see also Mirra Co. v. School Administrative District No. 35,* 251 F.3d 301, 304 (1st Cir.2001) ("Arbitration is a contractual matter, and no party may be forced to arbitrate a dispute unless she has expressly agreed to do so by contract."). The determination of whether the parties have formed an agreement to arbitrate is a matter of state contract law. *See* 9 U.S.C. § 2; *First Options of Chicago, Inc. v. Kaplan,* 514 U.S. 938, 944, 115 S.Ct. 1920, 131 L.Ed.2d 985 (1995). Moreover, a hearing justice's determination of "[w]hether a party has agreed to be bound by arbitration is a question of law subject to this Court's de novo review." *Stanley-Bostitch, Inc. v. Regenerative Environmental Equipment Co.,* 697 A.2d 323, 325 (R.I.1997) (citing *Providence Teachers' Union v. Providence School Committee,* 433 A.2d 202, 205 (R.I.1981)). . . .

We therefore evaluate whether plaintiffs are bound by the terms and conditions agreement by resorting to a careful review of the provisions of the U.C.C. Under U.C.C. § 2–204, contracts for the sale of goods may be formed "in any manner sufficient to show agreement, including conduct by both parties which recognizes the existence of such a contract." Tex. Bus. & Com.Code Ann. § 2.204 (Vernon 1994). The U.C.C. creates the assumption that, unless circumstances unambiguously demonstrate otherwise, the buyer is the offeror and the seller is the offeree. *See Klocek v. Gateway, Inc.,* 104 F.Supp.2d 1332, 1340 (D.Kan.2000). Moreover, U.C.C. § 2–206 provides in relevant part,

> "(a) Unless otherwise unambiguously indicated by the language or circumstances,

> "(1) an offer to make a contract shall be construed as inviting acceptance in any manner and by any medium reasonable in the circumstances;

> "(2) an order or other offer to buy goods for prompt or current shipment shall be construed as inviting acceptance either by a prompt promise to ship or by the prompt or current shipment of conforming or nonconforming goods * * *." Tex. Bus. & Com.Code Ann. § 2.206 (Vernon 1994).

If contract formation occurred at the moment Dell's sales agents processed the customer's credit card payment and agreed to ship the goods, as plaintiffs argue, then any additional terms would necessarily be treated as "[a]dditional [t]erms in [a]cceptance or [c]onfirmation" under U.C.C. § 2–207 or offers to modify the existing contract under U.C.C. § 2–209. Yet, the modern trend seems to favor placing the power of acceptance in the hands of the buyer after he or she receives goods containing a standard form statement of additional terms and conditions, provided the buyer retains the power to "accept or return" the product.

The eminent Judge Frank Easterbrook has authored what are widely considered to be the two leading cases on so-called "shrinkwrap" agreements. In *ProCD, Inc. v. Zeidenberg,* 86 F.3d 1447, 1452–53 (7th Cir.1996), the court challenged the traditional understanding of offer and acceptance in consumer transactions by holding that a buyer of software was bound by an agreement that was included within the packaging and later appeared when the buyer first used the software.[11] *Id.* The court first held that U.C.C. § 2–207 was inapplicable because in cases involving only one form, the "battle-of-the-forms" provision was irrelevant. *ProCD, Inc.,* 86 F.3d at 1452. It then proceeded to evaluate the agreement under U.C.C. § 2–204 and reasoned that "[a] vendor, as master of the offer, may invite acceptance by conduct, and may propose limitations on the kind of conduct that constitutes acceptance. A buyer may accept by performing the acts the vendor proposes to treat as acceptance." *ProCD, Inc.,* 86 F.3d at 1452. In

---

[11] Although not discussed in the appellate decision, the trial court indicated that the agreement included the language,

> "By using the discs and the listings licensed to you, you agree to be bound by the terms of this License. If you do not agree to the terms of this License, promptly return all copies of the software, listings that may have been exported, the discs and the User Guide to the place where you obtained it." *ProCD, Inc. v. Zeidenberg,* 908 F.Supp. 640, 644 (W.D.Wis.1996).

Hill v. Gateway 2000, Inc., 105 F.3d 1147, 1148–49 (7th Cir.1997),* the court expanded its earlier holding in *ProCD* beyond transactions involving software where the consumer is prompted to accept or decline the terms when he first uses the program. It determined that when a merchant delivers a product that includes additional terms and conditions, but expressly provides the consumer the right to either accept those terms or return the product for a refund within a reasonable time, a consumer who retains the goods beyond that period may be bound by the contract. *Id.* Judge Easterbrook explained,

> "Practical considerations support allowing vendors to enclose the full legal terms with their products. Cashiers cannot be expected to read legal documents to customers before ringing up sales. If the staff at the other end of the phone for direct-sales operations such as Gateway's had to read the four-page statement of terms before taking the buyer's credit card number, the droning voice would anesthetize rather than enlighten many potential buyers. Others would hang up in a rage over the waste of their time. And oral recitation would not avoid customers' assertions (whether true or feigned) that the clerk did not read term X to them, or that they did not remember or understand it." *Id.* at 1149.

The defendants argue that *ProCD* represents the majority view and we have found considerable support for their contention. *See, e.g., O'Quin v. Verizon Wireless,* 256 F.Supp.2d 512, 515–16 (M.D.La.2003) ("Terms and Conditions Pamphlet" binding where acceptance expressed by activation and use of wireless services as long as "opportunity to return"); *Bischoff v. DirecTV, Inc.,* 180 F.Supp.2d 1097, 1101 (C.D.Cal.2002) ("Customer Agreement" mailed to each customer along with the first billing statement valid when clearly advised "[i]f you do not accept these terms, please notify us immediately and we will cancel your service"); *Brower v. Gateway 2000, Inc.,* 246 A.D.2d 246, 676 N.Y.S.2d 569, 572 (N.Y.App.Div.1998) (arbitration clause of standard terms and conditions agreement valid where consumer informed that by keeping product beyond thirty days after delivery he was accepting terms); *M.A. Mortenson Co., v. Timberline Software Corp.,* 140 Wash.2d 568, 998 P.2d 305, 308 (2000) (adopting ProCD analysis but noting shrinkwrap agreement explicitly instructed consumers "IF YOU DO NOT AGREE TO THESE TERMS AND CONDITIONS, PROMPTLY RETURN * * * TO THE PLACE OF

---

* [Footnote by editors. Gateway's arbitration term required the arbitration be conducted in Chicago under the rules of the International Chamber of Commerce. The ICC rules required a party filing a claim of less than $50,000 to pay an advance fee of $4,000 half of which was not refundable even if the party prevailed. While the arbitration was conducted in Chicago, all correspondence regarding the arbitration had to be sent to ICC headquarters in France. See Brower v. Gateway 2000, Inc., 246 A.D.2d 246, 676 N.Y.S.2d 569 (1998) (holding provision requiring arbitration before the ICC to be unconscionable and remanding so the trial court could consider whether Gateway's substitution of arbitration before the American Arbitration Association cured the problem).]

PURCHASE AND YOUR PURCHASE PRICE WILL BE REFUNDED"). Moreover, as plaintiffs' counsel has initiated nationwide litigation, a number of sister jurisdictions have decided more or less the precise issue put before us in defendants' favor. For instance, in *Stenzel v. Dell, Inc.*, 870 A.2d 133 (Me.2005), the Maine Supreme Judicial Court reviewed a similar terms and conditions agreement sent to Dell customers that included the language,

> "By accepting delivery of the computer systems, related products, and/or services and support, and/or other products described on that invoice [, the customer] agrees to be bound by and accepts these terms and conditions. If for any reason Customer is not satisfied with a Dell-branded hardware system, Customer may return the system under the terms and conditions of Dell's Total Satisfaction Return Policy * * *." *Id,* at 140.

The court held that by "accepting delivery of the computers, and then failing to exercise their right to return the computers as provided by the agreement, [the plaintiffs] expressly manifested their assent to be bound by the agreement * * *." *Id; see also Carideo v. Dell, Inc.*, 520 F.Supp.2d 1241, 1244 (W.D.Wash.2007); *Omstead v. Dell, Inc.*, 473 F.Supp.2d 1018, 1025–26 (N.D.Cal.2007); *Adams v. Dell Computer Corp.*, No. CIV AC–06–089, 2006 WL 2670969 (S.D.Tex. Sept.18, 2006); *Sherr v. Dell Inc.*, No. 05 CV 10097(GBD) 2006 WL 2109436, *3 (S.D.N.Y. July 27, 2006) ("customer need only return the product according to the return policy in order to reject the Agreement"); *Falbe v. Dell, Inc.*, No. 04–C–1425, 2004 WL 1588243, *3 (N.D.Ill.2004) ("Our analysis begins, and could end, with * * * *Hill v. Gateway 2000, Inc.*").

Courts have not been universal in embracing the reasoning of *ProCD* and its progeny, however. In *Step-Saver Data Systems, Inc. v. Wyse Technology,* 939 F.2d 91, 98 (3d Cir.1991), the court determined that when parties exchange the shipment of goods for remuneration the existence of a contract is not in doubt; rather, any dispute relates solely to the nature of its terms. After deciding that U.C.C. § 2–207 applies to situations in which a party sends a confirmatory document that claims to establish additional terms of the contract, the court held that U.C.C. § 2–207 "establishes a legal rule that proceeding with a contract after receiving a writing that purports to define the terms of the parties's contract is not sufficient to establish the party's consent to the terms of the writing to the extent that the terms of the writing either add to, or differ from, the terms detailed in the parties's earlier writings or discussions." *Id.* at 99.[12] The court therefore held that a licensing agreement affixed to the packaging

---

[12] The official comment to U.C.C. § 2–207 indicates that the provision applies "where an agreement has been reached orally or by informal correspondence between the parties and is followed by one or both of the parties sending formal memoranda embodying the terms so far agreed upon and adding terms not discussed." U.C.C. § 2–207 Official Comment 1 (2001).

constituted a proposal for additional terms that was not binding unless expressly agreed to by the purchaser. *Id* at 100; *see also Klocek,* 104 F.Supp.2d at 1339, 1341 (finding buyer's "act of keeping the computer past five days was not sufficient to demonstrate that plaintiff expressly agreed to the Standard Terms" and criticizing the *Hill* court's summary dismissal of U.C.C. § 2–207 by stating "nothing in its language precludes application in a case which involves only one form"); *Licitra v. Gateway, Inc.,* 189 Misc.2d 721, 734 N.Y.S.2d 389, 396 (N.Y.Civ.Ct.2001) (construing arbitration clause of a shrinkwrap agreement as a proposal for additional terms under U.C.C. § 2–207 because it materially altered the existing agreement).

The Supreme Court of Oklahoma, which has also been drawn into this nationwide class-action suit against defendants, has rejected *Hill's* reasoning as well. *See Rogers,* 138 P.3d at 833. Although remanding the case to determine whether the arbitration provision was included in the parties' agreement, it noted,

> "The plaintiffs' accepting the computers and not returning them is consistent with a contract being formed at the time that the orders were placed and cannot be construed as acquiescing in the 'Terms and Conditions of Sale' document whether included with the invoice or acknowledgment or with the computer packaging. If the contracts were formed at the time the orders were placed, *see* U.C.C. § 2–206(1), the 'Terms and Conditions of Sale' document, including the arbitration provision, would be an additional term of the contracts under section 2–207. The arbitration provision would not be part of the contracts but proposals to add it as a term to the contracts." *Rogers,* 138 P.3d at 833 (citing U.C.C. § 2–207).[13]

After reviewing the case law pertaining to so-called "shrinkwrap" agreements, we are satisfied that the *ProCD* line of cases is better reasoned and more consistent with contemporary consumer transactions. It is simply unreasonable to expect a seller to apprise a consumer of every term and condition at the moment he or she makes a purchase. A modern consumer neither expects nor desires to wade through such minutia, particularly when making a purchase over the phone, where full disclosure of the terms would border on the sadistic. Nor do we believe that, after placing a

---

[13] It appears that the drafters of the Uniform Commercial Code were themselves flummoxed by this issue. Amended U.C.C. § 2–207, which, although not adopted, could provide some insight into any evolving consensus among commercial law scholars and practitioners, states in Official Comment 5,

> "The section omits any specific treatment of terms attached to the goods, or in or on the container in which the goods are delivered. This article takes no position on whether a court should follow the reasoning in *Step-Saver Data Systems, Inc. v. Wyse Technology,* 939 F.2d 91 (3d Cir.1991) and *Klocek v. Gateway, Inc.,* 104 F.Supp.2d 1332 (D.Kan.2000) (original 2–207 governs) or the contrary reasoning of *Hill v. Gateway* 2000, 105 F.3d 1147 (7th Cir.1997) (original 2–207 inapplicable)." Amended § 2–207, Comment 5 (2003).

telephone order for a computer, a reasonable consumer would believe that he or she has entered into a fully consummated agreement. *See Axelson, Inc. v. McEvoy-Willis, a Division of Smith International (North Sea), Ltd.,* 7 F.3d 1230, 1232–33 (5th Cir.1993) ("An offer is an act that leads the offeree reasonably to believe that assent (i.e., acceptance) will conclude the deal."). Rather, he or she is aware that with delivery comes a multitude of standard terms attendant to nearly every consumer transaction.

We therefore decline to adopt the minority view, as urged by plaintiffs, that a contract is fully formed when a buyer orders a product and the seller accepts payment and either ships or promises to ship. Instead, formation occurs when the consumer accepts the full terms after receiving a reasonable opportunity to refuse them. Yet in adopting the so-called "layered contracting"[14] theory of formation, we reiterate that the burden falls squarely on the seller to show that the buyer has accepted the seller's terms after delivery. Thus, the crucial question in this case is whether defendants reasonably invited acceptance by making clear in the terms and conditions agreement that (1) by accepting defendants' product the consumer was accepting the terms and conditions contained within and (2) the consumer could reject the terms and conditions by returning the product.

On the first question, defendants notified plaintiffs that "[b]y accepting delivery of the computer systems, related products, and/or services and support, and/or other products described on that invoice[,] You ('Customer') agrees to be bound by and accepts those terms and conditions." This language certainly informed plaintiffs that defendants intended to bind them to heretofore undisclosed terms and conditions, but it did not advise them of the period beyond which they will have indicated their assent to those terms. The defendants argue that the meaning of the term "accepting delivery" is apparent to a reasonable consumer. We are not so sure. *See Licitra,* 734 N.Y.S.2d at 392 ("All terms of the 'Agreement' should not be enforced merely because the consumer retains the equipment for 30 days after receipt, especially because it is unclear when the 30-day period to protest begins. Does it commence upon delivery of the goods to the carrier since the 'Agreement' states that title passes upon 'delivery to the carrier' * * * or does it commence upon receipt by the consumer? Is the time period stayed in the all too common situation where a parent buys the computer as a present for a student and does not give the gift for several weeks or is the clock ticking while the equipment sits in the box?"). "Acceptance of goods" has a technical meaning not easily discernable to the average consumer. A consumer may believe that simply by opening the

---

[14] This phrase is taken from the Supreme Court of Washington and is meant to denote that "while some contracts are formed and their terms fully defined at a single point in time, many transactions involve a rolling or layered process." *M.A. Mortenson Co. v. Timberline Software Corp.,* 140 Wash.2d 568, 998 P.2d 305, 313 n. 10 (2000) (quoting the Uniform Computer Information Transactions Act § 208 cmt. 3 (Approved Official Draft)).

package he or she has agreed to be bound by the terms and conditions contained therein. Indeed, many of the courts that have enforced so-called "approve-or-return" agreements cite language informing the consumer of a specific period after which he or she will have accepted the terms. *See, e.g., Hill,* 105 F.3d at 1148 (terms govern if consumer retains beyond thirty days); *Brower,* 676 N.Y.S.2d at 570 ("By keeping your Gateway 2000 computer system beyond thirty (30) days after the date of delivery, you accept the Terms and Conditions."). The more problematic issue, however, is whether plaintiffs were aware of their power to reject by returning the goods.

Significantly, the agreement sent to Ms. DeFontes, who is no longer a plaintiff in this case, contained additional language advising her of the method of rejection. The introductory provision of the terms and conditions agreement that defendants sent to her stated, "[i]f for any reason Customer is not satisfied with a Dell-branded hardware system, Customer may return the system under the terms and conditions of Dell's Total Satisfaction Return Policy * * *." In doing so, defendants explicitly contrasted acceptance of the terms with rejection of the goods, albeit while retaining some ambiguity whether rejection of defendants' proposed terms could reasonably be construed as dissatisfaction with "Dell-branded hardware." Many of the cases upholding shrinkwrap agreements cite explicit disclaimers advising consumers of their right to reject the terms. *See, e.g., ProCD, Inc. v. Zeidenberg,* 908 F.Supp. 640, 644 (W.D.Wis.1996) ("If you do not agree to the terms of this License, promptly return all copies of the software, listings that may have been exported, the discs and the User Guide to the place where you obtained it."); *Bischoff,* 180 F.Supp.2d at 1101 ("[i]f you do not accept these terms, please notify us immediately and we will cancel your service"); *M.A. Mortenson Co.,* 998 P.2d at 308 ("IF YOU DO NOT AGREE TO THESE TERMS AND CONDITIONS, PROMPTLY RETURN * * * TO THE PLACE OF PURCHASE AND YOUR PURCHASE PRICE WILL BE REFUNDED"). Such explicit language is also present in some of the foreign cases in which defendants have prevailed. *See, e.g., Sherr,* 2006 WL 2109436, at *1 ("[a]greement informs the consumer that by returning the product or refusing delivery in accordance with Dell's return policy, he can reject the terms and conditions"). Although the above language is significantly clearer, the terms and conditions agreement sent to Ms. DeFontes nevertheless made the important connection between acceptance of the terms by accepting delivery and rejection by returning the goods.[16]

That this language is absent in the documents sent to current plaintiffs Mr. Long and Ms. Ricci is troubling and raises the specter that they were unaware of both their power to reject and the method with which

---

[16] We do not decide today whether the disclaimer sent to Ms. DeFontes was sufficient to bind her to the terms and conditions.

to do so. The introductory provision that purportedly bound plaintiffs does not mention either the "Total Satisfaction Return Policy" or the thirty-day period in which a consumer may exercise his or her right to return the product. Rather, this policy is explained, if at all, in a distinct section of the terms and conditions agreement, which confusingly informed plaintiffs that "Dell Branded Hardware systems and parts that are purchased directly from Dell by an end-user Customer may be returned by Customer in accordance with Dell's 'Total Satisfaction Return Policy' in effect on the date of the invoice." Thus, the consumer is left to construe these provisions together and infer that his or her right to reject the terms extends beyond what would commonly be understood as the moment of delivery. This separate provision not only fails to establish a clear relationship between the consumer's acceptance of the terms by retaining the goods and his or her right to reject the terms by returning the product, but it further obscures the matter by forcing the consumer to refer to a separate document if he or she wants to discover the full terms and conditions of the "Total Satisfaction Return Policy." Even if the consumer reviews the total satisfaction return policy, we are not convinced that the policy clearly explains to a reasonable consumer that his or her right to return the product includes rejection of the terms and conditions agreement. We believe the hearing justice rightly concluded that although "Dell does provide a 'total satisfaction policy' whereby a customer may return the computer, this return policy does not mention the customer's ability to return based on their unwillingness to comply with the terms."

In reviewing the language of the terms and conditions agreement it cannot be said that it was reasonably apparent to the plaintiffs that they could reject the terms simply by returning the goods. We believe that too many inferential steps were required of the plaintiffs and too many of the relevant provisions were left ambiguous. We are not persuaded that a reasonably prudent offeree would understand that by keeping the Dell computer he or she was agreeing to be bound by the terms and conditions agreement and retained, for a specified time, the power to reject the terms by returning the product. Because we hold that the hearing justice properly denied the defendants' motion to compel arbitration on the ground that the plaintiffs did not agree to be bound by the terms and conditions agreement, we need not discuss any of the alternative grounds the hearing justice offered for denying the defendants' motion to compel arbitration. We must note, however, that the hearing justice found that the purported agreement "fails to bind Defendants in any genuine way" because it gave the defendants the right to change the terms of the agreement "without prior written notice at any time, in Dell's sole discretion." Although we recognize the existence of a formidable argument that such language rendered the purported agreement illusory, we shall leave the analysis of that argument for another day, in keeping with our general aversion towards reaching issues that prove unnecessary for the disposition of the case at bar. *See Irons v. Rhode Island Ethics Commission,* 973 A.2d 1124, 1135 (R.I.2009).

III

Conclusion

For the reasons set out above, the judgment of the Superior Court is affirmed. The papers of the case are returned to the Superior Court.

CHIEF JUSTICE SUTTELL and JUSTICE ROBINSON did not participate.

———

ProCD, Inc. v. Zeidenberg

86 F.3d 1447 (7th Cir.1996)

ProCD sold packaged software with a database of information compiled for more than 3,000 telephone directories. A lower-priced package was sold to the general public for personal use. A higher-priced package was sold to trade users. The manual and CD-ROM disks inside the lower-priced package included a license limiting the use of the application program and information in the database to non-commercial purposes. Zeidenberg purchased the lower-priced package at a retail outlet and began to sell the data over the internet. ProCD filed a lawsuit seeking an injunction against this activity based on Zeidenberg's violation of the license. The district court denied the injunction because the terms of the license did not appear on the outside of the package. Reversed.

(Easterbrook, J.) "Transactions in which the exchange of money precedes the communication of detailed terms are common. Consider the purchase of insurance. The buyer goes to an agent, who explains the essentials (amount of coverage, number of years) and remits the premium to the home office, which sends back a policy. On the district judge's understanding, the terms of the policy are irrelevant because the insured paid before receiving them. Yet the device of payment, often with a "binder" (so that the insurance takes effect immediately even though the home office reserves the right to withdraw coverage later), in advance of the policy, serves buyers' interests by accelerating effectiveness and reducing transactions costs. Or consider the purchase of an airline ticket. The traveler calls the carrier or an agent, is quoted a price, reserves a seat, pays, and gets a ticket, in that order. The ticket contains elaborate terms, which the traveler can reject by canceling the reservation. To use the ticket is to accept the terms, even terms that in retrospect are disadvantageous. See Carnival Cruise Lines, Inc. v. Shute, 499 U.S. 585, 111 S.Ct. 1522, 113 L.Ed.2d 622 (1991); see also Vimar Seguros y Reaseguros, S.A. v. M/V Sky Reefer, 515 U.S. 528, 115 S.Ct. 2322, 132 L.Ed.2d 462 (1995) (bills of lading). Just so with a ticket to a concert. The back of the ticket states that the patron promises not to record the concert; to attend is to agree. A theater that detects a violation will confiscate the tape and escort the violator to the exit. One could arrange things so that every concertgoer signs this promise before forking over the money, but that cumbersome way of doing things not only would lengthen queues and raise prices but also would scotch the sale of tickets by phone or electronic data service. . . .

"Some portions of the UCC impose additional requirements on the way parties agree on terms. A disclaimer of the implied warranty of merchantability must be "conspicuous." UCC § 2–316(2), incorporating UCC § 1–201(10). Promises to make firm offers, or to negate oral modifications, must be "separately signed." UCC §§ 2–205, 2–209(2). These special provisos reinforce the impression that, so far as the UCC is concerned, other terms may be as inconspicuous as the forum-selection clause on the back of the cruise ship ticket in *Carnival Lines*. Zeidenberg has not located any Wisconsin case—for that matter, any case in any state—holding that under the UCC the ordinary terms found in shrinkwrap licenses require any special prominence, or otherwise are to be undercut rather than enforced. In the end, the terms of the license are conceptually identical to the contents of the package. Just as no court would dream of saying that SelectPhone (trademark) must contain 3,100 phone books rather than 3,000, or must have data no more than 30 days old, or must sell for $100 rather than $150—although any of these changes would be welcomed by the customer, if all other things were held constant—so, we believe, Wisconsin would not let the buyer pick and choose among terms. Terms of use are no less a part of "the product" than are the size of the database and the speed with which the software compiles listings. Competition among vendors, not judicial revision of a package's contents, is how consumers are protected in a market economy. Digital Equipment Corp. v. Uniq Digital Technologies, Inc., 73 F.3d 756 (7th Cir.1996). ProCD has rivals, which may elect to compete by offering superior software, monthly updates, improved terms of use, lower price, or a better compromise among these elements. As we stressed above, adjusting terms in buyers' favor might help Matthew Zeidenberg today (he already has the software) but would lead to a response, such as a higher price, that might make consumers as a whole worse off. . . ."

Nguyen v. Barnes & Noble Inc.

763 F.3d 1171 (9th Cir. 2014)

Nguyen purchased two heavily discounted Hewlett-Packard Touchpads using Barnes & Noble's website during what was advertised as a "fire sale." He received an email confirming the transaction but the next day he received another email informing that his order had been cancelled due to unexpectedly high demand. Nguyen filed a lawsuit on behalf of himself and a putative class of consumers whose Touchpad orders had been cancelled. Barnes & Noble moved to compel arbitration invoking its "Terms of Use," which required claims be resolved by arbitration on an individual basis. The district court denied the motion. Affirmed.

(Noonan, J.) "Contracts formed on the Internet come primarily in two flavors: "clickwrap" (or "click-through") agreements, in which website users are required to click on an "I agree" box after being presented with a list of terms and conditions of use; and "browsewrap" agreements, where a website's terms and conditions of use are generally posted on the website via a hyperlink at the bottom of the screen. *See Register.com,* 356 F.3d at 428–30. Barnes & Noble's Terms of Use fall in the latter category.

"'Unlike a clickwrap agreement, a browsewrap agreement does not require the user to manifest assent to the terms and conditions expressly . . . [a] party instead gives his assent simply by using the website.' *Hines v. Overstock.com, Inc.,* 668 F.Supp.2d 362, 366–67 (E.D.N.Y.2009) (citation and quotation marks omitted) (alteration in original). Indeed, "in a pure—form browsewrap agreement, 'the website will contain a notice that—by merely using the services of, obtaining information from, or initiating applications within the website—the user is agreeing to and is bound by the site's terms of service.'" *Fteja v. Facebook, Inc.,* 841 F.Supp.2d 829, 837 (S.D.N.Y.2012) (quoting *United States v. Drew,* 259 F.R.D. 449, 462 n. 22 (C.D.Cal.2009)). Thus, "by visiting the website—something that the user has already done—the user agrees to the Terms of Use not listed on the site itself but available only by clicking a hyperlink." *Id.* "The defining feature of browsewrap agreements is that the user can continue to use the website or its services without visiting the page hosting the browsewrap agreement or even knowing that such a webpage exists." *Be In, Inc. v. Google Inc.,* No. 12–CV–03373–LHK, 2013 WL 5568706, at *6 (N.D.Cal. Oct. 9, 2013). "Because no affirmative action is required by the website user to agree to the terms of a contract other than his or her use of the website, the determination of the validity of the browsewrap contract depends on whether the user has actual or constructive knowledge of a website's terms and conditions." *Van Tassell v. United Mktg. Grp., LLC,* 795 F.Supp.2d 770, 790 (N.D.Ill.2011) (citing *Sw. Airlines Co. v. BoardFirst, LLC,* No. 06–CV–0891–B, 2007 WL 4823761, at *4 (N.D.Tex. Sept. 12, 2007)); *see also* Mark A. Lemley, *Terms of Use,* 91 Minn. L.Rev. 459, 477 (2006) ("Courts may be willing to overlook the utter absence of assent only when there are reasons to believe that the [website user] is aware of the [website owner's] terms.").

"Were there any evidence in the record that Nguyen had actual notice of the Terms of Use or was required to affirmatively acknowledge the Terms of Use before completing his online purchase, the outcome of this case might be different. Indeed, courts have consistently enforced browsewrap agreements where the user had actual notice of the agreement. . . .Courts have also been more willing to find the requisite notice for constructive assent where the browsewrap agreement resembles a clickwrap agreement—that is, where the user is required to affirmatively acknowledge the agreement before proceeding with use of the website. *See, e.g., Zaltz v. JDATE,* 952 F.Supp.2d 439, 451–52 (E.D.N.Y.2013)(enforcing forum selection clause where prospective members had to check box confirming that they both read and agreed to the website's Terms and Conditions of Service to obtain account); *Fteja,* 841 F.Supp.2d at 838–40 (enforcing forum selection clause in website's terms of service where a notice below the "Sign Up" button stated, "By clicking Sign Up, you are indicating that you have read and agree to the Terms of Service," and user had clicked "Sign Up").

"But where, as here, there is no evidence that the website user had actual knowledge of the agreement, the validity of the browsewrap agreement turns on whether the website puts a reasonably prudent user on inquiry notice of the terms of the contract. *Specht,* 306 F.3d at 30–31; *see also In re Zappos.com, Inc. Customer Data Sec. Breach Litig.,* 893 F.Supp.2d 1058, 1064 (D.Nev.2012). Whether a user has inquiry notice of a browsewrap agreement, in turn, depends on the design and content of the website and the agreement's webpage. *Google,* 2013 WL 5568706, at *6. Where the link to a website's terms of use is buried at the bottom of the page or tucked away in obscure corners of the website where users are unlikely to see it, courts have refused to enforce the browsewrap agreement. *See, e.g., Specht,* 306 F.3d at 23 (refusing to enforce terms of use that "would have become visible to plaintiffs only if they had scrolled down to the next screen"); *In re Zappos.com,* 893 F.Supp.2d at 1064 ("The Terms of Use is inconspicuous, buried in the middle to bottom of every Zappos.com webpage among many other links, and the website never directs a user to the Terms of Use."); *Van Tassell,* 795 F.Supp.2d at 792–93 (refusing to enforce arbitration clause in browsewrap agreement that was only noticeable after a "multi-step process" of clicking through non-obvious links); *Hines,* 668 F.Supp.2d at 367 (plaintiff "could not even see the link to [the terms and conditions] without scrolling down to the bottom of the screen—an action that was not required to effectuate her purchase"). On the other hand, where the website contains an explicit textual notice that continued use will act as a manifestation of the user's intent to be bound, courts have been more amenable to enforcing browsewrap agreements. *See, e.g., Cairo, Inc. v. Crossmedia Servs., Inc.,* No. 04–04825, 2005 WL 756610, at *2, *4–5 (N.D.Cal. Apr. 1, 2005) (enforcing forum selection clause in website's terms of use where every page on the website had a textual notice that read: "By continuing past this page and/or using this site, you agree to abide by the Terms of Use for this site, which prohibit commercial use of any information on this site"). *But see Pollstar v. Gigmania, Ltd.,* 170 F.Supp.2d 974, 981 (E.D.Cal.2000) (refusing to enforce browsewrap agreement where textual notice appeared in small gray print against a gray background). In short, the conspicuousness and placement of the "Terms of Use" hyperlink, other notices given to users of the terms of use, and the website's general design all contribute to whether a reasonably prudent user would have inquiry notice of a browsewrap agreement.

"Barnes & Noble argues that the placement of the "Terms of Use" hyperlink in the bottom left-hand corner of every page on the Barnes & Noble website, and its close proximity to the buttons a user must click on to complete an online purchase, is enough to place a reasonably prudent user on constructive notice. It is true that the location of the hyperlink on Barnes & Noble's website distinguishes this case from *Specht,* the leading authority on the enforceability of browsewrap terms under New York law. There, the Second Circuit refused to enforce an arbitration provision in a website's licensing terms where the hyperlink to the terms was located at the bottom of the page, hidden below the "Download" button that users had to click to initiate the software download. *See Specht,* 306 F.3d at 30. Then-Second Circuit Judge Sotomayor, writing for the panel, held that "a reference to the existence of license terms on a submerged screen is not sufficient to place consumers on inquiry or constructive notice of those terms." *Id.* at 32. By contrast, here the "Terms of Use" link appears either directly below the relevant button a user must click on to proceed in the checkout process or just a few inches away. On some pages, the content of the webpage is compact enough that a user can view the link without scrolling. On the remaining pages, the hyperlink is close enough to the "Proceed with Checkout" button that a user would have to bring the link within his field of vision in order to complete his order.

"But the proximity or conspicuousness of the hyperlink alone is not enough to give rise to constructive notice, and Barnes & Noble directs us to no case law that supports this proposition. The most analogous case the court was able to locate is *PDC Labs., Inc. v. Hach Co.,* an unpublished district court order cited by neither party. No. 09–1110, 2009 WL 2605270 (C.D.Ill. Aug. 25, 2009). There, the "Terms [and Conditions of Sale] were hyperlinked on three separate pages of the online . . . order process in underlined, blue, contrasting text." *Id.* at *3. The court held that "[t]his contrasting text is sufficient to be considered conspicuous," thereby placing a reasonable user on notice that the terms applied. *Id.* It also observed, however, that the terms' conspicuousness was reinforced by the language of the final checkout screen, which read, " 'STEP 4 of 4: *Review terms,* add any comments, and submit order,' " and was followed by a hyperlink to the Terms. *Id.* (emphasis added).

"As in *PDC,* the checkout screens here contained "Terms of Use" hyperlinks in underlined, color-contrasting text. But *PDC* is dissimilar in that the final screen on that website contained the phrase "Review terms." *PDC Labs.,* 2009 WL 2605270, at *3. This admonition makes *PDC* distinguishable, despite the court's explanation that the blue contrasting hyperlinks were sufficiently conspicuous on their own. That the *PDC* decision couched its holding in terms of procedural unconscionability rather than contract formation further distinguishes it from our case. *See id.*

"In light of the lack of controlling authority on point, and in keeping with courts' traditional reluctance to enforce browsewrap agreements against individual consumers, we therefore hold that where a website makes its terms of use available via a conspicuous hyperlink on every page of the website but otherwise provides no notice to users nor prompts them to take any affirmative action to demonstrate assent, even close proximity of the hyperlink to relevant buttons users must click on—without more—is insufficient to give rise to constructive notice. While failure to read a contract before agreeing to its terms does not relieve a party of its obligations under the contract, *Gillman v. Chase Manhattan Bank, N.A.,* 73 N.Y.2d 1, 11, 537 N.Y.S.2d 787, 534 N.E.2d 824 (1988), the onus must be on website owners to put users on notice of the terms to which they wish to bind consumers. Given the breadth of the range of technological savvy of online purchasers, consumers cannot be expected to ferret out hyperlinks to terms and conditions to which they have no reason to suspect they will be bound."

————

NOTE ON UNCONSCIONABILITY AND WAIVER OF ARBITRATION CLAUSES IN FORM CONTRACTS

Discover Bank v. Superior Court, 36 Cal.4th 148, 113 P.3d 1100, 30 Cal. Rptr. 76 (2005), held waiver of class arbitration in a consumer contract of adhesion unconscionable "in a setting in which disputes between the contracting parties predictably involve small amounts of damages, and when it is alleged that the party with the superior bargaining power has carried out a scheme to deliberately cheat large numbers of consumers out of individually small sums of money. . . . " The decision was abrogated by AT&T Mobility LLC v. Concepcion, 131 S.Ct. 1740, 179 L.E.2d 742 (2011), which held that the Federal Arbitration Act preempts the rule:

> California's Discover Bank rule similarly interferes with arbitration. Although the rule does not require classwide arbitration, it allows any party to a consumer contract to demand it ex post. The rule is limited to adhesion contracts. . . but the times in which consumer contracts were anything other than adhesive are long past. . . . Hill v. Gateway 2000, Inc., 105 F.3d 1147, 1149 (C.A.7 1997). The rule also requires that damages be predictably small, and that the consumer allege a scheme to cheat consumers. . . . The former requirement, however, is toothless and malleable (the Ninth Circuit has held that damages of $4,000 are sufficiently small. . .) and the latter has no limiting effect, as all that is required is an allegation.

State courts continue to evaluate arbitration clauses for unconscionability on a case-by-case basis, reading *Concepcion* to preclude only a "rule classifying most collective-arbitration waivers in consumer contracts as unconscionable." Saleemi v. Doctor's Associates, Inc., 176 Wash.2d 368, 292 P.3d 108 (2013).

————

SECTION 2. UCC RULES PROTECTING FORM-TAKERS

————

UCC §§ 1–201(10), 2–302, 2–314, 2–316, 2–719(2), 2–719(3)

[See Selected Source Materials Supplement]

————

MOSCATIELLO V. PITTSBURGH CONTRACTORS EQUIPMENT CO.

Superior Court of Pennsylvania, 1991.
407 Pa. Super. 363, 595 A.2d 1190.

HESTER, JUDGE: Pittsburgh Contractors Equipment Company ("PCEC") appeals from judgment entered on that portion of the order of August 21, 1990 entered in the Allegheny County Court of Common Pleas which denied the relief sought by PCEC in its post-trial motions. We find appellant's numerous allegations of trial court error to be without merit, and accordingly, we affirm the judgment.

This action arises out of a contract entered between appellant, PCEC, and appellee, Franco Moscatiello, i/a, t/d/b/a Moscatiello Construction Company ("Moscatiello"), for the purchase of a concrete paving machine ("paver") manufactured by Curbmaster, Inc. Approximately one month before the contract between PCEC and Moscatiello was executed in May, 1987, Franco Moscatiello and his superintendent, Jay Palino, met with the vice president of PCEC to discuss the purchase of the paver. At the time of the meeting, PCEC was aware that Moscatiello had been awarded a contract by the Pennsylvania Department of Transportation ("PennDot") to reconstruct a road, and that PennDot required that the concrete surface of the road be laid by a certain type of paving machine. The manufacturer of the paver, Curbmaster, also participated in these preliminary discussions. The vice president of Curbmaster had a telephone conversation with a representative of PCEC and Moscatiello in which he suggested that either of two machines manufactured by Curbmaster would be suitable for the job and acceptable to PennDot. Reproduced Record ("R.R.") at 92–93a, 340–41a, 432a, 492a.

On or about May 19, 1987, Mr. Palino, Moscatiello's superintendent, executed a contract on a form provided by PCEC for the purchase from PCEC of a Curbmaster concrete spreader-finisher machine for a total price of $85,125.42. PCEC's purchase agreement stated on the reverse side that no warranties were offered on equipment sold and that any implied warranties were excluded in favor of the manufacturer's offer of warranties. The contract also contained a provision which limited a buyer's remedy solely to return of the purchase price, less wear and use of the machine. In addition, all consequential and incidental damages were expressly excluded.

Moscatiello had no previous dealing with PCEC and was not on notice that the sales agreement relinquished warranties and limited damages. During the contract negotiations, neither PCEC's vice president nor the salesman in attendance directed Moscatiello's attention to the reverse side of the contract where the warranty exclusions were printed.

The paver was manufactured by Curbmaster at its plant in Iowa and shipped to Pittsburgh, arriving at Moscatiello's job site on June 15, 1987. When the paver arrived, it contained no warranty information from the manufacturer. It was alleged during trial that Curbmaster's warranty information was attached to Curbmaster's operations and parts manual, which was delivered to PCEC following execution of the sales contract between Curbmaster and PCEC. However, the trial court found that the manual which ultimately was delivered to Moscatiello did not contain Curbmaster's warranty exclusions and disclaimers. A Curbmaster employee was present when the paver arrived, assisted Moscatiello employees in assembling it, instructed Moscatiello employees on how to operate the machine, and was present when the machine was used for the first time. The Curbmaster representative never informed Moscatiello employees that the machine's warranties were limited or excluded.

According to the testimony of four witnesses during trial, from the time it was first used in June, 1987, to on or about November 12, 1987, when it was used last, the paver failed to lay concrete evenly. Furthermore, the product which resulted was unacceptable to PennDot. During the five-month period of the paver's operation, Moscatiello made numerous complaints to PCEC about the paver's failure to produce an acceptable product. During this period, PCEC and Curbmaster unsuccessfully attempted numerous times to remedy the defects in the machine. The machine finally was returned to Curbmaster in December, 1987. As a result of the paver's failure to perform its functions properly, Moscatiello incurred increased labor costs in order to produce a product acceptable to PennDot.

On February 8, 1988, Moscatiello filed a complaint against PCEC asserting breach of contract, breach of express warranty, breach of implied warranty of merchantability, and breach of implied warranty of fitness for a particular purpose. PCEC joined Curbmaster as an additional defendant, asserting breach of express warranty, breach of implied warranties of merchantability and fitness for a particular purpose, and negligence. By agreement of the parties, PCEC dismissed its negligence claim against Curbmaster and amended its complaint to add a claim against Curbmaster for breach of contract.

Following a bench trial, the trial court issued an opinion and order dated March 14, 1990, awarding $146,811.43 in damages, plus interest, to Moscatiello against PCEC and Curbmaster jointly. . . PCEC filed this timely appeal . . . .

PCEC first argues that the trial court erred in concluding that the disclaimer of warranties contained in the sales agreement was not conspicuous. PCEC contends that the disclaimer contained in the contract between Moscatiello and itself was a binding and effective disclaimer of all warranty liability, which consequently, precludes Moscatiello's claims of breach of warranties and breach of contract.

. . . [W]e concur with the trial court's determination that PCEC's disclaimer of warranties was inconspicuous and therefore ineffective as a bar to Moscatiello's breach of warranty claims.

Counts three and four of Moscatiello's complaint against PCEC consist of claims for breach of implied warranty of merchantability and for breach of implied warranty of fitness for a particular purpose. The Uniform Commercial Code ("U.C.C.") defines the implied warranty of merchantability as a warranty that the goods will pass without objection in the trade and are fit for the ordinary purposes for which such goods are used. 13 Pa.C.S.A. § 2314. Comment 11 to this section of the U.C.C. states that this warranty is so commonly taken for granted that its exclusion from a contract is recognized as a matter threatening surprise and therefore requiring special precaution. Thus, to exclude the implied warranty of merchantability, the exclusionary language must mention the term "merchantability" and be conspicuous. 13 Pa.C.S.A. § 2316(b). As noted in Comment 1 to section 2316(b), this section of the U.C.C. is designed to protect a buyer from unexpected and unbargained for language of disclaimer.

A term or clause is "conspicuous" when it is "so written that a reasonable person against whom it is to operate ought to have noticed it. . . Language in the body of a form is conspicuous if it is in larger or other contrasting type or color. . . " 13 Pa.C.S.A. § 1201. Comment 10 to section 1201 states that the test for conspicuousness is whether attention can reasonably be expected to be called to the exclusions. The primary object of the conspicuousness requirement is to avoid fine print waiver of rights by the buyer. *Greenspun v. American Adhesives, Inc.,* 320 F.Supp. 442 (E.D.Pa.1970).

The exclusionary clause involved herein is located on the reverse side of a standard sales contract. The front of the form contains blank lines in which are typed a customer's name, shipping instructions, detailed description of the machine, price breakdown, and payment terms. All of the information is individually typed on separate lines at least one quarter of an inch wide. Toward the bottom of the form, inside the margins for the price breakdown, is the phrase in capital letters: "TERMS AND CONDITIONS ON REVERSE SIDE ARE AN INTEGRAL PART OF THIS ORDER." Immediately below is a sentence containing the clause, in smaller type, "subject to the provisions hereof and conditions contained on reverse side hereof."

By contrast, the reverse side of the form contains eighteen numbered paragraphs which fill the page, top to bottom and side to side, in extremely small type, approximately one-sixteenth inch in height and one-fourth the size used on the front. The capital letters are slightly larger, but of the same color and in the same type style as the rest of the printing. The type used on the front of the contract is much larger and bolder than that used on the reverse side. The warranty disclaimer is buried in paragraph number sixteen at the bottom of the page. Though the operative language of the disclaimer is set forth in capital letters, the size of the type of even the capital letters is so minute that it simply does nothing to attract attention to the clause. As Moscatiello aptly observes, "to say that the print is 'fine' is an understatement." Appellee's brief at 12.

Upon our review of the agreement, we have no doubt, as the trial court stated, that PCEC's warranty disclaimer "did not adequately put Moscatiello on notice that substantial rights of theirs were being relinquished." Trial court opinion at 5. The disclaimer was set forth in some of the "finest" print this court ever has read. Even the language on the front of the contract referring to terms and conditions on the reverse side of the contract was inconspicuous as well as misleading. The letters are capitalized but are buried in the middle of the contract within the margins of the price breakdown of the goods. In addition, reference is made only to the "terms" and "conditions" on the reverse side rather than to the limitation on warranties and remedies available to the buyer. This language clearly does not meet the letter or the spirit of the U.C.C. requirements.

The evidence during trial was unequivocal that PCEC was fully familiar with the terms of the agreement, having employed it for many years, and had numerous opportunities throughout the purchase negotiations to notify Moscatiello of the exclusion of warranties and the limitation on potential remedies set forth on the reverse side of the contract. It is clear that PCEC failed to take advantage of those opportunities. Instead, as the trial court noted, PCEC "utilized a boiler-plate provision in a standard sales agreement to exclude important warranties that naturally arise in the course of any sale." Trial court opinion at 5. Section 2316 of the U.C.C. protects buyers such as Moscatiello from this type of disclaimer hidden deep within the illegible fine print on the reverse side of a standard sales contract, and that section invalidates such exclusionary language. Thus, we agree with the trial court's finding that the warranty disclaimer was ineffective, and we find no error in the trial court's decision to allow Moscatiello to pursue its cause of action for breach of implied warranty of merchantability.

We also concur with the trial court's finding that PCEC, in fact, did breach its implied warranty of merchantability. Our review of the record in accordance with our standard compels the conclusion that the machine in question could not "pass without objection in the trade under the contract description," nor was it "fit for the ordinary purposes for which such goods are used." 13 Pa.C.S.A. § 2314(b). From the first use of the paver, it failed to lay concrete evenly, which even a lay person would recognize as inadequate for its intended purpose. Further, PennDot's strict requirements regarding its paving were known to PCEC. Testimony during trial established that representatives from PCEC and the manufacturer, Curbmaster, devoted as many as twenty days on site attempting to make the paver perform the functions for which Moscatiello purchased it. They failed, and consequently, the machine was returned. Since the paver never conformed to the contract and obviously was not fit for the ordinary, let alone the specific, purposes for which it was sold, we find no error in the trial court's determination that PCEC breached its implied warranty of merchantability and that Moscatiello was entitled to recover damages from PCEC for that breach.

PCEC next argues that the trial court erred in failing to calculate the damages to which Moscatiello was entitled in a manner consistent with the limitation of remedies provision set forth in the sales agreement. Specifically, PCEC contends that Moscatiello is bound by the limitation of remedies provisions in the contract regardless of whether such provisions were conspicuous "inasmuch as any limitation is a term set forth in a contract executed by [Moscatiello]." Appellant's brief at 22. Moscatiello responds that the provisions in the contract which prohibit recovery of incidental and consequential damages are unconscionable, and therefore, the trial court was correct in refusing to enforce those provisions. We concur and consequently, find no error in the trial court's ruling.

Our examination begins with a review of the applicable sections of the U.C.C. Section 2714(c) provides that incidental or consequential damages may be recovered in an action for breach of contract or breach of warranty. 13 Pa.C.S.A. § 2714(c). Consequential damages include "any loss resulting from general or particular requirements and needs of which the seller at the time of contracting had reason to know . . . " 13 Pa.C.S.A. § 2715(b)(1). Consequential damages may be limited or excluded unless the limitation or exclusion is unconscionable. 13 Pa.C.S.A. § 2719(c). Section 2302 of the U.C.C. allows the court to refuse to enforce the contract as a whole or any single clause or group of clauses if permeated by unconscionability. 13 Pa.C.S.A. § 2302(a). The principle upon which this section rests is one of prevention of oppression and unfair surprise. 13 Pa.C.S.A. § 2302, Comment 1.

The verdict which Moscatiello received from the trial court included the sum of $64,567.93, representing the increased costs it incurred in laying concrete with the defective paver and interest on money borrowed by Moscatiello to purchase the machine. PCEC argues that this portion of the award is erroneous due to the existence of paragraphs seventeen and eighteen in the parties' sales contract which provide the following:

17. If the goods covered by this Order are new, Buyer and Vendor agree that there is no failure of an essential purpose of Buyer's exclusive and limited remedy so long as Vendor is willing and able to repair or replace any part which is not as warranted. If Vendor is not willing and able to repair or replace any such part or if for any reason it is determined that Buyer's exclusive and limited remedy has failed of its essential purpose, Buyer's sole and exclusive remedy shall then be to have its purchase price returned in exchange for the goods, less a reasonable charge for any use by Buyer.

18. It is agreed that Vendor shall not be liable for any incidental or consequential damages occasioned by the sale, possession, operation, maintenance or use of the goods or for any failure of the goods to operate under any claim of breach of warranty or contract, negligence, strict liability or otherwise.

A clause in a contract is considered unconscionable and unenforceable if there is "an absence of meaningful choice on the part of one of the parties together with contract terms which are unreasonably favorable to the other party." *Germantown Manufacturing Co. v. Rawlinson,* 341 Pa.Super. 42, 55, 491 A.2d 138, 145 (1985), quoting E.A. Farnsworth *Contracts* 314 (1982). In *Germantown,* we were asked to determine the enforceability of a confession of judgment clause which was buried, as were the contract provisions at issue here, within the fine print of boilerplate language of a standard form. In finding the clause unenforceable, we were guided by the following analysis contained in section 353 of J. Murray, *Murray on Contracts* (2d ed., 1974):

> Parties to a contract rarely consciously advert to any number of terms which are binding upon them. If such terms allocate the risks of the bargain in a manner which the parties should have reasonably expected, they are enforceable-they are, to use the expression of Karl Llewellyn, decent terms. If the terms of the contract suggest the reallocation of material risks, an attempted reallocation may be so extreme that regardless of apparent and genuine assent, a court will not enforce it. . . The parties will not be found to have agreed to an abnormal allocation of risk if the only evidence thereof is an inconspicuous provision on the boilerplate of a standard form. At a minimum, the reallocation must be physically manifested in a fashion comprehensible to the party against whom it is sought to be enforced. Finally, such party must have had a reasonable choice in relation to such reallocation.

Germantown Manufacturing Company v. Rawlinson, 341 Pa.Super. at 56–57, 491 A.2d at 146.

The question presented in the instant sales agreement, therefore, is whether Mr. Moscatiello and his superintendent reasonably should have expected that if the paver failed to perform as promised, they, rather than the seller, would be responsible for the economic losses which resulted. We cannot agree with appellant that appellee harbored any such expectation.

First, paragraphs seventeen and eighteen of the sales contract are, as appellee aptly states in his brief, "classic examples of physically inconspicuous provisions in the boilerplate of a standard form." Appellee's brief at 21. Neither Mr. Moscatiello nor Mr. Palino understood that buried in the fine print on the reverse side of the contract was a term that shifted to Moscatiello the risk of loss resulting from the purchase of a machine which was unable to perform the operations that it was designed to perform. Neither man was a dealer in concrete-spreader finishers or heavy equipment of any kind. Neither individual had ever dealt with PCEC on any previous occasion, and neither had any knowledge of the standard contracts or business practices of PCEC.

Thus, Moscatiello qualified as neither a merchant, as the term is defined in 13 Pa.C.S.A. § 2104, nor a substantial business concern skilled in the negotiation of sales contracts for goods. It is undisputed that PCEC was both. Courts have upheld limitation of damage provisions in sales contracts between merchants or experienced business concerns because there is no disparity between such entities in either bargaining power or sophistication. *See K & C, Inc. v. Westinghouse Electric Corp.*, 437 Pa. 303, 263 A.2d 390 (1970) (buyers were an experienced attorney and the owner of a used furniture business who dealt with the renovation and sale of the type of machines being purchased); *Chatlos Systems, Inc. v. National Cash Register Corp.*, 635 F.2d 1081 (3rd Cir.1980) (buyer was a manufacturer of complex electronic equipment who purchased a defective computer system).

Appellant places great reliance on *S. M. Wilson and Co. v. Smith International, Inc.*, 587 F.2d 1363 (9th Cir.1978), in support of its argument that the limitation of damages provisions were reasonable. However, just as in *K & C, Inc.* and *Chatlos*, the parties in *Wilson* held equal bargaining positions as experienced business concerns. Moreover, the limitation of damages provision in *Wilson* was agreed to specifically by the buyer during purchase negotiations between the parties, and the damage provision as well as the warranty disclaimer were conspicuously set forth in the contract between the parties.

Similarly, the limitation of damages provision upheld by the court in *Marr Enterprises, Inc. v. Lewis Refrigeration Co.*, 556 F.2d 951 (9th Cir.1977), also was set forth conspicuously in the contract between the parties. The contract provision at issue in the final case cited by appellant, *FMC Finance Corp. v. Murphree*, 632 F.2d 413 (5th Cir.1980), was a warranty disclaimer rather than a limitation of damage provision and therefore, is inapposite to the facts before us.

The contract provisions at issue in the cases cited by appellant are clearly distinguishable from the provisions contained in the contract between the parties herein. Each contract either involved experienced business concerns holding equal bargaining positions or the provision at issue was displayed in a very conspicuous manner in the contract. Appellee was not a dealer or manufacturer of heavy equipment of any kind, and he lacked any prior experience negotiating a contract for the purchase of this type of equipment with PCEC. He had no reason to expect that the contract he signed contained a clause that was buried in the fine print on the reverse side which shifted to him the risk of economic loss resulting from the purchase of a machine which was incapable of performing the job that it was designed to do.

In contrast, PCEC was a well-established dealer engaged in the sale, service, and support of construction equipment to area contractors. It had negotiated many other contracts for the purchase of this type of equipment and was familiar with the "conditions" on the reverse side of its own form which disclaimed warranties and limited damages. PCEC clearly held superior bargaining position with respect to Moscatiello. Moreover, the limitation of damages provisions were classic examples of physically inconspicuous provisions in the boilerplate language of a standard form. Thus, we find the numerous cases cited in appellant's brief inapplicable to the case at bar. Accordingly, we concur with appellee's contention that the limitation of damages provisions contained in its contract with PCEC are unconscionable, and we affirm the trial court's refusal to give effect to those provisions.

Appellant next argues that the integration clause contained in the contract between the parties operates as a waiver of appellee's objections to the terms and conditions of the agreement of sale. While we agree that the terms of an integrated agreement may not be contradicted by evidence of any prior agreement or of a contemporaneous oral agreement, an integration clause cannot validate an unconscionable or otherwise invalid contract provision. The remedies which the trial court afforded appellee were specifically provided to purchasers in the position of appellee by the legislature when it adopted the U.C.C. These remedies cannot be extinguished by the inclusion of an integration clause in a contract which contains invalid provisions. . . .

Judgment affirmed; appellant's request for assessment of attorneys' fees and costs remanded to the trial court; jurisdiction relinquished.

———

Pierce v. Catalina Yachts, Inc.

2 P.3d 618 (Alaska 2000)

Catalina sold a yacht to the Pierces. The contract included the limited warranty: "Catalina will repair or, at its option, pay for 100% of the labor and material necessary to repair" below-line water blisters. The contract included a separate disclaimer of liability for consequential damages. The Pierces sued after Catalina refused to honor the limited warranty, denying the seriousness of the problem. The Pierces prevailed at trial but their damages were limited to the cost of repair based on these contract terms. The Pierces appealed.

(Bryner, J.) "Courts construing U.C.C. subsection 719(b) agree that a limited warranty to repair 'fails of its essential purpose,' when the seller is either unwilling or unable to conform the goods to the contract. The policy behind the failure of essential purpose rule is to insure that the buyer has 'at least minimum adequate remedies.' Typically, a limited repair/replacement remedy fails of its essential purpose where (1) the seller is unsuccessful in repairing or replacing the defective part, regardless of good or bad faith; or (2) there is unreasonable delay in repairing or replacing defective components.

"Here, by specifically finding that the Pierces' boat experienced gel-coat blisters, that the Pierces gave Catalina timely notice of the problem, that Catalina thereafter breached its obligations under the limited gel-coat warranty, and that the Pierces could not have avoided their damages, the jury effectively determined that the gel-coat warranty had failed of its essential purpose. . .

"[W]hen a warranty fails, a separate provision barring consequential damages will survive under subsection 719(c) as long as the bar itself is not unconscionable. . .[1]

"In the present case, the nature of the Pierces' warranty and the circumstances surrounding Catalina's breach weigh heavily against enforcing the consequential damages bar. The contract at issue was a consumer sale, not a commercial transaction between sophisticated businesses with equivalent bargaining power. Catalina unilaterally drafted the damages bar and evidently included it in a preprinted standard limited warranty. Moreover, the jury's sizable award for the reasonable cost of repairing the boat's gel coat establishes that Catalina's breach deprived the Pierces of a substantial benefit of their bargain. Though some gel-coat blistering might have been foreseeable, a defect of this magnitude does not fit neatly 'within the realm of expectable losses.'

"But the decisive factor in this case is the nature of Catalina's breach, which caused the limited remedy to fail of its essential purpose. The jury specifically found that Catalina acted in bad faith in failing to honor its warranty. This finding virtually establishes a 'circumstance[ ] resulting in failure of performance that makes it unconscionable to enforce the parties'

---

[1]   The opinion characterizes this "case-by-case" analysis of a term excluding consequential damages as the majority approach while noting that some courts adopt a per se rule allowing for the recovery of consequential damages when a limited remedy fails under UCC § 2–719(2).

allocation of risk.' 'Because the jury found that Catalina consciously deprived the Pierces of their rights under the warranty, the company cannot conscionably demand to enforce its own warranty rights against the Pierces . . .

"This Court would be in an untenable position if it allowed the defendant to shelter itself behind one segment of the warranty when it has allegedly repudiated and ignored its very limited obligations under another segment of the same warranty, which alleged repudiation has caused the very need for relief which the defendant is attempting to avoid.

"Moreover, in light of Catalina's bad faith, allowing the company to enforce the consequential damages bar would conflict with the commercial code's imperative that '[e]very contract or duty in the code imposes an obligation of good faith in its performance or enforcement.' Finally, because it is self-evident that the Pierces did not bargain to assume the risk of a bad faith breach by Catalina, enforcing the bar against consequential damages would thwart AS 45.02.719's basic goal of implementing the parties' agreement."

SECTION 3. THE REASONABLE EXPECTATIONS DOCTRINE

RESTATEMENT, SECOND, CONTRACTS § 211

[See Selected Source Materials Supplement]

UNIDROIT PRINCIPLES OF INTERNATIONAL COMMERCIAL CONTRACTS ARTS. 2.1.19, 2.1.22

[See Selected Source Materials Supplement]

PRINCIPLES OF EUROPEAN CONTRACT LAW ART. 4.110

[See Selected Source Materials Supplement]

DARNER MOTOR SALES V. UNIVERSAL UNDERWRITERS

Supreme Court of Arizona, En Banc, 1984.
140 Ariz. 383, 682 P.2d 388.

FELDMAN, JUSTICE.

Darner Motor Sales, Inc., dba Darner Leasing Co. (Darner Motors), petitions for review of a memorandum decision of the court of appeals (Darner Motor Sales, Inc. v. Universal Underwriters Insurance Company, No. 1 CA–CIV 5796, filed February 22, 1983). That decision affirmed a summary judgment in favor of Universal Underwriters Insurance Company (Universal) and their agent, John Brent Doxsee (Doxsee), who were the third party defendants impleaded by Darner Motors. We granted review because we believe that the issues presented call into question the clarity and consistency of a large body of Arizona law dealing with insurance coverage. We have jurisdiction pursuant to Ariz. Const. Art. 6, § 5(3) and Rule 23, Rules of Civ.App.P., 17A A.R.S.

FACTS

Darner Motors is in the automobile sales, service and leasing business. Prior to transacting business with Universal, Darner Motors' various operations were insured under several policies issued by The Travelers Company (Travelers). In October of 1973, Doxsee, an insurance agent who was a full-time employee of Universal, contacted Joel Darner to solicit insurance business. The following month, Darner purchased a Universal "U-Drive policy" through Doxsee. This policy insured Darner Motors and the lessees of its cars for automobile liability risk. Darner Motors was covered in limits of $100,000 for any one injury and $300,000 (100/300) for all injuries arising out of any one accident. The lessees were covered in limits of 15/30. The rest of Darner Motors' business risks continued to be insured under a "dealership package policy" issued by Travelers.

It is unclear from the record, but this situation presumably continued until April of 1975, a renewal date of the Travelers policy. In April of 1975, Universal "picked up" the entire insurance "package" for Darner Motors' various business activities. This "package" consisted of a Universal "Unicover" policy which included coverage for garagekeeper's liability, premises liability, property coverage, crime coverage, customer car coverage, and plate glass insurance. The parties describe this as an "umbrella policy," so it is possible that, in addition to covering multiple risks, it also contained excess coverage over other policies which provided primary coverage.[1] In addition to the umbrella policy, Universal also

---

[1] It is difficult to tell just what was or was not insured under this "umbrella policy" since a copy of the policy is not part of the record, even though the coverage contained in that policy is the precise issue in the case.

renewed the U-Drive policy, which provided coverage to the lessees of Darner Motors.[2]

Substantial controversy exists with regard to many of the factual allegations. However, according to Darner, he informed Doxsee that renewal of lessee coverage was to be in the same limits as applied to Darner Motors in the original U-Drive policy. When the new U-Drive policy arrived after renewal in April of 1975, Darner examined it and noticed that the limits of coverage for lessees were 15/30. After reading this, Darner claims that he called Doxsee. He was concerned because his rental contract contained a representation of greater coverage (100/300) and because he felt that it would be better for his business operation if his lessees had the higher coverage. Darner told Doxsee that the liability limits of the U-Drive policy did not conform to their prior agreement, and asked Doxsee to come to Darner Motors and discuss the matter. Doxsee did call upon Mr. Darner at the latter's office. Although Doxsee could not recall the subsequent conversation, both Darner and his former sales manager, Jack Hadley, testified about the discussion. Their deposition testimony would support a finding that Doxsee told Darner not to worry about the limits because, although the U-Drive policy provided only 15/30 coverage, the all-risk clause of the umbrella policy would provide additional coverage to limits of 100/300.[3]

At some time after he received the U-Drive policy and, presumably, also after his discussions with Doxsee, Darner did receive a copy of the umbrella policy. That policy was evidently quite lengthy and forbidding. Darner admits never reading it; he explained this omission by pointing out that "it's like reading a book" and stating that, following his conversations with Doxsee, "I didn't think I needed to." Darner's office manager testified that she never really read the policy either and saw little need to do so in view of the fact that Doxsee would occasionally appear, remove pages from the loose-leaf binder and insert new pages. So far as the record shows, the printed, boiler-plate provisions contained in the loose-leaf type, "book length," all-risk policy were neither negotiated before nor discussed after the policy was delivered. The parties seem to have confined themselves to a discussion of the objectives that would be realized from the purchase of the policy rather than an attempt to negotiate the wording of the policy.

---

[2] Lessors are required to provide such insurance to their lessees, A.R.S. § 28–324. The statute also provides that if the lessor fails to do so, it is jointly and severally liable for all damages caused by the lessee while driving the leased vehicle.

[3] As might be expected, although Doxsee does not remember the substance of the conversation, he is quite sure he could have told Darner no such thing. Darner's testimony was impeached by evidence that he subsequently reduced the limits on his rental forms from 100/300 to 15/30. Darner explains this by stating that Doxsee told him that it was better to represent the coverage limits at the minimum required by the state so as to discourage plaintiffs' lawyers from pursuing claims for their badly injured clients. As in most such cases, who told what to whom is hotly contested, and there is much to be said for both versions of the facts.

Approximately twenty months after the conversation between Darner and Doxsee concerning coverage under the Universal policies, Darner Motors rented a car to Dwayne Crawford. The transaction was in the ordinary course of business, except that the form used for the rental agreement was the "old type," which contained a representation of coverage in the amount of 100/300. While driving the vehicle under this rental contract, Crawford negligently injured a pedestrian and caused severe injuries. The pedestrian sued Crawford, who looked to Universal for coverage. Universal claimed that lessee's coverage on the "U-Drive" policy was limited to 15/30. Crawford then sued Darner Motors under the rental agreement warranty that coverage was provided in limits of 100/300. Darner Motors called upon Universal to provide additional coverage under the umbrella policy. The umbrella policy did contain the higher limits, but Universal claimed that lessees were not parties "insured" as that term was defined in the all-risk policy. Universal was therefore unwilling to provide coverage in excess of the $15,000 limit of the U-Drive policy. Darner Motors then filed a third-party complaint, naming Universal and Doxsee as third party defendants.

Eventually, the pedestrian recovered $60,000 from Crawford. Universal paid $15,000 of this amount, and Darner Motors has either paid or is liable to Crawford for the remainder. Darner Motors claims that Universal and Doxsee are obligated to indemnify it against that loss. To support that contention, Darner Motors advances the following theories:

(1) Universal is estopped to deny coverage for lessees under the umbrella policy in amounts less than 100/300;

(2) The umbrella policy should be reformed so that it does contain such coverage;

(3) If no coverage is found through estoppel or reformation, then the loss incurred by Darner Motors was caused by the negligence of Universal and its agent, Doxsee, and should be borne by them;

(4) If no coverage exists by way of estoppel or reformation, then the loss incurred by Darner Motors is the result of fraud committed by Universal and its agent, Doxsee.

After considerable discovery, Universal and Doxsee moved for summary judgment, contending that there was no genuine issue of fact and that they were entitled to judgment as a matter of law. The motion was granted and judgment entered against Darner Motors. The court of appeals affirmed; pointing out that Darner Motors had not claimed that the umbrella policy was ambiguous, the court held that the insured's failure to read the policy prevented recovery on any theory, even though the contents of the policy did not comport with the representations of the insurance agent and those same representations were a part of the reason that the insured failed to read the policy.

The court of appeals stated that under Arizona law an insured who had received a copy of an unambiguous policy could not "expand the insurer's liability beyond the terms of the . . . policy issued. . . . " We believe this statement is too broad, though we acknowledge that the law is, at best, confused on this subject. In an attempt to bring some clarity and logic to the question, we have reviewed our cases and will discuss each of the theories advanced by Darner Motors. Before doing so, however, we must consider the inherent nature of an insurance contract and of the issues presented by the fact situation before us.

CONTRACT LAW AND INSURANCE POLICIES

Since this is an appeal from summary judgment, we must view the facts in the light most favorable to the party against whom judgment was taken. *Gulf Insurance Co. v. Grisham,* 125 Ariz. 123, 124, 613 P.2d 283, 284 (1980). Taking the facts in that light, the question we must decide is whether the courts will enforce an unambiguous provision contrary to the negotiated agreement made by the parties because, after the insurer's representations of coverage, the insured failed to read the insurance contract which was in his possession.[5]

Implicit in the reasoning of the court of appeals is the concept that the insurance policies purchased by Darner constitute *the* contract between Darner and Universal. Darner is considered to be bound by the terms contained within the documents. The court of appeals held:

> Because Mr. Darner received a copy of the umbrella policy and made no contention that it was ambiguous or confusing, he cannot expand the insurer's liability beyond the terms of the umbrella policy issued by Universal.

(slip op. at 7). Basic to this holding is the principle that the oral agreement between Doxsee and Darner cannot be shown to vary the terms of the insurance policy. This, indeed, was at one time the majority view. See cases cited in 12 Appleman, *Insurance Law and Practice* § 7155 (1981); similar language is contained in *Parks v. American Casualty Co. of Reading, Pa.,* 117 Ariz. 339, 572 P.2d 801 (1977); *Sellers v. Allstate Insurance Company,*

---

[5]   In characterizing the issue in this manner, we acknowledge that the insured did read the terms of the policy covering lessees and did discover the error in that policy. He was told by the agent that the umbrella policy provided the additional coverage. He did not read the provisions of the umbrella policy. Although that policy is not part of the record, we assume that it contains a clause or clauses defining the word "insured" in such a manner that lessees are excluded from the class of persons insured by the policy. We assume further that this definitional exclusion is clear and unambiguous. Therefore, it could have been found, read and understood by Darner. Of course we have no way of knowing that these assumptions are correct; however, it was the appellant's burden to make an adequate record on appeal. Since the appellant failed to offer the policy in evidence at the trial, we settle all factual uncertainty in favor of supporting the judgment of the trial court.

113 Ariz. 419, 422, 555 P.2d 1113, 1116 (1976); *see also Western Farm Bureau Mut. Ins. Co. v. Barela,* 79 N.M. 149, 441 P.2d 47 (1968). Some cases, including those from our own state, hold that since insurance policies are like other contracts, where the meaning and intent of the parties is "clear" from the words used in the instrument, the courts cannot "rewrite" the policy by considering the actual "words" used in striking the bargain. Thus, the rule of interpretation is stated to be that the intention of the parties as derived from the language used within the four corners of the instrument must prevail. *See, e.g., Rodemich v. State Farm Mutual Auto. Insurance Co.,* 130 Ariz. 538, 539, 637 P.2d 748, 749 (App.1981) (a vehicle which turned over and was damaged when the driver swerved to avoid an animal was not covered under the "upset" clause of a comprehensive risk policy because "upsets" resulting from attempts to avoid collision with animals were not covered unless there was actual contact). . . .

. . . Artificial results derived from application of ordinary rules of contract construction to insurance policies have made courts struggle to find some method of reaching a sensible resolution within the conceptual bounds of treating standardized, formal contracts as if they were traditional "agreements," reached by bargaining between the parties. This difficult task is often accomplished by the use of various constructs which enable courts to reach a desired result by giving lip service to traditional contract rules. One of the most prominent of these methods is the well recognized principle of resolving ambiguities against the insurer. *See Almadova v. State Farm Mutual Automobile Ins. Co.,* 133 Ariz. 81, 649 P.2d 284 (1982). The limitations of this principle have been discussed by Professor Robert Keeton, who comments that

> [t]he principle of resolving ambiguities against the draftsman is simply an inadequate explanation of the results of some cases. The conclusion is inescapable that courts have sometimes invented ambiguity where none existed, then resolved the invented ambiguity contrary to the plainly expressed terms of the contract document.

Keeton, *Insurance Law Rights at Variance with Policy Provisions,* 83 Harv.L.Rev. 961, 972 (1970) (footnotes omitted). Our court of appeals has attempted to avoid the problem of invented ambiguity by stating the principle that courts should not create ambiguities in order to rewrite the policy. Cf. *Barber v. Old Republic Life Ins. Co.,* 132 Ariz. 602, 604, 647 P.2d 1200, 1202 (App.1982) with *State Farm v. Gibbs, supra.* However, we also follow the rule of construction that where different jurisdictions reach different conclusions regarding the language of an insurance contract "ambiguity is established," *Federal Insurance Co. v. P.A.T. Homes, Inc.,* 113 Ariz. 136, 138, 547 P.2d 1050, 1052 (1976); thus, we may find ourselves justly criticized for accepting the inventions of other courts. It is also illogical to hold that an unexpected, unknown ambiguity in a clause which the parties did not negotiate, write or read should permit them to show the true terms of the agreement, but that the lack of such an ambiguity prevents them from so doing.

Such systems of logic—or illogic—have been criticized by Keeton, *supra,* and others for failing to recognize the realities of the insurance business and the methods used in modern insurance practice. *See, e.g., Zuckerman v. Transamerica Ins. Co.,* 133 Ariz. 139, 144–46, 650 P.2d 441, 446–48 (1982); *Harr v. Allstate Insurance Co.,* 54 N.J. 287, 301–04, 255 A.2d 208, 216–18 (1969); Restatement of Contracts (Second) § 211, comment b, and authorities cited in the reporter's note thereto; Abraham, *Judge-Made Law and Judge-Made Insurance: Honoring the Reasonable Expectations of the Insured,* 67 Va.L.Rev. (1981); Murray, *The Parol Evidence Process and Standardized Agreements under the Restatement (Second) of Contracts,* 123 U.Pa.L.Rev. 1342 (1975).

Abraham, *supra,* argues that "insurance law should be brought into the mainstream of our jurisprudence," and notes that "in many states, a principle authorizing the courts to honor the 'reasonable expectations' of the insured is emerging." *Id.* at 1151. "Emergence" is probably an inaccurate description of the use of the reasonable expectations test since, if correctly understood, that doctrine has long been a basic principle in the law of contracts.

> That portion of the field of law that is classified and described as the law of contracts attempts the realization of *reasonable expectations that have been induced* by the making of a promise.

1 Corbin, *Contracts* § 1, at 2 (1963) (emphasis supplied). We have previously recognized the doctrine of "reasonable expectations." *Zuckerman v. Transamerica Ins. Co.,* 133 Ariz. at 146, 650 P.2d at 448; *Sparks v. Republic Nat. Life Ins. Co.,* 132 Ariz. 529, 536–37, 647 P.2d 1127, 1134–35, *cert. denied,* 459 U.S. 1070, 74 L.Ed.2d 632, 103 S.Ct. 490 (1982). Of course, if not put in proper perspective, the reasonable expectations concept is quite troublesome, since most insureds develop a "reasonable expectation" that every loss will be covered by their policy. Therefore, the reasonable expectation concept must be limited by something more than the fervent hope usually engendered by loss. Such a limitation is easily found in the postulate contained in Corbin's work—that the expectations to be realized are those that "have been induced by the making of a promise." 1 Corbin, *supra* § 1 at 2.

We think it better, then, to start the analysis by attempting to determine what expectations have been induced. We note the concept that contracts are not merely printed words. The words, of course, are usually of paramount importance. However, other matters are also significant. 3 Corbin, *supra* §§ 538, 549. It is important to recognize that although the writing "may be coextensive with the agreement, it is not the agreement but only evidence thereof." Murray, *supra,* 123 U.Pa.L.Rev. at 1389. Murray adds that "if the writing is normally executed absent understanding of its fine print provisions, it is less worthy as evidence of the true agreement." *Id.* at 1373. Llewellyn puts the proposition another way:

> The fine print which has not been read has no business to cut under the reasonable meaning of those dickered terms which constitute the dominant and only real expression of agreement, but much of [the writing] commonly belongs in [the contract].

Llewellyn, *The Common Law Tradition* 370 (1960). Thus, Llewellyn concludes, "any contract with boiler-plate results in *two* several contracts: the *dickered* deal and the collateral one of *supplementary* boiler-plate." *Id.* at 371 (emphasis in original).

If we continue to look at an insurance policy as a contract between the insured and insurer, the foregoing analysis compels the conclusion that the problem is simply the application of the parol evidence rule. The traditional view of the law of contracts is that a written agreement adopted by the parties will be viewed as an integrated contract which binds those parties to the terms expressed within the four corners of the agreement. Thus, the parties may not vary or expand the agreement by introducing parol evidence to show understandings or antecedent agreements which are in some way contrary to the terms of the contract. *Restatement (Second) of Contracts* § 215. This rule is applied with varying degrees of exactitude to insurance policies. Cases from this state reflect that attitude. *See Sparks v. Republic Nat. Life Ins. Co., supra; Isaak v. Massachusetts Indemnity Life Ins. Co.,* 127 Ariz. 581, 623 P.2d 11 (1981); *Dairyland Mutual Ins. Co. v. Andersen,* 102 Ariz. 515, 433 P.2d 963 (1967); *but see Southern Casualty v. Hughes,* 33 Ariz. 206, 263 P. 584 (1928); *Ranger Insurance Co. v. Phillips,* 25 Ariz.App. 426, 544 P.2d 250 (1976).

When faced with harsh or illogical results, such as those produced by application of the parol evidence rule to most insurance contracts, the law usually reacts by recognizing exceptions which permit courts to avoid injustice. The ambiguity rule is, of course, one of those exceptions. Others, advanced with varying success, are the doctrines of waiver and estoppel. In our view, a better rationale is to be found by application of *established principles of contract law.* In so doing, however, we must remember that the usual insurance policy is a special kind of contract. It is largely adhesive; some terms are bargained for, but most terms consist of boilerplate, not bargained for, neither read nor understood by the buyer, and often not even fully understood by the selling agent. In contracts, as in other fields, the common law has evolved to accommodate the practices of the marketplace. Thus, in insurance law, as in other areas of contract law, the parol evidence rule has not been strictly applied to enforce an illusory "bargain" set forth in a *standardized contract* when that "bargain" was never really made and would, if applied, defeat the true agreement which was supposedly contained in the policy. *Sparks v. Republic National Life Insurance Co.,* 132 Ariz. at 537, 647 P.2d at 1135. *See also Zuckerman v. Transamerica Insurance Co.,* 133 Ariz. at 144, 650 P.2d at 446.

Sparks and *Zuckerman* reflect this court's attempt to bring some degree of logic and predictability into the field of insurance. What is needed, however, is recognition of a general rule of contract law. We believe that the current formulation of the *Restatement (Second) of Contracts* contains a workable resolution of the problem. The Restatement approach is basically a modification of the parol evidence rule when dealing with contracts containing boiler-plate provisions which are not negotiated, and often not even read by the parties.

Standardized Agreements

(1) Except as stated in Subsection (3), where a party to an agreement signs or otherwise manifests assent to a writing and has reason to believe that like writings are regularly used to embody terms of agreements of the same type, he adopts the writing as an integrated agreement with respect to the terms included in the writing.

(2) Such a writing is interpreted wherever reasonable as treating alike all those similarly situated, without regard to their knowledge or understanding of the standard terms of the writing.

(3) Where the other party has reason to believe that the party manifesting such assent would not do so if he knew that the writing contained a particular term, the term is not part of the agreement.

Restatement (Second) of Contracts § 211. We believe that the comments to this section of the Restatement support the wisdom of the rule formulated. Comment (a) points out that standardization of agreements is essential

> to a system of mass production and distribution. Scarce and costly time and skill can be devoted to a class of transactions rather than to details of individual transactions. . . . Sales personnel and customers are freed from attention to numberless variations and can focus on meaningful choice among a limited number of significant features: transaction-type, style, quantity, price, or the like. Operations are simplified and costs reduced, to the advantage of all concerned.

Subsections (1) and (2) of § 211 reflect the reality of the marketplace. Thus, those who make use of a standardized form of agreement neither expect nor desire their customers "to understand or even to read the standard terms." *Id.* comment (b). On the other hand, customers "trust to the good faith of the party using the form [and] . . . understand that they are assenting to the terms not read or not understood, subject to such limitations as the law may impose." *Id.* The limitations that the law may impose are that standard terms

> may be superseded by separately negotiated or added terms (§ 203), they are construed against the draftsman (§ 206), and they are subject to the overriding obligation of good faith (§ 205) and to the power of the court to refuse to enforce an unconscionable contract or term (§ 208).

Id. comment (c).[7]

Subsection (3) of § 211 is the Restatement's codification of and limitation on the "reasonable expectation" rule as applied to standardized agreements. The comment reads as follows:

> Although customers typically adhere to standardized agreements and are bound by them without even appearing to know the standard terms in detail, they are not bound to unknown terms which are beyond the range of reasonable expectation. . . . [An insured] who adheres to the [insurer's] standard terms does not assent to a term if the [insurer] has reason to believe that the [insured] would not have accepted the agreement if he had known that the agreement contained the particular term. Such a belief or assumption may be shown by the prior negotiations or inferred from the circumstances. Reason to believe may be inferred from the fact that the term is bizarre or oppressive, from the fact that it eviscerates the non-standard terms explicitly agreed to, or from the fact that it eliminates the dominant purpose of the transaction. The inference is reinforced if the adhering party never had an opportunity to read the term, or if it is illegible or otherwise hidden from view. This rule is closely related to the policy against unconscionable terms and the rule of interpretation against the draftsman.

Id. comment (f). We believe the analysis contained in the comments to the cited sections in the Restatement is a sensible rationale for interpretation of the usual type of insuring agreement.[8]

---

[7]   The Section numbers in this quote refer to sections in the Restatement (Second) of Contracts.

[8]   It would, of course, also be applicable to other transactions handled in a similar manner. We note, for example, that contracts for transport by rail, airline or bus; for rental of cars, trucks and other equipment; credit card and charge account "rules" and terms; bills of lading, invoices and many other commercial documents are "sold" or "made" in the same manner as most insurance policies. On the other hand, there are some insurance transactions which are still the product of negotiation which includes the terms of the policy. Such contracts are not affected by § 211 because it applies only to standardized agreements such as the average automobile, general liability, or fire policy.

This treatment of insurance law is neither radical nor new. All that is new in the "changed" Restatement is the articulation of the rule. Some cases long ago recognized the underlying principles. . . .

. . . Missing has been the articulation or formulation of some general rule to explain results of many past cases and to provide a pragmatic, honest approach to the resolution of future disputes. Hopefully, the adoption of § 211 of the Restatement as the rule for standardized contracts will provide greater predictability and uniformity of results—a benefit to both the insurance industry and the consumer.

In adopting this rule, we do not create a special field of contract law, we merely adopt a rule of integration which recognizes the method by which people do business. Indeed, the law pertaining to nonstandardized, negotiated contracts long ago began to move in the same direction. "Ordinary" contract law now recognizes that an agreement may be "partially integrated," or "completely integrated," depending upon "the degree to which the parties intended the writing to express their agreement." E. Farnsworth, *Contracts,* § 7.3 at 452 (1982). The relationship between the degree of integration and the application of the parol evidence rule has been the subject of much scholarly controversy. The authors of the leading contract treatises, Williston and Corbin, present differing views. "The point in dispute is whether the fact that the writing appears on its face to be a complete and exclusive statement of the terms of the agreement establishes conclusively that the agreement is completely integrated." Farnsworth, *supra* at 455. If it does, Williston would restrict interpretation to the four corners of the document. *Id.; See 4 Williston on Contracts* §§ 600A, 629, 633 (3d ed. 1961). Corbin argues that account should always be taken of all the surrounding circumstances to determine the extent of the integration *and* the interpretation of the agreement. Farnsworth, *supra* at 456; 3 Corbin, *supra,* § 582.

Recent decisions, the Uniform Commercial Code and the Restatement (Second) of Contracts have all favored Corbin's view. Farnsworth, *supra* at 453. *See also* Braucher, *Interpretation and Legal Effect in the Second Restatement of Contracts,* 81 Colum.L.Rev. 12 (1981). Arizona has followed the modern trend and adopted the Corbin view. . . .

It would be anomalous, indeed, to follow this view for contracts with bargained terms but to cling to the rejected rule in cases involving standardized form contracts. It would be even more anomalous if reasonable expectations induced by promises or conduct of a party are to be considered in determining integration or interpreting the words of a negotiated . . . agreement but disregarded when dealing with boilerplate, so that regardless of intent or even actual agreement, the parties are bound by provisions that were never discussed, examined, read or understood.

The general rule of contract interpretations adopted by the Restatement and based on Corbin's viewpoint is a modern view which takes into account the realities of present day commercial practice. See, Trakman, *Interpreting Contracts: A Common Law Dilemma,* 59 Canadian Bar Review 241 (1981). The rule which we adopt today for interpretation of standardized contracts recognizes modern commercial practice by business entities which use automated equipment to effect a large volume of transactions through use of standardized forms. It parallels the general rule which applies to all contracts by attempting to discover the intent of the parties, in so far as intent existed, and attempts to ascertain the real agreement so far as it was expressed or conveyed by implication. However, it recognizes that most provisions of standardized agreements are not the result of negotiation; often, neither customer nor salesperson are aware of the contract provisions. The rule adopted today recognizes reality and the needs of commerce; it allows businesses that use such forms to write their own contract. It charges the customer with knowledge that the contract being "purchased" is or contains a form applied to a vast number of transactions and includes terms which are unknown (or even unknowable); it binds the customer to such terms. However, the rule stops short of granting the drafter of the contract license to accomplish any result. It holds the drafter to good faith and terms which are conscionable; it requires drafting of provisions which can be understood if the customer does attempt to check on his rights; it does not give effect to boilerplate terms which are contrary to either the expressed agreement or the purpose of the transaction as known to the contracting parties. From the standpoint of the judicial system, the rule recognizes the true origin of standardized contract provisions, frees the courts from having to write a contract for the parties, and removes the temptation to create ambiguity or invent intent in order to reach a result.

The rule does not set a premium on failure to read. Those who negotiate their transactions will be held to the same rules as have previously obtained with regard to the duty to read. The rule which we adopt applies to contracts (or parts of contracts) made up of standardized forms which, because of the nature of the enterprise, customers will not be expected to read and over which they have no real power of negotiation.[9]

---

[9]　It cannot be seriously contended, for instance, that airline companies, car rental agencies, and the like expect their customers to line up, demand copies of the various instruments which set forth the "contract" and require explanations of the various terms. The usual "contract" for air transportation provides an example; it begins as follows:

Conditions of Contract

As used in this contract "ticket" means this passenger ticket and baggage check, of which these conditions and the notices form part, "carriage" is equivalent to "transportation", "carrier" means all air carriers that carry or undertake to carry the passenger or his baggage hereunder or perform any other service incidental to such air carriage, "Warsaw Convention" means the convention for the unification of certain rules relating to international carriage by air signed at Warsaw, 12th of October, 1929, or that

To apply the old rule and interpret such contracts according to the imagined intent of the parties is to perpetuate a fiction which can do no more than bring the law into ridicule. To those troubled by the change in the law, we point out that the fundamental change occurred first in business practice. The change in legal analysis does no more than reflect the change in methods of doing business. To acknowledge standardized contracts for what they are—rules written by commercial enterprises—and to enforce them as written, subject to those reasonable limitations provided by law, is to recognize the reality of the marketplace as it now exists, while imposing just limits on business practice. These, we think, have always been the proper functions of contract law. . . .

[The court also held that Darner might prevail on an equitable estoppel or reformation theory. As to estoppel, the court held: "if the fact finder determines that Darner and Doxsee did agree upon lessee's coverage in limits of 100/300, and if, by justifiably relying on Doxsee's assurances or for some other justifiable reason, Darner was unaware of the limitation in the umbrella policy, Universal would be estopped to assert the definitional exclusion which eliminates Darner's lessee from the class of persons insured." As to reformation, the court held the contract would be formed to be in accord with Darner's understanding if Darner could establish "Doxsee had knowledge of Darner's 'mistaken' understanding of the agreement."

As to Darner's negligence theory, the court held that an insurance agent owes a duty to the insured to exercise reasonable care, skill, and prudence in procuring insurance; that whether the insured's not reading the policies constitutes contributory negligence turns on the reasonableness of not reading the policies and relying on the agent's statements; and that the issue was one for the trier of fact. As to Darner's fraud theory, the court held that it could not say that the allegations on which the fraud count was based were wholly without merit.]

For the foregoing reasons we vacate the decision of the court of appeals and reverse the trial court's summary judgment as to the counts of equitable estoppel, reformation of the contract, negligent misrepresentation and fraud. Because of this disposition of the substantive matters, the court of appeals' award of attorney's fees is vacated.

GORDON, V.C.J., and HAYS, J., concur.

[The concurring opinion of Cameron, J., and the dissenting opinion of Holohan, C.J., are omitted.]

---

convention as amended at the Hague, 28th September, 1955, whichever may be applicable.

Uniform Passenger Ticket and Baggage Check, ATC version, printed on the back of the standard form of ticket in general use by airlines in the United States. Fortunately, we have not yet been required to interpret this contract by conjuring up some supposed intent of the passenger.

Gordinier v. Aetna Casualty & Surety Co.

154 Ariz. 266, 742 P.2d 277 (1987)

The Arizona Court here elaborated on *Darner* as follows: " ... As a synthesis of the cases and authorities demonstrates, Arizona courts will not enforce even unambiguous boilerplate terms in standardized insurance contracts in a *limited* variety of situations:

"1. Where the contract terms, although not ambiguous to the court, cannot be understood by the reasonably intelligent consumer who might check on his or her rights, the court will interpret them in light of the objective, reasonable expectations of the average insured (*see* ... *Wainscott v. Ossenkop,* 633 P.2d 237 (Alaska 1981) (application of "resident of same household" definition, while not technically ambiguous, defeats reasonable expectations of spouse));

"2. Where the insured did not receive full and adequate notice of the term in question, and the provision is either unusual or unexpected, or one that emasculates apparent coverage ... ;

"3. Where some activity which can be reasonably attributed to the insurer would create an objective impression of coverage in the mind of a reasonable insured ... ;

"4. Where some activity reasonably attributable to the insurer has induced a particular insured reasonably to believe that he has coverage, although such coverage is expressly and unambiguously denied by the policy. . . .

SECTION 4. COMPANY POLICY DOCUMENTS AS CONTRACTS

ANDERSON v. DOUGLAS & LOMASON COMPANY
Supreme Court of Iowa, 1995.
540 N.W.2d 277.

TERNUS, JUSTICE.

Defendant, Douglas & Lomason Company (DLC), discharged plaintiff, Terry Anderson, for taking a box of pencils. Anderson responded with a breach-of-contract action claiming DLC failed to follow progressive discipline policies contained in the employee handbook. The district court granted DLC's motion for summary judgment, which argued, in part, that the handbook did not constitute a contract. Anderson appealed.

Although we conclude progressive discipline policies meeting the requirements for a unilateral contract are enforceable, a disclaimer in the handbook given to Anderson prevented the policies from constituting a contract. Therefore, we affirm the district court's grant of summary judgment.

I. *Background Facts and Proceedings.*

On Anderson's first day of work at DLC he attended a six hour orientation session for new employees. He was informed that DLC had a progressive discipline policy and he was given a fifty-three page employee handbook which included these policies. Anderson read only the first few pages of the handbook; he admits he never read the provisions on progressive discipline.

DLC fired Anderson after three years of employment. His termination was based on an incident which occurred as he was leaving the plant one day. Company personnel stopped his pickup and asked to search it. Anderson gave permission and the workers found a box of company pencils. As a result, they also asked to search his home and garage. Anderson consented and a subsequent search revealed no company property. However, that same day, DLC asked Anderson to resign. He refused and was immediately fired.

Anderson responded by filing this breach-of-contract action against DLC. He claims DLC did not follow the progressive discipline policies outlined in its handbook for unauthorized possession of company property. These progressive discipline policies require a written warning for the first offense, a three-day suspension without pay for the second offense, and discharge for the third offense. Because this was not Anderson's third offense, he claims DLC could not fire him.

DLC filed a motion for summary judgment claiming the handbook did not constitute a contract and therefore Anderson was employed at-will. First, DLC contended the handbook was never communicated to or accepted by Anderson because he did not read it. Second, DLC argued the handbook was not definite enough to constitute an offer. DLC cited two reasons for its vagueness claim: the handbook contains no written guarantees that discharge will occur only for cause or under certain conditions—the rules are mere guidance; and the manual contains a written disclaimer. The district court granted the employer's summary judgment motion without explanation in a calendar entry.

II. *Scope of Review.*

We uphold summary judgment when the moving party shows no genuine issue of material fact exists and it is entitled to judgment as a matter of law. Iowa R.Civ.P. 237(c); *C-Thru Container Corp. v. Midland Mfg. Co.,* 533 N.W.2d 542, 544 (Iowa 1995). To decide if the moving party has met this burden, we review the record in the light most favorable to the party opposing summary judgment. *Hoffnagle v. McDonald's Corp.*, 522 N.W.2d 808, 811 (Iowa 1994).

III. *Indefinite Employment Contracts.*

The central issue presented by this dispute is whether DLC's issuance of a handbook created an employment contract. This question arises because Iowa employment relationships are presumed to be at-will: In the absence of a valid employment contract either party may terminate the relationship without consequence. *See Hunter v. Board of Trustees*, 481 N.W.2d 510, 513 (Iowa 1992). Indeed, the doctrine of employment at-will is merely a gap-filler, a judicially created presumption utilized when parties to an employment contract are silent as to duration. *Butler v. Walker Power, Inc.*, 137 N.H. 432, 629 A.2d 91, 93 (1993); *see also Sorenson v. Kennecott-Utah Copper Corp.*, 873 P.2d 1141, 1145 (Utah App.1994) (at-will rule is mere rule of contract construction); Richard A. Epstein, *In Defense of the Contract at Will*, U.Chi.L.Rev. 947, 951 (1984) ("[at-will] rule of construction [is] in response to the perennial question of gaps"). To understand our interpretation of employment contracts, particularly the nexus between the at-will doctrine and employee handbooks, we provide a brief overview.

A. *Development of employment at will.* The at-will presumption originated in English seasonal servant contract law. *See* Jay M. Feinman, *The Development of the Employment at Will Rule*, 20 Am.J.Legal Hist. 118, 118 (1976) (hereinafter "Feinman Article"). When parties remained silent as to the duration of service, the English courts filled the gap by presuming a certain duration and imposing a notice-of-termination requirement. 1 William Blackstone, *Commentaries on the Laws of England* 413 (U.Chi.Press 1979) ("If the hiring be general without any particular time limited, the law construes it to be a hiring for a year. . . . [Neither side can break the contract] without a quarter's warning.") (hereinafter "Blackstone"). The judicially created doctrine complemented statutes imposing a ban on leaving one's position or firing a worker before the end of the term and reflected the judiciary's concern for fairness between masters and seasonal servants. Feinman Article, 20 Am.J.Legal Hist. at 120; *see* Blackstone, at 413 (relationship continues "throughout all the revolutions of the respective seasons; as well as when there is work to be done, as when there is not").

The doctrine has never been static. As additional statutes were promulgated and the variety of employment situations far removed from the domestic environment increased, the English judiciary varied the amount of notice in accordance with the type of employment. Feinman Article, 20 Am.J.Legal Hist. at 121–22. "English law thus attempted to adapt to changing conditions and new situations. . . . " *Id.* at 121.

American courts relied heavily upon English precedent until the 1870s, when changing economic and social conditions prompted a dissolution of earlier law: the presumption of yearly hiring was seen as anachronistic and the concept of reasonable notice was disavowed. *Id.* at 125; *cf.* Richard J. Pratt, Comment, *Unilateral Modification of Employment Handbooks: Further Encroachments On the Employment-At-Will Doctrine,* 139 U.Pa.L.Rev. 197, 198–99 (1990) (hereinafter "Pratt Article"); Marla J. Weinstein, Comment, *The Limitations of Judicial Innovation: A Case Study of Wrongful Dismissal Litigation in Canada and the United States,* 14 Comp.Lab.L.J. 478 (1993) (comparing Canadian and American at-will jurisprudence; Canada retains the notice requirement). At this juncture, a new approach was suggested that changed the doctrine to a presumption of at-will employment:

> With us the rule is inflexible, that a general or indefinite hiring is *prima facie* a hiring at will, and if the servant seeks to make it out a yearly hiring, the burden is upon him to establish it by proof. . . . [I]t is an indefinite hiring and is determinable at the will of either party, and in this respect there is no distinction between domestic and other servants.

H.G. Wood, *A Treatise on the Law of Master & Servant* § 134, at 272 (1877). As the English presumption was a reflection of the economic and societal conditions in early Britain, Wood's rule was an outgrowth of prevailing American thought: ascendancy of freedom of contract, a reflection of the usual duration of employment contracts, and support for the development of advanced capitalism. Feinman Article, 20 Am.J.Legal Hist. at 130–31; *see also* Pratt Article, 139 U.Pa.L.Rev. at 199–201.

B. *Iowa jurisprudence.* Wood's version of employment at will quickly spread and was universally adopted. 1 Samuel Williston, *The Law of Contracts* § 39, at 61–62 (1920) (hereinafter "Williston"). Indeed, it is long established in Iowa case law. *Harrod v. Wineman,* 146 Iowa 718, 720, 125 N.W. 812, 813 (1910) ("it is held by an overwhelming weight of authority that a contract of indefinite employment may be abandoned at will by either party without incurring any liability"); *see also Fogel v. Trustees of Iowa College,* 446 N.W.2d 451, 455 (Iowa 1989); *Wolfe v. Graether,* 389 N.W.2d 643, 652 (Iowa 1986); *Harper v. Cedar Rapids Television Co.,* 244 N.W.2d 782, 791 (Iowa 1976).

Despite the universal acceptance of the employment-at-will doctrine, legislatures and courts have restricted its application. For example, federal labor law gave rise to union contracts that include just cause discharge provisions. Michael J. Phillips, *Disclaimers of Wrongful Discharge Liability: Time for a Crackdown,* 70 Wash.U.L.Q. 1131, 1134 (1992). Similarly, public employees are protected from arbitrary dismissal under civil service statutes. *E.g., City of Des Moines v. Civil Serv. Comm'n,* 540 N.W.2d 52, 58 (Iowa 1995); Iowa Code § 400.18 (1995).

Reflecting the perceived need to protect employees from the harshness of the at-will doctrine, courts began to erode the doctrine with exceptions. Richard Harrison Winters, Note, *Employee Handbooks & Employment-At-Will Contracts,* 1985 Duke L.J. 196, 199; *cf.* Lawrence E. Blades, *Employment at Will vs. Individual Freedom: On Limiting the Abusive Exercise of Employer Power,* 67 Colum.L.Rev. 1404 (1967). These exceptions generally fell within three categories: (1) discharges in violation of public policy, (2) discharges in violation of employee handbooks constituting a unilateral contract, and (3) discharges in violation of a covenant of good faith and fair dealing. Stephen F. Befort, *Employee Handbooks & the Legal Effect of Disclaimers,* 13 Indus.Rel.L.J. 326, 333–34 (1991/1992) (hereinafter "Befort Article"). However, Iowa's strong support of the at-will presumption is demonstrated by our reluctance to undermine the rule with exemptions. We have carved out only two narrow deviations: tort liability when a discharge is in clear violation of a "well-recognized and defined public policy of the State," *Springer v. Weeks & Leo Co.,* 429 N.W.2d 558, 560 (Iowa 1988), and employee handbooks that meet the requirements for a unilateral contract, *French v. Foods, Inc.,* 495 N.W.2d 768, 769–71 (Iowa 1993). We have consistently rejected recognition of a covenant of good faith and fair dealing. *E.g., id.* at 771; *Fogel,* 446 N.W.2d at 456–57.

Our prior handbook decisions concerned only "for-cause" provisions. However, we explicitly left room for future expansion: an employment handbook may guarantee an employee that discharge will occur "only for cause *or under certain conditions.*" *French,* 495 N.W.2d at 770; *accord Hunter,* 481 N.W.2d at 513; *Fogel,* 446 N.W.2d at 455. We now hold "or under certain conditions" to include progressive disciplinary procedures. Such provisions are enforceable if they are part of an employment contract. *Cf. Vaughn v. Ag Processing, Inc.,* 459 N.W.2d 627, 639 (Iowa 1990) ("We have recognized that written personnel policies providing terms *and procedures to be followed when discharging an employee* would be considered part of an at-will employee's employment contract.") (emphasis added); *Hamilton v. First Baptist Elderly Hous. Found.,* 436 N.W.2d 336, 340–41 (Iowa 1989) (considering whether personnel policies are part of the employment contract). We must now determine whether Anderson's handbook constitutes an enforceable contract. If it does not, we presume the parties intended a contract at will.

C. *Unilateral contract approach.* When considering whether a handbook creates a contract we utilize unilateral contract theory. *McBride v. City of Sioux City,* 444 N.W.2d 85, 90–91 (Iowa 1989). A unilateral contract consists of an offeror making a promise and an offeree rendering some performance as acceptance. *See Hunter,* 481 N.W.2d at 513; *see also*

1 E. Allan Farnsworth, *Farnsworth on Contracts* § 3.4, at 165 (1990) (hereinafter "Farnsworth"). An employee handbook is a unilateral contract when three elements are present: (1) the handbook is sufficiently definite in its terms to create an *offer;* (2) the handbook is communicated to and accepted by the employee so as to constitute *acceptance;* and (3) the employee provides *consideration. McBride,* 444 N.W.2d at 91.

As with any contract, the party who seeks recovery on the basis of a unilateral contract has the burden to prove the existence of a contract. *Hawkeye Land Co. v. Iowa Power & Light Co.,* 497 N.W.2d 480, 486 (Iowa App.1993). Therefore, Anderson has the burden to prove DLC's handbook created an enforceable contract. We begin our analysis with a discussion of the communication aspect of the acceptance element of Anderson's claim.

III. *Was the Employee Manual Communicated Even Though Anderson Never Read the Progressive Discipline Policies Upon Which He Now Relies?*

Anderson read only a few pages of the employee manual; he did not read the provisions on progressive discipline. DLC contends that under these circumstances, there can be no acceptance. We disagree. DLC distributed its employee handbook to new employees. We think Anderson's receipt of the handbook is sufficient communication.

A. *Traditional analysis: offeree must know of offer.* Under traditional contract analysis, an offer is not effective until it reaches the offeree. Farnsworth, § 3.10, at 212; Restatement (Second) of Contracts § 51, cmt. a (1981) ("it is ordinarily essential to the acceptance of the offer that the offeree know of the proposal made"); *cf. Iowa Malleable Iron Co. v. Iowa Employment Sec. Comm'n,* 195 N.W.2d 714, 718 (Iowa 1972) ("one cannot be deemed to have declined an offer never communicated to him"). The reason for the rule is clear: The offeree must know of the offer before there can be mutual assent. *Caldwell v. Cline,* 109 W.Va. 553, 554, 156 S.E. 55, 56 (1930); Farnsworth, § 3.10, at 212 ("This requirement has been reinforced by the insistence of the bargain theory of consideration that the acceptance be made in response to the offer.").

The most common illustration of the application of this rule is the general offer of a reward. John P. Dawson et al., *Cases & Comment on Contracts* 360 (5th ed. 1987). The reward-giver, or offeror, bargains for performance, not a reciprocal promise; sometimes the performance is rendered without knowledge of the offer. Some courts resolve this issue using the traditional law of contracts:

> there can be no contract unless the claimant when giving the desired information knew of the offer of the reward and acted with the intention of accepting such offer; otherwise the claimant gives the information not in the expectation of receiving a reward but rather out of a sense of public duty or other motive unconnected with the reward.

Glover v. Jewish War Veterans, 68 A.2d 233, 234 (D.C.1949); *see also Gadsden Times v. Doe,* 345 So.2d 1361, 1363–64 (Ala.Civ.App.1977); *Slattery v. Wells Fargo Armored Serv. Corp.,* 366 So.2d 157, 159 (Fla.Dist.App.1979); *Alexander v. Russo,* 1 Kan.App.2d 546, 571 P.2d 350, 358 (1977); *Braun v. Northeast Stations & Servs., Inc.,* 93 A.D.2d 994, 461 N.Y.S.2d 623, 624 (1983). Courts adopting this traditional approach do so because " 'it is impossible for an offeree actually to assent to an offer unless he knows of its existence.' " *Glover,* 68 A.2d at 234 (quoting Williston, § 33, at 47). On the other hand, one authority has suggested knowledge of a reward-offer need not be a prerequisite to acceptance:

> It is probable, indeed, that the chief reason for enforcing a promise is that it has induced the promisee to act in reliance upon it. One who has rendered a service without knowledge of an offered promise has not so acted. But the chief reason is not necessarily the only reason for enforcing a promise. If it seems fair to the courts to enforce a promise when the promisor has received the desired equivalent, even though the one rendering it knew nothing of the promise and rendered the service from other motives, there is no sufficient reason for refusing to call that enforceable promise a contract.

1 Joseph M. Perillo, *Corbin on Contracts* § 3.5, at 328 (rev. ed. 1993).

Iowa case law on rewards has not addressed this issue. However, we have adopted the traditional position with respect to unilateral contracts in general, that the offeree's performance "must have been induced by the promise made." *St. Peter v. Pioneer Theatre Corp.,* 227 Iowa 1391, 1401, 291 N.W. 164, 169 (1940). Nevertheless, for reasons that follow, we decline to follow the traditional requirement that knowledge of the offer is a prerequisite to acceptance *in the limited context of employee handbook cases.*

B.　*Employee handbooks: alteration of traditional rule.* Although we apply the traditional requirement of communication in ordinary contexts, an employment contract based upon an employee handbook "does not always follow the traditional model." Mark Pettit, Jr., *Modern Unilateral Contracts,* 63 B.U.L.Rev. 551, 583 (1983). We believe important policies, which are confined to employee handbook cases, dictate a narrow divergence.

Where a contract is based upon an employee handbook distributed to all employees, the contract is not an individually negotiated agreement; it is a standardized agreement between the employer and a class of employees. *Id.* We analogize to the interpretation of standardized contracts: "A standardized agreement 'is interpreted wherever reasonable as treating alike all those similarly situated, without regard to their knowledge or understanding of the standard terms of the writing.' "

Kinoshita v. Canadian P. Airlines, Ltd., 68 Haw. 594, 724 P.2d 110, 116–17 (1986) (quoting Restatement (Second) of Contracts § 211(2) (1981)).

Therefore, we hold it unnecessary that the particular employee seeking to enforce a promise made in an employee manual have knowledge of the promise. Although this holding is a departure from traditional 'bargain-theory' contract analysis, we think it produces "the salutary result that all employees, those who read the handbook and those who did not, are treated alike." E. Allan Farnsworth, *Developments in Contract Law During the 1980's: The Top Ten,* 41 Case W.Res.L.Rev. 203, 209 (1990). Moreover, our deviation from traditional contract theory is consistent with the spirit of the judicially created at-will presumption: It is a common law presumption created in response to statutory and societal demands.

Our decision also finds support in other jurisdictions. *E.g., Kinoshita,* 724 P.2d at 117 ("the plaintiffs' right to compel the company to live up to its promises does not turn on whether they received all of the communications addressed to the employees or not"); *Toussaint v. Blue Cross & Blue Shield,* 408 Mich. 579, 292 N.W.2d 880, 892 (1980) ("nor does it matter that the employee knows nothing of the particulars of the employer's policies and practices"); *Woolley v. Hoffmann-La Roche, Inc.,* 99 N.J. 284, 491 A.2d 1257, 1268 n. 10 (1985), *modified,* 101 N.J. 10, 499 A.2d 515 (1988) ("If reliance is not presumed, a strict contractual analysis might protect the rights of some employees and not the others. . . . [E]mployees neither had to read [the manual], know of its existence, or rely on it to benefit from its provisions any more than employees in a plant that is unionized have to read or rely on a collective-bargaining agreement in order to obtain its benefits."). Thus, the fact that Anderson did not read the employee manual does not prevent him from relying on the promises contained in the manual in this breach-of-contract action.

IV. *Did the Handbook's Progressive Discipline Procedures Constitute an Offer?*

We now consider whether DLC's handbook constituted an offer to Anderson to utilize progressive disciplinary procedures. We believe this aspect of the analysis should be conducted according to traditional contract theory.

A. *Offer.* All contracts must contain mutual assent; mode of assent is termed offer and acceptance. *Kristerin Dev. Co. v. Granson Inv.,* 394 N.W.2d 325, 330 (Iowa 1986); Restatement (Second) of Contracts § 22 (1981); *see also Service Employees Int'l Local No. 55 v. Cedar Rapids Community Sch. Dist.,* 222 N.W.2d 403, 408 (Iowa 1974). An offer is a "manifestation of willingness to enter into a bargain, so made as to justify another person in understanding that his assent to that bargain is invited and will conclude it." Restatement (Second) of Contracts § 24 (1981); *accord* Farnsworth, § 3.10, at 210 (offer is "a promise that is conditional on a manifestation of assent in the form of some action by the offeree and that confers upon the offeree the right to create a contract by taking that action").

We look for the existence of an offer objectively—not subjectively. *Cf. LaFontaine v. Developers & Builders, Inc.,* 261 Iowa 1177, 1183, 156 N.W.2d 651, 655 (1968) (existence of contract determined from words and circumstances). Judge Learned Hand explained this rule:

> A contract has, strictly speaking, nothing to do with the personal, or individual intent of the parties. A contract is an obligation attached by the mere force of law to certain acts of the parties, usually words, which ordinarily accompany and represent a known intent. If, however, it were proved by twenty bishops that either party, when he used the words, intended something else than the usual meaning which the law imposes upon them, he would still be held. . . .

Hotchkiss v. National City Bank, 200 F. 287, 293 (S.D.N.Y.1911), *aff'd sub nom. Ernst v. Mechanics' & Metals Nat'l Bank,* 201 F. 664 (2d Cir.1912), *aff'd sub nom. National City Bank v. Hotchkiss,* 231 U.S. 50, 34 S.Ct. 20, 58 L.Ed. 115 *and aff'd sub nom. Mechanics' & Metals Nat'l Bank v. Ernst,* 231 U.S. 60, 34 S.Ct. 22, 58 L.Ed. 121 (1913); *see also Embry v. Hargadine, McKittrick Dry Goods Co.,* 127 Mo.App. 383, 105 S.W. 777, 778 (1907) ("In so far as their intention is an influential element, it is only such intention as the words or acts of the parties indicate."). "The standard is what a normally constituted person would have understood [the words] to mean, when used in their actual setting." *New York Trust Co. v. Island Oil & Transp. Corp.,* 34 F.2d 655, 656 (2d Cir.1929) (Hand, J.); *cf. Deitrick v. Sinnott,* 189 Iowa 1002, 1010, 179 N.W. 424, 428 (1920) (cannot avoid contract because merely jesting if conduct and words were such as to warrant a reasonable person in believing that he was in earnest). We adopt the following analysis: "The test for an offer is whether it induces a reasonable belief in the recipient that he can, by accepting, bind the sender." *Architectural Metal Sys., Inc. v. Consolidated Sys., Inc.,* 58 F.3d 1227, 1229 (7th Cir.1995).

When objectively examining the handbook to determine intent to create an offer, we look for terms with precise meaning that provide certainty of performance. *Cf. Gildea v. Kapenis,* 402 N.W.2d 457, 459 (Iowa App.1987). This is a definiteness inquiry: if an offer is indefinite there is no intent to be bound. *See Architectural Metal Sys., Inc.,* 58 F.3d at 1229 ("A lack of essential detail would negate such a belief, since the sender could not reasonably be expected to empower the recipient to bind him to a contract of unknown terms. . . . [T]he recipient of a hopelessly vague offer should know that it was not intended to be an offer that could be made legally enforceable by being accepted.").

B.   *DLC's handbook is too vague to constitute an offer.* Here the issue is how a reasonable employee would construe DLC's handbook—a promise of progressive disciplinary procedures or mere guidance? The question resolves to whether the handbook's text was sufficiently definite to constitute an offer to apply certain procedures for discharge. *See Falczynski v. Amoco Oil Co.,* 533 N.W.2d 226, 235 (Iowa 1995). That is a question of law. *French,* 495 N.W.2d at 770; *Fogel,* 446 N.W.2d at 456.

DLC asserts the handbook was not definite enough to constitute an offer for two reasons: It claims there are no guarantees that the company will always follow the progressive discipline procedures, and the handbook includes a written disclaimer that expressly states there is no intent to create a contract. Therefore, DLC contends no offer existed for Anderson to accept.

1.   *Handbook language.* When considering whether a handbook is objectively definite to create a contract we consider its language and context. Our analysis of case law reveals three factors to guide this highly fact-intensive inquiry: (1) Is the handbook in general and the progressive disciplinary procedures in particular mere guidelines or a statement of policy, or are they directives? *See Boulay v. Impell Corp.,* 939 F.2d 480, 482 (7th Cir.1991) (language that was suggestive rather than mandatory lead to conclusion of no promise); *Johnson v. McDonnell Douglas Corp.,* 745 S.W.2d 661, 662 (Mo.1988) (en banc) ("The handbook was merely an informational statement of McDonnell's self-imposed policies"); (2) Is the language of the disciplinary procedures detailed and definite or general and vague? *See Hunt v. I.B.M. Mid America Employees Fed. Credit Union,* 384 N.W.2d 853, 856–58 (Minn.1986) (vague language fails to provide any detailed or definite disciplinary procedure); *Mecurio v. Therm-O-Disc, Inc.,* 92 Ohio App.3d 131, 634 N.E.2d 633, 637 (Ohio App.), *overruled on other grounds,* 68 Ohio St.3d 1410, 623 N.E.2d 566 (1993) ("From the plain terms of the [progressive discipline] policy . . . reasonable minds could conclude that an implied contract was created."); and (3) Does the employer have the power to alter the procedures at will or are they invariable? *See McDonnell Douglas Corp.,* 745 S.W.2d at 662 (handbook "provided that the rules were subject to change at any time"; thus, there was no contract); *Martin v. Capital Cities Media, Inc.,* 354 Pa.Super. 199, 511 A.2d 830, 838–39 (1986) (because employer could alter plan at will, no contract). We ask these questions to determine whether an employee is reasonably justified in understanding a commitment has been made. *See Bolling v. Clevepak Corp.,* 20 Ohio App.3d 113, 20 O.B.R. 146, 484 N.E.2d 1367, 1373 (1984).

Here, the text of the disciplinary procedures contains language of command: "The following action is prohibited, and the penalties for violation of these Shop Rules *shall* be as follows [progressive discipline steps are then listed]." (Emphasis added.) However, the introduction to the section of the handbook containing the disciplinary procedures states twice that the rules "have been designed for the *information and guidance* of all employees." (Emphasis added.) Second, the procedures themselves are fairly specific. There are four categories that describe in detail the offenses included in each category. In addition, the discipline for each category is also specific: for unauthorized possession of company property, the first offense requires a written warning, the second offense a three day unpaid suspension and the third offense results in discharge. Finally, DLC retained the power to alter the procedures at will. We need not decide whether these factors alone result in a sufficiently definite offer, however, because we must also consider the effect of DLC's disclaimer. *See Johnson v. Morton Thiokol, Inc.,* 818 P.2d 997, 1003 (Utah 1991) ("procedures in the handbook for terminating an employee must be read in light of the language in the disclaimer which clearly reserved the right to discharge for any reason").

2. *Handbook disclaimer.* A disclaimer can prevent the formation of a contract by clarifying the intent of the employer not to make an offer. Befort Article, 13 Indus.Rel.L.J. at 349; Chagares Article, 17 Hofstra L.Rev. at 378. "In the context of employee handbooks, the essential purpose of a disclaimer is to claim at-will status for the employment relationship by repudiating or denying liability for statements expressed in the handbook." Befort Article, 13 Indus.Rel.L.J. at 349. Although in theory disclaimers protect employers, many courts have imposed requirements that make it more difficult to give effect to them. *Id.*

For example, many jurisdictions require the disclaimer be "clear and conspicuous" to be enforceable and negate any contractual relationship between an employer and employee. Chagares Article, 17 Hofstra L.Rev. at 380; *see, e.g., Mace v. Charleston Area Medical Ctr. Found., Inc.,* 188 W.Va. 57, 63, 422 S.E.2d 624, 630 (1992) ("employee handbook which contains a clear and conspicuous disclaimer of job security will preserve the at-will status"). While we have never considered whether a disclaimer in an employee handbook must be clear and conspicuous, our court of appeals has implicitly endorsed a conspicuous requirement by holding a disclaimer "[p]rominently displayed in the first page" of a handbook prevented the formation of a contract. *Palmer v. Women's Christian Ass'n,* 485 N.W.2d 93, 95–96 (Iowa App.1992).

The requirement that a disclaimer be conspicuous has given rise to much litigation. Compare cases holding disclaimer clear and conspicuous, *Hein v. Kerr-McGee Coal Corp.,* 809 F.Supp. 84, 86–87 (D.Wyo.1990), *aff'd,* 956 F.2d 278 (10th Cir.1992) (disclaimer at beginning of handbook under heading "INTRODUCTION" which was one of two paragraphs on page, both of which were surrounded by open space); *Chambers v. Valley Nat'l Bank,* 721 F.Supp. 1128, 1131 (D.Ariz.1988) (disclaimer prominently displayed in bold print in introductory paragraph); *Nettles v. Techplan Corp.,* 704 F.Supp. 95, 98 (D.S.C.1988) (disclaimer of same type and color contained in separate paragraph on first page of manual); *Butler v. Westinghouse Elec. Corp.,* 690 F.Supp. 424, 429 (D.Md.1987) (disclaimer in bold print at front of handbook); *Investors Premium Corp. v. Burroughs Corp.,* 389 F.Supp. 39, 45 (D.S.C.1974) (clause set out in separate paragraph in capital letters); *Hanson v. New Technology, Inc.,* 594 So.2d 96, 99 (Ala.1992) (language found on first page of handbook); *Chesnick v. Saint Mary of Nazareth Hosp.,* 211 Ill.App.3d 593, 156 Ill.Dec. 69, 71, 570 N.E.2d 545, 547 (1991) (disclaimer on separate page signed by plaintiff); *Eldridge v. Evangelical Lutheran Good Samaritan Soc'y,* 417 N.W.2d 797, 800 (N.D.1987) (explicit disclaimer in closing statement located directly above signature of employee) with cases holding disclaimer not clear and conspicuous, *Durtsche v. American Colloid Co.,* 958 F.2d 1007, 1010 (10th Cir.1992) (disclaimer buried in glossary definition and no effort to highlight existence or effect of disclaimer); *Jimenez v. Colorado Interstate Gas Co.,* 690 F.Supp. 977, 980 (D.Wyo.1988) (disclaimer not set off in any way to attract attention, was placed under heading "GENERAL INSTRUCTIONS" and subheading "CONTENTS," was indistinct in print and type and had no border setting it apart from any other paragraph on page); *Hicks v. Methodist Medical Ctr.,* 229 Ill.App.3d 610, 170 Ill.Dec. 577, 579–80, 593 N.E.2d 119, 121–22 (1992) (disclaimer located on page thirty-eight of thirty-nine page manual; not highlighted, printed in capital letters nor in any way prominently displayed; was not entitled "Disclaimer," but was located in section headed "Revisions"); *Kumpf v. United Tel. Co.,* 311 S.C. 533, 429 S.E.2d 869, 872 (App.1993) (disclaimer located in "conclusion" section of handbook and not capitalized, in bold type, set apart with distinctive border nor in contrasting type or color). While the factual nature of the definiteness inquiry is partially to blame, too often such litigation is the product of illusory judicial standards. *See Sanchez v. Life Care Ctrs. of Am., Inc.,* 855 P.2d 1256, 1260 (Wyo.1993) ("This is yet another case to come before us in which an employer has tried to satisfy the court's secret concept of an adequate disclaimer in an employee handbook.") (Cardine, J., dissenting).

We think such uncertainty is unnecessary. A disclaimer should be considered in the same manner as any other language in the handbook to ascertain its impact on our search for the employer's intent. Therefore, we reject any special requirements for disclaimers; we simply examine the language and context of the disclaimer to decide whether a reasonable employee, reading the disclaimer, would understand it to mean that the employer has not assented to be bound by the handbook's provisions. *Cf. Bolling,* 484 N.E.2d at 1373 ("the employees . . . must be justified 'in understanding that a commitment has been made.'") (citations omitted); *Payne v. Sunnyside Community Hosp.,* 78 Wash.App. 34, 894 P.2d 1379, 1384 (1995) ("crucial question is whether the employee has a reasonable expectation the employer will follow the discipline procedure, based upon the language used").

Similar to our consideration of handbook language in general, we believe two factors guide our inquiry. First, is the disclaimer clear in its terms: does the disclaimer state that the handbook does not create any rights, or does not alter the at-will employment status? Second, is the coverage of the disclaimer unambiguous: what is the scope of its applicability? Here the disclaimer appears on page fifty-three, the last page of the handbook, two inches below the preceding paragraph:

This Employee Handbook is not intended to create any contractual rights in favor of you or the Company. The Company reserves the right to change the terms of this handbook at any time.

When examining the disclaimer we first consider the text employed. In no uncertain terms DLC's disclaimer states the handbook "is not intended to create *any* contractual rights." (Emphasis added.) *See Smoot v. Boise Cascade Corp.,* 942 F.2d 1408, 1411 (9th Cir.1991) ("the written materials also contain explicit disclaimers that preclude their forming the basis of an employment agreement"); *Shapiro v. Wells Fargo Realty Advisors,* 152 Cal.App.3d 467, 199 Cal.Rptr. 613, 616 (1984) (agreement stated that it did not confer a right to continued employment); *Tilbert v. Eagle Lock Co.,* 116 Conn. 357, 165 A. 205, 207 (1933) (death benefit plan said "it constitutes no contract with any Employee or any beneficiary, and confers no legal rights on" any party). We believe DLC's disclaimer is clear in its disavowal of any intent to create a contract.

Second, we examine the scope of the disclaimer. There is nothing about the location of DLC's disclaimer or the language used to suggest that the disclaimer does not apply to the progressive discipline policies. The disclaimer is found in the handbook itself and *289 unequivocally applies to the entire employee handbook.

We think a reasonable person reading the handbook could not believe that DLC has assented to be bound to the provisions contained in the manual. *See Smoot,* 942 F.2d at 1411 (finding employment at will as a matter of law: "Although [employer's] termination policies contain promises of specific treatment in specific situations, the written materials also contain explicit disclaimers that preclude their forming the basis of an employment agreement."). Thus, we hold DLC's handbook is not sufficiently definite to constitute a valid offer.

VI. *Summary.*

We hold as a matter of law no contract existed between Anderson and DLC. Anderson was employed at-will. Therefore, the trial court correctly granted summary judgment to DLC.

AFFIRMED.

———

Dyer v. Northwest Airlines Corporations

334 F.Supp.2d 1196 (D.N.D. 2004)

(Hovland, C.J.) "Following September 11, 2001, the National Aeronautical and Space Administration ("NASA") requested system-wide passenger data from Northwest Airlines for a three-month period in order to conduct research for use in airline security studies. Northwest Airlines complied and, unbeknownst to its customers, provided NASA with the names, addresses, credit card numbers, and travel itineraries of persons who had flown on Northwest Airlines between July and December 2001.

"The discovery of Northwest Airlines' disclosure of its customers' personal information triggered a wave of litigation. Eight class actions—seven in Minnesota and one in Tennessee—were filed in federal court prior to March 19, 2004. The seven Minnesota actions were later consolidated into a master file.

"The Plaintiffs initiated the above-entitled action in state court in North Dakota on March 19, 2004. The complaint alleges that Northwest Airlines' unauthorized disclosure of customers' personal information constituted a violation of the Electronic Communications Privacy Act ("ECPA"), 18 U.S.C. §§ 2702(a)(1) and (a)(3), and a breach of contract. . . .

"The Plaintiffs base their breach of contract claim on Northwest Airlines' alleged violation of the privacy policy posted on its website. Northwest Airlines contends that a policy posted on its website does not constitute a contract. In addition, Northwest Airlines argues that even if the policy did constitute a contract, the Plaintiffs claim fails because they have not alleged any contract damages.

"To sustain a breach of contract claim, the Plaintiffs must demonstrate (1) the existence of a contract; (2) breach of the contract; and (3) damages which flow from the breach. *United States v. Basin Elec. Power Co-op.*, 248 F.3d 781, 810 (8th Cir.2001) (applying North Dakota law). The plaintiff bears the burden of proving each element. *Id.*

"Having carefully reviewed the complaint, the Court finds the Plaintiffs' breach of contract claim fails as a matter of law. First, broad statements of company policy do not generally give rise to contract claims. See *Pratt v. Heartview Foundation*, 512 N.W.2d 675, 677 (N.D.1994); accord *Martens v. Minnesota Mining and Manu. Co.*, 616 N.W.2d 732, 740 (Minn.2000). As such, the alleged violation of the privacy policy at issue does not give rise to a contract claim. Second, nowhere in the complaint are the Plaintiffs alleged to have ever logged onto Northwest Airlines' website and accessed, read, understood, actually relied upon, or otherwise considered Northwest Airlines' privacy policy. Finally, even if the privacy policy was sufficiently definite and the Plaintiffs had alleged they did read the policy prior to providing personal information to Northwest Airlines, the Plaintiffs have failed to allege any contractual damages arising out of the alleged breach. A plaintiff cannot recover for a breach of contract claim without showing damages resulting from the breach. The Plaintiffs have failed to allege any facts relating to the breach of contract claim which support the conclusory statements they have suffered damages. The breach of contract claim is subject to dismissal as a matter of law."

PART 5

MISTAKE AND UNEXPECTED CIRCUMSTANCES

■ ■ ■

CHAPTER 17

MISTAKE

■ ■ ■

Suppose that A and B enter into a contract that is either based on or reflects some kind of mistake made by A, or by A and B jointly. After the mistake is discovered, A claims that because of the mistake the contract should either be unenforceable, if it has not been performed, or reversible, if it has been.

The problems raised by claims of this kind have been a source of persistent difficulty in contract law. In part this difficulty results from the complex nature of the underlying issues. Intuitively, there seems to be a serious tension between the concept that a mistake may be a ground for relief in contractual transactions, on the one hand, and such basic ideas of contract law as risk-shifting, the security of transactions, and rewards for knowledge, skill, and diligence, on the other. Much of the difficulty, however, results from the use of legal categories and doctrinal rules that are not based on a functional analysis.

This Chapter will consider four types of mistake: mechanical errors ("unilateral mistakes"), mistranscriptions, shared mistaken factual assumptions ("mutual mistakes"), and unshared mistaken factual assumptions (nondisclosure). (Another type of mistake, misunderstanding, has been considered in Chapter 8, Section 1, supra.)

SECTION 1. MECHANICAL ERRORS ("UNILATERAL MISTAKES")

A common kind of mistake in everyday life consists of physical blunders, like spilling coffee. This kind of mistake, although manifested externally, normally results from an error in the mechanics of an actor's internal machinery, such as a lapse of concentration, a loss of balance, or an error in hand-eye coordination. Such errors are almost invariably transient. If an actor spilled every cup of coffee he handled, we would not characterize his spills as mistakes, but instead would conclude that he had a disability.

A counterpart to transient physical blunders consists of intellectual blunders that result from transient errors in the mechanics of an actor's internal machinery. For example, as a result of a transient error in the mechanics of an actor's mental machinery, the actor may write "65" when he intends to write "56" or may incorrectly add a column of figures.

Mistakes of this kind—that is, physical or intellectual blunders that result from transient errors in the mechanics of an actor's internal machinery—may be thought of as *mechanical errors*. Mechanical errors resemble the kind of mistake sometimes made in the transcription of DNA. Almost invariably, that transcription is correct. Every once in a while, it goes transiently awry.

Although contract law does not use the term mechanical errors, virtually all cases that are categorized as involving unilateral mistakes are mechanical-error cases.

DePrince v. Starboard Cruise Services, Inc.

District Court of Appeal of Florida, 2015.
163 So.3d 586.

ROTHENBERG, J.

Thomas DePrince ("DePrince") appeals the trial court's order granting summary judgment in favor of Starboard Cruise Services, Inc. ("Starboard") on DePrince's claims against Starboard for breach of contract, specific performance, and conversion. Because we find that disputed issues of material fact remain to be resolved on all three counts of DePrince's complaint, we reverse and remand for further proceedings.

Historical Hollywood starlet Mae West once said, "I never worry about diets. The only carrots that interest me are the number of carats in a diamond." Thus, it appears quite likely that Ms. West would have been interested in the diamond in this case: a twenty carat diamond that Starboard offered to DePrince for a very low sum. As it turns out, the "too good to be true" price of the diamond was just that, and the price conveyed to DePrince was a mistake. Now DePrince wants his twenty carat diamond; Starboard wants out of its sales contract; and Starboard's supplier, who allegedly misquoted the price of the diamond upon which Starboard and DePrince relied, has not even been added as a party to the lawsuit. In short, this is truly a gem of a case.

FACTUAL BACKGROUND

DePrince embarked on a cruise from Miami in February 2013. During that cruise, DePrince visited an onboard jewelry shop that is wholly owned and operated by Starboard. When DePrince expressed some interest in a large loose diamond[1] and specified to the sales manager of the store, Mihai Rusan ("Rusan"), that the stone should be between 15 and 20 carats, Rusan, who had never dealt with a diamond of such magnitude, sent an email inquiry to Starboard's corporate office in Miami ("the Miami Office").

Starboard maintains a consignment agreement with a supplier, Sophia Fiori ("Fiori"), that allows Starboard to obtain gemstones and jewelry for sale in its onboard stores. The consignment agreement between Starboard and Fiori specifies, in relevant part:

> 3. Title to the Consigned Merchandise shall at all times remain with Consignor until the time of its sale to customers of Consignee, whereupon the Consigned Merchandise shall be deemed to have been purchased from Consignor by Consignee.

Upon receiving the email inquiry from Rusan, the Miami Office relayed the information to Fiori to determine whether Fiori could fill such an order should DePrince decide to purchase a diamond. Fiori responded to the Miami Office via email, informing Starboard that there were two diamonds of that size available. Fiori's email described the diamonds precisely as follows:

1. EMERALD CUT 20.64 carats D VVS2 GIA VG Price $235,000

2. EMERALD CUT 20.73 carats E VVS2 GIA EX EX FNT Price $245,000

The Miami Office relayed this information to Rusan via email exactly as Fiori had typed it. Rusan notified DePrince of the availability of the size of the diamond he was interested in purchasing and the pricing information contained in the email, telling him that the purchase prices for the diamonds were $235,000 and $245,000 respectively.

DePrince told Rusan that he was interested, but that he would like to take some time to think about the purchase. That night, DePrince spoke with his life partner, Vernon Crawford, a certified gemologist who was on the cruise with DePrince, and also DePrince's sister, Carolyn DePrince, who holds the highest available degree in gemology. Both advised DePrince against making the purchase, telling him that the sale price was too good to be true and that the price for a diamond that large should be at least $2 million.

DePrince, however, ignored their advice and opted to complete the transaction. DePrince returned to Starboard's onboard jewelry store and placed a special mail purchase order for the 20.64 carat diamond the next day. Rusan prepared and signed a one-page sales agreement that listed the total price for the diamond at $235,000 plus a $25 shipping charge.

---

[1] A "loose diamond" refers only to the gemstone itself, rather than a gemstone that is a component of a larger piece of jewelry.

DePrince made an initial down payment of $125,000 on the spot and paid the balance ($110,025) the next day. The parties agreed to have the diamond shipped to the Gemological Institute of America laboratory in New York so that a neutral gemologist could verify that the diamond that was shipped was the same one specified in the sales agreement.

Soon after the sale was completed, Starboard learned that Fiori's $235,000 price quote in the email was the **per carat** price for the diamond rather than the **total price** for the diamond ($4,850,400), and thus, Starboard had inadvertently contracted to sell the diamond to DePrince for less than 1/20th of the diamond's actual value. Five days after the sales agreement was executed, Starboard contacted DePrince via telephone to explain the situation, stating that the price on the sales agreement was "seriously in error" due to the mix-up in the email. Starboard offered discounted future cruise rates to DePrince to compensate him for the inconvenience, but DePrince demanded that the sale be completed as specified in the sales agreement. Starboard unilaterally reversed the charges on DePrince's credit card to refund him all the money he had paid and then repudiated the sales agreement, informing DePrince that it would not be shipping the diamond as they had originally agreed. These communications were memorialized in an email Starboard sent to DePrince after the phone call. The record does not disclose how Starboard dealt with the cancellation of the sale with regard to Fiori.

Thereafter, DePrince filed a complaint against Starboard alleging counts for specific performance, breach of contract, and conversion. Starboard answered and pleaded the affirmative defense of unilateral mistake, among others, claiming that Rusan had misquoted DePrince the total price of the diamond rather than the per carat price and that DePrince had known about the error the whole time due to his extensive experience with jewelry. Starboard also counterclaimed for a declaratory judgment that the sales agreement was unenforceable and for rescission of the contract.

Starboard moved for summary judgment on the ground that there had clearly been a unilateral mistake in the pricing, and, after hearing argument on that issue, the trial court granted summary judgment against DePrince on all his claims. Specifically, the trial court ruled at the summary judgment hearing:

> I don't find that the plaintiff has established that there were any actionable damages and I don't find that there was a valid and enforceable contract for either the breach of contract or the conversion count. Particularly as to conversion, I don't find that the plaintiff or the defendant ever—there's no record evidence that the plaintiff possessed the diamond, as opposed to remaining

in the possession of the vendor. I find, quite frankly, that it may be unconscionable to enforce this particular contract.

This appeal followed.

ANALYSIS

"[A] party moving for summary judgment must show conclusively the absence of any genuine issue of material fact and the court must draw every possible inference in favor of the party against whom a summary judgment is sought." *Moore v. Morris,* 475 So.2d 666, 668 (Fla.1985). Summary judgment is only appropriate when an examination of the facts in the light most favorable to the non-movant demonstrates that the movant is entitled to judgment as a matter of law. Fla. R. Civ. P. 1.510(c); *Volusia Cnty. v. Aberdeen at Ormond Beach, L.P.,* 760 So.2d 126, 130 (Fla.2000).

The trial court granted summary judgment against DePrince on his breach of contract action due to its finding that there had been a unilateral mistake of fact sufficient to rescind the otherwise-enforceable contract, enforcement of the contract would be "unconscionable," and DePrince had not alleged any actionable damages. On DePrince's claim for specific performance, the trial court found that the diamond was not unique and was therefore not the proper subject of the remedy of specific performance. And as to DePrince's conversion claim, the trial court granted summary judgment in Starboard's favor based on its finding that Starboard never had possession of the diamond.

We do not agree with the trial court that there are no genuine issues of material fact such that Starboard is entitled to judgment as a matter of law on any of these claims. Thus, Starboard was not entitled to summary judgment.

I.   Contract Formation and Enforcement

On appeal, Starboard has raised two defenses to the sales agreement's formation and enforcement. First and primarily, Starboard claims that a unilateral mistake of law prevents the contract from being formed. Second, Starboard summarily raised an unconscionability defense in its briefing and then pressed that point more extensively at oral argument. For the reasons that follow, neither of these arguments entitle Starboard to summary judgment on DePrince's breach of contract claim. Moreover, the trial court seemed to make a sua sponte finding that DePrince had not alleged any actionable damages to support his breach of contract claim. That ruling was also in error. We explain each of these theories at length because there appears to be a great deal of misunderstanding in each of these areas.

A. Unilateral Mistake

There are three potentially viable tests to determine whether a contract may be rescinded based on a unilateral mistake of fact: (1) A four-prong test requiring the highest burden of proof for the party seeking to avoid the contract; (2) a two-prong test requiring the lowest burden of proof for the party seeking to avoid the contract; and (3) a 3-prong disjunctive test that provides several more-flexible methods of establishing a unilateral mistake.

This Court's most recent decisions on this topic clearly articulated and reaffirmed the viability of the four-prong test to establish a unilateral mistake, *Rachid v. Perez,* 26 So.3d 70, 72 (Fla. 3d DCA 2010), and this panel—along with the trial court—is of course bound by that decision, *see State v. Washington,* 114 So.3d 182, 188–89 (Fla. 3d DCA 2012) ("This panel is not free to disregard, or recede from, [a prior decision from this Court]; only this Court, sitting en banc, may recede from an earlier opinion."). However, it matters not which test is applied at this stage of the proceedings because we find that the trial court's summary judgment order cannot be upheld due to a unilateral mistake of fact under any of these three formulations. Thus, the trial court's order granting summary judgment cannot be upheld based on a unilateral mistake of fact. We analyze each of these three tests in turn to clarify what appears to be a confusing area of the law with inconsistent application among Florida's district courts of appeal.

1. This Court's Four-Prong Test for Unilateral Mistakes of Fact

This Court has held that in order to rescind an otherwise-valid contract based on a unilateral mistake, the party seeking to avoid the contract must show:

> (1) [T]he mistake was induced by the party seeking to benefit from the mistake, (2) there is no negligence or want of due care on the part of the party seeking a return to the status quo, (3) denial of release from the agreement would be inequitable, and (4) the position of the opposing party has not so changed that granting the relief would be unjust.

Rachid, 26 So.3d at 72 (quoting *Lechuga v. Flanigan's Enters., Inc.,* 533 So.2d 856, 857 (Fla. 3d DCA 1988)); *Ali R. Ghahramani, M.D., P.A. v. Pablo A. Guzman, M.D., P.A.,* 768 So.2d 535, 537 n. 1 (Fla. 4th DCA 2000). Examining the facts as alleged and supported by DePrince, Starboard did not conclusively demonstrate either of the first two prongs of this analysis.[5]

---

[5] DePrince has not argued on appeal that the third or fourth prong has not been satisfied. He seems to agree that the transaction appears inequitable and that he has not changed his position in reliance on the purchase.

First, Starboard presented no evidence that DePrince induced it into making the pricing mistake. The primary focus of Starboard's argument, both at the summary judgment hearing and in its brief, was that DePrince must have known of the mistake in pricing due to his background as a former antiques and jewelry dealer and the advice he received from his gemologist partner and his sister. DePrince, however, denied that he knew there had been a pricing mistake in his affidavit, which is sufficient at the summary judgment phase of the proceedings to create a genuine issue of material fact. More importantly, we note that even if DePrince had known that the price he was quoted to purchase the diamond was in error, knowledge of an error is markedly different than inducement of that error. *See, e.g., Gemini Investors III, L.P. v. Nunez,* 78 So.3d 94, 97 (Fla. 3d DCA 2012) (explaining that fraudulent inducement requires that the party seeking to enforce the contract "(1) made a statement concerning a material fact, (2) knowing that the statement was false, (3) with intent that the [mistaken party] act on the false statement; and (4) the [mistaken party was] damaged as a result of [its] reasonable reliance on the false statement"). Because Starboard presented no evidence that the pricing mistake was induced by DePrince, the trial court clearly erred by granting summary judgment in Starboard's favor under the four-prong test.

Second, there is a factual dispute regarding the second prong of the unilateral mistake standard: that the party seeking to avoid the contract (Starboard) was not inexcusably negligent or failed to act with due care. DePrince avers in both his complaint and affidavit that Starboard did **not** act with due care when it sold him the diamond. Starboard claims it simply provided DePrince with the quote provided to it by Fiori, and that it did not act negligently. Thus, whether Starboard made a reasonable and understandable mistake or acted negligently in its handling of the sale is a disputed issue of fact, and, because questions involving reasonableness and negligence determinations are highly factual inquiries upon which reasonable people could disagree, they are rarely appropriately resolved on summary judgment. *Spadafora v. Carlo,* 569 So.2d 1329, 1331 (Fla. 2d DCA 1990). This case is no exception.

2.   *The Two-Prong Test for Unilateral Mistakes of Fact*

Although we have determined that Starboard has not satisfied its burden of meeting the four-prong test adopted by this Court to set aside a contract for unilateral mistake for purposes of summary judgment, Starboard contends that the two-prong test for pleading and proving a unilateral mistake is the test that should be applied. Starboard's argument is not wholly without merit, and in fact, numerous Florida cases have relied on the two-prong standard. Most recently, in *Garvin v. Tidwell,* the Fourth District Court of Appeal stated "that a trial court may rescind an agreement based on unilateral mistake if '(1) the mistake did not result from an inexcusable lack of due care, and (2) defendant's position did not so change in reliance that it would be unconscionable to set aside the agreement.' " 126 So.3d 1224, 1228 (Fla. 4th DCA 2012) (quoting *Stamato v. Stamato,* 818 So.2d 662, 664 (Fla. 4th DCA 2002)); *see also Fla. Ins. Guar. Ass'n v. Love,* 732 So.2d 456, 457 (Fla. 2d DCA 1999) (applying the same two-prong test); *U.S. Alliance Corp. v. Tobon,* 715 So.2d 1122, 1123 (Fla. 3d DCA 1998) (same); *BMW of N. Am., Inc. v. Krathen,* 471 So.2d 585, 588 (Fla. 4th DCA 1985) (same).

The two elements in the two-prong test are in substance nearly identical to two of the four prongs relied upon by this Court. Indeed, the four-prong test largely restates the two-prong test and adds the elements that "the mistake was induced by the party seeking to benefit from the mistake [and] ... denial of release from the agreement would be inequitable." *Rachid,* 26 So.3d at 72 (quoting *Lechuga,* 533 So.2d at 857). . . .

Most importantly in this case, however, is the fact that both the two- and the four-prong tests require that the party seeking to invoke a unilateral mistake of fact as an affirmative defense establish that he was not unduly negligent in forming the contract. As explained above, a genuine question of fact remains regarding whether Starboard was negligent in this case, thereby precluding summary judgment under the two-prong standard as well.

3.   *Florida's Jury Instruction for Unilateral Mistakes of Fact*

Lastly, although neither party initially argued for the application of the third test to establish unilateral mistake, Florida's new jury instruction, which was adopted in June 2013, *In re Standard Jury Instructions-Contract and Bus. Cases,* 116 So.3d 284, 324 (Fla.2013), pertaining to unilateral mistake states the test in yet another substantially different way:

To establish [the defense of unilateral mistake], (defendant) must prove all of the following:

1.   (Defendant) was mistaken about (insert description of mistake) at the time the parties made the contract;

2.   [The effect of the mistake is such that enforcement of the contract would be unconscionable]

[or]

[(Claimant) had reason to know of the mistake or [he][she][it] caused the mistake.]

and

3.   (Defendant) did not bear the risk of mistake. A party bears the risk of a mistake when

[the parties' agreement assigned the risk to [him][her][it]]

[or]

[[he][she][it] was aware, at the time the contract was made, that [he][she] [it] had only limited knowledge about the facts relating to the mistake but decided to proceed with the contract].

Fla. Std. Jury Instr. (Civ.) 416.26 (first alteration added).

This instruction is nearly identical to the formulation of the unilateral mistake defense found in the Restatement (Second) of Contracts. *See* Restatement (Second) of Contracts §§ 153, 154 (1979). However, this particular three-prong test has not been adopted or cited by any Florida decision to date. "Standard jury instructions are not binding precedent," although they can be quite persuasive and instructive "[i]n the absence of a definitive case." *BellSouth Telecomm., Inc. v. Meeks,* 863 So.2d 287, 292 (Fla.2003). In this instance, however, because there are definitive cases in this jurisdiction, we are bound by those cases. And in those cases, this Court clearly applied the four-prong test. *See Rachid,* 26 So.3d at 72; *Lechuga,* 533 So.2d at 857.

Even if jury instruction 416.26 was the law in Florida, Starboard should not have prevailed on its summary judgment motion. That is because even if DePrince had been aware of the mistake and enforcement of the contract would be unconscionable—either or both of which would satisfy the second prong of the analysis—the third prong requires that the party seeking to assert the unilateral mistake defense show that it did not bear the risk of the mistake. Fla. Std. Jury Instr. (Civ.) 416.26. A party can be found to bear the risk of its mistake if the contract expressly assigns that risk to the party or if that party is aware at the time of the contract's formation that it had only limited knowledge about the facts relating to the mistake but decided to proceed with the contract anyway. The contract in this case does not assign the risk to either party, and factual questions certainly remain as to whether Starboard should have known at the time it formed the contract that it had insufficient information to facilitate such an expensive transaction. Indeed, Rusan himself stated in his deposition that he had never dealt with a diamond this large. Because this factual question remains, summary judgment would also have been inappropriate under the new jury instruction.

To reiterate our position on unilateral mistakes of fact, this Court currently adheres to the four-prong test as stated in *Rachid* and *Lechuga.* There are at least two other tests—the two-prong test found primarily in other districts' case law and the three-prong test found in standard jury instruction 416.26—in Florida jurisprudence. The existence of three different tests has caused a great deal of confusion in the case law and to litigants and trial courts. However, under any of these three tests,

Starboard should not have prevailed on summary judgment based on its unilateral mistake of fact defense.

B.   Unconscionability as an element of Unilateral Mistake

Starboard also contends on appeal, and the trial court seemed to find, that the contract was unenforceable because the agreement was unconscionable. The independent affirmative defense of unconscionability requires that the party seeking to avoid enforcement of the contract prove both procedural and substantive unconscionability. *Kohl v. Bay Colony Club Condo., Inc.,* 398 So.2d 865, 867 (Fla. 4th DCA 1981). The procedural aspect of an unconscionability defense focuses on the parties to the contract and the circumstances surrounding the formation of the contract. In essence, procedural unconscionability requires proof that one party had such an extreme advantage with respect to bargaining power, experience, or some other important characteristic that the other party to the contract was not given a "meaningful choice" to refuse the contract terms. *Id.* at 868 (quoting *Bennett v. Behring Corp.,* 466 F.Supp. 689, 696 (S.D.Fla.1979)). Before finding that a contract is a product of procedural unconscionability, the court must examine all the details surrounding the formation of the contract-an incredibly factually intensive inquiry. *Gainesville Health Care Ctr., Inc. v. Weston,* 857 So.2d 278, 284 (Fla. 1st DCA 2003).

Conversely, the substantive aspect of an unconscionability defense focuses on the terms of the contract itself. To find that a contract is substantively unconscionable, a court must find that the terms are "so outrageously unfair as to shock the judicial conscience." *Id.* at 285 (quotation marks omitted). Resolving an unconscionability defense obviously requires a great deal of fact-finding regarding many aspects of the contract formation process; it should not be the subject of a trial court's gut feeling or whim, and it is rarely appropriately determined on summary judgment.

In this case, Starboard never asserted a full-fledged unconscionability defense in its motion for summary judgment. Rather, Starboard seems to assert "unconscionability" as an element or factor—it is unclear which—in establishing its unilateral mistake defense. The only portions of Starboard's summary judgment motion and answer brief that discuss unconscionability cite *Florida Cranes, Inc. v. Florida East Coast Properties, Inc.* for the proposition that "equity can correct a unilateral mistake where said mistake is committed by an employee of the appellant, and constitutes a simple but honest mistake which could lead to an unconscionable result." 324 So.2d 721, 722 (Fla. 3d DCA 1976). The use of the word "unconscionable" in the *Florida Cranes* decision is not in reference to the independent unconscionability defense explained above, however, but is merely a portion of the unilateral mistake analysis. Indeed, the word "unconscionable" is also used in the Florida Supreme Court's decision in

Krasnek, but only to explain that a trial court cannot grant relief based on a unilateral mistake if the party seeking to enforce the contract has changed its position in reliance on the contract. 174 So.2d at 543 (holding that a trial court cannot order rescission based on unilateral mistake unless "the respondent's position had not been so changed in reliance on the contract that it would be **unconscionable** to order rescission" (emphasis added)).

To the extent that Starboard relies on unconscionability as an independent affirmative defense to the contract—not as part of the unilateral mistake analysis—that defense was not properly before the trial court on summary judgment, and the trial court did not and could not make the requisite findings to warrant rescission on that basis. Indeed, the word "unconscionable," or any variation thereof, only appears one time in the hearing transcript—when the trial court found that it would be unconscionable to enforce the contract. And to the extent that Starboard relies on "unconscionability" as a way to establish its unilateral mistake defense, the "unconscionability" it has demonstrated is merely a necessary component to the four-prong (or two-prong) test to establish a unilateral mistake of fact, not a sufficient basis for relief in and of itself. Thus, the trial court erred in granting relief based on "unconscionability."

[The court's discussion of damages, specific performance, and the conversion claim are omitted.]

CONCLUSION

The trial court erred by granting summary judgment on all three of DePrince's claims. There remain genuine issues of material fact to be resolved, and Starboard has not demonstrated that it is entitled to judgment as a matter of law.

We also note that, for some inexplicable reason, Fiori has not been made a party to this suit. It is difficult to imagine how DePrince's and Starboard's rights and obligations can be completely established and redressed without Fiori's involvement, particularly if specific performance is found to be a proper remedy. Importantly, both parties in their briefs have at times suggested that Fiori is the party who was actually negligent by way of its price quote, which omitted a "per carat" designation. Fiori can undoubtedly shed light on who, if anyone, should shoulder the blame of the price mistake, as well as explain industry standards and its pattern of dealings with Starboard.

We therefore conclude that while some may claim that diamonds are forever, the same cannot be said of the trial court's summary judgment order.

Reversed and remanded.

———

In re UAL Corporation

411 F.3d 818 (2005))

UAL filed a motion to vacate on the ground of excusable neglect an order of the bankruptcy court that it had requested. UAL claimed that it had mistakenly elected not to abandon three airplane leases, as was its right under bankruptcy law, because it was unaware that it owed several million dollars on the leases. The bankruptcy court granted the motion. Affirmed, in an opinion drawing on the law of unilateral mistake.

(Posner, J.) "We agree with the bankruptcy court that this is a case of excusable neglect within the meaning of Rule 60(b). United's mistake in failing to abandon the leases was excusable, but not because their number and complexity and the 60-day deadline for sorting through them and figuring out which to abandon and which to keep made mistakes inevitable. That would make it a case not of excusable *neglect,* but of unavoidable error. See *Pioneer Investment Services Co. v. Brunswick Associates Limited Partnership,* 507 U.S. 380, 394–95, 113 S.Ct. 1489, 123 L.Ed.2d 74 (1993). United is a huge company represented by one of the nation's largest law firms (Kirkland & Ellis). Sixty days in which to sort through some 460 leases requires examining on average fewer than eight leases per day, and all that had to be determined was whether United owed any money on the lease; if it did, it would abandon the lease and if not, not.

"Had the beneficiaries of the mistake, the airplanes' owners, relied to their detriment on it, United would not be entitled to relief. *General Electric Capital Corp. v. Central Bank,* 49 F.3d 280, 284–86 (7th Cir.1995); *Equilease Corp. v. Hentz,* 634 F.2d 850, 854 (5th Cir.1981); *Strubbe v. Sonnenschein,* 299 F.2d 185, 192 (2d Cir.1962); *Bank of Naperville v. Catalano,* 86 Ill.App.3d 1005, 42 Ill.Dec. 63, 408 N.E.2d 441, 445–46 (1980). This is a general limitation on restitution unless restitution is sought against a defrauder or other wrongdoer; it is not a limitation that is special to mistake cases. See, e.g., *Amalgamated Ass'n of Street Electric Ry. & Motor Coach Employees of America v. Danielson,* 24 Wis.2d 33, 128 N.W.2d 9, 10–11 (1964); *Restatement of Restitution* § 69 (1937). But the owners do not argue that they relied . . . .

"Even without reliance, it can be argued that United is entitled to no relief because a unilateral mistake by a contract party, as distinct from a mutual mistake, is not a generally recognized excuse for failing to comply with the contract's terms. *Praxair, Inc. v. Hinshaw & Culbertson,* 235 F.3d 1028, 1034–35 (7th Cir.2000); II. E. Allan Farnsworth, *Contracts* § 9.4, p. 614 (3d ed.2004). But the qualification in "generally" is, as so often in law, critical. Nor is the qualification limited to trivial errors in the administration of a contract, as where one party pays the other the wrong amount because of a mistake in calculation. That by the way is a classic case for restitution even if the mistake was careless-always provided, however, that the payee had not relied on it, to his disadvantage if it is corrected. . . .

"Closest to the present case is a line of cases illustrated by *M.F. Kemper Construction Co. v. City of Los Angeles,* 37 Cal.2d 696, 235 P.2d 7 (1951); see also *Donovan v. RRL Corp,* 26 Cal.4th 261, 109 Cal.Rptr.2d 807, 27 P.3d 702, 714–17 (2001) .... As succinctly explained in *Donovan v. RRL Corp., supra,* 109 Cal.Rptr.2d 807, 27 P.3d at 715, "the plaintiff in *Kemper* inadvertently omitted a $301,769 item from its bid for the defendant city's public works project-approximately one-third of the total contract price. After discovering the mistake several hours later, the plaintiff immediately notified the city and subsequently withdrew its bid. Nevertheless, the city accepted the erroneous bid, contending that rescission of the offer was unavailable for the plaintiff's unilateral mistake." The court rejected the city's argument. When an innocent mistake can be rectified without harm to anyone (loss of a windfall is not the kind of harm that a court should endeavor to avert), it should be. Especially in a case such as this. If the mistake is not corrected, the cost will be borne not by its maker—United—but by creditors no less innocent than the airplanes' owners. A refusal to correct would serve no deterrent or punitive purpose; it would merely redistribute wealth among creditors capriciously. . . .

"The principle of the mistaken-bid cases must not be pressed too far. Otherwise the courts would be drowned in disputes over whether, for example, a seller had made a mistake in charging such a low price-had he studied market conditions more carefully he would have realized that the buyer would have been willing to pay more. Cases like *Kemper* and *Boise* distinguish between an obvious error, such as an error in computation, and an "error of judgment," which if a ground of restitution would make every contract party a kind of fiduciary of the opposing party, end arm's length bargaining, and make contractual obligations radically uncertain. The present case, however, is closer to the computation-error pole than to the error-of-judgment pole. Indeed, for all we know, it *was* a computation error that precipitated United's decision not to abandon the three leases."

RESTATEMENT, SECOND, CONTRACTS §§ 153, 154

[See Selected Source Materials Supplement]

NOTE ON UNILATERAL MISTAKE

It is sometimes said that relief for unilateral mistake will not be granted unless the parties "can be placed in status quo in the equity sense, i.e. rescission must not result in prejudice to the other party except for the loss of his bargain." James T. Taylor & Son, Inc. v. Arlington Independent School District, 160 Tex. 617, 335 S.W.2d 371 (1960). Taken literally, this would preclude relief when there has been *any* reliance by the nonmistaken party. Such a rule would be unnecessary to serve the purposes intended, and expressions like that in *James T. Taylor* should be read to mean that relief will not be granted unless the other party has either not relied *or* cannot be restored to his precontractual position by the award of reliance damages.

SECTION 2. MISTAKES IN TRANSCRIPTION; REFORMATION

TRAVELERS INS. CO. V. BAILEY
Supreme Court of Vermont, 1964.
124 Vt. 114, 197 A.2d 813.

BARNEY, JUSTICE. The plaintiff insurance company has come into equity asking for reformation of the annuity provisions of a life insurance policy on the basis of mistake. Thirty years after issuance of the original policy it tendered the defendant insured an amended policy which he refused. On trial, the chancellor found that the amended policy represented the true insuring agreement originally entered into by the parties and allowed reformation. The defendant appealed.

At the instance of his mother, the defendant, when nineteen, submitted an application to an agent of the plaintiff for a life insurance policy. The plan requested in the application was one insuring the defendant's life for five thousand dollars, with an annuity at age sixty-five for five hundred dollars a year for the balance of his life, ten years certain. When the application was accepted and the policy prepared in the home office of the plaintiff, the correct descriptive information was inserted on the wrong policy form. The printed portion of the form used yielded the correct life insurance contract, but produced an annuity obligation to pay five hundred dollars a month for life, one hundred months certain. The application was made a part of the policy, by its terms. In accordance with its usual practice, the plaintiff did not retain a copy of the policy itself but kept a record of the information permitting reproduction of the policy if the occasion demanded.

The premiums were regularly paid on the policy issued in 1931, and about the middle of 1961 the actual policy came into the possession of the defendant for the first time. The semi-annual premiums charged and paid were identical with the prescribed premium for five thousand dollars of life insurance with annuity at age sixty-five of five hundred dollars annually, with payment for ten years certain. This $40.90 semi-annual premium was applicable only to that policy plan, issued at the defendant's then age of nineteen, and no other. The plaintiff had no rate for and did not sell a policy for five thousand dollars life insurance with an annuity at age sixty-five of five hundred dollars monthly, payment for one hundred months certain.

After being told by a third party that his policy could not have the provisions he claimed for it, the defendant took the policy to the office of the defendant's agent that sold the policy and made inquiry. Shortly thereafter, in late 1961, the amended policy was tendered. There is no evidence that the defendant then knew that his original policy provided for an annuity payment larger than he was entitled to in view of the premium paid and the life insurance coverage purchased.

Vermont law, like that of many jurisdictions, imposes upon the party seeking reformation the duty of establishing, beyond a reasonable doubt, the true agreement to which the contract in question is to be reformed. deNeergaard v. Dillingham, 123 Vt. 327, 331, 187 A.2d 494. That this was accomplished, in the judgment of the chancellor, is demonstrated by this finding in particular:

> "The only agreement that the plaintiff and defendant made was for $5000 insurance with annuity of $500 per year at attained age 65, ten years certain."

Adequate evidentiary support for all findings of fact, including this one, made in this case by the chancellor, appears from the transcript of the evidence.

Indeed, in his appeal, the defendant does not question any of the findings relating to the facts already recited. His principal attack on the decision relates to the chancellor's finding that the mistake in issuing the policy furnished the defendant came about through no fault of the defendant, but solely through the negligence and inattention of the plaintiff. This, says the defendant, is a finding of unilateral mistake, and therefore, under the authority of New York Life Insurance Co. v. Kimball, 93 Vt. 147, 153, 106 A. 676, is not grounds for reformation. . . .

In [that case] Justice Miles commented . . . "The law of a case cannot be determined from a brief quotation of portions of the opinion separate from the facts of a case, especially where the law upon the subject has many exceptions, as in the subject now under consideration." This thought is particularly applicable to cases dealing with mistake and reformation. . . .

One variety of classification [of cases involving mistake] is suggested by the difference between a subsequent erroneous recording or transcription of a contract already in fact agreed to by the parties, and a mistake or misunderstanding [which] occurs while the parties are seeking to arrive at or believe they are arriving at an agreement. In the first case an agreement already exists, while in the second considerations of mutuality, together with knowledge of and responsibility for the mistake, weigh heavily in determining whether or not an enforceable agreement, or a right to relief, exists. Unfortunately, language appropriate to the second situation has sometimes been transposed to the first, where it may be both inappropriate and misleading. See 3 Corbin on Contracts § 608 (1960).

Where, as here, an antecedent contract has been established by the requisite measure of proof, equity will act to bring the erroneous writing into conformity with the true agreement. Burlington Building & Loan Ass'n v. Cummings, 111 Vt. 447, 453, 17 A.2d 319. On the basis of the maxim, "Equity regards that as done which ought to be done," equity will deal generously with the correction of mistakes. Stone v. Blake, 118 Vt. 424, 427, 110 A.2d 702, 704. This power has been regularly and frequently invoked in connection with real estate transactions, but there is nothing that requires that equity limit its application to that kind of case.

Other courts have exercised the equitable power of reformation in similar cases. In New England Mutual Life Insurance Co. v. Jones, D.C., 1 F.Supp. 984, a clerical mistake in the policy was discovered after the death of the insured when a double indemnity benefit claim for accidental death was made. The policy provided for double indemnity on the basis of the face amount of the policy, but in the blank space stating the obligation the figure $5000.00 had been entered. This considerably increased the double indemnity figure above that computed on the face amount of the policy. Premiums had been assessed and paid on the basis of the correct figure. Reformation was allowed.

In Stamen v. Metropolitan Life Insurance Co., 41 N.J.Super. 135, 124 A.2d 328, the insured received a policy, after a series of policy conversions, which inadvertently included a provision for disability benefits. The original application accepted by the company requested a policy without such provision, and the premiums had been assessed on the basis that no such benefits were payable. Reformation was allowed. . . .

Each of these cases speak of the reformation as justified either because there was "mutuality" of mistake or because the policy holder knew or ought to have known that there was a variation between the policy described in the accepted application and the one handed the insured. To insist on enforcement of the contract once knowledge of the error is acquired by the insured is held to be unconscionable, and classified as then a unilateral mistake known to the other party, which supports reformation. If the mistake exists in the writing unknown to both parties, it is classified as "mutual" and reformation is allowed.

Since these cases support reformation irrespective of the insured's knowledge of the existence of the mistake conferring a benefit on him beyond the bargain, talk of "mutual" or "unilateral" mistake seems to be of little help in this kind of situation. . . .

If, in this kind of case, talk of "mutuality" of mistake is unnecessary, much confusion can be avoided. Invariably, two mistakes are involved. There is a natural tendency to concentrate on the making of the clerical error in the writing as the critical mistake involved, when the true crucial error is mistaken belief of the parties about the correctness of the written instrument. When a test of "mutuality" is applied to the clerical error, the confusion is compounded, since the concern of the court should be with the belief or knowledge of the parties. The concept of "mutuality" adds nothing to the right to a remedy in this type of case. It is important as a concept in other, different, reformation situations. Applying to all the common linguistic label of "mutuality" gives to unlike situations an illusion of similarity. This invites the misapplication of principles, sound for one type of situation, to a different type, for which they are unsound.

Accordingly, we hold that where there has been established beyond a reasonable doubt a specific contractual agreement between parties, and a subsequent erroneous rendition of the terms of the agreement in a material particular, the party penalized by the error is entitled to reformation, if there has been no prejudicial change of position by the other party while ignorant of the mistake. If such change of position can equitably be taken into account and adjusted for in the decree, reformation may be possible even then. Mutual Life Ins. Co. of Baltimore v. Metzger, 167 Md. 27, 172 A. 610; see also Brown v. Lamphear, 35 Vt. 252. Mistakes generally occur through some carelessness, and failure to discover a mistake may be in some degree negligent, but unless some prejudice to the other party's rights under the true contract results, so as to make its enforcement inequitable, reformation will not be refused because of the presence of some negligence. Ward v. Lyman, 108 Vt. 464, 471, 188 A. 892; Mutual Life Insurance Co. of Baltimore v. Metzger, supra, 167 Md. 27, 30, 172 A. 610.

Change of position is raised as an issue by the defendant. It cannot be said that the defendant acted in reliance on the terms of the policy which, he testified, were not exactly known by him until he received the policy in 1961. But he argues that the mere passage of time, in this case thirty years, should overcome the chancellor's finding to the contrary and establish a change of position. But clearly this aging process was inevitable, and not a prejudicial act induced by the mistaken term in the policy. The defendant has not demonstrated that he was prejudiced by the existence of the error. Ward v. Lyman, supra, 108 Vt. 464, 471, 188 A. 892.

Reformation was properly granted.

Decree affirmed.

————

RESTATEMENT, SECOND, OF CONTRACTS § 155

[See Selected Source Materials Supplement]

————

Chimart Associates v. Paul

66 N.Y.2d 570, 498 N.Y.S.2d 344, 489 N.E.2d 231 (1986)

(Kaye, J.) "Because the thrust of a reformation claim is that a writing does not set forth the actual agreement of the parties, generally neither the parol evidence rule nor the Statute of Frauds applies to bar proof, in the form of parol or extrinsic evidence, of the claimed agreement. . . . However, this obviously recreates the very danger against which the parol evidence rule and Statute of Frauds were supposed to protect—the danger that a party, having agreed to a written contract that turns out to be disadvantageous, will falsely claim the existence of a different, oral contract. . . . To this end . . . reformation has been limited both substantively and procedurally. Substantively, for example, reformation based upon mistake is not available where the parties purposely contract based upon uncertain or contingent events. . . .

"Procedurally, there is a 'heavy presumption that a deliberately prepared and executed written instrument [manifests] the true intention of the parties' . . . and a correspondingly high order of evidence is required to overcome that presumption. . . . The proponent of reformation must 'show in no uncertain terms, not only that mistake or fraud exists, but exactly what was really agreed upon between the parties'. . . . "

————

SECTION 3. MUTUAL MISTAKES (SHARED MISTAKEN ASSUMPTIONS)

Another important type of mistake in contract law consists of a mistaken factual assumption about the present state of the world outside the mind of the actor who holds the assumption. Mistaken factual assumptions differ from mechanical errors, because they do not involve blunders that result from transient errors in a party's mental or physical machinery. They differ from mistranscriptions, because they do not turn on whether a writing is erroneous.

A mistaken factual assumption may either be shared by both parties to a contract or held by only one of the parties. Traditionally, shared mistaken factual assumptions have been treated under the heading of mutual mistake, meaning a mistake that is shared by both parties. This terminology fails to differentiate among shared mistakes according to their functional characteristics. Some kinds of shared mistakes should provide a basis for relief, while others should not. For example, if Team A trades Player P to Team B, and both teams share a mistake about just how fast or how strong P is, that mistake should not and would not give either team the right to rescind the trade. Even shared mistakes that should provide a basis for relief fall into different functional categories that require differing treatment. For example, in mistranscription cases the parties both mistakenly believe that the writing properly transcribes the bargain. The appropriate remedy here normally is reformation, not recission.

In short, that a mistake is shared is relevant but it is not critical. What is critical is the character of the shared mistake. That character is captured in the term *shared mistaken factual assumptions*.

In analyzing shared mistaken factual assumptions, it is useful to begin with assumptions that are made explicit in a contract. If a contract is explicitly based on a shared mistaken factual assumption, normally the mistake would furnish a basis for relief under a relatively straightforward interpretation of the language of the contract. For example, suppose A agrees to sell a plot of land, Tenacre, to B, and the contract provides, "This agreement is made on the assumption that Tenacre is zoned for commercial use." If it turns out that Tenacre is not zoned for commercial use, it is pretty clear that under the contract, B should be entitled to rescission.

Now suppose a shared mistaken factual assumption is tacit rather than explicit. The concept of a tacit assumption has been explicated as follows by Lon Fuller:

> Words like "intention," "assumption," "expectation" and "understanding" all seem to imply a conscious state involving an awareness of alternatives and a deliberate choice among them. It is, however, plain that there is a psychological state that can be described as a "tacit assumption", which does not involve a consciousness of alternatives. The absent-minded professor stepping from his office into the hall as he reads a book "assumes" that the floor of the hall will be there to receive him. His conduct is conditioned and directed by this assumption, even though the possibility that the floor has been removed does not "occur" to him, that is, is not present in his conscious mental processes.

A more colloquial expression that captures the concept of a tacit assumption is "taken for granted." A tacit assumption is so deeply embedded in an actor's mind that it simply doesn't occur to the actor to make the assumption explicit—any more than it occurs to Fuller's professor to think to himself, every time he is about to walk through a door, "Remember to check that the floor is still in place." Of course, if actors had infinite time and no costs, they would ransack their minds to think through every one of their tacit assumptions, and make each of those assumptions explicit. But actors do not have infinite time and they do have costs. Normally, it would be irrational for a potential contracting party to take the time to determine, and make explicit, every tacit assumption that he holds, because the costs of doing so would often approach or exceed the expected profit from the contract. It would also normally be virtually impossible to make such a determination. As Randy Barnett has stated:

> [When we add] to the infinity of knowledge about the present world the inherent uncertainty of future events ... we immediately can see that the seductive idea that a contract can ... articulate every contingency that might arise before ... performance is sheer fantasy. For this reason, contracts must be silent on an untold number of items. And many of these silent assumptions that underlie every agreement are as basic as the assumption that the sun will rise tomorrow. They are simply too basic to merit mention.

Randy E. Barnett, Contracts: Cases and Doctrine 1163 (2d ed. 1999).

———

SHERWOOD V. WALKER

Supreme Court of Michigan, 1887.
66 Mich. 568, 33 N.W. 919, 11 Am.St.Rep. 531.

MORSE, J. Replevin for a cow. Suit commenced in justice's court; judgment for plaintiff; appealed to circuit court of Wayne county, and verdict and judgment for plaintiff in that court. The defendants bring error, and set out 25 assignments of the same.

The main controversy depends upon the construction of a contract for the sale of the cow. The plaintiff claims that the title passed, and bases his action upon such claim. The defendants contend that the contract was executory, and by its terms no title to the animal was acquired by plaintiff. The defendants reside at Detroit, but are in business at Walkerville, Ontario, and have a farm at Greenfield, in Wayne county, upon which were some blooded cattle supposed to be barren as breeders. The Walkers are importers and breeders of polled Angus cattle. The plaintiff is a banker living at Plymouth, in Wayne county. He called upon the defendants at Walkerville for the purchase of some of their stock, but found none there that suited him. Meeting one of the defendants afterwards, he was informed that they had a few head upon their Greenfield farm. He was asked to go out and look at them, with the statement at the time that they were probably barren, and would not breed. May 5, 1886, plaintiff went out to Greenfield and saw the cattle. A few days thereafter, he called upon one of the defendants with the view of purchasing a cow, known as "Rose 2d of Aberlone." After considerable talk it was agreed that defendants would telephone Sherwood at his home in Plymouth in reference to the price. The second morning after this talk he was called up by telephone, and the terms of the sale were finally agreed upon. He was to pay five and one-half cents per pound, live weight, fifty pounds shrinkage. He was asked how he intended to take the cow home, and replied that he might ship her from King's cattle-yard. He requested defendants to confirm the sale in writing, which they did by sending him the following letter:

"Walkerville, May 15, 1886.

"T.C. Sherwood, President, etc.—Dear Sir: We confirm sale to you of the cow Rose 2d of Aberlone, lot 56 of our catalogue, at five and a half cents per pound, less fifty pounds shrink. We inclose herewith order on Mr. Graham for the cow. You might leave check with him, or mail to us here, as you prefer.

"YOURS TRULY,

HIRAM WALKER & SONS."

The order upon Graham enclosed in the letter read as follows:

"Walkerville, May 15, 1886.

"George Graham: You will please deliver at King's cattle-yard to Mr. T.C. Sherwood, Plymouth, the cow Rose 2d of Aberlone, lot 56 of our catalogue. Send halter with the cow, and have her weighed.

"YOURS TRULY,

HIRAM WALKER & SONS."

On the twenty-first of the same month the plaintiff went to defendants' farm at Greenfield, and presented the order and letter to Graham, who informed him that the defendants had instructed him not to deliver the cow. Soon after, the plaintiff tendered to Hiram Walker, one of the defendants, $80, and demanded the cow. Walker refused to take the money or deliver the cow. The plaintiff then instituted this suit. After he had secured possession of the cow under the writ of replevin, the plaintiff caused her to be weighed by the constable who served the writ, at a place other than King's cattle-yard. She weighed 1,420 pounds.

When the plaintiff, upon the trial in the circuit court, had submitted his proofs showing the above transaction, defendants moved to strike out and exclude the testimony from the case, for the reason that it was irrelevant and did not tend to show that the title to the cow passed, and that it showed that the contract of sale was merely executory. The court refused the motion, and an exception was taken.

The defendants then introduced evidence tending to show that at the time of the alleged sale it was believed by both the plaintiff and themselves that the cow was barren and would not breed; that she cost $850, and if not barren would be worth from $750 to $1,000; that after the date of the letter, and the order to Graham, the defendants were informed by said Graham that in his judgment the cow was with calf, and therefore they instructed him not to deliver her to plaintiff, and on the twentieth of May, 1886, telegraphed plaintiff what Graham thought about the cow being with calf, and that consequently they could not sell her. The cow had a calf in the month of October following.

On the nineteenth of May, the plaintiff wrote Graham as follows:

"Plymouth, May 19, 1886

"Mr. George Graham, Greenfield—Dear Sir: I have bought Rose or Lucy from Mr. Walker, and will be there for her Friday morning, nine or ten o'clock. Do not water her in the morning.

"YOURS, ETC., T.C. SHERWOOD"

Plaintiff explained the mention of the two cows in this letter by testifying that, when he wrote this letter, the order and letter of defendants was at his home, and, writing in a hurry, and being uncertain as to the name of the cow, and not wishing his cow watered, he thought it would do no harm to name them both, as his bill of sale would show which one he had purchased. Plaintiff also testified that he asked defendants to give him a price on the balance of their herd at Greenfield, as a friend thought of buying some, and received a letter dated May 17, 1886, in which they named the price of five cattle, including Lucy, at $90, and Rose 2d at $80. When he received the letter he called defendants up by telephone, and asked them why they put Rose 2d in the list, as he had already purchased her. They replied that they knew he had, but thought it would make no difference if plaintiff and his friend concluded to take the whole herd.

The foregoing is the substance of all the testimony in the case.

The circuit judge instructed the jury that if they believed the defendants, when they sent the order and letter to plaintiff, meant to pass the title to the cow, and that the cow was intended to be delivered to plaintiff, it did not matter whether the cow was weighed at any particular place, or by any particular person; and if the cow was weighed afterwards, as Sherwood testified, such weighing would be a sufficient compliance with the order. If they believed that defendants intended to pass the title by writing, it did not matter whether the cow was weighed before or after suit brought, and the plaintiff would be entitled to recover.

The defendants submitted a number of requests which were refused. The substance of them was that the cow was never delivered to plaintiff, and the title to her did not pass by the letter and order; and that under the contract, as evidenced by these writings, the title did not pass until the cow was weighed and her price thereby determined; and that, if the defendants only agreed to sell a cow that would not breed, then the barrenness of the cow was a condition precedent to passing title, and plaintiff cannot recover. The court also charged the jury that it was immaterial whether the cow was with calf or not. It will therefore be seen that the defendants claim that, as a matter of law, the title of this cow did not pass, and that the circuit judge erred in submitting the case to the jury, to be determined by them, upon the intent of the parties as to whether or not the title passed with the sending of the letter and order by the defendants to the plaintiff. . . .

It appears from the record that both parties supposed this cow was barren and would not breed, and she was sold by the pound for an insignificant sum as compared with her real value if a breeder. She was evidently sold and purchased on the relation of her value for beef, unless the plaintiff had learned of her true condition, and concealed such knowledge from the defendants. Before the plaintiff secured the possession of the animal, the defendants learned that she was with calf, and therefore of great value, and undertook to rescind the sale by refusing to deliver her. The question arises whether they had a right to do so. The circuit judge ruled that this fact did not avoid the sale and it made no difference whether she was barren or not. I am of the opinion that the court erred in this holding. I know that this is a close question, and the dividing line between the adjudicated cases is not easily discerned. But it must be considered as well settled that a party who has given an apparent consent to a contract of sale may refuse to execute it, or he may avoid it after it has been completed, if the assent was founded, or the contract made, upon the mistake of a material fact,—such as the subject-matter of the sale, the price, or some collateral fact materially inducing the agreement; and this can be done when the mistake is mutual. . . .

If there is a difference or misapprehension as to the substance of the thing bargained for; if the thing actually delivered or received is different in substance from the thing bargained for, and intended to be sold,—then there is no contract; but if it be only a difference in some quality or accident, even though the mistake may have been the actuating motive to the purchaser or seller, or both of them, yet the contract remains binding. "The difficulty in every case is to determine whether the mistake or misapprehension is as to the substance of the whole contract, going, as it were, to the root of the matter, or only to some point, even though a material point, an error as to which does not affect the substance of the whole consideration." Kennedy v. Panama, etc., Mail Co., L.R. 2 Q.B. 580, 588. It has been held, in accordance with the principles above stated, that where a horse is bought under the belief that he is sound, and both vendor and vendee honestly believe him to be sound, the purchaser must stand by his bargain, and pay the full price, unless there was a warranty.

It seems to me, however, in the case made by this record, that the mistake or misapprehension of the parties went to the whole substance of the agreement. If the cow was a breeder, she was worth at least $750; if barren, she was worth not over $80. The parties would not have made the contract of sale except upon the understanding and belief that she was incapable of breeding, and of no use as a cow. It is true she is now the identical animal that they thought her to be when the contract was made; there is no mistake as to the identity of the creature. Yet the mistake was not of the mere quality of the animal, but went to the very nature of the thing. A barren cow is substantially a different creature than a breeding one. There is as much difference between them for all purposes of use as there is between an ox and a cow that is capable of breeding and giving milk. If the mutual mistake had simply related to the fact whether she was with calf or not for one season, then it might have been a good sale, but the mistake affected the character of the animal for all time, and for its present and ultimate use. She was not in fact the animal, or the kind of animal, the defendants intended to sell or the plaintiff to buy. She was not a barren cow, and, if this fact had been known, there would have been no contract. The mistake affected the substance of the whole consideration, and it must be considered that there was no contract to sell or sale of the cow as she actually was. The thing sold and bought had in fact no existence. She was sold as a beef creature would be sold; she is in fact a breeding cow, and a valuable one. The court should have instructed the jury that if they found that the cow was sold, or contracted to be sold, upon the understanding of both parties that she was barren, and useless for the purpose of breeding, and that in fact she was not barren, but capable of breeding, then the defendants had a right to rescind, and refuse to deliver, and the verdict should be in their favor.

The judgment of the court below must be reversed, and a new trial granted, with costs of this court to defendants.

CAMPBELL, C.J., and CHAMPLIN, J., concurred.

SHERWOOD, J. (dissenting). I do not concur in the opinion given by my brethren in this case. . . .

As has already been stated by my brethren, the record shows that the plaintiff is a banker and a farmer as well, carrying on a farm, and raising the best breeds of stock, and lived in Plymouth, in the county of Wayne, 23 miles from Detroit; that the defendants lived in Detroit, and were also dealers in stock of the higher grades; that they had a farm at Walkerville, in Canada, and also one in Greenfield in said county of Wayne, and upon these farms the defendants kept their stock. The Greenfield farm was about 15 miles from the plaintiff's. In the spring of 1886 the plaintiff, learning that the defendants had some "polled Angus cattle" for sale, was desirous of purchasing some of that breed, and meeting the defendants, or some of them, at Walkerville, inquired about them, and was informed that they had none at Walkerville, "but had a few head left on their farm in Greenfield, and asked the plaintiff to go and see them, stating that in all probability they were sterile and would not breed." . . . The record further shows that the defendants, when they sold the cow, believed the cow was not with calf, and barren; that from what the plaintiff had been told by defendants (for it does not appear he had any other knowledge or facts from which he could form an opinion) he believed the cow was farrow, but still thought she could be made to breed. The foregoing shows the entire interview and treaty between the parties as to the sterility and qualities of the cow sold to the plaintiff. The cow had a calf in the month of October.

There is no question but that the defendants sold the cow representing her of the breed and quality they believed the cow to be, and that the purchaser so understood it. And the buyer purchased her believing her to be of the breed represented by the sellers, and possessing all the qualities stated, and even more. He believed she would breed. There is no pretense that the plaintiff bought the cow for beef, and there is nothing in the record indicating that he would have bought her at all only that he thought she might be made to breed. Under the foregoing facts,—and these are all that are contained in the record material to the contract,—it is held that because it turned out that the plaintiff was more correct in his judgment as to one quality of the cow than the defendants, and a quality, too, which could not by any possibility be positively known at the time by either party to exist, the contract may be annulled by the defendants at their pleasure. I know of no law, and have not been referred to any, which will justify any such holding, and I think the circuit judge was right in his construction of the contract between the parties.

It is claimed that a mutual mistake of a material fact was made by the parties when the contract of sale was made. There was no warranty in the case of the quality of the animal. When a mistaken fact is relied upon as ground for rescinding, such fact must not only exist at the time the contract is made, but must have been known to one or both of the parties. Where there is no warranty, there can be no mistake of fact when no such fact exists, or, if in existence, neither party knew of it, or could know of it; and that is precisely this case. If the owner of a Hambletonian horse had speeded him, and was only able to make him go a mile in three minutes, and should sell him to another, believing that was his greatest speed, for $300, when the purchaser believed he could go much faster, and made the purchase for that sum, and a few days thereafter, under more favorable circumstances, the horse was driven a mile in 2 min. 16 sec., and was found to be worth $20,000, I hardly think it would be held, either at law or in equity, by any one, that the seller in such case could rescind the contract. The same legal principles apply in each case.

In this case neither party knew the actual quality and condition of this cow at the time of the sale. The defendants say, or rather said, to the plaintiff, "they had a few head left on their farm in Greenfield, and asked plaintiff to go and see them, stating to plaintiff that in all probability they were sterile and would not breed." Plaintiff did go as requested, and found there these cows, including the one purchased, with a bull. The cow had been exposed, but neither knew she was with calf or whether she would breed. The defendants thought she would not, but the plaintiff says that he thought she could be made to breed, but believed she was not with calf. The defendants sold the cow for what they believed her to be, and the plaintiff bought her as he believed she was, after the statements made by the defendants. No conditions whatever were attached to the terms of sale by either party. It was in fact as absolute as it could well be made, and I know of no precedent as authority by which this court can alter the contract thus made by these parties in writing, and interpolate in it a condition by which, if the *defendants should be mistaken in their belief that the cow was barren,* she could be returned to them and their contract should be annulled. It is not the duty of courts to destroy contracts when called upon to enforce them, after they have been legally made. There was no mistake of any material fact by either of the parties in the case as would license the vendors to rescind. There was no difference between the parties, nor misapprehension, as to the substance of the thing bargained for, which was a cow supposed to be barren by one party, and believed not to be by the other. As to the quality of the animal, subsequently developed, both parties were equally ignorant, and as to this each party took his chances. If this were not the law, there would be no safety in purchasing this kind of stock.

I entirely agree with my brethren that the right to rescind occurs whenever "the thing actually delivered or received is different in substance from the thing bargained for, and intended to be sold; but if it be only a difference in some quality or accident, even though the misapprehension may have been the actuating motive" of the parties in making the contract, yet it will remain binding. In this case the cow sold was the one delivered. What might or might not happen to her after the sale formed no element in the contract. . . .

———

Nester v. Michigan Land & Iron Co.

69 Mich. 290, 37 N.W. 278 (1888)

In September 1885, Michigan Land entered into a written contract with Nester, under which Michigan Land sold to Nester all the merchantable pine on certain land. Michigan Land made no representation to Nester that it intended Nester to rely upon, or that he did rely upon, in making his purchase. Prior to the sale, Michigan Land's agent told Nester that if he purchased the timber he had to do so on the basis of his own estimate. Nester had such an estimate made, and knew that an estimate could not be made with any degree of certainty—to use the language of his estimate, that "it is all guesswork any way." After the purchase, Nester sued to reduce the purchase price by 50% on the ground that both parties were mistaken in their estimate of the quality of the timber on the land; that a large portion of the timber was unsound; and that in consequence of the amount of decayed timber, the yield of merchantable pine furnished only about half the quantity of such pine that was anticipated or estimated. The case was decided by the Michigan Supreme Court, one year after Sherwood v. Walker. The opinion was written by Judge Sherwood, who had dissented in Sherwood v. Walker, and then had become Chief Judge of the Court. Held, for Michigan Land.

"We know of no case which will sustain the complainant's case upon the facts before us. That of *Sherwood v. Walker* . . . will come the nearest to it of any referred to. That is, however, somewhat different upon its facts, and the rule applied in that case can never be resorted to except in a case where all the facts and circumstances are precisely the same as in that." There were no dissents.

———

Everett v. Estate of Sumstad

95 Wash.2d 853, 631 P.2d 366 (1981)

The Mitchells owned a small secondhand store. In August 1978, they attended Alexander's Auction, where they frequently shopped to obtain merchandise for their own use and for use as inventory in their business. At the auction, the Mitchells purchased for $50 a used safe that had a locked inside compartment. Several days after the auction, the Mitchells took the safe to a locksmith to have the locked compartment opened. The locksmith found $32,207 inside, and a controversy arose whether the Mitchells were entitled to the money. An affidavit of the Mitchells stated:

> [W]e saw that the top outer-most door with a combination lock was open, and that the inner door was locked shut. That inner door required a key to open, and we learned that the safe would have to be taken to a locksmith to get the inner door opened because no key was available. We also learned that the combination for the outer lock was unknown. The auctioneer told the bidders that both this and the other safe had come from an estate, that both were still locked, that neither had been opened, and that the required combinations and key were unavailable for either.

The auctioneer's affidavit stated:

> I told the crowd at the auction that [the safes] were from an estate, that they were still locked and had never been opened by me and that I didn't have the combinations.

Held, for the Mitchells.

> A sale is a consensual transaction. The subject matter which passes is to be determined by the intent of the parties as revealed by the terms of their agreement in light of the surrounding circumstances. . . .
>
> . . .Under these circumstances, we hold reasonable persons would conclude that the auctioneer manifested an objective intent to sell the safe and its contents and that the parties mutually assented

to enter into that sale of the safe and the contents of the locked compartment.

———

RESTATEMENT, SECOND, CONTRACTS §§ 151, 152, 154

[See Selected Source Materials Supplement]

———

UNIDROIT PRINCIPLES OF INTERNATIONAL COMMERCIAL CONTRACTS ARTS. 3.4, 3.5, 3.18

[See Selected Source Materials Supplement]

———

PRINCIPLES OF EUROPEAN CONTRACT LAW ART. 4.103

[See Selected Source Materials Supplement]

———

LENAWEE COUNTY BOARD OF HEALTH V. MESSERLY
Supreme Court of Michigan, 1982.
417 Mich. 17, 331 N.W.2d 203.

RYAN, JUSTICE.

In March of 1977, Carl and Nancy Pickles, appellees, purchased from appellants, William and Martha Messerly, a 600-square-foot tract of land upon which is located a three-unit apartment building. Shortly after the transaction was closed, the Lenawee County Board of Health condemned the property and obtained a permanent injunction which prohibits human habitation on the premises until the defective sewage system is brought into conformance with the Lenawee County sanitation code.

We are required to determine whether appellees should prevail in their attempt to avoid this land contract on the basis of mutual mistake and failure of consideration. We conclude that the parties did entertain a mutual misapprehension of fact, but that the circumstances of this case do not warrant rescission.

I

The facts of the case are not seriously in dispute. In 1971, the Messerlys acquired approximately one acre plus 600 square feet of land. A three-unit apartment building was situated upon the 600-square-foot portion. The trial court found that, prior to this transfer, the Messerlys' predecessor in title, Mr. Bloom, had installed a septic tank on the property without a permit and in violation of the applicable health code. The Messerlys used the building as an income investment property until 1973 when they sold it, upon [a] land contract, to James Barnes who likewise used it primarily as an income-producing investment.

Mr. and Mrs. Barnes, with the permission of the Messerlys, sold approximately one acre of the property in 1976, and the remaining 600 square feet and building were offered for sale soon thereafter when Mr. and Mrs. Barnes defaulted on their land contract. Mr. and Mrs. Pickles evidenced an interest in the property, but were dissatisfied with the terms of the Barnes-Messerly land contract. Consequently, to accommodate the Pickleses' preference to enter into a land contract directly with the Messerlys, Mr. and Mrs. Barnes executed a quit-claim deed which conveyed their interest in the property back to the Messerlys. After inspecting the property, Mr. and Mrs. Pickles executed a new land contract with the Messerlys on March 21, 1977. It provided for a purchase price of $25,500. A clause was added to the end of the land contract form which provides:

> "17. Purchaser has examined this property and agrees to accept same in its present condition. There are no other or additional written or oral understandings."

Five or six days later, when the Pickleses went to introduce themselves to the tenants, they discovered raw sewage seeping out of the ground. Tests conducted by a sanitation expert indicated the inadequacy of the sewage system. The Lenawee County Board of Health subsequently condemned the property and initiated this lawsuit in the Lenawee Circuit Court against the Messerlys as land contract vendors, and the Pickleses, as vendees, to obtain a permanent injunction proscribing human habitation of the premises until the property was brought into conformance with the Lenawee County sanitation code. The injunction was granted, and the Lenawee County Board of Health was permitted to withdraw from the lawsuit by stipulation of the parties.

When no payments were made on the land contract, the Messerlys filed a cross-complaint against the Pickleses seeking foreclosure, sale of the property, and a deficiency judgment. Mr. and Mrs. Pickles then counterclaimed for rescission against the Messerlys, and filed a third-party complaint against the Barneses, which incorporated, by reference, the allegations of the counterclaim against the Messerlys. In count one, Mr. and Mrs. Pickles alleged failure of consideration. Count two charged Mr. and Mrs. Barnes with willful concealment and misrepresentation as a result of their failure to disclose the condition of the sanitation system. Additionally, Mr. and Mrs. Pickles sought to hold the Messerlys liable in equity for the Barneses' alleged misrepresentation. The Pickleses prayed that the land contract be rescinded.

After a bench trial, the court concluded that the Pickleses had no cause of action against either the Messerlys or the Barneses as there was no fraud or misrepresentation. This ruling was predicated on the trial judge's conclusion that none of the parties knew of Mr. Bloom's earlier transgression or of the resultant problem with the septic system until it was discovered by the Pickleses, and that the sanitation problem was not caused by any of the parties. The trial court held that the property was purchased "as is", after inspection and, accordingly, its "negative * * * value cannot be blamed upon an innocent seller". Foreclosure was ordered against the Pickleses, together with a judgment against them in the amount of $25,943.09.[3]

Mr. and Mrs. Pickles appealed from the adverse judgment. The Court of Appeals unanimously affirmed the trial court's ruling with respect to Mr. and Mrs. Barnes but, in a two-to-one decision, reversed the finding of no cause of action on the Pickleses' claims against the Messerlys. *Lenawee County Board of Health v. Messerly,* 98 Mich.App. 478, 295 N.W.2d 903 (1980). It concluded that the mutual mistake between the Messerlys and the Pickleses went to a basic, as opposed to a collateral, element of the contract,[6] and that the parties intended to transfer income-producing rental property but, in actuality, the vendees paid $25,500 for an asset without value.[7]

We granted the Messerlys' application for leave to appeal. 411 Mich. 900 (1981).[8]

II

We must decide initially whether there was a mistaken belief entertained by one or both parties to the contract in dispute and, if so, the resultant legal significance.[9]

---

[3] The parties stipulated that this amount was due on the land contract, assuming that the contract was valid and enforceable.

[6] Mr. and Mrs. Pickles did not appeal the trial court's finding that there was no fraud or misrepresentation by the Messerlys or Mr. and Mrs. Barnes. Likewise, the propriety of that ruling is not before this Court today.

[7] The trial court found that the only way that the property could be put to residential use would be to pump and haul the sewage, a method which is economically unfeasible, as the cost of such a disposal system amounts to double the income generated by the property. There was speculation by the trial court that the adjoining land might be utilized to make the property suitable for residential use, but, in the absence of testimony directed at that point, the court refused to draw any conclusions. The trial court and the Court of Appeals both found that the property was valueless, or had a negative value.

[8] The Court of Appeals decision to affirm the trial court's finding of no cause of action against Mr. and Mrs. Barnes has not been appealed to this Court and, accordingly, the propriety of that ruling is not before us today.

[9] We emphasize that this is a bifurcated inquiry. Legal or equitable remedial measures are not mandated in every case in which a mutual mistake has been established.

A contractual mistake "is a belief that is not in accord with the facts". 1 Restatement Contracts, 2d, § 151, p. 383. The erroneous belief of one or both of the parties must relate to a fact in existence at the time the contract is executed. *Richardson Lumber Co. v. Hoey,* 219 Mich. 643, 189 N.W. 923 (1922); *Sherwood v. Walker,* 66 Mich. 568, 580, 33 N.W. 919 (1887) (Sherwood, J., dissenting). That is to say, the belief which is found to be in error may not be, in substance, a prediction as to a future occurrence or non-occurrence. *Henry v. Thomas,* 241 Ga. 360, 245 S.E.2d 646 (1978); *Hailpern v. Dryden,* 154 Colo. 231, 389 P.2d 590 (1964). But see *Denton v. Utley,* 350 Mich. 332, 86 N.W.2d 537 (1957).

The Court of Appeals concluded, after a *de novo* review of the record, that the parties were mistaken as to the income-producing capacity of the property in question. 98 Mich.App. 487–488, 295 N.W.2d 903. We agree. The vendors and the vendees each believed that the property transferred could be utilized as income-generating rental property. All of the parties subsequently learned that, in fact, the property was unsuitable for any residential use.

Appellants assert that there was no mistake in the contractual sense because the defect in the sewage system did not arise until after the contract was executed. The appellees respond that the Messerlys are confusing the date of the inception of the defect with the date upon which the defect was discovered.

This is essentially a factual dispute which the trial court failed to resolve directly. Nevertheless, we are empowered to draw factual inferences from the facts found by the trial court. GCR 1963, 865.1(6).

An examination of the record reveals that the septic system was defective prior to the date on which the land contract was executed. The Messerlys' grantor installed a nonconforming septic system without a permit prior to the transfer of the property to the Messerlys in 1971. Moreover, virtually undisputed testimony indicates that, assuming ideal soil conditions, 2,500 square feet of property is necessary to support a sewage system adequate to serve a three-family dwelling. Likewise, 750 square feet is mandated for a one-family home. Thus, the division of the parcel and sale of one acre of the property by Mr. and Mrs. Barnes in 1976 made it impossible to remedy the already illegal septic system within the confines of the 600-square-foot parcel.

Appellants do not dispute these underlying facts which give rise to an inference contrary to their contentions.

Having determined that when these parties entered into the land contract they were laboring under a mutual mistake of fact, we now direct our attention to a determination of the legal significance of that finding.

A contract may be rescinded because of a mutual misapprehension of the parties, but this remedy is granted only in the sound discretion of the court. *Harris v. Axline,* 323 Mich. 585, 36 N.W.2d 154 (1949). Appellants argue that the parties' mistake relates only to the quality or value of the real estate transferred, and that such mistakes are collateral to the agreement and do not justify rescission, citing *A & M Land Development Co. v. Miller,* 354 Mich. 681, 94 N.W.2d 197 (1959).

In that case, the plaintiff was the purchaser of 91 lots of real property. It sought partial rescission of the land contract when it was frustrated in its attempts to develop 42 of the lots because it could not obtain permits from the county health department to install septic tanks on these lots. This Court refused to allow rescission because the mistake, whether mutual or unilateral, related only to the value of the property. . . .

Appellees contend, on the other hand, that in this case the parties were mistaken as to the very nature of the character of the consideration and claim that the pervasive and essential quality of this mistake renders rescission appropriate. They cite in support of that view *Sherwood v. Walker,* 66 Mich. 568, 33 N.W. 919 (1887), the famous "barren cow" case. . . .

As the parties suggest, the foregoing precedent arguably distinguishes mistakes affecting the essence of the consideration from those which go to its quality or value, affording relief on a per se basis for the former but not the latter. See, *e.g., Lenawee County Board of Health v. Messerly,* 98 Mich.App. 478, 492, 295 N.W.2d 903 (1980) (Mackenzie, J., concurring in part).

However, the distinctions which may be drawn from *Sherwood* and *A & M Land Development Co.* do not provide a satisfactory analysis of the nature of a mistake sufficient to invalidate a contract. Often, a mistake relates to an underlying factual assumption which, when discovered, directly affects value, but simultaneously and materially affects the essence of the contractual consideration. It is disingenuous to label such a mistake collateral. *McKay v. Coleman,* 85 Mich. 60, 48 N.W. 203 (1891). Corbin, Contracts (One Vol. ed.), § 605, p. 551.

Appellant and appellee both mistakenly believed that the property which was the subject of their land contract would generate income as rental property. The fact that it could not be used for human habitation deprived the property of its income-earning potential and rendered it less valuable. However, this mistake, while directly and dramatically affecting the property's value, cannot accurately be characterized as collateral because it also affects the very essence of the consideration. "The thing sold and bought [income generating rental property] had in fact no existence". *Sherwood v. Walker,* 66 Mich. 578, 33 N.W. 919.

We find that the inexact and confusing distinction between contractual mistakes running to value and those touching the substance of the consideration serves only as an impediment to a clear and helpful analysis for the equitable resolution of cases in which mistake is alleged and proven. Accordingly, the holdings of *A & M Land Development Co.* and *Sherwood* with respect to the material or collateral nature of a mistake are limited to the facts of those cases.

Instead, we think the better-reasoned approach is a case-by-case analysis whereby rescission is indicated when the mistaken belief relates to a basic assumption of the parties upon which the contract is made, and which materially affects the agreed performances of the parties. *Denton v. Utley,* 350 Mich. 332, 86 N.W.2d 537 (1957); *Farhat v. Rassey,* 295 Mich. 349, 294 N.W. 707 (1940); *Richardson Lumber Co. v. Hoey,* 219 Mich. 643, 189 N.W. 923 (1922). 1 Restatement Contracts, 2d, § 152, pp. 385–386. Rescission is not available, however, to relieve a party who has assumed the risk of loss in connection with the mistake. *Denton v. Utley,* 350 Mich. 344–345, 86 N.W.2d 537; *Farhat v. Rassey,* 295 Mich. 352, 294 N.W. 707; Corbin, Contracts (One Vol. ed.), § 605, p. 552; 1 Restatement Contracts, 2d, §§ 152, 154, pp. 385–386, 402–406.

All of the parties to this contract erroneously assumed that the property transferred by the vendors to the vendees was suitable for human habitation and could be utilized to generate rental income. The fundamental nature of these assumptions is indicated by the fact that their invalidity changed the character of the property transferred, thereby frustrating, indeed precluding, Mr. and Mrs. Pickles' intended use of the real estate. Although the Pickleses are disadvantaged by enforcement of the contract, performance is advantageous to the Messerlys, as the property at issue is less valuable absent its income-earning potential. Nothing short of rescission can remedy the mistake. Thus, the parties' mistake as to a basic assumption materially affects the agreed performances of the parties.

Despite the significance of the mistake made by the parties, we reverse the Court of Appeals because we conclude that equity does not justify the remedy sought by Mr. and Mrs. Pickles.

Rescission is an equitable remedy which is granted only in the sound discretion of the court. *Harris v. Axline,* 323 Mich. 585, 36 N.W.2d 154 (1949); *Hathaway v. Hudson,* 256 Mich. 694, 239 N.W. 859 (1932). A court need not grant rescission in every case in which the mutual mistake relates to a basic assumption and materially affects the agreed performance of the parties.

In cases of mistake by two equally innocent parties, we are required, in the exercise of our equitable powers, to determine which blameless party should assume the loss resulting from the misapprehension they shared.[13] Normally that can only be done by drawing upon our "own notions of what is reasonable and just under all the surrounding circumstances".[14]

Equity suggests that, in this case, the risk should be allocated to the purchasers. We are guided to that conclusion, in part, by the standards announced in § 154 of the Restatement of Contracts 2d, for determining when a party bears the risk of mistake. . . . Section 154(a) suggests that the court should look first to whether the parties have agreed to the allocation of the risk between themselves. While there is no express assumption in the contract by either party of the risk of the property becoming uninhabitable, there was indeed some agreed allocation of the risk to the vendees by the incorporation of an "as is" clause into the contract which, we repeat, provided:

> "Purchaser has examined this property and agrees to accept same in its present condition. There are no other or additional written or oral understandings."

That is a persuasive indication that the parties considered that, as between them, such risk as related to the "present condition" of the property should lie with the purchaser. If the "as is" clause is to have any meaning at all, it must be interpreted to refer to those defects which were unknown at the time that the contract was executed.[15] Thus, the parties themselves assigned the risk of loss to Mr. and Mrs. Pickles.

We conclude that Mr. and Mrs. Pickles are not entitled to the equitable remedy of rescission and, accordingly, reverse the decision the Court of Appeals.

WILLIAMS, C.J., and COLEMAN, FITZGERALD, KAVANAGH and LEVIN, JJ., concur.

RILEY, J., not participating.

---

[13] This risk-of-loss analysis is absent in both *A & M Land Development Co.* and *Sherwood,* and this omission helps to explain, in part, the disparate treatment in the two cases. Had such an inquiry been undertaken in *Sherwood,* we believe that the result might have been different. Moreover, a determination as to which party assumed the risk in *A & M Land Development Co.* would have alleviated the need to characterize the mistake as collateral so as to justify the result denying rescission. Despite the absence of any inquiry as to the assumption of risk in those two leading cases, we find that there exists sufficient precedent to warrant such an analysis in future cases of mistake.

[14] *Hathaway v. Hudson,* 256 Mich. 702, 239 N.W. 859, quoting 9 C.J., p. 1161.

[15] An "as is" clause waives those implied warranties which accompany the sale of a new home, *Tibbitts v. Openshaw,* 18 Utah 2d 442, 425 P.2d 160 (1967), or the sale of goods. M.C.L. § 440.2316(3)(a); M.S.A. § 19.2316(3)(a). Since implied warranties protect against latent defects, an "as is" clause will impose upon the purchaser the assumption of the risk of latent defects, such as an inadequate sanitation system, even when there are no implied warranties.

UCC §§ 2–312, 2–313, 2–314, 2–315

[See Selected Source Materials Supplement]

SECTION 4. NONDISCLOSURE

HILL V. JONES

Arizona Court of Appeals, 1986.
151 Ariz. 81, 725 P.2d 1115.

MEYERSON, JUDGE.

Must the seller of a residence disclose to the buyer facts pertaining to past termite infestation? This is the primary question presented in this appeal. Plaintiffs Warren G. Hill and Gloria R. Hill (buyers) filed suit to rescind an agreement to purchase a residence. Buyers alleged that Ora G. Jones and Barbara R. Jones (sellers) had made misrepresentations concerning termite damage in the residence and had failed to disclose to them the existence of the damage and history of termite infestation in the residence. . . .

. . . The trial court granted summary judgment, finding that there was "no genuinely disputed issue of material fact and that the law favors the . . . defendants." . . . Buyers have appealed from the judgment and sellers have cross-appealed from the trial court's ruling on attorney's fees.

I. FACTS

In 1982, buyers entered into an agreement to purchase sellers' residence for $72,000. The agreement was entered after buyers made several visits to the home. The purchase agreement provided that sellers were to pay for and place in escrow a termite inspection report stating that the property was free from evidence of termite infestation. Escrow was scheduled to close two months later.

One of the central features of the house is a parquet teak floor covering the sunken living room, the dining room, the entryway and portions of the halls. On a subsequent visit to the house, and when sellers were present, buyers noticed a small "ripple" in the wood floor on the step leading up to the dining room from the sunken living room. Mr. Hill asked if the ripple could be termite damage. Mrs. Jones answered that it was water damage. A few years previously, a broken water heater in the house had in fact caused water damage in the area of the dining room and steps which necessitated that some repairs be made to the floor. No further discussion on the subject, however, took place between the parties at that time or afterwards.

Mr. Hill, through his job as maintenance supervisor at a school district, had seen similar "ripples" in wood which had turned out to be termite damage. Mr. Hill was not totally satisfied with Mrs. Jones's explanation, but he felt that the termite inspection report would reveal whether the ripple was due to termites or some other cause.

The termite inspection report stated that there was no visible evidence of infestation. The report failed to note the existence of physical damage or evidence of previous treatment. The realtor notified the parties that the property had passed the termite inspection. Apparently, neither party actually saw the report prior to close of escrow.

After moving into the house, buyers found a pamphlet left in one of the drawers entitled "Termites, the Silent Saboteurs." They learned from a neighbor that the house had some termite infestation in the past. Shortly after the close of escrow, Mrs. Hill noticed that the wood on the steps leading down to the sunken living room was crumbling. She called an exterminator who confirmed the existence of termite damage to the floor and steps and to wood columns in the house. The estimated cost of repairing the wood floor alone was approximately $5,000.

Through discovery after their lawsuit was filed, buyers learned the following. When sellers purchased the residence in 1974, they received two termite guarantees that had been given to the previous owner by Truly Nolen, as well as a diagram showing termite treatment at the residence that had taken place in 1963. The guarantees provided for semi-annual inspections and annual termite booster treatments. The accompanying diagram stated that the existing damage had not been repaired. The second guarantee, dated 1965, reinstated the earlier contract for inspection and treatment. Mr. Jones admitted that he read the guarantees when he received them. Sellers renewed the guarantees when they purchased the residence in 1974. They also paid the annual fee each year until they sold the home.

On two occasions during sellers' ownership of the house but while they were at their other residence in Minnesota, a neighbor noticed "streamers" evidencing live termites in the wood tile floor near the entryway. On both occasions, Truly Nolen gave a booster treatment for termites. On the second incident, Truly Nolen drilled through one of the wood tiles to treat for termites. The neighbor showed Mr. Jones the area where the damage and treatment had occurred. Sellers had also seen termites on the back fence and had replaced and treated portions of the fence.

Sellers did not mention any of this information to buyers prior to close of escrow. They did not mention the past termite infestation and treatment to the realtor or to the termite inspector. There was evidence of holes on the patio that had been drilled years previously to treat for termites. The inspector returned to the residence to determine why he had not found evidence of prior treatment and termite damage. He indicated that he had not seen the holes in the patio because of boxes stacked there. It is unclear whether the boxes had been placed there by buyers or sellers. He had not found the damage inside the house because a large plant, which buyers had purchased from sellers, covered the area. After investigating the second time, the inspector found the damage and evidence of past treatment. He acknowledged that this information should have appeared in the report. He complained, however, that he should have been told of any history of termite infestation and treatment before he performed his inspection and that it was customary for the inspector to be given such information.

Other evidence presented to the trial court was that during their numerous visits to the residence before close of escrow, buyers had unrestricted access to view and inspect the entire house. Both Mr. and Mrs. Hill had seen termite damage and were therefore familiar with what it might look like. Mr. Hill had seen termite damage on the fence at this property. Mrs. Hill had noticed the holes on the patio but claimed not to realize at the time what they were for. Buyers asked no questions about termites except when they asked if the "ripple" on the stairs was termite damage. Mrs. Hill admitted she was not "trying" to find problems with the house because she really wanted it. . . .

III. DUTY TO DISCLOSE

The principal legal question presented in this appeal is whether a seller has a duty to disclose to the buyer the existence of termite damage in a residential dwelling known to the seller, but not to the buyer, which materially affects the value of the property. For the reasons stated herein, we hold that such a duty exists.

This is not the place to trace the history of the doctrine of caveat emptor. Suffice it to say that its vitality has waned during the latter half of the 20th century. E.g., Richards v. Powercraft Homes, Inc., 139 Ariz. 242, 678 P.2d 427 (1984) (implied warranty of workmanship and habitability extends to subsequent buyers of homes); see generally Quashnock v. Frost, 299 Pa.Super. 9, 445 A.2d 121 (1982); Ollerman v. O'Rourke Co., 94 Wis.2d 17, 288 N.W.2d 95 (1980). The modern view is that a vendor has an affirmative duty to disclose material facts where:

    1.   Disclosure is necessary to prevent a previous assertion from being a misrepresentation or from being fraudulent or material;

    2.   Disclosure would correct a mistake of the other party as to a basic assumption on which that party is making the contract and if nondisclosure amounts to a failure to act in good faith and in accordance with reasonable standards of fair dealing;

3.   Disclosure would correct a mistake of the other party as to the contents or effect of a writing, evidencing or embodying an agreement in whole or in part;

4.   The other person is entitled to know the fact because of a relationship of trust and confidence between them.

Restatement (Second) of Contracts § 161 (1981) (Restatement); See Restatement (Second) of Torts § 551 (1977).

Arizona courts have long recognized that under certain circumstances there may be a "duty to speak." Van Buren v. Pima Community College Dist. Bd., 113 Ariz. 85, 87, 546 P.2d 821, 823 (1976); Batty v. Arizona State Dental Bd., 57 Ariz. 239, 254, 112 P.2d 870, 877 (1941). As the supreme court noted in the context of a confidential relationship, "[s]uppression of a material fact which a party is bound in good faith to disclose is equivalent to a false representation." Leigh v. Loyd, 74 Ariz. 84, 87, 244 P.2d 356, 358 (1952); National Housing Indus. Inc. v. E.L. Jones Dev. Co., 118 Ariz. 374, 379, 576 P.2d 1374, 1379 (1978).

Thus, the important question we must answer is whether under the facts of this case, buyers should have been permitted to present to the jury their claim that sellers were under a duty to disclose their (sellers') knowledge of termite infestation in the residence. This broader question involves two inquiries. First, must a seller of residential property advise the buyer of material facts within his knowledge pertaining to the value of the property? Second, may termite damage and the existence of past infestation constitute such material facts?

The doctrine imposing a duty to disclose is akin to the well-established contractual rules pertaining to relief from contracts based upon mistake. Although the law of contracts supports the finality of transactions, over the years courts have recognized that under certain limited circumstances it is unjust to strictly enforce the policy favoring finality. Thus, for example, even a unilateral mistake of one party to a transaction may justify rescission. Restatement § 153.

There is also a judicial policy promoting honesty and fair dealing in business relationships. This policy is expressed in the law of fraudulent and negligent misrepresentations. Where a misrepresentation is fraudulent or where a negligent misrepresentation is one of material fact, the policy of finality rightly gives way to the policy of promoting honest dealings between the parties. See Restatement § 164(1).

Under certain circumstances nondisclosure of a fact known to one party may be equivalent to the assertion that the fact does not exist. For example "[w]hen one conveys a false impression by the disclosure of some facts and the concealment of others, such concealment is in effect a false representation that what is disclosed is the whole truth." State v.

Coddington, 135 Ariz. 480, 481, 662 P.2d 155, 156 (App.1983). Thus, nondisclosure may be equated with and given the same legal effect as fraud and misrepresentation. One category of cases where this has been done involves the area of nondisclosure of material facts affecting the value of property, known to the seller but not reasonably capable of being known to the buyer.

Courts have formulated this "duty to disclose" in slightly different ways. For example, the Florida Supreme Court recently declared that "where the seller of a home knows of facts materially affecting the value of the property which are not readily observable and are not known to the buyer, the seller is under a duty to disclose them to the buyer." Johnson v. Davis, 480 So.2d 625, 629 (Fla.1985) (defective roof in three-year old home). In California, the rule has been stated this way:

> [W]here the seller knows of facts materially affecting the value or desirability of the property which are known or accessible only to him and also knows that such facts are not known to, or within the reach of the diligent attention and observation of the buyer, the seller is under a duty to disclose them to the buyer.

Lingsch v. Savage, 213 Cal.App.2d 729, 735, 29 Cal.Rptr. 201, 204 (1963); contra Ray v. Montgomery, 399 So.2d 230 (Ala.1980); see generally W. Prosser & W. Keeton, The Law of Torts § 106 (5th ed.1984). We find that the Florida formulation of the disclosure rule properly balances the legitimate interests of the parties in a transaction for the sale of a private residence and accordingly adopt it for such cases.

As can be seen, the rule requiring disclosure is invoked in the case of material facts.[3] Thus, we are led to the second inquiry—whether the existence of termite damage in a residential dwelling is the type of material fact which gives rise to the duty to disclose. The existence of termite damage and past termite infestation has been considered by other courts to be sufficiently material to warrant disclosure. See generally Annot., 22 A.L.R.3d 972 (1968). . . .

Although sellers have attempted to draw a distinction between live termites[4] and past infestation, the concept of materiality is an elastic one which is not limited by the termites' health. "A matter is material if it is one to which a reasonable person would attach importance in determining his choice of action in the transaction in question." Lynn v. Taylor, 7 Kan.App.2d at 371, 642 P.2d at 134–35. For example, termite damage

---

[3] Arizona has recognized that a duty to disclose may arise where the buyer makes an inquiry of the seller, regardless of whether or not the fact is material. Universal Inv. Co. v. Sahara Motor Inn, Inc., 127 Ariz. 213, 215, 619 P.2d 485, 487 (1980). The inquiry by buyers whether the ripple was termite damage imposed a duty upon sellers to disclose what information they knew concerning the existence of termite infestation in the residence.

[4] Sellers acknowledge that a duty of disclosure would exist if live termites were present. Obde v. Schlemeyer, 56 Wash.2d 449, 353 P.2d 672 (1960).

substantially affecting the structural soundness of the residence may be material even if there is no evidence of present infestation. Unless reasonable minds could not differ, materiality is a factual matter which must be determined by the trier of fact. The termite damage in this case may or may not be material. Accordingly, we conclude that buyers should be allowed to present their case to a jury.

Sellers argue that even assuming the existence of a duty to disclose, summary judgment was proper because the record shows that their "silence . . . did not induce or influence" the buyers. This is so, sellers contend, because Mr. Hill stated in his deposition that he intended to rely on the termite inspection report. But this argument begs the question. If sellers were fully aware of the extent of termite damage and if such information had been disclosed to buyers, a jury could accept Mr. Hill's testimony that had he known of the termite damage he would not have purchased the house.

Sellers further contend that buyers were put on notice of the possible existence of termite infestation and were therefore "chargeable with the knowledge which [an] inquiry, if made, would have revealed." Godfrey v. Navratil, 3 Ariz.App. 47, 51, 411 P.2d 470 (1966) (quoting Luke v. Smith, 13 Ariz. 155, 162, 108 P. 494, 496 (1910)). It is also true that "a party may . . . reasonably expect the other to take normal steps to inform himself and to draw his own conclusions." Restatement § 161 comment d. Under the facts of this case, the question of buyers' knowledge of the termite problem (or their diligence in attempting to inform themselves about the termite problem) should be left to the jury.[5]

. . . Reversed and remanded.

CONTRERAS, P.J., and YALE MCFATE, J. (Retired), concur.

––––––––––

RESTATEMENT, SECOND, CONTRACTS §§ 159, 161

[See Selected Source Materials Supplement]

––––––––––

RESTATEMENT, SECOND, CONTRACTS § 161, ILLUSTRATIONS 7, 10, 11

7.   A, seeking to induce B to make a contract to sell land, knows that B does not know that the land has appreciably increased in value because of a proposed shopping center but does not disclose this to B. B makes the

––––––––––

[5]   Sellers also contend that they had no knowledge of any existing termite damage in the house. An extended discussion of the facts on this point is unnecessary. Simply stated, the facts are in conflict on this issue.

contract. Since B's mistake is not one as to a basic assumption . . . A's non-disclosure is not equivalent to an assertion that the value of the land has not appreciably increased. . . . The contract is not voidable by B. . . .

10. A, seeking to induce B to make a contract to sell A land, learns from government surveys that the land contains valuable mineral deposits and knows that B does not know this, but does not disclose this to B. B makes the contract. A's non-disclosure does not amount to a failure to act in good faith and in accordance with reasonable standards of fair dealing and is therefore not equivalent to an assertion that the land does not contain valuable mineral deposits. The contract is not voidable by B.

11. The facts being otherwise as stated in Illustration 10, A learns of the valuable mineral deposits from trespassing on B's land and not from government surveys. A's non-disclosure is equivalent to an assertion that the land does not contain valuable mineral deposits, and this assertion is a misrepresentation. . . .

RESTATEMENT, SECOND, TORTS § 551, ILLUSTRATIONS 6, 8

6. A is a violin expert. He pays a casual visit to B's shop, where second-hand musical instruments are sold. He finds a violin which, by reason of his expert knowledge and experience, he immediately recognizes as a genuine Stradivarius, in good condition and worth at least $50,000. The violin is priced for sale at $100. Without disclosing his information or his identity, A buys the violin from B for $100. A is not liable to B. . . .

8. B has a shop in which he sells second-hand musical instruments. In it he offers for sale for $100 a violin, which he knows to be an imitation Stradivarius and worth at most $50. A enters the shop, looks at the violin and is overheard by B to say to his companion that he is sure that the instrument is a genuine Stradivarius. B says nothing, and A buys the violin for $100. B is not liable to A. . . .

CHAPTER 18

THE EFFECT OF UNEXPECTED CIRCUMSTANCES

■ ■ ■

INTRODUCTORY NOTE

The issue considered in this Chapter is when, and to what extent, unexpected circumstances bear on the parties' rights and duties under a contract. In many crucial respects, the modern legal rules that govern this issue are comparable to the rules that govern mutual mistake, in that both sets of rules focus on the effect of shared tacit assumptions that proved to be incorrect. A major difference between the two kinds of cases is practical: In general, mutual-mistake cases usually involve attempts to either rescind the contract, or justify nonperformance, before either party has done much under the contract. In contrast, in unexpected-circumstances cases the relevant circumstances usually become salient only after performance has begun. The legal treatment of unexpected-circumstances cases is often rendered more complex and difficult as a result of this practical difference.

The cases considered in this chapter are generally dealt with under the legal rubrics *impossibility*, *impracticability*, and *frustration*. Historically, the three doctrines arose in roughly that order: First, the courts recognized that impossibility might be a defense; next, that impracticability might be a defense; and finally, that frustration of the purpose of a contract might be a defense. In this Chapter, these three doctrines will be taken up more or less in that order ("more or less," because the doctrines overlap) under the general heading of unexpected circumstances.

TAYLOR V. CALDWELL
In the Queen's Bench, 1863.
3 Best & S. 826.

BLACKBURN, J. In this case the plaintiffs and defendants had, on May 27th, 1861, entered into a contract by which the defendants agreed to let the plaintiffs have the use of The Surrey Gardens and Music Hall on four days then to come, viz., June 17th, July 15th, August 5th, and August 19th, for the purpose of giving a series of four grand concerts, and day and night fêtes, at the Gardens and Hall on those days respectively; and the plaintiffs agreed to take the Gardens and Hall on those days, and pay £100 for each day.

The parties inaccurately call this a "letting," and the money to be paid, a "rent"; but the whole agreement is such as to show that the defendants were to retain the possession of the Hall and Gardens so that there was to be no demise of them, and that the contract was merely to give the plaintiffs the use of them on those days. Nothing, however, in our opinion, depends on this. The agreement then proceeds to set out various stipulations between the parties as to what each was to supply for these concerts and entertainments, and as to the manner in which they should be carried on. The effect of the whole is to show that the existence of the Music Hall in the Surrey Gardens in a state fit for a concert was essential for the fulfilment of the contract,—such entertainments as the parties contemplated in their agreement could not be given without it.

After the making of the agreement, and before the first day on which a concert was to be given, the Hall was destroyed by fire. This destruction, we must take it on the evidence, was without the fault of either party, and was so complete that in consequence the concerts could not be given as intended. And the question we have to decide is whether, under these circumstances, the loss which the plaintiffs have sustained is to fall upon the defendants. [The damages claimed in the declaration were for moneys paid by the plaintiffs in advertising the concerts and for sums expended and expenses incurred by them in preparing for the concerts.] The parties when framing their agreement evidently had not present to their minds the possibility of such a disaster, and have made no express stipulation with reference to it, so that the answer to the question must depend upon the general rules of law applicable to such a contract.

There seems no doubt that where there is a positive contract to do a thing, not in itself unlawful, the contractor must perform it or pay damages for not doing it, although in consequence of unforeseen accidents the performance of his contract has become unexpectedly burdensome or even impossible. The law is so laid down in 1 Roll.Abr. 450, Condition (G), and in the note (2) to Walton v. Waterhouse (2 Wms.Saund. 421a, 6th Ed.) and is recognized as the general rule by all the judges in the much discussed case of Hall v. Wright (E.B. & E. 746). But this rule is only applicable when the contract is positive and absolute, and not subject to any condition either express or implied; and there are authorities which, as we think, establish the principle that where, from the nature of the contract, it appears that the parties must from the beginning have known that it could not be fulfilled unless when the time for the fulfilment of the contract arrived some particular specified thing continued to exist, so that, when entering into the contract, they must have contemplated such continuing existence as the foundation of what was to be done; there, in the absence of any express or implied warranty that the thing shall exist, the contract is not to be construed as a positive contract, but as subject to an implied condition that the parties shall be excused in case, before breach, performance becomes impossible from the perishing of the thing without default of the contractor.

There seems little doubt that this implication tends to further the great object of making the legal construction such as to fulfill the intention of those who entered into the contract. For in the course of affairs men in making such contracts in general would, if it were brought to their minds, say that there should be such a condition. . . .

There is a class of contracts in which a person binds himself to do something which requires to be performed by him in person; and such promises, e.g. promises to marry, or promises to serve for a certain time, are never in practice qualified by an express exception of the death of the party; and therefore in such cases the contract is in terms broken if the promisor dies before fulfilment. Yet it was very early determined that, if the performance is personal, the executors are not liable; Hyde v. The Dean of Windsor (Cro.Eliz. 552, 553). See 2 Wms.Exors. 1560 (5th Ed.), where a very apt illustration is given. "Thus," says the learned author, "if an author undertakes to compose a work, and dies before completing it, his executors are discharged from this contract; for the undertaking is merely personal in its nature, and by the intervention of the contractor's death, has become impossible to be performed." For this he cites a dictum of Lord Lyndhurst in Marshall v. Broadhurst (1 Tyr. 348, 349) and a case mentioned by Patteson, J., in Wentworth v. Cock (10 A. & E. 42, 45–46). In Hall v. Wright (E.B. & E. 746, 749), Crompton, J., in his judgment, puts another case. "Where a contract depends upon personal skill, and the act of God renders it impossible, as, for instance, in the case of a painter employed to paint a picture who is struck blind, it may be that the performance might be excused."

It seems that in those cases the only ground on which the parties or their executors can be excused from the consequences of the breach of the contract, is, that from the nature of the contract there is an implied condition of the continued existence of the life of the contractor, and perhaps in the case of the painter, of his eyesight. In the instances just given the person, the continued existence of whose life is necessary to the fulfilment of the contract, is himself the contractor, but that does not seem in itself to be necessary to the application of the principle, as is illustrated by the following example. In the ordinary form of an apprentice deed, the apprentice binds himself in unqualified terms to "serve until the full end and term of seven years to be fully complete and ended," during which term it is covenanted that the apprentice his master "faithfully shall serve," and the father of the apprentice in equally unqualified terms binds himself for the performance by the apprentice of all and every covenant on his part. (See the form, 2 Chitty on Pleading, 370 [7th Ed.] by Greening.) It is undeniable that if the apprentice dies within the seven years, the covenant of the father that he shall perform his covenant to serve for seven years is not fulfilled, yet surely it cannot be that an action would lie against the father. Yet the only reason why it would not is that he is excused because of the apprentice's death.

These are instances where the implied condition is of the life of a human being, but there are others in which the same implication is made as to the continued existence of a thing. For example, where a contract of sale is made amounting to a bargain and sale, transferring presently the property in specific chattels, which are to be delivered by the vendor at a future day; there, if the chattels, without the fault of the vendor, perish in the interval, the purchaser must pay the price, and the vendor is excused from performing his contract to deliver, which has thus become impossible.

That this is the rule of the English law is established by the case of Rugg v. Minett (11 East, 210), where the article that perished before delivery was turpentine, and it was decided that the vendor was bound to refund the price of all those lots in which the property had not passed; but was entitled to retain without deduction the price of those lots in which the property had passed, though they were not delivered, and though in the conditions of sale, which are set out in the report, there was no express qualification of the promise to deliver on payment. It seems in that case rather to have been taken for granted than decided that the destruction of the thing sold before delivery excused the vendor from fulfilling his contract to deliver on payment. . . .

It may, we think, be safely asserted to be now English law, that in all contracts of loan of chattels or bailments if the performance of the promise of the borrower or bailee to return the things lent or bailed, becomes impossible because it has perished, this impossibility (if not arising from the fault of the borrower or bailee from some risk which he has taken upon himself) excuses the borrower or bailee from the performance of his promise to redeliver the chattel.

The great case of Coggs v. Bernard (1 Smith's L.C. 171 [5th Ed.] 2 L.Raym. 909) is now the leading case on the law of bailments, and Lord Holt, in that case, referred so much to the civil law that it might perhaps be thought that this principle was there derived direct from the civilians, and was not generally applicable in English law except in the case of bailments; but the case of Williams v. Lloyd (W. Jones, 179), above cited, shows that the same law had been already adopted by the English law as early as the Book of Assizes. The principle seems to us to be that, in contracts in which the performance depends on the continued existence of a given person or thing, a condition is implied that the impossibility of performance arising from the perishing of the person or thing shall excuse the performance.

In none of these cases is the promise in words other than positive, nor is there any express stipulation that the destruction of the person or thing shall excuse the performance; but that excuse is by law implied, because from the nature of the contract it is apparent that the parties contracted on the basis of the continued existence of the particular person or chattel. In the present case, looking at the whole contract, we find that the parties contracted on the basis of the continued existence of the Music Hall at the time when the concerts were to be given, that being essential to their performance.

We think, therefore, that the Music Hall having ceased to exist, without fault of either party, both parties are excused, the plaintiffs from taking the gardens and paying the money, the defendants from performing their promise to give the use of the Hall and Gardens and other things. Consequently the rule must be absolute to enter the verdict for the defendants.

Rule absolute.

TACIT ASSUMPTIONS—CONTINUED

In *Taylor v. Caldwell* the court says that when framing their agreement the parties "had not present to their minds the possibility" of a disaster affecting the Music Hall, and concludes that "the parties contracted on the basis of the continued existence" of the Hall.

Is there a contradiction here? The court seems to say that the parties did not think of the possibility of the Hall's burning and therefore assumed that it would not burn. But how can the parties assume that no fire will occur when the possibility of a fire was never present to their minds? If this possibility was not present to their minds, would it not be more accurate to say that they assumed nothing about a fire, either that it would or would not occur?

The difficulty here can be resolved through the concept of tacit assumptions, discussed in the previous Chapter. As pointed out in that Chapter, words like "intention," "assumption," "expectation" and "understanding" all seem to imply a *conscious* state involving an awareness of alternatives and a deliberate choice among them. However, there is a psychological state that can be described as a tacit assumption, which does not involve a consciousness of alternatives. In experiments with animals, the relative strength of such assumptions can be roughly measured. If a rat is trained for months to run through a particular maze, the sudden interposition of a barrier in one of the paths will have a very disruptive effect on its behavior. For some time after encountering the barrier, the rat will be likely to engage in random and apparently pointless behavior, running in circles, scratching itself, etc. The degree to which the barrier operates disruptively reflects the strength of the assumption made by the rat that the barrier would not be there. If the maze has been frequently changed, and the rat has only recently become accustomed to the maze's present form, the introduction of a barrier will act less disruptively. In such a case, after a relatively short period of random behavior the rat will begin to act purposively, will retrace its steps, seek other outlets, etc. In this situation the assumption that the path would not be obstructed has not been deeply etched into the rat's nervous system; the rat behaves as if it "half-expected" some such impediment.

In a similar way, where parties have entered into a contract, an unexpected obstacle to performance may operate disruptively in varying degrees, depending on the context. To one who has contracted to carry goods by truck over a road traversing a mountain pass, a landslide filling the pass may be a very disruptive and unexpected event. But one who contracts to build a road through the mountains might view the same event, occurring during the course of construction, as a temporary set-back and a challenge to her resourcefulness. One who contracts to deliver goods a year from now at a fixed price certainly takes into account the possibility of some inflation, but may feel that a ten-fold inflation is contrary to an assumption or expectation that price variations would occur within the normal range, and that this expectation was the foundation of the contract.

In spite of hopeful beginnings that promise a more comprehensive psychological treatment of human behavior, for the time being the only methods available for dealing with problems like that raised by *Taylor v. Caldwell* are essentially those resting on intuition and introspection. We "just know" that the burning of a music hall violates a tacit assumption of the parties who executed a contract for hiring it for a few days in the very near future; we "just know" that a two per cent increase in the price of beans does not violate a tacit assumption underlying a contract to deliver a ton of beans for a fixed price.

––––––

Ocean Tramp Tankers Corp. v. V/O Sovfracht

[1964] 2 Q.B. 226 (1963)

(Denning, M.R.). "It was originally said that the doctrine of frustration was based on an implied term. In short, that the parties, if they had foreseen the new situation, would have said to one another: 'If that happens, of course, it is all over between us.' But the theory of an implied term has now been discarded by everyone, or nearly everyone, for the simple reason that it does not represent the truth. The parties would not have said: 'It is all over between us.' They would have differed about what was to happen. Each would have sought to insert reservations or qualifications of one kind or another."

Mineral Park Land Co. v. Howard

172 Cal. 289, 156 P. 458 (1916)

Plaintiff owned certain land in a ravine. Defendants had made a contract with public authorities to construct a concrete bridge across the ravine. In August 1911, the parties made a contract under which plaintiff granted defendants the right to haul gravel and earth from its land, and defendants agreed to take from that land all the gravel and earth necessary for the fill and cement work on the bridge. Defendants used 101,000 cubic yards in this work but procured 50,869 of those cubic yards from persons other than plaintiff, and plaintiff sued for breach of contract. The trial court found as follows: Plaintiff's land contained earth and gravel far in excess of 101,000 cubic yards of earth and gravel, but only 50,131 of these cubic yards, the amount taken by defendants, was above the water level. No greater quantity could have been taken by ordinary means, but only by employing a steam dredger, and earth and gravel taken in this way could not have been used without first having been dried. Defendants removed all the earth and gravel from plaintiff's land "that was practical to take and remove from a financial standpoint." Any greater amount could have been taken only at an expense of 10 or 12 times the usual cost per yard. It was not "advantageous or practical" to have taken more material from plaintiff's land, although it was not impossible. Held, defendants were excused:

"... When [the parties] stipulated that all of the earth and gravel needed for this purpose should be taken from plaintiff's land, they contemplated and assumed that the land contained the requisite quantity, available for use. The defendants were not binding themselves to take what was not there. And, in determining whether the earth and gravel were "available," we must view the conditions in a practical and reasonable way. Although there was gravel on the land, it was so situated that the defendants could not take it by ordinary means, nor except at a prohibitive cost. To all fair intents then, it was impossible for defendants to take it.

"... A thing is impossible in legal contemplation when it is not practicable; and a thing is impracticable when it can only be done at an excessive and unreasonable cost." 1 Beach on Contr. § 216. We do not mean to intimate that the defendants could excuse themselves by showing the existence of conditions which would make the performance of their obligation more expensive than they had anticipated, or which would entail a loss upon them. But, where the difference in cost is so great as here, and has the effect, as found, of making performance impracticable, the situation is not different from that of a total absence of earth and gravel.

TRANSATLANTIC FINANCING CORP. v. UNITED STATES

United States Court of Appeals, District of Columbia Circuit, 1966.
363 F.2d 312.

Before DANAHER, WRIGHT and MCGOWAN, CIRCUIT JUDGES.

J. SKELLY WRIGHT, CIRCUIT JUDGE. This appeal involves a voyage charter between Transatlantic Financing Corporation, operator of the SS CHRISTOS, and the United States covering carriage of a full cargo of wheat from a United States Gulf port to a safe port in Iran. The District Court dismissed a libel filed by Transatlantic against the United States for costs attributable to the ship's diversion from the normal sea route caused by the closing of the Suez Canal. We affirm.

On July 26, 1956, the Government of Egypt nationalized the Suez Canal Company and took over operation of the Canal. On October 2, 1956, during the international crisis which resulted from the seizure, the voyage charter in suit was executed between representatives of Transatlantic and the United States. The charter indicated the termini of the voyage but not the route. On October 27, 1956, the SS CHRISTOS sailed from Galveston for Bandar Shapur, Iran, on a course which would have taken her through Gibraltar and the Suez Canal. On October 29, 1956, Israel invaded Egypt. On October 31, 1956, Great Britain and France invaded the Suez Canal Zone. On November 2, 1956, the Egyptian Government obstructed the Suez Canal with sunken vessels and closed it to traffic.

On or about November 7, 1956, Beckmann, representing Transatlantic, contacted Potosky, an employee of the United States Department of Agriculture, who appellant concedes was unauthorized to bind the Government, requesting instructions concerning disposition of the cargo and seeking an agreement for payment of additional compensation for a voyage around the Cape of Good Hope. Potosky advised Beckmann that Transatlantic was expected to perform the charter according to its terms, that he did not believe Transatlantic was entitled to additional compensation for a voyage around the Cape, but that Transatlantic was free to file such a claim. Following this discussion, the CHRISTOS changed course for the Cape of Good Hope and eventually arrived in Bandar Shapur on December 30, 1956.

Transatlantic's claim is based on the following train of argument. The charter was a contract for a voyage from a Gulf port to Iran. Admiralty principles and practices, especially stemming from the doctrine of deviation, require us to imply into the contract the term that the voyage was to be performed by the "usual and customary" route. The usual and customary route from Texas to Iran was, at the time of contract, via Suez, so the contract was for a voyage from Texas to Iran via Suez. When Suez was closed this contract became impossible to perform. Consequently, appellant's argument continues, when Transatlantic delivered the cargo by going around the Cape of Good Hope, in compliance with the Government's demand under claim of right, it conferred a benefit upon the United States for which it should be paid in *quantum meruit*.

The doctrine of impossibility of performance has gradually been freed from the earlier fictional and unrealistic strictures of such tests as the "implied term" and the parties' "contemplation." Page, The Development of the Doctrine of Impossibility of Performance, 18 Mich.L.Rev. 589, 596 (1920). See generally 6 Corbin, Contracts §§ 1320–1372 (rev. ed. 1962); 6 Williston, Contracts §§ 1931–1979 (rev. ed. 1938). It is now recognized that " 'A thing is impossible in legal contemplation when it is not practicable; and a thing is impracticable when it can only be done at an excessive and unreasonable cost.' " Mineral Park Land Co. v. Howard, 172 Cal. 289, 293, 156 P. 458, 460, L.R.A. 1916F, 1 (1916). Accord, Whelan v. Griffith Consumers Company, D.C.Mun.App., 170 A.2d 229 (1961); Restatement, Contracts § 454 (1932); Uniform Commercial Code (U.L.A.) § 2–615, comment 3. The doctrine ultimately represents the ever-shifting line, drawn by courts hopefully responsive to commercial practices and mores, at which the community's interest in having contracts enforced according to their terms is outweighed by the commercial senselessness of requiring performance.[1] When the issue is raised, the court is asked to construct a condition of performance based on the changed circumstances, a process which involves at least three reasonably definable steps. First, a contingency—something unexpected—must have occurred. Second, the risk of the unexpected occurrence must not have been allocated either by agreement or by custom. Finally, occurrence of the contingency must have rendered performance commercially impracticable.[3] Unless the court finds these three requirements satisfied, the plea of impossibility must fail.

The first requirement was met here. It seems reasonable, where no route is mentioned in a contract, to assume the parties expected performance by the usual and customary route at the time of contract. Since the usual and customary route from Texas to Iran at the time of contract[5] was through Suez, closure of the Canal made impossible the

---

[1]   While the impossibility issue rarely arises, as it has here, in a suit to recover the cost of an alternative method of performance, compare Annot., 84 A.L.R.2d 12, 19 (1962), there is nothing necessarily inconsistent in claiming commercial impracticability for the method of performance actually adopted; the concept of impracticability assumes performance was physically possible. Moreover, a rule making nonperformance a condition precedent to recovery would unjustifiably encourage disappointment of expectations.

[3]   Compare Uniform Commercial Code § 2–615 (a). . . .

[5]   . . . It may be that very often the availability of a customary route at the time of performance other than the route expected to be used at the time of contract should result in denial of relief under the impossibility theory; certainly if *no* customary route is available at the time of performance the contract is rendered impossible. But the same customarily used alternative route may be practicable in one set of circumstances and impracticable in another, as where the goods are unable to survive the extra journey. Moreover, . . . the alternative route, in our case around the Cape, may be practicable at some time during performance, for example while the vessel is still in the Atlantic Ocean, and impracticable at another time during performance, for example after the vessel has traversed most of the Mediterranean Sea. . . .

expected method of performance. But this unexpected development raises rather than resolves the impossibility issue, which turns additionally on whether the risk of the contingency's occurrence had been allocated and, if not, whether performance by alternative routes was rendered impracticable.

Proof that the risk of a contingency's occurrence has been allocated may be expressed in or implied from the agreement. Such proof may also be found in the surrounding circumstances, including custom and usages of the trade. See 6 Corbin, supra, § 1339, at 394–397; 6 Williston, supra, § 1948, at 5457–5458. The contract in this case does not expressly condition performance upon availability of the Suez route. Nor does it specify "via Suez" or, on the other hand, "via Suez or Cape of Good Hope." Nor are there provisions in the contract from which we may properly imply that the continued availability of Suez was a condition of performance.[8] Nor is there anything in custom or trade usage, or in the surrounding circumstances generally, which would support our constructing a condition of performance. The numerous cases requiring performance around the Cape when Suez was closed, see e.g., Ocean Tramp Tankers Corp. v. V/O Sovfracht (The Eugenia), [1964] 2 Q.B. 226, and cases cited therein, indicate that the Cape route is generally regarded as an alternative means of performance. So the implied expectation that the route would be via Suez is hardly adequate proof of an allocation to the promisee of the risk of closure. In some cases, even an express expectation may not amount to a condition of performance.[9] The doctrine of deviation supports our assumption that parties normally expect performance by the usual and customary route, but it adds nothing beyond this that is probative of an allocation of the risk.[10]

---

[8] The charter provides that the vessel is "in every way fitted for *the voyage*" (emphasis added), and the "P. & I. Bunker Deviation Clause" refers to "the contract voyage" and the "direct and/or customary route." Appellant argues that these provisions require implication of a voyage by the direct and customary route. Actually they prove only what we are willing to accept—that the parties expected the usual and customary route would be used. The provisions in no way condition performance upon nonoccurrence of this contingency. . . .

[9] [The court here quoted UCC § 2–614(1).]

[10] The deviation doctrine, drawn principally from admiralty insurance practice, implies into all relevant commercial instruments naming the termini of voyages the usual and customary route between those points. 1 Arnould, Marine Insurance and Average § 376, at 522 (10th ed. 1921). Insurance is cancelled when a ship unreasonably "deviates" from this course, for example by extending a voyage or by putting in at an irregular port, and the shipowner forfeits the protection of clauses of exception which might otherwise have protected him from his common law insurer's liability to cargo. See Gilmore & Black [on Admiralty] § 2–6, at 59–60. This practice, properly qualified see id. § 3–41, makes good sense, since insurance rates are computed on the basis of the implied course, and deviations in the course increasing the anticipated risk make the insurer's calculations meaningless. Arnould, supra, § 14, at 26. Thus the route, so far as insurance contracts are concerned, is crucial, whether express or implied. But even here, the implied term is not inflexible. Reasonable deviations do not result in loss of insurance, at least so long as established practice is followed . . . The doctrine's only relevance, therefore, is that it provides additional support for the assumption we willingly make that merchants agreeing to a voyage between two

If anything, the circumstances surrounding this contract indicate that the risk of the Canal's closure may be deemed to have been allocated to Transatlantic. We know or may safely assume that the parties were aware, as were most commercial men with interests affected by the Suez situation, see The Eugenia, supra, that the Canal might become a dangerous area. No doubt the tension affected freight rates, and it is arguable that the risk of closure became part of the dickered terms. Uniform Commercial Code § 2–615, comment 8. We do not deem the risk of closure so allocated, however. Foreseeability or even recognition of a risk does not necessarily prove its allocation.[11] Compare Uniform Commercial Code § 2–615, Comment 1; Restatement, Contracts § 457 (1932). Parties to a contract are not always able to provide for all the possibilities of which they are aware, sometimes because they cannot agree, often simply because they are too busy. Moreover, that some abnormal risk was contemplated is probative but does not necessarily establish an allocation of the risk of the contingency which actually occurs. In this case, for example, nationalization by Egypt of the Canal Corporation and formation of the Suez Users Group did not necessarily indicate that the Canal would be blocked even if a confrontation resulted.[12] The surrounding circumstances do indicate, however, a willingness by Transatlantic to assume abnormal risks, and this fact should legitimately cause us to judge the impracticability of performance by an alternative route in stricter terms than we would were the contingency unforeseen.

We turn then to the question whether occurrence of the contingency rendered performance commercially impracticable under the circumstances of this case. The goods shipped were not subject to harm from the longer, less temperate Southern route. The vessel and crew were fit to proceed around the Cape. Transatlantic was no less able than the United States to purchase insurance to cover the contingency's occurrence. If anything, it is more reasonable to expect owner-operators of vessels to insure against the hazards of war. They are in the best position to calculate the cost of performance by alternative routes (and therefore to estimate the amount of insurance required), and are undoubtedly sensitive to international troubles which uniquely affect the demand for and cost of their services. The only factor operating here in appellant's favor is the

---

points expect that the usual and customary route between those points will be used. The doctrine provides no evidence of an allocation of the risk of the route's unavailability.

[11] See Note, The Fetish of Impossibility in the Law of Contracts, 53 Colum.L.Rev. 94, 98 n. 23 (1953), suggesting that foreseeability is properly used "as a *factor* probative of assumption of the risk of impossibility." (Emphasis added.)

[12] Sources cited in the briefs indicate formation of the Suez Canal Users Association on October 1, 1956, was viewed in some quarters as an implied threat of force. See N.Y. Times, Oct. 2, 1956, p. 1, col. 1, noting, on the day the charter in this case was executed, that "Britain has declared her freedom to use force as a last resort if peaceful methods fail to achieve a satisfactory settlement." Secretary of State Dulles was able, however, to view the statement as evidence of the canal users' "dedication to a just and peaceful solution." The Suez Problem 369–370 (Department of State Pub.1956).

added expense, allegedly $43,972.00 above and beyond the contract price of $305,842.92, of extending a 10,000 mile voyage by approximately 3,000 miles. While it may be an overstatement to say that increased cost and difficulty of performance never constitute impracticability, to justify relief there must be more of a variation between expected cost and the cost of performing by an available alternative than is present in this case, where the promisor can legitimately be presumed to have accepted some degree of abnormal risk, and where impracticability is urged on the basis of added expense alone.

We conclude, therefore, as have most other courts considering related issues arising out of the Suez closure, that performance of this contract was not rendered legally impossible. Even if we agreed with appellant, its theory of relief seems untenable. When performance of a contract is deemed impossible it is a nullity. In the case of a charter party involving carriage of goods, the carrier may return to an appropriate port and unload its cargo, The Malcolm Baxter, Jr., 277 U.S. 323, 48 S.Ct. 516, 72 L.Ed. 901 (1928), subject of course to required steps to minimize damages. If the performance rendered has value, recovery in *quantum meruit* for the entire performance is proper. But here Transatlantic has collected its contract price, and now seeks *quantum meruit* relief for the additional expense of the trip around the Cape. If the contract is a nullity, Transatlantic's theory of relief should have been *quantum meruit* for the entire trip, rather than only for the extra expense. Transatlantic attempts to take its profit on the contract, and then force the Government to absorb the cost of the additional voyage. When impracticability without fault occurs, the law seeks an equitable solution, see 6 Corbin, supra, § 1321, and *quantum meruit* is one of its potent devices to achieve this end. There is no interest in casting the entire burden of commercial disaster on one party in order to preserve the other's profit. Apparently the contract price in this case was advantageous enough to deter appellant from taking a stance on damages consistent with its theory of liability. In any event, there is no basis for relief.

Affirmed.

Mishara Constr. Co. v. Transit-Mixed Concrete Corp.

365 Mass. 122, 310 N.E.2d 363 (1974)

"With respect to the requirement that performance must have been impracticable, the Official Code Comment to the section stresses that the reference is to 'commercial impracticability' as opposed to strict impossibility. G.L. c. 106, § 2–615, comments 3–4. This is not a radical departure from the common law of contracts as interpreted by this court. Although a strict rule was originally followed denying any excuse for accident or 'inevitable necessity,' e.g., Adams v. Nichols, 19 Pick. 275 (1837), it has long been assumed that circumstances drastically increasing the difficulty and expense of the contemplated performance may be within the compass of 'impossibility.' See Rowe v. Peabody, 207 Mass. 226, 233–234, 93 N.E. 604 (1911) (dictum); Fauci v. Denehy, 332 Mass. 691, 696–697, 127 N.E.2d 477 (1955). By adopting the term 'impracticability' rather than 'impossibility' the drafters of the Code appear to be in accord with Professor Williston who stated that 'the essence of the modern defense of impossibility is that the promised performance was at the making of the contract, or thereafter became, impracticable owing to some extreme or unreasonable difficulty, expense, injury, or loss involved, rather than that it is scientifically or actually impossible.' Williston, Contracts (Rev. ed.) § 1931 (1938). See Restatement: Contracts, § 454 (1932); Corbin, Contracts, § 1339 (1962).

"The second criterion of the excuse, that the intervening circumstance be one which the parties assumed would not occur, is also familiar to the law of Massachusetts. Baetjer v. New England Alcohol Co., 319 Mass. 592, 600, 66 N.E.2d 798 (1946). Boston Plate & Window Glass Co. v. John Bowen Co., Inc., 335 Mass. 697, 699–700, 141 N.E.2d 715 (1957). The rule is essentially aimed at the distribution of certain kinds of risks in the contractual relationship. By directing the inquiry to the time when the contract was first made, we really seek to determine whether the risk of the intervening circumstance was one which the parties may be taken to have assigned between themselves. It is, of course, the very essence of contract that it is directed at the elimination of some risks for each party in exchange for others. Each receives the certainty of price, quantity, and time, and assumes the risk of changing market prices, superior opportunity, or added costs. It is implicit in the doctrine of impossibility (and the companion rule of 'frustration of purpose') that certain risks are so unusual and have such severe consequences that they must have been beyond the scope of the assignment of risks inherent in the contract, that is, beyond the agreement made by the parties. To require performance in that case would be to grant the promisee an advantage for which he could not be said to have bargained in making the contract. 'The important question is whether an unanticipated circumstance has made performance of the promise vitally different from what should reasonably have been within the contemplation of both parties when they entered into the contract. If so, the risk should not fairly be thrown upon the promisor.' Williston, Contracts (Rev. ed.) § 1931 (1938). The emphasis in contracts governed by the Uniform Commercial Code is on the commercial context in which the agreement was made. The question is, given the commercial circumstances in which the parties dealt: Was the contingency which developed one which the parties could reasonably be thought to have foreseen as a real possibility which could affect performance? Was it one of that variety of risks which the parties were tacitly assigning to the promisor by their failure to provide for it explicitly? If it were, performance will be required. If it could not be so considered, performance is excused. The contract cannot be reasonably thought to govern in these circumstances, and the parties are both thrown upon the resources of the open market without the benefit of their contract."

———

UCC §§ 1–103, 2–509, 2–510, 2–613, 2–614, 2–615, 2–616
[See Selected Source Materials Supplement]

———

RESTATEMENT, SECOND, CONTRACTS §§ 261–272
[See Selected Source Materials Supplement]

———

CISG ARTS. 66–69
[See Selected Source Materials Supplement]

———

UNIDROIT PRINCIPLES OF INTERNATIONAL COMMERCIAL CONTRACTS ARTS. 6.2.1, 6.2.2, 6.2.3, 7.1.7
[See Selected Source Materials Supplement]

———

PRINCIPLES OF EUROPEAN CONTRACT LAW ARTS. 4.102, 6.111, 8.108
[See Selected Source Materials Supplement]

———

ALBRE MARBLE & TILE CO. v. JOHN BOWEN CO.
Supreme Judicial Court of Massachusetts, 1959.
338 Mass. 394, 155 N.E.2d 437.

Before SPALDING, WILLIAMS, COUNIHAN and WHITTEMORE, JJ.

SPALDING, JUSTICE. The declaration in this action of contract contains four counts. The plaintiff in counts 1 and 2 seeks damages for the defendant's alleged breach of two subcontracts under which the plaintiff agreed to supply labor and materials to the defendant as general contractor of the Chronic Disease Hospital and Nurses' Home in Boston.[1] In counts 3 and 4 the plaintiff seeks to recover the value of work and labor furnished by it to the defendant at the defendant's request. The defendant's substitute answer in defence to the first two counts states that the

---

[1]   Count 1 relates to tile work and count 2 relates to marble work.

performance of the subcontracts became impossible when the defendant's general contract with the Commonwealth was declared invalid by this court in Gifford v. Commissioner of Public Health, 328 Mass. 608, 105 N.E.2d 476. The defendant's answer to counts 3 and 4 (based on quantum meruit) states that no payment could be demanded because the plaintiff did not possess an architect's certificate for the work done. . . .

The defendant filed a motion, accompanied by an affidavit, for the immediate entry of judgment in its favor. . . . The plaintiff filed a counter affidavit. After hearing, the motion was allowed, and the plaintiff duly claimed an exception.

[The court concluded that the granting of defendant's motion for judgment on counts 1 and 2 was proper.]

We turn now to counts 3 and 4 by which the plaintiff seeks a recovery for the fair value of work and labor furnished to the defendant prior to the termination of the general contract. The plaintiff seeks recovery in count 3 for "preparation of samples, shop drawings, tests and affidavits" in connection with the tile work; in count 4 recovery for similar work in connection with the marble contract is sought.

The defendant in its affidavit maintains that the tile and marble work to be furnished by the plaintiff could not have been done until late in the construction process; that no tile or marble was actually installed in the building; and that the expenses incurred by the plaintiff prior to the time the general contract was declared invalid consisted solely of expenditures in preparation for performance. Relying on the decision in Young v. Chicopee, 186 Mass. 518, 72 N.E. 63, the defendant maintains that where a building contract has been rendered impossible of performance a plaintiff may not recover for expenses incurred in preparation for performance, but may recover only for the labor and materials "wrought into" the structure. Therefore, the defendant says, the plaintiff should take nothing here.

The plaintiff places its reliance upon a clause appearing in both contracts which provides in part: "It is agreed you [the plaintiff] will furnish and submit all necessary or required samples, shop drawings, tests, affidavits, etc., for approval, all as ordered or specified. . . . " The plaintiff in effect concedes that no labor or materials were actually wrought into the structure, but argues that the contract provision quoted above placed its preparatory efforts under the supervision of the defendant, and that this circumstance removes this case from the ambit of those decisions which apply the "wrought-in" principle. . . .

The problem of allocating losses where a building contract has been rendered impossible of performance by a supervening act not chargeable to either party is a vexed one. In situations where the part performance of one party measurably exceeds that of the other the tendency has been to allow recovery for the fair value of work done in the actual performance of the contract and to deny recovery for expenditures made in reliance upon the contract or in preparing to perform. This principle has sometimes been expressed in terms of "benefit" or "lack of benefit." In other words, recovery may be had only for those expenditures which, but for the supervening act, would have enured to the benefit of the defendant as contemplated by the contract. See, e.g. Young v. Chicopee, 186 Mass. 518, 520, 72 N.E. 63. The "wrought-in" principle applied in building contract cases is merely a variant of this principle. It has long been recognized that this theory is unworkable if the concept of benefit is applied literally. In M. Ahern Co. v. John Bowen Co. Inc., 334 Mass. 36, 41, 133 N.E.2d 484, 487, we quoted with approval the statement of Professor Williston that "It is enough that the defendant has actually received in part performance of the contract something for which when completed he had agreed to pay a price." Williston on Contracts (Rev. ed.) § 1976.

Although the matter of denial of reliance expenditures in impossibility situations seems to have been discussed but little in judicial opinions, it has, however, been the subject of critical comment by scholars. See Fuller and Perdue, The Reliance Interest in Contract Damages, 46 Yale L.J. 52, 373, 379–383. Note, 46 Mich.L.Rev. 401. In England the recent frustrated contracts legislation provides that the court may grant recovery for expenditures in reliance on the contract or in preparation to perform it where it appears *just to do so having regard to all the circumstances of the case*" (emphasis supplied). 6 & 7 George VI, c. 40.

We are of opinion that the plaintiff here may recover for those expenditures made pursuant to the specific request of the defendant as set forth in the contract clause quoted above. A combination of factors peculiar to this case justifies such a holding without laying down the broader principle that in every case recovery may be had for payments made or obligations reasonably incurred in preparation for performance of a contract where further performance is rendered impossible without fault by either party. See Boston Plate & Window Glass Co. v. John Bowen Co. Inc., 335 Mass. 697, 702, 141 N.E.2d 715.

The factors which determine the holding here are these: First, this is not a case of mere impossibility by reason of a supervening act. The opinion of this court in M. Ahern Co. v. John Bowen Co. Inc., 334 Mass. 36, 133 N.E.2d 484, points out that the defendant's involvement in creating the impossibility was greater than that of its subcontractors. The facts regarding the defendant's conduct are set forth in that opinion and need not be restated.* Although the defendant's conduct was not so culpable as to render it liable for breach of contract (Boston Plate & Window Glass Co. v. John Bowen Co. Inc., 335 Mass. 697, 141 N.E.2d 715), nevertheless, it was a contributing factor to a loss sustained by the plaintiff which as

---

* The defendant had presented its bid for the hospital construction project in such a manner as to cause the bid to appear to be the lowest although in fact it was not. (Footnote by ed.)

between the plaintiff and the defendant the latter ought to bear to the extent herein permitted.

We attach significance to the clause in the contract, which was prepared by the defendant, specifically requesting the plaintiff to submit samples, shop drawings, tests, affidavits, etc., to the defendant. This is not a case in which all efforts in preparation for performance were solely within the discretion and control of the subcontractor. We are mindful that in *Young v. Chicopee*, 186 Mass. 518, 72 N.E. 63, recovery of the value of materials brought to the construction site at the specific request of the defendant therein was denied. But in that case the supervening act rendering further performance impossible was a fire not shown to have been caused by the fault of either party. We are not disposed to extend that holding to a situation in which the defendant's fault is greater than the plaintiff's.

Moreover, the acts requested here by their very nature could not be "wrought into" the structure. In *Angus v. Scully*, 176 Mass. 357, 57 N.E. 674, 49 A.L.R. 562, recovery for the value of services rendered by house movers was allowed although the house was destroyed midway in the moving. The present case comes nearer to the rationale of the *Angus* case than to that of the *Young* case. . . .

We hold that the damages to be assessed are limited solely to the fair value of those acts done in conformity with the specific request of the defendant as contained in the contract. Expenses incurred prior to the execution of the contract, such as those arising out of preparing the plaintiff's bid, are not to be considered.

The plaintiff's exceptions as to counts 1 and 2 are overruled and are sustained as to counts 3 and 4; as to those counts the case is remanded to the Superior Court for further proceedings in conformity with this opinion. The appeal is dismissed.

So ordered.

NOTE ON THE EQUITABLE APPORTIONMENT OF LOSSES FOLLOWING IMPOSSIBILITY

Restatement First seemed to adopt the assumption that the reimbursement of reliance is not a proper function of the courts except in tort cases. As a corollary, it was assumed that in contract cases a court has a choice, subject to the applicable rules of law, of (1) denying relief; (2) granting relief measured by the value of the performance promised by the defendant; or (3) granting relief measured by the value of the benefit conferred by the plaintiff on the defendant. The possibility of measuring relief by the plaintiff's losses through reliance was completely passed over, except insofar as it crept in, perhaps unintentionally, in certain of the illustrative cases. As applied to unexpected-circumstances cases, this meant that courts had to go whole hog or none in dealing with the problem of remedies. It is difficult to see anything in the American case law that compelled that assumption. If a court has power to impose an obligation to return benefits, it would seem also to have power to impose equitable conditions and limitations on this obligation. If a court has power to relieve a person from a promise because of an unexpected event, it would seem also to have power to relieve the person on condition that she reimburse all or a part of the other party's reliance on the contract.

Restatement Second takes a considerably different view on this matter than Restatement First. Under Restatement Second Section 272:

> (1) In any case governed by the rules stated in this Chapter [Impracticability and Frustration], either party may have a claim for relief including restitution . . .

> (2) In any case governed by the rules stated in this Chapter, if those rules together with the rules stated in [the chapter on remedies] will not avoid injustice, the court may grant relief on such terms as justice requires, including protection of the parties' reliance interests.

To the same effect is Official Comment 6 to UCC Section 2–615 (the principal UCC section dealing with the problem of unexpected circumstances):

> In situations in which neither sense nor justice is served by either answer when the issue is posed in flat terms of "excuse" or "no excuse," adjustment under the various provisions of this Article is necessary, especially the sections on good faith, on insecurity and assurance and on the reading of all provisions in the light of their purposes, and the general policy of this Act to use equitable principles in furtherance of commercial standards and good faith.

KRELL V. HENRY

In the Court of Appeal, 1903.
[1903] 2 K.B. 740.

Appeal from a decision of DARLING, J.

The plaintiff, Paul Krell, sued the defendant, C.S. Henry, for £50, being the balance of a sum of £75, for which the defendant had agreed to hire a flat at 56A, Pall Mall on the days of June 26 and 27, for the purpose of viewing the processions to be held in connection with the coronation of His Majesty. The defendant denied his liability, and counterclaimed for the return of the sum of £25, which had been paid as a deposit, on the ground that, the processions not having taken place owing to the serious illness of the King, there had been a total failure of consideration for the contract entered into by him.

The facts, which were not disputed, were as follows. The plaintiff on leaving the country in March, 1902, left instructions with his solicitor to let his suite of chambers at 56A, Pall Mall on such terms and for such period (not exceeding six months) as he thought proper. On June 17, 1902, the defendant noticed an announcement in the windows of the plaintiff's flat to the effect that windows to view the coronation processions were to be let. The defendant interviewed the housekeeper on the subject, when it was pointed out to him what a good view of the procession could be obtained from the premises, and he eventually agreed with the housekeeper to take the suite for the two days in question for a sum of £75.

On June 20 the defendant wrote the following letter to the plaintiff's solicitor:—

"I am in receipt of yours of the 18th instant, inclosing form of agreement for the suite of chambers on the third floor at 56A, Pall Mall, which I have agreed to take for the two days, the 26th and 27th instant, for the sum of £75. For reasons given you I cannot enter into the agreement, but as arranged over the telephone I inclose herewith cheque for £25 as deposit, and will thank you to confirm to me that I shall have the entire use of these rooms during the days (not the nights) of the 26th and 27th instant. You may rely that every care will be taken of the premises and their contents. On the 24th inst. I will pay the balance, viz., £50, to complete the £75 agreed upon."

On the same day the defendant received the following reply from the plaintiff's solicitor:—

"I am in receipt of your letter of today's date inclosing cheque for £25 deposit on your agreeing to take Mr. Krell's chambers on the third floor at 56A, Pall Mall for the two days, the 26th and 27th June, and I confirm the agreement that you are to have the entire use of these rooms during the days (but not the nights), the balance, £50, to be paid to me on Tuesday next the 24th instant."

The processions not having taken place on the days originally appointed, namely, June 26 and 27, the defendant declined to pay the balance of £50 alleged to be due from him under the contract in writing of June 20 constituted by the above two letters. Hence the present action.

DARLING J., on August 11, 1902, held upon the authority of Taylor v. Caldwell and The Moorcock (1889, 14 P.D. 64), that there was an implied condition in the contract that the procession should take place, and gave judgment for the defendant on the claim and counterclaim.

The plaintiff appealed.

Spencer Bower, K.C., and Holman Gregory, for the plaintiff. In the contract nothing is said about the coronation procession, but it is admitted that both parties expected that there would be a procession, and that the price to be paid for the rooms was fixed with reference to the expected procession. Darling J. held that both the claim and the counterclaim were governed by Taylor v. Caldwell, and that there was an implied term in the contract that the procession should take place. It is submitted that the learned judge was wrong. If he was right, the result would be that in every case of this kind an unremunerated promisor will be in effect an insurer of the hopes and expectations of the promisee. . . . In order that the person who has contracted to pay the price should be excused from doing so, there must be (1) no default on his part; (2) either the physical extinction or the not coming into existence of the subject-matter of the contract; (3) the performance of the contract must have been thereby rendered impossible.

In the present case there has been no default on the part of the defendant. But there has been no physical extinction of the subject-matter, and the performance of the contract was quite possible. . . .

VAUGHAN WILLIAMS, L.J. read the following written judgment:—The real question in this case is the extent of the application in English law of the principle of the Roman law which has been adopted and acted on in many English decisions, and notably in the case of Taylor v. Caldwell. . . . It is said, on the one side, that the specified thing, state of things, or condition the continued existence of which is necessary for the fulfilment of the contract, so that the parties entering into the contract must have contemplated the continued existence of that thing, condition, or state of things as the foundation of what was to be done under the contract, is limited to things which are either the subject-matter of the contract or a condition or state of things, present or anticipated, which is expressly mentioned in the contract. But, on the other side, it is said that the condition or state of things need not be expressly specified, but that it is sufficient if that condition or state of things clearly appears by extrinsic evidence to have been assumed by the parties to be the foundation or basis of the contract, and the event which causes the impossibility is of such a character that it cannot reasonably be supposed to have been in the contemplation of the contracting parties when the contract was made. In such a case the contracting parties will not be held bound by the general words which, though large enough to include, were not used with reference to a possibility of a particular event rendering performance of the contract impossible. I do not think that the principle of the civil law as introduced into the English law is limited to cases in which the event causing the impossibility of performance is the destruction or nonexistence of some thing which is the subject-matter of the contract or of some condition or state of things expressly specified as a condition of it. I think that you first have to ascertain, not necessarily from the terms of the contract, but, if required, from necessary inferences, drawn from surrounding circumstances recognized by both contracting parties, what is the substance of the contract, and then to ask the question whether that substantial contract needs for its foundation the assumption of the existence of a particular state of things. If it does, this will limit the operation of the general words, and in such case, if the contract becomes impossible of performance by reason of the nonexistence of the state of things assumed by both contracting parties as the foundation of the contract, there will be no breach of the contract thus limited. . . .

In my judgment [in this case] the use of the rooms was let and taken for the purpose of seeing the Royal procession. It was not a demise of the rooms, or even an agreement to let and take the rooms. It is a licence to use rooms for a particular purpose and none other. And in my judgment the taking place of those processions on the days proclaimed along the proclaimed route, which passed 56A, Pall Mall, was regarded by both contracting parties as the foundation of the contract; and I think that it cannot reasonably be supposed to have been in the contemplation of the contracting parties, when the contract was made, that the coronation would not be held on the proclaimed days, or the processions not take place on those days along the proclaimed route; and I think that the words imposing on the defendant the obligation to accept and pay for the use of the rooms for the named days, although general and unconditional, were not used with reference to the possibility of the particular contingency which afterwards occurred.

It was suggested in the course of the argument that if the occurrence, on the proclaimed days, of the coronation and the procession in this case were the foundation of the contract, and if the general words are thereby limited or qualified, so that in the event of the non-occurrence of the coronation and procession along the proclaimed route they would discharge both parties from further performance of the contract, it would follow that if a cabman was engaged to take some one to Epsom on Derby Day at a suitable enhanced price for such a journey, say £10, both parties to the contract would be discharged in the contingency of the race at Epsom for some reason becoming impossible; but I do not think this follows, for I do not think that in the cab case the happening of the race would be the foundation of the contract. No doubt the purpose of the engager would be to go to see the Derby, and the price would be proportionately high; but the cab had no special qualifications for the purpose which led to the selection of the cab for this particular occasion. Any other cab would have done as well. Moreover, I think, that under the cab contract, the hirer, even if the race went off, could have said, "Drive me to Epsom; I will pay you the agreed sum; you have nothing to do with the purpose for which I hired the cab," and that if the cabman refused he would have been guilty of a breach of contract, there being nothing to qualify his promise to drive the hirer to Epsom on a particular day. Whereas in the case of the coronation, there is not merely the purpose of the hirer to see the coronation procession, but it is the coronation procession and the relative position of the rooms which is the basis of the contract as much for the lessor as the hirer; and I think that if the King, before the coronation day and after the contract, had died, the hirer could not have insisted on having the rooms on the days named. It could not in the cab case be reasonably said that seeing the Derby race was the foundation of the contract, as it was of the licence in this case. Whereas in the present case, where the rooms were offered and taken, by reason of their peculiar suitability from the position of the rooms for a view of the coronation procession, surely the view of the coronation procession was the foundation of the contract, which is a very different thing from the purpose of the man who engaged the cab—namely, to see the race—being held to be the foundation of the contract.

Each case must be judged by its own circumstances. In each case one must ask oneself, first, what, having regard to all the circumstances, was the foundation of the contract? Secondly, was the performance of the contract prevented? Thirdly, was the event which prevented the performance of the contract of such a character that it cannot reasonably be said to have been in the contemplation of the parties at the date of the contract? If all these questions are answered in the affirmative (as I think they should be in this case), I think both parties are discharged from further performance of the contract. . . .

This disposes of the plaintiff's claim for £50 unpaid balance of the price agreed to be paid for the use of the rooms. The defendant at one time set up a cross-claim for the return of the £25 he paid at the date of the contract. As that claim is now withdrawn it is unnecessary to say anything about it. . . . I think this appeal ought to be dismissed.

[The concurring opinions of Romer, L.J., and Stirling, L.J., are omitted.]

Appeal dismissed.

———

Wladis, Common Law and Uncommon Events: The Development of the Doctrine of Impossibility of Performance in English Contract Law

75 Geo.L.J. 1575, 1609, 1618 (1987)

"The facts giving rise to the coronation cases may be stated briefly: Edward VII was to be crowned on Thursday, June 26, 1902, in Westminster Abbey. There was to be a coronation procession that day between the royal residence at Buckingham Palace and the Abbey, and a lengthier one [on June 27] throughout the city of London. In addition, on Saturday, June 28, a naval review of the fleet was to take place. Flats were let, grandstands erected, and seats sold along the routes of the processions. Boats were also chartered to take the public to the naval review. However, during the morning of June 24 it was determined that Edward, who had been suffering from appendicitis, needed to undergo surgery. Later that day it was announced that the coronation would be postponed and the naval review not held. . . .

"... The coronation events were not canceled, but only postponed. The procession [scheduled for] June 26 eventually took place on August 9 and proceeded along the same route as had originally been planned. The procession scheduled for June 27 occurred on October 25 and followed as nearly as possible the original route. Even the naval review that had been canceled was rescheduled and held on August 16."

———

La Cumbre Golf & Country Club v. Santa Barbara Hotel Co.

205 Cal. 422, 271 P. 476 (1928)

Santa Barbara Hotel Co. owned and operated the Ambassador Hotel. Under a contract between Santa Barbara and the La Cumbre Golf and Country Club, La Cumbre extended privileges at its Club to guests at the Ambassador. In 1920, Santa Barbara wanted to purchase and operate a bus between the Ambassador and the Club, provided the golf privileges were extended over an additional period of time. Accordingly, the parties made a contract for a period ending December 31, 1923, under which La Cumbre agreed that it would grant all the privileges of membership to guests at the Ambassador, and Santa Barbara agreed to be responsible for the guests' greens fees and to pay La Cumbre $300 a month. In April 1921, the Ambassador burned down. Santa Barbara stopped making payments under the contract, and La Cumbre sued for the balance due, $7200. Held, for Santa Barbara. It was an implied condition of the contract that there would be guests in the Ambassador.

———

Chase Precast Corp. v. John J. Paonessa Co.

409 Mass. 371, 566 N.E.2d 603 (1991)

In 1982, the Commonwealth of Massachusetts, through the Department of Public Works (the Department), entered into two contracts with Paonessa for resurfacing and improvements on two stretches of Route 128. Part of each contract called for replacing a grass median strip between the north- and south-bound lanes with concrete surfacing and precast concrete median barriers. Paonessa then entered into two contracts with Chase, under which Chase was to supply 25,800 linear feet of precast concrete median barriers according to the Department's specifications. The quantity and type of barriers to be supplied were specified in two purchase orders prepared by Chase.

The highway reconstruction began in the spring of 1983. By late May, the Department was receiving protests from angry residents who objected to use of the concrete median barriers and removal of the grass median strip. Paonessa and Chase became aware of the protest around June 1. On June 6, a group of about 100 citizens filed an action in the Superior Court to stop installation of the concrete median barriers and other aspects of the work. On June 7, anticipating modification of the contracts by the Department, Paonessa notified Chase by letter to stop producing concrete barriers for the projects. Chase did so. On June 17, the Department and the citizens' group entered into a settlement which provided, in part, that no additional concrete median barriers would be installed. On June 23, the Department deleted the concrete-median-barriers item from its contracts with Paonessa.

Before stopping production on June 8, Chase had produced approximately one-half of the barriers required under its contracts with Paonessa, and had delivered most of these to the construction sites. Paonessa paid Chase, at the contract price, for all the barriers that Chase had produced. Chase suffered no out-of-pocket expense as a result of the cancellation of the remaining barriers.

Chase brought an action against Paonessa to recover its anticipated profit on the median barriers called for by its supply contracts with Paonessa but not produced. After a jury-waived trial, a Superior Court judge ruled for Paonessa on the basis of impossibility of performance. The Appeals Court affirmed, noting that the doctrine of frustration of purpose more accurately described the basis of the decision than the doctrine of impossibility. The Massachusetts Supreme Judicial Court agreed:

> Paonessa bore no responsibility for the department's elimination of the median barriers from the projects. Therefore, whether it can rely on the defense of frustration turns on whether elimination of the barriers was a risk allocated by the contracts to Paonessa. *Mishara Constr. Co., supra,* 365 Mass. [122,] at 129, 310 N.E.2d 363 [1974], articulates the relevant test:
>
> > "The question is, given the commercial circumstances in which the parties dealt: Was the contingency which developed one which the parties could reasonably be thought to have foreseen as a real possibility which could affect performance? Was it one of that variety of risks which the parties were tacitly assigning to the promisor by their failure to provide for it explicitly? If it was, performance will be required. If it could not be so considered, performance is excused."

This is a question for the trier of fact. *Id.* at 127, 130, 310 N.E.2d 363.

PART 6

CONDITIONS

■ ■ ■

Part VI of this book concerns conditions.

Chapter 19 concerns several doctrines that often are described as "constructive conditions." These doctrines are default rules that define when a breach by one party discharges the other party from her performance obligation under the contract, or at least allows the other party to suspend performance until the breach is cured.

Chapter 20 concerns express conditions. An express condition differs from a promise in that it imposes no obligation, but instead provides that a contracting party either does not come under a duty to perform unless a certain state of affairs exists, or is released from a duty to perform if a certain state of affairs exists.

———

CHAPTER 19

CONSTRUCTIVE CONDITIONS

■ ■ ■

This Chapter concerns a set of doctrines that often are described as constructive conditions. When a promise is subject to a condition, non-occurrence of the condition discharges the promisor from her obligation to perform the promise. Suppose A and B make a bargain in which A's achievement of objective x is of vital importance to B. B may encourage A to achieve x, and B may ensure she is not obligated to pay A as promised if x is not achieved, by making A's achievement of x a condition to B's payment obligation. Express conditions tend to be clearcut. B wants condition x to be clearly defined to avoid any dispute about her payment obligation if x is not achieved.

The rules considered in this Chapter generally are not clearcut. They are standards that generally ask a court to balance the risk B will suffer an uncompensated loss if she is not discharged from her obligation to perform her part of the bargain and the risk A will suffer forfeiture if B is discharged from her obligation. An important consideration is whether B can be made whole by a damage award so she will not suffer an uncompensated loss, if she is required to perform her part of the bargain while recovering damages. Another important consideration is whether A has acted in bad faith.

The rules considered in this Chapter rest on the premise that obligations under a contract generally are mutually dependent, so that if one party fails to perform in a substantial or material respect, then the other party is discharged from her obligation under the contract. It took a long time for the common law to come around to this point of view. For much of the history of the common law promises were assumed to be independent, in the absence of an express condition. The final break with the old view came in a decision by Mansfield in 1773, Kingston v. Preston, 2 Douglas 689, which established that to recover on a contract claim a plaintiff generally must allege substantial performance of her promise, or some excuse for her failure to perform, such as a material breach by the defendant.

———

SECTION 1. COMMON LAW DOCTRINES

This Section concerns common law doctrines that determine when one party's breach of contract discharges the other party from her performance obligation under the contract. The issue is framed as one of substantial performance when the question is whether a party who has rendered defective or partial performance is entitled to the contract price less damages. More precisely, the doctrine of substantial performance concerns the question when can a party who has breached a contract nevertheless bring suit under the contract. The doctrine of material breach concern when a party has the power to suspend performance or the power to terminate a contract because the other party has breached.

(A) SUBSTANTIAL PERFORMANCE

JACOB & YOUNGS V. KENT
Court of Appeals of New York, 1921.
230 N.Y. 239, 129 N.E. 889, 23 A.L.R. 1429.

CARDOZO, J. The plaintiff built a country residence for the defendant at a cost of upwards of $77,000, and now sues to recover a balance of $3,483.46, remaining unpaid. The work of construction ceased in June, 1914, and the defendant then began to occupy the dwelling. There was no complaint of defective performance until March, 1915. One of the specifications for the plumbing work provides that "all wrought-iron pipe must be well galvanized, lap welded pipe of the grade known as 'standard pipe' of Reading manufacture."

The defendant learned in March, 1915, that some of the pipe, instead of being made in Reading, was the product of other factories. The plaintiff was accordingly directed by the architect to do the work anew. The plumbing was then encased within the walls except in a few places where it had to be exposed. Obedience to the order meant more than the substitution of other pipe. It meant the demolition at great expense of substantial parts of the completed structure. The plaintiff left the work untouched, and asked for a certificate that the final payment was due. Refusal of the certificate was followed by this suit.

The evidence sustains a finding that the omission of the prescribed brand of pipe was neither fraudulent nor wilful. It was the result of the oversight and inattention of the plaintiff's subcontractor. Reading pipe is distinguished from Cohoes pipe and other brands only by the name of the manufacturer stamped upon it at intervals of between six and seven feet. Even the defendant's architect, though he inspected the pipe upon arrival, failed to notice the discrepancy. The plaintiff tried to show that the brands installed, though made by other manufacturers, were the same in quality, in appearance, in market value, and in cost as the brand stated in the contract—that they were indeed, the same thing, though manufactured in another place. The evidence was excluded, and a verdict directed for the defendant. The Appellate Division reversed, and granted a new trial.

We think the evidence, if admitted would have supplied some basis for the inference that the defect was insignificant in its relation to the project. The courts never say that one who makes a contract fills the measure of his duty by less than full performance. They do say, however, that an omission, both trivial and innocent, will sometimes be atoned for by allowance of the resulting damage, and will not always be the breach of a condition to be followed by a forfeiture. . . . The distinction is akin to that between dependent and independent promises, or between promises and conditions. Anson on Contracts (Corbin's Ed.) § 367; 2 Williston on Contracts, § 842. Some promises are so plainly independent that they can never by fair construction be conditions of one another. Rosenthal Paper Co. v. Nat. Folding Box & Paper Co., 226 N.Y. 313, 123 N.E. 766; Bogardus v. N.Y. Life Ins. Co., 101 N.Y. 328, 4 N.E. 522. Others are so plainly dependent that they must always be conditions. Others, though dependent and thus conditions when there is departure in point of substance, will be viewed as independent and collateral when the departure is insignificant. 2 Williston on Contracts, §§ 841, 842; Eastern Forge Co. v. Corbin, 182 Mass. 590, 592, 66 N.E. 419; Robinson v. Mollett, L.R., 7 Eng. & Ir.App. 802, 814; Miller v. Benjamin, 142 N.Y. 613, 37 N.E. 631. Considerations partly of justice and partly of presumable intention are to tell us whether this or that promise shall be placed in one class or in another. The simple and the uniform will call for different remedies from the multifarious and the intricate. The margin of departure within the range of normal expectation upon a sale of common chattels will vary from the margin to be expected upon a contract for the construction of a mansion or a "skyscraper." There will be harshness sometimes and oppression in the implication of a condition when the thing upon which labor has been expended is incapable of surrender because united to the land, and equity and reason in the implication of a like condition when the subject-matter, if defective, is in shape to be returned. From the conclusion that promises may not be treated as dependent to the extent of their uttermost minutiae without sacrifice of justice, the progress is a short one to the conclusion that they may not be so treated without a perversion of intention. Intention not otherwise revealed may be presumed to hold in contemplation the reasonable and probable. If something else is in view, it must not be left to implication. There will be no assumption of a purpose to visit venial faults with oppressive retribution.

Those who think more of symmetry and logic in the development of legal rules than of practical adaptation to the attainment of a just result will be troubled by a classification where the lines of division are so wavering and blurred. Something doubtless, may be said on the score of consistency and certainty in favor of a stricter standard. The courts have balanced such considerations against those of equity and fairness, and found the latter to be the weightier. The decisions in this state commit us to the liberal view, which is making its way, nowadays, in jurisdictions slow to welcome it. Dakin & Co. v. Lee, 1916, 1 K.B. 566, 579. Where the line is to be drawn between the important and the trivial cannot be settled by a formula. "In the nature of the case precise boundaries are impossible." 2 Williston on Contracts, § 841. The same omission may take on one aspect or another according to its setting. Substitution of equivalents may not have the same significance in fields of art on the one side and in those of mere utility on the other. Nowhere will change be tolerated, however, if it is so dominant or pervasive as in any real or substantial measure to frustrate the purpose of the contract. Crouch v. Gutmann, 134 N.Y. 45, 51, 31 N.E. 271, 30 Am.St.Rep. 608. There is no general license to install whatever, in the builder's judgment, may be regarded as "just as good." Easthampton L. & C. Co., Ltd. v. Worthington, 186 N.Y. 407, 412, 79 N.E. 323. The question is one of degree, to be answered, if there is doubt, by the triers of the facts (Crouch v. Gutmann; Woodward v. Fuller, supra), and, if the inferences are certain, by the judges of the law (Easthampton L. & C. Co., Ltd. v. Worthington, supra). We must weigh the purpose to be served, the desire to be gratified, the excuse for deviation from the letter, the cruelty of enforced adherence. Then only can we tell whether literal fulfillment is to be implied by law as a condition. This is not to say that the parties are not free by apt and certain words to effectuate a purpose that performance of every term shall be a condition of recovery. That question is not here. This is merely to say that the law will be slow to impute the purpose, in the silence of the parties, where the significance of the default is grievously out of proportion to the oppression of the forfeiture. The wilful transgressor must accept the penalty of his transgression. Schultze v. Goodstein, 180 N.Y. 248, 251, 73 N.E. 21; Desmond-Dunne Co. v. Friedman-Doscher Co., 162 N.Y. 486, 490, 56 N.E. 995. For him there is no occasion to mitigate the rigor of implied conditions. The transgressor whose default is unintentional and trivial may hope for mercy if he will offer atonement for his wrong. Spence v. Ham [163 N.Y. 220, 57 N.E. 412].

In the circumstances of this case, we think the measure of the allowance is not the cost of replacement, which would be great, but the difference in value, which would be either nominal or nothing. . . . It is true that in most cases the cost of replacement is the measure. Spence v. Ham, supra. The owner is entitled to the money which will permit him to complete, unless the cost of completion is grossly and unfairly out of proportion to the good to be attained. When that is true, the measure is the difference in value. . . .

The order should be affirmed, and judgment absolute directed in favor of the plaintiff upon the stipulation, with costs in all courts. . . .

[The dissenting opinion of McLaughlin, J. is omitted.]

———

R. Danzig, The Capability Problem in Contract Law

120–23 (1978)

"The contract [in Jacob & Youngs v. Kent] specified a standard of pipe [wrought iron] which cost 30% more than steel pipe—then the most widely used (and now the almost universally used) pipe. The makers of wrought iron pipe, however, claimed that the savings due to durability and low maintenance more than made up for the added expense. . . .

"The Reading Company was by its account the largest manufacturer of wrought iron pipe in the country. . . .

". . . According to a pipe wholesaler interviewed in New York City in 1975, genuine wrought iron pipe was manufactured in the pre-war period by four largely noncompeting companies: Reading, Cohoes, Byers and Southchester. According to this informant, all of these brands 'were of the same quality and price. The manufacturer's name would make absolutely no difference in pipe or in price.' . . .

"Why then was Reading Pipe specified? Apparently because it was the normal trade practice to assure wrought iron pipe quality by naming a manufacturer. In contemporary trade bulletins put out by Byers and Reading, prospective buyers were cautioned that some steel pipe manufacturers used iron pipe and often sold under misleading names like 'wrought pipe.' To avoid such inferior products, Byers warned: 'When wrought iron pipe is desired, the specifications often read "genuine wrought iron pipe" but as this does not always exclude wrought iron containing steel scrap, it is safer to mention the name of a manufacturer known not to use scrap.' "

———

Vincenzi v. Cerro

186 Conn. 612, 442 A.2d 1352 (1982)

(Shea, J.) "The principal claim of the defendants is that the doctrine of substantial performance was inapplicable in this case because the plaintiffs were guilty of a wilful or intentional breach of contract by failing to complete all of the work required. . . . We have in several cases approved the common statement that a contractor who is guilty of a 'wilful' breach cannot maintain an action upon the contract. . . . The contemporary view, however, is that even a conscious and intentional departure from the contract specifications will not necessarily defeat recovery, but may be considered as one of the several factors involved in deciding whether there has been full performance. 3A Corbin, Contract § 707; 2 Restatement (Second), Contracts § 237, comment D. The pertinent inquiry is not simply whether the breach was 'wilful' but whether the behavior of the party in default 'comports with standard of good faith and fair dealing.' 2 Restatement (Second), Contracts § 241(e); see comment f. Even an adverse conclusion on this point is not decisive but is to be weighted with other factors, such as the extent to which the owner will be deprived of a reasonably expected benefit and the extent to which the builder may suffer forfeiture, in deciding whether there has been substantial performance. Id.; see § 237, comment d."

O.W. Grun Roofing & Constr. Co. v. Cope

529 S.W.2d 258 (Tex.Civ.App.1975)

Grun agreed to install a new russet-colored shingle roof on Cope's home for $648. As actually installed, the roof had yellow streaks but was structurally sound. Cope refused to pay, and Grun filed a mechanic's lien. Cope then sued to set aside the lien and for damages equal to difference between (i) the $648 price under the contract with Grun and (ii) the cost of installing a new roof, which was 20% higher. The trial court set aside the lien and awarded Cope $123, based on the cost to install a new roof ($648 plus 20% for price increases). Affirmed:

> . . . It should not come as a shock to anyone to adopt a rule to the effect that a person has, particularly with respect to his home, to choose for himself and to contract for something which exactly satisfies that choice, and not to be compelled to accept something else. In the matter of homes and their decoration, as much as, if not more than, in many other fields, mere taste or preference, almost approaching whimsy, may be controlling with the homeowner, so that variations which might, under other circumstances, be considered trifling, may be inconsistent with that "substantial performance" on which liability to pay must be predicated. [M]ere incompleteness or deviations which may be easily supplied or remedied after the contractor has finished his work, and the cost of which to the owner is not excessive and readily ascertainable, present less cause for hesitation in concluding that the performance tendered constitutes substantial performance, since in such cases the owner can obtain complete satisfaction by merely spending some money and deducting the amount of such expenditure from the contract price.

> In the case before us there is evidence to support the conclusion that plaintiff can secure a roof of uniform coloring only by installing a completely new roof. We cannot say, as a matter of law, that the evidence establishes that in this case that a roof which so lacks uniformity in color as to give the appearance of a patch job serves essentially the same purpose as a roof of uniform color which has the appearance of being a new roof. We are not prepared to hold that a contractor who tenders a performance so deficient that it can be remedied only by completely redoing the work for which the contract

called has established, as a matter of law, that he has substantially performed his contractual obligation.

A recovery by Grun in quantum meruit for benefit conferred was denied:

> . . . [T]he evidence does not conclusively establish that plaintiff has received any benefit from defendant's defective performance. As already pointed out, there is evidence that plaintiff will have to install a completely new roof.

NOTE ON RESTITUTION IN FAVOR OF A PLAINTIFF IN DEFAULT

The quantum meruit claim brought by Grun alongside the claim for the contract price is part of the law of restitution or unjust enrichment. A party who partially performs a contract and then defaults has a claim in restitution to be compensated for the performance rendered, if the plaintiff can establish that the defendant otherwise would receive a windfall, i.e. be in a better position than the defendant would have been on full performance. The restitution claim can be brought by a defaulting purchaser of real property to recover a deposit when the purchaser can establish that the seller suffered a smaller loss as a result of the purchaser's breach. Usually this will be because the seller resells the property for the contract price, or an amount near the contract price. In a sale of goods, U.C.C. § 2–718(2) and (3) give a purchaser the right to recover a deposit if the seller cannot establish damages. A seller is allowed to retain part of the deposit as statutory liquidated damages (the lesser of $500 or 20 percent of the purchase price). Under both the common law rule and U.C.C. § 2–718(2), if the contract provides a deposit is forfeited as liquidated damages, then the rule on penalties determines the seller's right to retain the deposit.

In construction cases a contractor may bring a restitution claim alongside a claim for the contract price. To recover the contract price (less damages), the contractor must persuade the court that his performance satisfies the substantial performance test. The restitution claim gives the contractor a second chance at recovering some compensation for his work. From the perspective of the court, the consequence of finding the contractor's performance satisfies the substantial performance test is that this places the burden on the defendant to establish damages as an offset to the contract price. On the other hand, if the court finds the contractor's performance does not satisfy the substantial performance test, then this places the burden on the contractor to establish that the defendant would be unjustly enriched, if the defendant did not pay for the work done. The defendant can shield himself from a claim of substantial performance and a restitution claim by making his obligation to pay subject to a condition. The contractor would have to look to doctrines covered in Chapter 20 to excuse his nonfulfillment of a condition.

Vines v. Orchard Hills, Inc.

181 Conn. 501, 435 A.2d 1022 (1980)

(Peters, J.) "This case concerns the right of purchasers of real property, after their own default, to recover moneys paid at the time of execution of a valid contract of sale. The plaintiffs, Euel D. Vines and his wife Etta Vines, contracted, on July 11, 1973, to buy Unit No. 10, Orchard Hills Condominium, New Canaan, Connecticut, from the defendant Orchard Hills, Inc. for $78,800. On or before that date, they had paid the defendant $7880 as a down payment toward the purchase. Alleging that the sale of the property was never consummated, the plaintiffs sought to recover their down payment. . . .

". . . The purchasers decided not to take title to the condominium because Euel D. Vines was transferred by his employer to New Jersey; the Vines so informed the seller by a letter dated January 4, 1974. There has never been any claim that the seller has failed, in any respect, to conform to his obligations under the contract, nor does the complaint allege that the purchasers are legally excused from their performance under the contract. In short, it is the purchasers and not the seller whose breach precipitated the present cause of action. . . .

"The right of a contracting party, despite his default, to seek restitution for benefits conferred and allegedly unjustly retained has been much disputed in the legal literature and in the case law. . . . Although earlier cases often refused to permit a party to bring an action that could be said to be based on his own breach . . . many of the more recent cases support restitution in order to prevent unjust enrichment and to avoid forfeiture. . . .

"A variety of considerations, some practical and some theoretical, underlie this shift in attitude toward the plaintiff in breach. As Professor Corbin pointed out in his seminal article, 'The Right of a Defaulting Vendee to the Restitution of Installments Paid,' 40 Yale L.J. 1013 (1931), the anomalous result of denying any remedy to the plaintiff in breach is to punish more severely the person who has partially performed, often in good faith, than the person who has entirely disregarded his contractual obligations from the outset. Only partial performance triggers a claim for restitution, and partial performance will not, in the ordinary course of events, have been more injurious to the innocent party than total nonperformance. Recognition of a claim in restitution is, furthermore, consistent with the economic functions that the law of contracts is designed to serve. See Kessler & Gilmore, Contracts, pp. 4–6 (1970). The principal purpose of remedies for the breach of contract is to provide compensation for loss; see Restatement (Second), Contracts, c. 16, Introductory Note (Tent.Draft No. 14, 1979); Farnsworth, 'Legal Remedies for Breach of Contract,' 70 Colum.L.Rev. 1145 (1970); and therefore a party injured by breach of contract is entitled to retain nothing in excess of that sum which compensates him for the loss of his bargain. . . .

"Recognition that there are circumstances under which a defaulting purchaser may be entitled to restitution for benefits conferred upon the innocent seller of land is consistent with parallel developments elsewhere in the law of contracts. Judicial resistance to enforcement of forfeitures has of course long been commonplace, particularly with regard to contract clauses purporting to liquidate damages. See 5 Corbin, Contracts § 1058 (1964); 5 Williston, Contracts § 788 (3d Ed.1961). Despite the deference afforded by nineteenth-century courts to freedom of contract in other areas; see Weisbrod, The Boundaries of Utopia, pp. 165–67, 210–11 (1980); clauses that might impose forfeitures were invariably carefully scrutinized and frequently denounced as penal. . . .

". . . We . . . conclude that a purchaser whose breach is not willful has a restitutionary claim to recover moneys paid that unjustly enrich his seller. In this case, no one has alleged that the purchasers' breach, arising out of a transfer to a more distant place of employment, should be deemed to have been willful. . . .

"The purchaser's right to recover in restitution requires the purchaser to establish that the seller has been unjustly enriched. The purchaser must show more than that the contract has come to an end and that the seller retains moneys paid pursuant to the contract. To prove unjust enrichment, in the ordinary case, the purchaser, because he is the party in breach, must prove that the damages suffered by his seller are less than the moneys received from the purchaser. *Schwasnick v. Blandin, 65 F.2d 354, 358 (2d Cir.1933);* Kitchin v. Mori, 84 Nev. 181, 437 P.2d 865, 866 (1968). It may not be easy for the purchaser to prove the extent of the seller's damages, it may even be strategically advantageous for the seller to come forward with relevant evidence of the losses he has incurred and may expect to incur on account of the buyer's breach. Nonetheless, only if the breaching party satisfies his burden of proof that the innocent party has sustained a net gain may a claim for unjust enrichment be sustained. Dobbs, Remedies '12.14 (1973); 1 Palmer, Restitution § 5.4 (1978)."

RESTATEMENT, THIRD, RESTITUTION AND UNJUST ENRICHMENT § 36

[See Selected Source Materials Supplement]

(B) MATERIAL BREACH

This Section considers when breach gives a party the powers to withhold performance and to treat a contract as at an end ("terminate the contract") in the absence of an express condition. Under the Restatement a "material breach" gives a party the power to suspend performance while a "total breach" gives a party the power to terminate a contract. Often when the question is framed as one of material breach both parties will have failed to perform in a tit for tat way and each party will argue the other party's prior non-performance excuses their own responsive non-performance, which would allow them to recover contract damages for total breach. In this situation, each party will try to persuade the court the other was the first to materially breach, justifying their own responsive non-performance.

———

K & G Constr. Co. v. Harris

Court of Appeals of Maryland, 1960.
223 Md. 305, 164 A.2d 451.

Before BRUNE, C.J., and HENDERSON, HAMMOND, PRESCOTT and HORNEY, JJ.

PRESCOTT, JUDGE. Feeling aggrieved by the action of the trial judge of the Circuit Court for Prince George's County, sitting without a jury, in finding a judgment against it in favor of a subcontractor, the appellant, the general contractor on a construction project, appealed.[1]

The principal question presented is: Does a contractor, damaged by a subcontractor's failure to perform a portion of his work in a workmanlike manner, have a right, under the circumstances of this case, to withhold, in partial satisfaction of said damages, an installment payment, which, under the terms of the contract, was due the subcontractor, unless the negligent performance of his work excused its payment?

The appeal is presented on a case stated in accordance with Maryland Rule 826g.

The statement, in relevant part, is as follows:

"... K & G Construction Company, Inc. (hereinafter called Contractor), plaintiff and counter-defendant in the Circuit Court and appellant herein, was owner and general contractor of a housing subdivision project being constructed (herein called Project). Harris and Brooks (hereinafter called Subcontractor), defendants and counter-plaintiffs in the Circuit Court and appellees herein, entered into a contract with Contractor to do excavating and earth-moving work on the Project. Pertinent parts of the contract are set forth below:

---

[1] There are two appellees; the statement of the case refers to them as "subcontractor." We shall do likewise.

" 'Section 3. The Subcontractor agrees to complete the several portions and the whole of the work herein sublet by the time or times following:

" '(a) Without delay, as called for by the Contractor.

" '(b) It is expressly agreed that time is of the essence of this contract, and that the Contractor will have the right to terminate this contract and employ a substitute to perform the work in the event of delay on the part of Subcontractor, and Subcontractor agrees to indemnify the Contractor for any loss sustained thereby, provided, however, that nothing in this paragraph shall be construed to deprive Contractor of any rights or remedies it would otherwise have as to damage for delay.

" 'Section 4. (b)   Progress payments will be made each month during the performance of the work. Subcontractor will submit to Contractor, by the 25th of each month, a requisition for work performed during the preceding month. Contractor will pay these requisitions, less a retainer equal to ten per cent (10%), by the 10th of the months in which such requisitions are received.[2]

" '(c) No payments will be made under this contract until the insurance requirements of Sec. 9 hereof have been complied with. . . .

" 'Section 8. . . . All work shall be performed in a workmanlike manner, and in accordance with the best practices.

" 'Section 9. Subcontractor agrees to carry, during the progress of the work, . . . liability insurance against . . . property damage, in such amounts and with such companies as may be satisfactory to Contractor and shall provide Contractor with certificates showing the same to be in force.'

"While in the course of his employment by the Subcontractor on the Project, a bulldozer operator drove his machine too close to Contractor's house while grading the yard, causing the immediate collapse of a wall and other damage to the house. The resulting damage to contractor's house was $3,400.00. Subcontractor had complied with the insurance provision (Sec. 9) of the aforesaid contract. Subcontractor reported said damages to their liability insurance carrier. The Subcontractor and its insurance carrier refused to repair damage or compensate Contractor for damage to

---

[2]   This section is not a model for clarity.

the house, claiming that there was no liability on the part of the Subcontractor.

"Contractor gave no written notice to Subcontractor for any services rendered or materials furnished by the Contractor to the Subcontractor . . .

"Contractor was generally satisfied with Subcontractor's work and progress as required under Sections 3 and 8 of the contract until September 12, 1958, with the exception of the bulldozer accident of August 9, 1958.

"Subcontractor performed work under the contract during July, 1958, for which it submitted a requisition by the 25th of July, as required by the contract, for work done prior to the 25th of July, payable under the terms of the contract by Contractor on or before August 10, 1958. Contractor was current as to payments due under all preceding monthly requisitions from Subcontractor. The aforesaid bulldozer accident damaging Contractor's house occurred on August 9, 1958. Contractor refused to pay Subcontractor's requisition due on August 10, 1958, because the bulldozer damage to Contractor's house had not been repaired or paid for. Subcontractor continued to work on the project until the 12th of September, 1958, at which time they discontinued working on the project because of Contractor's refusal to pay the said work requisition and notified Contractor by registered letters of their position and willingness to return to the job, but only upon payment. At that time, September 12, 1958, the value of the work completed by Subcontractor on the project for which they had not been paid was $1,484.50

"Contractor later requested Subcontractor to return and complete work on the Project which Subcontractor refused to do because of nonpayment of work requisitions of July 25 and thereafter. Contractor's house was not repaired by Subcontractor nor compensation paid for the damage.

"It was stipulated that Subcontractor had completed work on the Project under the contract for which they had not been paid in the amount of $1,484.50 and that if they had completed the remaining work to be done under the contract, they would have made a profit of $1,340.00 on the remaining uncompleted portion of the contract. It was further stipulated that it cost the Contractor $450.00 above the contract price to have another excavating contractor complete remaining work required under the contract. It was the opinion of the Court that if judgment were in favor of the Subcontractor, it should be for the total amount of $2,824.50.

"... Contractor filed suit against the Subcontractor in two counts: (1), for the aforesaid bulldozer damage to Contractor's house, alleging negligence of the Subcontractor's bulldozer operator, and (2) for the $450.00 costs above the contract price in having another excavating subcontractor complete the uncompleted work in the contract. Subcontractor filed a counter-claim for recovery of work of the value of $1,484.50 for which they had not received payment and for loss of anticipated profits on uncompleted portion of work in the amount of $1,340.00. By agreement of the parties, the first count of Contractor's claim, i.e., for aforesaid bulldozer damage to Contractor's house, was submitted to jury who found in favor of Contractor in the amount of $3,400.00. Following the finding by the jury, the second count of the Contractor's claim and the counter-claims of the Subcontractor, by agreement of the parties, were submitted to the Court for determination, without jury. All of the facts recited herein above were stipulated to by the parties to the Court. Circuit Court Judge Fletcher found for counter-plaintiff Subcontractor in the amount of $2,824.50 from which Contractor has entered this appeal."

The $3,400 judgment has been paid.

It is immediately apparent that our decision turns upon the respective rights and liabilities of the parties under that portion of their contract whereby the subcontractor agreed to do the excavating and earth-moving work in "a workmanlike manner, and in accordance with the best practices," with time being of the essence of the contract, and the contractor agreed to make progress payments therefor on the 10th day of the months following the performance of the work by the subcontractor.[3] The subcontractor contends, of course, that when the contractor failed to make the payment due on August 10, 1958, he breached his contract and thereby released him (the subcontractor) from any further obligation to perform. The contractor, on the other hand, argues that the failure of the subcontractor to perform his work in a workmanlike manner constituted a material breach of the contract, which justified his refusal to make the August 10 payment; and, as there was no breach on his part, the subcontractor had no right to cease performance on September 12, and his refusal to continue work on the project constituted another breach, which rendered him liable to the contractor for damages. The vital question, more tersely stated, remains: Did the contractor have a right, under the

---

[3] The statement of the case does not show the exact terms concerning the remuneration to be paid the subcontractor. It does not disclose whether he was to be paid a total lump sum, by the cubic yard, by the day, or in some other manner. It does state that the excavation finally cost the contractor $450 more than the "contract price."

circumstances, to refuse to make the progress payment due on August 10, 1958?

. . . Promises are mutually dependent if the parties intend *performance* by one to be conditioned upon *performance* by the other, and, if they be mutually dependent, they may be (a) precedent, i.e., a promise that is to be performed before a corresponding promise on the part of the adversary party is to be performed, (b) subsequent, i.e., a corresponding promise that is not to be performed until the other party to the contract has performed a precedent covenant, or (c) concurrent, i.e., promises that are to be performed at the same time by each of the parties, who are respectively bound to perform each. . . .

. . . The modern rule, which seems to be of almost universal application, is that there is a presumption that mutual promises in a contract are dependent and are to be so regarded, whenever possible. . . .

Considering the presumption that promises and counter-promises are dependent and the statement of the case, we have no hesitation in holding that the promise and counter-promise under consideration here were mutually dependent, that is to say, the parties intended performance by one to be conditioned on performance by the other; and the subcontractor's promise was, by the explicit wording of the contract, precedent to the promise of payment, monthly, by the contractor. In Shapiro Engineering Corp. v. Francis O. Day Co., 215 Md. 373, 380, 137 A.2d 695, we stated that it is the general rule that where a total price for work is fixed by a contract, the work is not rendered divisible by progress payments. It would indeed present an unusual situation if we were to hold that a building contractor, who has obtained someone to do work for him and has agreed to pay each month for the work performed in the previous month, has to continue the monthly payments, irrespective of the degree of skill and care displayed in the performance of work, and his only recourse is by way of suit for ill-performance. If this were the law, it is conceivable, in fact, probable, that many contractors would become insolvent before they were able to complete their contracts. . . .

We hold that when the subcontractor's employee negligently damaged the contractor's wall, this constituted a breach of the subcontractor's promise to perform his work in a "workmanlike manner, and in accordance with the best practices." Gaybis v. Palm, 201 Md. 78, 85, 93 A.2d 269; Johnson v. Metcalfe, 209 Md. 537, 544, 121 A.2d 825; 17 C.J.S. Contracts § 515; Weiss v. Sheet Metal Fabricators, 206 Md. 195, 203, 110 A.2d 671. And there can be little doubt that the breach was material: the damage to the wall amounted to more than double the payment due on August 10. Speed v. Bailey, 153 Md. 655, 661, 662, 139 A. 534. 3A Corbin, Contracts, § 708, says: "The failure of a contractor's [in our case, the subcontractor's] performance to constitute 'substantial' performance may justify the owner [in our case, the contractor] in refusing to make a progress payment. . . . If the refusal to pay an installment is justified on the owner's [contractor's] part, the contractor [subcontractor] is not justified in abandoning work by reason of that refusal. His abandonment of the work will itself be a wrongful repudiation that goes to the essence, even if the defects in performance did not." See also Restatement, Contracts § 274; F.H. McGraw & Co. v. Sherman Plastering Co., D.C.Conn., 60 F.Supp. 504, 512, affirmed 2 Cir., 149 F.2d 301 . . . and compare Williston, op. cit., §§ 805, 841 and 842. Professor Corbin, in § 954, states further: "The unexcused failure of a contractor to render a promised performance when it is due is always a breach of contract . . . Such failure may be of such great importance as to constitute what has been called herein a 'total' breach. . . . For a failure of performance constituting such a 'total' breach, an action for remedies that are appropriate thereto is at once maintainable. Yet the injured party is not required to bring such action. He has the option of treating the non-performance as a 'partial' breach only. . . ." In permitting the subcontractor to proceed with work on the project after August 9, the contractor, obviously, treated the breach by the subcontractor as a partial one. As the promises were mutually dependent and the subcontractor had made a material breach in his performance, this justified the contractor in refusing to make the August 10 payment; hence, as the contractor was not in default, the subcontractor again breached the contract when he, on September 12, discontinued work on the project, which rendered him liable (by the express terms of the contract) to the contractor for his increased cost in having the excavating done—a stipulated amount of $450. Cf. Keystone Engineering Corp. v. Sutter, 196 Md. 620, 628, 78 A.2d 191. . . .

Judgment against the appellant reversed; and judgment entered in favor of the appellant against the appellees for $450, the appellees to pay the costs.

Bartlett v. Bartlett

465 S.W.3d 745 (2015)

William and Lori Bartlett's divorce decree included a provision that William would pay the college expenses of each of their two children "provided the child is a full-time student and maintains at least a "C" or equivalent grade point average . . . " Their son began Trinity College in August 2012. Lori sued William for breach of contract in 2012 when he refused to pay his son's expenses for the fall semester. At trial the son testified his grades dropped below a "C" average to 1.929 after the Spring semester of his freshman year but that after the Summer semester his average was at least a "C." The trial court held the agreement to pay college expenses was enforceable as a contract and that the son's failure to maintain a "C" average at the end of the Spring semester of his first year was not a material breach, discharging William from his obligation to pay college expenses for the year. The court of appeals affirmed, applying the factors in the Restatement.

In view of these factors, the record supports the trial court's deemed finding that any breach by the son was not material and did not excuse William's obligation to pay for expenses incurred before the breach. First, as the trial court expressly found, the son brought his GPA above a "C" average after the Summer 2013 semester. Thus, the son actually cured any failure to perform that occurred by his having a GPA below a "C" after the Spring 2013 semester. The trial court could have concluded that the son's behavior comported with standards of good faith and fair dealing, as he testified his grades dipped below a "C" average because his attendance suffered after surgery on his knee; he also was a football player for the university. Excusing William's performance as to all semesters (including the Fall 2012 semester for which the son's GPA was above a "C") would cause the son significant forfeiture. William was not deprived of the benefit he expected because his son remained a full time student toward a bachelor's degree at a university and maintained a GPA above a "C" by the time of trial. And there was evidence that William's refusal to fulfill his obligations under the agreement had nothing to do with the son's failure to maintain a "C" GPA for the Spring 2013 semester. There is no evidence that the son's one-semester lapse prevented William from making "substitute arrangements." Finally, the agreement itself does not require performance on a semester-by-semester basis, nor does it call for the forfeiture of obligations previously owed to the son (i.e., Fall 2012 expenses) for a breach occurring in a later semester. The agreement itself does not explicitly require the son to reimburse William for expenses incurred for a prior semester if the son ultimately does not obtain a "C" average in a later semester.

Frost, C.J., disagreed with this analysis, arguing that the son maintaining a "C" average was a condition to William's obligation to pay college expenses. He continued: "Even presuming for the sake of argument that a breach-of-contract analysis would be appropriate in this context, the failure to meet the grade requirement was material. . . . A "D" is not a "C." Saying the difference between a "D" and a "C" is immaterial is like saying that almost scoring a touchdown is the same as scoring a touchdown or that "second place" is no different than "first place." Grade-point averages, by nature, are precise measurements that set lines of demarcation between one performance category and the next. The metric reflects an exact and unforgiving standard. Anything that falls short of meeting it is a material failure."

———

RESTATEMENT, SECOND, CONTRACTS §§ 237, 241, 242

[See Selected Source Materials Supplement]

CISG ARTS. 25, 49

[See Selected Source Materials Supplement]

UNIDROIT PRINCIPLES OF INTERNATIONAL COMMERCIAL CONTRACTS ARTS. 7.3.1, 7.3.5, 7.3.6

[See Selected Source Materials Supplement]

PRINCIPLES OF EUROPEAN CONTRACT LAW ARTS. 9.301, 9.302, 9.305, 9.307–309

[See Selected Source Materials Supplement]

E. Allan Farnsworth, Contracts

§ 8.13 (4th ed. 2004)

"A contract is said to be divisible if the performances to be exchanged can be divided into corresponding pairs of part performances in such a way that a court will treat the parts of each pair as if the parties had agreed that they were equivalents. . . .

"Suppose, for example, that a builder has made a contract to build three houses at $100,000 each for a total price of $300,000. The builder breaks the contract by building only one of the houses and claims its price of $100,000. Will a court allow the builder to recover on the contract to build three houses, even though the builder has not substantially performed it? It will, if it regards the contract as divisible into three pairs of part performances, each pair consisting of the building of a house and the payment of $100,000. The builder is then entitled to recover $100,000 on the contract for the house that was built, less such damages as the owner can prove were suffered by the builder's breach in not building the other two. Indeed, if the contract is divisible, the builder is entitled to recover on the contract for building the first house even if performance of that part of the contract is only substantial. The builder's recovery will then be reduced by damages resulting from the defects in the first house as well as from the failure to build the other two houses.

"How does a court decide whether a contract is divisible? As the Supreme Court of Colorado warned that 'there is no set formula which furnishes a foolproof method for determining in a given case just which contracts are severable and which are entire.' The Restatement Second lays down two requirements: it must be possible to apportion the parties' performances into corresponding pairs of part performances; and it must be proper to regard the parts of each pair as agreed equivalents."

_____

NOTE ON ANTICIPATORY REPUDIATION

A declaration of an intent not to perform a contract in the future is described by UCC Section 2–610 as an "Anticipatory Repudiation." The Restatement addresses the topic under the heading "Prospective Non-Performance" in Sections 250 to 260. The reluctance to describe the conduct as simply a breach of contract reflects an old debate. Wells. J., pithly expressed one side of this debate in Daniels v. Newtown, 114 Mass. 530 (1874):

> A renunciation of the agreement, by declarations or inconsistent conduct, before the time of performance, may give cause for treating it as rescinded, and excuse the other party from making ready for performance on his part, or relieve him from the necessity of offering performance in order to enforce his rights. It may destroy all capacity of the party, so disavowing its obligations to assert rights under it afterwards, if the other party has acted upon such disavowal. But we are unable to see how it can of itself constitute a present violation of any legal rights of the other party, or confer upon him a present right of action. An executory contract ordinarily confers no title or interest in the subject matter of the agreement. Until the time arrives when, by the terms of the agreement, he is or might be entitled to its performance, he can suffer no injury or deprivation which can form a ground of damages. There is neither violation of right, nor loss upon which to found an action. . . .

The other side of this debate overcame this objection by implying a promise not to repudiate. Learned Hand, J., explained this solution in Equitable Trust Co. v. Western Pac. Ry., 244 Fed. 485, 501–502 (S.D.N.Y.1917), remanded for correction and affirmed, 250 Fed. 327 (2d Cir.), cert. denied 246 U.S. 672, 38 S.Ct. 423, 62 L.Ed. 932 (1918):

> [The basis of the doctrine of anticipatory breach] is that a promise to perform in the future by implication includes an engagement not deliberately to compromise the probability of performance. A promise is a verbal act designed as a reliance to the promisee, and so as a means to the forecast of his own conduct. Abstention from any deliberate act before the time of performance which makes impossible that reliance and that forecast ought surely to be included by implication. Such intermediate uncertainties as arise from the vicissitudes of the promisor's affairs are, of course, a part of the risk, but it is hard to see how, except by mere verbalism, it can be supposed that the promisor may within the terms of his undertaking gratuitously add to those uncertainties by announcing his purpose to default.

Today it is well established that a clear repudiation of a future performance obligation is a breach of contract. It is also well established that it gives rise to an immediate claim for damages. Issues remain. Among these issues is when words and conduct short of a clear repudiation of a future performance obligation will be treated as anticipatory repudiation.

WHOLESALE SAND & GRAVEL, INC. V. DECKER
Supreme Judicial Court of Maine, 1993.
630 A.2d 710.

Before WATHEN, C.J., and ROBERTS, GLASSMAN, CLIFFORD, COLLINS, RUDMAN and DANA, JJ.

ROBERTS, JUSTICE.

Wholesale Sand & Gravel, Inc., appeals from a judgment entered in the Superior Court (Sagadahoc County, *Lipez, J.*) in favor of James Decker on its claim for the breach of their contract. On appeal, Wholesale contends that the court erred in holding that its conduct constituted an anticipatory repudiation of the contract and in deciding the case on a defense that had not been raised in the pleadings. Finding no error, we affirm the judgment.

On June 13, 1989, James Decker and Wholesale Sand & Gravel, Inc., entered into a contract whereby Wholesale agreed to perform earth work, including the installation of a gravel driveway, on Decker's property in Bowdoin. The contract contained no provision specifying a completion date for the work. Indeed, the only time reference made in the contract was that payment was to be made within 90 days. Although Carl Goodenow, Wholesale's president, believed the company had 90 days within which to complete the work, he told Decker that the driveway portion of the work would be completed within one week.

Wholesale began work on the driveway on the weekend after the contract was executed and immediately experienced difficulty because of the wetness of the ground. In fact, Wholesale's bulldozer became stuck in the mud and had to be removed with a backhoe. Wholesale returned to the site the following weekend, when it attempted to stabilize the driveway site by hauling out mud and hauling in gravel. Because the ground was too wet to allow Wholesale to perform the work without substantially exceeding the contract price, Goodenow decided to wait for the ground to dry out before proceeding further.

On July 12, 1989, Decker contacted Goodenow concerning the lack of activity at the site and his urgent need to have the driveway completed. Goodenow responded that he would "get right on it." On July 19, Decker telephoned Goodenow to inquire again about the lack of activity and gave him one week in which to finish the driveway. Again, Goodenow said that he would "get right on it." On July 28, Decker called Goodenow for the purpose of terminating the contract. When Goodenow stated that he would be at the site the next day, Decker decided to give him one more chance. Goodenow, however, did not appear at the site and Decker subsequently terminated the contract. At that point, Goodenow believed Wholesale still had 45 days to complete the job. Decker, however, hired another contractor to finish the driveway and complete the excavation work.

Wholesale commenced this action against Decker by a complaint seeking damages for a breach of their contract. After a jury-waived trial, the court entered a judgment in favor of Decker. Although it found that a reasonable time for the completion of performance was 60 days, the court concluded that Wholesale's conduct constituted an anticipatory repudiation of the contract, permitting Decker to terminate the contract during the 60-day period. This timely appeal followed.

An anticipatory repudiation of a contract is "a definite and unequivocal manifestation of intention on the part of the repudiator that he will not render the promised performance when the time fixed for it in the contract arrives." 4 Corbin, *Corbin on Contracts* § 973 (1951); *Restatement (Second) of Contracts* § 250 (1979). The manifestation of an intention to repudiate a contract may be made and communicated by either words or conduct. *See* 4 Corbin § 973; *Restatement* § 250(b). The words or conduct evidencing such refusal or inability to perform, however, must be definite, unequivocal, and absolute. *See Martell Bros., Inc. v. Donbury, Inc.,* 577 A.2d 334, 337 n. 1 (Me.1990). Wholesale contends that the court erred in concluding that its conduct constituted an anticipatory repudiation of the contract. We disagree. After its second weekend of work at the site, Wholesale removed its equipment and did not return. Moreover, on two occasions Goodenow, responding to Decker's inquiries about the progress of the job, promised to get right to work but did not do so. Indeed, when confronted by the fact that Wholesale would be fired if he did not appear at the job site the following day, Goodenow promised that he would be at the site but did not appear. On this record it was reasonable for Decker to conclude that Wholesale would never complete its performance under the contract. We conclude therefore that the court properly found that Wholesale, through its conduct, manifested an unequivocal and definite inability or unwillingness to perform within a reasonable time. . . .

The entry is:

Judgment affirmed.

GLASSMAN, COLLINS, RUDMAN and DANA, JJ., concur.

WATHEN, CHIEF JUSTICE, with whom CLIFFORD, J., joins, dissenting.

I must respectfully dissent. In my judgment both this Court and the Superior Court misapply the doctrine of anticipatory repudiation. The record is devoid of any words or conduct on the part of plaintiff that distinctly, unequivocally, and absolutely evidence a refusal or inability to perform. *See Martell Bros., Inc. v. Donbury, Inc.,* 577 A.2d 334, 337 n. 1 (Me.1990). There was a disagreement between the parties as to how much time was allowed for performance, but it is clear that plaintiff expected to perform the contract as soon as circumstances permitted. The Superior Court found a repudiation of the contract even though the 60 days it found available for performance had not passed.

I would vacate the judgment.

———

Unique Systems, Inc. v. Zotos International, Inc.

622 F.2d 373 (8th Cir.1980)

On January 30, 1974, Lilja contracted to manufacture and sell to Zotos, for resale by Zotos, 15,000 hair-spray systems that Lilja would develop. In an amendment to the contract, the parties agreed that Zotos's stocking and distribution of the systems would commence in "month one," defined as a "mutually agreed date in the year 1974." Later, Zotos began to fear a softening of the market, and indicated that it would not proceed unless Lilja would agree to a market test of completed systems. In light of Zotos's refusal to proceed without the market-test period, Lilja considered the contract repudiated, and brought suit. Held, for Lilja.

"If a party to a contract demands of the other party a performance to which he has no right under the contract and states definitely that, unless his demand is complied with, he will not render his promised performance, an anticipatory repudiation has been committed. 4 Corbin, Contracts § 973 (1951). When Zotos told Lilja in August of 1975 that it would not proceed until market tests were performed with results subject to Zotos's approval, Zotos repudiated the contract and was in total breach. No market tests were required by the contract, a fact that Zotos admits that it knew."

———

Thermo Electron Corp. v. Schiavone Construction Co.

958 F.2d 1158 (1st Cir.1992)

" . . . Thermo repudiated only if it 'insist[ed] . . . upon terms' . . . to the point where that insistence 'amounts to a statement of intention not to perform except on conditions which go beyond the contract.' Restatement (Second) of Contracts § 250 cmt. b, at 273 (quoting U.C.C. § 2–610 cmt. 2) (emphasis added). Commentators have pointed out that there 'must be a definite and unequivocal manifestation of intention [not to render performance]. . . . A mere request for a change in the terms or a request for cancellation of the contract is not in itself enough to constitute a repudiation.' 4 Arthur L. Corbin, Corbin on Contracts § 973, at 905–06 (1951) (footnotes omitted). A party's statements or actions 'must be sufficiently positive to be reasonably understood as meaning that the breach will actually occur. A party's expressions of doubt as to its willingness or ability to perform do not constitute a repudiation.' E. Allan Farnsworth, Contracts § 8.21, at 663 (2d ed. 1990); accord Restatement (Second) of Contracts § 250 cmt. b, at 273."

———

SECTION 2. CONTRACTS FOR THE SALE OF GOODS

———

UCC §§ 2–508, 2–601, 2–608, 2–612

[See Selected Source Materials Supplement]

———

CISG ARTS. 35(1), 37, 45, 46, 48, 49

[See Selected Source Materials Supplement]

———

J. White & R. Summers, Uniform Commercial Code

§ 8–2 (5th ed. 2000)

"At the outset one should understand the significance of a self-help remedy which permits the buyer to return the goods to the seller (that is, rejection or revocation of acceptance). In these cases the buyer is freed from its obligation to pay the price, and the buyer has a right to recover that part of the price already paid. Moreover, except in unusual circumstances, the buyer need not resell the goods. One should understand the economic difference between the status of the buyer who has rejected and the status of the buyer who has accepted and sued for breach of warranty. The typical buyer who accepts and sues for breach of warranty under 2–714 will recover only for injury proximately resulting from defects in the goods at the time of sale. If, for example, the purchased automobile had a cracked piston that will cost $500 to repair (and the value of the car is so diminished by $500), buyer will recover that $500. On the other hand, if buyer rejects the goods, buyer is first recompensed for the losses resulting from the seller's failure to perform its end of the contract (for example, by a suit under 2–713 or 2–712); more important, buyer escapes the bargain, and throws any loss resulting from depreciation of the goods back upon the seller.

"The importance of goods oriented remedies can be illustrated by an example from a commodity market. Assume that the seller delivers 10,000 bushels of potatoes and that 100 of those bushels are rotten. If the buyer accepts the potatoes, it will have a cause of action under 2–714, and it will recover money approximately equivalent to the value of those 100 bushels. If, on the other hand, the buyer rejects the entire delivery, if the seller cannot cure, and if the price of the potatoes has fallen substantially, the buyer's rejection may save it thousands of dollars by allowing the purchase of conforming goods on the market at a much lower price than specified in the contract. Rejection avoids the economic injury of a bad bargain as well."

NOTE ON THE PERFECT-TENDER RULE AND THE UCC

Prior to the adoption of the Uniform Commercial Code, the doctrine of substantial performance was not applicable to contracts for the sale of goods. Instead, at least in theory and often in practice, a buyer could refuse to accept a delivery of goods that in any way failed to conform to the contract. This rule was known as the perfect-tender rule, because a buyer of goods could reject any tender of delivery that was not perfect. A leading case was Norrington v. Wright, 115 U.S. 188, 6 S.Ct. 12, 29 L.Ed. 366 (1885). UCC § 2–601 nominally preserves the perfect-tender rule for the sale of goods. However, other provisions of the UCC strip away much or most of the significance of this Section.

1. *Revocation of acceptance.* First, UCC § 2–601 applies only where a buyer rejects goods. It does not apply where the buyer accepts goods and then discovers a defect. Under UCC § 2–608, a buyer may revoke acceptance in such a case, but only if the nonconformity substantially impairs the value of the goods to her.

There are other limitations on the buyer's right to revoke acceptance under § 2–608, even if the nonconformity does substantially impair the value of the goods to him. If the buyer accepted the goods knowing that they were nonconforming, she can revoke her acceptance only if she accepted on the reasonable assumption that the nonconformity would be cured (for example, because the seller promised cure), and the nonconformity was not seasonably cured. If the buyer accepted the goods without knowing that they were nonconforming, she can revoke her acceptance only if her acceptance was reasonably induced either by the difficulty of discovering the defect before acceptance or by the seller's assurances.

2. *Installment contracts.* Section 2–601 is also inapplicable to installment contracts, that is, contracts that require or authorize the delivery of goods in separate lots, to be separately accepted. Such contracts are covered by Section 2–612. Under Section 2–612(2), a buyer normally can reject a nonconforming installment only if the nonconformity substantially impairs the value of the installment and cannot be cured. Furthermore, under Section 2–612(3) a buyer cannot treat the whole installment contract as breached on the ground of a nonconformity or default with respect to one or more installments,

unless those nonconformities or defaults substantially impair the value of the whole contract.

3. *Cure.* The perfect-tender rule is also significantly ameliorated by Section 2–508, the "cure" provision. Under Section 2–508(1), in the case of a single-delivery (non-installment) contract, if a tender of goods is rejected because it is nonconforming, and the time for performance has not yet expired, the seller may cure the defect by making a conforming delivery within the contract time. Even more significantly, under Section 2–508(2) if a tender of goods is rejected because it is nonconforming, and the seller had reasonable grounds to believe that the tender would be acceptable with a money allowance or otherwise, the seller has a further reasonable time to substitute a conforming tender even if the time for performance has expired.

4. *Good faith.* The obligation of good faith under the UCC requires "honesty in fact and the observance of reasonable commercial standards of fair dealing." The obligation and this definition are in Sections 1–304 and 1–201(20) of the 2001 version of the UCC. In the pre-2001 version of the UCC, Sections 1–203, 1–201(19), and 2–103(1)(b) required honesty of fact of everyone but only merchants to observe reasonable commercial standards. A buyer who seized on a minor defect to justify a rejection that was really based on the fact that the contract is no longer favorable to her might not satisfy this obligation. As stated in Printing Center of Texas, Inc. v. Supermind Publishing Co., 669 S.W.2d 779 (Tex.App.1984):

> Once the contract of the parties has been determined, the evidence must be reviewed to see if the right goods were tendered at the right time and place. If the evidence does establish nonconformity in some respect, the buyer is entitled to reject if he rejects in good faith. [UCC] § 1–203 provides that, "Every contract or duty within this Act imposes an obligation of good faith in its performance or enforcement." Since the rejection of goods is a matter of performance, the buyer is obligated to act in good faith when he rejects the goods. When the buyer is a merchant, his standard of good faith rejection requires honesty in fact and observance of reasonable commercial standards of fair dealing in the trade. [UCC § 2–103(2)]. . . . Evidence of circumstances which indicate that the buyer's motivation in rejecting the goods was to escape the bargain, rather than to avoid acceptance of a tender which in some respect impairs the value of the bargain to him, would support a finding of rejection in bad faith. Neumiller Farms Inc. v. Cornett, 368 So.2d 272 (Ala.1979). Thus, evidence of rejection of the goods on account of a minor defect in a falling market would in some instances be sufficient to support a finding that the buyer acted in bad faith when he rejected the goods.

––––––––

Ramirez v. Autosport

88 N.J. 277, 440 A.2d 1345 (1982)

"In the nineteenth century, sellers were required to deliver goods that complied exactly with the sales agreement. See Filley v. Pope, 115 U.S. 213, 220, 6 S.Ct. 19, 21, 29 L.Ed. 372, 373 (1885) (buyer not obliged to accept otherwise conforming scrap iron shipped to New Orleans from Leith, rather than Glasgow, Scotland, as required by contract); Columbia Iron Works & Dry-Dock Co. v. Douglas, 84 Md. 44, 47, 34 A. 1118, 1120–1121 (1896) (buyer who agreed to purchase steel scrap from United States cruisers not obliged to take any other kind of scrap). That rule, known as the 'perfect tender' rule, remained part of the law of sales well into the twentieth century. By the 1920's the doctrine was so entrenched in the law that Judge Learned Hand declared '[t]here is no room in commercial contracts for the doctrine of substantial performance.' Mitsubishi Goshi Kaisha v. J. Aaron & Co., Inc., 16 F.2d 185, 186 (2 Cir.1926).

"The harshness of the rule led courts to seek to ameliorate its effect and to bring the law of sales in closer harmony with the law of contracts, which allows rescission only for material breaches. LeRoy Dyal Co. v. Allen, 161 F.2d 152, 155 (4 Cir.1947). See 5 Corbin, Contracts § 1104 at 464 (1951); 12 Williston, Contracts § 1455 at 14 (3 ed. 1970). Nevertheless, a variation of the perfect tender rule appeared in the Uniform Sales Act. N.J.S.A. 46:30–75 (purchasers permitted to reject goods or rescind contracts for any breach of warranty). . . . The chief objection to the continuation of the perfect tender rule was that buyers in a declining market would reject goods for minor non-conformities and force the loss on surprised sellers. . . .

"To the extent that a buyer can reject goods for any nonconformity, the UCC retains the perfect tender rule. . . . Section 2–601 authorizes a buyer to reject goods if they 'or the tender of delivery fail in any respect to conform to the contract.' . . . The Code, however, mitigates the harshness of the perfect tender rule and balances the interests of buyer and seller."

T.W. OIL, INC. v. CONSOLIDATED EDISON CO.
Court of Appeals of New York, 1982.
57 N.Y.2d 574, 457 N.Y.S.2d 458, 443 N.E.2d 932.

FUCHSBERG, JUDGE.

In the first case to wend its way through our appellate courts on this question, we are asked, in the main, to decide whether a seller who, acting in good faith and without knowledge of any defect, tenders nonconforming goods to a buyer who properly rejects them, may avail itself of the cure provision of subdivision (2) of section 2–508 of the Uniform Commercial Code. We hold that, if seasonable notice be given, such a seller may offer to cure the defect within a reasonable period beyond the time when the contract was to be performed so long as it has acted in good faith and with a reasonable expectation that the original goods would be acceptable to the buyer.

The factual background against which we decide this appeal is based on either undisputed proof or express findings at Trial Term. In January, 1974, midst the fuel shortage produced by the oil embargo, the plaintiff (then known as Joc Oil USA, Inc.) purchased a cargo of fuel oil whose sulfur content was represented to it as no greater than 1%. While the oil was still at sea en route to the United States in the tanker *MT Khamsin,* plaintiff received a certificate from the foreign refinery at which it had been processed informing it that the sulfur content in fact was .52%. Thereafter, on January 24, the plaintiff entered into a written contract with the defendant (Con Ed) for the sale of this oil. The agreement was for delivery to take place between January 24 and January 30, payment being subject to a named independent testing agency's confirmation of quality and quantity. The contract, following a trade custom to round off specifications of sulfur content at, for instance, 1%, .5% or .3%, described that of the *Khamsin* oil as .5%. In the course of the negotiations, the plaintiff learned that Con Ed was then authorized to buy and burn oil with a sulfur content of up to 1% and would even mix oils containing more and less to maintain that figure.

When the vessel arrived, on January 25, its cargo was discharged into Con Ed storage tanks in Bayonne, New Jersey.[2] In due course, the independent testing people reported a sulfur content of .92%. On this basis, acting within a time frame whose reasonableness is not in question, on February 14 Con Ed rejected the shipment. Prompt negotiations to adjust the price failed; by February 20, plaintiff had offered a price reduction roughly responsive to the difference in sulfur reading, but Con Ed, though it could use the oil, rejected this proposition out of hand. It was insistent on paying no more than the latest prevailing price, which, in the volatile market that then existed, was some 25% below the level which prevailed when it agreed to buy the oil.

The very next day, February 21, plaintiff offered to cure the defect with a substitute shipment of conforming oil scheduled to arrive on the *S.S. Appollonian Victory* on February 28. Nevertheless, on February 22, the very day after the cure was proffered, Con Ed, adamant in its intention to avail itself of the intervening drop in prices, summarily rejected this proposal too. The two cargos were subsequently sold to third parties at the best price obtainable, first that of the *Appollonian* and, sometime later,

---

[2] The tanks already contained some other oil, but Con Ed appears to have had no concern over the admixture of the differing sulfur contents. In any event, the efficacy of the independent testing required by the contract was not impaired by the commingling.

after extraction from the tanks had been accomplished, that of the *Khamsin*.[3]

There ensued this action for breach of contract,[4] which, after a somewhat unconventional trial course, resulted in a nonjury decision for the plaintiff in the sum of $1,385,512.83, essentially the difference between the original contract price of $3,360,667.14 and the amount received by the plaintiff by way of resale of the *Khamsin* oil at what the court found as a matter of fact was a negotiated price which, under all the circumstances,[5] was reasonably procured in the open market. To arrive at this result, the Trial Judge, while ruling against other liability theories advanced by the plaintiff, which, in particular, included one charging the defendant with having failed to act in good faith in the negotiations for a price adjustment on the *Khamsin* oil (Uniform Commercial Code, § 1–203), decided as a matter of law that subdivision (2) of section 2–508 of the Uniform Commercial Code was available to the plaintiff even if it had no prior knowledge of the nonconformity. Finding that in fact plaintiff had no such belief at the time of the delivery, that what turned out to be a .92% sulfur content was "within the range of contemplation of reasonable acceptability" to Con. Ed., and that seasonable notice of an intention to cure was given, the court went on to hold that plaintiff's "reasonable and timely offer to cure" was improperly rejected (*sub nom. Joc Oil USA v. Consolidated Edison Co. of N.Y.*, 107 Misc.2d 376, 390, 434 N.Y.S.2d 623 [Shanley N. Egeth, J.]). The Appellate Division, 84 A.D.2d 970, 447 N.Y.S.2d 572, having unanimously affirmed the judgment entered on this decision, the case is now here by our leave (CPLR 5602, subd. [a], par. 1, cl. [i]).

In support of its quest for reversal, the defendant now asserts that the trial court erred . . . in failing to interpret subdivision (2) of section 2–508 of the Uniform Commercial Code to limit the availability of the right to cure after date of performance to cases in which the seller knowingly made a nonconforming tender and . . . in calculating damages on the basis of the resale of the nonconforming cargo rather than of the substitute offered to replace it. For the reasons which follow, we find [these assertions] unacceptable. . . .

. . . Fairly interpreted, did subdivision (2) of section 2–508 of the Uniform Commercial Code require Con Ed to accept the substitute

---

[3]   Most of the *Khamsin* oil was drained from the tanks and sold at $10.75 per barrel. The balance was retained by Con Ed in its mixed form at $10.45 per barrel. The original price in January had been $17.875 per barrel.

[4]   The plaintiff originally also sought an affirmative injunction to compel Con Ed to accept the *Khamsin* shipment or, alternatively, the *Appollonian* substitute. However, when a preliminary injunction was denied on the ground that the plaintiff had an adequate remedy at law, it amended its complaint to pursue the latter remedy alone.

[5]   These circumstances included the fact that the preliminary injunction was not denied until April so that, by the time the *Khamsin* oil was sold in May, almost three months had gone by since its rejection.

CONDITIONS

shipment plaintiff tendered? In approaching this question, we, of course, must remember that a seller's right to cure a defective tender, as allowed by both subdivisions of section 2–508, was intended to act as a meaningful limitation on the absolutism of the old perfect tender rule, under which, no leeway being allowed for any imperfections, there was, as one court put it, just "no room * * * for the doctrine of substantial performance" of commercial obligations (*Mitsubishi Goshi Kaisha v. Aron & Co.,* 16 F.2d 185, 186 [Learned Hand, J.]; see Note, Uniform Commercial Code, § 2–508; Seller's Right to Cure Non-Conforming Goods, 6 Rutgers—Camden L.J. 387–388).

In contrast, to meet the realities of the more impersonal business world of our day, the code, to avoid sharp dealing, expressly provides for the liberal construction of its remedial provisions (§ 1–102) so that "good faith" and the "observance of reasonable commercial standards of fair dealing" be the rule rather than the exception in trade (see § 2–103, subd. [1], par. [b]), "good faith" being defined as "honesty in fact in the conduct or transaction concerned" (Uniform Commercial Code, § 1–201, subd. [19]). As to section 2–508 in particular, the code's Official Comment advises that its mission is to safeguard the seller "against surprise as a result of sudden technicality on the buyer's part" (Uniform Commercial Code, § 2–106, Comment 2; see, also, Peters, Remedies for Breach of Contracts Relating to the Sale of Goods under the Uniform Commercial Code: A Roadmap for Article Two, 73 Yale L.J. 199, 210; 51 N.Y.Jur., Sales, § 101, p. 41).

Section 2–508 may be conveniently divided between provisions for cure offered when "the time for performance has not yet expired" (subd. [1]), a precode concept in this State (*Lowinson v. Newman,* 201 App.Div. 266, 194 N.Y.S. 253), and ones which, by newly introducing the possibility of a seller obtaining "a further reasonable time to substitute a conforming tender" (subd. [2]), also permit cure beyond the date set for performance. In its entirety the section reads as follows:

"(1) Where any tender or delivery by the seller is rejected because non-conforming and the time for performance has not yet expired, the seller may seasonably notify the buyer of his intention to cure and may then within the contract time make a conforming delivery.

"(2) Where the buyer rejects a non-conforming tender which the seller had reasonable grounds to believe would be acceptable with or without money allowance the seller may if he seasonably notifies the buyer have a further reasonable time to substitute a conforming tender."

Since we here confront circumstances in which the conforming tender came after the time of performance, we focus on subdivision (2). On its face, taking its conditions in the order in which they appear, for the statute to apply (1) a buyer must have rejected a nonconforming tender, (2) the seller must have had reasonable grounds to believe this tender would be acceptable (with or without money allowance), and (3) the seller must have "seasonably" notified the buyer of the intention to substitute a conforming tender within a reasonable time.[7]

In the present case, none of these presented a problem. The first one was easily met for it is unquestioned that, at .92%, the sulfur content of the *Khamsin* oil did not conform to the .5% specified in the contract and that it was rejected by Con Ed. The second, the reasonableness of the seller's belief that the original tender would be acceptable, was supported not only by unimpeached proof that the contract's .5% and the refinery certificate's .52% were trade equivalents, but by testimony that, by the time the contract was made, the plaintiff knew Con Ed burned fuel with a content of up to 1%, so that, with appropriate price adjustment, the *Khamsin* oil would have suited its needs even if, at delivery, it was, to the plaintiff's surprise, to test out at .92%. Further, the matter seems to have been put beyond dispute by the defendant's readiness to take the oil at the reduced market price on February 20. Surely, on such a record, the trial court cannot be faulted for having found as a fact that the second condition too had been established.

As to the third, the conforming state of the *Appollonian* oil is undisputed, the offer to tender it took place on February 21, only a day after Con Ed finally had rejected the *Khamsin* delivery and the *Appollonian* substitute then already was en route to the United States, where it was expected in a week and did arrive on March 4, only four days later than expected. Especially since Con Ed pleaded no prejudice (unless the drop in prices could be so regarded), it is almost impossible, given the flexibility of the Uniform Commercial Code definitions of "seasonable" and "reasonable" (n. 7, *supra*), to quarrel with the finding that the remaining requirements of the statute also had been met.

Thus lacking the support of the statute's literal language, the defendant nonetheless would have us limit its application to cases in which a seller *knowingly* makes a nonconforming tender which it has reason to believe the buyer will accept. For this proposition, it relies almost entirely on a critique in Nordstrom, Law of Sales (§ 105), which rationalizes that, since a seller who believes its tender is conforming would have no reason to think in terms of a reduction in the price of the goods, to allow such a seller to cure after the time for performance had passed would make the

---

[7]　Essentially a factual matter, "seasonable" is defined in subdivision (3) of section 1–204 of the Uniform Commercial Code as "at or within the time agreed or if no time is agreed at or within a reasonable time". At least equally factual in character, a "reasonable time" is left to depend on the "nature, purpose and circumstances" of any action which is to be taken (Uniform Commercial Code, § 1–204, subd. [2]).

statutory reference to a money allowance redundant.[8] Nordstrom, interestingly enough, finds it useful to buttress this position by the somewhat dire prediction, though backed by no empirical or other confirmation, that, unless the right to cure is confined to those whose nonconforming tenders are knowing ones, the incentive of sellers to timely deliver will be undermined. To this it also adds the somewhat moralistic note that a seller who is mistaken as to the quality of its goods does not merit additional time (Nordstrom, *loc. cit.*). Curiously, recognizing that the few decisions extant on this subject have adopted a position opposed to the one for which it contends, Con Ed seeks to treat these as exceptions rather than exemplars of the rule (e.g., *Wilson v. Scampoli,* 228 A.2d 848 (D.C.App.) [goods obtained by seller from their manufacturer in original carton resold unopened to purchaser; seller held within statute though it had no reason to believe the goods defective]; *Appleton State Bank v. Lee,* 33 Wis.2d 690, 148 N.W.2d 1 [seller mistakenly delivered sewing machine of wrong brand but otherwise identical to one sold; held that seller, though it did not know of its mistake, had a right to cure by substitution]).[9]

That the principle for which these cases stand goes far beyond their particular facts cannot be gainsaid. These holdings demonstrate that, in dealing with the application of subdivision (2) of section 2–508, courts have been concerned with the reasonableness of the seller's belief that the goods would be acceptable rather than with the seller's pretender knowledge or lack of knowledge of the defect (*Wilson v. Scampoli, supra;* compare *Zabriskie Chevrolet v. Smith,* 99 N.J.Super. 441, 240 A.2d 195).

It also is no surprise then that the aforementioned decisional history is a reflection of the mainstream of scholarly commentary on the subject. . . .

White and Summers, for instance, put it well, and bluntly. Stressing that the code intended cure to be "a remedy which should be carefully cultivated and developed by the courts" because it "offers the possibility of conforming the law to reasonable expectations and of thwarting the chiseler who seeks to escape from a bad bargain" . . ., the authors conclude, as do we, that a seller should have recourse to the relief afforded by

---

[8]   The premise for such an argument, which ignores the policy of the code to prevent buyers from using insubstantial remediable or price adjustable defects to free themselves from unprofitable bargains (Hawkland, Sales and Bulk Sales Under the Uniform Commercial Code, pp. 120–122), is that the words "with or without money allowance" apply only to sellers who believe their goods will be acceptable with such an allowance and not to sellers who believe their goods will be acceptable without such an allowance. But, since the words are part of a phrase which speaks of an otherwise unqualified belief that the goods will be acceptable, unless one strains for an opposite interpretation, we find insufficient reason to doubt that it intends to include both those who find a need to offer an allowance and those who do not.

[9]   The only New York case to deal with this section involved a seller who knowingly tendered a "newer and improved version of the model that was actually ordered" on the contract delivery date. The court held he had reasonable grounds to believe the buyer would accept the newer model (*Bartus v. Riccardi,* 55 Misc.2d 3, 284 N.Y.S.2d 222 [Utica City Ct., Hymes, J.]).

subdivision (2) of section 2–508 of the Uniform Commercial Code as long as it can establish that it had reasonable grounds, tested objectively, for its belief that the goods would be accepted (*ibid.,* at p 321). It goes without saying that the test of reasonableness, in this context, must encompass the concepts of "good faith" and "commercial standards of fair dealing" which permeate the code (Uniform Commercial Code, § 1–201, subd. [19] ; §§ 1–203, 2–103, subd. [1], par. [b]).

As to the damages issue raised by the defendant, we affirm without reaching the merits. At no stage of the proceedings before the trial court did the defendant object to the plaintiff's proposed method for their calculation. . . .

COOKE, C.J., and JASEN, GABRIELLI, JONES, WACHTLER and MEYER, JJ., concur.

Order affirmed.

————

Zabriskie Chevrolet v. Smith

99 N.J.Super. 441, 240 A.2d 195 (1968)

Zabriskie Chevrolet, a new-car dealership, sold a new 1966 Chevrolet to Smith. As soon as Smith's wife drove off from the dealership, it became evident that the car had very serious problems. As a result, Smith stopped payment on his check and notified Zabriskie that the sale was canceled. Zabriskie then towed the car back, determined that the transmission was defective, replaced the transmission with a transmission it removed from a car on its showroom floor, and asked Smith to take delivery of the repaired car under the contract. When Smith refused to take delivery, Zabriskie brought suit. Held, Zabriskie did not have a right to cure the defective delivery:

"A 'cure' which endeavors by substitution to tender a chattel not within the agreement or contemplation of the parties is invalid.

"For a majority of people the purchase of a new car is a major investment, rationalized by the peace of mind that flows from its dependability and safety. Once their faith is shaken, the vehicle loses not only its real value in their eyes, but becomes an instrument whose integrity is substantially impaired and whose operation is fraught with apprehension. The attempted cure in the present case was ineffective."

————

Manassas Autocars v. Couch

274 Va. 82, 645 S.E.2d 443 (2007)

The Couches agreed to purchase a new red minivan from Manassas Autocars. The dealership did not have the van in stock so they arranged to have one delivered from another dealership. When the Couches came to pick up the van and do paperwork to complete the purchase they noticed "a grey circular 'splotch' approximately seven to eight inches in diameter with a 'drip' mark streaking three to four inches down to the wheel well of the passenger side rear panel." The salesperson persuaded the Couches to take the van and return to the dealership later to have the stain removed. When the Couches brought the van in for the repair the dealership was unable to remove the stain. Without asking the Couches' permission, the dealership repainted the stained area. The Couches returned the van to the dealership as soon as they realized what had been done, stating they had purchased a new vehicle and not a repainted vehicle. The dealership had the van towed back to the Couches' home. The Couches also notified the lender of the revocation. Eventually the lender repossessed the van. When the Couches returned the van it had been driven approximately 1,100 miles. The Couches brought a claim for damages. The jury returned a verdict in favor of the Couches on the revocation claim and awarded damages. Held, affirmed:

Manassas claims that the trial court erred in denying its motions to strike the Couches' revocation claim because the evidence did not establish that the nonconformity substantially impaired the vehicle's value to the Couches. Specifically, Manassas argues that under *Gasque v. Mooers Motor Car Co.,* 227 Va. 154, 313 S.E.2d 384 (1984), the measure of substantial impairment of value to the buyer is not diminution in the value of the goods on the open market; rather, unless the evidence establishes otherwise, the usual and customary purpose of the goods—in this case, transportation—is presumed to be the reason for the purchase and the measure by which the value of the goods is determined. Considering this purpose, Manassas points out that there was no evidence that the nonconformity adversely affected the vehicle's "driveability." The only evidence offered at trial regarding value was the Couches' expert witness who testified that the repainting diminished the value of the vehicle by 20 percent. Manassas contends that the Couches therefore failed to carry their burden of proof on their revocation claim and the trial court erred in submitting this issue to the jury. We disagree with Manassas' proposed application of *Gasque.*

The plaintiffs in *Gasque* sought to revoke their acceptance of a new 1979 Fiat vehicle based on a number of problems such as a water leak, heater malfunction, inoperative clock and interior light, automatic choke problems, excessive oil consumption, loud vibrations, and other noises and rattles. The plaintiffs had driven the vehicle with these various defects for at least 4,500 miles prior to revocation, and the vehicle had been driven over 8,000 miles at the time of trial. The trial court struck the plaintiffs' evidence and entered judgment for the defendant dealer, holding that, under a 'driveability' test, there was no substantial diminution in the value of the vehicle to the plaintiffs and the plaintiffs did not notify the dealer of the revocation within a reasonable time.

On appeal to this Court, one issue was whether the "driveability" test used by the trial court was correct. The plaintiffs argued that the appropriate test was a subjective test, "under which the buyers need only persuade the fact-finder that their 'faith has been shaken' in the product." 227 Va. at 160, 313 S.E.2d at 389. We rejected this argument, holding that while a "driveability" test "would not be of universal application," the application of the test in that case was not erroneous "where the buyers failed to prove any need for the car beyond ordinary transportation." *Id.* at 161, 313 S.E.2d at 389.

The record in this case shows that Mr. Couch testified he wanted to purchase a new vehicle, not a repainted vehicle, and that the repainted vehicle was not the vehicle they purchased. Mrs. Couch testified that, if she had been told that Manassas intended to cure the defect in the vehicle by repainting it, she would not have given permission because she "purchased a vehicle at new car standards and if you paint it, then, it is no longer a new car." The Couches' expert witness then testified that the vehicle lost 20 percent of its value in its repainted condition.

This record thus demonstrates that the Couches intended to buy not only a means of transportation but a *new* vehicle. When the nonconforming condition was repaired by repainting, the value of the vehicle to the Couches—as a new vehicle—was impaired. The expert's testimony that the repainting caused a 20 percent decrease in value supports a determination that the impairment was substantial. Therefore the trial court did not err in submitting the Couches' revocation of acceptance claim to the jury.

———

CHAPTER 20

EXPRESS CONDITIONS

■ ■ ■

SECTION 1. INTRODUCTION

NOTE ON THE DIFFERENCE BETWEEN PROMISES AND CONDITIONS

Up to now, the materials in this casebook have chiefly concerned promises. This Chapter concerns another basic set of contractual building blocks— express conditions. As previously discussed, the term "express condition" normally refers to an explicit contractual provision that either: (1) A party to the contract does not come under a duty to perform unless and until some designated state of affairs occurs or fails to occur; or (2) If some designated state of affairs occurs or fails to occur, a party's duty to perform is suspended or terminated. For example, Corporation A may agree to merge with Corporation B, but only on condition that the Commissioner of Internal Revenue rules that the transaction will be tax-free. Or, C may agree to purchase D's house, but only on condition that a termite-inspection report shows no infestation.

Why would parties use an express condition rather than a promise? In some cases, it is because neither party is willing to promise that the state of affairs in question will occur. In the merger hypothetical, for example, neither A nor B would normally be willing to promise that the Commissioner will issue a favorable ruling. In the sale-of-the-house hypothetical, D may not know whether the house is infested with termites, and therefore may not be willing to promise that there is no infestation.

Another possible reason for using express conditions, rather than promises, is to avoid the doctrine of substantial performance. Under that doctrine, if A promises to perform construction for B according to agreed-upon specifications, a slight deviation from the specifications will render A liable to a claim for damages by B, but may not prevent A from holding B to his promise to pay for the job, with an offset for the damages. On the other hand, if the contract expressly states that it is a condition to B's liability to A that A's performance meets the designated specifications, then B's chance of escaping liability for the contract price because of a departure from the specifications is greatly improved. Similarly, if B wants to avoid having a court apply the doctrine of material breach to determine whether she may terminate a contract if A does not achieve a benchmark in performance, then B can make A's achievement of the benchmark a condition of her obligation under the contract.

In NPS LLC v. Minihane, Chapter 5 supra, a condition was coupled with a liquidated damage clause to give the New England Patriots the power to terminate a season ticket holder's multi-year license, and recover as liquidated damages the agreed annual fee for the balance of the term of the license, if a season ticket holder failed to pay the annual fee by a specified date.

As the next several cases illustrate, it is not always easy to determine whether a contractual provision is a promise or a condition. The issue whether a contractual provision is a promise or a condition is further confused by the fact that under modern contract terminology, where A and B have a contract, A's substantial performance of *his* promises may be an *implied condition* to B's obligation to perform *her* promises. The doctrines of substantial performance and material breach (taken up in Chapter 19, supra), are often described as constructive conditions.

The organization of this Chapter is as follows: Section 2 will explore the differences between the operation of promises and conditions. Section 3 concerns issues of interpretation in determining whether a contractual provision is a promise or a condition. Sections 4 and 5 concern the prevention doctrine, which denies effect to a condition when the obligor wrongfully prevents its fulfillment, and conditions of satisfaction, in which a duty to pay for a performance is made conditional on satisfaction with the performance. A common theme is the interplay of the duty of good faith with conditions. Section 6 concerns excuses for the nonfulfillment of conditions that do not turn on the obligor's misconduct or bad faith. Waiver of a condition was taken up in Chapter 14, supra.

SECTION 2. THE DISTINCTIONS BETWEEN THE OPERATION OF A PROMISE AND THE OPERATION OF A CONDITION

OPPENHEIMER & CO. V. OPPENHEIM, APPEL, DIXON & CO.

Court of Appeals of New York, 1995.
86 N.Y.2d 685, 660 N.E.2d 415, 636 N.Y.S.2d 734.

CIPARICK, JUSTICE.

The parties entered into a letter agreement setting forth certain conditions precedent to the formation and existence of a sublease between them. The agreement provided that there would be no sublease between the parties "unless and until" plaintiff delivered to defendant the prime landlord's written consent to certain "tenant work" on or before a specified deadline. If this condition did not occur, the sublease was to be deemed "null and void." Plaintiff provided only oral notice on the specified date. The issue presented is whether the doctrine of substantial performance applies to the facts of this case. We conclude it does not for the reasons that follow.

I.

In 1986, plaintiff Oppenheimer & Co. moved to the World Financial Center in Manhattan, a building constructed by Olympia & York Company (O & Y). At the time of its move, plaintiff had three years remaining on its existing lease for the 33rd floor of the building known as One New York Plaza. As an incentive to induce plaintiff's move, O & Y agreed to make the rental payments due under plaintiff's rental agreement in the event plaintiff was unable to sublease its prior space in One New York Plaza.

In December 1986, the parties to this action entered into a conditional letter agreement to sublease the 33rd floor. Defendant already leased space on the 29th floor of One New York Plaza and was seeking to expand its operations. The proposed sublease between the parties was attached to the letter agreement. The letter agreement provided that the proposed sublease would be executed only upon the satisfaction of certain conditions. Pursuant to paragraph 1(a) of the agreement, plaintiff was required to obtain "the Prime Landlord's written notice of confirmation, substantially to the effect that [defendant] is a subtenant of the Premises reasonably acceptable to Prime Landlord." If such written notice of confirmation were not obtained "on or before December 30, 1986, then this letter agreement and the Sublease shall be deemed null and void and of no further force and effect and neither party shall have any rights against nor obligations to the other."

Assuming satisfaction of the condition set forth in paragraph 1(a), defendant was required to submit to plaintiff, on or before January 2, 1987, its plans for "tenant work" involving construction of a telephone communication linkage system between the 29th and 33rd floors. Paragraph 4(c) of the letter agreement then obligated plaintiff to obtain the prime landlord's "written consent" to the proposed "tenant work" and deliver such consent to defendant on or before January 30, 1987. Furthermore, if defendant had not received the prime landlord's written consent by the agreed date, both the agreement and the sublease were to be deemed "null and void and of no further force and effect," and neither party was to have "any rights against nor obligations to the other." Paragraph 4(d) additionally provided that, notwithstanding satisfaction of the condition set forth in paragraph 1(a), the parties "agree not to execute and exchange the Sublease unless and until the conditions set forth in paragraph (c) above are timely satisfied."

The parties extended the letter agreement's deadlines in writing and plaintiff timely satisfied the first condition set forth in paragraph 1(a) pursuant to the modified deadline. However, plaintiff never delivered the prime landlord's written consent to the proposed tenant work on or before the modified final deadline of February 25, 1987. Rather, plaintiff's attorney telephoned defendant's attorney on February 25 and informed defendant that the prime landlord's consent had been secured. On February 26, defendant, through its attorney, informed plaintiff's attorney that the letter agreement and sublease were invalid for failure to timely deliver the prime landlord's written consent and that it would not agree to an extension of the deadline. The document embodying the prime landlord's written consent was eventually received by plaintiff on March 20, 1987, 23 days after expiration of paragraph 4(c)'s modified final deadline.

Plaintiff commenced this action for breach of contract, asserting that defendant waived and/or was estopped by virtue of its conduct[1] from insisting on physical delivery of the prime landlord's written consent by the February 25 deadline. Plaintiff further alleged in its complaint that it had substantially performed the conditions set forth in the letter agreement.

At the outset of trial, the court issued an order in *limine* barring any reference to substantial performance of the terms of the letter agreement. Nonetheless, during the course of trial, the court permitted the jury to consider the theory of substantial performance, and additionally charged the jury concerning substantial performance. Special interrogatories were submitted. The jury found that defendant had properly complied with the terms of the letter agreement, and answered in the negative the questions whether defendant failed to perform its obligations under the letter agreement concerning submission of plans for tenant work, whether defendant by its conduct waived the February 25 deadline for delivery by plaintiff of the landlord's written consent to tenant work, and whether defendant by its conduct was equitably estopped from requiring plaintiff's strict adherence to the February 25 deadline. Nonetheless, the jury answered in the affirmative the question, "Did plaintiff substantially perform the conditions set forth in the Letter Agreement?," and awarded plaintiff damages of $1.2 million.

Defendant moved for judgment notwithstanding the verdict. Supreme Court granted the motion, ruling as a matter of law that "the doctrine of substantial performance has no application to this dispute, where the Letter Agreement is free of all ambiguity in setting the deadline that plaintiff concededly did not honor." The Appellate Division reversed the judgment on the law and facts, and reinstated the jury verdict. The Court concluded that the question of substantial compliance was properly submitted to the jury and that the verdict should be reinstated because plaintiff's failure to deliver the prime landlord's written consent was inconsequential.

---

[1] Plaintiff argued that it could have met the deadline, but failed to do so only because defendant, acting in bad faith, induced plaintiff into delaying delivery of the landlord's consent. Plaintiff asserted that the parties had previously extended the agreement's deadlines as a matter of course.

This Court granted defendant's motion for leave to appeal and we now reverse.

II.

Defendant argues that no sublease or contractual relationship ever arose here because plaintiff failed to satisfy the condition set forth in paragraph 4(c) of the letter agreement. Defendant contends that the doctrine of substantial performance is not applicable to excuse plaintiff's failure to deliver the prime landlord's written consent to defendant on or before the date specified in the letter agreement and that the Appellate Division erred in holding to the contrary. Before addressing defendant's arguments and the decision of the court below, an understanding of certain relevant principles is helpful.

A condition precedent is "an act or event, other than a lapse of time, which, unless the condition is excused, must occur before a duty to perform a promise in the agreement arises" (Calamari and Perillo, Contracts § 11–2, at 438 [3d ed.]; see, Restatement [Second] of Contracts § 224; see also, Merritt Hill Vineyards v. Windy Hgts. Vineyard, 61 N.Y.2d 106, 112–113, 472 N.Y.S.2d 592, 460 N.E.2d 1077). Most conditions precedent describe acts or events which must occur before a party is obliged to perform a promise made pursuant to an existing contract, a situation to be distinguished conceptually from a condition precedent to the formation or existence of the contract itself (see, M.K. Metals v. Container Recovery Corp., 645 F.2d 583). In the latter situation, no contract arises "unless and until the condition occurs" (Calamari and Perillo, Contracts § 11–5, at 440 [3d ed]).

Conditions can be express or implied. Express conditions are those agreed to and imposed by the parties themselves. Implied or constructive conditions are those "imposed by law to do justice" (Calamari and Perillo, Contracts § 11–8, at 444 [3d ed]). Express conditions must be literally performed, whereas constructive conditions, which ordinarily arise from language of promise, are subject to the precept that substantial compliance is sufficient. The importance of the distinction has been explained by Professor Williston:

> "Since an express condition depends for its validity on the manifested intention of the parties, it has the same sanctity as the promise itself. Though the court may regret the harshness of such a condition, as it may regret the harshness of a promise, it must, nevertheless, generally enforce the will of the parties unless to do so will violate public policy. Where, however, the law itself has imposed the condition, in absence of or irrespective of the manifested intention of the parties, it can deal with its creation as it pleases, shaping the boundaries of the constructive condition in

such a way as to do justice and avoid hardship". (5 Williston, Contracts § 669, at 154 [3d ed].)

In determining whether a particular agreement makes an event a condition courts will interpret doubtful language as embodying a promise or constructive condition rather than an express condition. This interpretive preference is especially strong when a finding of express condition would increase the risk of forfeiture by the obligee (see, Restatement [Second] of Contracts § 227 [1]).

Interpretation as a means of reducing the risk of forfeiture cannot be employed if "the occurrence of the event as a condition is expressed in unmistakable language" (Restatement [Second] of Contracts § 229, comment a, at 185; see, § 227, comment b [where language is clear, "(t)he policy favoring freedom of contract requires that, within broad limits, the agreement of the parties should be honored even though forfeiture results"]). Nonetheless, the nonoccurrence of the condition may yet be excused by waiver, breach or forfeiture. The Restatement posits that "[t]o the extent that the non-occurrence of a condition would cause disproportionate forfeiture, a court may excuse the non-occurrence of that condition unless its occurrence was a material part of the agreed exchange" (Restatement [Second] of Contracts § 229).

Turning to the case at bar, it is undisputed that the critical language of paragraph 4(c) of the letter agreement unambiguously establishes an express condition precedent rather than a promise, as the parties employed the unmistakable language of condition ("if," "unless and until"). There is no doubt of the parties' intent and no occasion for interpreting the terms of the letter agreement other than as written.

Furthermore, plaintiff has never argued, and does not now contend, that the nonoccurrence of the condition set forth in paragraph 4(c) should be excused on the ground of forfeiture.[2] Rather, plaintiff's primary argument from the inception of this litigation has been that defendant waived or was equitably estopped from invoking paragraph 4(c). Plaintiff argued secondarily that it substantially complied with the express condition of delivery of written notice on or before February 25th in that it gave defendant oral notice of consent on the 25th.

Contrary to the decision of the Court below, we perceive no justifiable basis for applying the doctrine of substantial performance to the facts of this case. The flexible concept of substantial compliance "stands in sharp contrast to the requirement of strict compliance that protects a party that has taken the precaution of making its duty expressly conditional" (2 Farnsworth, Contracts § 8.12, at 415 [2d ed 1990]). If the parties "have

---

[2]   The Restatement defines the term "forfeiture" as "the denial of compensation that results when the obligee loses [its] right to the agreed exchange after [it] has relied substantially, as by preparation or performance on the expectation of that exchange" (§ 229, comment b).

made an event a condition of their agreement, there is no mitigating standard of materiality or substantiality applicable to the non-occurrence of that event" (Restatement [Second] of Contracts § 237, comment d, at 220). Substantial performance in this context is not sufficient, "and if relief is to be had under the contract, it must be through excuse of the non-occurrence of the condition to avoid forfeiture" (id.; see, Brown-Marx Assocs. v. Emigrant Sav. Bank, 703 F.2d 1361, 1367–1368 [11th Cir.]; see also, Childres, Conditions in the Law of Contracts, 45 NYU L.Rev. 33, 35).

Here, it is undisputed that plaintiff has not suffered a forfeiture or conferred a benefit upon defendant. Plaintiff alludes to a $1 million licensing fee it allegedly paid to the prime landlord for the purpose of securing the latter's consent to the subleasing of the premises. At no point, however, does plaintiff claim that this sum was forfeited or that it was expended for the purpose of accomplishing the sublease with defendant. It is further undisputed that O & Y, as an inducement to effect plaintiff's move to the World Financial Center, promised to indemnify plaintiff for damages resulting from failure to sublease the 33rd floor of One New York Plaza. Consequently, because the critical concern of forfeiture or unjust enrichment is simply not present in this case, we are not presented with an occasion to consider whether the doctrine of substantial performance is applicable, that is, whether the courts should intervene to excuse the nonoccurrence of a condition precedent to the formation of a contract.

The essence of the Appellate Division's holding is that the substantial performance doctrine is universally applicable to all categories of breach of contract, including the nonoccurrence of an express condition precedent. However, as discussed, substantial performance is ordinarily not applicable to excuse the nonoccurrence of an express condition precedent . . .

III.

In sum, the letter agreement provides in the clearest language that the parties did not intend to form a contract "unless and until" defendant received written notice of the prime landlord's consent on or before February 25, 1987. Defendant would lease the 33rd floor from plaintiff only on the condition that the landlord consent in writing to a telephone communication linkage system between the 29th and 33rd floors and to defendant's plans for construction effectuating that linkage. This matter was sufficiently important to defendant that it would not enter into the sublease "unless and until" the condition was satisfied. Inasmuch as we are not dealing here with a situation where plaintiff stands to suffer some forfeiture or undue hardship, we perceive no justification for engaging in a "materiality-of-the-nonoccurrence" analysis. To do so would simply frustrate the clearly expressed intention of the parties. Freedom of contract prevails in an arm's length transaction between sophisticated parties such as these, and in the absence of countervailing public policy concerns there is no reason to relieve them of the consequences of their bargain. If they are dissatisfied with the consequences of their agreement, "the time to say so [was] at the bargaining table" [Maxton Bldrs. v. Lo Galbo, 68 N.Y.2d 373, 509 N.Y.S.2d 507, 502 N.E.2d 184].

Finally, the issue of substantial performance was not for the jury to resolve in this case. A determination whether there has been substantial performance is to be answered, "if the inferences are certain, by the judges of the law" (Jacob & Youngs v. Kent, 230 N.Y. 239, 243, 129 N.E. 889 supra).

Accordingly, the order of the Appellate Division should be reversed, with costs, and the complaint dismissed.

CHIEF JUDGE KAYE, C.J., and JUDGES SIMONS, TITONE, BELLACOSA, SMITH and LEVINE, JJ., concur.

Order reversed, etc.

MERRITT HILL VINEYARDS, INC. v. WINDY HEIGHTS VINEYARD, INC.

Court of Appeals of New York, 1984.
61 N.Y.2d 106, 472 N.Y.S.2d 592, 460 N.E.2d 1077.

KAYE, JUDGE. . .

In September, 1981, plaintiff, Merritt Hill Vineyards, entered into a written agreement with defendants, Windy Heights Vineyard and its sole shareholder Leon Taylor, to purchase a majority stock interest in respondents' Yates County vineyard, and tendered a $15,000 deposit. The agreement provides that "[i]f the sale contemplated hereby does not close, Taylor shall retain the deposit as liquidated damages unless Taylor or Windy Heights failed to satisfy the conditions specified in Section 3 thereof." Section 3, in turn, lists several "conditions precedent" to which the obligation of purchaser to pay the purchase price and to complete the purchase is subject. Among the conditions are that, by the time of the closing, Windy Heights shall have obtained a title insurance policy in a form satisfactory to Merritt Hill, and Windy Heights and Merritt Hill shall have received confirmation from the Farmers Home Administration that certain mortgages on the vineyard are in effect and that the proposed sale does not constitute a default.

In April, 1982, at the closing, plaintiff discovered that neither the policy nor the confirmation had been issued. Plaintiff thereupon refused to close and demanded return of its deposit. When defendants did not return the deposit, plaintiff instituted this action, asserting two causes of action, one for return of the deposit, and one for approximately $26,000 in consequential damages allegedly suffered as a result of defendants' failure to perform.

Special Term denied plaintiff's motion for summary judgment on both causes of action. The Appellate Division unanimously reversed Special Term's order, granted plaintiff's motion for summary judgment as to the cause of action for return of the deposit, and . . . granted summary judgment in favor of defendants, dismissing plaintiff's second cause of action for consequential damages. Both plaintiff and defendants appealed from that decision. . . .

. . . [P]laintiff's right to return of its deposit or to consequential damages depends upon whether the undertaking to produce the policy and mortgage confirmation is a promise or a condition.

A promise is "a manifestation of intention to act or refrain from acting in a specified way, so made as to justify a promisee in understanding that a commitment has been made." (Restatement, Contracts 2d, § 2, subd. [1].) A *condition,* by comparison, is "an event, not certain to occur, which must occur, unless its non-occurrence is excused, before performance under a contract becomes due." (Restatement, Contracts 2d, § 224.) Here, the contract requirements of a title insurance policy and mortgage confirmation are expressed as conditions of plaintiff's performance rather than as promises by defendants. The requirements are contained in a section of the agreement entitled "Conditions Precedent to Purchaser's Obligation to Close," which provides that plaintiff's obligation to pay the purchase price and complete the purchase of the vineyard is "subject to" fulfillment of those requirements. No words of promise are employed.* Defendants' agreement to sell the stock of the vineyard, not those conditions, was the promise by defendants for which plaintiff's promise to pay the purchase price was exchanged.

Defendants' failure to fulfill the conditions of section 3 entitles plaintiff to a return of its deposit but not to consequential damages. While a contracting party's failure to fulfill a condition excuses performance by the other party whose performance is so conditioned, it is not, without an independent promise to perform the condition, a breach of contract subjecting the nonfulfilling party to liability for damages (Restatement, Contracts 2d, § 225, subds. [1], [3]; 3A Corbin, Contracts, § 663; 5 Williston,

---

*   Plaintiff contends that the failure to produce the policy and confirmation is also a breach of section 5, entitled "Representations, Warranties and Agreements." A provision may be both a condition and a promise, if the parties additionally promise to perform a condition as part of their bargain. Such a promise is not present here. The only provision of section 5 conceivably relevant is that "Windy Heights has good and marketable title to the Property and all other properties and assets * * * as of December 31, 1980". But this is quite different from the conditions of section 3 that a title insurance policy and mortgage confirmation be produced at the closing, which took place in April, 1982. Both the complaint and plaintiff's affidavits are premised on nonperformance of section 3 of the agreement, not section 5. [Footnote by the court.]

Contracts [Jaeger—3d ed.], § 665). This is in accord with the parties' expressed intent, for section 1 of their agreement provides that if defendants fail to satisfy the conditions of section 3 plaintiff's deposit will not be returned. It does not provide for payment of damages.

On the merits of this case the Appellate Division thus correctly determined that plaintiff was entitled to the return of its deposit but not to consequential damages.

Accordingly, the order of the Appellate Division should be affirmed.

COOKE, C.J., and JASEN, JONES, WACHTLER and MEYER, JJ., concur.

SIMONS, J., taking no part.

Order affirmed, without costs.

SECTION 3. PROBLEMS OF INTERPRETATION IN DISTINGUISHING BETWEEN CONDITIONS AND PROMISES

HOWARD v. FEDERAL CROP INSURANCE CORP.

United States Court of Appeals, Fourth Circuit, 1976.
540 F.2d 695.

Before RUSSELL, FIELD and WIDENER, CIRCUIT JUDGES.

WIDENER, CIRCUIT JUDGE:

Plaintiff-appellants sued to recover for losses to their 1973 tobacco crop due to alleged rain damage. The crops were insured by defendant-appellee, Federal Crop Insurance Corporation (FCIC). Suits were brought in a state court in North Carolina and removed to the United States District Court. The three suits are not distinguishable factually so far as we are concerned here and involve identical questions of law. They were combined for disposition in the district court and for appeal. The district court granted summary judgment for the defendant and dismissed all three actions. We remand for further proceedings. Since we find for the plaintiffs as to the construction of the policy, we express no opinion on the procedural questions.

Federal Crop Insurance Corporation, an agency of the United States, in 1973, issued three policies to the Howards, insuring their tobacco crops, to be grown on six farms, against weather damage and other hazards.

The Howards (plaintiffs) established production of tobacco on their acreage, and have alleged that their 1973 crop was extensively damaged by heavy rains, resulting in a gross loss to the three plaintiffs in excess of

$35,000. The plaintiffs harvested and sold the depleted crop and timely filed notice and proof of loss with FCIC, but, prior to inspection by the adjuster for FCIC, the Howards had either plowed or disked under the tobacco fields in question to prepare the same for sowing a cover crop of rye to preserve the soil. When the FCIC adjuster later inspected the fields, he found the stalks had been largely obscured or obliterated by plowing or disking and denied the claims, apparently on the ground that the plaintiffs had violated a portion of the policy which provides that the stalks on any acreage with respect to which a loss is claimed shall not be destroyed until the corporation makes an inspection.

The holding of the district court is best capsuled in its own words:

> "The inquiry here is whether compliance by the insureds with this provision of the policy was a condition precedent to the recovery. The court concludes that it was and that the failure of the insureds to comply worked a forfeiture of benefits for the alleged loss."

... Paragraph 5 of the tobacco endorsement is entitled *Claims*. Pertinent to this case are subparagraphs 5(b) and 5(f), which are as follows:

> "5(b) *It shall be a condition precedent* to the payment of any loss that the insured establish the production of the insured crop on a unit and that such loss has been directly caused by one or more of the hazards insured against during the insurance period for the crop year for which the loss is claimed, and furnish any other information regarding the manner and extent of loss as may be required by the Corporation. (Emphasis added)"

> "5(f) The tobacco stalks on any acreage of tobacco of types 11a, 11b, 12, 13, or 14 with respect to which a loss is claimed *shall not be destroyed until the Corporation makes an inspection.* (Emphasis added)"

The arguments of both parties are predicated upon the same two assumptions. First, if subparagraph 5(f) creates a condition precedent, its violation caused a forfeiture of plaintiffs' coverage. Second, if subparagraph 5(f) creates an obligation (variously called a promise or covenant) upon plaintiffs not to plow under the tobacco stalks, defendant may recover from plaintiffs (either in an original action, or, in this case, by a counterclaim, or as a matter of defense) for whatever damage it sustained because of the elimination of the stalks. However, a violation of subparagraph 5(f) would not, under the second premise, standing alone, cause a forfeiture of the policy.

Generally accepted law provides us with guidelines here. There is a general legal policy opposed to forfeitures. *United States v. One Ford Coach,* 307 U.S. 219, 226, 59 S.Ct. 861, 83 L.Ed. 1249 (1939); *Baca v.*

Commissioner of Internal Revenue, 326 F.2d 189, 191 (5th Cir.1963). Insurance policies are generally construed most strongly against the insurer. *Henderson v. Hartford Accident & Indemnity Co.,* 268 N.C. 129, 150 S.E.2d 17, 19 (1966). When it is doubtful whether words create a promise or a condition precedent, they will be construed as creating a promise. *Harris and Harris Const. Co. v. Crain and Denbo, Inc.,* 256 N.C. 110, 123 S.E.2d 590, 595 (1962). The provisions of a contract will not be construed as conditions precedent in the absence of language plainly requiring such construction. *Harris,* 123 S.E.2d at 596. And *Harris,* at 123 S.E.2d 590, 595, cites *Jones v. Palace Realty Co.,* 226 N.C. 303, 37 S.E.2d 906 (1946), and *Restatement of the Law, Contracts,* § 261.

Plaintiffs rely most strongly upon the fact that the term "condition precedent" is included in subparagraph 5(b) but not in subparagraph 5(f). It is true that whether a contract provision is construed as a condition or an obligation does not depend entirely upon whether the word "condition" is expressly used. Appleman, *Insurance Law and Practice* (1972), vol. 6A, § 4144. However, the persuasive force of plaintiffs' argument in this case is found in the use of the term "condition precedent" in subparagraph 5(b) but not in subparagraph 5(f). Thus, it is argued that the ancient maxim to be applied is that the expression of one thing is the exclusion of another. . . .

The *Restatement [First] of the Law of Contracts* states:

"§ 261. Interpretation of Doubtful Words as Promise or Condition.

Where it is doubtful whether words create a promise or an express condition, they are interpreted as creating a promise; but the same words may sometimes mean that one party promises a performance and that the other party's promise is conditional on that performance."

Two illustrations (one involving a promise, the other a condition) are used in the *Restatement:*

"2. A, an insurance company, issues to B a policy of insurance containing promises by A that are in terms conditional on the happening of certain events. The policy contains this clause: 'provided, in case differences shall arise touching any loss, *the matter shall be submitted to impartial arbitrators,* whose award shall be binding on the parties.' This is a promise to arbitrate and does not make an award a condition precedent of the insurer's duty to pay.

"3. A, an insurance company, issues to B an insurance policy in usual form containing this clause: 'In the event of disagreement as to the amount of loss it shall be ascertained by two appraisers and an umpire. The loss shall *not be payable until 60 days after the award of the appraisers when such an appraisal is required.'*

This provision is not merely a promise to arbitrate differences but makes an award a condition of the insurer's duty to pay in case of disagreement." (Emphasis added)

We believe that subparagraph 5(f) in the policy here under consideration fits illustration 2 rather than illustration 3. Illustration 2 specifies something to be done, whereas subparagraph 5(f) specifies something not to be done. Unlike illustration 3, subparagraph 5(f) does not state any conditions under which the insurance shall "not be payable," or use any words of like import. We hold that the district court erroneously held, on the motion for summary judgment, that subparagraph 5(f) established a condition precedent to plaintiffs' recovery which forfeited the coverage.

From our holding that defendant's motion for summary judgment was improperly allowed, it does not follow the plaintiffs' motion for summary judgment should have been granted, for if subparagraph 5(f) be not construed as a condition precedent, there are other questions of fact to be determined. At this point, we merely hold that the district court erred in holding, on the motion for summary judgment, that subparagraph 5(f) constituted a condition precedent with resulting forfeiture.

The explanation defendant makes for including subparagraph 5(f) in the tobacco endorsement is that it is necessary that the stalks remain standing in order for the Corporation to evaluate the extent of loss and to determine whether loss resulted from some cause not covered by the policy. However, was subparagraph 5(f) inserted because without it the Corporation's opportunities for proof would be more difficult, or because they would be impossible? Plaintiffs point out that the Tobacco Endorsement, with subparagraph 5(f), was adopted in 1970, and crop insurance goes back long before that date. Nothing is shown as to the Corporation's prior 1970 practice of evaluating losses. Such a showing might have a bearing upon establishing defendant's intention in including 5(f). Plaintiffs state, and defendant does not deny, that another division of the Department of Agriculture, or the North Carolina Department, urged that tobacco stalks be cut as soon as possible after harvesting as a means of pest control. Such an explanation might refute the idea that plaintiffs plowed under the stalks for any fraudulent purpose. Could these conflicting directives affect the reasonableness of plaintiffs' interpretation of defendant's prohibition upon plowing under the stalks prior to adjustment?

We express no opinion on these questions because they were not before the district court and are mentioned to us largely by way of argument rather than from the record. No question of ambiguity was raised in the court below or here and no question of the applicability of paragraph 5(c) to this case was alluded to other than in the defendant's pleadings, so we also do not reach those questions. Nothing we say here should preclude FCIC from asserting as a defense that the plowing or disking under of the stalks caused damage to FCIC if, for example, the amount of the loss was thereby made more difficult or impossible to ascertain whether the plowing or disking under was done with bad purpose or innocently. To repeat, our narrow holding is that merely plowing or disking under the stalks does not of itself operate to forfeit coverage under the policy.

The case is remanded for further proceedings not inconsistent with this opinion.

VACATED AND REMANDED.

RESTATEMENT, SECOND, CONTRACTS § 227

[See Selected Source Materials Supplement]

SECTION 4. PREVENTION; THE IMPLICATION OF A DUTY TO FULFILL A CONDITION

JOHNSON V. COSS
Supreme Court of South Dakota, 2003.
667 N.W.2d 701, 2003 SD 86.

ZINTER, JUSTICE. Lawrence Coss entered into an agreement to purchase George Johnson's, auto dealership. The agreement was conditioned on Ford Motor Company's transfer of its franchise from Johnson to Coss. After several months, Coss notified both Johnson and Ford that the agreement could not be completed because Coss could not meet Ford's franchise transfer requirements. Johnson subsequently commenced this action for breach of contract and breach of the covenant of good faith and fair dealing. The circuit court granted summary judgment for Johnson reasoning that Coss's actions prevented Ford's transfer of the franchise. Coss appeals. Because we find material issues of disputed fact relating to the cause of the failure to transfer the franchise, we reverse and remand.

FACTS AND PROCEDURAL HISTORY

On January 7, 2000, Johnson and Coss entered into an Asset Purchase Agreement for the sale of Johnson Ford Lincoln-Mercury, Inc. The sale included the dealership assets, the real estate upon which the car business was located, as well as the inventory, parts, and other related items.

The agreement was expressly conditioned upon Ford Motor Company's approval of the transfer of the Ford franchise from Johnson to Coss. Paragraph 16 of the agreement provided:

All transactions described in this agreement are subject to the consent and approval of Seller's franchisor, Ford Motor Company, and any of its subsidiaries or member companies. Transfer, or written approval of transfer, of the Ford Lincoln-Mercury franchise, is a condition precedent to closing of the transactions herein. In the event the consent and approval of Ford Motor Company or any other entity necessary to approve and effectively transfer the Ford Lincoln-Mercury franchise to Purchaser is not obtained, then this transaction in its entirety and this agreement in its entirety is null and void.

Paragraph 17 of the agreement also conditioned the agreement on: "[r]eceipt of the consent and approval [sic] the Corporation's franchisor, Ford Motor Company, in regard to the transfer of the Corporation's Ford Lincoln-Mercury franchise to Purchaser[.]"

Coss hired Steven Grodahl, an attorney and CPA, to assist Coss with the franchise transfer. According to Grodahl's affidavit in opposition to Johnson's motion for summary judgment, Ford identified several requirements that Coss needed to satisfy before Ford would approve the transfer. Those requirements included an on site manager that was approved by Ford. That manager was required to demonstrate, to Ford's satisfaction, the ability to operate a dealership successfully. The manager was also required to own a substantial interest in the business.

Viewing the facts most favorably to Coss as we must do on summary judgment, Grodahl indicated that Ford would not approve Coss as the manager/co-owner. Because Ford would not transfer the franchise if Coss were the sole owner, Coss decided that the success of the agreement depended upon finding a manager willing to run the day-to-day operations of the dealership. That person would also have to acquire a substantial ownership in the business.

Mark Goodrich was identified as such a manager/co-owner. Originally, Coss proposed a 50/50 ownership arrangement with Goodrich and a joint capitalization of $1 million. However, Ford indicated that they required a majority owner. Pursuant to that requirement, Coss revised the plan so that he would own 50.1% of the dealership. In addition to the ownership requirements, Ford required that the potential owners develop a New Dealer Operating Plan, and that each owner submit personal and financial information. Ford further advised that it would require an initial capitalization of $1.476 million instead of the $1 million Coss had initially proposed.

Grodahl's affidavit indicates that despite Coss's attempts to comply with these requirements, Coss could not meet them. Although it is undisputed that Ford did not issue a written denial of the transfer after a formal request by Coss, Grodahl asserted that it became clear after several conversations with Ford representatives that they would refuse to approve the transfer to Coss if a formal request were made. Consequently, Grodahl sent letters to Ford and Johnson informing them that, because Coss could not meet Ford's requirements, the agreement was null and void under paragraph 16.

After receiving Grodahl's letter, Johnson commenced this action against Coss. Johnson filed a motion for partial summary judgment on Count 1 (breach of contract) and Count 2 (breach of the covenant of good faith and fair dealing). Coss filed a cross motion for summary judgment. After a hearing, the circuit court granted partial summary judgment in favor of Johnson and denied judgment for Coss. The circuit court reasoned that: "the agreement was not performed and the transaction was not consummated according to its terms 'due to an act of the Purchaser,' and was not a result of the denial of the application by Ford Motor Co." Coss appeals . . . .

The dispositive issue in this appeal is whether the condition precedent (Ford's approval of the franchise transfer) failed because of an act for which Coss was legally responsible, or because of a discretionary act of Ford Motor Co. . . . Ford held the ultimate right to determine if the condition precedent was fulfilled by approval of the franchise transfer. By affidavit opposing summary judgment, Grodahl stated that the terms and conditions imposed by Ford could not be met. However, Johnson argues, and the circuit court concluded, that under the prevention doctrine, the failure of the condition precedent was caused by Coss, and therefore, Coss should be prevented from relying on the unfulfilled condition.

"The prevention doctrine . . . operates as an exception to the general rule that one has no duty to perform under a contract containing a condition precedent until the condition occurs." *Williston* § 39:4; *see also Moore Brothers Co. v. Brown & Root, Inc.*, 207 F.3d 717, 725 (4th Cir.2000). "[P]revention is similar to the concept of 'waiver by estoppel' in the context of excuses for nonperformance of contractual duties. An individual who prevents the occurrence of a condition may be said to be 'estopped' from benefiting from the fact that the condition precedent to his or her obligation failed to occur." *Williston* § 39:7. As the Restatement (Second) of Contracts explains:

> Where a duty of one party is subject to the occurrence of a condition, the additional duty of good faith and fair dealing imposed on him . . . may require some cooperation on his part, either by refraining from conduct that will prevent or hinder the occurrence of that condition or by taking affirmative steps to cause its occurrence. . . [N]on-performance of that duty when performance is due is a breach. . . [I]t has the further effect of excusing the non-occurrence of the condition itself, so that

performance of the duty that was originally subject to its occurrence can become due in spite of its non-occurrence.

Restatement (Second) of Contracts § 245 cmt. (a) (1981). Similarly, *Williston* explains that if a party to a contract hinders the occurrence of a condition precedent, that condition is waived.

If a promisor prevents or hinders the occurrence or fulfillment of a condition to his or her duty of performance, the condition is excused. In other words, "the nonoccurrence or nonperformance of a condition is excused where the failure of the condition is caused by the party against whom the condition operates to impose a duty." Accordingly, the liability of the promisor is fixed regardless of the failure to fulfill the condition.

Williston, § 39:4. (citing *Rohde v. Massachusetts Mut. Life Ins. Co.,* 632 F.2d 667 (6th Cir.1980)). "The prevention doctrine does not require proof that the condition would have occurred 'but for' the wrongful conduct of the promisor; instead it only requires that the conduct have 'contributed materially' to the non-occurrence of the condition." *Moore Brothers,* 207 F.3d at 725. "Whether interference by one party to a contract amounts to prevention so as to excuse performance by the other party and constitute a breach by the interfering party is a question of fact to be decided by the jury under all of the proved facts and circumstances." *Williston,* § 39:3.

Because this is a summary judgment under review, the question then is whether there are genuine issues of material fact whether Coss contributed materially to the failure of the condition. According to Grodahl's affidavit, one of Ford's requirements for transfer of the franchise was that the dealership be managed and operated by a person who could run the business, on site, on a day-to-day basis. That person had to demonstrate, to Ford's satisfaction, the ability to manage a dealership successfully. That person also had to have a substantial ownership interest in the business. According to Grodahl, Ford indicated that Coss was not acceptable or qualified for these purposes. Therefore, to satisfy the agreement's conditions precedent, it was reasonably necessary for Coss to locate a manager/co-owner who could meet Ford's requirement.

Although the trial court did not believe that Coss could rely on the Goodrich co-ownership arrangement to satisfy the condition precedent, that manager/co-owner contingency was envisioned by the agreement. Even before the agreement's execution, the parties were aware that Ford would require someone other than Coss to be the on-site manager. Consequently, in October 1999, Coss identified Goodrich as a potential co-owner and manager. In fact, Coss produced an October 25, 1999 letter from Coss's attorney to Goodrich outlining the potential co-owner relationship between Coss and Goodrich. That October letter emphasized that the "entire series of transactions [was] all contingent on Ford approving the transfer of the franchise." At that time, Coss proposed that he and Goodrich would each own a 50% interest in the business, and each would contribute $500,000 toward its initial capitalization.

However, following the execution of the agreement, Ben Waite, a Ford District Representative, advised Grodahl that Ford would not approve the ownership arrangement expressed in the October letter to Goodrich. Waite stated that one of the owners had to have a majority interest in the business. Pursuant to this requirement, Coss revised the plan so he would be the majority owner with the 50.1% interest in the business.

However, Waite also advised Grodahl that Ford required an initial capitalization of $1.476 million instead of the contemplated $1 million. According to Grodahl, even after this added capitalization requirement, Coss continued to work towards the consummation of the transaction and was willing to satisfy that requirement. Coss established a new South Dakota corporation called "21st Century Motor Company, Inc." to operate the business. Coss also submitted his completed personal and financial information. Waite later advised Grodahl that the information provided was sufficient for Ford's purposes.

Ultimately, however, Coss asserts that he could not comply with all of Ford's requirements for the franchise transfer. According to the Grodahl affidavit, "Ford imposed requirements relating to ownership and capitalization that Mark Goodrich and Lawrence Coss were unable to meet to Ford's satisfaction." Although there was no written rejection from Ford, Grodahl's affidavit asserted that Waite had verbally advised him of the requirements from which Ford would not deviate. The alleged fact that Coss, working with Goodrich, could not meet these requirements, led Coss to the conclusion that the conditions could not be met. We believe that these alleged facts were sufficient to create genuine issues of dispute whether Coss spent sufficient time, energy, and expense to satisfy the condition precedent. Under those circumstances, a trier of fact must determine whether Coss's conduct contributed materially to the failure to obtain Ford's approval. . . .

Johnson finally argues that Coss's failure to deposit $100,000 into an escrow account, as required by paragraph 9 of the agreement, demonstrates Coss's abandonment of the contract from the very beginning. However, Coss submitted evidence indicating that a check for that amount was outstanding. Moreover, even if there was a total failure to tender $100,000, that failure was only some evidence of Coss's abandonment of the contract, and Grodahl's affidavit raised other facts indicating that Coss did not intend to abandon the contract. Therefore, Coss's showing was sufficient to preclude summary judgment. Any alleged abandonment must ultimately be determined by trial.

Because Coss raised disputed issues of material fact concerning the cause of the failure of the condition precedent, we reverse the summary judgment and remand for further proceedings.

SECTION 5. CONDITIONS OF SATISFACTION

INTRODUCTORY NOTE

Often a contract provides that one party, A, need not pay for the performance of the other party, B, unless A is satisfied with the performance. The question then arises whether A may escape liability even though his dissatisfaction, while honest, is unreasonable. In the determination of this question, the following factors would probably be influential:

(1) The language used. Did the contract say, for example, that A must be "personally satisfied," or merely that the performance must be "satisfactory"?

(2) The degree to which it is possible to apply an objective standard to the performance in question. For example, there is a decided difference in this respect between a contract to install a furnace and a contract to paint a portrait. The inclination to interpret "satisfaction" as the actual personal satisfaction of A would obviously be stronger in the later case.

(3) The degree to which A will be enriched at B's expense if the contract is interpreted to require A's personal satisfaction. If A retains and uses in his house a furnace installed by B, and seeks to escape liability to pay anything for the furnace by declaring that he is not satisfied with its performance, the case would be a very strong one for B. Recovery in B's favor might be supported either on the basis of interpretation—the word "satisfaction" being interpreted to mean satisfaction of a reasonable person—or on the theory that one who has failed to comply with a condition may nevertheless recover the value of the benefit conferred on the other party. The case is less strong for B if he has, for example, painted a portrait under a contract whereby A is not to pay unless he is satisfied, and A refuses to accept the portrait. Here B has lost the value of his own performance, but A has not been enriched.

(4) The degree of forfeiture that will be imposed on B if A escapes liability to pay for B's performance.

The chief lesson that the draftsman should derive from the cases in this field is that even though the words used in the contract may seem clearly to imply that the actual, personal satisfaction of the defendant is a condition to his liability, in certain cases the courts may nevertheless construe the contract to require only such performance as would satisfy a reasonable person.

McCartney v. Badovinac

62 Colo. 76, 160 P. 190 (1916)

A diamond had been stolen from Mrs. Ragsdale. Her husband, Dr. Ragsdale, accused Mrs. McCartney of the theft. Mr. McCartney then hired Badovinac, a private detective, to investigate the affair. Badovinac was to receive $500 for his services when he had "to the satisfaction of the said McCartney" determined whether the diamond was stolen, and if so, who had taken it. Badovinac's investigations led him to the uncomforting conclusion that Mrs. McCartney had in fact stolen the diamond, and he put his proofs before McCartney. On McCartney's refusal to pay, Badovinac brought suit. The case was tried without a jury. The trial judge found that Badovinac had clearly established that Mrs. McCartney had taken the jewel. McCartney, however, testified on the stand that he was not satisfied that his wife was the thief. Held, McCartney's statement that he is not satisfied is not conclusive of the issue. On these facts the trial judge properly found that McCartney's answers on the stand were "a mere subterfuge and pretext." A judgment for Badovinac was affirmed.

MORIN BUILDING PRODUCTS CO. V. BAYSTONE CONSTRUCTION, INC.

United States Court of Appeals, Seventh Circuit, 1983.
717 F.2d 413.

Before POSNER and COFFEY, CIRCUIT JUDGES and FAIRCHILD, SENIOR CIRCUIT JUDGE.

POSNER, CIRCUIT JUDGE.

This appeal from a judgment for the plaintiff in a diversity suit requires us to interpret Indiana's common law of contracts. General Motors, which is not a party to this case, hired Baystone Construction, Inc., the defendant, to build an addition to a Chevrolet plant in Muncie, Indiana. Baystone hired Morin Building Products Company, the plaintiff, to supply and erect the aluminum walls for the addition. The contract required that the exterior siding of the walls be of "aluminum type 3003, not less than 18 B & S gauge, with a mill finish and stucco embossed surface texture to match finish and texture of existing metal siding." The contract also provided "that all work shall be done subject to the final approval of the Architect or Owner's [General Motors'] authorized agent, and his decision in matters relating to artistic effect shall be final, if within the terms of the Contract Documents"; and that "should any dispute arise as to the quality or fitness of materials or workmanship, the decision as to acceptability shall rest strictly with the Owner, based on the requirement that all work done or materials furnished shall be first class in every respect. What is usual or customary in erecting other buildings shall in no wise enter into any consideration or decision."

Morin put up the walls. But viewed in bright sunlight from an acute angle the exterior siding did not give the impression of having a uniform finish, and General Motors' representative rejected it. Baystone removed Morin's siding and hired another subcontractor to replace it. General Motors approved the replacement siding. Baystone refused to pay Morin the balance of the contract price ($23,000) and Morin brought this suit for the balance, and won.

The only issue on appeal is the correctness of a jury instruction which, after quoting the contractual provisions requiring that the owner (General Motors) be satisfied with the contractor's (Morin's) work, states: "Notwithstanding the apparent finality of the foregoing language, however, the general rule applying to satisfaction in the case of contracts for the construction of commercial buildings is that the satisfaction clause must be determined by objective criteria. Under this standard, the question is not whether the owner was satisfied in fact, but whether the owner, as a reasonable person, should have been satisfied with the materials and workmanship in question." There was much evidence that General Motors' rejection of Morin's exterior siding had been totally unreasonable. Not only was the lack of absolute uniformity in the finish of the walls a seemingly trivial defect given the strictly utilitarian purpose of the building that they enclosed, but it may have been inevitable; "mill finish sheet" is defined in the trade as "sheet having a nonuniform finish which may vary from sheet to sheet and within a sheet, and may not be entirely free from stains or oil." If the instruction was correct, so was the judgment. But if the instruction was incorrect—if the proper standard is not whether a reasonable man would have been satisfied with Morin's exterior siding but whether General Motors' authorized representative in fact was—then there must be a new trial to determine whether he really was dissatisfied, or whether he was not and the rejection therefore was in bad faith.

Some cases hold that if the contract provides that the seller's performance must be to the buyer's satisfaction, his rejection—however unreasonable—of the seller's performance is not a breach of the contract unless the rejection is in bad faith. See, e.g., *Stone Mountain Properties, Ltd. v. Helmer,* 139 Ga.App. 865, 869, 229 S.E.2d 779, 783 (1976). But most cases conform to the position stated in section 228 of the Restatement (Second) of Contracts (1979): if "it is practicable to determine whether a reasonable person in the position of the obligor would be satisfied, an interpretation is preferred under which the condition [that the obligor be satisfied with the obligee's performance] occurs if such a reasonable person in the position of the obligor would be satisfied." See Farnsworth, Contracts 556–59 (1982); Annot., 44 A.L.R.2d 1114, 1117, 1119–20 (1955). *Indiana Tri-City Plaza Bowl, Inc. v. Estate of Glueck,* 422 N.E.2d 670, 675

(Ind.App.1981), consistently with hints in earlier Indiana cases, see *Andis v. Personett,* 108 Ind. 202, 206, 9 N.E. 101, 103 (1886); *Semon, Bache & Co. v. Coppes, Zook & Mutschler Co.,* 35 Ind.App. 351, 355, 74 N.E. 41, 43 (1905), adopts the majority position as the law of Indiana.

We do not understand the majority position to be paternalistic; and paternalism would be out of place in a case such as this, where the subcontractor is a substantial multistate enterprise. The requirement of reasonableness is read into a contract not to protect the weaker party but to approximate what the parties would have expressly provided with respect to a contingency that they did not foresee, if they had foreseen it. Therefore the requirement is not read into every contract, because it is not always a reliable guide to the parties' intentions. In particular, the presumption that the performing party would not have wanted to put himself at the mercy of the paying party's whim is overcome when the nature of the performance contracted for is such that there are no objective standards to guide the court. It cannot be assumed in such a case that the parties would have wanted a court to second-guess the buyer's rejection. So "the reasonable person standard is employed when the contract involves commercial quality, operative fitness, or mechanical utility which other knowledgeable persons can judge.... The standard of good faith is employed when the contract involves personal aesthetics or fancy." *Indiana Tri-City Plaza Bowl, Inc. v. Estate of Glueck, supra,* 422 N.E.2d at 675; see also *Action Engineering v. Martin Marietta Aluminum,* 670 F.2d 456, 460–61 (3d Cir.1982).

We have to decide which category the contract between Baystone and Morin belongs in. The particular in which Morin's aluminum siding was found wanting was its appearance, which may seem quintessentially a matter of "personal aesthetics," or as the contract put it, "artistic effect." But it is easy to imagine situations where this would not be so. Suppose the manager of a steel plant rejected a shipment of pig iron because he did not think the pigs had a pretty shape. The reasonable-man standard would be applied even if the contract had an "acceptability shall rest strictly with the Owner" clause, for it would be fantastic to think that the iron supplier would have subjected his contract rights to the whimsy of the buyer's agent. At the other extreme would be a contract to paint a portrait, the buyer having reserved the right to reject the portrait if it did not satisfy him. Such a buyer wants a portrait that will please him rather than a jury, even a jury of connoisseurs, so the only question would be his good faith in rejecting the portrait. *Gibson v. Cranage,* 39 Mich. 49 (1878).

This case is closer to the first example than to the second. The building for which the aluminum siding was intended was a factory—not usually intended to be a thing of beauty. That aesthetic considerations were decidedly secondary to considerations of function and cost is suggested by the fact that the contract specified mill-finish aluminum, which is unpainted. There is much debate in the record over whether it is even possible to ensure a uniform finish within and among sheets, but it is at least clear that mill finish usually is not uniform. If General Motors and Baystone had wanted a uniform finish they would in all likelihood have ordered a painted siding. Whether Morin's siding achieved a reasonable uniformity amounting to satisfactory commercial quality was susceptible of objective judgment; in the language of the Restatement, a reasonableness standard was "practicable."

But this means only that a requirement of reasonableness would be read into this contract if it contained a standard owner's satisfaction clause, which it did not; and since the ultimate touchstone of decision must be the intent of the parties to the contract we must consider the actual language they used. The contract refers explicitly to "artistic effect," a choice of words that may seem deliberately designed to put the contract in the "personal aesthetics" category whatever an outside observer might think. But the reference appears as number 17 in a list of conditions in a general purpose form contract. And the words "artistic effect" are immediately followed by the qualifying phrase, "if within the terms of the Contract Documents," which suggests that the "artistic effect" clause is limited to contracts in which artistic effect is one of the things the buyer is aiming for; it is not clear that he was here. The other clause on which Baystone relies, relating to the quality or fitness of workmanship and materials, may seem all-encompassing, but it is qualified by the phrase, "based on the requirement that all work done or materials furnished shall be first class in every respect"—and it is not clear that Morin's were not. This clause also was not drafted for this contract; it was incorporated by reference to another form contract (the Chevrolet Division's "Contract General Conditions"), of which it is paragraph 35. We do not disparage form contracts, without which the commercial life of the nation would grind to a halt. But we are left with more than a suspicion that the artistic-effect and quality-fitness clauses in the form contract used here were not intended to cover the aesthetics of a mill-finish aluminum factory wall.

If we are right, Morin might prevail even under the minority position, which makes good faith the only standard but presupposes that the contract conditioned acceptance of performance on the buyer's satisfaction in the particular respect in which he was dissatisfied. Maybe this contract was not intended to allow General Motors to reject the aluminum siding on the basis of artistic effect. It would not follow that the contract put Morin under no obligations whatsoever with regard to uniformity of finish. The contract expressly required it to use aluminum having "a mill finish . . . to match finish . . . of existing metal siding." The jury was asked to decide whether a reasonable man would have found that Morin had used aluminum sufficiently uniform to satisfy the matching requirement. This was the right standard if, as we believe, the parties would have adopted it had they foreseen this dispute. It is unlikely that Morin intended to bind itself to a higher and perhaps unattainable standard of achieving whatever perfection of matching that General Motors' agent insisted on, or that General Motors would have required Baystone to submit to such a standard. Because it is difficult—maybe impossible—to achieve a uniform finish with mill-finish aluminum, Morin would have been running a considerable risk of rejection if it had agreed to such a condition, and it therefore could have been expected to demand a compensating increase in the contract price. This would have required General Motors to pay a premium to obtain a freedom of action that it could not have thought terribly important, since its objective was not aesthetic. If a uniform finish was important to it, it could have gotten such a finish by specifying painted siding.

All this is conjecture; we do not know how important the aesthetics were to General Motors when the contract was signed or how difficult it really would have been to obtain the uniformity of finish it desired. The fact that General Motors accepted the replacement siding proves little, for there is evidence that the replacement siding produced the same striped effect, when viewed from an acute angle in bright sunlight, that Morin's had. When in doubt on a difficult issue of state law it is only prudent to defer to the view of the district judge, *Murphy v. White Hen Pantry Co.,* 691 F.2d 350, 354 (7th Cir.1982), here an experienced Indiana lawyer who thought this the type of contract where the buyer cannot unreasonably withhold approval of the seller's performance.

Lest this conclusion be thought to strike at the foundations of freedom of contract, we repeat that if it appeared from the language or circumstances of the contract that the parties really intended General Motors to have the right to reject Morin's work for failure to satisfy the private aesthetic taste of General Motors' representative, the rejection would have been proper even if unreasonable. But the contract is ambiguous because of the qualifications with which the terms "artistic effect" and "decision as to acceptability" are hedged about, and the circumstances suggest that the parties probably did not intend to subject Morin's rights to aesthetic whim.

AFFIRMED.

_____

MATTEI v. HOPPER

[Chapter 2, supra]

_____

Fursmidt v. Hotel Abbey Holding Corp.

10 A.D.2d 447, 200 N.Y.S.2d 256 (1960)

On February 1, 1958, Fursmidt entered into a contract with a hotel, which provided that Fursmidt would furnish valet and laundry services to guests at the hotel for a three-year period, and would pay the hotel $325 per month for the valet-and-laundry franchise. The agreement provided that "it is distinctly understood and agreed that the services to be rendered by [Fursmidt] shall meet with the approval of the [hotel], who shall be the sole judge of the sufficiency and propriety of the services."

In September 1958, the hotel informed Fursmidt that he was to discontinue his services as of October 1, 1958. Fursmidt then sued for breach of contract. The hotel counterclaimed for damages that it said it sustained by reason of Fursmidt's failure to render adequate and proper service. The trial court charged the jury that it had to decide not only whether the hotel was in fact dissatisfied but also whether the dissatisfaction was reasonable. Judgment was rendered for Fursmidt. Reversed.

(Rabin, J.) "[A] literal construction of . . . 'satisfaction' provisions is made where the agreements provide for performance involving 'fancy, taste, sensibility, or judgment' of the party for whose benefit it was made. . . . Such a result obtains in cases calling for performance to one's satisfaction in the making of a garment, the giving of a course of instruction, the services of an orchestra, the making of recordings by a singer and the painting of a portrait. . . .

"The resolution of the issue here presented lies with the determination of whether the instant agreement is one relating to operative fitness, utility or marketability or one involving fancy, taste, sensibility or judgment. We find that it comes within the rules applicable to the latter class and thus conclude that the court erred in its charge. . . .

"[I]t appears that the primary and overriding objective of the defendant in entering into this agreement was to ensure to its guests proper, efficient, courteous and reasonable valet and laundry facilities as an integral part of the overall personal services rendered by the hotel to the end that the good will of the guests be retained. . . . No objective standards of reasonableness can be set up by which the effectiveness of the plaintiff's performance in achieving the effect sought can be measured. It is for that reason that in cases of this nature the honest judgment of the party rather than that of a jury is all that is required and it was in order to make sure that that would be the measure of performance that the defendant inserted in the contract that it was to be the sole judge. . . .

"It may very well be that the charge of the Court is correct for the purpose of determining whether the plaintiff breached the agreement so as to entitle the defendant to damages on its counterclaim as distinguished from its right to terminate the contract. Honest dissatisfaction on the part of the defendant, although entitling it to terminate will not, in and of itself, entitle it to recover damages on its counterclaim. Such determination will depend on the facts surrounding the manner of the plaintiff's performance in relation to what he was obliged to do under the agreement and accordingly we do not pass on that phase of the case at this time."

RESTATEMENT, SECOND, CONTRACTS § 227, ILLUSTRATIONS 5–8

"5. A contracts with B to repair B's building for $20,000, payment to be made 'on the satisfaction of C, B's architect, and the issuance of his certificate.' A makes the repairs, but C refuses to issue his certificate, and explains why he is not satisfied. Other experts in the field consider A's performance to be satisfactory and disagree with C's explanation. A has no claim against B. . . . If C is honestly not satisfied, B is under no duty to pay A, and it makes no difference if his dissatisfaction was not reasonable.

"6. The facts being otherwise as stated in Illustration 5, C refuses to issue his certificate although he admits that he is satisfied. A has a claim against B for $20,000. The quoted language will be interpreted so that the requirement of the certificate is merely evidentiary and the condition occurs when there is, as here, adequate evidence that C is honestly satisfied.

"7. The facts being otherwise as stated in Illustration 5, C does not make a proper inspection of the work and gives no reasons for his dissatisfaction. A has a claim against B for $20,000. In using the quoted language, A and B assumed that C would exercise an honest judgment and by failing to make a proper inspection, C did not exercise such a judgment. . . .

"8. The facts being otherwise as stated in Illustration "5, C makes a gross mistake with reference to the facts on which his refusal to give a certificate is based. A has a claim against B for $20,000. In using the quoted language, A and B assumed that C would exercise his judgment without a gross mistake as to the facts. . . . "

SECTION 6. EXCUSE

AETNA CASUALTY AND SURETY CO. v. MURPHY

Supreme Court of Connecticut, 1988.
206 Conn. 409, 538 A.2d 219.

PETERS, CHIEF JUSTICE.

The sole issue in this appeal is whether an insured who belatedly gives notice of an insurable claim can nonetheless recover on the insurance contract by rebutting the presumption that his delay has been prejudicial to the insurance carrier. The plaintiff, Aetna Casualty and Surety Company, brought an action against the defendant, George A. Murphy III, to recover for damage he allegedly caused to a building it had insured. The defendant then filed a third party complaint impleading his comprehensive liability insurer, Federal Insurance Company, Chubb Group of Insurance Companies (hereinafter Chubb), as third party defendant. Chubb successfully moved for summary judgment on the ground that Murphy, the defendant and third party plaintiff, had inexcusably and unreasonably delayed in complying with the notice provisions of the insurance contract. The defendant appeals from this judgment. We find no error.

The underlying facts are undisputed. The defendant, George A. Murphy III, a dentist, terminated a lease with Hopmeadow Professional Center Associates on or about November 30, 1982. The manner in which he had dismantled his office gave rise to a claim for damages to which the plaintiff, Aetna Casualty and Surety Company, became subrogated. Although served with the plaintiff's complaint on November 21, 1983, the defendant gave no notice of the existence of this claim to Chubb until January 10, 1986. The motion to implead Chubb as third party defendant was filed on May 14, 1986, and granted on June 2, 1986.

Chubb moved for summary judgment on its three special defenses,* alleging Murphy's noncompliance with the terms of his insurance policy. Its first claim was that it was entitled to judgment because Murphy had ignored two provisions in the Chubb policy imposing notice requirements on its policyholders. The first of these provisions states: "In the event of an occurrence, written notice . . . shall be given by or for the insured to the company . . . as soon as practicable." The other states: "If claim is made or suit is brought against the insured, the insured shall immediately forward to the company every demand, notice, summons, or other process received by him or his representative." In his answer to Chubb's special defenses,

---

* Chubb, the third party defendant, had filed three special defenses, although the trial court ruled on only one. The first special defense relied on Murphy's admitted failure to give written notice of loss as soon as practicable and to forward notice of the claim against him immediately upon its filing by the plaintiff. The second and third special defenses related to questions of coverage: whether the loss suffered by Murphy was excluded as having been "expected or intended from the standpoint of the insured" or as falling outside the policy definitions of "occurrence."

Murphy admitted his failure to comply with these provisions. Accordingly, his affidavit opposing summary judgment raised no question of fact but relied on his argument that, as a matter of law, an insurer may not deny coverage because of late notice without a showing, on its part, that it has been prejudiced by its insured's delay.

The trial court granted Chubb's motion for summary judgment on its first special defense. It found that Murphy's two year delay in giving notice to Chubb was inexcusable and unreasonable, and concluded that such a delay "voids coverage and insurer's duties under the contract [of insurance]. . . ."

On appeal, Murphy challenges only the trial court's conclusion of law. Despite his inexcusable and unreasonable delay in giving notice, he maintains that he is entitled to insurance coverage because Chubb has failed to allege or to show prejudice because of his late notice.

As Murphy concedes, the trial court's decision accurately reflects numerous holdings of this court that, absent waiver, an unexcused, unreasonable delay in notification constitutes a failure of condition that entirely discharges an insurance carrier from any further liability on its insurance contract. . . .

In our appraisal of the continued vitality of this line of cases, it is noteworthy that they do not reflect a searching analysis of what role prejudice, or its absence, should play in the enforcement of such standard clauses in insurance policies. That issue was put on the table, but not resolved, by a vigorous dissent in *Plasticrete Corporation v. American Policyholders Ins. Co.,* 184 Conn. 231, 240–44, 439 A.2d 968 (1981) (*Bogdanski, J.,* dissenting). The time has come for us to address it squarely.

We are confronted, in this case, by a conflict between two competing principles in the law of contracts. On the one hand, the law of contracts supports the principle that contracts should be enforced as written, and that contracting parties are bound by the contractual provisions to which they have given their assent. Among the provisions for which the parties may bargain are clauses that impose conditions upon contractual liability. "If the occurrence of a condition is required by the agreement of the parties, rather than as a matter of law, a rule of strict compliance traditionally applies." E. Farnsworth, Contracts (1982) § 8.3, p. 544; see *Grenier v. Compratt Construction Co.,* 189 Conn. 144, 148, 454 A.2d 1289 (1983); *Brauer v. Freccia,* 159 Conn. 289, 293–94, 268 A.2d 645 (1970); *Strimiska v. Yates,* 158 Conn. 179, 185–86, 257 A.2d 814 (1969). On the other hand, the rigor of this traditional principle of strict compliance has increasingly been tempered by the recognition that the occurrence of a condition may, in appropriate circumstances, be excused in order to avoid a 'disproportionate forfeiture.' See, e.g., 2 Restatement (Second), Contracts

(1981) § 229;** *Johnson Controls, Inc. v. Bowes,* 381 Mass. 278, 280, 409 N.E.2d 185 (1980); 3A A. Corbin, Contracts (1960 & Sup.1984) § 754; E. Farnsworth, supra, § 8.7, pp. 570–71; 5 S. Williston, Contracts (3d Ed. Jaeger 1961) §§ 769 through 811.

In numerous cases, this court has held that, especially in the absence of conduct that is "wilful," a contracting party may, despite his own departure from the specifications of his contract, enforce the obligations of the other party with whom he has dealt in good faith. In construction contracts, a builder's deviation from contract specifications, even if such a departure is conscious and intentional, will not totally defeat the right to recover in an action against the owner on the contract. *Grenier v. Compratt Construction Co.,* supra, 148–49, 454 A.2d 1289; *Vincenzi v. Cerro,* 186 Conn. 612, 615, 442 A.2d 1352 (1982). In contracts for the sale of real property, the fact that a contract states a date for performance does not necessarily make time of the essence. *Kakalik v. Bernardo,* 184 Conn. 386, 392, 439 A.2d 1016 (1981); see *Ravitch v. Stollman Poultry Farms, Inc.,* 165 Conn. 135, 148, 328 A.2d 711 (1973). A purchaser of real property does not, despite his knowing default, forfeit the right to seek restitution of sums of money earlier paid under the contract of sale, even when such payments are therein characterized as liquidated damages. *Vines v. Orchard Hills, Inc.,* 181 Conn. 501, 509, 435 A.2d 1022 (1980); *Pierce v. Staub,* 78 Conn. 459, 466, 62 A. 760 (1906). Finally, despite a failure to deliver contract goods, a seller need not pay an amount contractually designated as liquidated damages to a buyer who has suffered no damages attributable to the seller's breach. *Norwalk Door Closer Co. v. Eagle Lock & Screw Co.,* 153 Conn. 681, 689, 220 A.2d 263 (1966).

This case law demonstrates that, in appropriate circumstances, a contracting party, despite his own default, may be entitled to relief from the rigorous enforcement of contract provisions that would otherwise amount to a forfeiture. On the question of what circumstances warrant such relief, no better guidelines have ever been proffered than those articulated by Judge Benjamin Cardozo in the celebrated case of *Jacob &*

** The Restatement (Second) of Contracts (1981) § 229, entitled "Excuse of a Condition to Avoid Forfeiture," provides: "To the extent that the non-occurrence of a condition would cause disproportionate forfeiture, a court may excuse the non-occurrence of that condition unless its occurrence was a material part of the agreed exchange."

Comment b elaborates on the concept of "disproportionate forfeiture" as follows: "The rule stated in the present Section is, of necessity, a flexible one, and its application is within the sound discretion of the court. Here, as in § 227(1), 'forfeiture' is used to refer to the denial of compensation that results when the obligee loses his right to the agreed exchange after he has relied substantially, as by preparation or performance on the expectation of that exchange. See Comment b to § 227. The extent of the forfeiture in any particular case will depend on the extent of that denial of compensation. In determining whether the forfeiture is 'disproportionate,' a court must weigh the extent of the forfeiture by the obligee against the importance to the obligor of the risk from which he sought to be protected and the degree to which that protection will be lost if the non-occurrence of the condition is excused to the extent required to prevent forfeiture. *The character of the agreement may, as in the case of insurance agreements, affect the rigor with which the requirement is applied.*" (Emphasis added.)

Youngs, Inc. v. Kent, 230 N.Y. 239, 129 N.E. 889 (1921). Discussing the interpretation of contracts to ascertain how the parties intended to govern their contractual relationship, Cardozo first notes that "[t]here will be no assumption of a [contractual] purpose to visit venial faults with oppressive retribution." Id., 242, 129 N.E. 889. The opinion then continues: "Those who think more of symmetry and logic in the development of legal rules than of practical adaptation to the attainment of a just result will be troubled by a classification where the lines of division are so wavering and blurred. Something, doubtless, may be said on the score of consistency and certainty in favor of a stricter standard. The courts have balanced such considerations against those of equity and fairness, and found the latter to be the weightier. . . . Where the line is to be drawn between the important and the trivial cannot be settled by a formula. 'In the nature of the case precise boundaries are impossible' (2 Williston on Contracts, sec. 841). The same omission may take on one aspect or another according to its setting. . . . The question is one of degree, to be answered, if there is doubt, by the triers of the facts . . . and, if the inferences are certain, by the judges of the law. . . . We must weigh the purpose to be served, the desire to be gratified, the excuse for deviation from the letter, the cruelty of enforced adherence. Then only can we tell whether literal fulfilment is to be implied by law as a condition."*** Id., 242–43, 129 N.E. 889.

In the setting of this case, three considerations are central. First, the contractual provisions presently at issue are contained in an insurance policy that is a "contract of adhesion," the parties to this form contract having had no occasion to bargain about the consequences of delayed notice. Second, enforcement of these notice provisions will operate as a forfeiture because the insured will lose his insurance coverage without regard to his dutiful payment of insurance premiums. Third, the insurer's legitimate purpose of guaranteeing itself a fair opportunity to investigate accidents and claims can be protected without the forfeiture that results from presuming, irrebuttably, that late notice invariably prejudices the insurer.

There can be no question that the insurance policy in this case is a "contract of adhesion." That term was first introduced into American legal vocabulary by Professor Edwin Patterson, who noted that life insurance contracts are contracts of adhesion because "[t]he contract is drawn up by the insurer and the insured, who merely 'adheres' to it, has little choice as to its terms." E. Patterson, "The Delivery of a Life-Insurance Policy," 33

*** The court's opinion in *Jacob & Youngs, Inc. v. Kent,* 230 N.Y. 239, 243, 129 N.E. 889 (1921), suggests that the parties may, by express contractual language, "effectuate a purpose that performance of every term shall be a condition of recovery." That observation is not easy to reconcile with the fact that the record in the case discloses the existence of a clause specifically permitting rejection, whenever discovered, of any work of the contractor that failed "fully" to conform with contract specifications "in every respect." See J. Dawson, W. Harvey & S. Henderson, Contracts and Contract Remedies (4th Ed.1982) pp. 816–17.

Harv.L.Rev. 198, 222 (1919). Standardized contracts of insurance continue to be prime examples of contracts of adhesion, whose most salient feature is that they are not subject to the normal bargaining processes of ordinary contracts. *Nationwide Ins. Co. v. Gode,* 187 Conn. 386, 404, 446 A.2d 1059 (1982) (*Shea, J.,* dissenting); *Weaver Bros., Inc. v. Chappel,* 684 P.2d 123, 125 (Alaska 1984); *Cooper v. Government Employees Ins. Co.,* 51 N.J. 86, 93, 237 A.2d 870 (1968); *Great American Ins. Co. v. C.G. Tate Construction Co.,* 303 N.C. 387, 392–93, 279 S.E.2d 769 (1981); *Brakeman v. Potomac Ins. Co.,* 472 Pa. 66, 72–73, 371 A.2d 193 (1977); F. Kessler, "Contracts of Adhesion—Some Thoughts about Freedom of Contract," 43 Colum.L.Rev. 629, 631–32 (1943). The fact that the notice provisions in the Chubb insurance policy were an inconspicuous part of a printed form; cf. General Statutes §§ 42a–1–201 (10) and 42a–2–316 (2); supports the characterization of these clauses as a "contract of adhesion." Nothing in the record suggests that they were brought to Murphy's attention or that, if they had been, their terms would have been subject to negotiation.

It is equally clear that literal enforcement of the notice provisions in this case will discharge Chubb from any further liability to Murphy with regard to the present claims for insurance coverage. That indeed is the necessary purport of Chubb's special defense and the consequence of the trial court's ruling on its motion for summary judgment. The operative effect of noncompliance with the notice provisions is a forfeiture of the interests of the insured that is, in all likelihood, disproportionate. *Johnson Controls, Inc. v. Bowes,* supra, 381 Mass. at 280–81, 409 N.E.2d 185.

In determining whether an insured is entitled to relief from such a disproportionate forfeiture, loss of coverage must be weighed against an insurer's legitimate interest in protection from stale claims. "The purpose of a policy provision requiring the insured to give the company prompt notice of an accident or claim is to give the insurer an opportunity to make a timely and adequate investigation of all the circumstances. . . . And further, if the insurer is thus given the opportunity for a timely investigation, reasonable compromises and settlements may be made, thereby avoiding prolonged and unnecessary litigation." 8 J. Appleman, Insurance Law and Practice (Rev.Ed.1981) § 4731, pp. 2–5. If this legitimate purpose can be protected by something short of automatic enforcement of the notice provisions, then their strict enforcement is unwarranted.

In our judgment, a proper balance between the interests of the insurer and the insured requires a factual inquiry into whether, in the circumstances of a particular case, an insurer has been prejudiced by its insured's delay in giving notice of an event triggering insurance coverage. If it can be shown that the insurer suffered no material prejudice from the delay, the nonoccurrence of the condition of timely notice may be excused because it is not, in Restatement terms, "a material part of the agreed exchange." Literal enforcement of notice provisions when there is no prejudice is no more appropriate than literal enforcement of liquidated damages clauses when there are no damages. *Norwalk Door Closer Co. v. Eagle Lock & Screw Co.,* supra, 153 Conn. at 689, 220 A.2d 263.

A significant number of cases in other jurisdictions lend support to our conclusion that, absent a showing of material prejudice, an insured's failure to give timely notice does not discharge the insurer's continuing duty to provide insurance coverage. Most of these decisions place the burden of proof on the issue of prejudice on the insurer. . . . In a few jurisdictions, although prejudice from delay is presumed, that presumption is rebuttable if the insured can demonstrate an actual lack of material prejudice. . . . By contrast to these cases which afford some latitude for factual inquiry into prejudice, some jurisdictions continue to enforce delayed notice provisions literally. . . .

In light of existing related precedents in this jurisdiction, although we are persuaded that the existence or nonexistence of prejudice from delayed notice should be determined on a factual basis, the burden of establishing lack of prejudice must be borne by the insured. It is the insured who is seeking to be excused from the consequences of a contract provision with which he has concededly failed to comply. His position is akin to that of the defaulting purchaser of real property in *Vines v. Orchard Hills, Inc.,* supra, 181 Conn. at 510, 435 A.2d 1022, where we held that, "[t]o prove unjust enrichment, in the ordinary case, the purchaser, because he is the party in breach, must prove that the damages suffered by his seller are less than the moneys received from the purchaser. . . . It may not be easy for the purchaser to prove the extent of the seller's damages, it may even be strategically advantageous for the seller to come forward with relevant evidence of the losses he has incurred and may expect to incur on account of the buyer's breach. Nonetheless, only if the breaching party satisfies his burden of proof that the innocent party has sustained a net gain may a claim for unjust enrichment be sustained." Principles of unjust enrichment and restitution bear a family resemblance to those involved in considerations of forfeiture. Under both sets of principles, the law has come to permit a complainant to seek a fair allocation of profit and loss despite the complainant's own failure to comply fully with his contract obligations. The determination of what is fair, as a factual matter, must however depend upon a proper showing by the complainant who seeks this extraordinary relief.

Applying these principles to the present case, we conclude that the trial court was correct in granting summary judgment, although not for the reason upon which it relied. *A & H Corporation v. Bridgeport,* 180 Conn. 435, 443, 430 A.2d 25 (1980); *Favorite v. Miller,* 176 Conn. 310, 317, 407 A.2d 974 (1978). Chubb, the third party defendant, was not automatically discharged because of the delay of Murphy, the third party plaintiff, in giving notice of an insured occurrence. Chubb was, however, entitled to summary judgment because Murphy's affidavit opposing summary judgment contained no factual basis for a claim that Chubb had not been materially prejudiced by Murphy's delay.

There is no error.

In this opinion ARTHUR H. HEALEY, CALLAHAN and GLASS, JJ., concurred.

COVELLO, J., concurred in the result.

RESTATEMENT, SECOND, CONTRACTS § 229

[See Selected Source Materials Supplement]

RESTATEMENT, SECOND, CONTRACTS § 229, ILLUSTRATIONS 1, 2

1. A contracts to build a house for B, using pipe of Reading manufacture. In return, B agrees to pay $75,000 in progress payments, each payment to be made "on condition that no pipe other than that of Reading manufacture has been used." Without A's knowledge, a subcontractor mistakenly uses pipe of Cohoes manufacture which is identical in quality and is distinguishable only by the name of the manufacturer which is stamped on it. The mistake is not discovered until the house is completed, when replacement of the pipe will require destruction of substantial parts of the house. B refuses to pay the unpaid balance of $10,000. A court may conclude that the use of Reading rather than Cohoes pipe is so relatively unimportant to B that the forfeiture that would result from denying A the entire balance would be disproportionate, and may allow recovery by A subject to any claim for damages for A's breach of his duty to use Reading pipe.

2. A, an ocean carrier, carries B's goods under a contract providing that it is a condition of A's liability for damage to cargo that "written notice of claim for loss or damage must be given within 10 days after removal of goods." B's cargo is damaged during carriage and A knows of this. On removal of the goods, B notes in writing on the delivery record that the cargo is damaged, and five days later informs A over the telephone of a claim for that damage and invites A to participate in an inspection within the ten day period. A inspects the goods within the period, but B does not give written notice of its claim until 25 days after removal of the goods. Since the purpose of requiring the condition of written notice is to alert the carrier and enable it to make a prompt investigation, and since this

purpose had been served by the written notice of damage and the oral notice of claim, the court may excuse the non-occurrence of the condition to the extent required to allow recovery by B.

———

Great American Ins. Co. v. C.G. Tate Construction Co.

303 N.C. 387, 279 S.E.2d 769 (1981)

Great American issued a liability policy to C.G. Tate. Under the policy, Great American was obliged to defend and indemnify Tate in connection with an incident covered by a policy. It was a condition to this obligation that Tate notify Great American of such an incident "as soon as practicable." An automobile accident occurred which might have been covered by the policy. Tate believed its personnel had not been involved in causing the accident and therefore did not give notice to Great American as soon as practicable. Held, the provision should be construed according to the parties' reasonable expectations.

(Carlton, J.) ". . . [A]n unexcused delay by the insured in giving notice to the insurer of an accident does not relieve the insurer of its obligation to defend and indemnify unless the delay operates materially to prejudice the insurer's ability to investigate and defend. . . .

". . . . The terms of an insurance contract are not bargained for in the traditional sense. Insurance policies are offered on a take-it-or-leave-it basis and, frequently, the only term over which the insured has any say is the amount of coverage. Strict interpretation of the notice requirement leads to harsh results: failure to notify the insurer within a reasonable time, for whatever reason, relieves the insurer of its obligations to defend and indemnify, the essence of the contract, even though it may have suffered no prejudice whatsoever as a result of the delay. Rejection of the strict contractual approach means that the interpretation of the notice provision will be guided more by its purpose—the reason for its inclusion in the insurance contract—than by its seemingly conclusive terms. Additionally, adoption of the modern rule of reasonable expectations promotes the social function of insurance coverage: providing compensation for injuries sustained by innocent members of the public. The rule we adopt today has the advantages of promoting social policy and fulfilling the reasonable expectations of the purchaser while fully protecting the ability of the insurer to protect its own interests. . . .

"The rule we adopt today places the notice requirement in its proper context. No condition of timely notice will be given a greater scope than required to fulfill its purpose. Simply put, the scope of the condition precedent which will relieve an insurer of its obligations under an insurance contract, is only as broad as its purpose: to protect the ability of the insurer to defend by preserving its ability fully to investigate the accident, e.g., Peeler v. United States Casualty Co., 197 N.C. 286, 148 S.E. 261. If, under the circumstances of a particular case, the purpose behind the requirement has been met, the insurer will not be relieved of its obligations. If, on the other hand, the purpose of protecting the insurer's ability to defend has been frustrated, the insurer has no duty under the contract. This equitable approach to the interpretation of notice requirements in insurance contracts has the advantages of providing coverage whenever in the reasonable expectations of the parties it should exist and of protecting the insurer whenever failure strictly to comply with a condition has resulted in material prejudice."

————

RESTATEMENT, SECOND, CONTRACTS § 230

[See Selected Source Materials Supplement]

————

RESTATEMENT, SECOND, CONTRACTS § 230, ILLUSTRATIONS 1, 2

1.   A, an insurance company, insures the property of B under a policy providing that no recovery can be had if suit is not brought on the policy within two years after a loss. A loss occurs and B lets two years pass before bringing suit. A's duty to pay B for the loss is discharged and B cannot maintain the action on the policy.

2.   The facts being otherwise as stated in Illustration 1, B lives in a foreign country and is prevented by the outbreak of war from bringing suit against A for two years. A's duty to pay B for the loss is not discharged and B can maintain an action on the policy when the war is ended.

————

RESTATEMENT, SECOND, CONTRACTS § 271

[See Selected Source Materials Supplement]

————

RESTATEMENT, SECOND, CONTRACTS § 271, ILLUSTRATIONS 1, 2

1.   A contracts with B to repair B's building for $20,000, payment to be made "on the satisfaction of C, B's architect, and the issuance of his certificate." A properly makes the repairs, but C dies before he is able to give a certificate. Since presentation of the architect's certificate is not a material part of the agreed exchange and forfeiture would otherwise result, the occurrence of the condition is excused, and A has a claim against B for $20,000. . . .

2. A, an insurance company, issues to B a policy of accidental injury insurance which provides that notice within 14 days of an accident is a condition of A's duty. B is injured as a result of an accident covered by the policy but is so mentally deranged that he is unable to give notice for 20 days. B gives notice as soon as he is able. Since the giving of notice within 14 days is not a material part of the agreed exchange, and forfeiture would otherwise result, the non-occurrence of the condition is excused and B has a claim against A under the policy.

––––––––

Royal-Globe Insurance Co. v. Craven

411 Mass. 629, 585 N.E.2d 315 (1992)

(Abrams, J.) "The uninsured motorist policy in effect at the time of the accident requires notice to both the police and the insurer '[w]ithin [twenty-four] hours . . . if [the insured has] . . . been involved in a hit and run accident.' The judge concluded, however, that Craven [the insured] 'was in the intensive care unit during the first twenty-four hours [after the accident]' and could not be expected to notify the police and her insurance company within twenty-four hours. The judge ruled that Craven therefore was excused from the twenty-four hour notice requirement.

"Royal-Globe maintains that the judge's ruling on excuse was error because someone hired an attorney to represent Craven the morning of the accident. If Craven or someone acting on her behalf was able within twenty-four hours to engage a lawyer to represent her, Royal-Globe argues, it was error for the judge to conclude that Craven was excused from the twenty-four hour notice requirement. It is undisputed that Craven remained in intensive care for several days after the accident. The judge determined that to expect Craven to give notice while she was in intensive care would be 'unreasonable.' There was no error in that determination."

––––––––

APPENDIX

THE STATUTE OF FRAUDS

■ ■ ■

Analysis

Sec.

1. Introduction.
2. The Text of the Original Statute.
3. The Purpose of the Statute.
4. How It was Decided What Kinds of Contracts Should Be Required to Be in Writing.
5. American Variations on the English Theme.
6. Judicial Interpretations of the Various Subsections of the Statute of Frauds—Introduction.
7. Contracts for the Sale of an Interest in Land (Section 4(4)).
8. Contracts for the Sale of Goods.
9. Some Other Formal Requirements in the Uniform Commercial Code.
10. Agreements Not to Be Performed Within One Year from the Making Thereof (Section 4(5)).
11. The Suretyship Section (Section 4(2))—Generally.
12. The Suretyship Section Continued—"The Main Purpose Rule".
13. The Suretyship Section Continued—Miscellaneous Problems.
14. Promises Made by Executors and Administrators (Section 4(1)).
15. Contracts upon Consideration of Marriage (Section 4(3)).
16. What Kind of Writing Will Satisfy the Statute.
17. Electronic Contracting and the Statute of Frauds.
18. Claims Available for Breach of an Oral Contract Within the Statute—Introduction.
19. Restitution.
20. Part Performance.
21. Promissory Estoppel.
22. The Effect of Non-Compliance—Legal Consequences of the Unenforceable Agreement.
23. Oral Rescission.
24. Oral Modifications.
25. The Interaction of the Statute of Frauds with the Parol Evidence Rule.
26. The Interaction of the Statute of Frauds with the Remedy of Reformation.
27. Pleading and Procedural Problems in Connection with the Statute.
28. A Glance Backward and Ahead.

SECTION 1. INTRODUCTION

Under the Statute of Frauds, certain types of contracts are unenforceable against a party unless the contract is in writing, or evidenced by a writing (or, to use the terminology of the Statute, by a "memorandum") signed by the party to be charged, that is, the party sought to be held liable under the contract. (For ease of exposition, in the balance of this Appendix this requirement, where applicable, will be referred to simply as a requirement that a contract be in writing.) The purpose of this Appendix is to provide an introduction to problems that can arise under the Statute.

This Appendix is organized as follows: Sections 2–6 provide a general introduction to the Statute of Frauds. Sections 7–15 concern judicial interpretations of the provisions of the Statute that are most important in contract law (for example, provisions concerning contracts for the sale of an interest in land or for the sale of goods). The balance of this Appendix concerns exceptions to the Statute (that is, instances in which contracts of a type that are covered by the Statute are nevertheless enforceable in whole or in part even though not in writing) and miscellaneous problems, such as the interaction of the Statute of Frauds with certain other rules of other contract law.

This Appendix includes a number of Examples, in the form of hypothetical cases and their resolutions. The resolutions offered in the Examples are those that would normally be rendered in a typical American jurisdiction, although not necessarily in every jurisdiction.

A note on terminology: When a contract is of a type that is covered by the Statute, and is not in writing, the contract is said to be "within the Statute." However, when an exception to the Statute applies, the contract is said to be "taken out of the Statute" by virtue of the exception. Thus a contract that is within the Statute and is not in writing is unenforceable unless it is taken out of the Statute by an exception. If it is taken out of the Statute, the contract is enforceable although not in writing.

SECTION 2. THE TEXT OF THE ORIGINAL STATUTE

The original English Statute of Frauds was passed in 1677. Its title was "An Act for Prevention of Frauds and Perjuries." It contained twenty-five sections, and attempted to prevent fraud in the proof of many different kinds of legal transactions—not only in the area of contracts, but also in the areas of assignments, deeds to land, trusts, and wills. To insure a trustworthy memorial of what occurred, and thereby to prevent perjury, many sections of the Statute required a signed writing to make particular kinds of acts or transactions enforceable. In some cases an additional formality, such as attestation by witnesses, was required. In others, an alternative formality was permitted, such as providing that a will may be effectively revoked if it is canceled, torn, or obliterated by the testator or under his immediate direction. Certain sections of the Statute related to matters of procedure and land law that had only an indirect relation to the general object of the Statute.

The provisions of the original Statute that are chiefly relevant to contract law are Sections 4 and 17, reproduced below. In the balance of this Appendix, references to "the Statute of Frauds" or "the Statute" refer to those two sections and their modern counterparts. Spelling and punctuation have been modernized, and some liberties have been taken with the original in the paragraphing and numbering of subsections.

Section 4

And be it further enacted . . . that . . . no action shall be brought

> (1) whereby to charge any executor or administrator upon any special promise to answer damages out of his own estate; or

> (2) whereby to charge the defendant upon any special promise to answer for the debt, default or miscarriages of another person; or

> (3) to charge any person upon any agreement made upon consideration of marriage; or

> (4) upon any contract or sale of lands, tenements or hereditaments, or any interest in or concerning them; or

> (5) upon any agreement that is not to be performed within the space of one year from the making thereof;

unless the agreement upon which such action shall be brought, or some memorandum or note thereof, shall be in writing, and signed by the party to be charged therewith, or some other person thereunto by him lawfully authorized.

Section 17

[The "sale-of-goods" section]

And be it further enacted . . . that . . . no contract for the sale of any goods, wares or merchandises for the price of ten pounds sterling or upwards shall be allowed to be good, except

    (a) the buyer shall accept part of the goods so sold and actually receive the same; or

    (b) give something in earnest to bind the bargain or in part payment; or

    (c) that some note or memorandum in writing of the said bargain be made and signed by the parties to be charged by such contract or their agents thereunto lawfully authorized.

(Note that the Statute uses the terms "agreement" and "contract" interchangeably. The same usage will be followed in this Appendix.)

———

SECTION 3. THE PURPOSE OF THE STATUTE

Legislation that makes the enforceability of an act or transaction depend upon the observance of certain formalities may be adopted for a variety of reasons. In contract law, Austin discerned two principal reasons for requiring formalities: (1) "to provide evidence of the existence and purport of the contract, in case of controversy," and (2) "to prevent inconsiderate [not well-thought-through] engagements." J. Austin, Fragments—On Contracts, 2 Lectures on Jurisprudence 940 (4th ed., 1879).

Certainly the Statute of Frauds was intended to serve the first purpose. It was an act to prevent "frauds and perjuries," and stated in its preamble that it was aimed at "many fraudulent practices which are commonly endeavored to be upheld by perjury, and subornation of perjury." To handicap the plaintiff who might seek to establish a contract by perjured testimony, the Statute required him to base his case on a writing signed by the defendant. In this respect the purpose of the Statute was evidentiary. It sought a trustworthy memorial of the transaction and its terms.

On the other hand, it is clear that the Statute could also have had another purpose, that which Austin described as preventing "inconsiderate engagements." When a person is not bound unless and until she has signed a writing, a procedure has been established that will tend to prevent persons from slipping into legal undertakings without a full appreciation of what they are doing, because the writing may serve as a warning or deterrent against hasty action.

If the drafters of the Statute of Frauds had this second object in mind, they left no trace of it in the historical records of the time or in the language of the act they drew up. On the other hand, the judges who have interpreted the Statute have occasionally assumed that ensuring deliberation in the making of contracts was a collateral and secondary purpose of the Statute.

Thus in Warden v. Jones, 1857, 2 De.Gex & J. 76, 83–84, the court said, "The law has . . . wisely forbidden [oral proof of contracts in consideration of marriage]. Persons are so likely to be led into such promises inconsiderately, that the law has wisely required them to be manifested by writing." Expressions tending toward the same thought will be found in cases involving some other sections of the Statute, particularly the "suretyship" provision, section 4(2).

However, there are holdings that can only be justified on the view that the sole purpose of the Statute is to ensure reliable evidence of the contract. If the purpose of the Statute was to protect persons against hasty engagements, it would seem that the Statute could not be satisfied simply by a writing that repudiates the contract. Indeed, Restatement Second provides that in the case of a contract in consideration of marriage, "a subsequent writing does not satisfy the Statute unless made as a memorandum of the agreement," because "[t]he marriage provision . . . performs a cautionary function" as well as an evidentiary one. Restatement Second § 133, comment a. See also Restatement Second § 124, comment d. However, the general rule is that a writing that sets forth an earlier oral contract but repudiates the contract serves as a memorandum that satisfies the Statute. Restatement Second § 133.

Example No. 1:

As part of a land-development scheme, Susan Slide wanted to buy Blackacre, owned by Oliver Oakapple. Slide enters an agreement for the purchase of Blackacre for $40,000. This agreement is incorporated in an elaborate written contract, which Oakapple signs but Slide does not. When the development scheme collapses, Slide wishes to escape her obligation. Oakapple writes a letter to Slide reminding her of the contract, which he encloses, demanding performance. Slide returns the contract, with a letter that reads: "It is true that I entered an oral contract with you on the terms of the enclosed written document. However, the law requires that the contract or a memorandum of it be signed by the party to be charged therewith. You will note that I did not sign this contract, and therefore I am not bound by it. Hoping this incident will teach you some law, Yours truly, Susan Slide."

The decision will go for Oakapple. Slide has provided Oakapple with a signed memorandum of the contract, which will take the contract out of the Statute and permit a successful suit against her.

The conclusions in this Section may be summarized as follows: Everyone agrees that the primary purpose of the Statute of Frauds is to ensure reliable evidence of certain types of contracts on which suit is brought. Cases like *Example No. 1* indicate that the courts usually view the "memorandum" that is required by the Statute, in the absence of a written contract, not as a writing designed to warn a party against "inconsiderate engagements," but as a means of ensuring the existence of a contract and its terms. On the other hand, some cases discern, as a secondary purpose of the Statute, ensuring against hasty action, and this conception of the Statute may influence the interpretation of some of its provisions.

SECTION 4. HOW IT WAS DECIDED WHAT KINDS OF CONTRACTS SHOULD BE REQUIRED TO BE IN WRITING

The question addressed in this Section is, How did the drafters of the Statute of Frauds decide which contracts to include in their requirement of a writing and which to exclude? This question is closely related to that raised in the last Section, because we cannot know why the drafters included some contracts and left out others unless we know in general what objectives the drafters were trying to achieve.

Offhand, it might be thought that important and complex kinds of contracts would be covered by the Statute, and simple and unimportant kinds of contracts would not be. As applied to the modern business world, however, the Statute leaves out some very important and often complex kinds of contracts.

Example No. 2:

Bertram Builder and Teresa Turf enter an oral contract under which Builder promises to construct a commercial building according to certain plans and specifications, commencing work on January 1 and finishing by December 1, and Turf agrees to pay Builder $15 million for the job.

The enforceability of this oral agreement is unaffected by the Statute of Frauds, because it does not come within any of the Statute's sections. (If this seems hard to believe, read Sections 4 and 17 over again, which is a good idea at this point anyway.)

Example No. 3:

In the case supposed in *Example No. 2,* after the completion of the building, Turf enters into an agreement with the Rock of Ages Insurance Company, under which Rock of Ages insures the building for one year against fire in the amount of $15 million, and Turf agrees to pay a premium of $200,000.

This contract is also enforceable, although oral, because it too does not come within any of the Statute's sections.

If we were to attempt to retrace the actual mental processes of the drafters of the original Statute when they drew up their list, we would have to know much about the commercial and feudal practices of the time. We would also have to study closely the rules of procedure then prevailing, since the need for evidentiary safeguards in the proof of a particular type of transaction would depend in part on the procedural rules applied to suits founded on that transaction-type. Pursuing the same principle of inquiry, we would also have to ask similar questions about each American state when it adopted its Statute of Frauds, and decided either to accept the English original or to take the English Statute with certain changes or omissions. No one seriously contends that a scholarly inquiry of that sort would contribute much to a solution of the problem how the Statute ought to be construed today. A general analysis of the possible reasons for including the types of contracts that were enumerated in the original Statute may, however, be helpful.

Of contracts to sell land or any interests therein (section 4(4)), and of contracts "upon consideration of marriage" (section 4(3)), we can say that their inclusion is readily explained on the grounds that they are fairly important agreements, often rather complex in their terms. Contracts not to be performed within a year also look like important contracts, proof of which may require witnesses to stretch their memories over an uncomfortably long period if there is no written evidence of the contract. Similarly, Section 17, the sales-of-goods provision, explicitly made the importance of the contract, as measured in monetary terms, the test of whether a writing was required.

It is harder to explain why sections 4(1) and 4(2) were included. In general, these two sections mean that where a person is to be held as a surety or guarantor for another, she can only be charged on a writing that she has signed. (Section 4(1) covers the special case of an executor or administrator who undertakes to be surety on a debt of the deceased for which the estate is liable. See Section 14 of this Appendix.) A contract of suretyship is usually not a complicated contract; it generally amounts in effect to saying, "If he doesn't pay or perform, I will." On the other hand, the very simplicity of the agreement, and its vital importance to the surety, who often acts without compensation, may be a reason for taking steps to guard against perjury. In civil-law countries, provisions requiring the undertaking of a surety to be in writing are generally interpreted to have a cautionary purpose, on the theory that people are often drawn into becoming sureties without a full appreciation of what they are doing. There are occasional intimations of a similar view in discussions of the English Statute of Frauds or its American counterparts. Whatever intention the draftsmen of the original Statute may have harbored, it is certainly true that some of the judicial interpretations of the suretyship section would be easier to understand if we were free to assume that it had a cautionary or deterrent purpose. (See Section 12 of this Appendix.)

SECTION 5. AMERICAN VARIATIONS ON THE ENGLISH THEME

Ambit. All the American states except Louisiana, Maryland, and New Mexico copied Section 4 of the English Statute of Frauds, and in Maryland and New Mexico the Statute of Frauds is in force by judicial decision. See Restatement Second, ch. 5, Statutory Note. Some states originally omitted Section 17 from their Statutes of Frauds, but the substance of Section 17 was later incorporated in the Uniform Commercial Code. Other states have in a very few instances left out particular provisions of Section 4 of the original Statute, or more commonly have extended the requirement of a writing to transactions not included in the English Statute. One common extension requires a suit to recover a real estate broker's commission to be founded on a written agreement. A contract to make a will is sometimes required to be in writing. Many statutes require a promise to pay certain types of barred or discharged debts to be in writing.

Phraseology. Sometimes American enactments of the original statute introduce minor changes in phraseology. For example, instead of saying "no action shall be brought" on a specified type of oral contract (section 4 of the English Statute), or that the oral contract shall not "be allowed to be good" (section 17 of the English Statute), a Statute of Frauds may simply say that oral contracts of certain types shall be "void." Though the word "void" is probably not to be taken in a literal sense, its use may have some influence in the application of a Statute of Frauds. (See Section 22 of this Appendix.)

Another change sometimes introduced in American Statutes of Frauds is to say that "the contract" must be in writing, instead of following the language of the English Statute, which requires only that "the agreement" or "some memorandum or note thereof" be in writing. This change may be significant as destroying the efficacy of a memorandum executed for some purpose other than that of serving as a statement of the agreement. (See *Example No. 1.* Slide's letter is perhaps a memorandum of the agreement; it is certainly not "the contract.")

SECTION 6. JUDICIAL INTERPRETATIONS OF THE VARIOUS SUBSECTIONS OF THE STATUTE OF FRAUDS—INTRODUCTION

The best general guide to the judicial interpretation of the Statute of Frauds is to remember this simple truth: The courts have not favored the Statute of Frauds. Generally—although certainly not invariably—whenever the words of the Statute leave any leeway (and often when they do not), the courts have restricted its meaning and found ways of making an oral agreement enforceable.

Example No. 4:

Sally Smooth and Plastic Age, Inc., enter a written contract whereby Smooth is to work for Plastic Age for five years as Personnel Manager, at a salary of $30,000 a year. After Smooth has been on the job for one month, the parties orally rescind the contract and release each other from it. The next day Smooth repents of her decision and insists on her rights under the written contract. Her attorney argues as follows: This contract of employment fell within Section 4(5) of the Statute of Frauds, because it was not to be performed within one year from the time it was made. The Statute requires that the creation of such a contract be evidenced by a writing, and it is only logical that the same formality should be required for its rescission.

The decision would go for Plastic Age. The Statute of Frauds does not explicitly address the question of rescission, and as a general proposition rescission does not fall within the Statute, on the theory that a rescission does not call for the performance of any duties. (For exceptions to this proposition, see Section 23 of this Appendix.)

———

SECTION 7. CONTRACTS FOR THE SALE OF AN INTEREST IN LAND (SECTION 4(4))

Section 4(4) covers broadly and somewhat verbosely contracts for the sale of any kind of interest in land. The price, value, or extent of the interest is immaterial.

Example No. 5:

Jim Joad orally agrees with Jane Jukes that he will sell her his eroded tract, Redacre, for ten cents. The contract is within section 4(4) of the Statute of Frauds.

Test. In determining what constitutes an interest in land for purposes of the Statute of Frauds, the test applied is generally that furnished by the law of property. Restatement Second § 127.

Example No. 6:

To obtain a shortcut from his farm to the highway, Paul Pass wants the right to drive through Bilbo Block's land. The parties orally agree that in consideration of the payment of $1000, Pass shall have that right during his life. This contract falls within Section 4(4), because it is a contract for the sale of an interest in land. If the parties had called in a lawyer to draw up the papers for their transaction, the lawyer would have treated this right as an "easement," a familiar heading in books dealing with interests in land.

Example No. 7:

Richard Rocksie, a theatre proprietor, who owns his theatre and the land on which it rests, orally agrees with Julia Roberts that if she will attend the theater's opening night, he will give her a pass, good for life, to sit in seat F11, sixth-row center, for all future performances.

This contract is not within section 4(4). The right to sit in a certain seat during a theatrical performance would not be viewed generally as an interest in the land. No lawyer with a sense of linguistic proprieties would call this right an "easement."

Conveyances. The language of section 4(4) speaks of "any contract *or* sale" of lands. One might assume that this covers either a contract *to* convey, or a *present* conveyance by way of sale. Actually, however, present conveyances are covered by the first three sections of the Statute of Frauds, which have not been reproduced in this Appendix. Accordingly, it is safe to assume that despite its language, section 4(4) really means any contract for the sale of an interest in land, with the qualification that the term "contract or sale of lands . . . or any interest concerning them" is used here in a broad sense that includes contracts to devise land by will or to exchange land for something other than money, as well as the more common contract to convey land by deed in return for an agreed money price. (Restatement Second § 125, comments a, c, and Illustrations.)

Leases. In very general terms, the first three Sections of the original Statute state that a writing is necessary to create or transfer an interest in land, except that a tenancy at will and, under certain conditions, a lease not to exceed three years, may be created orally. The substance of these provisions is very generally carried over into American Statutes of Frauds, but the exception for oral short-term leases is usually reduced to either one year or two years.

SECTION 8. CONTRACTS FOR THE SALE OF GOODS

The basic provision. In this country, Section 17 of the Statute of Frauds (the sale-of-goods section) was eventually succeeded by UCC § 2–201:

§ 2–201. Formal Requirements; Statute of Frauds

(1) Except as otherwise provided in this section a contract for the sale of goods for the price of $500 or more is not enforceable by way of action or defense unless there is some writing sufficient to indicate that a contract for sale has been made between the parties and signed by the party against whom enforcement is sought or by his authorized agent or broker. A writing is not insufficient because it omits or incorrectly states a term agreed upon but the contract is not enforceable under this paragraph beyond the quantity of goods shown in such writing.

(2) Between merchants if within a reasonable time a writing in confirmation of the contract and sufficient against the sender is received and the party receiving it has reason to know its contents, it satisfies the requirements of subsection (1) against such party unless written notice of objection to its contents is given within 10 days after it is received.

(3) A contract which does not satisfy the requirements of subsection (1) but which is valid in other respects is enforceable

(a) if the goods are to be specially manufactured for the buyer and are not suitable for sale to others in the ordinary course of the seller's business and the seller, before notice of repudiation is received and under circumstances which reasonably indicate that the goods are for the buyer, has made either a substantial beginning of their manufacture or commitments for their procurement; or

(b) if the party against whom enforcement is sought admits in his pleading, testimony or otherwise in court that a contract for sale was made, but the contract is not enforceable under this provision beyond the quantity of goods admitted; or

(c) with respect to goods for which payment has been made and accepted or which have been received and accepted. . . .

Three points are worth noting at the outset.

First, UCC § 2–201 (1) relates only to the sale of "goods"—that is, physical property other than realty, or what the comment to the UCC calls "movables." It does not include sales of "choses in action" or other intangibles.

Second, the writing required by UCC § 2–201 (1) need only be "sufficient to indicate that a contract for sale has been made between the parties." There is no requirement that the writing either specify the kind of goods involved or state the price. Curiously, there is not even a requirement that the quantity of goods sold be stated, but this apparent looseness is illusory, because subsection (1) provides that "the contract is not enforceable . . . beyond the quantity of goods shown in such writing." Accordingly, if no quantity is shown the extent of enforcement is zero; if the oral agreement was for 1000 units, while the writing says 500 units, the contract is enforceable only to the extent of 500 units. (The UCC does not itself deal with the possibility of reforming the writing to correct a mistake. Presumably, if both parties intended the writing to state 1000 units, a court might in a proper case reform the memorandum, which then would become enforceable to the extent of 1000 units. See Section 25 of this Appendix.)

Third, UCC § 2–201 applies only if the price is $500 or more. However, if the price is $500 or more, and § 2–201 is not satisfied, the entire contract (not merely that portion of the contract in excess of $500) is unenforceable.

Exceptions. As indicated by introductory clause to UCC § 2–201, the basic requirement of section 2–201(1) is subject to several exceptions.

Part performance. Subsection (3)(c) provides that "A contract which does not satisfy the requirements of [section 2–201 (1)] but which is valid in other respects is enforceable . . . with respect to goods for which payment has been made and accepted or which have been received and accepted. . . . " Even in the absence of subsection (3)(c), if a buyer has accepted goods she would be liable for the value of the goods under the law of unjust enrichment. See Section 19 of this Appendix. The significance of subsection (3)(c) is that if seller sues under the law of unjust enrichment, he would be entitled to recover only the value of the goods at the time they were accepted by the buyer. In contrast, under subsection (3)(c) the seller can recover the contract price of the accepted goods.

Goods made specially to order. Suppose a patient orders a dental bridge from his dentist and orally agrees to pay a price of $2000. The dentist faithfully prepares the bridge to fit the patient's teeth, but when the time comes for installation of the bridge, the patient refuses to pay for it or to receive and accept it. If this contract was held to be a contract for the sale of goods, and unenforceable unless in writing, a serious injustice would be done to the dentist, who will obviously have some difficulty finding a market for the bridge that the patient rejected. Subsection (3)(a) deals with this problem by providing that "A contract which does not satisfy the requirements of [§ 2–201 (1)] but which is valid in other respects is enforceable . . . if [i] the goods are to be specially manufactured for the buyer and [ii] are not suitable for sale to others in the ordinary course of the seller's business and [iii] the seller, before notice of repudiation is received and under circumstances which reasonably indicate that the goods are for the buyer, has made either a substantial beginning of their manufacture or commitments for their procurement. . . . " (Subdivisions inserted by ed.)

Receipt of confirmation. Subsection (2) adds another exception to the requirement of a writing for a contract for the sale of goods, based upon modern methods of contracting. That subsection provides, "Between merchants if within a reasonable time a writing in confirmation of the contract and sufficient against the sender is received and the party receiving it has reason to know its contents, it satisfies the requirements of [§ 2–201 (1)] against such party unless written notice of objection to its contents is given within 10 days after it is received." Note that subsection (2) is confined to transactions between merchants. (For the UCC definition of "merchant," see UCC § 2–104(1).)

Admissions. Subsection (3)(b) provides that "A contract which does not satisfy the requirements of [§ 2–201 (1)] but which is valid in other respects is enforceable . . . if the party against whom enforcement is sought admits in his pleading, testimony or otherwise in court that a contract for sale was made, but the contract is not enforceable under this provision beyond the quantity of goods admitted. . . . " The weight of authority is that the admission may be involuntary as well as voluntary. Accordingly, under subsection 3(b) a plaintiff can bring suit on an oral contract and then try to make the defendant admit, in discovery proceedings or on cross-examination, that the oral contract was in fact made. Indeed, there is much authority that where a complaint is based on an oral contract for the sale of goods it should ordinarily not be dismissed on motion before the plaintiff has had the chance to depose the defendant, because the plaintiff should have an opportunity to elicit such an admission. See, e.g., ALA, Inc. v. CCAIR, Inc., 29 F.3d 855 (3d Cir. 1994) (decided under an analogous statute); Theta Products, Inc. v. Zippo Mfg. Co., 81 F. Supp. 2d 346 (D.R.I. 1999). This is as it should be. The Statute of Frauds is designed to protect against the danger that a plaintiff may, by perjury, establish a contract to the jury's satisfaction where there was no contract in fact. If the defendant *admits* the contract existed, the purpose of the Statute is satisfied. As stated in the *ALA* case:

> In order for [the admissions exception] to function, the plaintiff must have some opportunity to obtain an admission from the defendant. A Rule 12(b)(6) motion [for failure to state a claim on which relief can be granted], however, would derail the plaintiff's case pre-pleading and allow the defendant to defeat a cause of action on an oral contract before the plaintiff has any opportunity to seek an admission that a contract existed. Allowing a defendant

to dispose of a case on a Rule 12(b)(6) motion would eviscerate [the admissions exception] and potentially allow a defendant to avoid the obligations of an oral contract into which he or she actually entered.*

The following two Examples illustrate some of the problems of interpretation raised by UCC § 2–201:

Example No. 8:

Seller and Buyer enter an oral contract whereby Seller is to deliver 12,000 widgets over a twelve months' period, in twelve shipments of 1000 each. The agreed price is $1 per widget. The first ten shipments are accepted and paid for. After the eleventh shipment has been accepted, but before it has been paid for, Buyer repudiates the contract, refusing to pay for the eleventh shipment, and stating that he will not accept the final shipment for the twelfth month. Seller sues to recover $1000 due for the eleventh shipment and damages of $400 for Buyer's refusal to accept the final shipment. Buyer pleads UCC § 2–201 as a defense.

The cases would be resolved as follows: The contract involves the sale of goods, and therefore comes within § 2–201. The successive deliveries and payments made before Buyer repudiated the agreement do not take the entire contract out of the Statute, but only those deliveries and payments. Since Buyer has already paid for the first ten shipments, Seller is entitled to the price of the eleventh shipment—$1000. Seller cannot recover $400 as damages for Buyer's refusal to take the final delivery. Although the $400 in damages that Seller seeks is less than the $500 figure in § 2–201, that figure relates not to the amount of damages but to the total price set in the contract, which in this case was $12,000.

---

*   However, in DF Activities Corp. v. Brown, 851 F.2d 920 (7th Cir.1988), the court held that suit on an oral contact could be dismissed on summary judgement where the defendant by sworn affidavit denied that she ever agreed to sell the goods in question (a Frank Lloyd Wright chair) to the plaintiff:

"... When there is a bare motion to dismiss, or an answer, with no evidentiary materials, the possibility remains a live one that, if asked under oath whether a contract had been made, the defendant would admit it had been. The only way to test the proposition is for the plaintiff to take the defendant's deposition, or, if there is no discovery, to call the defendant as an adverse witness at trial. But where as in this case the defendant swears in an affidavit that there was no contract, we see no point in keeping the lawsuit alive. Of course the defendant may blurt out an admission in a deposition, but this is hardly likely, especially since by doing so he may be admitting to having perjured himself in his affidavit. Stranger things have happened, but remote possibilities do not warrant subjecting the parties and the judiciary to proceedings almost certain to be futile." (Footnote by ed.)

Example No. 9:

Seller and Buyer orally agree that Seller will deliver her used Camry to Buyer next Monday for an agreed price of $5000. Buyer pays Seller $500 with a promise to pay the remaining $4500 when the car is delivered. When Monday comes, Seller refuses to go through with the oral bargain. Buyer sues for damages.

Because a sale of goods is involved, the applicable provision is UCC § 2–201. According to subsection (3)(c), Buyer's rights are limited to the "goods for which payment has been made." This seems to suggest that Buyer is entitled to $500 worth of automobile. The cases are not unanimous, but under the weight of authority a down payment on an indivisible unit makes the entire contract enforceable, on the ground that the payment evidences the contract and identifies the party to be charged, and that in such cases there is no room for a dispute over quantity. White & Summers state: "Some courts have had to consider whether a down payment on a single nondivisible unit . . . indicates a contract and permits the party making the payment to prove and recover in full on his oral contract. A court might say that 2–201(3)(c) is not satisfied, because payment must be made in full with respect to the single unit. Williamson v. Martz, [11 Pa.D. & C.2d 33 (1958)], a Pennsylvania lower court case, so held. Other courts (correctly, in our opinion) have gone the other way. Lockwood v. Smigel [18 Cal.App.3d 800, 96 Cal.Rptr. 289 (1971)] is illustrative. There the court held that a $100 down payment on an $11,000 Rolls Royce brought 2–201(3)(c) into play and permitted the seller to try to prove his oral contract for the whole." J. White & R. Summers, Uniform Commercial Code § 2–5 (5th ed. 2000).

The CISG. So far, we have been dealing only with the provisions of the UCC that concern when a contract for the sale of goods must be in writing. Many international contracts for the sale of goods are governed by the CISG (Convention for the International Sale of Goods) rather than the UCC. Article 11 of the CISG provides that "A contract of sale need not be concluded in or evidenced by writing and is not subject to any other requirement as to form." See Dodge, Teaching the CISG in Contracts, 50 J. Leg. Ed. 72 (2000).

Amendments to the official version of UCC section 2–201. In 2003, the National Conference of Commissioners on State Laws and the American Law Institute, who are jointly responsible for promulgating and amending the Uniform Commercial Code, adopted a number of amendments to the official version of Article 2 of the Code. One of the amended sections is 2–201. Some of the amendments to this section are technical, but two are substantive. First, the threshold amount under section 2–201(1) is increased from $500 to $5,000. Second, a new subsection (4) provides, "A contract that is enforceable under this section is not unenforceable merely because it is not capable of being performed within one year or any other period after its making." As of early 2006, however, no state legislature has adopted the amended version of Article 2. Accordingly, the pre-2003 version of section 2–201 remains the governing law.

————

SECTION 9. SOME OTHER FORMAL REQUIREMENTS IN THE UNIFORM COMMERCIAL CODE

The UCC has several other provisions that bear on the requirement of a writing. In particular:

1. UCC § 9–203 provides that security interests in most types of collateral that are already not in the creditor's possession are enforceable only if described in a security agreement that is authenticated by the debtor.

2. UCC § 8–113 provides that "A contract or modification of a contract for the sale or purchase of a security is enforceable whether or not there is a writing signed or record authenticated by a party against whom enforcement is sought, even if the contract or modification is not capable of performance within one year of its making."

3. UCC § 1–206 ("Statute of Frauds for Kinds of Personal Property Not Otherwise Covered") provides:

(1) Except in the cases described in subsection (2) of this section a contract for the sale of personal property is not enforceable by way of action or defense beyond five thousand dollars in amount or value of remedy unless there is some writing which indicates that a contract for sale has been made between the parties at a defined or stated price, reasonably identifies the subject matter, and is signed by the party against whom enforcement is sought or by his authorized agent.

(2) Subsection (1) of this section does not apply to contracts for the sale of goods (Section 2–201) nor of securities (Section 8–113) nor of security agreements (Section 9–203).

Note that no matter how great is the price, UCC § 1–206 is only applicable if the value of the *remedy* is $5,000 or more.

In 2005, the National Conference of Commissioners on Uniform State Laws and the American Law Institute promulgated a revised version of Article 1 ("Revised Article 1"). Revised Article 1 drops section 1–206. A Legislative Note to Revised Article 1 explains the reasons for dropping section 1–206 as follows:

Former Section 1–206, a Statute of Frauds for sales of "kinds of personal property not otherwise covered," has been deleted. The other articles of the Uniform Commercial Code make individual determinations as to requirements for memorializing transactions within their scope, so that the primary effect of former Section 1–206 was to impose a writing requirement on sales transactions not otherwise governed by the UCC. Deletion of former Section 1–206 does not constitute a recommendation to legislatures as to whether such sales transactions should be covered by a Statute of Frauds; rather, it reflects a determination that there is no need for uniform commercial law to resolve that issue.

As of early 2006, only sixteen states have adopted the revised version of Article 1, so that in most states section 1–206 remains the law.

SECTION 10. AGREEMENTS NOT TO BE PERFORMED WITHIN ONE YEAR FROM THE MAKING THEREOF (SECTION 4(5))

Section 4(5) of the Statute of Frauds concerns actions "upon any agreement that is not to be performed within the space of one year from the making thereof."

To the casual reader, the language of section 4(5) contains no warning of the interpretation the courts have put on this section. It will be easier to understand this interpretation if one considers first the problem that faced courts that had to apply the section.

There was no mystery about the reason for requiring a signed writing in the case of a contract not to be performed within one year; in Holt's words, "the design of the statute was, not to trust to the memory of witnesses for a longer time than one year." Smith v. Westall, 1697, 1 Lord Raymond 317. The trouble lay, not in any obscurity of purpose, but in a failure to provide an apt means for effectuating that purpose.

In the first place, there is no direct relation between the time when a witness may be called to testify and the time that is required to perform the contract; a contract might be scheduled for completion within one month and yet first come into proof in court two years later. Furthermore, the drafters failed to ask themselves what should be done in the case of a contract as to which it is impossible to say in advance how much time its performance will require. For example, the performance of a contract to support A for life might be completed within a month if A died so soon, or might on the other hand stretch over decades if A were sufficiently long-lived. In a case coming up for decision shortly after the Statute was enacted, it was suggested that the validity of the contract should depend on the actual course of events. (Smith v. Westall, supra.) But this solution was never accepted, and could not be. Parties need to know from the outset, or at least as soon as trouble develops, whether they have a contract. To make the existence of a binding contract depend upon later events would invite all kinds of jockeying for position and produce an intolerable confusion.

The courts were, then, confronted with a statute that simply could not be applied in a way to carry out the likely conceived intention of its drafters. One stab at a solution that easily comes to mind is to measure expected duration for performance according to the expectation of the parties when they entered the contract. There are, in fact, a few cases that speak as if this were the governing principle, but this way out is scarcely acceptable. Where the time that will be required for performance is uncertain, there is usually no reason to suppose that the parties have made some calculation of probabilities and have in their minds some expected duration, such as six months or five years. Where a contract requires that A be supported for the rest of his life, the parties do not know how long A will live, and know that they do not know.

Accordingly, most courts have said that the applicability of Section 4(5) depends not on what actually happens, or on what the parties thought would happen, but on what *could have* happened. When the contract was entered, was there any *possibility* that it could have been performed within a year? If so, it is not within the Statute and is therefore enforceable although oral. Restatement Second § 130. As stated by Chief Justice Peters in C.R. Klewin, Inc. v. Flagship Properties, Inc., 220 Conn. 569, 600 A.2d 772 (1991):

> . . . [The] issue can be framed as follows: in the exclusion from the statute of frauds of all contracts except those "whose performance cannot possibly be completed within a year" . . . what meaning should be attributed to the word "possibly"? One construction of "possibly" would encompass only contracts whose completion within a year would be inconsistent with the express terms of the contract. An alternate construction would include as well contracts . . . in which, while no time period is expressly specified, it is . . . realistically impossible for performance to be completed within a year. We now hold that the former and not the latter is the correct interpretation. "The critical test . . . is whether 'by its terms' the agreement is not to be performed within a year, so that the statute will not apply where "the alleged agreement contain[s] [no] provision which directly or indirectly regulated the time for performance." Freedman v. Chemical Construction Corporation, 43 N.Y.2d 260, 265, 372 N.E.2d 12, 401 N.Y.S.2d 176 (1977). "It is the law of this state, as it is elsewhere, that a contract is not within this clause of the statute unless its terms are so

drawn that it cannot by any possibility be performed fully within one year." (Emphasis added.) Burkle v. Superflow Mfg. Co., . . . 137 Conn. at 492, 78 A.2d 698. . . .

We therefore hold that an oral contract that does not say, in express terms, that performance is to have a specific duration beyond one year is, as a matter of law. . . . enforceable because it is outside the prescriptive force of the statute regardless of how long completion of performance will actually take.

Similarly, in Freedman v. Chemical Construction Corp., 372 N.E.2d 12 (N.Y. 1977), the court said: "Subdivision 1 [of the Statute of Frauds] renders unenforceable an oral agreement which '(b)y its terms is not to be performed within one year from the making thereof.' True, as Chemical asserts, it was unlikely that Freedman's efforts to obtain the construction contract and Chemical's payment, due only upon completion of the plant, would occur within one year. In fact, Freedman admits it took over three years for his own performance and another six until the plant was built. It matters not, however, that it was unlikely or improbable that a $41 million plant would be constructed within one year. The critical test, instead, is whether 'by its terms' the agreement is not to be performed within a year. . . Since neither party has contended that the alleged agreement contained any provision which directly or indirectly regulated the time for performance, the agreement is not within the bar of subdivision 1."

Under this rule, an oral agreement to hire A for life is not within the Statute of Frauds, because there is a possibility that the agreement can be performed within a year through the death of A within that time. It is immaterial that in fact A lives and works on the job for twenty years. If A is then discharged, he can base a suit against the employer on proof of the oral agreement made years before, when he accepted employment. (*Warning.* In some states it is specifically provided that a contract that is not to be completed before the end of a lifetime *is* within the Statute. A few cases reach the same result. See, e.g., McInerney v. Charter Golf, Inc., 176 Ill.2d 482, 680 N.E.2d 1347 (1997), where the court so held over a vigorous dissent.)

What shall be said of a contract to employ A for ten years? Shall we say that such a contract is not within the Statute of Frauds because it would have been dissolved by the death of either party, and therefore might have been ended within the first year? The difficulty is that if this line of reasoning was accepted, it would be hard to find any contract to which the one-year provision would apply. In the case of almost any contract it is possible to imagine some cataclysmic event that might occur during the first year, preventing performance and excusing the parties from their obligations. Accordingly, the courts have generally distinguished between the time in which performance can possibly occur, on the one hand, and discharge or excuse from performance, on the other. Restatement Second § 130. On this basis, an agreement to hire an octogenarian for thirteen months is within the Statute of Frauds, and therefore unenforceable unless in writing, while an agreement to hire a healthy young person of twenty-one for life is not within the Statute, and therefore enforceable although oral. (Suppose the stated term of a contract is more than a year, but one or both parties are explicitly given the right to terminate the contract on three months' notice. Is the contract within the Statute? The cases are divided.)

The one-year provision has been heavily criticized in recent years. A good example is the decision of Judge Peters in *C.R. Klewin, supra*:

> Modern scholarly commentary has found much to criticize about the continued viability of the statute of frauds. The statute has been found wanting because it serves none of its purported functions very well; ... and because it permits or compels economically wasteful behavior. ... It is, however, the one-year provision ... that has caused the greatest puzzlement among commentators. As Professor Farnsworth observes, "of all the provisions of the statute, it is the most difficult to rationalize.
>
> > "If the one-year provision is based on the tendency of memory to fail and of evidence to go stale with the passage of time, it is ill-contrived because the one-year period does not run from the making of the contract to the proof of the making, but from the making of the contract to the completion of performance. If an oral contract that cannot be performed within a year is broken the day after its making, the provision applies though the terms of the contract are fresh in the minds of the parties. But if an oral contract that can be performed within a year is broken and suit is not brought until nearly six years (the usual statute of limitations for contract actions) after the breach, the provision does not apply, even though the terms of the contract are no longer fresh in the minds of the parties.
> >
> > "If the one-year provision is an attempt to separate significant contracts of long duration, for which writings should be required, from less significant contracts of short duration, for which writings are unnecessary, it is equally ill-contrived because the one-year period does not run from the commencement of performance to the completion of performance, but from the making of the contract to the completion of performance. If an oral contract to work for one day, 13 months from now, is broken, the provision applies, even though the duration of performance is only one day. But if an oral contract to work for a year beginning today is

broken, the provision does not apply, even though the duration of performance is a full year." 2 E. Farnsworth, Contracts (2d Ed.1990) § 6.4, pp. 110–11 (footnotes omitted). . . .

Historians have had difficulty accounting for the original inclusion of the one-year provision. Some years after its enactment, one English judge stated that "the design of the statute was, not to trust to the memory of witnesses for a longer time than one year." Smith v. Westall, 1 Ld.Raym. 316, 317, 91 Eng.Rep. 1106, 1107 (1697). That explanation is, however, unpersuasive, since, as Farnsworth notes, the language of the statute is ill suited to this purpose. One eminent historian suggested that because such contracts are continuing contracts, it might be very difficult to give evidence of their formation, inasmuch as the rules of evidence of that time prohibited testimony by the parties to an action or any person who had an interest in the litigation. 6 W. Holdsworth, [A History of English Law, p.] 392. That argument, however, proves too much, since it would apply equally to all oral contracts regardless of the duration of their performance. The most extensive recent study of the history of English contract law offers plausible explanations for all of the other provisions, but acknowledges that this one is "curious." A. Simpson, A History of the Common Law of Contract (1975) p. 612. . . .

In any case, the one-year provision no longer seems to serve any purpose very well, and today its only remaining effect is arbitrarily to forestall the adjudication of possibly meritorious claims. For this reason, the courts have for many years looked on the provision with disfavor, and have sought constructions that limited its application. . . .

SECTION 11.   THE SURETYSHIP SECTION (SECTION 4(2))—GENERALLY

Section 4(2) of the Statute of Frauds concerns actions "whereby to charge the defendant upon any special promise to answer for the debt, default or miscarriages of another person."

It is not easy to know just what the scope of section 4(2) was originally intended to be. There are many situations in which a person may, in varying degrees and under varying conditions, be bound to "answer for" another. The courts have construed this section so that a person does not "answer for" another within the meaning of the section unless his oral promise places him in the position of a surety or guarantor of the obligation of another person. Restatement Second § 112. A *surety* is a person who is liable for a debt or other obligation that a second person, the *principal,* owes to a third person, the *creditor,* in cases where the principal is primarily liable for the debt or obligation. In such cases, both the principal and the surety owe the same debt, or have the duty to perform the same obligation, and the creditor can sue either the principal or the surety if the principal defaults. However, the principal's obligation is primary, so that if the surety is forced to pay the debt or perform the obligation, she can sue the principal for indemnification.

Suretyship is often used to afford security to a creditor. For example, suppose Peter Prince wishes to borrow from Marvin Moneypenny, but Prince's credit is weak. Prince may then not only promise to repay the loan herself, but may also get Angela Answer, whose credit is stronger, to promise Moneypenny that she will repay the loan if Prince does not. Answer is then a surety for Prince's debt.

If a promisor is a surety or guarantor, then under section 4(2) the nature of the guaranteed obligation is not material. Thus an oral promise to answer for another's obligation that is based on a tort comes within the broad language that speaks of "the debt, default or miscarriages of another." Restatement Second § 112. But for the suretyship provision to be applicable, the other person must be under some obligation to the creditor, although even an imperfect obligation may suffice. See Section 13 of this Appendix.

Example No. 10:

Richard Rash buys a $100 suit from a tailor. Though he has no real or apparent authority from his uncle to charge the suit to him, Rash says to the tailor, "Charge the suit to my uncle, Milton Means. I will answer for him if he doesn't pay." Rash's promise is not within the Statute of Frauds, and is therefore enforceable although oral, because Means is under no obligation to the tailor, so that Rash is not the surety of another.

SECTION 12.   THE SURETYSHIP SECTION CONTINUED—"THE MAIN PURPOSE RULE"

It will be convenient to start this Section with a hypothetical case.

Example No. 11:

Manley Minus owes Charley Claim $1,000. Minus gives Claim a mortgage on Blackacre to secure his debt. Thereafter, Minus conveys Blackacre to Paula Owne, subject to the mortgage.

Owne does not assume Minus's obligation to pay off the mortgage. However, Minus promises Owne that he will pay off the mortgage and thereby release the mortgage lien on Blackacre. Minus fails to do so, and Claim brings a suit to foreclose the mortgage. To save her land, Owne orally promises Claim that if Claim will discontinue the suit, she, Owne, will stand in back of Minus's debt. Claim discontinues the suit but Owne refuses to honor her promise. When Claim sues Owne on the oral agreement, Owne pleads the Statute of Frauds, asserting that her promise to Claim was a promise to answer for the debt of another, namely, Minus.

A well-established line of authorities would hold that Owne's promise is not within the Statute, so that it is enforceable although oral. Although it is possible to predict with considerable assurance that *Example No. 11* would generally be decided as indicated, it is difficult to find any justification for the result in the language of the Statute.

If the Statute concerns an oral promise that makes the promisor a surety, Pawn is clearly becoming a surety for Minus. The only difference between Pawn's case and the usual case is that in making the promise Pawn was advancing her own interest by freeing her land from the threat of foreclosure.

If it were not for certain embarrassments that will be discussed in a minute, it might be possible to construct a rationale for the decision reached in cases like *Example No. 11* along the following lines: The suretyship provision of the Statute of Frauds is intended to perform a cautionary or deterrent function. The legislators were thinking of the typical victim of family or sentimental pressures, who says to the creditor, "Advance $1000 to my niece and I will see that it is paid," and who receives no financial advantage from the transaction. It was the legislators' intention to erect a legal safeguard on generous impulses. This section of the Statute is therefore inapplicable when the promisor undertakes to be surety to advance some business advantage of her own.

This simple explanation runs into two inconvenient facts: (1) It is generally assumed that the formalities prescribed by the Statute of Frauds normally serve an *evidentiary* rather than a *cautionary* purpose. (2) Although there is little case law on the subject, and that divided, it is generally asserted that the receipt of a monetary premium by a surety for undertaking the risk does not take the surety's oral promise out of the Statute, although a surety who receives such a premium is obviously making the promise to advance its own interests. See Restatement Second § 116.

The result is that in cases like *Example No. 11* we have a judicially established exception to the suretyship section whose rationale is doubtful.

Since the underlying basis for the exception is obscure, it is difficult to know just what its scope is. It has often been called "the main purpose rule," meaning that exception applies when the main purpose of the surety is to serve a pecuniary interest of her own. According to Restatement Second § 116, the question is whether the consideration given for the promise of the surety "is in fact or apparently desired by the promisor mainly for his own economic advantage, rather than in order to benefit the third person." However, the Restatement excepts from the exception—and thereby renders unenforceable—an oral promise (typically made by a guaranty company) to answer for the obligation of another where the consideration given the surety consists simply of a premium.

The "main purpose rule" is applied chiefly to two types of cases: (1) Those like *Example No. 11*, where the promisor is willing to become surety in order to save her own property from the assertion of a lien that secures the debtor's obligation. (2) Those in which the promisor, who steps forward as surety, has a pecuniary interest in the debtor's affairs and wishes to procure a breathing spell for him. The promisor may have a pecuniary interest in the debtor's affairs, and a corresponding interest in staving off suit by the creditor against the debtor, because she is herself a creditor; or because she is a shareholder in a debtor-corporation; or because the debtor is under contract to construct a building for her, the completion of which she does not want impeded; or for a great variety of other reasons. See Restatement Second § 116, illustrations.

———

SECTION 13. THE SURETYSHIP SECTION CONTINUED—MISCELLANEOUS PROBLEMS

The account just concluded covers the major surprises to be encountered in the judicial interpretation of Section 4(2). It omits several disputed issues that are mentioned briefly below.

1. A promise is within section 4(2) only if it is made *to the creditor*. If Prince is indebted to Moneypenny, and Answer promises *Prince* that she will pay off Prince's debt, the promise is not within the Statute, and is therefore enforceable although oral.

2. Often, a creditor deals with two or more persons without knowing what their internal relationship is. For example, Moneypenny may negotiate primarily with Prince, but at some stage of the negotiations, either at the outset or later, Answer come in alongside Prince as a person obligated on the agreement. Moneypenny may not know whether the funds that he is furnishing are to be used by Prince and Answer in some common venture, or whether one of the parties is merely lending his or her name and credit to the other. If the relationship of Prince and Answer to one

another is such that Answer is surety and Prince is principal debtor, then the oral promise of Answer is within section 4(2) if, but only if, Moneypenny knew or had reason to know of Answer's true position. Restatement Second §§ 112–113.

3. Even though Moneypenny knows in such a case that Answer is a surety, there is one situation where Answer may be held on her oral promise. This situation is illustrated by the case where Moneypenny renders services to Prince, and charges the services, with Answer's consent, to Answer and Prince as if they were jointly purchasing the services. Here, even though Moneypenny knows that Answer is lending her credit to Prince, it has been held that since Answer and Prince become joint debtors, Section 4(2) does not apply, and Answer is liable on her oral promise. Restatement Second § 113. (Since this rule is applicable only where the debt is joint, rather than either several or joint and several, the possibility of holding Answer on her oral promise may be affected by statutes, adopted in many states, that convert joint obligations into joint and several obligations.)

4. The principle that section 4(2) applies to the promise of a surety or guarantor gives rise to another kind of difficulty, illustrated in the following case. Moneypenny lends money to Prince on the oral promise of Answer to be surety. It is known to all concerned that Prince is under age, and therefore has the defense of infancy to any suit on the debt. Moneypenny argues that Answer's promise is not within Section 4(2), on the ground that since Prince legally owed nothing, Answer's obligation is not that of a surety. This argument has been accepted in some cases. Others have held that Answer is not liable on her oral promise, on the following line of reasoning: The debt of a minor may be affirmed, without new consideration, after the minor comes of age. The minor's obligation is therefore not "void" but "voidable." It is not a legal zero, but a legal something, although the minor has a defense unless when he comes of age he affirms the agreement. Since there is an imperfect (although unenforceable) obligation running from the minor to the creditor, a promisor who agrees to stand in back of the minor's undertaking is really a surety, and her promise is therefore within section 4(2).

SECTION 14. PROMISES MADE BY EXECUTORS AND ADMINISTRATORS (SECTION 4(1))

Section 4(1) of the Statute of Frauds concerns actions "to charge any executor or administrator upon any special promise to answer damages out of his own estate."

The case aimed at by section 4(1) is that where an executor or administrator of an estate promises a creditor of the decedent that if the decedent's estate proves insufficient to discharge the debt owed by the decedent, the executor or administrator will personally answer for it. Although the Statute speaks in terms of "any . . . promise" by an executor or administrator, in fact it covers only a promise by an executor or administrator to pay an *existing* debt of the estate—that is, in effect, a debt contracted by the decedent. A promise by an executor or administrator to personally pay a *fresh* debt contracted by her on the estate's behalf is not deemed within the Statute, on the theory that under principles of estate law the administrator or executor is primarily liable on such an obligation, rather than being liable merely as a surety. Restatement Second § 111.

Section 4(1) is quite unimportant. Few cases arise under it. In effect, it is a special case of suretyship, since the promise of the executor or administrator contemplated by Section 4(1) is a promise to answer for the debt of another, the "other" in this case being the decedent. The distinctions applied to such cases are similar to those developed under the suretyship provision. Restatement Second § 111.

SECTION 15. CONTRACTS UPON CONSIDERATION OF MARRIAGE (SECTION 4(3))

Section 4(3) of the Statute of Frauds concerns actions "to charge any person upon any agreement made upon consideration of marriage." The chief thing to know about the marriage section is that it does not apply to the case one would most expect it to be applied to, namely, a simple engagement by which two persons promise to marry each other. Such an agreement is a contract "to marry," not a contract "made upon consideration of marriage." At least, that is the way the courts interpret the Statute. Restatement Second § 124.

Conversely, even a promise running between the parents of the prospective spouses may not be "made upon consideration of marriage" within the meaning of the Statute, as the following Example shows.

Example No. 12:

Pater Primus, father of one prospective spouse, and Joan Secundus, mother of the other, exchange oral promises that if the marriage takes place they will each give $10,000 to the couple.

This agreement is not within section 4(3) of the Statute, because the consideration for the promise of each party is the promise of the other party, not the marriage. The occurrence of the marriage is merely the occasion for the parties' contributions to the couple, and a condition of their liability. Restatement Second § 124, Illus. 5.

The typical situation to which section 4(3) *does* apply is that of a "marriage settlement," in which a parent of a prospective spouse promises the prospective spouse to settle money or property on the couple upon their marriage. Similarly, if the prospective spouses make an oral contract with each other concerning their anticipated marriage, and the contract involves pecuniary features, such as a promise by one prospective spouse to convey certain sculptures to the other upon their marriage, the Statute of Frauds will apply, and all of the terms of the contract being intertwined, the contract as a whole becomes unenforceable.

As a by-point, it should be noted that there is considerable doubt whether a later writing, not intended as a statement of the contract itself, will satisfy section 4(3). See Section 3 of this Appendix.

SECTION 16.   WHAT KIND OF WRITING WILL SATISFY THE STATUTE

The issue, what type of writing is required to satisfy the Statute of Frauds, has become recast in recent years, because the broader concept of a *record* has for many purposes, including the Statute, replaced the narrower concept of a *writing*. That complication will be put aside for the moment, and discussed in the next Section of this Appendix. Much of the discussion in this Section will use the term "writing," because that is the traditional term used in Statute and in most of the cases. The discussion of the term "record" in the next Section will build on the discussion of the term "writing" in this Section, because most of the points made in this Section apply to a record as well.

The principal points to note are the following:

First. Unless the relevant Statute requires "the contract" to be in writing, the Statute is satisfied by almost any kind of signed document (using the term *document* extremely broadly, for present purposes only, to include both writings and records) that evidences the terms of the parties' agreement. This result follows from the language of section 4, which states, in effect, that there must either be a written contract *or* some memorandum or note *of* the contract.

Second. The requirement of a "signed" document does not mean that a document must be signed by the party in her own hand and with her full name. Any symbol used with an intent to authenticate a document will suffice. For instance, an "O.K." with initials is sufficient. Even a photocopied or computer-printed name will count as a signature if it reflects an intent to authenticate a document.

The UCC defines the term "signed" to include "any symbol executed or adopted by a party with present intention to authenticate a writing." UCC § 1–201 (39) (as in force in most states). The Comment states: "The inclusion of authentication in the definition of 'signed' is to make clear that as the term is used in [the Code] a complete signature is not necessary. Authentication may be printed, stamped, or written; it may be by initials or by thumbprint. It may be on any part of the document and in appropriate cases may be found in a billhead or letterhead. No catalog of possible authentications can be complete and the court must use common sense and commercial experience in passing upon these matters. The question always is whether the symbol was executed or adopted by the party with present intention to authenticate the writing."

Restatement Second is somewhat broader, in that it allows either actual or apparent intent to suffice. Restatement Second § 134. Farnsworth wrote similarly that the "modern test is whether the other party reasonably believes that the asserted signer's intention is to authenticate the writing as the asserted signer's own." E. Allan Farnsworth, Contracts, § 6.8 (4th ed. 2004). In Donovan v. RRL Corp., 26 Cal.4th 261, 27 P.3d 702 (Cal. 2001), the court held that "[w]hen an advertisement constitutes an offer, the printed name of the merchant is intended to authenticate the advertisement as that of the merchant. . . . In other words, where the advertisement reasonably justifies the recipient's understanding that the communication was intended as an offer, the offeror's intent to authenticate his or her name as a signature can be established from the face of the advertisement."

Third. If an agreement or memorandum is to satisfy the Statute, it must state the terms of the contract with reasonable adequacy. A document that failed to identify the parties, the subject-matter, and the essential terms would normally not be sufficient. On the other hand, the courts do not demand perfection, and some degree of ambiguity or ellipsis is not fatal.

Fourth. An adequate statement of the terms of the contract would normally reveal the consideration that made the promise or promises binding. However, it is not uncommon for a surety to guarantee a debt in writing without stating the consideration for her own undertaking as surety—which may be, for example, an advance made by the creditor to the debtor or an extension of time granted by the creditor to the debtor. An early English case construing section 4(2) of the Statute of Frauds declared such a memorandum to be fatally defective. Some American courts have followed this English decision; more have refused to. In 1856 the English law was changed by a statute that dispensed with the need for stating the consideration in a written guaranty.

In the United States there are a variety of statutes concerning whether the consideration must be stated to make a document effective. Some statutes say the consideration *must* be stated; some say the consideration need not be stated in a guaranty; some say the consideration need not be stated in any case. It is the last form of statute that gives the most difficulty. Does it mean, for example, that a written contract to sell land is effective although it makes no mention of the price, or states the price incorrectly? The cases are divided, but some have gone so far as to accept this conclusion. And note that the UCC Statute of Frauds, § 2–201, does not require the price to be stated in the writing. See *Ninth*, infra.

Fifth. Generally the document need not be signed by both parties, but only by the "party to be charged." This may result in a contract that can be enforced in one direction only.

Sixth. Even where no single document exists that is sufficient to satisfy the Statute, a memorandum that satisfies the statute may sometimes be obtained by piecing together several documents. If the documents are physically attached, or contain internal references to one another, there is no difficulty. More doubtful is the question whether piecing together is permissible where doing so rests entirely on oral evidence or general appearances. In Crabtree v. Elizabeth Arden Sales Corp., 305 N.Y. 48, 110 N.E.2d 551 (1953), the court stated:

> The statute of frauds does not require the "memorandum to be in one document. It may be pieced together out of separate writings, connected with one another either expressly or by the internal evidence of subject-matter and occasion." Marks v. Cowdin, supra, 226 N.Y. 138, 145, 128 N.E. 139, 141, see, also, 2 Williston, op. ct., p. 1671; Restatement, Contracts, § 208. subd. [a]. Where each of the separate writings has been subscribed by the party to be charged, little if any difficulty is encountered. See, e.g., Marks v. Cowdin, supra, 226 N.Y. 138, 144–145, 123 N.E. 139, 141. Where, however, some writings have been signed, and others have not—as in the case before us—there is basic disagreement as to what constitutes a sufficient connection permitting the unsigned papers to be considered as part or the statutory memorandum. The courts of some jurisdictions insist that there be a reference, of varying degrees of specificity, in the signed writing to that unsigned, and, if there is no such reference, they refuse to permit consideration of the latter in determining whether the memorandum satisfies the statute. See, e.g., Osborn v. Phelps, 19 Conn. 63; Hewett Grain & Provision Co. v. Spear, 222 Mich. 608, 193 N.W. 291. That conclusion is based upon a construction of the statute which requires that the connection between the writings and defendant's acknowledgment of the one not subscribed, appear from examination of the papers alone,

without the aid of parol evidence. The other position—which has gained increasing support over the years—is that a sufficient connection between the papers is established simply by a reference in them to the same subject matter or transaction. See, e.g., Frost v. Alward, 176 Cal. 691, 169 P. 379; Lerned v. Wannemacher, 9 Allen, 412, 91 Mass. 412. The statute is not pressed "to the extreme of a literal and rigid logic", Marks v. Cowdin, supra, 226 N.Y. 138, 144, 123 N.E. 139, 141, and oral testimony is admitted to show the connection between the documents and to establish the acquiescence, of the party to be charged, to the contents of the one unsigned. . . .

The view last expressed impresses us as the more sound, and, indeed—although several of our cases appear to have gone the other way, see, e.g., Newbery v. Wall, 65 N.Y. 484; Wilson v. Lewiston Mill Co., 150 N.Y. 314, 44 N.E. 959—this court has on a number of occasions approved the rule, and we now definitively adopt it, permitting the signed and unsigned writings to be read together, provided that they clearly refer to the same subject matter or transaction. . . .

Seventh. A memorandum may fail to satisfy the Statute of Frauds because it does not *correctly* state the agreement. Restatement Second § 131, comment g. (But note that UCC § 2–201 (1) specifically provides otherwise in the case of a sale of goods. See *Ninth*, below.)

Example No. 13:

On May 1, Frederick Firm and Quincy Qualm enter an oral agreement whereby Firm is to convey Dreamacre to Qualm on June 1, and on that date Qualm is to pay $50,000 cash as the full price of the land. On May 5 Qualm writes to Firm: "This is about the contract we entered on May 1, whereby you are to convey Dreamacre to me on June 1 and I am to pay $49,000. I heard a rumor that you had offered this land to someone else, and I want to know whether you are going through with our contract. Yours truly, Quincy Qualm." Before Firm can answer this letter, Qualm repudiates the contract. Firm sues Qualm for damages, asserting that Qualm's letter satisfies the Statute.

The letter might be held to be an insufficient memorandum, since it does not correctly state the terms of the oral agreement.

Lovers of paradox will observe: The Statute of Frauds finds its rationale in the untrustworthiness of oral agreements. Yet the document that the Statute requires may itself be impugned, and its effect destroyed, by showing that it does not correctly state the oral agreement.

Eighth. A principal will normally be bound by the signature of an authorized agent on the principal's behalf, even if the agent's authority is not in writing. In some states, however, a statute provides that if a contract signed by an agent is required to be in writing, the agent's authority must also be evidenced in a writing signed by the principal. The doctrine that such statutes embody is sometimes called the "equal-dignity rule"— meaning that the authority of an agent to enter into a contract on behalf of a principal must be evidenced by a formality equal to that required for the contract itself. Note that the equal-dignity rule is normally applicable only in states where it has been specifically adopted by statute.

Ninth. As regards contracts for the sale of goods, UCC § 2–201(1) changes this whole corner of Statute of Frauds law in a fairly substantial way. It will be recalled that under § 2–201(1):

> Except as otherwise provided in this section a contract for the sale of goods for the price of $500 or more is not enforceable by way of action or defense unless there is some writing sufficient to indicate that a contract for sale has been made between the parties and signed by the party against whom enforcement is sought or by his authorized agent or broker. A writing is not insufficient because it omits or incorrectly states a term agreed upon but the contract is not enforceable under this paragraph beyond the quantity of goods shown in such writing.

According to the Official Comment to this Section:

> . . . The required writing need not contain all the material terms of the contract and such material terms as are stated need not be precisely stated. All that is required is that the writing afford a basis for believing that the offered oral evidence rests on a real transaction. It may be written in lead pencil on a scratch pad. It need not indicate which party is the buyer and which the seller. The only term which must appear is the quantity term which need not be accurately stated but recovery is limited to the amount stated. The price, time and place of payment or delivery, the general quality of the goods, or any particular warranties may all be omitted.

> Special emphasis must be placed on the permissibility of omitting the price term in view of the insistence of some courts on the express inclusion of this term even where the parties have contracted on the basis of a published price list. In many valid contracts for sale the parties do not mention the price in express terms, the buyer being bound to pay and the seller to accept a reasonable price which the trier of the fact may well be trusted to determine. Again, frequently the price is not mentioned since the parties have based their agreement on a price list or catalogue

known to both of them and this list serves as an efficient safeguard against perjury. Finally, "market" prices and valuations that are current in the vicinity constitute a similar check. Thus if the price is not stated in the memorandum it can normally be supplied without danger of fraud. Of course if the "price" consists of goods rather than money the quantity of goods must be stated.

Only three definite and invariable requirements as to the memorandum are made by this subsection. First, it must evidence a contract for the sale of goods; second, it must be "signed," a word which includes any authentication which identifies the party to be charged; and third, it must specify a quantity.

In Howard Construction Co. v. Jeff-Coles Quarries, Inc., 669 S.W.2d 221 (Mo.App.1983), the court pointed out that UCC § 2–201(1) requires only "some writing sufficient to indicate that a contract for sale has been made," and. . . . one writer has suggested that the spirit of the comments seems to be that 'sufficient to indicate' is roughly equivalent to 'more probable than not.' . . . In other words, if it is more probable than not that the writing evidences a deal between the parties, then the writing should be found sufficient."

There is some division of authority concerning whether a purchase order or a sales order will by itself satisfy UCC § 2–201. A naked purchase order or sales order signed by one party is unlikely to meet the test of that section, because it does not provide evidence that a contract had been concluded. See Bazak International Corp. v. Mast Industries, 73 N.Y.2d 113, 538 N.Y.S.2d 503, 535 N.E.2d 633 (1989); Trilco Terminal v. Prebilt Corp., 167 N.J.Super. 449, 400 A.2d 1237 (Law Div.1979), aff'd, 174 N.J.Super. 24, 415 A.2d 356 (App.Div.1980). However, a purchase order or sales order that has more to it may satisfy § 2–201. For example, in *Bazak,* supra, the New York Court held that § 2–201 was satisfied by the purchase orders in that case, partly on the ground that the purchase orders had been sent by the seller from the premises of the buyer's parent company to the buyer's subsidiary. That fact, the court concluded, suggested that the purchase orders were not unsolicited, but instead reflected that an agreement had already been reached. Other courts have held that a purchase order suffices if it is signed by both parties, or can be matched with a document sent by the other party, or indicates that a down payment has been made. See Lonnie Hayes & Sons Staves, Inc. v. Bourbon Cooperage Co., 777 S.W.2d 940 (Ky.App.1989); Koenen v. Royal Buick Co., 162 Ariz. 376, 783 P.2d 822 (App.1989). Furthermore, UCC § 2–201(2) provides that "Between merchants if within a reasonable time a writing"—which could include a purchase order or sales order—"in confirmation of the contract and sufficient against the sender is received and the party receiving it has reason to know its contents, it satisfies the requirements of [section 2–201] against such party unless written notice of objection to its contents is given within 10 days after it is received."

Tenth. As shown in the next Section of the Appendix, two new statutes provide that for Statute of Frauds and many other purposes the requirement of a writing can normally be satisfied by a "record"—a term that includes both information that is inscribed on a tangible medium, such as a traditional writing on paper, and information that is stored in an electronic or other medium and is retrievable in perceivable form. Most of the issues considered in this Section of the Appendix, concerning the standards that a traditional writing must meet to satisfy the Statute of Frauds, also apply to the standards that a record other than a traditional writing must meet to satisfy the Statute.

SECTION 17.   ELECTRONIC CONTRACTING AND THE STATUTE OF FRAUDS

Within the last few years, the concept and term record has come into use in place of the concept and term *writing*. A *record* is defined slightly differently in different statutes, but at its core the term has the meaning given by section 2(13) of the Uniform Electronic Transactions Act, discussed below: "information that is inscribed on a tangible medium or that is stored in an electronic or other medium and is retrievable in perceivable form." In connection with the shift from *writing* to *record*, two important legislative developments have affected the issue of what kinds of records and signatures satisfy the Statute of Frauds.

UETA. First, the Uniform Electronics Transactions Act (UETA) was promulgated in 1999 by the National Conference of Commissioners on Uniform State Laws, and has been adopted by almost all the states. UETA § 7 provides as follows:

(a) A record or signature may not be denied legal effect or enforceability solely because it is in electronic form.

(b) A contract may not be denied legal effect or enforceability solely because an electronic record was used in its formation.

(c) If a law requires a record to be in writing, an electronic record satisfies the law.

(d) If a law requires a signature, an electronic signature satisfies the law.

The terms used in section 7 are defined in section 2. Section 2(13) provides that the term "record" means "information that is inscribed on a tangible medium or that is stored in an electronic or other medium and is retrievable in perceivable form." The Comment to section 2(13) states:

This is a standard definition designed to embrace all means of communicating or storing information except human memory. It includes any method for storing or communicating information, including "writings." A record need not be indestructible or permanent, but the term does not include oral or other communications which are not stored or preserved by some means. Information that has not been retained other than through human memory does not qualify as a record. As in the case of the terms "writing" or "written," the term "record" does not establish the purposes, permitted uses or legal effect which a record may have under any particular provision of substantive law.

Section 2(8) provides that the term "electronic signature" means "an electronic sound, symbol, or process attached to or logically associated with a record and executed or adopted by a person with the intent to sign the record." The Comment to section 2(8) states:

The idea of a signature is broad and not specifically defined. Whether any particular record is "signed" is a question of fact. Proof of that fact must be made under other applicable law. This Act simply assures that the signature may be accomplished through electronic means. No specific technology need be used in order to create a valid signature. One's voice on an answering machine may suffice if the requisite intention is present. Similarly, including one's name as part of an electronic mail communication also may suffice, as may the firm name on a facsimile. . . . In any case the critical element is the intention to execute or adopt the sound or symbol or process for the purpose of signing the related record. . . . It is that intention that is understood in the law as a part of the word "sign", without the need for a definition.

This Act establishes, to the greatest extent possible, the equivalency of electronic signatures and manual signatures. Therefore the term "signature" has been used to connote and convey that equivalency. . . .

This definition includes as an electronic signature the standard webpage click through process. For example, when a person orders goods or services through a vendor's website, the person will be required to provide information as part of a process which will result in receipt of the goods or services. When the customer ultimately gets to the last step and clicks "I agree," the person has adopted the process and has done so with the intent to associate the person with the record of that process. The actual effect of the electronic signature will be determined from all the

SEC. 17   THE STATUTE OF FRAUDS   809

surrounding circumstances[;] however, the person adopted a process which the circumstances indicate s/he intended to have the effect of getting the goods/services and being bound to pay for them. The adoption of the process carried the intent to do a legally significant act, the hallmark of a signature.

Another important aspect of this definition lies in the necessity that the electronic signature be linked or logically associated with the record. In the paper world, it is assumed that the symbol adopted by a party is attached to or located somewhere in the same paper that is intended to be authenticated, e.g., an allonge firmly attached to a promissory note, or the classic signature at the end of a long contract. These tangible manifestations do not exist in the electronic environment, and accordingly, this definition expressly provides that the symbol must in some way be linked to, or connected with, the electronic record being signed. . . .

The Illustrations to UETA § 7 exemplify how this section operates:

Illustration 1: A sends the following e-mail to B: "I hereby offer to buy widgets from you, delivery next Tuesday. /s/ A." B responds with the following e-mail: "I accept your offer to buy widgets for delivery next Tuesday. /s/ B." The e-mails may not be denied effect solely because they are electronic. In addition, the e-mails . . . qualify as records under the Statute of Frauds. However, because there is no quantity stated in either record, the parties' agreement would be unenforceable under existing UCC Section 2–201 (1).

Illustration 2: A sends the following e-mail to B: "I hereby offer to buy 100 widgets for $1000, delivery next Tuesday. /s/ A." B responds with the following e-mail: "I accept your offer to purchase 100 widgets for $1000, delivery next Tuesday. /s/ B." In this case the analysis is the same as in Illustration 1 except that here the records otherwise satisfy the requirements of UCC Section 2–201 (1). The transaction may not be denied legal effect solely because there is not a pen and ink "writing" or "signature".

E-Sign. The second major legislative development affecting records and signatures is the Electronic Signatures in Global and National Commerce Act ("E-Sign"). E-Sign is a federal statute which is generally comparable to UETA as regards the effect of electronic records and electronic signatures. Because E-Sign is a federal statute, it would normally preempt UETA. However, E-Sign specifically recognizes and avoids preempting UETA, and on the contrary, provides that with limited exceptions, states may preempt E-sign by adopting UETA. Because all but four states have adopted UETA, UETA generally takes precedence over E-Sign.

SECTION 18. CLAIMS AVAILABLE FOR BREACH OF AN ORAL CONTRACT WITHIN THE STATUTE—INTRODUCTION

This Section will consider the following question: A has allegedly entered an oral contract with B, and A has broken the contract after B acted upon it. Should B be given any recovery? This question is best approached if it is first put in general terms, without reference to specific provisions the Statute of Frauds. The basic opposing considerations that must be weighed in answering this question are: (1) the dangers involved in allowing B to try to establish the alledged oral contract in the absence of a writing to satisfy the statute; and (2) the possible hardship to B resulting from a denial of relief on the alleged oral contract.

To balance these opposing considerations, it is necessary to know the strength of the evidence of the alleged oral contract and the particular hardship of which B complains and the specific measure of relief that B demands. Sections 19 and 20 address two claims that were available under classical contract law for breach of an oral contract within the statute in a case in which A could otherwise assert a statute of frauds defense. These are a restitution claim and a claim under the doctrine of part performance. Section 21 addresses the promissory estoppel claim, which is broader and more flexible.

SECTION 19. RESTITUTION

It is well settled that normally B may recover the value of any benefits he conferred on A under an oral contract that falls within the Statute of Frauds.

Example No. 14:

Under an oral contract with Marian Means, Steven Smock, an artist, agrees to paint a mural in Means's home in exchange for a conveyance of Passacre. After full performance by Smock, Means refuses to give him a deed to Passacre.

Although this transaction is a contract for the sale of land within Section 4(4) of the Statute of Frauds, Smock can recover the value of the mural.

There are two explanations for reconciling this result with the Statute of Frauds. One explanation is normative; the other is doctrinal.

The normative explanation is that to allow a party to retain benefits that she has received under a contract that is unenforceable only because Smock cannot establish a writing to satisfy the statute of frauds is unjust and unnecessary. It is unjust because Means would be enriched at Smock's expense were recovery not allowed. It is unnecessary because the fact Smock painted the mural is strong evidence of a contract between Means and Smock, satisfying the evidentiary function of the Statute of Frauds.

The doctrinal explanation is that the Statute of Frauds only bars actions to enforce a contract, and doctrinally a suit for restitution is not an action to enforce the contract. Such an action is based not on contract law, but on an entirely separate body of law, the law of unjust enrichment and restitution. Correspondingly, the measure of recovery in a suit in restitution is basically different from the measure of recovery in a suit on the contract. In a suit on the contract, the plaintiff's recovery is measured by the value of the performance promised by the defendant. In *Example No. 14*, this would be the value of Passacre. In contrast, in a suit in restitution the plaintiff's recovery is measured by a reasonable price for the performance rendered. In *Example No. 14*, this would be a reasonable price for the work done on the mural.

The limitation of damages to a reasonable price for the performance rendered ameliorates the remaining evidentiary concern that Smock may misrepresent (or misremember) the price he was promised for painting the mural. Nevertheless, according to some authorities, in proving the value of the mural, Smock would be permitted to introduce evidence of the market value of Passacre. This evidence would be admitted on the theory that Means by her oral contract conceded that the mural, if properly done, would be equal in value to Passacre. Although in theory this concession or admission by Means is not conclusive, and is only relevant as tending to show how much the mural itself was worth, the practical result may be that Smock will recover the value of Passacre, just as if his suit was for breach of the oral agreement. This result could especially be anticipated if there was no satisfactory way of measuring the value of the mural or of Smock's services, while Passacre had a fairly definite market value, as by being a lot in a subdivision in which all lots were selling for $5,000 each.

Some cases allow the plaintiff to recover on a reasonable price for performance rendered at the request of the defendant even though the performance clearly did not enrich the defendant. See, e.g., Farash v. Sykes Datatronics, Inc., 59 N.Y.2d 500, 465 N.Y.S.2d 917, 452 N.E.2d 1245 (1983); Randolph v. Castle, 190 Ky. 776, 228 S.W. 418 (1921). Often the plaintiff pleads quantum meruit in these cases and does not refer to the law of unjust enrichment. This masks the oddity of recovery being non-benefit based. Restatement, Third, of Restitution and Unjust Enrichment § 31, comment *c* observes: "A straightforward account of such outcomes describes them in terms of promissory liability (circumventing unacceptable consequences of the Statute of Frauds), not as restitution based on unjust enrichment."

Caution: In one special case, a plaintiff who has conferred a benefit under an oral contract is not permitted the restitutionary recovery described in this Section. This is the case where the contract falls within one of the statutes, mentioned in Section 5 of this Appendix, that require a contract with a real-estate broker, involving a potential commission for the sale of real estate, to be in writing. A seller's engagement of a real-estate broker is usually in legal effect an offer for a unilateral contract (for example, a promise that the seller will pay a commission to the broker if the broker causes a sale to occur), and involves no explicit promise by the broker. Accordingly, the broker normally has no right to a commission unless and until he has performed his services in connection with the sale. Therefore, a statute that provides that real-estate commission contracts must be in writing is normally directed precisely against a suit by a broker to recover for services that the broker has performed. To allow restitutionary recovery for the value of such services would deprive such a statute of any real effect.

SECTION 20. PART PERFORMANCE

Courts, by a process extending over the centuries, have read into certain provisions of the Statute of Frauds exceptions under which the Statute becomes inapplicable, and the plaintiff can bring suit under the contract for expectation damages, where the contract has been fully or even partly performed on one side. The exact nature of the part-performance exceptions vary from provision to provision of the Statute. A summary of the law on this question follows.

Land Contracts

In the case of contracts for the sale of an interest in land ("land contracts"), a part-performance exception—perhaps more accurately, a part-performance-and-reliance exception—has become institutionalized and has been built into an imposing body of case law.

The traditional rules. Traditionally, the cases in this area make explicit two different considerations: (1) The equity in favor of a party who has acted under the oral contract and who will suffer hardship if the contract is not enforced. (2) The evidentiary value of acts of reliance or part performance in pointing to the existence of a contract. Because these considerations may appear in varying degrees, there are strict and liberal applications of the part-performance exception in this context. Furthermore, some decisions place greater weight on the evidentiary significance of acts of performance or reliance, while others place greater weight on the element of hardship.

In discussing the case law on the part-performance exception for land contracts, it is necessary to distinguish between acts under the contract by the *vendor* and acts under the contract by the *purchaser.*

A *vendor* is entitled to recover the price under an oral contract for the sale of land as soon as the vendor has actually conveyed the land to the purchaser. Restatement Second § 125(3). Thus the vendor can obtain the price promised by the purchaser, and with it the benefit of the vendor's oral bargain, instead of being thrown back upon either an action in restitution for the reasonable value of the land or a suit in equity to compel a reconveyance of the land (specific restitution).

Where it is the *purchaser* who acts under the oral contract, the law is more complicated. A good summary of the traditional rule in this area was set out in Restatement First § 197. That Section provided that an oral agreement for the sale of an interest in land becomes *specifically enforceable* if "the purchaser with the assent of the vendor (a) makes valuable improvements on the land, or (b) takes possession thereof or retains a possession thereof existing at the time of the bargain, and also pays a portion or all of the purchase price."

As indicated by Restatement First § 197, under the traditional rule payment of all or part of the purchase price does not alone make the contract enforceable, although there are some cases to the contrary. The theory is that such a payment does not identify the land sold. (However, the payment can be recovered in a suit for restitution.) Similarly, under the traditional rule the purchaser's act of taking possession does not alone make the contract enforceable by the plaintiff. The theory is that although taking possession may have evidentiary value as indicating some kind of agreement and identifying its object, taking possession is as consistent with a lease as with a sale, and may not always involve a serious change of position by the purchaser.

These limitations are by no means universally respected by the courts. In addition to some cases indicating that taking possession is sufficient, even without payment of the purchase price, there are many cases holding that the rendition of services over a long period will suffice to take the contract out of the Statute. This type of holding is found typically in "care-for-me-for-the-rest-of-my-life-and-you-can-have-the-farm-when-I-am-gone" contracts.

Concerning the traditional rule that certain acts by the purchaser under a land contract may make the contract specifically enforceable, the following points should be noted.

(1) This rule was developed by courts of equity, and therefore it is generally assumed to affect only the purchaser's right to specific performance, and not to give the purchaser a right to recover damages measured by the value of the land. Restatement Second § 129, Comment c. In contrast, the *vendor's* right to the price after conveying land under an oral contract is a right to sue at law.

(2) Generally it is the purchaser who, having made improvements or otherwise acted under the contract, brings suit for specific performance against the vendor. There are cases, however, holding that the same acts under the contract by the purchaser that will create in him a right to specific performance will also create a right to specific performance in the vendor. Here it is not the hardship to the plaintiff-vendor that makes the oral contract enforceable, but either (1) the evidentiary value of the purchaser's acts, or (2) a notion that if it is fair for the purchaser to enforce the contract, equality of treatment should allow the vendor to sue on the same set of facts.

(3) In a few jurisdictions, the courts have stated that they do not recognize the principle that part performance of an oral contract for the sale of an interest in land will make the contract specifically enforceable.

(4) There is a general tendency to very liberally enforce an oral contract that settles a disputed boundary. Where parties are in dispute or doubt about the boundary between their lands, and orally agree to settle the issue by running a fence or other marker along a designated line, generally the agreement becomes enforceable as soon as any action is taken under it. Restatement Second § 128(1).

The rule in Restatement Second. Restatement Second § 129 completely reconceptualizes and reformulates the part-performance exception for land contracts, by making the exception center on reliance. That section provides:

> A contract for the transfer of an interest in land may be specifically enforced notwithstanding failure to comply with the Statute of Frauds if it is established that the party seeking enforcement, in reasonable reliance on the contract and on the continuing assent of the party against whom enforcement is sought, has so changed his position that injustice can be avoided only by specific enforcement.

Whether the law in this area will shift to the rule stated in Restatement Second § 129 remains to be seen.

The One-Year Provision

Taking as a guide Restatement Second § 130 and many cases, the part-performance rule concerning the one-year provision—section 4(5)—is as follows: As soon as one side of the contract has been fully performed the promise of the other party becomes binding, whether or not that promise can be performed within one year. (The rationale of this rule is seldom discussed. Perhaps the explanation lies in the fact that difficulties intrinsic to section 4(5) had already compelled so much departure from the literal meaning of the section (see Section 10 of this Appendix) that the courts have felt free to take further liberties with its language in order to make its operation more equitable.) Piecing this principle together with the basic interpretation of section 4(5), it may be said that an oral contract is either not within or is taken out of the one-year provision if (1) the whole contract *could* have been performed within one year, although neither party has as yet fully performed or (2) one party has fully performed, no matter how long it took for performance to take place.

Caution: The case law is more ambiguous than the rule laid down by Restatement Second, and the general tendency of the law is less favorable to removing the oral contract from the Statute's one-year provision as a result of part performance. According to some cases, if the defendant's performance will require more than a year, the fact that the plaintiff has fully performed is immaterial. Under this view, the plaintiff's only relief is in restitution. Still other cases say that full performance on one side will take the contract out of the Statute only if that performance itself takes place within one year after the contract is made.

The Suretyship Section

Generally no exception to the Statute of Frauds is read into the suretyship section of the Statute in favor of a party who performs on the basis of an oral guaranty. For example, if Seller delivers goods to Buyer in reliance on Surety's oral promise to answer for Buyer's obligation to pay the price, Surety does not thereby become bound.

The Marriage Section

It is generally assumed that an oral contract upon consideration of marriage is not taken out of the Statute of Frauds simply because the marriage has taken place in reliance on the promise. (There are, however, cases enforcing the oral agreement where a serious change of position, involving acts in addition to marriage, has occurred.)

SECTION 21. PROMISSORY ESTOPPEL

Suppose a plaintiff seeks, not restitution for a benefit conferred under a contract that is unenforceable under the Statute of Frauds, but damages based on losses that he incurred in acting under the contract, which losses did not result in a benefit to the defendant. The issue here is not as clear-cut as it is in the case of a benefit conferred under a contract that is unenforceable under the Statute of Frauds.

Normatively, a rule that allowed a defendant to retain a benefit that has been conferred upon her under a contract that is unenforceable only because it is not in writing would be more shocking to the sense of justice than a rule that a defendant need not reimburse the plaintiff for his losses under such contract, where those losses did not result in a benefit to the defendant. (This is not to say that a rule of the second kind would be just; only that the injustice is less intense in the reliance case than in the restitution case.)

Doctrinally, unlike an action to recover the value of a benefit conferred, which is brought under the law of unjust enrichment and restitution, an action to recover reliance damages is a suit under contract law. Such an action therefore runs more squarely into the Statute of Frauds than an action to recover the value of a benefit conferred.

At least until recently, the prevailing view has been that it would be contrary to the Statute of Frauds to allow a recovery for losses from reliance on a contract that is unenforceable under the Statute when those losses did not benefit the defendant. It looked like that view was changing in the middle of the last century. Two of the leading cases are Monarco v. Lo Greco, 35 Cal.2d 621, 220 P.2d 737 (1950) and Alaska Airlines v. Stephenson, 217 F.2d 295 (9th Cir.1954).

In Monarco v. Lo Greco, Christie Lo Greco's mother and stepfather orally promised Christie that if he would stay on the family farm and help in its management, they would leave him the bulk of their property. Christie did as they asked, and the family farm prospered. However, Christie's stepfather left the property to his grandson. The court held for Christie, despite Section 4(4) of the Statute of Frauds (the land section) on the basis of Christie's reliance. The opinion qualified the reliance exception to the Statute of Frauds by stating that reliance was a ground for overcoming the Statute only "where either an unconscionable injury or unjust enrichment would result from refusal to enforce the contract."

In Alaska Airlines v. Stephenson, Alaska Airlines orally promised to give an airline pilot a two-year written contract as soon as the airline obtained a required certificate to fly between Seattle and Alaska. In reliance on this promise, the pilot let his right to return to his previous employer expire. The airline broke its promise. Here too the court held that the pilot's reliance overcame the Statute. See also, e.g., Alaska Democratic Party v. Rice, 934 P.2d 1313 (Alaska 1997).

Going one step further, Restatement Second § 139 gives full recognition to the reliance principle in the Statute of Frauds area. Furthermore, under the principle embodied in this section, a relying promisee may be entitled to expectation damages:

§ 139. Enforcement by Virtue of Action in Reliance

(1) A promise which the promisor should reasonably expect to induce action or forbearance on the part of the promisee or a third person and which does induce the action or forbearance is enforceable notwithstanding the Statute of Frauds if injustice can be avoided only by enforcement of the promise. The remedy granted for breach is to be limited as justice requires.

(2) In determining whether injustice can be avoided only by enforcement of the promise, the following circumstances are significant:

    (a) the availability and adequacy of other remedies, particularly cancellation and restitution;

    (b) the definite and substantial character of the action or forbearance in relation to the remedy sought;

    (c) the extent to which the action or forbearance corroborates evidence of the making and terms of the promise, or the making and terms are otherwise established by clear and convincing evidence;

    (d) the reasonableness of the action or forbearance;

    (e) the extent to which the action or forbearance was foreseeable by the promisor. . . .

Comment . . .

    d. Partial enforcement; particular remedies. The same factors which bear on whether any relief should be granted also bear on the character and extent of the remedy. In particular, the remedy of restitution is not ordinarily affected by the Statute of Frauds . . . ; where restitution is an adequate remedy, other remedies are not made available by the rule stated in this Section. Again, when specific enforcement is available . . . an ordinary action for damages is commonly less satisfactory, and justice then does not require enforcement in such an action. . . . In some cases it may be appropriate to measure relief by the extent of the promisee's reliance rather than by the terms of the promise. See § 90. . . .

A significant number of courts have refused to adopt a general reliance exception. See, e.g., Greaves v. Medical Imaging Systems, Inc., 124 Wash.2d 389, 879 P.2d 276 (1994)(holding court of appeals erred in relying on § 139). Some courts that adopt a reliance exception continue to qualify the exception in the same manner as *Monarco.* See, e.g., Classic Cheesecake Company, Inc. v. JP Morgan Chase Bank, N.A., 546 F.3d 839 (7th Cir. 2008)(Indiana law), chapter 11 supra. Other courts that adopt a reliance exception require the plaintiff to have relied on the defendant's promise to execute and deliver a writing that would satisfy the statute. See, e.g., Stearns v. Emery-Waterhouse Co., 596 A.2d 72 (Maine 1991); "Moore" Burger, Inc. v. Phillips Petroleum Co., 492 S.W.2d 934 (Tex. 1972).

The cases are divided on whether the reliance exception applies to UCC § 2–201. Some cases take the position that the exceptions in § 2–201 should be deemed to be exclusive of any others, partly to promote uniformity in the application of the Code. See, e.g., Renfroe v. Ladd, 701 S.W.2d 148 (Ky.App.1985); Lige Dickson Co. v. Union Oil Co., 96 Wash.2d 291, 635 P.2d 103 (1981). Other cases take the position that the reliance exception applies to cases that fall within § 2–201 because UCC § 1–103 provides that "Unless displaced by the particular provisions of this Act, the principles of law and equity, including . . . the law relative to . . . estoppel . . . or other validating or invalidating cause shall supplement its provisions." See, e.g., Allen M. Campbell Co. v. Virginia Metal Industries, 708 F.2d 930 (4th Cir.1983); Ralston Purina Co. v. McCollum, 271 Ark. 840, 611 S.W.2d 201 (1981).

SECTION 22. THE EFFECT OF NON-COMPLIANCE—LEGAL CONSEQUENCES OF THE UNENFORCEABLE AGREEMENT

It is a safe guess that the problem, what are the legal consequences of an agreement that is unenforceable under the Statute of Frauds, is one that never occurred to the drafters of the original Act. When they said in Section 4 that "no action shall be brought" on the oral contract, or in Section 17 that the oral contract shall not "be allowed to be good," they probably meant in both cases something roughly equivalent to: "the oral contract is not good." It is equally doubtful that those occasional American legislatures who changed the wording of the Statute to make the oral contract "void" had any clearer idea of what they were doing.

A contractual transaction between two persons may give rise to a multitude of legal consequences. It may, for example, make the participants guilty of a crime, transfer or affect rights, create duties, rebut the implication that property was transferred as a gift, furnish the substratum of moral obligation that will make a later promise enforceable, or create a relationship with which others cannot interfere without liability. Terms like "unenforceable," "void," and "voidable" are blind verbal jabs into a complex molecule of relationships. When they are used in legislation, it is the unhappy task of the courts to decide what changes in the structure of the molecule the words were intended to bring about and what changes are in keeping with the general purpose of the legislation.

Sometimes this task is easy, as in the next *Example*.

Example No. 15:

Gilbert Gore orally agrees with Catherine Cabal that he will murder Delbert Doom in return for a conveyance of Bloodacre. The agreement is discovered before it is carried out, and Gore is indicted for criminal conspiracy. The local Statute of Frauds makes any contract for the sale of an interest in land "void." Gore's attorney relies on dictionary definition of "void" as meaning "of no legal force or effect." He argues that since this contract was "void" it cannot have the legal effect of making his client guilty of a crime.

This argument would be rejected. Criminal liability is a matter that is beyond the purpose of the Statute of Frauds. Although in Gore's jurisdiction the Statute uses the word "void," that doesn't not mean that entering the oral contract has no legal consequences, but only that the oral contract will be deprived of those legal consequences that would be inconsistent with the purpose of the Statute.

Simple and obvious as is *Example No. 15*, it illustrates the basic difficulty the courts have faced in determining the legal effect of the unenforceable oral contract. What legal effects *are* inconsistent with the purpose of the Statute?

One generalization that holds fairly firm is that the Statute of Frauds affects only the legal relations of the contracting parties. Accordingly, that a contract is oral and therefore unenforceable between the parties makes it no less a binding contract so far as third persons are concerned. Restatement Second § 144. Accordingly, persuading a party to break an oral contract may constitute the tort of inducing breach of contract even though the contract is within the Statute.

The most knotty problem the courts have faced in this area has arisen in connection with suits for restitution.

Example No. 16:

Recall *Example No. 14:* Steven Smock orally agrees to paint a mural in Marian Means's home in return for Passacre. Smock paints the mural; Means conveys Passacre to him. Smock then sues Means for $10,000, based on the principle of unjust enrichment, alleging that the reasonable value of the mural is $15,000 and that he has so far only received a piece of land worth $5,000. Means pleads performance of the oral agreement. Smock replies by asserting that the oral agreement was within the Statute of Frauds and therefore without legal effect. He argues that when Means seeks to restrict Smock to the orally agreed price

820 APPENDIX SEC. 22

for her work, Means is in effect holding Smock to the agreement. If the contract cannot be enforced by the plaintiff, it ought to be unenforceable on behalf of the defendant.

Judgment would go for Means. Since she has paid the price orally agreed upon, there is no basis for a suit founded on a theory of unjust enrichment. Her use of the oral contract to show that she had paid the agreed price is not "enforcing" that contract. If Smock had presented the mural to her as a gift, Smock could not later change her mind and recover its value from Means. In such a case, Means could show an oral statement by Smock that his mural was to be given gratuitously. The fact that such a statement words would impose no liability on Smock to carry out the gift would be immaterial. In the same way here, the fact that suit could not have been brought on the oral contract is immaterial to Means's use of the contract to rebut the claim of unjust enrichment.

The result reached in *Example No. 16* is one that can be predicted with some assurance. Generally, a person may not undo an executed transaction simply because the contract under which he acts would not have been enforceable if it were an executory agreement. This would probably be true even if the Statute says that the oral contract is "void." Restatement Second § 145. The following case is more troublesome:

Example No. 17:

Quigley Quail orally agrees to serve Fiona Fast as secretary for six months, and Fast agrees to pay for Quail's services by conveying Penacre to him at the end of the six months' period. When Quail has served two months, he learns that his contract is unenforceable under section 4(4) of the Statute of Frauds (the land section). Quail brings suit for the reasonable value of two months' services. Fast asserts that she is willing to abide by the agreement, and that she stands ready to convey Penacre when Quail's work is finished. She argues that Quail's discontinuance of performance is a breach of the oral agreement that should disentitle him to relief. Quail argues that he should not be asked to complete his work under the contract when he has no assurance that Fast will in fact pay him. Restatement Second § 141(2) proposes, as a solution for this problem, that "[where] a party to a contract which is unenforceable against him refuses either to perform the contract or to sign a sufficient memorandum, the other party is justified in suspending any performance for which he has not already received the agreed return, and such a suspension is not a defense in an action for the value of performance rendered before the suspension."

SECTION 23. ORAL RESCISSION

The problem of the validity of an oral rescission arises chiefly in connection with the following situation: The original contract was in writing, and its terms were such as to bring it within the Statute of Frauds. In short, the contract had to be in writing—as it was—to be enforceable. The contract is then orally rescinded by the parties' mutual agreement. As a general proposition, in such cases the rescission is effective, on the theory that the rescission does not call for the performance of any duties, and therefore does not fall within any of the classes covered by the Statute. See *Example No. 4* in Section 6 of this Appendix; Restatement Second § 148 and comment a.

This general proposition requires two qualifications:

1. *Sale of land.* Where the rescinded contract is for the sale of land, and the original transaction was fully executed, the rescission itself effectively calls for a conveyance—albeit a reconveyance—and therefore falls within the Statute. Suppose the original contract was executory at the time the contract of rescission was entered into? Even here, there are cases saying that the rescission is ineffective unless in writing. The theory of these cases is that an executory contract to sell land creates a present property interest in the purchaser, so that a rescission of such a contract also involves the reconveyance of an interest in land. However, according to Restatement Second § 148, comment c, "[t]he prevailing rule"—which is adopted by Restatement Second—"is that an executory land contract may be rescinded orally like other contracts within the Statute. . . . "

2. *Sale of goods.* If the original contract was for the sale of goods, and title had already passed to the buyer, "rescission" is really a resale of the goods, and comes within UCC § 2–201 if the amount involved is sufficient. Restatement Second § 148, comment b and Illustration 2.

SECTION 24. ORAL MODIFICATIONS

Generally speaking, a modification of a contract falls within the Statute of Frauds if, but only if, the new agreement that results from putting together the original agreement and the modification is within the Statute. However, a special rule applies to modifications of contracts for the sale of goods, which are governed by UCC § 2–209 (3). That section provides:

> The requirements of the statute of frauds section of this Article (Section 2–201) must be satisfied if [a contract for the sale of goods] as modified is within its provisions.

Comment 3 adds:

> The Statute of Frauds provisions of this Article are expressly applied to modifications by subsection (3). Under those provisions the "delivery and acceptance" test is limited to the goods which have been accepted, that is, to the past. "Modification" for the future cannot therefore be conjured up by oral testimony if the price involved is $500.00 or more since such modification must be shown at least by an authenticated memo. And since a memo is limited in its effect to the quantity of goods set forth in it there is safeguard against oral evidence.

The Comment suggests that *any* modification of a contract for the sale of goods must be in writing. This position was taken in Zemco Mfg., Inc. v. Navistar Int'l Transp. Corp., 186 F.3d 815 (7th Cir. 1999), decided by the Seventh Circuit under Indiana law. In 1983, the parties entered into a written contract for the sale of parts. Originally, the contract was to last one year, but it was extended to 1987 by successive written agreements. After 1987, the parties orally agreed to extend the contract. Navistar argued that the oral contract extensions were unenforceable under the Statute of Frauds. The Seventh Circuit agreed:

> We begin our analysis of this question with [UCC] § 2–209 (3), which generally applies to contract modifications. It states that "[t]he requirements of the statute of frauds . . . must be satisfied if the contract as modified is within its provisions." . . . The interpretation of this provision . . . has generated controversy among courts and commentators. One view is that all contract modifications must be in writing; another view is that only modifications of terms that are required to be in writing under [UCC] § 2–201 must be in writing. Under the second view, the time extension would not need to be in writing because the length of a contract is not a type of term that needs to be in writing.

> Indiana courts have not interpreted the meaning of [UCC § 2–209 (3).] A substantial number of the courts in other jurisdictions that have considered identical UCC provisions have held that every contract modification must be in writing. . . . Although these courts have provided little analysis, they essentially interpret § 2–209(3) to mean that, if the post-modification contract fits within the terms of § 2–201 (i.e., it is a sale of goods for more than $500), then any modification of it must be in writing. . . .

> At least one court has held that the writing requirement for modifications applies only to either a change in consideration, or a change in a term that the UCC statute of frauds requires to be in writing. *See Costco Wholesale Corp. v. World Wide Licensing*

Corp., 78 Wash.App. 637, 898 P.2d 347, 351 & n. 5 (1995). This view also appears to be favored among commentators. The general theory behind this approach is that it would be anomalous, if not inconsistent, to require that a modification be in writing if the same term in the original contract could be proven by parol evidence. Moreover, proponents of this view argue, § 2–209 (3) explicitly invokes only the writing requirements contained in § 2–201—nothing less and nothing more. . . .

We need not decide in the abstract the correct interpretation of § 2–209 (3). Because the jurisdiction of the district court was based on the diversity of citizenship of the parties, it was obligated to apply the law of Indiana. . . . Although the Indiana courts have not spoken directly on the matter, we believe . . . that Indiana would follow the majority of jurisdictions and hold that the extension of the contract needed to be in writing. . . . [because there] is no suggestion in this record that Indiana would not follow the majority rule or that its courts would not consider important the goal of uniformity in the interpretation of the Commercial Code. . . . [T]he influential [Official Comment] suggests strongly that Indiana would require compliance with the statute of frauds in this case.

In contrast, White & Summers comment, "Assuming that a party can establish a modifying agreement, must one show that it was reduced to writing? Section 2–209 (3) states that '[t]he requirements of the statute of frauds section of this Article (2–201) must be satisfied if the contract as modified is within its provisions.' The impact of this provision is not clear. We see at least the following possible interpretations: (1) that if the original contract was within 2–201, any modification thereof must also be in writing; (2) that a modification must be in writing if the term it adds brings the entire deal within 2–201 for the first time, as where the price is modified from $400 to $500; (3) that a modification must be in writing if it falls in 2–201 on its own; (4) that the modification must be in writing if it changes the quantity term of an original agreement that fell within 2–201; and (5) some combination of the foregoing. Given the purposes of the basic statute of frauds section 2–201, we believe interpretations (2), (3), and (4) are each justified, subject, of course, to the exceptions in 2–201 itself and to any general supplemental principles of estoppel." J. White & R. Summers, Uniform Commercial Code § 1–6 (5th ed. 2000).

Finally there is emergent in this area another doctrine of part performance or reliance, according to which an oral modification becomes effective if action has been taken under it. Restatement Second § 150. In this connection, UCC § 2–209 (4) provides that an attempt at modification that does not satisfy § 2–209(3) can operate as a waiver, and § 2–209(5) provides that such a waiver cannot be retracted if retraction would be unjust in view of a material change of position in reliance on the waiver.

―――――――

SECTION 25.   THE INTERACTION OF THE STATUTE OF FRAUDS WITH THE PAROL EVIDENCE RULE

There is obvious similarity between the Statute of Frauds and the parol evidence rule, since both are concerned with oral evidence. However, the two rules have different functions, which give rise to differences in operation. The following points should be noted.

First. The parol evidence rule does not invalidate a later oral modification of a written agreement. The Statute of Frauds may. See Section 24 of this Appendix.

Second. The Statute of Frauds requires a writing and, where applicable, prevents the use of an oral agreement as the basis for suit. The parol evidence rule may exclude *written* as well as oral proof of an agreement.

Third. Unless the Statute of Frauds requires "the contract" to be in writing, it may be satisfied by writings that do not call into operation the parol evidence rule. Thus the Statute may often be satisfied by piecing together a series of informal letters. Such a series of letters would not ordinarily be construed as an "integration" of the contract, and therefore would not prevent the introduction of parol evidence.

Fourth. In litigation involving a written contract, one party may object that the contract is incomplete. The other party may then offer parol evidence to supply the apparent gap in the written contract. The admission of such evidence may raise two questions: (1) Is the testimony offered admissible under the parol evidence rule? (2) Is the gap in the written contract so serious that the writing fails to satisfy the Statute of Frauds, thus making the offered testimony legally irrelevant? These are different questions, the answers to which depend on distinct considerations.

Example No. 18:

Seller and Buyer sign a written contract covering the sale of certain land for $10,000. The contract is complete in every respect except that it does not identify or describe the land in any way, but merely says, "This contract covers the land that we have this day orally agreed shall be conveyed." Seller sues Buyer for breach of the contract. Buyer pleads the Statute of Frauds. Seller relies on the written contract as satisfying the Statute, while Buyer contends that the writing is insufficient because it does not describe the land sold. Seller answers by saying, "The parol evidence rule does not prevent introducing oral evidence showing what the land is. Therefore, I can supplement the written contract by parol evidence identifying the land intended to be conveyed. Hence the writing satisfies the Statute." Seller is right about the parol evidence rule, but wrong about the Statute of Frauds.

SECTION 26.   THE INTERACTION OF THE STATUTE OF FRAUDS WITH THE REMEDY OF REFORMATION

The interaction of the Statute of Frauds and the remedy of reformation can also raise problems. In considering this interaction, it would be well to start with a case where the Statute of Frauds is plainly not involved. C contracts to build a house for O in nine months. A written contract is drawn up and signed, which contains all the requisite terms except that through a typist's error the price is stated as $10,000 instead of the agreed figure of $100,000. Here, on clear proof that both parties understood the price to be $100,000, the court would order reformation. Would it make any difference if the contract had been one that was required by the Statute to be in writing? There is something disturbing about the idea of a court's rewriting a contract to make it conform to an oral agreement of a type that the Statute of Frauds declares to be legally unenforceable. Yet is there any real reason for disquietude here? After all, the basic purpose of the Statute is to obtain for certain transactions the security of a written document. In the case of the building contract the parties sought that security for themselves in a formal written contract signed by both of them. A court would not hesitate to rewrite that contract to make it conform to an intention plainly shared by both parties. Why should it make any difference if the contract were such that had it been wholly unwritten it would have been unenforceable? If the Statute is thought, as it often is, to be grounded in large measure on a distrust of juries, no jury is involved in the remedy of reformation, which in any event is granted only on clear and convincing proof.

Today it is generally accepted that the circumstance that a contract falls within the Statute of Frauds does not of itself bar the possibility of reformation. There are, however, substantial traces of discomfort in some cases concerning reformation of contracts that fall within the Statute:

(1) There is authority for restricting reformation of such contracts to situations where the party seeking reformation has seriously relied on the contract; reformation of the wholly executory agreement may be refused.

(2) Reformation may be denied where it concerns the central term of a contract that falls within the Statute of Frauds—for example, where a

written contract for the sale of land inadvertently omits any hint of what land is to be conveyed.

(3) Some cases say that the obligation expressed in a writing that failed within the Statute of Frauds can be "contracted" by reformation, but not "expanded."

SECTION 27. PLEADING AND PROCEDURAL PROBLEMS IN CONNECTION WITH THE STATUTE

What procedure must be followed to utilize the Statute of Frauds as a defense? A defendant who took the words "no action shall be brought" literally might decide to say nothing of the Statute in her pleading, wait until the plaintiff attempted to introduce evidence to prove the oral agreement, and then ask for a ruling that the offered proof was incompetent under the Statute. In most jurisdictions, however, such a course of action would forfeit a defense under the Statute, because a defendant's failure to plead the Statute will usually be treated as waiving it. Correspondingly, in many or most jurisdictions a defendant who wants to invoke the Statute must raise the Statute as a specially pleaded affirmative defense, and cannot simply rely on pleading a general denial or the like. A companion rule in most jurisdictions is that the Statute of Frauds cannot be raised for the first time on appeal.

SECTION 28. A GLANCE BACKWARD AND AHEAD

Little is known about the legislative deliberations by which the Statute of Frauds was reduced to the form in which it was finally enacted in 1677. We do know, however, the precise language of its original draft. In the bill as it was first introduced in the House of Lords in 1673, the provision relating to contracts read as follows:

And be it further enacted by Authority aforesaid that in all actions upon the case, actions of debt, or other personal actions which from and after the [blank] day of [blank] shall be commenced upon any assumpsit, promise, contract or agreement made, or supposed to be made, by parol and whereof no memorandum, note or memorial in writing shall be taken by the direction of the parties thereunto no greater damages shall at any time be recovered than the sum of [blank], any law or usage to the contrary notwithstanding.

Provided that this Act shall not extend to such actions or suits which shall or may be grounded upon contracts or agreements for wares sold or money lent or upon any *quantum meruit* or any other assumpsits or promises which are created by the construction or operation of law; but that all and every such actions shall and may be sued and prosecuted in such manner as the same might have been before the making of this Act, anything hereinbefore to the contrary notwithstanding.

In contrast with the legislation that was actually enacted, it should be noted that the original draft: (1) Required a written memorandum, note, or memorial "taken by direction of the parties" rather than a written agreement, or a memorandum or note thereof, signed by the party to be charged. (2) Did not attempt to separate off certain defined kinds of contracts as requiring a writing, but instead contemplated imposing (subject to the qualifications in the second paragraph) a limitation on the recovery that could be had on *any* kind of oral contract. (3) Provided generally in its last paragraph that even in the absence of a memorandum, an appropriate recovery might be had, without limit of amount, where the plaintiff had actually conferred a benefit on the defendant under the agreement, and brought suit for the value of the benefit. It is remarkable that except as to the sales-of-goods section this last qualification should have disappeared in the final legislation, so that the concept of recovery for benefit conferred had to be supplied, in a somewhat irregular way, by a judicial gloss on the Statute.

The question may well be raised whether the Lords would have done better by subsequent generations if they had stood by their original draft. It should be noted that UCC § 1–206, in the form adopted in most states, is similarly based on a limit on recovery for contracts to which it applies.

The question may also be raised whether the Statute of Frauds has not long since outlived its usefulness. The Statute was, from the beginning, badly drafted. Its authors plainly did not clearly think through the relation between the disease they sought to cure and the remedy they prescribed, most notably so with respect to contracts not to be performed within one year. Furthermore, the principles by which the authors of the Statute decided the question, what contracts deserved the protection of a writing, were based on the needs of the seventeenth century, not those of modern commerce. And the tangled web of judicial interpretation that has gathered about the words of the Statute through the centuries surely deserves to be called, as it was by a British writer, "filthily technical." To the laudatory comment that every line of the Statute is worth a subsidy, the apt rejoinder has been made that every line of it has cost a subsidy.

In 1954 the British Parliament repealed the provisions of the English Statute of Frauds concerning (1) special promises of executors or administrators, (2) agreements in consideration of marriage, (3) agreements not to be performed within one year, and (4) contracts for the sale of goods. This leaves in effect, from the original Statute, only a promise to be a surety for another and a contract for the sale of an interest in land. (As in this country, however, since the adoption of the original Statute of Frauds, England has enacted statutes requiring a signed writing for certain other special kinds of contracts.)

The Permanent Editorial Board for the UCC ["PEB"] Study Group on the Revision of Article 2 of the Uniform Commercial Code concluded that "Despite its ancient lineage, there is no persuasive evidence either that the statute of frauds has prevented fraud in the proof of the making of a contract or that its presence has channeled behavior toward more reliable forms of record keeping. . . . England repealed the statute of frauds for sales in 1953. Since [then] there has been little discussion and no reports about the impact, if any. In short, the statute of frauds has apparently sunk in England without an adverse trace." PEB Study Group Report on Article 2 at 50–51 (1990). Furthermore, Article 11 of the CISG provides: "A contract of sale need not be concluded in or evidenced by writing and is not subject to any other requirements as to form." Similarly, Unidroit Art. 1.2 provides that "Nothing in these Principles requires that a contract be concluded in or evidenced by writing. It may be proven by any means, including witnesses."

The PEB Study Group suggested that even if the Statute of Frauds requirement for the sale of goods was not repealed, the quantity requirement ought to be deleted and certain other changes ought to be made, including possibly the addition of a reliance exception. An ABA Task Force on the revision of Article 2 was divided on whether the Statute of Frauds in Article 2 should be repealed, but suggested that one alternative would be to require that an oral contract be proven by clear and convincing evidence, rather than merely a preponderance of the evidence. ABA Task Force Report on Article 2, 16 Del.J.Corp.Law 981, 1039 (1991). Through the late 1990s, the National Conference of Commissioners on Uniform State Law and the American Law Institute worked to produce a thoroughly revised version of Article 2. At one point in the drafting process, the proposed revision entirely dropped a Statute of Frauds provision for contracts for the sale of goods. At that point, Section 2–201 was entitled "No Formal Requirements." Section 2–201(a) then provided that "A contract or modification is enforceable, whether or not there is a record signed by the party against whom enforcement is sought, even if the contract or modification is not capable of performance within one year after its making." Later, however, a Statute of Frauds provision was reinstated in the proposed revision.

In the end, the attempt to produce a thorough revision of Article 2 was abandoned. Instead, in 2003 NCCUSL and the ALI promulgated limited amendments to Article 2. Among these amendments was a revision to section 2–201 that raised the price for which a writing is required, in the case of a contract for the sale of goods, from $500 to $5,000. As of early 2006, however, no state has adopted the amended version of Article 2.

———

INDEX

References are to Pages

ACCEPTANCE
Generally, 387–415
Conduct, acceptance by, 558
Crossed revocation and acceptance, 396–397
Delay or failure of transmission, 397
Electronic commerce, 399–400
Modes of acceptance, 387–415
Silence as acceptance, 403–417
Offer and Revocation, this index
Revocation of acceptance, 726
Silence as acceptance, 403–417
UCC, what constitutes acceptance under, 559–560
Variance between offer and acceptance, 360–361
When effective, 396–397

ANTICIPATORY BREACH
Breach and Response, this index

ASSENT
Generally, 297–461
Acceptance, this index
Good faith, duty to bargain in, 427–461
Implied-in-Law and Implied-in-Fact Contracts, this index
Indefiniteness, 427–461
Interpretation of Contracts, this index
Parol Evidence Rule, this index
Preliminary negotiations, 427–461

ASSIGNMENT AND NEGOTIATION
Preliminary negotiations, 427–461

BARGAIN
Consideration, bargain theory, 12
Good faith, duty to bargain in, 427–461
Legal duty, performance of, 120–138
Modification of contractual duties, 120–138
Mutuality, this index
Offer and Revocation, this index
Principle of bargain, 57–86
Reliance damages in bargain context, 265–271
Statute of frauds and right to value of bargain, 810–815
Theory, 12
Transacting at a distance, 396–399
Unconscionability, this index
Value of bargain and statute of frauds, 810–815
Waiver of contractual duties, 120–138

BREACH AND RESPONSE
Generally, 713–737
Ability to perform, 713–714
Failure of performance by once party as excuse for nonperformance by the other, 714–720
Material breach
Generally, 714–715
Order of performance
Restatement, 714
Remedies for Breach of Contract, this index

CERTAINTY
Damages, 224–233

CIRCUMSTANCES
Unexpected Circumstances, this index

CLASSICAL CONTRACT LAW
Mirror image rule, 360, 558
Offer and acceptance, 427
Unilateral contract, offer for, 376–378

COMMERCIAL CONTRACTS
Uniform Commercial Code, this index

COMPENSATION
Expectation and reliance conceptions, 37, 163–167

CONDITIONS
Generally, 739–774
Conditions precedent and conditions subsequent, distinction between, 748–752
Donative promises, conditional, 15–16
Excuse, 764–774
Interpretation problems in distinguishing between conditions and promises, 748–752
Operation of promise and operation of condition, difference between, 740–748
Promises and conditions, difference between
Generally, 739–740
Interpretation problems in distinguishing between, 748–752
Satisfaction, conditions of, 757–764

CONDUCT
Acceptance by, 559

CONSIDERATION
    Generally, 7–154
Bargain, this index
Civil law analogues, 471
Compensation, expectation and reliance
    conceptions, 37
Concept of, 14–16
Conditional donative promises, 15–16
Donative promises, simple, 9–16
Expectation interest, injury to, 37
Form, element of
        Generally, 16–24
    Seals, this index
Gifts, 14–16
Illusory promises, 112–114
Injury to reliance and expectation
    interests, 37
Lack of consideration, sealed instruments,
    23
Limits of contract, 139–154
Nominal consideration, 20–22
Past consideration, 42–56
Performance of legal duty, 120–138
Presumption of consideration, seal, 22
Reliance
        Generally, 25–42
    Damages, 38
    Injury to reliance interest, 37
    Opportunity costs, 38
    Out-of-pocket costs, 38
Remedies and consideration, 37–42
Seals, this index
Unenforceable obligation, when promise to
    discharge is binding, 42–43

COSTS
Opportunity costs, reimbursement, 38
Out-of-pocket costs, reimbursement, 38

COURSE OF DEALING
Role of, interpretation of contracts, 509–
    520

CURE
Substantial Performance, this index

DAMAGES
Certainty, 224–233
Donative promise, breach of, 39–41
Expectation Measure, this index
Foreseeability, 216–222
Introduction to contract damages, 157–167
Liquidated damages, 234–247
Reliance damages
        Generally, 163–167
    Bargain context, 265–271
    Note on, 277
Remedies, this index
Restitution Measure of Damages, this
    index
Sale of Goods, this index
Services Contracts, this index

DEALING
Course of dealing, interpretation of
    contracts, 509–520

DISCLOSURE
Requirement of, 671–677

DONATIVE PROMISES
    Generally, 9–16
Consideration, this index

EFFICIENT BREACH
Theory of, 288–294

ELECTRONIC COMMERCE
Offer and acceptance, 398

ELECTRONIC CONTRACTING
Statute of frauds, 807–810

EMPLOYMENT CONTRACTS
Specific performance, 262–263

E-SIGN
Generally, 809

**EUROPEAN CONTRACT LAW,
    PRINCIPLES OF**
Generally, 78–79

EVIDENCE
Parol Evidence Rule, this index
Presumption of consideration, seal, 22

EXCUSE
Express conditions, 765–774
Failure of performance by once party as
    excuse for nonperformance by the
    other, 714–720
Restatement of Contracts, 771–773

EXPECTATION INTEREST
Injury to, 37

**EXPECTATION MEASURE OF
    DAMAGES**
    Generally, 169–247
Certainty, 224–233
Foreseeability, 216–222
Liquidated damages, 234–247
New business rule, 228
Sale of Goods, this index
Services Contracts, this index

EXPRESS CONDITIONS
Conditions, this index

FORESEEABILITY
Expectation measure of damages, 216–222

FORM CONTRACTS
    Generally, 555–619
Acceptance under UCC, what constitutes,
    559–560
Basic issues, 557–576
Interpretation, 577–619
Knockout rule, 570
Mirror image rule, 557–558

Purchase order, 557
Sales order, 557
Unconscionability, 577–619
Uniform Commercial Code, acceptance, 559–560

FORMALITIES
Statute of frauds, 785

FORMATION
Acceptance, this index
Form Contracts, this index
Offer and Revocation, this index

GOOD FAITH
Bargaining in good faith, duty, 427–461
Perfect tender rule, 727–728
Performing in good faith, obligation
    Generally, 521–528
    Restatement, 528
    UCC, 529

GOODS
Sale of Goods, this index

HISTORICAL BACKGROUND
Specific performance, 249–250

ILLUSORY PROMISES
Generally, 112–114

IMPLIED-IN-LAW AND IMPLIED-IN-FACT CONTRACTS
Generally, 417–420

IMPOSSIBILITY
Unexpected Circumstances, this index

INALIENABILITY
Market inalienability, 152–154

INDEFINITENESS
Generally, 427–461

INJURY
What constitutes, 37

INSTALLMENT CONTRACTS
Substantial performance, 727

INTERPRETATION OF CONTRACTS
    Generally, 297–329
Dealing, course of, 509–520
Form contracts, 577–619
Language and the law, 319–321
Parol Evidence Rule, this index
Performance, course of, 509–520
Promises and conditions, interpretation
    problems in distinguishing between, 748–752
Purposive language, problems of
    interpreting, 319–329
Restatement, 317–319, 513–515
Subjective and objective elements
    Generally, 297–319
    Introductory note, 297–298

Trade usage, role of
    Generally, 509–520
    Written contract, as part of, 517–520

KNOCKOUT RULE
Conflicting terms in form contracts, 570

LAND SALES
Statute of Frauds, this index

LEGAL DUTY
Convention for the International Sale of
    Goods, 137
Performance as consideration, 120–138
United Nations Commission on
    International Trade Law, 137

LIMITS OF CONTRACT
Generally, 139–154

LIQUIDATED DAMAGES
    Generally, 234–247
Special judicial scrutiny, 240

MAILBOX RULE
When acceptance effective, 396–399

MEASURE OF DAMAGES
Expectation Measure of Damages, this
    index
Restitution Measure of Damages, this
    index

MIRROR IMAGE RULE
    Generally, 360
Form contracts, 558

MISTAKE
    Generally, 637–677
Factual assumption, mistaken, 654
Mechanical errors, 637–650
Mutual mistakes, 654–670
Nondisclosure, 671–676
Reformation, 650–654
Restatement, 676–677
Shared mistaken assumptions, 654–670
Tacit assumptions, 654–655, 683–684
Transcription, mistakes in, 650–654
Unilateral mistakes, 637–650

MODIFICATION
Contractual duties, 120–138
Oral modification, 821–824

MUTUAL MISTAKES
Generally, 653–670

MUTUALITY
Illusory promises, 112–114

NEGOTIATION
Assignment and Negotiation, this index

NEW BUSINESS RULE
Certainty of damages, 228

NONDISCLOSURE
Generally, 671–677

OFFER AND REVOCATION
Generally, 331–386
Acceptance, this index
Counter-offers, 348–361
Crossed revocation and acceptance, 396–397
Delay or failure of transmission, 397
Electronic commerce, 399–403
Lapse of offer, 348–361
Mailbox rule, 396–398
Mirror image rule, 360
Offer, what constitutes
Generally, 331–337
Record, note on concept of, 399
Rejection of offer
Generally, 348–361
Expressions by offeree, effect of, 353–354
Restatement of contracts, 359
Revocation
Generally, 361–386
Crossed revocation and acceptance, 396–397
Unilateral contract, offer for, 376–378
Transacting at a distance, 396–399
Variance between offer and acceptance, 360

OPPORTUNITY COSTS
Reimbursement, 38

ORAL CONTRACTS
Part performance of, or reliance on, oral contract within statute of frauds, 810

ORAL MODIFICATIONS
Generally, 821–824

ORAL RESCISSION
Generally, 821

ORGAN PURCHASES
Statutory prohibition, 151

OUT-OF-POCKET COSTS
Reimbursement, 38

PAROL EVIDENCE RULE
Generally, 463–495
Course of performance and course of dealing as part of written contract, 517–520
Interpretation of written contracts, 495–509
Trade usage as part of written contract, 517–520

PERFECT TENDER RULE
Generally, 727–729

PERFORMANCE
Ability to perform
Generally, 713–714
Breach and Response, this index
Course of performance, interpretation of contracts, 509–520
Express Conditions, this index

Good Faith, this index
Legal duty, performance as consideration, 120–138
Order of performance
Breach and Response, this index
Part performance of oral contract within statute of frauds, 810
Substantial Performance, this index

PRELIMINARY NEGOTIATIONS
Generally, 427–461

PRESUMPTIONS
Consideration, seal, 22

PURCHASE ORDERS
Form contracts, 557

REAL PROPERTY
Specific performance, contracts for sale of land, 261–263
Statute of Frauds, this index

RECORDS
Electronic records, 399

REFORMATION
Mistakes in transcription, 650–654

REIMBURSEMENT
Opportunity costs, 38
Reliance on oral contract, 815–818

RELIANCE
Consideration, this index
Damages, this index
Statute of Frauds, this index

REMEDIES FOR BREACH OF CONTRACT
Generally, 155–294
Consideration, contract remedies and, 37–42
Damages, this index
Efficient breach, theory of, 288–294
Specific Performance, this index

RESCISSION
Oral rescission, 821

RESTATEMENT OF CONTRACTS
Background and history, 11–12
Conditions of satisfaction, 764
Excuse, 771–773
Good faith performance, 529
Illusory promises, 117–119
Interpretation of contracts, 316–319, 513–515
Measure of damages, breach of donative promise, 38–41
Mistake, 676–677
Nominal consideration, 20–22
Offer and revocation, 357
Unilateral contracts, 376–378, 383–384

RESTITUTION MEASURE OF DAMAGES
Generally, 271–294
Benefits conferred under oral agreement, 810–812
Breach of contract, 272–273
Note on restitutionary damages, 277
Plaintiff in default, restitution in favor of, 711–720

REVOCATION
Offer and Revocation, this index

SALE OF GOODS
Damages for breach of contract
Generally, 187–204
Buyer, breach by, 199–204
Seller, breach by, 187–199
Form Contracts, this index
Installment contracts, 727
Perfect tender rule and UCC, 727–729
Revocation of acceptance, 727
Specific performance, traditional rule, 260–261
Statute of frauds
Generally, 785–789
Oral rescission, 821
Substantial performance, 726–737
UCC
Damages for breach of contract, 187
Substantial performance, 727–729

SATISFACTION
Conditions of satisfaction, 757–764

SEALS
Generally, 22–24
Abolishing distinction between sealed and unsealed instruments, 23
Historical background, 22–23
Presumption of consideration, 22
Statutory provisions, 23

SIGNATURES
E-Sign, 809

SILENCE
As acceptance, 403–417

SPECIFIC PERFORMANCE
Generally, 249–263
Employment contracts, 262–263
Goods, contracts for sale of, 260–261
Historical background, 249–251
Land, contracts for sale of, 261–263
Law and equity, relation of, 250

STANDARDIZED AGREEMENTS
Form Contracts, this index

STATUTE OF FRAUDS
Generally, 775–829
American variations, 782
Bargain principle and, 59
Correct statement of agreement, 807
Electronic contracting, 807–810
Formal requirements under UCC, 785
Kinds of writings that will satisfy statute, 801–807
Land, sale of interest in
Generally, 783–784
Oral rescission, 821
Value of bargain, right to, 812–814
Modifications, oral, 821–824
One year provision, 791–795, 814–815
Oral contracts
Part performance, below
Reliance, below
Oral modifications, 821–824
Original statute, 776–778
Part performance of oral contract within statute
Generally, 810
Piecing together several writings, 807
Purpose, 778–780
Real estate. Land, sale of interest in, above
Reliance on oral contract within statute
Generally, 810
Reimbursement for reliance, 815
Rescission, oral, 821
Restitution of benefits conferred under oral agreement, 810–812
Sale of Goods, this index

SUBSTANTIAL PERFORMANCE
Generally, 706–737
Capability problem in contract law, 709
Cure, perfect tender rule, 727
General principle, 706–711
Installment contracts, 727
Perfect tender rule, 727–729
Revocation of acceptance, 728
Sale of goods, contracts for, 726–737
UCC provisions, 727–729

TENDER
Perfect tender rule, 727–727

TRADE USAGE
Generally, 509–520
Written contract, trade usage as part of, 517–520

UNCONSCIONABILITY
Generally, 86–106
Form contracts, 577–618
UCC, 92–93

UNENFORCEABLE OBLIGATION
When promise to discharge is binding, 42–43

UNEXPECTED CIRCUMSTANCES
Generally, 679–702
Impossibility, development of doctrine, 700
Tacit assumptions, 683–684

UNIDROIT PRINCIPLES
Generally, 78

UNIFORM COMMERCIAL CODE
Damages for seller's breach of contract for
      sale of goods, 187
Form Contracts, this index
Formal requirements, 785
Good faith performance, 529
Offer and acceptance, variance between,
      360
Sale of Goods, this index
Unconscionability, 92–93

**UNIFORM ELECTRONIC
      TRANSACTIONS ACT**
Generally, 807–810

UNILATERAL CONTRACTS
Implied-in-law and implied-in-fact, 417–
      420
Offers for, 376–378
Restatement of Contracts, 376–378, 383–
      384

USAGE
Trade Usage, this index

WAIVER
Contractual duties, 120–138

WRITING
Statute of Frauds, this index